THE SOCIOLOGY OF CRIME AND DELINQUENCY

THE SOCIOLOGY OF CRIME AND DELINQUENCY

SECOND EDITION

Marvin E. Wolfgang
Leonard Savitz
Norman Johnston

New York · London · Sydney · Toronto
John Wiley & Sons, Inc.

Copyright © 1962, 1970, by John Wiley & Sons, Inc.

All rights reserved. No part of this book may be reproduced by any means, nor transmitted, nor translated into a machine language without the written permission of the publisher.

10 9 8 7 6 5 4 3 2 1

Library of Congress Catalogue Card Number: 73-96041

SBN 471-95954 5 (cloth) 471-95955 3 (paper)

Printed in the United States of America

Preface

In the seven years since the publication of the first edition of *The Sociology of Crime and Delinquency,* considerable changes have transpired in the field of criminology. The rate and the quality of the published literature has perceptibly increased. If we add to this the numerous reports, surveys, and materials flowing from the President's Commission on Law Enforcement and Administration of Justice, it becomes clear why about 60 percent of the material in the present edition of *The Sociology of Crime and Delinquency* and its companion volume, *The Sociology of Punishment and Correction,* is new. In this volume 34 of 63 items were not in the first edition. It was not our desire to replace any item with another more recent one merely because the latter was more current, although where currency and quality combine we have replaced older items. However, few articles, new to this edition, were published before 1962, and their inclusion now means that we believe them to be more cogent and current than we did in our earlier evaluation.

The purpose of *The Sociology of Crime and Delinquency* is to provide the student of criminology with ready access to some of the most important contemporary sociological literature in this field. The book should, therefore, be of value to students in any variety of undergraduate or graduate courses in criminology and delinquency and to their instructors.

This book, with *The Sociology of Punishment and Correction,* can be used as a text or as supplemental reading in an undergraduate criminology course. Some colleges and universities offer special courses in juvenile delinquency, and although both books can advantageously be used, because crime-causation studies usually involve juveniles, *The Sociology of Crime and Delinquency* is especially applicable to these courses.

We have not subscribed to the idea that the undergraduate student in criminology is interested merely in being entertained. Students today are more research oriented than ever before and are seeking knowledge that bears the imprint of the scientific approach. Criminology is a sufficiently colorful and intriguing field of study in itself to enlist the interest of capable minds without having to resort to devices designed to arouse attention. The scientific study of crime, although still close to its nascency, has been maturing toward a sophisticated level of theory and research. Isolated and reformistic in its early stages in America, criminology today embraces a broader framework of scientific attitude and inquiry. The table of contents will show that considerable attention has been given to articles and selections from books that are empirical, theoretical, or that contain detailed descriptive studies. For these reasons, the book can very profitably be used in graduate courses.

We have used some selections that are well known to scholars in the field and are considered traditional; they are traditional because they made substantial impacts or are contributions that have endured. We believe that students should become familiar with them. Substantive contributions involving different viewpoints and critiques of these positions have also been included. We have emphasized areas that involve problems of theory and research such as the meaning of criminology, criminal and delinquency statistics, the concept of *cause* in criminology, theories and their substantive support, and delineation of sub-fields of investigation. Most authors offer suggestions for research or provocative insights for further development of their theories. In these ways the student in advanced graduate study can not only become informed and more knowledgeable about criminology but also can have on hand some of the most meaningful critiques and encouragements for engaging in his own field studies and theoretical analyses.

Criminology courses in the United States are generally taught in departments of sociology. The editors of these selections and authors of the introductory remarks for each section are sociologists. Consequently, we have tried to keep the book (1) sociological, (2) contemporary in research, theory, and description (even though some of the articles are over twenty years old), and (3) empirical, whenever appropriate and possible.

The abundance of excellent sociological materials available reflects the primary orientation of American criminology. Historical studies, for example, such as may be found in *Pioneers in Criminology* (London: Stevens and Sons; Chicago: Quadrangle Press, 1960), form an important background for an understanding and perspective of contemporary research and thought. However, the inclusion of non-sociological, that is, biological and psychological, and historical studies would have resulted in a collection of prohibitive length unless important sociological contributions were sacrificed.

Although we characterize the present group of selections as contemporary, the ideas contained in a given work are always considered more important than their date of publication. Moreover, because much of the most pervasive and persuasively meaningful criminal sociology has been objective and empirical, we have concentrated on the research and analysis reflecting these values. If the discipline of criminology is an attempt to use the scientific approach, that is, attitudes and methods of empirical research, we believe that they should be represented in a book of readings. Many of the selections, therefore, consist of empirical research findings, details of which are not generally included in a standard textbook. We have also included theoretical discussions and purely descriptive material when they have made significant contributions to the study of crime and the criminal.

American criminology, like some other specialized areas of sociology, has been unnecessarily provincial. We have not entirely overcome this weakness. There were, for example, a variety of problems that prevented our using foreign-language material. Moreover, criminology in European countries is less sociologically oriented, being taught and studied mostly in schools of law or medicine or by governmental agencies having interests in legal and political ramifications. However, there are several selections in the book, written by scholars from abroad, which, we feel, should extend the students' perspective beyond national boundaries.

Neither all subjects nor all good articles and books within the selected subject areas could be included in a book of this size. Choice and compromise must always be made. We would have preferred to include more selections in some special areas. In those areas where there are few selections the material included represents the best available.

The brief section introductions written by the editors of the book are designed to bridge gaps between sections and individual selections. These introductory remarks briefly describe the selections without imposing any particular orientation on them. Section I, "The Meaning of Criminology," seeks to orient the student to an understanding of the scientific discipline embraced by criminology and to what is meant by the sociological approach in the study of crime causation. Some attention is given to the legal definitions of delinquency and crime, *mens rea,* felony, misdemeanor, principles of the first and second degree, accessories, etc. Whether "white collar crime" is in fact crime, a full discussion of sociological concepts such as conduct norms and culture conflict, an essay on the definition of the criminal, and a provocative analysis of whether "good men" are more perceptive of reality than are "bad men" are included in this section.

Rather than presenting the latest police, court, or prison statistics we are devoting Section II, "Criminal and Delinquency Statistics," to a discussion of the difficulties and limitations involved in a collection and analysis of statistics in criminology. Criminal statistics form a major basis for the development of the discipline and for much scientific research. More likely than in most fields, the sociologist working in criminology must rely upon legal concepts, administrative policy and procedure for many of his terms. Moreover, he often must use crude data collected by public authorities who are interested less in research than in administration. The foci of Section II are problems of the role and use of criminal statistics, undetected delinquent behavior, the victim's decision to report a crime to the police, the measurement of crime, and police practices which contaminate criminal statistics.

Section III, "The Concept of Cause," is concerned with the necessity of being alert to the meaning of social causation within a broad perspective, to the differences between causal and correlational forms of relationships, and to a discussion of the "multiple factor" approach. The question of what are the minimal requirements for an adequate system of analyzing causes is raised. Problems of predicting behavior of a supposedly "unique" individual are discussed, as is the need for some complex probabilistic model of causation to replace deterministic schemes.

One of the longest and most important sections of the book is Section IV, "Theory and Evidence." We present a theoretical statement on crime or delinquency and then offer an example of some supportive or nonsupportive research. The theory that crime is an "American way of life" for some segments of our population, at least, is examined in the light of recent evidence on La Cosa Nostra. The theory of culture conflict, in one form or another, is also subjected to some empirical examination, as is "differential association" and the "cultural transmission" models of Shaw and McKay. The anomic theories, culminating in the "opportunity" model, are either confirmed or severely attacked depending on which of several investigations is accepted. Walter Miller's theory, the subculture of violence, and the "containment theory" all find varying measures of empirical support.

In "The Social Structure" (Section V), Negro and crime and differentials in crime rates between Negroes and whites are some of the variables examined. Social class, a prime sociological variable, is the center of concern for several articles. The presumed criminogenic features of migration, school dropouts, broken homes, and the working mother are all examined. The control of religion over young males and the mass media's influence on the youthful population are the final topics in this section.

Although efforts to classify criminal behavior or criminal offenders have been unsuccessful generally and have not enjoyed widespread acceptance, some research studies and descriptions of distinct varieties of criminal activity have provided valuable insights about crime and the criminal. Section VI, "Selected Patterns of Criminal Activity," includes references to white collar crime as a product of our contemporary social values; crime on a business basis as a suborganization within society; theft that is a man's vocation; homicide that involves the contribution which the victim makes to his own victimization; sex offenses that are found in many varieties but with recognizable patterns of behavior; organized crime, its code and its cost to society in terms of corruption and economics; and contentions regarding the effects and legal consequences of the use of marihuana and other "soft" drugs.

The collection of writings in this book represents no doctrinaire position, and we have deliberately presented some opposing viewpoints to stimulate thought and discussion. We hope that *The Sociology of Crime and Delinquency* reflects the best of the framework which we have used; namely, contemporary sociological and empirical research and theory in criminology. Above all, we trust that the book will aid both teacher and student to think intelligently, constructively, and critically about this subject.

MARVIN E. WOLFGANG
LEONARD SAVITZ
NORMAN JOHNSTON

Contents

Section I / THE MEANING OF CRIMINOLOGY — 1
1. A Sociological Approach — 3
   THORSTEN SELLIN
2. The Normal and The Pathological — 11
   EMILE DURKHEIM
3. The Legal Definition of Crime and Criminals — 15
   WILLIAM L. MARSHALL & WILLIAM L. CLARK
4. The Legal Basis of Delinquency — 22
   THORSTEN SELLIN & MARVIN E. WOLFGANG
5. Is "White Collar Crime" Crime? — 32
   EDWIN H. SUTHERLAND
6. Who is the Criminal? — 41
   PAUL W. TAPPAN
7. Good Men, Bad Men, and the Perception of Reality — 49
   GWYNN NETTLER

Section II / CRIMINAL AND DELINQUENCY STATISTICS — 61
8. New Thinking in Criminal Statistics — 63
   LESLIE T. WILKINS
9. Crime, Victims, and the Police — 74
   PHILLIP H. ENNIS
10. Undetected Delinquent Behavior — 82
    MARTIN GOLD
11. Measuring Crime — 101
12. Abuses in Crime Reporting — 114

Section III / THE CONCEPT OF CAUSE — 117
13. Social Causation — 119
    ROBERT MacIVER
14. Multiple Factor Approaches — 123
    ALBERT K. COHEN

15. False Criteria of Causality   127
  TRAVIS HIRSCHI & HANAN C. SELVIN
16. The Unique Individual   141
  LESLIE T. WILKINS
17. The Concept of Cause in Criminology   147
  LESLIE T. WILKINS

Section IV / THEORY AND EVIDENCE   161

18. Crime as an American Way of Life   165
  DANIEL BELL
19. La Cosa Nostra   180
20. The Conflict of Conduct Norms   186
  THORSTEN SELLIN
21. The Conflict of Values in Delinquency Areas   190
  SOLOMON KOBRIN
22. Culture Conflict in Israel   199
  SHLOMO SHOHAM
23. Differential Association   208
  EDWIN H. SUTHERLAND
24. An Empirical Test of Differential Association Theory   211
  ALBERT J. REISS, JR., & A. LEWIS RHODES
25. Cultural Transmission   225
  CLIFFORD R. SHAW & HENRY D. McKAY
26. An Ecological Analysis of Chicago   233
  CLIFFORD R. SHAW & HENRY D. McKAY
27. Social Structure and Anomie   238
  ROBERT K. MERTON
28. An Ecological Analysis of Baltimore   247
  BERNARD LANDER
29. Issues in the Ecological Study of Delinquency   266
  ROBERT A. GORDON
30. The Delinquent Subculture   286
  ALBERT K. COHEN
31. Techniques of Delinquency   292
  GRESHAM M. SYKES & DAVID MATZA
32. Differential Opportunity Structure   300
  RICHARD A. CLOWARD & LLOYD E. OHLIN
33. Values and Gang Delinquency: A Study of Street-Corner Groups   319
  JAMES SHORT, JR. & FRED L. STRODTBECK
34. Dimensions of Current Gang Delinquency   340
  THOMAS M. GANNON

CONTENTS xi

35. Lower Class Culture as a Generating Milieu of Gang
    Delinquency   351
    WALTER B. MILLER
36. Violent Crimes in City Gangs   364
    WALTER B. MILLER
37. The Subculture of Violence   380
    MARVIN E. WOLFGANG AND FRANCO FERRACUTI
38. Violent Gang Organization   392
    LEWIS YABLONSKY
39. Containment Theory   401
    WALTER C. RECKLESS
40. Self-Concept Research   406
    SANDRA S. TANGRI & MICHAEL SCHWARTZ

Section V / THE SOCIAL STRUCTURE   417
41. The Negro and Crime   419
    GUY B. JOHNSON
42. Negro and White Crime Rates   430
    EARL R. MOSES
43. The Moynihan Report: The Negro Family and Crime
    United States Department of Labor, Office of Policy
    Planning and Research   440
44. Social Class and Delinquency   451
    JOHN P. CLARK & EUGENE P. WENNINGER
45. Middle Class Gangs   463
    HOWARD L. MYERHOFF & BARBARA G. MYERHOFF
46. Delinquency and Migration   473
    LEONARD SAVITZ
47. Delinquency, School Attendance and Dropout   481
    DELBERT S. ELLIOTT
48. The Broken Home and Male Delinquency   489
    LAWRENCE ROSEN
49. Working Mothers and Delinquency   496
    SHELDON & ELEANOR GLUECK
50. Religious Control and Delinquent Behavior   499
    THOMAS M. GANNON
51. Mass Media and Reported Delinquent Behavior:
    A Negative Case   509
    ERDWIN H. PFUHL, JR.

Section VI / SELECTED PATTERNS OF CRIMINAL ACTIVITY   525
52. The Incredible Electrical Conspiracy   529
    RICHARD AUSTIN SMITH

53.	Newspaper Publicity and the Electrical Conspiracy	549
54.	Murder, Inc.	551
	MEYER BERGER	
55.	Theft as a Way of Life	559
	EDWIN H. SUTHERLAND	
56.	Victim-Precipitated Criminal Homicide	569
	MARVIN E. WOLFGANG	
57.	Organized Crime: The Code and its Functions	579
58.	Gambling and Corruption	596
59.	Economics and Criminal Enterprise	613
	THOMAS C. SCHELLING	
60.	Sex Offenses: A Sociological Critique	626
	STANTON WHEELER	
61.	Forcible Rape	644
	MENACHEM AMIR	
62.	The Marihuana Problem	654
	ALFRED R. LINDESMITH	
63.	A Hierarchy of Drug Users	666
	ALAN G. SUTTER	

THE SOCIOLOGY
OF CRIME AND
DELINQUENCY

SECTION I

The Meaning of Criminology

THE DISCIPLINE OF CRIMINOLOGY HAS COME TO MEAN A VARIETY OF THINGS. In this book we have taken the position that criminology should be used "to designate only the body of *scientific* knowledge and the deliberate pursuit of such knowledge."[1] Within this framework there is no limit to the tools of analysis that can be employed because the statistical, historical, clinical, case study or other techniques may furnish important data and provide provocative theory that can contribute to the scientific study of crime and criminals. Thus, criminology herein refers to the use of scientific methods in the study and analysis of regularities, uniformities, patterns, and causal factors related to crime and criminals and the social reactions to both. As Sellin has pointed out, "The scientist aims at the discovery of constants in the relationships among certain defined facts [and] the technologist at the adaptation of knowledge to the social needs of the moment."[2] We are contending, therefore, that as useful as application of criminological research by social workers, probation officers, and others may be, such application is not necessarily criminology nor are these persons criminologists by reason of their occupational roles per se. But the acquisition of criminological knowledge is important to the practitioner if he is to bring new insights and a firm professional background into his functioning role and experiences.

Different approaches to the same subject matter are clearly present in almost all disciplines. Many contributions to the scientific study of crime, criminals, and the treatment of offenders have been made by such disciplines as biology, psychology, psychiatry, endocrinology, law, and anthropology. However, in the United States probably the most extensive and intensive analyses have been made within a sociological orientation. The predominantly biological and legal orientation of some European criminology that has long historical traditions and the American sociological orientation that is equally linked to its own historical continuity are simply different approaches to the scientific study of crime and the criminal. This

---

[1] Thorsten Sellin, *Culture Conflict and Crime*, New York: Social Science Research Council, 1938, p. 3.
[2] *Ibid.*

section and the remaining portions of the book concentrate on the sociological aspects of criminology, as in the first selection by Sellin, "A Sociological Approach to the Study of Crime Causation," which provides a point of departure for the rest of the book.

Although Emile Durkheim was not specifically a criminologist, he made cogent remarks about the sociological approach to an understanding of crime and punishment. In his view, crime is a normal phenomenon in any society characterized by heterogeneity and social change. Such a perspective has had both direct and indirect effects upon sociologists who are concerned with criminology, although Durkheim has not had similar effects upon those psychologists and psychiatrists who view the criminal as a manifestation of some type of pathology.

Knowing something about the legal definitions of crime, criminal, delinquency, and delinquent is fundamental to an understanding of the statutory norms that form part of the social process leading to the determination that a type of deviant conduct is designated as criminal. Therefore, because most of the crude data of criminological research are based upon violations of legal norms, we have included a brief selection from Marshall and Clark's *A Treatise on the Law of Crime*, in which some attention is given to the legal definitions of crime, mens rea, felony, misdemeanor, principles of the first and second degree, and so forth. Similarly, the Sellin and Wolfgang selection concisely indicates the broadness of the legal definition of delinquency and the variations of Juvenile Court jurisdictions in the United States.

The prevalent use of Sutherland's term "white collar crime" has led, since the 1930's, to a series of discussions and arguments about the definition of crime and the criminal. Although not challenging our fundamental position about the scientific nature of criminology, the debate is of consequence on a substantive level, for it raises questions about the sources of data for analysis and the relationship between social science and the law. Both Sellin and Sutherland agree that the sociological study of crime may embrace concepts broader than those found in the criminal law; analyses of conduct norms, culture conflict, differential association, and white collar crime extend the scientist's inquiry over a range of deviance not covered by the law. Tappan in "Who Is The Criminal?" disagrees with this position and restricts the study of crime and the criminal to a more narrow legal conceptualism. Nettler, finally, demonstrates the invalidity of the "popular thoughtway" that a criminal *must* be a sick human being, suffering from erroneous perceptions of the world around him. This selection suggests that the noncriminal may have a more inaccurate perception of what is "true" and thereby sharpens our own views about the criminal.

1. A SOCIOLOGICAL APPROACH

THORSTEN SELLIN

ONE OF THE MOST IMPORTANT ASPECTS OF criminology is the search for the "causes" of crime. The first problem arises in connection with the very concept of cause since the word "cause" has been applied to widely different concepts. An analysis of these concepts is hardly necessary. Science has abandoned the concept of cause except to denote a functional relationship between or among elements or facts. "When we speak of one thing being the cause of another," says Stewart, "all that we mean is that the two are constantly conjoined, so that when we see the one we may expect the other. These conjunctions we learn from experience alone."[1] A more recent writer voices nearly the same opinion.

The word *cause* in the scientific account of the world belongs only to the early stages in which small preliminary, approximate generalizations are being ascertained with a view to subsequent larger and more invariable laws. We may say 'arsenic causes death' so long as we are ignorant of the precise process by which the result is brought about.

But in a sufficiently advanced science, the word *'cause'* will not occur in any statement of invariable laws. There is, however, a somewhat rough and loose use of the word 'cause' which may be preserved. The approximate uniformities which lead to its pre-scientific employment may trun out to be true in all but very rare and exceptional circumstances, perhaps in all circumstances that actually occur. In such cases it is convenient to be able to speak of the antecedent event as the 'cause' and the subsequent event as the 'effect.' In this sense, provided it is realized that the sequence is not necessary and may have exceptions it is still possible to employ the words 'cause' and 'effect'. It is in this sense, and in this sense only, that we ... intend the words when we speak of one particular event as 'causing' another particular event, as we must sometimes do if we are to avoid intolerable circumlocutions.[2]

Adopting this view of the concept of causation, we understand by the "cause" of crime merely the necessary antecedents or conditions of criminal conduct. Research into the "causes" of crime becomes then a pursuit of these antecedents and the establishment of constants in their relations to criminal conduct. As it is with this particular aspect of criminological research that subsequent chapters will deal, it should be stated at the outset that the terms cause, causal, or causation (or etiology and etiological), will be frequently employed "to avoid intolerable circumlocutions," but that they are to be under-

►SOURCE: *Culture Conflict & Crime,* New York: Social Science Research Council, Bulletin 41, 1938, pp. 17–32. (Editorial adaptations) Reprinted by permission of the Social Science Research Council.

[1] Stewart, Dugald, *Elements of the Philosophy of the Human Mind,* Boston: James Munroe & Co. Vol. I, p. 53.

[2] Russell, Bertrand, "On the Notion of Cause with Application to the Free Will Problem." Lecture eight in his *Our Knowledge of the External World as a Field for Scientific Method in Philosophy.* London: Allen & Unwin, 1914. p. 220.

stood to signify merely the relationship to which reference has been made.

Most researchers on the causes of crime clearly indicate that criminology is still largely in the impressionistic, speculative stage of development. The conclusions of these researches remain hypotheses which require testing before their relevancy to etiological problems can be established. It is, therefore, proper to inquire whether or not the basic concepts underlying causation research are adequate.

The very foundation of studies in crime causation rests upon the definition of "crime" and "criminal." They are the subject matter of traditional criminology. Both are defined by law, but while the limitations which such definition imposes upon research has been lamented by the criminologist, it has not been seriously questioned. Even such astute critics of criminological research as Michael and Adler stated:

> We cannot make empirical investigations of crime and criminals unless we have some basis for differentiating criminal from other behavior and criminals from other persons, which is so precise and definite that we will not confuse them in our observations.... The most precise and least ambiguous definition of crime is that which defines it as behavior which is prohibited by the criminal code.... Not only is the legal definition of a crime precise and unambiguous, but it is the *only possible* definition of crime.[3]

These authors go even further in their interpretation of the concepts under discussion. While they recognize that a person who violates the criminal law thereby becomes a criminal, they add that "the most certain way...to distinguish criminals from non-criminals is in terms of those who have been convicted of crime and those who have not.... Both for practical and for theoretical purposes we must proceed as if that were true.... The criminologist is therefore quite justified in making the convict population the subject of his studies as he does." [4]

In a footnote in another section of their work, however, they raised a question which should be noted here and which they made no attempt to answer: "One of the crucial problems which confronts the criminologist is whether this manner of distinguishing criminals from non-criminals is significant for his purposes." [5] In designating this problem as a "crucial" one, the authors were undoubtedly right. It is *the* crucial problem. It is, furthermore, one to which little attention has been paid by criminologists. Criminology has become the study of crimes and criminals. The social demand for crime prevention and repression, the apparent precision of the legal definitions, and the availability of concrete data, collected during the law enforcement process have all aided in fixing the artificial boundaries of criminology. Such boundaries can not be recognized by science. Yet, specialization, a division of labor, is obviously necessary in research. "The scientific study of any field of phenomena," to quote George Catlin, "requires the general delimitation of that field," but that delimitation must "arise intrinsically from the nature of the subject matter and [must] not be of a purely fortuitous nature, based on some merely external similarities in what is observed." [6] The legal definitions which circumscribe criminological research fall into the class of "external similarities" mentioned. Criminologists have defined the phenomena, which they study "in terms of the most available...[data] thereby stultifying... [their] entire theoretical concepts," to para-

---

[3] Michael, Jerome and Adler, Mortimer J., *Crime, Law, and Social Science*. New York: Harcourt, Brace & Co. 1933. pp. 1-2 and note on p. 2.

[4] *Ibid.* p. 3.

[5] *Ibid.* p. 92.

[6] Catlin, George. "The Delimitation and Mensurability of Political Phenomena." *American Political Science Review*, 21:255–69. May 1937. The term "delimitation" is not to be interpreted as fixing the boundaries of any field or area of research, but as a manner of conceiving the intrinsic or natural properties of the objects studied.

phrase a statement by Frank Ross.[7] We shall attempt to show that the categories set up by the criminal law do not meet the demands of scientists because they are of "a fortuitous nature" and do not "arise intrinsically from the nature of the subject matter."

CRIME NORMS

Among the various instrumentalities which social groups have evolved to secure conformity in the conduct of their members, the criminal law occupies an important place, for its norms are binding upon all who live within the political boundaries of a state and are enforced through the coercive power of that state. The criminal law may be regarded as in part a body of rules, which prohibit specific forms of conduct and indicate punishments for violations. The character of these rules, the kind or type of conduct they prohibit, the nature of the sanction attached to their violation, etc. depend upon the character and interests of those groups in the population which influence legislation. In some states these groups may comprise the majority, in others a minority, but the social values which receive the protection of the criminal law are ultimately those which are treasured by dominant interest groups.[8] In democratic states this essential character of the criminal law is not so easy to discern as in states with other forms of government, but even in democracies the importance of strong minority interest groups can be seen shaping some part of the criminal law.

Our legislators [says Manuel Gamio, in discussing the penal law of Mexico] . . . make laws for the dominant minority, similar in race, tradition and civilization of the people of Europe . . . with the result that the laws are to a large degree copied from foreign patterns. . . . The social majorities, especially the indigenous peoples, remain outside the boundaries of these laws, which ignore their biological needs and the nature of their mental processes, their peculiar indo-hispanic culture, their economic status, aspirations and tendencies.[9]

Among the examples he cites the law which makes the religious and the "natural" or common-law marriages illegal. In the Valley of Teotihuacan, 73 percent of the marriages are illegal, due to no conscious violation but "for the social minority, for whom the laws were made the 'natural' union is abnormal, although for the social majority . . . these unions are perfectly normal."[10] Similar lack of congruence between the laws of a state and the moral ideas of different social groups within its population may be observed wherever the standards of the dominant groups are at variance with those of subjected or submissive ones.[11] The criminal norms, i.e. the conduct norms embodied in the criminal law, change as the values of the dominant groups are modified or as the vicissitudes of social growth cause a reconstitution of these groups themselves and shifts in the focus of power. Thus crimes of yesteryear may be legal conduct today, while crimes in one contemporary state may be legal conduct in another. This lesson of history makes it a safe prediction —an empirical generalization as well founded as any generalization in the natural sciences—that everything the criminal law of any state prohibits today, it will not prohibit at a given future time, unless complete social stagnation sets in, an experience unknown to the social historian.

As a matter of fact, the variability in the definition of crime—and consequently in the meaning attached to the noun "criminal"—is too familiar to the social scientists

---

[7] Ross, Frank. *Fields and Methods of Sociology.* Bernard, L. L. (ed.) 2nd Ed., New York: Farrar & Rhinehart, 1934. p. 463.

[8] This view has been most recently defended by Joseph A. Leighton in his *Social Philosophies in Conflict.* New York: D. Appleton-Century Co. 1937. See especially Ch. XXIV on "Law and Social Ethics."

[9] Gamio, Manuel. *Hacia un Mexico Nuevo.* Mexico City: Manuel Gamio. 1935. pp. 186–87.

[10] *Loc. cit.*

[11] [More specific illustrations may be found in Section V, Selection 30 (eds.)]

to require any demonstration. It should, however, raise in his mind the question of how such variability can permit the formulation of the universal categories required in all scientific research.

The unqualified acceptance of the legal definitions of the basic units or elements of criminological inquiry violates a fundamental criterion of science. The scientist must have freedom to define his own terms, based on the intrinsic character of his material and designating properties in that material which are assumed to be universal. There are indeed numerous instances where public policy, expressed in law, has temporarily restrained, frustrated, or fixed the social ends of scientific research in this or that field. There is also evidence to show the hampering effect which the weight of authority, ascribed to one or more scientists, has had upon the progress of research. In neither case, however, have scientists permitted non-scientists to define the basic *terms* of inquiry.

It should be emphasized at this point that the above comments do not imply that the criminal law or the data about crimes and criminals assembled in the process of its enforcement are not useful in scientific research. They are indeed a rich source for the scientist, but the application of scientific criteria to the selection and classification of these data independently of their *legal* form is essential to render them valuable to science. Nor is it claimed that the study of criminology as traditionally conceived has no value. On the contrary, the *social* value of such research may be at times very great even when the scientific validity of its conclusions is questionable. The results of such study may afford a basis for social action or public policy which is in harmony with dominant attitudes. They may furthermore give social prestige to the investigator and therefore have distinct value to him. What *is* claimed is that if a science of human conduct is to develop, the investigator in this field of research must rid himself of shackles which have been forged by the criminal law. If psychiatry had confined itself to the study of persons legally incompetent by criminal courts, it would no doubt have learned something about mental disease, but if courts had defined and thus classified various forms of mental disease for reasons to be sought in public policy; the psychiatrist would have learned little indeed. It is because he has insisted on defining his own terms that he is now so frequently in conflict with the law, which serves socially defined ends and is not concerned solely with what scientists do. The legislator and the administrator on the one hand, the scientist on the other, speak different languages, fundamentally irreconcilable. This is as it should be, for they are pursuing essentially different ends. The scientist has to have a language of his own in which everyday words, if they are employed, carry a specific meaning significant to him although to others they may have no such import. Confinement to the study of crime and criminals and the acceptance of the categories of specific forms of "crime" and "criminal" as laid down in law renders criminological research theoretically invalid from the point of view of science. The data of the criminal law and the data about crimes and criminals now subservient to legal categories must be "processed" by the scientist before he can use them.

CONDUCT NORMS

Man is born into a culture. He arrives biologically equipped to receive and to adapt knowledge about himself and his relationships to others. His first social contacts begin a life-long process of coordination during which he absorbs and adapts ideas which are transmitted to him formally or informally by instruction or precept. These ideas embody *meanings* attached to customs, beliefs, artifacts, and his own relationships to his fellow men and to social institutions. Looked upon as discrete units, these ideas may be regarded as *cultural elements,* which fit into patterns or configurations of ideas, which tend to become fixed into integrated systems of meanings. Embodied in the mind they become *personality elements,* and the sum total of all such elements may be conveniently called *personality,* as distinguished from the person's biological individuality or his inherited and acquired morphological and physiological traits. Personality then rests upon a biological foundation, which is of the greatest importance in the formation of personality. The biological make-up of an individual fixes limits to personality development, determines the character of the receptive and adaptive processes which transform cultural elements into personality elements, and influences the latter's expressions in social activity.

This definition of personality is not acceptable to all sociologists, not to mention the representatives of other disciplines. In a recent work Gordon W. Allport [12] analyzes no fewer than forty-eight definitions and then proposes one of his own. The one adopted above and previously used by W. I. Thomas, Ellsworth Faris, and others, he criticizes as being the result of a failure to realize that "personality is more than 'the subjective side of culture'—a truth that sociologists and cultural anthropologists with their one-sided studies of 'culture and personality' are likely to forget." [13] This critique assumes that psychologists *know* what personality is, when all that can be said is that for the purpose of psychological research, any sociological definition of personality is inadequate. For the same reason, sociologists insist on defining their own terms of inquiry. In studying social phenomena, they are compelled to pay attention to the person, but they see him primarily as the focus of group influences, a product of social conditioning, a social microcosm. If they prefer to use the term personality as the label for the "subjective aspect of culture," they may be criticized for contributing to the confusion of language by employing a term which is used in so many different senses that it makes rigid thinking difficult, but they can not be criticized for placing upon their inquiries the limitations imposed by their science. This does not mean that the sociologist is not interested in "the dynamic organization within the individual of those psycho-physical systems that determine his unique adjustment to his environment" [14] and that these "psycho-physical systems" can be left out of consideration in the study of social phenomena. It does mean, however, that sociologists are not prepared to investigate these "systems," since they are not psychologists or biologists; and that they have to rely on those scientists to define them. The value of such definitions to the sociologist can then be tested by him in his own way.

If all individuals were biologically alike and subjected to identical cultural influences, all personalities would be identical. If all individuals were biologically alike, but each subjected to different cultural influences, each would present unique personality configurations. Since with the possible exceptions of identical twins, no two individuals can be found that possess the same biological equipment, and since no two persons can ever be assumed to have been exposed to the same cultural influences, at least after the period of early infancy, each total personality is unique. Scientific research in the behavior field is therefore confronted with the problem of offering scientific descriptions of the growth and manifestations of unique personalities in unique biological individuals. The scientific method, however, is not applicable to the study of unique phenomena. It can only deal with classes, kinds, types. If a generalization were made on the basis

---

[12] *Personality: A Psychological Interpretation.* New York: Henry Holt & Co. 1937.
[13] *Ibid.* p. 372.
[14] *Ibid.,* p. 48.

of the findings in a study of a case assumed to be unique, the validity of that generalization could never be tested. Etiological research would be impossible if it could not assume that the data it employs may be grouped into classes, the units of which are identical or may at least be assumed to possess sufficient similarity to be classed together for research purposes.

Every person's existence may be regarded from one point of view at least as being made up of one choice after another. He is constantly faced with the need of deciding whether he should do this or do that. The vast majority of these choices are of an undramatic nature, involving the prosaic routine of daily life and so affected by habit that the deliberative element associated with the idea of "choice" has been submerged and the person's reaction has gradually become automatic. Such being the case, it is the new or the infrequently recurring situation in which he finds himself which most obviously calls into action the exercise of the will and compels him to balance against one another the various possible reactions which the life situation in question arouses, selecting the one he deems most suitable to him at the moment. Whether the manner in which a person responds in a life situation is the result of habit or of deliberation, his reaction may be regarded as an expression of his personality. The character of that reaction depends upon what the life situation involved *means* to him. Some of these situations, at least are sufficiently repetitious and socially so defined that they call for definite responses from the type of person who encounters them. There are attached to them, so to speak, norms which define the reaction or response which in a given person is approved or disapproved by the normative group. The social attitude of this group toward the various ways in which a person might act under certain circumstances has thus been crystallized into a rule, the violation of which arouses a group reaction. These rules or norms may be called *conduct norms*. All personal reaction or activity which they govern may be called *conduct*. The term behavior might well be reserved for all types of reactions—conduct then being a subtype—or for all types *not* defined as conduct.

Conduct, as defined above, can occur only in situations which are defined by some social group and governed by a rule of some sort. Furthermore, all conduct has been socially conditioned, since personality is a social product. Therefore, it is unwise from a scientific point of view to speak of anti-social as opposed to social conduct. These terms belong to the language of social reform. It would seem best, in order to avoid misunderstanding, to speak instead of *normal* and *abnormal conduct,* i.e. conduct in accord with or deviating from a conduct norm.

Conduct norms are the products of social life. Social groups place on the activity of their members certain restrictions which aim to insure the protection of social values which have been injured by unrestricted conduct. A conduct norm is originally an *ex post facto* rule. Generally speaking "breach is the mother of law" [15] and equally a mother of conduct norms.

Every person is identified with a number of social groups, each meeting some biologically conditioned or socially created need. Each of these groups is normative in the sense that within it there grow up norms of conduct applicable to situations created by that group's specific activities. As a member of a given group, a person is not only supposed to conform to the rules which it shares with other groups, but also to those which are peculiarly its own. A person who as a member of a family group—in turn the transmitting agency for the norms which governed the groups from which the parents came—possesses all its norms pertaining to conduct in routine life

---

[15] A phrase borrowed from Seagle, William. "Primitive Law and Professor Malinowski." *American Anthropologist.* 39:275–90. April-June 1937. p. 284.

situations, may also as a member of a play group, a work group, a political group, a religious group, etc., acquire norms which regulate specialized life situations and which sustain, weaken or even contradict the norms earlier incorporated in his personality. The more complex a culture becomes, the more likely it is that the number of normative groups which affect a person will be large, and the greater is the chance that the norms of these groups will fail to agree, no matter how much they may overlap as a result of a common acceptance of certain norms. A conflict of norms is said to exist when more or less divergent rules of conduct govern the specific life situation in which a person may find himself. The conduct norm of one group of which he is a part may permit one response to this situation, the norm of another group may permit perhaps the very opposite response.[16]

For every person, then, there is from the point of view of a given group of which he is a member, a normal (right) and an abnormal (wrong) way of reacting, the norm depending upon the social values of the group which formulated it. *Conduct norms are, therefore, found wherever social groups are found, i.e. universally. They are not the creation of any ONE normative group; they are not confined within political boundaries; they are not necessarily embodied in law.*

These facts lead to the inescapable conclusion that the study of conduct norms would afford a sounder basis for the development of scientific categories than a study of crimes as defined in the criminal law. Such study would involve the isolation and classification of norms into *universal categories,* transcending political and other boundaries, a necessity imposed by the logic of science. The study of how conduct norms develop, how they are related to each other and to other cultural elements, the study of changes and differentials in norm violations and the relationship of such violations to other cultural phenomena, are certainly questions which the sociologists by training and interest might regard as falling within his field. They are questions which scholars such as Lévy-Bruhl and Bayet would include within the framework of what the latter calls *ethology*—not to be confused with John Stuart Mill's characterology to which he gave the same label—or the discipline which attempts to formulate the scientific generalizations governing the structure, growth, and relationships of "moral facts"![17]

The need for finding some basis for criminological research which would extend beyond that of the law has been expressed before. Innumerable definitions of crime have been offered which if not read in their context would appear to go beyond the legal definition. Upon examination, however, almost all of them prove to be the legal norms clothed in a sociological language. Such is not the case, however, with the definition offered by Makarewicz, who can be said to use the term crime in the sense of a conduct norm. "A crime is an act by a member of a given social group, which by the rest of the members of that group is regarded as so injurious or as showing such a degree of antisocial attitude in the actor that the group publicly, overtly and collectively reacts by trying to abrogate some one of his rights (*Güter*)."[18] Znaniecki[19] also attempts to avoid the legal definition and in his latest work we find the following statement which presents his point of view.

---

[16] [For a more detailed treatment of the conflict of norms, see Selection 30 (eds.)]

[17] Cf. especially the introduction in Bayet, Albert. *Le suicide et la morale.* Paris: Alcan, 1922; also *La science des faits moraux.* Paris: Alcan, 1925, especially Ch. I on "L'éthologie" in which the author expresses his indebtedness to Lévy-Bruhl and the latter's work on *La morale et la science des moeurs,* published in 1903.

[18] Makarewicz, J. *Einführung in die Philosophie des Strafrechts.* Stuttgart: Enke, 1906. pp. 79–80.

[19] Znaniecki, Florian. "Social Research in Criminology." *Sociology and Social Research.* 12:207–22. March-April 1928.

Because a collective system has social validity in the eyes of each and all of those who share in it, because it is endowed with a special dignity which merely individual systems lack altogether, individual behavior which endangers a collective system and threatens to harm any of its elements appears quite different from an agression against an individual (unless, of course, such an agression hurts collective values as well as individual values). It is not only a harmful act, but an objectively evil act, a violation of social validity, an offense against the superior dignity of this collective system. . . . The best term to express the specific significance of such behavior is *crime*. We are aware that in using the word in this sense, we are giving it a much wider significance than it has in criminology. *But we believe, that it is desirable for criminology to put its investigations on a broader basis; for strictly speaking, it still lacks a proper theoretic basis.* . . . Legal qualifications are not founded on the results of previous research and not made for the purpose of future research; therefore they have no claim to be valid as scientific generalizations—nor even as heuristic hypotheses.[20]

This extension of the meaning of the term *crime* is not desirable. It is wiser to retain that term for the offenses made punishable by the criminal law and to use the term abnormal conduct for the violations of norms whether legal or not.

---

[20]Znaniecki, Florian. *Social Actions*. New York: Farrar & Rinehart. 1936. pp. 350–52. (The italics are mine.)

2. THE NORMAL AND THE PATHOLOGICAL

EMILE DURKHEIM

CRIME IS PRESENT NOT ONLY IN THE MAjority of societies of one particular species but in all societies of all types. There is no society that is not confronted with the problem of criminality. Its form changes; the acts thus characterized are not the same everywhere; but, everywhere and always, there have been men who have behaved in such a way as to draw upon themselves penal repression. If, in proportion as societies pass from the lower to the higher types, the rate of criminality, i.e., the relation between the yearly number of crimes and the population, tended to decline, it might be believed that crime, while still normal, is tending to lose this character of normality. But we have no reason to believe that such a regression is substantiated. Many facts would seem rather to indicate a movement in the opposite direction. From the beginning of the [nineteenth] century, statistics enable us to follow the course of criminality. It has everywhere increased. In France the increase is nearly 300 percent. There is, then no phenomenon that presents more indisputably all the symptoms of normality, since it appears closely connected with the conditions of all collective life. To make of crime a form of social morbidity would be to admit that morbidity is not something accidental, but, on the contrary, that in certain cases it grows out of the fundamental constitution of the living organism; it would result in wiping out all distinction between the physiological and the pathological. No doubt it is possible that crime itself will have abnormal forms, as, for example, when its rate is unusually high. This excess is, indeed, undoubtedly morbid in nature. What is normal, simply, is the existence of criminality, provided that it attains and does not exceed, for each social type, a certain level, which it is perhaps not impossible to fix in conformity with the preceding rules.[1]

Here we are, then, in the presence of a conclusion in appearance quite paradoxical. Let us make no mistake. To classify crime among the phenomena of normal sociology is not to say merely that it is an inevitable, although regrettable phenomenon, due to the incorrigible wickedness of men; it is to affirm that it is a factor in public health, an integral part of all healthy societies. This result is, at first glance, surprising enough to have puzzled even ourselves for a long time. Once this

▶SOURCE: *Rules of Sociological Method* [Eighth Edition, translated by Sarah A. Solvay and John H. Mueller and edited by George E. G. Catlin] Glencoe, Illinois: The Free Press, 1950, pp. 65–73. Reprinted by permission.

---

[1] From the fact that crime is a phenomenon of normal sociology, it does not follow that the criminal is an individual normally constituted from the biological and psychological points of view. The two questions are independent of each other. This independence will be better understood when we have shown, later on, the difference between psychological and sociological facts.

first surprise has been overcome, however, it is not difficult to find reasons explaining this normality and at the same time confirming it.

In the first place crime is normal because a society exempt from it is utterly impossible. Crime, we have shown elsewhere, consists of an act that offends certain very strong collective sentiments. In a society in which criminal acts are no longer committed, the sentiments they offend would have to be found without exception in all individual consciousnesses, and they must be found to exist with the same degree as sentiments contrary to them. Assuming that this condition could actually be realized, crime would not thereby disappear; it would only change its form, for the very cause which would thus dry up the sources of criminality would immediately open up new ones.

Indeed, for the collective sentiments which are protected by the penal law of a people at a specified moment of its history to take possession of the public conscience or for them to acquire a stronger hold where they have an insufficient grip, they must acquire an intensity greater than that which they had hitherto had. The community as a whole must experience them more vividly, for it can acquire from no other source the greater force necessary to control these individuals who formerly were the most refractory. For murderers to disappear, the horror of bloodshed must become greater in those social strata from which murderers are recruited; but, first it must become greater throughout the entire society. Moreover, the very absence of crime would directly contribute to produce this horror; because any sentiment seems much more respectable when it is always and uniformly respected.

One easily overlooks the consideration that these strong states of the common consciousness cannot be thus reinforced without reinforcing at the same time the more feeble states, whose violation previously gave birth to mere infraction of convention —since the weaker ones are only the prolongation, the attenuated form, of the stronger. Thus robbery and simple bad taste injure the same single altruistic sentiment, the respect for that which is another's. However, this same sentiment is less grievously offended by bad taste than by robbery; and since, in addition, the average consciousness has not sufficient intensity to react keenly to the bad taste, it is treated with greater tolerance. That is why the person guilty of bad taste is merely blamed, whereas the thief is punished. But, if this sentiment grows stronger, to the point of silencing in all consciousness the inclination which disposes man to steal, he will become more sensitive to the offenses which, until then, touched him but lightly. He will react against them, then, with more energy; they will be the object of greater opprobrium, which will transform certain of them from the simple moral faults that they were and give them the quality of crimes. For example, improper contracts, or contracts improperly executed, which only incur public blame or civil damages, will become offenses in law.

Imagine a society of saints, a perfect cloister of exemplary individuals. Crimes, properly so called, will there be unknown; but faults which appear venial to the layman will create there the same scandal that the ordinary offense does in ordinary consciousnesses. If, then, this society has the power to judge and punish, it will define these acts as criminal and will treat them as such. For the same reason, the perfect and upright man judges his smallest failings with a severity that the majority reserve for acts more truly in the nature of an offense. Formerly, acts of violence against persons were more frequent than they are today, because respect for individual dignity was less strong. As this has increased, these crimes have become more rare; and also, many acts violating this sentiment have been introduced into the penal law which were not included there in primitive times.[2]

In order to exhaust all the hypotheses logically possible, it will perhaps be asked why this unanimity does not extend to all collective sentiments without exception. Why should not even the most feeble sentiment gather enough energy to prevent all dissent? The moral consciousness of the society would be present in its entirety in all the individuals, with a vitality sufficient to prevent all acts offending it—the purely conventional faults as well as the crimes. But a uniformity so universal and absolute is utterly impossible; for the immediate physical milieu in which each one of us is placed, the hereditary antecedents, and the social influences vary from one individual to the next, and consequently diversify consciousness. It is impossible for all to be alike, if only because each one has his own organism and that these organisms occupy different areas in space. That is why, even among the lower peoples, where individual originality is very little developed, it nevertheless does exist.

Thus, since there cannot be a society in which the individuals do not differ more or less from the collective type, it is also inevitable that, among these divergences, there are some with a criminal character. What confers this character upon them is not the intrinsic quality of a given act but that definition which the collective conscience lends them. If the collective conscience is stronger, if it has enough authority practically to suppress these divergencies, it will also be more sensitive, more exacting; and, reacting against the slightest deviations with the energy it otherwise displays only against more considerable infractions, it will attribute to them the same gravity as formerly to crimes. In other words, it will designate them as criminal.

Crime is, then, necessary; it is bound up with the fundamental conditions of all social life, and by that very fact it is useful, because these conditions of which it is a part are themselves indispensable to the normal evolution of morality and law.

Indeed, it is no longer possible today to dispute the fact that law and morality vary from one social type to the next, nor that they change within the same type if the conditions of life are modified. But, in order that these transformations may be possible, the collective sentiments at the basis of morality must not be hostile to change, and consequently must have but moderate energy. If they were too strong, they would no longer be plastic. Every pattern is an obstacle to new patterns, to the extent that the first pattern is inflexible. The better a structure is articulated, the more it offers a healthy resistance to all modification; and this is equally true of functional, as of anatomical, organization. If there were no crimes, this condition could not have been fulfilled; for such a hypothesis presupposes that collective sentiments have arrived at a degree of intensity unexampled in history. Nothing is good indefinitely and to an unlimited extent. The authority which the moral conscience enjoys must not be excessive; otherwise no one would dare criticize it, and it would too easily congeal into an immutable form. To make progress, individual originality must be able to express itself. In order that the originality of the idealist whose dreams transcend his century may find expression, it is necessary that the originality of the criminal, who is below the level of his time, shall also be possible. One does not occur without the other.

Nor is this all. Aside from this indirect utility, it happens that crime itself plays a useful role in this evolution. Crime implies not only that the way remains open to necessary changes but that in certain cases it directly prepares these changes. Where crime exists, collective sentiments are sufficiently flexible to take on a new form, and crime sometimes helps to de-

---

[2] Calumny, insults, slander, fraud, etc.

termine the form they will take. How many times, indeed, it is only an anticipation of future morality—a step toward what will be! According to Athenian law, Socrates was a criminal, and his condemnation was no more than just. However, his crime, namely, the independence of his thought, rendered a service not only to humanity but to his country. It served to prepare a new morality and faith which the Athenians needed, since the traditions by which they had lived until then were no longer in harmony with the current conditions of life. Nor is the case of Socrates unique; it is reproduced periodically in history. It would never have been possible to establish the freedom of thought we now enjoy if the regulations prohibiting it had not been violated before being solemnly abrogated. At that time, however, the violation was a crime, since it was an offense against sentiments still very keen in the average conscience. And yet this crime was useful as a prelude to reforms which daily became more necessary. Liberal philosophy had as its precursors the heretics of all kinds who were justly punished by secular authorities during the entire course of the Middle Ages and until the eve of modern times.

From this point of view the fundamental facts of criminality present themselves to us in an entirely new light. Contrary to current ideas, the criminal no longer seems a totally unsociable being, a sort of parasitic element, a strange and unassimilable body, introduced into the midst of society.[3] On the contrary, he plays a definite role in social life. Crime, for its part, must no longer be conceived as an evil that cannot be too much suppressed. There is no occasion for self-congratulation when the crime rate drops noticeably below the average level, for we may be certain that this apparent progress is associated with some social disorder. Thus, the number of assault cases never falls so low as in times of want.[4] With the drop in the crime rate, and as a reaction to it, comes a revision, or the need of a revision in the theory of punishment. If, indeed, crime is a disease, its punishment is its remedy and cannot be otherwise conceived; thus, all the discussions it arouses bear on the point of determining what the punishment must be in order to fulfill this role of remedy. If crime is not pathological at all, the object of punishment cannot be to cure it, and its true function must be sought elsewhere.

---

[3] We have ourselves committed the error of speaking thus of the criminal, because of a failure to apply our rule (*Division du travail social*, pp. 395–96).

[4] Although crime is a fact of normal sociology, it does not follow that we must not abhor it. Pain itself has nothing desirable about it; the individual dislikes it as society does crime, and yet it is a function of normal physiology. Not only is it necessarily derived from the very constitution of every living organism, but it plays a useful role in life, for which reason it cannot be replaced. It would, then, be a singular distortion of our thought to present it as an apology for crime. We would not even think of protesting against such an interpretation, did we not know to what strange accusations and misunderstandings one exposes oneself when one undertakes to study moral facts objectively and to speak of them in a different language from that of the layman.

3. THE LEGAL DEFINITION OF CRIME AND CRIMINALS

WILLIAM L. MARSHALL
WILLIAM L. CLARK

DEFINITION OF CRIME

A crime is any act or omission prohibited by public law for the protection of the public, and made punishable by the state in a judicial proceeding in its own name.[1] It is a public wrong, as distinguished from a mere private wrong or civil injury to an individual.

The development of the law of crimes from private vengeance, when self-help was sanctioned, to the present day, when any taking of the law into one's own hands is frowned upon, is one of the more interesting developments in legal history. During the later centuries of this growth the concept of crime and of criminality has not altered greatly, although it is admitted that the concept of punishment has undergone severe and constant change. New crimes have been formulated during this period and on occasion punishment was changed to fit the criminal instead of the crime, but crime itself remained the same.

It is important to note that the foregoing definition requires the previous existence of a law to warrant public prosecution. This principle of *nullum crimen sine lege,* or *nullum poena sine lege,* has long been accepted in Ango-American jurisprudence, but in the recent past it has been discarded in Nazi Germany, Russia, and certain other countries which have allowed punishment if the act was considered by the court to be "dangerous to society." This principle, of course, also figured heavily in the trial of the war criminals after World War II.

As indicated from the above definition, crime concerns transgressions against the public order, rather than against the moral or private orders. It will be seen that mere intent is not punishable as it is believed to be under the general theory of Christian morality, and even though there be an act or an omission to act, as well as the criminal intent, it is still not a crime unless it offends the general public rather than a private person.

Care must be taken to consider the aforementioned definition of crime as a whole, for other definitions lacking some of its integral parts are fallacious because inac-

▶SOURCE: *A Treatise on the Law of Crimes,* Chicago: Callaghan, Callaghan and Company, 1952, pp. 1–13, 59–60, 160, 228, 230–231, 236, 239–240, 243. (Editorial adaptations.) Reprinted by permission.

[1] "A crime is any wrong which the government deems injurious to the public at large, and punishes through a judicial proceeding in its own name." 1 Bish. Crim. Law, § 32.

A crime, "in a general sense, implies any act done or omitted in violation of public law, and for which the person is liable to punishment by indictment, presentment, or impeachment." Smith v. Smith, 2 Sneed (Tenn.) 473.

curate or insufficiently extensive. Blackstone's definition—"An act committed or omitted in violation of a public law, either forbidding or commanding it," although frequently quoted with approval, is inaccurate. In the first place, it is not the "act omitted" that constitutes a crime, but the omission to act, and, in the second place, the term "public law" is too broad, for it includes many other laws besides those which define and punish crimes. An act is not necessarily a crime because it is prohibited by a public law. It is necessary to look further and ascertain the ground upon which the act is punished and by whom the punishment is imposed. To constitute a crime, it must be punished to protect the public, and it must be punished by the state or other sovereign power.

Violations of Municipal Ordinances. By the weight of authority, the violation of a municipal ordinance, enacted by a city under legislative authority, as in the case of ordinances prohibiting and punishing gaming, and the keeping of gaming houses, bawdy houses, etc., is not a crime, in the proper sense of the term, for such ordinances are not public laws, and the punishment for their violation is imposed by the municipality, and not by the state. Since such ordinances are not consider laws, it is usually held, where a state statute prohibits the same act forbidden by a municipal ordinance, that *both* the state and the municipality may punish whoever commits the offense.

PUBLIC AND PRIVATE WRONGS DISTINGUISHED

As indicated in the preceding section, the law does not take cognizance of offenses against the moral order unless they are prohibited by the legal order as well. In general, the law seeks to remedy private and public wrongs. A *private* wrong, otherwise termed a "tort" or "civil injury," is "an infringement or privation of the civil rights which belong to individuals, considered merely as individuals." A *public* wrong or "crime" is "a breach and violation of the public rights and duties due to the whole community, considered as a community, in its social aggregate capacity." It is a wrong that affects the whole community, and not merely individual members of the community, and therefore the public good requires the state to interfere and punish the wrongdoer. The punishment is imposed for the protection of the public, and not because of the injury to the individual. The latter must seek redress in a civil action. The crime arises when the restoration of the *status quo* is insufficient satisfaction for the offense, and it is believed that "the State should punish that man."

Illustrations. For example, if I go upon another man's land wrongfully, but without committing a breach of the peace, I commit a wrong which does not affect the other members of the community to such an extent as to require the state to punish me. I am merely liable in an action for damages by the individual whose rights I have infringed. This is not a public wrong, or crime, but a mere private wrong, or tort. On the same principle, it is a mere private wrong if I maintain a nuisance which affects a single individual only, or, a common law, if I obtain another man's property by a mere lie.

On the other hand, it is a public wrong, or crime, if I go upon another's land under such circumstances as to render me guilty of a breach of the public peace, or if I maintain a nuisance on or near a public highway, so as to affect all who pass, or in a thickly-settled community, so as to affect the whole community, or if I cheat another out of his property by using false weights or measures. In these cases the wrong affects the whole community to such an extent that the public welfare requires the state to interfere and punish me.

Crimes as Private Wrongs. Since the same act may be offensive to a private individual as well as to the public generally, it may be a tort as well as a crime. From early times this was true of the lesser offenses, but since the common punishment for the serious crimes was death and forfeiture of goods as a practical matter, no recovery for the tort was possible, but now civil recovery for the tort, arising out of the same act constituting the crime, is uniformly permitted.

The Distinguishing Characteristics. Since the same act may be both a crime and a civil injury—a crime for the purpose of a prosecution by the state, and a civil injury for the purpose of an action by the individual injured—it is obvious that the tendency of the act cannot be relied upon alone to determine in any particular case whether it is a crime, and whether the proceeding therefor is a criminal prosecution. The purpose and nature of the proceeding must be considered. As was said by Austin:

> The difference between crimes and civil injuries is not to be sought in a supposed difference between their tendencies, but in the difference between the mode wherein they are respectively pursued, or wherein the sanction is applied in the two cases. An offense which is pursued at the discretion of the injured party. or his representative, is a civil injury. An offense which is pursued by the sovereign, or by a subordinate of the sovereign is a crime.

Principles of Law Based upon This Distinction. It is well to bear in mind the distinction between public wrongs or crimes and mere private wrongs or civil injuries, for many important principles of law are based upon it. Thus, by reason of the fact that a crime is punished for the protection of the public, and not merely because of the injury to the individual, there are many acts which render the doer criminally responsible, notwithstanding the consent of the individual against whom they are committed. For the same reason, it is ordinarily no defense in a criminal prosecution to show that the individual particularly injured was himself committing or attempting to commit an offense, or that he was guilty of contributory negligence, or that he has settled with the wrongdoer, or condoned the offense, or recovered damages in a civil action.

CLASSIFICATION OF CRIMES

Crimes are divided into three classes or grades. These are:

1. Treason.
2. Felonies.
3. Misdemeanors.

The generic term "crime" includes all offenses against the public order. However, depending upon the grievousness of the offense, and the severity of the punishment therefor, crimes are commonly divided into three classes, treason, felonies, and misdemeanors.[2]

Treason. At common law, treason was divided into high treason and petit treason. *High* treason was the compassing of the king's death and aiding and comforting his enemies, the forging or counterfeiting of his coin, the counterfeiting of the privy seal, or the killing of the chancellor, or either of the king's justices; and *petit* treason was where a wife murdered her husband, an ecclesiastic his lord or ordinary, or a servant his master.

In this country, treason against the United States is defined by the constitution of the United States, and consists in the levying of war against the United States or

---

[2] The impeachment of President Johnson for "high crimes and misdemeanors" has generally been considered bad law as well as poor rhetoric. Blackstone speaks of "crimes and misdemeanors" (4 Bl. Comm. 5), and there are reported cases in which the distinction is made. This, however, is wrong. The term "crime" includes every offense, whether it be treason or felony, or merely a misdemeanor. Thus, in the case of In re Bergin, 31 Wis. 383, it was held that any wrong against the public which is punishable in a criminal proceeding prosecuted by the state in its own name, or in the name of the people, or of the sovereign, is a "crime," within the meaning of the constitutional prohibition against involuntary servitude, except as a punishment for a crime, and that the term, therefore, includes both felonies and misdemeanors.

adhering to their enemies, giving them aid and comfort. In state constitutions or statutes there are similar definitions of treason against the state. What was petit treason at common law is in this country simply murder or manslaughter, and a felony.

Felonies. The chief division of crimes is into *felonies* and *misdemeanors*. The distinction is of great importance.[3]

At *common law,* felonies were those offenses which occasioned forfeiture of the lands and goods of the offender, and to which might be added death or other punishment, according to the degree of guilt. Generally the punishment was death, in addition to such forfeiture, subject, however, to the benefit of clergy. The common-law felonies were murder, manslaughter, rape, sodomy, robbery, larceny, arson, burglary, and perhaps mayhem.

In this country there is no forfeiture of property on conviction of crime, but the distinction between felonies and misdemeanors is still recognized, and, as was stated above, it is very important. According to the weight of authority, in the absence of any statute on the subject, we recognize as felonies all those crimes, enumerated above, that were felonies at common law, and only those crimes, whatever might be the punishment imposed.

In addition to the common-law offenses which we have adopted from England, it is generally believed that statutory offenses created by the English Parliament before 1607, when Virginia was settled, are likewise considered crimes in America if such statutes are applicable to local conditions. Many states by statute have listed the early English statutes which are binding within the state.

By Statute. Many new felonies have, from time to time, been created by statute, and what were merely misdemeanors at common law have in some cases been raised to the grade of felony. Often felonies are created by declaring in express terms that the offense shall be deemed or taken to be a felony, but they may be created by implication. Thus, if a statute creating an offense provides for the punishment of accessaries as such, the offense must be deemed a felony, for, as we shall see, it is only in the case of felonies that there can be accessaries. Where the court or the jury is given the discretion to impose a fine or imprisonment in the penitentiary, a majority of the courts have held that such offenses so punished are felonies irrespective of what punishment is actually imposed. An offense cannot be considered as impliedly made a felony by statute, unless such an intention on the part of the legislature is clear, and the implication is a necessary one.

Offenses Punishable by Death or Confinement in State Prison. By statute in some states it is expressly declared that all offenses that *are punishable,* or that *may be punished,* by death, or by confinement in the state prison, are felonies. In a few states the confinement must be at hard labor. Some of the statutes apply only to the term "felony," when used in a statute.

Under such a statute, it is the *possible* punishment—the punishment that may be imposed—that determines whether an of-

---

[3] To show the importance of the distinction: In felonies there may be principals and accessaries. In misdemeanors all are principals. Unintentionally causing death in committing some felony is murder, while to unintentionally cause death in committing a misdemeanor is manslaughter only. To constitute burglary at common law, the house must be broken and entered with intent to commit a felony. Intent to commit a misdemeanor is not enough. In making an arrest for a felony, a warrant is not necessary, while it is generally necessary to authorize arrest for a misdemeanor. In making an arrest for a felony, but not in making an arrest for a misdemeanor, the accused may be killed, if he cannot otherwise be taken.

The distinction is also important as regards questions of procedure. Thus, in some jurisdictions, in the case of felonies, but not in the case of misdemeanors, the prosecution must be by indictment, and not by information or complaint, the accused must be present during the trial, and the indictment must expressly allege that the act was done "feloniously."

fense is a felony, and not the punishment that is actually imposed in a particular case.

Under the federal statutes a felony is an offense punishable by death or by imprisonment for more than one year.

Misdemeanors. All crimes that are not treasons or felonies are misdemeanors.

INFAMOUS CRIMES

The term "infamous" was applied at common law to crimes disqualifying convicts as witnesses. They included treason and felonies, and also forgery and other misdemeanors affecting, by falsehood and fraud, the administration of justice, such as perjury, conspiracy to falsely accuse one of crime, etc., but did not include cases of cheating, assault and battery, and other mere breaches of the peace, etc. It was the nature of the offense, and not the punishment, that rendered it infamous.

The disqualification of witnesses for this cause has been generally abolished or restricted to convictions for perjury. Federal and state constitutions and statutes generally provide that none shall be held to answer for an infamous crime except after presentment or indictment by a grand jury. An offense is now held to be infamous within such provisions according to whether the punishment which may be inflicted is capital or imprisonment in a penitentiary with or without hard labor. Where an accused public official would lose his right to hold his office of highway commissioner if convicted of the offense charged, the Illinois Supreme Court held that he was improperly tried upon an information, since he could be prosecuted only upon an indictment by a grand jury. Infamous crime is also a bar to certain rights of citizenship, such as holding public office, or becoming a juror or elector.

* * *

CRIMES MALA IN SE AND MALA PROHIBITA

Originally crimes were divided into those that were *mala in se,* or wrong in themselves, and those that were *mala prohibita,* or wrong merely because they were prohibited and punished by statute. Crimes *mala in se* included all common-law offenses, for the common law punished no act that was not wrong in itself. They included, in addition to felonies, all breaches of the public peace or order, injuries to person or property, outrages upon public decency or good morals, and wilful and corrupt breaches of official duty. Acts *mala prohibita* included any act forbidden by statute, but not otherwise wrong.

This distinction is obvious, but the use that is made of it is frequently unfounded, and even as early as 1822 an English judge said that the distinction had long since been exploded.

Presently it seems to get its greatest use by misinformed or lethargic courts who insert it as a prop to rationalize preconceived results.

CRIMINAL INTENT IN GENERAL

Necessity for a Criminal Intent or Mens Rea. It is a general rule, applicable both to common-law and to statutory crimes, that there is no crime unless there is a so-called criminal intent, often referred to as mens rea. The legislature, and infrequently the courts, however, may punish acts when the mind is entirely innocent, and on grounds of public policy may dispense with the necessity for a criminal intent in some cases.

Necessity for Criminal Intent or Mens Rea at Common Law. As has been seen earlier in this work, a crime consists in a *combination* of a criminal act and a criminal intent, or *mens rea*. The character of the criminal act will be considered in subsequent chapters; for the present, suffice it to say that it is a necessary ingredient of a crime. The other ingredient, that of intent, is likewise essential, although often thought otherwise. The maxim is, *"Actus non facit reum, nisi mens sit rea."* A wrongful act and a wrongful intent must concur. "It is a sacred principal of criminal jurisprudence," said the Tennessee court, "that the intention to commit the crime is of the essence of the crime, and to hold that a man shall be held criminally responsible for an offense, of the commission of which he was ignorant at the time, would be intolerable tyranny." It is because of this principle, as we shall presently see at some length, that the law does not punish children of tender age and insane persons, who, by reason of their mental incapacity, are incapable of understanding the nature of their acts, or of distinguishing between right and wrong, persons acting in good faith and without negligence under a mistake of fact, and persons under necessity for compulsion.

Mens Rea Defined. *Mens rea* is too often used synonymously with criminal intent. To preserve the integrity of any definition of *mens rea* it seems more prudent to say that *mens rea* is the nonphysical element which, combined with the act of the accused, makes up the crime charged. Most frequently it is the criminal intent, or the guilty mind, but since it may be supplied by criminal negligence which is oftentimes directly contrary to the intention of the actor, the term "intent" is not sufficiently inclusive. Courts and writers labeling *mens rea* simply as criminal intention frequently provide for the unintended acts by classifying them under the anomalous term of constructive intent. Thus is the confusion heightened.

Certain as is the requirement for *mens rea* its exact nature is uncertain and quite confusing. Professors Sayre and Perkins have written learnedly on this subject along with many other legal scholars who have expanded their treatment of this basic proposition to a greater extent than is possible in this text. To them reference is made for more exhaustive and more historical treatment.

* * *

NECESSITY FOR A CRIMINAL ACT

In General. To constitute a crime there must be a criminal act, as well as a criminal intent. The law does not punish a mere intent to commit a crime. There is a sufficient act, however,

1. Where a person solicits another to commit a felony, or in some jurisdictions a misdemeanor, though the other may not do so.
2. Where a person attempts to commit a crime, though he may not succeed in accomplishing his purpose.
3. Where two or more agree or conspire to commit a crime or do any other unlawful act, though no attempt may be made to carry out the conspiracy.

* * *

PRINCIPALS IN THE FIRST DEGREE

Definition. A principle in the first degree is the one who actually commits the crime, either by his own hand, or by an inanimate agency, or by an innocent human agent.

* * *

PRINCIPALS IN THE SECOND DEGREE

Definition. A principal in the second degree is one who is present when a felony is committed by another, and who aids or abets in its commission. To constitute one a principal in the second degree—

1. There must be a guilty principal in the first degree.
2. The principal in the second degree must be present when the offense is committed. But his presence may be constructive.
3. He must aid or abet the commission of the offense. Some participation is necessary, though it need not necessarily be active. Mere knowledge of the offense and mental approval is not enough.

* * *

ACCESSARIES BEFORE THE FACT

Definition. An accessary before the fact is one who procures, commands, or counsels the commission of a felony by another, but who is not present, either actually or constructively, when the felony is committed. To constitute one an accessary before the fact—

1. There must be a guilty principal in the first degree.
2. The accessary must be neither actually nor constructively present when the offense is committed.
3. There must be some participation by way of procurement, command, or counsel. Mere knowledge that the offense is to be committed, or even mental approval, is not enough.

* * *

ACCESSARIES AFTER THE FACT

Definition. An accessary after the fact is one who receives, relieves, comforts, or assists another personally, with knowledge that he has committed a felony. To constitute one an accessary after the fact—

1. A felony must have been committed, and it must have been complete at the time of the relief or assistance.
2. The accused must know that the felony has been committed by the person received, relieved, or assisted.
3. The assistance must be rendered to the felon personally.

4. Under the federal statute the aid must be given to hinder or prevent the apprehension, trial or punishment of the principal.

* * *

ACT FOR WHICH ACCOMPLICES ARE RESPONSIBLE

In General. As a general rule, no one can be punished as an aider or abettor, or as an accessary before the fact, for a crime, to the commission of which he has never expressly or impliedly given his consent.

But if a person joins in an attempt to commit one crime, by aiding, abetting, counseling, or commanding its commission, he is to be considered as assenting to any crime which is committed by his associates in the attempt to execute the common purpose, and which is a natural or probable consequence of said attempt.

To render one guilty of a crime as a principal in the second degree or accessary before the fact, the act must constitute a crime on the part of the person committing it. There must be a guilty principal in the first degree.

Acts for Which Accomplice Is Not Responsible. As stated above, it may be laid down as an undoubted general proposition that no man can be properly convicted of a crime as principal in the second degree or accessary before the fact if he never expressly or impliedly consented to the commission of the crime.

4. THE LEGAL BASIS OF DELINQUENCY

THORSTEN SELLIN
MARVIN E. WOLFGANG

A CLEAR DEFINITION OF FUNDAMENTAL CONcepts is a prime requisite for all research. Therefore, any study of delinquency must first establish the meaning of this term. This task has often been neglected by criminologists who have spent more time on examining the terms and concepts of the independent variables than of the dependent one—delinquency—which they have hoped to explain. As Mack has written: "It is impossible to undertake any such [etiological] research without having to decide first of all what you mean by delinquency. This is a condition which most textbooks and research papers acknowledge in their first paragraph and then go on to ignore."[1] The need for a definition of delinquency is equally stressed by Tappan, who states:

Certainly there is no more central question in this study and probably none more difficult to answer. Yet it is important to see the nature of delinquency as clearly as possible and to understand the problems that have impeded efforts at definition . . . , because on the interpretation of the term depend all those vital differences which set off the juvenile delinquent from the adult criminal at the one extreme and from the nonoffender at the other.[2]

These quotations may appear strange in view of the fact that definitions of delinquency exist in laws that provide the basis for dealing with juvenile offenders. It is these definitions that have been used in the compilation of official statistics about delinquency and delinquents, on which so many studies have relied, or in classifying delinquents, when the researcher has had access to the original records of public agencies. Indeed, innumerable variables have been statistically correlated with the events covered by the legal terms "crime" and "delinquency" and provocative theories about these phenomena have been formulated, but even in the most sophisticated researches little or no account has been taken of the great diversity of conduct represented, not only by the inclusive designation of "delinquency" but even by such legal categories as "offenses against the person," "offenses against property," criminal homicide, rape, robbery, burglary, larceny, and others. This, we think, is a cogent reason for the dissatisfaction with present definitions of juvenile delinquency and for the demand that something be

▶SOURCE: *The Measurement of Delinquincy*, New York: John Wiley & Sons, Inc., 1964, Chapter 6, pp. 71-86. Reprinted by permission of John Wiley & Sons and the authors.

---

[1] J. A. Mack, "Juvenile delinquency research: A criticism," *Sociol. Rev.* N.S. 3:47-64 (July 1955), p. 56.

[2] Paul W. Tappan, *Juvenile Delinquency* (613 pp. New York: McGraw Hll, 1949), p. 3. Quoted by permission of publisher.

done about it. But first, let us look at what the law calls delinquency.

This involves not only an examination of the specific statutes, which in creating juvenile courts also prescribed the scope of their jurisdiction in terms of the kinds of conduct and classes of juveniles affected, but also of the criminal law, since all juvenile court statutes in the United States provide that a child is a juvenile delinquent if he commits any act which would be a crime if done by an adult. Were delinquency limited to such conduct, our task would be simpler, but all jurisdictions, except the federal, label a variety of other forms of conduct as delinquency. Sussmann has listed all of them in the order of their frequency and has shown, for each state, which ones are specified.[3] They number thirty-four, varying from truancy, incorrigibility, and running away from home to using tobacco in any form. No state has adopted all of them, but Indiana leads with seventeen; Maine, at the other extreme, names but one—"growing up in idleness and crime." Some of them could equally well come under the heading of dependency or neglect because the distinctions are often difficult to draw. As a matter of fact, some states classify as delinquency a condition which other states define as dependency or neglect.

The problem is not limited to the United States, as is seen from the following statement:

> In many countries the meaning of juvenile delinquency is so broad that it embraces practically all manifestations of juvenile behavior. Under the influence of certain theories, juvenile delinquency is identified either with maladjustment or with forms of juvenile behavior which actually are more a reflection of poor living conditions or inadequate laws and regulations than a delinquent inclination. Thus, disobedience, stubbornness, lack of respect, being incorrigible, smoking without permission, collecting cigarette butts, hawking and the like are considered juvenile delinquency. Very often these "forms of delinquency" are hidden in statistical data under the vague term "other offenses." More often than would be desirable, the "offenders" are lumped together with real ones not only because services and institutions for them are not available but also because, according to some policies and practices, all of them are considered "maladjusted" and sent to the same institutions. The result is an artificial inflation of the juvenile delinquency problem and its "forms."[4]

Confusion results from these legal definitions of delinquency.

> It is reasonable to believe [says Tappan] that all, or at least a vast majority of, normal children sometimes indulge in forms of behavior that might come within the purview of the juvenile court. Whether a given child will get into trouble depends largely on the interpretation that is attached to his conduct and the willingness or ability of the parent to deal with it. Considering the broad scope of legal provisions on insubordination, "questionable behavior," "injuring or endangering the morals or health of himself or others," truancy, running away, trespassing, and petty theft, it would be difficult to find any paragons of virtue who would be wholly exonerated of delinquency, save through parental understanding and leniency.[5]

The lack of uniformity among jurisdictions makes comparative studies especially difficult. Although violations of criminal laws and ordinances are generally considered "delinquency" when committed by a juvenile, many states give exclusive jurisdiction to the criminal court if the violation is of a certain kind. This holds true for capital crimes in the federal code and in the laws of eleven states (Colorado, Georgia, Iowa, Maryland, Massachusetts, Minnesota, South Carolina, Tennessee, Delaware, Vermont, and West Virginia) and for crimes punishable by life impris-

---

[3] Frederick B. Sussmann, *Law of Juvenile Delinquency* (96 pp. New York: Oceana Publications, 1959), pp. 21-22.

[4] The Second United Nations Congress on The Prevention of Crime and the Treatment of Offenders (London, August 8–20, 1960). *New Forms of Juvenile Delinquency: Their Origin, Prevention and Treatment*. Report prepared by the Secretariat, A/Conf. 17/7.

[5] Paul W. Tappan, *op. cit.*, p. 32.

onment in the first eight of these mentioned; for murder in five states (Kansas, Louisiana, Montana, New Jersey, and Pennsylvania); for homicide (Texas); for manslaughter (Montana); for rape (Louisiana, Tennessee); for attempted rape (Louisiana); for crimes of violence (Illinois); for crimes punishable by more than ten years imprisonment (North Carolina); for imfamous crimes (Maine); for traffic law (Indiana, New Jersey) or motor vehicle law offenses (Rhode Island); and for "any crime" (Florida).[6] Juveniles prosecuted for these offenses in the jurisdictions just mentioned fall outside of "delinquency" properly speaking. In studies of the illegal conduct of juveniles, they would, of course, have to be included, but if they have not been processed by juvenile courts they do not figure in the records of these courts which have so often been the chief source of data for delinquency studies.

Comparative analysis of such studies is complicated by still another problem, namely the lack of a standard definition of who is capable of engaging in "delinquency," both as to age and sex. Considering the fifty-two jurisdictions—constituted of fifty states, the District of Columbia, and the federal government—anyone under 21 years of age can commit a "delinquency" and therefore be adjudged a juvenile delinquent in 4 of the jurisdictions; under 19 in 2; under 18 in 28; under 17 in 10; and under 16 in 8. This is true for both sexes, but in one state that has a maximum limit of 19 for males, the limit is 21 for females; in two states these maxima are respectively 16 and 18, and in five states, 17 and 18. The effect of these diverse age limits on interstate research is easy to imagine, unless comparable age and sex groups have been used (Table I).

[6] Based on Sussman, *op. cit.*, pp. 65–77, as adapted from Paul W. Tappan, "Children and youth in the criminal court," *Ann. Amer. Acad. polit. and soc. Sci.* 261:128–136 (January 1949), pp. 129–130.

Except for the jurisdictions mentioned earlier, no state has given criminal courts exclusive jurisdiction over juveniles, but most have given them concurrent jurisdiction, which means that a juvenile in these states may, under certain circumstances, be adjudged a criminal rather than a delinquent. The scope of this power varies greatly among the jurisdictions, as may be seen from the tabulation on page 75, which takes only juvenile males into consideration.[7]

Although it can be seen that more than half of the jurisdictions (28) limit delinquency to illegal conduct by those under 18 years of age, there could be substantial errors made, for instance, in comparing the results of studies made in the eleven states, in which any juvenile may be prosecuted for crime, with those made in the two states (New Hampshire and Virginia) where criminal courts have no jurisdiction at all over those under 18.

Table I

Where the original jurisdiction of the Juvenile Court extends to age	The Criminal Court has overlapping or concurrent jurisdiction over juveniles	
	above the age of	in_____ jurisdictions
21	11	1
	17	3
19	all ages	1
	14	1
18	all ages	11
	19–21	1
	11–21	1
	13	5
	15	8
	none	2
17	all ages	2
	9	1
	11	1
	15	1
	16	1
	none	4
16	all ages	2
	14	1
	none	5

[7] Compiled from Sussman, *ibid.*

In most states there is no lower age limit set for the adjudication of a child as delinquent; Mississippi and Texas place that limit at ten and New York at seven.[8]

Our brief discussion of how diversely "delinquency" and "delinquents" are defined in American statutes and how judicial administration may affect the assignment of an offense or an offender to the criminal or the delinquency area has been pursued to indicate one aspect of the difficulties involved in securing uniform and reliable data for the measurement of delinquency. Although these difficulties are especially great when data from different jurisdictions are involved, they are not absent in studies dealing with a single state or community. So long as the definition of delinquency in law in any jurisdiction includes so many ill-defined kinds of conduct and admits of the exercise of wide administrative discretion at all levels in handling juvenile offenders, the problem of standardization of data needed for measurement purposes will always face the student. Indeed, it has forced us, in the present research to develop a system of classifying delinquent acts which is in a sense independent of the labels attached to them by the law.

THE PENNSYLVANIA JUVENILE COURT ACT

The source documents used in our study are records of various kinds, compiled by the police of Philadelphia in connection with their routine enforcement of the law. So far as juveniles are concerned, such enforcement is circumscribed by what is considered to be delinquent conduct by the legislature of the Commonwealth of Pennsylvania and recorded in an act of June 2, 1933, Public Law 1433, with amendments of 1937, 1939, 1953. Section I, Subsection 2 and 4, contains the following definitions.

(2) The word "child," as used in this act, means a minor under the age of eighteen years.
(4) The words "delinquent child" include:
   (a) A child who has violated any law of the Commonwealth or ordinance of any city, borough or township;
   (b) A child who, by reason of being wayward or habitually disobedient, is uncontrolled by his or her parent, guardian, custodian, or legal representative;
   (c) A child who is habitually truant from school or home;
   (d) A child who habitually so deports himself or herself as to injure or endanger the morals or health of himself, herself, or others.

As can be seen, Section 1, Subsection 4a, defines delinquency as any act, which if committed by an adult would be a crime; and Subsections 4b, c, and define delinquency in terms of an age status and constituting acts or conditions that could not be attributed to an adult.

THE STANDARD JUVENILE COURT ACT

The definition of delinquency, such as the one used in the Pennsylvania statute, is no longer supported by leading authorities. It is challenged, in particular, by the drafters of the Standard Juvenile Court Act. The first edition of this Act was published by the National Probation Association in 1925. It was revised and reissued in 1928, 1933, 1943, 1949, and 1959. Prepared by the Committee on Standard Juvenile Court Act of the National Probation and Parole Association, in cooperation with the National Council of Juvenile Court Judges and the United States Children's Bureau, the new act emphasizes the basic concept in *parens patriae*. Under the act, Article 1, Sections 2e and 2f, a "child" is defined as a person under 18 years of age and a "minor" as any person under 21

---

[8] Sol Rubin, "The legal character of juvenile delinquency," *Ann. Amer. Acad. polit. and soc. Sci.*, 261:1–8 (January 1949), p. 6.

years of age. As in the 1943 and 1949 editions of the Act, the terms "delinquency" and "neglect" are avoided. Article 2, Section 8, Subsection 1 reads:

[Except as otherwise provided herein, the court shall have exclusive original jurisdiction in proceedings.]
1. Concerning any child who is alleged to have violated any federal, state, or local law or municipal ordinance, regardless of where the violation occurred; or any minor alleged to have violated any federal, state, or local law or municipal ordinance prior to having become 18 years of age. Such minor shall be dealt with under the provisions of this act relating to children. Jurisdiction may be taken by the court of the district where the minor is living or found, or where the offense is alleged to have occurred. When a minor 18 years of age or over already under the jurisdiction of the court is alleged to have violated any federal, state, or local law or municipal ordinance, the juvenile court shall have concurrent jurisdicition with the criminal court.[9]

This delimitation of the scope of juvenile delinquency has received recent support from two sources. The Second United Nations Congress on the Prevention of Crime and the Treatment of Offenders, London 1960, passed a resolution that stated: "The Congress considers that the scope of the problem of juvenile delinquency should not be unnecessarily inflated ... it recommends that the meaning of the term juvenile delinquency should be restricted as far as possible to violations of the criminal law." [10]

The New York Joint Legislative Committee on Court Reorganization, in its draft of a Family Court Act, has taken a similar stand:

"Juvenile delinquent" is defined in the proposed legislation as "a person over seven and less than sixteen years of age who does any act which, if done by an adult would constitute a crime, and requires supervision, treatment or confinement." This definition, considerably narrower than the current definition, accords with the common understanding.[11]

We believe that statistical collections and analyses in terms of the definitions of delinquency must adopt this delimitation if they are to provide a useful measurement or index of the volume, character or trend of delinquency.

Although the present research has had to depend on the definition of delinquency found in the Juvenile Court Act of Pennsylvania in selecting an appropriate sample of delinquent acts for analysis, we decided that it would be impossible to utilize the data on the "juvenile status" offenses in the construction of an index to delinquency. Such offenses are viewed by most writers only as predelinquent behavior or symptomatic of potential delinquent behavior. That is why it is often argued that they should not be labeled delinquency, and that is the chief reason behind the recommendations of the Standard Juvenile Court Act.

Truancy, for example, is a violation of a regulation requiring compulsory school attendance, but the explanation for truancy involves parental influence or lack of it or the failure of educational facilities and authorities to solve purely educational problems. To call the absence from classes delinquency places the truant in the same category with more serious violators of substantive legal codes. Shulman suggests: "Since chronic truancy often antedates serious delinquency by several years and may serve as a valuable warning signal of impending serious behavior disorder, we may raise the question of whether its formal handling as an aspect of juvenile delinquency is a proper one." [12]

---

[9] "Standard Juvenile Court Act," *National Probation and Parole Assoc. J.* 5:323–391 (October 1959), p. 344.

[10] See *Report Prepared by the Secretariat* (iv, 95 pp., New York: United Nations, 1961), p. 61.

[11] Joint Legislative Committee on Court Reorganization, II, "The Family Court Act," New York State, Daniel G. Albert, Chairman (Albany, N.Y., 1962), p. 6.

[12] Harry M. Shulman, *Juvenile Delinquency in American Society* (New York: Harper, 1961), p. 33.

The law presumes that children belong at home, and consequently a child who runs away from home is considered delinquent. But as in the case of incorrigibility and ungovernable behavior, the problems of family neglect are the important issues to be considered by the juvenile court in handling these children rather than behavior that constitutes serious and injurious threats to other members of the community.

Excluding these and similar acts from use in the measurement of delinquency and concentrating only on violations by juveniles of the law and ordinances that, were they committed by adults, would be considered crimes, reduce but do not eliminate the problem of legal definitions and classifications. The substantive content of the definitions of these offenses in the criminal law therefore has to be considered since it is common practice in official statistics of delinquency, especially in police statistics, to classify delinquents and their conduct in categories designated by labels derived from the criminal law.

The Labels of the Criminal Law. Since police agencies are entrusted with the enforcement of the criminal law, it is both obvious and natural that, in the investigation of offenses, they think in terms of the specific definitions of crime contained in the law. When a complaint is made and they investigate the incident, or when they observe an offense being committed, its objective characteristics lead them to call it burglary, robbery, larceny, etc. And when they prepare reports on the incidents on some standard forms, these labels are recorded and furnish the basis for later periodic tabulations of the number of different offenses the police have dealt with whether or not an offender is taken into custody. The result is that when juveniles are apprehended by the police, their offenses are not labeled "delinquency" but are given appropriate criminal designations or, in the case of juvenile status offenses, a specific designation supplied by the juvenile court law, such as truancy, runaway, incorrigibility, etc.

No police department, to our knowledge, publishes any statistics of juvenile *offenses*. Since most offenses are committed by unknown persons, those committed by juveniles can be segregated only when an apprehension is made. Even then, however, the practice is to publish only statistics of juvenile *delinquents* without reference to the number of offenses of different legal categories that have been "cleared" by their apprehension. In any event, such statistics are commonly relied on today as indicators of the movement and character of juvenile delinquency. Therefore, it becomes necessary to ask if (a) the criminal law labels best characterize delinquency and (b) if customary practices of statistical classification of juvenile offenses present the best picture of such delinquency.

Answers to these questions are complicated by the fact that the problems they involve are not independent of one another. The criminal law of a state may contain a very large number of distinctive crime designations, several hundreds of them, but when police departments record offenses with a view to their later inclusion in statistics, they are accustomed to use relatively few such designations and give the same label to a variety of offenses that resemble one another in some way. This practice has become more and more common and has been greatly stimulated by the formulation of the Uniform Classification of Offenses in the early 1930's. This classification is used in national statistics of offenses known to the police and of persons charged with offenses and published in *Uniform Crime Reports* issued by the FBI and based on reports now submitted by most civil police agencies in the United States. The classification, as slightly revised in 1958, contains 26 offense categories. Police agencies periodically submit reports to the FBI on standard forms containing these categories; and to facilitate the preparation of these reports the police now tend to label offenses not according to the more specific designations in the criminal law but by the code numbers and titles used in the Uniform Classification.

UNIFORM CLASSIFICATION OF OFFENSES

Part 1

1. Criminal homicide
   a. Murder and non-negligent manslaughter
   b. Manslaughter by negligence
2. Forcible rape
3. Robbery
4. Aggravated assault
5. Burglary—breaking or entering
6. Larceny-theft (except auto theft)
   a. $50 and over in value
   b. Under $50 in value
7. Auto theft

Part 2

8. Other assaults
9. Forgery and counterfeiting
10. Embezzlement and fraud
11. Stolen property: Buying, receiving, possessing
12. Weapons: Carrying, possessing, etc.
13. Prostitution and commercialized vice
14. Sex offenses (except forcible rape, prostitution, and commercialized vice)
15. Offenses against the family and children
16. Narcotic drug laws
17. Liquor laws (except drunkenness)
18. Drunkenness
19. Disorderly conduct
20. Vagrancy
21. Gambling
22. Driving while intoxicated
23. Violation of road and driving laws
24. Parking violations
25. Other violations of traffic and motor vehicle laws
26. All other offenses

Each of the titles in the above classification is derived from the criminal law but of necessity each covers a considerable variety of illegal conduct. When juvenile delinquency which violates the criminal law is subsumed under them, the result is a highly simplified and considerably distorted picture of that delinquency. A few illustrations will suffice. They will be limited largely to some of the titles of offenses which in *Uniform Crime Reports* are considered as "index crimes," that is, susceptible of use as a measurement of criminality. These are murder and non-negligent manslaughter, forcible rape, robbery, aggravated assault, burglary-breaking and entering, larceny or theft of property valued at 50 dollars or more, and auto theft (motor vehicle theft). It should be recalled that so far as juveniles are concerned, these titles are applicable only in descriptions of *offenses* attributable to juveniles or to *apprehended juveniles* charged with their commission.

Robbery. This title implies to most people that there is only one kind of robbery, that it is terrible and that it connotes taking something of value from a person, usually with violence. Yet, evidence points to significant differences in the quality of these acts.[13] As Beattie points out,

... there is no knowledge of the variation that has occurred in different types of robbery. Such increases or decreases as have been observed may be due to variations in armed robbery or in strong-arm robbery, which in some instances amounts to no more than drunk rolls. Reports are often received today that children have been engaged in hijacking coins from each other. These incidents have been reported as robberies.[14]

The victim-offender relationship is also important, by sex, age, and other variables. There is certainly a vast difference between a 16-year-old boy's forcing a gas station attendant at the point of a gun to give up money from the cash register and an eight-year-old boy's twisting the arm of another eight-year-old boy in the school corridor in order to take his lunch money. Both

---

[13] These differences in adult robberes have recently been examined in some detail by F. H. McClintock and Evelyn Gibson, *Robbery in London* (xix, 147 pp. London: Macmillan, 1961).

[14] *Crime in California 1958*, p. 18. See also Nochem S. Winnet, *Twenty-Five Years of Crime Prevention* (Philadelphia: Philadelphia Crime Association) *Annual Report 1956*, p. 1: "Hundreds of robberies were reported. An analysis showed many of them involved petty sums, one as low as ten cents, a tribute exacted by one school child from another."

acts are classified legally and statistically as robbery. This same kind of situation was referred to in the 1956 Annual Report of the Crime Prevention Association of Philadelphia:

> And again, what is "highway robbery"? In the thinking of the American people, this indeed is a serious offense. Yet we know of a case last year in which a 14-year-old boy approached another boy of similar age and demanded 15 cents; the boy accosted stated he had only a quarter. The "highway robber" took the quarter, had it changed and returned to the other boy 10 cents. *This offense is listed as highway robbery.* Another instance involved two boys who extorted 20 cents daily for a week from another boy as he went to and from school. This youthful highjacking was reported by the victim's parents to the police; charge against the two offenders — highway robbery. Now we must admit that such extortion and highjacking is nasty behavior but to call this highway robbery and still keep a straight face is naive.[15]

Burglary. Burglary is another example of the need for subclassifications, for while it is an offense that has shown a steady increase over the past years, we are never sure what kind of burglary has been increasing. The California Report has raised this same question: "Is the increase in safe burglary, large-scale residential and commercial burglary, or in just smallscale pilferings that are technically burglary? A large part of the latter could be the result of juvenile behavior. Under present classification methods, this question cannot be answered."[16] There are wide variations in the state statutes that define burglary. Although breaking into a locked car is defined as burglary in California and is reported thus in many instances, it is an offense that is often reported by many law enforcement agencies as petty theft and classified as larceny.

Some of these problems were raised in papers presented in 1960 before the Social Statistics Section of the American Statistical Association. It was pointed out, for example, that broad crime groupings are used to tally major offenses which differ according to some element in definition. The following cases were given as illustrations:

> (A) Two juveniles while on school vacation break into a neighbor's barn, steal some nails, a hammer, and a saw in order to build a treehouse nearby; (B) a prowler sneaks into an unoccupied bedroom and rummages for money or jewelry while the occupants are having dinner downstairs; (C) a team of thugs, armed and with heavy burglar tools force entrance into an office and attack a safe. Each of these cases is classified ordinarily as a "burglary" according to police statistical practices.[17]

Both from the viewpoint of police protective services and of threats of danger to life or property, these acts are clearly distinguishable, but the differential variables are hidden in formal statistical tabulations that use legal categories. Such factors as the presence or absence of violence to obtain entry, the legal or illegal presence of the offender at the scene of the crime, the amount of property loss or damage, etc., are totally neglected.

Assaults. The legal definitions of aggravated assaults, sexual assaults, rape, and similar offenses against the person each cover a variety of forms of conduct. The 1958 California report again suggests:

> ... because of the relationship of the parties or the conditions under which the assaults occurred, many altercations, largely domestic quarrels, characterized in reports as aggravated assault, do not seem to fall in the general area of felonious assault. There is need to sub-classify this type of offense in order to arrive at a true picture of assault.[18]

A New Jersey analysis of juvenile court cases a decade ago alluded to the same problem: "Personal injury, while having a higher percentage of dismissals as malicious

---

[15] *Ibid.*, p. 11.
[16] *Crime in California 1958*, p. 18.
[17] Edward V. Comber, "Discussion," *Proc. Social Statistics Section 1960*. (viii, 211 pp., Washington, D.C.: American Statistical Association, n.d., mimeo.); pp. 36–37.
[18] *Crime in California 1958*, p. 18.

mischief, does not carry comparable value under analysis. A majority of personal injury complaints were not assault cases per se—proper classification would be street fighting." [19] Moreover, the differences between a simple assault and battery and aggravated assault and battery are such that not only police variations but statutory provisions as well lend confusion rather than clarity to the classification problems. The legal nomenclature often distorts the true character of an attack on the person because of the difficulties of determining "grievous bodily harm" or extent of the injury and because suspects are often willing to confess to a simple assault or the police and courts are willing to accept a plea of guilty to a simple assault in order to obtain a conviction even when the more serious aggravated assault occurred.[20]

Rape. The categories of rape—even forcible rape—assault with attempt to ravish, sexual license, and sexual offenses generally fail to provide qualitative information on the broad range of activities and on the dimensions of seriousness or injury that may be involved in these acts. Forcible rape can range from violent and unprovoked attacks on women by strangers to a common pickup in a barroom that ends in greater sexual intimacy than the woman intended. The lines between forcible rape, statutory rape, fornication, and contributing to the delinquency of a minor are never clear from statistical tabulations that merely use these legal terms. Without examination of the detailed descriptions in police reports, the compilation of data in tabular form usually fail to represent important distinctions in the facts. As the United Nations Congress in 1960 reported on an attempt to collect international data on sex offenses: " 'Sexual license' was too vague. The replies do not always make clear what kind of offenses are referred to: Full sexual relations or sexual games between children? Relations between lovers, sexual promiscuity, dissolute behavior, prostitution?" [21]

Certainly there are vast differences in the types of offenses that are listed as "assault with intent to ravish." The conduct of a 16-year-old boy, who attacks a 30-year-old woman, drags her into a dark alley to assault her sexually but is thwarted by screams and the appearance of a police officer, is surely different from a 9-year-old boy's exploratory sexual curiosity with a neighbor girl aged 8. When she innocently tells her mother about the afternoon's adventure, and when the mother imagines horrendous things, calls the police, and has the boy arrested, this case like the previous one is listed as "assault with intent to ravish." Once again, Beattie has remarked:

Much has been said in recent years of the apparent growth of viciousness in certain types of crime. There is no basis upon which to determine whether or not there has been such a growth. There have been many cases that have received a great deal of publicity, but without careful classification, it cannot be known whether the impression is backed by fact.[22]

We believe that these illustrations suffice to show that the use of the broad titles of offenses derived from the Uniform Classification of Offenses for a description of delinquency chargeable to juveniles would be an unsatisfactory procedure that cannot provide sensitive measures of delinquency.

A second problem arises out of certain arbitrary practices of classifying and ordering offenses in official statistics of delinquency. These practices are directly attributable to the manner in which the Uniform Classification is applied in accord with the instructions governing its use. There are, of course, many ways of presenting offense statistics. The offenses involved

---

[19] *Children in New Jersey Courts 1953*, p. 24.

[20] See Donald J. Newman, "Pleading guilty for considerations: A study of bargain justice," *J. Crim. Law, Criminol., and Police Sci.*, 46:780–790, March–April, 1956.

[21] United Nations Congress, London, August 8–20, 1960, A/Conf. 17/6, p. 64.

[22] *Crime in California 1958*, p. 19.

could be listed alphabetically, or grouped in broad classes—for instance, offenses against the person, offenses against property, etc.—with appropriate subclasses, or grouped according to the Uniform Classification, to mention but a few patterns. For reasons already stated the last mentioned method is the most common one in American police statistics.

There are two built-in features of the use of this classification which reduce its value. First, an implicit hypothesis underlies it, namely that its 26 classes are arranged in decreasing order of seriousness. This hypothesis is not completely invalid. Certainly most offenses in Part 1 of the classification are more injurious than most of those in Part 2, but arson, kidnapping, abortion, blackmail and extortion, and malicious mischief now falling into the last class of "all other offenses," and simple assault and battery (item 8) and embezzlement and fraud (item 10) may in fact involve more personal injury or loss of property, for instance, than many of the offenses listed among the "index crimes" under rape, aggravated assault, burglary and larceny. Therefore, the present grouping of the offenses by the broad legal labels employed does not provide the best typology of offenses based on an hypothesis of degree of seriousness, not to mention the fact that it does not provide for differential weighting of the classes, nor of the great number of variants among the offenses included in any single class. One theft of fifty dollars is given as much weight as one homicide, and one such theft as much weight as one of $5000.[23]

Second, the manner in which the classification is used conceals a great deal of delinquency known to the police because it offers no possibility of counting all the *components* of a delinquent event. The problem does not arise in the case of uncomplicated events. A mere breaking and entering can be classified as burglary, but suppose that in committing this offense a juvenile also steals property of great value, and on being surprised, assaults and wounds the owner with a dangerous weapon. The instructions for classifying this total event require that only the offense highest in the order of the Uniform Classification be counted—in this instance, the aggravated assault and battery. This conceals both the burglary and the theft. If a juvenile holds up the occupants of an automobile, kills the driver, rapes his female companion, and steals her pocketbook, jewelry, and the car, this complex event must be counted as one non-negligent criminal homicide (item 1) and the rape and the thefts will be concealed. All kinds of other complex events could be cited to show that the manner in which offenses are commonly tabulated for statistical presentation results in an incomplete picture even of the delinquency known to the police.

The conclusion seems inescapable that when an offense is given, in official police statistics, a broad legal label which does not allow for adequate discriminatory separation and weighting of the variants covered by it, and when all but the hypothetically most serious component of a delinquency event are concealed by the procedure followed in scoring offenses, the resulting statistics are not adequate for the measurement of delinquency.

---

[23] For a more detailed discussion of these and related problems, see Marvin E. Wolfgang, "Uniform crime reports: A critical appraisal," *University of Pennsylvania Law Rev.* 111:708–738 (April 1963).

5. IS "WHITE COLLAR CRIME" CRIME?

EDWIN H. SUTHERLAND

THE ARGUMENT HAS BEEN MADE THAT BUSINESS and professional men commit crimes which should be brought within the scope of the theories of criminal behavior.[1] In order to secure evidence as to the prevalence of such white-collar crimes an analysis was made of the decisions by courts and commissions against the seventy largest industrial and mercantile corporations in the United States under four types of laws, namely, antitrust, false advertising, National Labor Relations, and infringement of patents, copyrights, and trademarks. This resulted in the finding that 547 such adverse decisions had been made, with an average of 7.8 decisions per corporation and with each corporation having at least 1. Although all of these were decisions that the behavior was unlawful, only 49 or 9 per cent of the total were made by criminal courts and were *ipso facto* decisions that the behavior was criminal. Since not all unlawful behavior is criminal behavior, these decisions can be used as a measure of criminal behavior only if the other 498 decisions can be shown to be decisions that the behavior of the corporations was criminal.

This is a problem in the legal definition of crime and involves two types of questions: May the word "crime" be applied to the behavior regarding which these decisions were made? If so, why is it not generally applied and why have not the criminologists regarded white-collar crime as cognate with other crime? The first question involves semantics; the second, interpretation or explanation.

A combination of two abstract criteria is generally regarded by legal scholars as necessary to define crime, namely, legal description of an act as socially injurious and legal provision of a penalty for the act.[2]

When the criterion of legally defined social injury as applied to these 547 decisions, the conclusion is reached that all the classes of behaviors regarding which the decisions were made are legally defined as socially injurious. This can be readily determined by the words in the statutes—"crime" or "misdemeanors" in some and "unfair," "discrimination," or "infringement" in all the others. The persons injured may be divided into two groups: first, a relatively small number of persons engaged in the

---

►SOURCE: *"Is 'White Collar Crime' Crime?" American Sociological Review (1945), 10:132–139.* Reprinted by permission.

[1] Edwin H. Sutherland, "White Collar Criminality," *American Sociological Review*, V (1940), 1–12; Edwin H. Sutherland, "Crime and Business," *Annals of the American Academy of Political and Social Science*, CCXVII (1941), 112–18.

[2] The most satisfactory analysis of the criteria of crime from the legal point of view may be found in the following papers by Jerome Hall: "Prolegomena to a Science of Criminal Law," *University of Pennsylvania Law Review*, LXXXIX (1941), 549–80; "Interrelations of Criminal Law and Torts," *Columbia Law Review*, XLIII (1943), 735–79, 967–1001; "Criminal Attempts—A Study of the Foundations of Criminal Liability," *Yale Law Review*, XLIX (1940), 789–840.

same occupation as the offenders or in related occupations and, second, the general public either as consumers or as constituents of the general social institutions which are affected by the violations of the laws. The anti-trust laws are designed to protect competitors and also to protect the institution of free competition as the regulator of the economic system and thereby to protect consumers against arbitrary prices and to protect the institution of democracy against the dangers of great concentration of wealth in the hands of monopolies. Laws against false advertising are designed to protect competitors against unfair competition and also to protect consumers against fraud. The National Labor Relations Law is designed to protect employees against coercion by employers and also to protect the general public against interferences with commerce caused by strikes and lockouts. The laws against infringements are designed to protect the owners of patents, copyrights, and trade-marks against deprivation of their property and against unfair competition, and also to protect the institution of patents and copyrights, which was established in order to "promote the progress of science and the useful arts." Violations of these laws are legally defined as injuries to the parties specified.

Each of these laws has a logical basis in the common law and is an adaptation of the common law to modern social organization. False advertising is related to common law fraud, and infringement to larceny. The National Labor Relations Law, as an attempt to prevent coercion, is related to the common-law prohibition of restrictions on freedom in the form of assault, false imprisonment, and extortion. For at least two centuries prior to the enactment of the modern antitrust laws the common law was moving against restraint of trade, monopoly, and unfair competition.

Each of the four laws provides a penal sanction and thus meets the second criterion in the definition of crime, and each of the adverse decisions under these four laws, except certain decisions under the infringement laws to be discussed later, is a decision that a crime was committed. This conclusion will be made more specific by analysis of the penal sanctions provided in the four laws.

The Sherman Antitrust Law states explicitly that a violation of the law is a misdemeanor. Three methods of enforcement of this law are provided, each of them involving procedures regarding misdemeanors. First, it may be enforced by the usual criminal prosecution, resulting in the imposition of fine or imprisonment. Second, the attorney general of the United States and the several district attorneys are given the "duty" of repressing and preventing violations of the law by petitions for injunctions, and violations of the injunctions are punishable as contempt of court. This method of enforcing a criminal law was an invention and, as will be described later, is the key to the interpretation of the differential implementation of the criminal law as applied to white-collar criminals. Third, parties who are injured by violations of the law are authorized to sue for damages, with a mandatory provision that the damages awarded be three times the damages suffered. These damages in excess of reparation are penalties for violation of the law. They are payable to the injured party in order to induce him to take the initiative in the enforcement of the criminal law and in this respect are similar to the earlier methods of private prosecutions under the criminal law. All three of these methods of enforcement are based on decisions that a criminal law was violated and therefore that a crime was committed; the decisions of a civil court or a court of equity as to these violations are as good evidence of criminal behavior as is the decision of a criminal court.

The Sherman Antitrust Law has been amended by the Federal Trade Commission Law, the Clayton Law, and several other laws. Some of these amendments define violations as crimes and provide the conventional penalties, but most of the amendments do not make the criminality explicit. A large proportion of the cases which are dealt with under these amendments could be dealt with, instead, under the original Sherman Law, which is explicitly a criminal law. In practice, the amendments are under the jurisdiction of the Federal Trade Commission, which has authority to make official decisions as to violations. The Commission has two principal sanctions under its control, namely, the stipulation and the cease-and-desist order. The Commission may, after the violation of the law has been proved, accept a stipulation from the corporation that it will not violate the law in the future. Such stipulations are customarily restricted to the minor or technical violations. If a stipulation is violated or if no stipulation is accepted, the Commission may issue a cease-and-desist order; this is equivalent to a court's injunction except that violation is not punishable as contempt. If the Commission's desist order is violated, the Commission may apply to the court for an injunction, the violation of which is punishable as contempt. By an amendment to the Federal Trade Commission Law in the Wheeler-Lea Act of 1938 an order of the Commission becomes "final" if not officially questioned within a specified time and thereafter its violation is punishable by a civil fine. Thus, although certain interim procedures may be used in the enforcement of the amendments to the antitrust law, fines or imprisonment for contempt are available if the interim procedures fail. In this respect the interim procedures are similar to probation in ordinary criminal cases. An unlawful act is not defined as criminal by the fact that it is punished, but by the fact that it is punishable. Larceny is as truly a crime when the thief is placed on probation as when he is committed to prison. The argument may be made that punishment for contempt of court is not punishment for violation of the original law and that, therefore, the original law does not contain a penal sanction. This reasoning is specious since the original law provides the injunction with its penalty as a part of the procedure for enforcement. Consequently all the decisions made under the amendments to the antitrust law are decisions that the corporations committed crimes.[3]

The laws regarding false advertising, as included in the decisions under consideration, are of two types. First, false advertising in the form of false labels is defined in the Pure Food and Drug Law as a misdemeanor and is punishable by a fine. Second, false advertising generally is defined in the Federal Trade Commission Act as unfair competition. Cases of the second type are under the jurisdiction of the Federal Trade Commission, which uses the same procedures as in antitrust cases. Penal sanctions are available in antitrust cases, as previously described, and are similarly available in these cases of false advertising. Thus, all of the decisions in false advertising cases are decisions that the corporations committed crimes.

The National Labor Relations Law of 1935 defines a violation as "unfair labor practice." The National Labor Relations Board is authorized to make official decisions as to violations of the law and, in case of violation, to issue desist orders and also to make certain remedial orders, such as reimbursement of employees who had been dismissed or demoted because of activities in collective bargaining. If an order is violated, the Board may apply to the court for enforcement and a violation of the order of the court is punishable as contempt. Thus, all of the decisions under this law, which is enforceable by penal sanctions, are decisions that crimes were committed.

The methods for the repression of in-

---

[3] Some of the antitrust decisions were made against meat packers under the Packers and Stockyards Act. The penal sanctions in this act are essentially the same as in the Federal Trade Commission Act.

fringements vary. Infringements of a copyright or a patented design are defined as misdemeanors, punishable by fines. No case of this type has been discovered against the seventy corporations. Other infringements are not explicitly defined in the statutes on patents, copyrights, and trademarks as crimes, and agents of the state are not authorized by these statutes to initiate actions against violators of the law. Nevertheless, infringements may be punished in either of two ways: First, agents of the State may initiate action against infringements under the Federal Trade Commission Law as unfair competition, and they do so, especially against infringements of copyrights and trademarks; these infringements are then punishable in the same sense as violations of the amendments to the antitrust laws. Second, the patent, copyright, and trademark statutes provide that the damages awarded to injured owners of those rights may be greater than (in one statute as much as threefold) the damages actually suffered. These additional damages are not mandatory, as in the Sherman Antitrust Law, but on the other hand they are not explicitly limited to wanton and malicious infringements. Three decisions against the seventy corporations under the patent law and one under the copyright law included awards of such additional damages and on that account were classified in the tabulation of decisions as evidence of criminal behavior of the corporations. The other decisions, 74 in number, in regard to infringements were classified as not conclusive evidence of criminal behavior and were discarded. However, in 20 of these 74 cases the decisions of the court contain evidence which would be sufficient to make a *prima facie* case in a criminal prosecution; evidence outside these decisions which may be found in the general descriptions of practices regarding patents, copyrights, and trademarks, justifies a belief that a very large proportion of the 74 cases did, in fact, involve willful infringement of property rights and might well have resulted in the imposition of a penalty if the injured party and the court had approached the behavior from the point of view of crime.

In the preceding discussion the penalties which are definitive of crime have been limited to fine, imprisonment, and punitive damages. In addition, the stipulation, the desist order, and the injunction, without reference to punishment for contempt, have the attributes of punishment. This is evident both in that they result in some suffering on the part of the corporation against which they are issued and also in that they are designed by legislators and administrators to produce suffering. The suffering is in the form of public shame, as illustrated in more extreme form in the colonial penalty of sewing the letter "T" on the clothing of the thief. The design is shown in the sequence of sanctions used by the Federal Trade Commission. The stipulation involves the least publicity and the least discomfort, and it is used for minor and technical violations. The desist order is used if the stipulation is violated and also if the violation of the law is appraised by the Commission as willful and major. This involves more public shame; this shame is somewhat mitigated by the statements made by corporations, in exculpation, that such orders are merely the acts of bureaucrats. Still more shameful to the corporation is an injunction issued by a court. The shame resulting from this order is sometimes mitigated and the corporation's face saved by taking a consent decree.[4] The corporation may insist that the consent decree is not an admission that it violated the law. For instance, the meat packers took a consent decree in an antitrust case in 1921, with the explanation that they had not knowingly violated any law and were consenting to the decree without attempting to defend themselves because they wished to co-operate with the government in every possible way.

---

[4] The consent decree may be taken for other reasons, especially because it cannot be used as evidence in other suits.

This patriotic motivation appeared questionable, however, after the packers fought during almost all of the next ten years for a modification of the decree. Although the sequence of stipulation, desist order, and injunction indicates that the variations in public shame are designed, these orders have other functions, as well, especially a remedial function and the clarification of the law in a particular complex situation.

The conclusion in this semantic portion of the discussion is that 473 of the 547 decisions are decisions that crimes were committed.

This conclusion may be questioned on the ground that the rules of proof and evidence used in reaching these decisions are not the same as those used in decisions regarding other crimes, especially that some of the agencies which rendered the decisions did not require proof of criminal intent and did not presume the accused to be innocent. These rules of criminal intent and presumption of innocence, however, are not required in all prosecutions under the regular penal code and the number of exceptions is increasing. In many states a person may be committed to prison without protection of one or both of these rules on charges of statutory rape, bigamy, adultery, passing bad checks, selling mortgaged property, defrauding a hotelkeeper, and other offenses.[5] Consequently the criteria which have been used in defining white-collar crimes are not categorically different from the criteria used in defining other crimes, for these rules are abrogated both in regard to white-collar crimes and other crimes, including some felonies. The proportion of decisions rendered against corporations without the protection of these rules is probably greater than the proportion rendered against other criminals, but a difference in proportion does not make the violations of law by corporations categorically different from the violations of laws by other criminals. Moreover, the difference in proportion, as the procedures actually operate, is not great. On the one side, many of the defendants in usual criminal cases, being in relative poverty, do not get good defense and consequently secure little benefit from these rules; on the other hand, the commissions come close to observing these rules of proof and evidence although they are not required to do so. This is illustrated by the procedure of the Federal Trade Commission in regard to advertisements. Each year it examines several hundred thousand advertisements and appraises about 50,000 of them as probably false. From the 50,000 it selects about 1,500 as patently false. For instance, an advertisement of gum-wood furniture as "mahogany" would seldom be an accidental error and would generally result from a state of mind which deviated from honesty by more than the natural tendency of humans beings to feel proud of their handiwork.

The preceding discussion has shown that these seventy corporations committed crimes according to 473 adverse decisions, and also has shown that the criminality of their behavior was not made obvious by the conventional procedures of the criminal law but was blurred and concealed by special procedures. This differential implementation of the law as applied to the crimes of corporations eliminates or at least minimizes the stigma of crime. Such differential implementation began with the Sherman Antitrust Law of 1890. As previously described, this law is explicitly a criminal law, and a violation of the law is a misdemeanor no matter what procedure is used. The customary policy would have been to rely entirely on criminal prosecution as the method of enforcement. But a clever invention was made in the provision of an injunction to enforce a criminal law; this was not only an invention but a direct reversal of previous case law. Also, private parties were encouraged by treble damages to enforce a criminal law by suits in civil courts. In either case, the defendant did not appear in the criminal court, and the

---

[5] Livingston Hall, "Statutory Law of Crimes, 1887–1936," *Harvard Law Review*, L (1937), 616–53.

fact that he had committed a crime did not appear in the face of the proceedings.

The Sherman Antitrust law, in this respect, became the model in practically all the subsequent procedures authorized to deal with the crimes of corporations. When the Federal Trade Commission bill and the Clayton bill were introduced in Congress, they contained the conventional criminal procedures; these were eliminated in committee discussions, and other procedures which did not carry the external symbols of criminal process were substituted. The violations of these laws are crimes, as has been shown above, but they are treated as though they were not crimes, with the effect and probably the intention of eliminating the stigma of crime.

This policy of eliminating the stigma of crime is illustrated in the following statement by Wendell Berge, at the time assistant to the head of the antitrust division of the Department of Justice, in a plea of abandonment of the criminal prosecution under the Sherman Antitrust Law and the authorization of civil procedures with civil fines as a substitute.

While civil penalties may be as severe in their financial effects as criminal penalties, yet they do not involve the stigma that attends indictment and conviction. Most of the defendants in antitrust cases are not criminals in the usual sense. There is no inherent reason why antitrust enforcement requires branding them as such.[6]

If a civil fine were substituted for a criminal fine, a violation of the antitrust law would be as truly a crime as it is now. The thing which would be eliminated would be the stigma of crime. Consequently, the stigma of crime has become a penalty in itself, which may be imposed in connection with other penalties or withheld, just as it is possible to combine imprisonment with a fine or have a fine without imprisonment. A civil fine is a financial penalty without the additional penalty of stigma, while a criminal fine is a financial penalty with the additional penalty of stigma.

When the stigma of crime is imposed as a penalty, it places the defendant in the category of criminals, and he becomes a criminal according to the popular stereotype of "the criminal." In primitive society "the criminal" was substantially the same as "the stranger," [7] while in modern society "the criminal" is a person of less esteemed cultural attainments. Seventy-five per cent of the persons committed to state prisons are probably not, aside from their unesteemed cultural attainments, "criminals in the usual sense of the word." It may be excellent policy to eliminate the stigma of crime in a large proportion of cases, but the question at hand is why the law has a different implementation for white-collar criminals than for others.

Three factors assist in explaining this differential implementation of the law, namely, the status of the businessman, the trend away from punishment, and relatively unorganized resentment of the public against white-collar criminals. Each of these will be described.

First, the methods used in the enforcement of any law are an adaption to the characteristics of the prospective violators of the law, as appraised by the legislators and the judicial and administrative personnel. The appraisals regarding businessmen, who are the prospective violators of the four laws under consideration, include a combination of fear and admiration. Those who are responsible for the system of criminal justice are afraid to antagonize businessmen; among other consequences, such antagonism may result in a reduction in contributions to the campaign funds needed to win the next election. Probably

---

[6] Wendell Berge, "Remedies Available to the Government under the Sherman Act," *Law and Contemporary Problems,* VII (1940), 111.

[7] On the role of the stranger in punitive justice, see Ellsworth Faris, "The Origin of Punishment," *International Journal of Ethics,* XXV (1914), 54–67; George H. Mead, "The Psychology of Punitive Justice," *American Journal of Sociology,* XXIII (1918), 577–602.

much more important is the cultural homogeneity of legislators, judges, and administrators with businessmen. Legislators admire and respect businessmen and cannot conceive of them as criminals; that is, businessmen do not conform to the popular stereotype of "the criminal." The Legislators are confident that these businessmen will conform as a result of very mild pressures.

This interpretation meets with considerable opposition from persons who insist that this is an egalitarian society in which all men are equal in the eyes of the law. It is not possible to give a complete demonstration of the validity of this interpretation, but four types of evidence are presented in the following paragraphs as partial demonstration.

The Department of Justice is authorized to use both criminal prosecutions and petitions in equity to enforce the Sherman Antitrust Law. The Department has selected the method of criminal prosecution in a larger proportion of cases against trade unions than of cases against corporations, although the law was enacted primarily because of fear of the corporations. From 1890 to 1929 the Department of Justice initiated 438 actions under this law with decisions favorable to the United States. Of the actions against business firms and associations of business firms, 27 per cent were criminal prosecutions, while of the actions against trade unions 71 per cent were criminal prosecutions.[8] This shows that the Department of Justice has been comparatively reluctant to use a method against business firms which carries with it the stigma of crime.

The method of criminal prosecution in enforcement of the Sherman Antitrust Law has varied from one presidential administration to another. It has seldom been used in the administrations of the presidents who are popularly appraised as friendly toward business, namely, McKinley, Harding, Coolidge, and Hoover.

Businessmen suffered their greatest loss of prestige in the depression which began in 1929. It was precisely in this period of low status of businessmen that the most strenuous efforts were made to enforce the old laws and enact new laws for the regulation of businessmen. The appropriations for this purpose were multiplied several times, and persons were selected for their vigor in administration of the laws. Of the 547 decisions against the seventy corporations during their life careers, which have averaged about forty years, 63 per cent were rendered in the period of 1935-43, that is, during the period of low status of businessmen.

The Federal Trade Commission Law states that a violation of the antitrust laws by a corporation shall be deemed to be, also, a violation by the officers and directors of the corporation. However, businessmen are practically never convicted as persons, and several cases have been reported, like the six per cent case against the automobile manufacturers, in which the corporation was convicted and the persons who directed the corporation were all acquitted.[9]

A second factor in the explanation of the differential implementation of the law as applied to white-collar criminals is the trend away from reliance on penal methods. This trend advanced more rapidly in the area of white-collar crimes than of other crimes because this area, due to the recency of the statutes, is least bound by precedents and also because of the status of businessmen. This trend is seen in the almost complete abandonment of the most extreme penalties of death and physical torture; in the supplanting of conventional penal methods by non-penal methods such as probation and the case-work methods which accompany

---

[8] Percentages compiled from cases listed in the report of the Department of Justice "Federal Antitrust Laws, 1938."

[9] The question may be asked, "If businessmen are so influential, why did they not retain the protection of the rules of the criminal procedure?" The answer is that they lost this protection, despite their status, on the principle that "You can't eat your cake and have it, too."

probation; and in the supplementing of penal methods by non-penal methods, as in the development of case-work and educational policies in prisons. These decreases in penal methods are explained by a series of social changes: the increased power of the lower socioeconomic class upon which previously most of the penalties were inflicted; the inclusion within the scope of the penal laws of a large part of the upper socioeconomic class as illustrated by traffic regulations; the increased social interaction among the classes, which has resulted in increased understanding and sympathy; the failure of penal methods to make substantial reductions in crime rates; and the weakening hold on the legal profession and others of the individualistic and hedonistic psychology which had placed great emphasis on pain in the control of behavior. To some extent overlapping those just mentioned is the fact that punishment, which was previously the chief reliance for control in the home, the school, and the church, has tended to disappear from those institutions, leaving the State without cultural support for its own penal methods.[10]

White-collar crime is similar to juvenile delinquency in respect to the differential implementation of the law. In both cases, the procedures of the criminal law are modified so that the stigma of crime will not attach to the offenders. The stigma of crime has been less completely eliminated from juvenile delinquents than from white-collar criminals because the procedures for the former are a less complete departure from conventional criminal procedures, because most juvenile delinquents come from a class with low social status, and because the juveniles have not organized to protect their good names. Since the juveniles have not been successfully freed from the stigma of crime they have been generally held to be within the scope of the theories of criminology and in fact provide a large part of the data for criminology; since the external symbols have been more successfully eliminated from white-collar crimes, white-collar crimes have generally not been included within these theories.

A third factor in the differential implementation of the law is the difference in the relation between the law and the mores in the area of white-collar crime. The laws under consideration are recent and do not have a firm foundation in public ethics or business ethics; in fact, certain rules of business ethics, such as contempt for the "price chiseler," are generally in conflict with the law. The crimes are not obvious, as are assault and battery, and can be appreciated readily only by persons who are expert in the occupations in which they occur. A corporation often violates a law for a decade or longer before the administrative agency becomes aware of the violation, and in the meantime the violation may have become accepted practice in the industry. The effects of a white-collar crime upon the public are diffused over a long period of time and perhaps over millions of people, with no person suffering much at a particular time. The public agencies of communication do not express and organize the moral sentiments of the community as to white-collar crimes, in part because the crimes are complicated and not easily presented as news, but probably in greater part because these agencies of communication are owned or controlled by the businessmen who violate the laws and because these agencies are themselves frequently charged with violations of the same laws. Public opinion in regard to picking pockets would not be well organized if most of the information regarding this crime came to the public directly from the pickpockets themselves.

This third factor, if properly limited, is a valid part of the explanation of the differential implementation of the law. It tends to be exaggerated and become the complete explanation in the form of a denial that white-collar crimes involve any moral cul-

---

[10] The trend away from penal methods suggests that the penal sanction may not be a completely adequate criterion in the definition of crime.

pability whatever. On that account it is desirable to state a few reasons why this factor is not the complete explanation.

The assertion is sometimes made that white-collar crimes are merely technical violations and involve no moral culpability, i.e., violation of the mores, whatever. In fact, these white-collar crimes, like other crimes, are distributed along a continuum in which the *mala in se* are at one extreme and the *mala prohibita* at the other.[11] None of the white-collar crimes is purely arbitrary, as is the regulation that one must drive on the right side of the street, which might equally well be that one must drive on the left side. The Sherman Antitrust Law, for instance, is regarded by many persons as an unwise law, and it may well be that some other policy would be preferable. It is questioned principally by persons who believe in a more collectivistic economic system, namely, the communists and the leaders of big business, while its support comes largely from an emotional ideology in favor of free enterprise which is held by farmers, wage-earners, small businessmen, and professional men. Therefore, as appraised by the majority of the population it is necessary for the preservation of American institutions, and its violation is a violation of strongly entrenched moral sentiments.

The sentimental reaction toward a particular white-collar crime is certainly different from that toward some other crimes. This difference is often exaggerated, especially as the reaction occurs in urban society. The characteristic reaction of the average citizen in the modern city toward burglary is apathy unless he or his immediate friends are victims or unless the case is very spectacular. The average citizen, reading in his morning paper that the home of an unknown person has been burglarized by another unknown person, has no appreciable increase in blood pressure. Fear and resentment develop in modern society primarily as the result of the accumulation of crimes as depicted in crime rates or in general descriptions, and this develops both as to white-collar crimes and other crimes.

Finally, although many laws have been enacted for the regulation of occupations other than business, such as agriculture or plumbing, the procedures used in the enforcement of those other laws are more nearly the same as the conventional criminal procedures, and law-violators in these other occupations are not so completely protected against the stigma of crime as are businessmen. The relation between the law and the mores tends to be circular. The mores are crystallized in the law, and each act of enforcement of the laws tends to reenforce the mores. The laws regarding white-collar crime, which conceal the criminality of the behavior, have been less effective than other laws in re-enforcement of the mores.

---

[11] An excellent discussion of this continuum is presented by Jerome Hall, *op. cit.*, 563–69.

6. WHO IS THE CRIMINAL?

PAUL W. TAPPAN

WHAT IS CRIME? AS A LAWYER-SOCIOLOGIST, the writer finds perturbing the current confusion on this important issue. Important because it delimits the subject matter of criminological investigation. A criminologist who strives to aid in formulating the beginnings of a science finds himself in an increasingly equivocal position. He studies the criminals convicted by the courts and is then confounded by the growing clamor that he is not studying the real criminal at all, but an insignificant proportion of non-representative and stupid unfortunates who happened to have become enmeshed in technical legal difficulties. It has become a fashion to maintain that the convicted population is no proper category for the empirical research of the criminologist. Ergo, the many studies of convicts which have been conducted by the orthodox, now presumably outmoded criminologists, have no real meaning for either descriptive or scientific purposes. Off with the old criminologies, on with the new orientations, the new horizons!

This position reflects in part at least the familiar suspicion and misunderstanding held by the layman sociologist toward the law. To a large extent it reveals the feeling among social scientists that not all antisocial conduct is proscribed by law (which is probably true), that not all conduct violative of the criminal code is truly antisocial, or is not so to any significant extent (which is also undoubtedly true). Among some students the opposition to the traditional definition of crime as law violation arises from their desire to discover and study wrongs which are absolute and eternal rather than mere violations of a statutory and case law system which vary in time and place; this is essentially the old metaphysical search for the law of nature. They consider the dynamic and relativistic nature of law to be a barrier to the growth of a scientific system of hypotheses possessing universal validity.[1]

▶SOURCE: *"Who Is the Criminal?"* American Sociological Review (February, 1947), 12:96–102. Reprinted by permission.

---

[1] The manner in which the legal definition of the criminal is avoided by prominent sociological scholars through amazingly loose, circumlocutory description may be instanced by this sort of definition: "Because a collective system has social validity in the eyes of each and all of those who share in it, because it is endowed with a special dignity which merely individual systems lack altogether, individual behavior which endangers a collective system and threatens to harm any of its elements appears quite different from an aggression against an individual (unless, of course, such an aggression hurts collective values as well as individual values). It is not only a harmful act, but an objectively evil act [sic!], a violation of social validity, an offense against the superior dignity of this collective system. . . . The best term to express the specific significance of such behavior is crime. We are aware that in using the word in this sense, we are giving it a much wider significance than it has in criminology. But we believe that it is desirable for criminology to put its

Recent protestants against the orthodox conceptions of crime and criminal are diverse in their views: they unite only in their denial of the allegedly legalistic and arbitrary doctrine that those convicted under the criminal law are the criminals of our society and in promoting the confusion as to their proper province of criminology. It is enough here to examine briefly a few of the current schisms with a view to the difficulties at which they arrive.

I

A number of criminologists today maintain that mere violation of the criminal law is an artificial criterion of criminality, that categories set up by the law do not meet the demands of scientists because they are of a "fortuitous nature" and do not "arise intrinsically from the nature of the subject matter."[2] The validity of this contention must depend, of course, upon what the nature of the subject matter is. These scholars suggest that, as a part of the general study of human behavior, criminology should concern itself broadly with all anti-social conduct, behavior injurious to society. We take it that anti-social conduct is essentially any sort of behavior which violates some social interest. What are these social interests? Which are weighty enough to merit the concern of the sociologist, to bear the odium of crime? What shall constitute a violation of them?—particularly where, as is so commonly true in our complicated and unintegrated society, these interests are themselves in conflict? Roscoe Pound's suggestive classification of the social interests served by law is valuable in a juristic framework, but it solves no problems for the sociologist who seeks to depart from legal standards in search of all manner of anti-social behavior.

However desirable may be the concept of socially injurious conduct for purposes of general normation or abstract description, it does not define what is injurious. It sets no standard. It does not discriminate cases, but merely invites the subjective value-judgments of the investigator. Until it is structurally embodied with distinct criteria or norms—as is now the case in the legal system—the notion of anti-social conduct is useless for purposes of research, even for the rawest empiricism. The emancipated criminologist reasons himself into a cul de sac: having decided that it is footless to study convicted offenders on the ground that this is an artificial category—though its membership is quite precisely ascertainable, he must now conclude that, in his lack of standards to determine anti-sociality, though this may be what he considers a real scientific category, its membership and its characteristics are unascertainable. Failing do define anti-social behavior in any fashion suitable to research, the criminologist may be deluded further into assuming that there is an absoluteness and permanence in this undefined category, lacking in the law. It is unwise for the social scientist ever to forget that all standards of social normation are relative, impermanent, variable. And that they do not, certainly the law does not, arise out of mere fortuity or artifice.[3]

---

[2] See, for example, Thorsten Sellin, *Culture Conflict and Crime,* pp. 20–21 (1938).

investigations on a broader basis; for strictly speaking, it still lacks a proper theoretic basis. . . . Legal qualifications are not founded on the results of previous research and not made for the purpose of future research; therefore they have no claim to be valid as scientific generalizations—nor even as heuristic hypotheses." Florian Znaniecki, "Social Research in Criminology," 12 *Sociology and Social Research* 207 (1928).

[3] An instance of this broadening of the concept of the criminal is the penchant among certain anthropologists to equate crime with taboo. See, especially, Bronislaw Malinowski, *Crime and Custom in Savage Society* (1936), and "A New Instrument for the Study of Law—Especially Primitive," 51 *Yale L. J.* 1237 (1944). Compare William Seagle, "Primitive Law and Professor Malinowski," 39 *American Anthropologist* 275 (1937), and *The Quest for Law* (1941). Karl Llewellyn and E. Adamson Hoebel, *The Cheyenne Way* (1941) and E. Adamson Hoebel, "Law and Anthropology," 32 *Virginia L. R.* 835 (1946).

II

In a differing approach certain other criminologists suggest that "conduct norms" rather than either crime or anti-social conduct should be studied.[4] There is an unquestionable need to pursue the investigation of general conduct norms and their violation. It is desirable to segregate the various classes of such norms, to determine relationships between them, to understand similarities and differences between them as to the norms themselves, their sources, methods of imposition of control, and their consequences. The subject matter of this field of social control is in a regrettably primitive state. It will be important to discover the individuals who belong within the several categories of norm violators established and to determine then what motivations operate to promote conformity or breach. So far as it may be determinable, we shall wish to know in what way these motivations may serve to insure conformity to different sets of conduct norms, how they may overlap and reinforce the norms or conflict and weaken the effectiveness of the norms.

We concur in the importance of the study of conduct norms and their violation and, more particularly, if we are to develop a science of human behavior, in the need for careful researches to determine the psychological and environmental variables which are associated etiologically with non-conformity to these norms. However, the importance of the more general subject matter of social control or "ethology" does not mean that the more specific study of the law-violator is non-significant. Indeed, the direction of progress in the field of social control seems to lie largely in the observation and analysis of more specific types of non-conformity to particular, specialized standards. We shall learn more by attempting to determine why some individuals take human life deliberately and with premeditation, why some take property by force and others by trick, than we shall in seeking at the start a universal formula to account for any and all behavior in breach of social interests. This broader knowledge of conduct norms may conceivably develop through induction, in its inevitably very generic terms, from the empirical data derived in the study of particular sorts of violations. Too, our more specific information about the factors which lie behind violations of precisely defined norms will be more useful in the technology of social control. Where legal standards require change to keep step with the changing requirements of a dynamic society, the sociologist may advocate —even as the legal profession does—the necessary statutory modifications, rather than assume that for sociological purposes the conduct he disapproves is already criminal, without legislative, political, or judicial intervention.

III

Another increasingly widespread and seductive movement to revolutionize the concepts of crime and criminal has developed around the currently fashionable dogma of "white collar crime." This is actually a particular school among those who contend that the criminologist should study anti-social behavior rather than law violation. The dominant contention of the group appears to be that the convict classes are merely our "petty" criminals, the few whose depredations against society have been on a small scale, who have blundered into difficulties with the police and courts through their ignorance and stupidity. The important criminals, those who do irreparable damage with impunity, deftly evade the machinery of justice, either by remaining "technically" within the law or by exercising their intelligence, financial prowess, or political connections in its violation. We seek a definition of the white collar criminal and find an amazing diversity, even among those flowing from

---

[4] Sellin, *op. cit.*, pp. 25 ff.

the same pen, and observe that characteristically they are loose, doctrinaire, and invective. When Professor Sutherland launched the term, it was applied to those individuals of upper socio-economic class who violate the criminal law, usually by breach of trust, in the ordinary course of their business activities.[5] This original usage accords with legal ideas of crime and points moreover to the significant and difficult problems of enforcement in the areas of business crimes, particularly where those violations are made criminal by recent statutory enactment. From this fruitful beginning the term has spread into vacuity, wide and handsome. We learn that the white collar criminal, may be the suave and deceptive merchant prince or "robber baron," that the existence of such crime may be determined readily "in casual conversation with a representative of an occupation by asking him, 'What crooked practices are found in your occupation?' " [6]

Confusion grows as we learn from another proponent of this concept that, "There are various phases of white-collar criminality that touch the lives of the common man almost daily. The large majority of them are operating within the letter and spirit of the law...." and that "In short, greed, not need, lies at the basis of white-collar crime." [7] Apparently the criminal may be law obedient but greedy; the specific quality of his crimes is far from clear.

Another avenue is taken in Professor Sutherland's more recent definition of crime as a "legal description of an act as socially injurious and legal provision of penalty for the act." [8] Here he has deemed the connotation of his term too narrow if confined to violations of the criminal code; he includes by a slight modification conduct violative of any law, civil or criminal, when it is "socially injurious."

In light of these definitions, the normative issue is pointed. Who should be considered the white collar criminal? It is the merchant who, out of greed, business acumen, or competitive motivations, breaches a trust with his consumer by "puffing his wares" beyond their merits, by pricing them beyond their value, or by ordinary advertising? Is it he who breaks trust with his employees in order to keep wages down, refusing to permit labor organization or to bargain collectively, and who is found guilty by a labor relations board of an unfair labor practice? May it be the white collar worker who breaches trust with his employers by inefficient performance at work, by sympathetic strike or secondary boycott? Or is it the merchandiser who violates ethics by under-cutting the prices of his fellow merchants? In general these acts do not violate the criminal law. All in some manner breach a trust for motives which a criminologist may (or may not) disapprove for one reason or another. All are within the framework of the norms of ordinary business practice. One seeks in vain for criteria to determine this white collar criminality. It is the conduct of one who wears a white collar and who indulges in occupational behavior to which some particular criminologist takes exception. It may easily be a term of propaganda. For purposes of empirical research or objective description, what is it?

Whether criminology aspires one day to become a science or a repository of reasonably accurate descriptive information, it cannot tolerate a nomenclature of such loose and variable usage. A special hazard exists in the employment of the term, "white collar criminal," in that it invites individual systems of private values to run riot in an area (economic ethics) where gross variation exists among criminologists as well as others. The rebel may enjoy a

---

[5] E. H. Sutherland, "Crime and Business," 217 *The Annals of the American Academy of Political and Social Science* 112 (1941).

[6] Sutherland, "White-Collar Criminality," 5 *American Sociological Review* 1 (1940).

[7] Harry Elmer Barnes and Negley K. Teeters, *New Horizons in Criminology*, pp. 42–43 (1943).

[8] Sutherland, "Is 'White-Collar Crime' Crime?" 10 *American Sociological Review* 132 (1945).

veritable orgy of delight in damning as criminal most anyone he pleases; one imagines that some experts would thus consign to the criminal classes any successful capitalistic business man; the reactionary or conservative, complacently viewing the occupational practices of the business world might find all in perfect order in this best of all possible worlds. The result may be fine indoctrination or catharsis achieved through blustering broadsides against the "existing system." It is not criminology. It is not social science. The terms "unfair," "infringement," "discrimination," "injury to society," and so on, employed by the white collar criminologists cannot, taken alone, differentiate criminal and non-criminal. Until refined to mean certain specific actions, they are merely epithets.

Vague, omnibus concepts defining crime are a blight upon either a legal system or a system of sociology that strives to be objective. They allow judge, administrator, or—conceivably—sociologist, in an undirected, freely operating discretion, to attribute the status "criminal" to any individual or class which he conceives nefarious. This can accomplish no desirable objective, either politically or sociologically.[9]

Worse than futile, it is courting disaster, political, economic, and social, to promulgate a system of justice in which the individual may be held criminal without having committed a crime, defined with some precision by statute and case law. To describe crime the sociologist, liké the lawyer-legislator, must do more than condemn conduct deviation in the abstract. He must avoid definitions predicated simply upon state of mind or social injury and determine what particular types of deviation, in what directions, and to what degree, shall be considered criminal. This is exactly what the criminal code today attempts to do, though imperfectly of course. More slowly and conservatively than many of us would wish: that is in the nature of legal institutions, as it is in other social institutions as well. But law has defined with greater clarity and precision the conduct which is criminal than our anti-legalistic criminologists promise to do; it has moreover promoted a stability, a security and dependability of justice through its exactness, its so-called technicalities, and its moderation in inspecting proposals for change.

IV

Having considered the conceptions of an innovating sociology in ascribing the terms "crime" and "criminal," let us state here the juristic view: Only those are criminals who have been adjudicated as such by the courts. Crime is an intentional act in violation of the criminal law (statutory and case law), committed without defense or excuse, and penalized by the state as a felony or misdemeanor. In studying the offender there can be no presumption that arrested, arraigned, indicted, or prosecuted persons are criminals unless they also be held guilty beyong a reasonable doubt of

---

[9] In the province of juvenile delinquency we may observe already the evil that flows from this sort of loose definition in applied sociology. In many jurisdictions, under broad statutory definition of delinquency, it has become common practice to adjudicate as delinquent any child deemed to be anti-social or a behavior problem. Instead of requiring sound systematic proof of specific reprehensible conduct, the courts can attach to children the odious label of delinquent through the evaluations and recommendations of overworked, undertrained case investigators who convey to the judge their hearsay testimony of neighborhood gossip and personal predilection. Thus these vaunted "socialized tribunals" sometimes become themselves a source of delinquent and criminal careers as they adjudge individuals who are innocent of proven wrong to a depraved offender's status through an administrative determination of something they know vaguely as antisocial conduct. See Introduction by Roscoe Pound of Pauline V. Young, *Social Treatment in Probation and Delinquency* (1937). See also Paul W. Tappan, *Delinquent Girls in Court* (1947) and "Treatment Without Trial," 24 *Social Forces*, 306 (1946).

a particular offense.[10] Even less than the unconvicted suspect can those individuals be considered criminal who have violated no law. Only those are criminals who have been selected by a clear substantive and a careful adjective law, such as obtains in our courts. The unconvicted offenders of whom the criminologist may wish to take cognizance are an important but unselected group; it has no specific membership presently ascertainable. Sociologists may strive, as does the legal profession, to perfect measures for more complete and accurate ascertainment of offenders, but it is futile simply to rail against a machinery of justice which is, and to a large extent must inevitably remain, something less than entirely accurate or efficient.

Criminal behavior as here defined fits very nicely into the sociologists' formulations of social control. Here we find *norms* of conduct, comparable to the mores, but considerably more distinct, precise, and detailed, as they are fashioned through statutory and case law. The *agencies* of this control, like the norms themselves, are more formal than is true in other types of control: the law depends for its instrumentation chiefly upon police, prosecutors, judges, juries, and the support of a favorable public opinion. The law has for its *sanctions* the specifically enumerated punitive measures set up by the state for breach, penalties which are additional to any of the sanctions which society exerts informally against the violator or norms which may overlap with laws. *Crime* is itself simply the breach of the legal norm, a violation within this particular category of social control; the criminal is, of course, the individual who has committed such acts of breach.

Much ink has been spilled on the extent of deterrent efficacy of the criminal law in social control. This is a matter which is not subject to demonstration in any exact and measurable fashion, any more than one can conclusively demonstrate the efficiency of a moral norm.[11] Certainly the degree of success in asserting a control, legal or moral, will vary with the particular norm itself, its instrumentation, the subject individuals, the time, the place, and the sanctions. The efficiency of legal control is sometimes confused by the fact that, in the common overlapping of crimes (particularly those *mala in se*) with moral standards, the norms and sanctions of each may operate in mutual support to produce conformity. Moreover, mere breach of norm is no evidence of the general failure of a social control system, but indication rather of the need for control. Thus the occurrence of theft and homicide does not mean that the law is ineffective, for one cannot tell how frequently such acts might occur in the absence of law and penal sanction. Where such acts are avoided, one may not appraise the relative efficacy of law and mores in prevention. When they occur, one cannot apportion blame, either in the individual case or in general, to failures of the legal and moral systems. The individual in society does undoubtedly conduct himself in reference to legal requirements. Living "beyond the law" has a quality independent of being non-conventional, immoral, sinful. Mr. Justice Holmes has shown that the "bad man of the law"—those who become our criminals—are motivated in part by disrespect for the law or, at the least, are inadequately restrained by its taboos.

From introspection and from objective analysis of criminal histories one can not but accept as axiomatic the thesis that the norms of criminal law and its sanctions do exert some measure of effective control

---

[10] The unconvicted suspect cannot be known as a violator of the law: to assume him so would be in derogation of our most basic political and ethical philosophies. In empirical research it would be quite inaccurate, obviously, to study all suspects or defendants as criminals.

[11] For a detailed consideration of the efficacy of legal norms, see Jerome Michael and Herbert Wechsler, "A Rationale of the Law of Homicide," 37 *Columbia Law Review* 701, 1261 (1937).

over human behavior; that this control is increased by moral, conventional, and traditional norms; and that the effectiveness of control norms is variable. It seems a fair inference from urban investigations that in our contemporary mass society, the legal system is becoming increasingly important in constraining behavior as primary group norms and sanctions deteriorate. Criminal law, crime, and the criminal become more significant subjects of sociological inquiry, therefore, as we strive to describe, understand, and control the uniformities and variability in culture.

We consider that the "white collar criminal," the violator of conduct norms, and the anti-social personality are not criminal in any sense meaningful to the social scientist unless he has violated a criminal statute. We cannot know him as such unless he has been properly convicted. He may be a boor, a sinner, a moral leper, or the devil incarnate, but he does not become a criminal through sociological name-calling unless politically constituted authority says he is. It is footless for the sociologist to confuse issues of definition, normation, etiology, sanction, agency and social effects by saying one thing and meaning another.

V

To conclude, we reiterate and defend the contention that crime, as legally defined, is a sociologically significant province of study. The view that it is not appears to be based upon either of two premises: 1. that offenders convicted under the criminal law are not representative of all criminals and 2. that criminal law violation (and, therefore, the criminal himself) is not significant to the sociologist because it is composed of a set of legal, nonsociological categories irrelevant to the understanding of group behavior and/or social control. Through these contentions to invalidate the traditional and legal frame of reference adopted by the criminologist, several considerations, briefly enumerated below, must be met.

1. Convicted criminals as a sample of law violators:

a. Adjudicated offenders represent the closest possible approximation to those who have in fact violated the law, carefully selected by the sieving of the due process of law; no other province of social control attempts to ascertain the breach of norms with such rigor and precision.

b. It is as futile to contend that this group should not be studied on the grounds that it is incomplete or non-representative as it would be to maintain that psychology should terminate its description, analysis, diagnosis, and treatment of deviants who cannot be completely representative as selected. Convicted persons are nearly all criminals. They offer large and varied samples of all types; their origins, traits, dynamics of development, and treatment influences can be studied profitably for purposes of description, understanding, and control. To be sure, they are not necessarily representative of all offenders; if characteristics observed among them are imputed to law violators generally, it must be with the qualification implied by the selective processes of discovery and adjudication.

c. Convicted criminals are important as a sociological category, furthermore, in that they have been exposed and respond to the influences of court contact, official punitive treatment, and public stigma as convicts.

2. The relevance of violation of the criminal law:

a. The criminal law establishes substantive norms of behavior, standards more clear cut, specific, and detailed than the norms in any other category of social controls.

b. The behavior prohibited has been considered significantly in derogation of group welfare by deliberative and representative assembly, formally constituted for the purpose of establishing such norms; nowhere else in the field of social control is there directed a comparable rational effort to elaborate standards conforming to the predominant needs, desires, and interests of the community.

c. There are legislative and juridical lags which reduce the social value of the legal norms; as an important characteristic of law, such lag does not reduce the relevance of law as a province of sociological inquiry. From a detached sociological view, the significant thing is not the absolute goodness or badness of the norms but the fact that these norms do control behavior. The sociologist is interested in the results of such control, the correlates of violation, and in the lags themselves.

d. Upon breach of these legal (and social) norms, the refractory are treated officially in punitive and/or rehabilitative ways, not for being generally anti-social, immoral, unconventional, or bad, but for violation of the specific legal norms of control.

e. Law becomes the peculiarly important and ultimate pressure toward conformity to minimum standards of conduct deemed essential to group welfare as other systems of norms and mechanics of control deteriorate.

f. Criminals, therefore, are a sociologically distinct group of violators of specific legal norms, subjected to official state treatment. They and the non-criminals respond, though differentially of course, to the standards, threats, and correctional devices established in this system of social control.

g. The norms, their violation, the mechanics of dealing with breach constitute major provinces of legal sociology. They are basic to the theoretical framework of sociological criminology.[12]

---

[12] For other expositions of this view, see articles by Jerome Hall: "Prolegomena to a Science of Criminal Law," 89 *University of Pennsylvania Law Review* 570 (1941); "Criminology and a Modern Penal Code," 27 *Journal of Criminal Law and Criminology* 4 (May-June, 1936); "Criminology," *Twentieth Century Sociology*, pp. 342–65 (1945).

7. GOOD MEN, BAD MEN, AND THE PERCEPTION OF REALITY

GWYNN NETTLER

WITH THE RISE OF A SCIENTIFIC DETERMINISM and the associated decline of free will and sin as explanations of deviant behavior, it has become popular to look upon "badness" as sickness. Research designed to increase our knowledge of prostitution, radicalism, homosexuality, dictatorship, race prejudice, crime and delinquency often makes the assumption, implicitly and explicitly, that evil is illness.[1]

►SOURCE: "Good Men, Bad Men, and the Perception of Reality," Sociometry (September 1961), 24:3:279–294. Reprinted by permission of Sociometry and the author.

---

[1] There is a tautological sense in which this is true: if illness is defined as anything bad that is caused.

For present purposes and euphony's sake I should like to use "evil," "bad," and "deviant" interchangeably, if it will be recognized that I do not believe that all deviation—even some of which offends society—is evil, and that what is evil according to classical standards includes much that is now acceptable.

This synonymy seems defensible in view of the orientation of Social Problems and Social Disorganization textbooks which, although they do not always say so directly, are "really" concerned with badness. And this remains true even when they are re-titled "Social Deviation," because it is only disapproved difference that one finds in the chapter headings. Thus one doesn't see nor expect discussions in these books of such deviations as being rich, powerful, beautiful, or creative, clear, and intelligent.

Thus saying, this paper will hereafter abandon the defense of placing quotation marks about these useful but fuzzy terms.

These assumptions have not gone unchallenged (10, 18, 35, 56, 65, 66), yet they flourish. Part of their viability flows from the "evil-causes-evil" fallacy (60, page 62), but these assumptions are sustained also in the vogue of psychoanalysis and by the ambiguities that reside in the idea of mental health, ambiguities into which prejudices have stepped. Attempts to define a "healthy personality" carry a load of personal preference and we are prone to call the man "sound" who behaves as we do, or as we like to think we behave (9). These preferences seem not merely idiosyncratic but also class-biased and ethnocentric.[2] They gather ideological support from the Platonic suggestion that goodness, truth, and beauty are the ultimate desirables and that they bear each other an intimate connection. Since this Platonism is part of the academic subculture in which most investigators have been steeped, there have been few dissident voices among sociologists (65) or humanists (37), although psychologists seem increasingly re-

---

[2] For example, Witmer and Kotinsky (71) write that ". . . to be happy and responsible is to be healthy in personality." The words "happy" and "responsible" are so glorious that one is loath to question their relevance to mental health, but they *are* suspect simply because we do not expect a man to be happy regardless of circumstance and "responsibility" does not specify for whom nor how nor under what conditions with what limits.

luctant to accept the vaunted relationship of health and goodness (19, 46, 59, 62, 63).

The hope that goodness is friendly to the truth, or, better, that knowing the truth will make us good, has been brewed into our definitions of the healthy man and the concoction then used to justify our values. The California study of the *Authoritarian Personality* is a prime example (1). Maslow makes the logic explicit:

> The neurotic is not only emotionally sick—he is cognitively *wrong!* If health and neurosis are, respectively, correct and incorrect perceptions of reality, propositions of fact and propositions of value merge in this area, and in principle, value propositions should then be empirically demonstrable rather than merely matters of taste or exhortation (36).

If the scientist can show that bad behavior is a symptom of sickness and if a measure of this sickness is a perverted picture of the world, then the equation of morality (ours) with correctness seems established and certain happy consequences may be inferred, for example:

1. That truth and utility are *not* at war, as Pareto and the inconsistent Plato believed.
2. That science can "prove" values and thus give them the underpinning they lost with the decline of religious authority.
3. That, since evil-is-sickness-is-error, therapy remains what some like to think it is: truth-giving.
4. That we good people are also more factually correct.

But what if these assumptions are questionable? What if evil is a way of responding to an imperfect world by actors with limited resources in a determinate situation? What shall we say to such a sensitive writer as Han Su-yin (Dr. Elizabeth K. Comber) when she tells us, "So I'm not a good woman. If I'd been a good woman, where would I be now? I'll tell you—dead!"? Finally, what will it mean for our notions of psychotherapy and sociotherapy if, in those cases where evil people see a different world from that observed by good men, the evil eye should prove the clearer?

Raising such a possibility is itself an invidious task, but just such a one as the professional student of society must undertake as part of the work of describing how people behave. To the objector who would resist the question and assume its answer in advance of test, the remainder must be given that the conflict between truth and utility is an old one and that, while it remains unresolved, it is of crucial importance for any theory of personal or social improvement. It must also be considered that, while as scientists we protest our preference for truth over error, as culture-bound thinkers we may favor lies when their credentials are of the right sort.

Raising the uncomfortable question of the healthfulness of bad actors may place us, as meliorists, in a "bind" because there are realities which, correctly perceived, are sickening, and we may have to choose between the "health" of the man who behaves badly because he sees accurately and the "health" of the man who behaves nicely because he has learned the popular ways of seeing falsely.

A PARTIAL EXAMINATION OF THE EVIL EYE

There is little doubt that bad people see the world differently from good. Many studies tell us so. Part of this perception involves preferences, tastes, self-conceptions and attitudes, but part of the difference in perception concerns how the world really is, and it is with this that we are concerned.

The differences in what good and bad people see "out there" share a generality because evil has been defined in socio-psychological research as deviation from a humanitarian, "progressive," middle-class, quasi-Christian,[3] Western-urban standard, so that it makes almost no difference which kind of badness one is inspecting—the kinds of belief about the world that allegedly differentiate the good and the bad man are of a persistent piece. In fact, one prominent study consciously explores the possibility that these evils are one morsel, as it attempts to relate political evil ("authoritarianism") to ethnic prejudice, crime, and psychic malfunction (1). What is crucial for present purposes is that these investigators believe the evil eye is astigmatic; they hold political evil (*their* conception) to be an ideology that fails as "... an objective appraisal of social reality, (and) tends to resemble a fantasy...." (1, page 845).

The purportedly fantastic world seen by the bad man is a jungle. And a jungle may be defined as a place where strength and cunning decide and win—not "humanness," "justice," "principle," nor any other ethnic than force and fraud. It is a place where each against all is truer than all for each or, even, each for himself alone.

Since the perceptions reported as marking off the bad man from the good have this generality, it is not necessary to use the findings of every study, nor to limit our search to one kind of wrong, in order to examine the relative acuity of good and evil perception. A sample of such studies dealing with delinquency (6, 22, 23), juvenile narcotic users (14), fascism (1), and ethnic prejudice (1, 2) has been taken. From the measures which these studies report as differentiating, with some degree of probability, the attitudes of good and bad people, *all* statements relating to "external fact" as opposed to self-evaluation or personal behavior have been listed. The literature has then been scanned for evidence, tentative and partial though it might be, that would permit a grading of these differentiating perceptions, using the bad person's view from his environment as the one to be tested, since it is he who is allegedly unhealthy and who eyes the world through need-distorted lenses.

In fairness to the investigators whose studies have been used, employment of their differentiating items should not be construed as meaning that these authors necessarily subscribe to the notion under question here—that badness is sickness, a symptom of which is a distorted perception of the world. The approach of certain of these investigators has been purely actuarial: what distinctions can be found that allow us to predict? But in other cases, notably those of Allport-Kramer and the Adorno group, the investigators do maintain that "good" perceptions are healthier and more accurate than evil ones.

The reality-perceptions of bad men, and one judge's estimate of their accuracy based on the sources cited, are listed below. To propose one's own estimate of perceptual accuracy is, of course, to run the risk of criticism *ad hominem* and the kind of "tele-psyching" to which even behavioral scientists are not immune. However, this study has been entered with the explicit assumption that socio-psychological observers assessing good and evil conduct and mental health may themselves be wearing class-ethnic blinkers, so that it would hardly be pertinent to put this matter to their vote. Since the present concern lies more heavily with being heuristic than with being right, it would seem sufficient only to make a probable guess as to the state of the "real world" as good and bad people differentially see it, and to cite one's grounds for his estimate.

Some Available Evidence. Ball (6) reports five statements that differentiate between delinquent and non-delinquent perceptions of the prevalence of stealing. The first reads:

"How many people would steal if they had a good chance?"

---

[3] The use of the qualifier, "quasi," is not flippant. Western society has moved a long way from the ideals and practices of a Christian community. For a statement of what the Christian mode would mean, see Jones (28) and Russell (54).

a. *The delinquent believes* "about half, most, or all."

b. *Estimate:* Probably accurate; much depends on the meaning of "good chance."

c. *Evidence:*

1. "... all employees of a chain-store were run through his (Keeler's) polygraph when the company complained it was losing more than one million dollars annually through petty thefts. Polygraph records indicated fully three out of four employees were pilfering funds. This and subsequent experiences led Keeler to pronounce a rather cynical dictum generally held by lie-detection experts today: '65 per cent of people who handle money take money....' " (17, pages, 154–155)

2. "Lie detector tests of employees of certain Chicago banks showed that 20 per cent had taken money or property, and in almost all cases the tests were supported by confessions. Similarly, lie detector tests of a cross section sample of the employees of a chain store indicated that about 75 per cent had taken money or merchandise from the store." (40)

3. "... the Comptroller of Currency reported that about three-fourths of the national banks examined in one period were violating the national banking laws and that dishonesty was found in 50.5 per cent of the national bank failures in the years 1865–1899, and 61.4 per cent in the years 1900–1919." (16, page 185)

4. "Undersecretary of the Treasury Fred A. Scribner, Jr., reported that a Treasury examination of 1956 income tax returns discovered that taxpayers had failed to report almost $4,500,000,000 of interest and dividends received during that year. ..." (55)

5. Investigators carefully dropped stamped, addressed postcards, letters, and letters bearing a lead coin simulating a 50-cent piece in various cities of the East and Midwest. Seventy-two per cent of the postcards were returned; 85 per cent of the blank letters; 54 per cent of the "coin-carrying" letters. "We conclude ... that the public at large is very strikingly altruistic, manifesting obligingness, consideration, and responsibility. A sharp decline in the reliability of the public sets in under the effects of suggestion of financial gain. One-third of the altruistically minded are converted to selfish behavior. It is probable that an even larger proportion of the public at large is unreliable in such a financial matter." (41)

6. "Hume said one could be sufficiently sure about certain aspects of human nature to predict with accuracy what would happen to a quantity of gold left unguarded in a populous place. On the basis of human experience in a free society one can now say the same of anything, of however little value, that is portable. For in all our centers of dense population any possessions left unguarded on the doorstep—roller skates, bicycles, baby carriages, appliances, garbage cans, tools, lawn mowers, trash receptacles and the like—disappear as if by magic." (33)

7. *Reader's Digest* Survey, 1941:
   Of 347 garages visited, 63 per cent were dishonest.
   Of 304 radio shops, 64 per cent were dishonest.
   Of 462 watchmakers, 49 per cent were dishonest (51).

A second of Ball's questions asks, *"Do you think many people have taken things at some time?"*

a. *The delinquent* again believes that "about half, most, or all" have.

b. *Estimate and Evidence:* There is little reliable evidence on this matter. However, one study of a non-criminal population is suggestive. Nettler (48) asked a heterogeneous sample of California residents these questions, among others, concerning their criminal conduct:

—"Since age 16, how many times have you taken hotel towels or blankets as souvenirs?"

—"Since age 16, how many times have you taken a newspaper from a stand without paying for it?"

—"Since age 16, how many times have you taken something from a store without paying for it?"

—"Since age 16, how many times have you kept money for yourself that belonged to someone else?"

—"Since age 16, how many times have you taken another's property such as fruit, tools, library books, or other unsecured objects?"

A majority of the respondents admitted anonymously to one or more of these crimes.

Ball reports three other statements that distinguish good and bad perception: "Do you think many people would steal from their friends?" "Do you think many people would steal from a store if they had a good chance?" "...from a school?" Lack of evidence prevents a test of these items.

Chein (14) found that juvenile narcotics users tend to see a different social world than children who are free of this habit:

"Most policemen treat people of all races the same."

a. *Narcotics user* denies.
b. *Estimate:* probably an accurate perception — in the environment in which the question was asked.
c. *Evidence:* (4; 7, pages 159, 164–165; 53; 60, pages 139–140; 64, page 95)

"Most policemen can be paid off."

a. *Narcotics user* agrees.
b. *Estimate and Evidence:* No one knows about "most policemen." But for evidence that this perception is not a fantasy, see (7, pages 245–246; 49, page 73; 60, pages 228–229, 383–389)

"The police often pick on people for no good reason."

a. *Narcotics user* agrees.
b. *Estimate and Evidence:* This must vary with race, class, and the police force. And no one knows, class by class, whether this is "often" true. But for evidence that this perception, again, is not a hallucination, see (7, page 750; 60, pages 331–341)

"I am sure that most of my friends would stand by me no matter what kind of trouble I got into."

a. *Narcotics user* denies.
b. *Estimate and Evidence:* Part of this is tautology; a "friend" is this kind of person.

Again, no one knows how much friendship there is in our society. And such as one finds probably varies socio-economically (13, pages 189–190; 34; 42, *passim*). "When you have no money, nobody takes an interest in you. I never had a friend. For six years it has been like that. We are living in filthy misery on the East Side — nobody can ever help us out of that." (25, page 17)

Jungles, by definition, are not friendly environments and we need to know their protean styles and their prevalence. It is more than one observer's judgment that friendship, as distinct from "cliqueship," is an abnormality on Manhattan's Seventh Avenue or San Francisco's Montgomery Street. And, if one talks as an industrial consultant to the $52-a-week girls straitened desk-after-desk in the offices of Megalopolitan Insurance, he will not be reassured that many abide in the warmth of friendship. Or enter academia and observe the rarity of love and charity. Some participants have described the Academy as a general jungle, a microcosm of the competitive, political, envious and even unhappy world we usually associate with the strivers in grey flannel (8, 39, 69)

"Everybody is just out for himself. Nobody really cares about anybody else."

a. *Narcotics user* agrees.
b. *Estimate and Evidence:* As worded, this seems patently false. *Some* people care for others, at least in some milieux.

But this too must be class linked and the delinquent's perception may give an accurate picture of his world.

Such a statement poses, and leaves unanswered, three important questions about people's concern for others:

1. Under what circumstances does altruism develop?
2. How many people do care about how many others? What is the *range* of love by ethnic group and socio-economic status?
3. What is the *quality* of this concern? Love

does not often come to us unalloyed. Portions of personal motivation, self-interest, ego are involved in altruism; the question is, "How much?" As Eric Hoffer has put it, "There is no doubt that in exchanging a self-centered for a selfless life we gain enormously in self-esteem."

As "concern for others" becomes a thing one does out of concern for himself—not to uphold self-principle, but to get something or somewhere—the delinquent's perception becomes more accurate. Perhaps he has put the emphasis on *"really* cares." Instance: involvement in a large community's welfare activities will impress one that many (how many)? of the civic-minded altruists do not "really" care for those they are helping. Their concern seems to this admittedly fallible observer sometimes to be a public expression that has status and recreational value, political, and even commercial value. Probably no one who has worked with charities and welfare agencies would dispute the existence (while he may debate the prevalance) of non-loving motives among board members, junior leaguers, service clubs, and other volunteer welfare-dispensers.

In the investigation by Hathaway and Monachesi (23) the following perceptions were found to distinguish predelinquent boys from others:

"My mother was a good woman."

a. *Predelinquent* denies.
b. *No evidence* available. A "good woman" is difficult to define.

"One or more members of my family is very nervous."

a. *Predelinquent* agrees.
b. *No evidence* in either direction.

"The man who had most to do with me when I was a child (such as my father, stepfather, etc.) was very strict with me."

a. *Predelinquent* agrees.
b. *Estimate:* probably true.
c. *Evidence:*
   1. Glueck's "Social Factors" Prediction Table (21, p. 260):

	Weighted Failure Score:
#1. Discipine of Boy by Father—	
Overstrict or erratic	71.8
Lax	59.8
Firm but kindly	9.3

2. Anderson (3) reports that parents ranked by psychometrics as high in dominance and low in affection had aggressive and rebellious children.
3. "On every item in the interview in which intensity of punishment was rated, the fathers of the high aggression boys punished more severely than the fathers of the low aggression boys" (67). (This finding is qualified by the possibility that judges may have rated non-verbal punishment as more severe than verbal. Personal communication from the investigator).

"When a man is with a woman he is usually thinking about things related to her sex."

a. *Predelinquents* affirm.
b. *Estimate and Evidence:* This may be a function of age, but otherwise . . . ? It may also vary with status and culture. Much depends on the meaning of "with a woman" and "thinking about things." But, if the delinquent's perception is widely inaccurate, then Hollywood, the ladies' magazines, and American advertisers are also wearing distorting spectacles.

"My parents have often objected to the kind of people I went around with."

a. *Predelinquent* admits.
b. *Estimate:* probably true.
c. *Evidence:* Chwast (15) cites many studies that affirm the relationship between delinquent behavior and parental rejection/disapproval.

Gough and Peterson's items (22) distinguishing those predisposed to crime from those more immune are largely attitudinal and self-descriptive. However, there are two categories of statement that deal with how the world "out there" is perceived; three items are concerned with how "jungley" it is and nine with family life.

The predelinquent is depicted by Gough and Peterson as believing that: *"I would* have been more successful if people had given me a fair chance"; "Life usually hands me a pretty raw deal"; and "A person is better off if he doesn't trust anyone."

For all of these statements there is thus far no conclusive evidence. These items are, of course, both "objective" and "subjective"—they carry a heavy load of interpretation of what has happened to one—but, for present purposes, it need only be indicated that the predelinquent, particularly if he comes from the lower classes, is probably not distorting his reality greatly. And, in validation of the delinquent perception, one can cite all manner of learned non-delinquent. For example, Charles Stockard, the noted zoologist, believed, erroneously, that "...man is the only animal that gives deliberately false signals to his kind," and George Bernard Shaw has been quoted as saying:

Man is the only animal of which I am thoroughly and cravenly afraid. I have never thought much of the courage of the lion-tamer. Inside the cage he is at least safe from other men. There is less harm in a well-fed lion. It has no ideals, no sect, no party, no nation, no class; in short, no reason for destroying anything it does not want to eat. (11)

Myers and Roberts (47) write of their class V (lowest status) patients, "They were reared in an environment where violence, aggression, hostility, and rebellion were accepted. (They)...received little warmth or affection."

David Riesman summarizes, "...the conditions of lower-class life do not encourage trust" (52)

The pre-criminal, according to Gough and Peterson, sees his family life as unsatisfactory and he is probably right. He believes:

"My family has objected to the kind of work I do, or plan to do."
"My parents were too strict with me when I was a child."
"My parents never really understood me."
"My home life as a child was less peaceful and quiet than those of most other people."
"My parents have often disapproved of my friends."
"I was often punished unfairly as a child."

And he denies that:

"My home life was always very pleasant."
"My parents have generally let me make my own decisions."
"The members of my family were always very close to each other."

The final form of the F (authoritarianism) scale devised by Adorno and associates (1) contains ten statements that describe how the world is or will be and to which the "fascist" subscribes. Of these ten items, one seems false, one true, and four might be correct depending upon the definitions adopted. For the remaining four statements no evidence is available.

Probably false: "Wars and social troubles may someday be ended by an earthquake or flood that will destroy the whole world."
Probably true: "Human nature being what it is, there will always be war and conflict."
See Hanson Baldwin (5) or Freud (20).
Possibly true, depending upon the definitions given:

"People can be divided into two distinct classes, the weak and the strong."

As with all defining statements, the "validity" of this one is a function of someone's purposes in making such a classification. While field theorists warn against such Aristotelian dichotomies, many scientists are convinced of the usefulness of dichotomous assumptions for certain purposes. See, for example, George Kelly (30).

"A person who has bad manners, habits, and breeding can hardly expect to get along with decent people."

As conventionally understood, this is probably a true statement; much depends on who one thinks is "decent."

"Most of our social problems would be solved if we could somehow get rid of the immoral, crooked, and feeble-minded people."

Since there is no agreed-upon roster of social problems, it is impossible to say how many problems would constitute "most." However, see any social problems text.

"*The wild sex life of the old Greeks and Romans was tame compared to some of the goings-on in this country, even in places where people might least expect it.*"

Comparative study of this nature seems insurmountably difficult, although challenging. See almost any issue of *Playboy, Confidential,* or the daily press. Also, Ben Hecht (24).

No evidence available:

"*If people would talk less and work more, everybody would be better off.*"

"*Most people don't realize how much our lives are controlled by plots hatched in secret places.*"

The words "plot" and "secret" make the statement difficult to evaluate; otherwise see Hunter (26) and Mills (42).

"*The businessman and the manufacturer are much more important to society than the artist and the professor.*"

"*Familiarity breeds contempt.*"

Most of the items in E (Ethnocentrism) scale devised by the same group of investigators (1, page 142) are too attitudinal and ambiguous to permit test, but one seems quite probably false, and two possibly true:

Probably false: "*The people who raise all the talk about putting Negroes on the same level as whites are mostly radical agitators trying to stir up conflicts.*"

Possibly true: "*The best guarantee of our national security is for America to have the biggest army and navy in the world and the secret of the atom bomb.*"

This item is dated. If its intent is read as of 1961, our government seems to be acting as if preparedness were "the best guarantee," even though American sociologists may not feel too secure in it.

Again, see Baldwin: "The right fist of all-out nuclear power must remain ready as a sanction to help ensure limited war" (5, page 43).

Or, Morgenstern: "The problem, the great problem, of our military planners is to organize and maintain armed forces capable of fighting any kind of war anywhere" (43).

"*The trouble with letting Jews into a nice neighborhood is that they gradually give it a typical Jewish atmosphere.*"

This offensive statement is emotionally loaded by the phrase, "The trouble with ..." and the adjective, "nice." If one discounts these attitudinal indicators and restricts the sentence to its factual representation, to the possibility of ethnic invasion and succession, it seems true in the larger metropolitan areas of the United States (70).

Ambiguous and No Evidence Available:

"*One trouble with Jewish businessmen is that they stick together and prevent other people from having a fair chance in competition.*"

"*There may be a few exceptions, but in general Jews are pretty much alike.*"

"*There is something different and strange about Jews; it's hard to tell what they are thinking and planning, and what makes them tick.*"

"*Manual labor and unskilled jobs seem to fit the Negro mentality and ability better than more skilled or responsible work.*"

"*Most Negroes would become overbearing and disagreeable if not kept in their place.*"

"*The worst danger to real Americanism during the last 50 years has come from foreign ideas and agitators.*"

"*America may not be perfect, but the American way has brought us about as close as human beings can get to a perfect society.*"

Allport and Kramer (2), testing Ichheiser's psychoanalytic hypothesis about anti-Semitism (27), find that anti-Semites are differentiated from the unprejudiced by their greater fear of swindlers than of gangsters. They say, "... those who are more afraid of swindlers also have higher prejudice scores in general. ($\chi^2 = 7.17$, significant at the 1 per cent level). Those who are more afraid of gangsters (may we not say, a more natural and normal fear?) are less prejudiced" (2, pages 33-34).

Allport and Kramer may choose to call the good man's greater fear of gangsters "natural and normal," whatever that means, but such honorific labelling does nothing to root this fear in a clearer perception of reality. Again, the good man, Allport and Kramer included, seems to be looking at the world through distorting spectacles, for the evidence is abundant that good and bad pepole alike are at least as apt to be defrauded by swindlers as bludgeoned by gangsters. Barnes and Teeters (7, page 69) call it a toss-up, but Nietzsche (32), White (68), and Bernard (12, page 36), among others, see fraud as the more common danger. Sutherland felt it probable that "... fraud is the most prevalent crime in America" (60, page 42), Schur calls swindling, "... a strongly entrenched national phenomenon...." (57, page 269), and Nettler (48) found "crimes of deceit" to be admitted anonymously by a majority of non-criminal population. Reference to works on white-collar crime (61) and confidence games (38) confirms the suspicion that Allport-Kramer and their unprejudiced subjects are less able to test the reality about them (in this department at least) than their evil respondents.

A Tally. It appears that good people see the world at least as inaccurately—to put it mildly—as bad ones. Any "score" here is subject to criticism and can only be offered tentatively. For, aside from the quarrels with one investigator's assessment of reality, even where he cites "evidence"

Table I. *A Tally of the Relative Accuracy of the Perceptions of Good and Bad Men*

TALLY I: ALL ITEMS

	Study							
	Ball	Chein	H-M	G-P	F-Scale	E-Scale	A-K	Total
Bad Man Accurate	2	5	3	9	5	2	1	27
Good Man Accurate	0	0	0	0	1	1	0	2
Evidence Lacking or Ambiguous	3	0	2	3	4	7	0	19
Total	5	5	5	12	10	10	1	48

TALLY II: FAMILY HISTORY ITEMS OMITTED "ROUGH" VERSION

	Ball	Chein	H-M	G-P	F-Scale	E-Scale	A-K	Total
Bad Man Accurate	2	5	1	0	5	2	1	16
Good Man Accurate	0	0	0	0	1	1	0	2
Evidence Lacking or Ambiguous	3	0	2	3	4	7	0	19
Total	5	5	3	3	10	10	1	37

TALLY III: FAMILY HISTORY ITEMS OMITTED "SOFT" VERSION

	Ball	Chein	H-M	G-P	F-Scale	E-Scale	A-K	Total
Bad Man Accurate	1 [a]	1 [b]	1	0	1 [c]	1 [d]	1	6
Good Man Accurate	0	0	0	0	1	1	0	2
Evidence Lacking or Ambiguous	4	4	2	3	8	8	0	29
Total	5	5	3	3	10	10	1	37

[a] Calls "many people have taken things" lacking in evidence.

[b] Considers only the delinquent negation of "most policemen treat people of all races the same" as an accurate perception in the environment in which the question was asked.

[c] Calls the four items judged "possible true" lacking in evidence.

[d] Calls the item about "Jews in nice neighborhoods" ambiguous and lacking in evidence.

for his view, there remains the possibility that good and bad men reside in different "real" worlds and, hence, where they differ they may be equally correct or incorrect. For this reason Table 1 presents three tallies: one of all 48 items as judged for approximation to actuality in the text above, and two tallies—a "rough" and a "soft" one —of the 37 items that remain after the family history items in the Gough-Peterson and Hathaway-Monachesi studies are discounted.

A reading of these 37 non-personal items shows that the possible residence of good and bad men in different "real" worlds does not explain all the differences in perception; a generalized view of the shared world remains and, from the items and evidence at hand, it cannot be concluded that the evil eye sees it poorly.

DISCUSSION

It has been argued that the conception of evil action as sickness is questionable. Particularly doubtful is the assumption that a prime symptom of the illness that generates badness is a false picture of the world. If this now seems obvious, one wonders how such an idea could have been given professional credence. A few sources of this intellectual infection may be suggested.

It would seem that the notion that bad people must be sick is the spawn of American pragmatic optimism (All problems are soluble if we but think; do something!) bred with the classic values of goodness, truth, and beauty in an atmosphere in which the prestige of religious explanation has been declining while that of popular psychologizing has been rising.

Having "advanced" beyond blaming the bad man for his moral depravity, the middle-class investigator proposes to treat him for his sickness. This proposal is emboldened by the optimistic assumption that goodness and health (which includes telling, seeking, and seeing the truth) are reciprocally related. With faith so set, it follows that evil may be cured, like other infirmities, and that an important part of the cure lies in the bad, sick man's taking psychotherapeutic exercises in correct perception—of what he has done, and why, and of how people "really" are as opposed to what he thought they were.

This tentative study calls into question this popular thoughtway. Bad actors may not be sick—at least no more so than good men—and, particularly, they may not suffer from perverted perception. Rather, if the present tally has validity, it is the good man who sees relatively inaccurately.

Two questions persist:

—How jungle-like is our society?
—To what extent is behavior a function of how one perceives his social world?

On the first question our "authorities" give conflicting answers. Freud advises that "Men are not only worse, but also better, than they think they are," but, another time, he writes, *"Homo homini lupus;* who has the courage to dispute it in the face of all the evidence in his own life and in history?" (20)

A philosopher reviewing a work on "New Knowledge in Human Values" asks its psychologist-editor, "If Maslow is right in saying that 'our deepest needs are *not* ... dangerous or evil or bad,' why are our surface appetites often so?" (58)

And Ortega tells us, "The very name, 'society,' as denoting groups of men who live together, is equivocal and utopian." (50)

Relative to the second question, disputes persist concerning the value of accurate perception (44).

—"It is not wholesome to live by illusion," Gordon Allport assures us.
—"Mankind cannot stand too much reality," T. S. Eliot replies.
—The golden virtues are ". . . love, truth, beauty, self-realization . . . (they) conduce to psychological health," Huston Smith retorts.
—But ". . . mental integrity may rest on the

capacity for denial, for sustained repression of truth," answers Philip Roche.

If more thorough investigations support present assumptions about the likely answers to our two questions, the result will be unfortunate for those of us who have learned to value truth. With the Existentialists, we may have to agree that some truths are sickening. And with Plato and the many religionists, we may have to agree that men need the control as well as the comfort of myth.

REFERENCES

1. Adorno, T. W., et. al., *The Authoritarian Personality*, New York: Harper, 1950.
2. Allport, G., and B. M. Kramer, "Some Roots of Prejudice," *Journal of Psychology*, 1946, 22, 9–39.
3. Anderson, J. P., "A Study of the Relationships Between Certain Aspects of Parental Behavior and the Attitudes and Behavior of Junior High School Students," *Contributions to Education*, *#809*, New York: Teachers College, Columbia University, 1940.
4. Axelrad, Sidney, "Negro and White Institutionalized Delinquents," *American Journal of Sociology*, 1952, 57, 569–574.
5. Baldwin, H. W., "Limited War," *The Atlantic Monthly*, May, 1959, 203, 35–43.
6. Ball, J. C., "Delinquent and Non-Delinquent Attitudes Toward the Prevalence of Stealing," *Journal of Criminal Law, Criminology, and Police Science*, 1957, 48, 259–274.
7. Barnes, H. E., and N. K. Teeters, *New Horizons in Criminology*, New York: Prentice-Hall, 1951.
8. Barr, Stringfellow, *Purely Academic*, New York: Simon and Schuster, 1958.
9. Barron, Frank, "Towards a Positive Definition of Psychological Health," paper read to the American Psychological Association, 1955.
10. Barron, M. L., *The Juvenile in Delinquent Society*, New York: Knopf, 1954.
11. Basso, H., "Foxy Like a Grandpa," *New Yorker*, 1949, 25, 109.
12. Bernard, L. L., *Social Control*, New York: Macmillan, 1939.
13. Broom, L., and P. Selznick, *Sociology*, Evanston: Row-Peterson, 1955.
14. Chein, I., "Narcotics Use Among Juveniles," *Social Work*, 1956, 1, 50–60.
15. Chwast, J., "Perceived Parental Attitudes and Pre-Delinquency," *Journal of Criminal Law, Criminology, and Police Science*, 1958, 49, 116–128.
16. Cressey, D. R., *Other People's Money*, Glencoe: Free Press, 1953.
17. Deutsch, A., *The Trouble with Cops*, Boston: Little, Brown, 1950.
18. Frank, L. K., *Society as the Patient*, New Brunswick: Rutgers University Press, 1948.
19. Freides, D., "Toward the Elimination of the Concept of Normality," *Journal of Consulting Psychology*, 1960, 24, 128–133.
20. Freud, S., *Civilization and Its Discontents*, New York: Doubleday, 1953, p. 61.
21. Glueck, S., and E. Glueck, *Unraveling Juvenile Delinquency*, Cambridge: Harvard University Press, 1950, pp. 257–262.
22. Gough, H., and D. R. Peterson, "The Identification and Measurement of Predispositional Factors in Crime and Delinquency: A First Report," paper read at the 1951 meeting of The Western Psychological Association.
23. Hathaway, S. R., and E. D. Monachesi, "The Personalities of Predelinquent Boys," *Journal of Criminal Law, Criminology, and Police Science*, 1957, 48, 149–163.
24. Hecht, B., "Sex in Hollywood," *Esquire*, 1954, 41, 35 and *passim*.
25. Hellersberg, E. F., *The Individual's Relation to Reality in Our Culture*, Springfield: Thomas, 1950.
26. Hunter, F., *Top Leadership, U.S.A.*, Chapel Hill: University of North Carolina Press, 1959.
27. Ichheiser, G., "Fear of Violence and Fear of Fraud, with Some Remarks on the Social Psychology of Anti-Semitism," *Sociometry*, 1944, 7, 376–383.
28. Jones, W. T., *A History of Western Philosophy*, New York: Harcourt, Brace, 1952, pp. 342–343.
29. Kahn, Jr., E. J., "Annals of Crime," *New Yorker*, 1959, 35, 122–153.
30. Kelly, G. A., *The Psychology of Personal Constructs*, New York: Norton, 1955, vol. I, pp. 109–110.
31. Lambert, W. W., L. M. Triandis, and M. Wolf, "Some Correlates of Belief in the Malevolence and Benevolence of Supernatural Beings: A Cross-Societal Study," *Journal of Abnormal and Social Psychology*, 1959, 58, 162–169.
32. Levy, O. (ed.) *The Complete Works of Friederich Nietzsche, vol. 7, Human, All-too-Human*, London: Fouilis, 1911, pp. 200–201.
33. Lundberg, F., *The Treason of the People*, New York: Harper 1954, p. 289.
34. Lynd, R. J., and H. Lynd, *Middletown*, New York: Harcourt, Brace, 1929, p. 272.

35. Masling, S. M., "How Neurotic is the Authoritarian?", *Journal of Abnormal and Social Psychology*, 1954, 49, 316–318.
36. Maslow, A. H., *Motivation and Personality*, New York: Harper, 1954, p. 204.
37. Maugham, S., *The Summing Up*, New York: Doubleday, 1938.
38. Maurer, D. W., *The Big Con*, New York: Bobbs-Merrill, 1940.
39. McCarthy, M., *The Groves of Academe*, New York: Harcourt, Brace, 1952.
40. McEvoy, F. P., "The Lie-Detector Goes Into Business," *Reader's Digest*, 1941, 38, 69–72.
41. Merritt, C. B. and E. G. Fowler, "The Pecuniary Honesty of the Public at Large," *Journal of Abnormal and Social Psychology*, 1948, 43, 90–93.
42. Mills, C. W., *The Power Elite*, New York: Oxford University Press, 1956.
43. Morgenstern, O., *The Question of National Defense*, New York: Random House, 1959.
44. Moore, W. E., and M. M. Tumin, "Some Social Functions of Ignorance," *American Sociological Review*, 1949, 14, 787–795.
45. Morris, C. W., *The Variety of Values*, Chicago: University of Chicago Press, 1956.
46. Mowrer, O. H., "Sin, the Lesser of Two Evils," *American Psychologist*, 1960, 15, 301–304.
47. Myers, J. K., and B. H. Roberts, *Family and Class Dynamics in Mental Illness*, New York: Wiley, 1959, page 253.
48. Nettler, G., "Antisocial Sentiment and Criminality," *American Sociological Review*, 1959, 24, 202–218.
49. Nossiter, B. D., "The Teamsters: Corrupt Policemen of an Unruly Industry," *Harper's*, 1959, 218, 70–76.
50. Ortega y Gasset, Jose, *Concord and Liberty*, New York: Norton, 1946, p. 24.
51. *Reader's Digest*, 1941, 38, July, August, September issues.
52. Riesman, D., "Political Communication and Social Structure in the United States," *Public Opinion Quarterly*, 1956, 20, 60.
53. Robison, S. M., *Juvenile Delinquency: Its Nature and Control*, New York: Holt-Dryden, 1960, p. 211.
54. Russell, B., *Why I Am Not a Christian*, New York: Simon and Schuster, 1957.
55. Sahlman, H., "Taxes: Evasion and Avoidance," *Commentary*, 1959, 28, 447–448.
56. Schuessler, K. F., and D. R. Cressey, "Personality Characteristics of Criminals," *American Journal of Sociology*, 1950, 55, 476–484.
57. Schur, E. M., "Sociological Analysis of Confidence Swindling," *Journal of Criminal Law, Criminology, and Police Science*, 1957, 48, 296–304.
58. Smith, H., review of A. H. Maslow (ed.), "New Knowledge of Human Values," *Saturday Review*, 1959, 42, 25.
59. Smith, M. B., "Research Strategies Toward a Conception of Positive Mental Health," *American Psychologist*, 1959, 14, 673–681.
60. Sutherland, E. H., and D. R. Cressey, *Principles of Criminology*, Philadelphia: Lippincott, 1955.
61. Sutherland, E. H., *White Collar Crime*, New York: Dryden, 1949.
62. Szaz, T. S., "The Myth of Mental Illness," *American Psychologist*, 1960, 15, 113–118.
63. Szaz, T. S., "Naming and the Myth of Mental Illness," *American Psychologist*, 1961, 16, 59–65.
64. Taft, D. R., *Criminology*, New York: Macmillan, 1950.
65. van den Haag, E., "Psychoanalysis and Its Discontents," in S. Hook (ed.), *Psychoanalysis, Scientific Method, and Philosophy*, New York: New York University Press, 1959.
66. Volkman, A. P., "Delinquent and Nondelinquent Personality," *Social Problems*, 1958–59, 6, 238–245.
67. Walder, L. O., "An Attempt at an Empirical Test of a Theory," in *The Application of Role and Learning Theories to the Study of the Development of Aggression in Children*, Washington: American Psychological Association, 1958.
68. White, L. A., *The Evolution of Culture*, New York: McGraw-Hill, 1959, pp. 346–347.
69. Williams, G., *Some of My Best Friends Are Professors*, New York: Abelard-Schuman, 1958.
70. Wirth, L., *The Ghetto*, Chicago: The University of Chicago Press, 1929.
71. Witmer, H. L., and R. Kotinsky, *Personality in the Making*, New York: Harper, 1952, p. xviii.

SECTION II

Criminal and Delinquency Statistics

IT IS NOT THE PURPOSE OF THIS SECTION TO PROVIDE THE LATEST CRIMINAL statistics, for the absolute numbers of officially recorded data change each year and are readily available in various public documents. Our aim is to promote insight and understanding of criminal and delinquency statistics; to help develop a critical awareness of the difficulties involved in the collection of basic data that are used in research and theory; to indicate the limitations imposed when it is necessary to rely upon data collected by and for public administrative authorities and when the scientific investigator has little control in the definition of terms, conceptual framework, or the error correction process.

Wilkins discusses the need for conceptual clarification as a necessary preliminary stage to the efficient collection of criminal statistics as well as citing some of the operational problems in data gathering. The crucial role of the victim in criminal statistics relates to his deciding whether to inform the police of a crime. Ennis' study is one of the most provocative investigations to emerge from the President's Commission on Law Enforcement. The selection by Gold, measuring undetected delinquency, claims to be free of the "selectivity" of police and court records and examines the inverse relationship of social status and delinquency. The article raises fundamental questions about delinquencies undetected by public authorities and the value of "self-report" delinquency instruments in the solving of these questions. "Measuring Crime" proposes a model criminal justice system and vividly illustrates the successive elimination of cases at the various stages of law involvement from crimes known to the police to imprisonment. An examination of the data indicates, among other things, that of 2,780,000 Index crimes known, less than 3 percent result in offenders being sentenced to prison. The difficulties of constructing a crime index are compounded by inefficiency or misrepresentation of record keeping by police departments. In the brief selection entitled "Abuses in Crime Reporting" these problems are clearly presented as having serious effects on our knowledge of the amount of real criminality in a community.

It should become clear that public announcements and many newspaper reports about "crime waves" and increases or decreases in the amount of delinquency must be subjected to careful critical appraisal before such statements can be considered valid. Two major concepts should be kept in mind throughout the section: validity and reliability. That criminal statistics should measure what they purport to measure raises questions about validity. Whether these statistics have a high degree of consistency and measure the same thing raises questions about reliability. The articles in this section seek to promote insight into an understanding of both these concepts.

8. NEW THINKING IN CRIMINAL STATISTICS

LESLIE T. WILKINS

THROUGHOUT THE WORLD THERE IS EVIDENCE of new thinking in social defense and criminology. There is new thinking, too, in the fields of statistics and population accounting. Many of the concepts developed in economics are having an influence on other aspects of social studies; the new concepts of operations research, theory of games, decision theory, communications and information theory are not without an impact upon many and diverse fields of inquiry.

The recently published (1964) work of Sellin and Wolfgang, *Measurement of Delinquency,* makes a major contribution to the new thinking in crime measurement by showing that there are concepts in criminology which may be scaled. But before they could develop this line of analysis they had to clear away many misconceptions of the past. While their approach is original, they are not alone in developing concepts of this kind. Indeed a new general line of thinking to which their work represents a major contribution may be seen in many Western countries.

The British Home Office and the Scottish Home Department recently established Departmental Committees to consider revision of *criminal statistics.* Although these Committees have not yet reported, permission has been granted for the publication of a paper presented to them by the author. At that time he was Deputy Director of Research in the Home Office, but the report was presented as a private and personal contribution at the request of the Committee. It may be of interest to make this document available in the same form as it was presented, but to relate some of the concepts to the work of Sellin and Wolfgang. It should be noted, however, that the British contribution did not involve experimental trials of ratings which are a central feature of the American book, but there are other features which may make the comparison of the two approaches of interest to others concerned with problems of crime measurement.

Following is the report which I prepared for *The Departmental Committee on Statistics:*

A NOTE ON STATISTICS OF CRIME, CRIMINALS AND COURT DECISIONS

1. The writer is of the opinion that the main problems concerning criminal statistics are not matters of detail but relate to quite fundamental concepts, and that ends must be closely examined before means may be considered.

2. Criminal statistics should provide basic information in many fields of study and guidance in many administrative and

▶SOURCE: *"New Thinking in Criminal Statistics," Journal of Criminal Law, Criminology, and Police Science* (September 1965), 56:3:277–284. Copyright 1965 by Northwestern University School of Law. Reprinted by special permission of the Journal of Criminal Law, Criminology and Police Science and the author.

legal processes. Consideration of the ends in any detail would involve a study of the concepts of several disciplines and the functions of the departments concerned. Such detailed analysis cannot be a practical consideration at this time. It is suggested, therefore, that the possibility of sequential change to meet changing needs should be specifically planned into any system that may be developed.[1]

3. This paper is divided into three parts. In the first some brief notes on basic concepts are set out. In the second the implications of the concepts are related to what appear to be the more important operational questions. The third section puts forward some opinions on possible outlines of solutions.

BASIC CONCEPTS

4. The primary function of criminal statistics is to provide quantitative classified information regarding both (a) crimes, and (b) criminals. That is to say, the data must cover: (a) descriptions of *events* which are identified as breaches of the law (as defined at the time and place of the event);[2] and (b) *decisions* made by authorised persons regarding *individuals* who are identified as associated with the criminal act, and, where possible, the consequences of such decisions.

5. The information may be presented in regard to *persons* or *events,* or persons x events, but it is essential that data relating to criminals (persons/decisions) are not confounded with data relating to crimes (events). It should, however, be possible to relate to persons without confusion.

The Concept of Crime

6. It is doubtful whether it is legitimate to discuss the concept of crime as though it was something which can be measured or counted. Certainly it is not possible to make valid inferences from any counts or measurements without reference to the changing norms of acceptable and unacceptable behaviour in different social groups at different times.[3] It is of course, possible to define crime as the summation over (Σ) the separate definitions of proscribed behaviour encoded in some form of law. The boundaries of different definitions do not, however, have a constant relationship to the consensus of public opinion or even of "informed public opinion". Thus, reported crime and recorded crime will differ and the gap between the two collectives will change as behaviour, which is perceived as socially acceptable or unacceptable, changes either in relation to space or time factors.

7. Socially acceptable events may, at some times and places be illegal (crimes), but these events will not be reported and will seldom stand any chance of being recorded. Further, socially unacceptable events which are not indictable offences, although reported, will not in present conditions be recorded as crimes.[4]

The Concept of Criminal

8. There is a possibility that some of the confusion of criminological concepts is semantic in origin. The term "criminal" is used both as an adjective and as a noun, but the relationship between the two meanings is not as close as is usual between similar adjectives and nouns. It may be

---

[1] The rating scale of Sellin and Wolfgang meets this criterion, as well as allowing for geographical differences in the concept of "seriousness" of crime.

[2] The concept of an "event" is stressed by Sellin and Wolfgang, (see Ch 9) for their purposes, as they remark, ". . . *events* [their italics also] not delinquent juveniles, . . . the major focal point for establishing an index."

[3] One of the more unexpected results of Sellin and Wolfgang's work is the extreme similarity between assessments of their events by different sectors of society. In view of their findings, this point, although still applicable, may not be so serious as it was previously considered to be.

[4] In England and Wales, the figures usually regarded as the index of crime are, in fact, "Indictable Offences known to the Police."

admitted by most persons that shoplifting is a "crime" (criminal act), but the one-time shoplifter is not regarded as a criminal; or if under prompting this is admitted, not as a "typical criminal."

9. Confusion exists between the concepts of morals, crimes and socially dysfunctional behaviour. Clearly "Criminal Statistics", as they exist at present, cannot be used to form any legitimate inferences about moral factors.[5]

10. In the remainder of this paper the term "criminal" will be used only as a *noun* to indicate a *person,* "crime" will be used only as a *noun* to describe *an event* defined by the law as such. Where adjectives are needed, other terms will be selected, but if necessary to make the meaning clear, the adjective "criminal" will be given in parenthesis. The term "Criminal Statistics" will not be used except to refer to the publication of that title, and quotation marks will be used. We shall refer to "statistics of crimes", "statistics of court procedures" and other types of statistical data as may seem appropriate.[6]

Information and Utility

11. Dr. W. H. Hammond has represented that the test of statistical information is utility.[7] This must be agreed. Indeed there is no meaning to the concept of information except with respect to a purpose. In administrative statistical data the value of information seems best to be assessed by tests related to decision making. The question, "What does the knowledge of fact x make it possible to do (decide) that would be impossible or impracticable without the knowledge of x?" provides a measure of utility. The difference between the utilities of the decisions is identically equal to the utility of the information x. That is to say, if the same decision would be made with a knowledge of x as without that knowledge, the utility of the information x is zero. The same type of measure may be used for assessment of the utility of degrees of precision. Thus, if a decision could be made with the same level of confidence, given either $x \pm 5\%$ or $x \pm 10\%$, then the cost of the reduction of the error term from $\pm 10\%$ to $\pm 5\%$ is a waste of resources. Similarly if information at intervals is as good a guide to decisions as continuous information, the cost of continuous collection should not be entertained.

12. Unfortunately, needs may arise in the future for information being generated today, but these needs and the attendant utilities may not now be predictable. Some form of insurance against future loss of utilities is, therefore, essential. How much investment should be placed in insurance against future needs is a difficult question, but it is possible to suggest logical methods for its consideration.

Types of Procedures for Collection of Statistical Data

13. The concept of utility is helpful in proposing a strategy for data collection and handling. Four types of processes are suggested: *1.* Continuous collection for all persons or all events (continuous census); *2.* Collection for all persons or events, but at intervals (census); *3.* Collection in respect of a sample of persons or events, as a continuous process (continuous sample); *4.* Collection in respect of a sample of persons or events for part time (interval sample). In general the cost of the operation will diminish from type *1* to type *4*.

Types of Information Sources

14. Any data which are not accessible to meet a need have no utility. The cost of

---

[5] Wilkins, *The Measurement of Crime*, Brit. J. Crimino (April, 1963).

[6] This point must be taken as agreed quite generally in theory. Although Sellin and Wolfgang do not use the same type of point of English usage, the separation of the concepts is basic to their work.

[7] Unpublished paper by Dr. Hammond of the Home Office Research Unit.

storage and retrieval are important considerations. Certainly no data should be collected twice, since the cost of storage and retrieval will, in all normal circumstances, be less than re-collection.

15. Statistical data are usually secondary information, and the basic material for collection process *1* will be information necessary for other purposes. Initially it may be supposed that any information considered necessary to facilitate decisions about individuals has potential value for statistical inference about groups of persons. The same may be said to apply to events. The problem regarding type *1* collection processes is to ensure cheap methods for storage and retrieval of existing information, and these processes should be linked with automatic collation, summation and analytical processes. Types *2* to *4* processes of collection might be appropriate where: (a) Data were available for the population (all cases or events) but the individual decisions made on the basis of this information were taken at a low level of authority and the storage of the information would be costly (e.g. minor motoring offences); and (b) The information was not secondary, that is, not regarded as necessary for other decisions for all individual persons or events.

Classification, Analysis and Interpretation

16. Information becomes statistical data after the processes of classification and summation, and it is usual to add procedures for analysis and interpretation. These processes may be applied to data which exist in some form for other purposes, or the same operations may be applied to other information collected with a view to a specific purpose. It will be obvious that a hard line cannot be drawn between statistical material and case material, nor between data collected for administrative, diagnostic or other purposes. Perhaps the statistical operation is distinct from the research operation upon data in that the former is not concerned with the *content* of case material, but only with the storage, retrieval and classification of information originating in the form of case papers. But the statistical system must be planned to be flexible so that it can incorporate the results of research into the continuing series. If the statistical system cannot accommodate changes, the utility of the system will diminish.

OPERATIONAL PROBLEMS

17. The concepts introduced briefly in the preceding section may now be related to what appear to the writer to be the more important problems.

Crime and Socially Dysfunctional Behaviour

Types of concept and types of action

18. The main problems which arise in considering the nature of the measurement of crime are due to confusion of the concept(s). Some see crime largely as a moral problem, others as socially dysfunctional behaviour, and many do not separate the two concepts; and there are other views emphasising different aspects of offensive behaviour. Because the social action regarded as necessary (or legitimate) differs according to the philosophy, the types of statistical data which would be required to provide the most appropriate information for one view or purpose would be different from that most suited to another. There is some ground common to the different philosophies, and this will be considered first. Later the particular views of the writer may become more obvious and intrusive.[8]

---

[8] Sellin and Wolfgang deal with the problem by omitting consideration of "sin", and selecting a list of Offences which relate to the "common ground". They also show that the amount of "common ground" is remarkably large.

Comparability over time and space

19. If the conventional definition of crime is accepted as an initial basis for discussion, it is not clear what purposes are well served. It must be assumed that the counts of "crimes" (events) are intended to give some measure of the concept of the total "criminality" in the country. But a general and usual purpose of counting procedures is to afford a basis of comparison over time or between places. But since any state may define any act as "criminal" by legislative action, crime rates between countries (or legal systems) cannot be compared. Some supranational definitions might be made covering *types of behaviour* (events) disapproved by all societies, or by all "Western democracies" or some other collective of societies, but this seems an improbable event. Even if it were possible, the standardisation of definitions would not be sufficient to ensure comparability. No one state or society can determine a universal definition of crime. The valid use of crime rates, since crime is defined by the law, is confined to within one legal system.

20. There are similar problems in comparisons over time within a legal system. The law changes, reflecting the dynamic state of society and hence the definitions of crime which are based on the legal system (some Σ, over defined action) also change. Besides the official changes in the law, certain legal definitions are broadly based [9] and are adaptable to changing conditions (e.g., the "legal fictions"). Any statistical data which relate to legal definitions contain the effects of problems of this system of definition.

21. Presumably legal definitions are designed to serve legal purposes, and they are not open to criticism because they do not function in an optimum way for other purposes. Among the legal purposes which these definitions serve, the more important may be the determination of guilt or innocence of the individual offender. The emphasis in a trial (or hearing) is on the individual in the dock and the facts of the case in relation to the law. None the less, it will be obvious that descriptions of behaviour may be set forth which relate to other frames of reference. A system of classifying "what actually happened," which is optimum for legal purposes, is not the only system of classifying what happened. Other purposes than the determination of guilt in which present day society may be equally interested may require other methods of description. Societies today use many forms of social incentives and deterrents to induce individual members to conform to social norms.

Multiple Classification

22. Standard methods of problem solving include the classification of incidents in different ways in order to facilitate different solutions and to provide means for the assessment of the probable outcome of changes in the situation under study. For example, it was found by operational research workers during the war that flying accidents were seldom due to one "cause" —there were usually two or more factors which, if not present, might have resulted in the accident not taking place. The statistical policy of the Directorate of Accident Prevention of the Royal Air Force was, therefore, to classify each accident according to *all* the abnormal features in the situation so that the likely effect of any modification could be assessed. If crime is multi-causal, then it may be argued that the absence of any one factor in a situation might have changed the probability of its outcome. Socially damaging incidents (crimes) may be described and defined in many ways (on the same basic informa-

---

[9] The phrase "broadly based" is used to cover the two types of source of variations, the one semantic and the other perceptual. Since these two factors interact and the resulting difficulties of comparison are similar, no distinction will be made in this note. Nominalist and realist philosophies, although relating to different research strategies, present similar problems in statistical data collection.

tion) to facilitate the many different approaches to control and investigation. In the case of fires we do not allow the identification of an arsonist to inhibit development of means to prevent fires or to minimise the damage when they occur from whatever cause. The fact that some person (criminal) can be blamed for (found guilty of) a socially damaging incident (crime) does not absolve society from seeking ways to prevent or minimise damage irrespective of the form it may take or the guilt of the offender.

23. The central problem in devising statistics of crimes is to find ways for classifying events (crimes) which maximise the power of the information for purposes of different specific social action. The criterion by which existing "Criminal Statistics" should be tested is their fitness for these purposes (actions). Indeed, this is a general criterion for testing any form of social statistics.

24. In the light of this criterion it seems that the current definitions of "crime" for purposes of counting "crimes (indictable offences) known to the police" must be considered unsatisfactory. It would seem to be a matter for informed opinion to decide whether at least one "crime index" should reflect closely the lay public's views of what constitutes a "crime" or a "serious crime." If a "democratic definition" is regarded as appropriate, techniques exist for its refinement. If the definition of "crime" does not reflect the lay public's views of what crime is, the publication of figures for lay consumption will, it follows, be misleading and social pressures will develop leading to unsatisfactory action strategies.[10]

---

[10] This is exactly the point addressed by Sellin and Wolfgang and, indeed, they show that the scaling by the lay public does not differ significantly from the scaling of those professionally concerned with crime in different capacities. The matter of an index for action, or different forms of information for different purposes is, however, a rather different issue.

Complaints and public opinion

25. It may be held that the "crime complaints" reflect the public's views and awareness of socially disapproved behaviour which exceeds a threshold value such that they consider that the police ought to do something about it. As a measure of the pressure of police work it may be that "complaints" provide a better index than "indictable offences." It is, of course, probable that the threshold value of disapproval for a constant event will change with time and from place to place; that complaints will reflect the public expectation of behaviour and that this will provide a relative rather than an absolute measure of "crime." This is true. It is true also of the concept of "crime", whether this be measured by reference to indictable offences or some other legal definition or collective of such definitions.

Two measures may be better than one

26. It may be possible to obtain a better measure of the phenomena which most people have in mind when they speak of crime if it were possible to make two distinct and different measurements—one relating to *reported behaviour* by some system such as now, and one relating to *reporting behaviour* on the part of the general public. By relating changes in *reported behaviour* ("crimes" or complaints) to changes in *reporting behaviour* a robust index seems to be possible.

27. Sample survey techniques could provide a measure of the changes in reporting behaviour by means of attitude scales or by means of subjective utility assessments.

28. Crimes which are not known to exist until investigation of other complaints lead to their discovery; crimes of which members of the public are unaware; crimes where there is no victim, may in some sense be "crimes", but they are of a different order from the majority of incidents which the layman considers to be "criminal" events. Crimes may, of course, be

discovered by the police in the course of their work, but the victims remain unknown, and there are crimes where the victim may be regarded as the whole of society. If the public is unaware of a crime, or does not believe the incident to be a "crime," no complaint will be made because no one can disapprove of an unknown event. But these types of incidents are rare and it is unlikely hat they will represent a large proportion of "serious crime." There are also very important distinctions in criminological thought between "socially defined criminals" and "law-made criminals." This distinction could be usefully retained and made patent, rather than obscured and neglected in the statistics.

29. It seems probable that the majority of "crimes (indictable offences) known to the police" are notified to the police by the victim, or, if a corporate body, by some authorised person representing the institution. (It is unfortunate that these facts are not known.) It would greatly assist the interpretation of any statistics of crimes (events) if rises and falls in the "crime index" could be related to different types of notification, or other ways whereby the events became "known."

Types of notification of "crimes"

30. It seems necessary to give consideration to whether (a) some classification of the method whereby the "crime" first became known should be standardised and applied to (i) all cases, or (ii) certain types of offences (e.g. violence against the person); and (b) where a number of *crimes* (e.g. continuous offences) become known by the same *report*, the number of crimes is less important than the number of separate reports.[11]

A NEW FOCUS FOR MEASURING "CRIME"

31. The writer would prefer to see more radical changes than those proposed in paragraph 30 above, but along the same general lines. The role of the victim in the concept of jurisprudence has diminished over the centuries, but public interest is today beginning to re-focus. It seems that consideration should be given to whether the emphasis in statistical data regarding crimes should not be moved from the abstract concept of crime (events) to the person or concept of the victim. Such a change would facilitate the solution of many intractable problems. It seems that more useful information for purposes of social action could be derived from data about victims and the nature of the event *suffered by them,* than from information regarding the concept of the crime or the criminal.

32. It may be thought that the main purpose of the administration and government in the field of crime is not to protect morals but to protect the victim. If so, then a need exists for data to assist in the direction of this task. At present there are no measures of the effect of legally proscribed ("criminal") acts on the victims. The number of offenders is known in terms of "statistical persons", but there is no information regarding even "statistical" victims.

33. It has been noted earlier that one test of the utility of any measures is that

---

[11] The problem of continuous offences is a difficult one which arises from the compulsion to count rather than measure events. Sellin and Wolfgang stress the number of separate *events.* For most of the offences included in their index this presents no real problem. It is possible to instruct persons to consider separately "each distinct robbery regardless of the number of victims", or to count each unlawful entry in the case of burglary. In the event of larceny there may be some problem in identification of "each distinct operation" (p. 293). But has a forger committed as many crimes or "events" as he has made false entries? Any counting system will present problems and some unsatisfactory assessments. It must be agreed, however, that the concept of an event avoids the even more unsatisfactory concept by which one event may be classified as one crime or almost any number, and some of the less serious incidents are capable of expansion to many breaches of law.

they can be used to compare different areas of the country. Indeed, rates which do not permit of valid comparisons cannot be justified in terms of any utility. It is suggested that a base which would give good comparability and measure what most people mean by "crime" would be *damage done or loss or injury sustained by actions known or believed to be illegal*. Not only would a measure of this kind enable geographical areas to be compared, but, and this seems even more important, comparisons could be made regarding the effects of different kinds of social evils. There are limited social resources to deal with social problems and these should be deployed with a strategy which maximises social utility. Social action strategies cannot be evaluated unless comparable data are available to assess different social needs. Scales exist whereby personal injury or death may be translated into social costs (e.g industrial injuries, road accidents etc.).

Action and Intentions

34. The proposal to measure "crime" by means of social cost factors involves a change of base from "what the offender tried to do" (intent) to what was the effect of his actions. This approach avoids many administrative (as distinct from philosophical) difficulties. The matter of intent is important in moral issues, but morals and social costs are not the same thing and should be separated in the statistics. The two concepts of what happened and what was intended should happen, should not be confounded in one figure which serves to illuminate neither the social nor the ethical matters. Intent is a concept which relates more to the actor than to the action, and the introduction of intent into the description of crimes (events) tends towards the same error as confusion of "crimes" (events) with criminals (persons). Perhaps the utility of this separation of concepts is best indicated by an example. An area (X) may exist which has exactly (n) criminals who commit (N) offences, and who have the same intent as in another area (Y) also with exactly (n) criminals and (N) offences. But area (X) may suffer less social damage than area (Y) because, say, criminals in area (X) are less competent. By present statistics the number of crimes and criminals in area (X) would be exactly the same as in area (Y) and they could not be distinguished in any way. But clearly appropriate social action in the two areas might be very different. Again, suppose that the lack of social damage in area (X) was due, not to lack of competence of the offenders, but to extra competence of the police force; it would seem that these and similar factors should be revealed rather than hidden by the concept of "intent."

35. It will be recognised that the approach proposed is related to "welfare economics"—a field of statistical, econometric and mathematical theory which has developed rapidly in the last decade. Using known methods, areas could be compared on many indices of crime if crime were considered in terms of the social cost. Changes in the value of money, different rates of economic development, local and general economic boom and depression and the like could be related to "crime" through the medium of social costing. Some experts in the United States are beginning to think along these lines, but the idea of social welfare costing does not find such a ready acceptance here. Although Sellin and Wolfgang reject the idea of expressing everything in terms of the dollar, it is only a simple linear transform which is lacking to convert their seriousness scale for crimes into a scale of subjective social costing. It is then only a small step from subjective assignment of costs to more rigorous methods of ascertaining values. No such schemes could be put into action immediately; pilot investigation would be necessary to work out an inexpensive system and to remove snags in the detailed planning. But such measures of the state of crime may be de-

veloped independently of statistics of criminals (persons) and court disposals (decisions).

Criminals

Persons and Decisions

36. The legal concept of intent and most matters of interest to jurisprudence fall to be considered in connection with statistics relating to criminals (persons) rather than to crimes (events). Clearly, an event has neither intent nor responsibility—these are attributes of *persons*. The statistical person must be a "real" person and not the statistical fiction of current "Criminal Statistics," where one person may be several statistical persons in any one year, and a guilty corporation is a male aged 25! The units in data concerning courts could, it is proposed, be more correctly discussed as "decision"—not person—statistics. Statistics of court decisions are not statistics of criminals (persons); the two concepts should be clearly separated. In assessment of court work the number of persons involved in the decisions may be important, but the main factor must be the number of decisions. Of course, the person (criminal) is *affected by* the court decisions, but the final decision, in cases where there are more than one, is the factor of most concern from the viewpoint of the person in the dock, and the value (utility) of the decision.

37. The decision process is itself important, but it is desirable to leave consideration of this until we have discussed the problems of statistics of criminals (persons). At present there is considerable overlap and duplication of records in the flow of information regarding criminals. For example, when an offender is disposed of by the court (a decision) the person's movements are determined by that decision, and information about these movements is required by two central and certain regional organisations. The Criminal Record Office (and perhaps regional C.R.O.s) may require information so that the offender's history may be brought up to date, and the Statistical Branch of the Home Office requires information for statutory purposes.

Criminal's Debt to Society—The Ledger Accounts

38. The operations required to provide information about offenders are very similar to those required by classical double-entry book-keeping, but the different "books" in the "Criminal Statistics" case are kept from different source material. The C.R.O. record and the Statistical Branch Offender Index are exactly similar to the ledger accounts and show the debit incurred by the offender to society, together with his payments (penalties). In the same way as modern book-keeping makes use of original documents for posting ledgers and the like, including the extracting of sales statistics, profit and loss accounts, balance sheets, etc., "Criminal Statistics" data could be derived from the *secondary use of original documents* without special effort having to be diverted for statistical purposes as such. Unlike book-keeping, social accounting need not always be concerned with recording all items of information, but sampling may be inserted at various stages of processing as an economy or expediting measure.

Multiple Use of Primary Documents

39. Cheap copying systems are now available and the multiple purposes to be served by the primary source material could be met by routine copying, and far better than by special creation of subsidiary primary source material. Such copying of primary documents would serve as the basis for varying sampling fractions, where the proportion of the population sampled was determined according to the expected utility of the information. The storage of the primary information would ensure that utility not now foreseen was safeguarded.

Court Decisions

Decisions and Outcomes

40. The work of the courts has interest in its own right and the interest should be served by the statistical data, without confounding with other interests. The source material may, of course, be complex, but it is the function of the statistical processing of the primary information to separate out the concepts for policy and action. It should not be necessary to raise special primary information in order to meet statistical needs in this sector.

41. The delays which occur in bringing offenders to trial, the frequency of appeals, the proportion of defended and undefended cases, the frequency with which offenders at different courts plead guilty, and many other factors affect the type of court work, but data on few of these matters are available in the current "Criminal Statistics."

42. Any decision, it may be thought, is intended to maximise the probability of an outcome which is desired by the decision maker. If this is so, the outcome of the treatment (decision) determined by the court is relevant and provides the link between statistics of criminals and statistics of court decisions. Data of this kind were specifically requested by the Streatfeild Committee. At present, such data as are available are obtained by specific "research" studies.

Inter-relation of Data—Crimes, Criminals and Decisions

43. Before it is possible to inter-relate the data covering different concepts it is, of course, necessary to differentiate them. The satisfactory integration into "Criminal Statistics" of data relating to crimes (events), criminals (persons) and courts (decisions), can be achieved only when it is possible to separate them. Information regarding "crime" should be related to the information about the criminal whenever possible, and both should be related to the court decisions. The court decision should be related to information regarding the outcome of the treatment, and so throughout. All the information required for statistical purposes is available in some form in a primary source document. The problem is in providing means for linking this material and in the design of an efficient means for the information to flow to those who have need of it. It is the writer's view that these problems are soluble cheaply and that better data could be obtained with less "paper work" for the police and other agencies concerned with action, than is at present the case.

44. It seems essential that at some *one place* there should exist a comprehensive record of offenders with a continuously maintained record of their offences (the "ledger accounts"). This place should be responsible for copying and supplying to other persons and agencies the information required—other agencies should not have to collect again data which could be copied. If no such comprehensive records exist, there will be no way for providing courts with the information they need or ways whereby treatments may be evaluated. If the documents are not in one place, the time and complexity of tracing the appropriate source will add to the cost and the full benefits of automation will not be obtained. It would seem that the requirement to provide information to the central agency (whatever form this might take) should be statutory.

(Part Three which discussed systems of documentation is not reproduced here since it is of limited interest).

Lord Kelvin is reported as saying, "When you can measure what you are speaking about and express it in numbers you know something about it, but when you cannot measure it, when you cannot express it in numbers, your knowledge is of a meagre and unsatisfactory kind". Measurement is developing rapidly in many branches of social science, and few would now wish to reverse this trend. There is a long way to go before a sound strategy of social action, policy and research can be developed, but the types of measure proposed by Sellin and Wolfgang in respect of criminality are adaptable to other fields and allow of comparisons in terms of perceived social utilities.

9. CRIME, VICTIMS, AND THE POLICE

PHILLIP H. ENNIS

"A SKID ROW DRUNK LYING IN A GUTTER IS crime. So is the killing of an unfaithful wife. A Cosa Nostra conspiracy to bribe public officials is crime. So is a strong-arm robbery...." So states the report of the President's Commission on Law Enforcement and Administration of Justice, commonly known as the Crime Commission report, in pointing out the diversity of crime. Our recent investigation at Chicago's National Opinion Research Center reveals that Americans are also frequent prey to incidents which may not fall firmly within the jurisdiction of criminal law, but which still leave the ordinary citizen with a strong sense of victimization—consumer frauds, landlord-tenant violations, and injury or property damage due to someone else's negligent driving.

With the aid of a new research method for estimating national crime rates (Figure 1) the Crime Commission study has now confirmed what many have claimed all along—that the rates for a wide range of personal crimes and property offenses are considerably higher than previous figures would indicate. Traditional studies have relied on the police blotter for information. The present research, devised and carried out by the National Opinion Research Center (NORC), tried a survey approach instead. Taking a random sample of 10,000 households during the summer of 1965, we asked people what crimes had been committed against them during the preceding year. The results—roughly 2,100 verified incidents—indicated that as many as half of the people interviewed were victims of offenses which they did not report to the police.

This finding raised several questions. How much did this very high incidence of unreported offenses alter the picture presented by the standard measures, notably the FBI's Uniform Crime Reports (UCR) index, based only on reported incidents? What was the situation with minor offenses, those not considered in the UCR index? What sorts of crimes tended to go unreported? And why did so many victims fail to contact the authorities? These were some of the issues we attempted to probe.

THE UNKNOWN VICTIMS

More than 20 percent of the households surveyed were criminally victimized during the preceding year. This figure includes about *twice as much* major crime as reported by the UCR index. The incidence of minor crimes—simple assaults, petty larcenies, malicious mischiefs, frauds, and so on—is even greater. According to our research, these are at least twice as frequent as major crimes. The UCR index includes seven major crimes, so the proliferation of petty offenses not taken into account by the index makes the discrepancy between

►SOURCE: *"Crime, Victims, and the Police," Trans-Action (June 1967), 4:7:36–44.* Reprinted by permission.

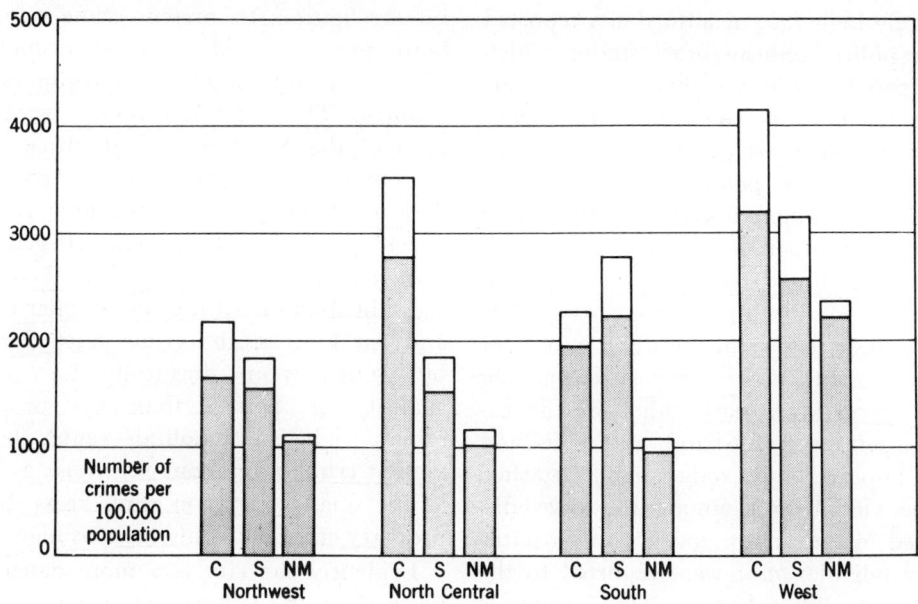

Figure 1. Regional crime rates by type of community.

Table I. *Estimated Rates of Major Crimes: 1965-1966*

Crime	NORC Sample: Estimated Rate per 100,000	Uniform Crime Reports, 1965: Individual or Residential Rates per 100,000
Homicide	3.0	5.1
Forcible rape	42.5	11.6
Robbery	94.0	61.4 [a]
Aggravated assault	218.3	106.6
Burglary	949.1	296.6 [a]
Larceny ($50+)	606.5	267.4 [a]
Car theft	206.2	226.0 [b]
Total	2,119.6	974.7

[a] The 1965 Uniform Crime Reports show for burglary and larcenies the number of residential and individual crimes. The overall rate per 100,000 population is therefore reduced by the proportion of these crimes that occurred to individuals. Since all robberies to individuals were included in the NORC sample regardless of whether the victim was acting as an individual or as part of an organization, the total UCR figure was used for comparison.

[b] The reduction of the UCR auto theft rate by 10 percent is based on the figures of the Automobile Manufacturers Association showing that 10 percent of all cars are owned by leasing-rental agencies and private and governmental fleets. The Chicago Police Department's auto theft personnel confirmed that about 7-10 percent of stolen cars recovered were from fleet, rental, and other nonindividually owned sources.

that index and the real crime picture even greater than a consideration of major offenses alone would indicate.

Table I compares our figures with the UCR rates for the seven major crimes upon which the index is based—homicide, forcible rape, robbery, aggravated assault, burglary, larceny (over $50), and auto theft. The homicide rate projected by the survey is very close to the UCR rate—not surprising since murder is the crime most likely to be discovered and reported.

The survey estimate of the car theft rate is puzzlingly low. This could be because people report their cars "stolen" to the police and then find that they themselves have "misplaced" the car or that someone else has merely "borrowed" it. They may either forget the incident when interviewed or be too embarrassed to mention it. The relatively high rate of auto thefts reported to the police confirms other studies which show people are more likely to notify the police in this case than they are if they are victims of most other crimes. It may also indicate that people think the police can or will do more about a car theft than about many other offenses.

The startling frequency of reported forcible rape, four times that of the UCR index, underscores the peculiar nature of this crime. It occurs very often among people who know each other—at the extreme, estranged husband and wife—and there appears to be some stigma attached to the victim. Yet among the cases discovered in the survey, too few to be statistically reliable, most were reported to the police. Do the police tend to downgrade the offense into an assault or a minor sex case or put it into some miscellaneous category? This is a well-known practice for certain other kinds of crime.

To what extent is crime concentrated in the urban environment? To what extent are there regional differences in crime rates? And to what extent are the poor, and especially Negroes, more or less likely to be victims of crime? Behind these questions lie alternative remedial measures, measures which range from city planning and antipoverty programs to the training and organization of police departments and the allocation of their resources throughout the nation.

THE WILD, WILD WEST

The NORC findings presented in the chart above give an overview of the crime rates for central cities in metropolitan areas, for their suburban environs, and for nonmetropolitan areas in the four main regions of the country. The chart shows the crime rate (per 100,000 population) for serious crimes against the person (homicide, rape, robbery, and aggravated assault) and serious crimes against property (burglary, larceny over $50, and vehicle theft).

The myth of the wild West is borne out by our figures. Its present crime rate, for both property and personal crimes, is higher than that of any other region of the country. The West has almost twice the rates of the Northeast for all three types of communities. The South, in contrast, does not appear to have the high rate of violent crime that is sometimes alleged.

As one moves from the central city to the suburbs and out into the smaller towns and rural areas, the crime rates decline, but much more drastically for crimes against the person than for property crimes. The metropolitan center has a violent crime rate about *five times* as high as the smaller city and rural areas, but a property crime rate only *twice* as high.

Evidently the city is a more dangerous place than the suburbs or a small town. Yet these figures require some qualification: About 40 percent of the aggravated assaults and rapes (constituting most of the serious crimes against the person) take place *within* the victim's home; and about 45 percent of all the serious crimes against the person are committed by someone familiar to the victim. Random "crime in the streets" by strangers is clearly *not* the main picture that emerges from these figures, even in the urban setting.

Who are the victims? Among lower income groups (under $6,000 per year) Negroes are almost twice as likely as whites to be victims of serious crimes of violence but only very slightly more likely to be victims of property crimes. Our figures show that, per 100,000 population, an estimated 748 low-income Negroes per year will be victims of criminal violence and 1,927 victims of property offenses, whereas the numbers for whites in the same income bracket are 402 and 1,829. The situation is exactly reversed for upper income groups. The wealthier Negro is not much more likely than the white to be a victim of a violent crime, but he is considerably more likely to have property stolen. His chances of losing property are 3,024 in 100,000,

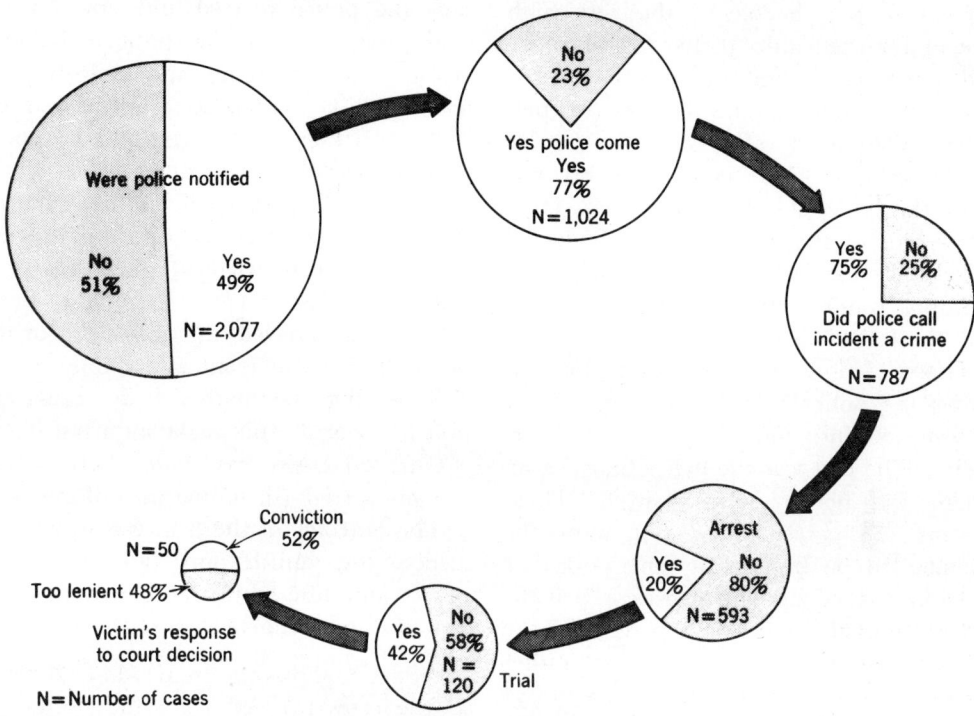

Figure 2. Attrition in the legal process. (N, number of cases.)

whereas the figure is only 1,765 for whites in the same income bracket. Burglary is the most common property crime against more affluent Negroes. The implication is that ghetto neighborhoods in which poor and richer Negroes live side by side make the latter more vulnerable to property losses than are higher income whites, who can live in more economically homogeneous areas.

Despite the fact then that per capita offense rates are generally acknowledged to be higher among Negroes than among whites, the incidence of whites being victimized by Negroes—an image frequently conjured up by the specter of "crime in the streets"—is relatively infrequent. Negroes tend instead to commit offenses against members of their own race. The same is true of whites. Further, to the extent that crime is interracial at all, Negroes are more likely to be victims of white offenders than vice versa. Our figures show that only 12 percent of the offenses against whites in our sample were committed by nonwhites, whereas 19 percent of the nonwhite victims reported that the persons who committed offenses against them were white.

WHO CALLS THE POLICE?

What happens when a person is victimized? How often are law enforcement and judicial authorities involved? What changes occur in the victim's attitude and behavior as a result of the incident?

If the "right thing" to do is to call the police when you have been a victim of a crime, and there is considerable pressure to do just that, why is it that half the victimizations were not reported to the police?

The more serious the crime, the more likely it is to be reported: 65 percent of the aggravated assaults in our sample were reported to the police, but only 46 percent of the simple assaults; 60 percent of the grand larcenies, but only 37 percent of the petty larcenies. Insurance recovery also appears to play a role in the very high rate of reported auto thefts (89 percent) and reported victimizations that are the result of automobile negligence (71 percent). Victims of offenses at the border of the criminal law apparently do not think the police should be involved. Only 10 percent of the consumer fraud victims called the police, whereas 26 percent of the ordinary fraud victims (mainly those of bad checks) did so.

Those victims who said they did not notify the police were asked why. Their reasons fell into four fairly distinct categories. The first was the belief that the incident was not a police matter. These victims (34 percent) did not want the offender to be harmed by the police or thought that the incident was a private, not a criminal, affair. Two percent of the nonreporting victims feared reprisal, either physically from the offender's friends or economically from cancellation of or increases in rates of insurance. Nine percent did not want to take the time or trouble to get involved with the police, did not know whether they should call the police, or were too confused to do so. Finally, a substantial 55 percent of the nonreporting victims failed to notify the authorities because of their attitudes toward police effectiveness. These people believed the police could not do anything about the incident, would not catch the offenders, or would not want to be bothered.

The distribution of these four types of reasons for failure to notify police varies by type of crime and by the social characteristics of the victim, but two points are clear. First, there is strong resistance to invoking the law enforcement process even in matters that are clearly criminal. Second, there is considerable skepticism as to the effectiveness of police action.

THE ATTRITION OF JUSTICE

A clue to this skepticism lies in the events which follow a call to the police. All the victims who reported an offense were asked how the police reacted and how far the case proceeded up the judicial ladder—arrest, trial, sentencing, and so forth. We have simplified the process into six stages:

Given a "real" victimization, the police were or were not notified.

Once notified, the police either came to the scene of the victimization (or in some other way acknowledged the event) or failed to do so.

Once they arrived, the police did or did not regard the incident as a crime.

Regarding the matter as a crime, the police did or did not make an arrest.

Once an arrest was made, there was or was not a trial (including plea of guilty).

The outcome of the trial was to free the suspect (or punish him "too leniently") or to find him guilty and give him the "proper" punishment.

Figure 2, shows the tremendous attrition as the cases proceed from the bottom of the "iceberg," the initial victimization, to the top, the trial and sentencing. Failure of the police to heed a call and their rejection of the incident as a crime account for a large proportion of this attrition. Also noteworthy are the low arrest and trial rates. Once the offender is brought to trial, however, the outcome appears more balanced. About half the offenders were treated too leniently in the victim's view, but the other half were convicted and given "proper" punishment.

SATISFACTION AND REVENGE

How do the victims feel about this truncated legal process? Do they feel that the situation is their own fault and accept it, or are they dissatisfied with the relatively frequent failure of the police to apprehend the offender? When the victims were asked their feelings about the outcome of the incident, only 18 percent said they were very satisfied; another 19 percent were somewhat satisfied; 24 percent were some-

Table II. *Degree of Satisfaction with Outcome of Offense*

Disposition of Case	Very Satisfied	Somewhat Satisfied	Somewhat Dissatisfied	Very Dissatisfied
No notification of police	13	18	28	41
Police did not respond to notification	22	22	18	38
Police did not consider incident a crime	24	26	24	26
Crime, but no arrest	20	23	27	30
Arrest, but no trial	33	21	22	24
Acquittal or too lenient penalty	17	13	26	44
Conviction and "proper" penalty	60	16	12	12

what dissatisfied; and 35 percent were very dissatisfied (4 percent gave no answer).

The level of satisfaction was closely related to how far the case went judicially. (See Table II.) People who did not call the police at all were the most dissatisfied. If they called and the police did not come, about the same percentage were very dissatisfied; but peculiarly, there were more who reported that they were satisfied. An arrest lowered the dissatisfaction level, but the dramatic differences appeared when the offender was brought to trial. If he was acquitted or given too lenient a penalty (in the victim's view), dissatisfaction ran high; if he was convicted and given the "proper" penalty, the victim was generally quite pleased. This suggests that the ordinary citizen's sense of justice includes a vengeful element—a desire for punishment over and above monetary compensation for loss. Advocates of rehabilitation rather than retribution for criminals might well take such public sentiments into account.

Quite independent of the judicial outcome of the case is its impact on the daily life and feelings of the victim and his family. Slightly more than 40 percent of the victims reported increased suspicion and distrustfulness along with intensified personal and household security measures. It appears that it is the unpredictability of the event and the sense of invasion by strangers rather than the seriousness of the crime that engenders this mistrust. With these strong feelings and the frequent lack of knowledge about the identity of the offender, victimization may well exacerbate existing prejudice against the groups typically blamed for social disorder and crime.

POLICE POPULARITY POLL

How does the public feel about the police? The survey asked all the crime victims and a comparably large sample of nonvictims a series of questions probing their attitudes on how well the local police do their job, how respectful they are toward the citizenry, and how honest they are. Items concerning the limits of police authority and exploring the functions of the police were also included.

Several conclusions emerged. Upper income groups are consistently more favorable in their evaluation of the police and are more in favor of augmenting their power than those with lower incomes. Negroes at all income levels show strong negative attitudes toward the police. (See Tables III and IV).

Table III shows rather clearly that Negroes, regardless of income, estimate police effectiveness lower than whites do, with Negro women being even more critical

Table III. *Positive Opinions on Local Police Effectiveness (Percentage who think police do an excellent or good job in enforcing the law)*

	White		Nonwhite	
Sex	Less than $6,000	$6,000 or More	Less than $6,000	$6,000 or More
Male	67	72	54	56
Female	66	74	39	43

than Negro men of the job the police are doing. Furthermore, Negroes show a smaller shift in attitude with increasing income than do whites, who are more favorable in their opinion of police effectiveness as their income rises.

Table IV shows that Negroes are also sharply more critical than whites are of police honesty. Here there are no income differences in attitude among white males. Women at higher income levels, both white and Negro, appear to be relatively less suspicious of police honesty. It is difficult to say how much these attitude differences are attributable to actual experience with police corruption and how much they express degrees of general hostility to the police. In either case the results indicate a more negative attitude toward the police among Negroes than among whites.

Table IV. *Opinions on the Honesty of Neighborhood Police (Percent)*

	Males			
	White		Nonwhite	
Police are ...	Less than $6,000	$6,000 or More	Less than $6,000	$6,000 or More
Almost all honest	65	67	33	33
Most honest, few corrupt	24	26	47	41
Almost all corrupt	3	1	9	19
Don't know	8	6	11	7
	Females			
	White		Nonwhite	
Police are ...	Less than $6,000	$6,000 or More	Less than $6,000	$6,000 or More
Almost all honest	57	65	24	35
Most honest, few corrupt	27	29	54	49
Almost all corrupt	2	0	10	4
Don't know	14	6	12	12

The next question probed a more personal attitude toward the police—their respectfulness toward "people like yourself." Almost 14 percent of the Negroes answered that it was "not so good." Less than 3 percent of the whites chose this response. This represents a much more critical attitude by Negroes than by whites, with hardly any differences by sex or income. There is some tendency, however, for very low income people of both races and sexes to feel that the police are not sufficiently respectful to them.

One further conclusion is more tentative. It appears that there is no *one* underlying attitude toward the police. The police have many and sometimes only slightly related jobs to do in society. For example, they have a role both in suppressing organized gambling and in maintaining civil order. Most people (73 percent) feel the police should stop gambling even though it brings a good deal of money into the community. A significant minority (21 percent) feel the police should act only on complaints, and only 2 percent said the police should not interfere with gambling at all. With respect to police control of demonstrations for civil and political rights, on the other hand, a slight majority (54 percent) say police should not interfere if the protests are peaceful; 40 percent say police should stop all demonstrations; and 3 percent feel demonstrations should be allowed under any and all circumstances. Negroes are much more permissive about demonstrations than whites, and somewhat more permissive about gambling. Among lower income Negroes there is a significant relation between permissiveness on gambling and a strong prodemonstration attitude. But whites show no such consistent attitudes on the two issues. They tend to favor police intervention in gambling but not in rights demonstrations.

A more dramatic example of discontinuities in attitudes toward police has to do with limitations on their power. A national cross-section of citizens was asked: "Recently some cities have added civilian review boards to their police departments. Some people say such boards offer the public needed protection against the police, and others say these boards are unnecessary and would interfere with good police work and morale. In general, would you be in favor of civilian review boards or opposed to them?"

In favor	45%
Opposed	35
Don't know	20

"Do you favor giving the police more power to question people, do you think they have enough power already, or would you like to see some of their power to question people curtailed?"

Police should have more power	52%
Have enough power already	43
Should curtail power	5

"The police sometimes have a hard time deciding if there is enough evidence to arrest a suspect. In general, do you think it is better for them to risk arresting an innocent person rather than letting the criminal get away, or is it better for them to be really sure they are getting the right person before they make an arrest?"

Risk arresting innocent	42%
Be really sure	58

"The Supreme Court has recently ruled that in criminal cases the police may not question a suspect without his lawyer being present, unless the suspect agrees to be questioned without a lawyer. Are you in favor of this Supreme Court decision or opposed to it?"

In favor	65%
Opposed	35

The significance of these results is their lack of consensus. On none of the questions is there overwhelming agreement or disagreement. Opinions are split almost in half, with the exception that hardly anyone is in favor of curtailing present police powers. The advocates of extending police authority in questioning suspects are almost balanced by those who think the police have enough power to do their job. Further, there is lack of internal agreement on the specific facets of the question. Being in favor of a civilian review board does not necessarily make a person support the Supreme Court decision on interrogation of suspects. Nor does a preference for having the police risk arresting the innocent rather than letting a criminal go free strongly predict being of granting more power to the police in questioning people.

It is not clear why attitudes toward the police are so scattered. Perhaps police power is too new an issue on the national scene to have its components hammered into a clear and cohesive whole. Local variations in police practices may also blur the situation. It appears we are only at the beginning of a long process of relocating the police in the political spectrum.

As the federal presence in local law enforcement enlarges, both the shape of crime and the nature of law enforcement itself will change. Accurate crime statistics will be essential in monitoring these changes and in evaluating the worth of new programs designed to protect the public from the growing threat of invasion and victimization by criminal acts.

10. UNDETECTED DELINQUENT BEHAVIOR*

MARTIN GOLD

STUDENTS OF JUVENILE DELINQUENCY AND practitioners who explore the research literature for help in treating delinquents have found that measurements of delinquency have been grievously inadequate. A youngster generally has been labeled "delinquent" either because he has been caught by the police or because his answers to questions about himself are similar to those of youngsters caught by the police.

Social scientists alert to this problem have developed various methods to measure delinquency directly from youngsters themselves, including field observation, self-administered questionnaires, and interviews. Results have been discrepant, as, for example, in studies of the relationship between juvenile delinquency and social status, a relationship upon which many theories of delinquency have been built.

This article introduces an interview method designed to find out from teenagers how many delinquent acts they have committed in the recent past and to discover other pertinent information about this behavior.

WHY COLLECT SUCH DATA?

Almost all of the research on delinquency begins in the official records of police, courts, and institutions. A large number of delinquent acts and the identities of children who committed them are unrecorded in these sources. In addition, they may not accurately reflect the distribution of delinquency by sex, social status, race, and other variables.

Murphy, Shirley, and Witmer,[1] for example, report that social agency records reveal what everyone suspected—that police never learn who committed most delinquent acts.

Furthermore, as demonstrated in one Michigan city, boys who live in poorer parts of town and are apprehended by police for delinquency are four to five times more likely to appear in some official record than boys from wealthier sections who commit the same kinds of of-

▶SOURCE: *"Undetected Delinquent Behavior",* Journal of Research in Crime and Delinquency *(January 1966), 13:1:27–46. Reprinted by permission.*

---

* The author wishes to thank Bert Greene, Donald Halsted, Safia Mohsen, and Margaret Simberg, who worked on various phases of this research; the Juvenile Division of the Flint Police Department and the Pupil Personnel Office of the Flint Public Schools, who gave invaluable assistance; and Dorwin Cartwright, Elizabeth Douvan, Ronald Lippitt, and Alvin Zander, who helped improve the manuscript.

This study was part of the Inter-Center Program on Children, Youth, and Family Life, which was directed by Ronald Lippitt and Stephen Withey. The research was supported by Grant M-09-109 from the National Institute of Mental Health.

[1] Fred J. Murphy, Mary W. Shirley, and Helen L. Witmer, "The Incidence of Hidden Delinquency," *American Journal of Orthopsychiatry*, October 1946, pp. 686–96.

fenses.[2] These same data show that, at each stage in the legal process from charging a boy with an offense to some sort of disposition in court, boys from different socio-economic backgrounds are treated differently, so that those eventually incarcerated in public institutions, that site of most of the research on delinquency, are selectively poorer boys.

Many well-known social-psychological and sociological theories of delinquency are grounded in data abstracted from official records.[3] These theories are built fundamentally on the finding that delinquency is related to socio-economic status, although the theoreticians recognize that this relationship may arise from the method by which the data are compiled. We need better data if we are to build and test theories more confidently.

Attempts have been made to collect data on delinquency independently of official records. Case histories in the files of social agencies have been one source of data,[4] but social agencies themselves contact a highly selective population, so their files do not adequately sample the population of American adolescents. Other investigators have administered anonymous questionnaires to samples of adolescents [5] and have produced findings which challenge the reality of the supposed relationship between socio-economic status and delinquency. Clark and Wenninger report:

> Our findings are similar to those of Nye-Short and Dentler-Monroe in that we failed to detect any significant differences in illegal behavior rates among the social classes of rural and small urban areas.[6]

On the other hand, Reiss and Rhodes [7] conducted personal interviews with boys in Nashville, Tenn., asking them if they had ever done something at one time or another for which they would have been arrested if they had been caught, and found that "delinquency rates, in general, vary inversely with ... the ascribed social status of the boy."

Because no investigation of undetected delinquency so far has sampled a large representative group of teen-age boys and girls and because results thus far have been so mixed, further work along these lines is indicated.

Beyond the need simply for accurate data on the extent and distribution of delinquency, descriptions of a large number of representative delinquent acts should give us further insight into the etiology of delinquency. For example, if we were able to distinguish the person who commits delinquent acts in the company of others from the one whose delinquency is solo behavior, we might be in a better position to sort out various motivations behind delinquency. Or, if we were able to determine precisely what it is that youngsters steal and what they do with the stolen goods, this information would help us distinguish between "utilitarian" and "malicious" forms of delinquency.

---

[2] Martin Gold, *Status Forces in Delinquent Boys* (Ann Arbor: University of Michigan, Institute for Social Research, 1963).

[3] Albert K. Cohen, *Delinquent Boys* (New York: Free Press, 1955); Richard Cloward and Lloyd Ohlin, *Delinquency and Opportunity* (New York: Free Press, 1960).

[4] Murphy et al., *supra* note 1; Sophia M. Robison, *Can Delinquency Be Measured?* (New York: Columbia University Press, 1936); Clifford R. Shaw and Henry D. McKay, *Juvenile Delinquency and Urban Areas* (Chicago: University of Chicago Press, 1942).

[5] John P. Clark and Eugene P. Wenninger, "Socio-Economic Class and Area as Correlates of Illegal Behavior among Juveniles," *American Sociological Review*, December 1962, pp. 826–34; Robert Dentler and Lawrence J. Monroe, "Early Adolescent Theft," *Amercan Sociological Review*, October 1961, pp. 733–43; Ivan E. Nye, *Family Relationships and Delinquent Behavior* (New York: Wiley, 1958); Austin L. Porterfield and Stanley C. Clifton, *Youth in Trouble* (Fort Worth, Tex.: Leo Potishman Foundation, 1946).

[6] Clark and Wenninger, *supra* note 5.

[7] Albert J. Reiss, Jr. and Albert L. Rhodes, "The Distribution of Juvenile Delinquency in the Social Class Structure," *American Sociological Review*, October 1961, pp. 720–32.

MEASUREMENT TECHNIQUE

The Sample. We aimed to study a representative set of teen-agers in Flint, Mich., an industrial city of 200,000 people. With the cooperation of the public school system, we selected at random a sample of six hundred from a list of almost all boys and girls thirteen through sixteen years old living in the school district, regardless of whether they were attending public or private schools or had dropped out of school altogether. We eventually interviewed 522 of them, or 87 percent of those originally selected. A look at the available demographic data on the 6 percent who refused to be interviewed and the 7 percent who had moved from Flint indicated that representativeness was not diminished by our inability to interview them. Table I describes the distribution of the sample by sex, race, and the occupation of the chief bread-winner in the family.

Introductory Procedure. We trained local college students in field interviewing techniques. Each interviewer was assigned to interview youngsters of the same sex and race as himself. Interviewers were instructed to turn back an assignment if they or members of their immediate family knew the youngster or the youngster's family.

After sending an initial letter to parents and youngsters announcing a study of what teen-agers do in their spare time, the interviewer arranged by telephone to drive the youngster to a community center, firehouse, or similar facility near his home so that all interviews could be taken under standardized conditions. We suspect that almost all of the thirty-eight refusals were attributable to parental objection to their son's or daughter's leaving the house with the interviewers, a practice we required so the youngster could be interviewed out of earshot of his family.

Table I. *Random Sample, by Sex, Race, and Occupation of Chief Breadwinner in Youth's Family*

| | Male | | | | Female | | | |
| | White | | Other | | White | | Other | |
Occupation (U.S. Census Categories)	%	No.	%	No.	%	No.	%	No.
Professional, technical, and kindred	4	23	—	—	4	21	—	—
Self-employed businessmen and artisans	3	15	*	2	3	18	—	—
Managers and officials	3	18	—	—	3	17	*	1
Clerical and sales	3	17	*	1	4	22	—	—
Craftsmen, foremen, and skilled workers	12	64	1	4	12	61	1	4
Operatives and kindred	9	46	7	35	10	53	5	25
Protective services: police, firemen, etc.	1	3	—	—	1	4	—	—
Laborers, service workers, and unskilled	1	6	2	11	2	11	1	6
Not ascertained	1	7	1	6	3	14	1	7
Total	38	199	11	59	42	221	8	43

* Less than .5%.

During the drive to the interviewing station, the interviewer revealed that the study was about delinquent behavior which may or may not have been detected. He assured the youngster of confidentiality and anonymity, and he stressed the importance of truthfulness. Then he explained the randomness of sample selection and offered the youngster an opportunity to withdraw from the study.

One boy asked to be returned home at this point. Of course, this does not necessarily mean that the rest were completely honest. Indeed, we know now that some were not.

We elected to employ the method of personal interview for two reasons. First, we wanted to obtain detailed descriptions of delinquent acts, to find out the *who, what, when, where, and how* of them. Such data are too complicated to get in a self-administered questionnaire.

Second, we suspected that, given a checklist, some youngsters might admit delinquent acts which would turn out not to be offenses at all, while others might overlook actual offenses. Probing by an interviewer on the spot could winnow out the misunderstandings and identify and draw out omissions. Indeed, our subsequent analysis of data shows, for example, that half of the acts of property destruction, one-fourth of the confidence games, and one-fifth of the personal assaults to which our sample initially admitted could not conceivably be called chargeable offenses. We found that such overreporting was sometimes related to other variables in which we were interested; for example, the proportion of confessions of accidental or trivial acts of property destruction was significantly higher among wealthier than among poorer white boys.

We also found that confession of one act sometimes led an interviewer to discover other related delinquencies; for example, about one-third of the thefts involved at least one other chargeable offense, as did 10 percent of the assaults.

The personal interview has an apparent disadvantage, however. It is reasonable to suppose that offenses would be concealed from an interviewer more frequently than from an anonymous, self-administered checklist. Later in this article we report a validity study of the personal interview method we used. It throws some light on concealment.

The interview began with the interviewer setting up a large sortboard in front of the respondent. Across the top was written "How often have you ...?" Under this heading were slots marked "Never," "More than three years ago," "In the last three years ... once, ... twice, ... three or more times." The slots were large enough to accept a 3 x 5 card.

The interviewer placed a packet of fifty-one 3 x 5 cards in front of the respondent: "First of all, I'm going to ask you to sort this pack of cards for me. On each card is a statement describing something a fellow or girl might have done, like the first one..."

Almost all respondents were able to sort their cards without further instructions. The fifty-one questions inquired about such activities as truancy or disbarment from school, trespass, damage, hitting father, lying, stealing, drinking beer, fighting, arson, smoking, taking a car, fornication, and carrying weapons. Questions on approved activities were also asked. These included mention on the school honor roll, helping charity drives, and working on the school newspaper.

The interviewer questioned the youngster about those offenses he admitted committing in the last three years. If the youngster indicated he had committed any particular offense more than once in that time, he was asked about each of the two most recent offenses of that kind. A standard form, administered to every respondent, elicited demographic and other data.

The questions asked about admitted offenses were essentially the same for all offenses, with only minor variations tailored for the specific kind of offense. Figure 1 reproduces the form appropriate to "taking some part of a car or gasoline."

It should be pointed out that, in Questions 5 and 5a ("Were you with anyone? Who were they?"), the respondent was not asked for the names of his delinquent companions, but only their age and sex and their relationship (close friends, acquaintances, etc.).

Take some part of a car, or gasoline
(If 3 or more times recently):
1. About how often do (did) you do this?
   Once a week or more _____ Two or three times a month _____ Once a month _____
   Once or twice every four months _____ Once or twice a year _____
   Other (specify) _____
2. Thinking of the last time you did this, what did you take?
3. Have we covered this in a previous question?
4. Where was this?
   4a. About how many blocks was that from your house?
       0-2 _____ 3-5 _____ 6-10 _____ 11-20 _____ 21 or more _____ 1 mile or more _____
   4b. Would you say this was in your neighborhood? Yes _____ No _____
5. Were you with anyone? Yes _____ No _____ (go to question 6)
   (if yes) 5a. Who were they?
            5b. Did you actually take part _____ or just watch _____?
6. Whose idea was it to do this? Mine _____ Everyone's agreement _____
   Other (specify) _____
7. How long had you been thinking about taking this before you took it?
8. Why did you take this (part of car, or gasoline)?
9. What did you do with it? (More than one may be checked.)
   Used it _____ Destroyed or discarded it _____ Another involved party used it _____
   Gave it to party not involved _____ Sold or traded it _____ Other (specify) _____
10. When did this happen?
    (a) Year _____ (b) Month _____ (c) Day M.___ Tu.___ W.___ Th.___ F.___ Sat.___ Sun.___
    (d) Time 5 a.m.-Noon _____ Noon-3 p.m. _____ 3 p.m.-6 p.m. _____
        6 p.m.-11 p.m. _____ 11 p.m.-5 a.m. _____
11. Did you tell anyone about it later? Yes _____ No _____ (go to Question 12)
    (if yes) 11a. How many adults and boys and girls did you tell?
             Adults _____ Boys _____ Girls _____
             11b. (if told adults) What relationship are these adults to you? _____
12. Did anyone catch you? Yes _____ No _____ (go to Question 13)
    (if yes) 12a. Who caught you? _____ 12b. How did they catch you? _____
             12c. What happened after you were caught? _____
13. Did your parents find out about it? Yes _____ No _____
    (if yes) 13a. How did they find out? _____ 13b. What did they do or say? _____

Figure 1. One section of the interview schedule.

The interview lasted from thirty-five minutes to over two hours, depending on the extent of the youngster's confessions. Average duration was about an hour and a half.

VALIDATION

A central problem in this sort of research is the extent of concealment by respondents.

Our interviewers were carefully selected and trained to gain the confidence of their respondents; our entire procedure was built around convincing youngsters of the scientific nature of the study; and we emphasized in many ways that confidentiality was assured. Nevertheless we expected that some proportion of youngsters would conceal offenses from us. Certain of them felt apprehensive about telling the complete truth. After all, said one boy, the interviewer would "have enough on me to send me up for thirty years." We did not know what proportion of our sample would conceal offenses; we did not know whether concealment would vary with factors like social status, race, and sex; and we did not know whether certain offenses would be concealed more often than others.

To study concealment we found it necessary to interview a criterion group, youngsters about whose delinquency we already had reliable information but who were not aware we had it. We managed eventually to interview 125 youngsters under these conditions.

Procedure. Our strategy was first to contact teenagers who seemed likely to have information about the delinquency of other boys and girls. We were introduced to these potential *informants* by teachers, youth workers, other interested adults, and by some informants themselves.

We explained the study to potential informants and asked them to help us by supplying names of boys and girls who they knew had committed delinquent acts for which they had not been caught, together with as much as they could tell us about these acts. We also asked them to tell us how they happened to know about the delinquencies they revealed to us, as we accepted no second-hand testimony. The only facts counted as reliable were those which the informants had witnessed themselves or which the delinquent himself had told them.

Over fifty potential informants were obtained, and more than forty of them agreed to cooperate. They were not all equally helpful. Some could not or would not give us any reliable information; others supplied us with as many as seven names along with complete descriptions of the delinquencies, often based on participant observation.

Table II describes the validation sample by categories of race, sex, and social status. The status distinction is primarily between blue-collar and white-collar workers. Because higher status Negroes are rare in Flint, few fell into our random sample of 522 teen-agers, so we did not at this time make any attempt to obtain a validating set of higher status Negro teen-agers.

An interviewer was assigned to a youngster in the validation sample without any prior knowledge of what offenses his respondent had committed; indeed, in most cases he was unaware that his respondent was not among the random sample. The interviewing procedure was the same as the one used with the random sample.

Our data on concealment came from comparisons of the responses of the 125 validating respondents with what our informants had already told us they had done. We considered a youngster a *truthteller* if he told us what our relevant informant had told us, or if he told us about more recent offenses of the same type, or if he told us about more serious offenses. A respondent was considered a *concealer* if he did not confess to an offense about which an informant had told us, or to any more recent similar offense, or to any more serious offense. Youngsters were categorized as *questionables* when they told us about offenses which were similar to but did not exactly match offenses about which we already had information. In such cases we were not certain whether something was being deliberately concealed or distorted or whether the memories of informants and respondents merely differed.

Results. Table III presents the findings of the validity check by the sex, race, and social status of respondents. Overall, 72 percent of the youngsters seemed to tell us everything which informants had told us; 17 percent appear to be outright concealers; the rest are *questionables*.

While the proportion of truthtellers differs somewhat from one category to an-

Table II. *Validation Sample*

Social Status	Male		Female		Total
	White	Other	White	Other	
Higher	19	—	14	—	
Lower	31	21	20	20	
	50	21	34	20	125

Table III. *Proportions of Truthtellers, Questionables, and Concealers, by Sex, and Social Status*

Sex	Race	Social Status	N	Truthtellers %	Questionables %	Concealers %
Boys	White	Higher	19	74	5	21
		Lower	31	71	23	6
	Negro	Lower	21	86	—	14
Girls	White	Higher	14	64	14	21
		Lower	20	75	10	15
	Negro	Lower	20	60	10	30
Total			125	72	11	17

other, no difference falls below the .20 chance probability level by the chi-square or Fisher Exact Test. We also wondered whether the more delinquent youngsters were more frequently the concealers. But a comparative check revealed no reliable differences.

Specific offenses most often concealed by the male validity sample were breaking and entering, property destruction, and carrying concealed weapons. Although many of each of these offenses were confessed, almost as many of those we had been told about were concealed as were confessed. For example, boys confessed to eighteen acts of breaking and entering about which we had no prior knowledge; but of the ten offenses of this kind about which we were quite certain, four were concealed.

Girls most frequently concealed breaking and entering, property destruction, unauthorized driving away, gangfighting, miscellaneous theft, and fornication.

Limitations. The validation study is far from foolproof. It is vulnerable in at least two respects:

First of all, the validation study, which is especially concerned with the problem of concealment, does not resolve the problem of exaggeration. We do not know to what extent teen-agers, and boys especially, want to project an image of at least moderate delinquency as a demonstration of daring and manliness. To check would require a criterion group for which we were certain not only of some of the offenses they had committed but also of some which they had not. We learned early in our study that teen-agers could not vouchsafe that even their closest friends had *not* committed any particular kind of offense.

One safeguard against exaggeration was the set of detailed questions we asked about each offense. It would have required an especially creative and quick-thinking youngster to fabricate offenses during his interview. In a few cases, interviewers did catch respondents in what may have been exaggeration: some concealed weapons turned out to be Boy Scout pocket knives; some gangfights were nothing more than minor playground scuffles; and some instances of auto theft were only quick spins around the block in the family car.

Although some exaggerations must still be distorting our data, we believe the distortion is quite minor.

Our use of informants—youngsters who are aware of the delinquencies of others—leads to a second possible source of vulnerability in the validation design, which is that we have no information about loners. Youngsters who commit their delinquent acts alone and tell no other youngster about them could not fall into our criterion group. We do not know how much loners are likely to conceal or how much they would gladly unburden, for the sake of science, to an accepting, interested young interviewer.

INDICES OF DELINQUENT BEHAVIOR

Measures of delinquent behavior are based on the confessions of the random sample of boys and girls, aged thirteen to sixteen, who lived in the Flint school district in 1960. Of the several indices of delinquency which have so far been constructed from these data, two—Index F and Index S—are currently employed in our analyses.

Index F. Index F draws data only from the detailed descriptions of delinquent acts which youngsters most seldom conceal—trespassing, assault, stealing a part of a car or gasoline, hitting father, hitting mother, drinking alcoholic beverages without parental knowledge or permission, running away from home, gangfighting, shoplifting, larceny, and fornication. This list covers a wide range of offenses, including offenses against persons (e.g., assault) and against property (e.g., theft); offenses generally believed to be more typical of boys (stealing a car part or gasoline) and more typical of girls (shoplifting); and offenses generally thought trivial (trespassing) as well as serious (hitting mother).

Since interviewers questioned respondents closely on no more than the two most recent offenses of each type, Index F is not as sensitive as other indices might be to the frequency of delinquent activity, but its correlations with indices which include a wider range of offenses and more information on frequency are .87 and higher.

The major advantage of Index F is that detailed information on the relevant offenses permitted exclusion of all those "offenses" which coders judged not to be chargeable by the police; that is, Index F includes only those offenses which in themselves would clearly have warranted police action if they had been detected. We noted in the first part of this paper that not all of the "offenses" to which youngsters confessed could reasonably be considered "delinquent acts"; 28 percent were not.

Index S. This index is based on a delinquency index devised by Sellin and Wolfgang,[8] which takes into account the *seriousness* of an offense as rated by university students, police officers, juvenile aid workers, and juvenile court judges. Each offense is weighted by some factor which reflects the seriousness with which that offense was regarded by the raters.

Our data were not collected in a way which allows precise application of the weights prescribed by Sellin and Wolfgang,

Figure 2. Offenses and weights assigned for seriousness on Index S.

Offense	*Weight*
Trespass	1
Threaten to assault	
Without a weapon	2
With a weapon	4
Property destruction	
Cost of estimated damage less than $50 or estimated cost not ascertained	1
Cost of estimated damage $50 or more	2
Assault, the effect requiring medical attention	4
Theft of part of a car or of gasoline	
Gasoline or inexpensive part (e.g., hub cap, antenna) or part not ascertained	1
More expensive part (e.g., jack, radio)	2
Theft, other	
Worth less than $50 or worth not ascertained	1
Worth $50 or more	2
Arson	2
Shoplifting	1
Driving away an auto without the owner's permission	2

(Modification of delinquency index by Sellin and Wolfgang.)

[8] Thorsten Sellin and Marvin E. Wolfgang, *The Measurement of Delinuency* (New York: Wiley, 1964).

for our data collection had begun before they had published their index. However, we found it possible to use an approximation of their index, assigning the weights to a set of nine offenses, as described in Figure 2.

Only those offenses were included for which interviewers had obtained detailed information because descriptions of the offenses, their chargeability, and the nature of items stolen or damaged were required in order to assign weights for seriousness.

Because the validation data show that youngsters fairly frequently conceal instances of property destruction and unauthorized driving away of an automobile, Index S in this respect may distort the absolute level of delinquency and the relative delinquency of youngsters in the sample.

Comparisons. Figure 3 presents the distributions of the two delinquency indices, each one a different way of organizing the youngsters' responses. A reader familiar with social scientific data will recognize the familiar J-shape of the curves generated by the distributions of the delinquency indices. Allport[9] has observed that this is just the shape of curve one should expect from data on deviations from recognized norms. That is, most people stick closely to the rules, and the curve drops off sharply

---

[9] Floyd H. Allport, "The J-curve Hypothesis of Conforming Behavior," *Journal of Social Psychology*, May 1934, pp. 141–83.

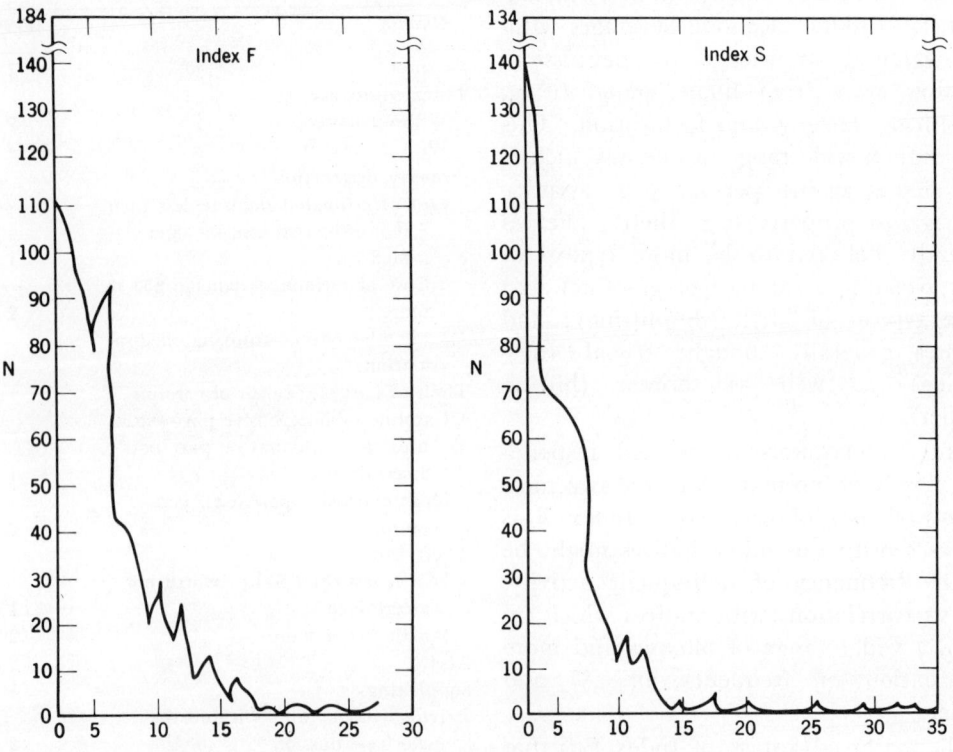

Figure 3. Frequency by distribution of scores on delinquency indices.

and bottoms out at its more deviant end. In this case, most youngsters are not very delinquent, either in the frequency or seriousness of their delinquent behaviour, and there are relatively few youngsters at the more delinquent ends of the curves.

The rank order (rho) correlation between these two indices is .68, a statistical reliable correlation ($p<.001$). These indices are highly correlated with one another as one might expect since they are both based largely on the same set of responses. However, correlations among several indices reveal that Index S, which takes into account a judgment of seriousness of the offense, stands somewhat apart from the others. Material presented later will demonstrate that the data on official records and the data collected from Negro boys turn out somewhat differently when seriousness is taken into account from when it is not. This difference makes Index S of special interest.

Illustrative Cases. The meaning of a score on a delinquency index will be more clear from the following examples of youngsters with different scores:

Case 115 (Index F=00; Index S=00). The respondent was a thirteen-year-old boy in the ninth grade. His mother and father are teachers. The boy is an active Boy Scout and an honor roll student. He was interviewed in October 1961.

He had played truant once, more than three years ago, and currently lies about his age when he goes to the movies so that he can get in for the children's price. "But the price is so high, I seldom go to the movies anymore," he said. "When I do, I save money on the ticket so I can buy popcorn and candy."

Case 297 (Index F=04; Index S=06). The subject here is a fifteen-year-old girl in the eighth grade. Her stepfather is a foreman for a beer distributor. She was interviewed in December 1961.

On December 6, 1958, her birthday, she ran away from home because her parents were fighting so much, and she said, "I got real nervous and scared." After wandering about Flint for hours, she went to her maternal grandmother's house, where her mother came to fetch her home.

Sometime in the summer of 1960 she and a friend went exploring in a house under construction. They found a case of beer, probably cached there by the workmen, and took it and some nails. They brought the loot to her stepfather, who spanked her soundly and made her take it all back.

In January 1961 she stole a phonograph record from a department store. Explaining her reason for this she said, "I wanted it and didn't have enough money with me."

In October 1961 she took some doll's clothes and three little bells from a department store. "I gave them to my little sister for a surprise," she reported.

Case 026 (Index F=14; Index S=15). This fifteen-year-old boy is in the eighth grade. His stepfather runs a baling machine in a container manufacturing plant; his mother works part-time as a salesclerk in a large department store downtown. He is on a basketball team in his junior high school and has been a class officer. He was interviewed in August 1962.

In May 1961 he and a friend entered a barn on a farm outside of Flint, played around in the hayloft awhile, then left.

In July he and some friends stole two hubcaps from cars parked outside a Flint dance hall and sold them.

In August he stole the net from a basketball hoop on a school playground and gave it to a friend for the hoop over his garage door.

On a Friday night that August he and some friends got into a fight with "some northside niggers."

Again in August he and some friends stole an air mattress, a portable icebox, a six-pack of beer, and the spark from the outboard motor of a boat left unattended at a pier. The boys drank the beer and divided the rest.

In September, he pulled his switchblade knife on "a big Italian boy" who had taken his notebook.

Later in September he and his friends pried open trunks of cars at the Armory parking lot and stole two tires, which were given to one of the group who had been driving them around in his car for several months.

In December he and some friends stole two cases of soda pop from a laundromat, drank what they wanted, and discarded the rest.

In January 1962 he shoplifted fishhooks, gloves, and two friendship rings from stores in a shopping center. "We had a kind of club like," he said, "and we decided to get this stuff."

During January he participated in two successive Saturday night drinking parties. At the first, he drank liquor at a friend's house when the friend's parents were not at home; at the second, he drank beer, bought by an older boy, in a car parked behind a school.

SOCIAL STATUS AND JUVENILE DELINQUENCY

We noted earlier that social scientists have long maintained that more lower-class youngsters are delinquent than are their middle-class peers. This relationship and the theories built from it have guided the major efforts to combat delinquency in action programs such as the current Federal War on Poverty, New York City's Mobilization for Youth, and the Chicago Boys Clubs Youth Development Project, all designed to alleviate in some way the condition of lower status life. There has, however, always been a persistent set of competent researchers who question the belief that lower status youngsters are the most serious and frequent offenders because of their lower status. They maintain that this relationship is only an artifact of the way data on delinquency are gathered. Probably a substantial portion of the American public shares these researchers' suspicions that the rich kids get away with delinquency and the poor kids get records.

Our measurement of undetected delinquency is free from the selectivity which exists in the records of police, courts, and social agencies. It allows us to examine the relationship between social status and delinquency; to see to what extent this selectivity does exist in the official records; and to determine to what extent official records truly reflect the actual distribution of delinquency among different social strata.

Our findings indicate that social status is indeed inversely related to juvenile delinquency, that more lower status youngsters commit delinquent acts more frequently than do higher status youngsters. However, the data allow us to be more specific about who among lower status youngsters are more likely to be delinquent and enable us to place important qualifications on the general statement of the relationship.

The Meaning of "Social Status." "Social status," as we use the term here, refers to the prestige hierarchy of occupations in our society. There is a great deal of agreement in the United States about the relative prestige of occupations [10] and a great deal of stability to the prestige hierarchy.[11] In this paper, a youngster's "status," unless otherwise qualified, refers to social status based on father's occupation.

The specific measure of status used here is O. D. Duncan's scale of occupations,[12] which is based on national studies of the prestige of occupations in the United States. These studies demonstrated that income and education are the two most

[10] Wellman L. Warner, M. Meeker, and K. Eels, *Social Class in America* (Chicago: Science Research Associates, 1949).

[11] Robert W. Hodge, Paul M. Siegel, and Peter H. Rossi, "Occupational Prestige in the United States, 1952–63," *American Journal of Sociology*, November 1964, pp. 286–302.

[12] Albert J. Reiss, Jr., Otis D. Duncan, Paul K. Hatt, and C. C. North, *Occupations and Social Status* (New York: Free Press, 1961).

important determinants of the prestige of an occupation. By computing the average income and level of education achieved by persons in each occupational category and making some adjustments for their ages, Duncan assigned a status score to a large number of occupations.

Selectivity in the Official Records. These data demonstrate that official records exaggerate the delinquent behavior of boys from lower status homes relative to their higher status peers. (Since only five of the 264 girls in the sample reported being caught by the police, the analyses of these data refer mainly to the boys.)

Police are more likely to record officially those offenses committed by lower status youngsters, the children of semi-skilled and unskilled men. Table IV documents this statement. Only about 3 percent of all the chargeable offenses reported by the youngsters in the sample resulted in police apprehension of the offender and, if the offender came from a higher status family police were more likely to handle the matter themselves without referring it to the court.

Some judgment by the police about the ability of a family to control its son's behavior is likely to be a major factor in determining whether official action will be taken. Lower status families as a group are judged less able to keep their sons out of trouble, so official action is more often taken.

Table IV. *Police Referral to Court of Offenses Committed by Lower Status Youngsters Compared with Offenses Committed by Middle Status Youngsters*

	Lower Status	Middle Status	Total
Station adjustment	20	20	40
Referred to court	11	2	13
Total	31	22	53
$x^2 = 3.52$	p<.10 (2t)		

Boys Only	Lower Status	Middle Status	Total
Station adjustment	18	19	37
Referred to court	9	2	11
Total	27	21	48
$x^2 = 3.79$	p<.10 (2t)		

Table V. *Relationship between Delinquency and Social Status (Boys Only) Demonstrated by Court Records*

Social Status	N	% Who Have Records
High (professionals, managers, etc.)	34	3
High middle (skilled workers, foremen, white collar, etc.)	104	9
Low middle (operatives, semiskilled, etc.)	79	14
Low (laborers, unskilled, etc.)	40	15
Total	257	11%

Partly as a result of this procedure, court records in Flint demonstrate the usual relationship between delinquency and social status: greater proportions of boys are adjudged delinquent as one goes from higher to lower status categories. The proportion listed in Table V, showing that four to five times more lower status boys are delinquent than higher status boys, is a common ratio in the delinquency literature.

Do Official Records Reflect the Amount of Delinquent Behavior? While official records are selective in a way which exaggerates the relative delinquency of lower status youngsters, they may nevertheless

Table VI. *Proportion of Boys at Each Level of Delinquency (Index S) Who Report Being Caught by Police at Least Once*

	Index S	N	% Report Caught
Low	0-2	83	7
	3-4	56	5
	5-8	60	26
High	9+	58	28
Total		257	16

$rpb = .32$
$p < .001$

Table VII. *Proportion of Boys at Each Level of Delinquency (Index F) Who Report Being Caught by Police at Least Once*

	Index F	N	% Report Caught
Low	0-1	52	2
	2-4	87	10
	5-7	62	12
High	8+	56	19
Total		257	16

$rpb = .40$
$p < .001$

approximate real delinquent behavior. For example, even though most juvenile offenses do not result in the apprehension of the offender and few juvenile offenders are on record with the authorities, the more delinquent youngsters may have been detected and recorded.

Only boys are included here in the analysis of the data since only five girls in the sample have official records, and only six report being caught by the police.

It is clear from the data in Tables VI and VII that the more delinquent boys are more likely to be caught by the police. Sixteen percent of the boys report being caught at least once; but, compared with the least delinquent boys, about four times as many of the most delinquent boys on Index S are caught, and about seventeen times as many when Index F is the measure of delinquency. Since Index F emphasizes frequency of offenses, while Index S emphasizes seriousness, these data suggest that frequency of offenses is a greater determinant of being caught than their seriousness. Erickson and Empey [13] come to the same conclusion on the basis of their data on Utah boys.

Do the figures on boys "booked" presented in Table X reflect degree of delinquency as the contact records do? The data show that about five times more of the most delinquent boys are booked than the least delinquent boys.

Furthermore, it seems that the seriousness of an offense is taken into account in the decision to book a boy. The data have shown that frequency is a greater determinant of apprehension than seriousness; data in Table VIII show that the most serious offenders, high on Index S, are about as likely to be booked as the most frequent offenders, high on Index F. Of course, most of the boys on one index are also high on the other. But although more of the frequent offenders are caught, no more of them are booked. Seriousness of the offense enters the decision to book.

It should be borne in mind that the majority of even the most delinquent boys are unknown to the police and the courts. This comes as no surprise to the police. The point is that the one-third or less of the most delinquent boys who are caught may be a highly selected group of youngsters; and the 16 percent of all the boys caught are not by any means equally delinquent or representative of delinquent boys. Researchers who generalize about

---

[13] Maynard L. Erickson and LaMar T. Empey, "Court Records, Undetected Delinquency and Decision-Making," *Journal of Criminal Law, Criminology and Police Science,* December 1963, pp. 456–69.

Table VIII. Proportion of Boys at Each Level of Delinquency Who Have Been Booked

	Index F				Index S		
	Level of Delinquent Behavior	N	% Booked		Level of Delinquent Behavior	N	% Booked
Low	0-1	52	4	Low	0-2	83	4
	2-4	87	9		3-4	56	5
	5-7	62	6		5-8	60	13
High	8+	56	21	High	9+	58	21
Total		257	10	Total		257	10
	rpb = .27				rpb = .25		
	p<.001				p<.001		

delinquents from apprehended or adjudged delinquents should be cautioned by these data.

Delinquent Behavior and Social Status. The data to be presented now demonstrate that there is indeed an inverse relationship between delinquent behavior and social status. However, this relationship exists only among boys. Tables 9 and 10 and Figures 4 and 5 present these data.

Both indices have been divided into four levels of delinquency for the purposes of

Table IX. Relationship between Delinquency (Index F) and Social Status by Race and Sex

Sex	Race	Social Status	N	Index F Mean	Rank Correlation τ	p-level of τ
Male	White	High	28	3.4		
			100	4.3		
			42	4.4		
		Low	25	7.6		
					−.12	<.01
	Nonwhite	High	37	4.9		
		Low	15	6.6		
					−.08	.37
Female	White	High	27	1.9		
			100	1.7		
			49	2.5		
		Low	34	2.0		
					.06	.16
	Nonwhite	High	21	1.3		
		Low	15	1.6		
					−.18	.09

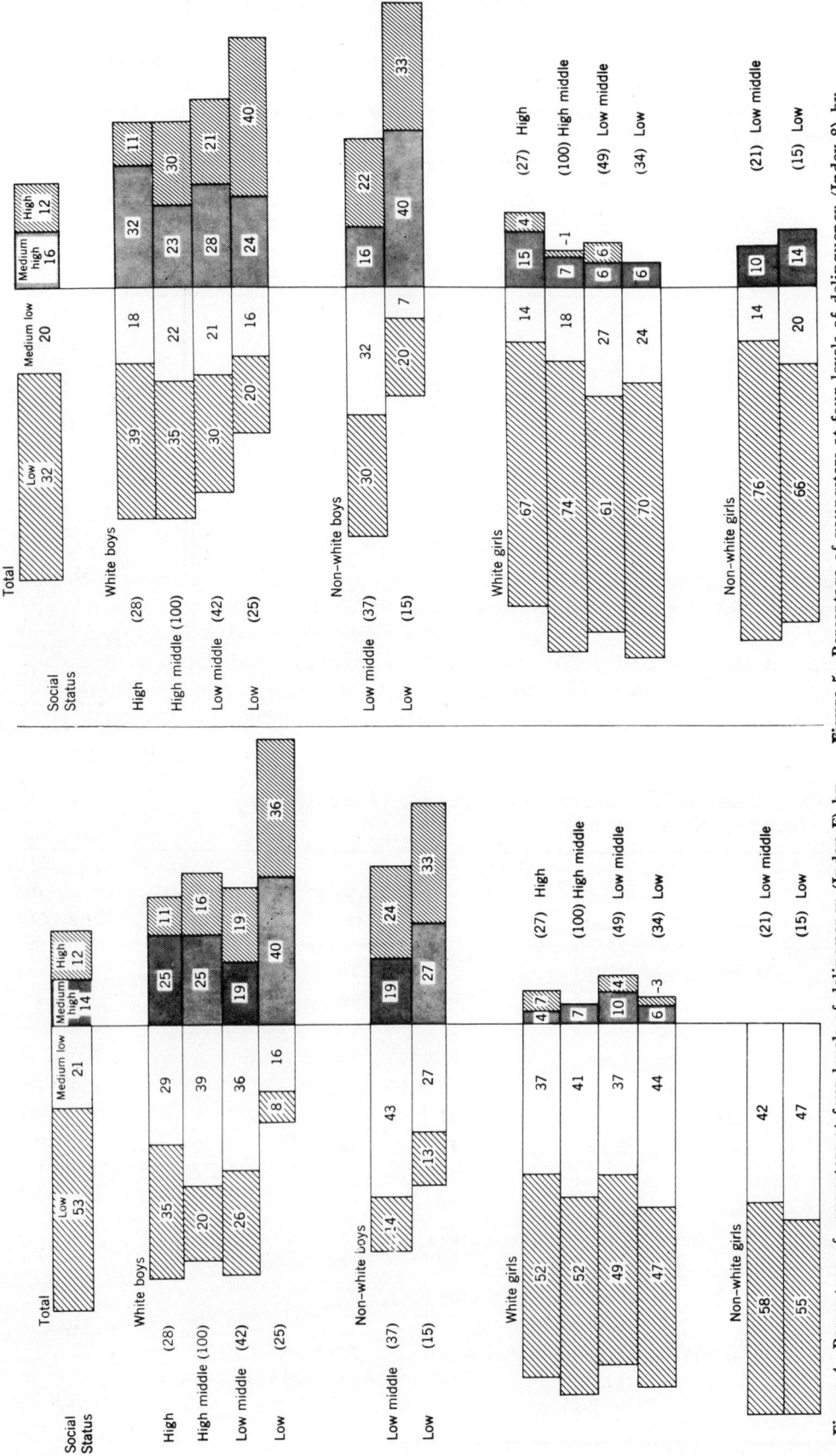

Figure 4. Percentage of youngsters at four levels of delinquency (Index F) by social status and by race and sex.

Figure 5. Percentage of youngsters at four levels of delinquency (Index 8) by social status and by race and sex.

Table X. *Relationship between Delinquency (Index S) and Social Status by Race and Sex*

Sex	Race	Social Status	N	Index S Mean	Rank Correlation τ	p-level of τ
Male	White	High	28	4.0		
			100	4.8		
			42	5.2		
		Low	25	8.3		
					−.12	<.01
	Nonwhite	High	37	5.3		
		Low	15	7.4		
					−.05	>.30
Female	White	High	27	2.1		
			100	1.7		
			49	2.6		
		Low	34	1.8		
					−.08	.09
	Nonwhite	High	21	1.8		
		Low	15	1.8		
					−.01	>.30

presenting the data as graphs. The lowest level of delinquency on both indices includes about 53 percent of the youngsters; the next to lowest, about 20 percent; the next to highest, about 15 percent; and the highest, about 12 percent.

Also, to make the data more clear, the measure of social status has been divided into four levels described in Table 5.

While the presentation of data is aided by so categorizing the measures, a more sensitive test of the relationship between social status and delinquency considers the complete order from high to low in both sets of measures. Kendall's rank order correlation is used here to measure the degree of their covariation.

The data reveal no reliable relationship between delinquency and social status among girls. Among white girls, 47 percent of the lowest status girls are in about the lower half of delinquency index F, compared with 52 percent of the highest status girls. Similarly, almost equal proportions of girls fall into the lower half of the sample on Index S. An inspection of the data on nonwhite, mostly Negro girls shows the same lack of relationship between delinquency and social status, although the comparison here is limited to the two lowest social status levels. These data contradict the relationship between girls' delinquency and their social status which emerges from official records.[14]

The pattern in the data on white boys is quite different from that for the girls. The proportion of lowest status boys climbs from 8 percent in the lowest delinquency category of Index F to 36 percent in the highest; the proportion of highest status boys falls from 35 percent in the lowest category to 11 percent in the highest category. The two middle status categories of white boys occupy intermediate positions on delinquency index F. The rank order correlation between social status and delinquency among white boys indicates that this relationship could have occurred merely by chance less than once in 100 times. White boys show the same pattern

---

[14] William I. Thomas, *The Unadjusted Girl* (Boston, Little, Brown, 1937); William W. Wattenberg, "Differences between Girl and Boy 'Repeaters,'" *Journal of Educational Psychology*, March 1953, pp. 137-46; William W. Wattenberg and Frank Saunders, "Recidivism among Girls," *Journal of Abnormal and Social Psychology*, May 1955, pp. 405-06.

on Index S (Figure 5). Figures 4 and 5 make clear that most of the relationship between social status and delinquency among white boys is accounted for by the greater delinquency of the lowest status white boys.

Among the nonwhite boys, the two delinquency indices produce somewhat different results. Neither index is correlated reliably with social status, but the range of social status among nonwhite boys is so truncated, effectively encompassing only the lowest three scores on the Duncan scale, that any rank correlation is limited by the data themselves. A comparison of the graphs in Figures 4 and 5 demonstrate that Index S, which takes seriousness of the offense into account, better discriminates between higher and lower status nonwhite boys than Index F does. Index S puts the proportions of lower status boys below the proportions of higher status boys at the less delinquent end of the index and above the higher status boys at the more delinquent end. Two-by-two chi-square analyses bear out the different patterns obtained by the two indices (Table XI): the chi-square result from Index F is reliable only at about the .40 level; from Index S, it is reliable at less than .05, more lower status boys being more delinquent. So it seems that, in frequency of delinquency, the sons of nonwhite unskilled workers do not differ much from the sons of nonwhite, semi-skilled workers; but, in seriousness of offense—as defined by white, middle-class judges—the former commit more serious offenses than the latter.

So we have found that delinquent behavior among boys is related to social status, just as the much criticized official records have demonstrated over and over again. It seems reasonable, then, to raise the question: why not continue to employ official records, at least to explore this relationship, rather than collect more expensive data?

One reason is that the official records exaggerate the differences in delinquency among boys of different status levels. They make social status, in the sense of the breadwinner's occupation, seem more important than it really is as far as researchers and practitioners are concerned. About five times more lowest than highest status boys appear in the official records; if records were complete and unselective, we estimate that the ratio would be closer to 1.5:1.

However, there is a sense in which the actual ratio of delinquent behavior specifically among boys is closer to 5:1 than 1.5:1 against the lowest status boys; that is, the official records come closer to a valid picture than does the estimate of unselective records. The data in Figures 4 and 5 show that three to four times more lowest status boys than highest status boys behave at the *highest* delinquency level on either index. If we consider these boys to be the ones who represent the most pressing social problem and therefore should be apprehended and given attention, then the official booking rates do not depart so far from truly representing differential delinquency among social status levels.

On the other hand, if we define the social problem to include the top two levels of delinquency, then the ratio of delinquents is only about 1.5:1 or 2:1 against the lowest status boys.

This kind of discussion exposes the greatest source of invalidity inherent in official records: youngsters are categorized as "delinquent" or not categorized at all. Some researchers have found this distinction too limiting, so they have distinguished between "sometime delinquents," who appear in the official records only once, and "repeaters."[15] We share the view of other researchers in this field that it is more useful to think of delinquency as a continuous rather than as a discrete variable. One of the major advantages of our method of

---

[15] Gold, *op. cit. supra* note 2; William W. Wattenberg, "A Comparison of Repeaters and Nonrepeaters among Boys in Trouble with Police in Detroit in 1946 and 1947," in Michigan Academy of Science, Arts, and Letters, *Papers 35*, 1949.

Table XI. *Relationship between Delinquency and Social Status among Nonwhite Males: Comparing Index F and Index S Measures*

	Index F Social Status				Index S Social Status		
Delinquency	Lower	Higher	Total	Delinquency	Lower	Higher	Total
Top 46%	9	16	25	Top 48%	11	14	25
Bottom 54%	6	21	27	Bottom 52%	4	23	27
Total	15	37		Total	15	37	
	$x^2 = .62$				$x^2 = 4.06$		
	$p < .30$				$p < .05$		

gathering data is that it permits us to measure delinquency in this way.

Finally, we should point out again that, according to our findings, official records are altogether invalid when they reflect a difference in degree of delinquency among social status levels for girls. It is true that our validation study revealed that girls tend to conceal fornication, an offense thought to account for a substantial portion of girls' delinquency. Nevertheless, the validation data give us no reason to believe that there are differences in concealment among social status levels. As far as we can tell from our data, delinquency among girls is not related to their social status.

Theoretical Implications. We noted near the beginning of this paper that major theories of delinquency are based on the inverse relationship between the degree of delinquency and social status. We noted, too, that the reality of this relationship has been questioned and that data have been produced to refute it.

On the basis of the data reported here, we conclude that the inverse relationship is indeed a fact among boys. (The theories of delinquency to which we have alluded have been implicitly, if not explicitly, limited to delinquency among boys.)

It seems that studies of undetected delinquency by interview methods consistently find a relationship with social status among boys,[16] while those which use self-administered checklists do not.[17] Perhaps the tendency we have found here for higher status youngsters more often to report nonchargeable behavior as delinquent obscures the relationship with social status in checklist data. Perhaps, in addition, social status itself is too roughly ascertained in a self-administered questionnaire.

Our data are limited to one city. However, we suspect that, in regard to delinquency, Flint is not different from any other community encompassing a fairly broad range of social status categories. We suspect that these same findings will hold not only for other urban communities but also for rural communities. We intend to do research on this problem.

Data presented here do not permit us to choose among the various theories of delinquency which are based on its relationship to social status.[18] The low correlation

---

[16] Maynard L. Erickson and LaMar T. Empey, "Class Position, Peers, and Delinquency," *Sociology and Social Research*, April 1965, pp. 268–82; Reiss and Rhodes, *supra* note 7.

[17] Clark and Wenninger, *supra* note 5; Dentler and Monroe, *supra* note 5; Jerome Himelhoch, "Socio-Economic Status and Delinquency in Rural New England" (paper read at the annual meeting of the American Sociological Association, Montreal, 1964); Nye, *op. cit. supra* note 5; Gerald J. Pine, *The Significance of the Relationships between Social Class Status, Social Mobility, and Delinquent Behavior*, unpublished doctoral dissertation, Boston University School of Education, 1963; Porterfield and Clifton, *op. cit. supra* note 5.

[18] Cohen, *op. cit. supra* note 3; Gold, *op. cit. supra* note 2; Cloward and Ohlin, *op. cit. supra* note 3; William C. Kvaraceus and Walter B. Miller, eds., *Delinquent Behavior: Culture and the Individual* (Washington, D.C.: National Education Association, 1959).

of delinquency with social status, however reliable that relationship is, suggests that it is time to examine empirically the links between social status and delinquency to see whether we can discover the more potent determinants to which social status is but a scant clue.

These data are only a small part of the total collected on this project. Data are now being organized around such topics as differences in sex, age, and race, the composition of delinquent groups, delinquent "loners," seasonal variations, the location of delinquent acts, types of delinquents, educational and vocational aspirations of youngsters related to their delinquency, school achievements, and so on.

As for girls, it seems that social scientists will have to search for theoretical bases different from a relationship with social status. Relatively little systematic research has been done on delinquency among girls;[19] the emphasis has been on emotional disturbance and family relationships. While this study has only a little to say about these factors, it will perhaps turn up enough new information about the nature of delinquency among girls to throw some light on the problem. Our data here already indicate that girls are far less delinquent than boys. Further analyses of data are proceeding.

[19] Ruth R. Morris, "Female Delinquency and Relational Problems," *Social Forces,* October 1964, pp. 82–89; Thomas, *supra* note 14; Wattenberg, *supra* note 14.

11. MEASURING CRIME

MEANS OF CRIME CONTROL BY THE CRIMINAL JUSTICE SYSTEM

THE CRIMINAL JUSTICE SYSTEM WORKS TO reduce crime in three basic ways: (1) *deterrence*, posing a threat of apprehension and consequent penalties; (2) *incapacitation*, removing individuals from places where they might commit further crimes or subjecting them to supervision that makes it difficult for them to do so; and (3) *rehabilitation*, treatment by correctional agencies.

Each of these methods is obviously extremely complex and our knowledge about them is very inadequate at present. Rehabilitation, for instance, appears in many cases to have been relatively ineffectual; limited data suggest that roughly one person in three released from prison will return and that over three-quarters of those once arrested will be subsequently arrested. Rehabilitation is an extremely complex task in which methods that succeed in one instance fail in another. Furthermore, gains in treatment may be easily offset by factors entirely unrelated to the criminal justice system, such as the inability of a released offender to get a job or the acquaintances he makes when he returns to the community.

Incarceration has inherent limitations as

▶SOURCE: *Task Force Report: Science and Technology, President's Commission on Law Enforcement and Administration of Justice, Washington, D.C.: 1967, pp. 55–64.*

a method for the general control of crime. Of all the Index crimes reported to the police, only about 25 percent are cleared by arrest. About 10-20 percent of the individuals arrested are sentenced to jail or prison. The jail terms are less than a year, and the average prison time is about one and a half years. So only a small percentage of the total possible crimes that could be committed on any given day are avoided by imprisonment.[1] Probation and parole supervision may also serve to some extent to incapacitate, but how much they do is clearly hard to measure and no data on their restraining effects exist at present.

The effects of deterrence are much more subtle and difficult to measure even than those of rehabilitative programs. One basic question is the degree to which deterrence is uniform over the population, or whether the population can be divided into identifiable classes with distinctly different responses to deterrence. In particular there is the question of whether people with criminal histories—those who were not deterred at least once in the past—are less deterred than those without such records. Another question is the extent to which the actions

---

[1] This means, neglecting the deterrent effects of imprisonment and the rehabilitative effects of associated correctional programs, and concentrating only on the removal effects of incarceration, that the amount of crime would increase by only a small percentage if there were no incarceration at all.

of the criminal justice system deters people from committing crime as compared to the extent to which they are deterred by things like general public opinion, the reactions of family and friends, religion and morality, and the fear of losing a job. Within the criminal justice system, it is not known in what measure deterrence is effected by the fear of being caught by the police, by the threat of a prison sentence, or by the stigma of a record. As difficult as these questions are they lie at the heart of the operation of the criminal justice system, and so must be addressed in a major research program involving analysis and experimentation. Until we begin, however, decisions will be based on intuition rather than on observed fact.

MEASURING CRIME

There are different ways of measuring the amount of crime, and they do not necessarily imply the same thing. Two basic directions can be taken. The first, determining the degree of public safety, is to measure the probability of a person in a certain category being a victim of a crime. The second, determining the extent of criminality within the society, is to measure the probability that an individual with specified characteristics will commit a crime.[2]

From the viewpoint of evaluating public safety, the absolute number of crimes fails to reflect accurately the victimization probability. If crimes increase in proportion to population increase, then there is no change in the gross victimization probability. Crime rate, the number of crimes per 100,000 population, measures victimization more accurately.

This same crime rate is often used as a measure of criminality. Different population groups differ in their propensity to commit crimes,[3] however. Crime rates are influenced by the age distribution of the population, by the extent of urbanization of the population, by the ethnic mix in different geographical regions, and many other demographic factors. Thus, crime rates could increase as a result of demographic changes (e.g., a decrease in the median age of the population) even without an increase in the criminality of any population subgroup.

Crime rates always measure the number of certain crimes divided by a measure of exposure. It is important that the exposure be defined in relation to the purpose for which the crime rate is to be used. For example, if we want to know how safe our 1964 Chevrolet is from theft, we are interested in the number of autos, or, even better, the number of 1964 Chevrolets stolen in our area each year per 100 autos. If we want to know how safe we are from robbery in a certain area, we are interested in the number of robberies in the area per year per 100 people in that area. If we want to know the chance of our son committing a crime this year, we are interested in the percentage of boys his age in the area who commit crimes in a year. The more finely the data can be divided, the more directly relevant it is to the question of interest. Most interpretations of crime statistics fail to identify the exposure rate associated with the intended interpretation.

Pervading all measures of crime is the inability to distinguish between changes in the amount of crime committed and the amount of crime reported. This difficulty is aggravated when the two are correlated, as they are in public reports of crime to the police. As the police became more effective in solving crimes and in recovering

---

[2] These problems have been treated by the Assessment Task Force and are discussed in detail in their report.

[3] The characteristics of those who commit crimes cannot be learned directly. The necessary approximation involves using the characteristics of arrestees. This introduces the possible bias that some types of criminals (e.g., the younger ones, the poorer ones, and the less intelligent ones) may be more likely to be arrested than others.

property, the reported rate might increase even though the actual rate might decline. This difficulty can be minimized by using several different approaches (e.g., victim surveys as well as police reports) to estimating the volume of crime. Even when there is a true change in crimes committed, it is extremely difficult to separate the results of actions by the criminal justice system from independent social changes, such as reduction in discrimination, economic improvement, or modifications in school systems.

Gross rates of victimization or commission of crimes, even if they could be obtained accurately and completely, would still fail to present an adequate picture of the magnitude of the crime problem. Each type of crime has a different degree of seriousness. The distribution of crimes among the different types is an important fact. In the District of Columbia, for example, the number of part I [4] crimes rose by 2,712 (8 percent) from 32,053 to 34,765 between 1965 and 1966. However, petty larceny, the least serious of the part I offenses, rose 2,729. There was a slight net decrease in both the number and the rate of the other, more serious, part I offenses.[5] Thus, it is difficult to say whether the crime problems grew more or less serious in Washington without measuring the relative seriousness of the different offenses.

FBI estimates of the index of crime are derived from an unweighted sum of the reported Index crimes. This Index is dominated by the far more prevalent crimes against property and is relatively insensitive to changes in the serious crimes against the person. Thus, murders could increase by 1,000 percent, but if auto theft fell by 10 percent, the Index would decline.

All crimes are not equally undesirable. Most people would be willing to tolerate a considerable amount of private gambling, or perhaps even shoplifting, if they could know that doing so would reduce the amount of street robberies. The trade-offs among different types of crime is an important consideration in allocating enforcement resources. Decisions, for example, on transferring detectives from the vice squad to the robbery squad should take into account the relative amounts of crime disutility they could reduce on each squad.

Crime derives its seriousness from many different effects. It is extremely difficult to assess these in order to determine their relative importance. One way of resolving these difficult issues is to measure public attitudes toward being a victim of different crimes, using a representative sample of individuals and applying scaling techniques. Some preliminary results have been obtained by Sellin & Wolfgang.[6] They asked a sample of people to weigh the seriousness of various crimes.[7] The concepts of utility theory can then be applied [8]

Table I. *Disutilities of Part I Crimes*

Type of Crime Ranked by UCR Seriousness	Estimated Average Disutility
1. Criminal homicide	400,000,000 [a]
2. Forcible rape	10,000,000 [a]
3. Robbery	10,000
4. Aggravated assault	20,000
5. Burglary	200
6. Larceny ($50 and over)	100
7. Auto theft	900
8. Larceny (under $50)	90

[a] The disutilities for criminal homicide and forcible rape are very crude estimates based on an extrapolation extending far beyond the region for which data were available concerning the functional form of the relationship between scale value and utility.

---

[4] Part I crimes are the Index crimes plus negligent manslaughter and larceny under $50.

[5] Report of the President's Commission on Crime in the District of Columbia, 1966, p. 24.

[6] The Measurement of Delinquency, Sellin & Wolfgang, J. Wiley & Sons, 1964.

[7] The crimes were defined so as to result in the amount of injury, property lost, property unrecovered, property damages, etc., typical of such crimes actually committed by juveniles.

[8] The Sellin-Wolfgang indexes for larceny crimes were translated into a utility scale based on the

to these values, resulting in estimated disutilities of each part I crime roughly as shown in table 10. This ranking of seriousness differs somewhat from the UCR ranking of seriousness which is also shown in Table I.

Thus, if a "rational person" strives to minimize his average disutility, then these numbers suggest that he is equally concerned about 1/200 probability of a burglary and 1/20,000 probability of an aggravated assault.[9]

These approaches, combined with those of Sellin and Wolfgang, could be used to develop an index of crime which more accurately reflects the total seriousness of crime than merely adding the offenses without attaching any weights to them.

In assessing the performance of the criminal justice system, the incidence of crimes must be balanced against the costs of crime control, including both the dollar costs, direct and indirect, and the social costs. One instrument for relating these cost and effectiveness measures is in a model of the criminal justice system (Chart 1).

A MODEL OF THE CRIMINAL JUSTICE SYSTEM

Form of a Model. The first step in developing a model of a generalized criminal justice system [10] is to describe in detail the events that occur as offenders are processed through the system. One such description, from the Commission's report, is illustrated in the next figure. Even this description is simplified, and differs from the real system in any particular jurisdiction. Transforming this description into a model involves the following steps:

(1) Aggregate a number of related processing stages consistent with the form of the available data. For example, the booking and initial appearance stages might be combined into a single one.

(2) Describe the probability that an arrested person is routed along the alternative paths out of each branching point in the diagram. This would include the proportion of individuals following each route as a function of the type of crime, characteristics of the individual such as age and prior criminal record, and characteristics of the processing stage.

(3) Attribute to each individual the costs of processing him at each stage.

(4) Determine the resources required to process the flow of individuals through each stage.

(5) For each possible route out of the system, describe the probability that an individual will again commit a crime as a function of his prior crime, his personal characteristics such as age, and the treatment provided.

(6) Translate these descriptions into computer language so that numerical results can be calculated.

(7) Collect data to estimate each of the model parameters in the above descriptions.

(8) Change the variables characterizing the system, and calculate the consequences of these changes on costs and on crimes.

A simplified version of the model which was developed by the Task Force following this process is shown in Figure 1. It can

---

monetary loss in the larceny. (For a definition of the utility scale and a discussion of its use in decision-making, see the classic work of John Von Neuman and Oscar Morganstern, Theory of Games and Economic Behavior, Princeton UP, 1948.) The other crimes were then interpolated onto this scale based on their Sellin-Wolfgang scale values.

[9] Of course, there are infinitely many possible scales of weights which are monotonic in seriousness. Since they are all monotonically related, maximizing "value" as measured on any one of the scales maximizes it on all of them. The unique feature of utilities as distinguished from other measures of "value," is that, roughly speaking, the marginal utility of an outcome is inversely proportional to the probability risk of its occurrence one is willing to take. This makes utilities particularly useful in analyses of decisions on actions directed at affecting the probabilities.

[10] The technical details are in "A Model of the Criminal Justice System," now in preparation. The report will be available from the Clearinghouse for Federal Scientific and Technical Information of the National Bureau of Standards.

be used to calculate what happens to arrested offenders as they flow through court and corrections subsystems. The analysis was restricted to the seven Index crimes and to offenders processed from committing them through either felony or juvenile court.

Each of the seven Index crimes was treated separately. The results for all the Index crimes were then totaled to obtain

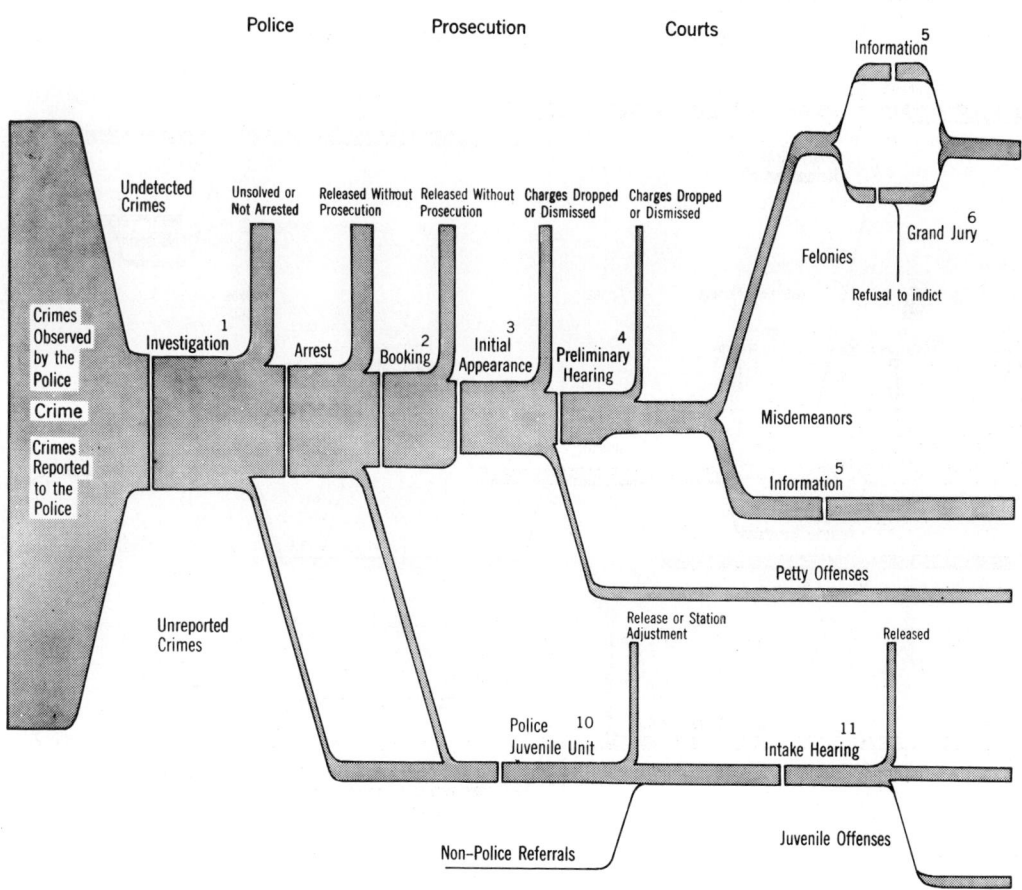

Chart 1. A general view of the criminal justice system. This chart seeks to present a simple yet comprehensive view of the movement of cases through the criminal justice system. Procedures in individual jurisdictions may vary from the pattern shown here. The differing weights of line indicate the relative volumes of cases disposed of at various points in the system, but this is only suggestive since no nationwide data of this sort exist. *1,* May continue until trial. *2,* Administrative record of arrest. First step at which temporary release on bail may be available. *3,* Before magistrate, commissioner, or justice of the peace. Formal notice of charge, advice of rights. Bail set. Summary trials for petty offenses usually conducted here without further processing. *4,* Preliminary testing of evidence against defendant. Charge may be reduced. No separate preliminary hearing for misdemeanors in some systems. *5,* Charge filed by prosecutor on basis of information submitted by police or citizens.

the costs incurred at each stage, and the number of people traveling each route shown in the figure. In order to make these calculations, data were gathered to describe operating procedures and costs. Often best estimates, approximations, or extrapolations to the whole country of data characteristic of specific jurisdictions had to suffice. Because of the gaps in the data, the numerical results must be viewed as

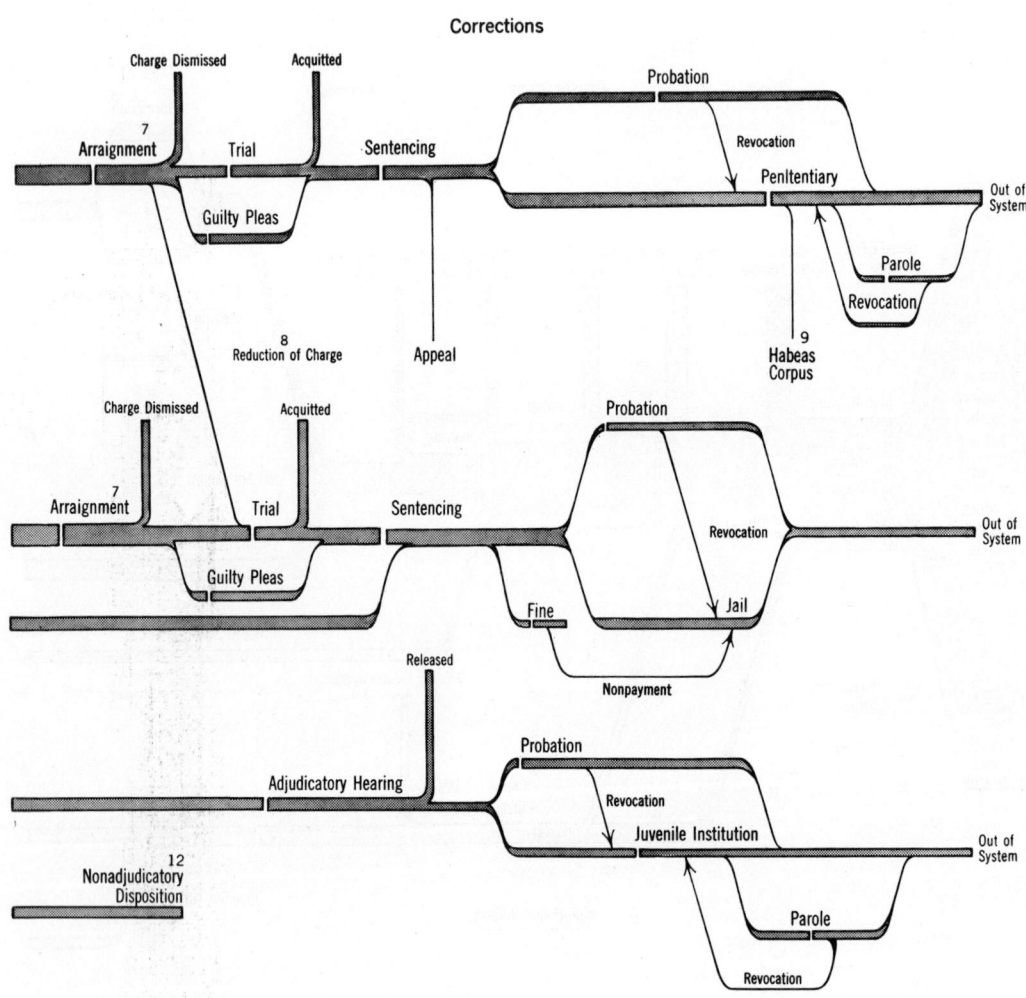

Alternative to grand jury indictment often used in felonies, almost always in misdemeanors. *6,* Reviews whether Government evidence sufficient to justify trial. Some states have no grand jury system; others seldom use it. *7,* Appearance for plea; defendant elects trial by judge or jury (if available); counsel for indigent usually appointed here in felonies. Often not at all in other cases. *8,* Charge may be reduced at any time prior to trial in return for plea of guilty or for other reasons. *9,* Challenge on constitutional grounds to legality of detention. May be sought at any point in process. *10,* Police often hold informal hearings, dismiss or adjust many cases without further processing. *11,* Probation officer decides desirability of further court action. *12,* Welfare agency, social services, counseling, medical care, etc., for cases where adjudicatory handling not needed.

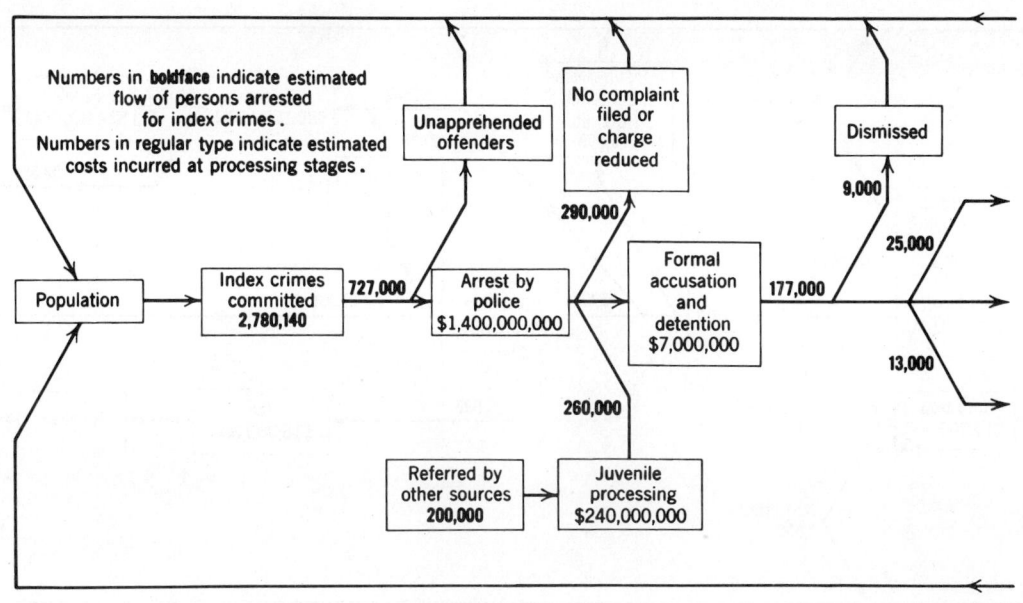

Figure 1. Criminal justice system model with estimates of flow of offenders and direct operating costs for index crimes in the United States in 1965. Data from Glaser (The Effectiveness of a Prison and Parole System; Bobbs Merrill: 1964) was used for the rearrest probabilities for those leaving corrections. The data for the other rearrest probabilities used in the model to derive criminal career patterns were tentative, but they are presented to illustrate the potential uses of the analysis and to give impetus to the collection of proper data for use in more definitive studies.

Data on crimes and arrests were based on data from the FBI "Uniform Crime Reports." [11] The probabilities describing the routing of offenders through each branching point were based on data from a sampling of State court reports for court and probation processing and on California [12] practices for correctional and juvenile processing.

As in all accounting, allocation of costs to crimes and to offenders often requires arbitrary judgments, especially in distributing fixed costs. Police costs were developed from information provided by the International Association of Chiefs of Police. They estimate that it would be reasonable to allocate 25 percent of patrol costs and 100 percent of detective costs to Index crimes.

Court costs were based on estimates in the District of Columbia of the time spent by the prosecutor and his staff, the judge and his staff, and witnesses and jurors on each type of crime as a function of the type of trial. Corrections costs were based on estimates by the Corrections Task Force of the cost per offender-year in prison and jail.

The costs for processing juveniles

---

[11] Federal Bureau of Investigation, U.S. Department of Justice, "Uniform Crime Reports for the United States," 1965, Washington, D.C.

[12] The reports from California provided the best published data on details of processing in the criminal justice system. The reports include: Bureau of Criminal Statistics, Division of Criminal Law and Enforcement, Department of Justice, State of California, "Crime in California, 1964." Administrative Statistics Section, Research Division, Department of Corrections State of California, "California Prisoners 1961, 1962, 1963," Sacramento, Calif. Bureau of Criminal Statistics, Division of Criminal Law and Enforcement, Department of Justice, State of California, "Delinquency and Probation in California, 1964."

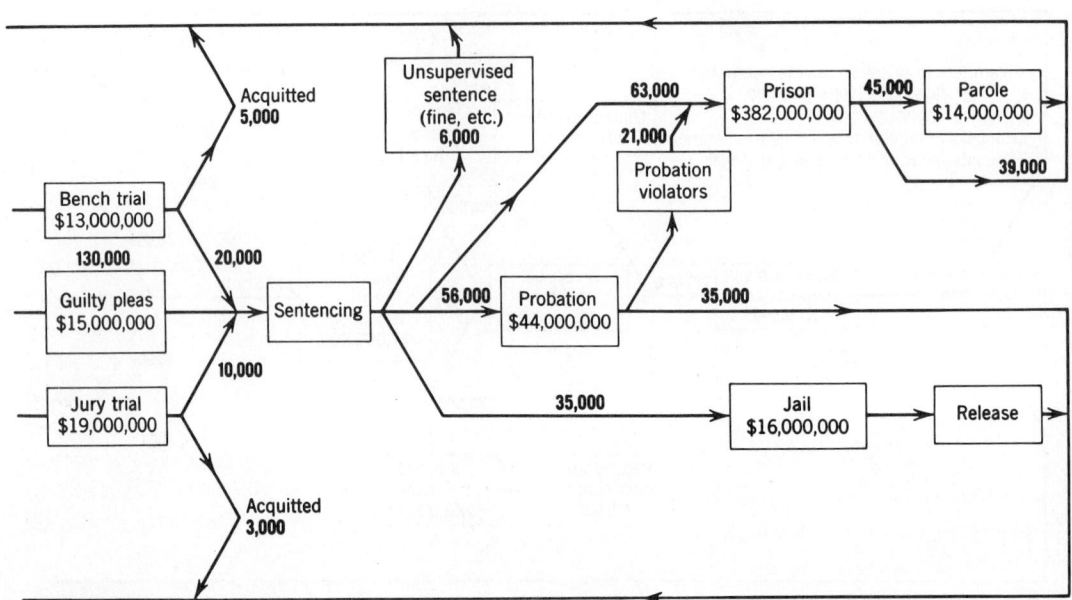

estimated so that the calculations would yield careers which approximated those in data collected by the Federal Bureau of Investigation and also give the closest approximation to arrest-age distributions given in the 1965 "Uniform Crime Report." For juveniles processed as such, the probabilities were assumed constant with age until they were processed as adults at age 18.

through courts and corrections are based on California costs and are underestimated since the only available cost data did not distinguish between the costs of processing juvenile Index crime offenders and other minor violators.

The cost calculations use an estimate of the processing time per case or offender. Hence, resource requirements can be easily calculated with data on the processing rate of each relevant resource: judges, prosecutors, probation officers, parole officers, prison guards, prison cells, etc.

The model can also be used to calculate the system's effectiveness in reducing crime by persons after they have been processed. At any stage in processing offenders can be released, dismissed, acquitted, discharged, or otherwise returned to the general population. When this happens, there is a chance of rearrest and reprocessing through the criminal justice system. This feedback feature permits the tracing of lifetime criminal career patterns—number of arrests, crimes arrested for, mean length of criminal careers—of individuals as they are recycled through the criminal justice system.

Calculating these criminal career patterns requires estimates of the probability of recidivism or recommission of crime for each type of offender leaving each processing stage. In the model, recidivism is related to offender variables, such as age and previous criminal history. It should also be related to variables characterizing the treatment (a person released by the police without being charged may have a different propensity to commit a new crime than one who is discharged from prison after serving a term) but such data are not now generally available.

There are many ways to measure recidivism. It would be desirable to know the probability of reversion to crime for

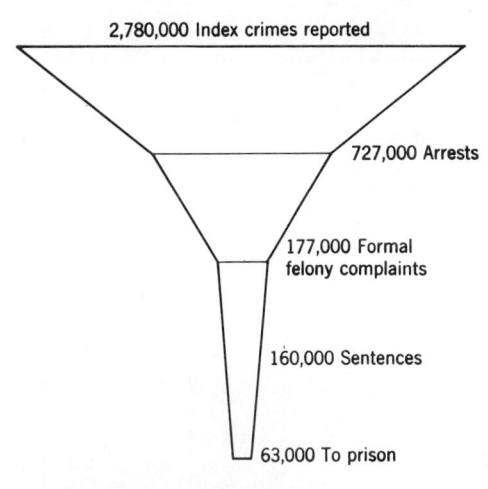

Figure 2. Funneling effect from reported crimes through prison sentence.

each type of offender as a function of the point of exit from the system. Unfortunately, direct data on reversion to crime would be impossible to develop because information on who committed an unsolved crime is impossible to obtain. Because of this difficulty, other measures of recidivism must be used. Some researchers, particularly those focusing on the corrections process, describe recidivism in terms of the probability that an offender released from corrections will be returned to corrections. This provides an underestimate of recidivism by those individuals because of the many opportunities for someone who committed a crime to drop out of the system, as illustrated by the funneling effect of Figure 2. For example, studies have shown that approximately one-third of the offenders released from prison will return. Typically, in the United States as a whole, 20 percent of individuals arrested for Index crimes are sentenced and only about 30 percent of these are sentenced to prison.

In the model, recidivism was measured at the point of rearrest. This brings into the sample a number of people arrested for crimes they did not commit, but reduces the error in ignoring people freed for legal or technical reasons even though they did commit the crime.

In this model, the probability that a person is rearrested was made to depend on his age, his previous crime, and on his exit point from the criminal justice system. These probabilities of rearrest were defined for each type of Index crime as decreasing constantly with age. The decrease is more rapid for some types of crime than for others.

The distributions of time lags between arrests were based on data from the FBI criminal careers study and on data from several jurisdictions. These data indicated that rearrest, if it happens, occurs within 5 years after release in about 99 percent of the cases and within 2 years in over 60 percent of the cases.

Another factor that must be included in a model to describe recidivism is the type of crime which a recidivist tends to commit. An individual's subsequent crimes are related to his previous crimes. The estimated array of these conditional probabilities for each of the seven Index crimes is shown in Table II. The table displays the chance of switching from each crime type to each other when rearrest occurs.

USES OF THE MODEL

Criminal Justice System Direct Operating Costs for Index Crimes. The direct costs of processing offenders at each stage were calculated for each Index crime on the basis of processing time and unit time costs. In Figure 3, the system costs for each kind of Index crime are distributed among the major cost components. Corrections costs account for a large portion of the total cost in murder and nonnegligent manslaughter (81 percent), forcible rape (42 percent), and robbery (42 percent). In all these crimes, police clearance rates tend to be high. For the property crimes, which have lower clearance rates, police costs are a much larger proportion, about 70 percent of the total costs. For all the Index crimes, the court costs are a very small portion of

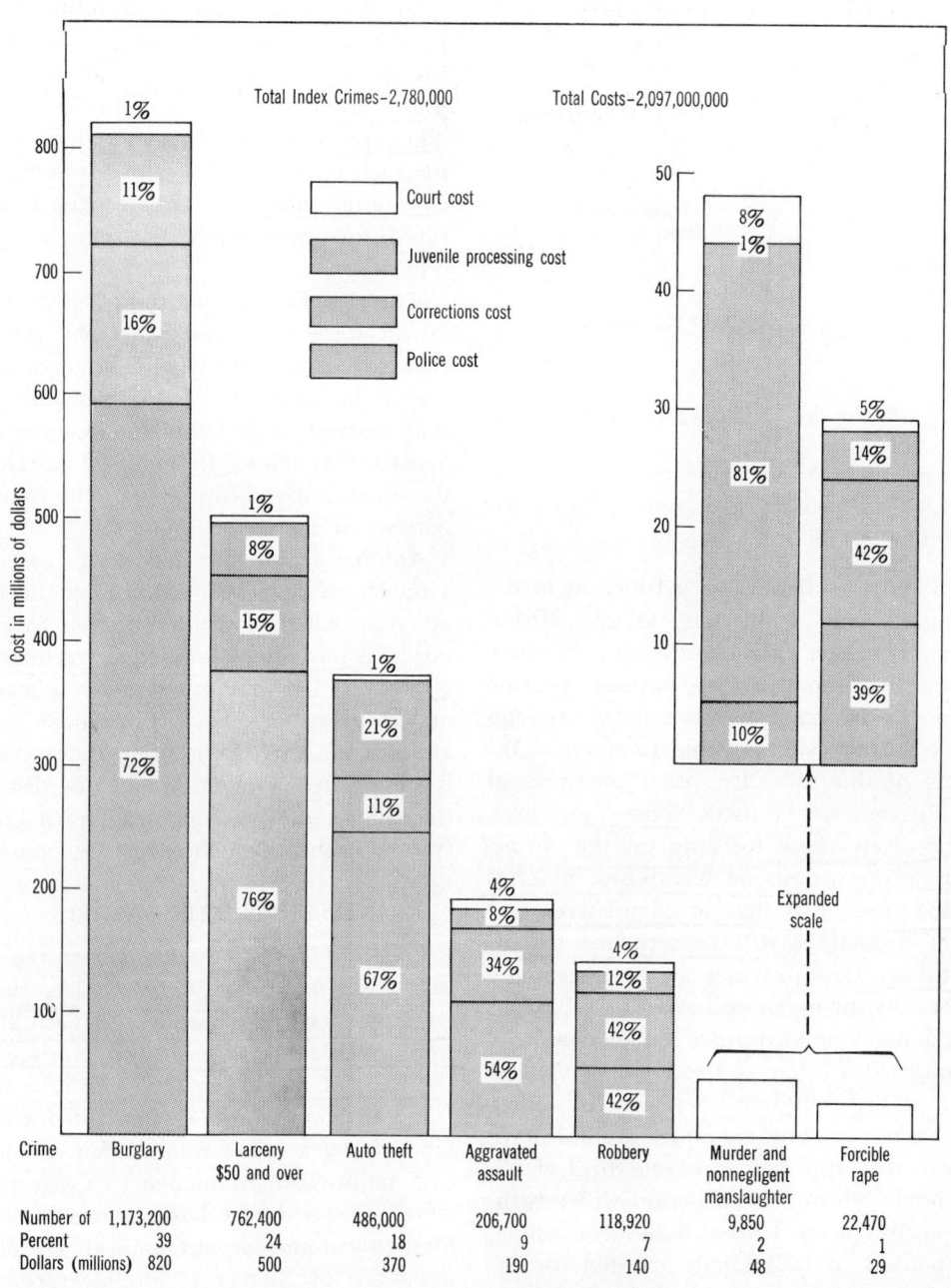

Figure 3. Estimated criminal justice system direct operating costs for United States Index crimes, 1965.

the total: 8 percent for murder, 4 to 5 percent for the other personal crimes, and 1 percent for the property crimes. Figure 4 shows how these costs are attributable to each of the 1965 Index crimes in the United States in 1965. It can be seen that the

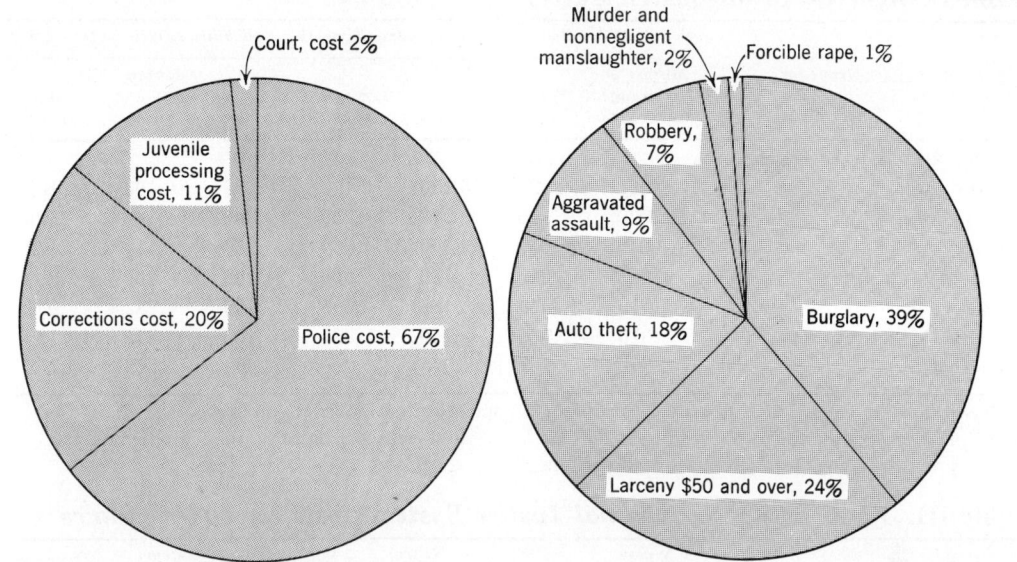

Figure 4. Estimated distribution of criminal justice system direct operating costs among major subsystem and types of Index crimes, 1965.

property crimes of burglary, larceny of $50 and over, and auto theft, which account for 87 percent of the Index crimes, also account for the bulk (81 percent) of the system costs for Index crimes. The figure also shows how these system costs for Index crimes are distributed among the major system components. Police costs are the largest (67 percent), followed by correctional programs (including probation) which account for 20 percent.

In Table III the system costs are presented as the cost per individual crime. Each reported Index crime costs the criminal justice system directly about $750. The cost per offender arrested, however, is about $3,000 since there are only about one-fourth as many arrests as Index crimes reported.

Another costing approach would omit the large amounts of police costs charged to the offenders, and charge them instead as fixed costs of the system. If offenders are not charged with any of the costs of police patrol, then the cost per offender arrested is reduced to about $1,000.

Criminal Careers. The criminal justice system pays a price for permitting a person to enter a life of crime. The cost is measured by the "criminal-career cost," or the total cost to the criminal justice system over the life of the offender for processing him. A simulated sample of 1,000 offenders, arrested for the first time at age 16,[13] was taken for each Index crime category, and the rearrest patterns over the Index crimes were computed using the rearrest matrix of probabilities which were given in Table II. The resulting criminal career patterns given in Table IV were derived. For example, 1,000 offenders arrested initially for robbery would accumulate during their lives: 50 arrests for murder, 70 for forcible rape, 800 more for robbery, 250 for aggravated assault, 1,400 for burglary, 730 for grand larceny, and 370 for auto theft—a total of 3,670 rearrests for Index crimes alone.

On the basis of these criminal career pattern results, the criminal-career costs were calculated to be about $12,000 per individual,[14] representing about 3 to 4 ar-

---

[13] Age 16 was chosen because the number of arrests for Index crimes peaks at this age.

[14] These estimates of current criminal career costs differ somewhat from those previously estimated by

Table II. Rearrest Crime-Switch Matrix [a]

	If Arrested Again for an Index Crime, the Probability It Will Be for—						
Last Index Arrest for	Murder and Nonnegligent Manslaughter	Forcible Rape	Robbery	Aggravated Assault	Burglary	Larceny ($50 and Over)	Auto Theft
Murder and nonnegligent manslaughter [b]	0.025	0.025	0.150	0.400	0.200	0.100	0.100
Forcible rape [b]	.020	.150	.110	.260	.200	.140	.120
Robbery	.015	.010	.350	.060	.350	.115	.100
Aggravated assault [b]	.025	.040	.150	.300	.085	.200	.200
Burglary	.010	.020	.135	.063	.459	.282	.031
Larceny ($50 and over)	.010	.020	.140	.025	.400	.275	.130
Auto theft	.010	.027	.045	.028	.390	.222	.278

[a] Based on data from Crime Revisited: Minnesota Board of Corrections; 1965 "Uniform Crime Reports," pp. 29-31; and Federal Bureau of Prisons, statistical tables, fiscal year 1965.
[b] Best estimates based on inadequate data.

Table III. Total 1965 U.S. Criminal Justice System Costs for Index Crimes [a]

Crime Type	Total System Costs (Millions of Dollars)	Number of Crimes	System Costs per Crime (Dollars)	Number of Arrests	System Costs per Arrest (Dollars)	Career Costs [b] (Dollars)
Willful homicide	48	9,850	4,900	9,400	5,100	12,600
Forcible rape	29	22,470	1,300	14,300	2,000	9,600
Robbery	140	118,920	1,200	54,300	2,600	13,500
Aggravated assault	190	206,700	920	108,000	1,800	13,500
Burglary	820	1,173,200	700	266,000	3,100	14,000
Larceny of $50 and over	500	762,400	660	144,000	3,500	11,900
Auto theft	370	486,600	760	131,000	2,800	11,000
All index crimes	2,097	2,780,140	750	727,000	2,900	[c] 12,200

[a] 100 percent of detective force costs and 25 percent of patrol force costs and court and corrections costs were allocated to Index crimes.
[b] Based on Index crimes with the 1st Index crime arrest occurring at age 16 for the indicated crime.
[c] Based on distribution of 1st arrests matched to distribution of arrests of individuals under 18 given in the 1965 "Uniform Crime Reports."

Table IV. Criminal Career Patterns for Index Crimes [a]

	Number of Lifetime Rearrests for—							
1,000 Initial Arrests at Age 16 for—	Murder and Nonnegligent Manslaughter	Forcible Rape	Robbery	Aggravated Assault	Burglary	Larceny ($50 and Over)	Auto Theft	Total Lifetime Rearrests
Murder and nonnegligent manslaughter	40	70	420	500	800	510	310	2,650
Forcible rape	40	200	380	380	810	540	320	2,670
Robbery	50	70	800	250	1,400	730	370	3,670
Aggravated assault	40	80	410	400	710	600	400	2,640
Burglary	40	80	560	250	1,500	900	280	3,610
Larceny ($50 and over)	30	60	430	160	1,100	700	310	2,790
Auto theft	30	70	330	150	1,100	650	400	2,730

[a] Based on calculations performed with the overall criminal justice system model with feedback loops.

rests for Index crimes per offender. This demonstrates the value of an investment in preventive programs that would avert criminal careers.

The model can also be used to examine the differences between the types of crimes for which first offenders are arrested and those for which repeaters are arrested. An example of such an examination is shown in table 5. The results are tabulated according to the order of seriousness used by the FBI in the UCR.

A typical distribution of 1,000 first arrests for Index offenses was taken. The criminal careers of these 1,000 individuals were then simulated by cycling through the model, taking the probabilities of rearrest over time, and the distribution among the Index crimes of each group or rearrested persons broken down according to the crime for which they were rearrested. The simulation showed an eventual accumulation of 3,010 subsequent arrests. These include a greater proportion of the more serious offenses than the 1,000 original offenses. For example, homicides, rapes, and robberies were several times more prevalent among the rearrests than among the first arrests. The less serious Index crimes of larceny and auto theft, on the other hand, became less prevalent.

These results, though only tentative, raise questions about why successive arrests appear to be for more serious crimes. This phenomenon may be due to the aging of the individuals, to the development of antisocial attitudes, or possibly even to reactions to treatment by the criminal justice system. It suggests the seriousness, in terms of escalating criminal conduct, of the problem of recidivism. A question to be explored is whether the rearrest probabilities and the crime-type distributions become worse for those who are processed further through the system. If that is the case, it may result either from differences among individuals who reach the various stages or from the treatment itself. Unfortunately, data to examine such basic questions do not now exist, but the questions are sufficiently important to warrant an intensive effort to collect the pertinent data, and ultimately, after hypotheses are developed, to conduct appropriate controlled experiments.

the Space-General Corp. ("Prevention and Control of Crime and Delinquency in California Final Report"; Space-General Corp.; July 29, 1965, pp. 65 ff.) largely because of several important differences in definitions. The Space-General analysis considered offenders rather than arrestees, thus necessitating fairly arbitrary estimates of the probability of not being caught after committing a crime. Furthermore, it considers repeated offenses only within the same type of crime (i.e., it used only the diagonal terms of the recidivism matrix). In addition the Space-General analysis treated repeated offenders as though they have infinite lives. This model used a probability of repeating that declined with age resulting in the limited criminal careers of 8 to 12 years. Finally, the Space-General analysis allocated all police costs, detective and patrol, to felony crimes. This model assigned only one-quarter of patrol costs to Index crimes.

Table V. *Average Distribution of First Arrests and Lifetime Rearrests for Index Crime Offenders*

Offense	First Arrests		Lifetime Rearrests		Percent Change in Proportion of Total
	Number [a]	Percent of Total	Number	Percent of Total	
Willful homicide	2	0.2	34	1.1	+450
Forcible rape	6	.6	68	2.3	+280
Robbery	33	3.3	458	15.2	+360
Aggravated assault	32	3.2	194	6.4	+100
Burglary	252	25.2	1,196	39.7	+60
Larceny of $50 and over	518	51.8	739	24.6	−50
Auto theft	157	15.7	321	10.7	−30
Total	1,000	100.0	3,010	100.0	----

[a] The distribution of the 1,000 first arrests is based on the distribution of arrests of indivduals under 18 given in the 1965 "Uniform Crime Reports."

12. ABUSES IN CRIME REPORTING

DURING 1933 THE NEW YORK CITY POLICE DEpartment began active participation in the Uniform Crime Reporting program and for some years the crime totals fell to lower and lower levels. Repeated efforts to secure a closer compliance with the established standards of crime reporting fell short of their objective because of a marked laxity in crime records control in this city, and an unfamiliarity with the use and value of such management tools. New York's crime returns were therefore excluded from national computations on the ground that they were incomplete, unreliable and misleading.

After months of critical examination of these questions by the press and by civic bodies, and a penetrating analysis of recording procedures by the office of the district attorney of New York County, a change in the police administration was followed in October 1950 by a quick reversal of earlier attitudes and a long postponed effort to comply with accepted standards and practical requirements. Since that time, the number of certain types of reported crimes has risen.

In the light of the figures tabulated during recent months the incompleteness of earlier compilations becomes apparent. Table I is a tabulation of selected offenses as reported by New York's police over the years. For the years 1934-1949 monthly averages are offered for comparison with current figures. In reviewing the data it should be remembered that the reported figures were intended to represent all offenses known to have been committed, as distinguished from the number of persons arrested, and that the tabulation is limited to four of the major offense classes which experience indicates are those most sensitive to changes in the quality of crime reporting in a given department.... In grand summary they amount to this: that reported robberies have risen by 400 percent, assaults with gun and knife by 200 percent, larcenies by 700 percent, while burglaries have risen to a level that is 13 times higher than that prevailing in 1948 and 1949.

Police officials were compelled to arrange the distribution of the force without the benefit of reasonably reliable figures as to the total volume of crime for the city as a whole, for the individual boroughs, divisions or precincts. Supervisory officers could not appraise the work of their subordinates in the affected categories and even the ultimate recovery of identifiable property was greatly impaired.

The most striking feature reflected in the charts and the tabulation is the amazing jump in the figures of October 1950. This rise in the number of reported offenses was in part the result of various changes in recording and forwarding practice in the police precincts; but it chiefly reflected the demand of the new police

►SOURCE: *Crime Records in Police Management: New York City, New York, The Institute of Public Administration, 1952, pp. 3–5, 10, 15–17. (Editorial adaptations.) Reprinted by permission.*

Table I. *Monthly Figures, 1934–1951*

Year		Robbery	Aggravated Assault	Burglary	Larceny
1934	Monthly Average	104	201	258	*
1935	Monthly Average	99	207	232	*
1936	Monthly Average	103	213	211	598
1937	Monthly Average	106	243	272	*
1938	Monthly Average	108	247	236	*
1939	Monthly Average	119	245	416	1,356
1940	Monthly Average	125	219	687	1,558
1941	Monthly Average	113	229	699	1,316
1942	Monthly Average	107	205	455	1,215
1943	Monthly Average	87	203	505	860
1944	Monthly Average	85	208	383	872
1945	Monthly Average	118	215	362	998
1946	Monthly Average	145	241	413	1,061
1947	Monthly Average	131	260	282	626
1948	Monthly Average	126	234	227	643
1949	Monthly Average	123	254	210	655
1950	January	156	292	234	720
	February	178	232	246	639
	March	161	239	213	651
	April	142	222	214	666
	May	145	264	175	423
	June	117	281	213	499
	July	127	281	214	315
	August	110	293	161	634
	September	128	230	242	738
	October	268	404	1,185	2,600
	November	396	492	2,000	3,845
	December	512	408	2,001	3,076
1951	January	427	371	1,594	2,431
	February	456	404	1,724	2,179
	March	492	408	1,832	2,456
	April	649	895	4,211	5,382
	May	615	729	3,031	5,613
	June	494	657	2,438	4,978
	July	512	655	2,456	4,542
	August	608	793	2,913	5,519
	September	576	701	2,524	5,151

* Not available.

commissioner that an honest record be compiled.

In most cases arising prior to October 1950 the information furnished by a complainant quickly found its way to a wastebasket. This practice was referred to cynically as "canning" a complaint or referring the matter to "Detective Can." For the most part those offenses that were recorded were entered initially in the detective bureau on a report form known as the DD-4 which was given a detective bureau serial number. A copy was forwarded to headquarters where a check was made for any missing numbers.

As an example of what can happen where real follow-up provided by headquarters control does not exist there is a case on

Table II. *Crime Rates*

	Murder	Robbery	Aggravated Assault	Burglary	Larceny	Auto Theft
New York City		11.4	19.4	16.4	45.6	63.1
January–June 1950	2.08	39.7	43.9	187.9	291.9	64.4
January–June 1951	1.42					
Other Cities Over 250,000 [a]		42.6	50.3	213.4	526.5	116.7
January–June 1951	3.21					

[a] *Uniform Crime Reports*, Vol. XXII, No. 1.

record during recent months where a man was brutally assaulted with a club and robbed in this city. The call to the police for an ambulance placed by someone passing by appears to have been recorded as a person injured in an auto accident, possibly because of the excitement of the person calling. In any event the ambulance arrived at the scene and removed the injured man to a hospital and when he was released 10 days later he inquired and found the police had no record of the assault and robbery. On the average, the chances of making an arrest in a robbery case is less than one out of two, but with a 10 day delay in starting the investigation, the chances are next to nothing.

This illustrative case demonstrates the need for a follow-up on ambulance cases and while a reasonably adequate control in this area will be provided in the recommendations which follow, it may be that the department will find it helpful to work out some arrangement with the hospitals so that in all ambulance cases a brief notation of the diagnosis on admission will be furnished the proposed central complaint room.

High as the crime totals now appear for New York City their enormity is more apparent than real. This is readily seen in the figures shown in Table II comparing the crime rates (number of offenses per 100,000 inhabitants) for the first half of 1950 and 1951 in New York with those of other cities in the country with population in excess of 250,000 for January-June 1951.

The crime figures currently being tabulated in New York are unquestionably a vast improvement over the obviously incomplete figures shown for the first half of 1950; however, it is clear from the figures that the 1951 rates are by no means high.

It is of particular significance to bring out here that in 1939 efforts in the general direction of complete crime reporting were made by way of instructions from headquarters but these instructions were not accompanied by any basic change in the reporting system that would provide headquarters with absolute administrative control. Thus in Table I we find some increase in the figures in 1939 in the burglary and larceny classes but the quality of reporting gradually deteriorated over the next decade to the point where the crime figures were no longer accepted for publication in the Uniform Crime Reports.

SECTION III

The Concept of Cause

THIS SECTION IS CONCERNED WITH THE NECESSITY OF BEING ALERT TO THE meaning of social causation, within causal and correlational forms of relationships, and to some refined problems raised by using prediction methods with "unique individuals." The "multiple factor" approach is analyzed and criticized by Cohen, while Hirschi and Selvin address themselves to the problem of minimum requirements for a scientifically adequate causal analysis. Being concerned with incorrect assertions of noncausality, they clearly demonstrate the falsity of six illegitimate criteria often raised in evaluating delinquency research.

The first article by Wilkins is especially lucid in communicating some of the methodological problems of probability theory to the statistically untrained layman. His comments on the complexity of human nature, the problem of the unique case, and the relationship between symbols and semantics are positive and constructive aids for understanding the meaning and importance of research designs that use operational definitions and control groups. This kind of understanding is necessary if we hope to achieve the goal of predicting deviant conduct or of measuring the outcome of any type of social action. In "The Concept of Cause in Criminology," Wilkins suggests that the concept of cause can be handled only within complex probabilistic systems, which should not be considered deterministic ones. He argues that we must, in time, abandon our predilection for deterministic schemes of human behavior (which have never "worked") for probabilistic ones which may ultimately prove productive.

There have been many arguments between proponents of "general theory" and "multiple factor" approaches. The basic question is whether it is more efficient and scientific to (a) collect data relevant to the general topic in the hope that some meaningful insights will emerge inductively and permit limited hypotheses suggesting specific data collection and factor analysis, and that accumulation of significant factors will develop a meaningful theory of delinquent and criminal behavior; or, (b) begin research with a meaningful general theory of delinquency and crime so that separate testable hypotheses, directed by and toward the theory, may reduce the number of variables (factors) to manageable size for an analysis that will test the validity of the hypotheses and, indirectly, of the general theory, so that in time the theory will mature by embracing a body of confirmed researches based on empirical data. It is suggested that every study undertaken with the multiple factor approach must limit the known universe of variables by *some* criteria of judgment, albeit implicit and without theoretical formulations. Because the search for data is partly a function of time, staff, financial resources, or simply the availability of kinds of data, some selective operation must occur. The limited selected factors collected, therefore, are prejudged to have some significant bearing on the dependent variable, delinquency or crime. *A posteriori* interpretation without a preceding guiding theory is, of course, much more random and perhaps is faced with more alternatives than interpretation of data collected in conjunction with hypotheses derived from a general theory. In any case, as Cohen suggests, the collection of multiple factors is not per se theory; but the selection of a limited number of factors for analysis nonetheless involves implicit assumptions.

Multiple factor adherents should: (1) state more explicitly the reasons for their choice of particular items for analysis; (2) attempt to arrange these reasons for delimited factor choice within an integrated and meaningful interrelationship of factors, for factors that remain outside the framework of the rationale for selection are meaningless even if correlated with the dependent variable; (3) seek to link previous unintegrated but highly correlated data to existing theory; or (4) produce new theory which their integrated data may provide. The generalizing theorists should: (1) examine and make more extensive use of analyses of data already collected by the multiple-factor approach in order to produce theory more closely linked to existing research; (2) specify more explicitly the range and parameters of their conceptualisms; (3) employ, wherever possible, the full complement of operational concepts in theories so that data can be gathered to support the theories directly; (4) provide wherever possible operational hypotheses that derive directly from the theory; (5) suggest the best sources and levels of quantitative and qualitative data that could be used to examine the specific components of the theory.

13. SOCIAL CAUSATION

ROBERT MacIVER

IT IS VAIN TO SEEK THE CAUSES OF CRIME AS such, of crime anywhere and everywhere. Crime is a legal category. The only thing that is alike in all crimes is that they are alike violations of law. In that sense the only cause of crime as such is the law itself. What is a crime in one country is no crime in another; what is a crime at one time is no crime at another. The law is forever changing, adding new crimes to the catalogue and cancelling former ones. It may even, as not infrequently happens in times of crisis or revolution, designate as the most heinous of crimes certain forms of behavior that were previously counted highly honorable. Since, then, crime varies with the law, the conditions that evoke it are equally variant. Moreover, the social conditions that increase the frequency of some categories of crime may diminish the frequency of others. Crime, then, is essentially relative. It has no inherent quality or property attaching to it as such, attaching to crime of all categories under all conditions. If indeed we do raise the question: Why crime? we are asking merely why people are so constituted that they violate laws under any conditions whatever. The question has no more specific significance than the question: Why human nature?

Since crime, as a category of social action, has no inherent universal property, we cannot expect to find, in the variety of persons who are convicted of crimes, any one psychological or physiological type, any character trait whatever that differentiates them all from other persons. The crime committer may be a maniac or a genius, a scoundrel or a patriot, a man without scruple or a man who puts his scruples above the law, a reckless exploiter or a man in desperate need. All attempts to find a physiognomy of crime have failed.[1] The vaguer attempts to find a particular mentality associated with lawbreaking are without warrant. The endless vicissitudes of circumstance, opportunity, and personal history preclude the expectation of any simple inclusive formula. There are, of course, criminal groups, gangs, habitual offenders who make a profession of crime under similar conditions, and these may well develop, like any other social or professional groups, their own distinctive traits.

These considerations reinforce the position we have already stated and which we shall develop more fully later on, that the

▶SOURCE: *Social Causation,* Boston: Ginn and Company, 1942, pp. 88–95. Reprinted by permission of Ginn and Company and the author.

[1] The most recent and most elaborate attempt is that of E. A. Hooton, *The American Criminal,* Cambridge, Massachusetts, 1939. See the searching criticism by Robert Merton and M. F. Ashley-Montagu, "Crime and the Anthropologist," *American Anthropologist* (July-September, 1940), Vol. 42, pp. 384–408.

only effective quest for causes is that which enquires into a specific difference between two or more comparable situations. The more determinate the difference and the more clearly comparable the situations, the more promising is the quest. If, for example, certain crimes are more in evidence during depressions than in better times, under the same social system, and if these crimes have a relative economic aspect, the problem is specific and easily attacked. But if there is a greater frequency of crime or of certain crimes among laborers than among business people, the problem is not yet demarcated, since many other conditions besides the mode of occupation distinguish the social groups to which laborers predominantly belong from the social groups to which business people predominantly belong. Or again, if there is a greater frequency of crime among bachelors than among married men, we cannot at once proceed to the question: Why does the marital condition act as a deterrent of crime? For there may very well be other factors than the married state distinguishing the unmarried, as a broad social category, from the married. First we must analyze our difference-revealing groups and situations to discover the grounds of their comparability, relative to the phenomenon under investigation. It is only when we have discovered in this way specific relations between crime and situation that we can hope to throw much light on any larger issues regarding the incidence of crime.

It is not unusual for writers on the subject of crime to be preoccupied with some types of crime and to explain crime in general by considerations drawn from the study of these types. We find this tendency in some authors who have made a particular study of gangs, and who consequently are apt to identify the gangster with the criminal. We should observe also that the expression "the criminal" has certain connotations that limit its application. A great number of those who commit crimes are not "criminals," as that term is usually understood. Hence even if we could explain why men become criminals, or habitual offenders within a certain range of crime, we would not have thereby explained why men commit crimes.

The opposite error, but one invoking a more flagrant confusion, is attributable to those who, in dealing with the causes of crime, are mainly concerned with moral explanations. Often they write as though crime itself were almost equivialent to wrong-doing or "immortality." We find this tendency in a number of writers who are content to refer crime to "bad homes," "vicious neighborhoods," "the weakening of the moral sense," "bad heredity," "lack of social control," "individualism," "egocentricity," "the decay of religious life," "the decline of social standards," and so forth. Such explanations are in the first instance vague and inconclusive. They introduce indeterminate principles as though they were determinate causes. If these principles explain anything—though they themselves require more definition and explanation than the phenomena to which they are applied—they explain a host of other things as much, and therefore as badly. But our objection at this point is that they fail to recognize the distinction between a moral category and a legal category. No one would deny that moral attitudes are involved in violations of the legal code. But we cannot assume that there is one characteristic type of moral attitude, describable as individualism, egocentricity, and so forth, that is peculiarly associated with the commission of crime. A crime is an infraction of a legal code that is not identical with any of the diverse moral codes of groups or individuals. The numerous conjectures of occasion, opportunity, personal experience, and socio-economic situation, to which acts of crime are responsive, make the appeal to any universal moral principle at best an inadequate and unilluminating explanation.

A simple correlation predicates no nexus between the correlated variables. It merely directs our enquiry in a particular direction. Where there is causation there is also correlation, but where there is correlation there may be no corresponding causation. Many things are happening and many things are changing at the same time. Some are causally independent, some are interdependent, some are alike dependent on the same larger causal scheme but not on one another. A correlation is a clue or a question mark. Its significance is what we can infer from it or what we may learn by following the lead it provides. Sometimes we can draw no inference, sometimes the lead peters out. Correlation techniques are extremely useful in many areas of investigation, both in the physical and in the social sciences, but their heuristic value is small where the correlated variables do not fall within or cannot be brought within a single coherent order. An illustration or two may suffice.

If bales of heavy dark wood and equally heavy bales of light colored aspen wood are compared (as to the relationship between weight and volume), then an influence of coloring on the weight might be disclosed which actually does not exist. The statistics of Russian compulsory fire insurance discloses a striking relationship between the average number of buildings destroyed in one conflagration in the country and the use or non-use of fire engines for its extinction: fires extinguished by a fire brigade furnished with a fire engine are, on the average, more destructive than others. To conclude from this that the destruction of fire engines constitutes the best means of reducing damage from fire would be . . . absurd.[2]

Why is this conclusion absurd? Not because it is inconsistent with other correlations. Established correlations cannot contradict one another, because they assert nothing regarding the relationship of the correlated variables. The conclusion is absurd because it is inconsistent with all the causal knowledge we already possess regarding the relationship of fire engines and fires. This illustration brings out the principle that the discovery of a correlation can serve only as the starting point for further investigation and analysis. This principle has a particular significance for the social sciences. We discover, for example, various correlations of social phenomena and physical phenomena. We discover, say, that the frequency of homicide is positively correlated with the summer rise of temperature. We cannot stop there. We certainly cannot conclude forthwith that summer heat is a cause of homicide. Nor again can we conclude that wintry weather is a cause of crimes against property. The nexus between summer heat and homicide, if one exists, is not immediate. We must seek for a more direct relation between homicide and certain ways of living, certain modes of behaving, that are associated, under certain conditions of civilization, with the season of hot weather. We may thus find a nexus that is not only more direct but also more understandable, more coherent with what knowledge we already possess regarding the responses of human beings to the conditions under which they live.[3]

The fallacy of this assumption is so simple that it ought to be immediately obvious, but it is committed rather frequently in studies of social causation. When a number of diverse factors are interactive and when a particular phenomenon is the result of their interactivity, we cannot treat them as though they were independent, homogeneous units each of which produces a measurable portion of their joint product. This crudely mechanistic assumption vitiates those investigations that seek to assess, often in precise quantitative terms, the role of the various components of a causal complex. It is present when writers list in order of priority or of importance the *diverse* causes they postulate for crime,

---

[2] A. A. Tschuprow, *Principles of the Mathematical Theory of Correlation* (London, 1939), p. 21.

[3] On this subject see the writer's book, *Society: A Textbook of Sociology* (New York, 1937), Chap. V.

unemployment, divorce, and other phenomena, the prevalence of which is subject to statistical measurement.

We have called this fallacy "mechanistic," meaning thereby it treats the various components of a social situation, or of any organized system, as though they were detachable, isolable, homogeneous, independently operative, and therefore susceptible of being added to or subtracted from the causal complex, increasing or decreasing the result by that amount. But even a slight acquaintance with mechanism itself should teach us to avoid this fallacy. We find writers who tell us that juvenile delinquency is due so much to this factor and so much to that and so much to this other. But no mechanic would make the mistake of saying that the carburetor contributed so much and the ignition system so much and the gasoline so much to the speed of the car.[4] If a car is an organization of parts and materials that interdependently determine its functioning, at least no less so is a society. Moreover, the conditions to which social phenomena are responsive belong to a variety of different orders, so as to make the comparative rating of factors within the causal complex even more incongruous. When we are faced with the problem of multiple order causation we must proceed upon entirely different lines. In due course we shall deal with it. For the present a simple illustration may suffice. Various studies have been made of fatigue as a cause of industrial accidents.[5] These have led in turn to researches into the causes of fatigue in industrial operations. Evidences have been adduced to show that, besides the physical factors lying in the nature of the work itself and of the working conditions and besides the physiological factors of the health and strength of the workers, there are also psycho-sociological factors, described in such terms as "morale," "emotional adjustment," "co-operative and non-co-operative attitudes," and so on.[6] The issue here raised is that the valuations and attitudes of the workers are *interactive* with the physical conditions in the causation of fatigue and that therefore neither set of factors can be independently assessed. If this is so for a localized physiological phenomenon such as industrial fatigue, how much more should we pause before attempting to attach any independent or absolute rating to the numerous factors involved in the wide-ranging social phenomenon of crime!

---

[4] It is of course another matter altogether to attribute to a change in any one factor, given the other factors as before, a difference, under stipulated conditions, in the result, say in the speed of the car. An important distinction between a mechanical unity and an organic or a social unity is that we can often change one factor in the former while keeping all the others wholly or practically unchanged.

[5] For example, Emery S. Bogardus, *The Relation of Fatigue to Industrial Accidents*, Chicago, 1912.

[6] An account of the conclusions to this effect of the Committee on Elimination of Fatigue in Industry is given by Donald A. Laird, "Work and Fatigue," *Scientific American* (1930), Vol. 143, pp. 24–26.

14. MULTIPLE FACTOR APPROACHES

ALBERT K. COHEN

MULTIPLE FACTOR APPROACHES TODAY ENJOY wide currency and respectability. The following quotation from a popular textbook in social disorganization is a representative example of multiple factor thinking:

> Elaborate investigations of delinquents give us conclusive evidence that there is no single pre-disposing factor leading inevitably to delinquent behavior. On the other hand, the delinquent child is generally a child handicapped not by one or two, but usually by seven or eight counts. We are safe in concluding that almost any child can overcome one or two handicaps, such as the death of one parent or poverty and poor health. However, if the child has a drunken unemployed father and an immoral mother, is mentally deficient, is taken out of school at an early age and put to work in a factory, and lives in a crowded home in a bad neighborhood, nearly every factor in his environment may seem to militate against him.[1]

William Healy set the pattern for research along multiple factor lines in his early work, *The Individual Delinquent*, published in 1915. In view of the manifest inadequacy of most earlier "single-factor"

▶SOURCE: *Juvenile Delinquency and the Social Structure (Ph.D. Thesis, Harvard University), 1951, pp. 5–13.*

[1] Mable A. Elliott and Francis E. Merrill *Social Disorganization*, Harper and Brothers, New York, 1941, p. 111. An almost identical passage appears in Martin H. Neumeyer *Juvenile Delinquency in Modern Society*, D. Van Nostrand Co., New York, 1949, p. 62.

theories, Healy was determined not to select for observation and study any preconceived set of factors but to note, in every case, every causal factor present, major and minor. This catholicism was conceived by Healy to be more scientific and more rigorously "empirical." This inaugurated a long series of multiple factor studies, each offering a long array of "causes." Of these perhaps the most influential has been Cyril Burt's *The Young Delinquent,* which produced "more than 170 distinct conditions ... every one of them conducive to childish misconduct."[1a] The average number of "subversive circumstances" per child was 9 or 10.[2] The following observations are not directed at any particular multiple factor studies but are general considerations of scientific method applicable to almost any study of this type.

Factors vs. Variables. A multiplicity of factors is not to be confused with a multiplicity of variables. Almost all scientific theories contain a multiplicity of variables. A variable is a logical universal; it is a characteristic or aspect with respect to which an object or event may vary, such as "velocity" or "size of income." Values of the variables are logical particulars; they are the logically possible different concrete circumstances which meet the criterion defining

[1a] Cyril Burt, *The Young Delinquent*, Fourth Edition. University of London Press, London, 1944, p. 600.

[2] *Ibid*, p. 602.

the variable, such as "30 miles per hour" or "5,000." A statement of fact is a report of an observation or a series of observations in terms of particular values of generalized variables. A statement of fact is not a theoretical explanation. A theoretical explanation is a demonstration that a particular concrete event, describable in terms of a statement of fact, is a logical inference from a theoretical proposition or system of propositions. A theoretical proposition is one which relates variations in one variable to variations in one or more other variables. The test of a theory is how well it approximates this ideal: that all verifiable statements of fact in terms of values of the variables of that theory be logical inferences from that theory. A satisfactory scientific explanation of an event does not require that a particular concrete circumstance or set of circumstances invariably accompany events like the one to be explained. Each event may well be accompanied by a unique configuration of circumstances which is in each case causally relevant since many different combinations of concrete circumstances may fit the conditions called for by the generalized theory. Explanation calls not for a *single factor* but for a *single theory* or system of theory applicable to all cases. It is not the attendant circumstances but the demonstration that the event and the attendant circumstances are a special case of generalized theory which constitutes an explanation.

A "factor" as here understood is not a variable; it is a particular concrete circumstance. A multiple factor approach is not a theory; it is an abdication of the quest for a theory. It simply asserts that this particular event is "caused" by this particular combination of concrete circumstances and that particular event by another combination of circumstances. This delinquency is caused by "bad neighborhood," "feeble-mindedness," and "drunken mother"; that delinquency is caused by "poverty," "broken home," "bad health," and "premature puberty." What makes these "causes" other than the fiat or "intuition" of the author? Nothing, if nothing more is offered. Probably, in many cases, the assertion that this complex of circumstances is causally related to that event rests upon implicit, inarticulate, "preconscious" theoretical assumptions in the mind of the author; but explanation lies precisely in making these theoretical assumptions explicit, showing their applicability to concretely or "phenotypically" different "special cases" of the general theory, and demonstrating that this particular complex of circumstances fits the conditions required by the theory.

This does not mean that the descriptive enumeration of circumstances attendant upon delinquent acts and their statistical summarization in the form of averages, percentages and correlations is not an important phase of research on the causation of delinquency or may not have other important applications. Every such verifiable statement of fact is a test case of the general theory, and a stimulus to formulation of a new theory or reformulation of the old if the theory does not "fit the facts." Of course such statistical analyses may have all sorts of actuarial uses without committing the users to any particular theoretical position.[4]

Assumption of Intrinsic Pathogenic Qualities. This assumption is really a corollary of the confusion of "factors" with "causes." Most approaches of this class implicitly or explicitly assume that each factor contains *within itself* a capacity to produce or to deter from delinquency, a fixed quantum, so to speak, of delinquent or anti-delinquent potential. From this follows the further assumption that the net effect of the total web of circumstances is

---

[4] See, for example, Sheldon and Eleanor T. Glueck, *One Thousand Juvenile Delinquents*, Harvard University Press, Cambridge, 1934, and *After-Conduct of Discharged Offenders*, Macmillan and Co., London, 1945, p. 18, n. 3; and Sheldon, Glueck "On the Causes of Crime", American Mercury, 29 (August, 1933), 436.

the sum of the pro-delinquent factors minus the sum of the anti-delinquent factors. Usually several pro-delinquent factors must conspire to produce a delinquent; the average child can overcome a few "handicaps." As Burt says, "it needs many coats of pitch to paint a thing thoroughly black."[5] Our quotation from Elliott and Merrill clearly illustrates this type of reasoning.

More specifically, this assumption implies (1) that the inherent pathogenic (or beneficent) tendency of each factor in the actor's milieu is independent of the other factors which accompany it and (2) that these tendencies are independent of the actor's personality or the meanings of the factors to the actor. There is no other conclusion to be drawn from a list of concrete circumstances labelled, without qualification, "causes of delinquency."

The failure to realize that the consequences of the presence of a factor are not determined by the intrinsic characteristics of the factor alone but by the total field in which it is embedded and by the actor's definition of the situation helps account for the inconclusive and conflicting results of numerous studies of the role of particular factors. Wattenberg's conclusions from his review of studies of delinquency and "only children" would apply with equal force to any other factor:

> One thing appears clear: The general "category" of "only child" is no good for psychological purposes. Differences in local customs, national or racial mores, and various other social and economic factors were largely uncontrolled in the studies reported. Such factors apparently can so change the meaning of being an only child or of having siblings that contrasting results are obtained.[6]

This does not merely mean that the pathogenic quality of a particular factor may be outweighed by some other factor; it means that inherently the factor possesses neither pathogenic nor any other quality.

The Evil-Causes-Evil Fallacy. What Kingsley Davis has called the "evil-causes-evil fallacy" characterizes most of the multiple factor approaches, though it is not inherent in the nature of the approach nor is it peculiar to it. This is the unconscious assumption that "evil" consequences have "evil" precedents, that "evil" precedents can have only "evil" consequences. This leads to a conspicuous feature of most of our textbooks of social pathology: for each "social problem" we find much the same catalogues of sordid and ugly circumstances, which any "decent citizen" would deplore, invoked as "causes."

Thus Lowell J. Carr finds the causes of delinquency in "deviation pressures." A deviation pressure is abstractly defined as anything in the environment that either blocks adjustment or turns adjustment in an anti-social direction."[7] How, in practice, do we determine whether a circumstance is a "deviation pressure"? Professor Carr takes up six areas or foci of deviation pressures. The first of these is "deviant homes."

> Physical and psychological normality are usually taken for granted in speaking of any normal home. Certainly a home that contains a chronic invalid or a feeble-minded person or a paranoid personality would hardly be called normal. Such a home would exert a definite deviation pressure on the behavior of its children. Insofar as any home departs from any of these characteristics—structural completeness, racial homogeneity, economic security, cultural conformity, physical and psychological normality, and functional adequacy—to that extent it is a deviant home and a center of definite deviation pressures.[8]

What are we to understand by "functional adequacy"?

---

[5] Burt, *op. cit.*, p. 600.
[6] William W. Wattenberg "Delinquency and Only Children: Study of a 'Category'," *Journal of Abnormal and Social Psychology*, 44 (July, 1949), 365.

[7] Lowell J. Carr *Delinquency Control*, Harper and Brothers, New York, 1941, p. 104.
[8] *Ibid.*, pp. 111–112.

It refers to the fact that the people in such a home carry on the process of interaction among themselves with a minimum of friction and a minimum of emotional frustration. In a functionally adequate home there is a minimum of parental rejection; a minimum of sibling rivalry; a minimum of inculcation of inferiority, escape from reality, self-pity, or any of the other attitudes that cripple and thwart the growing personality. A functionally adequate home encourages growth, confidence, frankness, respect for personality, ability to face reality. In short, a functionally adequate home is an *emotionally healthy home*.[9]

It is hard to resist the conclusion that if there is *anything* "wrong" with the home it may be assumed to be a deviation pressure. Though Carr emphatically asserts that all these situations are deviation pressures, he is but asserting what was to be proved. It is not self-evident nor has it been demonstrated that these situations "block adjustment or turn adjustment in an anti-social direction." What Carr has done is to enumerate for us the home conditions which he considers undesirable but he has begged the scientific question of demonstrating their criminogenic role.

An understanding of the "evil-causes-evil" fallacy calls for a brief excursion into the sociology of knowledge. An adequate appraisal of the current status of the study of social problems should note the part played by our value systems in blocking the scientific study of these problems. There is no reason why some of the things we hold to be most ugly, sinful and sordid may not be in part consequence, in part condition of what we most value, cherish and esteem. It is possible that some seemingly localized and uncomplicated problems may really be incapable of solution within the framework of the existing institutional order. Sociologists, being likewise citizens, tend to identify with that institutional order and to seek for the causes of social problems in factors which might be controlled or eliminated without impairing faith in the sanctity of our institutions or to seek them in factors which, though presumably uncontrollable, may be safely deplored without hurting anybody's feelings. This is one reason why we have been so slow to produce really penetrating analyses of the complex interdependence of social problems and the larger social system.[10]

---

[9] Carr, *op. ct.*, p. 112.

[10] This paragraph has been adapted from the writer's discussion of a paper by Francis E. Merrill, *American Sociological Review*, 13 (June, 1948), 259. See also Kingsley Davis, "Mental Hygiene and the Class Structure," *Psychiatry*, 1 (February, 1938) 55–65; Lawrence K. Frank "Social Problems," in *Society as the Patient*, Rutgers University Press, New Brunswick, 1948, pp. 10–20; and Richard C. Fuller "The Problem of Teaching Social Problems," *American Journal of Sociology*, 44 (November, 1938), 415–425.

15. FALSE CRITERIA OF CAUSALITY

TRAVIS HIRSCHI
HANAN C. SELVIN

SMOKING PER SE IS NOT A CAUSE OF LUNG CANCER. Evidence for this statement comes from the thousands of people who smoke and yet live normal, healthy lives. Lung cancer is simply unknown to the vast majority of smokers, even among those who smoke two or more packs a day. Whether smoking is a cause of lung cancer, then, depends upon the reaction of the lung tissues to the smoke inhaled. The important thing is not whether a person smokes, but how his lungs react to the smoke inhaled. These facts point to the danger of imputing causal significance to superficial variables. In essence, it is not smoking as such, but the carcinogenic elements in tobacco smoke that are the real causes of lung cancer.[1]

The task of determining whether such variables as broken homes, gang membership, or anomie are "causes" of delinquency benefits from a comparison with the more familiar problem of deciding whether cigarette smoking "causes" cancer. In both fields many statistical studies have shown strong relations between these presumed causes and the observed effects, but the critics of these studies often attack them as "merely statistical." This phrase has two meanings. To some critics it stands for the belief that only with experimental manipulation of the independent variables is a satisfactory causal inference possible. To others it is a brief way of saying that observing a statistical association between two phenomena is only the first step in plausibly inferring causality. Since no one proposes trying to give people cancer or to make them delinquent, the fruitful way toward better causal analyses in these two fields is to concentrate on improving the statistical approach.

In setting this task for ourselves we can begin with one area of agreement: all statistical analyses of causal relations in delinquency rest on observed associations between the independent and dependent variables. Beyond this there is less agreement. Following Hyman's reasoning,[2] we believe that these two additional criteria are the minimum requirements for an adequate causal analysis: (1) the independent variable is causally prior to the dependent variable (we shall refer to this as the criterion of "causal order"), and (2) the original association does not disappear when the influences of other variables causally prior to both of the original variables are removed ("lack of spuriousness").[3]

►SOURCE: "False Criteria of Causality in Delinquency," *Social Problems* (Winter, 1966), 13:3:254–268. Reprinted by permission.

[1] This is a manufactured "quotation"; its source will become obvious shortly.

[2] Herbert H. Hyman, *Survey Design and Analysis*. Glencoe, Illinois: The Free Press, 1955, chs. 5–7.

[3] Hyman appears to advocate another criterion as well: that a chain of intervening variables must link the independent and dependent variables of the original relation. We regard this as psychologically or theoretically desirable but not as part of the minimum methodological requirements for demonstrating causality in nonexperimental research.

The investigator who tries to meet these criteria does not have an easy time of it.[4] Our examination of statistical research on the causes of delinquency shows, however, that many investigators do not try to meet these criteria but instead invent one or another new criterion of causality—or, more often, of noncausality, perhaps because noncausality is easier to demonstrate. To establish causality one must forge a chain of three links (association, causal order, and lack of spuriousness), and the possibility that an antecedent variable not yet considered may account for the observed relation makes the third link inherently weak. To establish noncausality, one has only to break any one of these links.[5]

Despite the greater ease with which noncausality may be demonstrated, many assertions of noncausality in the delinquency literature turn out to be invalid. Some are invalid because the authors misuse statistical tools or misinterpret their findings. But many more are invalid because the authors invoke one or another false criterion of noncausality. Perhaps because assertions of noncausality are so easy to demonstrate, these invalid assertions have received a great deal of attention.

A clear assertion that certain variables long considered causes of delinquency are not really causes come from a 1960 *Report to The Congress:*

Many factors frequently cited as causes of delinquency are really only concomitants. They are not causes in the sense that if they were removed delinquency would decline. Among these factors are:
Broken homes.
Poverty.
Poor housing.
Lack of recreational facilities.
Poor physical health.
Race.
Working mothers.[6]

According to this report, all of these variables are statistically associated with delinquency, i.e., they are all "concomitants." To prove that they are not causes of delinquency it is necessary either to show that their relations with delinquency are spurious or that they are effects of delinquency rather than causes. Since all of these presumptive causes appear to precede delinquency, the only legitimate way to prove noncausality is to find an antecedent variable that accounts for the observed relations. None of the studies cited in the *Report* does this.[7] Instead, the assertion that broken homes, poverty, lack of recreational facilities, race, and working mothers are not causes of delinquency appears to be

---

[4] Hirschi and Selvin, *op. cit.*

[5] Popper calls this the asymmetry of verifiability and falsifiability. Karl R. Popper, *The Logic of Scientific Discovery*, New York: Basic Books, 1959, esp. pp. 27-48. For a fresh view of the verification-falsification controversy, see Thomas S. Kuhn, *The Structure of Scientific Revolutions*, Chicago: University of Chicago Press, 1962. Kuhn discusses Popper's views on pp. 145-146. Actually, it is harder to establish noncausality than our statement suggests, because of the possiblity of "spurious independence." This problem is discussed in Hirschi and Selvin, *op. cit.*, pp. 38-45, as "elaboration of a zero relation."

[6] U.S. Department of Health, Education, and Welfare, *Report to The Congress on Juvenile Delinquency*, United States Government Printing Office, 1960, p. 21. The conclusion that "poor housing" is not a cause of delinquency is based on Mildred Hartsough, *The Relation Between Housing and Delinquency*, Federal Emergency Administration of Public Works, Housing Division, 1936. The conclusion that "poor physical health" is not a cause is based on Edward Piper's "unpublished Children's Bureau manuscript summarizing the findings of numerous investigators on this subject." Since we have not examined these two works, the following conclusions do not apply to them.

[7] The works cited are: broken homes, Negly K. Teeters and John Otto Reinemann, *The Challenge of Delinquency*, New York: Prentice-Hall, 1950, pp. 149-154; poverty, Bernard Lander, *Toward an Understanding of Juvenile Delinquency*, New York: Columbia University Press, 1954; recreational facilities, Ethel Shanas and Catherine E. Dunning, *Recreation and Delinquency*, Chicago: Chicago Recreation Commission, 1942; race, Lander, *op. cit.*; working mothers, Eleanor E. Maccoby, "Children and Working Mothers," *Children*, 5 (May-June, 1958), pp. 83-89.

based on one or more of the following false "criteria":[8]

1. Insofar as a relation between two variables is not *perfect,* the relation is not causal.
    (a) Insofar as a factor is not a *necessary condition* for delinquency, it is not a cause of delinquency.
    (b) Insofar as a factor is not a *sufficient condition* for delinquency, it is not a cause of delinquency.
2. Insofar as a factor is not *"characteristic"* of delinquents, it is not a cause of delinquency.
3. If a relation between an independent variable and delinquency is found for a *single value of a situational or contextual factor,* then the situational or contextual factor cannot be a cause of delinquency.[9]
4. If a relation is observed between an independent variable and delinquency and if a psychological variable is suggested as *intervening* between these two variables, then the original relation is not causal.
5. *Measurable* variables are not causes.
6. If a relation between an independent variable and delinquency is *conditional* upon the value of other variables, the independent variable is not a cause of delinquency.

In our opinion, all of these criteria of noncausality are illegitimate. If they were systematically applied to any field of research, no relation would survive the test.

It is not clear in every case that the researcher himself reached the conclusion of noncausality or, if he did, that this conclusion was based on the false criteria discussed below. Maccoby's article, for example, contains a "conjectural explanation" of the relation between mother's employment and delinquency (i.e., without presenting any statistical evidence she suggests that the original relation came about through some antecedent variable), but it appears that the conclusion of noncausality in the *Report* is based on other statements in her work.

[9] All of the foregoing criteria are related to the "perfect relation" criterion in that they all require variation in delinquency that is unexplained by the "noncausal" variable. A more general statement of criterion 3 would be: "if variable X is related to delinquency when there is no variation in variable T, then variable T is not a cause of delinquency." In order for this criterion to be applicable, there must be some residual variation in delinquency after T has had its effect.

Some of them, however, have a superficial plausibility, both as stated or implied in the original works and as reformulated here. It will therefore be useful to consider in some detail just why these criteria are illegitimate and to see how they appear in delinquency research.

False Criterion 1. Insofar as a relation between two variables is not perfect, the relation is not causal.

Despite the preponderance of Negro delinquency, one must beware of imputing any causal significance to race per se. There is no *necessary* concomitance between the presence of Negroes and delinquency. In Census Tracts 9-1 and 20-2, with populations of 124 and 75 Negro juveniles, there were no recorded cases of delinquency during the study period. The rates of Negro delinquency also vary as widely as do the white rates indicating large differences in behavior patterns that are not a function or effect of race per se. It is also of interest to note that in at least 10% of the districts with substantial Negro juvenile populations, the Negro delinquency rate is lower than the corresponding white rate.[10]

There are three facts here (1) not all Negroes are delinquents; (2) the rates of Negro delinquency vary from place to place; (3) in some circumstances, Negroes are less likely than whites to be delinquent. These facts lead Lander to conclude that race has no causal significance in delinquency.

In each case the reasoning is the same: each fact is another way of saying that the statistical relation between race and de-

[10] Bernard Lander, *Towards an Understanding of Juvenile Delinquency,* New York: Columbia University Press, 1954, p. 32. Italics in original. An alternative interpretation of the assumptions implicit in this quotation is presented in the discussion of criterion 6, below.

Although both forms of this criterion fairly represent the reasoning involved in some claims of non-causality, and although both are false, the less explicit version in the text is superficially more plausible. This inverse relation between explicitness and plausibility is one reason for the kind of methodological explication presented here.

linquency is not perfect, and this apparently is enough to disqualify race as a cause. To see why this reasoning is invalid one has only to ask for the conditions under which race *could be* a cause of delinquency if this criterion were accepted. Suppose that the contrary of the first fact above were true, that *all* Negroes are delinquent. It would then follow necessarily that Negro delinquency rates would not vary from place to place (fact 2) and that the white rate would never be greater than the Negro rate (fact 3). Thus in order for race to have "any" causal significance, all Negroes must be delinquents (or all whites non-delinquents). In short, race must be perfectly related to delinquency.[11]

Now if an independent variable and a dependent variable are perfectly associated,[12] no other independent variable is needed: that is, perfect association implies single causation, and less-than-perfect association implies multiple causation. Rejecting as causes of delinquency those variables whose association with delinquency is less than perfect thus implies rejecting the principle of multiple-causation. Although there is nothing sacred about this principle, at least at the level of empirical research it is more viable than the principal of single causation. All studies show that more than one independent variable is needed to account for delinquency. In this field, as in others, perfect relations are virtually unknown. The researcher who finds a less-than-perfect relation between variable X and delinquency should not conclude that X is not a cause of delinquency, but merely that it is not the *only* cause.[13]

For example, suppose that tables like the following have been found for variables A, B, C, and D as well as for X (Table I).

Table I. *Delinquency by X, Where X Is Neither a Necessary Nor a Sufficient Condition for Delinquency, but May Be One of Several Causes*

	X	Not X
Delinquent	40	20
Nondelinquent	60	80

The researcher using the perfect relation criterion would have to conclude that none of the causes of delinquency has yet been discovered. Indeed, this criterion would force him to conclude that there are *no causes* of delinquency except *the* cause. The far-from-perfect relation between variable X and delinquency in the table above leads him to reject variable X as a cause of delinquency. Since variables A, B, C, and D are also far from perfectly related to delinquency, he must likewise reject them. Since it is unlikely that *the* cause of delinquency will ever be discovered by quantitative re-

---

[11] Strictly speaking, in this quotation Lander does not demand that race be perfectly related to delinquency, but only that all Negroes be delinquents (the sufficient conditions of criterion 1-b). Precedent for the "perfect relation" criterion of causality appears in a generally excellent critique of crime and delinquency research by Jerome Michael and Mortimer J. Adler published in 1933: "There is still another way of saying that none of the statistical findings derived from the quantitative data yields answers to etiological questions. The findings themselves show that every factor which can be seen to be in some way associated with criminality is also associated with non-criminality, and also that criminality is found in the absence of every factor with which it is also seen to be associated. In other words, what has been found is merely additional evidence of what we either knew or could have suspected, namely, that there is a plurality of related factors in this field." *Crime, Law and Social Science,* New York: Harcourt Brace, p. 53.

[12] "Perfect association" here means that all of the cases fall into the main diagonal of the table, that (in the 2 × 2 table) the independent variable is both a necessary and a sufficient cause of the dependent variable. Less stringent definitions of perfect association are considered in the following paragraphs. Since Lander deals with ecological correlations, he could reject race as a cause of delinquency even if it were perfectly related to delinquency at the census tract level, since the ecological and the individual correlations are not identical.

[13] We are assuming that the causal order and lack of spuriousness criteria are satisfied.

search, the researcher who accepts the perfect relation criterion should come to believe that such research is useless: all it can show is that there are *no* causes of delinquency.

False Criterion 1-a. Insofar as a factor is not a necessary condition for delinquency, it is not a cause of delinquency.

The "not necessary" (and of course the "not sufficient") argument against causation is a variant of the "perfect relation" criterion. A factor is a necessary condition for delinquency if it must be present for delinquency to occur—e.g., knowledge of the operation of an automobile is a necessary condition for auto theft (although all individuals charged with auto theft need not know how to drive a car). In the following table the independent variable X is a necessary (but not sufficient [14]) condition for delinquency (Table II).

Table II. *Delinquency by X, Where X Is a Necessary but Not Sufficient Condition for Delinquency*

	X	Not X
Delinquent	67	0
Nondelinquent	33	100

The strongest statement we can find in the work cited by the Children's Bureau in support of the contention that the broken home is not a cause of delinquency is the following:

We can leave this phase of the subject by stating that the phenomenon of the physically broken home is a cause of delinquent behavior is, in itself, not so important as was once believed. In essence, it is not that the home is broken, but rather that the home is inadequate, that really matters.[15]

This statement suggests that the broken home is not a necessary condition for delinquency (delinquents may come from intact but "inadequate" homes). The variable with which the broken home is compared, inadequacy, has all the attributes of a necessary condition for delinquency: a home that is "adequate" with respect to the prevention of delinquency will obviously produce no delinquent children. If, as appears to be the case, the relation between inadequacy and delinquency is a matter of definition, the comparison of this relation with the relation between the broken home and delinquency is simply an application of the illegitimate "necessary conditions" criterion. Compared to a necessary condition, the broken home is "not so important." Compared to some (or some *other*) *measure* of inadequacy, however, the broken home may be very important. For that matter, once "inadequacy" is empirically defined, the broken home may turn out to be one of its important causes. Thus the fact that the broken home is not a necessary condition for delinquency does not justify the statement that the broken home is "not [a cause of delinquency] in the sense that if [it] were removed delinquency would decline."[16]

False Criterion 1-b. Insofar as a factor is not a sufficient condition for delinquency, it is not a cause of delinquency.

A factor is a sufficient condition for delinquency if its presence is invariably followed by delinquency. Examples of sufficient conditions are hard to find in em-

---

[14] To say that X is a necessary condition for delinquency means that all delinquents are X (i.e., that the cell in the upper right of this table is zero); to say that X is a sufficient condition for delinquency implies that all X's are delinquent (i.e., that the cell in the lower left is zero); to say that X is a necessary and sufficient condition for delinquency means that all X's and no other persons are delinquent (i.e., that both cells in the minor diagonal of this table are zero).

[15] Teeters and Reinemann, *op. cit.*, p. 154.

[16] *Report to The Congress*, p. 21. Two additional illegitimate criteria of causality listed above are implicit in the quotation from Teeters and Reinemann. "Inadequacy of the home" could be treated as an intervening variable which interprets the relation between the broken home and delinquency (criterion 4) or as a theoretical variable of which the broken home is an indicator (criterion 5). These criteria are discussed below.

pirical research.[17] The nearest one comes to such conditions in delinquency research is in the use of predictive devices in which several factors taken together are virtually sufficient for delinquency.[18] (The fact that several variables are required even to approach sufficiency is of course one of the strongest arguments in favor of multiple causation.) Since sufficient conditions are rare, this unrealistic standard can be used against almost any imputation of causality.

First, however, let us make our position clear on the question. Poverty per se is not a cause of delinquency or criminal behavior; this statement is evidenced by the courage, fortitude, honesty, and moral stamina of thousands of parents who would rather starve than steal and who inculcate this attitude in their children. Even in the blighted neighborhoods of poverty and wretched housing conditions, crime and delinquency are simply nonexistent among most residents.[19]

Many mothers, and some fathers, who have lost their mates through separation, divorce, or death, are doing a splendid job of rearing their children.[20]

Our point of view is that the structure of the family *itself* does not cause delinquency. For example, the fact that a home is broken does not cause delinquency, but it is more difficult for a single parent to provide material needs, direct controls, and other important elements of family life.[21]

The error here lies in equating "not sufficient" with "not *a* cause." Even if every delinquent child were from an impoverished (or broken) home—that is, even if this factor were a necessary condition for delinquency—it would still be possible to show that poverty is not a sufficient condition for delinquency.

In order for the researcher to conclude that poverty is a cause of delinquency, it is not necessary that all or most of those who are poor become delinquent.[22] If it were, causal variables would be virtually impossible to find. From the standpoint of social action, this criterion can be particularly unfortunate. Suppose that poverty were a necessary but not sufficient condition for delinquency, as in the table on page 258. Advocates of the "not sufficient" criterion would be forced to conclude that, if poverty were removed, delinquency would not decline. As the table clearly shows, however, removal of poverty under these hypothetical conditions would *eliminate* delinquency!

To take another example, Wootton reports Carr-Saunders as finding that 28% of his delinquents and 16% of his controls came from broken homes and that this difference held in both London and the provinces. She quotes Carr-Saunders' "cautious" conclusion:

We can only point out that the broken home may have some influence on delinquency, though since we get control cases coming from broken homes, we cannot assert that there is a direct link between this factor and delinquency.[23]

---

[17] In his *Theory of Collective Behavior* (New York: The Free Press of Glencoe, 1963) Neil J. Smelser suggests sets of necessary conditions for riots, panics, and other forms of collective behavior; in this theory the entire set of necessary conditions for any one form of behavior is a sufficient condition for that form to occur.

[18] In the Gluecks' prediction table, those with scores of 400 or more have a 98.1% chance of delinquency. However, as Reiss has pointed out, the Gluecks *start* with a sample that is 50% delinquent. Had they started with a sample in which only 10% were delinquent, it would obviously have been more difficult to approach sufficiency. Sheldon Glueck and Eleanor Glueck, *Unraveling Juvenile Delinquency,* Cambridge: Harvard University Press, 1950, pp. 260–262; Albert J. Reiss, Jr., "Unraveling Juvenile Delinquency. II. An Appraisal of the Research Methods," *American Journal of Sociology,* 57:2, 1951, pp. 115–120.

[19] Teeters and Reinemann, *op. cit.,* p. 127.

[20] *Ibid.,* p. 154.

[21] F. Ivan Nye, *Family Relationships and Delinquent Behavior,* New York: John Wiley, 1958, p. 34. Italics in original.

[22] We are of course assuming throughout this discussion that the variables in question meet what we consider to be legitimate criteria of causality.

[23] Barbara Wootton, *Social Science and Social Pathology,* New York: Macmillan, 1959, p. 118.

Carr-Saunders' caution apparently stems from the "not sufficient" criterion, for unless the broken home is a sufficient condition for delinquency, there must be control cases (nondelinquents) from broken homes.

In each of these examples the attack on causality rests on the numbers in a single table. Since all of these tables show a non-zero relation, it seems to us that these researchers have misinterpreted the platitude "correlation is not causation." To us, this platitude means that one must go beyond the observed fact of association in order to demonstrate causality. To those who employ one or another variant of the perfect relation criterion, it appears to mean that there is something suspect in any numerical demonstration of association. Instead of being the first evidence for causality, an observed association becomes evidence against causality.

False Criterion 2. Insofar as a factor is not "characteristic" of delinquents, it is not a cause of delinquency.

Many correlation studies in delinquency may conquer all these hurdles and still fail to satisfy the vigorous demands of scientific causation. Frequently a group of delinquents is found to differ in a statistically significant way from a nondelinquent control group with which it is compared. Nevertheless, the differentiating trait may not be at all characteristic of the delinquent group. Suppose, for example, that a researcher compares 100 delinquent girls with 100 nondelinquent girls with respect to broken homes. He finds, let us say, that 10% of the nondelinquents come from broken homes, whereas this is true of 30% of the delinquent girls. Although the difference between the two groups is significant, the researcher has not demonstrated that the broken home is characteristic of delinquents. The fact is that 70% of them come from unbroken homes. Again, ecological studies showing a high correlation between residence in interstitial areas and delinquency, as compared with lower rates of delinquency in other areas, overlook the fact that even in the most marked interstitial area nine tenths of the children do not become delinquent.[24]

This argument is superficially plausible. If a factor is not characteristic, then it is apparently not important. But does "characteristic" mean "important"? No. Importance refers to the variation accounted for, to the size of the association, while "being characteristic" refers to only one of the conditional distributions (rows or columns) in the table (in the table on page 131, X is characteristic of delinquents because more than half of the delinquents are X). This is not enough to infer association, any more than the statement that 95% of the Negroes in some sample are illiterate can be taken to say anything about the association between race and illiteracy in that sample without a corresponding statement about the whites. In the following table, although Negroes are predominantly ("characteristically") illiterate, race has no effect on literacy, for the whites are equally likely to be illiterate.

| | Race | |
	Negro	White
Literate	5	5
Illiterate	95	95

More generally, even if a trait characterizes a large proportion of delinquents and also characterizes a large proportion of nondelinquents, it may be less important as a cause of delinquency than a trait that characterizes a much smaller proportion of delinquents. The strength of the relation is what matters—that is, the *difference* between delinquents and nondelinquents in the proportion having the trait (in other words, the difference between the conditional distributions of the dependent variable). In the quotation from Barron at the beginning of this section, would it make any difference for the imputation of causality if the proportions coming from

[24] Milton L. Barron, *The Juvenile in Delinquent Society*, New York: Knopf, 1954, pp. 86–87.

broken homes had been 40% for the nondelinquents and 60% for the delinquents, instead of 10 and 30%? Although broken homes would now be "characteristic" of delinquents, the percentage difference is the same as before. And the percentage difference would still be the same if the figures were 60 and 80%, but now broken homes would be characteristic of *both* nondelinquents and delinquents!

The "characteristic" criterion is thus statistically irrelevant to the task of assessing causality. It also appears to be inconsistent with the principle of multiple causation, to which Barron elsewhere subscribes.[25] If delinquency is really traceable to a plurality of causes," then some of these causes may well "characterize" a minority of delinquents. Furthermore, this "inconsistency" is empirical as well as logical: in survey data taken from ordinary populations it is rare to find that any group defined by more than three traits includes a majority of the cases.[26]

False Criterion 3. If a relation between an independent variable and delinquency is found for a single value of a situational or contextual factor, that situational or contextual factor cannot be a cause of delinquency.

---

[25] *Ibid.*, pp. 81–83.

[26] There are two reasons for this: the less-than-perfect association between individual traits and the fact that few traits are simple dichotomies. Of course, it is always possible to take the logical complement of a set of traits describing a minority and thus arrive at a set of traits that does "characterize" a group, but such artificial combinations have too much internal heterogeneity to be meaningful. What, for example, can one say of the delinquents who share the following set of traits: not Catholic, not middle class, not of average intelligence?

The problem of "characteristic" traits arises only when the dependent variable is inherently categorical (Democratic; member of a gang, an athletic club, or neither) or is treated as one (performs none, a few, or many delinquent acts). In other words, this criterion arises only in tabular analysis, not where some summary measure is used to describe the association between variables.

No investigation can establish the causal importance of variables that do not vary. This obvious fact should be even more obvious when the design of the study restricts it to single values of certain variables. Thus the researcher who restricts his sample to white Mormon boys cannot use his data to determine the importance of race, religious affiliation, or sex as causes of delinquency. Nevertheless, students of delinquency who discover either from research or logical analysis that an independent variable is related to delinquency in certain situations or contexts often conclude that these situational or contextual variables are not important causes of delinquency. Since personality or perceptual variables are related to delinquency in most kinds of social situations, social variables have suffered most from the application of this criterion:

Let the reader assume that a boy is returning home from school and sees an unexpected group of people at his doorstep, including a policeman, several neighbors, and some strangers. He may suppose that they have gathered to welcome him and congratulate him as the winner of a nationwide contest he entered several months ago. On the other hand, his supposition may be that they have discovered that he was one of several boys who broke some windows in the neighborhood on Halloween. If his interpretation is that they are a welcoming group he will respond one way; but if he feels that they have come to "get" him, his response is likely to be quite different. In either case he may be entirely wrong in his interpretation. *The important point, however, is that the external situation is relatively unimportant.* Rather, what the boy himself thinks of them [it] and how he interprets them [it] is the crucial factor in his response.[27]

There are at least three independent "variables" in this illustration: (1) the external situation—the group at the doorstep; (2) the boy's past behavior—entering a contest, breaking windows, etc.; (3) the boy's interpretation of the group's purpose.

---

[27] Barron, *op. cit.*, pp. 87–88. Italics added.

As Barron notes, variable (3) is obviously important in determining the boy's response. It does not follow from this, however, that variables (1) and (2) are unimportant. As a matter of fact, it is easy to see how variable (2), the boy's past behavior, could influence his interpretation of the group's purpose and thus affect his response. If he had not broken any windows in the neighborhood, for example, it is less likely that he would think that the group had come to "get" him, and it is therefore less likely that his response would be one of fear. Since Barron does not examine the relation between this situational variable and the response, he cannot make a legitimate statement about its causal importance.

Within the context of this illustration it is impossible to relate variable (1), the group at the doorstep, to the response. The reason for this is simple: this "variable" does not vary—it is fixed, given, constant. In order to assess the influence of a group at the doorstep (the external situation) on the response, it would be necessary to compare the effects of groups varying in size or composition. Suppose that there was no group at the doorstep. Presumably, if this were the case, the boy would feel neither fear nor joy. Barron restricts his examination of the relation between interpretation and response to a single situation, and on this basis concludes that what appears to be a necessary condition for the response is *relatively unimportant!*

In our opinion, it is sometimes better to say nothing about the effects of a variable whose range is restricted than to attempt to reach some idea of its importance with inadequate data. The first paragraph of the following statement suggests that its authors are completely aware of this problem. Nevertheless, the concluding paragraphs are misleading:

We recognized that the Cambridge-Somerville area represented a fairly restricted socioeconomic region. Although the bitter wave of the depression had passed, it had left in its wake large numbers of unemployed. Ten years after its onset, Cambridge and Somerville still showed the effects of the depression. Even the best neighborhoods in this study were lower middle class. Consequently, our results represent only a section of the class structure.

In our sample, however [*therefore*], there is not a *highly* significant relation between "delinquency areas," or subcultures, and crime. If we had predicted that every child who lived in the poorer Cambridge-Somerville areas would have committed a crime, we would have been more often wrong than right. Thus, current sociological theory, by itself, cannot explain why the majority of children, even those from the "worst" areas, never became delinquent.

Social factors, in our sample, were not strongly related to criminality. The fact that a child's neighborhood did not, by itself, exert an independently important influence may [*should not*] surprise social scientists. Undeniably, a slum neighborhood can mold a child's personality—but apparently only if other factors in his background make him susceptible to the sub-culture that surrounds him.[28]

False Criterion 4. If a relation is observed between an independent variable and delinquency and if a psychological variable is suggested as intervening between these two variables, then the original relation is not causal.

There appear to be two elements in this causal reasoning. One is the procedure of *conjectural interpretation.*[29] The other is

---

[28] William McCord and Joan McCord, *Origins of Crime*, New York: Columbia University Press, 1959, pp. 71 and 167.

In a study restricted to "known *offenders*" in which the dependent variable is the *seriousness* of the *first offense* Richard S. Sterne concludes: "Delinquency cannot be fruitfully controlled through broad programs to prevent divorce or other breaks in family life. The prevention of these would certainly decrease unhappiness, but it would not help to relieve the problem of delinquency." Since the range of the dependent variable, delinquency, is seriously reduced in a study restricted to *offenders*, such conclusions can not follow from the data. *Delinquent Conduct and Broken Homes*, New Haven: College and University Press, 1964, p. 96.

[29] Like conjectural explanation, this is an argument, unsupported by statistical data, that the relation between two variables would vanish if the

the confusion between *explanation,* in which an antecedent variable "explains away" an observed relation, and *interpretation,* in which an intervening variable links more tightly the two variables of the original relation. In short, the vanishing of the partial relations is assumed, not demonstrated, and this assumed statistical configuration is misconstrued.

This criterion is often encountered in a subtle form suggestive of social psychological theory:

The appropriate inference from the available data, on the basis of our present understanding of the nature of cause, is that whether poverty, broken homes, or working mothers are factors which cause delinquency depends upon the meaning the situation has for the child.[30]

It now appears that neither of these factors [the broken home and parental discipline] is so important in itself as is the child's reaction to them.[31]

A factor, whether personal or situational, does not become a cause unless and until it first becomes a motive.[32]

The appropriate inference about whether some factor is a cause of delinquency depends on the relation between that factor and delinquency (and possibly on other factors causally prior to both of these). All that can be determined about meanings, motives, or reactions that *follow from* the factor and *precede* delinquency can only strengthen the conclusion that the factor is a cause of delinquency, not weaken it.

A different example may make our argument clearer. *Given* the bombing of Pearl Harbor, the crucial factor in America's response to this situation was its interpretation of the meaning of this event. Is one to conclude, therefore, that the bombing of Pearl Harbor was relatively unimportant as a cause of America's entry into World War II? Intervening variables of this type are no less important than variables further removed from the dependent variable, but to limit analysis to them, to deny the importance of objective conditions, is to distort reality as much as do those who ignore intervening subjective states.[33]

This kind of mistaken causal inference can occur long after the original analysis of the data. A case in point is the inference in the *Report to The Congress*[34] that irregular employment of the mother does not cause delinquency. This inference appears to come from misreading Maccoby's reanalysis of the Gluecks' results.

Maccoby begins by noting that "the association between irregular employment and delinquency suggests at the outset that it may not be the mother's absence from home per se which creates adjustment problems for the children. Rather, the cause may be found in the conditions of the mother's employment or the family characteristics leading a mother to undertake outside employment."[35] She then lists several characteristics of the sporadically working mothers that might account for

---

effects of a third variable were removed; here however, the third variable "intervenes" causally between the original independent and dependent variables.

[30] Sophia Robison, *Juvenile Delinquency,* New York: Holt, Rinehart and Winston, 1961, p. 116.

[31] Paul W. Tappan, *Juvenile Delinquency,* New York: McGraw-Hill, 1949, p. 135.

[32] Sheldon and Eleanor Glueck, *Family Environment and Delinquency,* Boston: Houghton-Mifflin, 1962, p. 153. This statement is attributed to Bernard Glueck. No specific reference is provided.

[33] "Write your own life history, showing the factors *really* operative in you coming to college, contrasted with the external social and cultural factors of your situation." Barron, *op. cit.,* p. 89.

[34] *Op. cit.,* p. 21.

[35] Eleanor E. Maccoby, "Effects upon Children of Their Mothers' Outside Employment," in Norman W. Bell and Ezra F. Vogel (eds.), *A Modern Introduction to The Family,* Glencoe, Illinois: The Free Press, 1960, p. 523. In fairness to the Children's Bureau report, it should be mentioned that Maccoby's argument against the causality of the relation between mother's employment and delinquency has a stronger tone in the article cited there (see footnote 7) than in the version we have used as a source of quotations.

the greater likelihood of their children becoming delinquent. For example, many had a history of delinquency themselves. In our opinion, such conjectural "explanations" are legitimate guides to further study but, as Maccoby says, they leave the causal problem unsettled:

> It is a moot question, therefore, whether it is the mother's sporadic employment as such which conduced to delinquency in the sons; equally tenable is the interpretation that the emotionally disturbed and antisocial characteristics of the parents produced both a sporadic work pattern on the part of the mother and delinquent tendencies in the son.[36]

Maccoby's final step, and the one of greatest interest here, is to examine simultaneously the effects of mother's employment and mother's supervision on delinquency. From this examination she concludes:

> It can be seen that, whether the mother is working or not, the quality of the supervision her child receives is paramount. If the mother remains at home but does not keep track of where her child is and what he is doing, he is far more likely to become a delinquent (within this highly selected sample), than if he is closely watched. Furthermore, if a mother who works does arrange adequate care for the child in her absence, he is no more likely to be delinquent . . . than the adequately supervised child of a mother who does not work. But there is one more lesson to be learned from the data: among the working mothers, a majority did not in fact arrange adequate supervision for their children in their absence.[37]

It is clear, then, that regardless of the mother's employment status, supervision is related to delinquency. According to criterion 3, employment status is therefore not a cause of delinquency. It is also clear that when supervision is held relatively constant, the relation between employment status and delinquency disappears. According to criterion 4, employment status is therefore *not* a cause of delinquency. This appears to be the reasoning by which the authors of the *Report to The Congress* reject mother's employment as a cause of delinquency. But criterion 3 ignores the association between employment status and delinquency and is thus irrelevant. And criterion 4 treats what is probably best seen as an intervening variable as an antecedent variable and is thus a misconstruction of a legitimate criterion. Actually, the evidence that allows the user of criterion 4 to reach a conclusion of noncausality is, at least psychologically, evidence of *causality*. The disappearance of the relation between mother's employment and delinquency when supervision is held relatively constant makes the "How?" of the original relation clear: working mothers are less likely to provide adequate supervision for their children, and inadequately supervised children are more likely to become delinquent.

False Criterion 5. Measurable variables are not causes.

> In tract 11-1, and to a lesser extent to tract 11-2, the actual rate [of delinquency] is lower than the predicted rate. We suggest that these deviations [of the actual delinquency rate from the rate predicted from home ownership] point up the danger of imputing a causal significance to an index, per se, despite its statistical significance in a prediction formula. It is fallacious to impute causal significance to home ownership as such. In the present study, the author hypothesizes that the extent of home-ownership is probably highly correlated with, and hence constitutes a measure of community anomie.[38]

> As a preventive, "keeping youth busy," whether through compulsory education, drafting for service in the armed forces, providing fun through recreation or early employment, can, at best, only temporary postpone behavior that is symptomatic of more deep-seated or culturally oriented factors. . . . Merely "keeping idle hands occupied" touches only surface symptoms and overlooks underlying factors known to generate norm-violating behavior patterns.[39]

---

[36] *Ibid.*
[37] *Ibid.*, p. 524.
[38] Lander, *op. cit.*, p. 71.
[39] William C. Kvaraceus and Walter B. Miller, *Delinquent Behavior: Culture and the Individual*, National Education Association, 1959, p. 39.

The criterion of causation that, in effect, denies causal status to measurable variables occurs frequently in delinquency research. In the passages above, home ownership, compulsory education, military service, recreation, and early employment are all called into question as causes of delinquency. In their stead one finds as causes anomie and "deepseated or culturally oriented factors." The appeal to abstract as opposed to more directly measurable variables appears to be especially persuasive. Broad general concepts embrace such a variety of directly measurable variables that their causal efficacy becomes almost self evident. The broken home, for example, is no match for the "inadequate" home:

[T]he physically broken home as a cause of delinquent behavior is, in itself, not so important as was once believed. In essence, it is not that the home is broken, but rather that the home is inadequate, that really matters.[40]

The persuasiveness of these arguments against the causal efficacy of measurable variables has two additional sources: (1) their logical form resembles that of the legitimate criterion "lack of spuriousness"; (2) they are based on the seemingly obvious fact that "operational indices" (measures) do not *cause* the variations in other operational indices. Both of the following arguments can thus be brought against the assertion that, for example, home ownership causes delinquency.

Anomie causes delinquency. Home ownership is a measure of anomie. Anomie is thus the "source of variation" in both home ownership and delinquency. If the effects of anomie were removed, the observed relation between home ownership and delinquency would disappear. This observed relation is thus causally spurious.

Home ownership is used as an indicator of anomie, just as responses to questionnaire items are used as indicators of such things as "authoritarianism," "achievement motivation," and "religiosity." No one will argue that the responses to items on a questionnaire *cause* race hatred, long years of self-denial, or attendance at religious services. For the same reason, it is erroneous to think that home ownership "causes" delinquency.

Both of these arguments beg the question. As mentioned earlier, conjectural explanations, although legitimate guides to further study, leave the causal problem unsettled. The proposed "antecedent variable" may or *may not* actually account for the observed relation.

Our argument assumes that the proposed antecedent variable is directly measurable. In the cases cited here it is not. If the antecedent variable logic is accepted as appropriate in these cases, all relations between measurable variables and delinquency may be said to be causally spurious. If anomie can "explain away" the relation between *one* of its indicators and delinquency, it can explain away the relations between *all* of its indicators and delinquency.[41] No matter how closely a given indicator measures anomie, the indicator is not anomie, and thus not a cause of delinquency. The difficulty with these conjectural explanations is thus not that they may be false, but that they are *non-falsifiable*.[42]

The second argument against the causality of measurable variables over-looks the following point: it is one thing to use a measurable variable as an indicator of an-

---

[40] Teeters and Reinemann, *op. cit.*, p. 154.

[41] As would be expected, Lander succeeds in disposing of all the variables in his study as causes of delinquency—even those he says at some points are *"fundamentally* related to delinquency."

[42] While Lander throws out his measurable independent variables in favor of anomie, Kvaraceus and Miller throw out their measurable dependent variable in favor of "something else." "Series of normviolating behaviors, which run counter to legal codes and which are engaged in by youngsters [delinquency], are [is] only symptomatic of something else in the personal make-up of the individual, in his home and family, or in his cultural milieu." *Op. cit.*, p. 34. The result is the same, as the quotations suggest.

other, not directly measurable, variable; it is something else again to assume that the measurable variable is *only* an indicator. Not owning one's home may indeed be a useful indicator of anomie; it may, at the same time, be a potent cause of delinquency in its own right.

The user of the "measurable variables are not causes" criterion treats measurable variables as epiphenomena. He strips these variables of all their causal efficacy (and of all their meaning) by treating them merely as indexes, and by using such words as *per se, as such,* and *in itself.*[43] In so doing, he begs rather than answers the important question: Are these measurable variables causes of delinquency?

False Criterion 6. If the relation between an independent variable and delinquency is conditional upon the value of other variables, the independent variable is not a cause of delinquency.

The rates of Negro delinquency also vary as widely as do the white rates indicating large differences in behavior patterns that are not a function or effect of race per se. It is also of interest to note that in at least 10 percent of the districts with substantial Negro juvenile populations, the Negro delinquency rate is lower than the corresponding white rate.[44]

The appropriate inference from the available data, on the basis of our present understanding of the nature of cause, is that whether poverty, broken homes, or working mothers are factors which cause delinquency depends upon the meaning the situation has for the child.[45]

Both of these quotations make the same point: the association between an independent variable and delinquency depends on the value of a third variable. The original two-variable relation thus becomes a three-variable conditional relation. In the first quotation, the relation between race and delinquency is shown to depend on some (unspecified) property of census tracts. In the second quotation, each of three variables is said to "interact" with "the meaning of the situation" to cause delinquency.

One consequence of showing that certain variables are only conditionally related to delinquency is to invalidate what Albert K. Cohen has aptly named "the assumption of intrinsic pathogenic qualities"—the assumption that the causal efficacy of a variable is, or can be, independent of the value of other causal variables.[46] Invalidating this assumption, which Cohen shows to be widespread in the literature on delinquency, is a step in the right direction. As many of the quotations in this paper suggest, however, the discovery that a variable has no *intrinsic* pathogenic qualities has often led to the conclusion that it has no pathogenic qualities at all. The consequences of accepting this conclusion can be shown for delinquency research and theory.

Cloward and Ohlin's theory that delinquency is the product of lack of access to legitimate means *and* the availability of illegitimate means assumes, as Palmore and Hammond have shown,[47] that each of these states is a necessary condition for the other—i.e., that lack of access to legitimate and access to illegitimate means "interact" to produce delinquency. Now, if "conditional relations" are non-causal, neither lack of access to legitimate nor the availability of illegitimate means is a cause of delinquency, and one could manipulate either without affecting the delinquency rate.

Similarly absurd conclusions could be drawn from the results of empirical re-

---

[43] The appearance of these terms in the literature on delinquency almost invariably signals a logical difficulty.

[44] Lander, *op. cit.,* p. 32. This statement is quoted more fully above (see footnote 10).

[45] See footnote 30.

[46] "Multiple Factor Approaches," in Marvin E. Wolfgang et al. (eds.), *The Sociology of Crime and Delinquency,* New York: John Wiley, 1962, pp. 78–79.

[47] Erdman B. Palmore and Phillip E. Hammond, "Interacting Factors in Juvenile Delinquency," *American Sociological Review,* 29 (December, 1964), pp. 848–854.

search in delinquency, since all relations between independent variables and delinquency are at least conceivably conditional (the paucity of empirical generalizations produced by delinquency research as a whole shows that most of these relations have already actually been found to be conditional).[48]

Although conditional relations may be conceptually or statistically complicated and therefore psychologically unsatisfying, their discovery does not justify the conclusion that the variables involved are not causes of delinquency. In fact, the researcher who would grant causal status only to unconditional relations will end by granting it to none.

Any one of the criteria of causality discussed in this paper makes it possible to question the causality of most of the relations that have been or could be revealed by quantitative research. Some of these criteria stem from perfectionistic interpretations of legitimate criteria, others from misapplication of these legitimate criteria. Still others, especially the argument that a cause must be "characteristic" of delinquents, appear to result from practical considerations. (It would indeed be valuable to the practitioner if he could point to some easily identifiable trait as the "hallmark" of the delinquent.) Finally, one of these criteria is based on a mistaken notion of the relation between abstract concepts and measurable variable—a notion that only the former can be the causes of anything.

The implications of these standards of causality for practical efforts to reduce delinquency are devastating. Since nothing that can be pointed to in the practical world is a cause of delinquency (e.g., poverty, broken homes, lack of recreational facilities, working mothers), the practitioner is left with the task of combatting a nebulous "anomie" or an unmeasured "inadequacy of the home"; or else he must change the adolescent's interpretation of the "meaning" of events without at the same time changing the events themselves or the context in which they occur.

Mills has suggested that accepting the principle of multiple causation implies denying the possibility of radical change in the social structure.[49] Our analysis suggests that rejecting the principle of multiple causation implies denying the possibility of *any* change in the social structure—since, in this view, nothing causes anything.

---

[48] After reviewing the findings of twenty-one studies as they bear on the relations between twelve commonly used independent variables and delinquency, Barbara Wootton concludes: "All in all, therefore, this collection of studies, although chosen for its comparative methodological merit, produces only the most meager, and dubiously supported generalizations." *Op. cit.*, p. 134.

[49] C. Wright Mills, "The Professional Ideology of Social Pathologists," *American Journal of Sociology*, 44 (September, 1942), pp. 165–180, esp. pp. 171–172.

16. THE UNIQUE INDIVIDUAL

LESLIE WILKINS

THE UNIQUE INDIVIDUAL

THE OBJECTION STATES THAT PREDICTION IS useless (or dangerous?) because the individual is unique. Prediction is said to be either (or both) impossible or undesirable, and this argument rests on the complexity of human relationships. That the social and psychological make-up of man is complex is not denied. Nor is the argument that "only certain items matter" advanced from the statistical standpoint. While prediction methods lead to the simplification of the problem they do not approach by this route. Let us begin to show how this procedure is based by accepting the point that every individual is unique when we consider the complex of factors in his circumstances and make-up. Let us go further and claim that if we could measure any *one thing with sufficient accuracy* the individual would be unique, as we have already argued for height or weight. Since the "complexity" concept and the "accuracy" concept both lead to the concept of the unique individual, we will commence our discussion from the latter case because of its greater simplicity.

Our assumption of uniqueness from one

▶SOURCE: *"What is Prediction and is it Necessary in Evaluating Treatment?"* Report of a Conference on Research and Potential Application of Research in Probation, Parole and Delinquency Prediction, sponsored by the Citizens' Committee for Children of New York, Inc. and the Research Center, New York School of Social Work, Columbia University. (Mimeographed), pp. 23–34. (Editorial adaptations.)

accurate measurement may be related to the theorem of Dedekind which states that number is infinite—between any two numbers of which we can conceive there is always another number which may also be conceived. Now this is true, but the fact does not worry us. We operate with number sufficient for the purpose. For example we estimate circumferences of circles from their diameters using π, but we could raise the objection that the true value of π was unknown and also object that we could not exactly measure diameters. No one would regard this argument as of much value. We would use a value of π which, *having regard to the accuracy* with which we measured the diameter, would give results sufficiently accurate for estimating the circumference. This is our solution in physical problems. It might be claimed that our measuring instruments in this field are obviously highly accurate but the analogy cannot be rejected on these grounds. Not a hundred years ago the accuracy of measurement was often a limiting factor in the physical sciences, and at the frontiers of knowledge may be so today. If measurement is rejected outright there is little likelihood of it being improved; if it is accepted and its possibilities appreciated it is likely that advance will be made in the techniques of measurement. *This joint interplay of improvement in measurement techniques and the use of measurement is important in the social sciences also.* What we can do is limited by what we know and what we know is also limited by what we can do. With this point in mind let us look further into our analogue.

If we measure persons to the nearest inch we shall find many who are alike and can be classified together. This accuracy is sufficient for many purposes and inadequate for others. In general, if we are to take one characteristic at a time and to classify individuals into broad groups we shall find many alike. We cannot reject the utility of this principle, but it seems that this is what the critics of prediction are trying to do. They are claiming that the measurement is too coarse and that they could measure or describe much more accurately than the degree of accuracy we are utilizing. They claim, in fact, that they know (can show?) that they can describe individuals with such precision that they are seen to be unique, and go on to suggest that because we do not utilize this information our methods are incorrect. Logically they should surely also argue—number is infinite—I will not agree to use number which I know to be inaccurate! Clearly the concept of sufficient accuracy for utility must be accepted. This involves immediately the concept of use for a purpose. Our next point follows from this. Not only are different degrees of accuracy required for different purposes, but information which is useful for one purpose is not required for another. The number of measurements required as well as their accuracy depends on the complexity of the task.

This may seem obvious, but what follows from an acceptance of this obvious assessment of reasonable behavior is often rejected. Let us assume the acceptance of this argument insofar as we have stated:

(1) measurement is always approximate;
(2) the number and accuracy of measurements should depend on purpose.

Then it seems to follow that there is no point in demonstrating that individuals are unique nor that prediction methods use only a fraction of the information, or information which is inaccurate, without also showing that the omitted measurements of the items not accurately measured were (a) relevant, (b) not sufficiently accurate where both (a) and (b) apply *to a specific and limited purpose*. This should provide a dilemma for those opposing prediction on "uniqueness" grounds or on grounds of complexity which are similar. The proof of relevance and of the degree of accuracy with respect to a purpose can, it seems, only be found by the use of prediction methods. But there is a little more to it than that.

In prediction methods we do not necessarily seek a "meaningful" result (a subjectively satisfying explanation?) but a "powerful" result; we do not expect one classification to simple categories to suffice. There is a rationale behind the "small number of elements" to which the critics refer. The number is derived in two ways— one the trivial case which was appropriate to the Borstal study,[1] and the other, more general. In the Borstal study *all* the information which could be used was in fact used, and the resulting small number of elements condensed all the useful information available, where *"use"* was defined by the specification of the criteria. In the non-trivial case the procedure is one of balance. Let us again suppose that there is an infinity of "useful" facts; then each must contribute an infinitely small amount of information such that no method could be found of using it. More realistically we wish to find systems which could be used and which are found to apply in practice. Let us suppose we begin by finding one element which helps our purpose; we are better able to predict if we use this element and do not reject it. Then we wish to find others which will *not do again* the work

---

[1] Mannheim and L. T. Wilkins, *Prediction Methods in Relation to Borstal Training*, London: H.M.S.O., 1955.

already done by our first element, and *only* that part of the work.

In our search for more information we have the hard test of *use-for-purpose.* We wish to add categories and classifications or measurements that are useful, but we must also stop adding before the system breaks down. Similarly, we may wish to increase our accuracy of measurement, but there will come a point where increased accuracy becomes unnecessary—where the increase does not result in any significant increase in our control. Again, it must be stressed, for our single specific and unidimensional purpose.

That is not to say that we shall at that time have sufficient information for our purposes, but merely that the items of information which are candidates for inclusion cannot justify their claim to be included in terms of the work they will do towards the end purpose. We shall reject such information and seek other information *as a continuous process,* so that the area of our ignorance is gradually reduced. Any item may be a candidate for inclusion, irrespective of its "face validity." We shall not accept any abstract theory because it is convincing in itself; we shall decide to accept or reject it after we have investigated those concrete and practical consequences which can be directly tested by the contribution each item makes to the specific problem of specification or decision.

The process of finding items for test is related to problems in strategy. Each item may be considered in two dimensions which may be regarded as having a "cost" or "penalty" rating:

(1) The cost of testing the item if false.
(2) The cost (loss) of not testing the item if true.

If an item is likely to have a low rating on (2) and a low rating on (1) we may test it, but if we assess (2) as small and (1) as large, we shall not. It is here that social theory can help; it is here that we may seek a division of labor in the work—the grinding routine work—which is the major part of any science. The problem normally reduces to an evaluation of (2) since (1) is usually known with precision. Of course electronic computers have helped in reducing part of the cost of (1), but only for one aspect of cost; at some point we shall find our sample sizes are inadequate to test the data, and the cost of increased sample size is usually considerable. If we accept the selection procedure for equations which uses the most efficient solution (not necessarily the most "meaningful") we can operate more successfully, because we shall be rejecting items as new ones are added according to a simple arithmetical routine and the computer can make our decisions for us. If the item explains a significant amount of variance it will retain it; if not, our sample size is not greatly reduced [2] by the mere test and reject process. At some point [3] the contribution of further information will become so small *relative to our sample* size that we shall not be able to test its significance. Such items cannot be accepted on the grounds that (a) they are not tested and (b) their contribution could only be small. If we do not accept these limiting conditions we shall find no grounds for rejecting any item and will reduce the whole procedure to absurdity by being able to specify each case uniquely. In the scientific meaning of the word we cannot "explain" any unique case or once-for-all event, since any event which is unique or once-for-all can be no guide to future action.

One further point should, perhaps, be made before we proceed to deal briefly with

---

[2] Degrees of freedom in test and rejection procedures of this kind are lost, but the variance of the item is not a factor.

[3] The "stopping" procedure is the point of "efficiency" which we described elsewhere, but is only a part of the concept of efficiency. It is, however, the only part which concerns the objection to prediction methods on the grounds of complexity or uniqueness of case material.

the second part of the objection. The simplification process we have described above is possible only because we work to one specific purpose. We may, of course, select many objectives *one at a time* to extract different information from different or similar classifications. This piece-meal approach is essential to this method, indeed perhaps to all scientific method.[4] Thus items of information which might help to make an individual unique but which do not help any particular purpose *when that purpose is considered* may be *rejected,* but *accepted* when tested by their utility *for another purpose* or another criterion. We cannot set out to solve general problems by the scientific method—general solutions or "omnibus" laws can be made only when the necessary piece-by-piece research has proceeded far enough, and a genius of sufficient status is found to state the general law. A *completely general* solution should not be sought directly—indeed the information necessary would be so vast that we should reach again the concept of the unique individual. But this seems to involve a contradiction within itself. Prediction methods seek not *the* explanation, but *an* explanation which is operationally defined by the specification of a limited purpose and one purpose at a time in each "explanation." They *must,* therefore, use only a small number of elements and indeed, solutions which require a large number *cannot* be based on more than mere speculation. This is a hard fact of scientific life as we know it today.

Objectivity and Subjectivity. The objection has now, perhaps, lost much of its point, and we shall deal very briefly with the remaining statements. The objection continues, "through the necessity to employ objective factors prediction procedures lose touch with many significant intangible and dynamic features of personality frequently observed in the clinical situation. Successful prediction requires an understanding and assessment of the uniqueness of the individual."*

The last sentence contains its own refutation. If a case is unique what experience can the clinician use to guide him? If experience of the past is of any value at all then it can be applied only by observation of *similarities* not differences. It is not the uniqueness that concerns the clinician but the similarities between the particular case and prior cases in his or other people's experience. If this is so, then this is exactly the same as with the statistical procedures in the prediction method where experience is derived from the past and is analyzed and condensed systematically by known procedures rather than subjectively. Moreover statistical experience can be based on samples of the population which we know to be unbiased. A clinician has only his own sample to guide him with no guarantee of its lack of bias.

Is this criticism reduceable to a claim that a biased sample assessed subjectively provides better guidance than the procedures of the statistical method? If so, there is no denying the clinician's right to make such a claim in the name of faith and hope but not in the name of science or technology. It is certainly not acceptable to claim in the same breath that the past is no guide ("the case is unique") and that it is experience that counts.

But perhaps it may be conceded that when facts are being considered, statistical methods are acceptable, and stress might be laid on the importance of the "significant intangible features of personality frequently observed in the clinical situation." If these features are "intangible" how can we know that they exist? How in fact does the clinician take them into account? Can

---

[4] But theory has a very important role in the scientific method. The writer has gone into this aspect elsewhere. The omission from this discussion does not mean that theory is rejected—it too, is a useful tool.

* [Reference is here made to criticisms summarized by L. Ohlin, Paper prepared for the Third International Congress of Criminology, London, 1955, Preparatory Papers.—Editors].

they not be described in words? If not, are they more than the prejudices of the observer? If they are describable they may be dealt with statistically (although the statistician would reserve his right to introduce the *describer* as well as the *described* as a possible source of variance.) How do we know that these intangible features (if they exist) do not so overlap with observable, objective features that there would be no point in including them? Indeed we cannot test this until those who maintain that they can deal with these intangible features can reduce their claim to a set of hypotheses of a kind which can be tested.

Faith in intangibles, if coupled with a scientific attitude, is an essential challenge to further development. There is no wish to discourage faith but only to indicate that it is not a substitute for nor an answer to analytical methods. It might indicate where the next step forward in the scientific method might be made, and should stimulate effort towards further scientific endeavor, but not be used as a criticism of such endeavor. Science acknowledges the partial nature of knowledge and looks always for newer, better explanations, but cannot reduce its rigor.

Invention and Examination. In research we are concerned both with the formulation and testing of hypotheses. In the main the scientific method can say much about the latter aspect of research designs, but very little is known about the processes involved in the former operation. Indeed, apart from indicating the types of hypotheses which may be the more efficiently tested, research methods leave the matter of hypothesis formulation to the individual and provide no certain guidance. *Up to the point where a hypothesis is formed,* it is imagination and experience that count. Each research worker should know himself and his ways of thinking and recognize that source or sources of stimulation to invention which are for him the most fruitful.

Once hypotheses are formed, we have entered a world of communication and we can discuss techniques and share our experiences so that the concept of a body of scientific thought is meaningful. Accordingly, we do not criticize clinical approaches, intuitive approaches or any other approach *to hypothesis formation.* Hypotheses should be plentiful, but their mortality rate should also be high. A hypothesis should not be allowed to live beyond the point where it can be phrased in a way subject to test. If it survives the test its life should be extended until a better explanation—a more general or more powerful hypothesis—succeeds in passing appropriate tests. It follows that all informed persons should be able to agree upon the rigor of the tests and should also agree to accept the results so that the failed hypothesis is interred by agreement and does not appear again to waste research time.

From this it also follows that *communication of research findings is a part of the research method.* If research workers are unaware that certain theories have been tested, effort will be wasted not only in redundant testing but in the misdirection of thought processes. Unless such misdirection is part of a national defense system (where it is presumably desired to waste research effort of potential enemies) communication of both positive and negative results is an integral part of science.

Symbols and Semantics. This brings us to consider the second point. Those who do not favour the statistical or mathematical approach quite often object that the replacement of living individuals by mathematical symbols is essentially wrong. But such persons are prepared to read case papers which they believe are more "human" and more realistic. Clearly if a case is to be communicated from one case worker to another, then words must be used. Only in this way can one case worker learn from another. If this verbal communication of information is ignored, then each case worker must be assumed to begin from scratch and to act solely upon his own personal experience unmodified by the experience of others. The egoistic approach must, of course, be rejected. But the translation of events or emotional experiences into words represents a replacemen of the real things by symbols, namely words. It is then the claim that words are more effective systems of symbols than mathematical symbols. This is a hypothesis but it has not been demonstrated to be true. There is obviously no difference of kind if I write a description of an emotional experience in words in English or Latin, nor is there any difference of kind if I write the description as x, y or any other symbol. Words mean what by convention they have come to mean and the majority of words may be defined in other words. The effectiveness of words might be assessed by two criteria:

(a) How they convey meaning—are they effective for communication?
(b) How they allow of manipulation by the processes of logic—do they assist the thought processes?

A system of words with all (a) qualities and no (b) would be deficient over-all. The use of jargon which grows around any specialist study is an indication that normal language has been found to be deficient in either (a) or (b)—usually (a)—quality. The development of symbolic logic is an indication that some persons (not usually mathematicians) have found the redundancy and uncertainty of normal language inadequate for purpose (b). The use of mathematical models is another way of improving the efficiency of words for (b)

purposes. It will be clear, however, that there is no fundamental difference between the use of word-symbols to describe things and the use of abstract symbols. The difference exists mainly in that all persons have some knowledge of the use of words, for communication purposes and in general have found it possible to use the same system of symbols for (b) purposes also. The number of persons who "speak the language" is reduced when mathematical models are used and the coverage of communication is reduced, but nothing else need be lost. On the other hand, much is gained in that systems of operations built up over many centuries may be pressed into service once we can translate problems into this language.

If we require to *communicate* most effectively we should use the most common language consistent with the required degree of accuracy in communication. If we require to *use thought processes,* we should use any system of symbols which proves most effective. Some may choose one and others another. Eventually all researchers must submit to the trial by publication; they must be able to communicate their results so that a sufficient number of other qualified persons may examine their work. If we choose a system of symbolic logic to describe our thought processes we would be advised to use a system already in existence; if we choose mathematical models, we have chosen perhaps the most developed system of symbols where the largest number of persons will be able to follow our work without excessive background explanation of our system.

17. THE CONCEPT OF CAUSE IN CRIMINOLOGY

LESLIE T. WILKINS

FOR CENTURIES PHILOSOPHERS HAVE ARGUED regarding the concept of "cause." Most of this discussion has no practical significance for the social scientist of today, but recent developments in research methods do raise certain questions which are of importance, both in philosophical and practical terms.

To the layman it may seem that there are no issues worthy of attention—everybody knows what is meant by causation. Perhaps most persons can get along quite well with a simple notion of cause and effect, but not the scientist; certainly and especially not the social scientist. But, as is evidenced in the literature, most criminologists seem still prepared to talk about the "causes of crime." In consideration of this particular phrase, many express worries about the definition of their field of study as indicated by the term "crime" while few seem bothered about the concept of "cause." Nonetheless it is possible that the concept of "cause" is at least as important and open to discussion as is the concept of "crime." Perhaps the practical consequences of different perceptions and definitions of the former have a greater significance than varied perceptions of the latter.

The official wording of the enactment which established the British Home Office (Criminological) Research Unit charged it with the duty to "... conduct research into the causes of delinquency and the treatment of offenders and matters connected therewith." (See 77 (1) (b) Criminal Justice Act 1948). Everybody, it may be claimed, knows exactly what that phrase means, so why raise questions of no practical significance?

Elsewhere [1] the writer has argued the need for an operational approach to criminology and has shown little or no patience with hair-splitting arguments and definition polishing. Then why raise this issue now? The matter is raised only because it would seem to have practical significance in view of developments in certain other fields of scientific activity.

CONCEPTS AND TERMINOLOGY IN RELATION TO ACTION

How, it may be asked, can a matter of terminology be of serious practical significance? It is, of course, that pervasive concepts influence the nature of perception and thus the structure of thought and action. Consider, for example, the nature of actions based on the concepts of "responsibility," "free-will," and "rationality."

▶SOURCE: *"The Concept of Cause in Criminology", Issues in Criminology (Spring, 1968), 3:2: 147–165. Reprinted by permission.*

[1] Wilkins, L. T. (1962) Criminology—An Operations Research Approach; in *Society;* (Ed.) Welford: Routeledge and Kegan Paul.

A re-structuring of the concept of, say, responsibility or free-will would have considerable impact upon logical consequences in terms of legal action.

In the action of the courts much may depend upon a definition of a concept. Similarly for problem solving and the activities of scientists and those concerned with the asking of research questions in the field of criminology, the concept of "cause" is an important one. A re-structuring of the concept of cause could result in the re-structuring of the problems as they are now posed. In the solution of any problem, the formulation of the problem is always the main issue. A problem correctly formulated may be well on the way towards solution, whereas a problem not well formulated cannot be efficiently dealt with.

Ask a silly question and you get a silly answer! Are we in criminology, asking silly questions? Are we asking questions based on a formal concept which might now be modified? If so, what would be the form of the questions which might be asked, given the re-structuring of the basic concepts?

Few would doubt that we have, so far, found little of consequence which can assist us in dealing with problems of delinquency and crime. If then a re-structuring is possible, it might be that the new form of the questions which we may then be able to phrase in relation to our problems would be more amenable to analysis.

SCIENCE AND MORALS

The fact that criminology is a branch of social study closely related to law and even to moral concepts may explain some of the difficulties encountered in research methodology. Clearly the concepts of "cause and effect" are related to concepts of "determinism" and "free-will" and these in turn to the legal concepts of "responsibility" and "reasonable man." Fields of study further removed from moral and value questions may be able to ignore some of these philosophical difficulties. The concept of cause presents few difficulties for the engineer since the lay concept is adequate for most of the problems encountered in this field. Criminology cannot avoid the tackling of these philosophically difficult issues, because the questions with which it deals are made up from the semantic dust of these under-developed areas. Crime is a big concept and raises many problems of definition. We cannot study a thing or area which cannot be defined. If we do not know what "it" is, we cannot study "it," let alone find "its" causes.

If we can now remodel our concept of cause in order to bring our thinking more into line with that of other fields of inquiry, such a change of definition* may reflect upon the way we perceive the term "crime." Thus the combined concept "causes of crime" by which we denote one of our main fields of study may be reformed. It is easier to begin by considering the former term since in this analysis it is possible to refer to a wider range of experience and observation.

SOME QUESTIONS OF METHOD AND PHILOSOPHY

For the statement of some important questions in the area, your author is indebted to a distinguished Japanese criminologist who wrote, in part, as follows. "I feel that a new Queteletism or a new Lombrosian technique is making an appearance in our field, and that it is very different from the old techniques." "Could I," he asks, "have a direct answer to the questions?"

"1. what is the main difference between

---

* Re-structuring a concept is not exactly the same as redefining it; indeed the concept of a definition and the "defining act" may itself need to be re-structured. But the import of these factors may become more apparent as we proceed with the discussion.

the methodology of the natural sciences and the social sciences
2. so far as I know it is said that some fundamental ideas underlying scientific study have been changed, that, for example
   a. causal relations → probable relationships
   b. laws and rules → models
   c. research using large quantities of data → samples

Is this correct?"

It is not possible to answer or even to express an opinion on these questions in any simple terms. A question which raises complex issues can be discussed adequately only in terms of its complexity. The treatment to be given here will, therefore, be somewhat inadequate, but it is hoped to be able to indicate a line of thought which, if pursued by others, may lead towards a re-structuring of the concepts, and through this to a changed perception, in turn leading to a rephrasing of some of the puzzling issues of criminology today. What can be said here is only by way of a starting point —a sign-post pointing along a different road from that which has conventionally been traversed in criminological thought and research.

LAWS OF NATURE

Is the concept of "cause" to be replaced? If so by what? The scientist may now be able to deal with uncertainty by means of the calculus of probabilities, but is this only a technical matter? If we knew enough, should we be able to predict with precision? Is our uncertainty about, say, the weather an indication that we have not yet found the cause of the changes? Is the real world deterministic? These and many similar questions are, it is suggested, not very useful questions.

The concept of cause, like any other concept should be tested in terms of another concept, namely its utility. There are no laws "somewhere out there in the universe" which we may discover. The laws of science are sophisticated ideas expressed in some communicable form between scientists which, to their satisfaction, explain the way the world is arranged. The laws are statements made by man in a language which man has himself invented. We may use the terms in which the laws are stated to do things or to predict events. What is "out there" in the world is not the law, we do not know what is in fact out there. If we did know what was actually out there there would be no point in making any further inquiry. Thus the question of scientific method could not arise because there would be nothing to which to apply this methodology. There is no requirement or law of nature set up by man which nature is required to follow. We can pass laws affecting ourselves within our own power to enforce them, but laws of nature are not things which we can legislate about.

It is convenient to describe certain phenomena in certain ways for certain purposes. For certain purposes we may "set up" a "law of cause and effect" which supposes a deterministic system. This may, in some cases, be an adequate model, or we may set up a concept of probabilistic relationships and this may also be adequate for certain purposes. The language we select is *our* language—not the language of nature or God or other external influence. We make the laws; whether they are deterministic or probabilistic depends upon us and our purposes. A deterministic law may not reflect those features of the "thing" we wish to study with sufficient precision for a given purpose, and we might then change the law to a probabilistic one because this fits better those observations we can make.

THE CONCEPT OF SYSTEM

In a fairly general way we can describe the phenomena with which we are concerned in social science as *"systems."* This is a technical term central to any understanding of modern scientific methodology. This concept is a most valuable and fruitful one; and one which has already enabled much restructuring of the problems (and laws) used in many fields of scientific inquiry. It is as pervasive as the concept of cause and effect.

Before saying what is the current approach to "cause" and determinism it is necessary to take a little time to understand the special meaning now attributed to the term "system."

"A game of snooker," says Beer,[2] "is a *system,* whereas a single snooker ball is not. A car, a pair of scissors, an economy, a language and a quadratic equation..." are all systems. It is, of course, possible merely to point to a car or a pair of scissors as "things" thus denominated, but it is only when the ways in which the bits and pieces interact together are particularly noted that we have a reasonable basis for study. Such relationships constitute the "system" which makes a car or a pair of scissors. Linked with the concept of system is the concept of *"control"* which is defined as an attribute of any *system.*

The way which a *system* is conceptualised is determined by the scientist for his purposes. Again, as Beer observes, "a pair of scissors (is) a system. But the expanded system of a woman cutting with scissors is also a system—in turn part of a larger manufacturing system." In the other direction the pair of scissors is not the minimum system, although one blade is not very effective as a system for cutting cloth, and the single rivet would be useless for this purpose. Nonetheless, the rivet is a system of grains of steel and each grain contains an atomic system. The *definition* of *entities* as parts of systems is essential if we would consider the interaction affecting a single entity. In some ways a system of inter-related parts is a "thing" in itself. This is a somewhat complex concept but

an essential one if the new approach to scientific inquiry is to be appreciated.

Thus a "thing" which is defined as a *system* consists of elements (according to how far down the scale we wish to go). Let us say that there are (x) elements in a system conceived in the form in which we wish to study it, then there are $x(x-1)$ different relationships or possible states of the system. If we have a *very simple* system of seven elements, this has 42 relationships within itself. Suppose that this system is very, very simple indeed and that each of the relationships either is or is not, then the number of possible states of the system will be 2^{42}—about 4,000,000,000,000. Not such a simple system perhaps! But it is a deterministic system since we have defined it as such. We can specify all possible states: representation by computer is very simple, although perhaps difficult to imagine subjectively.

This type of analysis gives us a clue to a type of classification of a system indicated briefly above.

TYPES OF SYSTEMS AND MODELS

We may consider as a start the simple deterministic systems. These will have few interconnections and be completely predictable in their behavior. But clearly whether a system is simple or not depends upon how *we* choose to describe it. The game of snooker could belong to the class of deterministic systems since the angles of deflection (given a "perfect" table, "perfect" balls, "perfect" cues and a perfect player) are capable of precise calculation. A player playing such a "perfect" game could go on scoring to infinity! This is, therefore, not a very helpful way of looking at a game of snooker as played in any actual situation. The deterministic model is totally unsuited to almost any purpose, although of course it is possible to *imagine* a deterministic model for the game. (Imagination is not the issue in this aspect of our analysis.) Any such model might be

---

[2] Beer, S., *Cybernetics and Management.* John Wiley & Sons, 1964.

regarded as fairly simple in mathematical terms. The game, as played, bears no great relationship to the imagined "ideal" game. A probabilistic model is more realistic or more practical, since no other type of snooker game is possible for man. The probabilistic model is, thus, the only model which need concern us as a tool for research should we wish to do research into this game. Some other features of the game of snooker will later serve as illustrations of other matters.

There are, of course, complex deterministic systems, of which the best example may be the electronic computer as normally received. If a computer does not do exactly what it is predicted to do, then it has gone wrong. If we wish to include in our descriptive systems the possibility of failure, then the concept has to be changed to a probabilistic one for all practical purposes. At one level of conceptualisation it might be most useful to say that the computer is a deterministic system, at another level to say that it is a probabilistic system. Perhaps the universe of planets, suns and the like is a complex deterministic system, perhaps not. The *assumption that it is* (or may be perceived as) a deterministic system has led to a considerable ability to predict. The unpredictable aspect of the universe has been assumed to be due to factors not yet accounted for in the theory in "laws" as they can at present be stated. This has stimulated research and the concept of a deterministic system can, in this field of inquiry, show considerable "pay-off."

But whether the solar system *is* deterministic or not is a meaningless question. At the level of operation with which we are at present concerned, the methods of science applied in this field are rationally based. Whether the deterministic basis is the central tendency of large aggregates of probabilistic systems or not may belong to a belief system; it is not a matter for a system of knowledge.

It may be represented that if we postulate complete knowledge of any physical system, then complete and accurate prediction would be possible. This is both obvious, meaningless and useless. Some systems we are able to describe as deterministic, others we must describe as probabilistic, and indeed the same thing (like the game of snooker) looked at for different purposes may have to be changed from a deterministic to a probabilistic system. Such classifications—like "laws of nature"—are man-made classifications derived for his own purposes. The philosophy of AS IF must be invoked.[3] Some systems can be usefully studied AS IF they were deterministic, others may not usefully be studied thus. What they *are* is no concern of ours in determining our method for study. Information we do not possess we cannot use, and our information is certainly limited. What might or might not be the position were this not the case is irrelevant.

We may hold to certain beliefs about ultimates, and our beliefs may condition our perceptions. Some perceptions based on some systems of belief may be dysfunctional.

The usual basis for the belief in determinism is the assumption that what we perceive as probabilistic systems are only probabilistic because we do not have sufficient knowledge. This belief is closely related to the generally accepted concepts of "cause and effect." It is, however, obvious that there is no way for us to know whether the difference between deterministic systems where our knowledge is incomplete and "truly" probabilistic systems is "real" or not. Scientific methodology is not concerned with belief systems as such, but only with their consequences. Science is not religion, religion is not science. Let us then return to our consideration of scientific methodology.

We have, so far, seen how many variants may be found in an extremely simple deterministic system. Although some may

---

[3] Vaihinger, H. (1924) *The Philosophy of AS IF.* Barnes & Noble, 1935. Library.

think that the seven components example is far too simple, we have given the electronic computer as an example of deterministic systems. Continuously, however, we have had to keep glancing over our shoulder, as it were, at probabilistic systems. Before we discuss the probabilistic system in any detail it may be helpful to follow Beer's classification a little further.

It is possible to postulate an *exceedingly complex deterministic system*—so complex that it cannot be described. The computer does not fit this category no matter how large or complex since it can be constructed and predicted so long as it does not go wrong. But to postulate such an exceedingly complex system which is indescribable in detail is again meaningless, since when it is known to be deterministic it is no longer "exceedingly complex." Thus to postulate such types of systems is no more than a verbal device for blocking efficient practical thinking. Consider again the example of the solar system. If and when the solar system is known to be deterministic, then it must be known completely, and scientific inquiry will cease with respect to this area of our universe. At that time it will no longer be so complex that it is indescribable! Thus there can be no system which fits the category of *indescribably complex deterministic*. Before such systems can be known to be deterministic their behavior can be discussed only in terms of a probabilistic model.

Probabilistic systems cannot be simple in the meaning used here. Even the tossing of pennies, simple enough to perform, has results which are not predictable except in terms of fairly complex notions of probability. Assumptions may be made about what would happen if a person were to go on tossing pennies until infinity, and such notions may be useful although nobody could ever carry out the operation.

It is possible, then, to postulate *complex probabilistic systems*, but the most interesting category is that of the *exceedingly complex,* which although impossible in the deterministic case is perhaps the most usual in practical experience in the probabilistic form. Many systems in which we as social scientists are particularly interested are totally inaccessible to investigation by models which are perceived in terms of determinism. The category of complex probabilistic systems especially takes into account in the model the complexity in terms of the unknown, indescribable and even the imponderable. Such systems are typified by living processes and certain dynamic physical systems.

Consider for example the human brain. Once it is dead it is no longer a brain since the system is no longer operative. The brain can, nonetheless, be studied as a probabilistic system. How could it be otherwise since it has been calculated that the human brain contains 10,000,000,000 neurons and we know nothing about how they are connected. Remember the large number of different states of the very simple deterministic system of seven elements and then try to consider the number of states possible for 10^{10} neurons!

The important point of this discussion and the classification of systems is that each type of system, as we perceive it for our purposes, is amenable to different types of scientific methodology. Arguing that a system is *really* deterministic or really probabilistic will not help in re-structuring our knowledge of it. The structure of our perception must relate to our *information* (not our beliefs) and to our *purposes*.

Our problems, then, are concerned with finding an appropriate model which will enable us to discuss the system with which we are concerned. We may, of course, treat a *complex probabilistic system* as if it were *simple deterministic,* but if we do, our model will most likely fail to utilize the information we do possess to its greatest potential efficiency and we shall be able to explain little of the system. Moreover, our decisions based on the conclusions derived from our analysis of data relating to an inefficient analogue may well lead us to results which will be regretted. The deterministic model is generally unsafe in that it does not allow for the measurement of error. Even the simplest probabilistic models possess the safeguard that error (variance) is basic to the measurement and the inference, and estimation boundaries may be calculated. But we shall return to this point later after discussion of some other relevant issues in a more sophisticated way. Clearly the rejection of the *simple deterministic* model for the *complex or exceedingly complex probabilistic* model means that criminologists need a new armory of techniques, and that the descriptions of such techniques must themselves be somewhat complex.

SYSTEMS THEORY AND CRIMINOLOGICAL THEORY

For centuries, perhaps ever since man has committed his ideas to formal writing and before, crime has been one of the major themes of the drama and story. When the layman hears of crime his mental set is very much conditioned by storybook-land. The dramatic incident rather than the general state of deviant behavior influences thinking. This storybook-land mental set is not counteracted by the considerable insistence upon case histories by some serious students of human behavior. Jurisprudence emphasizes that "hard cases make bad law" but information available to the majority of persons interested in the phenomena of crime concerns the dramatic incident, if not the "hard case." It cannot be proved, but is is not unreasonable to suppose that more changes have been made in penal policy on the basis of information about one or two outstanding incidents than on the basis of carefully evaluated research analysis. The demand for the return of the death penalty in England was very strongly made when one person shot three policemen, although the average number of police lost in any one year throughout the whole country over a long period of years was less than a half (i.e., less than one every two years).

Scientific techniques should enable us to detach ourselves from the dramatic and enable us to focus upon ways for achieving socially desirable ends through careful analysis based on representative material.

It may be asked how the previous analysis which is only of a theoretical nature relates to practical research in relation to criminal and penal policy. In what ways are the commonly practiced methods of research regarded as inadequate or inaccurate?

Before methods which may be considered to be more powerful and rational are put forward, perhaps some current criminological theory should be noted. Research needs a basis in theory and the concepts briefly examined above should perhaps be specifically related to criminological theory. How then does the theory of systems relate to current theory in criminology?

No one believes that crime is a simple matter whatever is understood by the term "crime." Perhaps some of the actions taken in regard to criminals or crime lead to the valid deduction that we behave as if criminality were a very simple thing. Certainly the varieties of actions which are available for purposes of crime control are very limited. Nonetheless, few would expect to find a simple "cause." Indeed the most common so-called theory of crime causation is known as the "theory of multiple causation." There is no reason to repeat here the general argument which shows this concept to be futile if not absurd.[4] Rather let us examine the "theory" in the light of systems analysis. The main statement in this theory is that crime is a complex matter; perhaps this is the only statement of any meaning contained in this "theory." This statement must receive assent from all who have studied the subject. The statement is not clear and might be taken to mean that crime was a complex or ex-

---

[4] Wilkins, L. T., Juvenile Delinquency—A Critical Review: *J. Ed. Res.*: 5 (2) pp. 104–119.

ceedingly complex system. But the word "cause" has little significance unless it relates to a deterministic system. Thus we have a statement of belief masquerading as a theory, which in effect states (in terms of the classification system used here) only that "crime is a complex deterministic system."* But as we have attempted to demonstrate, there is no way for us to know whether a complex system is deterministic or probabilistic, although we may approach the problems involved AS IF it were either. In some aspects of the physical sciences and in astronomy the complex deterministic approach has been rewarding. Accordingly it would appear to be a rational strategy to continue utilizing *in these* areas models of the kind which in the past have demonstrated their power. Thus we are concerned with a *strategy;* with a method of approach; with a system of problem solving. Our choice of method has nothing to do with what is "true" which we shall not know, but with the methods available and with our assessment of the potential pay-off to be achieved by utilizing these methods. The information we possess regarding methods is relevant information regarding the selection of a strategy of methods. The methods we select are selected in accord with our basic philosophy, but only in a limiting case. We cannot, obviously, select for our purposes any method which is unknown. We will tend only to reject from known methods those which do not accord with our philosophy. Since we have no way of knowing whether a complex deterministic system is deterministic or probabilistic, this ignorance does not give us any sound rational basis for rejecting methods which may apply either to complex deterministic or probabilistic systems. Only if we can show that the system is probabilistic by showing that it is exceedingly complex can we use this prior information to throw doubt upon the efficiency of any deterministic model which we may use as (a) not a very powerful tool of analysis and (b) that it may have many pitfalls due to the excessive simplification of the concepts of the process which are involved. But we may obtain information by this type of model which may be of limited value although we must be extremely careful to keep our interpretation within the limits of the model and method.

If, in respect of our field of inquiry, in the past certain types of models have given a large pay-off we may consider investing more in these types of models than in others which have shown less pay-off. This is the basis for the defence of the use of models concordant with the view of the universe as a complex deterministic system; these models have worked well and enabled us to put man in space and to do many other things. The facility to predict which these methods have afforded provides the test of utility. The argument for the continued use of these methods relies upon the outcome of the past use of these methods, not the supposed nature of the unknown system of the universe.

Now consider criminology. Can we claim that the approach from models consistent with the belief in a complex deterministic system has worked well? How well can we predict the outcome of the treatment of offenders? What other decisions which we might make regarding crime have been facilitated by research? What types of models have tended to give the best pay-off so far? This is the kind of information we need if we are to make rational decisions regarding the selection of methods—not meaningless, useless, unscientific speculation about the real nature of crime or criminals.

A NOTE ON ANTI-SCIENCE

Perhaps we should make a brief reference to those who reject the scientific approach and assert that only human judgment can help with human problems. In-

---

* Some go on to describe other phenomena which suggest that they view crime as an exceedingly complex (deterministic!) system.

tuitive assessment of information, they claim, is superior to any other means for operating upon information. These types of arguments have been discussed in detail elsewhere and are dismissed by the majority of social scientists.[5] Moreover comparative studies have revealed the inaccuracy of the claim made.[6] However, the grounds for the rejection of these claims are worth examining again briefly here because the basis for our rational strategy for the selection of methods and models is the same whether the methods from which we select those to use include the antiscientific or only scientific methods. The method is not a justification for itself any more than the beliefs about the nature of the system provide rational grounds for the rejection or selection of methods of investigation of the system. The strategy of method selection relates to rational decisions made in relation to relevant information, namely information regarding methods and their pay-off, without regard to "real" nature.

The three components of rational decision-making may be applied in our attempt to work through to a strategy of methodology. A rational choice of a decision is the selection of that decision which, in the light of the available information, maximizes the probability of achieving the objective or maximizes the pay-off desired. In all practical cases there will be a limited number of possible, ethical decisions and the available information will also be limited. In the present case the decision to be selected is the decision to apply certain methods for a certain purpose. In more complex models the concept of cost can also be accommodated, but let us limit the consideration in this discussion. Clearly the boundary conditions around the decision-set are determined by the present limited state of knowledge with respect to methods; we can decide to use one or more of the known methods, or to use none. Although we may choose to do nothing something will happen by default, and we may consciously or unconsciously select to default. Doing nothing may be a completely rational action if this maximizes the probability of achieving the pay-off we desire. We can, of course, make rational decisions only in the light of information. What then is "information" in relation to the strategy of method selection? As yet we are not able to construct many formal solutions to the problem of strategy in criminological research. Perhaps we say that a rational choice, on our present information, is to select some form of scientific approach. We have evidence in many spheres that leads us to the reasonable belief that the scientific approach is likely to be valuable and some proofs of its superiority over intuitive systems in the criminological field. Whether this evidence is regarded as sufficiently convincing may still be open to some questioning. We have generated little information leading to a possibility of the development of a rational strategy of methodology. There is, as yet, no established science of science; there is no very sound basis for a strategy of methodology because the necessary information has not been systematically collected. The successful scientific (or even non-scientific) inquiry tends to be reported for its results, but few publications report the unsuccessful. In a rational strategy, information regarding attempts which are failures is as useful as information regarding success, indeed both types of information may be equally necessary. Nonetheless, if your author is correct in perceiving the problem as one of strategy, the angle from which the present situation is seen becomes drastically changed and we may be able to restructure many concepts and move forward to a more productve analysis of science itself in relation to social policy.

---

[5] Fink, A. E. (1962) Current Thinking In Parole Prediction. *J. Crime & Delinq.*: 8 (3).

[6] Meehl, P. E. (1956) *Clinical & Statistical Prediction:* U. of Minnesota, and London.

A SCIENCE OF SCIENCE?

Science, or the scientific method considered in the light of the foregoing argument may be seen itself as a "system." It follows, then, that the information we should seek should relate to methods, and perhaps even to beliefs about methods, but not to beliefs about the nature of the systems to which we propose to apply these methods, unless these beliefs relate directly to our selection of methods. That is to say, it is unless only to claim that the system under study is complex deterministic unless we can also show that the methods which relate to this type of system have been useful. Apart from this evidence (i.e., information generated by the use of different methods) there is no way of distinguishing the nature of the system. This is the very nature of our knowledge. Again, if we postulate that the system is exceedingly complex, then we have only probabilistic methods from which we may choose—others by definition do not model the concept of the system as stated.

In general, it would seem desirable to select mainly from methods which represent or can accommodate the postulated complexity of the field of study. These methods are generally of recent origin. There are grounds to believe that these will prove more profitable than methods which have known deficiencies. But as yet this is only a belief, since there is no evidence until information is generated by action. However, this belief system is of a different order from those belief systems which relate to beliefs about "the nature of things"—that is the things to be studied.

Beliefs about the power of different methods are beliefs about the probable results from human disciplined action in the carrying out of systematic processes of inquiry. These types of belief can be subject to continuous verification and modification as action develops, whereas beliefs about the "nature of things" are never open to verification as such. This is a most important distinction. The higher level of abstraction (if this is what this is) changes the nature of the style of acceptable proof. It does this by changing the nature of the hypotheses.

We have earlier seen that there are systems within systems (the scissors and the atoms) and now we see that there can be orders of systems; systems that, as it were control systems. (The term control in this case is not used in its technical cybernetic meaning.) The zero order systems may be regarded as systems of information. For example, the human body is a highly complex system, yet the glands, genes, D.N.A. exercise control in a most efficient manner.

CAUSE AND EFFECT RE-EXAMINED

The preceding slight excursion into the philosophy of systems provides the basis of justification for the approach now to be developed in relation to the concepts of cause and effect. The question was posed as to whether "cause and effect" models were totally unsatisfactory; whether the concept of "cause" had been replaced. If so, what basis for inquiry is proposed? Let us restate the problem of "cause" in a more sophisticated form as follows. Can simple deterministic models provide a fruitful line of investigation for problems in the field of criminology? The most obvious fact which may be stated which has relevance for this question is that to date, these are the models which have been most frequently used, and they have revealed a startling lack of pay-off. Can we gather any information as to why this has been so? Perhaps the answer lies to some extent in the observations of experienced persons in the operational fields associated with the discipline of criminology. Their experience may be useful and valid whereas their usual attempts at organizing their experience may be inadequate because it has not the support of a strong methodology. Perhaps the attempts to organize experience into inadequate models is the main factor in the lack of pay-off. This may be part of the explanation, since as we have already seen, there is a basic inconsistency in saying that criminal behavior is complex and then trying to organize that statement into a "cause-effect" system which is essentially simple. Moreover, it seems that simple probabilistic systems may not be very helpful except for limited aspects.

It may have already occurred to the reader that the examples given of "exceedingly complex systems" are more appropriate to the field of criminology, and (by definition) these may be discussed only in probabilistic terms. The system of law as a social control is an exceedingly complex system. There are many aspects of this system which we cannot even describe except perhaps in the broadest of general categories. Control by law in society is not a simple process of pain reflexes, although these can be complex enough! The economy of a country is an exceedingly complex system and the Bureau of the Budget is by no means a controller of the economy. Taxation may be raised and other fiscal measures may be taken, and these will have an impact upon the economy in a crude form. This guidance by trippings is better than no action to deal with unemployment, inflation and the like. But the system is not *controlled* in any detail. The actions of the Bureau are interventions in a process that has its own inbuilt controls through highly complex interconnections between its elements and sub-systems. These connections are not fully understood, but the disturbances to the system generated by legislative fiscal action have a probable effect on the general trends which can be predicted with a degree of precision.

SOME SPECIFIC EXAMPLES OF A FORM OF STRATEGY

Perhaps it should be emphasized that the strategy to which we have referred in the preceding paragraphs is only a strategy for the selection of models. This is, of course, by no means a complete strategy or policy for social research. In particular we have said nothing about the strategy which might apply in decisions regarding the effort to be put into the development of new methods, nor have we discussed the importance of the planning for some unplanned activity, and the systems of classification which should be designed to cut across the systems of classification.

Within the area of strategy of selection of appropriate methods for criminological research from among those methods which already exist, there are some questions which may be examined as an illustration of a means of approach. It may be noted that the acceptance of the concept of a strategy (rather than a concept of truth-seeking) restructures the problems. The old questions remain, but we may approach them somewhat differently.

It may be asked whether, in the light of the concept of a strategy for selection of methods, the simple or complex deterministic models might, in some cases at least, help with our understanding of some criminological problems, although the systems theory concept of such problems would classify them as probabilistic or exceedingly complex. Would not some such models simplify the situation as effectively as other models which in theory might be more appropriate? It would seem to be impossible to suggest that any general rule or law should apply; clearly to do so would destroy the basis of our own argument. There may be some cases where a simple or complex deterministic model may throw light upon a system which is exceedingly simplified thereby. In general, however, such models might be regarded as providing a poor strategy of investigation. The game of snooker which we have described as deterministic but so complex that in practical cases it may be conceived only as probabilistic, can provide an example. For some purposes it may be reasonable to use a deterministic model of the game. It may be that for purposes of introducing a novice to the principles of play in the initial stages, an explanation in terms of the basic mechanics and geometry would be helpful. But it is clear also to the novice that this model is not likely to be very representative of his play! The reader may find it interesting to speculate why we may expect the deterministic model to be helpful for some aspects of *teaching* and to consider how general this feature may be. It is also a worthwhile exercise to reflect upon the question of whether this feature does not also comment upon the ways in which the role of the teacher is perceived and the possible variety of different teaching and learning situations. To follow these thoughts would take us into a still different area of analysis which must not now be developed. However, the fact that so many other issues can arise directly from a consideration of systems demonstrates the power and pervasiveness of the idea.

One further observation may be appropriate before leaving this aspect of the discussion. The deterministic model of the game of snooker—the theory of geometry and mechanics—has very limited utility. Every player of snooker must have remarked after a poor miss "Good theory; execution poor!" Certainly after the initial explanation of the game using the deterministic model, a player would be unlikely to learn how further to improve his game by increasing his knowledge of mechanics or geometry. Rather he would be advised to observe experienced (but *imperfect!*) players and to practice as much as possible. There is another case where the deterministic model may be of some help in providing information. It is in cases of gross distortion of one factor. If, for example, the balls are clearly not round, or the player is blind, or the cues very much distorted, we could make some statements from the deterministic model. But a blind player, using bent cues and oval balls does not present a very good model of the game of snooker, interesting although it may be to postulate some outcomes! Minor distortions of more than one item would take us into a different model. If we wanted to know whether different tables had more effect than different balls or different cues, we would design a probabilistic model using replications and partition the observed variance and compare it with error variance due to higher order interactions. Classical analysis of variance would be a useful model as a start to the development of further and more detailed investigation.[7]

If we are interested in the learning process we would have to design experiments accordingly, using probabilistic models. Analysis of the factors most contributing to *effective learning* as observed in *practical situations* would doubtless help the snooker player to improve his game. The experienced player in an unfamiliar setting may test some of the factors of the game in subjective operational terms; he may throw the ball against the cushion and observe its travel, he may roll the cue along the table, and so on. By these processes he may be regarded as making observations and carrying out a kind of operational research. But no experienced player knows exactly how much a distorted cut, a rough table or a biased ball may affect his game, and he certainly cannot assess the joint contribution of any combination of these components. If any of these factors were found to be grossly distorted he would most likely refuse to play.

The analogue of the snooker game is capable of extension to few criminological problems. We may say, however, that in all problems in our field, it is the interactions between factors which concern us. If, then, in the simple game of snooker neither expert subjective judgment, including operational trials, nor deterministic models can deal with interactions, how much less likely are they to be adequate methods in our field? Thus, probabilistic models are normally the only kind that

---

[7] Any general statistical textbook; Analysis of Variance.

would seem to be indicated by rational strategy for the study of complex deterministic systems, at least for research if not for teaching purposes.

It may be asked, how simple must a deterministic system be before it ceases to be simple and has to be treated as complex. That is to say, when should probabilistic models be used for systems which we know cannot be specified completely in respect to all elements with which we are concerned. Assuming this to be a sensible question, it is again a question of strategy. For example, if we have access to large computers we may use them for simulating deterministic systems of some complexity. Cost will be another consideration. A cheaper but less accurate solution may be possible by use of probabilistic models and the cheaper solution may be equally effective in practice. There is no value in accuracy for its own sake. If an identical decision, say of social policy, would be made on the basis of information which was absolutely accurate and given information which had an error of $\pm 5\%$, then the extra money spent on obtaining the accuracy is wasted. Further, when we have obtained the detailed highly accurate data, these have to be appreciated by human intelligence. For these reasons also it may be a good strategy either to use probabilistic models from the start, or to use probability as a conditioning factor in the deterministic model and simulation program.

It is not possible here to go further into the matters of strategy or the differences between models to be selected for different purposes. The general complexity of research strategy may, however, have been demonstrated by this analysis.

RESEARCH PLANNING

The selection of the appropriate model for purposes of investigation of a particular question is a different matter from the strategy of control of research organizations. System theory, however, can contribute much to the ways in which research planning and the policy function may be profitably exercised. But this may be no more than briefly indicated here. It may be remarked that the raw material for research operations are people and ideas. Ideas are capable of being marshalled and manipulated in certain ways; people are a different matter altogether. We have not discussed people, and we have limited our attention to a narrow aspect of the content of ideas in the total research process.

It may be agreed that the complexity of research makes it no longer possible for one person to know all that can or even should be known in a quite limited area of one field of study. We need therefore, to discover ways for utilizing different skills together on our problems. We must seek systems for the division of labor with effective communication networks linking needs and resources for research. Research itself may be conceived as a complex or even exceedingly complex system.

Highly structured systems of organization, such as some governmental departments or the military may be suitable systems for dealing with some types of tasks; perhaps highly structured tasks. Unstructured problems and tasks such as those encountered in research work* cannot be dealt with efficiently or adequately if they are formulated in such a manner as enables them to be forced into a highly structured organizational system.

Questions which ask, implicitly or explicitly, how research should be *directed* may be poor questions. Rather we might ask how research can best be facilitated. How can the best results be obtained from the available resources of manpower and materials, and how may ideas and models be best utilized.

Research in the social field is a sub-system of the larger system, namely the social system. To conceptualize social research systems as independent of the systems of

---

* Research is not merely fact-finding activity.

social administration and policy is as unsound as it is to regard the research sub-system as having the same qualities as the policy and administrative systems. Sub-systems have their own characteristics and are often composed of different types of inter-connections from those of the larger systems. The sub-system of grains of steel in the system for cutting cloth, (the scissors referred to in an earlier example) are quite different forms of relationships. Knowledge about the one has little to contribute to knowledge of the other, yet they are both necessary forms of knowledge.

CONCLUSIONS

In the discussion regarding research methods one or two new terms or perhaps new concepts for some readers have been introduced. These terms are not new in the physical sciences and the operational research field. Indeed, in the analysis of systems, information and control processes many other useful concepts may be found. Linked with these concepts is a large body of knowledge regarding ways of operating with data derived from highly complex systems. These methods have been tested in applications to problems of automation and cybernation, from problems of man in space to problems of microbiology and neurology. The concepts of entropy, information, control, feed-back, mapping and many others have been so generally useful in such widely different fields of inquiry that it seems very difficult to believe that they would not be usefully developed in regard to the field of criminological investigation also. The purpose of this paper has been to encourage consideration of concepts of which there is little or no trace at present in the criminological literature, and to stimulate discussion.

SECTION IV

Theory and Evidence

IT MUST, BY THIS TIME, BE SOMETHING OF A TIRED CLICHE TO CONTEND THAT A sociological theory which is incapable of being tested empirically is merely a fruitless exercise in speculation. It is equally true that research which is devoid of theoretical implication is of extremely limited value and importance. Accordingly, this section, by far the largest in this volume, presents extensive selections from the more important recent theoretical statements in the field of criminology.

Each theory, in turn, is followed by one or more examples of relevant evidence supportive or destructive of the particular model. Certainly not all of the items listed as theories are equally sophisticated or logically derived. Bell's article is a sociologically oriented historical analysis of differential legitimate and illegitimate paths to success open to several immigrant groups in this country, while the "opportunity" theory of Cloward and Ohlin (derived from Merton, Cohen, Sykes and Matza, and perhaps Kobrin) is much more consistent with contemporary sociological requirements for adequate theory construction. Nevertheless, for our purposes, both are listed under the broad rubric of "theory." Similarly, the research presented ranges from the provocative but still inconclusive attempts to document the existence of La Cosa Nostra to Gordon's seemingly irrefutable attack on certain statistical techniques and assumptions sometimes used in ecological research.

Many commentators have suggested that America is probably the most criminal country in the world, and certainly a powerful case could be made to support that contention. What are the peculiarly criminogenic features of our culture? It is Bell's belief that for a certain segment of our population, criminality has become a normal way of life which absorbs a sizeable proportion of some late-arriving American immigrant groups, particularly, he thinks, the Italians. Crime offers them the most likely manner of attaining "success": the acquisition of large amounts of money. The Task Force on Organized Crime of the President's Commission on Law Enforcement and Administration of Justice argues that the core or organized crime in the United States today are 24 Italian "families" who collectively form what has come to be known as La Cosa Nostra.

One classical explanation for American criminality is offered by Sellin in his theory of culture conflict. A conflict between divergent value systems impinging upon many second generation immigrants has rendered some of them susceptible to crime and delinquency. Many of the ideas expressed in this selection have appeared in various forms in current theoretical systems. Kobrin's formulation of "The Conflict of Values in Delinquency Areas" is concerned with somewhat different dimensions of culture conflict. The integration of conventional and criminal value systems within certain parts of a city tends to produce one set of delinquency patterns while another area, characterized by maximum conflict between these two cultural systems, has a quite different distribution of deviant acts. Utilizing the differential crime rates among "new" and "old" immigrants in Israel, Shoham tests and seems to confirm, in this one instance at least, the association of culture conflict and crime.

The theory of differential association by Edwin Sutherland, built on the contention that criminal behavior is learned and is not genetic nor due to psychological maladjustment, is now a commonplace belief which implicitly requires a sociological-psychological frame-of-reference in the explication of delinquent and criminal behavior. "An Empirical Test of Differential Association Theory" by Riess and Rhodes, although mostly emphasizing the many difficulties in testing "inferences" to be derived from Sutherland's model, is not highly supportive of differential association as a viable explanation of delinquency.

Human ecology refers to the spatial distribution of population and became a significant feature of criminology shortly after the ecological approach was developed by Park and Burgess at the University of Chicago in the 1920's. Both as a theoretical model and as a research technique, ecological analyses of delinquency and crime in urban communities can be traced in the United States to the work of Shaw and McKay. The study of "social physics," which involved the use of geographic maps showing relationships between crime and selected social variables, began much earlier in the nineteenth century with the writings of Quetelet and Guerry. Shaw and McKay propound what has become known as the "cultural transmission" theory of delinquency which holds that within the most disorganized areas of our cities (ecological Zone II) crime has become a tradition which is transmitted from one generation to the next. The criminal, by his extravagant style of life and his visible display of many of the accoutrements of wealth, demonstrates his economic success and, hence, becomes a worthy model for ambitious youths.

Robert Merton perceived the problem of delinquency in terms of "anomie" whereby two noncooperating elements of American social structure (Means and Goals) have become dichotomized; and when in one mode of reaction the lower class boy rejects licit means but accepts economic goals, delinquency becomes his only solution. Lander's statistical study in Baltimore examines the concentric zone and gradient hypotheses, adds a new dimension with factor analysis, and hypothesizes an explanation of the differential delinquency rate in terms of the concept of anomie rather than the socio-economic conditions of an area. Lander's findings have been subjected to considerable attack in "Issues in the Ecological Study of Delinquency." Gordon concludes that the traditional socio-economic status indices of education and rent (nonanomic in Lander's view) are probably as highly correlated with delinquency as the two variables Landers thought uniquely clustered with delinquency.

Cohen has modified Merton's theory by dealing, in part, with the irrationality of much delinquent behavior and why it appears to be "malicious," "negativistic," and "nonutilitarian." His own solution, though somewhat devoid of substantive support, is highly persuasive. Sykes and Matza take issue with some of his explanations and suggest that delinquency is not the complete avoidance of middle class values, but that the delinquent must ultimately neutralize or rationalize much of his unconventional behavior. Finally, Cloward and Ohlin try, with some success, to combine the models of cultural transmission and of anomie. They argue that there is differential access to legitimate avenues to success, so that some segments of the population will turn to illegitimate opportunities for success. In urban areas, distinctive delinquent subcultures tend to arise: the integrated "criminal subculture" (representing a *modus vivendi* between conventional and deviant value systems), the "conflict subculture," and the "retreatist subculture" (largely consisting of "double failure" drug addicts). Parts of several anomic-based theories of delinquency, particularly those which are primarily related to lower class gang delinquency, are tested by Short and Strodtbeck, who find differential acceptance of middle class prescriptions and proscriptions among the groups they studied. Gannon's examination of the characteristics of a New York "defensive" gang is primarily oriented towards the role of status and status threats in gang conflicts and aggressions.

Walter Miller contends that the entire lower class has subcultural "focal concerns" which are divergent from those operating in the middle class and these generate value systems which are likely to produce gang delinquency. In his later article, Miller offers data on the behavior of 150 corner gangs to determine the amount and kinds of violence that is often attributed to city gangs.

Does there exist in our society, for some social groups, a subculture of violence—that is, a value system dependent on violence—demanding adherence to violence and penalizing deviations? Wolfgang and Ferracuti persuasively argue this is true. The violence endemic in certain urban settings is graphically described in "Violent Gang Organization." It is difficult to imagine a more frightening, and ultimately pathetic, personality than Yablonsky's depiction of the sociopathic, near-psychotic, highly inadequate gang leader. The social psychological model of delinquency causation known as Containment Theory is based on almost equal proportions of external and internal ("self") constraints. Several basic investigations of "self-concept research" are described and critized by Tangri and Schwartz.

18. CRIME AS AN AMERICAN WAY OF LIFE

DANIEL BELL

IN THE 1890's THE REVEREND DR. CHARLES Parkhurst, shocked at the open police protection afforded New York's bordellos, demanded a state inquiry. In the Lexow investigation that followed, the young and dashing William Travers Jerome staged a set of public hearings that created sensation after sensation. He badgered "Clubber" Williams, First Inspector of the Police Department, to account for wealth and property far greater than could have been saved on his salary; it was earned, the Clubber explained laconically, through land speculation "in Japan." Heavy-set Captain Schmittberger, the "collector" for the "Tenderloin precincts"—Broadway's fabulous concentration of hotels, theaters, restaurants, gaming houses, and saloons—related in detail how protection money was distributed among the police force. Crooks, policemen, public officials, businessmen, all paraded across the stage, each adding his chapter to a sordid story of corruption and crime. The upshot of these revelations was reform—the election of William L. Strong, a stalwart businessman, as mayor, and the naming of Theodore Roosevelt as police commissioner.

It did not last, of course, just as previous reform victories had not lasted. Yet the ritual drama was re-enacted. Twenty years ago the Seabury investigation in New York

▶SOURCE: *"Crime as an American Way of Life,"* *The Antioch Review (June, 1953), 13:131–154.* Reprinted by permission.

uncovered the tin-box brigade and the thirty-three little MacQuades. Jimmy Walker was ousted as Mayor and in came Fiorello La Guardia. Tom Dewey became district attorney, broke the industrial rackets, sent Lucky Luciano to jail and went to the Governor's chair in Albany. Then reform was again swallowed up in the insatiable maw of corruption until Kefauver and the young and dashing Rudolph Halley threw a new beam of light into the seemingly bottomless pit.

How explain this repetitious cycle? Obviously the simple moralistic distinction between "good guys" and "bad guys," so deep at the root of the reform impulse, bears little relation to the role of organized crime in American society. What, then, does?

II

Americans have had an extraordinary talent for compromise in politics and extremism in morality. The most shameless political deals (and "steals") have been rationalized as expedient and realistically necessary. Yet in no other country have there been such spectacular attempts to curb human appetites and brand them as illicit, and nowhere else such glaring failures. From the start America was at one and the same time a frontier community where "everything goes," and the fair country of the Blue Laws. At the turn of the century the cleavage developed between the Big City and the small-town conscience. Crime as a growing business was fed by the revenues from prostitution, liquor and gambling that a wide open urban society encouraged and which a middle-class Protestant ethos tried to suppress with a ferocity unmatched in any other civilized country. Catholic cultures rarely have imposed such restrictions, and have rarely suffered such excesses. Even in prim and proper Anglican England, prostitution is a commonplace of Piccadilly night life, and gambling one of the largest and most popular industries. In America the enforcement of public morals has been a continuing feature of our history.

Some truth may lie in Svend Ranulf's generalization that moral indignation is a peculiar fact of middle-class psychology and represents a disguised from of repressed envy. The larger truth lies perhaps in the brawling nature of American development and the social character of Crime. Crime, in many ways, is a Coney Island mirror, caricaturing the morals and manners of a society. The jungle quality of the American business community, particularly at the turn of the century, was reflected in the mode of "business" practiced by the coarse gangster elements, most of them from new immigrant families, who were "getting ahead," just as Horatio Alger had urged. In the older, Protestant tradition the intense acquisitiveness, such as that of Daniel Drew, was rationalized by a compulsive moral fervor. But the formal obeisance of the ruthless businessman in the workaday world to the church-going pieties of the Sabbath was one that the gangster could not make. Moreover, for the young criminal, hunting in the asphalt jungle of the crowded city, it was not the businessman with his wily manipulation of numbers but the "man with the gun" who was the American hero. "No amount of commercial prosperity," once wrote Teddy Roosevelt, "can supply the lack of the heroic virtues." The American was "the hunter, cowboy, frontiersman, the soldier, the naval hero." And in the crowded slums, the gangster. He was a man with a gun, acquiring by personal merit what was denied to him by complex orderings of a stratified society. And the duel with the law was the morality play *par excellence:* the gangster, with whom rides our own illicit desires, and the prosecutor, representing final judgment and the force of the law.

Yet all this was acted out in a wider context. The desires satisfied in extra-legal fashion were more than a hunger for the "forbidden fruits" of conventional morality. They also involved, in the complex and ever shifting structure of group, class and ethnic stratification, which is the warp and woof of America's "open" society, such "normal" goals as independence through a business of one's own, and such "moral" aspirations as the desire for social advancement and social prestige. For crime, in the language of the sociologists, has a "functional" role in the society, and the urban rackets—the illicit activity organized for continuing profit rather than individual illegal acts—is one of the queer ladders of social mobility in American life. Indeed, it is not too much to say that the whole question of organized crime in America cannot be understood unless one appreciates (1) the distinctive role of organized gambling as a function of a mass consumption economy; (2) the specific role of various immigrant groups as they one after another became involved in marginal business and crime; and (3) the relation of crime to the changing character of the urban political machines.

III

As a society changes, so does, in lagging fashion, its type of crime. As American society become more "organized," as the American businessman became more "civilized" and less "buccaneering," so did the American racketeer. And just as there were important changes in the structure of business enterprise, so the "institutionalized" criminal enterprise was transformed too.

In the America of the last fifty years the main drift of society has been toward the rationalization of industry, the domestication of the crude self-made captain of industry into the respectable man of manners, and the emergence of a mass-consumption economy. The most significant transformation in the field of "institutionalized" crime was the increasing relative importance of gambling as against other kinds of illegal activity. And, as a multi-billion-dollar business, gambling underwent a transition parallel to the changes in American enterprise as a whole. This parallel was exemplified in many ways: in gambling's industrial organization (e.g., the growth of a complex technology such as the national racing wire service and the minimization of risks by such techniques as lay-off betting); in its respectability, as was evidenced in the opening of smart and popular gambling casinos in resort towns and in "satellite" adjuncts to metropolitan areas; in its functional role in a mass-consumption economy (for sheer volume of money changing hands, nothing has ever surpassed this feverish activity of fifty million American adults); in the social acceptance of the gamblers in the important status world of sport and entertainment, i.e., "café society."

In seeking to "legitimize" itself, gambling had quite often actually become a force against older and more vicious forms of illegal activity. In 1946, for example, when a Chicago mobster, Pat Manno, went down to Dallas, Texas, to take over gambling in the area for the Accardo-Guzik combine, he reassured the sheriff as to his intent as follows: "Something I'm against, that's dope peddlers, pickpockets, hired killers. That's one thing I can't stomach, and that's one thing the fellows up there—the group won't stand for, things like that. They discourage it, they even go to headquarters and ask them why they don't do something about it."

Jimmy Cannon once reported that when the gambling raids started in Chicago, the "combine" protested that, in upsetting existing stable relations, the police were only opening the way for ambitious young punks and hoodlums to start trouble. Nor is there today, as there was twenty or even forty years ago, prostitution of major organized scope in the United States. Aside from the fact that manners and morals have changed, prostitution *as an industry* doesn't pay as well as gambling. Besides, its existence threatened the tacit moral acceptance and quasi-respectability that gamblers and gambling have secured in the American way of life. It was, as any operator in the field might tell you, "bad for business."

The criminal world of the last decade, its tone set by the captains of the gambling industry, is in startling contrast to the state of affairs in the two decades before. If a Kefauver report had been written then, the main "names" would have been Lepke and Gurrah, Dutch Schultz, Jack "Legs" Diamond, Lucky Luciano, and, reaching back a little further, Arnold Rothstein, the czar of the underworld. These men (with the exception of Luciano, who was involved in narcotics and prostitution) were in the main industrial racketeers. Rothstein, it is true, had a larger function: he was, as Frank Costello became later, the financier of the underworld—the pioneer big businessman of crime, who, understanding the logic of coordination, sought to *organize* crime as a source of regular income. His main interest in this direction was in industrial racketeering, and his entry was through labor disputes. At one time, employers in the garment trades hired Legs Diamond and his sluggers to break strikes, and the Communists, then in control of the cloakmakers union, hired one Little Orgie to protect the pickets and beat up the scabs; only later did both sides learn that Legs Diamond and Little Orgie were working for the same man, Rothstein.

Rothstein's chief successors, Lepke Buchalter and Gurrah Shapiro, were able, in the early '30's, to dominate sections of the men's and women's clothing industries, of painting, fur dressing, flour trucking, and other fields. In a highly chaotic and cut-throat industry such as clothing, the racketeer, paradoxically, played a stabilizing role by regulating competition and fixing prices. When the NRA came in and assumed this function, the businessman found that what had once been a quasi-economic service was now pure extortion, and he began to demand police action. In other types of racketeering, such as the trucking of perishable foods and water-front loading, where the racketeers entrenched themselves as middlemen—taking up, by default, a service that neither shippers nor truckers wanted to assume—a pattern of accommodation was roughly worked out and the rackets assumed a quasi-legal veneer. On the waterfront, old-time racketeers perform the necessary function of loading—but at an exorbitant price, and this monopoly was recognized by both the union and the shippers, and tacitly by government. (See my case study "The Last of the Business Rackets," in the June, 1951 issue of *Fortune*.)

But in the last decade and a half, industrial racketeering has not offered much in the way of opportunity. *Like American capitalism itself, crime shifted its emphasis from production to consumption.* The focus of crime became the direct exploitation of the citizen as consumer, largely through gambling. And while the protection of these huge revenues was inextricably linked to politics, the relation between gambling and "the mobs" became more complicated.

IV

Although it never showed up in the gross national product, gambling in the last decade was one of the largest industries in the United States. The Kefauver Committee estimated it as a twenty-billion-dollar business. This figure has been picked up and widely quoted, but in truth no one knows what the gambling "turnover" and "take" actually is, nor how much is bet legally (pari-mutuel, etc.) and how much illegally. In fact, the figure cited by the committee was arbitrary and arrived at quite sloppily. As one staff member said: "We had no real idea of the money spent. ... The California crime commission said twelve billion. Virgil Peterson of Chicago estimated thirty billion. We picked twenty billion as a balance between the two."

If comprehensive data are not available, we do know, from specific instances, the magnitude of many of the operations. Some indications can be seen from these items culled at random:

—James Carroll and M & G syndicate did a 20-million-dollar annual business in St. Louis. This was one of the two large books in the city.

—The S & G syndicate in Miami did a 26-million-dollar volume yearly; the total for all books in the Florida resort reached 40 millions.

—Slot machines were present in 69,786 establishments in 1951 (each paid $100 for a license to the Bureau of Internal Revenue); the usual average is three machines to a license, which would add up to 210,000 slot machines in operation in the United States. In legalized areas, where the betting is higher and more regular, the average gross "take" per machine is $50 a week.

—The largest policy wheel (i.e., "numbers") in Chicago's "Black Belt" reported taxable net profits for the four-year period from 1946 through 1949, after sizable deductions for "overhead," of $3,656,968. One of the large "white" wheels reported in 1947 a gross income of $2,317,000 and a net profit of $205,000. One CIO official estimated that perhaps 15 per cent of his union's lower echelon officials are involved in the numbers racket (a steward, free to roam a plant, is in a perfect situation for organizing bets).

If one considers the amount of betting on sports alone—an estimated six billion on baseball, a billion on football pools, another billion on basketball, six billion on horse racing—then Elmo Roper's judgment that "only the food, steel, auto, chemical, and machine-tool industries have a greater volume of business" does not seem too far-fetched.

While gambling has long flourished in the United States, the influx of the big mobsters into the industry—and its expansion—started in the '30's when repeal of Prohibition forced them to look about for new avenues of enterprise. Gambling, which had begun to flower under the nourishment of rising incomes, was the most lucrative field in sight. To a large extent the shift from bootlegging to gambling was a mere transfer of business operations. In the East, Frank Costello went into slot machines and the operation of a number of ritzy gambling casinos. He also became the "banker" for the Erickson "book," which "laid off" bets for other bookies. Joe Adonis, similarly, opened up a number of casinos, principally in New Jersey. Across the country, many other mobsters went into bookmaking. As other rackets diminished, and gambling, particularly horse-race betting, flourished in the '40's, a struggle erupted over the control of racing information.

Horse-race betting requires a peculiar industrial organization. The essential component is time. A bookie can operate only if he can get information on odds up to the very last minute before the race, so that he can "hedge" or "lay off" bets. With racing going on simultaneously on many tracks throughout the country, this information has to be obtained speedily and accurately. Thus, the racing wire is the nerve ganglion of race betting.

The racing-wire news service got started in the '20's through the genius of the late Moe Annenberg, who had made a fearful reputation for himself as Hearst's circulation manager in the rough-and-tumble Chicago newspaper wars. Annenberg conceived the idea of a telegraphic news service which would gather information from tracks and shoot it immediately to scratch sheets, horse parlors, and bookie joints. In some instances, track owners gave Annenberg the rights to send news from tracks; more often, the news was simply "stolen" by crews operating inside or near the tracks. So efficient did this news distribution system become, that in 1942, when a plane knocked out a vital telegraph circuit which served an Air Force field as well as the gamblers, the Continental Press managed to get its racing wire service for gamblers resumed in fifteen minutes, while it took the Fourth Army, which was responsible for the defense of the entire West Coast, something like three hours.

Annenberg built up a nationwide racing information chain that not only distributed wire news but controlled sub-outlets as well. In 1939, harassed by the Internal Revenue Bureau on income tax, and chivvied by the Justice Department for "monopolistic" control of the wire service, the tired and aging Annenberg simply walked out of the business. He did not sell his interest, or even seek to salvage some profit; he simply gave up. Yet, like any established and thriving institution, the enterprise continued, though on a decentralized basis. James Ragen, Annenberg's operations manager, and likewise a veteran of the old Chicago circulation wars, took over the national wire service through a dummy friend and renamed it the Continental Press Service.

The salient fact is that in the operation of the Annenberg and Ragen wire service, formally illegal as many of its subsidiary operations may have been (i.e., in "stealing" news, supplying information to bookies, etc.) gangsters played no part. It was a business, illicit, true, but primarily a business. The distinction between gamblers and gangsters, as we shall see, is a relevant one.

In 1946, the Chicago mob, whose main interest was in bookmaking rather than gambling casinos, began to move in on the wire monopoly. Following repeal, the Capone lieutenants had turned, like Lepke, to labor racketeering. Murray ("The Camel") Humphries muscled in on the teamsters, the operating engineers, and the cleaning-and-dyeing, laundry, and linen-supply industries. Through a small-time punk, Willie Bioff, and union official George Browne, Capone's chief successors, Frank ("The Enforcer") Nitti and Paul Ricca, came into control of the motion-picture union and proceeded to shake down the movie industry for fabulous sums in order to "avert strikes." In 1943, when the government moved in and smashed the industrial rackets, the remaining big shots, Charley Fischetti, Jake Guzik, and Tony Accardo decided to concentrate on gambling, and in particular began a drive to take over the racing wire.

In Chicago, the Guzik-Accardo gang, controlling a sub-distributor of the racing news service, began tapping Continental's wires. In Los Angeles, the head of the local distribution agency for Continental was beaten up by hoodlums working for Mickey Cohen and Joe Sica. Out of the blue appeared a new and competitive nationwide racing information and distribution service, known as Trans-American Publishing, the money for which was advanced by the Chicago mobs and Bugsy Siegel, who, at the time, held a monopoly of the bookmaking and wire-news service in Las Vegas. Many books pulled out of Continental and bought information from the new outfit, many hedged by buying from both. At the end of a year, however, the Capone mob's wire had lost about $200,000. Ragen felt that violence would erupt and went to the Cook County district attorney and told him that his life had been threatened by his rivals. Ragen knew his competitors. In June 1946 he was killed by a blast from a shotgun.

Thereafter, the Capone mob abandoned Trans-American and got a "piece" of Continental. Through their new control of the national racing-wire monopoly, the Capone mob began to muscle in on the lucrative Miami gambling business run by the so-called S & G syndicate. For a long time S & G's monopoly over bookmaking had been so complete that when New York gambler Frank Erickson bought a three months' bookmaking concession at the expensive Roney Plaza Hotel, for $45,000, the local police, in a highly publicized raid, swooped down on the hotel; the next year the Roney Plaza was again using local talent. The Capone group, however, was tougher. They demanded an interest in Miami bookmaking, and, when refused, began organizing a syndicate of their own, persuading some bookies at the big hotels to join them. Florida Governor Warren's crime investigator appeared—a friend, it seemed, of old Chicago dog-track operator William Johnston, who had contributed $100,000 to the Governor's campaign fund —and began raiding bookie points, but only those that were affiliated with S & G. Then S & G, which had been buying its racing news from the local distributor of Continental Press, found its service abruptly shut off. For a few days the syndicate sought to bootleg information from New Orleans, but found itself limping along. After ten days' war of attrition, the five S & G partners found themselves with a sixth partner, who, for a token "investmen" of $20,000 entered a Miami business that grossed $26,000,000 in one year.

V

While Americans made gambling illegal, they did not in their hearts think of it as wicked—even the churches benefited from the bingo and lottery crazes. So they gambled—and gamblers flourished. Against this open canvas, the indignant tones of Senator Wiley and the shocked righteousness of Senator Tobey during the Kefauver investigation rang oddly. Yet it was probably this very tone of surprise that gave the activity of the Kefauver Committee its piquant quality. Here were some Senators who seemingly did not know the facts of life, as most Americans did. Here, in the person of Senator Tobey, was the old New England Puritan conscience poking around in industrial America, in a world it had made but never seen. Here was old-fashioned moral indignation, at a time when cynicism was rampart in public life.

Commendable as such moralistic fervor was, it did not make for intelligent discrimination of fact. Throughout the Kefauver hearings, for example, there ran the presumption that all gamblers, were invariably gangsters. This was true of Chicago's Accardo-Guzik combine, which in the past had its fingers in many kinds of rackets. It was not nearly so true to many of the large gamblers in America, most of whom had the feeling that they were satisfying a basic American urge for sport and looked upon their calling with no greater sense of guilt than did many bootleggers. After all, Sherman Billingsley did start out as a speak-easy proprietor, as did the Kreindlers of the "21" Club; and today the Stork Club and the former Jack and Charlie's are the most fashionable night and dining spots in America (one prominent patron of the Stork Club: J. Edgar Hoover).

The S & G syndicate in Miami, for example (led by Harold Salvey, Jules Levitt, Charles Friedman, Sam Cohen, and Edward (Eddie Luckey) Rosenbaum was simply a master pool of some two hundred bookies that arranged for telephone service, handled "protection," acted as bankers for those who needed ready cash on hard-hit books, and, in short, functioned somewhat analogously to the large factoring corporations in the textile field or the credit companies in the auto industry. Yet to Kefauver, these S & G men were "slippery and arrogant characters.... Salvey, for instance, was an old-time bookie who told us he had done nothing except engage in bookmaking or finance other bookmakers for twenty years." When, as a result of committee publicity and the newly found purity of the Miami police, the S & G syndicate went out of business, it was, as the combine's lawyer told Kefauver, because the "boys" were weary of being painted "the worst monsters in the world." "It is true," Cohen acknowledged, "that they had been law violators." But they had never done anything worse than gambling, and "to fight the world isn't worth it."

Most intriguing of all were the opinions of James J. Carroll, the St. Louis "betting commissioner," who for years had been widely quoted on the sports pages of the country as setting odds on the Kentucky Derby winter book and the baseball pennant races. Senator Wiley, speaking like the prosecutor in Camus's novel, *The Stranger,* became the voice of official morality:

SENATOR WILEY: Have you any children?
MR. CARROLL: Yes, I have a boy.
SENATOR WILEY: How old is he?
MR. CARROLL: Thirty-three.
SENATOR WILEY: Does he gamble?
MR. CARROLL: No.
SENATOR WILEY: Would you like to see him grow up and become a gambler, either professional or amateur?
MR. CARROLL: No...
SENATOR WILEY: All right. Is your son interested in your business?
MR. CARROLL: No, he is a manufacturer.
SENATOR WILEY: Why do you not get him into the business?
MR. CARROLL: Well, psychologically a great many people are unsuited for gambling.

Retreating from this gambit, the Senator sought to pin Carroll down on his contributions to political campaigns:

SENATOR WILEY: Now this morning I asked you whether you contributed any money for political candidates or parties, and you said not more than $200 at any one time. I presume that does not indicate the total of your contributions in any one campaign, does it?
MR. CARROLL: Well, it might, might not, Senator. I have been an "againster" in many instances. I am a reader of *The Nation* for fifty years and they have advertisements calling for contributions for differ-

ent candidates, different cause.... They carried an advertisement for George Norris; I contributed, I think, to that, and to the elder La Follette.

Carroll, who admitted to having been in the betting business since 1899, was the sophisticated—but not immoral!—counterpoint to moralist Wiley. Here was a man without the stigmata of the underworld or underground; he was worldly, cynical of official rhetoric, jaundiced about people's motives, he was—an "againster" who believed that "all gambling legislation originates or stems from some group or some individual seeking special interests for himself or his cause."

Asked why people gamble, Carroll distilled his experiences of fifty years with a remark that deserves a place in American social history: "I really don't know how to answer the question," he said. "I think gambling is a biological necessity for certain types. I think it is the quality that gives substance to their daydreams."

In a sense, the entire Kefauver materials, unintentionally, seem to document that remark. For what the Committee revealed time and time again was a picture of gambling as a basic institution in American life, flourishing openly and accepted widely. In many of the small towns, the gambling joint is as open as a liquor establishment. The town of Havana, in Mason County, Illinois, felt miffed when Governor Adlai Stevenson intervened against local gambling. In 1950, the town had raised $15,000 of its $50,000 budget by making friendly raids on the gambling houses every month and having the owners pay fines. "With the gambling fines cut off," grumbled Mayor Clarence Chester, "the next year is going to be tough."

Apart from the gamblers, there were the mobsters. But what Senator Kefauver and company failed to understand was that the mobsters, like the gamblers, and like the entire gangdom generally, were seeking to become quasi-respectable and establish a place for themselves in American life. For the mobsters, by and large, had immigrant roots, and crime, as the pattern showed, was a route of social ascent and place in American life.

VI

The mobsters were able, where they wished, to "muscle in" on the gambling business because the established gamblers were wholly vulnerable, not being able to call on the law for protection. The Senators, however, refusing to make any distinction between a gambler and a gangster, found it convenient to talk loosely of a nationwide conspiracy of "illegal" elements. Senator Kefauver asserted that a "nationwide crime syndicate does exist in the United States, despite the protestations of a strangely assorted company of criminals, self-serving politicians, plain blind fools, and others who may be honestly misguided, that there is no such combine." The Senate Committee report states the matter more dogmatically: "There is a nationwide crime syndicate known as the Mafia.... Its leaders are usually found in control of the most lucrative rackets in their cities. There are indications of a centralized direction and control of these rackets.... The Mafia is the cement that helps to bind the Costello-Adonis-Lansky syndicate of New York and the Accardo-Guzik-Fischetti syndicate of Chicago.... These groups have kept in touch with Luciano since his deportation from the country."

Unfortunately for a good story—and the existence of the Mafia would be a whale of a story—neither the Senate Crime Committee in its testimony, nor Kefauver in his book, presented any real evidence that the Mafia exists as a functioning organization. One finds police officials asserting before the Kefauver committee their *belief* in the Mafia; the Narcotics Bureau *thinks* that a worldwide dope ring allegedly run by Luciano is part of the Mafia; but the only other "evidence" presented—aside from the incredulous responses both of Senator Kefauver and Rudolph Halley when nearly all the Italian gangsters asserted that they didn't know about the Mafia—is that certain crimes bear "the earmarks of the Mafia."

The legend of the Mafia has been fostered in recent years largely by the peephole writing team of Jack Lait and Lee Mortimer. In their *Chicago Confidential,* they rattled off a series of names and titles that made the organization sound like a rival to an Amos and Andy Kingfish society. Few serious reporters, however, give it much credence. Burton Turkus, the Brooklyn prosecutor who broke up the "Murder, Inc." ring, denies the existence of the Mafia. Nor could Senator Kefauver even make out much of a case for his picture of a national crime syndicate. He is forced to admit that "as it exists today [it] is an elusive and furtive but nonetheless tangible thing," and that "its organization and machinations are not always easy to pinpoint." His "evidence" that many gangsters congregate at certain times of the year in such places as Hot Springs, Arkansas, in itself does not prove much; people "in the trade" usually do, and as the loquacious late Willie Moretti of New Jersey said, in explaining how he had met the late Al Capone at a race track, "Listen, well-charactered people you don't need introductions to; you just meet automatically."

Why did the Senate Crime Committee pump so hard for its theory of the Mafia and a national crime syndicate? In part, they may have been misled by their own hearsay. The Senate Committee was not in the position to do original research, and its staff, both legal and investigative, was incredibly small. Senator Kefauver had begun the investigation with the attitude that with so much smoke there must be a raging fire. But smoke can also mean a smoke screen. Mob activities is a field in which busy gossip and exaggeration flourish even more readily than in a radical political sect.

There is, as well, in the American temper, a feeling that "somewhere," "somebody" is pulling all the complicated strings to which this jumbled world dances. In politics the labor image is "Wall Street," or "Big Business"; while the business stereotype was the "New Dealers." In the field of crime, the side-of-the-mouth lowdown was "Costello."

The salient reason, perhaps, why the Kefauver Committee was taken in by its own myth of an omnipotent Mafia and a despotic Costello was its failure to assimilate and understand three of the more relevant sociological facts about institutionalized crime in its relation to the political life of large urban communities in America, namely: (1) the rise of the American Italian community, as part of the inevitable process of ethnic succession, to positions of importance in politics, a process that has been occurring independently but almost simultaneously in most cities with large Italian constituencies—New York, Chicago, Kansas City, Los Angeles; (2) the fact that there are individual Italians who play prominent, often leading roles today in gambling and in the mobs; and (3) the fact that Italian gamblers and mobsters often possessed "status" within the Italian community itself and a "pull" in city politics.[1] These three items are indeed related—but not so as to form a "plot."

---

[1] Toward the end of his hearings, Senator Kefauver read a telegram from an indignant citizen of Italian descent, protesting against the impression the committee had created that organized crime in America was a distinctly Italian enterprise. The Senator took the occasion to state the obvious: that there are racketeers who are Italian does not mean that Italians are racketeers. However, it may be argued that to the extent the Kefauver Committee fell for the line about crime in America being organized and controlled by the Mafia, it did foster such a misunderstanding. Perhaps this is also the place to point out that insofar as the relation of ethnic groups and ethnic problems to illicit and quasi-legal activities is piously ignored, the field is left open to the kind of vicious sensationalism practiced by Mortimer and Lait.

VII

The Italian community has achieved wealth and political influence much later and in a harder way than previous immigrant groups. Early Jewish wealth, that of the German Jews of the late nineteenth century, was made largely in banking and merchandising. To that extent, the dominant group in the Jewish community was outside of, and independent of, the urban political machines. Later Jewish wealth, among the East European immigrants, was built in the garment trades, though with some involvement with the Jewish gangster, who was typically an industrial racketeer (Arnold Rothstein, Lepke and Gurrah, etc.). Among Jewish lawyers, a small minority, such as the "Tammany lawyer" (like the protagonist of Sam Ornitz's *Haunch, Paunch* and *Jowl*) rose through politics and occasionally touched the fringes of crime. Most of the Jewish lawyers, by and large the communal leaders, climbed rapidly, however, in the opportunities that established and legitimate Jewish wealth provided. Irish immigrant wealth in the northern urban centers, concentrated largely in construction, trucking and the waterfront, has, to a substantial extent, been wealth accumulated in and through political alliance, e.g. favoritism in city contracts.[2] Control of the politics of the city thus has been crucial for the continuance of Irish political wealth. This alliance of Irish immigrant wealth and politics has been reciprocal; many noted Irish political figures lent their names as important window-dressing for business corporations (Al Smith, for example, who helped form the U.S. Trucking Corporation, whose executive head for many years was William J. McCormack, the alleged "Mr. Big" of the New York waterfront) while Irish businessmen have lent their wealth to further the careers of Irish politicians. Irish mobsters have rarely achieved status in the Irish community, but have served as integral arms of the politicians, as strong-arm men on election day.

The Italians found the more obvious big city paths from rags to riches pre-empted. In part this was due to the character of the early Italian immigration. Most of them were unskilled and from rural stock. Jacob Riis could remark in the '90's, "the Italian comes in at the bottom and stays there." These dispossessed agricultural laborers found jobs as ditch-diggers, on the railroads as section hands, along the docks, in the service occupations, as shoemakers, barbers, garment workers, and stayed there. Many were fleeced by the "padrone" system, a few achieved wealth from truck farming, wine growing, and marketing produce; but this "marginal wealth" was not the source of coherent and stable political power.

Significantly, although the number of Italians in the U.S. is about a third as high as the number of Irish, and of the 30,000,000 Catholic communicants in the United States, about half are of Irish descent and a sixth of Italian, there is not one Italian bishop among the hundred Catholic bishops in this country, or one Italian archbishop among the 21 archbishops. The Irish have a virtual monopoly. This is a factor related to the politics of the American church; but the condition also is possible because there is not significant or sufficient wealth among Italian Americans to force some parity.

The children of the immigrants, the second and third generation, became wise in the ways of the urban slums. Excluded from the political ladder—in the early '30's there were almost no Italians on the city payroll in top jobs, nor in books of the period can one find discussion of Italian

---

[2] A fact which should occasion little shock if one recalls that in the nineteenth century American railroads virtually stole 190,000,000 acres of land by bribing Congressmen, and that more recently such scandals as the Teapot Dome oil grabs during the Harding administration, consummated, as the Supreme Court said, "by means of conspiracy, fraud and bribery," reached to the very doors of the White House.

political leaders—finding few open routes to wealth, some turned to illicit ways. In the children's court statistics of the 1930's, the largest group of delinquents were the Italian; nor were there any Italian communal or social agencies to cope with these problems. Yet it was, oddly enough, the quondam racketeer, seeking to become respectable, who provided one of the major supports for the drive to win a political voice for Italians in the power structure of the urban political machines.

This rise of the Italian political bloc was connected, at least in the major northern urban centers, to another important development which tended to make the traditional relation between the politician and the protected or tolerated illicit operator more close than it had been in the past. This is the fact that the urban political machines had to evolve new forms of fund-raising since the big business contributions, which once went heavily into municipal politics, now—with the shift in the locus of power—go largely into national affairs. (The ensuing corruption in national politics, as recent Congressional investigations show, is no petty matter; the scruples of businessmen do not seem much superior to those of the gamblers.) One way urban political machines raised their money resembled that of the large corporations which are no longer dependent on Wall Street: by self-financing—that is, by "taxing" the large number of municipal employees who bargain collectively with City Hall for their wage increases. So the firemen's union contributed money to O'Dwyer's campaign.

A second method was taxing the gamblers. The classic example, as *Life* reported, was Jersey City, where a top lieutenant of the Hague machine spent his full time screening applicants for unofficial bookmaking licenses. If found acceptable, the applicant was given a "location," usually the house or store of a loyal precinct worker, who kicked into the machine treasury a high proportion of the large rent exacted. The one thousand bookies and their one thousand landlords in Jersey City formed the hard core of the political machine that sweated and bled to get out the votes for Hague.

A third source for the financing of these machines was the new, and often illegally earned, Italian wealth. This is well illustrated by the career of Costello and his emergence as a political power in New York. Here the ruling motive has been the search for an entrée—for oneself and one's ethnic group—into the ruling circles of the big city.

Frank Costello made his money originally in bootlegging. After repeal, his big break came when Huey Long, desperate for ready cash to fight the old-line political machines, invited Costello to install slot machines in Louisiana. Costello did, and he flourished. Together with Dandy Phil Kastel, he also opened the Beverly Club, an elegant gambling establishment just outside New Orleans, at which have appeared some of the top entertainers in America. Subsequently, Costello invested his money in New York real estate (including 79 Wall Street, which he later sold), the Copacabana night club, and a leading brand of Scotch whiskey.

Costello's political opportunity came when a money-hungry Tammany, starved by lack of patronage from Roosevelt and La Guardia, turned to him for financial support. The Italian community in New York has for years nursed a grievance against the Irish and, to a lesser extent, the Jewish political groups for monopolizing political power. They complained about the lack of judicial jobs, the small number —usually one—of Italian Congressmen, the lack of representation on the state tickets. But the Italians lacked the means to make their ambitions a reality. Although they formed a large voting bloc, there was rarely sufficient wealth to finance political clubs. Italian immigrants, largely poor peasants from Southern Italy and Sicily, lacked the mercantile experience of the Jews, and the political experience gained in the seventy-five-year history of Irish immigration.

During the Prohibition years, the Italian racketeers had made certain political contacts in order to gain protection. Costello, always the compromiser and fixer rather than the muscle-man, was the first to establish relations with Jimmy Hines, the powerful leader of the West Side in Tammany Hall. But his rival, Lucky Luciano, suspicious of the Irish, and seeking more direct power, backed and elected Al Marinelli for district leader on the Lower West Side. Marinelli in 1932 was the only Italian leader inside Tammany Hall. Later, he was joined by Dr. Paul Sarubbi, a partner of Johnny Torrio in a large, legitimate liquor concern. Certainly, Costello and Luciano represented no "unified" move by the Italians as a whole for power; within the Italian community there are as many divisions as in any other group. What is significant is that different Italians, for different reasons, and in various fashions, were achieving influence for the first time. Marinelli became county clerk of New York and a leading power in Tammany. In 1937, after being blasted by Tom Dewey, then running for district attorney, as a "political ally of thieves... and big-shot racketeers," Marinelli was removed from office by Governor Lehman. The subsequent conviction by Dewey of Luciano and Hines, and the election of La Guardia, left most of the Tammany clubs financially weak and foundering. This was the moment Costello made his move. In a few years, by judicious financing, he controlled a block of "Italian" leaders in the Hall—as well as some Irish on the upper West Side, and some Jewish leaders on the East Side—and was able to influence the selection of a number of Italian judges. The most notable incident, revealed by a wire tap on Costello's phone, was the "Thank you, Francisco" call in 1943 by Supreme Court nominee Thomas Aurelio, who gave Costello full credit for his nomination.

It was not only Tammany that was eager to accept campaign contributions from newly rich Italians, even though some of these *nouveaux riches* had "arrived" through bootlegging and gambling. Fiorello La Guardia, the wiliest mind that Melting Pot politics has ever produced, understood in the early '30's where much of his covert support came from. (So, too, did Vito Marcantonio, an apt pupil of the master: Marcantonio has consistently made deals with Italian leaders of Tammany Hall—in 1943 he supported Aurelio, and refused to repudiate him even when the Democratic Party formally did). Joe Adonis, who had built a political following during the late '20's, when he ran a popular speakeasy, aided La Guardia financially to a considerable extent in 1933. "The Democrats haven't recognized the Italians," Adonis told a friend. "There is no reason for the Italians to support anybody but La Guardia; the Jews have played ball with the Democrats and haven't gotten much out of it. They know it now. They will vote for La Guardia. So will the Italians."

Adonis played his cards shrewdly. He supported La Guardia, but also a number of Democrats for local and judicial posts, and became a power in the Brooklyn area. His restaurant was frequented by Kenny Sutherland, the Coney Island Democratic leader; Irwin Steingut, the Democratic minority leader in Albany; Anthony DiGiovanni, later a Councilman; William O'Dwyer, and Jim Moran. But, in 1937, Adonis made the mistake of supporting Royal Copeland against La Guardia, and the irate Fiorello finally drove Adonis out of New York.[3]

---

[3] Adonis, and associate Willie Moretti, moved across the river to Bergen County, New Jersey, where, together with the quondam racketeer Abner, "Longie" Zwillman, he became one of the political powers in the state. Gambling flourished in Bergen County for almost a decade but after the Kefauver investigation the state was forced to act. A special inquiry in 1953 headed by Nelson Stamler, revealed that Moretti had paid $286,000 to an aide of

La Guardia later turned his ire against Costello, too. Yet Costello survived and reached the peak of his influence in 1942, when he was instrumental in electing Michael Kennedy leader of Tammany Hall. Despite the Aurelio fiasco, which first brought Costello into notoriety, he still had sufficient power in the Hall to swing votes for Hugo Rogers as Tammany leader in 1945, and had a tight grip on some districts as late as 1948. In those years many a Tammany leader came hat in hand to Costello's apartment, or sought him out on the golf links, to obtain the nomination for a judicial post.

During this period, other Italian political leaders were also coming to the fore. Generoso Pope, whose Colonial Sand and Stone Company began to prosper through political contacts, became an important political figure, especially when his purchase of the two largest Italian-language dailies (later merged into one), and of a radio station, gave him almost a monopoly of channels to Italian-speaking opinion of the city. Through Generoso Pope, and through Costello, the Italians became a major political force in New York.

That the urban machines, largely Democratic, have financed their heavy campaign costs in this fashion rather than having to turn to the "moneyed interests," explains in some part why these machines were able, in part, to support the New and Fair Deals without suffering the pressures they might have been subjected to had their source of money supply been the business groups. Although he has never publicly revealed his political convictions, it is likely that Frank Costello was a fervent admirer of Franklin D. Roosevelt and his efforts to aid the common man. The basic measures of the New Deal, which most Americans today agree were necessary for the public good, would not have been possible without the support of the "corrupt" big-city machines.

VIII

There is little question that men of Italian origin appeared in most of the leading roles in the high drama of gambling and mobs, just as twenty years ago the children of East European Jews were the most prominent figures in organized crime, and before that individuals of Irish descent were similarly prominent. To some extent statistical accident and the tendency of newspapers to emphasize the few sensational figures gives a greater illusion about the domination of illicit activities by a single ethnic group than all the facts warrant. In many cities, particularly in the South and on the West Coast, the mob and gambling fraternity consisted of many other groups, and often, predominantly, native white Protestants. Yet it is clear that in the major northern urban centers there was a distinct ethnic sequence in the modes of obtaining illicit wealth, and that uniquely in the case of the recent Italian elements, the former bootleggers and gamblers provided considerable leverage for the growth of political influence as well. A substantial number of Italian judges sitting on the bench in New York today are indebted in one fashion or another to Costello; so too are many Italian district leaders—as well as some Jewish and Irish politicians. And the motive in establishing Italian political prestige in New York was generous rather than scheming for personal advantage. For Costello it was largely a case of ethnic pride. As in earlier American eras, organized illegality became a stepladder of social ascent.

To the world at large, the news and pictures of Frank Sinatra, for example, mingling with former Italian mobsters could come somewhat as a shock. Yet to Sinatra, and to many Italians, these were men who had grown up in their neighborhoods, and who were, in some instances,

---

Governor Driscoll for "protection" and that the Republican state committee had accepted a $25,000 "loan" from gambler Joseph Bozzo, an associate of Zwillman.

bywords in the community for their helpfulness and their charities. The early Italian gangsters were hoodlums—rough, unlettered, and young (Al Capone was only twenty-nine at the height of his power). Those who survived learned to adapt. By now they are men of middle age or older. They learned to dress conservatively. Their homes are in respectable suburbs. They sent their children to good schools and had sought to avoid publicity.[4] Costello even went to a psychiatrist in his efforts to overcome a painful feeling of inferiority in the world of manners.

As happens with all "new" money in American society, the rough and ready contractors, the construction people, trucking entrepreneurs, as well as racketeers, polished up their manners and sought recognition and respectability in their own ethnic as well as in the general community. The "shanty" Irish became the "lace curtain" Irish, and then moved out for wider recognition.[5] Sometimes acceptance came first in established "American" society, and this was a certificate for later recognition by the ethnic community, a process well illustrated by the belated acceptance in established Negro society of such figures as Sugar Ray Robinson and Joe Louis, as well as leading popular entertainers.

Yet, after all, the foundation of many a distinguished older American fortune was laid by sharp practices and morally reprehensible methods. The pioneers of American capitalism were not graduated from Harvard's School of Business Administration. The early settlers and founding fathers, as well as those who "won the west" and built up cattle, mining and other fortunes, often did so by shady speculations and a not inconsiderable amount of violence. They ignored, circumvented or stretched the law when it stood in the way of America's destiny, and their own—or, were themselves the law when it served their purposes. This has not prevented them and their descendants from feeling proper moral outrage when under the changed circumstances of the crowded urban environments later comers pursued equally ruthless tactics.

IX

Ironically, the social development which made possible the rise to political influence sounds, too, the knell of the Italian gangster. For it is the growing number of Italians with professional training and legitimate business success that both prompts and permits the Italian group to wield increasing political influence; and increasingly it is the professionals and businessmen who provide models for Italian youth today, models that hardly existed twenty years ago. Ironically, the headlines and exposés of "crime" of the Italian "gangsters" came years after the fact. Many of the top "crime" figures long ago had forsworn violence, and even their income, in large part, was derived from legitimate investments (real estate in the case of Costello, motor haulage and auto dealer franchises in the case of Adonis) or from such quasi-legitimate but socially respectable

---

[4] Except at times by being overly neighborly, like Tony Accardo who, at Yuletide 1949, in his elegant River Forest home, decorated a 40-foot tree on his lawn and beneath it set a wooden Santa and reindeer, while around the yard, on tracks, electrically operated skating figures zipped merrily around while a loud speaker poured out Christmas carols. The next Christmas, the Accardo lawn was darkened; Tony was on the lam from Kefauver.

[5] The role of ethnic pride in corralling minority group votes is one of the oldest pieces of wisdom in American politics; but what is more remarkable is the persistence of this identification through second and third generation descendants, a fact which, as Samuel Lubell noted in his *Future of American Politics,* was one of the explanatory keys to political behavior in recent elections. Although the Irish bloc as a solid Democratic bloc is beginning to crack, particularly as middle-class status impels individuals to identify more strongly with the G.O.P., the nomination in Massachusetts of Jack Kennedy for the United States Senate created a tremendous solidarity among Irish voters and Kennedy was elected over Lodge although Eisenhower swept the state.

sources as gambling casinos. Hence society's "retribution" in the jail sentences for Costello and Adonis was little more than a trumped-up morality that disguised a social hyprocrisy.

Apart from these considerations, what of the larger context of crime and the American way of life? The passing of the Fair Deal signalizes, oddly, the passing of an older pattern of illicit activities. The gambling fever of the past decade and a half was part of the flush and exuberance of rising incomes, and was characteristic largely of new upper-middle class rich having a first fling at conspicuous consumption. This upper-middle class rich, a significant new stratum in American life (not rich in the nineteenth century sense of enormous wealth, but largely middle-sized businessmen and entrepreneurs of the service and luxury trades—the "tertiary economy" in Colin Clark's phrase—who by the tax laws have achieved sizable incomes often much higher than the managers of the super-giant corporations) were the chief patrons of the munificent gambling casinos. During the war decade when travel was difficult, gambling and the lush resorts provided important outlets for this social class. Now they are settling down, learning about Europe and culture. The petty gambling, the betting and bingo which relieve the tedium of small town life, of the expectation among the urban slum dwellers of winning a sizable sum by a "lucky number" or a "lucky horse" goes on. To quote Bernard Baruch: "You can't stop people from gambling on horses. And why should you prohibit a man from backing his own judgment? It's another form of personal initiative." But the lush profits are passing from gambling, as the costs of coordination rise. And in the future it is likely that gambling, like prostitution, winning tacit acceptance as a necessary fact, will continue on a decentralized, small entrepreneur basis.

But passing, too, is a political pattern, the system of political "bosses" which in its reciprocal relation provided "protection" for and was fed from crime. The collapse of the "boss" system was a product of the Roosevelt era. Twenty years ago Jim Farley's task was simple; he had to work only on some key state bosses. Now there is no longer such an animal. New Jersey Democracy was once ruled by Frank Hague; now there are five or six men each top dog, for the moment, in his part of the state or faction of the party. Within the urban centers, the old Irish-dominated political machines in New York, Boston, Newark, and Chicago have fallen apart. The decentralization of the metropolitan centers, the growth of suburbs and satellite towns, the break-up of old ecological patterns of slum and transient belts, the rise of functional groups, the increasing middle-class character of American life, all contribute to this decline.

With the rationalization and absorption of some illicit activities into the structure of the economy, the passing of an older generation that had established a hegemony over crime, the general rise of minority groups to social position, and the break-up of the urban boss system, the pattern of crime we have discussed is passing as well. Crime, of course, remains as long as passion and the desire for gain remain. But big, organized city crime, as we have known it for the past seventy-five years, was based on more than these universal motives. It was based on certain characteristics of the American economy, American ethnic groups, and American politics. The changes in all these areas means that it too, in the form we have known it, is at an end.

19. LA COSA NOSTRA

NATIONAL SCOPE OF ORGANIZED CRIME

IN 1951 THE KEFAUVER COMMITTEE DECLARED that a nationwide crime syndicate known as the Mafia operated in many large cities and that the leaders of the Mafia usually controlled the most lucrative rackets in their cities.[1]

In 1957, 20 of organized crime's top leaders were convicted (later reversed on appeal)[2] of a criminal charge arising from a meeting at Apalachin, N.Y. At the sentencing the judge stated that they had sought to corrupt and infiltrate the political mainstreams of the country, that they had led double lives of crime and respectability, and that their probation reports read "like a tale of horrors."

Today the core of organized crime in the United States consists of 24 groups operating as criminal cartels in large cities across the Nation. Their membership is exclusively men of Italian descent, they are in frequent communication with each other, and their smooth functioning is insured by a national body of overseers.[3] To date, only the Federal Bureau of Investigation has been able to document fully the national scope of these groups, and FBI intelligence indicates that the organization as a whole has changed its name from the Mafia to La Cosa Nostra.

In 1966 J. Edgar Hoover told a House of Representatives Appropriations Subcommittee:

La Cosa Nostra is the largest organization of the criminal underworld in this country, very closely organized and strictly disciplined. They have committed almost every crime under the sun...

La Cosa Nostra is a criminal fraternity whose membership is Italian either by birth or national origin, and it has been found to control major racket activities in many of our larger metropolitan areas, often working in concert with criminals representing other ethnic backgrounds.

It operates on a nationwide basis, with international implications, and until recent years it carried on its activities with almost complete secrecy. It functions as a criminal cartel, adhering to its own body of "law" and "justice" and, in so doing, thwarts and usurps the authority of legally constituted judicial bodies...[4]

In individual cities, the local core group may also be known as the "outfit," the

▶SOURCE: *Task Force Report: Organized Crime, President's Commission on Law Enforcement and Administration of Justice, Washington, D.C.: 1967, pp. 6–10.*

[1] Kefauver Comm., *3d Interim Rep.*, S. Rep. No. 307, 82d Cong., 1st Sess. 150 (1951).

[2] United States v. Bufalino, 285 F.2d 408 (2d Cir. 1960).

[3] See testimony of J. Edgar Hoover, *Hearings Before the Subcomm. on Dep'ts of State Justice and Commerce, the Judiciary, and Related Agencies Appropriations of the House Comm. on Appropriations*, 89th Cong., 2d Sess. (1966) at 272–74.

[4] *Id.* at 272.

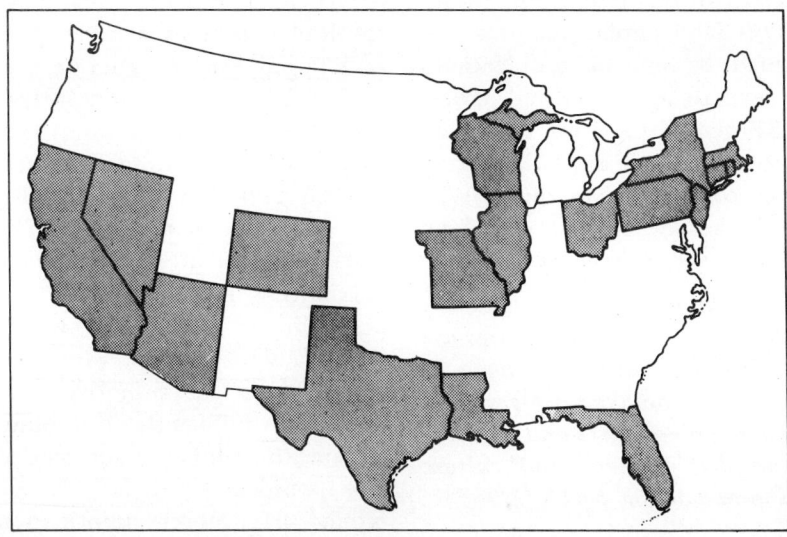

Figure 1. States in which organized crime core group members both reside and operate.

"syndicate," or the "mob." [5] These 24 groups work with and control other racket groups, whose leaders are of various ethnic derivations. In addition, the thousands of employees who perform the street-level functions of organized crime's gambling, usury, and other illegal activities represent a cross section of the Nation's population groups.

The present confederation of organized crime groups arose after Prohibition, during which Italian, German, Irish, and Jewish groups had competed with one another in racket operations. The Italian groups were successful in switching their enterprises from prostitution and bootlegging to gambling, extortion, and other illegal activities. They consolidated their power through murder and violence.[6]

Today, members of the 24 core groups reside and are active in the States shown on the map (Figure 1). The scope and effect of their criminal operations and penetration of legitimate businesses vary from area to area. The wealthiest and most influential core groups operate in States including New York, New Jersey, Illinois, Florida, Louisiana, Nevada, Michigan, and Rhode Island.[7] Not shown on the map are many States in which members of core groups control criminal activity even though they do not reside there. For example, a variety of illegal activities in New England is controlled from Rhode Island.[8]

Recognition of the common ethnic tie of the 5,000 or more members of organized crime's core groups [9] is essential to understanding the structure of these groups today. Some have been concerned that past identification of Cosa Nostra's ethnic char-

---

[5] See testimony of former New York City Police Comm'r Michael J. Murphy, McClellan, *Narcotics Hearings*, 88th Cong., 1st Sess., pt. 1, at 63 (1963); testimony of Capt. William Duffy, *id.* pt. 2, at 506; Office of the N.Y. Counsel to the Governor, Combating Organized Crime—A Report of the 1965 Oyster Bay, New York, Conferences on Combating Organized Crime 24 (1966).

[6] See generally Organized Crime in America 147–224 (Tyler ed. 1962).

[7] Information submitted to Commission by a Federal agency.

[8] *Ibid.*

[9] Testimony of J. Edgar Hoover, *Hearings Before the Subcomm. on Dep'ts of State, Justice, and Commerce, the Judiciary, and Related Agencies Appropriations of the House Comm. on Appropriations*, 89th Cong., 2d Sess. 273 (1966).

acter has reflected on Italian-Americans generally. This false implication was eloquently refuted by one of the Nation's outstanding experts on organized crime, Sgt. Ralph Salerno of the New York City Police Department. When an Italian-American racketeer complained to him, "Why does it have to be one of your own kind that hurts you?", Sgt. Salerno answered:

> I'm not your kind and you're not my kind. My manners, morals, and mores are not yours. The only thing we have in common is that we both spring from an Italian heritage and culture—and you are the traitor to that heritage and culture which I am proud to be part of.[10]

Organized crime in its totality thus consists of these 24 groups allied with other racket enterprises to form a loose confederation operating in large and small cities. In the core groups, because of their permanency of form, strength of organization and ability to control other racketeer operations, resides the power that organized crime has in America today.

INTERNAL STRUCTURE [11]

Each of the 24 groups is known as a "family," with membership varying from as many as 700 men to as few as 20. Most cities with organized crime have only one family; New York City has five. Each family can participate in the full range of activities in which organized crime generally is known to engage. Family organization is rationally designed with an integrated set of positions geared to maximize profits. Like any large corporation, the organization functions regardless of personnel changes, and no individual—not even the leader—is indispensable. If he dies or goes to jail, business goes on.

The heirarchical structure of the families resembles that of the Mafia groups that have operated for almost a century on the island of Sicily. Each family is headed by one man, the "boss," whose primary functions are maintaining order and maximizing profits. Subject only to the possibility of being overruled by the national advisory group, which will be discussed below, his authority in all matters relating to his family is absolute.

Beneath each boss is an "underboss," the vice president or deputy director of the family. He collects information for the boss; he relays messages to him and passes his instructions down to his own underlings. In the absence of the boss, the underboss acts for him.

On the same level as the underboss, but operating in a staff capacity, is the *consigliere*, who is a counselor, or adviser. Often an elder member of the family who has partially retired from a career in crime, he gives advice to family members, including the boss and underboss, and thereby enjoys considerable influence and power.

Below the level of the underboss are the *caporegime*, some of whom serve as buffers between the top members of the family and the lower-echelon personnel. To maintain their insulation from the police, the leaders of the hierarchy (particularly the boss) avoid direct communication with the workers. All commands, information, complaints, and money flow back and forth through a trusted go-between. A *caporegima* fulfilling this buffer capacity, however, unlike the underboss, does not make decisions or assume any of the authority of his boss.

Other *caporegime* serve as chiefs of operating units. The number of men supervised in each unit varies with the size and activities of particular families. Often the *caporegima* has one or two associates who work closely with him, carrying orders, in-

---

[10] Grutzner, City Police Expert on Mafia Retiring from Force, N.Y. Times, Jan. 21, 1967, p. 65, col. 3.

[11] For an extensive discussion of the internal structure of the organized crime groups, see Cressey, *The Functions and Structure of Criminal Syndicates*, Sept. 1966, at 31–40, printed as appendix A of *Task Force Report: Organized Crime*. See also McClellan, *Narcotics Hearings*, 88th Cong., 1st Sess., pts. 1 & 2 (1963), 1st & 2d Sess., pts. 3 & 4 (1963–64), 2d Sess., pt. 5 (1964).

formation, and money to the men who belong to his unit. From a business standpoint, the *caporegima* is analogous to plant supervisor or sales manager.

The lowest level "members" of a family are the *soldati*, the soldiers or "button" men who report to the *caporegime*. A soldier may operate a particular illicit enterprise, *e.g.*, a loan-sharking operation, a dice game, a lottery, a bookmaking operation, a smuggling operation, on a commission basis, or he may "own" the enterprise and pay a portion of its profit to the organization, in return for the right to operate. Partnerships are common between two or more soldiers and between soldiers and men higher up in the hierarchy. Some soldiers and most upper-echelon family members have interests in more than one business.

Beneath the soldiers in the hierarchy are large numbers of employees and commission agents who are not members of the family and are not necessarily of Italian descent. These are the people who do most of the actual work in the various enterprises. They have no buffers or other insulation from law enforcement. They take bets, drive trucks, answer telephones, sell narcotics, tend the stills, work in the legitimate businesses. For example, in a major lottery business that operated in Negro neighborhoods in Chicago, the workers were Negroes; the bankers for the lottery were Japanese-Americans; but the game, including the banking operation, was licensed, for a fee, by a family member.[12]

The structure and activities of a typical family are shown in Figure 2.

There are at least two aspects of organized crime that characterize it as a unique form of criminal activity. The first is the element of corruption. The second is the element of enforcement, which is necessary for the maintenance of both internal discipline and the regularity of business transactions. In the hierarchy of organized crime there are positions for people fulfilling both of these functions. But neither is essential to the long-term operation of other types of criminal groups. The members of a pickpocket troupe or check-passing ring, for example, are likely to take punitive action against any member who holds out more than his share of the spoils, or betrays the group to the police; but they do not recruit or train for a well-established position of "enforcer."

Organized crime groups, on the other hand, are believed to contain one or more fixed positions for "enforcers," whose duty it is to maintain organizational integrity by arranging for the maiming and killing of recalcitrant members. And there is a position for a "corrupter," whose function is to establish relationships with those public officials and other influential persons whose assistance is necessary to achieve the organization's goals.[13] By including these positions within its organization, each criminal cartel, or "family," becomes a government [14] as well as a business.

The highest ruling body of the 24 families is the "commission." This body serves as a combination legislature, supreme court, board of directors, and arbitration board; its principal functions are judicial. Family members look to the commission as the ultimate authority on organizational and jurisdictional disputes. It is composed of the bosses of the Nation's most powerful families but has authority over all 24. The composition of the commission varies from

---

[12] Information submitted to Commission by a Federal agency.

[13] Federal agency intelligence indicates that the *consigiliere* frequently acts as the "corrupter." In this connection, the Kefauver Committee underscored the sinister influence Frank Costello exercised upon the New York County Democratic organization. Kefauver Comm., *3d Interim Rep.*, S. Rep. No. 307, 82d Cong., 1st Sess. 143–44 (1951).

[14] "[I]n effect organized crime constitutes a kind of private government whose power rivals and often supplants that of elected public government." Moynihan, *The Private Government of Organized Crime,* The Reporter, July 6, 1961, p. 10.

184   THEORY AND EVIDENCE

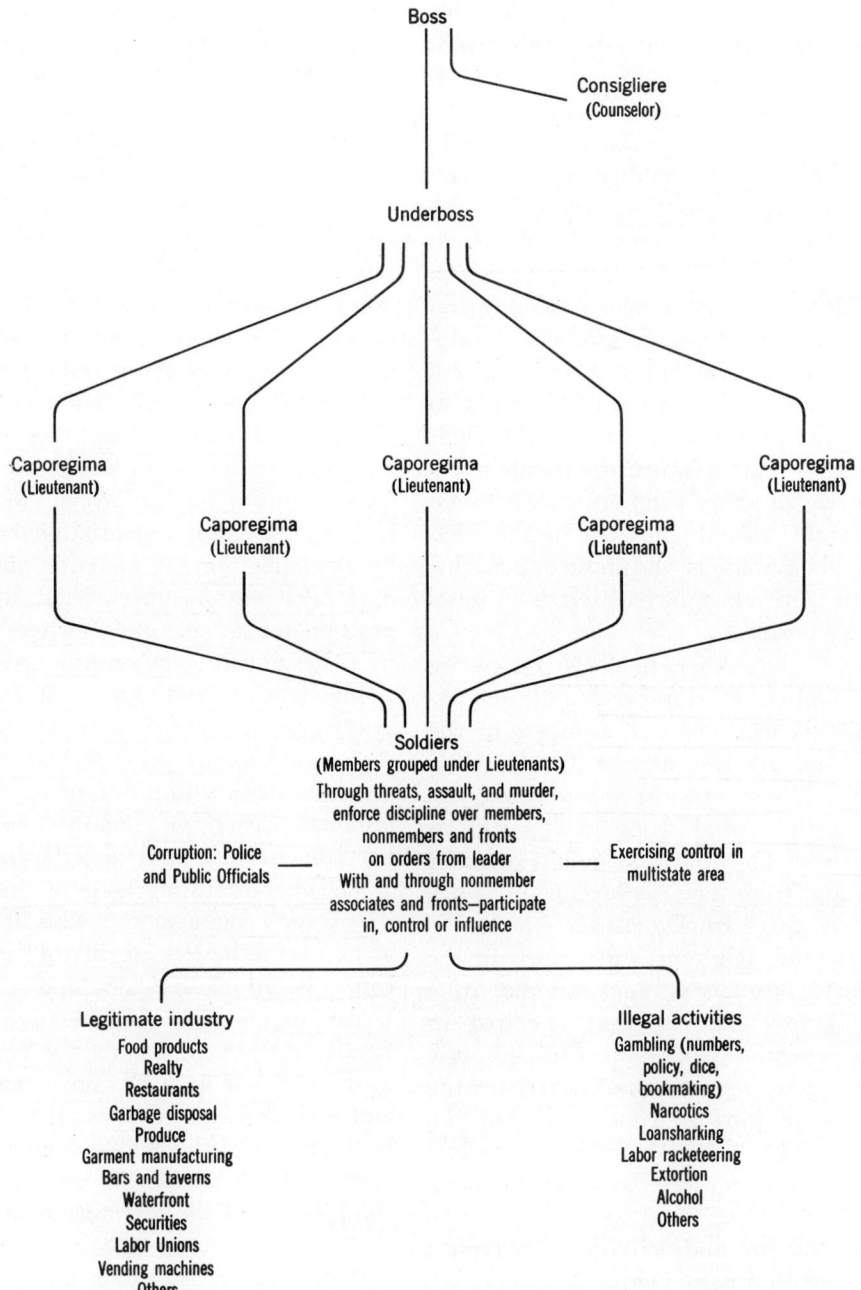

Figure 2. An organized crime family.

9 to 12 men. According to current information, there are presently 9 families represented, 5 from New York City and 1 each from Philadelphia, Buffalo, Detroit, and Chicago.[15]

The commission is not a representative legislative assembly or an elected judicial body. Members of this council do not regard each other as equals. Those with long tenure on the commission and those who head large families, or possess unusual wealth, exercise greater authority and receive utmost respect. The balance of power on this nationwide council rests with the leaders of New York's 5 families. They have always served on the commission and consider New York as at least the unofficial headquarters of the entire organization.

In recent years organized crime has become increasingly diversified and sophisticated. One consequence appears to be significant organizational restructuring. As in any organization, authority in organized crime may derive either from rank based on incumbency in a high position or from expertise based on possession of technical knowledge and skill. Traditionally, organized crime groups, like totalitarian governments, have maintained discipline through the unthinking acceptance of orders by underlings who have respected the rank of their superiors. However, since 1931, organized crime has gained power and respectability by moving out of bootlegging and prostitution and into gambling, usury, and control of legitimate business. Its need for expertise, based on technical knowledge and skill, has increased. Currently both the structure and operation of illicit enterprises reveal some indecision brought about by attempting to follow both patterns at the same time. Organized crime's "experts" are not fungible, or interchangeable, like the "soldiers" and street workers, and since experts are included within an organization, discipline and structure inevitably assume new forms. It may be awareness of these facts that is leading many family members to send their sons to universities to learn business administration skills.

As the bosses realize that they cannot handle the complicated problems of business and finance alone, their authority will be delegated. Decisionmaking will be decentralized, and individual freedom of action will tend to increase. New problems of discipline and authority may occur if greater emphasis on expertise within the ranks denies unskilled members of the families an opportunity to rise to positions of leadership. The unthinking acceptance of rank authority may be difficult to maintain when experts are placed above long-term, loyal soldiers. Primarily because of fear of infiltration by law enforcement, many of the families have not admitted new members for several years. That fact plus the increasing employment of personnel with specialized and expert functions may blur the lines between membership and nonmembership. In organized crime, internal rebellion would not take the form of strikes and picketing. It would bring a new wave of internal violence.

---

[15] Information submitted to Commission by a Federal agency.

20. THE CONFLICT OF CONDUCT NORMS

THORSTEN SELLIN

CONFLICTS OF CULTURAL CODES

CONFLICTS OF CONDUCT NORMS MAY ARISE IN a different manner from that just described. There are social groups on the surface of the earth which possess complexes of conduct norms which, due to differences in the mode of life and the social values evolved by these groups, appear to set them apart from other groups in many or most respects. We may expect conflicts of norms when the rural dweller moves to the city, but we assume that he has absorbed the basic norms of the culture which comprises both town and country. How much greater is not the conflict likely to be when Orient and Occident meet, or when the Corsican mountaineer is transplanted to the lower East Side of New York. Conflicts of cultures are inevitable when the norms of one cultural or subcultural area migrate to or come in contact with those of another, and it is interesting to note that most of the specific researches on culture conflict and delinquency have been concerned with this aspect of conflict rather than the one mentioned earlier.

Conflicts between the norms of divergent cultural codes may arise

(1) when these codes clash on the border of contiguous culture areas;
(2) when, as may be the case with legal norms, the law of one cultural group is extended to cover the territory of another; or
(3) when members of one cultural group migrate to another.[1]

Speck, for instance, notes that

Where the bands popularly known as Montagnais have come more and more into contact with Whites, their reputation has fallen lower among the traders, who have known them through commercial relationships within that period. The accusation is made that they have become less honest in connection with their debts, less trustworthy with property, less truthful, and more inclined to alcoholism and sexual freedom as contacts with the frontier towns have become easier for them. Richard White reports in 1933 unusual instances of Naskapi breaking into traders' store houses.[2]

Similar illustrations abound in the works of the cultural anthropologists. We need only to recall the effect on the American Indian of the culture conflicts induced by our policy of acculturation by guile and force. In this instance, it was not merely

▶SOURCE: *Culture Conflict and Crime,* New York: Social Science Research Council, 1938, pp. 63–70. Reprinted by permission of the Social Science Research Council.

[1] This is unfortunately not the whole story, for with the rapid growth of impersonal communication, the written (press, literature) and the spoken word (radio, talkie), knowledge concerning divergent conduct norms no longer grows solely out of direct personal contact with their carriers. And out of such conflicts grow some violations of customs and of law which would not have occurred without them.

[2] Speck, Frank G. "Ethical Attributes of the Labrador Indians," *American Anthropologist,* N.S. 35:559–94. October-December, 1933. P. 559.

contact wtih the white man's culture, his religion, his business methods, and his liquor, which weakened the tribal mores. In addition, the Indian became subject to the white man's law and this brought conflicts as well, as has always been the case when legal norms have been imposed upon a group previously ignorant of them. Maunier,[3] in discussing the diffusion of French law in Algeria, recently stated:

In introducing the *Code Pénal* in our colonies, as we do, we transform into offenses the ancient usages of the inhabitants which their customs permitted or imposed. Thus, among the Khabyles of Algeria, the killing of adulterous wives is ritual murder committed by the father or brother of the wife and not by her husband, as elsewhere. The woman having been sold by her family to her husband's family, the honor of her relatives is soiled by her infidelity. Her father or brother has the right and the duty to kill her in order to cleanse by her blood the honor of her relatives. Murder in revenge is also a duty, from family to family, in case of murder of or even in case of insults to a relative: the vendetta, called the *rekba* in Khabylian, is imposed by the law of honor. But these are crimes in French law! Murder for revenge, being premeditated and planned, is assassination, punishable by death! . . . What happens, then, often when our authorities pursue the criminal, guilty of an offense against public safety as well as against morality: public enemy of the French order, but who has acted in accord with a respected custom? The witnesses of the assassination, who are his relatives, or neighbors, fail to lay charges against the assassin; when they are questioned, they pretend to know nothing; and the pursuit is therefore useless. A French magistrate has been able to speak of the conspiracy of silence among the Algerians; a conspiracy aiming to preserve traditions, always followed and obeyed, against their violation by our power. This is the tragic aspect of the conflict of laws. A recent decree forbids the husband among the Khabyles to profit arbitrarily by the power given him according to this law to repudiate his wife, demanding that her new husband pay an exhorbitant price for her—this is the custom of the *lefdi*. Earlier, one who married a repudiated wife paid nothing to the former husband. It appears that the first who tried to avail himself of the new law was killed for violating the old custom. The abolition of the ancient law does not always occur without protest or opposition. That which is a crime was a duty; and the order which we cause to reign is sometimes established to the detriment of "superstition"; it is the gods and the spirits, it is believed, that would punish any one who fails to revenge his honor.

When Soviet law was extended to Siberia, similar effects were observed. Anossow[4] and Wirschubski[5] both relate that women among the Siberian tribes, who in obedience to the law, laid aside their veils were killed by their relatives for violating one of the most sacred norms of their tribes.

The relations between delinquency and the migration of the members of one cultural group to the area of another will be discussed later in this chapter.

We have noted that culture conflicts are the natural outgrowth of processes of social differentiation, which produce an infinity of social groupings, each with its own definitions of life situations, its own interpretations of social relationships, its own ignorance or misunderstanding of the social values of other groups. The transformation of a culture from a homogeneous and well-integrated type to a heterogeneous and disintegrated type is therefore accompanied by an increase of conflict situations. Conversely, the operation of integrating processes will reduce the number of conflict

---

[3] Maunier, René. "La diffusion du droit français en Algérie." Harvard Tercentenary Publications, *Independence, Convergence, and Borrowing in Institutions, Thought, and Art.* Cambridge: Harvard University Press, 1937. Pp. 84–85.

[4] Anossow, J. J. "Die volkstümlichen Verbrechen im Strafkodex der USSR." *Monatsschrift für Kriminalpsychologie und Strafrechtsreform.* 24: 534–37. September 1933.

[5] Wirschubski, Gregor. "Der Schutz der Sittlichkeit im Sowjetstrafrecht." *Zeitschrift für die gesamte Strafrechtswissenschaft.* 51:317–28. 1931.

situations. Such conflicts within a changing culture may be distinguished from those created when different cultural systems come in contact with one another, regardless of the character or stage of development of these systems. In either case, the conduct of members of a group involved in the conflict of codes will in some respects be judged abnormal by the other group.

THE STUDY OF CULTURE CONFLICTS

In the study of culture conflicts, some scholars have been concerned with the effect of such conflicts on the conduct of specific persons, an approach which is naturally preferred by psychologists and psychiatrists and by sociologists who have used the life history technique. These scholars view the conflict as internal. Wirth [6] states categorically that a culture "conflict can be said to be a factor in delinquency only if the individual feels it or acts as if it were present." Culture conflict is mental conflict, but the character of this conflict is viewed differently by the various disciplines which use this term. Freudian psychiatrists [7] regard it as a struggle between deeply rooted biological urges which demand expression and the culturally created rules which give rise to inhibitive mechanisms which thwart this expression and drive them below the conscious level of the mind, whence they rise either by ruse in some socially acceptable disguise, as abnormal conduct when the inhibiting mechanism breaks down, or as neuroses when it works too well. The sociologist, on the other hand, thinks of mental conflict as being primarily the clash between antagonistic conduct norms incorporated in personality. "Mental conflict in the person," says Burgess in discussing the case presented by Shaw in *The Jack-Roller*, "may always be explained in terms of the conflict of divergent cultures." [8]

If this view is accepted, sociological research on culture conflict and its relationships to abnormal conduct would have to be strictly limited to a study of the personality of cultural hybrids. Significant studies could be conducted only by the life-history case technique applied to persons in whom the conflict is internalized, appropriate control groups being utilized, of course. [Only studies of persons falling within the "reduced group resistance" category (III) in the schema presented in Sellin's Ch. II would produce theological generalizations of relevancy to the prom of causation. *Eds.*]

The absence of mental conflict, in the sociological sense, may, however, be well studied in terms of culture conflict. An example may make this clear. A few years ago a Sicilian father in New Jersey killed the sixteen-year-old seducer of his daughter, expressing surprise at his arrest since he had merely defended his family honor in a traditional way. In this case a mental conflict in the sociological sense did not exist. The conflict was external and occurred between cultural codes or norms. We may assume that where such conflicts occur violations of norms will arise merely because persons who have absorbed the norms of one cultural group or area migrate to another and that such conflict will continue so long as the acculturation process has not been completed. [See subcategories [b] and [c] in schema in Sellin's Ch. II. *Eds.*] Only then may the violations be regarded in terms of mental conflict.

---

[6] Wirth, Louis. "Culture Conflict and Misconduct." *Social Forces*. 9:484–92. June 1931. P. 490. Cf. Allport, Floyd H. "Culture Conflict versus the Individual as Factors in Delinquency." *Ibid.* Pp. 493–97.

[7] White, William A. *Crime and Criminals*. New York: Farrar & Rinehart. 1933. Healy, William. *Mental Conflict and Misconduct*. Boston: Little, Brown & Co. 1917. Alexander, Franz and Healy, William. *Roots of Crime*. New York: Alfred A. Knopf. 1935.

[8] Burgess, Ernest W. in Clifford R. Shaw's *The Jack-Roller*. Chicago: University of Chicago Press. 1930. Pp. 184–197, p. 186.

If culture conflict may be regarded as sometimes personalized, or mental, and sometimes as occurring entirely in an impersonal way solely as a conflict of group codes, it is obvious that research should not be confined to the investigation of mental conflicts and that contrary to Wirth's categorical statement that it is impossible to demonstrate the existence of a culture conflict "objectively . . . by a comparison between two cultural codes," [9] this procedure has not only a definite function, but may be carried out by researches employing techniques which are familiar to the sociologist.

The emphasis on the life history technique has grown out of the assumption that "the experiences of one person at the same time reveals the life activities of his group" and that "habit in the individual is an expression of custom in society." [10] This is undoubtedly one valid approach. Through it we may hope to discover generalizations of a scientific nature by studying persons who (1) have drawn their norms of conduct from a variety of groups with conflicting norms, or who (2) possess norms drawn from a group whose code is in conflict with that of the group which judges the conduct. In the former case alone can we speak of mental or internal culture conflict; in the latter, the conflict is external.

If the conduct norms of a group are, with reference to a given life situation, inconsistent, or if two groups possess inconsistent norms, we may assume that the members of these various groups will individually reflect such group attitudes. Paraphrasing Burgess, the experiences of a group will reveal the life activities of its members. While these norms can, no doubt, be best established by a study of a sufficient number of representative group members, they may for some groups at least be fixed with sufficient certainty to serve research purposes by a study of the social institutions, the administration of justice, the novel, the drama, the press, and other expressions of group attitudes. The identification of the groups in question having been made, it might be possible to determine to what extent such conflicts are reflected in the conduct of their members. Comparative studies based on the violation rates of the members of such groups, the trends of such rates, etc., would dominate this approach to the problem.

In conclusion, then, culture conflict may be studied either as mental conflict or as a conflict of cultural codes. The criminologist will naturally tend to concentrate on such conflicts between legal and nonlegal conduct norms. The concept of conflict fails to give him more than a general framework of reference for research. In practice, it has, however, become nearly synonymous with conflicts between the norms of cultural systems or areas. Most researches which have employed it have been done on immigrant or race groups in the United States, perhaps due to the ease with which such groups may be identified, the existence of more statistical data recognizing such groupings, and the conspicuous differences between some immigrant norms and our norms.

---

[9] Wirth, Louis. *Op. cit.* P. 490. It should be noted that Wirth also states that culture should be studied "on the objective side" and that "the sociologist is not primarily interested in personality but in culture."

[10] Burgess, Ernest W. *Op. cit.* P. 186.

21. THE CONFLICT OF VALUES IN DELINQUENCY AREAS

SOLOMON KOBRIN

THE CIRCUMSTANCE THAT LESS THAN ONE-quarter of the boys in the urban areas of high rates of delinquents are brought into the juvenile court charged as delinquents appears to invalidate the hypothesis that in the disorganized city areas delinquency is primarily a product of cultural rather than of personality or psychological processes.[1] Some of the official statistics of delinquency seem to suggest that most children conform to the legal norms of the wider society even in those urban areas where the culture of the local community is relatively favorable to the transmission of delinquent conduct patterns.[2] These statistics therefore leave the inference that even in this situation variables other than culture are of possibly greater importance in delinquency causation than the customary sociological explanations would concede.

While the literature of juvenile delinquency is replete with discussions of the inadequacy of delinquency statistics in general as a basis for measuring the extent of officially proscribed behavior in the larger administrative areas,[3] the present

▶SOURCE: "The Conflict of Values in Delinquency Areas," *American Sociological Review* (October, 1951), 16:653–661. Reprinted by permission.

[1] The ecological studies of Shaw and McKay in Chicago show that the proportion of juvenile court age boys on whom delinquency petitions were filed in the highest rate square mile areas were: for the 1917–1923 series, 19.4 per cent; for the 1927–1933 series, 18.9 per cent; and for the 1934–1940 series, 21.8 per cent. C. R. Shaw and Henry D. McKay, *Juvenile Delinquency and Urban Areas*, Chicago: University of Chicago Press, 1942, pp. 53 and 59. The figure for the 1934–1940 series is based on unpublished material by the same authors.

[2] Tappan observes that these statistics indicate that "most people living in such associations and under such social and psychological influences as those of the deteriorated slum do not violate the law." Paul W. Tappan, *Juvenile Delinquency*, New York: McGraw-Hill Book Co., 1949, p. 142. The ambivalence of many students in this field regarding the validity of delinquency statistics as a basis for judgments about the extent of proscribed behavior among children is revealed in the same author's assertion which appears earlier in the same work that "statistical data on the volume of delinquency give no valid picture of its actual extent." *Ibid.*, p. 37.

[3] Among recent evaluations of this problem are: Negley K. Teeters and John O. Reinemann, *The Challenge of Delinquency*, New York: Prentice-Hall, Inc., 1950, pp. 12–19; and Paul W. Tappan, *op. cit.*, pp. 31–52. Relevant discussion is also provided in Sophia M. Robison, "Wanted—An Index of Crime and Delinquency," *Proceedings*, American Prison Association, 1945, pp. 203–212; Edward E. Schwartz, "Statistics of Juvenile Delinquency in the United States," *The Annals*, 261 (1949), 9–20; I. Richard Perlman, "The Meaning of Juvenile Delinquency Statistics," *Federal Probation*, September, 1949, 63–67, F. J. Murphy, M. M. Shirley, and H. L. Witmer, "The Incidence of Hidden Delinquency," *American Journal of Orthopsychiatry*, 16 (1946), 685–696; and W. S. Robinson, "Ecological Correlations and the Behavior of Individuals" *American Sociological Review*, 15 (June 1950), 351–357.

paper will attempt to provide a demonstration of the inadequacies of these statistics with respect to the extent of delinquent behavior in the urban slum areas. This is deemed necessary only because the high proportion of official non-delinquency in these areas is sometimes construed as vital evidence bearing on the nature of the problem of delinquency. In addition, an attempt will be made to formulate a hypothesis with reference to delinquency in the high rate urban areas consistent with the statistical evidence of its extent in such areas, and to subject this hypothesis to preliminary examination in terms of certain widely observed features both of slum delinquency and its enveloping social structure.

I

As is well known, enumerations of delinquents based on different measures of delinquency produce different impressions of its extent. With increasing degrees of inclusiveness these measures range from commitments to training schools and other custodial institutions, through official and unofficial juvenile court cases, to police complaint cases. On the grounds of either accuracy or completeness no conclusive arguments may be adduced for regarding any of these enumerations as perferable, since each may serve to measure accurately a defined level of deviational behavior, or official action, or both.[4]

Thus, the range of possible enumerations of delinquents in the high rate areas may be illustrated by the data from one representative jurisdiction. During the seven-year period 1927-1933 the rate of commitment per 100 boys of juvenile court age residing in Chicago in the ten square mile areas with highest rates was 6.1.[5] In the highest rate square mile area this rate was 9.2. During the same period the rate of official court delinquents in the ten square mile areas of highest rates was 14.6, with a rate of 18.9 in the top square mile area.

In contrast to both commitments and juvenile court appearances, police complaint cases, as may be anticipated, include in the delinquent classification a considerably larger proportion of boys residing in urban delinquency areas. Thus, the Chicago data show that the average rate of delinquents based on police complaints for the ten square mile areas of highest rates for the year 1926 was 20.6. In this police series the top area had a rate of 26.6.[6] However, these rates are not computed on the basis of the seven-year period of age eligibility, and therefore do not parallel rates of commitments or court appearances. To restore comparability between the rates of police complaints here presented and rates of commitments and court appearances it is necessary to multiply by seven the annual rate given. Since the data for the police series do not eliminate duplications of individuals, the multiplication required would result in a rate which exceeds the total age eligible boy population of these areas. Unfortunately, a count of unduplicated individuals who became police cases in the ten highest rate areas of Chicago is not available for 1926.

However, such a count is available for an area of moderate rates for the standard seven-year period of juvenile court eligibility. A count of the unduplicated juveniles dealt with by the police during the 1927-1933 period disclosed that the police complaint rate for this area was 28.8, as compared to an average annual rate of police cases of 9.2 for the area. This in-

---

[4] Insofar as any of these measures may be assumed to bear a constant ratio to the total volume of proscribed behavior they may be used as indexes of delinquency. These indexes, in turn, may be validly used only to gain a picture of the relative volume of delinquency in subdivisons of the same juvenile court jurisdiction during a period of time when administrative practices remain unchanged.

[5] Clifford R. Shaw and Henry D. McKay, *op. cit.*, p. 70.

[6] From police data available in the Sociology Department, Illinois Institute for Juvenile Research.

dicates that the proportion of unduplicated individuals who become police cases during their seven-year period of eligibility is approximately three times larger than the rate of police cases for a single given year. Since the rate of police cases for the ten highest rate areas in Chicago in the single year 1926 was 20.6, the suggested relative magnitudes of single and seven-year rates indicate that the rate of police cases for the top ten square mile areas in Chicago during the seven-year period centering on 1926 was 65.9.[7] This is the proportion of individuals who, as they moved from their first to their seventh year of age eligibility, engaged in misbehavior serious enough to warrant recorded police attention. And this is the rate which is more nearly comparable, in terms of the basis of computation, to the rates of commitment and court appearance of 6.1 and 14.6 respectively, cited above. Thus, it is evident that when the most inclusive measure based on official records is used, not one-fifth but almost two-thirds of the boys in delinquency areas may be regarded as official delinquents.

The validity of such official cases for the measurement of delinquency rests not only on its inclusiveness of all official delinquents, but on its capacity to mark out as well a homogeneous segment of the juvenile population which is consistently delinquent in terms of behavior content. It is of course with reference to the latter function that the official statistics of delinquency are more severely limited. After making the distinction between the types of measures discussed, and concluding that police complaints probably represent the most inclusive measure, we are still confronted with the question whether the group thus identified is a distinctively delinquent group in contrast to the balance of the juvenile population. In other words, does even this inclusive measure include all juveniles who engage in delinquent activity? The answer, of course, is that it

---
[7] Ibid.

does not, since it is well known that many delinquent juveniles who are never apprehended are known to social agencies, neighbors, friends, and associates.

Even if a defensible division of boys between delinquent and non-delinquent could be made, the prognostic value of the concept "delinquent," in its official sense, would still be uncertain. This is indicated by the findings of a recent follow-up of the careers of 83 public school boys who in 1929 resided in one of Chicago's delinquency areas. The individuals in this group were ascertained to be without records of appearances before the juvenile court prior to 1929. In 1949 an examination of their records of law violations during their adult careers revealed that 51 percent of this group had been arrested for offenses other than infraction of the traffic laws. While a sample of 69 boys with juvenile court records drawn from the same neighborhood during the same year exhibited an adult arrest rate of 75 percent, illustrative of the tendency of juvenile courts to deal primarily with the more serious and persistent offenders, the fact remains that over half the boys in the group of putative non-delinquents became adult offenders.[8]

It is altogether unlikely that these individuals stoutly resisted influences in the direction of delinquency during their youth only to succumb as adults. It is more reasonable to assume that as children, they too engaged in delinquent activity, but perhaps less persistently or with greater success in avoiding detection and treatment in the court. If the terms "delinquent" and "non-delinquent" had dependable descriptive value the large proportion of boys who were non-delinquent officially would not have appeared as adult offenders.

Taken together, the data presented above indicate that enumerations of de-

---
[8] Unpublished materials available in the Sociology Department, Illinois Institute for Juvenile Research.

linquents in urban areas of high rates of delinquents exhibit a wide range. It is clear that (a) assertions of the preponderance of non-delinquency in these areas are based on relative uninclusive official records, and (b) the more inclusive official records indicate the proportion of delinquents to be approximately two-thirds of the age eligibles. Moreover, even so inclusive a category as police complaint cases cannot be regarded as including the total number of offenders, since the police neither know of all offenses committed nor apprehend all offenders.

II

These observations suggest that delinquency is widely diffused in the urban high rate areas and therefore represents normative behavior which, like all normative behavior, generates a systematic scheme of values and institutional forms for its expression. The statistics of delinquency also indicate that a significantly large number of boys in these areas are free of the kind of involvement in delinquent practices which ordinarily results in the acquisition of a police record or in the development of adult criminality. With respect to the careers of these individuals it seems necessary to assume the ultimate dominance of the norms of conventional society. Thus, a duality of conduct norms in the high rate areas rather than the hegemony of either conventional or criminal value systems may be regarded as the fundamental sociological fact in the culture of these communities.[9]

[9] This view is related both to Sutherland's concept of "differential association" and to Sellin's emphasis on the primacy of culture conflict, in one form or another, in the etiology of crime. E. H. Sutherland, *Principles of Criminology*, New York: J. B. Lippincott Co., 1939; and T. Sellin, *Culture Conflict and Crime*, New York: Social Science Research Council, 1938. The present discussion may be regarded, in fact, as an effort to identify and describe with a modicum of detail some of the coordinates of culture conflict in the urban delinquency area, and to mark out one type of problem involved in "associating differentially."

This conclusion is suggested largely by the statistics of delinquency. Its validity may be subjected to further examination by using it in an attempt to explain selected aspects of the problem of delinquency in the high rate urban areas.

(a) *The Variability of Behavior Status in the Delinquency Area.* The facts indicate that in areas of high rates of delinquents there are not only many boys who engage in delinquent activity without becoming official delinquents, but that a substantial number of boys who do possess police and court records become conventional and law-abiding adults. Moreover, there is evidence that of those who are without juvenile records, many become adult offenders. These apparent reversals of career lines are incomprehensible except on the assumption that the individual participates simultaneously in both criminal and conventional value systems. Observation of the social experiences of young persons in the delinquency areas supports this assumption and indicates that the simultaneous participation occurs in two ways.[10]

First, groupings of boys based on play interests frequently include at any given moment of time three types of individuals

[10] Concern with the social and psychological processes resulting in delinquent careers has led to a relative neglect of those aspects of the life of the "submerged" urban areas which center on the conventional and traditional institutions of the wider community. However, the presence of an emphatic strain of conventionality in these areas is indicated in W. F. Whyte, *Street Corner Society*, Chicago: University of Chicago Press, 1943. Ample reflection of the impact of such institutions and agencies as schools, police, social settlements, and churches may be found in C. R. Shaw and H. D. McKay, "Social Factors in Juvenile Delinquency," *Report on the Causes of Crime*, Vol. II, National Commission on Law Observance and Enforcement, Washington, D.C., 1931; and C. R. Shaw *et al., Brothers in Crime*, Chicago: University of Chicago Press, 1938. There exists, in addition, a large if popular biographical literature detailing the rise of children of poor immigrant families to positions of prominence, power, and wealth within conventional hierarchies.

with reference to delinquent conduct: those who at the time are occasionally delinquent; those who at the time are actively and persistently delinquent; and those who at the time refrain completely from delinquent activity. In terms of propinquity and opportunity for association, delinquents have many contacts with non-delinquents and vice versa. The play of influence with respect to the development of values and goals is simultaneously exerted in both directions, even though delinquents may be expected to have more frequent and more intimate contacts with other delinquents than with non-delinquents.

Second, taken from the standpoint of the developmental pattern of the individual, marked variability is encountered, particularly in the younger age groups, with respect to the degree of delinquent activity in which the individual is involved from time to time. Thus, the same person, either within the same group or in a succession of groups, may interchangeably occupy the role of persistent delinquent, occasional delinquent, or non-delinquent. He is thus provided an opportunity to experience in a direct and personal manner the full meaning of the alternative value systems implicit in each mode of conduct.

Simultaneous participation in the conventional and criminal value systems in either of the ways indicated is not inconsistent with the fact that over a long period of time persons in delinquency areas who come to occupy either the conventional or the delinquent role will develop more intimate associations and relationships with persons of the same role traits. As a result, progressive alienation from either the criminal or the conventional value scheme ensues, and the person may come in time to live more completely in terms of one rather than in terms of the other value scheme.

These observations emphasize the inadequacy, for purposes of either description or analysis, of designating boys in delinquency areas as delinquent or non-delinquent. In a real sense they are neither and they are both. The world of meanings in which they must find their way is an amalgam compounded in widely varying proportions of two implicitly inharmonious codes of conduct. As an amalgam of this character the world of the delinquency area represents an experience for the growing child which is qualitatively different from either the conventional world of the middle class child or the world of the child reared in an outcast society. It is, in fact, a world in which, because of its two scale value orientation, boys move readily between the delinquent and the non-delinquent classifications. Thus, when applied to the boy who resides in an urban area of high rate of delinquents, the term "non-delinquent" becomes ambiguous. This designation has stable meaning primarily in the social world of those who are conventional and law-abiding.

(b) *Varieties of Delinquency Areas.* The culture of delinquency areas and specific group patterns of delinquency in these areas may be regarded as in large part determined by the character of the interaction between the conventional and the criminal value systems. This fact suggests the possibility of a typology of delinquency areas based on variations in the relationship between these two systems.

Delinquency areas exhibit important differences in the degree to which integration between the conventional and criminal value systems is achieved.[11] Areas

---

[11] Competing value systems tend to accommodate to one another by mutual incorporation of elements common to or compatible with each. The criminal culture shares with the conventional culture the goal of a large and assured money income, and like the conventional culture utilizes the flexible processes of politics to achieve this goal. The use of the political process by organized crime entails the development of relationships with functionaries of the established power structure which

range from those in which the integration is well advanced to those in which it is minimal. The two polar types on this continuum may be briefly described.

In areas where the two systems are highly integrated adult violative activity tends to be systematic and organized. This tendency is revealed in the development in these areas of groups of adults engaged in the promotion and management of consistently profitable illegal enterprises. Leaders in these enterprises frequently maintain membership in such conventional institutions of their local communities as churches, fraternal and mutual benefit societies, and political parties. While participation in the political party organizations is usually required by the character of their occupational activity, participation in churches and the other social organizations of the community represents a spontaneous quest for status in the social structure within which they have become acculturated. Within this framework the influence of each of the two value systems is reciprocal, the leaders of illegal enterprise participating in the primary orientation of the conventional elements in the population, and the latter through their participation in a local power structure sustained in large part by illicit activity, participating perforce in the alternate, criminal value system.

The stable position of illicit enterprise in the adult society of the community is reflected in the character of delinquent conduct on the part of children. While delinquency in all high rate areas is intrinsically disorderly in that it is unrelated to official programs for the education of the young, in the type of community under discussion boys may more or less realistically recognize the potentialities for personal progress in the local society through success in delinquency. In a general way, therefore, delinquent activity in these areas constitutes a training ground for the acquisition of skill in the use of violence, concealment of offense, evasion of detection and arrest, and the purchase of immunity from punishment. Those who come to excel in these respects are frequently noted and valued by adult leaders in the rackets who are confronted, as are the leaders of all income-producing enterprises, with problems of the recruitment of competent personnel.

As a consequence of this situation delinquency tends to occur within a partial framework of social controls, insofar as delinquent activity in these areas represents a tolerated means for the acquisition of an approved role and status. Thus, while delinquent activity here possesses the usual characteristics of violence and destructiveness, there tend to develop effective limits of permissible activity in this direction. Delinquency is, in other words, encompassed and contained within a local social structure, and is marginally but palpably related to that structure.

The contrasting polar type of delinquency area is characterized principally by the absence of systematic and organized adult activity in violation of law, despite the fact that many adults in these areas commit violations. The presence of violators as adult models in the community legitimizes activity in opposition to law from the point of view of delinquent juveniles. In this situation conventional and criminal systems of values are not merely not integrated, but are in extreme and open opposition to one another. As a consequence, the delinquency in areas of this type tends to be unrestrained by controls originating *at any point* in the adult social structure.

---

transcend the symbiotic precisely because both the goal and in general form the methods of achieving the goal are truly shared by representatives of both cultures. The term "integration" as used in this connection denotes a situation in which such relationships are firmly established. When these relationships are haphazard, occasional, or undependable it appears logical to conceptualize such a situation as representing only partial integration.

Areas of this type are frequently produced by drastic changes in the class, ethnic, or racial characteristics of its population. Such transitions, as is well known, tend to devitalize the older institutions of the area, and to introduce a period during which institutional and other controls are at a minimum. During these interim periods the bearers of the conventional culture and its value system are without the customary institutional machinery, and therefore in effect partially demobilized with reference to the diffusion of their value system. In these conditions the alternative criminal value system is able to gain both ground and vigor, and to persist on the local scene without effective opposition.

Because adult crime in this type of area is itself unorganized, its value system remains implicit and hence incapable of generating norms which function effectively on a group-wise basis. As a result, juvenile violators readily escape not merely the controls of the conventional persons in the community, but those of adult violators as well. It should be noted that the emergence of group norms on the part of persistent and systematic violators in the contemporary urban milieu is usually accompanied by regularized and dependable accommodations with such representatives of the wider society as police and politicians. It is at this point that the implicit value system of criminality becomes explicit, moves toward integration with conventionality, and undergoes an enhancement of its capacity to exert control over the behavior of violators.

In areas where such integration is absent the delinquencies of juveniles tend to acquire a wild, untrammelled character. Delinquents in this kind of situation more frequently exhibit the personality traits of the social type sometimes referred to as the hoodlum. Both individually and in groups violent physical combat is engaged in for its own sake, almost as a form of recreation. Here groups of delinquents may be seen as excluded, isolated conflict groups dedicated to an unending battle against all forms of constraint. The escape from controls originating in any social structure, other than that provided by unstable groupings of the delinquents themselves, is here complete.

All delinquency areas fall somewhere between the polar types described. Moreover, changes in the character of a given delinquency area may be explained in terms of changes in the degree of integration existing from time to time between the criminal and the conventional value systems. It is, in fact, the specific form of the interaction between these opposing value systems which helps to explain the character of juvenile group activity in specific delinquency areas, as well as changes in these activities in either a criminal or a conventional direction.

Thus, duality of value orientation in the high rate urban areas may be regarded as a fundamental property of a wide variety of specific community situations. While delinquency areas may move toward or away from the integration of these opposing systems of values, the basic character of the social life of these communities appears to be determined in large part by the explicit presence of this duality.

(c) *Personality of the Delinquent and Conflicting Value Systems.* Juvenile groupings based on common interest in the pursuit of delinquent activity develop a body of shared attitudes which may be regarded as making up a distinctive culture. In a thoughtful analysis of the origin of this culture, Albert K. Cohen [12] has suggested that it arises in a framework of lower socioeconomic class status in which many persons are unable, in terms either of achievement or the disciplining of behavior necessary for achievement, to acquire the symbols of success current in the conven-

---

[12] Thesis statement submitted to Department of Human Relations, Harvard University, 1949.

tional, respectable, and dominant middle class culture of the wider society.[13] As a result, young persons are exposed to the invidious judgments of those who, within the range of social contacts of the lower-class child, represent and exemplify the norms of middle-class culture. Such persons, moreover, symbolize, by virtue both of their roles and their class position, the power and prestige of the wider society in which the lower-class area is set.[14] One of several adjustive responses available to young males in this situation is to reject the imputation of inferiority and degradation by emphasizing those activities and personal traits which distinguish them from striving, upward mobile persons. The common response inaugurates new norms of conduct out of which develop the distinctive criteria of status in the delinquent group. Thus, a coherent social milieu is created in which status is distributed according to success in attacking the symbols of middle-class respectability. Since property represents a central symbol of merit and virtue in the culture of this class, stealing and destructiveness become a principal though not the only form taken by the attack.

This analysis constitutes a framework within which personality process and culture process may be in part related for purposes of understanding the delinquent as a person. This analysis also throws light on a further aspect of the conflict of value systems which has been seen as an essential characteristic of delinquency areas.

The aggressively hostile response of the young male in the delinquency area to his devaluation by representatives of the conventional culture arises entirely from the fact that the criteria of status in the conventional culture have validity for him. This is indicated not in the hostile response as such, but in certain sentiments and emotions which accompany the hostility. These associated sentiments are reflected in the acts of defiance and contempt which frequently accompany ordinary depredations of property. Nowhere is this more apparent than in the not uncommon burglaries of schools in delinquency areas in which the delinquent escapade is sometimes crowned, as it were, by defecating upon the school principal's desk. This supreme gesture of defiance and contempt can be understood as an effort on the part of the delinquents to counteract their own impulses to accept and accede to the superior status of such representatives of the conventional order as school principals. In a sense, such an act is a dramatically exaggerated denial of a system of values which the delinquent has at least partially introjected, but which for the sake of preserving a tolerable self-image he must reject. In this interplay of attitudinal elements the vigor of the rejection of the value system is the measure of its hold upon the person. In other words, the mood of rebellion which characterizes these young males is created not alone by the negative judgments of the surrogates of middle-class culture, but by the negative self-judgment as well.

Such overtones of rebellion, on the other hand, do not characterize members of subculture groups who are totally excluded from participation in the dominant culture of the wider society. For example, those groups which live by systematic depredations upon property, like the criminal castes of India or the professional thieves of our own society, are relatively impervious to the negative judgments of conventional persons, and do not ordinarily resort

---

[13] The relation of social structure to the delinquency of the high rate urban areas is lucidly analyzed in Robert K. Merton, "Social Structure and Anomie," in *Social Theory and Social Structure,* Glencoe: The Free Press, 1949, pp. 134–140.

[14] The significance of the social class identification of teachers for their attitudes toward lowerclass children is in part indicated in W. Lloyd Warner, *Democracy in Jonesville,* New York: Harper & Brothers, 1949, pp. 208–210.

to the kind of behavior described.[15] Their devaluation and rejection by conventional society is not transmuted into self-rejection, since their criteria of worthiness diverge sharply from those encountered in conventional society. In contrast, the young male who occupies the role of delinquent in the delinquency area resorts to purposive destructiveness exaggerates the differences between himself and conventional persons precisely because he cannot exclude from his system of values the conventional criteria of personal worth. His delinquency may hence be seen as a defensive adaptation in which he creates an opposing system of values, since by virtue of his lower-class culture background he remains relatively unequipped to move toward the goals explicit in the middle-class culture of the wider society.

The general conclusions suggested by these observations are (a) that a delinquent subculture originates in a setting of cross-group hostility; (b) that this subculture is a groupwise elaboration of individual adaptations serving ego-defense needs; and (c) that the conflict of cultures generated in this situation is reflected on its social psychological side in the introjection by the delinquent of a dual value orientation as exhibited principally in the delinquent's aggressive destructiveness.[16]

SUMMARY

Analysis of the problem of the causation of delinquency in urban areas of high rates of delinquents is frequently confused by allusions to statistical data which suggest that, while the proportion of delinquents in these areas is high, this class nonetheless represents a distinct minority of the age eligible population. Examination of delinquency statistics indicates that no conclusive judgments regarding this matter may be made on the basis of these statistics.

On the other hand, the statistics do support the proposition that urban areas of high rates of delinquents are characterized by a duality of conduct norms rather than by the dominance of either a conventional or a criminal culture.

This hypothesis appears to be useful in explaining the variability of behavior status on the part of boys in delinquency areas; in constructing a typology of delinquency areas based on degrees of integration of opposing value schemes; and in accounting for certain psychological mechanisms involved in the origin and persistence of the subculture of the delinquent boys' gang.

---

[15] M. Kennedy, *Criminal Tribes of the Bombay Presidency*, Bombay, 1908; E. H. Sutherland, *The Professional Thief,* Chicago: University of Chicago Press, 1937.

[16] Discussions of this problem in the psychoanalytic literature, illuminating and suggestive as they are, do not deal explicitly with those variables related to delinquency which originate in intergroup relations. Thus Aichhorn covers the customary range of etiologies when he observes that the child may become delinquent when his psychic apparatus is defective, when he develops defects in the superego or conscience functions of personality as a result of distorting or shocking experiences in his family relationships, or when, as in the instance of the gang boy or child of delinquent parents, he acquires an ego-ideal which is socially unacceptable. August Aichhorn, *Wayward Youth,* New York: The Viking Press, 1935, pp. 222–225. The problem of etiology is further complicated when we consider the effect upon normal personality of constraints to identify with models defined by the subculture as hostile and inimical.

22. CULTURE CONFLICT IN ISRAEL

SHLOMO SHOHAM

IT HAS BEEN RECOGNIZED THAT A BASIC DIStinction should be made between the etiology of crime as a social phenomenon inherent in a given society and the process (i.e., the "recruiting") by which a certain individual becomes a criminal or commits a criminal act. The latter is studied from the point of view of the individual, whereas the former is regarded from the point of view of the group, community, or nation and is expressed in crime *rates*.[1] It should be mentioned that most efforts in criminology from the "positive school" on were directed at the explanation of crime on the personal level. But with the development of modern sociology and especially the so-called "formal school of sociology," which was mostly concerned with forms of human interaction,[2] more attention was given to the phenomenon of crime on the social level. The concept of conflict, which is one form of interaction,[3] was thus utilized by some American sociologists to explain the defferential crime rates in given communities.[4]

One of the most lucid adaptations of the idea of conflict to crime causation was carried out by Sellin in his monograph *On Culture Conflict and Crime*.[5] Sellin pointed out that the conflict relevant for criminological research is the clash between conduct norms brought about "as by-products of a cultural growth process—the growth of civilization—as the result of the migration of conduct norms from one culture complex or area to another. However produced, they are sometimes studied as mental conflicts[6] and sometimes as the clash of cultural codes."[7]

It should be pointed out that the concept of culture-conflict as expounded by Sellin

▶SOURCE: "The Application of the 'Culture-Conflict' Hypothesis to the Criminality of Immigrants in Israel," *Journal of Criminal Law, Criminology, and Police Science* (June 1962), 53:2:207–214. Copyright 1962 by The Northwestern University School of Law. Reprinted by special permission of the Journal of Criminal Law, Criminology, and Police Science and the author.

[1] See Sutherland, The Sutherland Papers 11 (Cohen, Lindesmith & Schuessler ed. 1956).
[2] See Park & Burgess, Introduction to the Science of Sociology (1942).
[3] See Simmel, *The Sociology of Conflict*, 9 Am. J. Sociology 490 (1903–1904).

[4] See Sutherland, *Crime and the Conflict Process*, 13 J. Juvenile Research 38 (1929); 2 Thomas & Znaniecki, The Polish Peasant in Europe and America 1753–55 (Knoph ed. 1927); Kobrin, *The Conflict of Values in Delinquency Areas*, 16 Am. Sociological Rev. 653 (1951).
[5] Sellin, On Culture Conflict and Crime (Social Science Research Council 1938).
[6] It seems that the idea of culture conflict as mental conflict has influenced Sutherland in formulating his differential association theory, which presumably explains criminal behavior on the personal level. This idea seems inherent in his statement that "a person becomes delinquent because of an excess of definitions favorable to violation of law over definitions unfavorable to violation of law." Sutherland, *op. cit. supra* note 1, at 20. See also *id.* at 9.
[7] Sellin, *op. cit. supra* note 5, at 58.

is intrinsically different from the concept of conflict as used by the formal school of sociology. Shaw and Mckay, for instance, used the concept of culture conflict to explain social "disorganization" which ensues from *group* conflict.[8] The same meaning was apparently given to culture-conflict (on the social level) by Sutherland when he spoke about "differential group organization," brought about when "several criminals perfect an organization and with organization their crimes increase in frequency and seriousness; in the course of time this arouses a narrower or a broader group which organizes itself against crime, and this tends to reduce crimes. *The crime rate at a particular time is a resultant of these opposed organizations*".[9]

But here apparently something is amiss, because obviously the *whole* volume of crimes in a given community cannot be explained by "differential group organization." It explains no doubt the rate of *organized* or professional crime, but surely it does not account for the rates of crimes of passion and isolated crimes in a given community. In contrast, Sellin's exposition of culture-conflict as a conflict of *conduct norms*, not only among different groups but also within the group itself and between the individual and his group, may account for the sum total of crimes in a given community.[10] In other words the higher the volume of clashes among the legal norms, folkways, and values in a given community, the higher the crime rate. It should be stressed however that this hypothesis has not yet been fully tested.

CULTURE-CONFLICT, IMMIGRATION, AND CRIME IN THE U.S.A.

The phenomenon of culture-conflict on the social level may be observed no doubt in the general growth of civilization and especially in the clashes of norms and values resulting from industrialization and urbanization of various communities. But the study of the conflict process in these instances is highly problematic from the methodological point of view, and the sheer length of time involved makes the possibility of comprehensive research highly remote. Most of the research on culture-conflict and crime has therefore dealt wtih the clashes among divergent cultural codes and especially the conflict between the conduct norms of immigrant groups and the norms prevailing in the receiving country.[11] It is only natural that much of the research in this field has been carried out in the U.S.A., which was until recently a country experiencing mass immigration.[12]

The results of the research on the problem of immigration and crime carried out in the U.S.A. have been more often contradictory than consistant. This of course may be partly attributed to the heterogeneity of methodology employed by the various investigators. It is possible nonetheless to summarize some of the more conspicuous findings of this research as follows:

A. The crime rate of the immigrants taken as a group was at first believed to be lower than the crime rate of the native group.[13] But then it was realized that foreign-born criminal groups are, on the average, older than native-born criminal

---

[8] Shaw & McKay, Juvenile Delinquency and Urban Areas (1942).

[9] Sutherland, *op. cit. supra* note 1, at 21.

[10] Sellin, *op. cit. supra* note 5, at 66 *et seq.*

[11] *Id.* at 70. As to the possible impact of immigration on deviant behaviour, see Eisenstadt, The Absorption of Immigrants 20 *et seq.* (London 1954).

[12] The first law that restricted the flow of mass immigration to the United States was the National Origins Law of 1924. From then onwards the restrictive legislation became tighter, and after passage of the McCarran-Walter Act of 1952, immigration to the United States became quantitatively insignificant.

[13] Nat'l Com'n on Law Observance and Enforcement, Report on Crime and the Foreign-Born (1931).

groups with native parentage,[14] and a study by Van Vechten [15] indeed revealed that, when compared on the basis of age, the criminality of immigrants exceeded the criminality of native-born whites by a ratio of ten to nine.

B. There is a wide difference in the extent and nature of the criminality of immigrants from different countries of origin and different ethnic groups.[16]

C. Immigrants presumably have a higher crime rate in the U.S.A. than in their countries of origin.[17] It should be stressed however that there is no conclusive evidence to this effect due to the differences between the definitions of "crime" and "offence" in the countries of origin and in the United States.

D. There is a marked consensus among the various investigators that the crime rate of native-born (or those who immigrated very young) of foreign-born parents is considerably higher than the rates of either the foreign-born or the relevant age groups of native-born of native parentage.[18]

However a very important exception, relevant to the culture-conflict hypothesis, should be noted. The delinquency rate of juveniles with immigrant parentage is considerably lower in immigrant communities which display a strong primary-group control of their members, have inner cohesion, and practice flexible but not weak home control over the young.[19] Taft, while commenting on these findings, says:

> Some immigrants have been protected against crime by life in the ghettos of our cities and in homogeneous immigrant colonies in rural areas. There they have established fairly effective institutions and primary relations. . . . Immigrants who only gradually give over their old world patterns of behavior are in general seldom seen in our criminal courts. [The immigrant thus] becomes assimilated more slowly possibly, but much more effectively. Not nonassimilation but overrapid Americanization spells crime.[20]

In other words the danger of culture-conflict is most imminent when the original norms and values of the immigrant have disintegrated rapidly, and a cultural vacuum or chaos is created. The immigrant group is not yet ready, or time is insufficient, for an orderly absorption of the norms and values of the receiving group. The younger generation is therefore more susceptible to the criminogenic "street-culture." In contrast, a slow and gradual absorption of the culture of the receiving group, accompanied by a gradual replacement of the original norms and values, causes not a clash or conflict but a synthesis which enhances the observance of the acquired norms rather than their breach.

IMMIGRATION AND CRIME IN ISRAEL

The study of the relation between immigration and crime in Israel is complicated by the fact that Israel is quite unique from the demographic point of view. The flow of Jewish immigration to the country has been almost continuous (with marked fluctuations of course) from the beginning

---

[14] Stofflet, A Study of National and Cultural Difference in Criminal Tendency (No. 185 Archives of Psychology 1935).

[15] Van Vechten, *Criminality of the Foreign Born*, Proceedings of the Seventieth Annual Congress of Correction of the Am. Prison Ass'n 505 (1940).

[16] Nat'l Com'n on Law Observance and Enforcement, *op. cit. supra* note 13, at 109; Dept. of Commerce, Bureau of the Census, Prisoners in State and Federal Prisons and Reformatories 28 (1934); Wood, *Minority Group Criminality and Cultural Integration*, 37 J. Crim. L. & C. 498 (1947).

[17] Thomas & Znaniecki, *op. cit. supra* note 4; Young, The Pilgrims of Russian Town (1932).

[18] Young, *op. cit. supra* note 17, at 209–10; Van Vechten, *supra* note 15; Ross, *Crime and the Native-Born Sons of European Immigrants*, 28 J. Crim. L. & C. 208 (1937); W. C. Smith, Americans in Process 8 (1937).

[19] Lind, *The Ghetto and the Slum,* 9 Social Forces 206 (1930); W. C. Smith, *op. cit. supra* note 18, at 214; Hayner, *Delinquency Areas in the Puget Sound Region*, 39 Am. J. Sociology 319 (1933).

[20] Taft, Criminology 159–60 (3d ed. 1956).

of the century to this present day. After the creation of the State of Israel in 1948, the flow of mass immigration greatly increased, but even before 1948 the Jewish community in Palestine was basically immigrant. Eisenstadt thus says:

> The Yishuv (i.e., the Jewish community in Palestine) was not merely an immigrant-absorbing community. More probably, than any other modern absorbing country . . . it was also a community which immigrants had created. The time-span between the establishment of its first institutional outlines and the influx of waves of immigrants was very short, sometimes almost non-existant, and its institutional structure was in continuous formation and development while these various waves were entering.[21]

The most conspicuous fact about Jewish immigration to Israel is that at the establishment of the state, on the 14th of May 1948, there were 649,633 Jews in the country. Within nine years (i.e. until the end of 1957) 896,355 [22] new immigrants had arrived and had to be absorbed by the former, who were clearly a minority from the quantitive point of view. The flow of immigration after May 1948 may be divided into three periods:

1948–1951—period of mass immigration.
1952–1954—period of a relative decline in immigration.
1955–1957—renewal of immigration (especially from Europe and North Africa).

A rough idea of the great variety of ethnic groups among the immigrants, the differences in their cultural backgrounds, and the extent of conflict among the various conduct-norms liable to ensue may be surmised from Table I. This table shows the distribution of Jewish immigrants by country of birth. The right column shows the origin of "old" immigrants (arrival before May 1948); the middle column shows the origin of "new" immigrants (arrival

[21] Eisenstadt, op. cit. supra note 11, at 46.
[22] Statistical Abstract of Israel 1957–58, table 2, at 7, table 5, at 59.

Table I. Distribution of Jewish Immigrants by Country of Birth[23]

Country of Birth	Percentage of Immigrants After 1948	Number of Immigrants After 1948	Number of Immigrants Before 1948
All Countries	100.0	896,655	452,158
Asia	29.6	259,648	40,776
Turkey	4.4	38,071	8,277
Iran	14.2	125,413	7,995
Iraq	3.3	29,528	3,536
Yemen	6.2	45,781	14,566
Aden	0.4	3,448	1,272
India	0.7	6,069	72
Other countries	1.4	11,338	5,058
Africa	25.2	221,500	4,033
Tunisia, Algeria, Morocco and Tangier	17.6	154,905	904
Liberya	3.7	32,849	873
Union of South Africa	0.1	982	259
Other countries	3.8	32,764	1,907
Europe	44.3	388,458	377,487
U.S.S.R.	1.4	11,994	52,350
Poland	15.8	136,620	170,127
Rumania	14.0	123,562	41,105
Bulgaria	4.4	38,559	7,057
Yugoslavia	0.9	7,842	1,944
Greece	0.3	2,579	8,767
Germany	1.0	8,908	52,951
Austria	0.3	2,906	7,748
Czechoslovakia	2.2	19,161	16,794
Hungary	2.6	23,263	10,342
U.K.	0.3	2,500	1,574
Netherlands	0.2	1,434	1,208
France	0.5	3,769	1,637
Italy	0.2	1,510	1,554
Other countries	0.4	3,611	2,329
America and Oceana	0.9	7,330	7,579
U.S.	0.3	1,987	6,635
Canada	0.0	363	316
Argentina	0.3	2,766	238
Other countries in America	0.3	2,039	318
Australia and New Zealand	0.0	175	72
Not stated	—	19,419	22,283

[23] Id., table 6, at 60.

Table II. *Percentage of Adult Immigrant Offenders Among Total Offender Population for the Years 1951-1957*

Year	1951	1952	1953	1954	1955	1956	1957
Percentage of immigrant offenders	60.7	65.7	67.1	65.8	66.2	68.9	66.7

after May 1948); and the left column shows the distribution of the latter in percentages.

It is necessary to point out a demographic fact concerning the Jewish community both in Palestine and in the State of Israel which will be highly relevant in our later analysis of data concerning the criminality of immigrants. This is the apparent dichotomy of oriental and so-called Sephardic Jews, and the Jews, mostly of European descent, known as Ashkenazi Jews. The Sephardic Jews trace their origin to the Jewish community expelled from Spain in 1492. These were probably a small nucleus of the Jews who lived in Palestine before the beginning of immigration at the end of the 19th century and whose origin cannot be clearly ascertained.[24] The oriental Jews are those who immigrated to Palestine and to Israel from eastern countries and especially from the regions formerly included in the Ottoman Empire.[25] The economic and educational standard of the oriental Jews is as a rule lower than the standard of Jews of European origin.

The Criminality of Adult "New" Immigrants. Our definition of "new" immigrants as those Jews who entered the country after the establishment of the state in May 1948 may seem quite arbitrary, and indeed from many aspects it is. It may be justified, nevertheless, for our purposes if we bear in mind that the rate of Jewish immigration to Palestine during the Second World War and the last years of the British mandate is quite low when compared with the mass immigration during the first years of the state. There are also grounds to believe that absorption of the "old" immigrants by the receiving community was much more effective,[26] and their integration quicker, than that of the "new" immigrants.

Table II shows the percentage of immigrant adult offenders (15 years of age and above) among the total population of offenders convicted of "serious"[27] offences.

The average percentage of "new" immigrants among the total population for the years 1953–1957 was approximately 60%, whereas the average percentage of adult immigrant offenders among the total population of immigrants for the same years was 67.2%, i.e., an excess of more than 7%. When we compare the ratio of these percentages with the ratio between the criminality of the native-born (including the pre-1948 immigrants) and their percentage of the total population, we observe that the criminality of adult "new" immigrants in Israel exceeds the criminality of the native-born (and the "old" immigrants) at the rate of 4 to 3 (or 10 to 7.5)[28] We may conclude that this rate is quite high if we bear in mind Van Vechten's findings concerning the relevant rate in the United States, which was 10 to 9.[29]

---

[24] See Poliak, The Jews of Palestine at the War's End 12 *et seq.* (Palestine 1945) (in Hebrew).

[25] See Eisenstadt, *op. cit. supra* note 11, at 90.

[26] *Id.* at 58 *et seq.*

[27] Minor offences, i.e., assaults, brawls, and offences against poilce regulations (contravention), were not included.

[28] The rates have been computed from "raw" data received from the Central Bureau of Statistics, Israel.

[29] Van Vechten, *supra* note 15, at 505–16. The shortcomings of this comparison are obvious, because Van Vechten compared the criminality of *all* the foreign born with that of the native born. If we had done the same, and based our comparison on the corresponding age groups, the criminality of our foreign born would have been much higher than that of the native born, but for our present purposes the rate as computed above is adequate because our main concern is with the criminality of immigrants who entered the country after 1948.

An interesting comparison may be made among the rates of serious offences committed by immigrants from the various continents. The rates were computed from data collected in 1957, which were the best data available. These rates were, for serious offences per 1000 immigrants from Africa, 13; Asia, 10; and from Europe and America, 5.

It should be mentioned that the overwhelming majority of immigrants from Africa have come from North Africa.[30] They belong to the "Moghrebite" community, and they have as a rule an ethnic and cultural background quite distinct from that of the rest of the oriental Jews. The Asian Jews belong mostly to the category of "oriental" Jews, whereas the relatively few American immigrants are mostly of European origin or parentage. The clue to these differential crime rates may quite possibly be found in the culture-conflict hypothesis, because as we have already mentioned the general cultural, economic, and educational standards of the North African and Asian immigrants are relatively low. It may be that the clash between the cultural codes, norms, and values of these immigrants and those of the receiving community causes a relative increase in the crime rate of these immigrants.[31] Note the relatively low rate of criminality of the European and American immigrants, whose general cultural and educational standards were similar or nearer to the standard of the receiving community.

Another aspect of the culture-conflict hypothesis may be studied by analyzing the types of offences committed by the various immigrant groups.[32]

Table III. *Distribution of Adult Immigrant Offenders According to Type of Offence (in Percentages)*

	Europe and America	Africa	Asia
Offences against public order	18	16	16
Offences against the person	26	30	27
Offences against morality	2	2	2
Offences against property	25	27	26
Burglary	2	2	1
Arson and Damage to Property	6	10	9
Forgery and embezzlement	2	1	1
Miscellaneous	19	12	18
Total	100%	100%	100%

The first impression one receives from Table III is the relative preponderance of the more serious offences among the African immigrants, because the item 'Miscellaneous" usually refers to the less serious offences, and this item is quite low among the Africans. Another is the high percentage among the Africans of offences against the person. It is permissible to add to this type the offences of arson and damage to property, inasmuch as the latter are committed as a rule out of violence and aggression and not for the sake of pecuniary gain. The resulting sum is 40% for the Africans, but only 32% for the Europeans. These figures may indicate the existence of a cultural tradition among the African immigrants of settling disputes by violence, a method of "self-help" which may have been more or less accepted conduct in their countries of origin. It should be stressed however that these comparisons provide only a suggestion for further research to

---

[30] See Table I.

[31] Eisenstadt has said, "The ... disorganization of the immigrant group, instability of social relations, and of various types of norm-breaking, juvenile delinquency, crime etc. is strongest among those groups whose cultural and educational standards are much lower than those of the absorbing society." *Op. cit. supra* note 11, at 260–61.

[32] This has been done in many researches carried out in the United States in order to determine what offences are characteristic to the criminals in the various immigrant groups. See Taft, Criminology 154 *et seq.* (3d ed. 1956).

determine whether the excess of violence among the North African offenders is embedded in the mores of their countries of origin, or whether some special attributes of their communities of origin or the receiving community hindered the process of integration, thereby causing real or illusory feelings of discrimination and increased violence. Whatever the case, our rough and to be sure quite superficial analysis of the data indicates that further research into the problem of culture-conflict as related to immigration and crime in Israel may bear fruitful implications concerning the etiology of crime.

Juvenile Delinquents of Immigrant Parentage. It has already been mentioned that the main problem of culture-conflict with respect to crime and immigration arises with the second generation. The native-born of immigrant parentage, or those who came very young, are the most prone to suffer from the effects of their parents' immigration.

The conduct norms of their parents diverge as a rule from the prevailing norms in the receiving country. The process of integration may also injure and sometimes shatter the social and economic status of the head of the family. This and other effects of the process of integration may weaken the cohesion of the family unit and thus hamper the family control over the young. The oriental Jewish father, however poor he may be, is always the omnipotent pater-familias. But when he comes to Israel, the different social set-up may prevent him from fully exercising his former status, he may be given a job not to his liking, and the different living conditions may shatter his previous convictions and leave him in a state of confusion in which he cannot exercise proper control over his family. The youngster may also realize that his father is not the omnipotent patriarch he was supposed to be, and sometimes when he comes home from school he may see his father signing a document with his ink stained thumb.

All these factors presumably increase the susceptibility of the children of immigrant parents to absorb the so-called "street-culture" and to become juvenile delinquents.[33]

Table IV shows the rates of Jewish juvenile delinquency.[35] The middle column shows the rates per 100,000 inhabitants, and the right column shows the

Table IV. *Rates of Juvenile Delinquency in Israel for the Years 1949–1959*[34]

Year	Absolute Numbers	Rate per 100,000 of the Population	Percentage in the Age Groups
1949	1000	99	0.68
1950	1147	95	0.67
1951	1300	93	0.66
1952	1500	103	0.74
1953	1541	103	0.75
1954	2072	136	0.96
1955	2471	155	1.06
1956	2623	157	1.06
1957	2933	166	1.03
1958	3407	188	1.08
1959	4089	220	1.32

percentage of delinquents in their age group. It is obvious that the rate of juvenile delinquency in Israel has been rising constantly.

We may ask whether this increase is

---

[33] As to the possible impact of these factors on juvenile delinquency see Shaw & McKay, Report on Social Factors in Juvenile Delinquency (Report No. 13, 2 Report on the Causes of Crime, National Commission on Law Observance and Enforcement 1937); Drucker & Hexter, Children Astray (1923); 1 Thomas & Znaniecki, op. cit. supra note 4, at 711; Abrahamson, *Family Tension Basic Cause of Criminal Behavior*, 40 J. Crim. L. & C. 330 (1949); Kobrin, *The Conflict of Values in Delinquency Areas*, 16 Am. Soc. Rev. 653 (1951).

[34] Source: The Juvenile Probation Service, The Ministry of Social Welfare, Israel.

[35] The relevant age groups are 9–16 for boys and 9–18 for girls. Children below 9 are not criminally responsible, whereas boys above 16 and girls above 18 are considered adults.

linked with immigration, or more precisely, what is the relative role of immigrant delinquents?[36] In the last two years for which data is available, the rates of immigrant delinquents per 100,000 new immigrants were 311 in 1958 and 282 in 1957, whereas the rates for the total population were 188 and 166 respectively. The ratio for both years is 10 "new" immigrant delinquents for 6 of the total population. It should be mentioned that immigrant families as a rule have more children than the older population, but this fact cannot decrease the significance of the unusually high rate of immigrant delinquency or of the possible application of the culture-conflict hypothesis.

Some relevant conclusions may also be drawn from the reports of the regional probation officers for the years 1957-58.[37] These reports, although not based on refined statistical analysis, contain valuable observations based on daily contact with the population of the region and its delinquents. For example, the regional probation officer for the Tel-Aviv area reports that there are nine main centres of delinquency in his area, seven of which are wholly or mainly inhabited by "new" immigrants. The probation officer of Haifa reports that the greatest delinquency rate in his area is in Tira, which is a large settlement near Haifa wholly inhabited by "new" immigrants. The highest rate of delinquency in the whole country was recorded in the rural region of the Jerusalem area. The population of this region is composed entirely of "new" immigrants. The rates per 100,000 inhibitants in that region were 455 in 1957 and 355 in 1958, whereas the corresponding rates for the town of Jerusalem were only 189 and 279 respectively.

Recent data as to the ethnic origin differentiation of delinquency are not available as yet. The latest findings in this context are the data examined by the Agranat Committee on Juvenile Delinquency in Israel.[38] This committee examined the delinquency rates for the years 1951-1953 and found a great preponderance of delinquency among the oriental Jews over the delinquency among the European Jews. This conclusion applied not only to new immigrants but also to "old" immigrants native-born. The committee concluded:

> The process of the social and cultural integration of the oriental immigrant boy is seemingly accompanied by internal and external conflicts which result inter-alia in delinquency. The delinquency proneness of these boys is augmenting the more the receiving community refrains from guiding and helping them to find their place in the new society. In that case a boy may develop a feeling that he is being discriminated against; the delinquency proneness therefore increases with the accumulation of real or illusory discrimination and failure experiences with the result that the rate of delinquency of the oriental boy increases the longer his stay in the country. The European boy on the other hand shows a better capacity of adaptation to the environment irrespective of the fact whether the receiving community is fully prepared to assist him in the process of integration or not, the latter is therefore less prone to seek anti-social substitutes of satisfaction and consequently the longer he stays in the country the less his susceptibility of turning delinquent.[39]

The committee states however that due to insufficient statistical data this conclusion should be regarded as a working hypothesis only to be confirmed or refuted by further research. It states however that, "primafacie the cultural differences (i.e., oriental-European) have a greater causal signifi-

---

[36] The rates for *native*-born delinquents of immigrant parentage could not be determined. The necessary data are not yet fully available, inasmuch as criminal responsibility begins at the age of 9, and "new" immigrants are those who entered the country after 1948.

[37] Ministry of Social Welfare, Juvenile Probation Service Report (1958).

[38] Juvenile Delinquency in Israel (Ministry of Justice 1956).

[39] *Id.* at 19.

cance than the sheer fact of immigration."[40]

It may be worthwhile to point out that according to the basic premises of the culture-conflict hypothesis, immigration and different ethnic origin are actually two aspects of the same thing. A clash of conduct norms with a resultant increase in crime may result from the conflict of norms and values among individuals and groups, within a given community, who have different cultural definitions due to different cultural traditions and backgrounds. But the same clash may result when members of one cultural group migrate to a community having a different culture.[41] The chances are that when a vast array of groups of different cultural traditions meet—not in a mutual country of origin, but through migration to a new country—the degree of culture-conflict, with the resultant crime and delinquency rates, will be higher among the new groups than among members of the receiving community, even though the receiving community is composed of divergent ethnic and cultural groups. This point, of primary importance for our present purposes, was partly confirmed by the data presented in this paper. The relative causal significance of immigration and different ethnic origins to the etiology of culture conflct—important as it is—is really not relevant for our present purposes. The committee has pointed out that a comparison between the relevant data of two years (i.e., 1951 and 1953) was not sufficient for conclusive results. We

may add that the time span between 1948–49 (the beginning of new immigration) and 1951 or 1953 was not long enough for the process of culture-conflict to crystalize its effects on the nature and rates of delinquency among the immigrants; moreover there was not yet any native-born second generation to be studied, and we have seen that one of the major points in the culture-conflict hypothesis concerns the second generation. A wide and thorough research into the problem of the impact of immigration on crime and delinquency in Israel, if undertaken now, will have at its disposal the relevant data from the last decade, including the 9–15 age group of the native-born second generation.

CONCLUSION

The purpose of this paper is to state the problem of culture-conflict and crime in relation to the criminality of immigrants in Israel. The criminality and delinquency of "new" immigrants tends to be considerably higher then the criminality and delinquency of the native-born and "old" immigrants. Differential crime and delinquency rates are also apparent between the European and the oriental Jews, the rates of the latter tending to be higher. We may state therefore that these primary findings call for further research into the nature and extent of culture-conflict and crime in Israel in relation to the "new" immigrants. The vast array of ethnic groups among the immigrants, the diversity of their cultural traditions, and the special social structure of the receiving community afford a unique opportunity to test one of the basic issues of the etiology of crime on the social level.

---

[40] *Ibid.*

[41] See Sellin, *op. cit. supra* note 5, at 63.

23. DIFFERENTIAL ASSOCIATION

EDWIN H. SUTHERLAND

THE SCIENTIFIC EXPLANATION OF A PHEnomenon may be stated either in terms of the factors which are operating at the moment of the occurrence of a phenomenon or in terms of the processes operating in the earlier history of that phenomenon. In the first case the explanation is mechanistic, in the second historical or genetic; both are usable. The physical and biological scientists favor the first of these methods, and it would probably be superior as an explanation of criminal behavior. Efforts at explanations of the mechanistic type have been notably unsuccessful, perhaps largely because they have been concentrated on the attempt to isolate personal and social pathologies. Work from this point of view has, at least, resulted in the conclusion that the immediate factors in criminal behavior lie in the person-situation complex. Person and situation are not factors exclusive of each other, for the situation which is important is the situation as defined by the person who is involved. The tendencies and inhibitions at the moment of the criminal behavior are, to be sure, largely a product of the earlier history of the person, but the expression of these tendencies and inhibitions is a reaction to the immediate situation as defined by the person. The

►SOURCE: *Principles of Criminology* (4th Edition) Philadelphia: J. B. Lippincott Company, 1947, pp. 5–7, reprinted in Sutherland Papers, Albert Cohen et. al. Bloomington: Indiana University Press, 1956, pp. 7–12. Reprinted by permission.

situation operates in many ways, of which perhaps the least important is the provision of an opportunity for a criminal act. A thief may steal from a fruit stand when the owner is not in sight but refrain when the owner is in sight; a bank burglar may attack a bank which is poorly protected but refrain from attacking a bank protected by watchmen and burglar alarms. A corporation which manufactures automobiles seldom or never violates the Pure Food and Drug Law, but a meat-packing corporation violates this law with great frequency.

The second type of explanation of criminal behavior is made in terms of the life experience of a person and is a historical or genetic explanation of criminal behavior. This, to be sure, assumes a situation to be defined by the person in terms of the inclinations and abilities which the person has acquired up to that date. The following paragraphs state such a genetic theory [i.e., the theory of differential association] of criminal behavior on the assumption that a criminal act occurs when a situation appropriate for it, as defined by a person, is present.

(1) *Criminal behavior is learned*. Negatively, this means that criminal behavior is not inherited, as such; also, the person who is not already trained in crime does not invent criminal behavior, just as a person does not make mechanical inventions unless he has had training in mechanics.

(2) *Criminal behavior is learned in interaction with other persons in a process of communication.* This communication is verbal in many respects but includes also "the communication of gestures."

(3) *The principal part of the learning of criminal behavior occurs within intimate personal groups.* Negatively, this means that the impersonal agencies of communication, such as picture shows and newspapers, play a relatively unimportant part in the genesis of criminal behavior.

(4) *When criminal behavior is learned, the learning includes* (a) *techniques of committing the crime, which are sometimes very complicated, sometimes very simple;* (b) *the specific direction of motives, drives, rationalizations, and attitudes.*

(5) *The specific direction of motives and drives is learned from definitions of legal codes as favorable and unfavorable.* In some societies an individual is surrounded by persons who invariably define the legal codes as rules to be observed, whereas in others he is surrounded by persons whose definitions are favorable to the violation of the legal codes. In our American society these definitions are almost always mixed, and consequently we have culture conflict in relation to the legal codes.

(6) *A person becomes delinquent because of an excess of definitions favorable to violation of law over definitions unfavorable to violation of law.* This is the principle of differential association. It refers to both criminal and anti-criminal associations and has to do with counteracting forces. When persons become criminals, they do so because of contacts with criminal patterns and also because of isolation from anti-criminal patterns. Any person inevitably assimilates the surrounding culture unless other patterns are in conflict; a Southerner does not pronounce "r" because other Southerners do not pronounce "r." Negatively, this proposition of differential association means that associations which are neutral so far as crime is concerned have little or no effect on the genesis of criminal behavior. Much of the experience of a person is neutral in this sense, e.g., learning to brush one's teeth. This behavior has no negative or positive effect on criminal behavior except as it may be related to associations which are concerned with the legal codes. This neutral behavior is important especially as an occupier of the time of a child so that he is not in contact with criminal behavior during the time he is engaged in neutral behavior.

(7) *Differential associations may vary in frequency, duration, priority, and intensity.* This means that associations with criminal behavior and also associations with anti-criminal behavior vary in those respects. "Frequency" and "duration" as modalities of associations are obvious and need no explanation. "Priority" is assumed to be important in the sense that lawful behavior developed in early childhood may persist throughout life, and also that delinquent behavior developed in early childhood may persist throughout life. This tendency, however, has not been adequately demonstrated, and priority seems to be important principally through its selective influence. "Intensity" is not precisely defined, but it has to do with such things as the prestige of the source of a criminal or anti-criminal pattern and with emotional reactions related to the associations. In a precise description of the criminal behavior of a person these modalities would be stated in quantitative form and a mathematical ratio be reached. A formula in this sense has not been developed, and the development of such a formula would be extremely difficult.

(8) *The process of learning criminal behavior by association with criminal and anti-criminal patterns involves all of the mechanisms that are involved in any other learning.* Negatively, this means that the learning of criminal behavior is not restricted to the process of imitation. A person who is seduced, for instance, learns criminal behavior by association, but this

process would not ordinarily be described as imitation.

(9) *Though criminal behavior is an expression of general needs and values, it is not explained by those general needs and values since non-criminal behavior is an expression of the same needs and values.* Thieves generally steal in order to secure money, but likewise honest laborers work in order to secure money. The attempts by many scholars to explain criminal behavior by general drives and values, such as the happiness principle, striving for social status, the money motive, or frustration, have been and must continue to be futile since they explain lawful behavior as completely as they explain criminal behavior. They are similar to respiration, which is necessary for any behavior but which does not differentiate criminal from non-criminal behavior.

It is not necessary, on this level of discussion, to explain why a person has the associations which he has; this certainly involves a complex of many things. In an area where the delinquency rate is high a boy who is sociable, gregarious, active, and athletic is very likely to come in contact with the other boys in the neighborhood, learn delinquent behavior from them, and become a gangster; in the same neighborhood the psychopathic boy who is isolated, introvert, and inert may remain at home, not become acquainted with the other boys in the neighborhood, and not become delinquent. In another situation, the sociable, athletic, aggressive boy may become a member of a scout troop and not become involved in delinquent behavior. The person's associations are determined in a general context of social organization. A child is ordinarily reared in a family; the place of residence of the family is determined largely by family income; and the delinquency rate is in many respects related to the rental value of the houses. Many other factors enter into this social organization, including many personal group relationships.

The preceding explanation of criminal behavior was stated from the point of view of the person who engages in criminal behavior. It is also possible to state theories of criminal behavior from the point of view of the community, nation, or other group. The problem, when thus stated, is generally concerned with crime rates and involves a comparison of the crime rates of various groups or the crime rates of a particular group at different times. One of the best explanations of crime rates from this point of view is that a high crime rate is due to social disorganization. The term "social disorganization" is not entirely satisfactory, and it seems preferable to substitute for it the term "differential social organization." The postulate on which this theory is based, regardless of the name, is that crime is rooted in the social organization and is an expression of that social organization. A group may be organized for criminal behavior or organized against criminal behavior. Most communities are organized both for criminal and anti-criminal behavior, and in that sense the crime rate is an expression of the differential group organization. Differential group organization as an explanation of a crime rate must be consistent with the explanation of the criminal behavior of the person, since the crime rate is a summary statement of the number of persons in the group who commit crimes and the frequency with which they commit crimes.

24. AN EMPIRICAL TEST OF DIFFERENTIAL ASSOCIATION THEORY

ALBERT J. RIESS, JR.
A. LEWIS RHODES

A BASIC POSTULATE IN SOCIOLOGICAL WRITING about delinquents is that delinquent behavior is essentially group behavior. Sociologists have shown that groups enter into delinquent activity in a number of ways. Beckenridge and Abbott were among the first to point out that not only are most delinquent offenses committed in groups but that most lone offenders are influenced by companions.[1] Somewhat later, Shaw and Meyer[2] and Shaw and McKay[3] estimated the extent to which juvenile delinquency is group activity, showing that less than 20 percent are lone offenders in juvenile court samples. Shaw and McKay also showed that the modal size of offending groups is two and three participants, and that not all group delinquency is committed by well organized gangs.[4] More recently Enyon and Reckless demonstrated that companionship is usually present at the onset of admitted delinquency as well as in officially recorded delinquency.[5] These studies for the United States and similar ones in other countries clearly establish that most delinquent behavior is committed as group activity.

Following Sutherland, many sociologists reason that delinquent behavior is genetically a function of learning delinquency through association with delinquents within intimate personal groups.[6] That this hypothesis is not demonstrated is troublesome to some sociologists[7] and a basis for criticism by others.[8] Criticism of

▶SOURCE: "An Empirical Test of Differential Association Theory", Journal of Research in Crime and Delinquency (January 1964), 1:1:5–18. Reprinted by permission.

[1] Sophonisba P. Breckinridge and Edith Abbot, *The Delinquent Child and the Home,* New York: The Russell Sage Foundation, 1917, pp. 34–35.

[2] Clifford R. Shaw and Earl D. Meyer, "The Juveline Delinquent," in *The Illinois Crime Survey,* Illinois Association for Criminal Justice, 1929, p. 662.

[3] Clifford R. Shaw and Henry D. McKay, "Social Factors in Juvenile Delinquency: A Study of the Community, the Family, and the Gang in Relation to Delinquent Behavior," National Commission on Law Observance and Enforcement, *Report on the Causes of Crime,* Washington, D.C.: USGPO, 1931, Volume II, No. 13, Chapter VI, esp. pp. 194–199.

[4] *Ibid.,* p. 195.

[5] Thomas G. Enyon and Walter C. Reckless, "Companionships at Delinquency Onset," *The British Journal of Criminology,* 2 (October, 1961), 167–68.

[6] Albert Cohen, Alfred Lindesmith and Karl Schuessler, *The Sutherland Papers,* Bloomington: Indiana University Press, 1956, pp. 8–11.

[7] Donald R. Cressey, "Epidemiology and Individual Conduct: A Case from Criminology," *Pacific Sociological Review,* 3 (Fall, 1960), and James F. Short, Jr., "Differential Association as a Hypothesis: Problems of Empirical Testing," *Social Problems,* 8 (Summer, 1960), pp. 14–25.

[8] The most pointed criticism has been made by the Gluecks. Sheldon and Eleanor Glueck, *Unraveling Juvenile Delinquency,* Cambridge: Harvard University Press, 1950, pp. 146–149 and 163–164. See also Marshall Clinard, "Criminological Research," in Robert K. Merton, Leonard Broom and Leonard S. Cottrell, Jr. (eds.), *Sociology Today:*

the hypothesis rests on a logical argument that empirical evidence of association in delinquent acts merely demonstrates concomitance of behavior, whereas a temporal sequence of the effects of association must be demonstrated.[9]

It is one thing to demonstrate that most delinquents associate with other delinquents, participate with them in delinquent activity or are members of a group where others are delinquent and that conforming boys and girls generally associate with other conformers, or belong to groups where behavior is essentially conforming to societal norms. It is quite another to demonstrate that delinquent behavior occurs after induction into a delinquent group, or that delinquency occurs as group activity after a group is formed. Apart from the methodological issues raised by a causal demonstration of group effects on individual behavior and the nature of criteria for an adequate test of differential association theory, there are problems of conceptualizing group effects and operationalizing concepts in differential association theory.

TESTING THE THEORY

Sutherland never explicitly formulated his hypothesis of differential association in operational terms and Short questions whether it lends itself to operationalization without reformulation.[10] Short, however, devised a test of differential association theory to show that the frequency, duration, priority and intensity of association with delinquent and anti-delinquent culture and behavior varies among delinquent and nondelinquent groups. He defined intensity of association as a subject's perception of the delinquency of his best friends and concludes that, among his

---

Problems and Prospects. New York: Basic Books, Inc., 1959, Chapter 23.

[9] Sheldon Glueck, "Theory and Fact in Criminology," *British Journal of Delinquency,* 7 (July, 1956), 92–109.

[10] James F. Short, Jr., *op. cit.,* p. 17.

operational measures of differential association, this measure of intensity is most consistently and strongly related to the delinquency of youth.[11] Short's test rests on a *subject's definition* of best friends as delinquent. The main purpose of this paper is to make a test similar to Short's on the effect of intensity of association, using, however, data on the *actual delinquency* known and reported by a boy and his best friends. We propose to examine whether the probability of an individual engaging in several different kinds of delinquent acts is associated with his close friends also having engaged in these acts. It should be apparent that a failure to demonstrate that one's close friends have delinquent behavior patterns similar to one's own in no way contradicts or supports the hypothesis that most delinquent behavior occurs as group activity. Rather, it would simply put in doubt the judgment that boys who engage in a kind of delinquent activity are generally also in *intimate* association with one another.

Sutherland's differential association hypothesis holds that variation in frequency, duration, priority and intensity of association with delinquent behavior patterns accounts for delinquent behavior. The homophily hypothesis holds that one is likely to select as best friends those whose values and behavior are similar to one's own [12] while coalition theory argues that all other things being equal, constraints on members who deviate from the expectations of the group lead to their behaving in conformity with these standards.[13]

---

[11] James F. Short, Jr., *op. cit.,* p. 18.

[12] Paul F. Lazarsfeld and Robert K. Merton, "Friendship as Social Process: A Substantive and Methodological Analysis," in Morroe Berger, et. al., *Freedom and Control in Modern Society,* New York: D. Van Nostrand Co., Inc., esp. footnote 19.

[13] John W. Thibaut and Harold H. Kelley, *The Social Psychology of Groups,* New York: John W. Wiley, Inc., 1959, pp. 208 and 210, and L. Festinger and J. Thibaut, "Interpersonal Communication in Small Groups," *Journal of Abnormal and Social Psychology,* XLVI (1951), 92–100.

Though not explicitly stated in any theory, both group selection and group constraint hypotheses lead to the same conclusion: one's close friends should have a delinquency history similar to one's own.

It is apparent, however, that there is considerable variation over time in the cliques to which an adolescent belongs, in whom he will select as his best friends, and in the kinds of delinquent activity in which he will engage. Shaw pointed out, for example, that Sidney in the course of his delinquent career from 7 to 17 years of age was officially known to have been involved in delinquency with 11 different companions, representing three distinct groups whose activities and traditions were delinquent in character, and that he was never implicated in any offense with more than three delinquents.[14] Recognizing that current best friends are not necessarily companions from past delinquent association, it seems consistent with differential association theory to argue that, if current best friends comprise a salient primary group, and if past behavior serves as a basis for mutual communication and action within it (which it need not), then boys currently in intense association with one another should show similar patterns of delinquency. Assuming that specific techniques for committing delinquent acts are communicated in primary association, it follows that all, or none, of the boys in close friendship triads should report committing a given kind of offense. Within a triadic friendship group, there should be no dyads committing a given type of offense, since group constraint should produce homogeneity in behavior. It should be clear that whether or not boys in close friendship groups show similarity in delinquent behavior because they select one another on this basis, or as a result of association, failure to show that delinquency histories of boys in close friendship groups are the same casts doubt at least upon the *specificity* of any learned delinquent behavior in intense association with others. Since Sutherland did not restrict this hypothesis to lower class delinquents, behavioral homophily should hold regardless of social class.[15]

To show that one's close friends are also delinquent is not to show that they have an effect on all of one's delinquent activity. Shaw and McKay early showed that stealing is more likely to be a group offense than are offenses against the home and school.[16] Enyon and Reckless have gone further to show that companionship characterizes first participation in some kind of offenses more than in others. Companions were present in 100 percent of boys' first involvement in gang fights but only 56 percent of the cases of first running away from home.[17] While our study cannot demonstrate the precise effect of friendship on delinquency patterns, it investigates the extent to which there is covariation in a boy's delinquent behavior and that of his friends for different kinds of delinquent behavior.

Sociological theories on delinquent subcultures that are consistent with Sutherland's differential association hypothesis postulate that members of delinquent subcultures become highly dependent upon one another, particularly for status gratification. As Short points out, it follows that members of such groups, having a more intense association with one another, should show greater similarity in their patterns of delinquency than do members of other delinquent groups.[18] Cohen's general theory of delinquent subcultures

---

[14] Clifford R. Shaw and Henry D. McKay, *op. cit.*, p. 221.

[15] *The Sutherland Papers, op. cit.*, p. 19, pp. 32–33 and pp. 58–59.

[16] Clifford R. Shaw and Henry D. McKay, *op. cit.*, pp. 195–196.

[17] Thomas G. Enyon and Walter C. Reckless, *op. cit.*, Table 3, p. 170.

[18] James F. Short, Jr., *op. cit.*, p. 17.

holds that subcultural delinquent groups should be homogeneous in behavior for a variety of delinquent offenses against property and persons. It is implicit in his theory that middle class boys will show less similarity and versatility in their delinquency.[19] Miller holds that delinquency is endemic in lower class culture. It would be consistent with his theory to argue that delinquent behavior of lower class boys is independent of the commission of the act by other members of the group.[20]

THE INVESTIGATION

The investigation was designed to gather information on the actual delinquent behavior of boys in close friendship cliques. A sample of 378 boys was drawn from a base population of all white males between the ages of 12 and 16 who were registered in one of 45 public, private or parochial junior or senior high schools in Davidson County, Tennessee during the 1957 school year. Strata were designed so as to select disproportionately lower- and middle-class delinquent boys.[21]

Each clique is a triad composed of a boy selected in the stratified probability sample of 378 boys and his two closest friends. Given a large population from which the sample of boys was drawn, only a few sample cases chose the same "closest" friends. Effects of overlapping friendship choice or of pyramiding therefore are negligible. Information was gathered for 299 triads and 79 dyads. The dyads are pairs where a boy selected only one "best friend." Data are presented in this paper only for the 299 triads. Each step was replicated for the 79 dyads and the results are similar where the number of dyads makes comparison possible.

The index person in each triad was classified into one of seven conforming or delinquent types.[22] The career-*oriented delinquent* is the most delinquent person in the classification schema. He is oriented toward the adult criminal world and maintains contact with adult criminals. The largest group of delinquents are *peer-oriented* and directed in their goals and behavior. The lone delinquent is our *nonconforming isolate*. There are four types of conforming boys. The *conforming nonachiever* is comparable to William Whyte's "corner boy" and the *conforming achiever* to his "college boy," if social class attributes are disregarded.[23] The *hyperconformer* disregards conventional for strict conformity while the *conforming isolate* is outside the clique system. Peer-oriented delinquents, conforming nonachievers, and achievers are divided into white-collar and blue-collar status based on father's occupation.[24]

The dependent variable, self-reported delinquent behavior, was measured by asking each boy how often he had done any of the following things, whether alone or with others, and by inquiring about the conditions related to it: taken little things worth less than $2? $2 to $50? more than $50? purposely damaged or destroyed property? taken a car without the owner's permission or knowledge? beat up somebody

---

[19] Albert K. Cohen, *Delinquent Boys: The Culture of the Gang*, Glencoe: The Free Press, 1955, pp. 157–169.

[20] Walter Miller, "The Impact of a 'Total Community' Delinquency Control Project," *Social Problems*, 10 (Fall, 1962), 169–191.

[21] This is a more efficient sample design inasmuch as delinquency is a relatively low incidence phenomenon in the general population. The methodological problems encountered in dealing with a low incidence phenomenon in a population have been discussed in Daniel Glaser, "Differential Association and Criminological Prediction," *Social Problems*, 8 (Summer, 1960), p. 7, and Albert J. Reiss, Jr., "Unraveling Juvenile Delinquency II: An Appraisal of the Research Methods," *American Journal of Sociology*, 57 (September, 1951), 118–119.

[22] Albert J. Reiss, Jr. and A. Lewis Rhodes, "The Distribution of Juvenile Delinquency in the Social Class Structure," *American Sociological Review*, 26 (October, 1961), Chart I.

[23] William F. Whyte, *Street Corner Society*, Chicago: University of Chicago Press, 1937.

[24] Albert J. Reiss, Jr. and A. Lewis Rhodes, *op. cit.*, pp. 721–722.

bad enough to be arrested?[25] Self-reports include virtually all cases of officially recorded delinquency. Only delinquent acts committed after age 10 are data for this paper.

Self-reported delinquent acts were tabulated for each of the six categories of delinquent act for the 299 triads arranged in the 10 types of conforming-delinquent, SES groups.[26] This tabulation provided information on kind of delinquent behavior reported by none, one, two or all members of the triad in each of the 10 conforming-delinquent groups. A model was then constructed to give the expected delinquent behavior composition of the triad, using the actual rate of delinquency for the sample of boys for estimation purposes. The model is based on the expansion of the binomial.[27] Our use of the binomial ignores variability in response patterns by friendship choice, e.g. $+$ (original) $-$ (first best friend) $+$ (second best friend) and $++-$ or $-++$ are all treated as two boys expected (or actual) to commit the act. This disregard of response order seems warranted for we cannot determine whether the original subject models his behavior on that of his two closest friends, or whether he chooses friends who have similar behavior, or whether they copy his behavior.

The observed distribution of boys in triads reporting they committed an act of delinquency is then compared with the expected distribution. The chi square test of goodness of fit is used to test the significance of the departure of the observed measure from the hypothetical one of the binomial.[28] Occasionally, the conventional test of the significance of difference between two proportions is used to test whether there is any significant difference in the number of observed and expected triads where all members of the triad reported committing the act.

Very briefly, this paper attempts to shed light on three closely related questions that are germane to propositions about the group nature of delinquency and the empirical testing of differential association theory: (1) Does the probability of an individual committing kinds of delinquent acts depend upon his close friends committing these acts? (2) Is there variation in dependence upon friends committing delinquent acts among different kinds of delinquent behavior? (3) Is the probability of committing a delinquent act less dependent upon one's friends committing the act in some kinds of conforming or delinquent groups than in others?

FINDINGS

Boys generally choose boys as close friends whose law-abiding or delinquent behavior is similar to their own. Table I answers our first question in comparing reported delinquent behavior of boys in triads with that expected from the proportion of boys in the sample who reported committing specific kinds of delinquency. For each kind of delinquent behavior, *the probability of an individual committing a specific delinquent act depends upon the commissions of the act by other members of the friendship triad.* More of the triads in Table I than expected from the binominal are made up of boys, all or none of

---

[25] Readers will note the similarity of these questions with the Nye-Short delinquency scale items: Ivan F. Nye and James F. Short, Jr., "Scaling Delinquent Behavior," *American Sociological Review*, 22 (June, 1957), 326–331.

[26] The authors express their appreciation to NAL, State University of Iowa for use of the IBM 650. A special program for rapid tabulation of response patterns in triads was developed for this study.

[27] $f(x) = \left(\frac{3!}{x!\,(3-x)!}\right) p^x (q)^{3-x}$

where x is the number of boys expected to commit the act (0, 1, 2 or 3); $_p$ is the proportion of the subgroup reporting commission of the act; $_q$ is the proportion of the subgroup not reporting commission of the act.

[28] No test was made if the expected frequency in any cell was less than two or less than five in two cells of a 2 × 3 table.

whom engaged in the same kind of delinquent act. The more serious the offense, the greater the difference between observed and expected proportions of triads where *all* of the boys committed the same kind of delinquent offense. Confidence in the finding that the probability for a boy committing a delinquent act is not independent of the behavior of his close friends is increased with the observation that fewer of the triads than expected have only one boy reporting he engaged in the delinquent activity. Table II restates the conclusion in a way that aids the interpretation. For each kind of act, significantly more of the original sociometric subjects who reported the offense, than of those who did not, have friends who also committed the act.

Nonetheless, Tables I and II make apparent considerable variation in delinquent behavior homophily of close friendship triads. Of the triads in Table I where at least one boy reported committing auto theft or assault, three-fifths have only one

Table I. *Observed (f), Expected $(f_e)^1$ and Sum of Expected $(f_\Sigma)^2$ for Conforming-Delinquent Subgroups. Number of White Male Triads Classified by Number of Males in Each Triad Who Reported Delinquent Behavior One or More Times for Six Kinds of Delinquent Behavior*

Kind of Delinquent Behavior	Per Cent Reporting Behavior	Number in Triad Reporting Delinquent Behavior				Number of Triads	$P(x^2)$ a
		0	1	2	3		
Auto theft	12						<.001
f_e		204	83	11*	1*	299	
f		229	42	17	11	299	
f_Σ		227	43	19	10	299	
Theft over $50	12						<.001
f_e		204	84	11*	1*	299	
f		236	31	18	14	299	
f_Σ		232	37	19	11	299	
Theft: $2-$50	18						<.001
f_e		111	130	51	7	299	
f		161	65	36	37	299	
f_Σ		150	78	44	27	299	
Assault	28						<.001
f_e		168	107	23*	2*	299	
f		200	61	18	20	299	
f_Σ		189	74	26	10	299	
Vandalism b	—b						<.001
f_e		44	116	103	31	294	
f		75	84	78	57	294	
f_Σ		60	103	86	45	294	
Theft under $2 b	—b						<.001
f_e		27	98	120	49	294	
f		52	80	77	85	294	
f_Σ		42	88	97	67	294	

[1] Expected frequencies are calculated for the binomial using the proportion of boys in the sample who reported committing each kind of delinquency.
[2] Expected frequencies were calculated for the binomial for each of 10 conforming-delinquent subgroups. The sum of these expected values is reported here.
a x^2 computed for actual (f) with expected (f_e) values only.
b Offense committed two or more times.
* Cell frequencies combined for computation of x^2.

Table II. *Per Cent of Triads with Number of Friends Committing Delinquent Act by Original Subject's Delinquent Behavior, for Six Kinds of Delinquent Behavior*

Original Subject's Delinquent Act	Number of Friends Committing Same Kind of Act				$P(x^2)$
	0	1	2	Total	
Auto theft					
Yes	45	28	27	40	.001
No	88	9	3	259	
Theft over $50					
Yes	29	29	42	34	.001
No	89	8	3	265	
Theft: $2-$50					
Yes	24	32	44	84	.001
No	75	21	4	215	
Assault					
Yes	35	27	38	52	.001
No	81	17	2	247	
Vandalism					
Yes	16	41	43	134	.001
No	47	39	14	160	
Theft under $2					
Yes	9	37	54	158	.001
No	38	48	14	136	

boy reporting he committed the act. By way of contrast, but one-fourth of the triads where at least one boy committed an act of vandalism and one in five for petty larceny are made up of boys where only one reported committing the act. Original sociometric subjects in Table II are more likely to choose boys as friends who also committed acts of vandalism or theft under two dollars than they are to have chosen boys as friends who also committed acts of auto larceny or assault, when they report having done these things. We must conclude in answer to our second question that although, in the aggregate, commission of a kind of delinquent act is not independent of the commission of the act by other members of a close friendship triad, the correlation varies with kind of delinquent behavior and is far from perfect for any kind.

We know from previous studies that roughly four-fifths of all boys arrested for delinquency had associates in the offense for which they were arrested, and that at least that high a proportion of delinquent boys have as close friends boys who have committed some kind of delinquent act. We must conclude then, that close friendship choices are more closely correlated with delinquency *per se* than with specialization or engagement in all specific kinds of delinquency.

Attention has been called to the ambiguity in formulation of Sutherland's differential association theory rendering difficult both operationalization of the theory and deductions from it. An altogether literal deduction from Sutherland's theory, though he never made it, is that either all or none of the boys in a close friendship triad should report committing the same kind of offense. It is immediately apparent from inspection of Tables I and II that there is a substantial number of triads where only one or two members of the triad committed the same kind of delinquent act, thereby calling into question any postulate about the homogeneity of law-violative behavior in triads through differential association. Let us assume, however, as does a variant of coalition theory, that when two members of a triad engage in a given kind of behavior, the third member is under strong pressure to do likewise.[29] We would expect, then, that there should be relatively few, if any, close friendship triads with only two members engaging in delinquent behavior. Expressing the triads where *all* members commit the same kind of delinquent act as a percent of all triads where two or three members commit the act, the following distribution results; auto theft (65 percent); theft over $50 (64 percent); theft $2-$50 (80 percent); assault (83 percent); vandalism (71 percent); theft under $2 (82 percent). The distribution supports the contention

---
[29] See footnote 13.

that there is pressure toward uniformity of behavior in these triads. In two-thirds or more of the triads, for each kind of delinquent offense, all members report they committed the act, i.e., if more than one did it, it was probably three. There remained, nonetheless, a substantial minority of triads in which only two members committed the same kind of delinquency. The more serious offenses are least likely to show triadic uniformity.

Thus far two main ways of accounting for the observed distribution of delinquent associates in close friendship triads have been introduced. We first examined whether the sample of triads was a sample drawn from a binomial based on the rate of a specified kind of delinquency, and we concluded that the departure of the observed distribution from the binomial exceeded that ordinarily encountered in random sampling. The probability of an individual committing a specific kind of delinquent act depends upon the commission of the act by other members of the friendship triad. We then examined whether the sample of triads conformed to predictions from Sutherland's differential association theory or coalition theory. Inasmuch as there was a substantial number of triads with only one or two members reporting they engaged in a specific kind of delinquent behavior, we are led to question the postulate that differential association is a necessary and sufficient condition explaining delinquency. Table III summarizes these comparisons and is a convenient way of raising the further question whether the observed distribution of triads departs more from the random distribution than the expected one based on the differential association hypothesis. Although no test of statistical significance is employed, it seems clear that the observed distribution is closer to the binomial than to the expected distribution based on the differential association hypothesis.

Table III. *Comparison of Reported Behavior in 299 Delinquent Triads (f) with Random Expectation (f_e) and Number Expected under Differential Association Effect on Behavior of Original Member of Sociometric Triad $(f_d)^2$ for Six Kinds of Delinquent Behavior*

Type of Delinquency and Number in Triad Committing Act	f_e^1	f	f_d^2
Auto theft			
3	*	11	40
2 or 1	95	59	0
0	204	229	259
Theft over $50			
3	*	14	34
2 or 1	95	49	0
0	204	236	265
Theft: $2-$50			
3	7	37	84
2 or 1	181	101	0
0	112	161	215
Assault			
3	2	20	52
2 or 1	129	79	0
0	168	200	247
Vandalism			
3	121	138	220
2 or 1	172	151	0
0	5	10	79
Theft under $2			
3	49	85	158
2 or 1	218	157	0
0	27	52	136

[1] The proportion of boys in the sample who reported each kind of delinquency is used to set up the binomial of triads.
[2] The expected values for differential association are the marginal frequencies of original subjects committing and not committing a specific kind of delinquent act.
* Less than one case.

The reciprocation of sociometric choices, the delinquency orientation and behavior of boys chosen as close friends, and the content and seriousness of a boy's delinquent offenses were the main criteria in classifying a boy into a particularly conforming or delinquent type in our study. The *type* and *content* of the delinquent offenses of his close friends were not used as criteria in classifying a boy into a particular group. Although classification of a boy and his friends into a conforming or delinquent subtype then is not independent of classification by type of delinquent behavior, there still can be considerable variation in the delinquent behavior among the members of a triad within any kind of delinquent group. Given the possibility of variation in type and content of delinquent offense within a triad, we compared the triads in each subtype of conforming or delinquent group to see whether boys in each subtype chose as close friends boys who committed acts of delinquency similar to their own. Table IV compares the reported behavior of boys in each subtype of conforming or delinquent triad with the behavior expected from the proportion of boys in each type who reported committing each kind of act. Such comparisons should permit us to learn whether membership in a specific kind of conforming or delinquent group has any effect upon one's delinquent behavior independent of the rate of delinquency within that type of group.

Inspection of Table IV shows that there is little significant variation between observed and expected values for any of the conforming-delinquent groups. The answer to our third question then is that selection of close friends who commit a specific kind of act within a given type of conforming-delinquent group is largely a function of the rate of that kind of delinquency within each group. The more boys there are committing any kind of offense in a type of group, the more likely one is to have groups in which all members commit that kind of offense. Put in another way, our classification of boys into conforming and delinquent types of groups accounts in large part for the tendency for boys to choose as close friends boys who commit delinquent acts similar to their own. This can be seen by turning again to Table I where we observe that the sum of the expected values for the conforming-delinquent subgroups is remarkably like that observed for all triads, particularly for the serious offenses of auto theft and theft over $50. These two types of offenses are more clearly concentrated in the career- and peer-oriented delinquent types, of course. The similarity between the sum of the expected values for subgroups and the actual behavior reported within triads is less marked for the less serious offenses, offenses which occur quite frequently in most conforming and delinquent groups.

These observations (a summary of which is aided by comparing the f and fΣ values in Table I) suggest that a model of random selection accounts for subcultural or career-oriented delinquents associating most frequently with boys who commit delinquent acts similar to their own, given our classification of them into that type of delinquent group. This finding, of course, should not obscure the fact that the classification system does discriminate among types of conforming and delinquent boys. Career-oriented delinquents are easily distinguished from all other types by the fact that for every kind of offense, at least two-thirds of the triads are made up of boys who committed the same kind of offense. There are significantly more career-oriented triads in which all members engaged in every kind of offense than in any other type of delinquent group except that peer-oriented white-collar delinquents have significantly more triads in which all members committed theft under two dollars.

We have shown that for each kind of delinquent behavior reported in this study, the probability of an individual committing a specific act of delinquency is dependent upon the commission of the act by other members of the triad. Except for Sutherland's original formulation of differential association theory, most contemporary sociological theories emphasize a qualitative difference between middle

Table IV. Observed (f) and Expected (f_e)² Number of White Male Triads Classified by Number of Males in Each Triad who Reported Delinquent Behavior for Each of Six Kinds of Delinquency in Each Type of Conforming-Delinquent Subgroup

Type of Conforming or Delinquent Group	Kind of Delinquent Act and Number in Triad Reporting Committing Act																							
	Theft under $2 More than Once				Vandalism More than Once				Theft: $2-$50 Once or More				Assault Once or More				Theft over $50 Once or More				Auto theft Once or More			
	0	1	2	3	0	1	2	3	0	1	2	3	0	1	2	3	0	1	2	3	0	1	2	3
Career oriented: B.C.																								
f_e	*	3	12	17†	*	4	13	15	*	2	11	19	1	7	14	10†	1	6	14	11	1	8	14	9
f	1	4	7	20	3	2	9	18	*	3	10	19	2	9	7	14	2	6	11	13	4	5	12	11
Peer oriented: B.C.																								
f_e	1	7	19	16	2	12	19	10	7	19	16	4	22	19	5	*	27	16	3	*	29	14	2	*
f	1	10	13	19	4	8	22	9	9	18	12	7	24	15	5	2	28	15	2	1	28	17	1	0
Peer oriented: W.C.																								
f_e	0	0	0	9	*	2	2	6	*	2	4	3	3	4	2	*	3	4	2	*	5	3	1	*
f	0	0	0	9	0	0	3	6	1	1	3	4	3	4	2	0	4	1	4		5	3	1	0
Conf. Non-achv: B.C.																								
f_e	10	29	27	8	16	32	21	5	42	27	6	*	55	18	2	*	69	6	*	*	69	6	*	*
f	15	23	24	12	19	29	18	8	45	22	5	3	59	12	2	2	70	4	1	0	68	6	1	0
Conf. Non-achv: W.C.																								
f_e	1	4	12	12	1	8	13	7	9	13	6	1	18	9	2	*	27	2	*	*	18	9	2	*
f	1	4	11	13	2	9	9	9	12	9	4	4	21	5	1	2	27	2	0	0	19	8	2	0
Nonconf. isolate																								
f_e	1	2	3	1	1	3	2	1	6	1	0	0	4	2	1	0	7	0	0	0	7	0	0	0
f		4	1	2	2	2	2	1	6	1	0	0	5	1	1	0	7	0	0	0	7	0	0	0
Conf. achiever: B.C.																								
f_e	8	10	4	*	10	9	3	*	19	3	*	*	17	5	0	0	22	2	0	0	22	0	0	0
f	8	9	4	1	11	8	2	1	20	1	1	0	17	5	0	0	22	0	0	0	22	0	0	0
Conf. achiever: W.C.																								
f_e	10	21	16	4†	17	23	10	1	40	10	1	0	45	6	0	0	49	2	0	0	48	3	*	0
f	14	17	12	8	22	16	8	5	41	9	1	0	45	6	0	0	49	2	0	0	48	3	0	0
Conf. isolate																								
f_e	6	8	3	0	6	8	3	0	17	1	0	0	15	3	0	0	17	1	0	0	18	0	0	0
f	7	6	3	1	6	6	5	0	17	1	0	0	15	3	0	0	17	1	0	0	18	0	0	0
Hyperconformer																								
f_e	5	4	1	0	7	3	0	0	10	0	0	0	9	1	0	0	10	0	0	0	10	0	0	0
f	5	3	2	0	6	4	0	0	10	0	0	0	9	1	0	0	10	0	0	0	10	0	0	0

Table V. *Observed (f) and Expected (f_e)[1] Number of White Male Triads Classified by Number of Males in Each Triad who Reported Delinquent Behavior for Six Kinds of Delinquent Behavior, Controlling on Social Class of Original Subject in Each Triad*

Kind of Delinquent Behavior	Number in Triad Reporting Delinquent Behavior by Social Class									
	White Collar Triads					Blue Collar Triads				
	0	1	2	3	$P(x^2)$	0	1	2	3	$P(x^2)$
Done One or More Times										
Auto theft										
f_e	72	16	1	*		100	61	13	1	
f	72	14	3	0	p > .90	122	28	14	11	p < .001
Theft over $50										
f_e	76	12	1	*		96	64	14	1	
f	80	5	4	0	p > .20	122	25	14	14	p < .001
Assault										
f_e	65	22	2	*		80	72	21	2	
f	69	15	3	2	p > .30	102	41	14	18	p < .001
Theft: $2-$50										
f_e	42	36	10	1		46	77	44	8	
f	54	19	8	8	p < .001	74	44	28	29	p < .001
Done More than Once										
Vandalism										
f_e	13	36	31	9		22	64	64	21	
f	24	25	20	20	p < .001	37	47	51	36	p < .001
Theft under $2										
f_e	6	27	38	18		13	52	73	33	
f	15	21	23	30	p < .001	25	46	48	52	p < .001

* Expected frequency is less than one case.
[1] The proportion of boys in each social class subgroup who reported committing each kind of delinquency is used to set up the binomial of triads for each social class subgroup.

and lower class delinquency. In Table V we ask whether the finding that a boy's delinquent behavior depends upon his close friends engaging in it is independent of the social class status of the boys. It clearly is not for all types of offenses. Among blue-collar boys, the probability of a boy engaging in any specific kind of delinquency depends upon his close friends engaging in it but among white-collar boys this is true only for theft involving amounts of less than $50 or for vandalism. Apparently when middle class delinquent boys engage in serious delinquent behavior it is relatively independent of their close friendship choices.

Our interviews with subjects were structured so as to avoid mention by name of close friends in delinquency. To do so would violate peer norms about "squealers" and at times jeopardize rapport. Many respondents nevertheless volunteered names of their co-participants for delinquent acts in which they had associates and these were usually persons mentioned as "closest friends." Each respondent was explicitly asked for each reported delinquent offense whether he was (always, usually, sometimes or never) alone (or with one or more persons) when committing it. Table VI presents this information only for those triads in which all members reported committing

Table VI. *Per Cent of Triads Where All Boys Admit Delinquent Acts in Which All Boys Also Indicate Commission of Act with Someone Else, by Kind of Act and Type of Triad*

Type of Conforming or Delinquent Triad	Theft <$2 Once or More		Vandalism Once or More		Theft: $2-$50 Once or More		Assault Once or More		Theft >$50 Once or More		Auto Theft Once or More	
	Per Cent	Number	Per Cent	Number	Per Cent	Number	Per Cent	Number	Per Cent	Number	Per Cent	Number
Career Oriented: B.C.	45	22	86	21	74	19	79	14	100	13	82	11
Peer Oriented: B.C.	45	29	74	19	43	7	50	2	0	1	0	0
Peer Oriented: W.C.	22	9	100	7	75	4	0	0	0	0	0	0
Conf. non-achv: B.C.	32	25	80	20	67	3	0	2	0	0	0	0
Conf. non-achv: W.C.	42	19	92	13	100	4	50	2	0	0	0	0
Non-conf. isolate	20	5	100	3	0	0	0	0	0	0	0	0
Conf. achiever: B.C.	0	6	80	5	0	0	0	0	0	0	0	0
Conf. achiever: W.C.	5	19	80	10	0	0	0	0	0	0	0	0
Conf. isolate	25	4	100	2	0	0	0	0	0	0	0	0
Hyperconformer	0	0	0	0	0	0	0	0	0	0	0	0

a specific kind of delinquent act. The objective is to investigate whether unanimous reporting of engaging in a kind of delinquent behavior in a triad means they engaged in the behavior as group activity. Evidently this is not always the case. It is apparent that, for close friendship groups where all members committed the same kind of act, participants are most likely to report vandalism as group activity and least likely to report theft under $2 as group activity. This finding is consistent with that of Enyon and Reckless on the percentage of cases in which companions were present at first occurrence of admitted delinquency, it being higher for acts of vandalism (91 percent) than for taking things under $2 (69 percent).[30]

If attention is directed to variation in group involvement in delinquency among our conforming-delinquent types of triads, there is substantial evidence that only career-oriented delinquents report group involvement for all types of offense other than theft under $2. The career-oriented delinquent is apparently most likely to commit his offenses with accomplices.

[30] Thomas G. Enyon and Walter C. Reckless, *op. cit.*, Table 4.

SUMMARY AND CONCLUSIONS

The main question for this paper was whether boys in close friendship groups have the same specific patterns of delinquent behavior. The reported delinquent behavior of boys in close friendship triads was compared with that expected for six kinds of delinquent behavior. Two different ways of accounting for the observed distribution were examined.

The first compares the observed delinquent behavior of boys in triads with a binomial based on the rate for each kind of delinquency in the population. We concluded that the probability for an individual committing a specific kind of delinquent act depends upon the commission of the act by other members of the triad. This dependence upon close friends engaging in delinquent activity is not independent of the social class status of boys for all kinds of offenses, however. Among blue-collar boys, the probability of a boy engaging in any of the six kinds of delinquency depends upon his close friends engaging in it but among white-collar boys this is true only for the less serious offenses.

The second comparison asks whether behavior of boys in triads departs from predictions from Sutherland's differential association theory or coalition theory that there be uniform conformity in conforming groups and uniformity of specific kinds of delinquent behavior in delinquent groups. We concluded there is considerable departure from this explanatory model even when only those groups are considered where at least two boys engaged in the same kind of delinquency. The observed distribution of delinquency in close friendship triads departs somewhat less from the random than the differential association model, at least for the more serious offenses.

There is in fact considerable variation in the delinquent behavior homophily of friendship triads. The degree to which commission of a kind of delinquent act depends upon its commission by other members of the triad varies considerably by type of delinquency. Vandalism and petty larceny, the more common offenses, are commonly committed by two or three members of the triad while a majority of the triads where at least one member committed auto theft or assault are made up of only one member committing the offense. Behavioral homophily in triads does not mean that boys always or usually commit these offenses together, since there is evidence that theft under $2 is least likely to involve group activity. Two things seem evident from these findings, that delinquent behavior homophily in close friendship triads does not necessarily involve association in the commission of offenses and that some offenses are more clearly group activity than others.

Our classification of boys into conforming and delinquent subgroups accounts in large part for the selection of close friends who commit delinquent acts similar to one's own. While career-oriented delinquent boys generally have the highest proportion of triads where boys commit the same kind of delinquent act, they also have the highest overall rate of delinquency for each kind of act. The main problem is to account for the higher rate of delinquency among these boys. Certainly the effect of one's close friends on delinquency does not appear to be a sufficient reason to account for this higher rate since a substantial minority of career-oriented delinquent boys are in close friendship triads where at least one other boy does not commit the same kind of offense and the convergence of boys who commit the same kind of delinquent act in close friendship triads is not greater than that one would expect from the rate of delinquency among these boys.

This study cannot be construed as a test of the genetic formulation of the differential association hypothesis. To the extent that the findings of this study are valid and our logical inferences correctly drawn, however, they may be disappointing to proponents of differential association theory. The association of boys with the *same kind* of delinquent behavior in close friendship triads while somewhat greater than chance is well below what one would expect from the learning hypothesis in differential association theory and the results are not independent of social class. Close friendship choices are more closely correlated with delinquency *per se* than with participation in specific patterns of delinquency presumably learned from others.

The results also cannot be interpreted as clearly supporting one of the major theories of delinquent behavior over that of another, though some postulates in these theories seem supported over others. The main sociological theories of subcultural delinquency such as those of Cohen and Walter Miller postulating differences between lower and middle class gang behavior find some support in this study. Delinquency among middle class boys, particularly for the more serious delinquent offenses, is independent of friendship choices while among lower class boys the probability of committing any kind of delinquent activity is related to the delinquent activity of one's close friends. The fact that selection of close friends who commit specific kinds of delinquency within each type of conforming-delinquent group is largely a function of the rate of delinquency within each group lends support to Walter Miller's contention that delinquency is endemic in lower class culture. Nonetheless, if Miller is correct, convergence of delinquent patterns of behavior in friendship groups should not exceed chance since he argues that the pressures toward deviance come from outside the immediate peer group. The fact that the probability of a lower class boy's committing any specific kind of delinquency is dependent upon the commission of the act by other members of the group therefore is at odds with Miller's formulation. The model of differential association seems even a less powerful one in accounting for our observed patterns of behavior in close friendship triads than does Miller's formulation, however.

The fact that a substantial proportion of career-oriented delinquent boys do show a marked similarity in delinquent activity, particularly for the more serious offenses, is consistent with Cohen's formulation emphasizing the versatility of delinquency among subcultural delinquents. That some of these groups may be specialized in specific kinds of delinquent activity was not investigated.

This study perhaps only serves to emphasize the difficulty in testing inferences from differential association theory. It perhaps is unnecessary to repeat what is already well stated, that we need to operationalize the hypothesis in such a way as to test the relationship of association with delinquent others through crime. Of considerable importance, however, in future research would be an investigation of the "deviant" cases which do not conform to expectations of the differential association model. How can one account for the fact that all members of delinquent groups do not conform to the same patterns of delinquency? Why are some members of close friendship groups delinquent and not others? What are the patterns of recruitment to peer groups and how stable is peer group structure?

25. CULTURAL TRANSMISSION

CLIFFORD R. SHAW
HENRY D. McKAY

DIFFERENTIAL SYSTEMS OF VALUES

IN GENERAL, THE MORE SUBTLE DIFFERENCES between types of communities in Chicago may be encompassed within the general proposition that in the areas of low rates of delinquents there is more or less uniformity, consistency, and universality of conventional values and attitudes with respect to child care, conformity to law, and related matters; whereas in the high-rate areas systems of competing and conflicting moral values have developed. Even though in the latter situation conventional traditions and institutions are dominant, delinquency has developed as a powerful competing way of life. It derives its impelling force in the boy's life from the fact that it provides a means of securing economic gain, prestige, and other human satisfactions and is embodied in delinquent groups and criminal organizations, many of which have great influence, power, and prestige.

In the areas of high economic status where the rates of delinquents are low there is, in general, a similarity in the attitudes of the residents with reference to conventional values, as has been said, especially those related to the welfare of children. This is illustrated by the practical unanimity of opinion as to the desirability of education and constructive leisure-time activities and of the need for a general health program. It is shown, too, in the subtle, yet easily recognizable, pressure exerted upon children to keep them engaged in conventional activities, and in the resistance offered by the community to behavior which threatens the conventional values. It does not follow that all the activities participated in by members of the community are lawful; but, since any unlawful pursuits are likely to be carried out in other parts of the city, children living in the low-rate communities are, on the whole, insulated from direct contact with these deviant forms of adult behavior.

In the middle-class areas and the areas of high economic status, moreover, the similarity of attitudes and values as to social control is expressed in institutions and voluntary associations designed to perpetuate and protect these values. Among these may be included such organizations as the parent-teachers associations, women's clubs, service clubs, churches, neighborhood centers, and the like. Where these institutions represent dominant values, the child is exposed to, and participates in a significant way in one mode of life only. While he may have knowledge of alternatives, they are not integral parts of the system in which he participates.

In contrast, the areas of low economic

▶SOURCE: *Juvenile Delinquency and Urban Areas*, Chicago: University of Chicago Press, 1942, pp. 164–170, 435–441. (Editorial adaptations.) Copyright 1942, University of Chicago Press. Reprinted by permission.

status, where the rates of delinquents are high, are characterized by wide diversity in norms and standards of behavior. The moral values range from those that are strictly conventional to those in direct opposition to conventionality as symbolized by the family, the church, and other institutions common to our general society. The deviant values are symbolized by groups and institutions ranging from adult criminal gangs engaged in theft and the marketing of stolen goods, on the one hand, to quasi-legitimate businesses and the rackets through which partial or complete control of legitimate business is sometimes exercised, on the other. Thus, within the same community, theft may be defined as right and proper in some groups and as immoral, improper, and undesirable in others. In some groups wealth and prestige are secured through acts of skill and courage in the delinquent or criminal world, while in neighboring groups any attempt to achieve distinction in this manner would result in extreme disapprobation. Two conflicting systems of economic activity here present roughly equivalent opportunities for employment and for promotion. Evidence of success in the criminal world is indicated by the presence of adult criminals whose clothes and automobiles indicate unmistakably that they have prospered in their chosen fields. The values missed and the greater risks incurred are not so clearly apparent to the young.

Children living in such communities are exposed to a variety of contradictory standards and forms of behavior rather than to a relatively consistent and conventional pattern.[1] More than one type of moral institution and education are available to them. A boy may be familiar with, or exposed to, either the system of conventional activities or the system of criminal activities, or both. Similarly, he may participate in the activities of groups which engage mainly in delinquent activities, those concerned with conventional pursuits, or those which alternate between the two worlds. His attitudes and habits will be formed largely in accordance with the extent to which he participates in and becomes identified with one or the other of these several types of groups.

Conflicts of values necessarily arise when boys are brought in contact with so many forms of conduct not reconcilable with conventional morality as expressed in church and school. A boy may be found guilty of delinquency in the court, which represents the values of the larger society, for an act which has had at least tacit approval in the community in which he lives. It is perhaps common knowledge in the neighborhood that public funds are embezzled and that favors and special consideration can be received from some public officials through the payment of stipulated sums; the boys assume that all officials can be influenced in this way. They are familiar with the location of illegal institutions in the community and with the procedures through which such institutions are opened and kept in operation; they know where stolen goods can be sold and the kinds of merchandise for which there is a ready market; they know what the rackets are; and they see in fine clothes, expensive cars, and other lavish expenditures the evidences of wealth among those who openly engage in illegal activities. All boys in the city have some knowledge of these activities; but in the inner-city areas they are known intimately, in terms of personal relationships, while in other sections they enter the child's experience through more impersonal forms of communication, such as motion pictures, the newspaper, and the radio.

Other types of evidence tending to support the existence of diverse systems of

---

[1] Edwin H. Sutherland has called this process "differential association." See E. H. Sutherland, *Principles of Criminology* (Chicago: J. B. Lippincott Co., 1939), chap. I.

values in various areas are to be found in the data on delinquency and crime. In the previous chapter, variations by local areas in the number and rates of adult offenders were presented. When translated into its significance for children, the presence of a large number of adult criminals in certain areas means that children there are in contact with crime as a career and with the criminal way of life, symbolized by organized crime. In this type of organization can be seen the delegation of authority, the division of labor, the specialization of function, and all the other characteristics common to well-organized business institutions wherever found.

Similarly, the delinquency data presented graphically on spot maps and rate maps in the preceding pages give plausibility to the existence of a coherent system of values supporting delinquent acts. In making these interpretations it should be remembered that delinquency is essentially group behavior. A study of boys brought into the Juvenile Court of Cook County during the year of 1928 [2] revealed that 81.8 percent of these boys committed the offenses for which they were brought to court as members of groups. And when the offenses were limited to stealing, it was found that 89 percent of all offenders were taken to court as group or gang members. In many additional cases where the boy actually committed his offense alone, the influence of companions was, nevertheless, apparent. This point is illustrated in certain cases of boys charged with stealing from members of their own families, where the theft clearly reflects the influence and instigation of companions, and in instances where the problems of the boy charged with incorrigibility reveal conflicting values, those of the family competing with those of the delinquent group for his allegiance.

The heavy concentration of delinquency in certain areas means, therefore, that boys living in these areas are in contact not only with individuals who engage in proscribed activity but also with groups which sanction such behavior and exert pressure upon their members to conform to group standards. Examination of the distribution map reveals that, in contrast with the areas of concentration of delinquents, there are many other communities where the cases are so widely dispersed that the chances of a boy's having intimate contact with other delinquents or with delinquent groups are comparatively slight.

The importance of the concentration of delinquents is seen most clearly when the effect is viewed in a temporal perspective. The maps representing distribution of delinquents at successive periods indicate that, year after year, decade after decade, the same areas have been characterized by these concentrations. This means that delinquent boys in these areas have contact not only with other delinquents who are their contemporaries but also with older offenders, who in turn had contact with delinquents preceding them, and so on back to the earliest history of the neighborhood. This contact means that the traditions of delinquency can be and are transmitted down through successive generations of boys, in much the same way that language and other social forms are transmitted.

The cumulative effect of this transmission of tradition is seen in two kinds of data, which will be presented here only very briefly. The first is a study of offenses, which reveals that certain types of delinquency have tended to characterize certain city areas. The execution of each type involves techniques which must be learned from others who have participated in the same activity. Each involves specialization of function, and each has its own terminology and standards of behavior. Jack-

---

[2] Clifford R. Shaw and Henry D. McKay, *Social Factors in Juvenile Delinquency*. Vol. II of *Report on the Causes of Crime*, National Commission on Law Observance and Enforcement, Report No. 13 (Washington, D.C.: U.S. Government Printing Office, 1931), pp. 191–99.

rolling, shoplifting, stealing from junkmen, and stealing automobiles are examples of offenses with well-developed techniques, passed on by one generation to the next.

The second body of evidence on the effects of the continuity of tradition within delinquent groups comprises the results of a study of the contacts between delinquents, made through the use of official records.[3] The names of boys who appeared together in court were taken, and the range of their association with other boys whose names appeared in the same records was then analyzed and charted. It was found that some members of each delinquent group had participated in offenses in the company of other older boys, and so on, backward in time in an unbroken continuity as far as the records were available. The continuity thus traced is roughly comparable to that which might be established among baseball players through their appearance in official line-ups or regularly scheduled games. In baseball it is known that the techniques are transmitted through practice in back yards, playgrounds, sand lots, and in other places where boys congregate. Similarly in the case of delinquency traditions, if an unbroken continuity can be traced through formal institutions such as the Juvenile Court, the actual contacts among delinquents in the community must be numerous, continuous, and vital.

The way in which boys are inducted into unconventional behavior has been revealed by large numbers of case studies of youths living in areas where the rates of delinquents are high. Through the boy's own life-story the wide range of contacts with other boys has been revealed. These stories indicate how at early ages the boys took part with older boys in delinquent activities, and how, as they themselves acquired experience, they initiated others into the same pursuits. These cases reveal also the steps through which members are incorporated into the delinquent group organization. Often at early ages boys engage in malicious mischief and simple acts of stealing. As their careers develop, they become involved in more serious offenses, and finally become skilled workmen or specialists in some particular field of criminal activity. In each of these phases the boy is supported by the sanction and the approbation of the delinquent group to which he belongs.

SUMMARY AND INTERPRETATION

It is clear from the data that there is a direct relationship between conditions existing in local communities of American cities and differential rates of delinquents and criminals. Communities with high rates have social and economic characteristics which differentiate them from communities with low rates. Delinquency—particularly group delinquency, which constitutes a preponderance of all officially recorded offenses committed by boys and young men—has its roots in the dynamic life of the community.

It is recognized that the data may be interpreted from many different points of view. However, the high degree of consistency in the association between delinquency and other characteristics of the community not only sustains the conclusion that delinquent behavior is related dynamically to the community but also appears to establish that all community characteristics, including delinquency, are products of the operation of general processes more or less common to American cities. Moreover, the fact that in Chicago the rates of delinquents for many years have remained relatively constant in the areas adjacent to centers of commerce and heavy industry, despite successive changes in the nativity and nationality composition of the population, supports emphatically

---
[3] "Contacts between Successive Generations of Delinquent Boys in a Low-Income Area in Chicago" (unpublished study by the Department of Sociology, Illinois Institute for Juvenile Research 1940).

the conclusion that the delinquency-producing factors are inherent in the community.

From the data available it appears that local variations in the conduct of children, as revealed in differential rates of delinquents, reflect the differences in social values, norms, and attitudes to which the children are exposed. In some parts of the city attitudes which support and sanction delinquency are, it seems, sufficiently extensive and dynamic to become the controlling forces in the development of delinquent careers among relatively large number of boys and young men. These are the low-income areas, where delinquency has developed in the form of a social tradition, inseparable from the life of the local community.

This tradition is manifested in many different ways. It becomes meaningful to the child through the conduct, speech, gestures, and attitudes of persons with whom he has contact. Of particular importance is the child's intimate association with predatory gangs or other forms of delinquent and criminal organization. Through his contacts with these groups and by virtue of his participation in their activities he learns the techniques of stealing, becomes involved in binding relationships with his companions in delinquency, and acquires the attitudes appropriate to his position as a member of such groups. To use the words of Frank Tannenbaum: "It is the group that sets the pattern, provides the stimulus, gives the rewards in glory and companionship, offers the protection and loyalty, and, most of all, gives the criminal life its ethical content without which it cannot persist." [4]

In these communities many children encounter competing systems of values. Their community, which provides most of the social forms in terms of their life will be organized, presents conflicting possibilities.

A career in delinquency and crime is one alternative, which often becomes real and enticing to the boy because it offers the promise of economic gain, prestige, and companionship and because he becomes acquainted with it through relationships with persons whose esteem and approbation are vital to his security and to the achievement of satisfactory status. In this situation the delinquent group may become both the incentive and the mechanism for initiating the boys into a career of delinquency and crime and for sustaining him in such a career, once he has embarked upon it.

In cases of group delinquency it may be said, therefore, that from the point of view of the delinquent's immediate social world, he is not necessarily disorganized, maladjusted, or anti-social. Within the limits of his social world and in terms of its norms and expectations, he may be a highly organized and well-adjusted person.

The residential communities of higher economic status, where the proportion of persons dealt with as delinquents and criminals is relatively low, stand in sharp contrast to the situation described above. Here the norms and values of the child's social world are more or less uniformly and consistently conventional. Generally speaking, the boy who grows up in this situation is not faced with the problem of making a choice between conflicting systems of moral values. Throughout the range of his contacts in the community he encounters similar attitudes of approval or disapproval. Cases of delinquency are relatively few and sporadic. The system of conventional values in the community is sufficiently pervasive and powerful to control and organize effectively, with few exceptions, the lives of most children and young people.

In both these types of communities the dominant system of values is conventional. In the first, however, a powerful competing system of delinquency values exists; whereas in the second, such a system, if it

---

[4] *Crime and the Community* (New York: Ginn & Co., 1938), p. 475.

exists at all, is not sufficiently extensive and powerful to exercise a strong influence in the lives of many children. Most of the communities of the city fall between these two extremes and represent gradations in the extent to which delinquency has become an established way of life.

It is important to ask what the forces are which give rise to these significant differences in the organized values in different communities. Under what conditions do the conventional forces in the community become so weakened as to tolerate the development of a conflicting system of criminal values? Under what conditions is the conventional community capable of maintaining its integrity and exercising such control over the lives of its members as to check the development of the competing system? Obviously, any discussion of this question at present must be tentative. The data, however, afford a basis for consideration of certain points which may be significant.

It may be observed, in the first instance, that the variations in rates of officially recorded delinquents in communities of the city correspond very closely with variations in economic status. The communities with the highest rates of delinquents are occupied by those segments of the population whose position is most disadvantageous in relation to the distribution of economic, social, and cultural values. Of all the communities in the city, these have the fewest facilities for acquiring the economic goods indicative of status and success in our conventional culture. Residence in the community is in itself an indication of inferior status, from the standpoint of persons residing in the more prosperous areas. It is a handicap in securing employment and in making satisfactory advancement in industry and the professions. Fewer opportunities are provided for securing the training, education, and contacts which facilitate advancement in the fields of business, industry, and the professions.

The communities with the lowest rates of delinquents, on the other hand, occupy a relatively high position in relation to the economic and social hierarchy of the city. Here the residents are relatively much more secure; and adequate provision is offered to young people for securing the material possessions symbolic of success and the education, training, and personal contacts which facilitate their advancement in the conventional careers they may pursue.

Despite these marked differences in the relative position of people in different communities, children and young people in all areas, both rich and poor, are exposed to the luxury values and success patterns of our culture. In school and elsewhere they are also exposed to ideas of equality, freedom, and individual enterprise. Among children and young people residing in low-income areas, interests in acquiring material goods and enhancing personal status are developed which are often difficult to realize by legitimate means because of limited access to the necessary facilities and opportunities.

This disparity in the facilities available to people in different communities for achieving a satisfactory position of social security and prestige is particularly important in relation to delinquency and crime in the urban world. In the city, relationships are largely impersonal. Because of the anonymity in urban life, the individual is freed from much of the scrutiny and control which characterize life in primary-group situations in small towns and rural communities. Personal status and the status of one's community are, to a very great extent, determined by economic achievement. Superior status depends not so much on character as on the possession of those goods and values which symbolize success. Hence, the kind of clothes one wears, the automobile one drives, the type of building in which one lives, and the physical character of one's community become of great importance to the person. To a large degree these are the symbols of his position—the external evidences of the extent to which he has succeeded in the struggle for a living. The urban world, with its anonymity, its greater freedom, the more impersonal character of its relationships, and the varied assortment of economic, social, and cultural backgrounds in its communities, provides a general setting particularly conducive to the development of deviations in moral norms and behavior practices.

In the low-income areas, where there is the greatest deprivation and frustration, where, in the history of the city, immigrant and migrant groups have brought together the widest variety of divergent cultural traditions and institutions, and where there exists the greatest disparity between the social values to which the people aspire and the availability of facilities for acquiring these values in conventional ways, the development of crime as an organized way of life is most marked. Crime, in this situation, may be regarded as one of the means employed by people to acquire, or to attempt to acquire, the economic and social values generally idealized in our culture, which persons in other circumstances acquire by conventional means. While the origin of this tradition of crime is obscure, it can be said that its development in the history of the community has been facilitated by the fact that many persons have, as a result of their criminal activities, greatly improved their economic and social status. Their clothes, cars, and other possessions are unmistakable evidence of this fact. That many of these persons also acquire influence and power in politics and elsewhere is so well known that it does not need elaboration at this point. The power and affluence achieved, at least temporarily, by many persons involved in crime and illegal rackets are well known to the children and youth of the community and are important in determining the character of their ideals.

It may be said, therefore, that the existence of a powerful system of criminal values and relationships in low-income urban areas is the product of accumulative process extending back into the history of the community and of the city. It is related both to the general character of the urban world and to the fact that the population in these communities has long occupied a disadvantageous position. It has developed in somewhat the same way as have all social traditions, that is, as a means of satisfying certain felt needs within the limits of a particular social and economic framework.

It should be observed that, while the tradition of delinquency and crime is thus a powerful force in certain communities, it is only a part of the community's system of values. As was pointed out previously, the dominant tradition in every community is conventional, even in those having the highest rates of delinquents. The traditionally conventional values are embodied in the family, the church, the school, and many other such institutions and organizations. Since the dominant tradition in the community is conventional, more persons pursue law-abiding careers than careers of delinquency and crime, as might be expected.

In communities occupied by Orientals, even those communities located in the most deteriorated sections of our large cities, the solidarity of Old World cultures and institutions has been preserved to such a marked extent that control of the child is still sufficiently effective to keep at a minimum delinquency and other forms of deviant behavior. As Professor Hayner has pointed out in his chapter on five cities of the Pacific Northwest, the close integration of the Oriental family, the feeling of group responsibility for the behavior of the child, and the desire of these groups to maintain a good reputation in American communities have all been important elements in preserving this cultural solidarity.

It is the assumption of this study that many factors are important in determining whether a particular child will become involved in delinquency, even in those communities in which a system of delinquent and criminal values exists. Individual and personality differences, as well as differences in family relationships and in contacts with other institutions and groups, no doubt influence greatly his acceptance or rejection of opportunities to engage in delinquent activities. It may be said, however, that if the delinquency tradition were not present and the boys were not thus exposed to it, a preponderance of those who become delinquent in low-income areas would find their satisfactions in activities other than delinquency.

In conclusion, it is not assumed that this theoretical proposition applies to all cases of officially proscribed behavior. It applies primarily to those delinquent activities which become embodied in groups and social organizations. For the most part, these are offenses against property, which comprise a very large proportion of all the cases of boys coming to the attention of the courts.

26. AN ECOLOGICAL ANALYSIS OF CHICAGO

CLIFFORD R. SHAW
HENRY D. McKAY

THE 1900–1906 JUVENILE COURT SERIES

Series Studied and Types of Offenses. This includes series 8,056 male delinquents brought into the Juvenile Court of Cook County from Chicago during 1900–1906 (the first 7 years of the Juvenile Court's existence). By comparing this series with that for 1927–33 it will be possible to determine the extent to which variations in the rates correspond and the extent to which changes in rates can be related to changes in the physical or social characteristics of the local areas.

The age distribution of the boys in the 1900–1906 series indicates that, on the whole, they were a little younger than those in the more recent series. At that time the upper age limit in the Juvenile Court was 15 instead of 16, and a somewhat larger number of boys were under 10 years of age (6.1 percent). The highest frequencies were in ages 13, 14, and 15. With regard to offenses, it seems probable that some boys were taken to court in these earlier years on charges for which no petitions would be filed by the police probation officers at the present time. This is indicated both by the fact that the number of cases in court was greater in proportion to the population than at present and by the fact that the classification of offenses indicated a somewhat higher proportion of less serious charges.

Distribution of Delinquents. In this series, as in those previously discussed, it will be noted that a preponderance of the delinquent boys lived either in areas adjacent to the central business and industrial district or along the two forks of the Chicago River, Back of the Yards, or in South Chicago, with relatively few in other outlying areas.

While this series exhibits the same general configuration found in the other, there are two noticeable variations. First, the concentrations are somewhat more restricted and closer to the central business district and to the industrial centers than in the later series. This is to be expected, since many of the areas used for residential purposes in this early period have since been depopulated by expanding industry and commerce. Second, on this map there are relatively few delinquents in the areas east of State Street, south from the Loop. These areas, it will be remembered, contained many delinquents in the 1917–23 map and were also areas of heavy concentration in 1927–33.

Rates of Delinquents. The population upon which rates were calculated was secured by combining into 106 comparable areas the 1,200 enumeration districts of 1900 and the 431 census tracts of 1910 and

▶SOURCE: *Juvenile Delinquency and Urban Areas*, Chicago: University of Chicago Press, 1942, pp. 60–61, 63–68. (Editorial adaptations.) Copyright 1942, University of Chicago Press. Reprinted by permission.

computing the yearly increase or decrease of population in each. The population for the midyear of this series was then estimated from the age 10–15 male population in 1910. The areas for which rates are presented are practically the same as those used in the 1917–23 juvenile court series, except that in 7 instances it was necessary to construct combinations of the 113 areas in order to secure a larger population in districts which were sparsely settled at that time.

The rates in this series range from 0.6 to 29.8. The median is 4.9 and the rate for the city as a whole 8.4. Four areas have rates of 20.0 and over; 7 have rates of 15.0 or over; and 12 have rates of 12.0 or over. At the other extreme, 3 areas have rates of less than 1.0, and 12 of less than 2.0.

The 4 areas with highest rates are all immediately adjacent to the Loop, and other high-rate areas are in the Stock Yards district and in South Chicago. The areas with low rates, on the other hand, are located, for the most part, near the city's periphery. As compared to rate maps for subsequent series, it can be seen that the areas with very high rates are somewhat more closely concentrated around the central business district. This is especially noticeable south from the Loop and east of State Street, where, after the first 2 miles, the rates of delinquents are below the average for the city as a whole.

COMPARISONS AMONG JUVENILE COURT SERIES
(1927–33, 1917–23, AND 1900–1906)

Three methods will be employed to determine the extent to which the variations in rates of delinquents in the several time series correspond: (1) comparisons by zones, (2) area comparisons and correlations, and (3) extent of concentration.

Rates by Zones. Rates of delinquents were calculated for each of 5 zones drawn at 2-mile intervals, with a focal point in the heart of the central business district. These rates were computed on the basis of the number of delinquents and the total aged 10–16 male population in each zone.[1]

It should be borne in mind that zone rates of delinquents are presented chiefly because of their theoretical value. They show the variations in rates more conceptually and idealistically than do the rates for smaller units. The number of zones used for this purpose is not important, as it is not assumed that there are actual zones in the city or sharp dividing lines between those presented. It is assumed, rather, that a more or less continuous variation exists between the rates of delinquents in the areas close to the center of the city and those outlying and that any arbitrary number of zones will exhibit this difference satisfactorily.

Inspection of the rate maps indicates that there are wide differentials among the rates of delinquents for the square miles within each zone, just as there are among rates for census tracts within each square-mile area. These fluctuations do not greatly affect the general trend, however; in fact, it is because the zone rates eliminate the fluctuations evident for smaller areas and present the general tendencies that they are interesting and important.

Maps *A*, *B*, and *C*, Figure 1, shows rates of delinquents by 5 complete zones, and also by the north and south halves of the city separately, for the three juvenile court series that have been presented. On the same figure are given the critical ratios between the rates in outer and inner zones, which are so great that clearly they could not be due to chance alone. The critical ratios for adjacent zones (not shown) are also strategically significant in every instance.

---

[1] When a square-mile area was divided by one of the concentric circles, the aged 10–16 population and the number of delinquents allocated to each zone corresponded to the proportion of the area which fell in each.

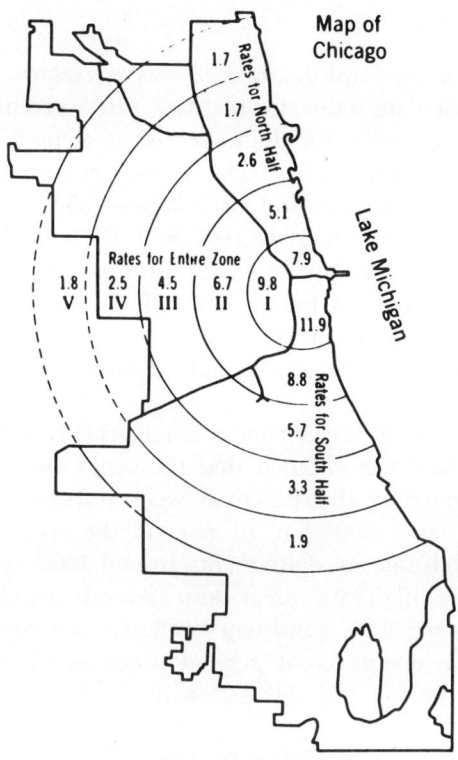

A. Zone rates of male juvenile delinquents, 1927-33 series

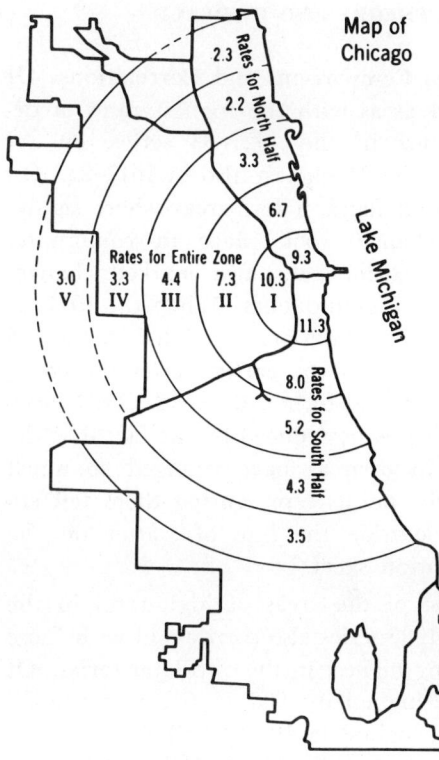

B. Zone rates of male juvenile delinquents, 1917-23 series

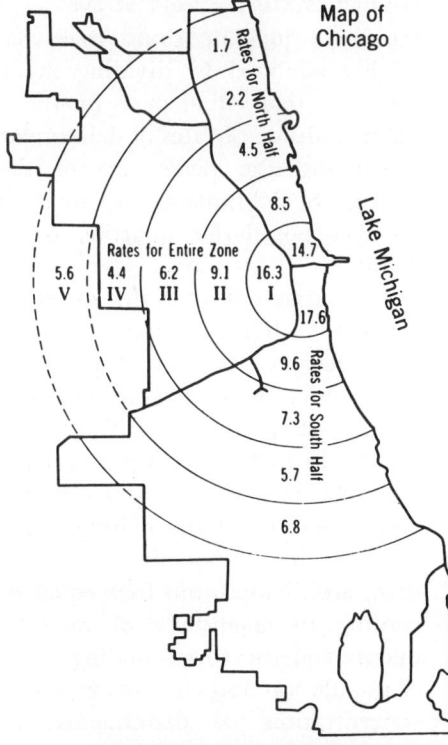

C. Zone rates of male juvenile delinquents, 1900-1906 series

Fig. 1.—Zone Maps for three juvenile court series.

Critical Ratios of Selected Zone Rates

Juvenile Court Series (Individuals)

Zones	Difference	Standard Error of the Difference	Critical Ratio
\multicolumn{4}{c}{A. 1927-33}			
1 and 4..	7.3	.301	24.2
1 and 5..	8.0	.302	26.5
2 and 4..	4.2	.142	29.6
2 and 5..	4.9	.142	34.5
\multicolumn{4}{c}{B. 1917-23}			
1 and 4..	7.0	.293	23.9
1 and 5..	7.3	.314	23.2
2 and 4..	4.0	.162	24.7
2 and 5..	4.3	.196	21.9
\multicolumn{4}{c}{C. 1900-1906}			
1 and 4..	11.9	.371	32.1
1 and 5..	10.7	.467	22.9
2 and 4..	4.7	.241	19.5
2 and 5..	3.5	.371	9.4

Area Comparisons and Correlations. Of the 24 areas with the highest rates of delinquents in the 1927–33 series, 20 are among the 24 highest also in 1917–23. On the other hand, a few areas where significant changes took place in community characteristics show also marked changes in rates of delinquents. When the 1917–23 and 1927–33 rates are correlated by the 113 areas used for the earlier series the coefficient is found to be .70 ± .02. This coefficient is greatly reduced by the fact that the rates in 6 areas have changed so much that the points representing them fell entirely outside the line of scatter on the correlation sheet.

Most of the areas of high rates in the 1900–1906 series also correspond with those ranking highest in the two later series. Of the 12 highest in 1900–1906, 9 were among the 12 highest in 1927–33. Three of the 5 highest-rate areas in the latter series, but not in the former, are the same 3 found among the high-rate areas as of 1917–23. Although some new areas appear among those with high rates in the more recent series. It is significant to note that all 12 of the areas of highest rates in the 1900–1906 series are among the areas of high rates in 1927–33. Because of these areas, the correspondence between the series is even more clearly seen when comparisons involving a larger number of areas are made. Of the 25 areas with the highest rates of delinquents in the 1900–1906 series, 19 are included among the 25 highest in the 1917–23 series, and 18 among the 25 highest in 1927–33, even though these series are separated by approximately 2 and 3 decades, respectively. This is especially significant in view of the fact that the nationality composition of the population has changed completely in some of these neighborhoods.

A more general statement of the relationship is found when the rates in the 1900–1906 series are correlated with those for each of the other juvenile court series. To accomplish this, it was necessary to calculate rates in the two later juvenile court series for the same 106 areas used in the early series. The coefficient secured for 1900–1906 and 1917–23 was .85 ± .04, and that for 1900–1906 and 1927–33 was .61 ± .04. In the latter case the coefficient was reduced by the few values which fell far out of the line of scatter, indicating areas where considerable change had occurred.

These coefficients are remarkably high when it is recalled that the series are separated by about 20 to 30 years, respectively. They reveal that, in general, the areas of high rates of delinquents around 1900 were the high-rate areas also several decades later. This consistency reflects once more the operation of general processes of distribution and segregation in the life of the city.

Extent of Concentration. The distribution of delinquents in relation to male population 10–16 years of age for each of the three juvenile court series has been further analyzed by dividing the population into four equal parts on the basis of the magnitude of rates of delinquents, then calculating the percentage of the total number of delinquents and total city area for each population quartile, as shown in Table I.

It is apparent that the quarter of the population living in the areas of highest rates occupied only 19.2 percent of the geographic area of the city in the 1927–33 series, 17.8 percent in 1917–23, and 13.1 percent in 1900–1906. Yet, in each instance this quarter of the population produced about one-half of the delinquents.

When the delinquents in each series, in turn, are divided into four equal parts according to magnitude of rate of delinquents and the corresponding distribution of population and city area is analyzed, the concentration of delinquents is again clearly evident (see Table II).

Table II shows that the upper quarter of the delinquents, living in high-rate

Table I. *Percentage of Delinquents and of City Area are for Quartiles of Male Population Age 10–16, When Areas are Ranked by Rate of Delinquents: Three Juvenile Court Series*

Quartiles of Population	Percentage of Delinquents			Percentage of City Area		
	1927–33	1917–23	1900–1906	1927–33	1917–23	1900–1906
Upper one-four in high-rate areas	54.3	46.1	47.3	19.2	17.8	13.1
Second one-fourth	23.9	27.3	26.6	19.4	24.8	12.1
Third one-fourth	14.6	17.7	17.4	32.3	27.1	21.7
Lower one-fourth, in low-rate areas	7.2	8.9	8.7	29.1	30.3	53.1

areas, represented only 7.7 percent of the population in the 1927–33 series, 10.9 percent as of 1917–23, and 10.6 percent in 1900–1906; and occupied respectively only 5.5, 6.0, and 3.7 percent of the total city area. At the opposite extreme, the one-fourth of the delinquents in the areas of lowest rates came from 54.2 percent of the population and 63.9 percent of the area in 1927–33, 48 percent of the population and 55.5 percent of the area a decade earlier, and 48.7 percent of the population and 68.4 percent of the area in 1900–1906.

Table II. *Percentage of Male Population Aged 10–16 and of City Area for Quartiles of Delinquents when Areas are Ranked by Rate of Delinquents: Three Juvenile Court Series*

Quartiles of Delinquents	Percentage of Population			Percentage of City Area		
	1927–33	1917–23	1900–1906	1927–33	1917–23	1900–1906
Upper one-fourth, from high-rate areas	7.7	10.9	10.6	5.5	6.0	3.7
Second one-fourth	13.8	12.1	16.6	8.6	11.1	10.1
Third one-fourth	24.3	29.0	24.1	22.0	27.4	17.8
Lower one-fourth, from low-rate areas	54.2	48.0	48.7	63.9	55.5	68.4

27. SOCIAL STRUCTURE AND ANOMIE

ROBERT K. MERTON

THERE PERSISTS A NOTABLE TENDENCY IN SOciological theory to attribute the malfunctioning of social structure primarily to those of man's imperious biological drives which are not adequately restrained by social control. In this view, the social order is solely a device for "impulse management" and the "social processing" of tensions. These impulses which break through social control, be it noted, are held to be biologically derived. Nonconformity is assumed to be rooted in original nature.[1] Conformity is by implication the result of an utilitarian calculus or unreasoned conditioning. This point of view, whatever its other deficiencies, clearly begs one question. It provides no basis for determining the nonbiological conditions which induce deviations from prescribed patterns of conduct. In this paper, it will be suggested that certain phases of social structure generate the circumstances in which infringement of social codes constitute a "normal" response.[2]

▶SOURCE: "Social Structure and Anomie," *American Sociological Review (October, 1938), 3:672–682.* Reprinted by permission.

The conceptual scheme to be outlined is designed to provide a coherent, systematic approach to the study of socio-cultural sources of deviate behavior. Our primary aim lies in discovering how some social structures *exert a definite pressure* upon certain persons in the society to engage in nonconformist rather than conformist conduct. The many ramifications of the scheme cannot all be discussed; the problems mentioned outnumber those explicitly treated.

Among the elements of social and cultural structure, two are important for our purposes. These are analytically separable although they merge imperceptibly in concrete situations. The first consists of culturally defined goals, purposes, and interests. It comprises a frame of aspirational reference. These goals are more or less integrated and involve varying degrees of prestige and sentiment. They constitute a basic, but not the exclusive, component of what Linton aptly has called "designs for group living." Some of these cultural aspirations are related to the original drives of man, but they are not determined

---

[1] E.g., Ernest Jones, *Social Aspects of Psychoanalysis*, 28, London, 1924. If the Freudian notion is a variety of the "original sin" dogma, then the interpretation advanced in this paper may be called the doctrine of "socially derived sin."

[2] "Normal" in the sense of a culturally oriented, if not approved, response. The statement does not deny the relevance of biological and personality differences which may be significantly involved in the *incidence* of deviate conduct. Our focus of interest is the social and cultural matrix; hence we abstract from other factors. It is in this sense, I take it, that James S. Plant speaks of the "normal reaction of normal people to abnormal conditions." See his *Personality and the Cultural Pattern*, 248, New York, 1937.

by them. The second phase of the social structure defines, regulates, and controls the acceptable modes of achieving these goals. Every social group invariably couples its scale of desired ends with moral or institutional regulation of permissible and required procedures for attaining these ends. These regulatory norms and moral imperatives do not necessarily coincide with technical or efficiency norms. Many procedures which form the standpoint of *particular individuals* would be most efficient in securing desired values, e.g., illicit oil-stock schemes, theft, fraud, are ruled out of the institutional area of permitted conduct. The choice of expedients is limited by the institutional norms.

To say that these two elements, culture goals and institutional norms, operate jointly is not to say that the ranges of alternative behaviors and aims bear some constant relation to one another. The emphasis upon certain goals may vary independently of the degree of emphasis upon institutional means. There may develop a disproportionate, at times, a virtually exclusive, stress upon the value of specific goals, involving relatively slight concern with the institutionally appropriate modes of attaining these goals. The limiting case in this direction is reached when the range of alternative procedures is limited only by the technical rather than institutional considerations. Any and all devices which promise attainment of the all important goal would be permitted in this hypothetical polar case.[3] This constitutes one type of cultural malintegration. A second polar type is found in groups where activities originally conceived as instrumental are transmuted into ends in themselves. The original purposes are forgotten and ritualistic adherence to institutionally prescribed conduct becomes virtually obsessive.[4] Stability is largely ensured while change is flouted. The range of alternative behaviors is severely limited. There develops a tradition-bound, sacred society characterized by neophobia. The occupational psychosis of the bureaucrat may be cited as a case in point. Finally, there are the intermediate types of groups where a balance between culture goals and institutional means is maintained. These are the significantly integrated and relatively stable, though changing, groups.

An effective equilibrium between the two phases of the social structure is maintained as long as satisfactions accrue to individuals who conform to both constraints, viz., satisfactions from the achievement of the goals and satisfactions emerging directly from the institutionally canalized modes of striving to attain these ends. Success, in such equilibrated cases, is twofold. Success is reckoned in terms of the product and in terms of the process, in terms of the outcome and in terms of activities. Continuing satisfactions must derive from sheer *participation* in a com-

---

[3] Contemporary American culture has been said to tend in this direction. See André Siegfried, *America Comes of Age*, 26–37, New York, 1927. The alleged extreme (?) emphasis on the goals of monetary success and material prosperity leads to dominant concern with technological and social instruments designed to produced the desired result, inasmuch as institutional controls become of secondary importance. In such a situation, innovation flourishes as the *range of means* employed is broadened. In a sense, then, there occurs the paradoxical emergence of "materialists" from an "idealistic" orientation. Cf. Durkheim's analysis of the cultural conditions which predispose toward crime and innovation, both of which are aimed toward efficiency, not moral norms. Durkheim was one of the first to see that "contrairement aux idées courantes le criminel n' apparait plus comme un être radicalement insociable, comme une sorte d'élément parasitaire, de corps étranger et inassimilable, introduit au sein de la société; c'est un agent régulier de la vie sociale." See *Les Régles de la Méthode Sociologique*, 86–89, Paris, 1927.

[4] Such ritualism may be associated with a mythology which rationalizes these actions so that they appear to retain their status as means, but the dominant pressure is in the direction of strict ritualistic conformity, irrespective of such rationalizations. In this sense, ritual has proceeded farthest when such rationalizations are not even called forth.

petitive order as well as from eclipsing one's competitors if the order itself is to be sustained. The occasional sacrifices involved in institutionalized conduct must be compensated by socialized rewards. The distribution of statuses and roles through competition must be so organized that positive incentives for conformity to roles and adherence to status obligations are provided *for every position* within the distributive order. Aberrant conduct, therefore, may be viewed as a symptom of dissociation between culturally defined aspirations and socially structured means.

Of the types of groups which result from the independent variation of the two phases of the social structure, we shall be primarily concerned with the first, namely, that involving a disproportionate accent on goals. This statement must be recast in a proper perspective. In no group is there an absence of regulatory codes governing conduct, yet groups do vary in the degree to which these folkways, mores, and institutional controls are effectively integrated with the more diffuse goals which are part of the culture matrix. Emotional convictions may cluster about the complex of socially acclaimed ends, meanwhile shifting their support from the culturally defined implementation of these ends. As we shall see, certain aspects of the social structure may generate countermores and antisocial behavior precisely because of differential emphases on goals and regulations. In the extreme case, the latter may be so vitiated by the goal-emphasis that the range of behavior is limited only by considerations of technical expediency. The sole significant question then becomes, which available means is most efficient in netting the socially approved value?[5] The technically most feasible procedure, whether legitimate or not, is preferred to the institutionally prescribed conduct. As this process continues, the integration of the society becomes tenuous and anomie ensues.

Thus, in competitive athletics, when the aim of victory is shorn of its institutional trappings and success in contests becomes construed as "winning the game" rather than "winning through circumscribed modes of activity," a premium is implicitly set upon the use of illegitimate but technically efficient means. The star of the opposing football team is surreptitiously slugged; the wrestler furtively incapacitates his opponent through ingenious but illicit techniques; university alumni covertly subsidize "students" whose talents are largely confined to the athletic field. The emphasis on the goal has so attenuated the satisfactions deriving from sheer participation in the competitive activity that these satisfactions are virtually confined to a successful outcome. Through the same process, tension generated by the desire to win in a poker game is relieved by successfully dealing oneself four aces, or when the cult of success has become completely dominant, by sagaciously shuffling the cards in a game of solitaire. The faint twinge of uneasiness in the last instance and the surreptitous nature of public delicts indicate clearly that the institutional rules of the game *are known* to those who evade them, but that the emotional supports of these rules are largely vitiated by cultural exaggeration of the success-goal.[6] They are microcosmic images of the social macrocosm.

---

[5] In this connection, one may see the relevance of Elton Mayo's paraphrase of the title of Tawney's well known book. "Actually the problem *is not that of the sickness of an acquisitive society; it is that of the acquisitiveness of a sick society.*" *Human Problems of an Industrial Civilization*, 153, New York, 1933. Mayo deals with the process through which wealth comes to be a symbol of social achievement. He sees this as arising from a state of anomie. We are considering the unintegrated monetary-success goals as an element in producing anomie. A complete analysis would involve both phases of this system of interdependent variables.

[6] It is unlikely that interiorized norms are completely eliminated. Whatever residuum persists will induce personality tensions and conflict. The

Of course, this process is not restricted to the realm of sport. The process whereby exaltation of the end generates a *literal demoralization,* i.e., a deinstitutionalization, of the means is one which characterizes many [7] groups in which the two phases of the social structure are not highly integrated. The extreme emphasis upon the accumulation of wealth as a symbol of success [8] in our own society militates against the completely effective control of institutionally regulated modes of acquiring a fortune.[9] Fraud, corruption, vice, crime, in short, the entire catalogue of proscribed behavior, becomes increasingly common when the emphasis on the *culturally induced* success-goal becomes divorced from a coordinated institutional emphasis. This observation is of crucial theoretical importance in examining the doctrine that antisocial behavior most frequently derives from biological drives breaking through the restraints imposed by society. The difference is one between a strictly utilitarian interpretation which conceives man's ends as random and an analysis which finds these ends deriving from the basic values of the culture.[10]

Our analysis can scarcely stop at this juncture. We must turn to other aspects of the social structure if we are to deal with the social genesis of the varying rates and types of deviate behavior characteristic of different societies. Thus far, we have sketched three ideal types of social orders constituted by distinctive patterns of relations between culture ends and means. Turning from these types of *culture patterning,* we find five logically possible, alternative modes of adjustment or adaptation *by individuals* within the culture-bearing society or group.[11] These are schematically presented in the following table, where $(+)$ signifies "acceptance," $(-)$ signifies "elimination" and $(\pm)$ signifies "rejection and substitution of new goals and standards."

	Culture Goals	Institutionalized Means
I. Conformity	$+$	$+$
II. Innovation	$+$	$-$
III. Ritualism	$-$	$+$
VI. Retreatism	$-$	$-$
V. Rebellion [12]	$\pm$	$\pm$

---

process involves a certain degree of ambivalence. A manifest rejection of the institutional norms is coupled with some latent retention of their emotional correlates. "Guilt feelings," "sense of sin," "pangs of conscience" are obvious manifestations of this unrelieved tension; symbolic adherence to the nominally repudiated values or rationalizations constitute a more subtle variety of tensional release.

[7] "Many," and not all, unintegrated groups, for the reason already mentioned. In groups where the primary emphasis shifts to institutional means, i.e., when the range of alternatives is very limited, the outcome is a type of ritualism rather than anomie.

[8] Money has several peculiarities which render it particularly apt to become a symbol of prestige divorced from institutional controls. As Simmel emphasized, money is highly abstract and impersonal. However acquired, through fraud or institutionally, it can be used to purchase the same goods and services. The anonymity of metropolitan culture, in conjunction with this peculiarity of money, permits wealth, the sources of which may be unknown to the community in which the plutocrat lives, to serve as a symbol of status.

[9] The emphasis upon wealth as a success-symbol is possibly reflected in the use of the term "fortune" to refer to a stock of accumulated wealth. This meaning becomes common in the late sixteenth century (Spenser and Shakespeare). A similar usage of the Latin *fortuna* comes into prominence during the first century B.C. Both these periods were marked by the rise to prestige and power of the "bourgeoisie."

[10] See Kingsley Davis, "Mental Hygiene and the Class Structure," *Psychiatry,* 1928, I, esp. 62–63; Talcott Parsons, *The Structure of Social Action,* 59–60, New York, 1937.

[11] This is a level intermediate between the two planes distinguished by Edward Sapir; namely, culture patterns and personal habit systems. See his "Contribution of Psychiatry to an Understanding of Behavior in Society," *Amer. J. Sociol.,* 1937, 42: 862–70.

[12] This fifth alternative is on a plane clearly different from that of the others. It represents a *transitional* response which seeks to *institutionalize*

Our discussion of the relation between these alternative responses and other phases of the social structure must be prefaced by the observation that persons may shift from one alternative to another as they engage in different social activities. These categories refer to role adjustments in specific situations, not to personality *in toto*. To treat the development of this process in various spheres of conduct would introduce a complexity unmanageable within the confines of this paper. For this reason, we shall be concerned primarily with economic activity in the broad sense, "the production, exchange, distribution and consumption of goods and services" in our competitive society, wherein wealth has taken on a highly symbolic cast. Our task is to search out some of the factors which exert pressure upon individuals to engage in certain of these logically possible alternative responses. This choice, as we shall see, is far from random.

In every society, Adaptation I (conformity to both culture goals and means) is the most common and widely diffused. Were this not so, the stability and continuity of the society could not be maintained. The mesh of expectancies which constitutes every social order is sustained by the modal behavior of its members falling within the first category. Conventional role behavior oriented toward the basic values of the group is the rule rather than the exception. It is this fact alone which permits us to speak of a human aggregate as comprising a group or society.

Conversely, Adaptation IV (rejection of goals and means) is the least common. Persons who adjust" (or maladjust) in this fashion are, strictly speaking, *in* the society but not *of* it. Sociologically, these constitute the true "aliens." Not sharing the common frame of orientation, they can be included within the societal population merely in a functional sense. In this category are *some* of the activities of psychotics, psychoneurotics, chronic autists, pariahs, outcasts, vagrants, vagabonds, tramps, chronic drunkards and drug addicts.[13] These have relinquished, in certain spheres of activity, the culturally defined goals, involving complete aim-inhibition in the polar case, and their adjustments are not in accord with institutional norms. This is not to say that in some cases the source of their behavioral adjustments is not in part the very social structure which they have in effect repudiated nor that their very existence within a social area does not constitute a problem for the socialized population.

This mode of "adjustment" occurs, as far as structural sources are concerned, when both the culture goals and institutionalized procedures have been assimilated thoroughly by the individual and imbued with affect and high positive value, but where those institutionalized procedures which promise a measure of successful attainment of the goals are not available to the individual. In such instances, there results a twofold mental conflict insofar as the moral obligation for adopting institutional means conflict with the pressure to resort to illegitimate means (which may attain the goal) and inasmuch as the individual is shut off from means which are both legitimate *and* effective. The competitive order is maintained, but the frustrated and handicapped individual who

new procedures oriented toward revamped cultural goals shared by the members of the society. It thus involves efforts to *change* the existing structure rather than to perform accommodative actions *within* this structure, and introduces additional problems with which we are not at the moment concerned.

[13] Obviously, this is an elliptical statement. These individuals may maintain some orientation to the values of their particular differentiated groupings within the larger society or, in part, of the conventional society itself. Insofar as they do so, their conduct cannot be classified in the "passive rejection" category (IV). Nels Anderson's description of the behavior and attitudes of the bum, for example, can readily be recast in terms of our analytical scheme. See *The Hobo*, 93–98, *et passim*, Chicago, 1923.

cannot cope with this order drops out. Defeatism, quietism and resignation are manifested in escape mechanisms which ultimately lead the individual to "escape" from the requirements of the society. It is an expedient which arises from continued failure to attain the goal by legitimate measures and from an inability to adopt the illegitimate route because of internalized prohibitions and institutionalized compulsives, *during which process the supreme value of the success-goal has as yet not been renounced*. The conflict is resolved by eliminating *both* precipitating elements, the goals and means. The escape is complete, the conflict is eliminated and the individual is socialized.

Be it noted that where frustration derives from the inaccessibility of effective institutional means for attaining economic or any other type of highly valued "success," that Adaptations II, III and V (innovation, ritualism and rebellion) are also possible. The result will be determined by the particular personality, and thus, the *particular* cultural background, involved. Inadequate socialization will result in the innovation response whereby the conflict and frustration are eliminated by relinquishing the institutional means and retaining the success-aspiration; an extreme assimilation of institutional demands will lead to ritualism wherein the goal is dropped as beyond one's reach but conformity to the mores persists; and rebellion occurs when emancipation from the reigning standards, due to frustration or to marginalist perspectives, leads to the attempt to introduce a "new social order."

Our major concern is with the illegitimacy adjustment. This involves the use of coventionally proscribed but frequently effective means of attaining at least the simulacrum of culturally defined success,— wealth, power, and the like. As we have seen, this adjustment occurs when the individual has assimilated the cultural emphasis on success without equally internalizing the morally prescribed norms governing means for its attainment. The question arises, Which phases of our social structure predispose toward this mode of adjustment? We may examine a concrete instance, effectively analyzed by Lohman,[14] which provides a clue to the answer. Lohman has shown that specialized areas of vice in the near north side of Chicago constitute a "normal" response to a situation where the cultural emphasis upon pecuniary success has been absorbed, but where there is little access to conventional and legitimate means for attaining such success. The conventional occupational opportunities of persons in this area are almost completely limited to manual labor. Given our cultural stigmatization of manual labor, and its correlate, the prestige of white collar work, it is clear that the result is a stain toward innovational practices. The limitation of opportunity to unskilled labor and the resultant low income can not compete *in terms of conventional standards of achievement* with the high income from organized vice.

For our purposes, this situation involves two important features. First, such antisocial behavior is in a sense "called forth" by certain conventional values of the culture *and* by the class structure involving differential access to the approved opportunities for legitimate, prestige-bearing pursuit of the culture goals. The lack of high integration between the means-and-end elements of the cultural pattern and the particular class structure combine to favor a heightened frequency of antisocial conduct in such groups. The second consideration is of equal significance. Recourse to the first of the alternative responses, legitimate effort, is limited by the fact that actual advance toward desired success-symbols through conventional channels is, despite our persisting open-class

---

[14] Joseph D. Lohman, "The Participant Observer in Community Studies," *Amer. Sociol. Rev.*, 1937, 2:890-98.

ideology,[15] relatively rare and difficult for those handicapped by little formal education and few economic resources. The dominant pressure of group standards of success is, therefore, on the gradual attenuation of legitimate, but by and large ineffective, strivings and the increasing use of illegitimate, but more or less effective, expedients of vice and crime. The cultural demands made on persons in this situation are incompatible. On the one hand, they are asked to orient their conduct toward the prospect of accumulating wealth and on the other, they are largely denied effective opportunities to do so institutionally. The consequences of such structural inconsistency are psychopathological personality, and/or antisocial conduct, and/or revolutionary activities. The equilibrium between culturally designated means and ends becomes highly unstable with the progressive emphasis on attaining the prestige-laden ends by any means whatsoever. Within this context, Capone represents the triumph of amoral intelligence over morally prescribed "failure," when the channels of vertical mobility are closed or narrowed [16] *in a society which places a high premium on economic affluence and social ascent for* all *its members.*[17]

This last qualification is of primary importance. It suggests that other phases of the social structure besides the extreme emphasis on pecuniary success, must be considered if we are to understand the social sources of antisocial behavior. A high frequency of deviate behavior is not generated simply by "lack of opportunity" or by this exaggerated pecuniary emphasis. A comparatively rigidified class structure, a feudalistic or caste order, may limit such opportunities far beyond the point which obtains in our society today. It is only when a system of cultural values extols, virtually above all else, certain *common* symbols of success *for the population at large* while its social structure rigorously restricts or completely eliminates access to approved modes of acquiring these symbols *for a considerable part of the same population,* that antisocial behavior ensues on a considerable scale. In other words, our egalitarian ideology denies by implication

---

[15] The shifting historical role of this ideology is a profitable subject for exploration. The "office-boy-to-president" stereotype was once in approximate accord with the facts. Such vertical mobility was probably more common then than now, when the class structure is more rigid. (See the following note.) The ideology largely persists, however, possibly because it still performs a useful function for maintaining the *status quo.* For insofar as it is accepted by the "masses," it constitutes a useful sop for those who might rebel against the entire structure, were this consoling hope removed. This ideology now serves to lessen the probability of Adaptation V. In short, the role of this notion has changed from that of an approximately valid empirical theorem to that of an ideology, in Mannheim's sense.

[16] There is a growing body of evidence, though none of it is clearly conclusive, to the effect that our class structure is becoming rigidified and that vertical mobility is declining. Taussig and Joslyn found that American business leaders are being *increasingly* recruited from the upper ranks of our society. The Lynds have also found a "diminished chance to get ahead" for the working classes in Middletown. Manifestly, these objective changes are not alone significant; the individual's subjective evaluation of the situation is a major determinant of the response. The extent to which this change in opportunity for social mobility has been recognized by the least advantaged classes is still conjectural, although the Lynds present some suggestive materials. The writer suggests that a case in point is the increasing frequency of cartoons which observe in a tragi-comic vein that "my old man says everybody can't be President. He says if ya can get three days a week steady on W.P.A. work ya ain't doin' so bad either." See F. W. Taussig and C. S. Joslyn, *American Business Leaders,* New York, 1932; R. S. and H. M. Lynd, *Middletown in Transition,* 67 ff., chap. 12, New York, 1937.

[17] The role of the Negro in this respect is of considerable theoretical interest. Certain elements of the Negro population have assimilated the dominant caste's values of pecuniary success and social advancement, but they also recognize that social ascent is at present restricted to their own caste almost exclusively. The pressures upon the Negro which would otherwise derive from the structural inconsistencies we have noticed are hence not identical with those upon lower class whites. See

the existence of noncompeting groups and individuals in the pursuit of pecuniary success. The same body of success-symbols is held to be desirable for all. These goals are held to *transcend class lines*, not to be bounded by them, yet the actual social organization is such that there exist class differentials in the accessibility of these *common* success-symbols. Frustration and thwarted aspiration lead to the search for avenues of escape from a culturally induced intolerable situation; or unrelieved ambition may eventuate in illicit attempts to acquire the dominant values.[18] The American stress on pecuniary success and ambitiousness for all thus invites exaggerated anxieties, hostilities, neuroses and antisocial behavior.

This theoretical analysis may go far toward explaining the varying correlations between crime and poverty.[19] Poverty is not an isolated variable. It is one of a complex and interdependent social and cultural variables. When viewed in such a context, it represents quite different states of affairs. Poverty as such, and consequent limitation of opportunity, are not sufficient to induce a conspicuously high rate of criminal behavior. Even the often mentioned "poverty in the midst of plenty" will not necessarily lead to this result. Only insofar as poverty and associated disadvantages in competition for the culture values approved for *all* members of the society is linked with the assimilation of a cultural emphasis on momentary accumulation as a symbol of success is antisocial conduct a "normal" outcome. Thus, poverty is less highly correlated with crime in southeastern Europe than in the United States. The possibilities of vertical mobility in these European areas would seem to be fewer than in this country, so that neither poverty *per se* nor its association with limited opportunity is sufficient to account for the varying correlations. It is only when the full configuration is considered, poverty, limited opportunity and a commonly shared system of success symbols, that we can explain the higher association between poverty and crime in our society than in others where rigidified class structure is coupled with *differential class symbols of achievement*.

In societies such as our own, then, the pressure of prestige-bearing success tends to eliminate the effective social constraint over means employed to this end. "The-end-justifies-the-means" doctrine becomes a guiding tenet for action when the cultural structure unduly exalts the end and the social organization unduly limits possible recourse to approved means. Otherwise put, this notion and associated behavior reflect a lack of cultural coordination. In international relations, the effects of this lack of integration are notoriously apparent. An emphasis upon national power is not readily coordinated with an inept organization of legitimate, i.e., internationally defined and accepted, means for attaining this goal. The result is a tendency toward the abrogation of international

---

Kingsley Davis, *op. cit.*, 63; John Dollard, *Caste and Class in a Southern Town*, 66 ff., New Haven, 1936; Donald Young, *American Minority Peoples*, 581, New York, 1932.

[18] The psychical coordinates of these processes have been partly established by the experimental evidence concerning *Anspruchsniveaus* and levels of performance. See Kurt Lewin, *Vorsatz, Wille und Bedurfnis*, Berlin, 1926; N. F. Hoppe, "Erfolg und Misserfolg," *Psychol. Forschung*, 1930, 14:1-63; Jerome D. Frank, "Individual Differences in Certain Aspects of the Level of Aspiration," *Amer. J. Psychol.*, 1935, 47:119-28.

[19] Standard criminology texts summarize the data in this field. Our scheme of analysis may serve to resolve some of the theoretical contradictions which P. A. Sorokin indicates. For example, "not everywhere nor always do the poor show a greater proportion of crime . . . many poorer countries have had less crime than the richer countries . . . The [economic] improvement in the second half of the nineteenth century, and the beginning of the twentieth, has not been followed by a decrease of crime." See his *Contemporary Sociological Theories*, 560-61, New York, 1928. The crucial point is, however, that poverty has varying social significance in different social structures, as we shall see. Hence, one would not expect a linear correlation between crime and poverty.

law, treaties become scraps of paper, "undeclared warfare" serves as a technical evasion, the bombing of civilian populations is rationalized,[20] just as the same societal situation induces the same sway of illegitimacy among individuals.

The social order we have described necessarily produces this "strain toward dissolution." The pressure of such an order is upon outdoing one's competitors. The choice of means within the ambit of institutional control will persist as long as the sentiments supporting a competitive system, i.e., deriving from the possibility of outranking competitors and hence enjoying the favorable response of others, are distributed throughout the entire system of activities and are not confined merely to the final result. A stable social structure demands a balanced distribution of affect among it various segments. When there occurs a shift of emphasis from the satisfactions deriving from competition itself to almost exclusive concern with successful competition, the resultant stress leads to the breakdown of the regulatory structure.[21] With the resulting attenuation of the institutional imperatives, there occurs an approximation of the situation erroneously held by utilitarians to be typical of society generally wherein calculations of advantage and fear of punishment are the sole regulating agencies. In such situations, as Hobbes observed, force and fraud come to constitute the sole virtues in view of their relative efficiency in attaining goals,— which were for him, of course, not culturally derived.

It should be apparent that the foregoing discussion is not pitched on a moralistic plane. Whatever the sentiments of the writer or reader concerning the ethical desirability of coordinating the means-and-goals phases of the social structure, one must agree that lack of such coordination leads to anomie. Insofar as one of the most general functions of social organizations is to provide a basis for calculability and regularity of behavior, it is increasingly limited in effectiveness as these elements of the structure become dissociated. At the extreme, predictability virtually disappears and what may be properly termed cultural chaos or anomie intervenes.

This statement, being brief, is also incomplete. It has not included an exhaustive treatment of the various structural elements which predispose toward one rather than another of the alternative responses open to individuals; it has neglected, but not denied the relevance of, the factors determining the specific incidence of these responses; it has not enumerated the various concrete responses which are constituted by combinations of specific values of the analytical variables; it has omitted, or included only by implication, any consideration of the social functions performed by illicit responses; it has not tested the full explanatory power of the analytical scheme by examining a large number of group variations in the frequency of deviate and conformist behavior; it has not adequately dealt with rebellious conduct which seeks to refashion the social framework radically; it has not examined the relevance of cultural conflict for an analysis of culture-goal and institutional-means malintegration. It is suggested that these and related problems may be profitably analyzed by this scheme.

---

[20] See M. W. Royse, *Aerial Bombardment and the International Regulation of War,* New York, 1928.

[21] Since our primary concern is with the sociocultural aspects of this problem, the psychological correlates have been only implicitly considered. See Karen Horney, *The Neurotic Personality of Our Time,* New York, 1937, for a psychological discussion of this process.

28. AN ECOLOGICAL ANALYSIS OF BALTIMORE

BERNARD LANDER

The Concentric Zone Hypothesis. Delinquency rates were calculated for each of the seven zones secured by drawing a series of seven concentric circles one mile apart with the intersection of Baltimore and Charles Streets, in the heart of the central business district, as the focal point.[1]

Table I. *Number of Delinquents, Population, Delinquency Rate for Both Races, Sexes, Aged 6–17 by One Mile Zones—Baltimore: 1939–1942*

Zone	Number of Delinquents	Population 6–17	Delinquency Rate
1	1,669	16,427	10.2
2	3,648	59,786	6.1
3	1,041	38,475	2.7
4	354	17,629	2.0
5	249	14,323	1.7
6	201	9,772	2.1
7	31	2,089	1.5
	7,193	158,501	

The examination of Table I reveals a preliminary confirmation of the Burgess'

▶SOURCE: *Towards An Understanding of Juvenile Delinquency New York: Columbia University Press, 1954, pp. 23–43 and 77–90. (Editorial adaptations.) Reprinted by permission.*

[1] When a census tract was divided by one of the concentric circles, the number of persons and delinquents, aged 6–17, was allocated to each zone corresponding to the proportion of the tract in each zone.

concentric zone hypothesis. The highest delinquency rates are found in the innermost zone in the zones surrounding it. However, the Burgess assumption of a continued and regular decline in the delinquency rate with progression from the innermost to the outermost zone does not find confirmation in Baltimore's zonal delinquency rates. The delinquency rate declines precipitously from 10.2 per 100 in Zone 1 to 6.1 in Zone 2 and 2.7 in Zone 3. Beyond Zone 3 the delinquency rate remains substantially the same for the remaining four zones.

A review of Table II indicates that the white delinquency rate decreases from 5.2 per 100 in the innermost zone to 4.3 in Zone 2 and 2.4 in Zone 3. Beyond this zone, the delinquency rate remains substantially the same for the other four zones. For the Negro group, the delinquency Zones 5 and 6 are higher than the rates in Zones 3 and 4. The rates in Zone 5 and 6 are more than twice as large as the delinquency rate in Zone 4. The small number of Negroes in these areas may however limit the significance of these aberrations from the concentric zone hypothesis.

The zonal hypothesis may lead to a considerable over-simplification of the actual pattern of the spatial distribution of delinquency. For example, in the innermost zones may be found a range in the delinquency rate from 20.8 per 100 to 1.1—virtually the entire range for the city as a whole. Census Tracts 25–5 and 25–6,

Table II. *Number of Delinquents, Population, Delinquency Rate for Specified Population Groups, Both Sexes, Aged 6–17 by One Mile Zones—Baltimore: 1939–1942*

	White			Negro		
Zone	Number of Delinquents	Population 6–17	Delinquency Rate	Number of Delinquents	Population 6–17	Delinquency Rate
1	399	7,718	5.17	1,270	8,709	14.58
2	1,610	37,790	4.26	2,038	21,996	9.27
3	843	35,550	2.37	198	2,925	6.77
4	343	17,327	1.98	11	302	3.64
5	227	14,045	1.62	22	278	7.91
6	188	9,602	1.96	13	170	7.65
7	31	2,089	1.48			
Total	3,641	124,121		3,552	34,380	

geographically removed 5 miles or more from the city center, are characterized by delinquency rates of 5.7 and 7.3—i.e., more than 7 times the delinquency rates of several tracts located within a one or two mile radius of the city center. An examination of the map also suggests that each zone contains a wide range of delinquency rates including both districts of high and low delinquency frequencies.

The preliminary examination of the data indicates that the concentric zone hypothesis over-simplifies the spatial distribution of delinquency in Baltimore and tends to obscure the wide range of rates within each zone. It does not however necessarily preclude the significance or importance of the ecological patterning or geographical distance from the city center, per se, as factors in the prediction and/or understanding of the differential delinquency rate. Other data which have direct bearing on this problem will be presented below.

Juvenile Delinquency and Propinquity to Industrial-Use Zoned Areas. The relationship between delinquency and the presence of, or proximity to, industry requires additional analysis and clarification. An examination of this relationship clearly reveals that there is no necessary concomitance between these two variables.

The juvenile delinquency rates in several industrial districts are considerably higher than the Baltimore census tract delinquency mean which is 4.2 per hundred for the entire study period. In contrast, some of the city's lowest delinquency rates occur in or near to industrial sections— Tracts 25–2, 25–4, 24–1 and 24–2, are cases in point. The delinquency rate in the latter two tracts is 1.1 for the four year study period, despite the fact that more than 50% of this area is zoned and used for industrial purposes. Omitting Tract 4–2 which is predominantly a commercial-use and only slightly an industrial-use zone, the mean census tract delinquency rate for 18 areas in which less than 50% of the tract is zoned for industrial-use is 4.8. In the 7 districts in which 50% or more of the tract is industrially zoned, the mean census tract delinquency rate is only 3.9—a lower delinquency rate mean than that of the city at large. Of the 25 tracts which are in part or predominantly zoned for industrial-use, only 2 are found in the 15 highest ranking delinquency areas and only 6 among the areas in the first quartile.

It is not directly clear whether the high delinquency rates in some industrial areas are effects of the presence of industry (and/or the ecological process of change in land-use) or whether they may be accounted for by the socio-economic variables studied in this monograph. As indicated previously, the presence of a low delinquency rate in an industrial-use zone does not in itself deny the possible significance of the presence of industry in the explanation of the differential delinquency rate. If an adequate quantitative index were available for this factor, the utilization of the factor analysis and the partial correlation techniques to be described below may provide an answer to these questions. However, the analysis of the distribution of errors in predicting delinquency from the variables analyzed in the regression equation, may help clarify the nature of the association between propinquity to industry per se and the delinquency rate.

It is germane to note that the distribution of industry in Baltimore does not conform to Burgess' zonal hypothesis. In Chicago and in other urban communities, studied by Burgess and his associates, the primary industrial areas are located in or near the center of the city. Zone I, in this conceptual scheme, is the central business and industrial district; Zone II, the zone in transition, or slum area, in the throes of change from residence to business and industry; Zone III, the zone of workmen's homes; Zone IV, the residential zone; and Zone V, the commuters zone, beyond the city limits. In contrast, in Baltimore only 50% of the districts in which industry is located or which are zoned for industry is found within Zones I and II. Several of Baltimore's most important industrial centers are located in Wards 25 and 26. These areas are several miles distant from the city center and are included in Zones 5 and 6. In Tracts 25-5 and 25-6 more than 80% of the available land is zoned and/or used for industrial purposes.

Juvenile Delinquency and Propinquity to Commercial-Use Zoned Areas. The mean census tract rate for 12 areas predominantly or in part commercially zoned is 9.0—almost twice the mean for the city

Table III. *Mean Rates of Delinquency for Census Tracts Grouped According to Percentage Increase or Decrease of Population, Baltimore: 1939–1942*

Percentage Increase or Decrease of Population, 1930–1940	Mean Rate of Delinquency 1939–1942
Decreasing	
20–39	13.1*
0–19	4.5
Increasing	
0–19	4.7
20–39	4.5
40 and over	1.3

* Only one census tract.

at large. One half of these tracts are among Baltimore's 15 ranking delinquency areas.

The association between a commercial-use zone and the delinquency rate needs further analysis, however; this will be provided in a later section. The need for additional analysis is indicated by the fact that in 4 of these 12 districts, the delinquency rate is much below the city mean. In one tract the rate is close to zero, only .1 for the four year period.

Juvenile Delinquency and Population Change. Since 1900 there has been a marked population decrease in the areas of delinquency concentration but there has been a different pattern of population changes. From 1930 to 1940 there have been no marked population decreases in the ranking delinquency areas. As a matter of fact, in many of the sections there have been population increases. In Census Tract 17-5, third ranking delinquency area, the population has increased 20% during this decade. Generally these have been areas with large concentrations of Negro population.

The correlation coefficient between the delinquency rate and the percentage of population increase (or decrease) is $r = -.12$, this coefficient being below the .05 significance level. Thus, in contrast to the findings of Shaw and his associates in

Chicago and other American cities, the relationship between the delinquency rate and the population change of an area is not statistically significant in Baltimore.

Table III, also, illustrates the findings of the correlational analysis. With the exception of areas with a population increase of 40% or more and the one tract in which the population decrease is more than 20%, there is no concomitance between population change and the delinquency rate.

What are the correlations between the social and economic indices studied by census tracts and the corresponding juvenile delinquency rates?

Juvenile Delinquency and Education. The correlation coefficient between the juvenile delinquency rate and median years of education is $r = -.51$.

An analysis of the scatter diagram suggests that the association between juvenile delinquency and education is not linear. As the delinquency rate increases from 1% to 4%, there is a marked decline in educational level. In areas with delinquency rates higher than 4%, the decline of educational level is much more gradual per unit change in years of education. As one moves towards the areas of highest delinquency, there appears what seems to be a surprising increase in formal schooling. However, data which will be presented below indicate that this last mentioned relationship is not statistically significant.

An examination of Table IV, also, points to a high degree of association between the educational level of a population group, the rent it pays, and the physical conditions and over-crowding of its homes. Further analysis is, therefore, essential to measure the relationship between schooling and delinquency when the influence of other social and economic factors is eliminated.

Juvenile Delinquency and Median Rentals. Juvenile delinquency rates vary inversely with the economic status of a neighborhood, as measured by its median monthly rent. The zero order correlation obtained between these two variables is $r = -.53$.

The lowest rentals are paid in Wards 2 and 3 of the Southeastern Health District, in Census Tract 4–2, in Ward 1, just outside the central business section, in Ward 22 of southwest Baltimore, just south of the central commercial zone, and in Census Tract 25–6.

Table IV indicates a high degree of intercorrelation between rentals, education, substandard housing and home ownership. The correlation of rentals and non-whites is significant, but not as high as one would expect in view of the Negroes' depressed socio-economic position. It is a result of the discrimination against Negroes in housing, which compels them to pay higher rentals than whites for similar housing.

A study of the scatter diagram indicates a curvilinear relationship between juvenile delinquency and rent. As the juvenile delinquency rate increases beyond 3.5, the per unit decrease in rents—as associated with a per unit increase in the juvenile delinquency rate—is gradualized.

In this connection, it is of interest to note that Census Tract 3–1, with a median estimated or contract monthly rental of $11.96 (the second lowest median rental in the city), possesses a much lower rate of juvenile delinquency than one might predict on the basis of its economic characteristics. Of the homes in this section, 75% are substandard. Only 3 of the 155 tracts have a greater percentage of substandard homes. The inhabitants of this tract attained a median of only 4.3 years of education—the least educated census tract population in the whole city. Of all occupied units in Baltimore, 94% had radios; in Census Tract 3–1, only 69.5% had them—the lowest percentage in the city. This neighborhood has the lowest percentage of homes without central heating, and 60% of its homes are either with outside or no toilet facilities at all; 8.15% of its homes are over-crowded (i.e., with more than 1.51 persons per room). Thus, this census tract is a very

Table IV. *Zero Order Correlations between the Juvenile Delinquency Rate and Specified Variables, Baltimore: 1939–1942*

	Education	Rent	Overcrowding	Nonwhite	Homes Owners-occupied	Substandard Housing	Foreign born	Juvenile Delinquency
Education		+.89	−.71	−.41	+.39	−.76	−.12	−.51
Rent	+.89		−.68	−.34	+.47	−.73	−.13	+.53
Overcrowding	−.71	−.68		+.69	−.72	+.86	−.01	+.73
Nonwhite	−.41	−.34	+.69		−.76	+.58	−.32	+.70
Homes Owner-occupied	+.39	+.47	−.72	−.76		−.67	+.12	−.80
Substandard Housing	−.76	−.73	+.86	+.58	−.67		+.07	+.69
Foreign born	−.12	−.13	−.01	−.32	+.12	+.07		−.16

For 155 observations r = ±.1576 is significant on the .05 significance level, and r = ±.2063 on the .01 level.

blighted neighborhood, with indices which mark it as one of Baltimore's most economically depressed sections. Yet it is not among the ranking juvenile delinquency areas. There are no special agencies operating in this district to lower the official rate artificially. This area is but one of many examples of the complexity of the problem of causation of juvenile delinquency, and illustrates the difficulty of trying to explain the variation of juvenile delinquency rates on the basis of pure economic determinism.

Juvenile Delinquency among Negroes. Negroes in Baltimore, as in many other American cities, contribute a disproportionate amount of juvenile delinquency. During the 1939–1942 study period, Negro children comprised 49% of Baltimore's delinquents although they constituted only, approximately, 20% of the juvenile group in the general population. This high proportion of Negro delinquency is reflected in a high correlation coefficient, r = +.70, expressing the concomitance between the delinquency rate and the percentage of Negroes.

The apparent magnitude of the Negro delinquency problem is even more precisely indicated in the analysis of Negro male delinquency rates for the 10–15 age category. In almost all of the tracts with 100 or more Negro boys, aged 10–15, the delinquency rate was 20 per 100 or more. In Tract 12–5, 95% of the 14–15 age group were allegedly delinquent. In Tracts 17–1, 4–2, and 12–4, respectively, 87%, 75% and 70% of the 14–15 age group were in court during the study period on official delinquency petitions.

Despite the preponderance of Negro delinquency, one must beware of imputing any causal significance to race per se. There is no *necessary* concomitance between the presence of Negroes and delinquency. In Census Tracts 9–1 and 20–2, with populations of 124 and 75 Negro juveniles, there were no recorded cases of delinquency during the study period. The rates of Negro delinquency also vary as widely as do the white rates indicating large differences in behavior patterns that are not a function or effect of race per se. It is also of interest to note that in at least 10% of the districts with substantial Negro juvenile populations, the Negro delinquency rate is lower than the corresponding white rate. In Tracts 13–3 and 18–2, the Negro rate is approximately one half as large as the corresponding white rate.

Table IV indicates a high correlation between the percentage of Negroes in a census tract and such socio-economic indices as over-crowding, substandard housing, the rate of juvenile delinquency and especially the percentage of homes owner-occupied. The latter correlation is r = —.76. Further analysis is thus necessary to unravel the extent to which the high correlation between the presence of Negroes and the delinquency rate is a function or consequence of the presence of Negroes as such or a reflection of the fact that in American urban centers Negroes live preponderantly in areas characterized by socio-economic and cultural factors more substantially and fundamentally associated with the prediction and/or understanding of the differential delinquency rate.

An inspection of the scatter diagram clearly indicates a highly curvilinear relationship between percentage of Negroes and delinquency rates. The proportion of Negroes remains almost constant as the delinquency rate increases from 0.0 to 5.0. It increases precipitously as the delinquency rate continues to increase from 5.0.

Despite the high concomitance between the presence of Negroes and the delinquency rate (r = +.70), a very interesting contrast is provided when an analysis is made of the concomitance between the purely Negro delinquency rate and the percentage of Negroes. In the latter instance, there is an *inverse* but insignificant relationship. The correlation between these two variables is r = —.19. The following table illustrates more effectively than a linear correlation coefficient the nature of this relationship. It suggests a positive correlation between the percentage of Negroes and the Negro delinquency rate as the proportion of Negroes in an area increases from 0.0 to 50%; a negative correlation between these two variables as the proportion of Negroes in a tract increases from 50% to 100%.

Areas were classified into six groups upon the basis of the Negro proportion of the population. The large majority of Balti-

Table V. *Number and Rate of Negro Juvenile Delinquency for Areas Grouped by Percentage of Negroes, Baltimore: 1939–1942*

Percentage of Negroes	Negro Delinquency Rate	Number of Negro Delinquents	Negro Population (Aged 6–17)
0– 9.9	8.10	153	1,891
10– 29.9	13.39	439	3,277
30– 49.9	13.75	461	3,353
50– 69.9	10.42	688	6,601
70– 89.9	12.33	1,056	8,563
90–100	7.06	755	10,695
Total		3,552	34,380

more's Negro population and delinquents were located in tracts with Negro percentages of 50% or more.

The delinquency rate increases from 8 per 100 in sections with 0–9.9% Negroes to 13 and 14 per 100 in areas with 10–29.9% and 30–49.9% Negroes. However, as the Negro population proportion increases beyond 50%, the Negro delinquency rate tends to decrease, with the areas of 90% or more Negro population concentration being characterized by the lowest delinquency rates. Thus in the most solidly populated Negro areas, the Negro delinquency rate is the lowest.

The following tables present the Negro and white delinquency rates for areas grouped by the percentages of Negroes.

A comparison of Tables V and VI indicates a generally similar pattern in the variations of Negro and white delinquency rates in relation to the proportion of Negroes in an area.

A review of the zero order correlations or a tabular presentation of the association between two variables provides only a superficial analysis of the "real" relationship. It is of value as it presents an entering wedge for deeper and more fundamental analysis. Additional data and analyses are therefore presented later in this study on the nature

Table VI. *Number and Rate of White Juvenile Delinquency for Areas Grouped by Percentage of Negroes, Baltimore: 1939-1942*

Percentage of Negroes	White Delinquency Rate	Number of White Delinquents	White Population (Aged 6–17)
0– 9.9	2.40	2,462	102,371
10– 29.9	5.36	663	12,375
30– 49.9	5.74	247	4,302
50– 69.9	5.15	162	3,146
70– 89.9	6.39	92	1,439
90–100	3.07	15	488
Total		3,641	124,121

of the association between the percentage of Negroes and the delinquency rate and their relations to the other socio-economic variables studied.

Juvenile Delinquency and Home Ownership. In the table of zero order correlations, (Table IV) juvenile delinquency is most highly associated with this variable— $r = -.80$. The relationship, however, is markedly curvilinear.

The smallest percentages of owner-occupied homes are found in the central business district, and in the adjoining Negro areas. Table IV also shows the significant correlation of home ownership with all other variables—with the exception of percentage foreign-born.

Juvenile Delinquency and Over-Crowding. The correlation coefficient between delinquency and over-crowding is $r = +.73$ and reflects a high degree of association between these variables. This is the second highest zero order correlation obtained in the study. This variable is also highly associated with the other indices.

Juvenile Delinquency and Substandard Housing. The Baltimore data tentatively support the findings of other studies, emphasizing the higher incidence of delinquency in "slums" or in areas characterized by a high percentage of substandard housing. The correlation coefficient is $r = +.69$.

Juvenile Delinquency and Percentage Foreign-Born. The correlation coefficient between the delinquency rate and the percentage of foreign-born is $r = -.16$. The percentage foreign-born is thus not significantly associated with juvenile delinquency at the .01 significance level, but does become significant at the .05 level— all values above $r \pm .1576$ being reliable. On the .01 level all correlation coefficients under $r = \pm .2063$ are not significant. Otherwise, the percentage of foreign-born is significantly correlated only with the percentage non-white ($r = -.32$); the greater the concentration of Negroes in an area, the smaller the proportion of foreign-born.

The 1903 Federal Slum Survey found delinquency concentrated primarily in foreign-born sections. In 1940 delinquency was a characteristic of areas inhabited by native born. In that year, only two of the 2,130 delinquency hearings involved foreign-born children; only 6% involved children of foreign-born or mixed parentage—and at the time 15% of Baltimore's native white population were of foreign-born or mixed parentage. Although the latter statistics are not entirely comparable, they suggest that neither the foreign-born element nor their children contribute more than a proportionate share to the Juvenile Court docket. These facts indicate the falsity of the hypothesis of a positive and necessary relationship between nationality as such and crime. In 1903, the foreign-born groups were economically and socially depressed. In general, they lived in highly mobile and culturally heterogeneous areas. By 1940 many of these groups were well integrated culturally and economically into the Baltimore community and had long left the homes in which they had originally settled. As their social and economic position improved and became stabilized, their delinquency rates decreased correspondingly. It is of interest to note that the correlation coefficient actually indicated an *inverse* relationship between delinquency and the presence of the foreign-born group.

In terms of the study of zero order correlations, the following variables stand out, in order of importance, in their association with juvenile delinquency:

1. Percentage of Homes Owner-occupied —.80
2. Percentage of Over-crowding +.73
3. Percentage of Non-whites +.70
4. Percentage of Substandard Housing +.69
5. Median Rentals —.53
6. Median School Years of Education —.51
7. Percentage of Foreign-born —.16

Some Limitations of the Correlation Coefficient. In the social sciences the use of the correlation coefficient is widespread. It is a useful tool if interpreted with full cognizance of its serious limitations.

1. The derivation of the product-moment correlation coefficient assumes a linear relationship between two variables. It assumes a constant average unit change in variable X with an approximately identical unit change in variable Y in the entire universe of their association. Actually, in social science data, the relationship is frequently not linear. In the present study, as is reported later, the correlations between variables were substantially changed when adjustments were made for the curvilinearity of the data. As statistical analysis is carried beyond the computation of zero order correlations, the curvilinear component of the data may materially affect the statistical results and their interpretation.

Furthermore, the assumption of linear correlation may obscure important variations in sub-classes of the data. The following data are presented as examples:

a. High negative correlations were found between percentage non-white and median monthly rent; also between the former and median school years of education. Actually these two high negative correlation coefficients obscure the fact that a breakdown of the data points to an interesting positive relationship between education, or rent, and percentage non-white as the concentration of Negroes increases beyond 90% of the total population. This fact, while interesting in itself, is of even greater importance in terms of the light it throws on the nature of the relationships between the levels of education, rent, and the percentage of Negroes in an area. The analysis of additional data suggests that areas of greatest Negro concentration are also characterized by lower delinquency rates.

b. The analysis of the concomitance between the Negro delinquency rate and the percentage of Negroes yielded a low inverse correlation between these variables. In actuality as was pointed out earlier, this correlation coefficient obscures a conflict in the nature of the association. As the proportion of Negroes in a community increases from 0 to 50%, the association between the Negro delinquency rate and the percentage of Negroes is a positive one; as the Negro concentration increases beyond 50%, the Negro delinquency rate becomes negatively correlated with the percentage of Negroes in an area.

c. Another illustration that may be of interest is indicated in Sullenger's studies of the relation of delinquency to mobility in Omaha.[2] Sullenger states that, "Where the mobility is large the delinquency is also large; and where there is little mobility, there is little delinquency." In more recent study [3] in Omaha of the relation of mobility to delinquency, Sullenger reaches a markedly different conclusion of the relationship of these two variables. Sullenger's recent study implies that a derived correlation coefficient would obscure the actual

---

[2] T. Earl Sullenger, *Social Determinants in Juvenile Delinquency,* New York, J. Wiley & Sons, 1936, pp. 179–80. (Out of print.)

[3] T. Earl Sullenger, "The Social Significance of Mobility," *American Journal of Sociology,* May, 1950, pp. 559–64.

nature of the concomitance between mobility and delinquency. The findings of the Omaha research indicated two distinct subgroups. Horizontal mobility is both a stabilizing and an unstabilizing influence on social relations. When the intra-urban mobility is accompanied by vertical mobility, stability generally follows a low delinquency rate. On the other hand, high rates of horizontal mobility unaccompanied by vertical mobility were associated with a high incidence of instability, unrest, and crime.

2. A correlation coefficient does not imply any causal nexus. It merely measures a concomitance. Maller's finding that 42% of delinquents were found by the New York City Board of Health to be suffering from malnutrition as compared with an average of 19% for the city as a whole does not imply therefore either that malnutrition is a cause of delinquency or that delinquency is a cause of malnutrition. Similarly Dexter's finding that there is a close association between the weather in New York City and Denver and the incidence of special types of crimes does not in itself necessarily reflect a causal relation. Unfortunately many studies on the basis of the discovery of a correlation between delinquency and such variables as population density, population change, poverty, presence of foreign-born or Negroes, physical type, endocrine gland balance, housing conditions, comic book sales, etc., have assumed a causal relationship between a specific variable and delinquency.

Ezekiel provides an interesting illustration of how completely adventitious a high correlation may be.[4]

If the number of automobiles moving down Sixteenth Street in Washington, D. C., for each 15 minute period through a given 12 hours is correlated with the height of the water in the Potomac River during each of the same periods, a definite correlation will be obtained. On some days this correlation would be so high that its probable error would indicate that it would be very unlikely that it could have occurred by chance. However, if on the basis of this correlation one were to attempt to forecast the flow of traffic from the height of the water, he would find his forecast sadly in error if he made it for another day when the street was closed for traffic repairs, when the water was high because of a flood, or when the moon was in a different phase. This is a case in which it is perfectly obvious that there is no direct causal relation between the two phenomena. Yet there is real correlation between them because they both are influenced, though very remotely, by the same sequence of cosmic events. The rising and the setting of the sun have a very definite influence on the movements of persons and therefore on the flow of traffic, whereas the rising and the setting of the moon likewise have a definite influence on the height of the water. Washington is so close to the ocean, and has so low an elevation, that the Potomac River has a definite ebb and flood of tide. There is a certain specific though complex relation between the rising and setting of the sun and of the moon. This relation is changing constantly from day to day. This illustrates a case in which real and significant correlation between two variables reflects causation by a common factor or factors, yet gives no inference as to direct causal connections. Many similar cases are met with in practical work in which the correlation between two variables is due to both being influenced by certain common causes although neither may in any conceivable way influence the other.

3. Sociological problems seldom involve a simple relationship between A and B, but usually involve a relationship between A, B, C, D, and other factors. As Burgess has noted, delinquency is associated with many socio-economic variables and these variables must also be more or less intercorrelated.[5] Data to be reported later in this study suggest the dangers in the all-too-frequent utilization of the zero order cor-

---

[4] Mordecai Ezekiel, *Methods of Correlation Analysis,* New York, J. Wiley & Sons, second edition, 1941, p. 451. (Out of print.)

[5] Shaw and McKay, *Juvenile Delinquency and Urban Areas,* Introduction XI.

relation table as a basis for definitive interpretation. Actually despite a high and significant zero order correlation coefficient between delinquency and a specific variable, when the other factors are held constant and their influences eliminated, the relationship may prove to be low and not significant. On the other hand, a variable which is only slightly associated with delinquency in the zero order correlation table may prove to be associated in an important fashion after the partial correlations have been computed.

A similar difficulty besets those criminologists who because delinquency is so highly associated with many factors substitute a multiple factor theory for an attempt at the formulation of a universal explanation of criminal behavior. "The adherents of this multiple factor 'theory' treat all factors as coordinate except that some are found to have a greater degree of statistical association with criminal behavior than others." [6] The adherents of this theory make no attempt to determine the factors that are basically related to delinquency and those that are merely adventitious and/or symptomatic, having no *real* relation to the understanding or prediction of delinquency, but are merely found together with other factors which are meaningful in the understanding of the etiology of delinquency or statistically significant in the prediction of the delinquency rate. Thus in putting forward an explanation of crime, Lombroso compiled the following factors: "Meteorological and climatic influences, mountain formation, race, civilization or barbarism, density of population, the ease of obtaining subsistence, alcoholism, education, wealth, religion, early training, heredity not only of certain characteristics but of criminality, age, sex, civil status, unemployment, prison, sense impression, imitation, suggestion." [7]

P. S. Florence, in his "Statistical Method" cites an example of erroneous generalization due to the failure to use partial association or selection.

The contention that most people die in their beds and that therefore a bed is the most unhealthy of places is a familiar example of failure to apply partial association. Going to bed is a usual consequence of being ill and dying occurs after a period of illness. Both phenomena are normal results of illness and to obtain a scientific proof it would be necessary to select only cases of illness and within the universe of illnesses to see whether those going to bed really die in greater proportion than those not going to bed.[8]

Durkheim, in his study of suicide, shows in an imaginative fashion the need for partial correlation and the danger of imputing causal significance to zero order correlations. Durkheim found, for example, that: (1) the rates of suicide are higher among Protestants than among Catholics, the rate for the former being in some instances two or three times as high as the rate for the latter; (2) the rates of suicide are higher in the summer than in the winter; (3) the suicide rate is higher in urban than in rural areas; (4) the suicide rate is higher among the single and the divorced persons than among the married; (5) and among the married persons it is higher among those who have no children.

Durkheim points out that we must not infer from these data that the difference of religion explains the differential rates among Catholics and Protestants. The theology of the Protestant religion is as antagonistic to suicide as is Catholicism. In actuality, Durkheim notes that the religious group with the lowest rate of suicide, the Jews, is the very one with fewest formal proscriptions against suicide and with the least emphasis on immortality.

---

[6] Edwin H. Sutherland, *Principles of Criminology*, Fourth Rev. Edition, Phila., J. B. Lippincott, 1947, pp. 56–8.

[7] R. M. MacIver, *Social Causation*, New York, Ginn & Company, 1942, p. 83.

---

[8] P. S. Florence, *The Statistical Method in Economics and Political Science*, New York, Harcourt, Brace & Co., 1929, p. 205.

Furthermore the shifting suicide rates among Jews emphasizes the significance of a factor other than religion in the explanation of the differential suicide rate. In the middle of the nineteenth century the suicide rate for Jews in Germany was even lower than that of the Catholics, whereas, in the twentieth century the Jewish rate exceeded even the Protestant rate. Neither should we infer that the climatic factor as such determines or explains the fact that the suicide rate is higher in the summer than in the winter.

In a highly imaginative, although nonstatistical method, Durkheim emphasizes the importance of "partialing-out" or holding constant the condition associated with being Catholic or Protestant, with one's marital status, with the season of the year, with living in urban or rural areas, that has relevance and is conducive to or deterrent of suicide. Durkheim advances the hypothesis that the relevant condition was the degree of social cohesion. The Catholic church group is *as a social group* more closely knit, and more cohesive than the Protestant church group. Marriage, parenthood, and rural life also make for closer social cohesion and integration. They protect the individual against the sense of social isolation. The analysis of the seasonal rates also indicates that it is not climate or temperature, as such, which affects the suicide rate but that with the coming of spring and summer, human activities and modes of living change. According to Durkheim, the length of the day influences the rhythm of social life. The longer day and the season of the year makes for more intense and active participation in social events and this in turn tends to deepen the already existing sense of social isolation which occurs in some individuals. The person experiencing a sense of social isolation feels his isolation much more deeply in the city center than if he were in a deserted district.

Thus, it is not weather, religion, area of residence, marital state, per se, that are causal factors of suicide. The aforementioned variables are all also highly correlated with the presence or lack of socially integrating conditions. The rate of suicide thus varies with the degree of social cohesion. In his study, Durkheim substituted for the zero order correlation coefficient as a basis for causal explanation a "partial correlation" analysis (utilizing statistical logic but no statistical formulas).

4. Professor W. S. Robinson demonstrates that ecological correlations cannot be used as substitutes for individual correlations. Correlations based on the "properties of areas as such" cannot be reasonably assumed to be equal to corresponding correlations based on the characteristics of individuals. Thus, the interpretation of the analysis of the differential delinquency rate in the present study has relevance only as it provides an explanation for the variations in delinquency rates between census tracts. Robinson's demonstration provides another indication that personal disorganization may not be taken to be merely a reflection of social disorganization....[9]

To what extent can the statistical measures and their results help in understanding the differential juvenile delinquency rate?

Our findings and their bearing on the *understanding* of the differential delinquency rate must be interpreted in the light of the statistical limitations outlined earlier in this study, as well as the additional following limitations:

The statistical findings in themselves do not supply the answer to the causal basis of the differential delinquency rate, but do provide a map which if analyzed with care and caution, may suggest some directions and answers. They enable us to

---

[9] *Cf.*, W. S. Robinson, "Ecological Correlations and the Behavior of Individuals," *American Sociological Review*, 15 (June 1950), pp. 551–57 also Herbert Menzel, "Comment on Robinson's Ecological Correlations and the Behavior of Individuals," *American Sociological Review*, 15 (October 1950), p. 674.

test and suggest hypotheses. Statistical techniques and their results are effective aids in the quest for understanding. At best, however, they provide only clues, and if used without caution may in many instances even be misleading. Methodologically, we have stressed in each stage of the study the very different conclusions we would have reached had we stopped earlier in our statistical analysis.

In this study, we have dealt primarily with prediction, rather than with causation. With the exception of the fatcor analysis, our statistical techniques have primarily dealt with the discovery of the independent variables that are statistically significant in predicting the differential delinquency rate. Yet, even successful prediction does not guarantee understanding. Prediction is based on the description of a statistically significant concomitant relationship between two or more variables. It does not tell us *why* this relationship exists or what it represents.[10]

Prediction and causation, while closely related, are separate goals of sociological research. In prediction study, we examine each factor in terms of *how much* it contributes to the variance of the dependent variable. In a causation study, our primary interest is not how much each factor contributes to the computation of a rate, but how the factors interact and are meaningfully related to differentials in the dependent variable.

The statistical analysis of the data available to us has a static character. It provides a snapshot of a relationship frozen in time. Causation, however, is dynamic. A study of causation entails an examination of the interaction of forces and resistances in the social situation—and in the individual—as they make for the acceptance or rejection of the norms of society with regard to juvenile conduct.

Professor Louis Guttman cites several examples of the fallacy of identifying the study of regression with the analysis of causation. He argues that,

> The absurdity of such interpretations, when based on no other considerations, can be shown in a number of ways. First, the regression coefficients may vary considerably with the insertion of one or more new variates into the regression or with the removal of one or more variates. There is nothing in the statistical theory as such which will explain such changes in terms of causation. Or consider the case where the Xj are linearly dependent. Then there is an infinite number of different sets of regression coefficients that will yield the same y'. There is nothing in the statistical theory as such which will select a particular set to be meaningful for the data.[11]

MAJOR STATISTICAL FINDINGS AND THEIR INTERPRETATION

Housing. The findings of this monograph confirm the many studies that have indicated a close correspondence between the delinquency rate and the housing characteristics of an area. In Baltimore, the zero order correlations between overcrowding, substandard housing conditions, and the juvenile delinquency rate are $r = +.73$ and $+.69$.

On the basis of similar zero order correlation coefficients, many investigators have argued that bad housing has a direct causal effect on the delinquency rate. The implication has been: "Remove the slums and you remove the social ills!"[12]

More careful analysis however indicates the insufficiency of this interpretation. The fact that in ranking delinquency areas there is a frequency of overcrowding and bad housing does not in itself suggest a causal nexus to any greater extent than the frequency of tuberculosis or child mortality in these areas suggest these variables as causal bases of the delinquency rate. Fur-

---

[10] For fuller discussion see R. M. MacIver, *Social Causation*, pp. 156–205, 383.

[11] Social Science Research Council, *The Prediction of Personal Adjustment*, Bulletin XLI, New York, 1941, pp. 288–9.

[12] John P. Dean, "The Myth of Housing Reform," *The American Journal of Sociology*, April 1949, pp. 271–88.

thermore, causation is not established unless we can indicate *how* the physical aspects of housing are related to the delinquency rate and *why* there is so much less delinquency in many rural areas or urban communities characterized in terms of our housing standards by primitive and very much substandard housing. It is germane to note here that several tracts, namely, Tracts 1–4 and 2–3 in which 84% or more of the homes are substandard, are not even included in the group of tracts comprising the first quartile of the ranking delinquency areas. In Tract 25–6, 98% of the housing is substandard, the median estimated or contract monthly rental of $11.81 is the lowest in the city, more than 80% of the area is zoned for industry, and the residential district is almost completely surrounded by heavy industry, yet there are 25 tracts in Baltimore with higher delinquency rates. As a matter of fact, in this study, the indices of partial correlation between overcrowding, substandard housing, and delinquency are reduced to zero when the other variables are held constant and their influence eliminated. Despite the high zero order correlation coefficients, the partial correlations suggest that there is no *real* or substantive relationship between the delinquency rate and the physical aspects of housing as such. The findings of the regression analysis in this respect are also amply confirmed by the factor analysis. On the other hand, our regression analysis indicates that home-ownership is significantly associated even on the .01 significance level with the presence of juvenile delinquency. We have hypothesized the frequency of home-ownership in Baltimore as a measure of community stability. The factor analysis also confirms the existence of a fundamental relationship between delinquency and social stability as measured by home-ownership and the lack of such a relationship with housing as measured by its physical or economic aspects. Thus, the primary significance of housing in the understanding of delinquency is not in its physical aspects or merely in the area's economic position in the city which its rentals reflect, but primarily and fundamentally in its social aspects as a measure of or contributor to social stability or *anomie*.

Other Socio-economic Variables. The zero order correlation between the median years schooling of a tract's population and its delinquency rate is $r = -.51$, and between median rentals and delinquency, $r = -.53$. The regression analysis and the factor analysis, however, clearly indicate that these variables are not fundamentally related to the prediction and/or understanding of juvenile delinquency.

Our analysis deals with the varying *area* rates. It is in this context that we find that economic variables are not significant in the prediction and understanding of the differential delinquency rate. As we have emphasized earlier these findings bear no necessary implication for a study of the prediction or understanding of the conduct patterns of a specific individual. The findings of this study do not gainsay the possible significance of any or all the variables studied as direct or indirect determinants of the behavior of individuals. Thus, one may well argue the hypothesis that poverty may compel the individual to live in the kind of community in which other factors conducive to delinquency operate. Presumably, however, if such variables as poverty do enter into the determination of individual behavior with respect to delinquency, they do so in different ways, for different individuals —i.e., the fact of poverty presumably has different significance and differing consequences for different individuals. Else one would expect them to show up significantly in the area statistics. Individual differences in response to such variables as poverty would tend to cancel one another out and, hence, to disappear in the area statistics. For an understanding of the total causal analysis of juvenile delinquency there is need for a study of the determinants of individual conduct as they operate in and interact with the social situation.

Population Composition. In Chicago and other American urban areas, Shaw found that high rates of delinquency characterized areas populated by large concentrations of foreign-born groups. This finding is not true for Baltimore. As a matter of fact there is if anything an *inverse* relationship between delinquency and the presence of foreign-born groups. The zero order correlation, r = —.16, is significant on the .05 significance level. The 1903 Federal Slum Survey found delinquency concentrated primarily in sections populated by the foreign-born; in 1940, delinquency was a characteristic of areas inhabited by the native-born. In 1940, many of the foreign-born groups were well integrated culturally and economically into the Baltimore community and were characterized by a high degree of home-ownership and social stability. At least two of these ethnic groups, the Jews and the Chinese, were characterized by almost a complete absence of any recorded delinquency. During the study period, it was the Negro, a native-born group, that contributed a large proportion of Baltimore's recorded crime and delinquency.

During the 1939-1942 study period, Negro children comprised 49% of Baltimore's delinquents although they only constituted approximately 20% of the comparable age grouping in the general population. In the regression and factor analysis the percentage of Negroes in a tract is significantly related to the prediction and understanding of the differential delinquency rate. On the basis of these analyses one might erroneously impute a causal significance to race per se. However, the following evidence amply supports the hypothesis that race as such is not a significant factor in the understanding of delinquency.

The racial factor does not explain the wide variation in Negro delinquency rates. This rate varies as widely as does the white rate, indicating large differences in behavior patterns that cannot be ascribed as an effect of race per se. It is also of interest to note that the Negro delinquency rate increases from 8% in areas in which the Negro population concentration is less than 10% of the total population to 13 and 14% in tracts with 10–29.9 and 30–49.9 Negro population percentages. However as the Negro population concentration increases beyond 50%, the Negro delinquency rate decreases to 7% in areas with 90% or more Negro population. Thus, in the areas with the greatest Negro population proportion, the Negro delinquency rate is lowest. A similar pattern of delinquency frequency also characterizes the white group in relation to the proportion of Negroes.

The net regression line which describes the relationship between the presence of Negroes and the delinquency rate when the influence of the other variables is eliminated also indicates a similar pattern. As the Negro proportion of the total tract population increases to 50%, the delinquency rate increases. As the percentage of Negroes increases beyond 50%, the delinquency rate correspondingly decreases. Thus, when other factors are held constant, delinquency rates in Baltimore are highest in areas of maximum racial heterogeneity. In areas of total Negro occupancy the delinquency rate is no higher than in similar areas of total white occupancy. This does not necessarily mean that high rates of delinquency are inevitable in racially heterogeneous areas. It means simply that under the conditions of racial heterogeneity found in Baltimore, such heterogeneity is associated with factors that effect an increased delinquency rate. The factor analysis suggests that, in Baltimore, the percentage of Negroes in an area is best viewed in the grouping of variables which define the *anomic* factor. The examination of the regression analysis, however, further suggests that the percentage of Negroes in an area is a curvilinear correlate of the *anomic* factor. Areas of maximum racial heterogeneity are characterized by the largest extent of social instability and *anomie*. In the areas of maximum Negro population concentration there is observable a corresponding increase of social stability and a decrease in delinquency.

Furthermore, there are many areas in which the Negro delinquency rate is substantially lower than the corresponding white rate. In two tracts with a population of approximately 200 Negro juveniles there were no recorded cases of delinquency during the study period.

The evidence cited amply demonstrates that Negro delinquency is not a function or effect of race as such but is a reflection of social instability. In sections characterized by *anomie,* the Negro delinquency rate is high; in areas of social stability, the Negro delinquency rate is of the same order as the corresponding white rate. Also, in Baltimore many Negroes, as a result of factors other than their race. are subject to the effects of *anomie.*

The Concentric Zone and Gradient Hypotheses. Many studies of the distribution and etiology of delinquency and other social pathologies have been stimulated by and prepared within the framework of the Park and Burgess ecological hypotheses. Burgess, in his introduction to Shaw's *Juvenile Delinquency and Urban Areas,* finds confirmation of his theories in the data presented in this volume on the distribution of delinquency in Chicago and other American urban communities.

We summarize below the findings of the present study which relate to these hypotheses.

1. (a) The location of industrial land use sections in Baltimore does not conform to the Burgess zonal hypothesis. There is no general tendency of heavy industry to surround or to be located near the central business district. As a matter of fact, the most important industrial concentrations are found in the outlying sections of the city. Tracts 25–5 and 25–6 which are almost completely zoned for industrial-use are located in Baltimore's outermost zones. It is also germane to note that important industrial concentrations are found in each of the zones that comprise the city of Baltimore.

(b) The delinquency rates in or near several industrial areas are considerably higher than the city mean rate. This is in conformity with the Burgess-Shaw hypothesis. Strikingly at variance with this hypothesis, however, is the fact that some of the city's lowest delinquency rates occur in or near industrial areas. Also, in the seven tracts in which the major land use or zoning is industrial, the mean tract delinquency rate is lower than the city's delinquency mean. On the other hand, the mean delinquency rate for the twelve tracts which are predominantly or in part zoned for commercial use is almost twice the mean for the city at large.

(c) According to the zonal hypothesis, the central business and industrial section is surrounded by the zone in transition, or slum area which is characterized by the greatest frequency of delinquency, bad housing and poverty. The following concentric district is the zone of workingmen's homes.

The findings of this monograph suggest that zones in transition from residence to business and industry are not limited to the innermost zones but are also found in the city's peripheral districts. Also, that areas characterized by poverty, bad housing and workingmen's homes while frequently near the center of the city are found in every zone. Baltimore's lowest rentals and most substandard housing is found in Ward 25 in the city's outskirts.

Furthermore, Baltimore's so-called "zone in transition," in the years 1939–42, contained districts with very high delinquency rates, but also areas in which the delinquency rate is close to zero; the wealthy or socially elite and the criminal or prostitute frequently living within a stone's throw of each other.

(d) Shaw allocates the central and basic

role in the understanding of the differential delinquency rate to the "invasion" of residential neighborhoods by business and industry in the process of city growth. In this study we have calculated and plotted the residual errors in order to analyse the significance of such factors of the delinquency rate, measures of which had not been included in the regressions equation. The examination of the distribution of the residual errors indicates that in many instances, especially in tracts adjoining retail commercial concentrations, the higher actual than predicted delinquency rates may suggest the influence of actual or impending changes in land-use as a causal factor of the delinquency rate. On the other hand, the majority of the tracts in the so-called "areas in transition" are characterized by predicted delinquency rates which are higher than the actual rates. In other words in the majority of tracts within the "zones of transition," there is no evidence to suggest that the delinquency rate is a function of the "invasion" of industry or commerce. We do not wish to deny the importance of changes in land-use in the understanding and/or prediction of the delinquency rate. The "invasion" by industry or commerce of a residential neighborhood may, undoubtedly, in many instances weaken the social controls or consensus of the area and thus affect its delinquency rate. But our findings do not support a hypothesis which gives this factor the central role in the explanation of the differential delinquency rate. As Professor R. M. MacIver states, "Delinquency rates are correlated with other conditions and processes besides the invasion of residential communities by business and industry."[13]

The findings of this study do support Shaw's thesis, "that delinquent behavior is related dynamically to the community and that because of the anonymity in urban life, the individual is freed from much of the scrutiny and control which characterize life in primary group situations in small towns and rural communities."[14] But our findings do not support (at least in the case of Baltimore) Shaw's hypothesis that the processes of city growth, as such, provide the basic explanation of a city's wide variations in delinquency rates.

2. (a) An examination of the zonal distribution rates superficially and in a general fashion supports the Burgess gradient hypothesis. Zone 1 is characterized by the highest delinquency rate. There is decrease—although it is not a *regular* one—in the delinquency rate with progression from Zone 1 to Zone 7. The delinquency rate is 10.2 in Zone 1, 6.1 in Zone 2, and then it declines preciptously to 2.7 in Zone 3. Beyond Zone 3, it remains substantially the same for the remaining zones. For the Negro group, the delinquency rates in Zones 6 and 7 are substantially higher than the delinquency rate in zone 4 and a little higher than the delinquency rate in Zone 3.

An examination of the distribution of delinquency rates by census tracts shows that the zonal hypothesis oversimplifies the actual pattern of delinquency distribution. Each zone includes high and low delinquency rate areas. Within Zone 1, for example, the delinquency rates vary widely; from a high of 20.8 to a low of 1.1. The emphasis on the study of delinquency by zonal rates also tends to obscure the more meaningful analysis of the mosaic of rates within each zone, the search for the explanation of the wide variation in the delinquency rates of contiguous areas.

(b) The Baltimore zonal areas cannot be designated as "natural areas." They are not characterized by a homogeneity of cultural and economic characteristics. Although low rental areas are found near the city center, they are by no means confined there but are found in every zone. As noted earlier, some of Baltimore's lowest

---

[13] R. M. MacIver, *op. cit.*, p. 379.

[14] Clifford R. Shaw and Henry D. McKay, *Juvenile Delinquency in Urban Areas*, Chicago, University of Chicago, 1942, pp. 435-8.

rental areas are found in the city's peripheral zone. In contrast, some of the city's highest rental districts are found in Zone 1. Similarly, with regards to the median years of schooling, in the inner zone are found tracts characterized by the city's highest and lowest educational medians. Census tracts 3-1 and 3-2 are characterized by populations with educational medians of 4.3 and 4.5 years. Tracts 11-1 and 11-2, immediately north of the central business district, are characterized by educational medians of 12.2 years. Only 7 of the 155 tracts which comprise Baltimore are characterized by populations with higher educational medians.

The data of this study also indicate that we cannot apply to Baltimore the attempt by Burgess to designate the successive zones as the zone of transition, the zone of workingmen's homes, the zone of the middle-class dwellers, and the commuters zone. Concentric zones in Baltimore are not characterized by any homogeneity in land-use. Workingmen's and middle-class homes are found in all zones. Industrial concentrations are not confined to the inner zones, but are also found in the so-called commuters zone.

(3) We find no support for the assumption that seems to be more or less tacit in the work of some ecologists that physical space or locale per se is an independent or causal factor in the predictions or understanding of delinquency. The examination of the distribution of the residual errors also indicates that there is no systematic patterning or concentration of errors of predictions on the basis of the variables we have found to be significant in Baltimore which might suggest the influence of a spatial variable per se on the delinquency rate. The analysis of delinquency in terms of its spatial distribution may nevertheless still be a valuable heuristic device in terms of Quinn's recommendation that, "In such studies the spatial distribution affords only a beginning clue that suggests critical problems of a non-spatial nature." [15]

(4) The factor analysis based on the correlations among the variables indicates that there are *two* independent and underlying factors. This finding contrasts with Burgess' assumption of one general basic factor, namely, social disorganization of which delinquency, poverty, bad housing and tuberculosis are equally manifestations. The basic factors in our study are closely associated with each other but are nonetheless different in character. Our evidence indicates that "social disorganization" (we prefer the concept "anomie") is perhaps a basic underlying factor of delinquency, but that this factor is not sufficient to account for a complex matrix of social interrelationships. A second, independently operating, factor is socio-economic in character.

SUMMARY AND INTERPRETATION

Our statistical measures indicate the importance of the fact that the surface associations between variables do not necessarily suggest fundamental or substantive relationships. The correlational and regression analyses suggest that the association between delinquency and poverty, bad housing, room density, propinquity to the city center, etc. are only surface relationships. The only variables that continued to be significant in the prediction of the delinquency rate when other variables are held constant are the home ownership and Negro population concentration indices. The factor analysis and additional statistical techniques described above, however, indicate the further danger of taking these variables in themselves as causal factors of the delinquency rate. The percentage of home-ownership is not a *necessary* component of the explanation or understanding of the differential delinquency rate. Home-ownership is an index of stability and the

[15] James A. Quinn, *Human Ecology*, New York, Prentice-Hall, 1950, p. 405.

lack of home-ownership in an area does not in iteslf cause delinquency. Furthermore, in a city like New York City with many apartment houses areas, home-ownership may not even be an adequate index of a factor that is really significant.

In our search for the understanding of the differential delinquency rate, we suggest that the nearer the explanation of this social phenomenon is to the direct motivation of behavior, the nearer it is to being an adequate explanation of the deviant behavior. We hypothesize an explanation of the differential delinquency rate in terms of the concept of *anomie*. When the *group norms* are no longer binding or valid in an area or for a population subgroup, in so far as individual behavior is likely to lead to deviant behavior. Delinquency is a function of the stability and acceptance of the group norms with legal sanctions and the consequent effectiveness of the social controls in securing conforming juvenile behavior.

If our search for scientific understanding has led us to return to the beginning of the circle (our explanation may perhaps be interpreted as saying that delinquency is due to a breakdown or lack of respect for law and order—a sheer tautology), we hope nonetheless that it has thrown some light on the dynamics involved in the etiology of delinquency. After all, our breakdown of social norms is here seen in the interrelationships of a number of variables. Also, it is evident that a number of variables that appear to be significant are not actually so and are functionally not involved in the interpretation of the underlying factor of delinquency.

The factor analysis indicates, and this finding is supported by our correlational analysis, that the delinquency rate is fundamentally related only to the *anomie* and not specifically to the socio-economic conditions of an area. The delinquency rate in a *stable* community will be low in spite of its being characterized by bad housing, poverty and propinquity to the city center. On the other hand, one would expect a high delinquency rate in an area characterized by normlessness and social instability. In such sections there is a deficiency in the traditional social controls which maintain conventional behavior in stable communities.

Emile Durkheim was one of the earliest sociologists to suggest that a differential crime rate is a reflection of differential degrees of social cohesion and the corresponding social control. Durkheim stresses that the breakdown of social cohesion frees the individual from the pressure of public opinion and the informal social controls which, in more solidary groups, operate to secure conformity to the norms of conventional behavior. [16]

In a stable community a child is born and raised in a context of established norms which are supported by a social consensus. He tends to interiorize these norms, and they contribute to the establishment of his psychological field of needs, goals and motivations. Generally, the child acts to satisfy his needs in a manner which has the approval of society. If he acts in a deviant fashion, formal and informal controls—including his own ego with its interiorized norms—act to deter the child from further deviant conduct.

Unstable community conditions and the consequent weakening of social controls that are congruent with the dominant culture provide fertile ground for the emergence of variant norms and group standards. It is erroneous to conceive of high delinquency areas as being devoid of norms and group controls or standards. Sherif's "Psychology of Social Norms" and the studies of Clifford Shaw and Frederic Thrasher indicate the existence of norms and standards in those areas. The controls and mores of a gang are highly regulatory of the behavior of its members. However, these norms may not be congruent with those of the larger society.

---

[16] E. Durkheim, *Division of Labor in Society*, translated by George Simpson, New York, The Macmillan Co., 1933, pp. 297–301.

A deeper understanding of the differential juvenile delinquency rate will necessitate further research on *how* community stability or instability is meaningful and dynamically related to the differential behavior of various types of individual children. Community or situational factors ultimately influence the delinquency rate only as they affect the needs, values, goals and behavior of individual children.

29. ISSUES IN THE ECOLOGICAL STUDY OF DELINQUENCY

ROBERT A. GORDON

EVER SINCE ITS APPEARANCE IN 1954, LANDER'S *Towards an Understanding of Juvenile Delinquency* has drawn much attention.[1] The major thesis of Lander's study, based upon multivariate analyses of ecological data, was that juvenile delinquency rates over a four-year period in the city of Baltimore were related in only a superficial sense to census tract variables indicative of socioeconomic status. Lander claimed to show that, in actuality, the juvenile delinquency rates in question were not related to socioeconomic status at all, but rather to the variables: percentage of homes owner-occupied, and percentage nonwhite. Since these latter variables seemed to him to be more identifiable with degrees of social integration than with degrees of socioeconomic status, Lander was led to conclude that his data favored an "anomie theory" explanation of delinquency rather than one based upon some kind of economic determinism.

Both types of theory have a long tradition in sociology, and both have their special adherents. It was only natural that the overall reaction to Lander's study be one of ambivalence. On the one hand, the study appeared to support the existence of the more elusive and therefore more glamorous variable, anomie. On the other hand, it denied a relation with the most concrete and most solidly established of all sociological variables, namely, socioeconomic status. This denial ran counter both to much statistical evidence and to intuition, and thus placed in doubt one of the few strong relations with delinquency that sociologists had been able to identify. As a result, sociologists have been at once fascinated with and suspicious of Lander's conclusion.

The two most ambitious re-examinations of Lander's findings to appear thus far have been by Bordua and by Chilton.[2] Bordua, employing data for Detroit, raised a number of questions concerning the original study, in the course of attempting to replicate some of Lander's analyses. Somewhat cautiously, he concluded that

▶SOURCE: "Issues in the Ecological Study of Delinquency," *American Sociological Review* (December, 1967), 32:6:927–944. Reprinted by permission.

[1] Bernard Lander, *Towards an Understanding of Juvenile Delinquency*, New York: Columbia University Press, 1954.

[2] David J. Bordua, "Juvenile Delinquency and 'Anomie': An Attempt at Replication," *Social Problems*, 6 (1958–1959), pp. 230–238; Roland J. Chilton, "Continuity in Delinquency Area Research: A Comparison of Studies for Baltimore, Detroit, and Indianapolis," *American Sociological Review*, 29 (February, 1964), pp. 71–83. Somewhat related papers are those by Kenneth Polk, "Juvenile Delinquency and Social Areas," *Social Problems*, 5 (1957–58), pp. 214–217; Bernard L. Bloom, "A Census Tract Analysis of Socially Deviant Behaviors," *Multivariate Behavioral Research*, 1 (1966), pp. 307–320; and Desmond S. Cartwright and Kenneth I. Howard, "Multivariate Analysis of Gang Delinquency: I. Ecologic Influences," *Multivariate Behavioral Research*, 1 (1966), pp. 321–371.

the Lander interpretations were essentially confirmed for Detroit. Chilton incorporated both Lander's and Bordua's data into an almost total replication, adding data for a third city, Indianapolis. On the basis of his analysis, he severely questioned the utility of Lander's anomie explanation. His main criticism, and potentially the most damaging one, was that Lander had confused the signs of the factor loadings of four of his variables, and that, as a result, his factor analysis could no longer support the interpretation that his variables gave rise to an anomie factor and a socioeconomic factor, with delinquency being more closely related to the anomie factor. This criticism alone would probably have been sufficient to discredit Lander's theory and to remove whatever doubt that theory had raised concerning the proposition that delinquency and socioeconomic status were related. At a time when resources are being committed on an unprecedented scale against poverty, partly on the justification that social ills such as crime and delinquency have a socioeconomic basis, it is certainly important that sociologists be correct about the facts of this particular relationship. Unfortunately Chilton's criticism of Lander on this point, and on other points as well, is mistaken. However, there are other important faults in Lander's procedures that completely invalidate his conclusions. The purpose of this paper, therefore, is to describe these mistakes, and others appearing in the studies by Bordua and Chilton, so that this particular erroneous challenge to the hypothesis of a relationship between delinquency and socioeconomic status may finally be laid to rest.

LANDER'S FACTOR ANALYSIS

Although not first in order of appearance in Lander's study, it is convenient to discuss his factor analysis before the other analyses. He performed a centroid factor analysis of seven census variables and the juvenile delinquency rate for census tracts in Baltimore. The census data were obtained from the 1940 census, and the delinquency data were for the years 1939 to 1942. From the resulting correlation matrix, he extracted two factors by the centroid method. These two factors, at this point, were unrotated and orthogonal. Lander gave no indication that he even considered an orthogonal rotation; instead, he apparently proceeded directly to an oblique solution that was no doubt intended to pass one of the two factor axes through the center of each of the two major clusters of variables in his plot. However, this is not what actually occurred. To understand what went wrong, we must refer to Table I, which is adapted from Lander's Table XII, on page 53 of his book, and to Figure 1, which is equivalent (except for certain additions) to his Graph I, on his page 54.

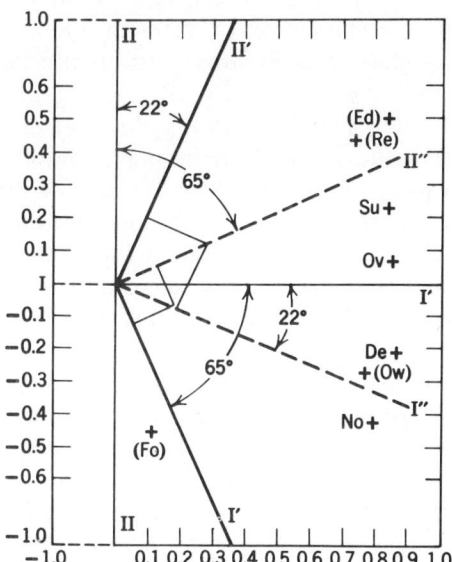

Figure 1.

Ed = Education
Re = Rent
Su = Substandard Housing
Ov = Overcrowded
De = Delinquency
Ow = Owner-Occupancy
No = Nonwhite
Fo = Foreign-Born

Table I. *Lander's Factor Analysis, With Correct Oblique Solution*

Variable	Lander's Centroid Solution		Lander's Oblique Solution		Correct Oblique Solution	
	I	II	"Anomie"	"SES"	I	II
Delinquency rate	.84	−.23	.56	.11	.87	.67
Low education	.76	.53	−.16	.78	.51	.92
Low rent	.75	.50	−.14	.75	.51	.90
Overcrowding	.90	.11	.28	.44	.80	.86
Substandard housing	.87	.25	.14	.56	.71	.90
Low owner occup.	.81	−.30	.62	.03	.86	.61
Nonwhite	.78	−.40	.70	−.08	.88	.54
Few foreign-born	.10	−.47	.47	−.40	.27	−.10
Transformation matrices for each oblique solution	−	−	.423	.375	.927	.906
	−	−	−.906	.927	−.375	.423

Since Lander did not indicate the oblique factors on his plot, we must conjecture to some degree how he intended to rotate his factors. If one were of the opinion that an oblique solution was desirable for these data, it seems logical that one would aim to pass vectors near or through the two major clusters in Figure 1. In attempting to understand Lander's results, we ourselves drew such lines on his plot, and then later found each of their angles of rotation to be within one degree of one or the other of the angles of rotation indicated by the sine and cosine values of his transformation matrix. This suggests that his choice of oblique solution was also ours. To further confirm that this choice was also Lander's natural choice, we submitted unidentified plots, on irregularly trimmed paper, to two experienced factor analysts, with the request that they draw the oblique solutions they would recommend.[3] The plots they were shown displayed no axes at all, merely eight unnamed variables located with respect to each other and to an origin, with the length of a unit vector indicated. Both offered oblique solutions that came within a few degrees of our reconstruction of Lander's intentions, thus upholding the reasonableness of our conjecture.

It is important to establish what must have been his intention here, because his transformation matrix does not yield the solution toward which we surmise that he was aiming. To obtain that solution, it would have been necessary to rotate his centroid factor I 65 degrees, and his centroid factor II 22 degrees. Unfortunately, the transformation matrix he employed—which does yield the values of his oblique factor matrix—accomplished the wrong rotation; the angles of rotation were the same, but they applied to the wrong factors. (Note the interchange of rows and columns in the two transformation matrices in Table I.) It was a peculiar property of this mistake that gave rise to the erroneous interpretation Lander placed upon the resultant oblique factor structure. Because he wanted to rotate centroid I 22 degrees in order to maximize the loadings of one cluster on I, but instead rotated centroid II 22 degrees in the same direction, and because centroid II was orthogonal to (90 degrees from) centroid I to begin with, he inadvertently created an oblique factor II that was exactly orthogonal to (90 degrees from) his target factor or, in other words, one that would *minimize* the loadings of that factor's cluster of variables on

---
[3] We are grateful for the help of Kenneth I. Howard and Jack Sawyer in this task.

oblique factor II. For the same reasons, an identical outcome was obtained for oblique factor I, with the result that rather than maximizing the loadings of its target cluster of variables, each oblique factor *minimizes* the loadings of the *other* cluster. This accounts for the fact that the socioeconomic variables of median rent and median education show negligible loadings on the oblique anomie factor and, especially, that the delinquency rate has a negligible loading on the oblique socioeconomic factor. In the case of a rotational solution with these properties, only variables that lie distant from the center of their cluster (and at the same distance from the origin as the cluster itself) can possibly have substantial loadings on both factors simultaneously (if we may be permitted an overly simple but essentially correct characterization). In Lander's data, there were no such variables.

However unlikely, it is still possible that Lander actually intended the oblique solution be achieved. In this event, we would have to challenge the principles underlying such a solution. This is quite easy to do. The rotational criterion implicit in his actual procedure amounts to determining a rotation by setting in advance what a given factor *is not* (what variables should not load on it); what it is would then turn out to be a composite of whatever variables remain. The sterility of this procedure may be grasped immediately by imagining what the outcome would be if it were applied to the case in which there was but a single cluster. In this event the factor would be aimed at nothing. That such a criterion would represent a radical departure from accepted principles is witnessed by the consensus among the three factor analysts (including ourselves) who independently rotated Lander's factors, and by authoritative texts.[4] Furthermore, Lander appears to have understood that the oblique solution he was aiming at would produce two positively correlated oblique factors, because he twice represents this correlation—correct in absolute value—as being positive.[5] In actuality, the two oblique factors of his solution are negatively correlated, with a value of -0.68.

Thinking that the correlation between his oblique factors was strongly positive in combination with the factor structure derived from a solution in which their correlation was instead strongly negative, Lander was led to conclude that the factor loadings represented a more fundamental aspect of his data than the strong zero-order correlations observed between delinquency and the socioeconomic variables, and that these more superficial zero-order relations were produced, and thereby accounted for, by the presumed positive correlation between the factors. Thus Lander stated:

> The factor analysis clearly demonstrates that delinquency in Baltimore is fundamentally related to the *stability* or *anomie* of an area and is not a function of nor is it basically associated with the economic characteristics of an area.
> ... The correlation between the *anomic* and the *socioeconomic* factors is, as one would expect from the inspection of graph I, high (.684). It provides an explanation of the fact that delinquency is so highly correlated with the socioeconomic properties of a tract. The association between the factors however is statistical.[6]

This interpretation is, of course, completely erroneous. Had he employed the correct transformation matrix, he would have obtained the loadings of the variables on two oblique factors that were substantially positively correlated in fact and, as is usually the case in such circumstances, his variables, including the juvenile delinquency rate, would have displayed high loadings on both factors. In addition, it

---

[4] See, for example, Harry H. Harman, *Modern Factor Analysis*, Chicago: University of Chicago Press, 1960, p. 265.

[5] Lander, *op. cit.*, pp. 53 and 59.
[6] *Ibid.*, p. 59.

would have been obvious that both factors were highly saturated with SES, and his anomie explanation would not have arisen. This can be seen in Table I, which presents the correct transformation matrix and the oblique factor structure it produces, and in Figure 1, where the correct oblique factors are indicated by broken lines. In our opinion, because of the high correlation between its factors, the oblique solution adds little to our understanding of this particular set of data, but that is beside the point—had he obtained this solution, Lander would not have been misled.

We postpone consideration of a possible orthogonal rotation until after our discussion of Chilton's article.

THE PARTIALLING FALLACY

Another of Lander's analyses consisted of obtaining the sixth-order partial correlation coefficients between the delinquency rate and each census variable in turn, holding the remaining census variables "constant."[7] Table II presents Lander's sixth-order partials, together with the zero-order correlations, of each variable with delinquency. His partials seem to have been subject to computational errors; Table II also provides recalculated partials, derived from his matrix of correlations.[8] It is clear at a glance that even the corrected partials are almost all much lower

---

[7] *Ibid.*, p. 46.

[8] With the exception of those involving delinquency, these zero-order correlations were themselves checked, starting with the original census data. Only minor discrepancies were found; for the sake of comparability, Lander's values were retained throughout this paper, unless otherwise stated. The delinquency rate data could be only approximated, however, by four class intervals, read from Map I in Lander's Appendix D with the aid of a magnifying glass. The resulting correlations with delinquency were close enough to Lander's to permit using the values that he calculated with reasonable security, especially since the remaining correlations had all been verified.

One strong indication that the partial correlations were in error was the fact that four of them display

then the zero-order correlations, so low in fact as to be not significantly different from zero in all but one case. Lander went on to introduce curvilinear components for four of the variables, in effect creating four new variables, and when these four were also incorporated into the partialling operation, he obtained a new set of correlations that were now tenth-order partials; however, out of respect for their violation of the assumption of linearity of regression, these new correlations were called "indices of partial correlation." Among these tenth-order partials, the two highest appear for the variables percentage nonwhite and percentage of homes owner-occupied. Lander drew the following conclusion from these results:

In the zero order correlation table, the juvenile delinquency rate is highly correlated with substandard housing and with residential overcrowding. In the partial correlation analysis, when the influence of other variables studied is eliminated, instead of positive correlations between these variables and delinquency of $r = +.69$ and $+.73$, we have derived coefficients of partial correlations of .0052 and .0079 as describing the *real* relationship between these variables and delinquency; and when adjustment is made for the curvilinearity of the data the partial correlations are reduced in both instances to .0000. [Actually, in his table, the correlation for homes overcrowded rises to .0090, but the point is trivial]. This indicates that, despite the high correlation coefficients, there is no substantive relationship between these two variables and delinquency when all other factors are held constant and their influence eliminated. We

---

reversals of sign. Although it is possible to reverse the sign of a zero-order relationship in partialling, this is extremely rare in practice, since it requires an unlikely combination of correlations. For this to have happened not once but four times, as his fgures seem to indicate, is most improbable. By the same reasoning, it is unlikely that all of the unreversed partials would be as close to zero as his figures show, because this places them on the threshold of a reversal of sign. Just as it is difficult to find data that would produce a sign reversal, it is difficult to find data that would entirely obliterate a strong zero-order relationship.

Table II. *Zero-Order and Sixth-Order Partial Correlations between Delinquency and Independent Variables, and Multiple Correlations with Other Independent Variables*

Variable	Zero-Order	Lander's Sixth-Order	Correct Sixth-Order	Multiple Correlation With Other Six	Squared Multiple Correlation
Median education	−.51	.0055	−.06	.93	.87
Median rent	−.53	.0003	−.02	.92	.84
Overcrowded	.73	.0079	.10	.90	.81
Substandard housing	.69	.0052	.08	.90	.81
Owner occupancy	−.80	.1764	−.43 [a]	.87	.75
Nonwhite	.70	.0086	.08	.86	.73
Foreign born	−.16	.0213	−.15	.47	.22

[a] Of the partial correlations, only the one for owner occupancy is significant: $p<.001$.

also cite the presented data to emphasize the danger of attaching great importance to interpretations based on zero order correlation analysis.[9]

We have here one of the clearer examples of an error that is not rare in sociology. The introduction of a control variable into a relationship implies the existence of a theoretical context, although in practice the context itself is often left unspecified. When experienced researchers fail to state the theoretical context explicitly, it is because they feel that it is sufficiently obvious to the reader. Often they are right. Some researchers, however, have been misled by this silence, and they are unaware of how necessary it is to be conscious of the theoretical implications underlying any partialling operation. As though to emphasize this aspect of the process, Kendall and Lazarsfeld, their classic exposition of the logic of partialling operations with categoric data, referred to the control variable as the "test" variable —clearly, a hypothesis is to be tested, and a hypothesis implies the existence of a theoretical context.[10] Some researchers, however, engage in what is actually atheoretical partialling, as though the only hypothesis to be tested were the purely statistical one of whether the zero-order relationship could survive the application of any conceivable control. The object, of course, is not simply to destroy an observed relationship, but rather to see whether it can be destroyed using as a control a variable that has been hypothesized to be potentially relevant and conceptually distinct within the theoretical context in which one is operating. However, without a theory, there is no way of telling what is conceptually distinct and what is not. Consequently, variables are often introduced as controls that are not meaningfully different in terms of what would constitute an appropriate theory. These variables so closely approach being identical with one of the variables already in the zero-order relationship that controlling for them becomes tantamount to partialling that relationship out of itself. This is exactly what Lander has done by taking a series of variables, many of which are important indicators of SES, and partialling all combinations of n-1 of them out of the relationship of the nth with delinquency. Under the circumstances, controlling for any one of them would be a mistake; controlling for them all approximates—in

---

[9] Lander, *op. cit.*, pp. 46–47. We have not checked the values of his tenth-order partial correlations.

[10] Patricia L. Kendall and Paul F. Lazarsfeld, "Problems of Survey Analysis," Robert K. Merton and Paul F. Lazarsfeld, eds., *Continuities in Social Research; Studies in the Scope and Method of "The American Soldier,"* Glencoe, Ill.: Free Press, 1950, 133–196.

view of the high multiple correlation that must obtain between any one of them and all of the rest—using as a control a variable that is almost perfectly correlated with at least one of the two in the zero-order relationship. (For the multiple correlation of each of his independent variables with the rest, see Table II.) In view of this, it is not surprising that the partial correlation coefficients in Lander's analysis turn out to be so small.

In reports of sociological research, it is not uncommon to find presented all of the possible highest-order partial correlations between each of a set of independent variables and the same dependent variable. Apparently, this practice also draws its inspiration from the Kendall and Lazarsfeld paper. However, the procedures advocated there are quite different in their logic. All of them *assume* knowledge concerning the presumed causal priority of the variables; they were never intended to provide that knowledge. Roughly, they ask, "Is variable A causally prior to B, or is it irrelevant?" and not, "Is variable A causally prior to B or is B causally prior to A?" Yet it appears to be the latter question that researchers are addressing when they calculate all possible partials to see which variable will emerge with the largest partial. There is nothing in the Kendall and Lazarsfeld paper to justify using each independent variable in turn as the test variable for each other independent variable. For one thing, the outcome of such a procedure is strongly influenced by small sampling or measurement errors when the independent variables are themselves highly correlated.[11] Moreover, not all covariation is necessarily spurious. Controlling for valid covariation makes as much sense as controlling for a parallel form of the same measuring instrument. Presenting all possible highest-order partials is a sure indication that the researcher has not thought through the theoretical connections among his variables. Once committed to such a mechanical procedure, he is quite apt to control for variables whose covariation is largely valid. Finally, there is no rule for attributing controlled covariation to the influence of one rather than another of the independent variables, regardless of the disparity in size between their partial correlations. Although the temptation to commit the partialling fallacy is greater in the case of continuous data—where it is more convenient to obtain partials of a high order—it must be emphasized that all control procedures are equally susceptible, including those for categoric data and for experiments.

An important property of this procedure of obtaining all possible highest-order partials is that the variables emerging with the largest partials will be those that are least redundantly represented in the set. Conceivably, these could even be the variables that show the poorest zero-order associations (although this happens not to be the case in Lander's analysis). In Lander's case, racial composition and owner occupancy were less redundantly represented than variables that were good indicators of SES and, as a result, the better indicators of SES wiped each other out. Inasmuch as racial composition and owner occupancy were also the highest-loading variables, along with delinquency, on his supposed anomie factor, their higher partials in the present analysis must have strongly reinforced Lander's interpretation of his mistaken oblique rotation.

One could argue, of course, that median education *is* different from median rent and that it is reasonable to examine the relationship between either variable and delinquency free of the effects of the other variable. This is true as far as it goes, but it implies a theoretical focus that is much narrower and much more highly specialized than the one with which Lander

---

[11] For an excellent discussion of this point, see H. M. Blalock, Jr., "Correlated Independent Variables: The Problem of Multicollinearity," *Social Forces*, 42 (December, 1963), pp. 233–237.

was properly concerned. This smaller question should not be confused with a hypothesis concerning the relationship between SES and delinquency when one has two or more equally valid indicators of SES. For example, one might wish to inspect for some reason the partial correlations between quantitative ability and verbal ability on the one hand and academic achievement on the other, but this would be a poor way to test whether ability in general is related to academic achievement. Clearly, the partialling operation implies distinctness between the control and zero-order variables, although there are different levels of distinctness. If the theoretical context is left implicit, the investigator may find that he has committed himself to a theory—or a level of distinctness—that he did not intend and that he would not support upon deeper consideration.

It is important to note that it is only the unusual explicitness with which Lander declared his intentions that enables us to criticize his methods so confidently. All too often, investigators are so unclear in their own minds as to why they are partialling that it is impossible to determine their intended level of distinctness. In this way they enjoy the methodological security of the microscopic level of distinctness, in that one is always entitled to examine a partial if he wishes, while leaving their readers with impressions concerning the macroscopic level. Should one call attention to their indiscriminate partialling, they are apt to find themselves suddenly convinced that they had intended the narrower focus all along. Potential critics are naturally unwilling to take a stand when the question of whether there is even an issue is itself so slippery. As a result, sociology that is conceptually blurred accumulates, unchallenged, in the literature.

The reasoning underlying the partialling fallacy is reduced to the absurd, incidentally, when we realize that one could calculate all possible highest-order partials between the variables of a highly interrelated set and erroneously conclude, when the low partials fail to be significantly different from zero, that none of them was related to any other one.

LANDER'S MULTIPLE REGRESSION ANALYSIS

Lander also performed several multiple regression analyses. The first of these employed all seven census variables as linear predictors of delinquency. This analysis was immediately rejected, however, in favor of a second that incorporated, in addition, curvilinear (quadratic) components for four of the variables.[12] His purpose in these analyses was not simply to see how well he could predict the dependent variable, but also to examine the standardized regression coefficients as indicators of the relative importance of the variables. He next tested the second set of regression coefficients for statistical significance, and found that only four were significant. These four were the coefficients of the linear and quadratic components of the same two variables that had stood out from the rest in the partial correlation study: percentage nonwhite and percentage of homes owner-occupied. At this point Lander concluded, "Of all the variables studied, only the percentage of homes owner-occupied and percentage of Negroes in an area are fundamentally related to the delinquency rate and can be characterized as statistically significant predicting variables" [13] He then introduced just these two predictors into a third, multiple curvilinear, analysis, in which all of the coefficients were statistically significant.[14] Thus, yet a third time, his analysis conveyed the impression that the delinquency rate was associated with these particular two variables rather than with the

---

[12] Lander, *op. cit.*, p. 48.
[13] *Ibid.*, p. 62.
[14] *Ibid.*

variables that were more obviously socioeconomic in nature.

This type of analysis can lead easily to other, perhaps more insidious, versions of the partialling fallacy. We have indicated that to the degree the variables of a set are highly interrelated or numerous and conceptually similar, we approach being able to produce a partial correlation coefficient of zero between any two of them by controlling for the rest. Similar circumstances affect the partial regression coefficient in nearly the same way. This comes about in the following manner.

As redundant independent variables are successively introduced into a regression problem, their common predictive value gets averaged, in a weighted manner, over all of their regression coefficients. As a result, all of their regression coefficients decline in absolute value. At the same time, the multiple correlation increases only a trivial amount with each new variable, reflecting the fact that little new information is being added. That the multiple correlation cannot decrease indicates that the common predictive value is conserved, although it does get spread out over more and more regression coefficients, each becoming smaller and smaller as new redundant variables are fed into the problem.

Continuing with our examination of the regression coefficient, we note that if at any point a new variable is added that is uncorrelated with previous independent variables, then the regression coefficients of the previous variables will be unaffected. Of course, it would be possible then to add more variables that are redundant with respect to this new variable, but not redundant with respect to the earlier set, so that the regression coefficient of the new variable is reduced, but not those of the earlier variables.

The argument developed above helps us to realize that among the independent variables there could occur two or more subsets of variables, the members of which were redundant (strongly correlated) with variables in the same subset, but relatively independent (weakly correlated) with respect to variables in other subsets. It becomes immediately apparent that, under these circumstances, the relative size of a variable's regression coefficient depends to a considerable extent upon the *number* of other variables in its subset. If all variables were redundant to the same degree with others in their subset, unrelated to the same degree with variables in other subsets, and all were equally related to the dependent variable, then differences in the sizes of the regression coefficients between the variables of one subset and those of another subset would depend entirely upon the relative numbers of variables in the two subsets. These conditions are, of course, quite special, but they serve to bring into sharp relief processes that operate as well in the analysis of real data.

A subset, for example, can be thought of as representing a particular domain of content (or an underlying factor). In the case of Lander's data, the two domains of content can be partitioned into two major subsets, one containing the four SES variables and the other the two anomie variables. (The remaining variable, foreign born, falls outside of both clusters, and it may be ignored for our purposes, since its correlation with delinquency is too low for it to act as an important subset composed of but a single variable.) Within the SES subset, the average absolute correlation is .77; within the anomie subset it is .76. Although the four variables of the SES subset have lower correlations with delinquency, on the average, than the two anomie variables, thus departing slightly from our ideal example, it is nevertheless true that the potential importance of the SES variables is completely obscured by the fact that there are so many of them. This is borne out by the fact that each of the SES variables, when included by itself in a regression analysis with either just the linear or both the linear and quadratic components of the two anomie variables, yields a regression coefficient that is significant at the .001 level. Thus, it is the *number* of SES variables, rather than the superiority of the anomie variables, that causes the regression coefficients of the former not to be significant in Lander's analysis. The supposed "importance" of variables thus turns out to be inversely related to the frequency with which their domain has been sampled.

By the same logic, we can understand what is wrong with Bordua's attempt (repeated by Chilton) to test Lander's hypothesis by adding to the regression two new variables, median income and an index for unrelated individuals, deemed to be representative of each type of factor, SES and anomie, respectively.[15] Bordua reasoned that if Lander were correct, the regression coefficient of the new anomie variable would be larger than the regression coefficient of the new SES variable or, possibly, the first would be significant and the second not. However, if these new variables were truly typical of their respective domains, the outcome could not possibly be otherwise. If one pie is to be divided among a larger number and another pie among a smaller number, no matter how often we add one to the number for each pie, it will never alter the fact that the portions from the first pie will be smaller than those from the second.

THE CONSTRUCT VALIDITY OF ANOMIE

Campbell and Fiske have proposed certain criteria to be satisfied whenever it is claimed that a particular set of measurements represents a particular theoretical construct.[16] Among these is the simple but powerful requirement that different measurements of the same construct correlate more highly with one another than with measurements of alternative constructs.

If one studies the correlation matrices for all three sets of data—Lander's, Bordua's and Chilton's—it can be seen that the putative anomie variable (nonwhite and homes owner-occupied) do not constitute a genuine construct in terms of this criterion, although the SES variables do.[17] For Detroit and Indianapolis, the anomie variables split apart, in that their highest correlations are not with each other. For Detroit, the variable most correlated with nonwhite is foreign born (-0.73), and with homes owner-occupied it is substandard housing (-0.64); for Indianapolis, nonwhite correlates most with over-crowded ($+0.46$), and homes owner-occupied with overcrowded (-0.56). This, in not a single instance out of four possible ones does an anomie variable have its highest correlation with another anomie variable in the other two cities. However, in all three replications each SES variable always has its highest correlation with another SES variable.

Furthermore, the correlation between the two anomie variables declines drastically. Whereas it was -0.76 for Baltimore, it drops to -0.43 for Detroit and to -0.26 for Indianapolis. In contrast, the mean absolute correlations between the four SES variables are 0.77, 0.60, and 0.79 for the three cities, respectively. We see, therefore, that in two of the cities the anomie variables are substantially more highly correlated with other variables than they are with each other. Thus, quite aside from the question of whether nonwhite and homes owner-occupied approximate our intuitive conception of what is meant by anomie, there is no evidence whatsoever that these two variables jointly define any theoretical construct at all that is uniquely different from what is measured by other variables in the analysis.

---

[15] Bordua, *op. cit.*, pp. 232–235; Chilton *op. cit.*, pp. 74–75.

[16] Donald T. Campbell and Donald W. Fiske, "Convergent and Discriminant Validation by the Multitrait-Multimethod Matrix," *Psychological Bulletin*, 56 (1959), pp. 81–105.

[17] All three correlation matrices appear in Chilton, *op. cit.*, p. 73.

CHILTON'S STUDY

In an attempt to reduce the data for all three cities to some common basis, Chilton performed new factor analyses for each city. In each of these analyses, he retained and rotated four factors—far too many for only eight variables. This is reflected in the appearance of unmistakable specific factors in several of the solutions, and corroborated by the fact that eigenvalues drop below 1.0 beyond the second factor in all three analyses.[18]

Chilton then noted that, in his factor analysis for Baltimore, the variables were grouped differently from their arrangement in Lander's original two-factor, unrotated centroid analysis. Thinking that the discrepancy might have resulted from his own use of a principal-axis solution, Chilton refactored the Baltimore data by the centroid method. Again, four factors were extracted, and these were presented both in rotated and unrotated form. Again seeming discrepancies were noted between Lander's solution and his own. In an effort to check these last results, he reconstructed the correlation matrix from both sets of factor loadings, his own and Lander's, and found that his solution led to a better approximation of the original correlations than did Lander's. He concluded that this was because Lander had erroneously reversed the signs of the loadings of four variables.[19]

However, Lander was right and Chilton wrong. First of all, there is never that much difference between centroid and principal-axis solutions. All of the discrepancies between factor solutions noted by Chilton are due in part to the natural differences between rotated and unrotated solutions, and in the main to the difference between the number of factors in Chilton's rotated analyses and the number employed by Lander. Because he extracted so many factors beyond the two that the data can barely support, Chilton's common factors show no stability and decompose rapidly under rotation. Furthermore, to the extent that the original correlations were more nearly reproduced using his own factor loadings rather than Lander's, it is entirely due to the contribution of the additional variance accounted for by the two extra factors in Chilton's four-factor solution. Possibly there was also some confusion of signs at this point because of Lander's having reversed four of his variables.

Lander reflected these four variables in order to save space in plotting them in his Graph I. The reflection is indicated, somewhat obscurely to be sure, by the minus signs to the left of his variable numbers in his centroid solution, and by actual changes in the names of his variables in his oblique solution.[20] In view of these changes, the signs of his loadings are all quite correct. Chilton's statement to the contrary notwithstanding, one can reverse any number of variables at any time, so long as the appropriate sign changes are carried through all of the factors. This Lander did.

The first two factors of Chilton's unrotated centroid solution should correspond exactly with Lander's centroid analysis, and they do—when certain facts are taken into account. One of these is that Chilton's factor II is a total reflection of Lander's factor II. (It is always permissible to reflect an entire factor.) In order to see that the two solutions are identical, it is necessary therefore to reflect Chilton's factor II, and then to make all of the sign changes in both factors as dictated by Lander's reversal of four variables. It

---

[18] On 1.0 as the criterion for stopping, see Harman, *op. cit.*, p. 363. On the appearance of specific factors, see the discussion and citations in Kenneth I. Howard and Robert A. Gordon, "Empirical Note on the 'Number of Factors' Problem in Factor Analysis," *Psychological Reports,* 12, No. 1 (1963), pp. 247–250, and the erratum, *loc. cit.*, No. 2 (1963). When eigenvalues drop below 1.0, factors cease to account for as much variance as a single variable, and so no data reduction is achieved.

[19] Chilton, *op. cit.*, p. 76.

[20] Lander, *op. cit.*, p. 53.

was probably this fortuitous reflection of factor II between the two analyses that led Chilton to name as the confused variables not the four that Lander reversed, but the four that he did not reverse. Ideally, Chilton should have considered whether any reflections were required to facilitate comparisons between the analyses before attempting to interpret the results. It should be emphasized that there is no substantive issue involved in any of these points of dispute between Lander and Chilton, with the possible exception of how many factors are appropriate.

One final point concerning the factor analyses remains to be corrected. Chilton, like Lander, wished to present a picture of two of his factors in as little space as possible (see his Graph 1). Therefore he treated negative signs on the abscissa as though they were positive, and included a brief explanation of what he had done. This is an extremely undesirable solution to the space problem. In effect, it folds over some of the variables, and moves them into an adjacent quadrant. Their presence there has no substantive or mathematical significance, and it leads to the fact that Chilton himself was misled confused interpretations, as witnessed by by his own device into stating that "the graphic plot upon which part of the original interpretation was based now presents a very different picture. Delinquency may be said to cluster with rent, education, and percent nonwhite, two of which were interpreted as indicators of an economic factor in the original Baltimore analysis."[21] Actually, rent and education belong either one quadrant to the left or one quadrant down, depending on how they were reflected. Other variables in his diagram, similarly treated, should also be relocated. As we indicated before, this analysis is actually identical with Lander's, and no interpretations not common to both are justified. If one wishes to save space in plotting factors, the appropriate variables should be reflected 180 degrees, which moves them through two quadrants (for two factors) and preserves their mathematical and substantive meaning.

INTERPRETATION OF FACTORS AND THE PROBLEM OF MIXED CUTTING POINTS

We have already indicated why we feel that no more than two factors can be supported by the three sets of census tract variables. It is also our opinion that the two factors in Lander's unrotated orthogonal centroid solution are best interpreted as two aspects of socioeconomic status, one giving more emphasis to economics and the other to race (just as verbal and quantitative skills might define two aspects of intellectual ability.) This organization of the variables emerges even more sharply when the first two principal components for each of the three cities are rotated to an orthogonal varimax solution. In all three cases, foreign born and nonwhite define the race factor, with strong help in Baltimore from owner occupancy.[22] These factor loadings appear in Table III. Coefficients of factorial similarity, in Table IV, show that the economic factor is highly invariant for all three cities, and that the

---

[21] Chilton, *op. cit.*, p. 76.

[22] The Detroit and Indianapolis data are for 1950. Therefore, the shift of owner occupancy away from the race factor for those cities probably reflects the improvement in the economic position of Negroes during the intervening decade. For urban Maryland only 10 percent of the nonwhite dwelling units were owner-occupied in 1940. This was less than half of the nonwhite rates of either urban Michigan or Indiana at *that* time. Furthermore, the owner-occupancy rates in general increased markedly in all three places during the next decade, more so for nonwhites than whites. This indicates that the 1940 Baltimore nonwhites were just much poorer than the 1950 nonwhites of the other two cities. On the economic position of nonwhites at the two points in time, see *Statistical Abstract of the United States, 1952*, p. 270. On owner occupancy, see U.S. Department of Commerce, Bureau of the Census, *Census of Housing: 1950, Vol. I: General Characteristics*, Washington, D.C.: U.S. Government Printing Office, 1953, Table 3.

Table III. *Orthogonal Varimax Rotations from Principal Axes Solutions; Baltimore, Detroit, and Indianapolis*

	Baltimore		Detroit		Indianapolis	
Variable	I	II	I	II	I	II
Delinquency rate	−.58	−.67	−.49	−.64	−.91	−.15
Median education	.91	.06	.86	.19	.71	.51
Median rent	.90	.06	.89	−.02	.60	.59
Overcrowded	−.79	−.47	−.55	−.67	−.88	−.32
Substandard housing	−.86	−.35	−.63	−.58	−.86	−.42
Owner occupancy	.52	.71	.62	.42	.76	−.19
Nonwhite	−.38	−.82	−.26	−.81	−.32	−.64
Foreign born	−.38	.70	−.10	.90	−.09	.81

race factor is highly invariant for all but Indianapolis, where it is nevertheless easily recognizable.[23] Except for Indianapolis, where it fails to load on race, delinquency loads strongly on both factors.

Despite the effort by Lander and others to see in some of these variables something other than socioeconomic status, it is obvious that—with the possible exception of foreign born—they all share heavily in that concept. This viewpoint is supported by the very high loadings that all of the variables except foreign born received on their first principal components. Excluding foreign born, the *smallest* such loading was 0.76 for Baltimore, 0.62 for Detroit, and 0.59 for Indianapolis. On this basis alone, a strong argument could be made for applying a general factor interpretation to all three sets of data. The general factor interpretation, furthermore, is also consistent with the fact that the coefficients of similarity (Table IV) between all of the factors are never small.[24] Thus, even the interpretation of the rotated two-factor solutions would have to be tempered by this consideration and, consequently, regardless of their preferences among these equally tenable alternative solutions, the factor analysts should all have arrived at pretty much the same substantive conclusions concerning the particular sets of correlations under study. As it happens, a somewhat different set of correlations would have been more appropriate in each case, but before showing this let us first note certain characteristics of the present analyses.

It is true that plots of the three analyses show owner occupancy—one of Lander's anomie variables—consistently diametrical to delinquency. However, Lander gave far too much emphasis to the possibility that the stabilizing influence of home ownership prevents delinquency, and not enough to the opposite interpretation, according to which a low owner occupancy rate may be merely an index of delinquency itself. Those who can afford to own property can generally afford to choose where they will live—and they will probably choose to live outside of areas with high delinquency rates, if only in the interests of their children.

Not easily seen from the table of loadings, but obvious when the variables are plotted, is the fact that, besides owner occupancy (when reflected), overcrowding and substandard housing are most consist-

---

[23] On the use of this coefficient, see Harman, *op. cit.*, pp. 257–260. Values as low as 0.94 previously have been accepted as indicating factors that are congruent, while one of 0.46 has been rejected as being too low for congruence.

[24] In performing the rotation of Lander's centroid factors without knowing the substance of the problem, Sawyer commented that a general factor would do very well, except for foreign born. The general factor interpretation looks even better, as would be expected, for the principal axes solutions (which were not available to him).

Table IV. *Coefficients of Factorial Similarity*

Factors	Baltimore		Detroit		Indianapolis	
	I	II	I	II	I	II
Baltimore I	—	.51	.98	.52	.95	.55
Baltimore II	—	—	.56	.96	.69	.64
Detroit I	—	—	—	.54	.94	.60
Detroit II	—	—	—	—	.68	.75
Indianapolis I	—	—	—	—	—	.53
Indianapolis II	—	—	—	—	—	—

ently in the greatest proximity to delinquency.[25] This results from the high zero-order correlations that these variables, in comparison to the other variables, particularly the more obviously socioeconomic ones of education and rent, have with delinquency. Anyone seeking a theoretical construct different from SES in these data might be inclined to see evidence for it in this somewhat poorer showing made by the education and rent measures in all three cities. Moreover, similar findings exist for other cities.

For San Diego, Polk found that a socioeconomic index based on occupation and education was correlated more weakly with delinquency than was a measure of ethnic status.[26] Bloom has presented correlations for an unnamed city that show median school years completed and median family income less related to delinquency than was the percentage of the white population with Spanish surnames.[27] And, in their examination of census tract data for the neighborhoods of sixteen gangs in Chicago, Cartwright and Howard report:

... whereas it has previously been found that higher delinquency rates are associated with lower rent, lesser educational attainment, more residential mobility and more overcrowding, such associations are not found with gang neighborhoods in the present study.[28]

Paradoxically, overcrowding now makes its appearance in this list as one of the variables failing to correlate with delinquency.

To say the least, these repeated failures of the quintessential indexes of socioeconomic status to correlate as well with delinquency as other variables is inconvenient to the argument that the other variables are also essentially themselves measures of socioeconomic status. Fortunately, it can be demonstrated that the inconsistencies between the two kinds of variable for the case of Baltimore, for which we possess the required data, are completely artifactual. There is no reason to think that the same explanation would not apply as well to the data from the remaining cities.

Even among high-delinquency census tracts, one rarely encounters delinquency rates much greater than 20 percent.[29]

---

[25] The less preferred centroid solutions show overcrowding and substandard housing farther from delinquency than they really are. As a result, our Figure 1 gives a somewhat misleading picture of the locations of these variables in comparison to the solutions based on principal axes.

[26] Polk, *op. cit.*

[27] Bloom, *op. cit.*, p. 316.

[28] *Op. cit.*, p. 358.

[29] To some degree these rates depend on the age range under consideration. Rates based on the narrower 12–16-year-old range, for example, which is weighted more heavily by peak rate ages of 14, 15, and 16, can reach 30 percent. For typical figures in the wider age ranges, for example 7–20, see the data for Negro Harlem in Harlem Youth Opportunities Unlimited, Inc., *Youth in the Ghetto*, New York: Harlem Youth Opportunities Unlimited, Inc., 1964, pp. 36 and 140. A prevalence rate of 20.7 percent for boys has been estimated for the Lexington, Kentucky area by John C. Ball, Alan Ross, and Alice Simpson. See their "Incidence and Estimated Prevalence of Recorded Delinquency in a Metropolitan Area," *American Sociological Review*, 29 (February, 1964), pp. 90–93. They also cite a num-

Therefore, if delinquency were perfectly correlated with socioeconomic status, at most only the lowest 20 percent of the households on any index of SES would be implicated. An index that is expressed as a percentage would be sensitive to the proportion of persons of critically low SES (low enough to be delinquent) in a tract, so long as the index was dichotomized at a point in its range close to the delinquent-nondelinquent boundary. If the point at which it was dichotomized is remote from that boundary, e.g., the proportion with incomes under a million dollars, it will, of course, be insensitive. More generally, if the information concerning a dependent variable is concentrated in one tail of the distribution of an independent variable, the full strength of the association will not be revealed unless the independent variable is dichotomized at the optimal point, in the tail.

There principles are so well-known that considerable care is exercised, usually, in choosing an at least intuitively appropriate cutting point for categoric census data that must be dichotomized. Indeed, census data are rarely dichotomized except with an end in mind which implicitly governs the choice of cutting point. In some cases there is no choice of cutting point, e.g., percentage non-white; in others one has been established by the Census Bureau, e.g., percentage overcrowded; whereas in others a good precedent is lacking and the investigator must do what he thinks is best with the available categories, e.g., Lander's substandard housing, apparently.

With respect to truly continuous variables, e.g., income, rent, or education, the situation is somewhat different. In their case, the purposes to which the information may be put are so various that the Census Bureau provides a measure of central tendency—which best summarizes the entire distribution. Because of open-ended categories at the extremes of these distributions, the measure chosen is usually the median rather than the mean. As a result, it has become common practice in the case of these variables to employ the conveniently available median.

Unlike percentages based upon appropriate cutting points, measures of central tendency, and especially the median, are insensitive to conditions in the tails of their distributions. Consequently, by employing both percentages and medians in multivariate studies of a phenomenon, such as delinquency, that is concentrated in the lower tail of the distribution of any index of SES, investigators have been using indexes with mixed cutting points for their independent variables, some of which carry much more information about the lower tail of their distribution than others.

To some degree, this adherence to medians when they are available may be motivated by the feeling that it would be improper to exploit the vagaries of data by searching for cutting points that would yield stronger associations. However, the chance inflation of a correlation by this means is probably trivial in magnitude when the question is one of choosing between adjacent cutting points that are equally appropriate theoretically. In contrast, when the cutting point is arbitrarily assigned, it is much more apt to be remote from the one that is both theoretically appropriate and statistically optimal, and hence the effect on the measure of association is more likely to be drastic. Furthermore, in the absence of information that would enable one to narrow down the range of choices to those cutting points that would be theoretically appropriate, more or less, the best estimate of an appropriate cutting point is probably the one that is statistically optimal.

In the studies by Lander and his followers, both education and rent are median-based indexes, whereas the other variables

---

ber of observed rates, some of which are much higher than 20 percent. However, our thesis depends mainly on the typical delinquency rate for an area, not on the maximum rate, and it can accommodate rates much higher than the 20 percent level we employ for the sake of argument.

—that we contend are also measures of SES —derive from percentages based on dichotomization close to the lower tails of their distributions. This accounts for the lower correlations of education and rent with delinquency. According to Lander's median-based indexes, education and rent are correlated −0.54 and −0.55 with delinquency.[30] However, by redefining education as "the proportion with less than five years of grade school," and rent as "the proportion paying less than $15.00 monthly rent," these correlations undergo spectacular rises to 0.72 and 0.73, respectively —each accounting for an additional 23 percent of the variance of delinquency. Their new absolute values are now approximately of the same order of magnitude as the correlations with delinquency of overcrowding (+0.75), substandard housing (+0.74), and owner-occupancy (−0.78), and they are higher than that of nonwhite (+0.67), which was one of Lander's anomie variables.[31]

The correlations between both education and rent and the remaining variables also increase in absolute value, so that when the new correlation matrix is factor analyzed, factor I, even after rotation, contains the highest loadings of *all* of the variables except foreign born.[32] This rotated factor differs very little from the first principal component in this analysis, so that it continues to support the interpretation of a general factor that is unmistakably based upon socioeconomic status. Instead of having its highest loading on the second factor—as it did even in our revision of Lander's analysis—delinquency now loads practically exclusively on this SES factor. (See Table V and compare it with Table II.) Factor II, which is brought out somewhat more clearly by the rotation, remains a race factor (or, if you will, a native-born factor).

The question naturally arises as to whether cutting points that are more nearly optimal could be found for the other variables, so that their correlations with delinquency would increase too. Of the other variables, only overcrowding and substandard housing offer the conceptual freedom for possible redefinition. However, none of the other logical cutting points for these variables increased their correlations with delinquency. They only decreased them. Given the available categories, their definitions were already optimal.

Although Polk's SES variables were not based on medians, the evidence that this same explanation applies to his San Diego data is strong. The operational definitions he employed were those introduced by Shevky and Bell in another study.[33] They divided education at "completion of the eighth grade," so that the cutting point used by Polk was four grades higher than the one we found optimal for Baltimore. Their second SES variable was based on the proportion of persons employed as "craftsmen, foremen, and kindred workers," "operatives and kindred workers," or "laborers, except mine." This formulation excludes service workers and private household workers, occupational categories that are lower in status than many of those included and which contain 11.8 percent of the San Diego civilian labor force. Even more importantly, it excludes the unemployed, who constituted an additional 7.9 percent of the 1950 San Diego civilian labor force. Needless to say, the presence of this last group in particular is critical to any delineation of a segment of

---

[30] To make the comparisons fairer, the correlations given here are based on our raw data, rather than Lander's published values, from which they differ slightly. See fn. 8.

[31] The correlation of owner occupancy with delinquency (reversed in sign) is significantly greater than that for education at the 0.05 level, using a one-tailed test. The difference between the owner occupancy and rent correlations with delinquency is not significant.

[32] Again, two factors were justified. One principal component accounted for 67 percent of the variance, two for 84 percent.

[33] Eshref Shevky and Wendell Bell, *Social Area Analysis* Stanford: Stanford University Press, 1955.

Table V. *Factor Analysis of Baltimore Data with Education and Rent Revised, and Revised Correlations*

	Orthogonal Varimax			Revised Correlations With Remaining Variables	
Variable	SES	Race	h²	Educ.	Rent
Delinquency rate	−.86	−.23	.79	.72	.73
Low education	−.94	.19	.91	—	.87
Low rent	−.91	.18	.87	.87	—
Overcrowded	−.92	−.10	.85	.84	.79
Substandard housing	−.93	.05	.87	.88	.90
Owner occupancy	.80	.36	.77	−.62	−.62
Nonwhite	−.69	−.56	.79	.58	.46
Foreign born	−.11	.91	.85	.26	.18

population of extremely low socioeconomic status. It appears that Polk's categories did not embrace the full lower range of the SES distribution.

Furthermore, the optimal cutting points for education and rent for Baltimore in 1940 included 16 and 14 percent of the reported population, respectively, whereas Polk's categories for education and occupation, applied to San Diego in 1950, included 28 and 34 percent of the population at risk, respectively. These percentages alone indicate that his categories were quite broad, and therefore that he was operating much more closely to the center of the SES distribution than may be warranted for predicting delinquency.

Finally, his actual SES index represented a composite of his occupation and education variables, so that the greater disadvantages of the occupation variable were visited upon the education variable. Although it cannot be assumed that the cutting points that prove optimal for one time and place will be the same as those for another time and place, it does seem likely, in view of the breadth of his categories, that Polk's ethnic status index, which correlated more highly with delinquency than his SES index, was actually the more valid indicator of extremely low socioeconomic status. Only 8.9 percent of San Diego's population fell into the ethnic category, as it was defined by Shevky and Bell. Negroes and Mexicans, whom it contains, comprised 4.5 and 1.2 percent, respectively, of the population, for a total of 5.7 percent. The much narrower ethnic category probably focused on persons of much lower status than those singled out by the SES index; the latter was not only broader in range, but was also shifted toward the center of the distribution by the exclusion of groups at the lower ends of its continuum.

In Bloom's study median-based measures of SES were again presented along with a percentage-based ethnic variable, and no further comment is necessary. The Cartwright and Howard study, it should be emphasized, was not intended as an exact replication of Lander's work, and any implications common to both types of study must be cautiously drawn. In their investigation, they were comparing certain gang neighborhoods with the entire city, controlling only for race. Consequently, their associations are apt to appear weaker than those from correlational studies of delinquency rates over all census tracts; any interpretation of their null findings especially must carry this qualification. Over and above this, however, we strongly suspect that it was mainly their use of medians in measuring rent, education, and overcrowding that accounts for the failure of these variables to produce differences. It is instructive to note that they shifted away from the percentage-based definition of overcrowding employed by Lander in favor of median persons per room and per dwelling unit. This shift coincides with the paradoxical first appearance of overcrowding among those variables showing weaker associations. Despite these ambiguities, it should be added, Cartwright and Howard were quite definite in concluding that their gang neighborhoods were of lower socioeconomic status.

We admit that we too were surprised to find that the effect of different cutting points on Lander's data was so strong. Clearly, the importance of choosing appropriate cutting points deserves great emphasis. In the future, it is recommended that investigators working with data like these select only the optimal cutting points for each of their independent variables with respect to a given dependent variable. This will necessitate a rather laborious searching procedure that is not now a standard step in data analysis. We suspect that it will prove especially crucial in the case of ecological correlations, where a badly chosen cutting point can cost information in every observation.

Our own experience has shown that it is better to pick a point between existing categories of a variable, and to calculate the percentage to one side of that, than to employ the value of the category that a particular percentile falls in. Because category boundaries are so broad, the location of a given percentile cannot be determined precisely enough; accordingly this solution yields lower correlations than the other. We call attention to this because it would naturally occur to investigators to assign a uniform percentile to all of their independent variables in the hope of making all of their cutting points comparable, both within a study and across different studies.

Some variables are, of course, defined intrinsically, and must be used as they stand: nonwhite is a good example. Whether to accept a given definition or to operationally redefine a variable will in most cases be quite clear, but there will be some occasions that require a judicious decision. Variables expressed in categories not all of which are distinctly ordered with respect to each other also pose a problem that can be resolved perhaps only somewhat arbitrarily.

CONCLUSION

Barring the appearance of surprising new data, there should no longer be any question about the ecological relations among these variables—particularly the one between SES and official delinquency rates. We have seen, for Baltimore, that when the optimal cutting points are used, the more traditional SES indexes of education and rent approach within a few points the correlations of the other indexes with delinquency. It is not unlikely that other data will continue to show this separation of a few points and perhaps, as a result, generate speculation as to its cause. In closing, therefore, it is worthwhile to call attention to possible reasons why the correlations observed between education and rent, on the one hand, and delinquency on the other, might be depressed slightly below those of the other variables that have been studied. Probably the most important of these reasons is the failure of measures like education and rent to be calibrated in the same way for Negroes and for whites.

In the case of education, the gap that widens between the performances of Negro and of white children as they progress through public school means that formally equivalent amounts of schooling, in years, do not imply equal competence in the competition for socioeconomic status.[34]

[34] This trend is documented for Harlem in *Youth in the Ghetto, op. cit.*, pp. 168–195, and for the country at large in James S. Coleman *el al., Equality of Educational Opportunity*, Washington: U.S. Government Printing Office, 1966, pp. 220–275.

This would be especially true for Negroes whose education was received in the rural South prior to their moving to those cities in which they were found at the times of the 1940 and 1950 censuses.[35] On top of this, the validity of formal education as an index of SES is further undermined by discrimination in employment. Thus Levenson and McDill, whose data are recent, report that even when there is good reason to believe that education is constant in quality, Negro high school graduates trained for a given vocation have substantially lower earnings than their white counterparts, although employment rates for the two groups are practically the same.[36]

Indexes based on rent present similar problems. In their analysis of 1950 Chicago data, the Duncans report that artificial restrictions upon his access to the housing market force the Negro to pay more than the white for housing of a given quality. They state:

> One thing seems quite clear: non-whites get less desirable housing for a given rent than do whites. . . . a much larger proportion of non-whites than of whites occupy dwelling units that either lack a private bath, are in a dilapidated structure, or fail to meet acknowledged housing standards in both these respects. In 1950, over half, or 53 percent, of non-white households, as against 15 percent of white households, lived in units with no private bath or which were dilapidated. This difference prevailed despite the fact that non-white median rental was only slightly below white median rental. . . .
>
> . . . Partly in order to pool incomes and partly because of the limited housing supply, Negroes resort to doubling-up of families and incorporation of non-family members into their households. . . . and the Negro household must more often endure a crowding of the dwelling unit to a degree that is generally recognized as undesirable.[37]

The import of these passages concerning the validity of rent as opposed to either substandard housing, overcrowding, or by implication owner-occupancy, as an index of socioeconomic status is clear. Shevky and Bell have also pointed to problems associated with rent and an index, the most important of which is probably the existence of rent controls; at the time of the 1950 census these were still in force, and somewhat spottily at that, thus compounding the difficulty.[38]

We see then that there are reasons for expecting a bit more error in predicting a style-of-life variable that is correlated with race, such as delinquency, from SES indexes based upon formalistic criteria, such as education measured in years, or rent, than from indexes in which present life-style is immanent, such as overcrowding and substandard housing. Until such a time as these reasons can be safely discounted, it would be unwise to conclude on the basis of small differences in correlation that the independent variables in question differ from each other in any fundamental sense.

Finally, it should be emphasized that this paper has been concerned with the empirical issue of whether delinquency is related to socioeconomic status or not, and not with the mechanisms of that relationship. The effect of the revised cutting points on education and rent, and the nature of the variables, such as overcrowding, that already possessed optimal cutting points, indicate that it is the extremely low end of the SES range that is most relevant. The advantage of having this established is that the many known concomitants of low SES become more worthy of investigation in the search for mechanisms.

This finding also contains a warning

---

[35] Coleman *et al., op. cit.,* pp. 219–220.

[36] Bernard Levenson and Mary S. McDill, "Vocational Graduates in Auto Mechanics: A Follow-up Study of Negro and White Youth," *Phylon,* 27, (1966), pp. 347–357.

[37] Otis Dudley Duncan and Beverly Duncan, *The Negro Population of Chicago: A Study of Residential Succession,* Chicago: University of Chicago Press, 1957, pp. 81–84.

[38] *Op. cit.,* pp. 23–24.

concerning the conduct of anti-poverty programs. It suggests that, in order to decrease delinquency, for example, it is necessary to reach the very bottom-most stratum in every census tract. Simply pumping money into low-income areas may result in helping needy people, but they may not be the ones chiefly responsible for the high social pathology indexes from which intervention against poverty now derives its main political justification. To the extent that programs fail to reach this lowest stratum—however successfully they are at assisting the more accessible higher-stratum poor—they will fail to alleviate the more intractable and socially visible consequences of poverty. Certainly there is much to be said, on humanitarian grounds alone, for directing limited resources toward the people best able to take advantage of them. Undoubtedly, this serves to prevent even higher pathology rates in the future. Nonetheless, there remains the possibility that the failure of programs to materially reduce delinquency and eliminate hard-core poverty will trigger political reactions that make it impossible to gain support for efforts that would benefit the very poorest. For these people's own misery to be used to legitimate help for someone else, and in a manner that diminishes their own chances of eventually receiving help themselves, would be the ultimate exploitation.

30. THE DELINQUENT SUBCULTURE

ALBERT K. COHEN

THE COMMON EXPRESSION, "JUVENILE crime," has unfortunate and misleading connotations. It suggests that we have two kinds of criminals, young and old, but only one kind of crime. It suggests that crime has it meanings and its motives which are much the same for young and old; that the young differ from the old as the apprentice and the master differ at the same trade; that we distinguish the young from the old only because the young are less "set in their ways," less "confirmed" in the same criminal habits, more amenable to treatment and more deserving, because of their tender age, of special consideration.

The problem of the relationship between juvenile delinquency and adult crime has many facets. To what extent are the offenses of children and adults distributed among the same legal categories, "burglary," "larceny," "vehicle-taking," and so forth? To what extent, even when the offenses are legally identical, do these acts have the same meaning for children and adults? To what extent are the careers of adult criminals continuations of careers of juvenile delinquency? We cannot solve these problems here, but we want to emphasize the danger of making facile and unproven assumptions. If we assume that "crime is crime," that child and adult criminals are practitioners of the same

▶SOURCE: *Delinquent Boys*, Glencoe: The Free Press, 1955, pp. 24–32. Reprinted by permission.

trade, and if our assumptions are false, then the road to error is wide and clear. Easily and unconsciously, we may impute a whole host of notions concerning the nature of crime and its causes, derived from our knowledge and fancies about adult crime, to a large realm of behavior to which these notions are irrelevant. It is better to make no such assumptions; it is better to look at juvenile delinquency with a fresh eye and try to explain what we see.

What we see when we look at the delinquent subculture (and we must not even assume that this describes *all juvenile* crime) is that it is *non-utilitarian, malicious* and *negativistic*.

We usually assume that when people steal things, they steal because they want them. They may want them because they can eat them, wear them or otherwise use them; or because they can sell them; or even—if we are given to a psychoanalytic turn of mind—because on some deep symbolic level they substitute or stand for something unconsciously desired but forbidden. All of these explanations have this in common, that they assume that the stealing is a means to an end, namely, the possession of some object of value, and that it is, in this sense, rational and "utilitarian." However, the fact cannot be blinked—and this fact is of crucial importance in defining our problem—that much gang stealing has no such motivation at all,

Even where the value of the object stolen is itself a motivating consideration, the stolen sweets are often sweeter than those acquired by more legitimate and prosaic means. In homelier language, stealing "for the hell of it" and apart from considerations of gain and profit is a valued activity to which attaches glory, prowess and profound satisfaction. There is no accounting in rational and utilitarian terms for the effort expended and the danger run in stealing things which are often discarded, destroyed or casually given away. A group of boys enters a store where each takes a hat, a ball or a light bulb. They then move on to another store where these things are covertly exchanged for like articles. Then they move on to other stores to continue the game indefinitely. They steal a basket of peaches, desultorily munch on a few of them and leave the rest to spoil. They steal clothes they cannot wear and toys they will not use. Unquestionably, most delinquents are from the more "needy" and "underprivileged" classes, and unquestionably many things are stolen because they are intrinsically valued. However, a humane and compassionate regard for their economic disabilities should not blind us to the fact that stealing is not merely an alternative means to the acquisition of objects otherwise difficult of attainment.[1]

Can we then account for this stealing by simply describing it as another form of recreation, play or sport? Surely it is that, but why is this form of play so attractive to some and so unappealing to others? Mountain climbing, chess, pinball, number pools and bingo are also different kinds of recreation. Each of us, child or adult, can choose from a host of alternative means for satisfying our common "need" for recreation. But every choice expresses a preference, and every preference reflects something about the chooser or his circumstances that endows the object of his choice with some special quality or virtue. The choice is not self-explanatory nor is it arbitrary or random. Each form of recreation is distributed in a characteristic way among the age, sex and social class sectors of our population. The explanation of these distributions and of the way they change is often puzzling, sometimes fascinating and rarely platitudinous.

By the same logic, it is an imperfect answer to our problem to say: "Stealing is but another way of satisfying the universal desire for status." Nothing is more obvious from numberless case histories of subcultural delinquents that they steal to achieve recognition and to avoid isolation or opprobrium. This is an important insight and part of the foundation on which we shall build. But the question still haunts

---

[1] See H. M. Tiebout and M. E. Kirkpatrick, "Psychiatric Factors in Stealing," *American Journal of Orthopsychiatry*, II (April, 1932), 114–123, which discusses, in an exceptionally lucid manner, the distinction between motivating factors which center around the acquisition of the object and those which center around the commission of the act itself.

The non-utilitarian nature of juvenile delinquency has been noted by many students. ". . . while older offenders may have definitely crystallized beliefs about profitable returns from antisocial conduct, it is very clear that in childhood and in earlier youth delinquency is certainly not entered into as a paying proposition in any ordinary sense." William Healy and Augusta F. Bronner, *op. cit.*, p. 22. "The juvenile property offender's thefts, at least at the start, are usually 'for fun' and not for gain." Paul Tappan, *Juvenile Delinquency* (New York: McGraw Hill Book Company, 1949), p. 143.

"Stealing, the leading predatory activity of the adolescent gang, is as much a result of the sport motive as of a desire for revenue." Frederic M. Thrasher, *The Gang* (Chicago: University of Chicago Press, 1936), p. 143. "In its early stages, delinquency is clearly a form of play." Henry D. McKay, "The Neighborhood and Child Conduct," *Annals of the American Academy of Political and Social Science*, CCLXI (January, 1949), 37. See also Barbara Bellow, Milton L. Blum, Kenneth B. Clark, et al., "Prejudice in Seaside," *Human Relations*, I (1947), 15–16 and Sophia M. Robison, Nathan Cohen and Murray Sachs, "An Unsolved Problem in Group Relations," *Journal of Educational Psychology*, XX (November, 1946), 154–162. The last cited paper is an excellent description of the nonutilitarian, malicious and negativistic quality of the delinquent subculture and is the clearest statement in the

us: "Why is stealing a claim to status in one group and a degrading blot in another?"

If stealing itself is not motivated by rational, utilitarian considerations, still less are the manifold other activities which constitute the delinquent's repertoire. Throughout there is a kind of *malice* apparent, an enjoyment in the discomfiture of others, a delight in the defiance of taboos itself. Thrasher quotes one gang delinquent:

> We did all kinds of dirty tricks for fun. We'd see a sign, "Please keep the streets clean," but we'd tear it down and say, "We don't feel like keeping it clean." One day we put a can of glue in the engine of a man's car. We would always tear things down. That would make us laugh and feel good, to have so many jokes.[2]

The gang exhibits this gratuitous hostility toward nongang peers as well as adults. Apart from its more dramatic manifestations in the form of gang wars, there is keen delight in terrorizing "good" children, in driving them from playgrounds and gyms for which the gang itself may have little use, and in general in making themselves obnoxious to the virtuous. The same spirit is evident in playing hookey and in misbehavior in school. The teacher and her rules are not merely something onerous to be evaded. They are to be *flouted*. There is an element of active spite and malice, contempt and ridicule, challenge and defiance, exquisitely symbolized, in an incident described to the writer by Henry D. McKay, of defecating on the teacher's desk.[3]

All this suggests also the intention of our term "negativistic." The delinquent subculture is not only a set of rules, a design for living which is different from or indifferent to or even in conflict with the norms of the "respectable" adult society. It would appear at least plausible that it is defined by its "negative polarity" to those norms. That is, the delinquent subculture takes its norms from the larger culture but turns them upside down. The delinquent's conduct is right, by the standards of his subculture, precisely *because* it is wrong by the norms of the larger culture.[4] "Malicious" and "negativistic" are foreign to the delinquent's vocabulary but he will often assure us, sometimes ruefully, sometimes with a touch of glee or even pride, that he is "just plain mean."

In describing what might be called the "spirit" of the delinquent culture, we have suggested also its *versatility*. Of the "antisocial" activities of the delinquent gangs, stealing, of course, looms largest. Stealing itself can be, and for the gang usually is, a diversified occupation. It may steal milk bottles, candy, fruit, pencils, sports equipment and cars; it may steal from drunks, homes, stores, schools and filling stations.

---

literature that a satisfactory theory of delinquency must make sense of these facts.

[2] Frederick M. Thrasher, *The Gang* (Chicago: University of Chicago Press, 1936), pp. 94–95.

[3] To justify the characterization of the delinquent subculture as "malicious" by multiplying citations from authorities would be empty pedantry. The malice is evident in any detailed description of juvenile gang life. We commend in particular, however, the cited works of Thrasher, Shaw and McKay and Robison *et al.* One aspect of this "gratuitous hostility" deserves special mention, however, for the benefit of those who see in the provision of facilities for "wholesome recreation" some magical therapeutic virtue. "On entering a playground or a gym the first activity of gang members is to disrupt and interrupt whatever activities are going on. Nongang members flee, and when the coast is clear the gang plays desultorily on the apparatus or carries on horseplay." Sophia Robison *et. al., op. cit.,* p. 159. See, to the same effect, the excellent little book by Kenneth H. Rogers, *Street Gangs in Toronto* (Toronto: The Ryerson Press, 1945), pp. 18–19.

[4] Shaw and McKay, in their *Social Factors in Juvenile Delinquency*, p. 241, come very close to making this point quite explicitly: "In fact the standards of these groups may represent a complete reversal of the standards and norms of conventional society. Types of conduct which result in personal degradation and dishonor in a conventional group, serve to enhance and elevate the personal prestige and status of a member of the delinquent group."

No gang runs the whole gamut but neither is it likely to "specialize" as do many adult criminal gangs and "solitary" delinquents. More to our point, however, is the fact that stealing tends to go hand-in-hand with "other property offenses," "malicious mischief," "vandalism," "trespass," and truancy. This quality of versatility and the fusion of versatility and malice are manifest in the following quotation:

We would get some milk bottles in front of the grocery store and break them in somebody's hallway. Then we would break windows or get some garbage cans and throw them down someone's front stairs. After doing all this dirty work and running through alleys and yards, we'd go over to a grocery store. There, some of the boys would hide in a hallway while I would get a basket of grapes. When the man came after me, why the boys would jump out of their places and each grab a basket of grapes.[5]

Dozens of young offenders, after relating to the writer this delinquent episode and that, have summarized: "I guess we was just ornery." A generalized, diversified, protean "orneriness," not this or that specialized delinquent pursuit seems best to describe the vocation of the delinquent gang.[6]

---

[5] Clifford R. Shaw and Henry D. McKay, *Social Factors in Juvenile Delinquency*, Vol. II of National Commission on Law Observance and Enforcement, *Report on the Causes of Crime* (Washington: U.S. Government Printing Office, 1931), p. 18.

[6] *Federal Probation*, XVIII (March, 1954), 3–16 contains an extremely valuable symposium on vandalism, which highlights all of the characteristics we have imputed to the delinquent subculture. In the belief that no generalization can convey the flavor and scope of this subculture as well as a simple but massive enumeration, we quote at length from Joseph E. Murphy's contribution, pp. 8–9.

Studies of the complaints made by citizens and public officials reveal that hardly any property is safe from this form of aggression. Schools are often the object of attack by vandals. Windows are broken; records, books, desks, typewriters, supplies, and other equipment are stolen or destroyed. Public property of all types appears to offer peculiar allurement to children bent on destruction. Parks, playgrounds, highway signs, and markers are frequently defaced or destroyed. Trees, shrubs, flowers, benches, and other equipment suffer in like manner. Autoists are constantly reporting the slashing or releasing of air from tires, broken windows, stolen accessories. Golf clubs complain that benches, markers, flags, even expensive and difficult-to-replace putting greens are defaced, broken or uprooted. Libraries report the theft and destruction of books and other equipment. Railroads complain of and demand protection from the destruction of freight car seals, theft of property, willful and deliberate throwing of stones at passenger car windows, tampering with rails and switches. Vacant houses are always the particular delight of children seeking outlets for destructive instincts; windows are broken, plumbing and hardware stolen, destroyed, or rendered unusable. Gasoline operators report pumps and other service equipment stolen, broken, or destroyed. Theatre managers, frequently in the "better" neighborhoods, complain of the slashing of seats, willful damaging of toilet facilities, even the burning of rugs, carpets, etc.

Recently the Newark *Evening News*, commenting editorially on the problem of vandalism in New York City housing projects, stated "housing authorities complain of the tearing out of steel banisters, incinerator openings, and mail boxes, damaging of elevators, defacing walls, smashing windows and light bulbs, stealing nozzles of fire hoses, destroying trees and benches on the project's grounds and occasionally plundering and setting fire to parked cars. Moreover, gangs have terrorized not only tenants but also the three hundred unarmed watchmen hired to protect the property."

This quotation places "stealing" in the context of a host of other manifestations of the protean "orneriness" of which we have spoken. The implication is strong that the fact that an object is "stolen" rather than destroyed or damaged is, from the standpoint of motivation, almost incidental. J. P. Shalloo, *ibid.*, pp. 6–7, states in a forceful way the problem which this creates for criminological theory: "Delinquency and crime are, and have been regarded as, purposeful behavior. But wanton and vicious destruction of property both public and private by teen-age hoodlums reveals no purpose, no rhyme, no reason. . . . These are not the actions of thoughtless youth. These are actions based upon a calculated contempt for the rights of others . . ."

It is widely believed that vandalism, on the scale we know it today, is a relatively recent phenomenon. Douglas H. MacNeil, *ibid.*, p. 16, observes that, although vandalism is a form of delinquency which has been neglected by social scientists, there is little reason to believe that it has increased spectacularly, if at all, in recent years. Apparently it is and it has been for many years part and parcel, indeed the very spirit, of the delinquent subculture.

In connection with the versatility of the delin-

Another characteristic of the subculture of the delinquent gang is *short-run hedonism*. There is little interest in long-run goals, in planning activities and budgeting time, or in activities involving knowledge and skills to be acquired only through practice, deliberation and study. The members of the gang typically congregate, with no specific activity in mind, at some street corner, candy store or other regular rendezvous. They "hang around," "rough-housing," "chewing the fat," and "waiting for something to turn up." They may respond impulsively to somebody's suggestion to play ball, go swimming, engage in some sort of mischief, or do something else that offers excitement. They do not take kindly to organized and supervised recreation, which subjects them to a regime of schedules and impersonal rules. They are impatient, impetuous and out for "fun," with little heed to the remoter gains and costs. It is to be noted that this short-run hedonism is not inherently delinquent and indeed it would be a serious error to think of the delinquent gang as dedicated solely to the cultivation of juvenile crime. Even in the most seriously delinquent gang only a small fraction of the "fun" is specifically and intrinsically delinquent. Furthermore, short-run hedonism is not characteristic of delinquent groups alone. On the contrary, it is common throughout the social class from which delinquents characteristically come. However, in the delinquent gang it reaches its finest flower. It is the fabric, as it were, of which delinquency is the most brilliant and spectacular thread.[7]

Another characteristic not peculiar to the delinquent gang but a conspicuous ingredient of its culture is an emphasis on *group autonomy*, or intolerance of restraint except from the informal pressures within the group itself. Relations with gang members tend to be intensely solidary and imperious. Relations with other groups tend to be indifferent, hostile or rebellious. Gang members are unusually resistant to the efforts of home, school and other agencies to regulate, not only their delinquent activities, but any activities carried on within the group, and to efforts to compete with the gang for the time and other resources of its members. It may be argued that the resistance of gang members to the authority of the home may not be a result of their membership in gangs but that membership in gangs, on the contrary, is a result of ineffective family supervision, the breakdown of parental authority and the hostility of the child toward the parents; in short, that the delinquent gang recruits members who have already achieved autonomy. Certainly a previous breakdown in family controls facilitates

---

quent subculture, it should be noted that truancy is also institutionalized in the delinquent gang. In Lester E. Hewitt and Richard L. Jenkins, *Fundamental Patterns of Maladjustment* (published by the State of Illinois, no date), p. 94, habitual truancy is found to have a tetrachoric coefficient of correlation of .10 with the "unsocialized aggressive" syndrome, −.08 with the "overinhibited behavior" syndrome and .75 with the "socialized delinquent" syndrome. These findings are of special interest because the latter syndrome corresponds closely to what we have called the delinquent subculture. For summaries of studies on the relationship between truancy and other forms of delinquency see Norman Fenton, *The Delinquent Boy and the Correctional School* (Claremont, California: Claremont Colleges Guidance Center 1935), pp. 66–69 and William Kvaraceus, *Juvenile Delinquency and the School* (Yonkers-on-Hudson: World Book Company, 1945), pp. 144–146.

[7] See the splendid report on "Working with a Street Gang" in Sylvan S. Furman (ed.), *Reaching the Unreached* (New York: New York City Youth Board, 1952), pp. 112–121. On this quality of short-run hedonism we quote, p. 13:

One boy once told me, "Now, for example, you take an average day. What happens? We come down to the restaurant and we sit in the restaurant, and sit and sit. All right, say, er . . . after a couple of hours in the restaurant, maybe we'll go to a poolroom, shoot a little pool, that's if somebody's got the money. O.K., a little pool, come back. By this time the restaurant is closed. We go in the candy store, sit around the candy store for a while, and that's it, that's all we do, man."

See also Barbara Bellow *et al., op. cit.*, pp. 4–15, and Ruth Topping, "Treatment of the Pseudo-Social Boy," *American Journal of Orthopsychiatry*, XIII (April, 1943), p. 353.

recruitment into delinquent gangs. But we are not speaking of the autonomy, the emancipation of *individuals*. It is not the individual delinquent but the gang that is autonomous. For many of our subcultural delinquents the claims of the home are very real and very compelling. The point is that the gang is a separate, distinct and often irresistible focus of attraction, loyalty and solidarity. The claims of the home versus the claims of the gang may present a real dilemma, and in such cases the breakdown of family controls is as much a casualty as a cause of gang membership.[8]

---

[8] The solidarity of the gang and the dependence of its members upon one another are especially well described in Barbara Bellow *et. al., op. cit.,* p. 16 and Sophia Robison *et al., op. cit.,* p. 158.

31. TECHNIQUES OF DELINQUENCY

GRESHAM M. SYKES
DAVID MATZA

IN ATTEMPTING TO UNCOVER THE ROOTS OF juvenile delinquency, the social scientist has long since ceased to search for devils in the mind or stigma of the body. It is now largely agreed that delinquent behavior, like most social behavior, is learned and that it is learned in the process of social interaction.

The classic statement of this position is found in Sutherland's theory of differential association, which asserts that criminal or delinquent behavior involves the learning of (a) techniques of committing crimes and (b) motives, drives, rationalizations, and attitudes favorable to the violation of law.[1] Unfortunately, the specific content of what is learned—as opposed to the process by which it is learned—has received relatively little attention in either theory or research. Perhaps the single strongest school of thought on the nature of this content has centered on the idea of a delinquent sub-culture. The basic characteristic of the delinquent sub-culture, it is argued, is a system of values that represents an inversion of the values held by respectable, law-abiding society. The world of the delinquent is the world of the law-abiding turned upside down and its norms constitute a countervailing force directed against the conforming social order. Cohen[2] sees the process of developing a delinquent sub-culture as a matter of building, maintaining, and reinforcing a code for behavior which exists by opposition, which stands in point by point contradiction to dominant values, particularly those of the middle class. Cohen's portrayal of delinquency is executed with a good deal of sophistication, and he carefully avoids overly simple explanations such as those based on the principle of "follow the leader" or easy generalizations about "emotional disturbances." Furthermore, he does not accept the delinquent sub-culture as something given, but instead systematically examines the function of delinquent values as a viable solution to the lower-class, male child's problems in the area of social status. Yet in spite of its virtues, this image of juvenile delinquency as a form of behavior based on competing or countervailing values and norms appears to suffer from a number of serious defects. It is the nature of these defects and a possible alternative or modified explanation for a large portion of juvenile delinquency with which this paper is concerned.

▶SOURCE: *"Techniques of Neutralization: A Theory of Delinquency," American Sociological Review (December, 1957), 22:664–670. Reprinted by permission.*

[1] E. H. Sutherland, *Principles of Criminology*, revised by D. R. Cressey, Chicago: Lippincott, 1955, pp. 77–80.

[2] Albert K. Cohen, *Delinquent Boys*, Glencoe, Ill.: The Free Press, 1955.

The difficulties in viewing delinquent behavior as springing from a set of deviant values and norms—as arising, that is to say, from a situation in which the delinquent defines his delinquency as "right"—are both empirical and theoretical. In the first place, if there existed in fact a delinquent sub-culture such that the delinquent viewed his illegal behavior as morally correct, we could reasonably suppose that he would exhibit no feelings of guilt or shame at detection or confinement. Instead, the major reaction would tend in the direction of indignation or a sense of martyrdom.[3] It is true that some delinquents do react in the latter fashion, although the sense of martyrdom often seems to be based on the fact that others "get away with it" and indignation appears to be directed against the chance events or lack of skill that led to apprehension. More important, however, is the fact that there is a good deal of evidence suggesting that many delinquents *do* experience a sense of guilt or shame, and its outward expression is not to be dismissed as a purely manipulative gesture to appease those in authority. Much of this evidence is, to be sure, of a clinical nature or in the form of impressionistic judgments of those who must deal first hand with the youthful offender. Assigning a weight to such evidence calls for caution, but it cannot be ignored if we are to avoid the gross stereotype of the juvenile delinquent as a hardened gangster in miniature.

In the second place, observers have noted that the juvenile delinquent frequently accords admiration and respect to law-abiding persons. The "really honest" person is often revered, and if the delinquent is sometimes overly keen to detect hypocrisy in those who conform, unquestioned probity is likely to win his approval. A fierce attachment to a humble, pious mother or a forgiving, upright priest (the former, according to many observers, is often encountered in both juvenile delinquents and adult criminals) might be dismissed as rank sentimentality, but at least it is clear that the delinquent does not necessarily regard those who abide by the legal rules as immoral. In a similar vein, it can be noted that the juvenile delinquent may exhibit great resentment if illegal behavior is imputed to "significant others" in his immediate social environment or to heroes in the world of sport and entertainment. In other words, if the delinquent does hold to a set of values and norms that stand in complete opposition to those of respectable society, his norm-holding is of a peculiar sort. While supposedly thoroughly committed to the deviant system of the delinquent sub-culture, he would appear to recognize the moral validity of the dominant normative system in many instances.[4]

In the third place, there is much evidence that juvenile delinquents often draw a sharp line between those who can be victimized and those who cannot. Certain social groups are not to be viewed as "fair game" in the performance of supposedly approved delinquent acts while others warrant a variety of attacks. In general, the potentiality for victimization would seem to be a function of the social distance between the juvenile delinquent and others and thus we find implicit maxims in the world of the delinquent such as

---

[3] This form of reaction among the adherents of a deviant subculture who fully believe in the "rightfulness" of their behavior and who are captured and punished by the agencies of the dominant social order can be illustrated, perhaps, by groups such as Jehovah's Witnesses, early Christian sects, nationalist movements in colonial areas, and conscientious objectors during World Wars I and II.

[4] As Weber has pointed out, a thief may recognize the legitimacy of legal rules without accepting their moral validity. Cf. Max Weber, *The Theory of Social and Economic Organization* (translated by A. M. Henderson and Talcott Parsons), New York: Oxford University Press, 1947, p. 125. We are arguing here, however, that the juvenile delinquent frequently recognizes *both* the legitimacy of the dominant social order and its moral "rightness."

"don't steal from friends" or "don't commit vandalism against a church of your own faith." [5] This is all rather obvious, but the implications have not received sufficient attention. The fact that supposedly valued behavior tends to be directed against disvalued social groups hints that the "wrongfulness" of such delinquent behavior is more widely recognized by delinquents than the literature has indicated. When the pool of victims is limited by consideration of kinship, friendship, ethnic group, social class, age, sex, etc., we have reason to suspect that the virtue of delinquency is far from unquestioned.

In the fourth place, it is doubtful if many juvenile delinquents are totally immune from the demands for conformity made by the dominant social order. There is a strong likelihood that the family of the delinquent will agree with respectable society that delinquency is wrong, even though the family may be engaged in a variety of illegal activities. That is, the parental posture conducive to delinquency is not apt to be a positive prodding. Whatever may be the influence of parental example, what might be called the "Fagin" pattern of socialization into delinquency is probably rare. Furthermore, as Redl has indicated, the idea that certain neighborhoods are completely delinquent, offering the child a model for delinquent behavior without reservations, is simply not supported by the data.[6]

The fact that a child is punished by parents, school officials, and agencies of the legal system for his delinquency may, as a number of observers have cynically noted, suggest to the child that he should be more careful not to get caught. There is an equal or greater probability, however, that the child will internalize the demands for conformity. This is not to say that demands for conformity cannot be counteracted. In fact, as we shall see shortly, an understanding of how internal and external demands for conformity are neutralized may be crucial for understanding delinquent behavior. But it is to say that a complete denial of the validity of demands for conformity and the substitution of a new normative system is improbable, in light of the child's or adolescent's dependency on adults and enrichment by adults inherent in his status in the social structure. No matter how deeply enmeshed in patterns of delinquency he may be and no matter how much this involvement may outweigh his association with the law-abiding, he cannot escape the condemnation of his deviance. Somehow the demands for conformity must be met and answered; they cannot be ignored as part of an alien system of values and norms.

In short, the theoretical viewpoint that sees juvenile delinquency as a form of behavior based on the values and norms of a deviant sub-culture in precisely the same way as law-abiding behavior is based on the values and norms of the larger society is open to serious doubt. The fact that the world of the delinquent is embedded in the larger world of those who conform cannot be overlooked nor can the delinquent be equated with an adult thoroughly socialized into an alternative way of life. Instead, the juvenile delinquent would appear to be at least partially committed to the dominant social order in that he frequently exhibits guilt or shame when he violates its proscriptions, accords approval to certain conforming figures, and distinguishes between appropriate and inappropriate targets for his deviance. It is to an explanation for the apparently paradoxical fact of his delinquency that we now turn.

As Morris Cohen once said, one of the most fascinating problems about human

---

[5] Thrasher's account of the "Itschkies"—a juvenile gang composed of Jewish boys—and the immunity from "rolling" enjoyed by Jewish drunkards is a good illustration. Cf. F. Thrasher, *The Gang*, Chicago: The University of Chicago Press, 1947, p. 315.

[6] Cf. Solomon Kobrin, "The Conflict of Values in Delinquency Areas," *American Sociological Review*, 16 (October, 1951), pp. 653–661.

behavior is why men violate the laws which they believe. This is the problem that confronts us when we attempt to explain why delinquency occurs despite a greater or lesser commitment to the usages of conformity. A basic clue is offered by the fact that social rules or norms calling for valued behavior seldom if ever take the form of categorical imperatives. Rather, values or norms appear as *qualified* guides for action, limited in their applicability in terms of time, place, persons, and social circumstances. The moral injunction against killing, for example, does not apply to the enemy during combat in time of war, although a captured enemy comes once again under the prohibition. Similarly, the taking and distributing of scarce goods in a time of acute social need is felt by many to be right, although under other circumstances private property is held inviolable. The normative system of a society, then, is marked by what Williams has termed *flexibility;* it does not consist of a body of rules held to be binding under all conditions.[7]

This flexibility is, in fact, an integral part of the criminal law in that measures for "defenses to crimes" are provided in pleas such as non-age, necessity, insanity, drunkenness, compulsion, self-defense, and so on. The individual can avoid moral culpability for his criminal action—and thus avoid the negative sanctions of society—if he can prove that criminal intent was lacking. It is our argument that much delinquency is based on what is essentially an unrecognized extension of defenses to crimes, in the form of justifications for deviance that are seen as valid by the delinquent but not by the legal system or society at large.

These justifications are commonly described as rationalizations. They are viewed as following deviant behavior and as protecting the individual from self-blame and the blame of others after the act. But there is also reason to believe that they precede deviant behavior and make deviant behavior possible. It is this possibility that Sutherland mentioned only in passing and that other writers have failed to exploit from the viewpoint of sociological theory. Disapproval flowing from internalized norms and conforming others in the social environment is neutralized, turned back, or deflected in advance. Social controls that serve to check or inhibit deviant motivational patterns are rendered inoperative, and the individual is freed to engage in delinquency without serious damage to his self image. In this sense, the delinquent both has his cake and eats it too, for he remains committed to the dominant normative system and yet so qualifies its imperatives that violations are "acceptable" if not "right." Thus the delinquent represents not a radical opposition to law-abiding society but something more like an apologetic failure, often more sinned against than sinning in his own eyes. We call these justifications of deviant behavior *techniques of neutralization;* and we believe these techniques make up a crucial component of Sutherland's "definitions favorable to the violation of law." It is by learning these techniques that the juvenile becomes delinquent, rather than by learning moral imperatives, values or attitudes standing in direct contradiction to those of the dominant society. In analyzing these techniques, we have found it convenient to divide them into five major types.

The Denial of Responsibility. In so far as the delinquent can define himself as lacking responsibility for his deviant actions, the disapproval of self or others is sharply reduced in effectiveness as a restraining influence. As Justice Holmes has said, even a dog distinguishes between being stumbled over and being kicked, and modern society is no less careful to draw a line between injuries that are unintentional, i.e., where responsibility is lacking, and those that are intentional. As a technique of neutralization, however, the denial of responsibility extends much further than

---

[7] Cf. Robin Williams, Jr., *American Society*, New York: Knopf, 1951, p. 28.

the claim that deviant acts are an "accident" or some similar negation of personal accountability. It may also be asserted that delinquent acts are due to forces outside of the individual and beyond his control such as unloving parents, bad companions, or a slum neighborhood. In effect, the delinquent approaches a "billiard ball" conception of himself in which he sees himself as helplessly propelled into new situations. From a psychodynamic viewpoint, this orientation toward one's own actions may represent a profound alienation from self, but it is important to stress the fact that interpretations of responsibility are cultural constructs and not merely idiosyncratic beliefs. The similarity between this mode of justifying illegal behavior assumed by the delinquent and the implications of a "sociological" frame of reference or a "humane" jurisprudence is readily apparent.[8] It is not the validity of this orientation that concerns us here, but its function of deflecting blame attached to violations of social norms and its relative independence of a particular personality structure.[9] By learning to view himself as more acted upon than acting, the delinquent prepares the way for deviance from the dominant normative system without the necessity of a formal assault on the norms themselves.

The Denial of Injury. A second major technique of neutralization centers on the injury or harm involved in the delinquent act. The criminal law has long made a distinction between crimes which are *mala in se* and *mala prohibita*—that is between acts that are wrong in themselves and acts that are illegal but not immoral—and the delinquent can make the same kind of distinction in evaluating the wrongfulness of his behavior. For the delinquent, however, wrongfulness may turn on the question of whether or not anyone has clearly been hurt by his deviance, and this matter is open to a variety of interpretations. Vandalism, for example, may be defined by the delinquent simply as "mischief"—after all, it may be claimed, the persons whose property has been destroyed can well afford it. Similarly, auto theft may be viewed as "borrowing," and gang fighting may be seen as a private quarrel, and agreed upon duel between two willing parties, and thus of no concern to the community at large. We are not suggesting that this technique of neutralization, labelled the denial of injury, involves an explicit dialectic. Rather, we are arguing that the delinquent frequently, and in a hazy fashion, feels that his behavior does not really cause any great harm despite the fact that it runs counter to law. Just as the link between the individual and his acts may be broken by the denial of responsibility, so may the link between acts and their consequences be broken by the denial of injury. Since society sometimes agrees with the delinquent, e.g., in matters such as truancy, "pranks," and so on, it merely reaffirms the idea that the delinquent's neutralization of social controls by means of qualifying the norms is an extension of common practice rather than a gesture of complete opposition.

The Denial of the Victim. Even if the delinquent accepts the responsibility for his deviant actions and is willing to admit that his deviant actions involve an injury or hurt, the moral indignation of self and others may be neutralized by an insistence that the injury is not wrong in light of the circumstances. The injury, it may be claimed, is not really an injury; rather, it is a form of rightful retaliation or punishment. By a subtle alchemy the delinquent moves himself into the position of an avenger and the victim is transformed into a wrong-doer. Assaults on homosexuals or suspected homosexuals, attacks on members

---

[8] A number of observers have wryly noted that many delinquents seem to show a surprising awareness of sociological and psychological explanations for their behavior and are quick to point out the causal role of their poor environment.

[9] It is possible, of course, that certain personality structures can accept some techniques of neutralization more readily than others, but this question remains largely unexplored.

of minority groups who are said to have gotten "out of place," vandalism as revenge on an unfair teacher or school official, thefts from a "crooked" store owner—all may be hurts inflicted on a transgressor, in the eyes of the delinquent. As Orwell has pointed out, the type of criminal admired by the general public has probably changed over the course of years and Raffles no longer serves as a hero;[10] but Robin Hood, and his latter day derivatives such as the tough detective seeking justice outside the law, still capture the popular imagination, and the delinquent may view his acts as part of a similar role.

To deny the existence of the victim, then, by transforming him into a person deserving injury is an extreme form of a phenomenon we have mentioned before, namely, the delinquent's recognition of appropriate and inappropriate targets for his delinquent acts. In addition, however, the existence of the victim may be denied for the delinquent, in a somewhat different sense, by the circumstances of the delinquent act itself. Insofar as the victim is physically absent, unknown or a vague abstraction (as is often the case in delinquent acts committed against property), the awareness of the victim's existence is weakened. Internalized norms and anticipations of the reactions of others must somehow be activated, if they are to serve as guides for behavior; and it is possible that a diminished awareness of the victim plays an important part in determining whether or not this process is set in motion.

The Condemnation of the Condemners. A fourth technique of neutralization would appear to involve a condemnation of the condemners or, as McCorkle and Korn have phrased it, a rejection of the rejectors.[11] The delinquent shifts the focus of attention from his own deviant acts to the motives of his violations. His condemners, he may claim, are hypocrites, deviants in disguise, or impelled by personal spite. This orientation toward the conforming world may be of particular importance when it hardens into a bitter cynicism directed against those assigned the task of enforcing or expressing the norms of the dominant society. Police, it may be said, are corrupt, stupid, and brutal. Teachers always show favoritism and parents always "take it out" on their children. By a slight extension, the rewards of conformity—such as material success—become a matter of pull or luck, thus decreasing still further the stature of those who stand on the side of the law-abiding. The validity of this jaundiced viewpoint is not so important as its function in turning back or deflecting the negative sanctions attached to violations of the norms. The delinquent, in effect, has changed the subject of the conversation in the dialogue between his own deviant impulses and the reactions of others; and by attacking others, the wrongfulness of his own behavior is more easily repressed or lost to view.

The Appeal to Higher Loyalties. Fifth, and last, internal and external social controls may be neutralized by sacrificing the demands of the larger society for the demands of the smaller social groups to which the delinquent belongs such as the sibling pair, the gang, or the friendship clique. It is important to note that the delinquent does not necessarily repudiate the imperatives of the dominant normative system, despite his failure to follow them. Rather, the delinquent may see himself as caught up in a dilemma that must be resolved, unfortunately, at the cost of violating the law. One aspect of this situation has been studied by Stouffer and Toby in their research on the conflict between particularistic and universalistic demands, between the claims of friendship and general social obligations, and their results suggest that "it is possible to classify people according to a predisposition to select one or the

---

[10] George Orwell, *Dickens, Dali, and Others*, New York: Reynal, 1946.

[11] Lloyd W. McCorkle and Richard Korn, "Resocialization Within Walls," *The Annals of the American Academy of Political and Social Science*, 293 (May, 1954), pp. 88–98.

other horn of a dilemma in role conflict."[12] For our purposes, however, the most important point is that deviation from certain norms may occur not because the norms are rejected but because other norms, held to be more pressing or involving a higher loyalty, are accorded precedence. Indeed, it is the fact that both sets of norms are believed in that gives meaning to our concepts of dilemma and role conflict.

The conflict between the claims of friendship and the claims of law, or a similar dilemma, has of course long been recognized by the social scientist (and the novelist) as a common human problem. If the juvenile delinquent frequently resolves his dilemma by insisting that he must "always help a buddy" or "never squeal on a friend," even when it throws him into serious difficulties with the dominant social order, his choice remains familiar to the supposedly law-abiding. The delinquent is unusual, perhaps, in the extent to which he is able to see the fact that he acts in behalf of the smaller social groups to which he belongs as a justification for violations of society's norms, but it is a matter of degree rather than of kind.

"I didn't mean it." "I didn't really hurt anybody." "They had it coming to them." "Everybody's picking on me." "I didn't do if for myself." These slogans or their variants, we hypothesize, prepare the juvenile for delinquent acts. These "definitions of the situation" represent tangential or glancing blows at the dominant normative system rather than the creation of an opposing ideology; and they are extensions of patterns of thought prevalent in society rather than something created *de novo*.

Techniques of neutralization may not be powerful enough to fully shield the individual from the force of his own internalized values and the reactions of conforming others, for as we have pointed out, juvenile delinquents often appear to suffer from feelings of guilt and shame when called into account for their deviant behavior. And some delinquents may be so isolated from the world of conformity that techniques of neutralization need not be called into play. Nonetheless, we would argue that techniques of neutralization are critical in lessening the effectiveness of social controls and that they lie behind a large share of delinquent behavior. Empirical research in this area is scattered and fragmentary at the present time, but the work of Redl,[13] Cressey,[14] and others has supplied a body of significant data that has done much to clarify the theoretical issues and enlarge the fund of supporting evidence. Two lines of investigation seem to be critical at this stage. First, there is need for more knowledge concerning the differential distribution of techniques of neutralization, as operative patterns of thought, by age, sex, social class, ethnic group, etc. On *a priori* grounds it might be assumed that these justifications for deviance will be more readily seized by segments of society for whom a discrepancy between common social ideals and social practice is most apparent. It is also possible however, that the habit of "bending" the dominant normative system—if not "breaking" it—cuts across our cruder social categories and is to be traced primarily to patterns of social interaction within the familial circle. Second, there is a need for a greater understanding of the internal structure of techniques of neutralization, as a system of beliefs and attitudes, and its relationship to various types of delinquent behavior. Certain techniques of neutralization would appear to be better adapted to particular deviant acts than to others, as we have suggested, for example, in the case of offenses against property and the denial of the victim.

---

[12] See Samuel A. Stouffer and Jackson Toby, "Role Conflict and Personality," in *Toward a General Theory of Action*, edited by Talcott Parsons and Edward A. Shils, Cambridge: Harvard University Press, 1951, p. 494.

[13] See Fritz Redl and David Wineman, *Children Who Hate*, Glencoe: The Free Press, 1956.

[14] See D. R. Cressey, *Other People's Money*, Glencoe: The Free Press, 1953.

But the issue remains far from clear and stands in need of more information.

In any case, techniques of neutralization appear to offer a promising line of research in enlarging and systematizing the theoretical grasp of juvenile delinquency. As more information is uncovered concerning techniques of neutralization, their origins, and their consequences, both juvenile delinquency in particular, and deviation from normative systems in general may be illuminated.

32. DIFFERENTIAL OPPORTUNITY STRUCTURE

RICHARD A. CLOWARD
LLOYD E. OHLIN

THE AVAILABILITY OF ILLEGITIMATE MEANS

SOCIAL NORMS ARE TWO-SIDED. A PRESCRIPtion implies the existence of a prohibition, and *vice versa*. To advocate honesty is to demarcate and condemn a set of actions which are dishonest. In other words, norms that define legitimate practices also implicitly define illegitimate practices. One purpose of norms, in fact, is to delineate the boundary between legitimate and illegitimate practices. In setting the boundary, in segregating and classifying various types of behavior, they make us aware not only of behavior that is regarded as right and proper but also of behavior that is said to be wrong and improper. Thus the criminal who engages in theft or fraud does not invent a new way of life; the possibility of employing alternative means is acknowledged, tacitly at least, by the norms of the culture.

This tendency for proscribed alternatives to be implicit in every prescription, and *vice versa*, although widely recognized, is nevertheless a reef upon which many a theory of delinquency has foundered. Much of the criminological literature assumes, for example, that one may explain a criminal act simply by accounting for

▶SOURCE: *Delinquency and Opportunity*, Glencoe: The Free Press, 1961, pp. 145–152; 161–186. Reprinted by permission.

the individual's readiness to employ illegal alternatives of which his culture, through its norms, has already made him generally aware. Such explanations are quite unsatisfactory, however, for they ignore a host of questions regarding the *relative availability* of illegal alternatives to various potential criminals. The aspiration to be a physician is hardly enough to explain the fact of becoming a physician; there is much that transpires between the aspiration and the achievement. This is no less true of the person who wants to be a successful criminal. Having decided that he "can't make it legitimately," he cannot simply choose among an array of illegitimate means, all equally available to him. As we have noted earlier, it is assumed in the theory of anomie that access to conventional means is differentially distributed, that some individuals, because of their social class, enjoy certain advantages that are denied to those elsewhere in the class structure. For example, there are variations in the degree to which members of various classes are fully exposed to and thus acquire the values, knowledge, and skills that facilitate upward mobility. It should not be startling, therefore, to suggest that there are socially structured variations in the availability of illegitimate means as well. In connection with delinquent subcultures, we shall be concerned principally with differentials in access to illegitimate means within the lower class.

Many sociologists have alluded to differentials in access to illegitimate means without explicitly incorporating this variable into a theory of deviant behavior. This is particularly true of scholars in the "Chicago tradition" of criminology. Two closely related theoretical perspectives emerged from this school. The theory of "cultural transmission," advanced by Clifford R. Shaw and Henry D. McKay, focuses on the development in some urban neighborhoods of a criminal tradition that persists from one generation to another despite constant changes in population.[1] In the theory of "differential association," Edwin H. Sutherland described the processes by which criminal values are taken over by the individual.[2] He asserted that criminal behavior is learned, and that it is learned in interaction with others who have already incorporated criminal values. Thus the first theory stresses the value systems of different areas; the second, the systems of social relationships that facilitate or impede the acquisition of these values.

Scholars in the Chicago tradition, who emphasized the processes involved in learning to be criminal, were actually pointing to differentials in the availability of illegal means—although they did not explicitly recognize this variable in their analysis. This can perhaps best be seen by examining Sutherland's classic work, *The Professional Thief*. "An inclination to steal," according to Sutherland, "is not a sufficient explanation to the genesis of the professional thief."[3] The "self-made" thief, lacking knowledge of the ways of securing immunity from prosecution and similar techniques of defense, "would quickly land in prison; . . . a person can be a professional thief only if he is recognized and received as such by other professional thieves." But recognition is not freely accorded: "Selection and tutelage are the two necessary elements in the process of acquiring recognition as a professional thief. . . . A person cannot acquire recognition as a professional thief until he has had tutelage in professional theft, *and tutelage is given only a few persons selected from the total population.*" For one thing, "the person must be appreciated by the professional thieves. He must be appraised as having an adequate equipment of wits, front, talking-ability, honesty, reliability, nerve and determination." Furthermore, the aspirant is judged by high standards of performance, for only "a very small percentage of those who start on this process ever reach the stage of professional thief. . . ." Thus motivation and pressures toward deviance do not fully account for deviant behavior any more than motivation and pressures toward conformity account for conforming behavior. The individual must have access to a learning environment and, once having been trained, must be allowed to perform his role. Roles, whether conforming or deviant in content, are not necessarily freely available; access to them depends upon a variety of factors, such as one's socioeconomic position, age, sex, ethnic affiliation, personality characteristics, and the like. The potential thief, like the potential physician, finds that access to his goal is governed by many criteria other than merit and motivation.

What we are asserting is that access to illegitimate roles is not freely available to all, as is commonly assumed. Only those neighborhoods in which crime flourishes as a stable, indigenous institution are fertile

---

[1] See esp. C.R. Shaw, *The Jack-Roller* (Chicago: University of Chicago Press, 1930); Shaw, *The Natural History of a Delinquent Career* (Chicago: University of Chicago Press, 1931); Shaw et al., *Delinquency Areas* (Chicago: University of Chicago Press, 1940); and Shaw and H. D. McKay, *Juvenile Delinquency and Urban Areas* (Chicago: University of Chicago Press, 1942).

[2] E. H. Sutherland, ed., *The Professional Thief* (Chicago: University of Chicago Press, 1937); and Sutherland, *Principles of Criminology*, 4th Ed. (Philadelphia: Lippincott, 1947).

[3] All quotations on this page are from *The Professional Thief*, pp. 211–13. Emphasis added.

criminal learning environments for the young. Because these environments afford integration of different age-levels of offender, selected young people are exposed to "differential association" through which tutelage is provided and criminal values and skills are acquired. To be prepared for the role may not, however, ensure that the individual will ever discharge it. One important limitation is that more youngsters are recruited into these patterns of differential associations than the adult criminal structure can possibly absorb. Since there is a surplus of contenders for these elite positions, criteria and mechanisms of selection must be evolved. Hence a certain proportion of those who aspire may not be permitted to engage in the behavior for which they have prepared themselves.

Thus we conclude that access to illegitimate roles, no less than access to legitimate roles, is limited by both social and psychological factors. We shall here be concerned primarily with socially structured differentials in illegitimate opportunities. Such differentials, we contend, have much to do with the type of delinquent subculture that develops.

LEARNING AND PERFORMANCE STRUCTURES

Our use of the term "opportunities," legitimate or illegitimate, implies access to both learning and performance structures. That is, the individual must have access to appropriate environments for the acquisition of the values and skills associated with the performance of a particular role, and he must be supported in the performance of the role once he has learned it.

Tannenbaum, several decades ago, vividly expressed the point that criminal role performance, no less than conventional role performance, presupposes a patterned set of relationships through which the requisite values and skills are transmitted by established practitioners to aspiring youth:

It takes a long time to make a good criminal, many years of specialized training and much preparation. But training is something that is given to people. People learn in a community where the materials and the knowledge are to be had. A craft needs an atmosphere saturated with purpose and promise. The community provides the attitudes, the point of view, the philosophy of life, the example, the motive, the contacts, the friendships, the incentives. No child brings those into the world. He finds them here and available for use and elaboration. The community gives the criminal his materials and habits, just as it gives the doctor, the lawyer, the teacher, and the candlestick-maker theirs.[4]

Sutherland systematized this general point of view, asserting that opportunity consists, at least in part, of learning structures. Thus "criminal behavior is learned" and, furthermore, it is learned "in interaction with other persons in a process of communication." However, he conceded that the differential-association theory does not constitute a full explanation of criminal behavior. In a paper circulated in 1944, he noted that "criminal behavior is partially a function of opportunities to commit [*i.e.*, to perform] specific classes of crime, such as embezzlement, bank burglary, or illicit heterosexual intercourse." Therefore, "while opportunity may be partially a function of association with criminal patterns and of the specialized techniques thus acquired, it is not determined entirely in that manner, and consequently differential association is not the sufficient cause of criminal behavior."[5]

To Sutherland, then, illegitimate opportunity included conditions favorable to the performance of a criminal role as well as conditions favorable to the learning of such a role (differential associations). These conditions, we suggest, depend upon

---

[4] Frank Tannenbaum, "The Professional Criminal," *The Century*, Vol. 110 (May-Oct. 1925), p. 577.

[5] See A. K. Cohen, Alfred Lindesmith, and Karl Schuessler, eds., *The Sutherland Papers* (Bloomington, Ind.: Indiana University Press, 1956), pp. 31–35.

certain features of the social structure of the community in which delinquency arises.

DIFFERENTIAL OPPORTUNITY: A HYPOTHESIS

We believe that each individual occupies a position in both legitimate and illegitimate opportunity structures. This is a new way of defining the situation. The theory of anomie views the individual primarily in terms of the legitimate opportunity structure. It poses questions regarding differentials in access to legitimates routes to success-goals; at the same time it assumes either that illegitimate avenues to success-goals are freely available or that differentials in their availability are of little significance. This tendency may be seen in the following statement by Merton:

> Several researchers have shown that specialized areas of vice and crime constitute a "normal" response to a situation where the cultural emphasis upon pecuniary success has been absorbed, but where there is little access to conventional and legitimate means for becoming successful. The occupational opportunities of people in these areas are largely confined to manual labor and the lesser white-collar jobs. Given the American stigmatization of manual labor *which has been found to hold rather uniformly for all social classes,* and the absence of realistic opportunities for advancement beyond this level, the result is a marked tendency toward deviant behavior. The status of unskilled labor and the consequent low income cannot readily compete *in terms of established standards of worth* with the promises of power and high income from organized vice, rackets and crime. . . . [Such a situation] leads toward the gradual attenuation of legitimate, but by and large ineffectual, strivings and the increasing use of illegitimate, but more or less effective, expedients.[6]

The cultural-transmission and differential-association tradition, on the other hand, assumes that access to illegitimate means is variable, but it does not recognize the significance of comparable differentials in access to legitimate means. Sutherland's "ninth proposition" in the theory of differential association states:

> Though criminal behavior is an expression of general needs and values, it is not explained by those general needs and values since noncriminal behavior is an expression of the same needs and values. Thieves generally steal in order to secure money, but likewise honest laborers work in order to secure money. The attempts by many scholars to explain criminal behavior by general drives and values, such as the happiness principle, striving for social status, the money motive, or frustration, have been and must continue to be futile since they explain lawful behavior as completely as they explain criminal behavior.[7]

In this statement, Sutherland appears to assume that people have equal and free access to legitimate means regardless of their social position. At the very least, he does not treat access to legitimate means as variable. It is, of course, perfectly true that "striving for social status," "the money motive," and other socially approved drives do not fully account for either deviant or conforming behavior. But if goal-oriented behavior occurs under conditions in which there are socially structured obstacles to the satisfaction of these drives by legitimate means, the resulting pressures, we contend, might lead to deviance.

The concept of differential opportunity structures permit us to unite the theory of anomie, which recognizes the concept of differentials in access to legitimate means, and the "Chicago tradition," in which the concept of differentials in access to illegitimate means is implicit. We can now look at the individual, not simply in relation to one or the other system of means, but in relation to both legitimate and illegiti-

---

[6] R. K. Merton, *Social Theory and Social Structure*, Rev. and Enl. Ed. (Glencoe, Ill.: Free Press, 1957), pp. 145–46.

[7] *Principles of Criminology, op. cit.*, pp. 7–8.

mate systems. This approach permits us to ask, for example, how the relative availability of illegitimate opportunities affects the resolution of adjustment problems leading to deviant behavior. We believe that the way in which these problems are resolved may depend upon the kind of support for one or another type of illegitimate activity that is given at different points in the social structure. If, in a given social location, illegal or criminal means are not readily available, then we should not expect a criminal subculture to develop among adolescents. By the same logic, we should expect the manipulation of violence to become a primary avenue to higher status only in areas where the means of violence are not denied to the young. To give a third example, drug addiction and participation in subcultures organized around the consumption of drugs presuppose that persons can secure access to drugs and knowledge about how to use them. In some parts of the social structure, this would be very difficult; in others, very easy. In short, there are marked differences from one part of the social structure to another in the types of illegitimate adaptation that are available to persons in search of solutions to problems of adjustment arising from the restricted availability of legitimate means.[8] In this sense, then, we can think of individuals as being located in two opportunity structures—one legitimate, the other illegitimate. Given limited access to success-goals by legitimate means, the nature of the delinquent response that may result will vary according to the availability of various illegitimate means....[9]

We come now to the question of the specific social conditions that make for the emergence of distinctive delinquent subcultures. Throughout this analysis, we shall make extensive use of the concepts of social organization developed in the preceding chapter: namely, integration of different age-levels of offenders, and integration of carriers of conventional and deviant values. Delinquent responses vary from one neighborhood to another, we believe, according to the articulation of these structures in the neighborhood. Our object here is to show more precisely how various forms of neighborhood integration affect the development of subcultural content.

THE CRIMINAL SUBCULTURE

The criminal subculture, like the conflict and retreatist adaptations, requires a specialized environment if it is to flourish. Among the environmental supports of a criminal style of life are integration of offenders at various age-levels and close integration of the carriers of conventional and illegitimate values.

Integration of Age-Levels. Nowhere in the criminological literature is the concept of integration between different age-levels of offender made more explicit than in discussions of criminal learning. Most criminologists agree that criminal behavior presupposes patterned sets of relationships through which the requisite values and

---

[8] For an example of restrictions on access to illegitimate roles, note the impact of racial definitions in the following case: "I was greeted by two prisoners who were to be my cell buddies. Ernest was a first offender, charged with being a 'holdup' man. Bill, the other buddy, was an old offender, going through the machinery of becoming a habitual criminal, in and out of jail.... The first thing they asked me was, 'What are you in for?' I said, 'Jack-rolling.' The hardened one (Bill) looked at me with a superior air and said, 'A hoodlum, eh? An ordinary sneak thief. Not willing to leave jack-rolling to the niggers, eh? That's all they're good for. Kid, jack-rolling's not a white man's job.' I could see that he was disgusted with me, and I was too scared to say anything." (Shaw, *The Jack-Roller, op. cit.*, p. 101).

[9] For a discussion of the way in which the availability of illegitimate means influences the adaptations of inmates to prison life, see R. A. Cloward, "Social Control in the Prison," *Theoretical Studies in Social Organization of the Prison*, Bulletin No. 15 (New York: Social Science Research Council, March 1960), pp. 20–48.

skills are communicated or transmitted from one age-level to another. What, then, are some of the specific components of systems organized for the socialization of potential criminals?

Criminal Role-Models. The lower class is not without its own distinctive and indigenous illegitimate success-models. Many accounts in the literature suggest that lower-class adults who have achieved success by illegitimate means not only are highly visible to young people in slum areas but often are willing to establish relationships with these youth.

> Every boy has some ideal he looks up to and admires. His ideal may be Babe Ruth, Jack Dempsey, or Al Capone. When I was twelve, we moved into a neighborhood with a lot of gangsters. They were all swell dressers and had big cars and carried "gats." Us kids saw these swell guys and mingled with them in the cigar store on the corner. Jack Gurney was the one in the mob that I had a fancy to. He used to take my sis out and that way I saw him often. He was in the stick-up rackets before he was in the beer rackets, and he was a swell dresser and had lots of dough. . . . I liked to be near and felt stuck up over the other guys because he came to my home to see my sis.[10]

Just as the middle-class youth, as a consequence of intimate relationships with, say, a banker or a businessman, may aspire to *become* a banker or a businessman, so the lower-class youth may be associated with and aspire to become a "policy king": " 'I want to be a big shot. . . . Have all the guys look up to me. Have a couple of Lincolns, lots of broads, and all the coppers licking my shoes.' "[11] The crucial point here is that success-goals are not equally available to persons in different positions in the social structure. To the extent that social-class lines act as barriers to interaction between persons in different social strata, conventional success-models may not be salient for lower-class youth. The successful criminal, on the other hand, may be an intimate, personal figure in the fabric of the lower-class area. Hence one of the forces leading to rational, disciplined, crime-oriented delinquency may be the availability of criminal success-models.

Age-Grading of Criminal Learning and Performance. The process by which the young acquire the values and skills prerequisite for a stable criminal career has been described in many studies. The central mechanism in the learning process is integration of different age-levels of offender. In an extensive study of a criminal gang on the Lower East Side of New York City, Bloch and Niederhoffer found that

> . . . the Pirates [a group of young adults] was actually the central organizing committee, the party headquarters for the youthful delinquents in the area. They held regular conferences with the delegates from outlying districts to outline strategy. . . . The younger Corner Boys [a gang of adolescents in the same vicinity] who . . . were trying to join with the older Pirates . . . were on a probationary status. If they showed signs of promise, a couple of them were allowed to accompany the Pirates on tours of exploration to look over the terrain around the next job."[12]

At the pinnacle of this age-graded system stood an adult, Paulie.

> Paulie had real prestige in the gang. His was the final say in all important decisions. Older than the other members [of the Pirates] by seven or eight years, he maintained a certain air of mystery. . . . From talks with more garrulous members, it was learned that Paulie was the mastermind behind some of the gang's most impressive coups.[13]

The basis of Paulie's prestige in the gang is apparent in the following account of

---

[10] C. R. Shaw, "Juvenile Delinquency—A Group Tradition," *Bulletin of the State University of Iowa*, No. 23, N. S. No. 700, 1933, p. 8.

[11] *Ibid.*, p. 9.

[12] H. H. Bloch and Arthur Niederhoffer, *The Gang: A Study in Adolescent Behavior* (New York: Philosophical Library, 1958), pp. 198–99.

[13] *Ibid.*, p. 201.

his relationship with the full-fledged adult criminal world:

From his contacts, information was obtained as to the most inviting locations to burglarize. It was he who developed the strategy and outlined the major stages of each campaign of burglary or robbery. . . . Another vital duty which he performed was to get rid of the considerable loot, which might consist of jewelry, clothing, tools, or currency in large denominations. His contact with professional gangsters, fences, bookies, made him an ideal choice for this function.[14]

Learning alone, as we have said, does not ensure that the individual can or will perform the role for which he has been prepared. The social structure must also support the actual performance of the role. To say that the individual must have the opportunity to discharge a stable criminal role as well as to prepare for it does not mean that role-preparation necessarily takes place in one stage and role-performance in a succeeding stage. The apprentice may be afforded opportunities to play out a particular role at various points in the learning process.

When we were shoplifting we always made a game of it. For example, we might gamble on who could steal the most caps in a day, or who could steal in the presence of a detective and then get away. This was the best part of the game. I would go into a store to steal a cap, by trying one on when the clerk was not watching, walk out of the store, leaving the old cap. With the new cap on my head I would go into another store, do the same thing as in the other store, getting a new hat and leaving the one I had taken from the other place. I might do this all day. . . . It was the fun I wanted, not the hat. I kept this up for months and *then began to sell the things to a man on the West Side. It was at this time that I began to steal for gain.*[15]

This quotation illustrates how delinquent role-preparation and role-performance may be integrated even at the "play-group"

stage of illegitimate learning. The child has an opportunity to actually perform illegitimate roles because such activity finds support in his immediate neighborhood milieu. The rewards—monetary and other—of successful learning and performance are immediate and gratifying at each age level.

Integration of Values. Unless the carriers of criminal and conventional values are closely bound to one another, stable criminal roles cannot develop. The criminal, like the occupant of a controversial role, must establish relationships with other categories of persons, all of whom contribute in one way or another to the successful performance of criminal activity. As Tannenbaum says, "The development of the criminal career requires and finds in the immediate environment other supporting elements in addition to the active 'criminal gangs'; to develop the career requires the support of middlemen. These may be junk men, fences, lawyers, bondsmen, 'backers,' as they are called."[16] The intricate systems of relationship between these legitimate and illegitimate persons constitute the type of environment in which the juvenile criminal subculture can come into being.[17]

An excellent example of the way in which the content of a delinquent subculture is affected by its location in a particular milieu is afforded by the "fence," a dealer in stolen goods who is found in some but not all lower-class neighborhoods. Relationships between such middlemen and criminals are not confined to adult offenders; numerous accounts of lower-class life suggest not only that relationships form between fences and youngsters but also that the fence is a crucial element in the struc-

---

[14] *Ibid.*

[15] Shaw, *op. cit.*, p. 3. Emphasis added.

[16] Frank Tannenbaum, *Crime and the Community* (New York: Columbia University Press, 1938), p. 60.

[17] In this connection, see R. A. Cloward, "Social Control in the Prison," *Theoretical Studies of the Social Organization of the Prison,* Bulletin No. 15 (New York: Social Science Research Council, March 1960), pp. 20–48, which illustrates similar forms of integration in a penal setting.

ture of illegitimate opportunity. He often caters to and encourages delinquent activities among the young. He may even exert controls leading the young to orient their stealing in the most lucrative and least risky directions. The same point may be made of junk dealers in some areas, racketeers who permit minors to run errands, and other occupants of illegitimate or semilegitimate roles.

As the apprentice criminal passes from one status to another in the illegitimate opportunity system, we should expect him to develop an ever-widening set of relationships with members of the semilegitimate and legitimate world. For example, a delinquent who is rising in the structure might begin to come into contact with mature criminals, law-enforcement officials, politicians, bail bondsmen, "fixers," and the like. As his activities become integrated with the activities of these persons, his knowledge of the illegitimate world is deepened, new skills are acquired, and the opportunity to engage in new types of illegitimate activity enhanced. Unless he can form these relationships, the possibility of a stable, protected criminal style of life is effectively precluded.

The type of environment that encourages a criminal orientation among delinquents is, then, characterized by close integration of the carriers of conventional and illegitimate values. The *content* of the delinquent subculture is a more or less direct response to the local milieu in which it emerges. And it is the "integrated" neighborhood, we suggest, that produces the criminal type of delinquent subculture.

Structural Integration and Social Control. Delinquent behavior generally exhibits a component of aggressiveness. Even youth in neighborhoods that are favorable learning environments for criminal careers are likely to engage in some "bopping" and other forms of violence. Hence one feature of delinquency that must be explained is its tendency toward aggressive behavior. However, aggressiveness is not the primary component of all delinquent behavior; it is much more characteristic of some delinquent groups than of others. Therefore, we must also concern ourselves with the conditions under which the aggressive component becomes ascendant.

The importance of assessing the relative dominance of expressive and instrumental components in delinquent patterns is often overlooked. Cohen, for example, stresses the aggressive or expressive aspect of delinquent behavior, remarking that "it is non-utilitarian, malicious and negativistic," although he also asserts that these traits may not characterize all delinquency. Cohen's tendency to neglect relatively non-aggressive aspects of delinquency is related to his failure to take into account the relationships between delinquent behavior and adult criminality. However, *depending upon the presence or absence of those integrative relationships,* behavior that appears to be "non-utilitarian" in achieving access to conventional roles may possess considerable utility for securing access to criminal roles. Furthermore, these integrated systems may have important consequences for social control.

To the extent that delinquents take as their primary reference group older and more sophisticated gang boys, or even fully acculturated criminals or racketeers, dramatic instances of "malicious, negativistic" behavior may represent efforts to express solidarity with the norms of the criminal world. Delinquents who so behave in an attempt to win acceptance by older criminals may be engaging in a familiar sociological process; namely, overconformity to the norms of a group to which they aspire but do not belong. By such overconformity to the norms of the criminal world, delinquents seek to dramatize their eligibility for membership. To an observer oriented toward conventional values, aggressive behavior of this kind might appear to be purposeless. However, from the perspective of the carriers of deviant values, conspicuous defiance of conventional values may validate the "rightness" of the aspirant. Once he has been defined as "right," he may then be selected for further socialization and preparation for mature criminal activity.

Once the delinquent has successfully demonstrated his eligibility for acceptance by persons higher in the criminal structure, social controls are exerted to suppress undisciplined, expressive behavior; there is no place in organized crime for the impulsive, unpredictable individual. A dramatic illustration of the emphasis upon instrumental performance is offered by the case of Murder, Inc. Abe Reles, a former member of the syndicate who turned state's evidence, made certain comments about Murder, Inc., which illustrate perfectly Max Weber's famous characterization of the norms governing role performance and interpersonal relationships in bureaucratic organizations: *"Sine ira et studio"* ("without anger or passion").

The crime trust, Reles insists, never commits murder out of passion, excitement, jealousy, personal revenge, or any of the usual motives which prompt private, unorganized murder. It kills impersonally, and solely for business considerations. Even business rivalry, he adds, is not the usual motive, unless "somebody gets too balky or somebody steps right on top of you." No gangster may kill on his own initiative; every murder must be ordered by the leaders at the top, and it must serve the welfare of the organization. . . . The crime trust insists that that murder must be a business matter, organized by the chiefs in conference and carried out in a disciplined way. "It's a real business all the way through," Reles explains. "It just happens to be that kind of business, but nobody is allowed to kill from personal grievance. There's got to be a good business reason, and top men of the combination must give their okay." [18]

The pressure for rational role performance in the adult criminal world is exerted downward, we suggest, through interconnected systems of age-graded statuses. At each point in this illegitimate hierarchy, instrumental rather than expressive behavior is emphasized. In their description of the Pirates, for example, Bloch and Niederhoffer observe that Paulie, the adult mastermind of the gang, avoided expressive behavior: "The younger Pirates might indulge in wild adolescent antics. Paulie remained aloof." [19] Paulie symbolized a mode of life in which reason, discipline, and foresight were uppermost. To the extent that younger members of the gang identified with him, they were constrained to adopt a similar posture. Rico, the leader of a gang described in a recent book by Harrison Salisbury, can be characterized in much the same way:

This youngster was the most successful kid in the neighborhood. He was a dope pusher. Some weeks he made as much as $200. He used his influence in some surprising ways. He persuaded the gang members to stop bopping because he was afraid it would bring on police intervention and interfere with his drug sales. He flatly refused to sell dope to boys and kicked out of the gang any kid who started to use drugs. He sold only to adults. With his money he brought jackets for the gang, took care of hospital bills of members, paid for the rent on his mother's flat, paid most of the family expenses and sometimes spent sixty dollars to buy a coat as a present for one of his boys.[20]

The same analysis helps to explain a puzzling aspect of delinquent behavior; namely, the apparent disregard delinquents sometimes exhibit for stolen objects. Some theorists have concluded from this that the ends of stealing are not utilitarian, that delinquents do not steal because they need or want the objects in question or for any other rational reason. Cohen, for example, asserts that "were the participant in the

---

[18] Joseph Freeman, "Murder Monopoly: The Inside Story of a Crime Trust," *The Nation*, Vol. 150, No. 21 (May 25, 1940), p. 648. This is but one of many sources in which the bureaucratization of crime is discussed.

[19] Bloch and Niederhoffer, *op. cit.*, p. 201.

[20] H. E. Salisbury, *The Shook-up Generation* (New York: Harper & Bros., 1958), p. 176.

delinquent subculture merely employing illicit means to the end of acquiring economic goods, he would show more respect for the goods he has thus acquired." [21] Hence, Cohen concludes, the bulk of stealing among delinquents is "for the hell of it" rather than for economic gain. Whether stealing is expressive or instrumental may depend, however, on the social context in which it occurs. Where criminal opportunities exist, it may be argued that stealing is a way of expressing solidarity with the carriers of criminal values and, further, that it is a way of acquiring the various concrete skills necessary before the potential criminal can gain full acceptance in the group to which he aspires. That is, a certain amount of stealing may be motivated less by immediate need for the objects in question than by a need to acquire skill in the arts of theft. When practice in theft is the implicit purpose, the manner of disposing of stolen goods is unimportant. Similarly, the status accruing to the pickpocket who can negotiate a "left-front-breech" derives not so much from the immediate profit attaching to this maneuver as from the fact that it marks the individual as a master craftsman. In other words, where criminal learning environments and opportunity structures exist, stealing beyond immediate economic needs may constitute anticipatory socialization. But where these structures do not exist, such stealing may be simply an expressive act of defiance of conventional values.

Shaw pointed to a related aspect of the social control of delinquent behavior. Noting the prestige ordering of criminal activities, he commented on the way in which such definitions once internalized, tend to regulate the behavior of delinquents:

It is a matter of significance to note . . . that there is a general tendency among older delinquents and criminals to look with contempt upon the person who specializes in any form of petty stealing. The common thief is not distinguished for manual dexterity and accomplishment, like the pickpocket or mobsman, nor for courage, ingenuity and skill, like the burglar, but is characterized by low cunning and stealth—hence the term "sneak thief." . . . It is possible that the stigma attaching to petty stealing among members of older delinquent groups is one factor which gives impetus to the young delinquent's desire to abandon such forms of petty delinquency as stealing junk, vegetables, breaking into freight cars . . . and to become identified with older groups engaged in such crimes as larceny of automobiles and robbery with a gun, both of which are accredited "rackets" among older delinquents. . . .[22]

To the extent that an area has an age-graded criminal structure in which juvenile delinquents can become enmeshed, we suggest that the norms governing adult criminal-role performance filter down, becoming significant principles in the life-organization of the young. The youngster who has come into contact with such an age-graded structure and who has won initial acceptance by older and more sophisticated delinquents will be less likely to engage in malicious, destructive behavior than in disciplined, instrumental, career-oriented behavior. In this way the adult criminal system exerts controls over the behavior of delinquents. Referring to urban areas characterized by integration of different age-levels of offender, Kobrin makes an observation that tends to bear out our theoretical scheme:

. . . delinquency tends to occur within a partial framework of social controls, insofar as delinquent activity in these areas represents a tolerated means for the acquisition of an approved role and status. Thus, while delinquent activity here possesses the usual characteristics of violence and destructiveness, there tend to develop effective limits of permissible activity in this direction. Delinquency is, in other words, encompassed and contained within

---

[21] A. K. Cohen, *Delinquent Boys: The Culture of the Gang* (Glencoe, Ill.: Free Press, 1955), p. 36.

[22] Shaw, *op. cit.*, p. 10.

a local structure, and is marginally but palpably related to that structure.[23]

In summary, the criminal subculture is likely to arise in a neighborhood milieu characterized by close bonds between different age-levels of offender, and between criminal and conventional elements. As a consequence of these integrative relationships, a new opportunity structure emerges which provides alternative avenues to success-goals. Hence the pressures generated by restrictions on legitimate access to success-goals are drained off. Social controls over the conduct of the young are effectively exercised, limiting expressive behavior and constraining the discontented to adopt instrumental, if criminalistic styles of life.

THE CONFLICT SUBCULTURE

Because youngsters caught up in the conflict subculture often endanger their own lives and the lives of others and cause considerable property damage, the conflict form of delinquency is a source of great public concern. Its prevalence, therefore, is probably exaggerated. There is no evidence to suggest that the conflict subculture is more widespread than the other subcultures, but the nature of its activities makes it more visible and thus attracts public attention. As a consequence, many people erroneously equate "delinquency" and "conflict behavior." But whatever its prevalence, the conflict subculture is of both theoretical and social importance, and calls for explanation.

Earlier in this book, we questioned the common belief that slum areas, because they are slums, are necessarily disorganized. We pointed to forms of integration which give some slum areas unity and cohesion. Areas in which these integrative structures are found, we suggested, tend to be characterized by criminal rather than conflict or retreatist subcultures. But not all slums are integrated. Some lower-class urban neighborhoods lack unity and cohesiveness. Because the prerequisites for the emergence of stable systems of social relations are not present, a state of social disorganization prevails.

The many forces making for instability in the social organization of some slum areas include high rates of vertical and geographic mobility; massive housing projects in which "site tenants" are not accorded priority in occupancy, so that traditional residents are dispersed and "strangers" re-assembled; and changing land use, as in the case of residential areas that are encroached upon by the expansion of adjacent commercial or industrial areas. Forces of this kind keep a community off balance, for tentative efforts to develop social organization are quickly checked. Transiency and instability become the over-riding features of social life.

Transiency and instability, in combination, produce powerful pressures for violent behavior among the young in these areas. First, an unorganized community cannot provide access to legitimate channels to success-goals, and thus discontent among the young with their life-chances is heightened. Secondly, access to stable criminal opportunity systems is also restricted, for disorganized neighborhoods do not develop integration of different age-levels of offender or integration of carriers of criminal and conventional values. The young in short, are relatively deprived of *both* conventional and criminal opportunity. Finally, social controls are weak in such communities. These conditions, we believe, lead to the emergence of conflict subcultures.

Social Disorganization and Opportunity. Communities that are unable to develop conventional forms of social organization are also unable to provide legitimate modes of access to culturally valued success-goals. The disorganized slum is a world populated with failures, with the outcasts of

---

[23] Solomon Kobrin, "The Conflict of Values in Delinquency Areas." *American Sociological Review*, Vol. 16 (Oct. 1951), p. 657.

the larger society. Here families orient themselves not toward the future but toward the present, not toward social advancement but toward survival. The adult community, being disorganized, cannot provide the resources and opportunities that are required if the young are to move upward in the social order.

Just as the unintegrated slum cannot mobilize legitimate resources for the young, neither can it provide them with access to stable criminal careers, for illegitimate learning and opportunity structures do not develop. The disorganized slum, populated in part by failures in the conventional world, also contains the outcasts of the criminal world. This is not to say that crime is nonexistent in such areas, but what crime there is tends to be individualistic, unorganized, petty, poorly paid, and unprotected. This is the haunt of the small-time thief, the grifter, the pimp, the jackroller, the unsophisticated "con" man, the pickpocket who is all thumbs, and others who cannot graduate beyond "heisting" candy stores or "busting" gas stations. Since they are unorganized and without financial resources, criminals in these areas cannot purchase immunity from prosecution; they have neither the money nor the political contacts to "put in the fix." Hence they are harassed by the police, and many of them spend the better part of their lives in prison. The organized criminal world is generally able to protect itself against such harassment, prosecution, and imprisonment. But professional crime and organized rackets, like any business enterprise, can thrive only in a stable, predictable, and integrated environment. In this sense, then, the unintegrated area does not constitute a promising launching site for lucrative and protected criminal careers. Because such areas fail to develop criminal learning environments and opportunity structures, stable criminal subcultures cannot emerge.

Social Disorganization and Social Control. As we have noted, social controls originate in both the conventional and the illegitimate sectors of the stable slum area. But this is apparently not the case in the disorganized slum. The basic disorganization of the conventional institutional structure makes it impossible for controls to originate there. At the same time, Kobrin asserts, "Because adult crime in this type of area is itself unorganized, its value system remains implicit and hence incapable of generating norms which function effectively on a groupwide basis." Hence juvenile violators readily escape not merely the controls of conventional persons in the community but those of adult violators as well." Under such conditions,

... [the] delinquencies of juveniles tend to acquire a wild, untrammelled character. Delinquents in this kind of situation more frequently exhibit the personality traits of the social type sometimes referred to as the hoodlum. Both individually and in groups, violent physical combat is engaged in for its own sake, almost as a form of recreation. Here groups of delinquents may be seen as excluded, isolated conflict groups dedicated to an unending battle against all forms of constraint. The escape from controls originating in any social structure, other than that provided by unstable groupings of the delinquents themselves, is here complete.[24]

Unlike Kobrin, we do not attribute conflict behavior in unorganized urban areas to the absence of controls alone. The young in such areas are also exposed to acute frustrations, arising from conditions in which access to success-goals is blocked by the absence of any institutionalized channels, legitimate or illegitimate. They are deprived not only of conventional opportunity but also of criminal routes to the "big money." In other words, precisely when frustrations are maximized, social controls are weakened. Social controls and channels to success-goals are generally related: where opportunities exist, patterns

---

[24] *Ibid.*, p. 658.

of control will be found; where opportunities are absent, patterns of social control are likely to be absent too. The association of these two features of social organization is a logical implication.

Social Disorganization and Violence. Those adolescents in disorganized urban areas who are oriented toward achieving higher position but are cut off from institutionalized channels, criminal as well as legitimate, must rely upon their own resources for solving this problem of adjustment. Under these conditions, tendencies toward aberrant behavior become intensified and magnified. The adolescents seize upon the manipulation of violence as a route to status not only because it provides a way of expressing pent-up angers and frustrations but also because they are not cut off from access to violent means by vicissitudes of birth. In the world of violence, such attributes as race, socioeconomic position, age, and the like are irrelevant; personal worth is judged on the basis of qualities that are available to all who would cultivate them. The principal prerequisites for success are "guts" and the capacity to endure pain. One doesn't need "connections," "pull," or elaborate technical skills in order to achieve "rep." The essence of the warrior adjustment is an expressed feeling-state: "heart." The acquisition of status is not simply a consequence of skill in the use of violence or of physical strength but depends, rather, on one's willingness to risk injury or death in the search for "rep." A physically immature boy may find a place among the warrior elite if, when provoked, he will run such risks, thus demonstrating "heart."

As long as conventional and criminal opportunity structures remain closed, violence continues unchecked. The bulk of aggressive behavior appears to be channeled into gang warfare; success in street combat assures the group that its "turf" will not be invaded, that its girls will not be molested, that its members will otherwise be treated deferentially by young and old in the local community. *If new opportunity structures are opened, however, violence tends to be relinquished.* Indeed, the success of certain efforts to discourage violent aggressive behavior among warrior gangs has resulted precisely from the fact that some powerful group has responded deferentially to these gangs. (The group is powerful because it can provide, or at least hold out the promise of providing, channels to higher position, such as jobs, education, and the like.) The most dramatic illustration of this process may be seen in programs conducted by social group workers who attach themselves to street gangs. Several points should be noted about the results of these programs.

First, violent behavior among street gangs appears to diminish rapidly once a social worker establishes liaison with them. Reporting on the outcome of detached-worker programs in Boston, for example, Miller notes, "One of the earliest and most evident changes . . . was that groups worked with directly [by social workers] relinquished active participation in the [established] network of conflict groups. . . ."[25] The reduction in conflict may reflect the skill of the social workers, but another explanation may be that *the advent of the street-gang worker symbolized the end of social rejection and the beginning of social accommodation.* To the extent that violence represents an effort to win deference, one would logically expect it to diminish once that end has been achieved.

Secondly, a detached-worker program, once initiated, tends to give rise to increased violence among groups to which workers have *not* been provided. In the Boston experience, to the extent that they interpreted having a street-club worker as an act of social deference, gangs came to compete for this prestige symbol. As Miller

---

[25] This quotation and those that follow are from W. B. Miller, "The Impact of a Community Group Work Program on Delinquent Corner Groups," *Social Service Review*, Vol. 31, No. 4 (Dec. 1957), pp. 390–406.

notes, "During later phases of the Program [there was] an upsurge in gang fights involving Program groups.... These conflicts did not involve Program groups fighting one another but represented for the most part attacks on Program groups by corner groups in adjacent areas which did not have an area worker." Miller suggests that such attacks took place in part because "the outside groups knew that Program groups were given a social worker in the first place because they were trouble-some; so they reasoned. 'They were bad, and they got a social worker; if we're bad enough now, we'll get a social worker, too.'" An attack by an outside gang on a Program gang was not, therefore, simply an expression of the traditional hostility of one gang toward another but an attempt on the part of the non-Program gang to win "rep." Thus Miller is led to observe, "A program aiming to 'clean up' the gang situation in a single section of the city cannot count on limiting its influence to that section but must anticipate the fact that its very success in its home district may increase difficulties in adjacent areas." This suggests that programs aimed at curbing violence constitute a new opportunity structure in which gangs compete for social deference from the conventional world.

Finally, a resurgence of violent behavior may be observed when the liaison between the street worker and the gang is terminated if the members of the gang have not been successfully incorporated in a conventional opportunity system. Continuing to lack conventional economic opportunity, the gang fears the loss of the one form of recognition it has achieved from conventional society, symbolized by the street worker. Hence the group may reassert the old patterns of violence in order to retain the social worker. Under these conditions, the conventional society will continue to accommodate to the group for fear that to do otherwise would result in renewed violence, as indeed it so often does. A successful street-gang program, in short, is one in which detached workers can create channels to legitimate opportunity; where such channels cannot be opened up, the gang will temporize with violence only as long as a street worker maintains liaison with them.

In summary, severe limitations on both conventional and criminal opportunity intensify frustrations and position discontent. Discontent is heightened further under conditions in which social control is relaxed, for the area lacking integration between age-levels of offender and between carriers of conventional and criminal values cannot generate pressures to contain frustrations among the young. These are the circumstances, we suggest, in which adolescents turn to violence in search of status. Violence comes to be ascendant, in short, under conditions of relative detachment from all institutionalized systems of opportunity and social control.

THE RETREATIST SUBCULTURE

The consumption of drugs—one of the most serious forms of retreatist behavior—has become a severe problem among adolescents and young adults, particularly in lower-class urban areas. By and large, drug use in these areas has been attributed to rapid geographic mobility, inadequate social controls, and other manifestations of social disorganization. In this section, we shall suggest a hypothesis that may open up new avenues of inquiry in regard to the growing problem of drug use among the young.

Pressures Leading to Retreatist Subcultures. Retreatism is often conceived as an isolated adaptation, characterized by a breakdown in relationships with other persons. Indeed, this is frequently true, as in the case of psychotics. The drug-user, however, must become affiliated with others, if only to secure access to a steady supply of drugs. Just as stable criminal activity cannot be explained by reference to motivation alone, neither can stable drug use be fully explained in this way. Opportunity to use drugs must also be present. But such opportunities are restricted. As Becker notes, the illegal distribution of drugs is limited to "sources which are not available to the ordinary person. In order for a person to begin marihuana use, he must begin participation in some group through which these sources of supply become available to him."[26]

Because of these restrictions on the availability of drugs, new users must become affiliated with old users. They must learn the lore of drug use, the skills required in making appropriate "connections," the controls which govern the purchase of drugs (*e.g.*, drugs will not generally be made available to anyone until he is "defined as a person who can safely be trusted to buy drugs without endangering anyone else"), and the like. As this process of socialization proceeds, the individual "is considered more trustworthy, [and] the necessary knowledge and introductions to dealers [then become] available to him." According to Becker, the "processes by which people are emancipated from the larger set of controls *and become responsive to those of the subculture*" are "important factors in the genesis of deviant behavior."[27] The drug-user, in other words, must be understood not only in terms of his personality and the social structure, which create a readiness to engage in drug use, but also in terms of the new patterns of associations and values to which he is exposed as he seeks access to drugs. The more the individual is caught in this web of associations, the more likely that he will persist in drug use, for he has become incorporated in a subculture that exerts control over his behavior.

Despite these pressures toward subcultural formation, it is probably also true that the resulting ties among addicts are not so solidary as those among participants in criminal and conflict subcultures. Addiction is in many ways an individualistic adaptation, for the "kick" is essentially a private experience. The compelling need for the drug is also a divisive force, for it leads to intense competition among addicts for money. Forces of this kind thus limit the relative cohesion which can develop among users.

"Double Failure" and Drug Use. We turn now to a discussion of the social conditions which give rise to retreatist reactions such as drug use among adolescents. According to Metron,

Retreatism arises from continued failure to near the goal by legitimate measures and from an inability to use the illegitimate route because of internalized prohibitions, this process occurring while the supreme value of the success-goal has not yet been renounced. The conflict is resolved by abandoning both precipitating elements, the goals and the norms. The escape is complete, the conflict is eliminated and the individual is asocialized.[28]

Thus he identifies two principal factors in the emergence of retreatist adaptations: (1) continued failure to reach culturally approved goals by legitimate means, and (2) inability to employ illegitimate alternatives because of internalized prohibitions. We take it that "internalized prohibitions" have to do with the individual's attitudes toward norms. Retreatists, ac-

---

[26] H. S. Becker, "Marihuana Use and Social Control," *Social Problems*, Vol. 3, No. 1 (July 1955), pp. 36–37.

[27] *Ibid., p. 35.* Emphasis added.

[28] R. K. Merton, *Social Theory and Social Structure*, Rev. and Enl. Ed. (Glencoe, Ill.: Free Press, 1957), pp. 153–54. For discussions of drug use among juveniles, see D. L. Gerard and Conon Kornetsky, "Adolescent Opiate Addiction—A Study of Control and Addict Subjects," *Psychiatric Quarterly*, Vol. 29 (April 1955), pp. 457–86; Isidor Chein *et al.*, *Studies of Narcotics Use Among Juveniles* (New York University, Research Center for Human Relations, mimeographed, Jan. 1956); Harold Finestone, "Cats, Kicks, and Color," *Social Problems*, Vol. 5, No. 1 (July 1957), pp. 3–13; and D. M. Wilmer, Eva Rosenfeld, R. S. Lee, D. L. Gerard, and Isidor Chein, "Heroin Use and Street Gangs," *Criminal Law, Criminology and Police Science*, Vol. 48, No. 4 (Nov.–Dec. 1957), pp. 399–409.

cording to Merton, do not call into question the legitimacy of existing institutional arrangements—a process which might then be followed by the use of illegitimate alternatives. Rather, they call into question their own adequacy, locating blame for their dilemma in personal deficiencies. One way of resolving the intense anxiety and guilt which ensue is to withdraw, to retreat, to abandon the struggle.

This definition of the processes giving rise to retreatist behavior is useful in connection with some types of retreatism, but it does not, we believe, fit the facts of drug use among lower-class adolescents. It is true that some youthful addicts appear to experience strong constraints on the use of illegitimate means; the great majority of drug-users, however, had a history of delinquency before becoming addicted. In these cases, unfavorable attitudes toward conventional norms are evident. Hence we conclude that internalized prohibitions, or favorable attitudes toward conventional norms, may not be a necessary condition for the emergence of retreatist behavior.

If internalized prohibitions are not a necessary component of the process by which retreatism is generated, then how are we to account for such behavior? We have noted that there are differentials in access both to illegitimate means; not all of those who seek to attain success-goals by prohibited routes are permitted to proceed. There are probably many lower-class adolescents oriented toward success in the criminal world who fail; similarly, many who would like to acquire proficiency in the use of violence also fail. We might ask, therefore, what the response would be among those faced with failure in the use of both legitimate and illegitimate means. We suggest that persons who experience this "double failure" are likely to move into a retreatist pattern of behavior. That is, retreatist behavior may arise as a consequence of limitations on the use of illegitimate means, whether the limitations are internalized prohibitions or socially structured barriers. For our purpose, the two types of restriction are functional equivalents. Thus we may amend Merton's statement as follows:

Retreatism arises from continued failure to near the goal by legitimate measures and from an inability to use the illegitimate route because of internalized prohibitions *or socially structured barriers,* this process occurring while the supreme value of the success-goal has not yet been renounced.

This hypothesis permits us to define two general classes of retreatist: those who are subject to internalized prohibitions on the use of illegitimate means, and those who seek success-goals by prohibited routes but do not succeed. If we now introduce a distinction between illegitimate opportunity structures based on the manipulative use of violence and those based on essentially criminal means, such as fraud, theft, and extortion, we can identify four classes of retreatist.

Types I and II both arise in the manner described by Merton—that is, as a consequence of internalized restrictions on the use of illegitimate means. The two types differ only with respect to the content of the internalized restraints. In type II, it is the use of criminal means that is precluded; in type I, it is the use of violence. Resort to illegitimate means, violent or criminal, apparently evokes extreme guilt and anxiety among persons in these categories; such persons are therefore effectively cut off from criminal or violent routes to higher status. For persons of types III and IV, access to illegitimate routes is limited by socially structured barriers. They are not restrained by internal prohibiitions; they would employ illegitimate means if these were available to them.

Generally speaking, it has been found that most drug addicts have a history of delinquent activity prior to becoming addicted. In Kobrin's research, conducted in Chicago, "Persons who become herion users were found to have engaged in delin-

Retreatist Adaptations

Basis of Illegitimate Opportunity Structure	Restrictions on Use of Illegitimate Means	
	Internalized Prohibitions	Socially Structured Barriers
Violence	I	III
Criminal Means	II	IV

quency *in a group-supported and habitual form* either prior to their use of drugs or simultaneously with their developing interest in drugs.[29] And from a study of drug addicts in California, "A very significant tentative conclusion [was reached]: namely, that the use of drugs follows criminal activity and criminal association rather than the other way around, which is often thought to be the case."[30] In other words, adolescents who are engaged in group-supported delinquency of the criminal or conflict type may eventually turn to drug use. Indeed, entire gangs sometimes shift from either criminal or conflict to retreatist adaptations.

We view these shifts in adaptations as responses to restrictions on the use of illegitimate means. Such restrictions, as we have seen, are always operative; not all who would acquire success by violence or criminal means are permitted to do so. It is our contention that retreatist behavior emerges among some lower-class adolescents because they have failed to find a place for themselves in criminal or conflict subcultures. Consider the case of competition for membership in conflict gangs. To the extent that conflict activity —"bopping," street-fighting, "rumbling," and the like—is tolerated, it represents an alternative means by which adolescents in many relatively disorganized urban areas may acquire status. Those who excel in the manipulation of violence may acquire "rep" within the group to which they belong and respect from other adolescent groups in the vicinity and from the adult world. In areas which do not offer criminal opportunities, the use of violence may be the only available avenue to prestige. But prestige is, by definition, scarce—just as scarce among adolescents who seek to acquire it by violence as it is elsewhere in the society. Not only do juvenile gangs compete vigorously with one another, but within each gang there is a continual struggle for prestigeful positions. Thus some gangs will acquire "rep" and others will fail; some persons will become upwardly mobile in conflict groups and others will remain on the periphery.

If the adolescent "failure" then turns to drugs as a solution to his status dilemma, his relationships with his peers become all the more attenuated. Habitual drug use is not generally a valued activity among juvenile gangs. Ordinarily the drug-user, if he persists in such behavior, tends to become completely disassociated from the group. Once disassociated, he may develop an even greater reliance upon drugs as a solution to status deprivations. Thus adolescent drug-users may be "double failures" who are restrained from participating in other delinquent modes of adaptation because access to these illegitimate structures is limited.

Our hypothesis states that adolescents who are double failures are more vulnerable than others to retreatist behavior; it does not imply that *all* double failures will subsequently become retreatists. Some will respond to failure by adopting a law-abiding lower-class style of life—the "corner

---

[29] Solomon Kobrin, *Drug Addiction Among Young Persons in Chicago* (Illinois Institute for Juvenile Research, Oct. 1953), p. 6. Harold Finestone, in a study of the relationship between addicts and criminal status, comments: "The impression gained from interviewing . . . was that these addicts were petty thieves and petty 'operators' who, status-wise, were at the bottom of the criminal population of the underworld." "Narcotics and Criminality," *Law and Contemporary Problems*, Vol. 22, No. 1 [Winter 1957], pp. 69–85).

[30] *Narcotics in California* (Board of Corrections, State of California, Feb. 18, 1959), p. 9.

boy" adaptation. It may be that those who become retreatists are incapable of revising their aspirations downward to correspond to reality. Some of those who shift to a corner-boy adaptation may not have held high aspirations initially. It has frequently been observed that some adolescents affiliate with delinquent groups simply for protection in gang-ridden areas; they are motivated not by frustration so much as by the "instinct of self-preservation." In a less hostile environment, they might simply have made a corner-boy adjustment in the first place. But for those who continue to exhibit high aspirations under conditions of double failure, retreatism is the expected result.

Sequences of Adaptation. Access to success-goals by illegitimate means diminishes as the lower-class adolescent approaches adulthood. Illegitimate avenues to higher status that were available during early adolescence become more restricted in later adolescence. These new limitations intensify frustration and so create pressures toward withdrawal or retreatist reactions.

With regard to criminal means, late adolescence is a crucial turning point, for it is during this period that the selection of candidates for stable adult criminal roles takes place. It is probably true that more youngsters are exposed to criminal learning environments during adolescence than can possibly be absorbed by the adult criminal structure. Because of variations in personality characteristics, criminal proficiency, and capacity to make "the right connections," or simply because of luck, some persons will find this avenue to higher status open and some will find it closed off. In effect, the latter face a dead end. Some delinquents, therefore, must cope with abrupt discontinuity in role-preparation and role-performance which may lead to retreatist responses.

In the case of conflict patterns, a similar process takes place. As adolescents near adulthood, excellence in the manipulation of violence no longer brings high status.

Quite the contrary, it generally evokes extreme negative sanctions. What was defined as permissible or tolerable behavior during adolescence tends to be sharply proscribed in adulthood. New expectations are imposed, expectations of "growing up," of taking on adult responsibilities in the economic, familial, and community spheres. The effectiveness with which these definitions are imposed is attested by the tendency among fighting gangs to decide that conflict is, in the final analysis, simply "kid stuff":

> As the group grows older, two things happen. Sports, hell raising, and gang fights become "kid stuff" and are given up. In the normal course of events, the youthful preoccupations are replaced with the more individual concerns about work, future, a "steady" girl, and the like.[31]

In other words, powerful community expectations emerge which have the consequence of closing off access to previously useful means of overcoming status deprivations. Strains are experienced, and retreatist behavior may result.

As we have noted, adolescents who experience pressures leading to retreatist reactions are often restrained by their peers. Adolescent gangs usually devalue drug use (except on an experimental basis or for the sake of novelty) and impose negative sanctions upon those who become "hooked." The very existence of the gang discourages the potential user:

> The activities of the gang offer a measure of shared status, a measure of security and a sense of belonging. The boys do not have to face life alone—the group protects them. Escape into drugs is not necessary as yet.[32]

In the post-adolescent period, however, the cohesiveness of the peer group usually weakens. Those who have the requisite skills and opportunities begin to make the transition to adulthood, assuming conventional occupational and kinship roles. As

---

[31] Wilmer *et al., op. cit.*, p. 409.
[32] *Ibid.*

the solidarity of the group declines, it can no longer satisfy the needs or control the behavior of those who continue to rely upon it. These members may try to reverse the trend toward disintegration and, failing this, turn to drugs:

> This group organized five years ago for self-protection against other fighting groups in the area. Recently, as the majority grew cool to bopping, a group of three boys broke off in open conflict with the president; *soon after, these three started using heroin and acting "down with the cats."* They continue making efforts to get the gang back to fights. . . . The three users are still out and it is unlikely that they will be readmitted.[33]

---

[33] *Ibid.*, p. 405. Emphasis added.

For some adolescents, the peer group is the primary avenue to status as well as the primary source of constraints on behavior. For these youngsters, the post-adolescent period, during which the group may disintegrate or shift its orientation, is one in which social controls are weakened precisely when tensions are heightened.

Whether the sequence of adaptations is from criminal to retreatist or from conflict to retreatist, we suggest that limitations on legitimate and illegitimate opportunity combine to produce intense pressures toward retreatist behavior. When both systems of means are simultaneously restricted, it is not strange that some persons become detached from the social structure, abandoning cultural goals and efforts to achieve them by any means.

33. VALUES AND GANG DELINQUENCY: A STUDY OF STREET-CORNER GROUPS

JAMES SHORT, JR.
FRED L. STRODTBECK

THREE RECENT THEORIES OF JUVENILE-GANG delinquency view values as an important link in a causal chain leading from social status to illegitimate behavior.[1] The theories are seemingly in agreement as to what they mean by "values," and they differ only slightly in the content of the values which they ascribe to members of three relatively distinct social categories: lower class gang, lower class non-gang, and middle class non-gang. There are, however, important differences between the theories in the assumptions underlying these values. As a result, competing, if not always mutually exclusive, hypotheses are implied. This chapter attempts to further refine thinking in this area by empirically testing some hypotheses that might reasonably be deduced from the three theories. Accordingly, relevant data gathered from both Negro and white adolescent members of each of the social categories are presented.

▶SOURCE: *Group Process and Gang Delinquency,* Chicago: University of Chicago Press, 1965, pp. 47-76. Copyright 1965 by the University of Chicago Press. Reprinted by permission.

[1] These theoretical statements are by Albert K. Cohen, *Delinquent Boys* (Glencoe: The Free Press, 1955); Walter B. Miller, "Lower Class Culture as a Generating Milieu of Gang Delinquency," *Journal of Social Issues,* XIV (1958), 5-19; and Richard A. Cloward and Lloyd E. Ohlin, *Delinquency and Opportunity* (Glencoe: The Free Press, 1960). For further elaboration of the Cohen point of view see Albert K. Cohen and James F. Short, Jr., "Research in Delinquent Subcultures," *Journal of Social Issues,* XIV (1958), 20-37. Miller brings his viewpoint to bear on empirical data in Walter B. Miller, Hildred Geertz, and Henry S. G. Cutter, "Aggression in a Boys' Street-Corner Group," *Psychiatry,* XXIV (1961), 283-98.

THE SAMPLE

Samples of Negro and white males were drawn from each of the following social categories, making a total of six populations under study.

Gang. The gang boys studied are members of nine Negro and six white gangs assigned workers by the Program for Detached Workers of the YMCA of Metropolitan Chicago. The samples contain 163 Negroes and 58 whites, and constitute from a third to a half of the total membership of these gangs. Police record data were obtained for all nine Negro gangs and four of the six white gangs.[2] For the total memberships, the number of offenses known to the police per boy averaged 3.17 for Negroes and 2.91 for whites; for boys in the samples these figures are 3.28 and 3.39, respectively. Thus, boys from whom data were collected do not appear to be less delinquent than the average member of their gangs. A comparison of the ages of

[2] The police record search was conducted by John M. Wise, who furnished the data upon which these figures are based (see his "A Comparison of Sources of Data as Indexes of Delinquent Behavior," unpublished Master's thesis, University of Chicago, 1962).

boys in the samples with those not included reveals that the included Negroes are 0.57 years, and the included whites 0.16 years younger than members of their gangs not included. A check of rosters of gang members prepared in advance of collecting these data gave no sign that detached workers were able to produce only their more tractable gang boys for research. If newspaper headlines are any criterion, these gangs include all but one of the most notorious in Chicago during 1960–61.

Lower Class. Boys residing in the same neighborhoods as the gang boys but not themselves members of gangs were contacted through Y's and settlement houses. Six Negro and two white groups or clubs constitute the samples, for a total of sixty-nine Negroes and thirty-seven whites. The search of police records revealed these boys to have had a moderate amount of official involvement in delinquency, indicating that these samples are not composed of boys who are unusually good. The mean number of offenses per boy known to the police was 0.33 for Negroes and 0.22 for whites.

Middle Class. Non-gang middle class boys were reached through two YMCA's known to serve a middle class clientele and located in areas of Chicago judged to be middle class according to conventional demographic criteria. A total of twenty-four Negro and forty-one white boys—from two Negro and two white clubs—is included. Just one boy within each race was known to police for delinquent activity, for a combined total of three offenses, all minor; the corresponding means were 0.08 for Negroes and 0.03 for whites. No examples of a middle class gang could be found locally.

The Sample as a Whole. Mean ages and standard deviations for the six samples, in years, are shown in Table I. The white gang sample includes the two oldest persons, one 24.4 and one 26 years old. Although most of the age differences between samples were statistically significant, an examination of the correlations between

Table I. *Mean Ages and Standard Deviations for Six Samples*

Group	Mean Age	Standard Deviation
	Negro	
Gang	17.2	1.9
Lower class	16.5	1.4
Middle class	17.3	0.9
	White	
Gang	18.2	2.1
Lower class	16.8	1.1
Middle class	16.1	1.2

the main data and age indicated that none of the interpretations to be presented could be accounted for by differences in age.[3] Although all the gang boys are definitely lower class, for convenience this report will distinguished the gang from non-gang lower class samples by the use of the terms "gang" and "lower class," respectively.

THE INSTRUMENT AND PROCEDURES

The data were gathered by means of a semantic differential, which consists of a number of seven-point, bipolar, adjectival scales against which any set of concepts or descriptive images may be rated.[4]

---

[3] Some selected 1960 Census statistics for the Chicago community areas and tracts from which these samples were drawn are presented in a table (Table A), which is one of three tables (indicated by alphabetic references in this chapter) that, along with certain methodological notes, have been deposited with the American Documentation Institute. For a discussion of the examination of relations with age, see Note A. Order Document No. 7468 from ADI Auxiliary Publications Project, Photoduplication Service, Library of Congress, Washington 25, D.C., remitting in advance $1.25 for 35-mm. microfilm or $1.25 for 6 × 8-inch photocopies. Make checks payable to Chief, Photoduplication Service, Library of Congress.

[4] See Charles E. Osgood, George J. Suci, and Percy H. Tannenbaum, *The Measurement of Meaning* (Urbana: University of Illinois Press, 1957).

This instrument measures what Osgood terms "connotative meaning" which, for a variety of populations, has been found to have two main orthogonal dimensions when a large number of scales and concepts are administered and the scales then intercorrelated and factor-analyzed. To obtain adequate measures of these dimensions, only a small number of scales, found to have high correlations with the appropriate dimensions, are required.

A score for a dimension is obtained by averaging the appropriate scale values, which ranged from one to seven. These dimensions and the corresponding scales used in this study are:

Evaluation	Potency
clean-dirty	hard-soft
good-bad	large-small
kind-cruel	strong-weak
fair-unfair	brave-cowardly
pleasant-unpleasant	rugged-delicate

Three additional scales, derived from Miller's "focal concerns" of lower class culture, were also included. These were "smart-sucker," "lucky-unlucky," and "exciting life-boring life."[5]

The images (see Table II) to be rated were chosen to represent salient examples of instrumental or dominant goal activity, leisure-time activity, and ethical orientation for each of five theoretically significant subcultures—middle class, lower class, conflict, criminal, and retreatist.[6] Leisure activity appeared to be essentially the same for three of the subcultures, and is therefore represented for all three by a single image.

Although they do not figure prominently in this analysis, the three aspects of subcultural roles did provide a basis for sampling widely within each domain. Of the four additional images included because of their theoretical interest, only the one identified by the label "GIRL" requires comment. This image was included to furnish responses relevant to sexual demonstrations of masculinity. Hopefully, images were phrased so as to be concrete as possible and yet personify the values hypothesized to distinguish the subcultures.

Administration of the semantic differential to small numbers of subjects at a time took place in an old, rather shabby onetime apartment building, where the subjects were fed hot dogs and soft drinks. The tester was quite permissive toward all departures from normally decorous behavior that did not jeopardize the validity of measures. Considerable care was taken to explain directions and check the boys' responses. A few boys, unable to read, had the semantic differential read to them as they responded.

Seventeen factor analyses of the evaluation and potency scales, performed for seventeen of the gangs and clubs studied, revealed evaluation and potency factors for all six populations matching those previously found by Osgood.[7] This rules out all but the most ingenious and most coincidentally patterned types of deliberately meaningless, falsified responding. It also justifies the scoring procedure.

STATISTICAL TREATMENT

The data consist of the mean scores for both evaluation (Table III) and the "smart-sucker" scale (Table V) accorded to each of the seventeen images by each of the six populations. Three-way (image by race by social category) analyses of variance (Tables B and C) have indicated high levels of over-all significance for these data.[8] The sources of this significance are

---

[5] Miller, op. cit., p. 6.

[6] The last three subcultures refer to types of delinquent gangs postulated by Cohen and Short, op. cit., and by Cloward and Ohlin, op. cit.

[7] See Robert A. Gordon, "The Generality of Semantic Differential Factors and Scales in Six American Subcultures," unpublished Master's thesis, University of Chicago, 1962.

[8] American Documentation Institute, op. cit. For a justification of the use of parametric statistics

Table II. *Semantic-Differential Images*

Subculture	Label	Images: "Someone who . . ."
Middle class:		
Dominant goal activity	GRAD	works for good grades at school
Leisure activity	READ	likes to read good books
Ethical orientation	SAVE	saves his money
Lower class:		
Dominant goal activity	SJOB	has a steady job washing and greasing cars
Leisure activity	HANG	likes to spend his spare time hanging on the corner with his friends
Ethical orientation	SHAR	shares his money with his friends
Conflict:		
Dominant goal activity	TUFF	is a good fighter with a tough reputation
Leisure activity	HANG	(see lower class)
Ethical orientation	STIK	sticks by his friends in a fight
Criminal:		
Dominant goal activity	FENC	knows where to sell what he steals
Leisure activity	HANG	(see lower class)
Ethical orientation	CONN	has good connections to avoid trouble with the law
Retreatist:		
Dominant goal activity	PIMP	makes easy money by pimping and other illegal hustles
Leisure activity	DRUG	gets his kicks by using drugs
Ethical orientation	COOL	stays cool and keeps to himself
Additional images	GIRL	makes out with every girl he wants
	SELF	Myself as I usually am
	IEGO	Myself as I would like to be
	GANG	is a member of (enter group name or if none, "your friendship group")

investigated further by comparing all six of the individual sample means for an image with each other, using two-tailed *t*-tests. Although this procedure carries a high risk of a Type I error [9]—because it inevitably compares the most extreme values in any set of six—it was felt that, because differences are theoretically more interesting here than similarities, this method is preferable to alternative tests having high risk of a Type II error. Important additional constraints upon interpretation are exerted, however, by (1) the fact that the three social categories are ordered with respect to presumed similarity (gang, lower class, middle class); (2) the presence of data for two races. Thus, any ordering of the data which is similar to that of the three categories, and which appears in both races, will strongly supplement the presence of statistical significance. This organization of the data has the advantage of possibly suggesting attitudinal trends in American society that may prove to be more useful in understanding delinquency than single comparisons holding constant race or class.

with semantic-differential data, see either Note B, *ibid.*, or Robert A. Gordon, "Values and Gang Delinquency," unpublished Ph.D dissertation, University of Chicago, 1963.

[9] See Thomas A. Ryan, "Multiple Comparisons in Psychological Research," *Psychological Bulletin*, LVI (1959), 26–47.

INFERENCES FROM THEORIES

Cohen. As an explanation of juvenile-gang delinquency, the hypothesis of a reaction formation against the standards of middle class society has been proposed by Albert K. Cohen. According to Cohen, reaction formation serves as a defense against the anxiety of status frustration, common to lower class youth and especially severe for those who join gangs. Although Cohen's theory holds that the wholesale repudiation of middle class values "does its job of problem-solving most effectively when it is adopted as a group solution," [10] and that "group interaction is a sort of catalyst which releases potentialities not otherwise visible," [11] thus seeming at times to leave unsettled the question of whether private values are similarly affected, the logic of the mechanism of reaction formation requires that middle class values be submerged in the consciousness of individuals as well as in the culture of the group. His point seems to be that the group experience, in which individuals come together with the common problem of status frustration, is necessary for the full unfolding and elaboration of a latent common solution, namely, total repudiation of middle class standards. Once exposed to the mutual self-recognitions and reinforcements of collective acting out, negative attitudes that were only latent in the individual's value processes become manifest. It is reasonable to expect that the resulting modification in values, while undoubtedly subject to intensification during group interaction, remains as a relatively enduring feature of an individual's personality, even when he is apart from the group. This interpretation is consistent with Cohen's emphasis upon the over-reactive quality of much delinquent behavior. Thus, although Cohen's theory asserts that middle class values are in fact internalized by gang boys, he clearly implies that they persist only as a repressed and unacknowledged source of anxiety.[12]

An instrument as baldly direct as the semantic differential would not be expected to bypass such a firmly established system of neurotic defenses. Accordingly, the explicit and highly developed negativism described by Cohen should characterize the conscious private values of the gang boy and be reflected in his evaluation of middle class images. As it was constructed, the instrument afforded subjects an opportunity to express bitterness and contempt toward rather tempting middle class figures (see GRAD, READ, and SAVE in Table II); they had only to avail themselves of the negativistic ends of the evaluative scales. Hence, if the hypothesis of reaction formation is correct, these evaluation scores for gang boys should be low.

In contrast, gang boys should evaluate images that are antithetical to middle class morality higher than the middle class images. This follows from Cohen's statement: "The hall-mark of the delinquent subculture is the explicit and wholesale repudiation of middle class standards and the adoption of their very antithesis." [13] Strictly speaking, only TUFF meets Cohen's specifications that the negativism of the reaction formation is also non-utilitarian. Yet, it would seem that FENC, CONN, PIMP and GIRL are sufficiently violative of middle class expectations to serve also as vehicles for the expression of negativism so presumably global (DRUG is perhaps too special a case to merit consideration). Whereas Cohen asserts that utility does not constitute the chief motivation of delinquent-gang boys, there is nevertheless nothing in his theory to suggest that such negativism would be inhibited if it happened to lead to a utilitarian end. For these reasons all of these images should be evaluated higher than the middle class images, but special attention should be paid to TUFF. The gang boys should also evaluate those images higher than do middle class boys.

Although not directly connected with the reaction-formation hypothesis, at least two of the lower class images, SHAR and HANG,

---

[10] Cohen, *op. cit.*, pp. 134-35.
[11] *Ibid.*, p. 136.
[12] *Ibid.*, p. 132.

[13] *Ibid.*, p. 129.

according to Cohen should be acceptable to the gang boys; the first, because it represents the lower class ethic of reciprocity, and the second, because it is an activity favored by both stable lower class and delinquent boys. Whether gang boys would perceive the third lower class image, SJOB, as but another form of subservience to middle class standards rather than as an admissible lower class occupation is not indicated in Cohen's theory.

Miller. The proposition that the lower class possesses a relatively distinct and autonomous value system is suggested, although not stated explicitly, by Walter B. Miller.[14] He does, however, clearly assert that the delinquent acts of lower class gang members have as their "dominant component of motivation" the "directed attempt by the actor to adhere to forms of behavior, and to achieve standards of value as they are defined by that community," [15] the reference being to the lower class community. He characterizes these standards as "focal concerns," and it is clear that, although they may be present to some degree in other strata, they receive radically different emphasis in the lower class than they might in the middle class. While it follows from this that lower class and gang values emphasize elements not emphasized in middle class values, Miller leaves unclear the weighting that lower class and gang values would accord to elements that do receive great emphasis in the middle class (unless one is willing to conclude that Miller intends his description of lower class values to be practically exhaustive, in which case elements emphasized in the middle class would be absent entirely from lower class culture). Despite this ambiguity, it seems reasonable to infer the following expectations from Miller's statement: lower class and gang boys should (1) not evaluate the middle class images as high as do middle class boys, (2) evaluate lower class images higher than middle class images, (3) evaluate the lower class images higher than do the middle class boys, (4) evaluate images that accord with lower class focal concerns, such as the retreatist, conflict, and criminal images, higher than do middle class boys.

Miller and others [16] also postulate the existence of a sex-identity problem for lower class males growing out of early socialization experiences in households in which adult male figures are not consistently present. According to this "female-based household" hypothesis, attempts by lower class males to achieve masculine identity are characterized by an exaggerated emphasis on sexual and aggressive exploits. Three images offer possibilities for testing this hypothesis: TUFF, GIRL, and PIMP, the last because it emphasizes a relationship with women in which the woman is controlled, exploited, and degraded. It was hypothesized that the order of evaluation of these images would run Gang>Lower Class>Middle Class and Negro>White within each of the three social levels. These orderings simply reflect the extent to which female-based households were assumed to occur in the family histories of members of each social category.

Because the focal concerns have themselves a dimensional character—consider, for example, *toughness, smartness,* and *excitement*—along which behaviors may be implicitly ordered, it might be questioned whether the evaluative responses of lower class respondents should reflect the same ordering. Miller, however, makes it quite clear that he expects evaluation and desirability to be linear functions of the focal concerns, rather than orthogonal to them, giving as one reason for preferring to speak of "focal concerns" rather than "values" his feeling that the former is neutral with respect to the implied direction of positive evaluation.[17] This indicates

---

[14] *Op. cit.*
[15] *Ibid.,* p. 5.
[16] E.g., Roger V. Burton and John W. M. Whiting, "The Absent Father and Cross-Sex Identity," *Merrill-Palmer Quarterly,* VII (1961), 85–95.
[17] *Op. cit.,* p. 7.

that the two run generally parallel to each other in his thinking.

Cloward and Ohlin. Two fundamental orientations of lower class youth have been distinguished by Richard A. Cloward and Lloyd E. Ohlin.[18] One is based upon attitude toward membership in the middle class, the other upon attitude toward improvement in one's economic position; a person may desire either, both, or none of these two objectives. The possible combinations of indifference or aspiration toward these objectives yield a typology—inspired by Merton's typology [19] of individual adaptation—of four kinds of lower class youth. Cloward and Ohlin hold that it is from Type III of their typology, those indifferent toward membership in the middle class but eager for improvement in their economic position, that the "principal constituents of delinquent subcultures" are drawn.[20] When legitimate avenues of opportunity are blocked for such boys, delinquent subcultures of different types emerge according to the pattern of illegitimate opportunities locally available.

It will be noted, however, that the middle class images used in the semantic differential appear to stand for striving, self-improvement, and sacrifice a more than for the "big cars," "flashy clothes," and "swell dames," that Cloward and Ohlin suggest epitomize the goals of Type III youth.[21] Therefore, insofar as the middle class images represent the style of life characteristic of actual membership rather than simply middle class economic position, it may be inferred that delinquents would be relatively cool toward them. Accordingly, they should evaluate GRAD, READ, and SAVE lower than does the middle class sample. But if they do evaluate the middle class images high it can be argued on a fortiori grounds that they would also evaluate images standing for middle class consumption patterns high. Indeed, despite the typology, it would be surprising if anyone did not. Thus, if gang boys evaluate the images GRAD, READ, and SAVE high it would constitute a conservative test in favor of Cloward and Ohlin's hypothesis concerning their attitudes toward economic position. But simultaneously this would bring into question either the separate existence of the two orientations on which the typology is founded or the supposition that gang delinquents emerge mainly from Type III. (It may be that if presented with them, gang members would evaluate images representing middle class consumption patterns extremely high, higher even than GRAD, READ, and SAVE, and higher also than would middle class boys. If so, there would then be reason to continue to regard the two orientations as relatively independent and distinct.) In either case it would then seem that the emphasis which Cloward and Ohlin give to exclusively economic motivation may require qualification.

Hypotheses concerning the deviant subcultural images are complicated by the fact that, according to Cloward and Ohlin, members of gangs would be expected to endorse highly the images standing for the subcultural adaptation into which their own gang best fits. There is thus no reason to believe that a gang boy would evaluate all deviant subculture adaptations high. Since this chapter makes no attempt to distinguish gangs according to this subcultural typology, any hypothesis dealing with the evaluation of illegitimate images by gang boys must be regarded as tentative. In general, it might be hypothesized that gang boys would evaluate illegitimate images higher than non-gang boys.

TYPES OF COMPARISON AND SUMMARY OF HYPOTHESES

Types of Comparisons. Implicit in the inferences from theory are two types of comparisons concerning the image means

---

[18] *Op. cit.*, pp. 90–97.
[19] Robert K. Merton, "Social Structure and Anomie," *Social Theory and Social Structure* (Glencoe: The Free Press, 1957).
[20] *Op. cit.*, p. 96.
[21] *Ibid.*

Table III. *Evaluation Means*

Images	Negro			White		
	Gang	Lower Class	Middle Class	Gang	Lower Class	Middle Class
Middle class:						
GRAD	5.58	5.72	5.68	5.35	5.79	5.61
READ	5.33	5.48	5.30	5.30	5.34	5.54
SAVE	5.30	5.33	5.18	5.12	5.17	5.15
Lower class:						
SJOB	4.25	4.26	3.93	4.26	3.71	3.60
HANG	4.05	4.29	3.52	4.23	4.02	2.98
SHAR	5.38	5.51	5.52	5.03	5.28	5.39
Conflict:						
TUFF	3.38	3.33	2.42	3.59	3.52	2.56
STIK	4.65	4.75	4.58	4.61	4.92	4.41
Criminal:						
FENC	3.03	2.53	2.38	2.88	2.18	2.31
CONN	4.22	3.62	3.28	3.98	2.99	2.40
Retreatist:						
PIMP	3.49	3.04	2.67	2.59	2.02	1.76
DRUG	2.65	2.70	2.09	2.46	2.04	2.39
COOL	4.85	4.72	4.55	5.03	4.78	4.57
Additional:						
GIRL	5.32	5.09	4.96	4.32	4.24	3.52
IEGO	5.84	6.23	6.35	5.75	6.28	6.40
GANG	4.63	5.24	5.92	4.56	5.00	5.81
SELF	5.26	5.64	5.92	4.88	5.24	5.50
LSD: [a]						
$p = .05$	0.17	0.16	0.17	0.21	0.20	0.17
DSD:						
$p = .05$	0.38	0.55	0.99	0.58	0.86	0.60
$p = .01$	0.50	0.73	1.34	0.77	1.15	0.80

[a] For each column lowest significant differences (LSD) are such that any lower are not significant; definitely significant differences (DSD) are such that any equal or higher are significant at the given level.

in Tables III and V. One compares the six populations for a single image to detect *differentials between populations for the same image;* this comparison focuses on one *row* of a table. The other type of comparison examines different images for the same population to detect *differences in relative level of the images;* it focuses on one *column*. All of the comparisons for rows have been made, and the results are presented in Tables IV and VI. Each image affords 15 possible comparisons between the 6 populations, for a total of 255 comparisons for all 17 images in each table. Of the 255 for evaluation, for example, 103 (over 40 percent) were statistically significant, many at a very high level. The greater attention will be paid to these row comparisons. However, some reference will be made to column comparisons, which, when especially relevant, have been calculated.[22] As an aid to interpretation, the range of potential significance for column comparisons has been given in Tables III and V, with figures below each column

---

[22] Such tests, which apply to several observations on the same sample, take into account the correlation between observations.

showing the magnitude of the smallest difference possibly significant at the .05 level, as well as the smallest difference definitely significant at the .05 and .01 levels. All differences less than the former are not significant; all equal to or greater than the latter are. These boundaries tend to be extreme. On the average, a difference intermediate between these limits would probably mark the threshold of significance.

Summary of Hypotheses. On the basis of quite different assumptions, each of the theories leads to the expectation that gang boys will evaluate deviant or illegitimate images higher than do middle class boys (Cohen's theory because of reaction formation, Miller's because these images correspond to the focal concerns of lower class culture, and Cloward and Ohlin's because the images represent adaptations to the relative unavailability of legitimate opportunities for members of the lower class), but only Cohen's theory carries the stronger implication that gang boys will value deviant images even higher than the middle class images. All three theories imply that middle class values, as represented in the middle class images, are not endorsed as highly by gang boys as by middle class boys. A careful reading of these theories has led to the following explicit hypotheses:

1. Gang boys evaluate the middle class images lower than illegitimate images such as PIMP, FENC, CONN, GIRL, and TUFF (Cohen). A column comparison.

2. Gang boys evaluate the middle class images lower than do lower class and middle class boys (Cohen). A row comparison.

3. Gang and lower class boys evaluate the middle class images lower than do middle class boys (Miller). A row comparison.

4. Gang boys evaluate the middle class images lower than do middle class boys (Cloward and Ohlin). A row comparison.

5. Gang boys evaluate SHAR and HANG higher than the middle class images (Cohen). A column comparison.

6. Gang and lower class boys evaluate lower class images higher than middle class images (Miller). A column comparison.

7. Gang and lower class boys evaluate lower class images higher than do the middle class boys (Miller). A row comparison.

8. PIMP, GIRL, and TUFF are evaluated higher (a) by Negroes than whites, (b) by gang boys than lower class and middle class boys, and (c) by lower class boys than middle class boys (Miller and others). All row comparisons.

9. Gang boys evaluate illegitimate images higher than do non-gang boys (Cohen; Cloward and Ohlin). A row comparison.

10. Gang and lower class boys evaluate illegitimate images higher than do middle class boys (Miller). A row comparison.

DATA AND INTERPRETATION

The images are discussed in the order in which they figure in the hypotheses. This leads first to a discussion of the middle class images (where the distinction between the moral validity and the legitimacy of norms is involved in an effort to account for the findings). The remaining images are discussed in clusters bearing upon particular hypotheses and interpretations suggested by regularities in the data.

Middle Class Images. Of forty-five differences between the six populations in evaluation of the middle class images, only two were significant (see Tables III and IV. Both Negro lower class and white lower class boys evaluated GRAD higher than did white gang boys, in both instances at the .05 level. This is almost precisely the number of significant findings out of forty-five totally independent tests (which these are not) to be expected at this level on the basis of chance alone. In view of the high risk of a Type I error in this statistical treatment, it is fair to describe the picture presented by these data as one of overwhelming homogeneity. *All six populations evaluated images representing salient features of a middle class style of life equally highly.*

Furthermore, no image representing the other four subcultures was evaluated significantly higher than the middle class images by any one of the six populations. Of the sixty means for non-middle class subcultural images, five were slightly higher than some of the means for middle class images. In every such instance the image involved was SHAR, standing for lower class reciprocity, an image that could not be characterized as illegitimate.

In fact, the middle class images were evaluated significantly higher by every one of the populations than nearly all other subcultural images, especially those that are unquestionably illegitimate.[23] None of the theories would have led one to expect these findings.

An explanation of the disparity between the theories and these particular data might be found in the distinction between moral validity and legitimacy. Cloward and Ohlin, for example, speak of "the legitimacy of social rules," which may be questioned by members of a socially disadvantaged population quite apart from their "moral validity." They assert that gang members no longer accord legitimacy to middle class norms because of social barriers obstructing their access to the opportunities implied by the norms.[24] Cohen, too, recognizes the importance of legitimacy when he states:

> For the child who temporizes with middle class morality, overt aggression and even the conscious recognition of his own hostile impulses are inhibited, for he acknowledges the *legitimacy* of the rules in terms of which he is stigmatized. For the child who breaks clean with middle class morality, on the other hand, there are no moral inhibitions on the free expression of aggression against the sources of his frustration.[25]

Even Miller may be responding to the legitimacy aspect of attitudes toward norms when he asserts that lower class culture is relatively autonomous. If it were true that the evaluation dimension reflects moral validity rather than legitimacy, these data would not constitute a proper test of the theories.

It seems reasonable to infer that anyone who complies with norms that lack legitimacy from the viewpoint of someone else faces the prospect of being branded a "sucker," that is, someone who is taken in and fooled by superficial appearances. This line of reasoning, coupled with Miller's assurances that "smartness," in exactly this sense, is a criterion of behavior to which lower class and gang members are sensitive, led to the "smart-sucker" scale as a measure of legitimacy.[26]

It might be argued that the "smart-sucker" scale is subject to being construed as an "intelligent-unintelligent" scale, and that since the three middle class images suggest rather cerebral types of performance, all the boys will rate these images high on smartness. On the other hand, the scale was always read aloud to the boys as part of an example of how to fill out the instrument: "Is he smart? Or is he a sucker?" Calling attention in this way to the presence of "sucker" at one end of the scale should be effective in defining its dimensionality, especially, according to to Miller, for lower class and gang boys. Since these are the boys who presumably are motivated to withhold legitimacy from such images, the combination of this motivation with their sensitivity should be

---

[23] As checked by means of the definitely significant difference (see Table III).

[24] Cloward and Ohlin, *op. cit.*, pp. 16–20, 136–37.

[25] *Op. cit.*, p. 132.

[26] This interpretation is not without its problems, for while "sucker" is pejorative it does not necessarily connote illegitimacy. It may be smart (in a "conning" sense) to do something, but for other reasons a person might be considered a sucker to do it. Our use of the smartness scale as a measure of legitimacy provides an opportunity for additional theoretical assessment with the data on the basis of the argument that is developed. (J.F.S.)

Table IV. *Images Evaluated Significantly Higher by Row Sample than by Column Sample (.05 Level or Better)*[a]

	Negro			White		
	Gang	Lower Class	Middle Class	Gang	Lower Class	Middle Class

Negro

Gang		FENC* CONN* PIMP	SJOB HANG* TUFF*** FENC* CONN* PIMP** DRUG	SHAR PIMP*** GIRL*** SELF	SJOB* FENC*** CONN*** PIMP*** DRUG* GIRL**	SJOB*** HANG*** TUFF*** FENC*** CONN*** PIMP*** GIRL***
Lower class	*IEGO* GANG** SELF*		HANG** TUFF** DRUG	GRAD SHAR* PIMP GIRL** *IEGO* *GANG* SELF***	SJOB* CONN PIMP** DRUG* GIRL* SELF	SJOB** HANG*** TUFF** CONN*** PIMP*** GIRL***
Middle class	*IEGO* GANG*** SELF**	GANG**		SHAR GIRL *IEGO* GANG*** SELF***	PIMP GIRL GANG*** SELF*	HANG CONN* PIMP** GIRL*** SELF

White

Gang			SJOB HANG* TUFF*** FENC CONN		SJOB* FENC* CONN*** PIMP	SJOB** HANG*** TUFF*** FENC* CONN*** PIMP*** COOL GIRL**
Lower class		*IEGO*	TUFF**	GRAD *IEGO*		HANG*** TUFF** STIK CONN GIRL
Middle class		IEGO*** GANG***	GANG**	*IEGO* GANG*** SELF**	GANG**	

[a] Italicized images are significant for evaluation, but not for smartness. Compare with Table VI.
* $p < .01$.
** $p < .001$.
*** $p < .0001$.

reflected in differential responses, even (or perhaps especially) if the middle class boys, lacking both the sensitivity and motivation, construe the scale as an intelligence measure.[27] Actually, there is no reason to suppose that middle class boys would not understand quite well a continuum delineated by "smart" and "sucker."

But the hypotheses placed in question by the evaluative findings enjoy only a brief respite. The smartness scores for all three middle class images for all populations are also virtually identical. Of forty-five comparisons, only one is significant; Negro middle class boys rated SAVE smarter than white lower class boys, at the .05 level (see Tables V and VI). The smartness ratings of middle class images by all populations are higher than those for any other subcultural image. Some readers may note that both gang samples rated READ noticeably lower on smartness than members of the other populations (the differences are not significant), and also that the three strata of both races were ordered for GRAD so that gang boys are lowest and middle class boys highest. However, this

[27] For a more thorough discussion of this point see American Documentation Institute, *op. cit.*, Note C.

Table V. *Smartness Means*

	Negro			White		
Images	Gang	Lower Class	Middle Class	Gang	Lower Class	Middle Class
Middle class:						
GRAD	6.35	6.61	6.58	6.43	6.54	6.66
READ	6.03	6.22	6.21	6.07	6.27	6.22
SAVE	6.37	6.49	6.67	6.55	6.03	6.29
Lower class:						
SJOB	4.99	4.70	4.17	4.69	4.30	4.10
HANG	4.34	3.99	3.17	4.40	4.14	2.61
SHAR	4.59	4.72	3.12	3.97	3.54	4.12
Conflict:						
TUFF	4.15	4.03	3.21	4.79	3.86	3.27
STIK	5.20	5.51	4.96	5.64	5.46	4.98
Criminal:						
FENC	4.99	4.38	3.75	4.98	3.24	3.15
CONN	5.75	5.33	4.96	5.71	3.70	3.80
Retreatist:						
PIMP	4.39	3.57	3.62	3.69	2.08	1.61
DRUG	2.37	2.04	1.17	1.93	1.19	1.15
COOL	5.63	5.26	4.12	5.90	4.54	3.76
Additional:						
GIRL	6.08	5.59	5.75	5.24	4.46	3.83
IEGO	6.21	6.45	6.33	6.64	6.43	6.76
GANG	5.58	5.71	6.00	5.40	5.43	6.05
SELF	5.79	5.49	5.75	5.14	5.14	5.63
LSD:[a]						
p = .05	0.20	0.14	0.11	0.24	0.22	0.13
DSD:						
p = .05	0.54	0.84	1.69	0.93	1.27	1.08
p = .01	0.72	1.12	2.29	1.23	1.71	1.44

[a] For each column lowest significant differences (LSD) are such that any lower are not significant; definitely significant differences (DSD) are such that any equal or higher are significant at the given level.

Table VI. *Images Rated Significantly Smarter by Row Sample than by Column Sample (.05 Lever or Better)*[a]

		Negro			White	
	Gang	Lower Class	Middle Class	Gang	Lower Class	Middle Class
Negro						
Gang		PIMP* *GIRL*	SJOB* HANG** SHAR*** TUFF* FENC DRUG*** COOL**	SHAR PIMP GIRL* SELF*	SJOB* SHAR* FENC*** CONN*** PIMP*** DRUG*** COOL* GIRL*** SELF*	SJOB** HANG*** TUFF* FENC*** CONN*** PIMP*** DRUG*** COOL*** GIRL***
Lower class			HANG SHAR*** TUFF DRUG*** COOL*	SHAR	SHAR* FENC CONN** PIMP*** DRUG** GIRL*	SJOB HANG*** TUFF FENC* CONN PIMP*** DRUG*** COOL***
Middle class				GANG SELF	*SAVE* *CONN* PIMP* GIRL* *GANG* *SELF*	GIRL*** CONN PIMP*** GIRL***
White						
Gang	TUFF IEGO*	*TUFF* *COOL*	HANG* SHAR TUFF*** STIK FENC DRUG* COOL***		*TUFF* FENC** CONN*** PIMP*** DRUG* COOL**	SJOB HANG*** TUFF*** *STIK* FENC*** CONN*** PIMP*** DRUG*
Lower class			HANG			COOL*** HANG***
Middle class	IEGO*** GANG*	*IEGO* *GANG*	SHAR	GANG* SELF	*IEGO* GANG* *SELF*	

[a] Italicized images are significant for smartness, but not for evaluation. Compare with Table IV.
* $p < .01$.
** $p < .001$.
*** $p < .0001$.

ordering is offset by the fact that both gang samples rated the third image, SAVE, higher than the white middle class boys. While slightly suggestive, this evidence falls short of the dramatic differences that the Cloward-Ohlin theory would seem to require, especially in view of the absolutely high ratings of these images as compared to the deviant images for all six populations. On the basis of significance tests, one must conclude that there is evidence of neither differential nor low legitimation of the behaviors represented by the middle class images by any population.

A sharp difference is to be noted between the smartness ratings, for all populations, of SHAR and SAVE; this difference was *not* reflected in the evaluation scores. All populations feel that it is much smarter to save than to share, while five out of six evaluated SHAR higher than SAVE. (All six smartness differences between SHAR and SAVE are significant at the .0001 level.) Smartness is thus a more sensitive indicator than evaluation of behavior that a person would actually endorse after a realistic appraisal of its material consequences and the justice of its attendant social expectations. Hence its use as a measure of legitimacy in the sense intended by Cloward and Ohlin appears to be justified. Intuitively, it would seem that if the smartness score registers the difference in utility of the behaviors represented by SAVE and SHAR, it should also reflect any tendency by gang boys to view the middle class behaviors as deficient in utility.

Hypotheses 1 through 4 are not supported by these data. And even when "legitimate" is substituted for "evaluate" in these hypotheses, they are still not supported by data based on "smartness" as a measure of legitimacy.

Lower Class Images. Hypotheses 5, 6, and 7 all deal with lower class images. Contrary to hypothesis 5, neither white nor Negro gang boys evaluated SHAR and HANG higher than middle class images. Contrary to hypothesis 6, neither gang nor lower class boys evaluated any of the lower class images significantly higher than any of the middle class images.

Before interpreting these results, the relevant row comparisons for hypothesis 7, involving SHAR, SJOB, and HANG, must be considered. The evaluation means for SHAR show no interpretable pattern (although all Negro samples evaluated sharing significantly higher than white gang boys). However, both gang samples evaluated SJOB and HANG significantly higher than both middle class samples; both lower class samples evaluated HANG significantly higher than their racially matched middle class sample; and the Negro lower class evaluated both SJOB and HANG significantly higher than the white middle class.

Joined with the patterns of these data, these significant findings strongly support hypothesis 7, derived from Miller. In effect, this supports Miller's general contention that the values of the lower class are distinguishable from those of the middle class. The failure of hypotheses 5 and 6 suggests that these differences are based more heavily on attitudes toward lower class norms than on those toward middle class norms.

These findings suggest that the idea of sharing money with friends taps a set of normative expectations that is more nearly universal than those associated with work and leisure, so that SHAR differentiates the samples only when the smartness scores, raising considerations of legitimacy or practicality, are inspected. As a matter of general interest, attention is called to the fact that gang boys of both races—together with Negro lower class boys—evaluated and legitimated higher than anyone else the idea of having a humble job in a gasoline station.

The Nature of the Remaining Images. The remaining subcultural images (plus GIRL) were chosen to represent behaviors that the theories hypothesize as deviant alternatives to a respectable style of life, either middle class or lower class. Not all of these behaviors are technically illegal or necessarily indicative of antisocial intent. The behavior described by COOL and STIK is intrinsically innocuous, and in the latter case even commendable. TUFF and GIRL, if perhaps more clearly at variance with middle class codes, nevertheless entail no necessary legal violation. And DRUG suggests behavior that, although illegal, is often more self-injurious than harmful to others. As a result, although the images were employed principally to aid in the identification of delinquent subcultures among gangs, they also represent points in what might be regarded—from a middle class standpoint—as the middle and lower ranges of an evaluative continuum. It is in this range of such a continuum that the most striking differences between samples appear.

Some Consistent Racial Differences and Masculinity. Inspection of the main diagonal of the upper right quadrant (which compares the races holding social level relatively constant) of Table IV discloses three images that Negro boys evaluated significantly higher than white boys within each one of the three social levels. These images are PIMP, GIRL, and SELF. The consistent reappearance of this constellation is slightly suggestive of a narcisic syndrome among Negro adolescent males. That two of these images figure in the sex-identity hypothesis supplements rather than precludes this possible interpretation. However, the higher evaluation of SELF by Negroes (GANG follows the same pattern) could also be a defense against low racial self-esteem, such as was recently suggested by James W. Vander Zanden.[28] Sexual self-indulgence, narcism, and defensive self-esteem all tend to shade into one another, and to disentangle these concepts would require more discriminating measures. Although tentative, such interpretations are of interest, however, in view of E. Franklin Frazier's description of Negro middle class males as tending to "cultivate their 'personalities,'" a phrase suggestive of narcisic concern, and evidence that Negroes spend more for food, clothing, and automobiles than whites at the same income level.[29] Negro consumer habits are apt to be attributed to their lack of other economic outlets and status-seeking, but it may be that such behavior reflects a deeper and more pervasive kind of self-indulgence (perhaps also compensatory) that manifests itself also in non-economic behavior.

Frazier's observations are especially reassuring concerning findings, for example, for PIMP and GIRL, that show the Negro middle class to be deviant in some respects from the white middle class and perhaps even from white gang boys. Although hypothesis 8 predicted such results between the two middle class samples, the magnitude of the differences at first aroused strong misgivings as to the representativeness of the Negro middle class sample.

Nevertheless, the data are consistent with other information indicating that these Negro middle class boys were definitely active sexually. Their sexual success is easy to account for in view of their strong competitive position, based on polish, money, and cars, and the sexual permissiveness of Negro lower class girls. Probably, it is difficult for Negro middle class girls to compete under these conditions without becoming themselves sexually accessible.

An impression of the sexual activity of these boys can be gained from an incident which occurred after one of the testing sessions. One boy raised his hand politely to inquire whether they could now ask the testers some questions. Anticipating curiosity about the tests, the tester invited

---

[28] See his "The Non-violent Resistance Movement against Segregation," *American Journal of Sociology*, LXVIII (1963), 544–50, and the literature cited there.

[29] See *Black Bourgeoisie* (Glencoe: The Free Press, 1957), p. 220. On the Negro consumer see, e.g., "The Negro Market," *Time*, February 9, 1962, pp. 80–81.

any questions the boys might wish to pose. The first question, put with sincere concern, was "If you do it (sexual intercourse) too much, is it true that you give out young?" The question drew little laughter.

Final doubts concerning the possible representativeness of this sample were then erased by Frazier, whose description of the Negro middle class emphasizes mediocre aspirations (the boys spoke of being physical education teachers, not doctors or lawyers), overcommitment to material satisfactions (they dressed extremely well, and arrived driving their own family cars), sexual promiscuity (already indicated), and involvement in recreation (one admitted, all *we* do is party").[30] Everything pictured by Frazier seems to fit, even down to the fact that the two clubs to which these boys belonged were the only groups to refer to themselves by Greek-letter names and to order "pledges" around in a semi-autocratic manner.

In interpreting the racial differences, however, it must be kept in mind that the Negroes in each social category really are socioeconomically lower than the whites in the corresponding category (see Table V).

Turning to the sex-identity hypothesis proper, all the various predictions from that compound hypothesis hold for the evaluative patterns of PIMP and GIRL; most of them are statistically significant as well. Furthermore, the mean scores for these two images display similar gradients, running from left to right across all six populations in Table III. In each case Negro gang boys are highest, each succeeding sample being lower until white middle class boys appear as the lowest. Both race and social level thus produce differences in the evaluation of PIMP and GIRL that accord with the sex-identity hypothesis; quite unexpected, however, is the finding that at every social level the Negro boys evaluated these two images higher than *any* sample of white boys.

With slight exceptions, the pattern for smartness of these two images is much the same. One noteworthy change is that non-gang Negro boys drop slightly below white gang boys in the legitimation of PIMP; since this places all non-gang boys now lower than all gang boys it suggests that the non-gang Negroes have reservations about pimping and illegal "hustling" that are not reflected in their evaluation of PIMP.

The third image included in the masculinity hypothesis was TUFF. This image was evaluated significantly higher by gang and lower class boys of both races than by either of the middle class samples. Within each stratum, the whites were higher, although not significantly so. This is contrary to the expectation stated in hypothesis 8 that the Negroes would evaluate TUFF higher at each social level, as they did PIMP and GIRL. However, since both gang samples also evaluated TUFF higher than did their racially matched lower class samples—although not significantly—the strata are ordered in accordance with the hypothesis. The smartness ratings produced a similar ordering of strata, but no sign of consistently higher ratings by Negroes. In fact, white gang boys legitimated TUFF significantly higher than Negro gang boys; this is the only instance in which a deviant image received a significantly higher rating from white gang boys than from Negro gang boys.

While it is felt that the preponderance of this evidence is consistent with the hypothesis dealing with problems of sex identity (though by no means proving it), the failure of TUFF to parallel the differences for race exhibited by PIMP and GIRL is puzzling. Whether sex identity or simply subcultural norms are responsible, these results suggest a degree of independence between attitudes toward the sexual and the aggressive expression of masculinity.[31] (It is interesting to note that between

---

[30] *Op. cit.*

[31] A plausible case for race differences in sexual permissiveness may be derived from the comparison of sex norms as described for Negro gang boys and

PIMP and TUFF, Negro gang boys favor PIMP, whereas white gang boys significantly favor TUFF at the .0001 level for evaluation and the .01 level for smartness.) Vander Zanden has also called attention to the historical necessity for Negroes to suppress aggression; possibly this accounts for the fact that for TUFF five out of six comparisons of evaluation and smartness means, within stratum, show Negroes lower than whites, despite the tendency for Negroes to be generally more tolerant than whites toward the other deviant images.[32]

The Narcotics Image. Of all images, DRUG received the lowest evaluation from both gang samples, and the lowest legitimation from everyone. (Both lower strata Negro samples evaluated DRUG significantly higher than Negro middle class and white lower class boys, and both gang samples and the Negro lower class legitimated it significantly higher than all three remaining populations.)

In view of the consistently low tolerance shown toward most other deviant images by the white middle class, their evaluation of DRUG seems rather high compared to the Negro middle class and the white lower class. However, these three samples are virtually identical in rejecting DRUG's legitimacy; here, the white middle class accords it the lowest smartness score in the entire table. Personal knowledge gained in working with the white middle class boys suggest that their relatively higher evaluation score may be a reflection of sophisticated compassion. If so, this provides another indication of meaningful independence between the two scores.

Criminal Images, Utility, and Legitimacy. The two images representing the criminal subculture were FENC and CONN. With minor imperfections, both of these images manifest a gradient that appears repeatedly among the deviant images for both evaluation and smartness: Gang > Lower Class > Middle Class. (Perfect examples of this gradient may be noted for PIMP, GIRL, and COOL.) Negro gang boys evaluated FENC and CONN significantly higher than all four non-gang samples; white gang boys evaluated them higher than all non-gang boys except those in the Negro lower class. Both gang samples, and the Negro lower class, legitimated FENC and CONN significantly higher than the non-gang whites. The Negro middle class evaluated and legitimated CONN significantly higher than the white middle class.

The two criminal images are among those that differentiate gang boys from lower class boys: PIMP, FENC, and CONN for both races and, in addition, SJOB for whites. The gang and lower class Negroes both evaluated SJOB at virtually the same high level. These four images have in common a utilitarian emphasis, indicating that the role of material gain in the values of gang boys is by no means negligible. That gang members do not repudiate the possibility of legitimate gain is indicated by the presence of SJOB. The prominence of the illegitimately gainful images suggests, however, that a choice between legal and illegal means is determined to a lesser degree in favor of legal means for gang boys than for lower class boys.

It can be shown, too, that the consideration of legitimacy or practicality appears even more conducive than that of evaluation to a choice of illegal means, especially for gang boys. For example, all six samples *evaluated* SJOB significantly higher than FENC (each at the .0001 level). However, only the non-gang whites *legitimated* SJOB significantly higher than FENC (white lower class, .01; white middle class, .02), while Negro gang boys now tied the two images,

---

the Negro middle class, on the one hand, and the white lower class, on the other. For Negro gang boys see Chapter 2. For the Negro middle class see Frazier, *op. cit.* For somewhat dated accounts of the white lower class as contrasted with the white middle class see William Foote Whyte, "A Slum Sex Code," *American Journal of Sociology*, XLIX (1943), 24–31, and Arnold W. Green, "The 'Cult of Personality' and Sexual Relations," *Psychiatry*, IV (1941), 343–48.

[32] *Op. cit.*, pp. 545–46.

and white gang boys legitimated FENC higher than SJOB.

A similarly revealing comparison concerns SJOB and CONN. SJOB was evaluated significantly higher than CONN by all four non-gang samples (Negro and white lower class, .01; Negro middle class, .05; white middle class, .001), and the gang samples showed the same tendency. However, except for the non-gang whites, all samples legitimated SJOB and CONN in reverse order, with both gang samples now rating CONN significantly higher than SJOB (Negro gang, .0001; white gang, .001; and Negro lower class, .10).

Not only the respectable image, SJOB, declines relative to criminal images when the basis of comparison is shifted to smartness. The conflict image, TUFF, follows the same pattern, thus indicating that it is not respectability per se that is the determinant, but rather differential practicality or utility. All samples evaluated TUFF higher than FENC; for the four lower strata these differences are significant (Negro and white lower class and white gang, .0001; Negro gang, .01). This order of the images is reversed for smartness by all but the non-gang whites, with the Negro gang sample now attaining significance (.001) in the new direction.

These last findings corroborate the importance that Miller attaches to smartness and Cloward and Ohlin to legitimacy. In some respects, however, they are not fully congruent with the expectations generated by these theorists. The tendency for smartness to rearrange the orderings of images for the Negro middle class, but not for the white lower class—in the examples given above—is not consistent with Miller's locating the salience of this dimension chiefly in the lower class. And the finding that gang boys grant greater legitimacy to deviant images, while not withdrawing legitimacy from middle class images, does not accord with Cloward and Ohlin's emphasis on middle class norms as sensitive to considerations of legitimacy. Their contention would now seem to apply to middle class proscriptive norms, but not to middle class prescriptive norms.

A quick review of the statistical findings and patterns for deviant images will indicate that hypotheses 9 and 10 are supported, and in this respect all three theories are correct. However, where none of the theories specified differences between each possible pairing of the three social levels, these data strongly indicate a gradient for attitudes toward deviant behaviors, such that the acceptability of these behaviors is inversely related to social level.

Another Gradient. The images GANG, SELF, and IEGO display a social level gradient opposite to that for deviant images; the higher the level, the more highly these three images are evaluated (see Tables 3.4 and 3.6 for significance levels). For the image GANG, this trend suggests that the gang is not the close-knit, highly cohesive entity which some might expect.[33] Conceivably, the trend for IEGO reflects superego strength.

The images SELF and IEGO serve to indicate the direction of preference for these scores, thus ruling out the possibility that gang boys completely invert the evaluative dimension while continuing to describe behavior verbally much as middle class people might. All six samples wanted to be significantly better (Negro middle class, .001; all others, .0001) and smarter (Negro gang, .01; Negro middle class, .10; all others, .001) than they usually are. An analysis of the five individual evaluative scales for seventeen of the groups making up the total sample showed this directionality for SELF and IEGO to prevail throughout, with the scale "good-bad" always contributing its proportionate share of the gain within each of the six samples.

---

[33] Yablonsky has also called into question the cohesiveness of gangs (see Lewis Yablonsky, "The Delinquent Gang as a Near-Group," *Social Problems*, VII [Fall, 1959], 108–17).

DISCUSSION

The finding that delinquent boys order behaviors as to their goodness much the same as do non-delinquents is not new, having been demonstrated as early as 1940 by Ruth Bishop.[34] Although Bishop was able to show that both delinquent and non-delinquent populations divide good from bad behaviors at the same neutral point, her technique leaves one in doubt as to whether her data reflect the affective preferences of her populations or merely their equal ability to perform a cognitive judgment task.[35]

Osgood, however, has come to the conclusion after years of experience that semantic differential responses have an affective character, apparently coinciding in dimensionality with universal dimensions of affective meaning applicable to all sensory modalities. He also feels that these dimensions typify ways in which people respond or react to their environment, rather than ways in which they receive and organize incoming stimuli.[36] This would seem to imply a greater relevance for behavior than if semantic differential responses merely recorded the passive categorizing of external stimuli. In addition, the global connotative richness of the five evaluative scales, the direction of the differences between IEGO and SELF, and the fact that for college students rating Morris' "ways to live" on a semantic differential, the correlation between a heavily evaluative factor and perference was .66 for individual scores and .93 for group means [37]

—all indicate strongly that evaluation and preference are closely related.

Although such considerations do much to clarify the meaning of the observed responses, it is nevertheless difficult to comprehend their full significance until the data are tied into a complex net of additional evidence. For despite the specificity of the images, the behaviors they represent were necessarily judged entirely apart from the contexts in which they are normally encountered by members of the six populations. The responses, therefore, must be viewed as having an "in principle" quality,[38] which, from the standpoint of assessing values, is not at all inappropriate, although it does imply that the information so obtained may be seriously incomplete for the purpose of explaining behavior. For example, some of the populations may view their own *real* school experiences in a highly unfavorable light, for a variety of both objective and subjective reasons, and yet maintain an essentially positive attitude toward the idea of education in general. This does not imply that it is any less important to know what these more abstract attitudes are.

The data imply that acceptance of middle class prescriptive norms (the middle class images) is quite general, while middle class proscriptive norms (the deviant images) either decline in force or are rejected more strongly as social level goes down. The former alternative suggests a weakening of inhibitory mechanisms as social level declines, perhaps ultimately traceable to a superego construct, such as was suggested by the IEGO gradient for evaluation. The latter alternative, or rejection, raises somewhat more strongly the possibility of a "rationally" motivated

---

[34] "Points of Neutrality in Social Attitudes of Delinquents and Non-Delinquents," *Psychometrika*, V (1940), 35–45.

[35] The ambiguities involved in making this determination are discussed by Warren S. Torgerson, *Theory and Methods of Scaling* (New York: John Wiley & Sons, 1958), pp. 48–49.

[36] Charles E. Osgood, "Studies on the Generality of Affective Meaning Systems," *American Psychologist*, XVII (January, 1962), 10–28.

[37] Charles E. Osgood, Edward E. Ware, and Charles Morris, "Analysis of the Connotative Meanings of a Variety of Human Values as Ex-

pressed by American College Students," *Journal of Abnormal and Social Psychology*, LXII (1961), 62–3.

[38] This "in principle" quality corresponds to the idea of "potential demand" in values as used by Cyril S. Belshaw, who elaborates further its implications for behavior ("The Identification of Values in Anthropology," *American Journal of Sociology*, LXIV [1959], 555–62).

choice, as indicated by the sensitivity of the images CONN and FENC to the practical emphasis of smartness for gang boys. The two alternatives need not be mutually exclusive.

In any case, the delicacy of the prescriptive-proscriptive balance achieved in their evaluations by gang boys raises the question of whether it indicates ambivalence toward middle class culture as a whole of the sort claimed by Cohen. Certainly, that would be a plausible interpretation. However, given that the hypothesis of reaction formation does not seem to be supported,[39] and that ambivalence can be said to exist whenever competing alternatives are present, the concept of ambivalence by itself lacks explanatory force.

In addition, it remains to be demonstrated that gang boys perceive legitimate and illegitimate behaviors as being in some sense mutually exclusive, so that a choice of one has strong implications for their realization of the other. Without such a demonstration, even equal evaluation of both kinds of behavior would not constitute sufficient evidence for ambivalence.

The implication in these data that gang boys evaluate highest behavior that appears as remote from their actual conduct as that depicted by GRAD, READ, and SAVE will undoubtedly strike many persons as an absurdity. Certainly, if the finding is valid, three separate theoretical formulations failed to make sufficient allowance for the meaningfulness of middle class values to members of gangs. To others, the apparent pervasiveness of middle class values in American life may come as no surprise; Cloward and Ohlin, it will be recalled, actually postulated that gang boys share middle class consumption values, although, contrary to this chapter's indications, they also held that middle class norms are not legitimated by gang boys.

Miller has given reason to believe that he would dismiss these findings as indicative merely of "official" ideals.[40]

A number of points, bearing also on the more general problem of accounting for the disparity between theories and these findings, can be made in response to such a criticism. For one thing, the allegation that gang boys mirror official ideals in their responses is consistent neither with the finding that they rated images which are highly deviant, such as PIMP, significantly higher than non-gang boys, nor with the social-level gradients for deviant images.

A second point concerns both the role of values in social theory and the methodology by means of which values are identified. Unless it is to be seriously maintained that values strictly determine behavior, or vice versa, one must be prepared for findings such as these. The discrepancy between these findings and the values reported for lower class culture (with respect to middle class values) by Miller may be related to his anthropological methodology. The anthropologist often assesses values by inferring them from extended observation of a population's spontaneous behavior, including verbal behavior. Since Miller has described the focal concerns as more readily derivable from direct observation than values, and also reflecting "actual behavior," it follows that this was also his method.[41]

When studying an entire primitive society in this way one can be fairly certain of having witnessed the full range of behavior that members of that society hold in high regard, given the relatively constant constraints of the physical environment. However, when this method is applied to subcultures contained within a single society, it is apt to lead to fallacious results; for, in such an instance, the values of the populations studied can never be reported as other than those implied by their behavior.

---

[39] For other evidence against the reaction formation hypothesis see Albert J. Reiss, Jr., and Albert Lewis Rhodes, "Delinquency and Social Class Structure," *American Sociological Review*, XXVI (1961), p. 729.

[40] *Op. cit.*, p. 7.
[41] *Ibid.*

Within a complex society, the existence of a differentiated segment of population may result from the operation of processes that constrain behavior in ways independent of, and in addition to, the constraints imposed by the values of that particular segment's members. To deny this is to favor an overly simple model of society. Such constraining processes can be either external or internal to a subculture. The limitation on opportunity that the larger society imposes or certain minority groups would be an example, from the Merton tradition, of an external constraint. The hypothesized female-dominated household would be an internal constraint. This hypothesis asserts that within lower class culture there exists a self-maintaining process that leads males to behave in self-defeating ways; this, in turn implies the frustration of tendencies to behave in ways that may actually be held in high regard.

Not even the anthropologist's use of verbal behavior, especially public or spontaneous verbal behavior, is free from this criticism if it is granted that what members of a subculture verbalize may itself reflect or even constitute a basis for their being differentiated from the larger population, despite their own deepest preferences. This criticism gains plausibility when it is noted that behaviors readily available to gang and lower class members and hence visible to the anthropologist, such as criminality, promiscuity, and pimping, are ones upon which Miller and the semantic differential are in accord; behaviors whose realization may be limited for lower class persons—as represented by the middle class images—are ones over which Miller and the semantic differential disagree.

In view of the unexpected nature of some of these findings, additional efforts to test their validity are being undertaken. If they are valid, the interpretations that may prove most important to the refinement of delinquency theory are the following: (1) For all six populations, the endorsement "in principle" of middle class prescriptive norms is uniformly high. (2) Gang, lower class, and middle class boys differ most in their attitudes toward behaviors proscribed by the middle class, and they tend to be ordered as listed with respect to their tolerance toward these behaviors. (3) Legitimacy or practicality as measured by a "smart-sucker" scale, seems to be a meaningful basis for distinguishing behavior. There is some evidence that gang boys, more than older boys, may be led by this distinction to a choice of criminal behavior over legitimately gainful behavior. (4) The hypothesis of a sex-identity problem for lower class and gang boys appears worth pursuing further.

Since these interpretations are not derived from true probability samples, it will be necessary for readers to employ discretion in applying them to other universes. A consideration of the degree to which other universes might reasonably be expected to differ in these respects from this chapter's samples should be of some guidance.

It is anticipated that the implications of these findings will be better understood if their further development is deferred until other relevant data have been analyzed.

34. DIMENSIONS OF CURRENT GANG DELINQUENCY

THOMAS M. GANNON

IT HAS OFTEN BEEN OBSERVED THAT THE gang of today is not like the gang of yesterday. The factual and mythical exploits described in Asbury's *The Gangs of New York* as well as the intriguing "natural histories" compiled by the "Chicago school"—Shaw, McKay, Thrasher, et al.—give accounts of gang behavior that differ in important respects from delinquency as it has been hypothesized to exist today.[1] Recent literature has focused on the "specialization" of current delinquent activity, the heightened use of lethal weapons in group conflict, and the emergence of more "retreatist" characteristics of gang life, especially the use of narcotics. Theoretically, delinquency is seen as rooted less in community tradition and "fun," and more in frustration and protest or even in the serious business of achieving manhood.[2] There also appears to be a decline in large-scale gang conflict, the splintering of highly organized gangs into smaller cliques, and increased social skills and aspirations among many of the individuals involved in these groups.

The present research into the types of groups serviced by the street club workers of the New York City Youth Board found evidence of the beginnings of a more sophisticated type of delinquent group. The structure of these groups has been taking shape almost imperceptibly over the past several years in New York City and deserves explicit recognition and closer observation. The following analysis is based on a participant observation and questionnaire study of the Youth Board's

▶SOURCE: *"Dimensions of Current Gang Delinquency,"* Journal of Research in Crime and Delinquency *(January, 1967) 4:2:119–131. Reprinted by permission.*

---

[1] Herbert Asbury, *The Gangs of New York* (New York: Alfred A. Knopf, 1927); Clifford R. Shaw, *The Jack Roller* (Chicago: University of Chicago Press, 1930); Clifford R. Shaw and Maurice E. Moore, *The Natural History of a Delinquent Career* (Chicago: University of Chicago Press, 1931); Clifford R. Shaw and Henry D. McKay, *Juvenile Delinquency and Urban Areas* (Chicago: University of Chicago Press, 1956); Frederic M. Thrasher, *The Gang* (Chicago: University of Chicago Press, 1936); cf. James F. Short, Jr. and Fred L. Strodtbeck, *Group Process and Gang Delinquency* (Chicago: University of Chicago Press, 1966), pp. 77–78.

[2] Albert K. Cohen, *Delinquent Boys: The Culture of the Gang* (New York: Free Press, 1955); Albert K. Cohen and James F. Short, Jr., "Research in Delinquent Subcultures," *Journal of Social Issues*, July 1958, pp. 20–37; Richard A. Cloward and Lloyd E. Ohlin, *Delinquency and Opportunity* (New York: Free Press, 1960); Walter B. Miller, "Lower Class Culture as a Generating Milieu of Gang Delinquency," *Journal of Social Issues*, July 1958, pp. 5–19; David J. Bordua, "Some Comments on Theories of Group Delinquency," *Sociological Inquiry*, Spring 1962, pp. 245–60; Gilbert Geis, *Juvenile Gangs* (Washington, D.C.: President's Committee on Juvenile Delinquency, 1965).

street club project, the Council of Social and Athletic Clubs (CSAC).[3]

Questionnaires were sent to the entire CSAC staff; the personal interviews were used more as interpretative aids than as statistical data for the study. Specifically, over half the unit offices (55 percent) were visited with concentration, and a third (33.6 percent) of the workers were interviewed at length and accompanied on the job. Eighty of the 11 workers returned the questionnaire (72 percent), and it is on these returns that the statistical findings are based.

To reconcile the various theoretical viewpoints on gang delinquency would require greater precision than the present study could attempt to obtain. Consequently, the different aspects of deviance analyzed have been grouped under the term "gang delinquency," avoiding for the moment the knotty problem of specifying the nature of subcultural or "contracultural" delinquency or the problem of defining delinquent subculture.[4] For our purposes, it seems more important to delineate the broad structure and function of the groups now serviced by the Youth Board.

Gathering data entirely from the street workers has certain limitations. Kobrin has clearly indicated the value and unique contribution such data can have for sociological analysis. Nevertheless, from the viewpoint of the individual worker, it is easy to arrive at many misconceptions of the type of group the agency services, since he sees only a selected number of groups and their activity cannot be as easily defined in its natural environment as it might in a more controlled setting. In the end we would agree with Kobrin that "fruitful observation of such groups is possible only when the observer is accepted by the subjects in a role which they perceive as meaningful in relation to their needs and problems."[5]

Altogether, the eighty street workers who responded to the questionnaire serviced 113 groups directly and 109 groups indirectly. Over two-thirds of the street workers (66.3 percent) serviced one group directly, whereas twenty-seven were assigned to two or three direct-service groups. Over two-fifths of the workers (46.3 percent) provided indirect service to one group, one-fifth (21.3 percent) to two groups, and 13.7 percent to three or more groups. For practical purposes, indirect service means that the Youth Board worker keeps aware of the general activities of certain groups that are known to him, especially if these activities might involve conflict with his or another group. These boys may or may not participate in the worker's programs. Only one-fifth of the street workers today operate on a one-to-one relationship with a single delinquent group. In summary, the Youth Board is currently in contact with over 3,100 boys in the high delinquency areas of New York.

STRUCTURE AND ORGANIZATION OF THE GROUP

Traditionally, the Youth Board has distinguished four types of adolescent groups with which it has come into contact.

(1) The *corner group* develops in a particular spot; its members usually grow up together and continue to hang around as a group, talking or engaging in some joint

---

[3] The present investigation is part of a larger study of the changing role of street work and was undertaken while the author was a Research Associate with the New York City Youth Board. Appreciation is due Maude M. Craig and Mary Koval for their active support and critical suggestions during the course of the study, and to Erminie C. Lacey for tabulating the statistical data.

[4] Robert K. Merton, "The Socio-Cultural Environment and Anomie," *New Perspectives for Research on Juvenile Delinquency*, Helen L. Witmer and Ruth Kotinsky, eds. (Washington, D.C.: U.S. Children's Bureau, 1956).

[5] Solomon Kobrin, "Sociological Aspects of the Development of a Street Corner Group: an Exploratory Study," *American Journal of Orthopsychiatry*, October 1961, p. 685. See also, Short and Strodtbeck, *op. cit. supra* note 1, pp. 8–10.

activity. Together they normally display little antisocial behavior.

(2) The *social club* almost always organizes around some common interest (e.g. baseball, basketball, jazz) and, like the corner group, is seldom involved in any serious group delinquency.

(3) The *conflict group* might begin either as a corner or social group, but becomes involved in serious conflict with other groups. This conflict may be due to the need for protection or the desire for aggression. As a rule the group has weapons and an organizational structure designed for conflict.

(4) The *thoroughly delinquent and pathological group,* totally committed to continuous violent activity,[6] resembles what Short has called the "hustling" group organized for the purpose of economic gain through nonlegitimate means, or Cloward and Ohlin's "criminal gang" whose primary activities are centered around rational, systematic, economically-motivated criminal activity.[7]

The Youth Board has been mainly concerned with the third type of adolescent group. Fighting potential varies not only in degree from one gang to another, but also in the form of conflict. An aggressive gang is involved in considerable initiation of conflict with rival gangs and in reputation- and status-seeking. A defensive group, on the other hand, seeks to maintain its identity without initiating conflict with other groups. It will usually prefer to settle provocations through peaceful means and to employ violent retaliation for only the most severe attack. Even this retaliation will often be carried on without weapons and may be followed by increased self-isolation from other gangs in the community.

This distinction between aggressive (or "fighting") gangs and defensive gangs became important in the present study when we inquired into the types of groups presently receiving street service.[8] As Table I indicates, over half the workers (53.8 percent) would describe their groups as defensive, less than one-sixth (15.0 percent) as fighting gangs, and almost one-third (31.2 percent) as corner-social. These findings substantiate those of the 1964 survey of the CSAC which found that the groups serviced by the street workers were organized and structured to meet needs other than aggression.[9] All aggressive behavior is certainly not absent in the defensive, corner, and social groups, but fighting does not constitute their main activity.

Table I. *Distribution by Type of Groups Serviced by Youth Board*

Type of Group	Number	Percent
Defensive	43	53.8
Fighting	12	15.0
Corner	18	22.5
Social	7	8.7
Total	80	100.0

Probing further the structure of the gangs, we find almost all of the workers (88.8 percent) reporting that the distinction between "core" and "peripheral" membership was still valid for their groups and most indicated that the groups have splintered into smaller cliques numbering from three to fifteen members. These cliques are usually part of a larger, more

---

[6] New York City Youth Board, *Reaching the Fighting Gang,* (New York: New York City Youth Board, 1960), pp. 14–16.

[7] J. F. Short, Jr., introduction to the abridged version of Thrasher, *op. cit. supra* note 1, p. xlvi; also Cloward and Ohlin, *op. cit. supra* note 2, p. 20.

[8] For a development of this distinction, see Thomas M. Gannon, S. J., "Emergence of the 'Defensive' Gang," *Federal Probation,* December 1966, pp. 44–48.

[9] Elliott Bovelle, George Beschner, James Norton, and Robert Rothenberg, eds., *Survey of the Street Club Project* (Research Report, New York City Youth Board, 1964), pp. 13–14.

Table II. *Ethnic Composition of the Groups**

Ethnic Composition	Number	Percent
Puerto Rican	29	36.2
Negro	28	35.0
Negro and Puerto Rican	10	12.5
White	9	11.3
Negro and White	2	2.5
Puerto Rican and White	2	2.5
Total	80	100.0

* The boys range in age from thirteen to nineteen years, with the lower limit for the defensive gang closer to fifteen years of age. As indicated in Table 2, most of these groups (over four-fifths) are either Negro, Puerto Rican, or a combination of the two.

loosely organized group of about thirty-five boys of which 28.0 percent are core members.

Over one-third of the workers (36.4 percent) reported a relatively strong leadership in their groups, with a president, titles, and division of labor, while 63.6 percent reported an informal leadership structure. Approximately one-half (53.3 percent) indicated a significant relationship to some older or other group, with 40 percent relating to an older group, 13.3 percent to another group. Twenty-three percent of the workers felt that their groups could be structurally classified as independent, self-contained units; 24 percent said that their groups had splintered into smaller cliques with only a loose relationship to other groups. In terms of general group cohesion, however, more than half the workers (54.5 percent) would label their groups loosely knit.

Regarding educational and employment status, the members of these groups—fighting or defensive—display very similar characteristics. During the fall and winter months the workers reported that less than half their boys are in school (46.4 percent), just over one-quarter (27.4 percent) are employed; the remainder (26.4 percent) seem to do nothing. During the summer, the "do-nothing" rate increases slightly (32.4 percent); the number in school understandably drops (12.6 percent); and many more boys are employed (55.0 percent). The increased rate of summer employment probably is due to the city's push for additional summer job opportunities as well as to the Youth Board's summer "crash programs."

The number of gang boys in school is impressive. Since these figures represent youngsters who are able to remain in school, there is reason to believe that the Youth Board is no longer working only with boys who "have left school at the minimum age . . . and, who, while in school, were chronically truant." [10] However, the present findings indicate little variation in the number of those "seemingly doing nothing" reported in the 1964 CSAC survey (25 percent versus 26.6 percent). More interesting is the strong similarity (Table III) between fighting and defensive groups. The social groups represent different patterns of school attendance and employment: 68.2 percent are in school and 10.6 percent are seemingly doing nothing during the school year; 76.9 percent are employed and only 17.4 percent do nothing during the summer.

GROUP FORMATION AND MAINTENANCE

Why do youngsters join and continue to belong to these groups? In order to understand this question, the worker must be able to perceive both the uniqueness of his groups and the ways in which the group functions to satisfy the needs and solve the problems of its members. According to current theories of gang delinquency, it does not seem much fun to be a gang delinquent. Thrasher's boys enjoyed being chased by the police, shooting dice, skipping school, and rolling drunks. Miller's

---

[10] New York City Youth Board, *op. cit. supra* note 6, p. 55.

Table III. *School Attendance and Employment*

Type of Employment	Fighting Group	Defensive Group	Corner Group	Social Group	Fighting and Defensive
Winter and Fall:					
Usually employed	27.6	27.4	28.0	21.2	27.4
In school	41.9	45.1	43.3	68.2	44.4
Seemingly doing nothing	30.5	27.5	28.7	10.6	28.2
Total	100.0	100.0	100.0	100.0	100.0
Summer Months:					
Usually employed	54.5	55.3	61.3	76.9	55.0
In school	9.7	13.3	7.5	5.7	12.6
Seemingly doing nothing	35.8	31.4	31.2	17.4	32.4
Total	100.0	100.0	100.0	100.0	100.0

boys have a little fun and excitement, but it seems somewhat desperate. For Cohen, and Cloward and Ohlin, the gang boys are driven into deviance by grim economic stress, status deprivation, and psychological necessity. Individuals always try to solve their problems in a satisfactory manner; for adolescents, this often takes the form of a "group" solution. The choice of a group and its importance to the members will usually depend on the way in which they perceive its relevance to their own situation. What factors appear most relevant?

Since over two-thirds of the workers (68.4 percent) reported that there had been more than one worker assigned to the group since the Youth Board began its service, it seemed more productive to inquire why the CSAC initiated service to these groups and why the workers felt the group remains together, than to inquire when the group first formed. Most of the workers (90.9 percent) reported that their group first received service because of its history of aggressive antisocial behavior. Only 10.8 percent mentioned increased problems in the area (other than gang fighting) and 4.1 percent indicated that a growing narcotics problem brought the worker into the area. One worker reported that the group had requested a worker.

As Table IV reveals, most of the workers (93.8 percent) felt their group stayed together because they lived in the same area. The next most common (70 percent) reason given for maintaining the group was the homogeneity of problems in school, home, or in the neighborhood. This gives more empirical substance to Cohen's observation that a delinquent subculture forms as a group solution to common problems of frustration.[11] Strongly reminiscent of Thrasher's analysis, the third most common factor (68.8 percent) contributing to group maintenance was the fact that the boys are friends. The need for protection was the reason for staying together for three-fifths of the groups with similarity of interests.

Comparing the fighting and defensive groups on these items, one finds that the fighting group is more often maintained because of the need for protection, because the boys have similar problems in school, family, or neighborhood, and because an older delinquent group is attractive to them. They are less often held together by similar interests or ethnic background.

We have already mentioned the current tendency for larger groups to split into smaller cliques. Short and Strodtbeck have

---

[11] Cohen, *op. cit. supra* note 2, pp. 132–33.

Table IV. Reasons Given by Workers for Group Maintenance

Worker's Responses*	Number	Percent
Live in the same area	75	93.8
Have same problems in school, family, neighborhood, etc.	56	70.0
Are friends	55	68.8
Feel need for protection	49	61.3
Have same interests	48	60.0
Attracted by older delinquent group in the area	23	28.8
All use or experiment with narcotics	16	20.0
Want to fight	7	8.8
Other reasons (ethnic rivalry, delinquent tradition, etc.)	4	5.0

* Each worker may have one or more responses.

pointed out in their study of delinquent groups:

"Data from a large, white street-corner group without *discernible delinquency specialization* . . . also suggest that "criminal cliques" may develop within such groups. In the observed case, a clique of eight boys formed exclusively around rationally directed theft activities—auto stripping, burglary, shoplifting, etc. This clique did not hang together on the corner, but met in one another's homes. When on the corner, they hung with members of the larger groups. They participated in the general hanging and drinking patterns, and in occasional altercations with various adults as part of this larger group, but not as a *distinguishable clique. Only in their pattern of theft activities were they a clique*." [12]

Our own data indicate that over three-fourths (76 percent) of the workers have observed such clique formation. Unlike the case referred to by Short and Strodtbeck, however, these cliques formed around a number of delinquent activities: narcotics (in first place), theft (second), and illicit sex (third), with small proportions indicating drinking and gambling.

[12] Short and Strodtbeck, *op. cit. supra* note 1, p. 98.

PATTERNS OF DEVIANT BEHAVIOR

A distinction has been made between groups which the street workers service directly and those serviced indirectly. Although all the preceding statistics have referred exclusively to directly serviced groups, the distinction becomes useful when discussing patterns of deviance. Two-fifths of the workers indicated that the direct-service groups are more aggressive than the groups serviced indirectly; the same number reported lessened involvement in criminal activity; and two-thirds indicated a decrease in gang fighting in their direct-service group. Less than one-third (32.3 percent) however, considered the direct-service groups more deviant and more than one-third saw the direct service groups as more formally organized.

The majority of workers (69.3 percent) reported that the direct-service groups demanded more time and energy. This is understandable in view of the workers' assignments; most would feel that they were not doing their job properly if they devoted the same time to both types of groups. Still, one might expect that the directly serviced groups would display more reason for attention in terms of aggressiveness and overall deviance.

More specifically, how did the workers assess the group's deviance? Interviews with the workers, rather than replies to the research questionnaire, revealed that 62 percent of the workers felt drinking to be the most prominent deviant characteristic; 47.6 percent listed stealing (burglary, petty theft) in first place; only 18.4 percent specified auto theft. Experimenting with narcotics was most commonly reported (68.2 percent). (No distinction here was made between use of marijuana, glue-sniffing, "pep" pills, etc.). A much smaller number (14.3 percent) indicated that a number of group members were addicted to more serious forms of narcotics.

Thirty percent listed gambling (cards, dice, numbers) as the most common deviance; 21.8 percent, school problems (truancy, dropout, school adjustment); and 18.8 percent, illicit sex activities.

When assessing these figures, it is important to recall that no attempt was made to discover the number of boys in each group who engaged in these activities. The findings of Short and Strodtbeck concerning the incidence of certain behavior among individual gang boys review this aspect in greater detail.[13] We were interested in a more general picture of the patterns of deviance perceived by the street workers as most characteristic of their groups. From this vantage point, most of the groups appear to have significant involvement in narcotics experimentation, excessive drinking, stealing, and gambling. Parallel to this, almost all workers reported that members of their group had been arrested at some time and/or had served time in a jail or reformatory.

On the other hand, it is also important to know what kinds of relatively "constructive" behavior these groups display. In enumerating the types of social activity most often pursued by the groups, hanging around on the street (socializing, group "bull-sessions," etc.) was most frequent (87.6 percent); dating and dancing rated second (64.3 percent); sports activities were third (46.2 percent). An interesting subject for further research would be the degree to which factors of deviance and constructive activity were related within the same group, as well as the various clusters of deviance which tended to exist together in different group types.

The measure of social conflict in a community, and the amount of socially imposed frustration in achieving society's established goals and rewards, have long been viewed as significant indicators of deviance. Since all the youths serviced by the Youth Board come from neighborhoods which lack cohesiveness and unity and where transiency and instability become the over-riding features of social life, there are obvious and powerful pressures for violent behavior.[14] As Cloward and Ohlin have observed:

... an unorganized community cannot provide access to legitimate channels to success-goals, and thus discontent among the youth with their life-chances is heightened. Secondly, access to stable criminal opportunity systems is also restricted, for disorganized neighborhoods do not develop different age-levels of offender or integration of carriers of criminal and conventional values. The young, in short, are relatively deprived of *both* conventional and criminal opportunities. Finally, social controls are weak in such communities. These conditions, we believe, lead to the emergence of conflict subcultures.[15]

One cannot reasonably expect an absence of group conflict in the day-to-day street corner activities of these youths. It is more relevant, therefore, to examine the form this group conflict assumes.

Over the past year, almost three-fourths (74.7 percent) of the workers reported that their groups were involved in some conflicts with members of other groups even though there has been a parallel trend of decreasing gang fights (68.9 percent). On analysis this is found to be an average of 3.1 conflicts per group. During the same period 59 percent of the workers reported some serious intragroup conflicts (2.5 per group), and more workers (80.6 percent) reported some serious conflicts with persons other than rival gang members. A "serious" conflict was defined as a fight with weapons between two or more members of opposing or allied groups or with individuals not affiliated with a group,

---

[13] Short and Strodtbeck, *op. cit. supra* note 1, pp. 87–93.

[14] *Cf.* "Delinquency in Youth Board Neighborhoods," Research Report, New York City Youth Board, August 1965; also "Socio-Economic Factors for the Twenty-Nine Youth Board Neighborhoods," Research Report, New York City Youth Board, November 1963.

[15] Cloward and Ohlin, *op. cit. supra* note 2, p. 172.

Table V. *Incidence of Conflict Reported by Group Workers*

Number of Conflicts	Fighting Group		Defensive Group		Corner Group		Social Group		All Groups	
	No.	%	No.	%	No.	%	No.	%	No.	%
Serious Conflicts with Other Groups										
Total responses	12	100.0	42	100.0	18	100.0	7	100.0	79	100.0
None	—	——	5	11.9	10	55.6	5	71.4	20	25.3
Some	12	100.0	37	88.1	8	44.4	2	28.6	59	74.7
Conflicts per group	79	6.6	136	3.2	24	1.3	2	0.3	241	3.1
Serious Intragroup Conflicts										
Total responses	12	——	42	——	17	——	7	——	78	——
None	2	11.7	10	23.8	14	82.4	6	85.7	32	41.0
Some	10	88.3	32	76.2	3	17.6	1	14.3	46	59.0
Conflicts per group	56	4.7	132	3.1	6	0.4	1	0.1	195	2.5
Conflicts with Other Persons										
Total responses	12	——	42	——	16	——	7	——	77	——
None	—	——	7	16.7	5	41.2	3	42.9	15	19.5
Some	12	100.0	35	83.3	11	68.8	4	57.1	62	80.6
Conflicts per group	80	6.7	233	5.5	32	2.0	9	1.3	354	4.6

which results in serious injury and possible arrest.

The type of conflict most often reported by workers with fighting or defensive groups was serious conflict with other groups (Table V); similar numbers report group involvement in serious conflict with persons other than gang members. The corner and social groups, however, seem to be involved in more conflicts with non-gang youths than in either intragroup or intergroup conflicts. As expected, the per-

Table VI. *Comparison between Worker-Reported Provocations to Group Conflict in 1964 and 1965 Surveys (Percent)*

Provocations to Conflict	Most often		Sometimes		Seldom	
	1964*	1965*	1964	1965	1964	1965
Drinking	40.6	42.0	46.9	50.7	10.9	7.2
Girls	26.6	34.8	39.1	40.6	20.3	24.6
Neighborhood group differences	37.5	34.8	34.4	31.9	10.7	7.3
Racial tension	45.3	30.6	34.4	24.2	31.3	45.2
Individual reprisals	25.0	21.2	56.7	50.0	21.9	28.8
"Sounding"	28.1	25.4	45.3	46.0	31.3	28.6
Price of liquor or drugs	18.8	9.4	34.4	29.7	51.6	60.9

* In this table, the total numbers for the 1964 survey were N = 64; for the 1965 study, the totals were as follows: drinking (N = 69), girls (N = 69); neighborhood group differences (N = 51), racial tension (N = 62), individual reprisals (N = 66), "sounding" (N = 63), price of liquor/drugs (N = 64).

centage of conflict involvement, as well as the number of conflicts reported per respondent, generally decreases from the fighting and defensive groups to the corner and social groups. These findings substantiate those of the 1964 CSAC survey which found a trend toward less group conflict over the preceding two-year period.

Any gang fight or intergroup conflict is almost always the result of provocation which mobilizes the groups or individuals within these groups. Provocations are usually exterior but, without an interior sensitivity to such situations, they would have little meaning. As the Sherifs observe:

> There may be cases in which the realistic basis for conflict is so over-generalized by members as to justify aggression on anyone who is not a group member. . . . Still, realistic factors and the group basis of violence and aggression should be considered in formulating proposals of what to do to prevent occurrence.[16]

The current data show the rank order of provocations (Table VI): drinking, girls, neighborhood group differences, "sounding," individual membership reprisals, racial tension, and arguments over the price of drugs or liquor. These findings contradict those of the 1964 CSAC survey which found that, in the preceding two years, nearly one-half of the group conflicts reported by the workers had developed because of racial tension or involvement over girls. The present data, as well as the research staff's interview experience, does not support this emphasis on racial tension. That such tension exists is unquestionable; whether it currently figures significantly in conflict provocations has not been determined.

As indicated in Table VII, the most common form of conflict reported by the workers was defensive fighting. The groups also tend to become involved in individual skirmishes, spontaneous fighting, and "japping" attacks. It is interesting that planned rumbles rank fourth as one of the least common forms of group conflict.

The Sherifs have observed: "A major concern of every group studied which engaged in violence against other groups and their members was avoidance of conflict."[17] In their research findings, this concern was frequently discussed and translated into appropriate precautions just as observable as planning an attack and easier to observe than actual violence. The present data support these findings; over two-thirds (67.1 percent) of the workers reported that boys in their groups often discussed with them their desire not to fight. More of the respondents (73.8 percent) indicated that the boys often discussed getting out of the neighborhood. Understandably, defensive groups were more apt to discuss their desire not to fight than were fighting groups (71.4 percent versus 58.3 percent); the fighting groups, on the other hand, more often discussed getting out of the neighborhood (83.3 percent versus 72.1 percent).

The workers reported that discussions with the boys more often concerned getting ahead in life, getting a job as a youth worker or social worker, and questions about the danger of pregnancy of girl friends than the use of marijuana or how to get rid of a weapon.

IMPLICATIONS FOR GROUP NORMS

The shift in fighting patterns raises an interesting question about the function which conflict plays within the status system of the group. According to Matza, the distinctive feature of the "spirit" of delinquency is the celebration of prowess.[18] Prowess can add considerably to the adventurous element of life as well as to

---

[16] Muzafer and Carolyn Sherif, *Reference Groups: Explorations into Conformity and Deviation of Adolescents* (New York: Harper & Row, 1964), p. 230.

[17] Sherif and Sherif, *op. cit. supra* note 16, p. 231.
[18] David Matza, "Subterranean Traditions of Youth," *Annals of the American Academy of Political and Social Science*, November 1961, p. 107.

Table VII. Distribution of Types of Conflict of Youth Board Groups

Forms of Conflict	Most Often		Sometimes		Seldom	
	No.	%	No.	%	No.	%
Spontaneous fights	27	40.3	25	37.3	15	22.2
Individual skirmishes	21	32.8	28	43.8	15	23.4
Defensive fighting	19	29.2	33	50.8	13	20.0
Planned rumbles	14	22.2	19	30.2	30	47.6
Japping attacks	13	20.3	28	43.8	23	35.9

Table VIII. Issues Discussed with Workers

Subject Discussed	Yes		No or not sure	
	No.	%	No.	%
How to get rid of a weapon	34	48.8	41	52.1
Pregnancy	64	81.0	15	19.0
Getting ahead in life	75	93.8	5	6.2
Getting out of the neighborhood	59	73.8	21	26.2
Desire not to fight	53	67.1	26	32.9
Use of marijuana	57	71.3	23	28.7
Getting job as youth or social worker	71	91.0	7	9.0

the success of one's reputation in the group. In this sense aggression is closely linked with the idea of prowess. The code of the "warrior" calls for aggressive manliness, a reluctance to accept a slight on one's honor. Such a code is reflected in the delinquent's esteem for "heart" (the ratio between bravery and fighting ability).

In the defensive group fighting skills continue to run high as a status symbol, but with the decrease in gang warfare a member's reputation tends to rest on his fighting *potential* rather than on his proved victories. With more of the boys interested in getting jobs, staying in school, and "getting ahead," status begins to be measured also in terms of a job, weekly salary, future plans, and one's involvement with the larger society. Given the fact that all these boys come from the lower-class culture where toughness is virtually connatural with social prestige, aggression and violence as motivating factors will never be wholly absent. What is more surprising is the emergence of the desire to get ahead, to have a stake in society. This trend, which is reflected in all our data of the defensive group, runs counter to the fatalism and lack of concern with legitimate achievement attributed to the lower-class boy.[19]

DIMENSIONS OF SOCIAL DISABILITY

In his classic analysis of street-corner society, William Whyte comments:

The stable composition of the group and the lack of social assurance on the part of its members contribute toward producing a very high rate of social interaction within the group. The group structure is a product of this interaction. . . . Out of such interaction there arises a system of mutual obligations which is fundamental to group cohesion.[20]

Whyte attributes the corner boy's lack of social assurance to their limited range of social experiences, with attendant rigidity in behavior.

While the workers in the present study

---

[19] Miller, *op. cit. supra* note 2, p. 9; see also Arthur Pearl, "Youth in Lower Class Settings," *Problems of Youth,* Sherif and Sherif, eds. (Chicago: Aldine, 1965), pp. 89–109.

[20] William F. Whyte, *Street Corner Society* (Chicago: University of Chicago Press, 1955), p. 256.

report the existence of some deficiency in social skills (lack of social "know-how" and social assurance), the contributing factors appear slightly different. First, as Short and Strodtbeck point out, the lack cannot be attributed to the intensity and rigidity of interaction patterns with their own group.[21] The workers unanimously report that in their groups these patterns are not stable enough to produce rigidity. However, there can be little doubt that gang boys lack the variety of experience which increases their ability to adapt to new situations such as an organized athletic team or a new job.

Most of the workers (92.2 percent) reported that their boys are able to move freely in the area, but only 36.4 percent felt that these same boys could move freely outside their neighborhood. Seventy percent considered that their groups spoke at least passable English; 64.9 percent reported that their groups could be aware of appointment times if they wanted to be, and 37.7 percent could keep track of money and save if they wished to purchase something.

Generally, 59.5 percent felt that their boys showed increased interest in school and employment, which correlates with the school and employment rates mentioned earlier. Over half of the workers (55.4 percent) indicated an overall increase in their group's social skills and over half (55.8 percent) reported that their boys get along relatively well with their peers. Although quite favorable, this last finding indicates a certain ambivalence on the part of gang members regarding their own group; this ambivalence appears more revealingly in the boys' tendency (observed during interviews with them) to endorse such apparently conflicting statements as: "Friends are generally more trouble than they are worth" and "You can only be really alive when you are with friends."[22] When the underlying tone of aggression noted earlier is considered, it becomes clearer that the fear of threat seems to hang over even the closest of group friendships and further substantiation is given to the observations of Short and Strodtbeck that the gang is hardly the stable and rewarding web of relationships it is often assumed to be.[23]

SUMMARY

The present analysis has shown that the average group serviced by the New York City Youth Board's street workers is the defensive gang of about thirty-five members, ten of whom can be classified as "hard core." The group ranges in age from thirteen to nineteen years, is either Puerto Rican or Negro, and displays a rather loosely knit structure, informal leadership, and some relationship to an older or other group. More boys are in school or employed than are seemingly doing nothing. Aggression as a principal mechanism of group maintenance has considerably declined. Group cohesion has lessened while the group's tolerance for other forms of deviant behavior (e.g., use of narcotics) has increased. The boys seem most concerned with getting a job, getting ahead, or a girl friend's pregnancy, and express a stronger desire to stay away from fighting. Group conflicts most often are directed toward members of other groups. These are usually provoked by drinking, girls, and neighborhood group differences.

Aggressive skills continue to rank high as group status symbols. Similarly, the groups display extreme sensitivity to any kind of status threat. In terms of social skills, the boys now seem to do better than they did at the outset of the project. Many of the groups can function both within and outside the area. Nevertheless, to equate this increased social ability with middle-class adolescent styles of life would be a misconception of the still bleak and treacherous existence experienced by current delinquent groups.

---

[21] Short and Strodtbeck, *op. cit. supra* note 1, p. 218.
[22] *Ibid.*, p. 221.
[23] *Ibid., p.* 231.

35. LOWER CLASS CULTURE AS A GENERATING MILIEU OF GANG DELINQUENCY

WALTER B. MILLER

THE ETIOLOGY OF DELINQUENCY HAS LONG been a controversial issue, and is particularly so at present. As new frames of reference for explaining human behavior have been added to traditional theories, some authors have adopted the practice of citing the major postulates of each school of thought as they pertain to delinquency, and going on to state that causality must be conceived in terms of the dynamic interaction of a complex combination of variables on many levels. The major sets of etiological factors currently adduced to explain delinquency are, in simplified terms, the physiological (delinquency results from organic pathology), the psychodynamic (delinquency is a "behavioral disorder" resulting primarily from emotional disturbance generated by a defective mother-child relationship), and the environmental (delinquency is the producer of disruptive forces, "disorganization," in the actor's physical or social environment).

This paper selects one particular kind of "delinquency"[1]—law-violating acts committed by members of adolescent street corner groups in lower class communities—and attempts to show that the dominant component of motivation underlying these acts consists in a directed attempt by the actor to adhere to forms of behavior, and to achieve standards of value as they are defined within that community. It takes as a premise that the motivation of behavior in this situation can be approached most productively by attempting to understand the nature of cultural forces impinging on the acting individual as they are perceived *by the actor himself*—although by no means only that segment of these forces of which the actor is consciously aware—rather than as they are perceived and evaluated from the reference position of another cultural system. In the case of "gang" delinquency, the cultural system which exerts the most direct influence on behavior is that of the lower class community itself—a long-established, distinctively patterned tradition with an integrity of its own—rather than a so-called "delinquent subculture" which has arisen through conflict with middle class culture and is oriented to the deliberate violation of middle class norms.

The bulk of the substantive data on which the following material is based was

▶SOURCE: *"Lower Class Culture as a Generating Milieu of Gang Delinquency," Journal of Social Issues (1958), 14:5–19. Reprinted by permission.*

[1] The complex issues involved in deriving a definition of "delinquency" cannot be discussed here. The term "delinquent" is used in this paper to characterize behavior or acts committed by individuals within specified age limits which if known to official authorities could result in legal action. The concept of a "delinquent" individual has little or no utility in the approach used here; rather, specified types of *acts* which may be committed rarely or frequently by few or many individuals are characterized as "delinquent."

collected in connection with a service-research project in the control of gang delinquency. During the service aspect of the project, which lasted for three years, seven trained social workers maintained contact with twenty-one corner group units in a "slum" district of a large eastern city for periods of time ranging from ten to thirty months. Groups were Negro and white, male and female, and in early, middle, and late adolescence. Over eight thousand pages of direct observational data on behavior patterns of group members and other community residents were collected; almost daily contact was maintained for a total time period of about thirteen worker years. Data include workers' contact reports, participant observation reports by the writer—a cultural anthropologist—and direct tape recordings of group activities and discussions.[2]

FOCAL CONCERNS OF LOWER CLASS CULTURE

There is a substantial segment of present-day American society whose way of life, values, and characteristic patterns of behavior are the product of a distinctive cultural system which may be termed "lower class." Evidence indicates that this cultural system is becoming increasingly distinctive, and that the size of the group which shares this tradition is increasing.[3]

[2] A three year research project is being financed under National Institutes of Health Grant M–1414, and administered through the Boston University School of Social Work. The primary research effort has subjected all collected material to a uniform data-coding process. All information bearing on some seventy areas of behavior (behavior in reference to school, police, theft, assault, sex, collective athletics, etc.) is extracted from the records, recorded on coded data cards, and filed under relevant categories. Analysis of these data aims to ascertain the actual nature of customary behavior in these areas, and the extent to which the social work effort was able to effect behavioral changes.

[3] Between 40 and 60 percent of all Americans are directly influenced by lower class culture, with about 15 percent, or twenty-five million, com-

The lower class way of life, in common with that of all distinctive cultural groups, is characterized by a set of focal concerns —areas or issues which command widespread and persistent attention and a high degree of emotional involvement. The specific concerns cited here, while by no means confined to the American lower classes, constitute a distinctive *patterning* of concerns which differs significantly, both in rank order and weighting from that of American middle class culture. Table I presents a highly schematic and simplified listing of six of the major concerns of lower class culture. Each is conceived as a "dimension" within which a fairly wide and varied range of alternative behavior patterns may be followed by different individuals under different situations. They are listed roughly in order of the degree of *explicit* attention accorded each, and, in this sense represent a weighted ranking of concerns. The "perceived alternatives" represent polar positions which define certain parameters within each dimension. As will be explained in more detail, it is necessary in relating the influence of these "concerns" to the motivation of delinquent behavior to specify *which* of its aspects is oriented to, whether orientation is *overt* or *covert, positive* (conforming to or seeking the aspect), or *negative* (rejecting or seeking to avoid the aspect).

The concept "focal concern" is used here in preference to the concept "value" for

prising the "hard core" lower class group—defined primarily by its use of the "female-based" household as the basic form of child-rearing unit and of the "serial monogamy" mating pattern as the primary form of marriage. The term "lower class culture" as used here refers most specifically to the way of life of the "hard core" group; systematic research in this area would probably reveal at least four to six major subtypes of lower class culture, for some of which the "concerns" presented here would be differently weighted, especially for those subtypes in which "law-abiding" behavior has a high overt valuation. It is impossible within the compass of this short paper to make the finer intracultural distinctions which a more accurate presentation would require.

Table I. *Focal Concerns of Lower Class Culture*

Area	Perceived Alternatives (state, quality, condition)	
1. Trouble:	law-abiding behavior	law-violating behavior
2. Toughness:	physical prowess, skill; "masculinity"; fearlessness, bravery, daring	weakness, ineptitude; effeminacy; timidity, cowardice, caution
3. Smartness:	ability to outsmart, dupe, "con"; gaining money by "wits"; shrewdness, adroitness in repartee	gullibility, "con-ability"; gaining money by hard work; slowness, dull-wittedness, verbal maladroitness
4. Excitement:	thrill; risk, danger; change, activity	boredom; "deadness," safeness; sameness, passivity
5. Fate:	favored by fortune, being "lucky"	ill-omened, being "unlucky"
6. Autonomy:	freedom from external constraint; freedom from superordinate authority; independence	presence of external constraint; presence of strong authority; dependency, being "cared for"

several interrelated reasons: (1) It is more readily derivable from direct field observation. (2) It is descriptively neutral—permitting independent consideration of positive and negative valences as varying under different conditions, whereas "value" carries a built-in positive valence. (3) It makes possible more refined analysis of subcultural differences, since it reflects actual behavior, whereas "value" tends to wash out intracultural differences since it is colored by notions of the "official" ideal.

Trouble. Concern over "trouble" is a dominant feature of lower class culture. The concept has various shades of meaning; "trouble" in one of its aspects represents a situation or a kind of behavior which results in unwelcome or complicating involvement with official authorities or agencies of middle class society. "Getting into trouble" and "staying out of trouble" represent major issues for male and female, adults and children. For men, "trouble" frequently involves fighting or sexual adventures while drinking; for women, sexual involvement with disadvantageous consequences. Expressed desire to avoid behavior which violates moral or legal norms is often based less on an explicit commitment to "official" moral or legal standards than on a desire to avoid "getting into trouble," e.g., the complicating consequences of the action.

The dominant concern over "trouble" involves a distinction of critical importance for the lower class community—that between "law-abiding" and "non-law-abiding" behavior. There is a high degree of sensitivity as to where each person stands in relation to these two classes of activity. Whereas in the middle class community a major dimension for evaluating a person's status is "achievement" and its external symbols, in the lower class, personal status is very frequently gauged along the law-abiding-non-law-abiding dimension. A mother will evaluate the suitability of her daughter's boyfriend less on the basis of his achievement potential than on the basis of his innate "trouble" potential. This sensitive awareness of the opposition of "trouble-producing" and "non-trouble-producing" behavior represents both a major basis for deriving status distinctions, and an internalized conflict potential for the individual.

As in the case of other focal concerns, which of two perceived alternatives—"law-abiding" or "non-law-abiding"—is valued varies according to the individual and the circumstances; in many instances there is an overt commitment to the "law-abiding" alternative, but a covert commitment to the "non-law-abiding." In certain situations, "getting into trouble" is overtly recognized as prestige-conferring; for example, membership in certain adult and adolescent primary groupings ("gangs") is contingent on having demonstrated an explicit commitment to the law-violating alternative. It is most important to note that the choice between "law-abiding" and non-law-abiding" behavior is still a choice *within* lower class culture; the distinction between the policeman and the criminal, the outlaw and the sheriff, involves primarily this one dimension; in other respects they have a high community of interests. Not infrequently brothers raised in an identical cultural milieu will become police and criminals respectively.

For a substantial segment of the lower class population "getting into trouble" is not in itself overtly defined as prestige-conferring, but is implicitly recognized as a means to other valued ends, e.g., the covertly valued desire to be "cared for" and subject to external constraint, or the overtly valued state of excitement or risk. Very frequently "getting into trouble" is multi-functional, and achieves several sets of valued ends.

Toughness. The concept of "toughness" in lower class culture represents a compound combination of qualities or states. Among its most important components are physical prowess, evidenced both by demonstrated possession of strength and endurance and athletic skill; "masculinity," symbolized by a distinctive complex of acts and avoidances (bodily tatooing; absence of sentimentality; non-concern with "art," "literature," conceptualization of women as conquest objects, etc.); and bravery in the face of physical threat. The model for the "tough guy"—hard, fearless, undemonstrative, skilled in physical combat—is represented by the movie gangster of the thirties, the "private eye," and the movie cowboy.

The genesis of the intense concern over "toughness" in lower class culture is probably related to the fact that a significant proportion of lower class males are reared in a predominantly female household, and lack a consistently present male figure with whom to identify and from whom to learn essential components of a "male" role. Since women serve as a primary object of identification during pre-adolescent years, the almost obsessive lower class concern with "masculinity" probably resembles a type of compulsive reaction-formation. A concern over homosexuality runs like a persistent thread through lower class culture. This is manifested by the institutionalized practice of baiting "queers," often accompanied by violent physical attacks, an expressed contempt for "softness" or frills, and the use of the local term for "homosexual" as a generalized pejorative epithet (e.g., higher class individuals or upwardly mobile peers are frequently characterized as "fags" or "queers"). The distinction between "overt" and "covert" orientation to aspects of an area of concern is especially important in regard to "toughness." A positive overt evaluation of behavior defined as "effeminate" would be out of the question for a lower class male; however, built into lower class culture is a range of devices which permit men to adopt behaviors and concerns which in other cultural milieux fall within the province of women, and at the same time to be defined as "tough" and manly. For example, lower class men can be professional short-order cooks in a diner and still be regarded as "tough." The highly intimate circumstances of the street corner gang involve the recurrent expression of strongly affectionate feelings towards other men. Such expressions, however, are disguised as their opposite, taking the form of ostensibly aggressive verbal and physical interaction (kidding, "ranking," roughhousing, etc.).

3) **Smartness.** "Smartness," as conceptualized in lower class culture, involves the capacity to outsmart, outfox, outwit, dupe, "take," "con" another or others, and the concomitant capacity to avoid being outwitted, "taken," or duped oneself. In its essence, smartness involves the capacity to achieve a valued entity—material goods, personal status—through a maximum use of mental agility and a minimum use of physical effort. This capacity has an extremely long tradition in lower class culture, and is highly valued. Lower class culture can be characterized as "non-intellectual" only if intellectualism is defined specifically in terms of control over a particular body of formally learned knowledge involving "culture" (art, literature, "good" music, etc.), a generalized perspective on the past and present conditions of our own and other societies, and other areas of knowledge imparted by formal educational institutions. This particular type of mental attainment is, in general, overtly disvalued and frequently associated with effeminancy; "smartness" in the lower class sense, however, is highly valued.

The lower class child learns and practices the use of this skill in the street corner situation. Individuals continually practice duping and outwitting one another through recurrent card games and other forms of gambling, mutual exchanges of insults, and "testing" for mutual "con-ability." Those who demonstrate competence in this skill are accorded considerable prestige. Leadership roles in the corner group are frequently allocated according to demonstrated capacity in the two areas of "smartness" and "toughness"; the ideal leader combines both, but the "smart" leader is often accorded more prestige than the "tough" one—reflecting a general lower class respect for "brain" in the "smartness" sense.[4]

The model of the "smart" person is represented in popular media by the card shark, the professional gambler, the "con" artist, the promoter. A conceptual distinction is made between two kinds of people: "suckers," easy marks, "lushes," dupes, who work for their money and are legitimate targets of exploitation; and sharp operators, the "brainy" ones, who live by their wits and "getting" from the suckers by mental adroitness.

Involved in the syndrome of capacities related to "smartness" is a dominant emphasis in lower class culture on ingenious aggressive repartee. This skill, learned and practiced in the context of the corner group, ranges in form from the widely prevalent semi-ritualized teasing, kidding, razzing "ranking," so characteristic of male peer group interaction, to the highly ritualized type of mutual insult interchange known as "the dirty dozens," "the dozens," "playing house," and other terms. This highly patterned cultural form is practiced on its most advanced level in adult male Negro society, but less polished variants are found throughout lower class culture—practiced, for example, by white children, male and female, as young as four or five. In essence, "doin' the dozens" involves two antagonists who vie with each other in the exchange of increasingly inflammatory insults, with incestuous and perverted sexual relations with the mother a dominant theme. In this form of insult interchange, as well as on other less ritualized occasions for joking, semi-serious, and serious mutual invective, a very high premium is placed on ingenuity, hair-trigger responsiveness, inventiveness, and the acute exercise of mental faculties.

4) **Excitement.** For many lower class individuals the rhythm of life fluctuates between periods of relatively routine or repetitive activity and sought situations of great emotional stimulation. Many of the

---

[4] The "brains-brawn" set of capacities are often paired in lower class folk lore or accounts of lower class life, e.g., "Brer Fox" and "Brer Bear" in the Uncle Remus stories, or George and Lennie in "Of Mice and Men."

most characteristic features of lower class life are related to the search for excitement or "thrill." Involved here are the highly prevalent use of alcohol by both sexes and the widespread use of gambling of all kinds —playing the numbers, betting on horse races, dice, cards. The quest for excitement finds what is perhaps its most vivid expression in the highly patterned practice of the recurrent "night on the town." This practice, designated by various terms in different areas ("honky-tonkin'"; "goin' out on the town"; "bar hoppin'"), involves a patterned set of activities in which alcohol, music, and sexual adventuring are major components. A group or individual sets out to "make the rounds" of various bars or night clubs. Drinking continues progressively throughout the evening. Men seek to "pick up" women, and women play the risky game of entertaining sexual advances. Fights between men involving women, gambling, and claims of physical prowess, in various combinations, are frequent consequences of a night of making the rounds. The explosive potential of this type of adventuring with sex and aggression, frequently leading to "trouble," is semi-explicitly sought by the individual. Since there is always a good likelihood that being out on the town will eventuate in fights, etc., the practice involves elements of sought risk and desired danger.

Counterbalancing the "flirting with danger" aspect of the "excitement" concern is the prevalence in lower class culture of other well established patterns of activity which involve long periods of relative inaction, or passivity. The term "hanging out" in lower class culture refers to extended periods of standing around, often with peer mates, doing what is defined as "nothing," "shooting the breeze," etc. A definite periodicity exists in the pattern of activity relating to the two aspects of the "excitement" dimension. For many lower class individuals the venture into the high risk world of alcohol, sex, and fighting occurs regularly once a week, with interim periods devoted to accommodating to possible consequences of these periods, along with recurrent resolves not to become so involved again.

Fate. Related to the quest for excitement is the concern with fate, fortune, or luck. Here also a distinction is made between two states—being "lucky" or "in luck," and being unlucky or jinxed. Many lower class individuals feel that their lives are subject to a set of forces over which they have relatively little control. These are not directly equated with the supernatural forces of formally organized religion, but relate more to a concept of "destiny," or man as a pawn of magical powers. Not infrequently this often implicit world view is associated with a conception of the ultimate futility of directed effort towards a goal: if the cards are right, or the dice good to you, or if your lucky number comes up, things will go your way; if luck is against you, it's not worth trying. The concept of performing semi-magical rituals so that one's "luck will change" is prevalent; one hopes that as a result he will move from the state of being "unlucky" to that of being "lucky." The element of fantasy plays an important part in this area. Related to and complementing the notion that "only suckers work" (Smartness) is the idea that once things start going your way, relatively independent of your own effort, all good things will come to you. Achieving great material rewards (big cars, big houses, a roll of cash to flash in a fancy night club), valued in lower class as well as in other parts of American culture, is a recurrent theme in lower class fantasy and folk lore; the cocaine dreams of Willie the Weeper or Minnie the Moocher present the components of this fantasy in vivid detail.

The prevalence in the lower class community of many forms of gambling, mentioned in connection with the "excitement" dimension, is also relevant here. Through cards and pool which involve skill, and thus both "toughness" and "smartness"; or through race horse betting, involving "smartness"; or through playing the numbers, involving predominantly "luck," one may make a big killing with a minimum of directed and persistent effort within conventional occupational channels. Gambling in its many forms illustrates the fact that many of the persistent features of lower class culture are multifunctional—serving a range of desired ends at the same time. Describing some of the incentives behind gambling has involved mention of all the focal concerns cited so far—Toughness, Smartness, and Excitement, in addition to Fate.

Autonomy. The extent and nature of control over the behavior of the individual—an important concern in most cultures—has a special significance and is distinctively patterned in lower class culture. The discrepancy between what is overtly valued and what is covertly sought is particularly striking in this area. On the overt level there is a strong and frequently expressed resentment of the idea of external controls, restrictions on behavior, and unjust or coercive authority. "No one's gonna push *me* around," or "I'm gonna tell him he can take the job and shove it...." are commonly expressed sentiments. Similar explicit attitudes are maintained to systems of behavior-restricting rules, insofar as these are perceived as representing the injunctions, and bearing the sanctions of superordinate authority. In addition, in lower class culture a close conceptual connection is made between "authority" and "nurturance." To be restrictively or firmly controlled is to be cared for. Thus the overtly negative evaluation of superordinate authority frequently extends as well to nuturance, care, or protection. The desire for personal independence is often expressed in such terms as "I don't need *nobody* to take care of me. I can take care of myself!" Actual patterns of behavior, however, reveal a marked discrepancy between expressed sentiment and what is covertly valued. Many lower class people appear to seek out highly restrictive social environments wherein stringent external controls are maintained over their behavior. Such institutions as the armed forces, the mental hospital, the disciplinary school, the prison or correctional institution, provide environments which incorporate a strict and detailed set of rules defining and limiting behavior, and enforced by an authority system which controls and applies coercive sanctions for deviances from these rules. While under the jurisdiction of such systems, the lower class person generally expresses to his peers continual resentment of the coercive, unjust, and arbitrary exercise of authority. Having been released, or having escaped from these milieux, however, he will often act in such a way as to insure recommitment, or choose recommitment voluntarily after a temporary period of "freedom."

Lower class patients in mental hospitals will exercise considerable ingenuity to insure continued commitment while voicing the desire to get out; delinquent boys will frequently "run" from a correctional institution to activate efforts to return them; to be caught and returned means that one is cared for. Since "being controlled" is equated with "being cared for," attempts are frequently made to "test" the severity or strictness of superordinate authority to see if it remains firm. If intended or executed rebellion produces swift and firm punitive sanctions, the individual is reassured, at the same time that he is complaining bitterly at the injustice of being caught and punished. Some environmental milieux, having been tested in this fashion for the "firmness" of their coercive sanctions, are rejected, ostensibly for being too strict, actually for not being strict enough. This is frequently so in the case of "problematic" behavior by lower class youngsters in the public schools, which generally cannot command the coercive controls implicitly sought by the individual.

A similar discrepancy between what is overtly and covertly desired is found in the area of dependence-independence. The pose of tough rebellious independence often assumed by the lower class person frequently conceals powerful dependency cravings. These are manifested primarily by obliquely expressed resentment when "care" is not forthcoming rather than by expressed satisfaction when it is. The concern over autonomy-dependency is related both to "trouble" and 'fate." Insofar as the lower class individual feels that his behavior is controlled by forces which often propel him into "trouble" in the face of an explicit determination to avoid it, there is an implied appeal to "save me from myself." A solution appears to lie in arranging things so that his behavior will be coercively restricted by an externally imposed set of controls strong enough to forcibly restrain his inexplicable inclination to get in trouble. The periodicity observed in connection with the "excitement" dimension is also relevant here; after involvement in trouble-producing behavior (assault, sexual adventure, a "drunk"), the individual will actively seek a locus of imposed control (his wife, prison, a restrictive job); after a given period of subjection to this control, resentment against it mounts, leading to a "break away" and a search for involvement in further "trouble."

FOCAL CONCERNS OF THE LOWER CLASS ADOLESCENT STREET CORNER GROUP

The one-sex peer group is a highly prevalent and significant structural form in the lower class community. There is a strong probability that the prevalence and stability of this type of unit is directly related to the prevalence of a stabilized type of lower class child-rearing unit—the "female-based" household. This is a nuclear kin unit in which a male parent is either absent from the household, present only sporadically, or, when present, only minimally or inconsistently involved in the support and rearing of children. This unit usually consists of one or more females of child-bearing age and their offspring. The females are frequently related to one another by blood or marriage ties, and the unit often includes two or more generations of women, e.g., the mother and/or aunt of the principal child-bearing female.

The nature of social groupings in the lower class community may be clarified if we make the assumption that it is the *one-sex peer unit* rather than the two-parent family unit which represents the most significant relational unit for both sexes in lower class communities. Lower class society may be pictured as comprising a set of age-graded one-sex groups which constitute the major psychic focus and reference group for those over twelve or thirteen. Men and women of mating age leave these groups periodically to form temporary marital alliances, but these lack stability, and after varying periods of "trying out" the two-sex family arrangement, gravitate back to the more "comfortable" one-sex grouping, whose members exert strong pressure on the individual *not* to disrupt the group by adopting a two-sex household pattern of life.[5] Membership in a stable and solidary peer unit is vital to the lower class individual precisely to the extent to which a range of essential functions—psychological, educational, and others—are not provided by the "family" unit.

The adolescent street corner group represents the adolescent variant of this lower class structural form. What has been called the "delinquent gang" is one subtype of this form, defined on the basis of frequency of participation in law-violating activity; this subtype should not be considered a legitimate unit of study per se, but rather as one particular variant of the adolescent street corner group. The "hanging" peer group is a unit of particular importance for the adolescent male. In many cases it

[5] Further data on the female-based household unit (estimated as comprising about 15 per cent of all American "families") and the role of one-sex groupings in lower class culture are contained in Walter B. Miller, Implications of Urban Lower Class Culture for Social Work. *Social Service Review*, 1959, *33*, No. 3.

is the most stable and solidary primary group he has ever belonged to; for boys reared in female-based households the corner group provides the first real opportunity to learn essential aspects of the male role in the context of peers facing similar problems of sex-role identification.

The form and functions of the adolescent corner group operate as a selective mechanism in recruiting members. The activity patterns of the group require a high level of intra-group solidarity; individual members must possess a good capacity for subordinating individual desires to general group interests as well as the capacity for intimate and persisting interaction. Thus highly "disturbed" individuals, or those who cannot tolerate consistently imposed sanctions on "deviant" behavior cannot remain accepted members; the group itself will extrude those whose behavior exceeds limits defined as "normal." This selective process produces a type of group whose members possess to an unusually high degree both the *capacity* and *motivation* to conform to perceived cultural norms, so that the nature of the system of norms and values oriented to is a particularly influential component of motivation.

Focal concerns of the male adolescent corner group are those of the general cultural milieu in which it functions. As would be expected, the relative weighting and importance of these concerns pattern somewhat differently for adolescents than for adults. The nature of this patterning centers around two additional "concerns" of particular importance to this group—concern with "belonging," and with "status." These may be conceptualized as being on a higher level of abstraction than concerns previously cited, since "status" and "belonging" are achieved *via* cited concern areas of Toughness, etc.

Belonging. Since the corner group fulfills essential functions for the individual, being a member in good standing of the group is of vital importance for its members. A continuing concern over who is "in" and who is not involves the citation and detailed discussion of highly refined criteria for "in-group" membership. The phrase "he hangs with us" means "he is accepted as a member in good standing by current consensus"; conversely, "he don't hang with us" means he is not so accepted. One achieves "belonging" primarily by demonstrating knowledge of and a determination to adhere to the system of standards and valued qualities defined by the group. One maintains membership by acting in conformity with valued aspects of Toughness, Smartness, Autonomy, etc. In those instances where conforming to norms of this reference group at the same time violates norms of other reference groups (e.g., middle class adults, institutional "officials"), immediate reference group norms are much more compelling since violation risks involving the group's most powerful sanction: exclusion.

Status. In common with most adolescents in American society, the lower class corner group manifests a dominant concern with status. What differentiates this type of group from others, however, is the particular set of criteria and weighting thereof by which "status" is defined. In general, status is achieved and maintained by demonstrated possession of the valued qualities of lower class culture—Toughness, Smartness, expressed resistance to authority, daring, etc. It is important to stress once more that the individual orients to these concerns *as they are defined within lower class society;* e.g., the status-conferring potential of "smartness" in the sense of scholastic achievement generally ranges from negligible to negative.

The concern with "status" is manifested in a variety of ways. Intragroup status is a continued concern, and is derived and tested constantly by means of a set of status-ranking activities; the intra-group "pecking order" is constantly at issue. One gains status within the group by demonstrated superiority in Toughness (physical prowess, bravery, skill in athletics and games such as pool and cards), Smartness (skill in repartee, capacity to "dupe" fellow group members), and the like. The term "ranking," used to refer to the pattern of intra-group aggressive repartee, indicates awareness of the fact that this is one device for establishing the intra-group status hierarchy.

The concern over status in the adolescent corner group involves in particular the component of "adultness," the intense desire to be seen as "grown up," and a corresponding aversion to "kid stuff." "Adult" status is defined less in terms of the assumption of "adult" responsibility than in terms of certain external symbols of adult status—a car, ready cash, and, in particular, a perceived "freedom" to drink, smoke, and gamble as one wishes and to come and go without restrictions. The desire to be seen as "adult" is often a more significant component of much involvement in illegal drinking, gambling, and automobile driving than the explicit enjoyment of the acts as such.

The intensity of the corner group member's desire to be seen as "adult" is sufficiently great that he feels called upon to demonstrate qualities associated with adultness (Toughness, Smartness, Autonomy) to a much greater degree than a lower class adult. This means that he will seek out and utilize those avenues to these qualities which he perceives as available with greater intensity than an adult and less regard for their "legitimacy." In this sense the adolescent variant of lower class culture represents a maximization of an intensified manifestation of many of its most characteristic features.

Concern over status is also manifested in reference to other street corner groups. The term "rep" used in this regard is especially significant, and has broad connotations. In its most frequent and explicit connotation, "rep" refers to the "toughness" of the corner group as a whole relative to that of other groups; a "pecking order" also exists among the several corner groups in a given interactional area, and there is a common perception that the safety or security of the group and all its members depends on maintaining a solid "rep" for toughness vis-a-vis other groups. This motive is most frequently advanced as a reason for involvement in gang fights: "We can't chicken out on this fight; our rep would be shot!"; this implies that the group would be relegated to the bottom of the status ladder and become a helpless and recurrent target of external attack.

On the other hand, there is implicit in the concept of "rep" the recognition that "rep" has or may have a dual basis—corresponding to the two aspects of the "trouble" dimension. It is recognized that group as well as individual status can be based on both "law-abiding" and "law-violating" behavior. The situational resolution of the persisting conflict between the "law-abiding" and "law-violating" bases of status comprises a vital set of dynamics in determining whether a "delinquent" mode of behavior will be adopted by a group, under what circumstances, and how persistently. The determinants of this choice are evidently highly complex and fluid, and rest on a range of factors including the presence and perceptual immediacy of different community reference-group loci (e.g., professional criminals, police, clergy, teachers, settlement house workers), the personality structures and "needs" of group members, the presence in the community of social work, recreation, or educational programs which can facilitate utilization of the "law-abiding" basis of status, and so on.

What remains constant is the critical importance of "status" both for the members of the group as individuals and for the group as a whole insofar as members perceive their individual destinies as linked to the destiny of the group, and the fact that action geared to attain status is much more acutely oriented to the fact of status itself than to the legality or illegality, morality or immorality of the means used to achieve it.

LOWER CLASS CULTURE AND THE MOTIVATION OF DELINQUENT BEHAVIOR

The customary set of activities of the adolescent street corner group includes activities which are in violation of laws and ordinances of the legal code. Most of these center around assault and theft of various types (the gang fight; auto theft; assault on an individual; petty pilfering and shoplifting; "mugging"; pocket-book theft). Members of street corner gangs are well aware of the law-violating nature of these acts; they are not psychopaths, nor physically or mentally "defective"; in fact, since the corner group supports and enforces a rigorous set of standards which demand a high degree of fitness and personal competence, it tends to recruit from the most "able" members of the community.

Why, then, is the commission of crimes a customary feature of gang activity? The most general answer is that the commission of crimes by members of adolescent street corner groups is motivated primarily by the attempt to achieve ends, states, or conditions, which are valued, and to avoid those that are disvalued within their most meaningful cultural milieu, through those culturally available avenues which appear as the most feasible means of attaining those ends.

The operation of these influences is well illustrated by the gang fight—a prevalent and characteristic type of corner group delinquency. This type of activity comprises a highly stylized and culturally patterned set of sequences. Although details vary under different circumstances, the following events are generally included. A member or several members of group A "trespass" on the claimed territory of group B. While there they commit an act or acts which group B defines as a violation of its rightful privileges, an affront to their honor, or a challenge to their "rep." Frequently this act involves advances to a girl associated with group B; it may occur at a dance or party; sometimes the mere act of "trespass" is seen as deliberate provocation. Members of group B then assaults members of group A, if they are caught while still in B's territory. Assaulted members of group A return to their "home" territory and recount to members of their group details of the incident, stressing the insufficient nature of the provocation ("I just *looked* at her! Hardly even said anything!"), and the unfair circumstances of the assault ("About *twenty* guys jumped just the *two* of us!"). The highly colored account is acutely inflammatory; group A, perceiving its honor violated and its "rep" threatened, feels obligated to retaliate in force. Sessions of detailed planning now occur; allies are recruited if the size of group A and its potential allies appears to necessitate larger numbers; strategy is plotted, and messengers dispatched. Since the prospect of a gang fight is frightening to even the "toughest" group members, a constant rehearsal of the provocative incident or incidents and the essentially evil nature of the opponents accompanies the planning process to bolster possibly weakening motivation to fight. The excursion into "enemy" territory sometimes results in a full scale fight; more often group B cannot be found, or the police appear and stop the fight, "tipped off" by an anonymous informant. When this occurs, group members express disgust and disappointment; secretly there is much relief; their honor has been avenged without incurring injury; often the anonymous tipster is a member of one of the involved groups.

The basic elements of this type of delinquency are sufficiently stabilized and recurrent as to constitute an essentially ritualized pattern, resembling both in structure and expressed motives for action classic forms such as the European "duel," the American Indian tribal war, and the Celtic clan feud. Although the arousing and "acting out" of individual aggressive emotions are inevitably involved in the gang fight, neither its form nor motivational dynamics can be adequately handled within a predominantly personality-focused frame of reference.

It would be possible to develop in considerable detail the processes by which the commission of a range of illegal acts is either explicitly supported by, implicitly demanded by, or not materially inhibited by factors relating to the focal concerns of lower class culture. In place of such a development, the following three statements condense in general terms the operation of these processes:

1. Following cultural practices which comprise essential elements of the total life pattern of lower class culture automatically violates certain legal norms.
2. In instances where alternate avenues to similar objectives are available, the non-law-abiding avenue frequently provides a relatively greater and more immediate return for a relatively smaller investment of energy.
3. The "demanded" response to certain situations recurrently engendered within lower class culture involves the commission of illegal acts.

The primary thesis of this paper is that the dominant component of the motivation of "delinquent" behavior engaged in by members of lower class corner groups involves a positive effort to achieve states, conditions, or qualities valued within the actor's most significant cultural milieu. If "conformity to immediate reference group values" is the major component of motivation of "delinquent" behavior by gang members, why is such behavior frequently referred to as negativistic, malicious, or rebellious? Albert Cohen, for example, in *Delinquent Boys* (Glencoe: Free Press, 1955) describes behavior which violates school rules as comprising elements of "active spite and malice, contempt and ridicule, challenge and defiance." He ascribes to the gang "keen delight in terrorizing 'good' children, and in general making themselves obnoxious to the virtuous." A recent national conference on social work with "hard-to-reach" groups characterized lower class corner groups as "youth groups in conflict with the culture of their (*sic*) communities." Such characterizations are obviously the result of taking the middle class community and its institutions as an implicit point of reference.

A large body of systematically interrelated attitudes, practices, behaviors, and values characteristic of lower class culture are designed to support and maintain the basic features of the lower class way of life. In areas where these differ from features of middle class culture, action oriented to the achievement and maintenance of the lower class system may violate norms of middle class culture and be perceived as deliberately non-conforming or malicious by an observer strongly cathected to middle class norms. This does not mean, however, that violation of the middle class norm is the dominant component of motivation; it is a by-product of action primarily oriented to the lower class system. The standards of lower class culture cannot be seen merely as a reverse function of middle class culture—as middle class standards "turned upside down"; lower class culture is a distinctive tradition many centuries old with an integrity of its own.

From the viewpoint of the acting individual, functioning within a field of well-structured cultural forces, the relative impact of "conforming" and "rejective" elements in the motivation of gang delinquency is weighted preponderantly on the conforming side. Rejective or rebellious elements are inevitably involved, but their influence during the actual commission of delinquent acts is relatively small compared to the influence of pressures to achieve what is valued by the actor's most immediate reference groups. Expressed awareness by the actor of the element of rebellion often represents only that aspect of motivation of which he is explicitly conscious; the deepest and most compelling components of motivation—adherence to highly meaningful group standards of Toughness, Smartness, Excitement, etc.—are often unconsciously patterned. No cultural pattern as well-established as the practice of illegal acts by members of lower class corner groups could persist if buttressed primarily by negative, hostile, or rejective motives; its principal motivational support, as in the case of any persisting cultural tradition, derives from a positive effort to achieve what is valued within that tradition, and to conform to its explicit and implicit norms.

36. VIOLENT CRIMES IN CITY GANGS

WALTER MILLER

THE 1960's HAVE WITNESSED A REMARKABLE upsurge of public concern over violence in the United States. The mass media flash before the public a vivid and multi-varied kaleidoscope of images of violence. Little attention is paid to those who question the assumption that the United States is experiencing an unparalleled epidemic of violence, who point out that other periods in the past may have been equally violent or more so; that troops were required to subdue rioting farmers in 1790, rioting tax-protesters in 1794, rioting laborers in the 1870's and 1880's, and rioting railroad workers in 1877; that race riots killed fifty people in St. Louis in 1917 and erupted in twenty-six other cities soon after; that fifty-seven whites were killed in a slave uprising in 1831; that the Plug Uglies, Dead Rabbits, and other street gangs virtually ruled parts of New York for close to forty years; that rival bootleg mobs engaged in armed warfare in Chicago and elsewhere during the Capone era; and that the number killed in the 1863 draft riots in New York was estimated at up to 1,000 men. Nevertheless, however much one may question the conviction that the United States today is engulfed in unprecedented violence, one can scarcely question the ascendancy of the *belief* that it is. It is this belief that moves men to action—action whose consequences are just as real as if the validity of the belief were incontrovertible.

Close to the core of the public imagery of violence is the urban street gang. The imagery evokes tableaux of sinister adolescent wolf packs prowling the darkened streets of the city intent on evil-doing, of grinning gangs of teenagers tormenting old ladies in wheelchairs and ganging up on hated and envied honor students, and of brutal bands of black-jacketed motorcyclists sweeping through quiet towns in orgies of terror and destruction. The substance of this image and its basic components of human cruelty, brutal sadism, and a delight in violence for its own sake have become conventionalized within the subculture of professional writers. The tradition received strong impetus in the public entertainment of the early 1950's with Marlon Brando and his black-jacketed motorcycle thugs, gathered momentum with the insolent and sadistic high-schoolers of *The Blackboard Jungle,* and achieved the status of an established ingredient of American folklore with the Sharks and Jets of the *West Side Story*.

What is the reality behind these images? Is the street gang fierce and romantic like the Sharks and Jets? Is it a tough but good-hearted bunch of rough and ready guys like the "Gang that Sang Heart of my Heart"? Or is it brutal and ruthless like

▶SOURCE: *"Violent Crimes in City Gangs,"* The Annals of the American Academy of Political and Social Science (March 1966), 364:97–112. Reprinted by permission.

the motorcyclist in *The Wild Ones?* In many instances where an area of interest engages both scholars and the public, most of the public embrace one set of conceptions and most scholars, another. This is not so in the case of the street gang; there is almost as much divergence with the ranks of scholars as there is between the scholars and the public.

One recent book on gangs contains these statements:

> Violence [is] the core spirit of the modern gang. . . . The gang boy . . . makes unprovoked violence . . . [senseless rather than premeditated] . . . the major activity or dream of his life. . . . The gang trades in violence. Brutality is basic to its system.[1]

Another recent work presents a different picture:

> The very few [gang] boys who persist in extreme aggression or other dangerous exploits are regarded generally as "crazy" by the other boys. . . . Our conservative estimate is that not more than one in five instances of potential violence actually result in serious consequences. . . . For average Negro gang boys the probability of an arrest for involvement in instances of potential violence is probably no greater than .04.[2]

A third important work states:

> In [a] second type [of delinquent gang or subculture] violence is the keynote. . . . The immediate aim in the world of fighting gangs is to acquire a reputation for toughness and destructive violence. . . . In the world of violence such attributes as race, socioeconomic position, age, and the like, are irrelevant.[3]

What is the reality behind these differences? The question is readily raised, but is not, unfortunately, readily answered.

---

[1] L. Yablonsky, *The Violent Gang* (New York: The Macmillan Company, 1963), pp. 4, 6.

[2] J. F. Short and F. L. Strodtbeck, *Group Process and Gang Delinquency* (Chicago: University of Chicago Press, 1965), pp. 224, 258.

[3] F. A. Cloward and L. E. Ohlin, *Delinquency and Opportunity: A Theory of Delinquent Gangs* (Glencoe, Ill.: Free Press, 1960), pp. 20, 24.

There exists in this area of high general interest a surprising dearth of reliable information. It is quite possible that discrepancies between the statements of scholars arise from the fact that each is referring to different kinds of gangs in different kinds of neighborhoods in different kinds of cities. We simply do not know. Lacking the information necessary to make general statements as to the nature of violence in the American city gang, it becomes obvious that one major need in a series of careful empirical studies of particular gangs in a range of cities and a variety of neighborhoods. The present paper is an attempt to present such information for one inner-city neighborhood, "Midcity," in a major eastern city," "Port City."

WHAT ARE "VIOLENT" CRIMES?

The term "violence" is highly charged. Like many terms which carry strong opprobrium, it is applied with little discrimination to a wide range of things which meet with general disapproval. Included in this broad net are phenomena such as toy advertising on television, boxing, rock-and-roll music and the mannerisms of its performers, fictional private detectives, and modern art. Used in this fashion the scope of the term becomes so broad as to vitiate its utility severely. Adding the term "crimes" to the designation substantially narrows its focus. It is at once apparent that not all "violence" is criminal (warfare, football, surgery, wrecking cars for scrap), but it is less apparent to some that not all crime is violent. In fact, the great bulk of adolescent crime consists of nonviolent forms of theft and statute violations such as truancy and running away. In the present report "violent crimes" are defined as *legally proscribed acts whose primary object is the deliberate use of force to inflict injury on persons or objects, and, under some circumstances, the stated intention to engage in such acts.* While the scope of this paper prevents discussion of numerous complex issues involved in this definition, for example, the role of "threat of force" as criminally culpable, an idea of the kinds of acts included under the definition may be obtained directly by referring to Tables 3 and 4, pages 373 and 107. Table 3 delineates sixteen forms of "violent" offenses directed at persons and objects, and Table 4 delineates fourteen legal categories. It is to these forms that the term "violent crimes" will apply.

CIRCUMSTANCES AND METHODS OF STUDY

Conclusions presented in subsequent sections are based on research findings of an extensive study of youth gangs in "Midcity," a central-city slum district of 100,000 persons. Information was obtained on some 150 corner gangs, numbering about 4,500 males and females, aged twelve to twenty, in the middle and late 1950's. Selected for more detailed study were twenty-one of these gangs numbering about 70 members; selection was based primarily on their reputation as the "toughest" in the city. Study data of many kinds were obtained from numerous sources, but the great bulk of data was derived from the detailed field records of workers who were in direct daily contact with gang members for periods averaging two years per gang. Seven of these gangs, numbering 205 members (four white male gangs, one Negro male, one white female, one Negro female) were subject to the most intensive field observation, and are designated "intensive observation" gangs. Findings presented here are based primarily on the experience of these seven, along with that of fourteen male gangs numbering 293 members (including the five intensive-observation male gangs) whose criminal records were obtained from the state central criminal records division.

Detailed qualitative information on the daily behavior of gang members in sixty "behavioral areas" (for example, sexual behavior, family behavior, and theft) was collected and analyzed; however, the bulk of the findings presented here will be quantitative in nature, due to requirements of brevity.[4] Present findings are based primarily on three kinds of data: (1) *Field-recorded behavior*—all actions and sentiments recorded for the seven intensive observation gangs which relate to assault (N = 1,600); (2) *Field-recorded crimes*—all recorded instances of illegal acts of assault and property damage engaged in by members of the same gangs (N = 228); and (3) *Court-recorded crimes*—all charges of assaultive or property damage offenses recorded by court officials for members of the fourteen male gangs between the ages of seven and twenty-seven (N = 138).

The analysis distinguishes four major characteristics of gangs: age, sex, race, and social status. Of the seven intensive-observation gangs, five were male (N = 155) and two, female (N = 50); none of the fourteen court-record gangs was female. Five of the intensive-observation gangs were white (N = 127) and two, Negro (N = 78); eight of the court-record gangs were white (N = 169) and six, Negro (N = 124). The ethnic-religious status of the white gangs was multinational Catholic (Irish-Italian, with Irish dominant, some French, and Slavic). Social status was determined by a relatively complex method based on a combination of educational, occupational, and other criteria (for example, parents' occupation, gang members' occupation, gang members' education, and families' welfare experience).[5] On the basis of these criteria all gangs were designated "lower class." Three levels *within* the lower class were delineated and were

---

[4] Qualitative data on the nature of "violent" and other forms of gang behavior which convey a notion of its "flavor" and life-context will be presented in W. B. Miller, *City Gangs* (New York: John Wiley & Sons, forthcoming).

[5] Details of this method are presented in *City Gangs, op. cit.*

designated, from highest to lowest, Lower Class I, II, and III. Gangs analyzed in the present paper belong to levels II and III; the former level is designated "higher" status, and the latter, "lower." It should be kept in mind that the terms "higher" and "lower" in this context refer to the lowest and next-lowest of three intra-lower-class social-status levels.[6]

THE PATTERNING OF VIOLENT CRIMES IN CITY GANGS

Study data make it possible to address a set of questions central to any consideration of the reality of violent crime in city gangs. How prevalent are violent crimes, both in absolute terms and relative to other forms of crime? What proportion of gang members engage in violent crimes? Is individual or collective participation more common? Are those most active in such crimes more likely to be younger or older? white or Negro? male or female? higher or lower in social status? What forms do violent crimes take, and which forms are most prevalent? Who and what are the targets of violent crimes? How serious are they? How does violence figure in the daily lives of gang members?

The following sections present data bearing on each of these questions, based on the experience of Midcity gangs in the 1950's. The first section bears on the last of the questions just cited: What was the role of assaultive behavior in the daily lives of gang members?

Assault-Oriented Behavior. Approximately 1,600 actions and sentiments relating to assaultive behavior were recorded by field workers during the course of their work with the seven "intensive observation" gangs—a period averaging two years per gang.[7]

This number comprised about 3 percent of a total of about 54,000 actions and sentiments oriented to some sixty behavioral areas (for example, sexual behavior, drinking behavior, theft, and police-oriented behavior). Assault-oriented behavior was relatively common, ranking ninth among sixty behavioral areas. A substantial portion of this behavior, however, took the form of words rather than deeds; for example, while the total number of assault-oriented actions and sentiments was over two and a half times as great as those relating to theft, the actual number of "arrestable" incidents of assault was less than half the number of theft incidents. This finding is concordant with others which depict the area of assaultive behavior as one characterized by considerably more smoke than fire.

About one half (821) of the 1,600 actions and sentiments were categorized as "approved" or "disapproved" with reference to a specified set of evaluative standards of middle-class adults;[8] the remainder

---

[6] IBM processing of court-recorded offenses and preliminary analyses of field-recorded assault behavior and illegal incidents was done by Dr. Robert Stanfield, University of Massachusetts; additional data analysis by Donald Zall, Midcity Delinquency Research Project. Some of the specific figures in the tables may be slightly altered in the larger report; such alterations will not, however, affect the substance of the findings. The research was supported under the National Institute of Health's Grant M–1414, and administered by the Boston University School of Social Work.

[7] The definition of "violent crimes" used here would call for an analysis at this point of behavior oriented to both assault and property destruction. However, the type of data-processing necessary to an integrated analysis of these two behavioral forms has not been done for "property damage," so that the present section is based almost entirely on behavior involving persons rather than persons and property. Behavior involving property damage was relatively infrequent; 265 actions and sentiments were recorded, ranking this form of behavior forty-fifth of sixty forms; vandalistic behavior was about one-sixth as common as assaultive behavior, a ratio paralleled in officially recorded data (cf. Table 4). Most subsequent sections will utilize findings based on both assault and property damage.

[8] Examples of *approved actions:* "acting to forestall threatened fighting" and "agreeing to settle disputes by means other than physical violence"; *disapproved actions:* "participating in gang-fighting" and "carrying weapons"; *approved sentiments:*

were categorized as "evaluatively neutral." There were approximately thirty "disapproved" assault-oriented actions for every instance of "arrestable" assault, and five instances of arrestable assault for every court appearance on assault changes. Males engaged in assault-oriented behavior far more frequently than females (males 6.3 events per month, females 1.4), and younger males more frequently than older.

Information concerning both actions and sentiments relating to assault—data not generally available—revealed both similarities and differences in the patterning of these two levels of behavior. Expressed sentiments concerning assaultive behavior were about one and a half times as common as actual actions; in this respect, assault was unique among analyzed forms of behavior, since, in every other case, recorded actions were more common than sentiments, for example, theft behavior (actions 1.5 times sentiments) and family-oriented behavior (actions 2.2 times sentiments). The majority of actions and sentiments (70 percent) were "disapproved" with reference to adult middle-class standards; actions and sentiments were "concordant" in this respect, in that both ran counter to middle-class standards by similar proportions (actions, 74 percent disapproved and sentiments, 68 percent). This concordance contrasted with other forms of behavior: in sexual behavior, the level of disapproved action was substantially higher than that of disapproved sentiment; in family-oriented behavior, the level of disapproved sentiment, substantially higher than that of action.

Separate analyses were made of behavior oriented to "individual" assault (mostly fights between two persons) and "collective" assault (mostly gang fighting). With regard to individual assault, the number of actions and the number of sentiments were approximately equal (181 actions, 187 sentiments); in the case of collective assault, in contrast, there was almost twice as much talk as action (239 sentiments, 124 actions). Sentiments with respect both to individual and collective assault were supportive of disapproved behavior, but collective assault received less support than individual. Behavior *opposing* disapproved assault showed an interesting pattern; specific actions aimed to inhibit or forestall collective assault were over twice as common as actions opposing individual assault. Gang members thus appeared to be considerably more reluctant to engage in collective than in individual fighting; the former was dangerous and frightening, with uncontrolled escalation a predictable risk, while much of the latter involved relatively mild set-to's between peers within the "controlled" context of gang interaction.

Assault-oriented behavior, in summary, was relatively common, but a substantial part of this behavior entails words rather than deeds. Both actions and sentiments ran counter to conventional middle-class adult standards, with these two levels of behavior concordant in this respect. Insofar as there did exist an element of assault-inhibiting behavior, it was manifested in connection with collective rather than individual assault. This provides evidence for the existence within the gang of a set of "natural" forces operating to control collective assault, a phenomenon to be discussed further.

Frequency of Violent Crime. The wide currency of an image of violence as a dominant occupation and preoccupation of street gangs grants special importance to the question of the actual prevalence of violent crimes. How frequently did gang members engage in illegal acts of assault and property damage? Table I shows that members of the five intensive-observation male gangs, on the basis of field records of known offenses, were involved in violent crimes at a rate of somewhat under one

---

"arguing against involvement in gang fighting" and "opposing the use of weapons"; *disapproved sentiments:* "defining fighting prowess as an essential virtue" and "perceiving fighting as inevitable."

Table I. *Frequency of Violent Crimes by Male Gang Members (by Race and Social Status)*

Race and Social Status	Five Intensive-Observation Gangs			Fourteen Court-Record Gangs		
	Number of Individuals	Number of Involvements [a]	Rate [b]	Number of Individuals	Number of Charges [c]	Rate [d]
White L.C. III	66	154	8.4	97	81	8.3
Negro L.C. III	—[e]	—	—	58	39	6.7
White L.C. II	50	40	1.5	72	10	1.4
Negro L.C. II	39	34	2.5	66	8	1.2
	155	228	4.7	293	138	4.7

L.C.III (8.4) = L.C.II (2.0) × 4.2   L.C.III (7.7) = L.C.II (1.3) × 5.9
White (5.4) = Negro (2.5) × 2.1   White (5.4) = Negro (3.8) × 1.4

[a] No incidents assault and property damage × number of participants.
[b] Involvements per 10 individuals per ten-month period.
[c] Charges on fourteen categories of assault and property-damage offenses (see Table IV).
[d] Charges per ten individuals ages seven through eighteen.
[e] Not included in study population.

offense for each two boys per ten-month period, and that the fourteen male gangs, on the basis of court-recorded offenses, were charged with "violent" crimes at a rate of somewhat under one charge for each two boys during the twelve-year period from ages seven through eighteen.[9] The

[9] Four types of "unit" figure in this and following tables. These are: (1) *Incidents:* An illegal incident is a behavioral event or sequence of events adjudged by a coder to provide a sound basis for arrest if known to authorities. Information as to most incidents was obtained from field records. In the case of assault incidents, this definition ruled out a fair number of moderately to fairly serious instances of actual or intended assault which involved members of the same gang or occurred under circumstances deemed unlikely to produce arrest even if known. (2) *Involvements:* Incidents multiplied by number of participants, for example: two gang members fight two others—one incident, four involvements. (3) *Court Appearances:* The appearance in court of a gang member on a "new" charge or charges (excluded are rehearings, appeals, and the like). (4) *Court Charges:* Appearances multiplied by number of separate charges, for example, an individual's being charged at one appearance with breaking and entering, possession of burglars' tools, and conspiracy to commit larceny counts as three "charges." The "violent crime" charges of Table 1 represent fourteen categories of offense involving actual or threatened injury to persons or objects. The fourteen offense designations appear in Table 4, and were condensed from forty categories of police-blotter designations.

228 "violent offense" involvements comprised 24 percent of all categories of illegal involvements (assault 17 percent, property damage 7 percent), with assault about one-half as common as theft, the most common offense, and property damage about one-quarter as common. The 138 court charges comprised 17 percent of all categories of charge (assault charges 11 percent, property damage 6 percent) with assault charges about one-third as common as theft, the most common charge, and property damage about one-fifth as common. The total number of "violence-oriented" actions and sentiments examined in the previous section comprised something under 4 percent of actions and sentiments oriented to sixty behavioral areas (assault-oriented behavior, 3.2 percent; property-damage-oriented, 0.5 percent).

These figures would indicate that violence and violent crimes did not play a dominant role in the lives of Midcity gangs. The cumulative figures taken alone—228 known offenses by 155 boys during a period of approximately two years, and 138 court charges for 293 boys during a twelve-year age span—would appear to indicate a fairly high "absolute" volume of violent crime. If, however, the volume of such crime is compared with that of other forms—with "violent" behavior, both actional and verbal, comprising less than 4 per cent of all recorded behavior, field-recorded "violent" offenses comprising less than one-quarter of all known offenses, and court charges of violent crimes less than one-fifth of all charges—violence appears neither as a dominant preoccupation of city gangs nor as a dominant form of criminal activity. Moreover, one should bear in mind that these rates apply to young people of the most "violent" sex, during the most "violent" years of their lives, during a time when they were members of the toughest gangs in the toughest section of the city.

Race and Social Status. The relative importance of race and social status is indicated in Table I, with field-recorded and court-recorded data showing close correspondence. Of the two characteristics, social status is clearly more important. Lower-status gang members (Lower Class III) engaged in field-recorded acts of illegal violence four times as often as those of higher status (Lower Class II) and were charged in court six times as often. White and Negro rates, in contrast, differ by a factor of two or less. The finding that boys of lower educational and occupational status both engaged in and were arrested for violent crimes to a substantially greater degree than those of higher status is not particularly surprising, and conforms to much research which shows that those of lower social status are likely to be more active in criminal behavior. What is noteworthy is the fact that differences of this magnitude appear in a situation where status differences are as small, relatively, as those between Lower Class II and III. One might expect, for example, substantial differences between college boys and high school drop-outs, but the existence of differences on the order of four to six times between groups *within* the lower class suggests that even relatively small social-status differences among laboring-class populations can be associated with relatively large differences in criminal behavior.

Table I findings relating to race runs counter to those of many studies which show Negroes to be more "violent" than whites and to engage more actively in violent crimes. Comparing similar-status white and Negro gangs in Midcity shows that racial differences were relatively unimportant, and that, insofar as there were differences, it was the whites rather than the Negroes who were more likely both to engage in and to be arrested for violent crimes. White gang members engaged in field-recorded acts of illegal violence twice as often as Negro gang members and were charged in court one and a half times as often. These data, moreover, do not support a contention that Negroes who engage in crime to a degree similar to that of whites tend to be arrested to a greater degree. The one instance where Negro rates exceed those of whites is in the case of field-recorded crimes for higher status gangs (white rate 1.5, Negro 2.5).[10] Court data, however, show that the Negro boys, with a *higher* rate of field-recorded crime, have a slightly *lower* rate of court-recorded crime. An explanation of these findings cannot be undertaken here; for present purposes it is sufficient to note that carefully collected data from one major American city do not support the notion that Negroes are more violent than whites at *similar social status levels,* nor the notion that high Negro arrest rates are invariably a consequence of the discriminatory application of justice by prejudiced white policemen and judges.

Age and Violent Crime. Was there any relationship between the age of gang mem-

---

[10] This ratio obtains for males only; calculations which include the girls' gangs show higher rates for whites in this category as well as the others. Data on field-recorded crimes on the female gangs are not included in Table I for purposes of comparability with court data; there were too few court-recorded offenses for females to make analysis practicable. At the time the field data were collected (1954–1957) Negroes comprised about 35 percent of the population of Midcity; court data cover the years up to 1964, at which time Negroes comprised about 55 percent of the population.

Table II. *Frequency of Violent Crimes by Age: 14 Male Gangs (N = 293): Court Charges (N = 229)*

Age	Number of Individuals	Number of Charges [a]	Rate [b]	Assault Charges [c]	Rate	Property Damage Charges [d]	Rate
8	293	—	—	—	—	—	—
9	293	—	—	—	—	—	—
10	293	1	0.3	1	0.3	—	—
11	293	7	2.4	2	0.7	5	1.7
12	293	—	—	—	—	—	—
13	293	6	2.0	1	0.3	5	1.7
14	293	16	5.5	12	4.1	4	1.4
15	293	19	6.5	14	4.8	5	1.7
16	293	26	8.9	21	7.2	5	1.7
17	293	25	8.5	21	7.2	5	1.7
18	293	27	9.2	23	7.8	3	1.0
19	293	21	7.2	18	6.1	3	1.0
20	293	22	7.5	21	7.2	1	0.3
21	293	20	6.8	19	6.5	1	0.3
22	292	9	3.1	8	2.7	1	0.3
23	281	10	3.5	8	2.8	2	0.7
24	247	5	2.0	4	1.6	1	0.4
25	191	7	3.7	6	3.1	1	0.5
26	155	5	3.2	5	3.2	—	—
27	95	3	3.1	3	3.2	—	—

[a] Charges on fourteen categories of offense (see Table IV).
[b] Charges per 100 individuals per year of age.
[c] Categories 1, 3, 4, 5, 5, 7, 8, 9, 13, and 14, Table IV.
[d] Categories 2, 10, 13, 12, Table IV.

bers and their propensity to engage in violent crimes? Table II shows a clear and regular relationship between age and offense-frequency. The yearly rate of changes rises quite steadily between the ages of 12 and 18, reaches a peak of about 9 charges per 100 boys at age 18, then drops off quite rapidly to age 22, leveling off thereafter to a relatively low rate of about 3 charges per 100 boys per year. The bulk of court action (82 percent of 229 charges) involved assaultive rather than property-damage offenses. The latter were proportionately more prevalent during the 11–13 age period, after which the former constitute a clear majority.

The age-patterning of theft-connected versus nontheft-connected violence and of intended versus actual violence was also determined. Violence in connection with theft—almost invariably the threat than the use thereof—constituted a relatively small proportion of all charges (14 percent), occurring primarily during the 15–21 age period. Court action based on the threat or intention to use violence rather than on its actual use comprised about one-quarter of all charges, becoming steadily more common between the ages of thirteen and twenty, and less common thereafter. At age twenty the number of charges based on the threat of violence was exactly equal to the number based on actual violence.

These data indicate quite clearly that involvement in violent crimes was a relatively transient phenomenon of adolescence, and did not presage a continuing pattern of similar involvement in adulthood. It should also be noted that these findings do not support an image of violent crimes as erratically impulsive, uncontrolled, and unpredictable. The fact that the practice of violent crime by gang members showed so regular and so predictable a relationship to age would indicate that violence was a "controlled" form of behavior—subject to a set of shared conceptions as to which forms were appropriate, and how often they were appropriate, at different age levels.

Participation in Assaultive Crime. What proportion of gang members engaged in assaultive crimes?[11] During the two-year period of field observation, 53 of the 205 intensive-contact gang members (26 percent) were known to have engaged in illegal acts of assault—50 out of 155 males (32 percent), and 3 out of 50 females (6 percent). Male-participation figures ranged from 22 percent for the higher status gangs to 42 percent for the lower. "Heavy" participants (four or more crimes) comprised only 4 percent (six males, no females) of all gang members. During the same period nineteen gang members (all males) appeared in court on assault charges—about 12 percent of the male gang members. While there is little doubt that some gang members also engaged in assaultive crimes that were known neither to field workers nor officials, the fact that three-quarters of the gang members and two-thirds of the males were *not* known to have engaged in assaultive crimes during the observation period and that 88 percent of the males and 100 percent of the females did not appear in court on charges of assaultive crimes strengthens the previous conclusion that assault was not a dominant form of gang activity.

A related question concerns the relative prevalence of individual and collective assault. One image of gang violence depicts gang members as cowardly when alone, daring to attack others only when bolstered by a clear numerical superiority. Study data give little support to this image. Fifty-one percent of recorded assault incidents involved either one-to-one engagements or engagements in which a single gang member confronted more than one antagonist. As will be shown in the discussion of "targets," a good proportion of the targets of collective assault were also groups rather than individuals. Some instances of the "ganging-up" phenomenon did occur, but they were relatively infrequent.

The Character of Violent Crime. What was the character of violent crime in Midcity gangs? Violent crimes, like other forms of gang behavior, consist of a multiplicity of particular events, varying considerably in form and circumstance. Any classification based on a single system does not account for the diversity of violence. The following sections use five ways of categorizing violent crimes: (1) *forms of crime directed at persons* (distinctions based on age, gang membership, and collectivity of actors and targets); (2) *forms of crime directed at objects* (distinctions based on mode of inflicting damage); (3) *forms of crime directed at persons and objects* (based on official classifications); (4) *targets of crime directed at persons* (distinctions based on age, sex, race, gang membership, collectivity); and '5) *targets of crime directed at objects* (distinctions based on identity of object).

Table III (column 1) shows the distribution of eleven specific forms of field-recorded assault directed at persons. In three-quarters of all incidents participants on both sides were peers of the same sex. In 60 per cent of the incidents, gang members acted in groups; in 40 per cent as individuals. Fifty-one per cent of the incidents involved collective engagements between same-sex peers. The most common form was the collective engagement between members of different gangs; it constituted one-third of all forms and was three times as common as the next most common form. Few of these engagements were full-scale massed-encounter gang

---
[11] Findings do not include data on property damage. See footnote 7.

Table III. *Forms of Violent Crime: Field-Recorded Offenses: Seven Intensive-Observation Gangs (N = 205): Incidents (N = 125)*

Person—Directed	Number of Incidents	% Known Forms	Object—Directed	Number of Incidents	% All Forms
1. Collective engagement: different gangs	27	32.9	1. Damaging via body blow, other body action	10	27.0
2. Assault by individual on individual adult, same sex	9	11.0	2. Throwing of missile (stone, brick, etc.)	10	27.0
3. Two-person engagement: different gangs	6	7.3	3. Scratching, marking, defacing, object or edifice	8	21.6
4. Two-person engagement: gang member, nongang peer	6	7.3	4. Setting fire to object or edifice	4	10.8
5. Two-person engagement: intragang	5	6.1	5. Damaging via explosive	1	2.7
6. Collective assault on same sex peer, non-gang-member	5	6.1	6. Other	4	10.8
7. Threatened collective assault on adult	5	6.1		37	100.0
8. Assault by individual on group	4	4.9			
9. Assault by individual on female peer	4	4.9			
10. Participation in general disturbance, riot	3	3.6			
11. Collective assault on same-sex peer, member of other gang	2	2.4			
12. Other	6	7.3			
13. Form Unknown	6	—			
	88	99.9			

fights; most were brief strike-and-fall-back forays by small guerrilla bands. Assault on male adults, the second most common form (11 percent), involved, for the most part the threat or use of force in connection with theft (for example, "mugging," or threatening a cab-driver with a knife) or attacks on policemen trying to make an arrest. It should be noted that those forms of gang assault which most alarm the public were rare. No case of assault on an adult woman, either by individuals or groups, was recorded. In three of the four instances of sexual assault on a female peer, the victim was either a past or present girl friend of the attacker. Only three incidents involving general rioting were recorded; two were prison riots and the third, a riot on a Sunday excursion boat.

The character of violent crimes acted on by the courts parallels that of field-recorded crimes. Table IV shows the distribution of fourteen categories of offense for 293 gang members during the age period from late childhood to early adulthood. Charges based on assault (187) were five and a half times as common as charges on property damage (42). About one-third of all assault

Table IV. *Forms of Violent Crime: Court-Recorded Offenses: 14 Male Gangs (N = 293): Court Charges through Age 27 (N = 229)*

Offense	Number	Percentage
1. Assault and battery: no weapon	75	32.7
2. Property damage	36	15.7
3. Affray	27	11.8
4. Theft-connected threat of force: no weapon	22	9.6
5. Possession of weapon	18	7.9
6. Assault, with weapon	18	7.9
7. Theft-connected threat of force: with weapon	11	4.8
8. Assault, threat of	8	3.5
9. Sexual assault	8	3.5
10. Arson	6	2.5
11. Property damage, threat of	—	—
12. Arson, threat of	—	—
13. Manslaughter	—	—
14. Murder	—	—
	229	100.0

charges involved the threat rather than the direct use of force. The most common charge was "assault and battery," including, primarily, various kinds of unarmed engagements such as street fighting and barroom brawls. The more "serious" forms of assaultive crime were among the less prevalent: armed assault, 8 percent; armed robbery, 5 percent; sexual assault, 4 percent. Not one of the 293 gang members appeared in court on charges of either murder or manslaughter between the ages of seven and twenty-seven.

The use of weapons and the inflicting of injury are two indications that violent crimes are of the more serious kind. Weapons were employed in a minority of cases of assault, actual or threatened, figuring in 16 of the 88 field-recorded offenses, and about 55 of the 187 court offenses.[12] In the

[12] On the basis of field-recorded data it was estimated that about one-quarter of "Affray" charges involved sticks or other weapons.

16 field-recorded incidents in which weapons were used to threaten or injure, 9 involved knives, 4, an object used as a club (baseball bat, pool cue), and 3, missiles (rocks, balls). In none of the 88 incidents was a firearm of any description used. The bulk of assaultive incidents, then, involved the direct use of the unarmed body; this finding accords with others in failing to support the notion that gang members engage in assault only when fortified by superior resources.

Serious injuries consequent on assault were also relatively uncommon. There were twenty-seven known injuries to all participants in the eighty-eight incidents of assault; most of these were minor cuts, scratches, and bruises. The most serious injury was a fractured skull inflicted by a crutch wielded during a small-scale set-to between two gangs. There were also two other skull injuries, three cases of broken bones, three broken noses, and one shoulder dislocation (incurred during a fight between girls). While these injuries were serious enough for those who sustained them, it could not be said that the totality of person-directed violence by Midcity gang members incurred any serious cost in maimed bodies. The average week-end of highway driving in and around Port City produces more serious body injuries than two years of violent crimes by Midcity gangs.

Data on modes of property damage similarly reflect a pattern of involvement in the less serious forms. As shown in Table 3, in ten of the thirty-seven field-recorded incidents the body was used directly to inflict damage (punching out a window, Breaking fences for slats); another ten involved common kinds of missile-throwing (brick through store window). Most of the "defacing" acts were not particularly destructive, for example, scratching the name of the gang on a store wall. Fire-setting was confined to relatively small objects, for example, trash barrels. No instance was recorded of viciously destructive forms of vandalism such as desecration of churches or cemeteries or bombing of residences. The one case where explosives were used involved the igniting of rifle cartridge powder in a variety store. Of the forty-two cases of court-charged property-destruction, only six involved arson; the actual nature of vandalistic acts was not specified in the legal designations.

Targets of Violent Crime. While much gang violence took the form of "engagements with" rather than "attacks on" other persons, additional insight may be gained by viewing the gang members as "actors," and asking: "What categories of person were targets of gang assault, and what kinds of physical objects targets of damage?" One image of gang violence already mentioned sees the act of "ganging up" on solitary and defenseless victims as a dominant gang practice; another sees racial antagonism as a major element in gang violence. What do these data show?

Table V shows the distribution of 88 field-recorded incidents of assault for 13 categories of target, and 43 incidents of damage for 6 categories.[13]

Of 77 targets of assault whose identity was known, a substantial majority (73 percent) were persons of the same age and sex category as the gang members, and a substantial majority (71 percent), of the same race. One-half of all targets were peers of the same age, sex, and race category. On initial inspection the data seem to grant substance to the "ganging up" notion; 44 of 77 targets (57 percent) were individuals. Reference to Table 3, however, shows that 34 of these incidents were assaults on individuals *by* individuals; of the remaining 10, 4 were adult males (police, mugging victims) and one, the female member of a couple robbed at knife point. The remaining 5 were same-sex peers, some of whom were members of rival gangs. There was no recorded instance of collective assault on a child, on old men or women, or on females by males. There was no instance of an attack on a white female by a Negro male. Partly balancing the five cases of collective assault on lone peers were three instances in which a lone gang member took on a group.

These data thus grant virtually no support of the notion that favored targets of gang attacks are the weak, the solitary, the defenseless, and the innocent; in most cases assaulters and assaultees were evenly matched; the bulk of assaultive incidents involved contests between peers in which the preservation and defense of gang honor was a central issue. Some support is given to the notion of radical friction; 30 percent of all targets were of a different race, and radical antagonism played some part in these encounters. On the other hand, of thirty-three instances of collective assault, a majority (55 percent) involved antagonists of the same race.

Physical objects and facilities suffering damage by gang members were largely those which they used and frequented in the course of daily life. Most damage was inflicted on public and semipublic facilities, little on private residences or other property. There was no evidence of "ideological" vandalism (stoning embassies, painting swastikas on synagogues). Most damage was deliberate, but some additional amount was a semiaccidental consequence of the profligate effusion of body energy so characteristic of male adolescents (breaking a store window in course of a scuffle). Little of the deliberately inflicted property damage represented a diffuse outpouring of accumulated hostility against arbitrary objects; in most cases the gang members injured the possession or properties of particular persons who had angered them, as a concrete expression of that anger (defacing automobile of mother responsible for having gang member committed to correctional institution; breaking windows of settlement house after ejection therefrom). There was thus little evidence of "senseless" destruction; most property damage was directed and responsive.

---

[13] Findings are based on field-recorded data only; official offense designations seldom specify targets.

Table V. *Targets of Violent Crime: Field-Recorded Offenses: Seven Intensive-Observation Gangs (N = 205): Incidents (N = 125)*

Persons	Number of Incidents	% Known Targets	Objects	Number of Incidents	% All Targets
1. Groups of adolescents, other gangs, same sex, race	18	23.4	1. Stores, commercial facilities: premises, equipment	11	29.7
2. Groups of adolescents, other gangs, same sex, different race	12	15.5	2. Semipublic facilities: social agencies, gyms, etc.	10	27.0
3. Individual adults, same sex, same race	12	15.5	3. Automobiles	8	21.6
4. Individual adolescents, other gangs, same sex, same race	8	10.4	4. Public facilities: schools, public transportation, etc.	5	13.5
5. Individual adolescents, nongang, same sex, race	6	7.8	5. Private houses: premises, furnishings	3	8.1
6. Individual adolescents, nongang, different sex, same race	4	5.2		37	99.9
7. Individual adolescents, nongang, same sex, different race	4	5.2			
8. Individual adults, same sex, different race	4	5.2			
9. Individual adolescents, own gang	3	3.9			
10. Groups of adolescents, own gang	3	3.9			
11. Individual adolescents, nongang, same sex, different race	2	2.6			
12. Individual adults, different sex, same race	1	1.3			
13. Target unknown	11	—			
	88	99.9			

Gang Fighting. An important form of gang violence is the gang fight; fiction and drama often depict gang fighting or gang wars as a central feature of gang life (for example, *West Side Story*). The Midcity study conceptualized a fully developed gang fight as involving four stages: initial provocation, initial attack, strategy-planning and mobilization, and counterattack.[14] During the study period, members of the intensive-observation gangs participated in situations involving some combination of these stages fifteen times. Despite intensive efforts by prowar agitators and

[14] A description of the gang fight as a form of gang behavior is included in W. B. Miller, "Lower-Class Culture as a Generating Milieu of Gang Delinquency," *Journal of Social Issues*, Vol. XXXI, No. 4 (December 1957), pp. 17, 18.

elaborate preparations for war, only one of these situations eventuated in full-scale conflict; in the other fourteen, one or both sides found a way to avoid open battle. A major objective of gang members was to put themselves in the posture of fighting without actually having to fight. The gangs utilized a variety of techniques to maintain their reputation as proud men, unable to tolerate an affront to honor, without having to confront the dangerous and frightening reality of massed antagonists. Among these were the "fair fight" (two champions represent their gangs *a la* David and Goliath); clandestine informing of police by prospective combatants; *reluctantly* accepting mediation by social workers.

Despite the very low ratio of actual to threatened fighting, a short-term observer swept up in the bustle and flurry of fight-oriented activity, and ignorant of the essentially ritualistic nature of much of this activity, might gain a strong impression of a great deal of actual violence. In this area, as in others, detailed observation of gangs over extended periods revealed that gang fighting resembled other forms of gang violence in showing much more smoke than fire.

THE PROBLEM OF GANG VIOLENCE

The picture of gang violence which emerges from the study of Midcity gangs differs markedly from the conventional imagery as well as from that presented by some scholars. How is this difference to be explained? The most obvious possibility is that Midcity gangs were somehow atypical of gangs in Port City, and of the "true" American street gang. In important respects the gangs were *not* representative of those in Port City, having been selected on the basis of their reputation as the "toughest" in the city, and were thus *more* violent than the average Port City gang. The possibility remains, in the absence of information equivalent in scope and detail to that presented here, that Port City gangs were atypical of, and less violent than, gangs in other cities. I would like in this connection to offer my personal opinion, based on ten years of contact with gang workers and researchers from all parts of the country, that Midcity gangs were in fact *quite* typical of "tough" gangs in Chicago, Brooklyn, Philadelphia, Detroit, and similar cities, and represent the "reality" of gang violence much more accurately than "the Wild Ones" or the Egyptian Kings, represented as the prototypical "violent gang" in a well-known television program.

Even if one grants that actual city gangs are far less violent than those manufactured by the mass media and that the public fear of gangs has been unduly aroused by exaggerated images, the problem of gang violence is still a real one. However one may argue that all social groups need outlets for violence and that gang violence may serve to siphon off accumulated aggression in a "functional" or necessary way, the fact remains that members of Midcity gangs repeatedly violated the law in using force to effect theft, in fighting, and in inflicting damage on property as regular and routine pursuits of adolescence. *Customary* engagement in illegal violence by a substantial sector of the population, however much milder than generally pictured, constitutes an important threat to the internal order of any large urbanized society, a threat which must be coped with. What clues are offered by the research findings of the Midcity study as to the problem of gang violence and its control?

First, a brief summary of what it *was*. Violence as a concern occupied a fairly important place in the daily lives of gang members, but was distinguished among all forms of behavior in the degree to which concern took the form of talk rather than action. Violent crime as such was fairly common during middle and late adolescence, but, relative to other forms of crime, was not dominant. Most violent crimes were directed at persons, few at property.

Only a small minority of gang members was active in violent crimes. Race had little to do with the frequency of involvement in violent crimes, but social status figured prominently. The practice of violent crimes was an essentially transient phenomenon of male adolescence, reaching a peak at the age when concern with attaining adult manhood was at a peak. While the nature of minor forms showed considerable variation, the large bulk of violent crime in Midcity gangs consisted in unarmed physical encounters between male antagonists—either in the classic form of combat skirmishes between small bands of warriors or the equally classic form of direct combative engagement between two males.

Next, a brief summary of what it was *not*. Violence was not a dominant activity of the gangs, nor a central reason for their existence. Violent crime was not a racial phenomenon—either in the sense that racial antagonisms played a major role in gang conflict, or that Negroes were more violent, or that resentment of racial injustice was a major incentive for violence. It was not "ganging up" by malicious sadists on the weak, the innocent, the solitary. It did not victimize adult females. With few exceptions, violent crimes fell into the "less serious" category, with the extreme or shocking crimes rare.

One way of summarizing the character of violent crime in Midcity gangs is to make a distinction between two kinds of violence—"means" violence and "end" violence. The concept of violence as a "means" involves the notion of a resort to violence when other means of attaining a desired objective have failed. Those who undertake violence in this context represent their involvement as distasteful but necessary—an attitude epitomized in the parental slogan, "It hurts me more than it does you." The concept of violence as an "end" involves the notion of eager recourse to violence for its own sake—epitomized in the mythical Irishman who says, "What a grand party! Let's start a fight!" The distinction is illustrated by concepts of two kinds of policeman—the one who with great reluctance resorts to force in order to make an arrest and the "brutal" policeman who inflicts violence unnecessarily and repeatedly for pure pleasure. It is obvious that "pure" cases of either means- or end-violence are rare or nonexistent; the "purest" means-violence may involve some personal gratification, and the "purest" end-violence can be seen as instrumental to other ends.

In the public mind, means-violence is unfortunate but sometimes necessary; it is the spectacle of end-violence which stirs deep indignation. Much of the public outrage over gang violence arises from the fact that it has been falsely represented, with great success, as pure end-violence ("senseless," "violence for its own sake") when it is largely, in fact, means-violence.

What are the "ends" toward which gang violence is a means, and how is one to evaluate the legitmacy of these ends? Most scholars of gangs agree that these ends are predominantly ideological rather than material, and revolve on the concepts of prestige and honor. Gang members fight to secure and defend their honor as males; to secure and defend the reputation of their local area and the honor of their women; to show that an affront to their pride and dignity demands retaliation.[15] Combat between males is a major means for attaining these ends.

It happens that great nations engage in national wars for almost identical reasons. It also happens, ironically, that during this period of national concern over gang violence our nation is pursuing, in the international arena, very similar ends by very similar means. At root, the solution to the problem of gang violence lies in the dis-

---

[15] The centrality of "honor" as a motive is evidenced by the fact that the "detached worker" method of working with gangs has achieved its clearest successes in preventing gang fights by the technique of furnishing would-be combatants with various means of avoiding direct conflict without sacrificing honor.

covery of a way of providing for men the means of attaining cherished objectives—personal honor, prestige, defense against perceived threats to one's homeland—without resort to violence. When men have found a solution to this problem they will at the same time have solved the problem of violent crimes in city gangs.

37. THE SUBCULTURE OF VIOLENCE

MARVIN E. WOLFGANG
FRANCO FERRACUTI

THE CULTURAL CONTEXT

LIKE ALL HUMAN BEHAVIOR, HOMICIDE AND other violent assaultive crimes must be viewed in terms of the cultural context from which they spring. De Champneuf, Guerry, Quetelet early in the nineteenth century, and Durkheim later, led the way toward emphasizing the necessity to examine the *physique sociale,* or social phenomena characterized by 'externality', if the scientist is to understand or interpret crime, suicide, prostitution, and other deviant behavior. Without promulgating a sociological fatalism, analysis of broad macroscopic correlates in this way may obscure the dynamic elements of the phenomenon and result in the empirical hiatus and fallacious association to which Selvin refers (1). Yet, because of wide individual variations, the clinical, idiosyncratic approach does not necessarily aid in arriving at Weber's *Verstehen,* or meaningful adequate understanding of regularities, uniformities, or patterns of interaction. And it is this kind of understanding we seek when we examine either deviation from, or conformity to, a normative social system.

Sociological contributions have made almost commonplace, since Durkheim, the fact that deviant conduct is not evenly distributed throughout the social structure.

►SOURCE: *The Subculture of Violence,* London: Tavistick, 1967, pp. 150–163. Reprinted by permission.

There is much empirical evidence that class position, ethnicity, occupational status, and other social variables are effective indicators for predicting rates of different kinds of deviance. Studies in ecology perform a valuable service for examining the phenomenology and distribution of aggression, but only inferentially point to the importance of the system of norms. Anomie, whether defined as the absence of norms (which is a doubtful conceptualization) or the conflict of norms (either normative goals or means), (2) or whether redefined by Powell (3) as 'meaningless', does not coincide with most empirical evidence on homicide. Acceptance of the concept of anomie would imply that marginal individuals who harbor psychic anomie that reflects (or causes) social anomie have the highest rates of homicides. Available data seem to reject this contention.

Anomie as culture conflict, or conflict of norms, suggests, as we have in the last section, that there is one segment (the prevailing middle-class value system) of a given culture whose value system is the antithesis of, or in conflict with, another, smaller, segment of the same culture. This conceptualism of anomie is a useful tool for referring to subcultures as ideal types, or mental constructs. But to transfer this norm-conflict approach from the social to the individual level, theoretically making the individual a repository of culture conflict, again does not conform to the patterns of known psychological and sociological data. This latter approach would be forced to hypothesize that socially mobile individuals and families would be most frequently involved in homicide, or that persons moving from a formerly embraced subvalue system to the predominant communal value system would commit this form of violent deviation in the greatest numbers. There are no homicide data that show high rates of homicides among persons manifesting higher social aspirations in terms of mobility. It should also be mentioned that anomie, as a concept, does not easily lend itself to psychological study (4).

That there is a conflict of value systems, we agree. That is, there is a conflict between a prevailing culture value and some subcultural entity. But commission of homicide by actors from the subculture at variance with the prevailing culture cannot be adequately explained in terms of frustration due to failure to attain normative-goals of the latter, in terms of inability to succeed with normative-procedures (means) for attaining those goals, nor in terms of an individual psychological condition of anomie. Homicide is most prevalent, or the highest rates of homicide occur, among a relatively homogeneous subcultural group in any large urban community. Similar prevalent rates can be found in some rural areas. The value system of this group, we are contending, constitutes a subculture of violence. From a psychological viewpoint, we might hypothesize that the greater the degree of integration of the individual into this subculture, the higher the probability that his behavior will be violent in a variety of situations. From the sociological side, there should be a direct relationship between rates of homicide and the extent to which the subculture of violence represents a cluster of values around the theme of violence.

Except for war, probably the most highly reportable, socially visible, and serious form of violence is expressed in criminal homicide. Data show that in the United States rates are highest among males, non-whites, and the young adult ages. Rates for most serious crimes, particularly against the person, are highest in these same groups. In a Philadelphia study of 588 criminal homicides (5), for example, non-white males aged 20–24 had a rate of 92 per 100,000 compared with 3.4 for white males of the same ages. Females consistently had lower rates than males in their respective race groups (non-white females, 9.3; white females, 0.4, in the same study), although it should be noted, as we shall discuss later, that non-white females have higher rates than white males.

It is possible to multiply these specific findings in any variety of ways; and although a subcultural affinity to violence appears to be principally present in large urban communities and increasingly in the adolescent population, some typical evidence of this phenomenon can be found, for example, in rural areas and among other adult groups. For example, a particular, very structured, subculture of this kind can be found in Sardinia, in the central mountain area of the island. Pigliaru has conducted a brilliant analysis of the people from this area and their criminal behavior, commonly known as the *vendetta barbaricina* (6).

In Colombia, the well known *violencia* has been raging for the last 15 years, causing deaths of a total estimated between 200,000 and 300,000 (7). The homicide rate in several areas has been among the highest in the world, and homicide has been the leading cause of death for Colombian males aged between 15 and 45. Several causes, some political, initially associated with the rise of this phenomenon continue to exist, and, among them, a subcultural transmission of violence is believed to play an important role. More will be said later about the subcultural traditions of violence in Sardinia, Columbia, and elsewhere.

We suggest that, by identifying the groups with the highest rates of homicide, we should find in the most intense degree a subculture of violence; and, having focused on these groups, we should subsequently examine the value system of their subculture, the importance of human life in the scale of values, the kinds of expected reaction to certain types of stimulus, perceptual differences in the evaluation of stimuli, and the general personality structure of the subcultural actors. In the Philadelphia study it was pointed out that:

> ... the significance of a jostle, a slightly derogatory remark, or the appearance of a weapon in the hands of an adversary are stimuli differentially perceived and interpreted by Negroes and whites, males and females. Social expectations of response in particular types of social interaction result in differential "definitions of the situation." A male is usually expected to defend the name and honor of his mother, the virtue of womanhood ... and to accept no derogation about his race (even from a member of his own race), his age, or his masculinity. Quick resort to physical combat as a measure of daring, courage, or defense of status appears to be a cultural expression, especially for lower socio-economic class males of both races. When such a culture norm response is elicited from an individual engaged in social interplay with others who harbor the same response mechanism, physical assaults, altercations, and violent domestic quarrels that result in homicide are likely to be common. The upper-middle and upper social class value system defines subcultural mores, and considers many of the social and personal stimuli that evoke a combative reaction in the lower classes as "trivial." Thus, there exists a cultural antipathy between many folk rationalizations of the lower class, and of males of both races, on the one hand, and the middle-class legal norms under which they live, on the other (8).

This kind of analysis, combined with other data about delinquency, the lower-class social structure, its value system, and its emphasis on aggression, suggest the thesis of a violent subculture, or by pushing the normative aspects a little further, a *subculture of violence*. Among many juvenile gangs, as has repeatedly been pointed out, there are violent feuds, meetings, territorial fights, and the use of violence to prove 'heart', to maintain or to acquire 'rep' (9).

Physical aggression is often seen as a demonstration of masculinity and toughness. We might argue that this emphasis on showing masculinity through aggression is not always supported by data. If homicide is any index at all of physical aggression, we must remember that in the Philadelphia data non-white females have rates often two to four times higher than the rates of white males. Violent behavior appears more dependent on cultural differences than on sex differences, traditionally considered of paramount importance in the expression of aggression. It could be argued, of course, that in a more matriarchal role than that of her white counterpart, the Negro female both enjoys and suffers more of the male role as head of the household, as parental authority and supervisor; that this imposed role makes her more aggressive, more male-like, more willing and more likely to respond violently. Because most of the victims of Negro female homicide offenders are Negro males, the Negro female may be striking out aggressively against the inadequate male protector whom she desperately wants but often cannot find or hold (10).

It appears valid to suggest that there are, in a heterogeneous population, differences in ideas and attitudes toward the use of violence and that these differences can be observed through variables related to social class and possibly through psychological correlates. There is evidence that modes of control of expressions of aggression in children vary among the social classes (11). Lower-class boys, for example, appear more likely to be oriented toward direct expression of aggression than are middle-class boys. The type of punishment meted out by parents to misbehaving children is related to this class orientation toward aggression. Lower-class mothers report that they or their husbands are likely to strike their children or threaten to strike them, whereas middle-class mothers report that their type of punishment is psychological rather than physical; and boys who are punished physically express aggression more directly than those who are punished psychologically. As Martin Gold (12) has suggested, the middle-class child is more likely to turn his aggression inward; in the extreme and as an adult he will commit suicide. But the lower-class child is more accustomed to a parent-child relationship which during punishment is for the moment that of attacker and attacked. The target for aggression, then, is external; aggression is directed toward others (13).

The existence of a subculture of violence is partly demonstrated by examination of the social groups and individuals who experience the highest rates of manifest violence. This examination need not be confined to the study of one national or ethnic group. On the contrary, the existence of a subculture of violence could perhaps receive even cross-cultural confirmation. Criminal homicide is the most acute and highly reportable example of this type of violence, but some circularity of thought is obvious in the effort to specify the dependent variable (homicide), and also to infer the independent variable (the existence of a subculture of violence). The highest rates of rape, aggravated assaults, persistency in arrests for assaults (recidivism) among these groups with high rates of homicide are, however, empirical addenda to the postulation of a subculture of violence. Residential propinquity of these same groups reinforces the sociopsychological impact which the integration of this subculture engenders. Sutherland's thesis of 'differential association', or a psychological reformulation of the same theory in terms of learning process, could effectively be employed to describe more fully this impact in its intensity, duration, repetition, and frequency. The more thoroughly integrated the individual is into this subculture, the more intensely he embraces its prescriptions of behavior, its conduct norms, and integrates them into his personality structure. The degree of integration may be measured partly and crudely by public records of contact with the law, so high arrest rates, particularly high rates of assault crimes and high rates of recidivism for assault crimes among groups that form the subculture of violence, may indicate allegiance to the values of violence.

We have said that overt physical violence often becomes a common subculturally expected response to certain stimuli. However, it is not merely rigid conformity to the demands and expectations of other persons, as Henry and Short (14) seem to suggest, that results in the high probability of homicide. Excessive, compulsive, or apathetic conformity of middle-class individuals to the value system of their social group is a widely recognized cultural malady. Our concern is with the value elements of violence as an integral component of the subculture which experiences high rates of homicide. It is conformity to *this* set of values, and not rigid conformity *per se*, that gives important meaning to the subculture of violence.

If violence is a common subcultural response to certain stimuli, penalties should exist for deviation from *this* norm. The comparatively nonviolent individual may be ostracized (15), but if social interaction must occur because of residential propinquity to others sharing in a subculture of violence, he is most likely to be treated with disdain or indifference. One who previously was considered a member of the ingroup, but who has rebelled or retreated from the subculture, is now an out-group member, a possible threat, and one for the group to avoid. Alienation or avoidance takes him out of the normal reach of most homicide attacks, which are highly personal offenses occurring with great frequency among friends, relatives, and associates. If social interaction continues, however, the deviant from the subculture of violence who fails to respond to a potentially violent situation, may find himself a victim of an adversary who continues to conform to the violence values.

It is not far-fetched to suggest that a whole culture may accept a value set dependent upon violence, demand or encourage adherence to violence, and penalize deviation. During periods of war the whole nation accepts the principle of violence against the enemy. The nonviolent citizen drafted into military service may adopt values associated with violence as an intimately internalized re-enforcement for his newly acquired rationalization to kill. War involves selective killing of an out-group enemy, and in this respect may be viewed as different from most forms of homicide. Criminal homicide may be either 'selective' or non-discriminate slaying, although the literature on homicide consistently reveals its intragroup nature. However, as in wartime combat between opposing individuals when an 'it-was-either-him-or-me' situation arises, similar attitudes and reactions occur among participants in homicide. It may be relevant to point out that in the Philadelphia study of criminal homicide, 65 per cent of the offenders and 47 percent of the victims had previous arrest records. Homicide, it appears, is often a situation not unlike that of confrontations in wartime combat, in which two individuals committed to the value of violence came together, and in which chance, prowess, or possession of a particular weapon dictates the identity of the slayer and of the slain. The peaceful noncombatant in both sets of circumstances is penalized, because of the allelomimetic behavior of the group supporting violence, by his being ostracized as an outgroup member, and he is thereby segregated (imprisoned, in wartime, as a conscientious objector) from his original group. If he is not segregated, but continues to interact with his original group in the public street or on the front line that represents the culture of violence, he may fall victim to the shot or stab from one of the group who still embraces the value of violence.

An internal need for aggression and a readiness to use violence by the individual who belongs to a subculture of violence should find their psychological foundation in personality traits and in attitudes which can, through careful studies, be assessed in such a way as to lead to a differential psychology of these subjects. Psychological tests have been repeatedly employed to study the differential characteristics of criminals; and if a theoretical frame of reference involving a subculture of violence is used, it should be possible to sharpen the discriminatory power of these tests. The fact that a subject belongs to a specific subculture (in our case, a deviant one), defined by the ready use of violence, should, among other consequences, cause the subject to adopt a differential perception of his environment and its stimuli. Variations in the surrounding world, the continuous challenges and daily frustrations which are faced and solved by the adaptive mechanism of the individual, have a greater chance of being perceived and reacted upon, in a subculture of violence, as menacing, aggressive stimuli which call for immediate defense and counter-aggression. This hypothesis lends itself to objective study through appropriate psychological methodologies. The word of Stagner (16) on industrial conflict exemplifies a similar approach in a different field. This perceptual approach is of great importance in view of studies on the physiology of aggression, which seem to show the need of outside stimulation in order to elicit aggressive behavior (17). This point will be discussed in more detail in the next chapter.

Confronted with many descriptive and test statistics, with some validated hypotheses and some confirmed replications of propositions regarding aggressive crime in psychological and sociological studies, interpretative analysis leading to the building of a theory is a normal functional aspect of the scientific method.

But there are two common and inherent dangers of an interpretative analysis that yields a thesis in an early stage of formulation, such as our thesis of a subculture of violence. These are: (*a*) the danger of going beyond the confines of empirical data which have been collected in response to some stated hypothesis; and (*b*) the danger of interpretation that produces generalizations emerging inductively from the data and that results in tautologous reasoning. Relative to the first type of danger, the social scientist incurs the risk of 'impressionistic', 'speculative' thinking, or of using previous peripheral research and trying to link it to his own data by theoretical ties that often result in knotted confusion typically calling for further research, the *caveat* of both 'good' and 'poor' analyses. Relative to the second danger, the limitations and problems of tautologies are too well known to be elaborated here. We hope that these two approaches to interpretation are herein combined in degrees that avoid compounding the fallacies of both, but that unite the benefits of each. We have made an effort to stay within the limits imposed by known empirical facts and not to become lost in speculative reasoning that combines accumulated, but unrelated, facts for which there is no empirically supportive link.

We have said that overt use of force or violence, either in interpersonal relationships or in group interaction, is generally viewed as a reflection of basic values that stand apart from the dominant, the central, or the parent culture. Our hypothesis is that this overt (and often illicit) expression of violence (of which homicide is only the most extreme) is part of a subcultural normative system, and that this system is reflected in the psychological traits of the subculture participants. In the light of our discussion of the caution to be exercised in interpretative analysis, in order to tighten the logic of this analysis, and to support the thesis of a subculture of violence, we offer the following corollary propositions:

1. No subculture can be totally different from or totally in conflict with the society of which it is a part. A subculture of violence is not entirely an expression of violence, for there must be interlocking value elements shared with the dominant culture. It should not be necessary to contend that violent aggression is the predominant mode of expression in order to show that the value system is set apart as subcultural. When violence occurs in the dominant culture, it is usually legitimized, but most often is vicarious and a part of phantasy. Moreover, subcultural variations, we have earlier suggested, may be viewed as quantitative and relative. The extent of difference from the larger culture and the degree of intensity, which violence as a subcultural theme may possess, are variables that could and should be measured by known socio-psychological techniques (18). At present, we are required to rely almost entirely upon expressions of violence in conduct of various forms—parent–child relationships, parental discipline, domestic quarrels, street fights, delinquent conflict gangs, criminal records of assaultive behavior, criminal homicide, etc.—but the number of psychometrically oriented studies in criminology is steadily increasing in both quantity and sophistication, and from them a reliable differential psychology of homicides should emerge to match current sociological research.

2. To establish the existence of a subculture of violence does not require that the actors sharing in these basic value elements should express violence in all situations. The normative system designates that in some types of social interaction a violent and physically aggressive response is either expected or required of all members sharing in that system of values. That the actors' behavior expectations occur in more than one situation is obvious. There is a variety of circumstances in which homicide occurs, and the history of past aggressive crimes in high proportions, both in the victims and in the offenders, attests to the multisituational character of the use of violence and to its interpersonal characteristics (19). But, obviously, persons living in a subcultural milieu designated as a subculture of violence cannot and do not engage in violence continuously, otherwise normal social functioning would be virtually impossible. We are merely suggesting, for example, that ready access to weapons in this milieu may become essential for protection against others who respond in similarly violent ways in certain situations, and that the carrying of knives or other protective devices becomes a common symbol of willingness to participate in violence, to expect violence, and to be ready for its retaliation (20).

3. The potential resort or willingness to resort to violence in a variety of situations emphasizes the penetrating and diffusive character of this culture theme. The number and kinds of situations in which an individual uses violence may be viewed as an index of the extent to which he has assimilated the values associated with violence. This index should also be reflected by quantitative differences in a variety of psychological dimensions, from differential perception of violent stimuli to different value expressions in questionnaire-type instruments. The range of violence from minor assault to fatal injury, or certainly the maximum of violence expected, is rarely made explicit for all situations to which an individual may be exposed. Overt violence may even occasionally be a chance result of events. But clearly this range and variability of behavioral expressions of aggression suggest the importance of psychological dimensions in measuring adherence to a subculture of violence.

4. The subcultural ethos of violence may be shared by all ages in a sub-society, but this ethos is most prominent in a limited age group, ranging from late adolescence to middle age. We are not suggesting that a particular ethnic, sex, or age group all share in common the use of potential threats of violence. We are contending merely that the known empirical distribution of conduct, which expresses the sharing of this violence theme, shows greatest localization, incidence, and frequency in limited sub-groups and reflects differences in learning about violence as a problem-solving mechanism.

5. The counter-norm is nonviolence. Violation of expected and required violence is most likely to result in ostracism from the group. Alienation of some kind, depending on the range of violence expectations that are unmet, seems to be a form of punitive action most feasible to this subculture. The juvenile who fails to live up to the conflict gang's requirements is pushed outside the group. The adult male who does not defend his honor or his female companion will be socially emasculated. The 'coward' is forced to move out of the territory, to find new friends and make new alliances. Membership is lost in the subsociety sharing the cluster of attitudes positively associated with violence. If forced withdrawal or voluntary retreat are not acceptable modes of response to engaging in the counter-norm, then execution, as is reputed to occur in organized crime, may be the extreme punitive measure.

6. The development of favorable attitudes toward, and the use of, violence in a subculture usually involve learned behavior and a process of differential learning (21), association (22), or identification (23). Not all persons exposed—even equally exposed—to the presence of a subculture of violence absorb and share in the values in equal portions. Differential personality variables must be considered in an integrated social-psychological approach to an understanding of the subcultural aspects of violence. We have taken the position that aggression is a learned response, socially facilitated and integrated, as a habit, in more or less permanent form, among the personality characteristics of the aggressor. Aggression, from a psychological standpoint, has been defined by Buss as 'the delivery of noxious stimuli in an interpersonal context' (24). Aggression seems to possess two major classes of reinforcers: the pain and injury inflicted upon the victim and its extrinsic rewards (25). Both are present in a subculture of violence, and their mechanism of action is facilitated by the social support that the aggressor receives in his group. The relationship between aggression, anger, and hostility is complicated by the habit characteristics of the first, the drive state of the second, and the attitudinal interpretative nature of the third. Obviously, the immediacy and the short temporal sequence of anger with its autonomic components make it difficult to study a criminal population that is some distance removed from the anger-provoked event. Hostility, although amenable to easier assessment, does not give a clear indication or measure of physical attack because of its predominantly verbal aspects. However, it may dispose to or prepare for aggression (26).

Aggression, in its physical manifest form, remains the most criminologically relevant aspect in a study of violent assaultive behavior. If violent aggression is a habit and possesses permanent or quasi-permanent personality trait characteristics, it should be amenable to psychological assessment through appropriate diagnostic techniques. Among the several alternative diagnostic methodologies, those based on a perceptual approach seem to be able, according to the existing literature (27), to elicit signs and symptoms of behavioral aggression, demonstrating the existence of this 'habit' and/or trait in the personality of the subject being tested. Obviously, the same set of techniques being used to diagnose the trait of aggression can be used to assess the presence of major psychopathology, which might, in a restricted number of cases, have caused 'aggressive behavior' outside, or in spite of, any cultural or subcultural allegiance.

7. *The use of violence in a subculture is not necessarily viewed as illicit conduct and the users therefore do not have to deal with feelings of guilt about their aggression.* Violence can become a part of the life style, the theme of solving difficult problems or problem situations. It should be stressed that the problems and situations to which we refer arise mostly within the subculture, for violence is used mostly between persons and groups who themselves rely upon the same supportive values and norms. A carrier and user of violence will not be burdened by conscious guilt, then, because generally he is not attacking the representatives of the non-violent culture, and because the recipient of this violence may be described by similar class status, occupational, residential, age, and other attribute categories which characterize the subuniverse of the collectivity sharing in the subculture of violence. Even law-abiding members of the local subculture area may not view various expressions of violence as menacing or immoral. Furthermore, when the attacked see their assaulters as agents of the same kind of aggression they themselves represent, violent retaliation is readily legitimized by a situationally specific rationale, as well as by the generally normative supports for violence.

Probably no single theory will ever explain the variety of observable violent behavior. However, the subculture-of-violence approach offers, we believe, the advantage of bringing together psychological and sociological constructs to aid in the explanation of the concentration of violence in specific socio-economic groups and ecological areas.

Some questions may arise about the genesis of an assumed subculture of violence. The theoretical formulation describes what is believed to be a condition that may exist in varying manifestations from organized crime, delinquent gangs, political subdivisions, and subsets of a lower-class culture. How these variations arise and from what base, are issues that have not been raised and that would require research to describe. Moreover, the literature on the sociology of conflict, derived principally from Simmel (28), on the social psychology of conflict (29), and on the more specific topic of the sociology of violence (30) would have to be carefully examined. That there may be some universal derivatives is neither asserted nor denied. One could argue (1) that there is a biological base for aggressive behavior which may, unless conditioned against it, manifest itself in physical violence; (2) that, in Hegelian terms, each culture thesis contains its contraculture antithesis, that to develop into a central culture, nonviolence within must be a dominant theme, and that therefore a subtheme of violence in some form is an invariable consequence. We do not find either of these propositions tenable, and there is considerable evidence to contradict both.

Even without returning philosophically to a discussion of man's pre-political or pre-societal state, a more temporally localized question of genesis may be raised. The descriptions current in subcultural theorizing in general sociology or sociological criminology are limited principally to a modern urban setting, although applications of these theories could conceivably be made to the criminal machinations in such culture periods as Renaissance Florence. At present, we create no new statement of the genesis of a subculture of violence, nor do we find it necessary to adopt a single position. The beginning could be a Cohen-like negative reaction that turned into regularized, institutionalized patterns of prescription. Sufficient communication of dominant culture values, norms, goals, and means is, of course, implicitly assumed if some subset of the population is to react negatively. The existence of violent (illegitimate) means also requires that some of the goals (or symbols of goals) of the dominant culture shall have been communicated to subcultural groups in sufficient strength for them to introject and to desire them and, if thwarted in their pursuit of them, to seek them by whatever illegal means are available. The Cloward-Ohlin formulation is, in this context, an equally useful hypothesis for the genesis of a subculture of violence. Miller's idea of a 'generating milieu does not assume—or perhaps even denies—the communication of most middle-class values to the lower class. Especially relevant to our present interest would be communication of attitudes toward the use of violence. Communication should, perhaps, be distinguished from absorption or introjection of culture values. Communication seems to imply transmission cognitively, to suggest that the recipients have conscious awareness of the existence of things. Absorption, or introjection, refers to conative aspects and goes beyond communication in its power to affect personalities. A value becomes part of the individual's attitudinal set or predisposition to act, and must be more than communicated to be an integral element in a prepotent tendency to respond to stimuli. It might be said that, both in Cohen's and in Cloward-Ohlin's conceptualizations, middle-class values are communicated but not absorbed as part of the personality or idioverse of those individuals who deviate. In Miller's schema, communication from middle to lower class is not required. A considerable degree of isolation of the latter class is even inferred, suggesting that the lower-class ethic has a developmental history and continuity of its own.

We are not prepared to assert how a subculture of violence arises. Perhaps there are several ways in different cultural settings. It may be that even within the same culture a collective conscience and allegiance to the use of violence develop into a subculture from the combination of more than one birth process, i.e. as a negative reaction to the communication of goals from the parent culture, as a positive reaction to this communication coupled with a willingness to use negative means, and as a positive absorption of an indigenous set of subcultural values that, as a system of interlocking values, are the antithesis of the main culture themes.

Whatever may be the circumstances creating any subculture at variance, the problems before us at present are those requiring more precision in defining a subculture, fuller descriptions and measurements of normative systems, and research designed to test hypotheses about subcultures through psychological, sociological, and other disciplinary methods. In the present chapter we have tried to provide an outline of how some of these problems might be resolved. We have used the conceptualization of a subculture of violence as a point of theoretical departure for an integrated sociological and psychological approach to definition, description, and measurement. It now seems appropriate to examine in more detail some of the relevant theory and data on homicide and other assaultive offenses in order to show how these formulations and empirical facts may lead into and be embraced or rejected by the thesis of a subculture of violence.

REFERENCES

1. Hanan C. Selvin, 'Durkheim's *Suicide* and Problems of Empirical Research', *American Journal of Sociology* (1958) **63**:607–619.

2. Robert K. Merton, *Social Theory and Social Structure*, Glencoe, Ill.: The Free Press, 1949, pp. 131–194.

3. E. H. Powell, 'Occupational Status and Suicide: Toward a Redefinition of Anomie', *American Sociological Review* (1958) **23**:131–139. See also the latest book publication which discusses the major notions, research, and inferences of anomie: Marshall Clinard (ed.) *Anomie and Deviant Behavior: A Discussion and Critique*, New York: The Free Press of Glencoe, 1964.

4. What is meant by psychological anomie can be a number of different constructs. For example, MacIver gives a psychological definition of anomie which describes psychopathological syndromes resulting from loss of sense of social cohesion [R. M. MacIver, *The Ramparts We Guard*, New York: Macmillan, 1950]. Ansbacher (H. L. Ansbacher, 'Anomie, the Sociologist's Conception of Lack of Social Interest', *Ind. Psychol. Newsletter* (1956) **5**:11–12, 3–5) has equated this to Adler's lack of social interest [A. Adler, *Social Interest*, New York: Putnam, 1939]. Merton defines psychological anomie as a counterpart of, and not a substitute for, sociological anomie [Merton, *op. cit.*], and, indeed, it would be difficult to exclude a psychological correlate to such a pervading concept as sociological anomie. The difficulty rests with its integration into other meaningful personality constructs and with its reliable measurement. Srole's scale [L. Srole, 'Anomie, Authoritarianism and Prejudice', *American Journal of Sociology* (1956) **62**:63–67; L. Srole, 'Social Integration and Certain Corollaries: An Exploratory Study', *American Sociological Review* (1956) **21**:709–716] has had so far a very limited application and its use is difficult in groups characterized by low educational level.

   For an expository analysis of anomie as a psychological concept, see Stephen H. Davol and Gunars Reimanis, 'The Role of Anomie as a Psychological Concept', *Journal of Individual Psychology* (1959) **15**:215–225.

5. Marvin E. Wolfgang, *Patterns in Criminal Homicide*, Philadelphia, Pennsylvania: University of Pennsylvania Press, 1958.

6. A Pigliaru, *La vendetta barbaricina come ordinamento giuridico*, Milano: Giuffrè, 1959.

   For an amazing report on the whole small town, Albanova, near Rome, that is devoted to the use of violence, see Giulio Frisoli, 'La pistola regalo di battesimo', *Epoca* (February 27, 1965), and Giulio Frisoli and Pietro Zullino, 'Il segreto di Albanova, *Epoca* (March 7, 1965).

7. G. Guzman Campos, O. Fals Borda, and E. Umaña Luna, *'La Violencia en Colombia: Estudio de un proceso social'*, Bogotá: Tercer Mundo, 1962.

8. Wolfgang, *Patterns in Criminal Homicide*, pp. 188–189.

9. We have elsewhere, in Chapter II, referred to the many studies of delinquency that discuss these matters. For recent items, see especially Lewis Yablonsky, *The Violent Gang*, New York: Macmillan, 1962; also, Dorothy Hayes and Russell Hogrefe, 'Group Sanction and Restraints Related to Use of Violence in Teenagers', paper read at the 41st annual meeting of the American Orthopsychiatric Association, Chicago, Illinois, March 20, 1964.

10. For an especially insightful comment that aided our thinking on this topic, see Otto Pollak, 'Our Social Values and Juvenile Delinquency', *The Quarterly of the Pennsylvania Association on Probation, Parole and Correction* (September, 1964) **21**:12–22.

11. There is an abundant literature on the combined topics of child-rearing practices, physical aggression, and social class. Among the earlier works, particularly useful are R. R. Sears, *Survey of Objective Studies of Psychoanalytical Concepts*, Bulletin 51, New York: Social Science Research Council, 1943; A. Davis and R. J. Havighurst, 'Racial Class and Color Difference in Child Rearing', *American Sociological Review* (1946) 11:698–710; J. H. S. Bossard, *The Sociology of Child Development*, New York: Harper and Brothers, 1948.

    Several specific references of special use in our concern with the transmission of values related to violence or physical aggression include:

    Charles McArthur, 'Personality Differences Between Middle and Upper Classes', *Journal of Abnormal and Social Psychology* (1955) 50:247–254.

    Clyde R. White, 'Social Class Differences in the Use of Leisure', *American Journal of Sociology* (1955) 61:145–151.

    O. G. Brim, 'Parent-Child Relations as a Social System: I. Parent and Child Roles', *Child Development* (1957) 28:342–364.

    Joel B. Montague and Edgar G. Epps, 'Attitudes Toward Social Mobility as Revealed by Samples of Negro and White Boys', *Pacific Sociological Review* (1958) 1:81–84.

    Lawrence Kohlberg, 'Status as Perspective on Society: An Interpretation of Class Differences in Children's Moral Judgments', paper delivered at the Society for Research in Child Development Symposium on Moral Process, Bethesda, Maryland, March 21, 1959.

    Melvin L. Kohn, 'Social Class and Parent-Child Relationships: An Interpretation', *American Journal of Sociology* (1963) 68:471–480.

    Louis Kriesberg, 'The Relationship Between Socio-Economic Rank and Behavior', *Social Problems* (1963) 10:334–353.

    Hyman Rodman, 'The Lower-Class Value Stretch', *Social Forces* (1963) 42:205–215.

    John C. Leggett, 'Uprootedness and Working-Class Consciousness', *American Journal of Sociology* (1963) 68:682–692.

    C. R. Roger, 'Toward a Modern Approach to Values: The Valuing Process in the Mature Person', *Journal of Abnormal and Social Psychology* (1964), 68:160–167.

    Leigh Minturn and William W. Lambert, *Mothers of Six Cultures*, New York: Wiley, 1964, especially Chapter 7, 'Aggression Training: Mother-Directed Aggression', pp. 136–162.

    Kathryn P. Johnson and Gerald R. Leslie, 'Methodological Notes on Research in Childrearing and Social Class', paper presented to the annual meeting of the American Sociological Association, Montreal, August, 1964.

    Excellent summaries of the literature in current works are found in Paul Henry Mussen (ed.) *Handbook of Research Methods in Child Development*, New York: Wiley, 1960; in Martin L. Holffman and Lois W. Hoffman, *Review of Child Development Research*, Vol. I, New York: Russell Sage Foundation, 1964; and in the rich bibliography noted in John J. Honigmann and Richard J. Preston, 'Recent Developments in Culture and Personality', Supplement to *The Annals of the American Academy of Political and Social Science* (July, 1964) 354:153–162.

    All of the recent literature we have been able to examine from anthropology, psychology, and sociology buttressed the general position of our thesis regarding class, punishment, and aggression.

12. Martin Gold, 'Suicide, Homicide and the Socialization of Aggression', *American Journal of Sociology* (May, 1958) 63:651–661.

13. *Ibid.*

14. This is different from the 'strength of the relational system' discussed by Henry and Short in their provocative analysis (Andrew F. Henry and James F. Short, Jr., *Suicide and Homicide*, Glencoe, Ill.: The Free Press, 1954, pp. 16–18, 91–92, 124–125). Relative to the Henry and Short suggestion, see Wolfgang, *Patterns in Criminal Homicide*, pp. 278–279. The attempt of Gibbs and Martin to measure Durkheim's reference to 'degree of integration' is a competent analysis of the problem, but a subculture of violence integrated around a given value item or value system may require quite different indices of integration than those to which these authors refer (Jack P. Gibbs and Walter T. Martin, 'A Theory of Status Integration and Its Relationship to Suicide, *American Sociological Review* (April, 1958) 23:140–147.

15. Robert J. Smith, 'The Japanese World Community: Norms, Sanctions, and Ostracism', *American Anthropologist* (1961) 63:522–533. Withdrawal from the group may be by the deviant's own design and desire, or by response to the reaction of the group, Cf. Robert A. Dentler and Kai T. Erikson, 'The Functions of Deviance in Groups', *Social Problems* (Fall 1959) 7:98–107.

16. Ross Stagner, *Psychology of Industrial Con-*

flict, New York: Wiley, 1956.

17. See, for example, John Paul Scott, *Aggression,* Chicago: University of Chicago Press, 1958, pp. 44–64.

18. For the concept of subculture to have psychological validity, psychologically meaningful differences should, of course, be evident in subjects belonging to the subculture of violence. From a diagnostic point of view, a number of signs and indicators, of both psychometric and projective type, can be used. The differential perception of violent stimuli can be used as an indicator. Partial studies in this direction are those of Shelley and Toch (E. L. V. Shelley and H. Toch, 'The Perception of Violence As an Indicator of Adjustment in Institutionalized Offenders', *Journal of Criminal Law, Criminology and Police Science,* (1962) **53**:463–469).

19. The Philadelphia study (Wolfgang, *Patterns in Criminal Homiicde*) showed that 65 percent of the offenders and 47 percent of the victims had a previous police record of arrests and that 75 percent of these arrests were for aggravated assaults. Here, then, is a situation in homicide often not unlike that of combat in which two persons committed to the value of violence come together and in which chance often dictates the identity of the slayer and of the slain.

20. A recent study (L. G. Schultz, 'Why the Negro Carries Weapons', *Journal of Criminal Law, Criminology and Police Science* (1962) **53**:476–483) on weapon-carrying suggests that this habit is related, within the colored population, to lower-class status, rural origin from the South, and prior criminal record.

21. As previously mentioned, differential reactions to conditioning may be the cause of differential adherence to the subculture by equally exposed subjects.

22. Alternative hypotheses make use of the concept of differential association (Edwin H. Sutherland and Donald E. Cressey, *Principles of Criminology,* Philadelphia: Lippincott, 1955).

23. Differential identification has been presented as a more psychologically meaningful alternative to simple association (Daniel Glaser, 'Criminality Theories and Behavioral Images', *American Journal of Sociology* (1956) **5**:433–444).

24. A. H. Buss, *The Psychology of Aggression,* New York: Wiley, 1961, pp. 1–2.

25. *Ibid.,* pp. 2–4.

26. *Ibid.,* Chapter I, *passim.*

27. For an analysis of relevant literature on diagnostic psychological instruments, see Buss, *op. cit.,* Chapters VIII and IX. For discussion of a preventive psychiatric system, see Leon D. Hankoff, 'Prevention of Violence', paper read at the annual meeting of the Association for the Psychiatric Treatment of Offenders, New York, May 7, 1964.

28. *The Sociology of Georg Simmel* (translated, edited, and with an introduction by Kurt H. Wolff), Glencoe, Ill.: The Free Press, 1950; *Georg Simmel, 1858–1918* (edited by Kurt H. Wolff), Columbus, Ohio: Ohio State University Press, 1959; Georg Simmel, *Conflict and the Web of Group Affiliations* (translated by Kurt H. Wolff and Reinhard Bendix), New York: The Free Press of Glencoe, 1964 paperback edition; Lewis Coser, *The Functions of Social Conflict,* Glencoe, Ill.: The Free Press, 1956; *The Nature of Human Conflict,* (edited by Elton B. McNeil) Englewood Cliffs, N.J.: Prentice-Hall, 1965.

29. The issues of *The Journal of Conflict Resolution* are, of course, pertinent. Relative to our main concern with violence, see especially Rolf Dahrendorf, 'Toward a Theory of Social Conflict', *Journal of Conflict Resolution* (1958) **2**: 170–183; the entire issue entitled 'The Anthropology of Conflict', *Journal of Conflict Resolution* (1961), Volume V, Number 1.

30. For an early provocative discussion of violence from a sociological viewpoint and as a tool of social protest against the Establishment, as a proletarian technique to threaten the existing institutions of society, see Georges Sorel, *Reflections on Violence* (the original French text appeared in 1906).

For recent general references to the sociology of violence, see:

Joseph S. Roucek, 'The Sociology of Violence', *Journal of Human Relations* (1957) **5**:9–21.

David Marlowe, 'Commitment, Contract, Group Boundaries and Conflict', reprinted from *Science and Psychoanalysis* (Masserman), New York: Grune & Stratton, 1963, pp. 43–55.

E. V. Walter, 'Violence and the Process of Terror', *American Sociological Review* (1964) **29**:248–257.

Jessie Bernard, 'Some Current Conceptualizations in the Field of Conflict', *American Journal of Sociology* (1965) **70**:442–454.

Austin L. Porterfield, *Cultures of Violence,* Fort Worth, Texas: Leo Potishman, 1965.

There is a growing concern in peace research with what has been called 'the sociology of nonviolence'. For a review of these ideas, see Martin Oppenheimer, 'Towards a Sociology of Nonviolence', paper read at the Eastern Sociological Society meeting, Boston, April 11, 1964.

38. VIOLENT GANG ORGANIZATION

LEWIS YABLONSKY

THE VIOLENT-GANG MEMBER HAS BEEN DE-scribed as a sociopathic personality characterized by a limited social conscience, inability to identify with others, with a tendency to be egocentric and exploitative in his general relations with others. The next important issue to be assessed in the development of the original assumptions about violent gangs centers around the nature of the relationship system of the violent gang. This can best be illuminated by attempting to answer the question: What are the structure and function of relationships in the violent gang? The working hypothesis that attempts to deal with this issue may be roughly stated as follows: Owing to the sociopathic defective social ability of its membership, violent-gang organization is characterized by limited group cohesion and different levels of commitment to the organization; and membership has a different meaning for each participant. Violent gangs tend to be only partially organized into a type of "near group." In order to appraise the nature of violent-gang structure, several important themes of its organization require closer attention and explanation. In particular the meanings of *membership* and *leadership* reveal a great deal about the nature of violent-gang organization.

▶SOURCE: *The Violent Gang*, New York: Macmillan, 1962, pp. 206–221. Reprinted by permission of Macmillan and the author.

SOME SIGNIFICANT THEMES OF VIOLENT-GANG ORGANIZATION

The Nature of Gang "Membership." Sociopathic youths join violent gangs for a variety of individualized, personal reasons. In some respects each youth has his own special motive for violent-gang membership, and this can be related to the intensity of his gang affiliation. The gang boy's degree of emotional involvement in the gang is indicated by his level of participation, which may be either core or marginal. The more sociopathic youth tends to be a core member, and the less pathological youth tends to be somewhat more marginal. Unlike participation in more defined groups, the amorphous quality of violent-gang organization provides the possibility for the sociopathic member to perceive the gang, especially its size, in his own particular way and to utilize it for adjusting a variety of individual problems.

Core Members. The core category includes both the leaders, who are at the center of the gang's structure, and the most dedicated and involved members. These central members know each other in face-to-face relationships, live in the same neighborhood, hang around the same corner, play together, fight among themselves, sound on each other, worry together, and plan gang strategy for warfare. The solidarity of the core members is much greater than that of the outer ring of more marginal gang participants. Gang membership is close to the core members lifeline of activity, and to them the gang constitutes their primary world. Their ego strength, position in the world, and any status or pleasure they enjoy are tied to gang activity. Their turf and activities, particularly the gang's violence, give meaning to their existence. The core gang members is easy to identify by his tremendous degree of around-the-clock involvement. This is not so with the more marginal gang member.

Marginal Members At the second level of overall violent-gang membership (and emotional involvement) are marginal members. Their participation in gang activities takes several forms: Category I—the sociopathic youth with immediate emotional problems; Category II—the sociopathic violence-dominated youth who is seeking his kicks through violence; and Category III—the "mythical member."

Marginal Members: Category I. The marginal member who joins the violent gang to resolve his immediate emotional state and needs does not usually know most other gang members. His closest friends are not core gang members, nor does he identify closely with the many real and imagined problems the gang consistently has with other gangs. This type of marginal member appears at gang-war discussions and battles at those times when he has a temporary need for violent behavior that he believes may be satisfied through gang activity.

One such marginal member of the Egyptian Kings went along the night of the murder because, "I just had a fight with my old man and I was mad at everybody." Another went along, as he put it, "for old time's sake." He never really "belonged" to the Kings nor was he defined by himself or others as a gang member. To reiterate his reason for participation:

I was walking uptown with a couple of friends and we ran into Magician [one of the Egyptian King gang leaders] and them there. They asked us if we wanted to go to a fight, and we said yes. When he asked me if I wanted to go to a fight, I couldn't say no. I mean, I could say no, but for old time's sake, I said yes.

Marginal Members: Category II. Other youths who may be included in the category of marginal gang membership are the sociopathic individuals almost *always* ready to fight with any available gang. They seek out violence or provoke it simply as they describe it: "for kicks or action." They are not necessarily members of any particular violent gang, yet are in some respects members of all. They join gangs because for them it is a convenient and easily accessible opportunity for violence. When the gang, as an instrument, is not appropriate they "roll their own" form of violence (for example, the three stomp slayers who kicked a man to death for "whistling a song we didn't like"). For example, in one typical pattern utilized by this type of gang boy, he will approach a stranger with the taunt, "What did you say about my mother?" An assault is then delivered upon the victim before he can respond to the question, which, of course, has no appropriate answer for preventing the attack. Some muggings (robbery combined with assault) are carried out by this type of gang member, not for money but for violent kicks. Such boys are "members" of all gangs and at the same moment "members" of none. If there is the possibility for violence, cloaked in the "rationality" and "legitimacy" of gang assault, they "join."

Marginal Members: Category III. A third category of marginal gang member may have no clear personal awareness of his membership. His essential "membership qualification" is to be identified as such by a core member. On many occasions during tours of the upper West Side with core gang leaders, particularly at times of gang-war stress, practically every boy seen by the leaders was identified as a gang member. At every corner where there was a collection of boys hanging around (a common sight in New York) the leaders pointed out members. Such "illusionary members" were identified essentially to satisfy the leaders' needs to "possess" a large membership. The leaders were not consciously lying; the imagined membership was part of their fantasy world.

In summary, the marginal, second-level gang "members" can be divided into three essential categories: gang "people" who exist in actuality and "join" to work out temporary violent needs; the continuous violence seekers; and gang "people" who exist in the fantasies and distorted conceptions dreamed up by core members in their efforts to reassure themselves of strength and power.

Miscellaneous Gang "Members". Some gang-war participants (who become "gang members" through identification by official agencies) defy categorization. The youth who arrives at the scene of a rumble simply out of curiosity and then gets arrested illustrates this type of gang "member," one difficult to count and categorize.

The following more detailed case illustrates this miscellaneous category more specifically. A youth who had no affiliation in any way with either the Balkans, Scorpions, or Villains "participated" in the June gang-war battle and was arrested at the scene as a gang member. According to his story, the evening of the fight he had nothing else to do, heard about the rumble, and decided that he would "make the scene just to see what was happening." On his way to the gang fight (at Grant's Tomb), he thought it might be a good idea to invite a few friends: "Just to be safe—like, man, who knows what's shakin'?" This, of course, increased the final number of youths arriving at the scene of the gang fight, since there were other boys who apparently did the same. He denied (and I had no reason to disbelieve him) "belonging" to either of the gangs, and the same applied to his friends. His arrest at the scene of "battle" was on two charges—disorderly conduct and possession of weapons.

I asked him: "Why did you carry the knife and zip gun when you went to the gang fight if you did not belong to either of the gangs and intended to be, as you say, a peaceful observer?" His response was: "Man, are you crazy?... I'm not going to a rumble without packin'." He took along weapons for protection in the event he was attacked. The possibility of his being attacked in the somewhat confused situation involving hundreds of youths, who had no clear idea of what they were doing at the rumble, was paradoxically quite good. Therefore (within his framework of reasoning) he was correct in taking along weapons for self-protection.

This type of rationale characterizes much "marginal" gang membership. The problem remains, however, that what may in fact be a confused situation involving miscellaneous youths with marginal membership and varied motives is too often defined by observers as a case of two highly mechanized and organized gang groups battling each other over territory. They project organization onto the gang and membership status onto a fellow curiosity seeker.

Another example of this difficult category of marginal membership is revealed by a different "gang war" incident. A clearly psychologically disturbed youth (this boy had been in the Bellevue Hospital Psychiatric Ward on several occasions) manifested his emotional disorder by stabbing another boy in the neighborhood. When arrested and questioned about committing the offense, he continually maintained that he had carried out his assault against the other boy (who was definitely not a gang member) because, "We had to get even with the bastards." He rationalized his individual act of assault by claiming to be a member of a gang getting even with a "rival" gang, which was "out to get him." For this disturbed youth, membership in the malleable violent gang organization became both his syndrome and rationale for violence.

It may be that such common psychotic syndromes as believing to be Napoleon, God, or Christ, and similar patterns so popular over the years, have been replaced on city streets by the rationale of gang membership (a rationale too often mistakenly accepted at "face value" by gang workers and authorities). Not only is the gang a convenient excuse for violence, but, as previously indicated, some disturbed youths find this behavior rewarded, nationally accepted, and aggrandized by many representatives of society. Public officials, such as police officers and social workers, in their interpretation of a violent incident, may thus help structure an individualistic act by one youth into a "gang war" explanation because it is to them and the gang youth himself a more logical reason for a difficult-to-define, senseless act. This error can result from a misconceived image of the violent gang and the complex meaning of membership.

There is some indication that the following typical "gang incident" involving mistaken identity is a case in point (*New York Daily Mirror,* June 30, 1959):

TWO TEEN GANGSTERS HELD IN "MISTAKE" SHOOTING

Two members of a shoot-first-and-ask-questions-later teen-age gang were arrested yesterday, charged with seriously wounding another youth with a shotgun.

The victim, police said, was not even a member of the rival gang the assailants were hunting to avenge an attack two weeks ago on one of their members.

Juan Melendez, 19—known as "Angel"—of 40 Ave. D, and Samuel Carrion, 18—known as "Ace"—of 70 E. 99th St., were held on charges of felonious assault and Sullivan Law violation. A third youth known as "The Fat Man" is still being hunted.

Their victim, Robert Castro, 19, of 636 E. Fifth St., is in serious condition in Bellevue Hospital with shotgun wounds in the back and elbow.

According to police, Castro and a friend, Abdul Zukur, 18, of 230 Clinton St., were walking on Madison St. at 12:10 A.M. yesterday after rehearsing with a singing group, when Melendez and the two others jumped them and began beating them.

"Are you Dragons?" one asked, and without waiting for an answer police said Melendez pulled the shotgun from under his coat and let go two blasts. One missed. The other hit Castro.

An hour later Patrolmen Lester Sloan and Solomon Meadero of the Clinton St. Station nabbed Melendez carrying a shotgun. They said he admitted seeking revenge for "The Sportsmen" on a rival gang, "The Dragons."

This type of gang incident is most apt to be an individual act of aggression, rationalized as gang revenge by "Angel" and "Ace," and erroneously accepted as a gang act by the police and public.

Some Varied Functions of Gang Membership. Violent gang membership has an adaptable, chameleon characteristic. A youth can belong one day and quit the next without the necessity of telling anyone. It is often possible to take the gang boy's emotional temperature by asking him daily whether he is a Dragon or a King. It is somewhat comparable to asking him, "How do you feel today?"

This individualized emotional interpretation helps reveal the function of gang membership. Some boys say that the gang is organized for protection and that one role of a gang member is to fight—how, when, with whom, and for what reason he is to fight are seldom clear, and answers vary from member to member. One gang boy may define himself more specifically as a protector of the younger boys in the neighborhood. Another defines his role in the gang as a response to prejudice: "We're going to get all those guys who call us Spicks." Still others say their participation in the gang was forced upon them against their will by a vaguely defined seducer. There appears to be no clear consensus of role expectation in violent gang membership, and this conveniently enables each gang boy to project his own definition onto the meaning of his "membership."

Despite the different degrees of participation ("core" and "marginal"), and the individualized interpretations of gang membership, a unifying bond among gang members is the belief that through gang membership they acquire prestige and status. It is also quite clear that the vagueness that surrounds the delineation of gang membership and organization enables the gang member to fulfill many varied needs. If qualifications for membership were more exact, most members, especially the more sociopathic leaders, would be unable to participate, for they lack the ability to assume the social responsibilities required for more structured normal organizations. As indicated, the acts of violence as "rites of passage" for participation in this type of gang demand limited ability and training. The violent gang is thus a human collectivity where even the most socially deficient youth is able to play some membership role.

Some youths clinging to membership in this diffuse human organization sometimes employ violence simply to maintain a human affiliation. Many gang members act out violence as part of their emotional disturbance, however, most gang members use violence to enjoy "a feeling of belonging" and keep their rep, both aspects of membership. The Kings expressed their varied needs for gang membership in their own fashion:

I didn't want to be different.

I didn't want to be like . . . you know, different from the other guys. Like they hit him, I hit him. In other words, I didn't want to show myself as a punk.

It makes you feel like a big shot.

It makes you feel like a big shot. You know, some guys think they're big shots and all that. They think, you know, they got the power to do everything they feel like doing. They say, like "I wanna stab a guy," and then the other guy says, "Oh, I wouldn't dare do that." You know, he thinks I'm acting like a big shot. That's the way he feels. He probably thinks in his mind, "Oh, he probably won't do that." Then, when we go to a fight, you know, he finds out what I do.

For selfishness

Momentarily I started to thinking about it inside; then I have my mind made up, I'm not going to be in no gang. Then I go on inside. Something comes up here come all my friends coming to me. Like I said before, I'm intelligent and so forth. They be coming to me—they talk to me about what they gonna do. Like, "Man, we'll go out here and kill this guy." I say, "Yeah." They kept on talkin'. I said, "Man, I just gotta go with you." Myself, I don't want to go, but when they start talkin' about what they gonna do, I say, "No, he isn't gonna take over my rep. I ain't gonna let him be known more than me." And I go ahead just for selfishness.

For a build-up

If I would of got the knife, I would have stabbed him. That would have gave me more of a build-up. People would have respected me for what I've done and things like that. They would say, "There goes a cold killer."

For some youths being a cold-killer "member" of a gang is better than being a lone "violent psycho." The violent gang with its minimal demands and its grand alliances provides the sociopathic youth with some minimal "sense of belonging." He "belongs" because it may be the only type of human organization whose demands are minimal enough for his sociopathic ability to participate. However different this "belonging" may be compared to other groups, it is still a form of participation and, in its unique fashion, "membership."

THE VIOLENT-GANG LEADER

According to Moreno, the leader is a function of the group, and the leadership pattern reveals something about the nature of the group being led.

Leadership is a function of group structure. The form it takes depends upon the constellation of the particular group. The power index of a leader depends upon the power indices of the individuals who are attracted to and influenced by him. Their indices are again expressed by the number of individuals who are attracted to and dominated by them. The power index of the leader is, however, also dependent upon the psychological communication networks to which his referents belong and the position which the networks themselves have within the entire collective within which his leadership is in operation.[1]

The core sociopath in the violent gang is generally the leader. Contrary to many widely held misconceptions that these leaders could become "captains of industry if only their energies were redirected," the gang leader appears as a socially ineffectual youth incapable of transferring his leadership ability and functioning to more demanding social groups. The low-level expectations of the violent gang, with its minimal social requirements, is appropriate to the leader's ability. Given his undersocialized personality attributes, he could only be a leader of a violent gang.

THE GANG LEADER'S "MASK OF SANITY" [2]

The violent-gang leader obsessively needs the gang, and provides it with its basic cohesive force. In a gang of some thirty boys there may be five or six core leaders who desperately rely on the gang to build and maintain their rep. They mold the gang's image and work to keep the "members" involved in violent action. The enlistment of new members (by force), plotting, and talking about gang warfare fills most of their waking hours. The gang is central to their existence.

The gang leader's age, revealed as five to ten years older than that of gang members, provides a clue to his pathological nature. A twenty- or twenty-five-year-old person leading a group of fourteen- or fifteen-year-old youths in a fantasy world of power and violence would appear to have problems. (If he was dealing with concrete objectives such as stealing for personal gain, as in the *delinquent gang,* his leadership would have greater rationality.) In addition to the sociopathic personality emerging from the "disorganized slum," gang leaders, in depth interviews, reveal the feeling that they are attempting to relive, at an older age, a "powerful" role which they were unable to fulfill during youth. Gang leadership appears as an important fulfillment of the disturbed youth's childhood dreams of glory—a regressive effort to achieve now what he failed at earlier in life.

The gang leader deprived of his gang appears as a pathetic figure. Loco and Duke, after the demise of the Kings and Balkans, bore some resemblance to Coleridge's "Ancient Mariner," mumbling stories about events and conditions no longer appropriate or relevant. The loss of their gang leaves the leader almost physically shaken—somewhat like a drug addict without a "shot."

Leading a violent gang is a more highly desirable pathological syndrome than many other patterns that are viewed with greater opprobrium The person who is in a position to accept this "face" for his pathology is not generally considered "crazy." Even more advantageous is the fact that he takes on a public role glorified by some popular "American heroes" of the past, such as Capone and Dillinger.

Currently, a cloak of social immunity and even aggrandizement is provided for *pathological violence* of the Western heroes on TV. Interestingly, these "modern" television heroes enacting brutal violence are found almost equally on both sides of the law. The "good guy," sheriff, or lawman is as sociopathic and enjoys his violence as much as the Robin Hood type of outlaw. Within this media context, the violence role is justified and aggrandized by any flimsy pretext of a story line. The form of violence depicted is not really important

---

[1] J. L. Moreno, *Who Shall Survive?* (New York: Beacon House, 1952).

[2] This expression is taken from Harvey Cleckley's classic volume *The Mask of Sanity.* In his discussion he makes the cogent point that many deviant persons, who appear normal on the surface, when stripped of their "mask of sanity" reveal the psychopath beneath.

as long as the violent hero is not clearly described as "sick" or psychotic. (For example, it would be difficult to imagine a Western psychologist telling the "Gunslinger" or Elliott Ness, "You really are disinterested in law enforcement; you simply love to assault and torture criminals because you are a sick man.")

Although the current violent-gang leader appears to be at a considerable social distance from the "Western violent hero," the underlying structure of his violence in the social scheme has some similarity. *He assumes a popular role socially supported, and his violent behavior is often aggrandized rather than stigmatized with a pathological label.*

The notion of gang size as a symbol of power reveals another facet of the leader's pathological perceptions and needs. In the course of a one-hour interview, the gang leader may manipulate gang size, affiliations, and territory in accord with his cyclical emotions. In such interviews, gang membership will jump, according to the leader's estimate, from 100 to 4,000; alliances from five brother gangs to sixty; and territorial control from ten square blocks to jurisdiction over all the boroughs of New York City, New Jersey, and part of Philadelphia.

Gang leaders act out a standard pattern to demonstrate their ability to mobilize vast gang forces. An illustration of two gang leaders in a standard street-corner conference (attended by several silent constituents from each gang) reveals the meaning of this "numbers game" to the gang leader. One leader will brag how he can muster 2,000 "people" from various boroughs to help him and his gang fight the other leader's gang. In turn, the other leader claims he can muster 3,000 "people." Gang size increases at a ridiculous rate. Later, when the leaders were interviewed separately, both admitted lying. Yet in the moment of lying neither showed any strong indication to invalidate the other leader's story, since such a refutation might induce a challenge and invalidate his own story. Thus, there is an unspoken pact among violent-gang leaders to accept each other's story—a kind of mutual distortion society to bolster each leader's gang ego and rep. Their roles interlock in a grand illusion that helps to satiate their needs for power and status. (This process of mutual acceptance of fantasy is a common practice among some mental patients.)

Duke's Hitlerlike five-year plan for expansion of the Balkan forces gives some further clues to the quality of mythical divisions and alliances so characteristic of the gang leader's fantasy world:

Each division must pay 50 cents a week dues per member and each and every club that we take over by war must pay $1.00 per person per week or they must supply us with fighting men in case we need them. For every club that joins willingly we will fight for them 100% and they pay only the dues that a member would pay and they will be given all advantages a member of our club could be given. . . . Cars will be bought for each division. . . .

The first clique that we are going to try to take over are the Villains. The second group will be the Braves. The third is what is left of the Scorpions, Rebels, Knights, Saxons, and Vultures and then the Dragons, and then we will move up to 150th St. and down to 105th St. from 8th Ave. to Riverside Drive. We will let the Harlem Syndicate alone for now, also the Anzacs, Saints, Rebels, Sea Hawks, Knights. Our aim is to take over all clubs in the 20th, 24th and 30th precinct [police], leaving alone only those listed. The plan is a five-year plan at which time we hope to have at least 500 people in each precinct.

Duke's grand-alliance fantasies pervaded all boroughs of New York. The exaggeration of gang networks throughout the city is of course not complete fantasy. It has some measure of rational explanation and is hinged to real social conditions. Since the families of gang boys are transient, a Dragon or Balkan moving to another neighborhood may "organize" another "division." He probably does not, but brags that he has when he visits his old neighborhood. This gives the local gang leader further fuel for claiming more extended alliances. Thus, alliances or brother gangs are, essentially, psychological weapons that give the leader and his gang some feeling of security and a readily available threat he can use on adversaries, real or imagined. Moreover, attacking enemy gangs and syndicates, for example "the invading Dragons," are usable "concrete" enemies to be feared by paranoid youths who already manifest some feelings of being persecuted.

The fear of attack by a mass gang syndicate, which they cannot concretely identify, also gives the gang leader an enemy or problem that may serve as a convenient excuse for not facing immediate responsibilities of school, work, or duty to his family—responsibilities he is incapable of fulfilling adequately in any case. In his delusionary world he is involved with hordes of brother gangs, and too many "important" dangers and problems exist for him to cope with the meaningless and mundane responsibilities of day-to-day life.

The institutionalized violent-gang leader pattern of "drafting" reveals another dimension of the leader's "social mask." The drafting procedure is essentially a pattern of coercion. Getting another youth to "join" or "belong" to the gang becomes an end in itself rather than a means to an end. The process, which usually involves assault, coercion, or threatening violence upon another youth, under the guise of getting him to join, tends to satisfy many emotional needs of the leader. He is not truly concerned with acquiring another gang member, since the meaning of membership is at best vague; however, acting in this power role, forcing another youth to do something against his will becomes meaningful to his personal needs. The leader often implements initiation rites created on the spot for his personal gratification. These might include sadistic torture, cigarette burnings, a simple assault, or the practical act of extortion by collecting "loot" in the form of "club dues."

In the process of "drafting," the leader accomplishes several goals at once. He asserts the strength and identity of "his gang"; he achieves greater power by adding a new member (if only theoretically); he has a "legitimate" opportunity for acting out violence and domination.

Despite the overt appearance of bravado displayed before his gang, the gang leader when alone expresses deep feelings of inadequacy. His senseless violence is often a quick, sudden effort at releasing himself from fear, in part as an effort continually to prove to himself and the boys around him that "he isn't afraid and he isn't yellow." The leader fears self-exposure: "Jack, I'm scared—I'll admit it; you're always scared. The cops—your own boys—someone's liable to make you look like a punk. I can't stand to look like a punk so I keep fighting."

A counterpoint to the fearful, disturbed gang leader is the less sociopathic youth from the same difficult neighborhood, who has the resources to resist violent-gang coercion: "Man, I don't need to always be beating up on people to prove I'm a big man. Loco and all those guys know I can take any of them.... When they sound on me and give me this drafting and bopping bullshit, I laugh in their face."

Within some violent gangs such youths with adequate leadership potential for constructive activities exist, but they are generally marginal members. Often such a marginal-level gang member emerges as a leader when part of the gang membership able to do so shifts to and participates in some constructive activity (for example, a dance, baseball, and so on). They may also appear as leaders in deviant but demanding activities of the violent gang; the reigning leader remains the most violent core member.[3]

---

[3] The gang social worker, attempting to redirect a gang into constructive activities, is more apt to deal with the marginal, less sociopathic leader than with the violent-gang leader, who is not so easily amenable to redirection into nonviolent construc-

The Violent-Gang Model. One of the violent-gang leader's vital functions for gang membership is to serve as a symbol of idealized violence. Cast in his violent role, he is a shining example for core gang followers. The leader, in their view, has "heart," and will pull a trigger, swing a bat, or wield a knife without any expression of fear or, most important, regret. As a prototype of the violent gang, the leader is thus an ideal model. Free-floating violence, pure and unencumbered by social restrictions, conscience, or regret, is the goal.

Beneath these fantasies of power, the leader has delusions of being persecuted. Rather than accept responsibility for his own feelings of extreme hostility, he projects the blame for his violent tendencies onto others, sometimes society in general, but primarily other gangs. The leader maintains an attitude of "Let's get them before they get us." Combined with the needs of other disturbed gang members the result is mob action at a rumble. Such gang-war episodes, provoked by the leaders, produce a pattern of hysteria and group contagion characteristic of the leader's personality. This "disturbed-leader pattern," interaction with other susceptible youths, and an opportune situation provide the active ingredients for a "senseless" violent-gang killing. The leader thus embodies in his sociopathic self the idealized attributes of violent-gang organization.

---

tive activities. This situation, in part, explains why some youth workers perceive the gang leader as a more stable personality. The real leader of gang violence remains in the background, only to emerge when the gang bursts into violent activity.

39. CONTAINMENT THEORY

WALTER C. RECKLESS

BEHAVIORAL SCIENTISTS, SUCH AS PSYCHIatrists, psychologists, and sociologists, have had great difficulty in identifying the operation of various factors or conditions, assumed to be directly related to crime and delinquency. It has been almost impossible to isolate and measure the influence of conditions or factors on behavior of people generally.

The status of knowledge about the "etiology" of crime was so bad thirty years ago that it led two behavioral scientists to conclude: "The absurdity of any attempt to draw etiological conclusions from the findings of criminological research is so patent as not to warrant further discussion."[1] Progress has been made in criminological research and scholarship since that time but not enough to negate the above evaluation of Michael and Adler.

In 1940 the author suggested that criminologists should abandon the search for a general theory of crime causation and look for alternative approaches which are more realistic and appropriate.[2] Dissatisfaction with the application of the concept of causation to criminal behavior was expressed also by L. Radzinowicz at the Second United Nations Congress on the Prevention of Crime and Treatment of Offenders, London, August 1960.

It is quite likely that causation is not a

▶SOURCE: *"A Non-Causal Explanation: Containment Theory,"* Exerpta Criminologica (March/April, 1962) 1:2:131–134. Reprinted by permission of the Exerpta Medica Foundation and the author.

valid concept to apply to human behavior such as crime and delinquency, and that a general theory of causation, which has validity for all or a large part of crime and delinquency, for various samples of offenders and nonoffenders in various environments, is even more unrealistic, inspite of heroic efforts on the part of criminologists to search for a valid general theory.

The author proposes that criminologists formulate hypotheses about or explanations of delinquent and criminal behavior which do not require the concept of cause or a combination of causes. Containment theory is suggested as a substitute for causal theory. The following statement supplements three recently published statements of the theory.[3]

COMPONENTS OF EXTERNAL AND INTERNAL CONTAINMENT

The assumption is that there is a containing external social structure which holds individuals in line and that there is also an internal buffer which protects people against deviation of the social and legal norms. The two containments act as a defense against deviating from the legal and social norms, as an insulation against pressures and pulls, as a protection against demoralization and seduction. If there are "causes" which lead to deviant behavior, they are negated, neutralized, rendered impotent, or are paired by the two containing buffers.

In a mobile, industrialized, urban society such as exists in the United States and large parts of Northern and Western Europe, external containment will be found to reside principally in the family and other supportive groups in which individuals actively participate. In times past, the clan, the neighborhood, the village, the caste, the tribe, the sect have acted as supportive external buffers for the individual, in addition to the family. However, containment which exists for individuals within the family and other supportive groups of modern urban, industrialized society consists of one or more of the following components:

1. A role structure which provides scope for the individual.

2. A set of reasonable limits and responsibilities for members.

3. An opportunity for the individual to achieve a status.

4. Cohesion among members, including joint activity and togetherness.

5. Sense of belongingness (identification with the group).

6. Identification with one or more persons within the group.

7. Provision for supplying alternative ways and means of satisfaction (when one or more ways are closed).

Internal containment consists of "self" components—those having to do with the strength of the self as an operating person. It is composed of:

1. A favorable image of self in relation to other persons, groups, and institutions.

2. An awareness of being an inner directed, goal oriented person.

3. A high level of frustration tolerance.

4. Strongly internalized morals and ethics.

5. Well developed ego and super ego (in the sense of Fritz Redl,[4] as the control and management system of behavior).

A STATEMENT OF PROBABILITY

The components of the two containing systems are not causes. They are buffers or insulations against pressures, pulls, and pushes. They withstand the pressures, pulls, and pushes. When they are absent or weak, the person is likely to deviate from accepted social and legal norms, and is vulnerable for committing an unofficial (unreported) and/or official (reported) delinquency or crime. When the two containing systems are strong, the individual will not deviate from the legal and social norms and will not be an unofficial or official offender.

Containment theory not only describes noncausal buffers against deviation but it also describes probability. What are the chances (probability) that official delinquency and crime (reported deviation of the legal norms) will occur or appear in an individual, with such and such assessment of his inner and outer containment. Obviously, individuals who can be classified as strong-strong (strong in external and strong in internal containment) will have a very low probability of committing crime or delinquency (becoming a legal deviant); whereas individuals who are classified as weak-weak (weak in external and weak in internal containment) will have a very high probability of committing crime and delinquency.

The writer is quite prepared to admit that of the two containing buffers against deviation, the inner containment is the more important in the mobile, industrialized settings of modern society. This is because individuals in such societies spend much of their time away from the family and other supportive groups which can contain them. As a result they must rely more on their own inner strength to function competently. It is also probable that the outer is operationally more important than the inner containing buffer in less mobile, less industrialized societies where the clan, the caste, the tribe, the village retain their effectiveness or in the modern,

Scheme 1. *Probabilities of Deviancy in Mobile, Industrialized, Urban Societies*

	Inner Containment (put to a test in everyday living)	
External Containment	Strong	Weak
Strong	Very Low	Medium to Moderately High
Weak	Moderately Low	Very High

intensively managed, communistic societies. In such societies the strength of the self, away from a circumscribed social structure, is not put to a test and we really do not know how strong it is or how well it can manage alone.

ASSESSMENT OF INDIVIDUALS

The assumption is that individuals of various samples can be assessed for the strength or weakness of their outer and inner containment by methods which are at least equal to, if not superior to, an ordinary physical examination or the schedule of information used by life insurance companies in computing the risk of an applicant. An evaluation or assessment of the external containment can be reliably made by a trained sociologist, psychologist, or social worker, working under an expert. And it should be possible for two or more investigators to obtain independently the same rating of the external containment of an individual, as a result of a field investigation. In the not too distant future, it should be possible for sociologists to develop a reliable and valid check list or a scale to measure the strength of external containment, which would help to standardize the assessments.

Likewise, an assessment of internal containment can be made reliably by competent psychiatrists, psychologists, or sociologists. Psychologists have already validated several personality scales and some of them could be used for measuring the strength of the self. It would be no large task for research psychologists, psychiatrists, or sociologists, familiar with measurement techniques, to validate a scale which tests several components of strength of self. Even without the aid of a measuring instrument, psychologists, psychiatrists, and sociologists could make a fairly reliable clinical evaluation of the inner containment, in term of the components listed above, through interview with the individual. And two or more equally trained experts could arrive at the same assessment of the self of an individual independently.

Known groups of juvenile and adult offenders can be assessed according to the two containing systems and comparisons can be made with the assessments of comparable groups (for age, sex, class, religion, etc.) of known nonoffenders. Preadolescent children can be assessed, say at 12 years of age, and records of official delinquency and adult crime could be cleared for this experimental sample until 21 years of age. Then inner and outer containment could be related to the absence of delinquency and crime, to the early onset and late onset (when they do occur), to continuation in

Scheme 2. *Probabilities of Deviancy in Less Advanced and in Highly Managed Societies*

	Inner Containment (probably not put to actual test)	
External Containment	Strong	Weak
Strong	Very Low	Moderately Low
Weak	Medium to Moderately High	Very High

delinquency and crime once having begun, etc.

ADVANTAGES IN USE OF CONTAINMENT THEORY

Apart from the research application of the theory, there are several distinct advantages and realistic aspects in the use of containment theory. In the first place, it applies equally well to modal conformity,[1] to unofficial nonconformity (undetected and unreported deviation against social norms), to unofficial (unreported) and official (reported) deviation against the legal norms (crime and delinquency). Secondly, research methods can be developed to implement the theory and to make the assessments of both containing buffers. Thirdly, psychiatrists, psychologists, and sociologists have commonly shared interests in the various components of outer and inner containment. They could very readily join hands in research; could very readily form a research team with such a mutually shared orientation; they could very readily supplement and verify each other's work. Fourthly, containment theory is a good operational theory for treatment of offenders and the prevention of crime and delinquency. Institutional programs and probation and aftercare service could seek to build up the strength of the self and reconstruct an outer containing buffer for holding individual offenders in line. Assessments of outer and inner containment in the preadolescent ages could provide the means of early case spotting of vulnerable children, so that parents, school, and welfare agencies might make special effort to overcome the trend toward delinquency and crime. Special programs to reach vulnerable youth could focus upon implanting a stronger inner insulation against deviancy as well as developing supportive outer containments.

MIDDLE RANGE THEORY

Perhaps the most realistic aspect of the theory, from a scholarly and research point of view, is that it is a middle range theory. It does not apply to crime or delinquency at the extremes. It does not apply to crime or delinquency which is the result of overpowering internal pushes, such as compulsions, the illogical propensity for infantile gratification, manias, fugues, panics, hallucinations, paranoidal tendencies. The self as a controlling agent of the person, if it is strong enough, can cope with ordinary restlessness, ordinary disappointments, ordinary frustration, ordinary desires, but the self as specified in the inner containing buffer cannot contain abnormally strong internal pushes.

Likewise, containment theory does not apply to the other extreme, where begging, predatory activities, criminal pursuits are part of the prevailing way of life, such as the criminal tribes of India, the Gypsies of Europe, illegal whisky making in the Appalachian region of the United States, families who live by begging, etc. Persons inherit these criminal pursuits socially. Their prevalence is the natural order of events, since there are no alternate or competing modes of gaining a living. What needs to be explained in such instances is failure on the part of some members of these groups to follow the mode. Opium smoking among males in certain countries of Southeast Asia, gambling among Chinese migrants before World War I, abduction of marriageable females in the Punjab of former days, use of the machette for defense of personal honor in several Latin American countries, smuggling among coastal villagers or mountain villagers on a frontier, stealing of goats and sheep from neighboring flocks in the Near East have been prevalent enough to be considered in the same category of accepted pursuits or activities, which need no explanation in

---

[1] It is assumed that people are very infrequently saints and that most conforming people err sometimes; however, they are modally (prevalently) conformists.

terms of deviancy. Some sociological criminologists have referred to such general pursuits and activities as "criminogenic patterns".

In between the extremes of abnormal pushes and criminogenic (widely practised) activities, is the large middle territory of delinquency and crime, which needs explanation, because it represents legal and social deviation. Consequently, a theory such as containment theory is needed to explain deviation from the legal and social norms as well as modal conformity to these norms.

One final reality aspect is also apparent in the use and application of Containment Theory. The microcosm reflects the macrocosm. The individual case mirrors the general formulation. In the actual research application of containment theory, each case in the various criminal or noncriminal samples must be assessed in terms of external and internal containment. It would be difficult to identify, uncover, or assess the presence or absence of the components of Lombroso's, Feri's, Tarde's, Bonger's, von Hentig's, Exner's, or Sutherland's theories in individual case records of various samples of criminal and noncriminal populations. In these instances, and many others could be mentioned, one cannot get the microcosm to reflect the macrocosm.

REFERENCES

1. Jerome Michael and Mortimer J. Adler, *Crime, Law and Social Science*, New York, 1933, p. 169.
2. Walter C. Reckless, *Criminal Behavior*, New York, 1940, p. 255.
3. The first statement of "Containment Theory" is found in the third edition of the author's textbook on criminology, *The Crime Problem*, New York, 1961, Chapter 18; the second, in an article entitled "Halttheorie", which was published in *Monatschrift für Kriminologie und Strafrechtsreform*, Vol. 44, June 1961, pp. 1–14; the third, in *Federal Probation*, Vol. 25, No. 4, December 1961.
4. Fritz Redl and David Wineman, *Children who Hate*, Chicago, 1951, pp. 74–140.

40. SELF-CONCEPT RESEARCH

SANDRA S. TANGRI
MICHAEL SCHWARTZ

A WIDE VARIETY OF VARIABLES HAVE BEEN related to delinquency rates. These include demographic variables,[1] social structural variables,[2] variables having to do with perception of the social structures,[3] and occasionally personality variables.[4] In a recent paper by Himelhoch,[5] the point is made, without much elaboration, that personality variables may indeed be necessary for an adequate prediction scheme in delinquency research. He makes a plea in his paper for multi-level analyses which ought to include at one time variables of structure, perception of structure, and personality.

▶SOURCE: *"Delinquency Research and the Self-Concept Variable," Journal of Criminal Law, Criminology and Police Science (June 1967), 58:2:182–190.* Copyright 1967 by Northwestern University School of Law. Reprinted by special permission of The Journal of Criminal Law, Criminology and Police Science and the authors.

[1] See especially Chilton, *Continuity in Delinquency Area Research: A Comparison of Studies for Baltimore, Detroit, and Indianapolis,* 29 Am. Soc. Rev., 71–83 (1964).

[2] For example, see Cloward & Ohlin, Delinquency and Opportunity (1960).

[3] See Short, Jr., Rivera & Tennyson, *Perceived Opportunities, Gang Membership and Delinquency,* 30 Am. Soc. Rev., 56–67 (1965).

[4] Reckless, Dinitz & Murray, Self-Concept and an Insulator Against Delinquency, 21 Am. Soc. Rev. 744–746 (1956).

[5] Himelhoch, Delinquency and Opportunity: An End and A Beginning of Theory, Gouldner & Miller, Eds., Applied Sociology, 189–206 (1965).

A case can be made for engaging in such research on a number of counts. In the first place, while structural variables seem to be the primary focus in delinquency research carried on by sociologists, the results of their studies can by no means be taken as heartening. For example, in a recent paper by Westie and Turk, in which they examine the question of the relationship of social class to delinquency, they point out that it is quite possible to support findings which indicate more delinquency in the lower class than the middle class, more delinquency in the middle class than the lower class, or no differences by class, on the basis of both current research and theory.[6] Similarly, those studies which relate demographic variables to delinquency rates do not by any means achieve the same results.

While some students of delinquency have been able to find that delinquents and non-delinquents have differing perceptions of the structure which they confront, in no case has it been determined that those perceptions precede delinquency or non-delinquency or are a consequence of delinquency or non-delinquency. That very criticism can be made of studies which claim to discriminate between delinquents and non-delinquents on the basis of personality measures, although studies of per-

[6] Westie & Turk, *A Strategy for Research on Social Class and Delinquency,* 56 J. Crim. L., C. & P. S. 454–462 (1965).

sonality variables and delinquency are most uncommon in the sociological literature.

Apparently the major point, which is not made with the strength necessary in Himelhoch's paper, is that delinquency research has reached a stage where study designs ought to include variables at all of the levels we have mentioned, and that designs aimed at discriminating between groups are, at this stage, less important than are designs aimed at determining the amount of variance which can be accounted for in delinquency and non-delinquency by variables at a number of levels of analysis. In other words, we are now due for designs in delinquency research which are analysis of variance designs.

If the ambiguity and contradictions in our univariate forms of an analysis are ever to be understood, then it seems that the analysis of variance design is one which ought to be employed. It does have the virtue of giving the researcher an indication of the ways in which the interactions of variables from different levels of analysis combine to account for delinquency, and it seems that there is every indication that an understanding of the interaction effects of these variables may prove to be vastly more fruitful than a continued pursuit of univariate studies.

As Himelhoch has argued, however, sociologists concerned with delinquency research seem either to ignore variables at the level of personality, or to take them as given. Variables of personality seem to be in the domain of the psychologists and therefore out of the realm of the sociologist's competence or research concern. Perhaps that is a great error. There is available in our discipline a tradition of thought in the realm of personality and socialization which is not only respectable but also growing in measurement sophistication and applicability in empirical research. That is, of course, the tradition of symbolic interactionism.

Some sociologists have, in the past, investigated personality of self variables, keeping constant the social structural variables. Most important and impressive among these studies are the ones conducted by Professor Reckless and his associates, in which self-concept is viewed as a variable which seems effective in insulating boys against delinquency or in making them more vulnerable. Because this research has been so widely quoted and reprinted, and because it is practically the only research by sociologists in the area of delinquency which claims to handle variables of personality and self, it is wise, we believe, to undertake a thoroughgoing analysis of those researches, their designs, and the findings in order to determine what sociologists have been able to learn about delinquency and personality, as well as to determine what remains to be done in that area.

The behavior of the non-delinquent in a high delinquency area has occasioned a good deal of interest because of its possible implications for policies of social control. None of the studies by the Reckless group, however, draw such implications although they all claim to have discovered a crucial variable which differentiates delinquents and non-delinquents, and delinquents who have and have not been in contact with legal authorities as offenders. They do suggest that "self theory seems . . . to be the best operational basis for designing effective prevention and treatment measures" [7] This proposal is elaborated no further. As they state, the crucial variable is self-concept or "self-evaluation":

> It is proposed that a socially appropriate or inappropriate concept of self and other is the basic component that steers the youthful person away from or toward delinquency and that those appropriate or inappropriate concepts represent differential response to various environments and confrontations of delinquent patterns.[8]

In this discussion we shall review the methodology and detailed results of several studies, and attempt to evaluate the extent

---

[7] Reckless, Dinitz & Kay, *The Self Component in Potential Delinquency and Non-Delinquency*, 22 Am. Soc. Rev., 570 (1957).
[8] *Ibid*, p. 569.

to which these impose certain restrictions on the broad interpretation quoted above.

THE ORIGINAL STUDY: SELF CONCEPT AS AN INSULATOR AGAINST DELINQUENCY [9]

This was the first of the series of articles on the problem and deals exclusively with the boys whom we shall refer to as "good boys".

For this study, all thirty sixth-grade teachers in schools located in the highest white delinquency areas of Columbus, Ohio, were asked to nominate those white boys who would not, in their opinion, ever experience police or juvenile court contact; and the teachers were asked to give their reasons. Half of those eligible were nominated (i.e., 192). Of those, 51 students (27.3%) could not be located because of summer vacation. Of the remaining 141 boys, sixteen (11.3%) already had records and were eliminated from the sample. This left 125 "good boys"—and their mothers—who were interviewed. Each boy was administered the delinquency proness (DE) and social responsibility (RE) scales of Gough's California Personality Inventory (CPI); a questionnaire on his occupational preference (the data from which do not appear among the results); and each was asked questions about his concept of himself, his family, and his interpersonal relations.

The results obtained for the "good boys" were: (1) Low scores on the DE scale and high scores on the RE scale; (2) "self-evaluations" which were law-abiding and obedient; and (3) very favorable perceptions of family interaction, and lack of resentment of close family (mother) supervision; (4) these families were maritally, residentially, and economically stable. The authors concluded: "Insulation against delinquency is an ongoing process reflecting internalization of non-delinquent values and conformity to the expectations of significant others".

---
[9] Reckless, Dinitz & Murray, *op cit supra* note 4.

Critique

1. The first and obvious problem is that, without knowing parallel results on a control group of so-called "bad boys", we cannot conclude that these results actually differentiate the two populations. Since this comparison is subsequently made at the time of a later study, we shall postpone further discussion of this issue.

2. Insofar as the term "insulation" implies present and/or future predictiveness as to actual delinquent behavior, the following difficulties arise:

(a) It is perhaps a truism to point out that court records do not contain evidence of all law-violating behavior, and particularly in the case of minors. Therefore, it is probably safe to guess that the previous offenders constituting 11.3% of the "good boys" is an undestimate. It is about half the proportion of previous offenders found among the "bad boys".

(b) Since these boys were only 12 years old at this time, it would be more reasonable to look for a correlation between present "self-concept" and future "delinquency". Most of these boys (99 out of 125) were relocated in school four years later (at age 16), and four of them had been in "contact" with the police or juvenile court or both, one time each during the intervening years. Even this interval might be questioned as to whether it provides an adequate time span in which to validate actual "insulation". Together with the 16 "good boys" who were eliminated for this reason from the original sample, this makes 20 boys, or 14.4% of the 141 nominated "good boys" who were originally located.

(c) What is required is a comparison of the proportion of "contacts" among those scoring like "good boys" and those scoring like "bad boys" on the DE and RE scales from both actual groups of "good boys" and "bad boys" as nominated by the teachers. The analysis is not made anywhere, and is precluded by the exclusion of the 16 "contact" cases from the study of "good boys".

3. There is some clarification needed as to the use of teacher's nominations in this design. We have already seen that there is not a perfect correlation between the teacher's evaluations of the boys and their actual (non-) delinquency, as operationally defined in this study.

(a) If the authors wanted to investigate that relationship, they would not have eliminated 11.3% of the "good boys" who had already experienced "contact" with juvenile court or police. Such an investigation would have shed an interesting sidelight on why, in spite of being capable of making a good impression, these boys also had police or court records. What if they had turned out to have relatively positive self-concepts instead of relatively negative ones—contrary to the author's later assumption? We would be in a much better position to evaluate the author's conclusion if they had elected to gather these data. On the other hand, it must be pointed out that the authors were presumably not interested in investigating this relationship. From their point of view, it could be argued that there is no need for a perfect correlation. The assumption is only that you have a little better chance of getting a pure non-delinquent sample if you have two criteria; that the delinquent who can slip by one of them is less likely to slip by both.

(b) Nevertheless, the margin of uncertainty about the meaning of the teachers' nominations is magnified by the fact that only one-half of the eligible students were nominated. Who are the remaining boys? We wonder how many of those not nominated as "good boys" and with no "contact" experience would have been found to have poor self-concepts? And how many of these would have had "contact" with the police or juvenile court? Conversely, we wonder how many of those not nominated but with no "contact" would have been found to have poor self-concepts. The magnitudes involved are certainly great enough to reverse or eliminate the reported relationships.

The fact remains, however, that if we are really interested in determining the effect of the self-concept upon delinquency vulnerability, then we ought not look for delinquent and non-delinquent groups, but rather for groups with clearly good and clearly bad self-concepts. How those would be distributed between later delinquent and non-delinquent groups would better determine the effect of self-concept as independent variable, upon delinquency as the dependent one. Clearly, a major issue in much of this research has to do with the delineation of the experimental variables. If self-concept is an "insulator against delinquency", this implies that self-concept is an independent variable. But the research causes confusion because self-concept is treated as the dependent variable.

(c) There is some reason to feel uneasy also about the fairly high percentage (27.3%) of "good boys" who could not be located (i.e., 51 out of 192). This is particularly so when we compare the similar percentage for the "bad boys" nominated in the later study: 6.5% (or 7 out of 108). Thus, the original population of "good boys" (192) has been reduced by 34.9% (51 + 16 = 67), whereas no comparable shrinkage occurred in the "bad boy" population.

4. Our most serious concern, however, is with the instruments used to evaluate self-concept.

(a) In terms of the most elementary Meadian psychology, the relationship between frame of reference and self-evaluation, i.e., the correlation between teachers' nominations and the boys' responses to CPI items is not surprising. The CPI items obviously are drawn from a middle-class frame of reference, as are the teachers' impressions. They do not sample from an alternative frame of reference, in which positive instead of negative values might be placed on the same response. But we do know whether a revised scoring procedure in itself could be sensibly interpreted. Therefore, we would prefer to substitute a less culture-bound measure such as the semantic differential, in which the individual is free to operate in terms of any (unspecified) frame of reference. (We will have more to say about this problem presently, in some general comments.)

(b) Viewed in this light, one might hypothesize that because of this frame of reference, boys who are nominated as "good" will continue to test positive on the CPI, until they are caught in a delinquent act, at which time—and not until—the middle-class frame of reference would operate to devalue their behavior, and supposedly that part of their self-concept. Unfortunately, no such separate analysis was made.

THE "GOOD BOYS" FOUR YEARS LATER [10]

Some of the questions raised in the previous section about the interpretation of the "insulation" of the "good boys" in these studies may now be answered. Of the original 125 on whom data had been collected, only 103 boys (82.4%) were relocated, now age 16, but only 99 of them were still in school. The others were not retested. These boys' homeroom teachers were again requested to nominate the boys as (a) ones who would not experience difficulty with the law, (b) ones who would get into trouble, or (c) ones about whom the teacher was unsure, and why. Each of the boys was again checked through police and juvenile court files "for official or unofficial violation behavior in the intervening years", and their school records were checked. Their mothers or mother-surrogates were again interviewed.

The results were as follows: Ninety-five of the boys were again nominated by their teachers as unlikely to get into trouble

[10] Scarpitti, Murray, Dinitz & Reckless, *The "Good" Boy in a High Delinquency Area: Four Years Later,* 25 Am. Soc. Rev. 555–558 (1960).

with the law. The reasons indicated "quietness", "good family", and "good student". Four of these boys had become known to the police or juvenile court, or both—one time each during the intervening years. Ninety-six boys were enrolled in the academic program, although they showed a more or less normal distribution scholastically and in attendance (in which respect there had been no significant change over time). Ninety-eight expected to finish high school. Ninety-one remained aloof from boys in trouble with the law. The families of these boys, who were found in the original study to be typical of the families in the school areas in terms of father's occupation, were not nearly as residentially mobile as anticipated. (A separate analysis comparing the respondents who remained in the high delinquency areas with those who had achieved upward mobility revealed no significant difference on any of the indices included.) The boys' responses on the tests "and, apparently, in behavior as well", were consistent with their earlier performances.

On an additional measure, the Short-Nye seven-item scale of admitted delinquent behavior, "The good boys appear almost angelic". The authors question, however, the reliability of this result because they were unable to replicate the Short-Nye scale in any of their own more recent studies and because of the lack of anonymity of the boys, ". . . and their younger age". The boys' reports on their families were again favorable, somewhat more so than previously.

Critique

1. Now it is somewhat more clear that self-concept is the independent variable and that delinquency is the dependent one. At least it is clear if one keeps the first paper in mind. Of greatest interest is the finding that most of the "good boys" located again are still in school (99/103 = 96.1%), and all but three are in the academic program. We wonder if this might not imply that the factor differentiating good from bad

boys is ability to perform adequately in school. Glueck's findings on comparative intelligence between the normal and reformatory population would tend to support this interpretation: "It will be seen that the reformatory population contains a considerable excess of dull, borderline, and feebleminded groups." [11]

2. There are, however, several reasons why this interpretation may be unwarranted:

(a) The later studies do not give information on how many of the "bad boys" similarly remained in school (and in an academic program).

(b) Even if we found the proportion to be radically different, it would be quite reasonable to argue that this was because of their delinquency, lack of motivation, rejection by their teachers, or any one of a number of other factors than intelligence *per se*. However, it might have been helpful for narrowing the possible interpretations to have such a measure, providing it too wasn't class-biased.

(c) Of the boys still in school, half were still in the compulsory attendance age bracket.

3. In the relocation of the "good boys", 22 of the original sample were lost. Although this is three times as many as were lost from the "bad boy" sample, because of the fact that the original nominees from the population were almost 50% more for the "good boys" than for the "bad boys", it means in effect that the retested samples were approximately in the same proportions to the original populations for both groups: $99/141 = 70.2\%$ of the "good boys" and $70/101 = 69.3\%$ of the "bad boys."

4. We are also faced again with the questionable interpretation of the teachers' nominations. Why were they again asked to nominate each boy as a likely or unlikely candidate for trouble?

(a) In this case they were not choosing the boys out of the total class; if they had, perhaps fewer would have been nominated as "good boys".

(b) We do not know whether the four "good boys" still in school but not renominated were nominated as likely to get into trouble, or whether in their case the teacher was "unsure" (an additional category not previously used).

(c) It is interesting to point out that the four boys who had police or court contact in the intervening years are not these four (who were *not* renominated), but are among those the teachers again nominated as unlikely to get into trouble.

(d) It is not clear whether these are the only boys out of those relocated who had been "in trouble", or whether they are the only ones out of those still in school. If the latter is the case, and it appears to be, then there remains some question about the "insulation" of the four boys *not* in school.

(e) We are left with 95 "good boys" (67.4%) out of the original 141 nominated and tested about whom we can way with some (but not absolute) confidence that they have not been delinquent. Because of the unfortunate reporting of data, we cannot determine the comparable figure for the "bad boys." We know there were 20 offenders among the original "good boys" at the end of the study, but we don't know how many there were among the "bad boys" (because some of the earlier and later offenders may be the same boys).

THE SELF COMPONENT IN POTENTIAL DELINQUENCY AND NON-DELINQUENCY;[12] A SELF-GRADIENT AMONG POTENTIAL DELINQUENTS [13]

The sample of potential delinquents were nominated a year after the "good boy" stuly by 37 sixth-grade teachers in the

---

[11] Glueck, S. & E., Five Hundred Criminal Careers, 156 (1939).

[12] Reckless, Dinitz & Kay, *op cit supra* note 7.

[13] Dinitz, Reckless & Kay, *A Self-Gradient Among Potential Delinquents*, 49 J. Crim. L., C. & P. S. 230–233 (1958).

same 20 schools in a white high delinquency area in Columbus, Ohio. Approximately one-fourth (108) of those eligible were nominated as "headed for police and juvenile court contact". Apparently population growth in the area had increased the white sixth-grade population by about 13% (from ca. 384 to ca. 432) and the number of sixth-grade teachers by 23% (from 30 to 37) (There may have been a greater increase in the area's Negro population than in its white population). Only seven of these boys could not be located; the remaining 101, and their mothers, were interviewed. A check of the police and juvenile court files revealed that 24 of these twelve-year-old boys (23%) were already on record for previous offenses which ranged from charges of incorrigibility to theft.

The results, when compared with the first study, were as follows: The "bad boy" scores... were significantly higher on the DE and lower on the RE scales than those made by the 'good boys' of the first study. Indeed, this mean delinquency vulnerability score was higher than that achieved by any of the non-delinquents and non-disciplinary sample subjects treated in other studies. Similarly, the mean social responsibility score was lower than those recorded in other studies for all but prisoners, delinquents, and school disciplinary cases. These scores seem to validate the judgments of the teachers in selecting these boys as ones who would get into future difficulties with the law.

Not only do these scales appear to differentiate between the potentially delinquent and non-delinquent, but even more importantly they were found to descriminate within the sample of nominated delinquents between those boys who had and those who had not experienced previous court contact... These differences between the contact and non-contact groups on both sides were statistically significant.[14]

---

[14] *Ibid*, p. 231.

Critique

(We shall not repeat the points already discussed as part of the preceding sections.)

1. Adding to the confusion of possible interpretations already mentioned is the fact that the samples were not "designed" in a parallel manner. It will be recalled that in order to isolate "a truly non-delinquent group" for the first study, the investigators discarded sixteen cases (11.3%) of the "good boys" who could be located. This procedure would lead one to think that the interest was in fact correlating certain psychological patterns with behavioral patterns. However, we find that in the second study no such "purity" is attempted, and the 77 boys (76.8% of the 101 "bad boys" located) who did *not* have records for previous offenses were retained in the sample. Had the parallel operation been carried out, the "truly delinquent" group would have been considerably smaller, thus altering the statistical results of the measure. However, it should be pointed out that this type of attrition would have led to more, rather than less, significant results. The problem, therefore, is not the validity of the statistics, but rather the *interpretation* in comparing two non-parallel groups.

2. The second most critical point to make is that there is further contamination of variables due to the fact that the teachers' knowledge of the boys' involvement with the law "undoubtedly influenced" their nominations. Therefore, we have neither an independent "nomination variable" nor independent behavior variable. (We shall subsequently discuss the possible contamination of the third and critical variable, the test and interview responses.)

3. Although it is not possible to infer *a priori* whether any bias in sampling occurred because of the increase in number of teachers participating (37 as against 30 in the first study), it should be noted that there were large teacher differences in the number of "bad boys" nominated. In some

classrooms 60% of the eligible boys were nominated, whereas nine teachers nominated no one. (There was an average of 11.7 white boys per class, out of whom an average of 2.9 were nominated as headed for trouble.) These differences may reflect school policy to segregate potential disrupters, but we do not know.

We should point out that the statement that "these scores seem to validate the judgment of the teachers in selecting these boys as ones who would get into future difficulties with the law" implies some "validation" of the teachers' nominations against the nominees' later (future) actual behavior. This interpretation clearly may be unwarranted insofar as the only relationship being described is that teachers' nominations succeeded in creating two groups (at two different times) whose average scores on the DE and RE scales were significantly different. Moreover, we do not know how many of the same teachers were involved in both tests.

5. With respect to the comparisons of the "contact cases" and "non-contact cases", the conclusion that "it is apparent that the contact cases in many respects seem to be confirmed in their delinquent self-concepts to a greater extent than are the others" is justified in light of the results. What is not warranted, however, is the investigators' projected *evaluation* of his self-concept as a negative one to the boys being studied. A delinquent self-concept is not necessarily a negative concept.

DELINQUENCY VULNERABILITY [15]

The follow-up study four years later of the "bad boys" succeeded in relocating 70 boys, now 16 years old. We know nothing of how many were in school or in an academic program, and there is no report of second set of teachers' nominations. Twenty-seven (38.6%) of these seventy boys "had had serious and frequent contact with the court during the four-year interlude. These 27 boys averaged slightly more than three contacts with the court, involving separate complaints for delinquency". However, we do not know how many (if any) of these 27 are the same boys (24 of them) who had already had records at the time of the first testing, or whether they are different boys from the original population. As was mentioned earlier, both the "good" and "bad" follow-up samples are approximately the same proportion of the originally located, but untested, nominee groups. The "good" group lost 11.3% of its boys before testing began because of their delinquency records, whereas none of the located "bad boys" was dropped. The "bad" group, on the other hand, diminished proportionately more in size between the first and second testing, which may be considered more serious because it was an *uncontrolled* shrinkage of the *tested* population. The result is that the "good" follow-ups constitute 82.4% of their originally tested group and the "bad" follow-up constitute only 69.3% of theirs. Results of the second follow-up indicated that the "bad boys" mean score on the DE scale had not changed (it was 23.6 and at second testing was 23.4), and was still significantly "worse" than the "good boys" (whose mean score was 14.2, and at the second testing 13.6). The authors also note that "whereas the individual scores of the 70 'bad' boys on the DE scale at age 16 correlated with their scores at 12 years of age to the extent of $r = .78$", the "coefficient of correlation (r) of the DE scores for the boys in the 'good' cohort at 16 and at 12 years of age was only .15". They do not attempt to give any explanation for this difference in the groups' longitudinal stability. Certainly this is a most important finding and requires further understanding.

GENERAL COMMENTS

There are criticisms which pertain to the series of studies as a whole, and which are so important as to restrict severely the

---
[15] Dinitz, Scarpitti & Reckless, *Delinquency Vulnerability: A Cross-Group and Longitudinal Analysis*, 27 Am. Soc. Rev. 515–517 (1962).

authors' interpretations given, even if all the foregoing is deemed irrelevant or incorrect. Of major concern to us are the measures which were used to define operationally the boys' self-concepts. In the first place, it is not made quite clear in the original studies whether the conclusions with regard to self-concept are based on the Gough (DE and RE) CPI Scales, or whether the conclusion is based on the boys' answers to questions about their expectations of getting into trouble, or whether it was based on attitude items such as whether "any real trouble persons have with the law can be 'fixed' if they know the right people", whether it had to do with their descriptions of their home life or the degree to which they and their mothers (or mother-surrogates) seemed to agree.

It would be helpful in deciding which items are appropriate to a self-concept measure to differentiate between questions of *fact* and questions of *evaluation*. It is our opinion that only the latter is relevant to self-concept. Therefore, insofar as the boy states facts as he perceives them about his present behavior, the age and delinquency of his companions, "activity level" (whatever that is), whether he relies more on his friends or his parents for advice, etc., he tells us nothing about whether he thinks these are good or bad things, i.e., how these reflect on him personally and in his own judgment. Even in his judgment about the likelihood of his getting into trouble in the future, we do not know whether 1) this is self-criticism, 2) a badge of bravado, or 3) whether the prediction is accurate.

If we look at the operational definitions which are more ambiguously stated in the later studies, we see that they consist primarily of these kinds of statements:

On a nine-item quasi-scale or inventory, which measures the boys' favorable or unfavorable *projections of self in reference to getting into trouble with the law,* the cohort of 103 sixteen-year-old insulated slum boys showed an average score of 15.8. In this instance, the inventory was scored from 10 for the most favorable answers to 19 for the most unfavorable answers on all nine items. The 70 vulnerable 16-year-old slum boys scored an average of 18.9 on this quasi-scale.[16]

Could not these results be regarded as a statistically reasonable prediction by the boys of future events based on their respective past histories? Could it not be possible that the "bad boys" take some pride in their "record" and consider it a necessary adjunct to their self-image to be "tough" and "in trouble"?

Later in the same article quoted above, the following operational definition is given:

Regarding favorable or unfavorable concepts of self as measured by responses to questions such as "up to now, do you think things have gone your way?" or "do you feel that grown ups are usually against you?" or "do you expect to get an even break from people in the future?" there was no major change in the percentage distribution of the responses of the two cohorts at age 12 and at age 16. The good cohort had a very high percentage of favorable responses and the bad cohort a low percentage favorable responses. On all three questions listed above, the percentage of favorable responses for the 103 good boys at age 16 was 90. For the 70 bad boys at 16 the percentage of favorable responses on the first of the above listed questions was 50; on the second, 29; on the third, 30.[17]

It is reasonable again to ask whether the "bad boys" responses are not simply realistic reflections of the fact that these same boys "... who had already been in trouble with the law defined themselves significantly more often than the others as likely candidates for getting into future difficulties with the police and the courts" [18]

Does it not reflect the fact that their mothers think so too; and that their

---

[16] *Ibid*, p. 516. (Emphasis added.)
[17] *Ibid*, p. 517.
[18] Dinitz, Reckless & Kay, *op cit supra* note 7, at p. 232.

teachers think so? Is it not just another way of saying that their "family affectional relationships" are not satisfactory? But, does it also necessarily mean that these boys have no recourse but to accept these negative evaluations of *these* others *as their own evaluations of themselves?* We would argue that this is not the case, but that these boys look elsewhere for positive self-reflection, and that they may find it in their friends, which is the meaning of their seeking advice from friends more than from parents. A major problem appears to be that the authors may have selected sets of others for the boys, i.e., mother and teacher, both of whom are not significant "others" from the boys' own points of view.[19]

In summary, we would say that these studies have demonstrated:

1. That there is a certain amount of agreement between teachers and parents on the likelihood of certain boys getting into trouble; it has not demonstrated that this consensus agrees with either present or future actual experience.
2. That boys are aware of the judgments their elders make of them; it has not demonstrated the boys' acceptances of these evaluations of them as their own.
3. That this is true for the so-called "good boys" as well as the "bad boys"; and we still do not know whether the former think well of themselves and the latter do not.

The primary problem that is raised by Reckless' treatment of self is this: from any collection of questionnaire or interview responses, what kinds of conclusions can we draw about the self? It is not enough to say that these responses represent the subject's self. Since almost anything one can say may have some bearing on the self, we must have rules for extracting that aspect or implication of the statement relevant to self; otherwise we have no basis for distinguishing self from non-self, for everything is self. And that is the trouble with these studies. If everything is self, then self becomes another word for everything and its value is destroyed! A general hodgepodge of items from the CPI, questions asked to mother, son and teacher all thrown into the pot of self seems to destroy the meaning of self for research usage.

Vastly improved measurement in all of sociology is necessary. But adequate self-concept measurement is a dire necessity. We do not wish, however, to belabor the point. This research represents an important contribution to delinquency theory as well as to general social psychology. The papers have been reprinted in numbers of books of readings. It has been our experience that teachers, school administrators, public officials concerned with youth problems and others are very much aware of the Reckless *et al.* studies and in some cases try to operate in terms of these findings. But it would seem that there are some problems with this work which require adequate investigation. Nevertheless, Professor Reckless has opened an important door.

Our second comment in general has to do with the interpretation of the correspondence between the two studies. It will be remembered that the two cohorts were examined a year apart and taken from the same schools. They were not done contemporaneously. This may have had the advantage of avoiding invidious comparisons between the two groups of boys. However, in order to have confidence in the lack of bias on the part of the *investigators who administered the tests and interviewed the parents,* we would have to know whether or not they knew which cohort they were interviewing. In light of the fact that the data on the students in the good cohort were published soon after the data on the bad cohort were collected, (which means, in effect, that the results were known sometime earlier), and con-

---

[19] Schwartz & Tangri, *A Note on Self-Concept As An Insulator Against Delinquency,* 30 Am. Soc. Rev. 922–926 (1965).

sidering the fact that all these studies have been done by substantially the same group of investigators, we are inclined to believe that the investigators' own interviewers knew which cohort was which *while they were collecting data.*

Finally, we would point out that a theoretical link is missing from this research. Why should poor self-concept leave the individual vulnerable to delinquency? It might be argued, for example, that a poor self-concept ought to produce behavior more in conformity with the demands of significant others like mother or teacher. Or does poor self-concept lead to rejecting the rejectors and subsequent attributions of significance to those others who prove rewarding to the self (say delinquent peers)?

Is it enough to indicate that more nominated "bad boys" than "good boys" become delinquent, even though the number of "bad boys" who become delinquent is less than 50% of the total nominated. In short, we are not yet convinced that "self-concept" is a major contributor to the variance in delinquent behavior. No small part of our skepticism arises from the atheoretical orientation of the Reckless work.

Even if all the foregoing criticism of this research were to be determined to be incorrect, the fact of the matter is that until this same form of research is undertaken in a somewhat more sophisticated way and a design is formed which includes not only self variables but also structural and cognitive (such as perception of structure) variables, and until the interaction effects from all of these levels as well as the main effects of each are understood, then it will continue to be impossible to develop predictive accuracy with reference to juvenile delinquency.

SECTION

V

The Social Structure

RACE AND CLASS ARE STANDARD DEMOGRAPHIC FACTORS USED IN THE SOCIOlogical analysis of crime and delinquency. These segmental aspects of population are analyzed in the descriptive studies found in this section. Johnson's article discusses the extent and kind of Negro participation in crime and draws inferences about their treatment and involvement in the legal processes. Moses attempts to equate Negro and white residential areas in Baltimore, according to certain ecologic correlates, and then proceeds to examine differences in the crime rates between Negroes and whites. Moses' study is almost unique in the field and provides an interesting analysis with somewhat controversial interpretations of the data.

The Department of Labor issued a survey of *The Negro Family*, commonly known as the Moynihan Report, which has become one of the most highly debated and savagely attacked governmental documents issued in recent decades. The section on "The Negro Family and Crime," while neatly summarizing much of the relevant research, heavily emphasizes inherent structural problems in matriarchal family units in America.

The relationship between socioeconomic class and delinquency is certainly not a simple or consistent one, as Clark and Wenniger demonstrate. Nevertheless, some positive correlation seems to exist between serious delinquencies and lower class urban life. The organization, values, interactions, and deviant activities of "Middle Class Gangs" in suburban Los Angeles seems to give substance to the view of Matza and Sykes that the deviant nature of juvenile delinquency has been much overstated in contemporary criminological theory.

The Philadelphia study of delinquency and migration is included in this section because the author has used one of the areas of the city with the highest rate of delinquency. This study is an analysis of migration relative to delinquency rates during the juvenile years of exposure to the environmental influences of the area. That the native-born Philadelphia group more frequently became delinquent than did the migrant group is a conclusion with many ramifications.

It is widely assumed that formal education is, without argument, a major weapon against delinquency. Yet the manner in which the American educational institution may have within it certain unanticipated criminogenic consequences is carefully investigated by Delbert Elliot.

The importance of the family setting in the socialization and personality development of the child is well recognized. If we assume that most criminality is not due to some physiological or psychological anomaly, then the significance of the family in the etiology of the criminal becomes obvious. Most studies have dealt with family pathologies, and the child coming from a "wholesome" family is given little attention. The major concern is with the broken home; that is, a home with one parent missing due to death, desertion, or divorce. There are more subtle family situations, however, that are seldom dealt with, such as the parent who is present but continuously engenders hostility. Is this not a psychologically broken home? If the father is in the army or is a traveling salesman, is this not also a broken home? If the home is broken and the mother takes a paramour, is this necessarily harmful for the child? He may at least have an adequate father figure upon which to structure his own male role.

The matriarchal family, as Parsons has noted, poses major problems for the young male in the family because the father is not present to offer a model of expected adult behavior. The boy, in consequence, may become overly-aggressive in order to demonstrate his doubted masculinity. Rosen's analysis of eleven major studies of juvenile delinquency and broken homes reveals a generally weak relationship between the two variables and offers several possible explanations why this may be so.

Although not a broken home according to most definitions, the home with a working mother is often thought to produce delinquent children. In "Working Mothers and Delinquency," some empirical data are presented relative to this problem.

As Gannon states, the relationship of religion and delinquency has long intrigued social scientists. As a good social scientist, he examines empirically the attitudes, values, and religious practices of Catholic male delinquents in order to gain some insight into why religion failed to prevent delinquency in his subject population.

The contention that the mass media, particularly television, somehow develop latent delinquent tendencies in many young viewers is put to the test by Pfuhl. His findings give little comfort to those who search for a simple and "easy" solution to the complex problem of delinquency.

41. THE NEGRO AND CRIME

GUY B. JOHNSON

MOST DISCUSSIONS OF NEGRO CRIMES HAVE been concerned with the biases and the inadequacies of criminal statistics as a measure of the actual criminality of the Negro, or with an "explanation" of the Negro's high crime rates. Sellin has aptly said:

It is unfortunate that the belief in the Negro's excessive criminality has made students of Negro crime expend so much energy in attempts to verify the charge. Attention has thus been diverted from much more fundamental matters, such as the causes of crime and the relationship of the Negro to our agencies of justice.[1]

The present discussion proposes to deal with the problem primarily from the standpoint of the causation of Negro criminal behavior and the relation of the Negro to the administation of justice.

SOME ASSUMPTIONS

We shall assume in this discussion that the most fruitful approach to the question of why social groups may differ in the number or distribution of criminal acts

▶SOURCE: *"The Negro and Crime," The Annals of the American Academy of Political and Social Science (September, 1941) 271:93–104. Reprinted with minor corrections by the author.*

[1] Thorsten Sellin, "The Negro and the Problem of Law Observance and Administration in the Light of Social Research," in Charles S. Johnson, *The Negro in American Civilization* (New York, 1939), p. 451.

which they commit is to inquire into their social interrelations and into the ways in which their social environments differ. We shall assume, further, that the fundamental causes of crime in the Negro are the same as in any other group and that the simple fact of race is not sufficient in itself to explain any important group differences in criminal behavior. We readily grant the possibility that the Negro differs from the white man in temperament or *psyche,* but we assume that by no stretch of the imagination can such a factor be a primary determinant of the amount or nature of crime. Still further, we shall assume that, in view of the advanced stage of the process of acculturation in the United States, culture conflict arising from the clash of the Negro's African heritage with his European heritage is not vital enough to be regarded as an important causative factor in Negro crime.

The most important fact about the relation of the Negro to American society is his subordinate social status. In the South his social position is so rigidly defined as to constitute a caste position, and even in the North and the West, in spite of a certain amount of equality with respect to "civil rights," the Negro is generally subjected to social ostracism and economic discriminations. An analysis of the role of the Negro's social status in the causation of Negro crime will therefore form the burden of our discussion.

CASTE AND HISTORICAL FACTORS

Of all the ethnic groups that have come to this country, the Negro is the only one to experience the degradation of slavery and a persistent status of subordination. Slavery in a sense dehumanized the Negro. It disrupted his native culture and taught him the rudiments of white civilization, but it did not permit him to develop as a whole man. It prevented the development of three things which are generally considered essential for normal group life: stable family relations, stable economic organization, and stable community life. Furthermore, slavery nurtured a set of habits and attitudes which still afflict many thousands of Negroes. Among these are lack of self-respect, lack of self-confidence, a distaste for hard work, a habit of dependence upon white friends, lack of regard for the property of others, a feeling that "the white folks owe us a living," a distrust of the white man's law, and a tendency to "let tomorrow take care of itself."

Emancipation did not mean the end of caste relations, nor did it mean the beginning of an opportunity for the Negro to compete on even terms with other men in the struggle for existence. His cultural retardation, his social and economic disabilities, must be attributed in large measure to historical factors reinforced by the continuing vicious circle of caste barriers. The difference, then, between the experience of the Negro and the experience of other ethnic groups in American society is not merely one of degree but is actually a difference in kind—a fact which certainly has some connection with the incidence of social conditions which are associated with crime.

CASTE AND ECONOMIC FACTORS

The exact relation of economic factors to crime causation is still in dispute, but there is general agreement that they play an important role either as primary or associated factors. Certainly there is a general expectation that the underprivileged economic classes will contribute unduly to the total amount of delinquency.

Economic factors must not be considered merely in the restricted sense of their relation to crimes against property. Their ramifications extend into every sphere of life. There is the whole question of the effect of being born into a barren, dull, underprivileged, lower-class household, of the effect of this upon the choices which a child can make, of the relation of this sort of environment to the personality, attitudes, and philosophy of life which he will develop.

If economic factors have something to do with crime, it is obvious that the force with which they impinge upon the Negro's behavior is much greater than for any other large group in the population. It goes without saying that the Negro is the Nation's Economic Problem Group Number One. The bulk of Negro wage earners scarcely accomplish the satisfaction of the elemental needs for food, shelter, and clothing. In all sections of the country race prejudice or caste attitudes have conditioned the Negro's jobs and wages, his working conditions, his relation to labor unions, his vocational training, his choice of a place to live, and his use of political power as a protection against exploitation. Comfort, home ownership, job security, and the enjoyment of "the finer things of life" are absolutely out of the realm of possibility for the majority of Negro families. On any scale of economic adequacy or inadequacy—measured, e.g., in terms of number unemployed, number on relief, number in unskilled occupations, number in professional work, income levels—the Negro would have to be rated as from two to four times worse off than the white man.

CASTE AND SOCIAL DISORGANIZATION

If it were possible to compute some sort of objective index of social disorder as a basis for predicting probable crime ratios, there can be little doubt that the index for the Negro would be higher than that for any other large group in the Nation. Economic factors and cultural retardation play their part in Negro personal and community disorganization just as they do for other groups, but there are certain ways in which caste status differentially affects the relation of the Negro community to the larger society. For example, there is the well-known fact, almost as true of the North and the West as of the South, that the Negro cannot live where he pleases. Various immigrant groups have come in, lived a "ghetto" existence for a time, and have "graduated" from these areas. Not so with the Negro. Race prejudice tends to make of him a *permanent* "ghetto" dweller. There is the further fact, particularly true in the South, that the Negro community is virtually without political power and thus cannot obtain an equitable share of the benefits and protection of government.

Since the highest Negro crime rates occur in urban areas, the relation of the city to Negro social disorder is a subject which merits much closer study than it has yet had. Ecological studies have demonstrated the relation of "delinquency areas" to the structure and the growth processes of the city.[2] Disorganized areas are selective in that they are populated by people who occupy the lowest social and economic level, and their relation to the larger urban configuration makes it impossible for them to stabilize, to achieve a moral order or a sense of community *esprit de corps*. Vice, crime, and social disorder become traditional. The Negro is our greatest slum dweller, and because of race prejudice his slums have persisted with little change. When one remembers that nearly 90 percent of all Negroes in the North and the West are urban dwellers and that in all probability about 90 percent of these live in or adjacent to disorganized areas, the implications for crime causation are rather startling.

CASTE AND THE ADMINISTRATION OF JUSTICE

Let us bear in mind that the process of the administration of justice is not merely a process which by its unevenness may distort the statistics of crime, but is also an aspect of the caste relationship itself and may therefore have a direct bearing on the causes of Negro crime. In this brief article we can do little more than outline the problem and suggest types of relevant data.

Caste Definition of Crime. There are many acts which are rarely if ever considered crimes when done by white persons but which are frequently defined as crimes when committed by Negroes. In the South the caste definition of crime has the sanction of both law and custom. Numerous laws concerning segregation, vagrancy, labor, etc., create a wide range of possible "crimes" which Negroes can commit. Capital punishment is applied to Negro offenders with relatively greater frequency than to whites, and it is common knowledge that "first degree burglary" is defined as a capital crime in several states as a threat to Negro offenders who enter a white residence after dark.

Quite aside from specific law, every conflict situation between a white person and a Negro has the possibility of being defined arbitrarily as a Negro crime or of leading up step by step to the commission of an actual offense. Forgetting to say "Mister" to a white man, "looking at" a white woman, entering the wrong waiting room, "sassing" the landlord, disputing a white man's word, taking the wrong seat on a bus or street car,[3] riding a Pullman car—

---

[2] See for example, Clifford R. Shaw, *et al.*, *Delinquency Areas* (Chicago, 1929), pp. 204–6; and Shaw and McKay, "Social Factors in Juvenile Delinquency," National Commission on Law Observance and Enforcement, *Report on the Causes of Crime* (Washington, 1931), Vol. 2.

[3] Motor buses and street cars are especially productive of unpleasant incidents because the color line is movable. The law usually provides that Negroes shall fill seats from the rear forward, and

these are some of the things which may define a dangerous situation. If the Negro persists in being "insolent" or aggressive, anything from abusive language to homicide may occur, but whatever occurs is likely to be to his own disadvantage. The exact amount of "crime" arising from violations of caste etiquette is a problem which future research will have to determine. Inspection of southern crime statistics shows relatively few offenses booked under "violation of segregation laws," but the writer is convinced, from years of observation and from illustrative cases obtained from Negro acquaintances, that in the South such cases considerably swell the number of Negro offenses booked under "creating a disturbance on a public vehicle," "resisting arrest," "assault," "felonious assault," "manslaughter," and "murder.'[4]

Scapegoats and Frame-Ups. The status of the Negro, particularly in the South, exposes him to the danger of being blamed for crimes committed by whites and of being framed by white criminals. The following types of situations are known to occur:[5] (1) A white person may commit a crime under such circumstances that suspicion will likely fall upon *some* Negro. A special variety of this is the white man's trick of blackening his face before committing his crime. (2) A white person may deliberately arrange a situation so that the guilt of a *particular* Negro will almost inevitably be taken for granted. Sometimes the scheme includes slaying the Negro so as to clinch his guilt and to keep him from talking. (3) A white woman may try to avoid the consequences of sexual delinquency by raising the cry that she has been raped by a Negro.[6] A man-hunt ensues and a Negro is "identified." The Negro may be lynched or legally convicted, while the woman obtains a legal abortion and thus saves her "honor." Sometimes her paramour is a Negro. (4) A neurotic woman may "imagine" that she has been raped by a Negro, or she may interpret some innocent action as an insult or "attack" by a Negro.

The exact incidence of these situations will probably never be known, because they come to light only when they *fail* to work. It is significant, however, that such things do happen, and to the extent that they succeed they are an absolute exaggeration of the Negro's *actual* criminality.

The Police. The police have an especially strategic position in the administration of justice. Variations in their activities can produce fluctuations in arrest statistics which have no relation to the number of

---

drivers may take it on themselves to try to see that no Negro moves forward one row until the rear seat or row is filled. For an example of an offense growing out of this kind of situation in North Carolina, see Charles S. Mangum, Jr., *The Legal Status of the Negro* (Chapel Hill, 1940), pp. 212–13. For a detailed account of a Virginia episode leading to the arrest of a young Negro couple, see Harold Garfinkel, "Color Trouble," *Opportunity*, Vol. XVIII (May 1940), pp. 144–52. Incidentally, this "story" was selected for inclusion in O'Brien's *Best Short Stories of 1940*. Perhaps truth is *stronger* than fiction!

[4] Such cases do occur in the North, but probably with much less frequency. Last year the writer encountered an instance in an Ohio city. A young Negro woman was standing in line to try to purchase theater tickets to "Gone with the Wind." A young white man approached her, saying, "Why don't you get out? You know you are not wanted here," and gave her a shove. She tried to stand her ground, but in a moment was arrested for "creating a public disturbance." Our investigation convinced us that the theater manager, wishing to impress upon Negroes the fact that they were not welcome, deliberately provoked the affair.

[5] For various examples, see Monroe N. Work (Ed.), *Negro Year Book* (1931–32), pp. 289–92; (1938–39), p. 147; and "Burnt Cork and Crime," a pamphlet issued by the Southern Commission on Interracial Co-operation, Atlanta, n. d. (copyright, 1935).

[6] The notorious Ben Bess case is a good example of the injustice which can be done to Negro men by white women. In 1928 a South Carolina white woman confessed that she had sent an innocent Negro, Ben Bess, to prison on a false charge of rape. Her confession was itself a violation of caste patterns, and pressure was put upon her to get her to repudiate her statement. Finally, in 1929, Bess was pardoned. He had served thirteen years in prison! See *Negro Year Book* (1931–32), p. 292.

offenses actually committed. By mistreatment or brutality toward any group or class of people they can even provoke or stimulate the commission of crime. The Negro is more exposed to the misuse of police power than any other group.

The police custom of arresting Negroes on slight suspicion or of staging mass "roundups" of Negroes is definitely related to the Negro's lack of security and his inability to exert pressure against such abuses. Police pretty generally feel that in making arrests, handling witnesses, and obtaining confessions they can use brute force against Negroes with impunity. In some places in the South, law officers and magistrates are engaged in a sort of "racket" which involves the rounding up of Negroes on trivial charges for the sake of earning fees. More commonly, however, the police wink at a good deal of petty crime and disorder in Negro communities. Their attitude is: "We can't attempt to control everything that goes on among the Negroes. As long as they keep their hell-raising to themselves and don't let it get too noticeable, we'd rather leave them alone."

In the interplay of behavior between the police and Negro suspects, there is a reciprocal expectation of violence.[7] The police too quickly use gun or club, and Negroes—especially those with reputations as "bad niggers"—are keyed to a desperate shoot-first-or-you'll get-shot psychology. Thus what starts out to be merely a questioning or an arrest for a misdemeanor may suddenly turn into violence and a charge of murder against the Negro.

The experiences of Negroes as victims of police mistreatment or as victims of unpunished depredations within the Negro community must give rise to considerable bitterness and a feeling that the law is unjust. These experiences and attitudes deserve careful study, for they are undoubtedly contributory to both the real and the apparent criminality of Negroes.

The Courts. The faults and the weaknesses of our courts are well known, particularly with respect to the functioning of juries and prosecutors and the existence of class differentials in the disposition of criminal cases. It is further well known that the Negro's chances of access to bail, to efficient legal counsel, to payment of cash fines instead of jail terms, to appeals, and to all other legal advantages is on the average very much lower than the chance of the white man. When a Negro goes into court he goes with the consciousness that the whole courtroom process is in the hands of "the opposite race"—white judge, white jurors, white attorneys, white guards, white everything, except perhaps some of the witnesses and spectators. Moreover, in the lower courts, especially in the South and in Negro intraracial cases, Negro defendants and witnesses are frequently subjected to gross insult and are made the brunt of various sorts of horseplay and coarse humor. Conditions such as these undoubtedly affect the statistical picture of crime, the efficiency of law enforcement, and the attitudes and motives which enter into the causation of crime.

Discussions of Negro crime almost inevitably get around to the question of whether Negro offenders are more readily convicted and whether they are given longer sentences than whites. It is impossible to obtain a clear-cut answer from judicial statistics at present, for these statistics are especially weak for the southern states and they rarely present us with the necessary data, namely, the details of dispositions by offense, race, and sex. Furthermore, the evidence draw from such compilations as have been made is sometimes confusing and contradictory. For example, if a national compilation [8] of length of sentences by race for ten important offense

---

[7] In this connection, see H. C. Brearley, *Homicide in the United States* (Chapel Hill, 1932), pp. 65–68, 101–2.

[8] See, for example, *Prisoners in State and Federal Prisons and Reformatories, 1931 and 1932*, Bureau of the Census (1934), Table 19, p. 21.

categories shows that the average definite sentence for Negroes is actually lower than for whites in six of the ten categories, what is one to think when one feels positively that there *are* racial differentials in the dispositions of cases in the courts? The answer, we believe, is not as difficult as it might seem at first glance, and at this point we wish to present a hypothesis and some supporting data.

Our hypothesis is simply that differentials in the treatment of Negro offenders in southern courts do exist but are obscured by the fact that conventional crime statistics take into account only the race of the *offender.* If caste values and attitudes mean anything at all, they mean that offenses by or against Negroes will be defined not so much in terms of their intrinsic seriousness as in terms of their importance in the eyes of the dominant group. Obviously the murder of a white person by a Negro and the murder of a Negro by a Negro are not at all the same kind of murder from the standpoint of the upper caste's scale of values, yet in crime statistics they are thrown together. Therefore, instead of two categories of offenders, Negro and white, we really need four offender-victim categories, and they would probably rank in seriousness from high to low as follows: (1) Negro versus white, (2) white versus white, (3) Negro versus Negro, (4) white versus Negro. It is our contention that, in the South at least, the Negro versus Negro offenses are treated with undue leniency, while the Negro versus white offenses are treated with undue severity. There are complicating factors, of course, such as sex, age, "goodness" or "badness" of the Negro offender, and the interest of white persons for or against the offender, but on the whole, if our hypothesis is correct, the differentials which we have suggested should show up in mass statistics based on offender-victim categories.

The probability that Negro intraracial offenses are treated with greater leniency than Negro interracial offenses has been mentioned by numerous writers, but no one has offered any definitive quantitative data on the subject. A thorough test of the hypothesis which we have sketched involves tremendous difficultise, because ordinary judicial statistics are of no use for this purpose. However, we have been able to secure some data which serve to check the hypothesis in a preliminary way with respect to one very important offense, namely, homicide. Table I presents data by offender-victim groups on the dispositions of murder indictments [9] in Richmond, Virginia, 1930–39, in five counties in North Carolina, 1930–40, and in Fulton County, Georgia, for the twenty-month period from February 1938 through September 1939.[10]

One thing which stands out in Table I is the preponderance of Negro in-group murders and the relatively small number of interracial murders. Computing percentages from the first column, one sees that Negro versus Negro cases account for 88 percent of the murder indictments in Richmond, 91 percent in Fulton County, Georgia, and 75 percent in the North Carolina counties. The differences in the percent convicted in the N–N and the W–W groups are not consistent, for in the North Carolint series the percent convicted in the N–N group is actually higher

[9] Cases of "manslaughter by automobile" have been excluded.

[10] Detailed analysis of these and other data will be presented in a forthcoming article on the Negro and homicide, to be published in *Social Forces.* Collecting data of this sort is an arduous task involving use of trial records, indictments, warrants, and sometimes newspapers, as well as interviews with court clerks and police. I am deeply indebted to the following persons for the collection of the basic data: Dr. Olive Stone, William and Mary College, Richmond, Virginia, for the Richmond material; Dr. Arthur Raper, Atlanta, Georgia, for the Fulton County material; and Mr. Harold Garfinkel, graduate student at the University of North Carolina, for the North Carolina material. The North Carolina counties used are Alamance, Caswell, Orange, Durham, and Guilford. The first three are "rural" counties, the other two are "urban," containing the cities of Durham and Greensboro respectively.

Table I. *Dispositions of Murder Indictments, by Race of Offender and Victim (Abbreviations: N = Negro; W = White; N–W = Negro versus White, etc.)*

Place and Offender-Victim Category	Total Indictments	Nol Prossed or Acquitted	Convicted		Sentences					Percent of Total Convicted		
			Number	Percent	Death	Life	20 Years to Life	10 to 19 Years	Under 10 Years	Life or Death Sentence	Less than 20 Years	Less than 10 Years
Richmond, Va.												
N–N	194	53	141	72.6	0	8	31	43	59	5.6	72.2	41.8
N–W	5	0	5	100.0	0	5	0	0	0	100.0	0	0
W–W	20	5	15	75.0	1	3	3	1	7	26.6	53.3	46.6
W–N	1	0	1	a	0	0	0	0	1	0	a	a
Total	220	58	162	73.6	1	16	34	44	67	10.5	68.5	41.3
Five N. C. Counties												
N–N	247	46	201	81.4	11	1	38	46	105	5.9	75.1	52.2
N–W	19	2	17	89.5	6	2	4	0	5	47.0	29.4	29.4
W–W	61	19	42	68.9	8	2	8	2	22	23.8	57.1	52.4
W–N	3	1	2	a	0	0	0	1	1	0	a	a
Total	330	68	262	79.4	25	5	50	49	133	11.4	69.5	50.7
Fulton County, Ga.												
N–N	87	21	66	75.8								
N–W	1	0	1	a	Details omitted because of small number of cases							
W–W	5	0	5	100.0								
W–N	2	2	0	a								
Total	95	23	72	75.8								

a Percent not shown because of small number of cases.

than in the W–W group. However, the conviction rates in the N–N groups are consistently lower than in the N–W groups. Perhaps the most striking thing as far as sentences are concerned is the tendency not to apply the death or life sentences to the N–N convictions. Thus in Richmond, of 141 N–N slayers convicted, not one received the death penalty and only 8 (5.6 percent) received life sentences. In the North Carolina series, of 201 N–N slayers convicted, 11 received the death penalty and one a life sentence, or a total of 5.9 percent of these two types of sentences. The contrast between these sentences and the sentences given to the N–W slayers is striking. If the percent receiving death or life sentences is a good index of severity, the data fit neatly into our ranking of offenses as stated above. If the percent receiving sentences of less than 20 years is a fair index of general leniency in sentences for murder, the data again tend to bear out our hypothesis. If the percent receiving sentences of less than 10 years be used as as index of extreme leniency, the picture is not so clear-cut. The differences between N–N slayers and N–W slayers remain, but the W–W group apparently has as good a chance as the N–N group of drawing these extremely light sentences. However, the fact cannot be disputed that the number of Negro in-group slayers is relatively very large and that the majority of them escape the more severe sentences and thus have a high expectation of regaining their freedom. To a considerable extent they can

Table II. *Death Sentences and Executions for Murder in North Carolina, 1933–39*[11]

Offender Group	Sentenced	Commuted	Executed Number	Executed Percent
Race of Offender Only:				
Negro	81	23	58	71.6
White	42	13	29	69.0
Race of Offender and Victim:				
N–N	45	16	29	64.4
N–W	36	7	29	80.5
W–W	41	13	28	68.3
W–N	1	0	1 [a]	—

[a] This was a very exceptional execution. It created much comment and was said to be the first such case in the state since Reconstruction days. It involved a particularly brutal murder of a respectable old Negro by a low-class white man, and there was strong public sentiment in favor of the execution.

literally "get away with murder" if they kill other Negroes.

Table II pursues the problem a bit further. It deals with death sentences for murder in North Carolina for the period 1933–39 and the extent to which they are actually executed. When the data are tabulated merely by race of offender they show that 71.6 percent of the Negroes and 69 percent of the whites get executed.[12] But when they are tabulated by offender-victim groupings the picture is different, for 80.5 percent of the Negro versus white offenders are executed, as against only 64.4 percent of the Negro versus Negro offenders.

The data presented here point toward a partial confirmation of our hypothesis, at least in so far as the crime of murder is concerned. Certainly they point toward a fruitful area for further research, and they suggest very strongly that judicial statistics would be far more interesting as well as more useful if a number of courts could be persuaded to experiment with racial offender-victim records.

Studies of less serious offenses than murder would probably show more clear-cut evidence of extremes of leniency in Negro in-group offenses. The implications with regard to the relation of the courts to the causation of Negro crime are clear. The courts, like the police, are dealing out a double standard of justice. Numerous Negro intraracial offenses probably go unpunished or are punished so lightly that offenders feel a real contempt for the law, while the certainty of severe punishment in Negro versus white cases cannot help but make the Negro feel that justice is not entirely color-blind. Undue leniency gives comfort to the disorderly and criminal element, promotes recidivism, and nurtures careers of crime. There is the further implication that if these differentials are very slight in the North, as seems likely, then northern statistics of Negro crime reflect actual Negro criminality in the North better than southern statistics reflect actual Negro criminality in the South, and the statistics are therefore not safe indices of regional differences.

Prison Experience. There can be no doubt that jails and prisons are to some extent breeding places for crime. Prison systems in the South are especially backward, and the caste position of the Negro

---

[11] I am indebted to Mr. G. K. Brown, formerly connected with the North Carolina State Prison Department, now at St. Lawrence University, for the collection of the data in this table.

[12] In this connection, see also the execution data for nine southern states collected by the writer for Charles S. Mangum, Jr., and published in Mangum, *op. cit.*, p. 369. The data are not shown according to offender-victim categories, but they show some striking racial differentials in the ratio of executions to death sentences.

exposes him to the worst which prison experience has to offer. Segregation of prisoners opens the way for all sorts of differentials in accommodations and treatment.[13] The lack of institutions for women and juvenile Negro offenders, the herding together of youthful offenders and hardened criminals, and the turning loose of numerous defective or insane prisoners because of lack of accommodations are all directly related to the crime potential of the Negro group. If there is hard, backbreaking work to be done, it is taken for granted that Negro prisoners will do it. The chain-gang system, which is still used in most of the southern states for highway work, is particularly hard on Negro prisoners. Terrible "accidents," such as the burning of twenty men in a truck cage because they were trying to warm themselves by setting fire to some gasoline, or two convicts' suffering the amputation of their feet after they were frozen during solitary confinement in a cage on a cold night, have a way of happening to Negro convicts almost exclusively. Guards are white, of course, and they share the prejudices of their race. Most of them in their dealings with Negro prisoners are all too quick to use the lash, to use solitary confinement on starvation diet, and to shoot to kill.

There is every reason to believe that the prisons "graduate" an unusually high proportion of Negroes who have been brutalized and have become hopelessly embittered toward society in general and the white man in particular. In this connection it is important to remember that relatively more Negroes than whites get exposed to the "educative" influences of jail, chain gang, and prison for the simple reason that they are unable to escape this experience by paying cash fines.

Release from Prison. Aside from execution, death in prison, and escape, prisoners may be released by serving out their time, by being pardoned, and by being paroled. Most Negro prisoners probably serve out their time, with certain allowances for good behavior. But since many Negroes who have committed serious crimes are serving light sentences because their crimes were against other Negroes, there is a quick turnover, so to speak, of prisoners who are potentially dangerous. This would be a factor making for recidivsm among Negroes.

As for pardons, Negroes do not share equitably for the simple reason that as a rule they cannot exert the amount of political pressure which all too frequently is needed in obtaining a pardon. There is some evidence that Negroes are discriminated against in the use of parole as a method of release and rehabilitation. This fact, of course, might actually tend to reduce recidivism by reducing the span of freedom of individual offenders. Much more important for our present purposes is the question of the *selection* of such Negro prisoners as *are* given the benefit of parole. Are they selected with a view to the best interests of the parolee and of society? Our general observations point to a decided negative answer. Too many cases fit into the following pattern: The sporty Negro butler for a wealthy white man is circumspect in his work but is considered something of a "menace" by his fellow Negroes. He deliberately murders a Negro girl who has spurned his attentions. Being ably defended by his employer, he receives a light sentence for manslaughter, and he has scarcely begun to serve this when his employer obtains his parole because he is anxious not to lose the Negro's services.

A recent study of parole in Alabama reveals something of the workings of the system in that state. Letters such as the following are "samples of many received by the Parole Bureau":

I can use a Negro full time ... will see that he has something to eat, and can keep him at

---

[13] For a recent survey of institutional facilities, see Mangum, *op. cit.*, Chap. IX, "Charitable and Penal Institutions."

work all the time clearing land, cutting wood, and helping cultivate the land....

I am in need of a Negro farm hand and I am depending on one from you. And if you have one for me, you may write what prison I can get him and when....

I understand that the state is letting out prisoners on parole, if so I would like to get a Negro named G—————— W—————.[14]

It seems highly probable that the dominant factor is not the best interest of the individual offender or the welfare of society, but the immediate interest of some white person.

CASTE IN RELATION TO ATTITUDES AND MOTIVES

Criminal conduct, except for accidental or unintentional crimes, is ultimately a matter of personal attitude and motivation. What are the implications of caste status for the motivation of Negro offenses against white people? First, it is well to emphasize the point that many Negro offenses are unintentional in that they get defined as crime only because there is an upper caste to define them as such.

It is scarcely necessary to prove that the frustrations involved in being a Negro in a white-dominated society put the Negro under severe emotional strain and give rise to impulses of hate and revenge. These impulses are undoubtedly related to the causes of crime. Most of the sudden and violent attacks by Negroes on white persons—landlords, bosses, police, prison guards, etc.—are explicable only as the final explosion of emotional tensions which have accumulated over a period of time. But it is not only in violent attacks that hate and revenge play a part. Arson, burglary, injury to livestock, petty thieving, etc., may be direct expressions of revenge; and it is altogether probable that some of the sexual assaults of Negro men on white women have definite overtones of revenge.[15]

No doubt much of the crime of Negroes against whites is merely crime which is motivated in the ordinary way and which happens to involve white persons. However, we would adopt the tentative conclusion that hate and revenge play a dominant role in some of the crimes of Negroes against whites and are contributory motives in many other offenses.

After all, a very large proportion of Negro crime takes place within Negro communities and involves the persons of interests of Negro victims. What role does caste status play in the motivation of such offenses? Let us outline our thesis briefly. First, the frustrations involved in being a Negro bear most heavily upon the members of the Negro lower class. Here one finds people who are utterly hopeless and degraded. They have nothing and know that they will never have anything. Their style of life fits very well into the common white stereotypes of Negroes—shiftless, lazy, impulsive, hypersensual, etc. They contribute the bulk of Negro crime, and their personalities and motives are inseparably tied up with their roles as lower-class members of a subordinate race. They let off most of the "steam" of their frustrated desires among their own group.[16]

Second, social institutions and community controls do not operate with sufficient strength in the Negro lower class to repress the disorganizing influences or to inhibit the rather free letting off of emotional "steam." Violence, for example, becomes almost a positive value and has a high expectancy. The "bad man," the bully, the gambler, the "pistol toter," the pimp, the rowdy woman—all thrive because there are so many of them that they constitute a veritable society of their own. Naturally they thrive best of all in the great Negro "ghettos" of our large cities.

---

[14] J. Herman Johnson, "Parole in Alabama," *Social Forces*, Vol. 18 (March 1940), pp. 388–89.

[15] Cf. John Dollard, *Class and Caste in a Southern Town* (New Haven, 1937), Chap. XIV, "Negro Aggression Against Whites."

[16] *Ibid.*, Chap. XIII, "Aggression Within the Negro Group."

Third, there is lacking, in the South certainly and perhaps to some extent elsewhere, a tradition of strict and impartial justice in Negro versus Negro offenses. The double standard of justice lends positive sanction to violence and other misconduct within the Negro community. The saying that "Negro life is cheap" is tragically real, for even murder is sometimes condoned—one might almost say blessed—by the white man's machinery of justice.

CONCLUSION

The position of the Negro in American society, with all that this means in terms of subordination, frustration, economic insecurity, and incomplete participation, enters significantly into almost every possible aspect of Negro crime causation. Indeed, it is so important as to constitute virtually a special and major set of sociological and psychological factors which can "explain" Negro crime in so far as it needs special explanation.

The administration of justice itself is from beginning to end so much a part of the whole system of Negro-white social relations that it must be viewed not only as a process which discriminates against Negroes and thus biases the statistics of crime, but also as a direct and indirect causative factor in the production of Negro crime.

Our survey of the factors which might be expected to affect Negro criminality lends strength to the presumption that the Negro crime rate is actually considerably higher than the white. We have taken note of several ways in which caste factors bias the statistics to the disadvantage of the Negro, but we have pointed out that compensating factors probably operate, in the South at least, so that it may be that crime statistics, as bad as they are, do not grossly exaggerate the actual criminality of the Negro.

In so far as certain special conditions or characteristics in the usual statistical picture need explanation—for example, that Negroes have higher crime rates than whites, that Negro offenders are younger than white offenders on the average, that Negro women have a relatively high criminality, that Negro crime distributions emphasize petty offenses against property and crimes of personal violence, that Negroes are more likely than whites to be recidivists, etc.—they would all seem to find sufficient explanation in the implications of the caste factors which have been discussed here.

42. NEGRO AND WHITE CRIME RATES

EARL R. MOSES

STUDENTS OF CRIME COMMONLY AGREE THAT Negroes in urban centers contribute a disproportionate share of juvenile delinquency and crime when compared with their proportion of the total population. This does not mean, however, that Negroes are innately predisposed toward crime.

THE PROBLEM OF COMPARING CRIME RATES BETWEEN NEGROES AND WHITES

Comparisons generally made of criminality between Negroes and whites are not comparisons of similar things. Edwin H. Sutherland, for example, gives no credence to innate disposition toward criminality based on the biology of race.[1]

This study compares four socio-economically equated areas: two Negro and two white areas. These are geographically distributed so that there are contiguous white and Negro areas, yet each contiguous group is located in different parts of the city (Baltimore, Maryland.)

▶SOURCE: *"Differentials in Crime Rates between Negroes and Whites Based on Comparisons of Four Socio-Economically Equated Areas," American Sociological Review (August, 1947), 12:411–420.* Reprinted by permission.

[1] For the delineation of other factors which may operate to make for criminality among Negroes see, Edward H. Sutherland, *Principles of Criminology*, Lippincott, 1939, p. 133.

Our primary equation pattern is the equation of communities, based on comparable socio-economic status. These four communities have striking resemblances as to physical characteristics, i.e., architectural pattern of housing, age of dwellings, size of lots, and streets lighted by gas. Physical deterioration is evident in all four areas. A secondary equation pattern is that of persons living in the areas based on occupations.

THE EQUATION OF AREAS

We will describe the characteristics of the equated areas; show their geographic location and population characteristics; state the indices used in equating the areas; delineate the socio-economic characteristics of the areas; and, finally, note the socio-economic characteristics common to all areas.[2] For the area locations, see map

[2] Acknowledgment herewith is given the following: Mr. Wallace Reidt, Assistant Managing Director, The Criminal Justice Commission, Baltimore, for use of the records of that organization dealing with felony cases during 1940; Dr. W. Thurber Fales, Director, Statistical Section, Baltimore City Health Department, for making valuable suggestions regarding the selection of areas used in this study, and for making available data on health conditions and juvenile delinquency; Mr. Isadore Seeman, Director, Bureau of Vital Records, for compiling these data; to four Morgan State College students, Misses Pauline Bates, Mildred McGlotten, Mildred Reynolds, and Mrs. Willodyne S. Gaston, for clerical assistance; and, to Dr. Thorsten Sellin,

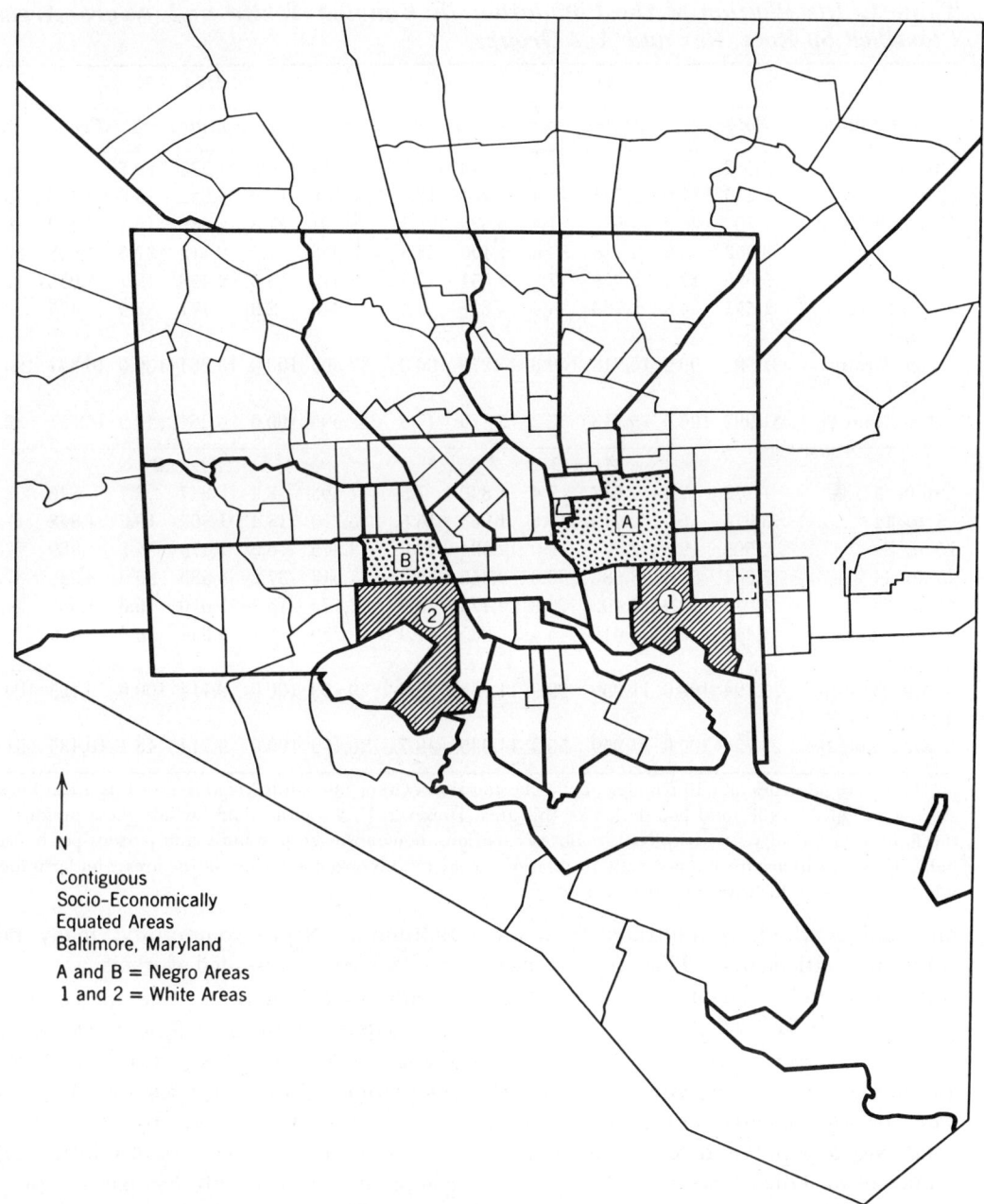

Contiguous
Socio-Economically
Equated Areas
Baltimore, Maryland
A and B = Negro Areas
1 and 2 = White Areas

above. The white areas are designated as Area 1 and Area 2; the Negro areas as Area A and Area B, being respectively located contiguous to Area 1 and Area 2.

---

of the University of Pennsylvania, is due a special measure of thanks for his guidance throughout the period of the study.

Population Characteristics. Population characteristics of the areas follow (see Figure 1).

Area 1. White, principally of foreign-born extraction. Poland contributes the largest population of foreign birth; Russia, second, although numerically far smaller than those from Poland; a few Germans

Table I. *Distribution of the Population in Equated White and Negro Areas, Classified by Race, Sex and Age Groups*

Age Groups	Area 1						Area A [a]					
	Total	%	Male	%	Female	%	Total	%	Male	%	Female	%
Under 5	2,412	7.5	1,234	7.4	1,178	7.7	3,118	9.5	1,572	9.7	1,546	9.5
5 to 14	5,455	17.0	2,751	16.4	2,704	17.7	6,168	18.9	3,032	18.6	3,136	19.2
15 to 24	7,107	22.2	3,585	21.4	3,522	23.1	5,791	17.8	2,619	16.1	3,172	19.4
25 to 44	9,852	30.8	5,446	32.6	4,406	28.8	12,055	37.0	6,112	37.6	5,943	36.4
45 to 64	5,620	17.6	2,969	17.8	2,651	17.3	4,517	13.9	2,458	15.1	2,059	12.6
65 and over	1,551	4.8	733	4.4	818	5.4	946	2.9	471	2.9	475	2.9
Totals:												
Age Groups	31,997	99.9	16,718	100.0	15,279	100.0	32,595	100.0	16,264	100.0	16,331	100.0
Totals:												
Race and Sex	31,997	100.0	16,718	52.2	15,279	47.8	32,595	100.0	16,264	49.9	16,331	50.1
	Area 2						Area B					
Under 5	1,772	7.4	882	7.4	890	7.5	1,693	8.4	847	8.7	846	8.1
5 to 14	3,976	16.7	2,013	16.8	1,963	16.6	3,710	18.4	1,862	19.2	1,848	17.6
15 to 24	4,595	19.3	2,271	19.0	2,324	19.6	3,345	16.6	1,476	15.2	1,869	17.8
25 to 44	7,041	29.6	3,686	30.8	3,355	28.3	7,517	37.2	3,585	36.9	3,932	37.5
45 to 64	4,970	20.9	2,492	20.8	2,478	20.9	3,175	15.7	1,610	16.6	1,565	14.9
65 and over	1,440	6.1	615	5.1	825	7.0	759	3.7	334	3.4	425	4.1
Totals:												
Age Groups	23,794	100.0	11,959	99.9	11,835	99.9	20,199	100.0	9,714	100.0	10,485	100.0
Totals:												
Race and Sex	23,794	100.0	11,959	50.3	11,835	49.7	20,199	100.0	9,714	48.1	10,485	51.9

[a] There are 36 males and 10 females in the classification "Other non-white" who live in this area. These are not included in the total population of this area. However, U. S. Census data include these persons in the figures on school years completed, major occupations, home ownership, rentals, and persons per household. These additions are unimportant in relation to the total Negro population in the area. Similar minor additions are true likewise for Area B.

and Italians who have infiltrated from surrounding settlements. This area is near water-front industrial areas, and its white population is 31,997.[3]

Area A. Negro; popularly called "East Baltimore"; many migrants, as authenticated by governmental and school statistics; total Negro population 32,595; a predominance of unskilled workers.

Area 2. White, primarily of foreign-born extraction; white population 23,795. Lithuania dominates the foreign-born, Russia and Germany next, and a few are from Ireland, Italy, Poland, Greece, etc.

Area B. Negro; total Negro population 20,199; part of the popularly called "West Baltimore" Negro community; many migrants; mostly unskilled workers.

Indices of Equation. The indices used to equate the four areas follow: (1) Race: Predominance of either a white or Negro population; (2) similar sex distributions; (3) similar distributions by age groups; (4) own or rent place of dwelling; (5) comparable rentals; (6) comparable property valuations of owner groups; (7) major occupational patterns; (8) years of schooling completed; and (9) number of persons in household.

Equating the Areas. The following comparative data for contiguous areas establish, in the writer's opinion, enough similarities to justify them as being equated areas, even though some variations appear.

[3] All population data are based on the U. S. Census, 1940, unless otherwise specifically stated.

DISTRIBUTION BY RACE, SEX AND AGE GROUPS

The comparative data in Table I summarize the distribution of population by race,[4] sex and age groups, and generally show them to be similar. The fluctuations at several age group levels are to be expected since the white population represents a settlement of long residence, while many among the Negroes represent a relative recent migrant population, including parents and their children. Fewer persons in the upper age levels among Negroes than among the whites may be accounted for not only by high mortality rates among Negroes in congested areas, but also in the non-migration of an elderly age group into the areas.

---

[4] In Areas 1 and 2 the Negro population and all data pertaining to them have been excluded from the figures presented in this study. Similar exclusions for the white population have been made in Areas A and B. Thus the data presented correspond to the racial type composing the given area. Negroes and whites often may live in the same census tract, but in different sections of it. Because of the segregated pattern of residence in Baltimore there is virtually no overlapping as to residence in the four areas used in this study.

HOME OWNERSHIP AND TENANT OCCUPANCY

Table II shows comparative data by areas on home ownership, tenant occupancy, rents, and valuations of owned homes. The median gross monthly rent appeared to be the best index available for these areas. It was not possible on this item to exclude data on Negroes in white areas, but a check showed only a small number of Negroes in the census tracts composing each white area. Valuation of homes occupied by owners are careful estimates. Some inadequacy as to availability of data, and the lack of completely homogeneous data by race probably influenced to some extent the average valuation figure given in the table.

Although the total occupied units are reasonably comparable, a wide variations in owner-occupied units is seen between Areas 1 and 2, compared with Areas A and B. The differences favor the white areas. This reflects the longer residence in their areas, plus, perhaps, larger accumulated savings, more freedom in buying as opposed to residence in restricted areas, and greater ease in financing home purchase.

Table II. *Comparative Data by Areas on Home Ownership, Tenant Occupancy, Rentals, and Valuations of Owned Property*

Areas	Total Occupied Units	Owner Occupied Units	%	Tenant Occupied Units	Median Gross Monthly Rent (Dollars)	Average Monthly	Average Valuation of Home (Dollars)
1	8,095	3,685	45.5	4,410	17.68		2,009
A	8,060	381	4.7	7,679	22.80		2,145 [a]
2	6,228	2,191	35.2	4,037	22.80		1,864 [b]
B	4,754	278	5.8	4,476	23.75		2,386 [c]
City-wide						25.82	
White household						28.14 [d]	
Non-white household						19.46	

[a] Not available for Negroes only.
[b] Estimated average.
[c] Estimated average; also not available for Negroes only.
[d] *Redevelopment of Blighted Residential Areas in Baltimore,* Commission on City Plan, July 1, 1945, p. 21.

434   THE SOCIAL STRUCTURE

Table III. *Major Occupational Patterns in the Four Areas*

Areas	Professional Workers			Craftsmen, Foremen and Kindred Workers			Domestic Service Workers			Laborers		
	Total	*Male*	*Female*	*Total*	*Male*	*Female*	*Total*	*Male*	*Female*	*Total*	*Male*	*Female*
1	257	143	114	2,055	1,911	144	79	4	75	2,123	2,008	115
A	133	84	49	451	442	9	2,498	66	2,432	4,544	4,479	65
2	142	75	67	1,766	1,662	104	127	2	125	844	812	32
B	155	73	82	235	230	5	2,437	116	2,321	2,437	2,364	73

This is worth noting since all the areas in this study represent low socio-economic indices compared with the city as a whole.

Comparison of median gross rents for the several areas shows Negroes paying higher rents than whites. These differentials conform to the alleged fact that Negroes pay higher rents than whites for comparable dwellings. This is not in conflict with the fact that the city-wide averages show Negroes pay much lower rents than whites. It must be remembered that the city-wide averages include wide extremes of economic sufficiency and, likewise, wide differences in rent. Thus the city-wide averages are not comparable to rents paid in these areas.

MAJOR OCCUPATIONAL PATTERNS

Table III shows the occupations in which most of the gainful workers are employed. Employment is comparatively negligible in categories other than those listed. The figures show two patterns pertinent to this study: (1) persons engaged in professional work are decidedly in the minority in all four areas; and (2) although occupational dominance is at the lowest occupational levels, the white workers are one step up the occupational ladder above Negroes. White males predominate as craftsmen, foremen, and kindred workers; Negro males predominate as laborers. The large number of Negro females employed have a virtual monopoly as domestic service workers.

YEARS OF SCHOOLING COMPLETED

The average adult has had a sixth grade education or less. The median years of schooling completed for persons 25 years and over are:

Areas	Median School Male	Years Completed Female
1	6.7	6.0
A	5.3	5.9
2	4.6	4.4
B	6.1	6.5

NUMBER OF PERSONS IN HOUSEHOLD

The size of the household is comparable in all areas. Either no average is shown,

Median number of persons in household

Areas	All Occupied Units	Owner-Occupied Units	Tenant-Occupied Units
1	3.39	4.08	2.94
A	3.92	Inadequate data	Inadequate data
2	3.32	3.46	3.27
B	3.45	3.71 (Estimated)	3.10 (Estimated)

or an estimated average is given for the subclassifications in the Negro areas. Census tract data were not available "where the base is less than 100."

OTHER QUASI-EQUATION INDICES

Additional data were collected relative to the equating of areas to the state of repair of dwellings, proportion of homes with a radio, pattern of refrigeration (ice or mechanical), and pattern of heating (central heating unit or not). In all areas, (1) a substantial number of houses needed repairs; (2) there was a preponderant use of ice for refrigeration; (3) radios were present in a substantial proportion of homes (83.6 percent or more); and (4) a preponderant lack of a central heating unit. The disparity between the presence or absence of a central heating plant was far greater in Areas 1 and A than Areas 2 and B.

The data in Table IV show selected indices of health status in the four areas. These data cover a five year period. This span of time makes for relative stabilization of figures and rates, compared with fluctuations which may be evident in data compiled for any one year. Moreover, attention is called to the fact that the midpoint of the period is 1940, which is prior to the heavy migration of workers and their families into Baltimore during the war years. Thus the data show a relatively normal pattern of health conditions prior to the greater congestion of population incident to the war period. A careful examination of these data show more unfavorable health conditions in Areas A and B, than in Areas 1 and 2, but they also reveal a similar low health status in all areas.

Summary of Characteristics of the Areas. The characteristics which either are common to all areas, or are similar in contiguous areas are summarized below.

SIMILARITIES

1. Each area is relatively homogeneous as to racial population. Because of the segregated pattern of residence in Baltimore there is virtually no overlapping as to residence. Moreover, the numerical similarity in the total population in each of the contiguous areas is close enough to be used for comparative purposes.

2. In spite of some differences which were noted earlier, there is a similarity in the distributions by sex and age groups in contiguous areas.

3. Contiguous areas have a comparable number of total dwelling units occupied. This numerical similarity is markedly close in Areas 1 and A.

4. Occupational dominance in all areas is in the lower occupational levels.

5. All areas are characterized by a low educational status of adults, the educational status being below the 7th grade.

Table IV. *Indices of Health Status in the Four Areas*[a]

Areas	Live Births (1938–1942)	Infant Deaths (1938–1942)	Infant Death Rate per 1,000 Live Births: 1938–1942	New Cases of Tuberculosis Reported (1938–1942)	Tuberculosis Case Rate per 10,000 Population: 1938–1942
1	2,965	137	46.2	306	19.1
A	3,999	257	64.3	736	45.1
2	2,333	128	54.9	195	16.3
B	2,333	164	70.3	462	45.7

[a] Data compiled by the Bureau of Vital Statistics of the Baltimore City Health Department. Data shown are figures and rates compiled by white and non-white in each area. See footnote 1, page 6, and footnote 1 Table I, page 7.

436   THE SOCIAL STRUCTURE

6. The size of household is comparable in all areas.

7. Data of quasi-equation indices show additional points of low socio-economic status comparable to data showing equation of areas. Similarly, low health status is evident in all these areas. It may be added, however, that although data reveal comparable low standards, conditions are somewhat less favorable in Negro areas than in the corresponding white areas.

DIFFERENCES

Characteristic differences between the white and Negro areas are summarized below.

1. The white populations are predominantly of foreign-born extraction. They are a settled population of long residence in their areas. On the other hand, there is a large element of migrants in the two Negro populations.[5] The difference in settlement patterns make for some differences in age group distributions, though not wide enough to invalidate comparisons between contiguous areas.

2. Home ownership is greater among the whites than among the Negroes. Conversely, the Negroes are a larger tenant group.

3. Negroes pay somewhat higher rents than whites for comparable dwelling units.

4. The whites are one step up the occupational ladder above Negroes, although occupational dominance in all areas is at the lowest occupational levels.

The materials presented above show that the areas in this study have homogeneous populations, and also that they are socio-economically equated areas. These areas, moreover, are below the city-wide average as to socio-economic status. Furthermore, they are areas characterized by urban blight. Based on these equatings as to externalities, we thus assume equal planes of living in these areas. Having established the equation of areas, we turn now to an examination of crime rates in these equated areas.

DIFFERENTIALS IN CRIME RATES IN EQUATED AREAS

Do differentials in crime rates persist even in face of the equation of areas? Felonies committed during 1940 will be our chief index to the extent of crime in these equated areas. Felonies may be divided into two groups: (1) felonies reported to the police and where the victim is known, but the offender is unknown or not apprehended; and (2) felonies reported to the police, where both the victim and the accused are known; where the accused has been brought to trial, either in 1940 or subsequently; and, where a definite judicial disposition has been made of the case. Cases within the second group are used herein.

Cases of felony for the year 1940 have been selected for several reasons. First, the 1940 U. S. Census data were used for the socio-economic equation of areas. Second, it was desirable to select a year prior to the heavy migration into Baltimore incident to the war period. This allowed for an assumed relative normal pattern of criminal behavior in Baltimore. Finally, felony cases were selected also because they are the more serious types of criminal behavior, requiring more careful investigations than misdemeanors. Thus it was felt that though fewer cases in number than for misdemeanors, felony cases would represent a fairly reliable index to the extent of criminality in a given year.

Crime Rates. Table V shows the extent of crime in the four areas during 1940. It will be noted that the crime rate for Area 1

---

[5] Dr. W. Thurber Fales writes: "Natural increase therefore accounted for 51.8 percent of the increase in the white population and 14.9 percent of the increase in the non-white population. The remainder of the increase between the 1930 and 1940 census is due to migration into the City. Since only 14.9 percent of the net increase for colored population was accounted for by natural increase, it is obvious that the immigration to the City has been much more pronounced for the Negro than for the white population." *The Councillor,* June, 1941.

Table V. *Persons Accused of Felonies During 1940, Classified by Area (Race) and Sex, and Showing Area Rates of Felonious Crime*

Areas	Males		Females	
	Accused Persons	Area Rate [a]	Accused Persons	Area Rate [a]
1	25	2.36	—	—
A	153	15.11	23	2.34
2	17	2.21	—	—
B	76	12.47	5	0.74

[a] The area rate is a ratio, expressed in thousands, between the number of accused persons in relation to the area population 21 years of age and over, classified by race and sex. Although some under 21 years of age were charged with a felony, the proportion of such cases compared with those 21 years of age and over was not unduly large. The maximum age in this series was 59. Since census data are not available for the exact age groups of persons younger than 21 which correspond to those under 21 who had committed felonies, it was judged that a valid ratio would be obtained by including the cases under 21 since there were adults in the population figures who were over 59 years of age.

is 2.36 compared with 15.11 for Area A. Similarly, the rate for Area 2 is 2.21 compared with 12.47 for Area B. There were no felonies committed by white females in Areas 1 and 2 to compare with those committed by Negro females in Areas A and B. Several striking differences are evident. In the first place, differences in crime rates persist even in equated areas. Secondly, there is a wide difference in these rates. Finally, the rates among the Negro females correspond more closely to the rates for the white males, than do the rates when comparing white males with Negro males.

Juvenile delinquency rates also are higher in the Negro areas than in the white areas. Juvenile delinquency rates per 1,000 of population, ages 6–17, for the years 1939–1942, inclusive, were computed for these areas. The rate for Area 1 was 14.4, for Area A, 26.7, for Area 2, 22.0, and for Area B, 28.4. Differentials in rates persist in juvenile delinquency even as in felonies, although less markedly so.

Types of Offenses. Crimes committed by persons living in one of the four areas, without regard to the place where the crime was committed, were canvassed, classified by areas and by sex. Space limitation necessitates a summary of these findings. A striking fact evident in the figures is that all murder and manslaughter offenses were committed by Negroes. Indeed, when the offenses are classified according to "crimes against persons" and "crimes involving property" more than 40.0 percent of the crimes in Area A, and more than 50.0 percent of those in Area B are crimes against persons, such as murder, manslaughter, rape, and aggravated assault. It is of value to note that, though fewer in number, the offenses in 13 categories other than murder and manslaughter in Areas 1 and 2 correspond roughly to a pattern similar to that in Areas A and B. But even with a general similarity one important difference may be noted, namely, that in Areas A and B some crimes against persons involved loss of life, whereas there was no such outcome in crimes in Areas 1 and 2.

Multiple Felonies. There were few cases of clear recidivism for 1940. Instead, there were cases where the same person committed more than one offense prior to arrest, and where trial and sentence covered the several different acts. It should be kept in mind that penalties inflicted for felonies often would insure incarceration for periods longer than one year. Persons involved in the 1940 cases thus either may have been or subsequently may have become recidivists. Our analysis concerns only the cases for one year. Hence we refer to multiple felonies rather than recidivism.

Multiple felonies occurred most frequently in Area A. The nature of the offenses, number of persons involved, and the time element in each case are summarized in the data which follow. Sample cases only are presented.

Area A. One act of burglary; one person; a second act of burglary, involving the same person and one other person; second act occurred 3 months later than the first act. Short sentence served for first act prior to commission of second act.

Area 2. Four separate acts, involving the same person. One act of assault, and 1 assault to rape act on the same day. Similarly, on the next day 1 act of assault, and 1 assault to rape act. Four separate victims; 2 separate acts each day.

Area B. Three separate acts of burglary; same 2 persons involved; two acts one day, third act on the succeeding day.

Convictions. The felony cases for 1940 were canvassed with reference to their disposition by the court. This was done to determine whether or not wide differences were evident in convictions in Areas 1 and 2 compared with convictions in Areas A and B. It was found that 17.0 percent of the cases in Area A, and 17.3 percent of the cases in Area B were found "Not Guilty." In Area 1 only 1 person was found "Not Guilty," while in Area 2, 17.6 percent were so found.

Attention is called to the fact that percentages determined for Areas 1 and 2 are not to be regarded as equally valid as those for Areas A and B since there are far fewer cases in Areas 1 and 2 than in Areas A and B. But even in face of this limitation, based on an examination of the proportions convicted to the total cases in each area, there is no reason to even suspect that Negroes were more readily convicted than whites. This is important since it rules out an element of policy as influencing the higher crime rates in Areas A and B than in Areas 1 and 2.

TENTATIVE FINDINGS AND CONCLUSIONS

The basic assumption with which we started in this study is that most comparisons of crime rates do not take into account differences in socio-economic status between the groups compared. Thus we equated contiguous areas to determine if differentials in crime rates persisted after equation. Felony cases during 1940 were used as an index to criminality. Crime rates in the 2 Negro areas continued to be higher than in the 2 white areas.

The primary equation pattern was the equating of communities, with reference to socio-economic status. There was also a relative equation of persons, based principally on the predominance of low status occupations. Thus, there was on the one hand, an equation based on externalities, viz., housing, and urban blight, and, on the other hand, an equating of population with the consequent assumption of equal planes of living.

That these areas are equated will hardly be seriously questioned. However, one recognizes that the equation is basically the equating of objective aspects of the areas. This fails to take into account subjective aspects, such as cultural meanings, which are basic to behavior patterns characteristic of a group. Even though holding to the validity of an equation of externalities, it is questionable whether or not a high degree of equation of subjective factors is obtainable.

Regarding criminal behavior in these areas we noted that there was no evidence of a policy whereby conviction rates were unfavorable to Negroes. Moreover, there was evidence of a general similarity in the patterns of offenses between Negroes and whites, although among the Negroes were concentrated the offenses involving loss of life. In light of these facts the validity of the determination of crime rates is judged equally valid as the equation of areas.

Although there was a basic similarity in the equation pattern, there were also some differences which were judged to be significant in their implications. Of these, the most significant variation was the fact that although both groups were predominantly in low occupational lines, the whites in Areas 1 and 2 were one step up the occupational ladder over the Negroes in Areas A and B. This fact raises the question as to whether or not the relatively fixed occupational status of the Negro does not reflect itself in a differential in the plane of living even though white and Negro areas are equated as to externalities and the relative equation of persons.

Homicides are more prevalent among Negroes. One alleged prevalent mode of behavior among Negroes is that of carrying knives and guns. If one accepts this as widespread, one accepts the accompanying alleged attitude of "security" borne of having a weapon. The presence of weapons often leads to their use, more than likely resulting in high homicide rates. Another stereotyped conception of behavior among Negroes is that of an enhanced prestige among the Negro criminal growing out of being considered a "bad" man. Fear of such a person often leads either to a bullying attitude, or the challenging of such behavior; aggravated assault or homicide frequently being the outcome.

While one cannot accept the foregoing stereotyped modes of behavior as the explanation of higher crime rates among Negroes, neither can one deny that in many cases these are factors conducive to criminal behavior. A more reasoned explanation is to be found in the poverty of life in the deteriorated areas inhabited by them. One recognizes this poverty on every hand and in a variety of its manifestations. Because of it, life in these areas has been reduced largely to organic survival; and the reflex of this is an organic plane of living. The poverty is more than economic; it is pervasive in character: bad housing, overcrowding, restricted areas of settlement, limited outlets of expression, as in recreation, restricted employment opportunities, etc. On every hand the Negro is hedged in by racial proscriptions.

The white areas have a population characterized by low economic status and a foreign-born extraction, but they are also a population of long residence in these areas, in contrast to a Negro population predominantly of relative recent migration. The Negroes with generally fewer resources have correspondingly heavier economic drains on their limited means than a comparable socio-economic status white population (e.g., Negroes generally pay higher rents than whites for comparable houses). Based on longer residence, wider occupational opportunities, easier financing of purchasing houses, etc., home ownership is far greater among the whites than Negroes.

Due to a low socio-economic status, accentuated by racial proscriptions, the Negroes in these areas, even as elsewhere, do not have a freedom of wholesome expression comparable to that of a similarly situated white group. Out of these and similar conditions arise elements conducive to greater criminality, as well as other forms of pathology, among the Negro population. It is out of community situations comparable to those just indicated that there develops a characteristic mode of behavior which is conducive to the emergence of the Negro criminal.

43. THE MOYNIHAN REPORT: THE NEGRO FAMILY AND CRIME

THAT THE NEGRO AMERICAN HAS SURVIVED at all is extraordinary—a lesser people might simply have died out, as indeed others have. That the Negro community has not only survived, but in this political generation has entered national affairs as a moderate, humane, and constructive national force is the highest testament to the healing powers of the democratic ideal and the creative vitality of the Negro people.

But it may not be supposed that the Negro American community has not paid a fearful price for the incredible mistreatment to which it has been subjected over the past three centuries.

In essence, the Negro community has been forced into a matriarchal structure which, because it is so out of line with the rest of the American society, seriously retards the progress of the group as a whole, and imposes a crushing burden on the Negro male and, in consequence, on a great many Negro women as well.

There is, presumably, no special reason why a society in which males are dominant in family relationships is to be preferred to a matriarchal arrangement. However, it is clearly a disadvantage for a minority group to be operating on one principle, while the great majority of the population,

▶SOURCE: *The Negro Family,* United States Department of Labor, Office of Planning and Research, Washington, D.C.: March 1965, pp. 29–40, 52–53.

and the one with the most advantages to begin with, is operating on another. This is the present situation of the Negro. Ours is a society which presumes male leadership in private and public affairs. The arrangements of society facilitate such leadership and reward it. A subculture, such as that of the Negro American, in which this is not the pattern, is placed at a distinct disadvantage.

Here an earlier word of caution should be repeated. There is much evidence that a considerable number of Negro families have managed to break out of the tangle of pathology and to establish themselves as stable, effective units, living according to patterns of American society in general. E. Franklin Frazier has suggested that the middle-class Negro American family is, if anything, more patriarchal and protective of its children than the general run of such families (1). Given equal opportunities, the children of these families will perform as well or better than their white peers. They need no help from anyone, and ask none.

While this phenomenon is not easily measured, one index is that middle-class Negroes have even fewer children than middle-class whites, indicating a desire to conserve the advances they have made and to insure that their children do as well or better. Negro women who marry early to uneducated laborers have more children than white women in the same situation; Negro women who marry at the common age for the middle class to educated men doing technical or professional work have only four-fifths as many children as their white counterparts.

It might be estimated that as much as half of the Negro community falls into the middle class. However, the remaining half is in desperate and deteriorating circumstances. Moreover, because of housing segregation it is immensely difficult for the stable half to escape from the cultural influences of the unstable one. The children of middle-class Negroes often as not must grow up in, or next to the slums, an experience almost unknown to white middle-class children. They are therefore constantly exposed to the pathology of the disturbed group and constantly in danger of being drawn into it. It is for this reason that the propositions put forth in this study may be thought of as having a more or less general application.

In a word, most Negro youth are in *danger* of being caught up in the tangle of pathology that affects their world, and probably a majority are so entrapped. Many of those who escape do so for one generation only: as things now are, their children may have to run the gauntlet all over again. That is not the least vicious aspect of the world that white America has made for the Negro.

Obviously, not every instance of social pathology afflicting the Negro community can be traced to the weakness of family structure. If, for example, organized crime in the Negro community were not largely controlled by whites, there would be more capital accumulation among Negroes, and therefore probably more Negro business enterprises. If it were not for the hostility and fear many whites exhibit towards Negroes, they in turn would be less afflicted by hostility and fear and so on. There is no one Negro community. There is no one Negro problem. There is no one solution. Nonetheless, at the center of the tangle of pathology is the weakness of the family structure. Once or twice removed, it will be found to be the principal source of most of the aberrant, inadequate, or antisocial behavior that did not establish, but now serves to perpetuate the cycle of poverty and deprivation.

It was by destroying the Negro family under slavery that white America broke the will of the Negro people. Although that will has reasserted itself in our time, it is a resurgence doomed to frustration unless the viability of the Negro family is restored.

MATRIARCHY

A fundamental fact of Negro American family life is the often reversed roles of husband and wife.

Robert O. Blood, Jr. and Donald M. Wolfe, in a study of Detroit families, note that "Negro husbands have unusually low power," (2) and while this is characteristic of all low income families, the pattern pervades the Negro social structure: "the

Children Born per Woman Age 35 to 44: Wives of Uneducated Laborers Who Married Young, Compared with Wives of Educated Professional Workers who Married After Age 21, White and Nonwhite, 1960[a]

	Children per Woman	
	White	Nonwhite
Wives married at age 14 to 21 to husbands who are laborers and did not go to high school	3.8	4.7
Wives married at age 22 or over to husbands who are professional or technical workers and have completed 1 year or more of college	2.4	1.9

[a] Wives married only once, with husbands present.

Source: 1960 Census, *Women by Number of Children ever Born*, PC (2) 3A, Tables 39 and 40, pp. 199–238.

cumulative result of discrimination in jobs ..., the segregated housing, and the poor schooling of Negro men" (3). In 44 percent of the Negro families studied, the wife was dominant, as against 20 percent of white wives. "Whereas the majority of white families are equalitarian, the largest percentage of Negro families are dominated by the wife" (4).

The matriarchal pattern of so many Negro families reinforces itself over the generations. This process begins with education. Although the gap appears to be closing at the moment, for a long while, Negro females were better educated than Negro males, and this remains true today for the Negro population as a whole.

Educational Attainment of the Civilian Noninstitutional Population 18 Years of Age and Over, March 1964

Color and Sex	Median School Years Completed
White:	
Male	12.1
Female	12.1
Nonwhite:	
Male	9.2
Female	10.0

Source: Bureau of Labor Statistics, unpublished data.

The difference in educational attainment between nonwhite men and women in the labor force is even greater; men lag 1.1 years behind women.

The disparity in educational attainment of male and female youth age 16 to 21 who were out of school in February 1963, is striking. Among the nonwhite males, 66.3 percent were not high school graduates, compared with 55.0 percent of the females. A similar difference existed at the college level, with 4.5 percent of the males having completed 1 to 3 years of college compared with 7.3 percent of the females.

The poorer performance of the male in school exists from the very beginning, and the magnitude of the difference was documented by the 1960 Census in statistics on the number of children who have fallen one or more grades below the typical grade for children of the same age. The boys have more frequently fallen behind at every age level. (White boys also lag behind white girls, but at a differential of 1 to 6 percentage points.)

Percent of Nonwhite Youth Enrolled in School Who are 1 or More Grades Below Mode for Age, by Sex, 1960

Age	Male	Female
7 to 9 years old	7.8	5.8
10 to 13 years old	25.0	17.1
14 and 15 years old	35.5	24.8
16 and 17 years old	39.4	27.2
18 and 19 years old	57.3	46.0

Source: 1960 Census, *School Enrollment,* PC(2) 5A, Table 3, p. 24.

In 1960, 39 percent of all white persons 25 years of age and over who had completed 4 or more years of college were women. Fifty-three percent of the nonwhites who had attained this level were women.

However, the gap is closing. By October 1963, there were slightly more Negro men in college than women. Among whites there were almost twice as many men as women enrolled.

There is much evidence that Negro females are better students than their male counterparts.

Daniel Thompson of Dillard University, in a private communication on January 9, 1965, writes:

As low as is the aspirational level among lower class Negro girls, it is considerably higher than among the boys. For example, I have examined the honor rolls in Negro high schools for about 10 years. As a rule, from 75 to 90 percent of all Negro honor students are girls.

Dr. Thompson reports that 70 percent of all applications for the National Achievement Scholarship Program financed by the Ford Foundation for outstanding Negro high school graduates are girls, despite special efforts by high school principals to submit the names of boys.

Fall Enrollment of Civilian Noninstitutional Population in College by Color and Sex—October 1963 (in Thousands)

Color and Sex	Population, age 14–34 October 1, 1963	Number Enrolled	Percent of Youth, Age 14–34
Nonwhite			
Male	2,884	149	5.2
Female	3,372	137	4.1
White			
Male	21,700	2,599	12.0
Female	20,613	1,451	7.0

Source: U.S. Bureau of the Census, *Current Population Reports,* Series P-20, No. 129 July 24, 1964, Tables 1, 5.

The finalists for this new program for outstanding Negro students were recently announced. Based on an inspection of the names, only about 43 percent of all the 639 finalists were male. (However, in the regular National Merit Scholarship program, males received 67 percent of the 1964 scholarship awards.)

Inevitably, these disparities have carried over to the area of employment and income.

In 1 out of 4 Negro families where the husband is present, is an earner, and someone else in the family works, the husband is not the principal earner. The comparable figure for whites is 18 percent.

More important, it is clear that Negro females have established a strong position for themselves in white collar and professional employment, precisely the areas of the economy which are growing most rapidly, and to which the highest prestige is accorded.

The President's Committee on Equal Employment Opportunity, making a preliminary report on employment in 1964 of over 16,000 companies with nearly 5 million employees, revealed this pattern with dramatic emphasis (see Figure 1).

In this work force, Negro males outnumber Negro females by a ratio of 4 to 1. Yet Negro males represent only 1.2 percent of all males in white collar occupations, while Negro females represent 3.1 percent of the total female white collar work force. Negro males represent 1.1 percent of all male professionals, whereas Negro females represent roughly 6 percent of all female professionals. Again, in technician occupations, Negro males represent 2.1 percent of all male technicians while Negro females represent roughly 10 percent of all female technicians. It would appear therefore that there are proportionately 4 times as many Negro females in significant white collar jobs than Negro males.

Although it is evident that office and clerical jobs account for approximately 50 percent of all Negro female white collar workers, it is significant that 6 out of every 100 Negro females are in professional jobs. This is substantially similar to the rate of all females in such jobs. Approximately 7 out of every 100 Negro females are in technician jobs. This exceeds the proportion of all females in technician jobs—approximately 5 out of every 100.

Negro females in skilled jobs are almost the same as that of all females in such jobs. Nine out of every 100 Negro males are in skilled occupations while 21 out of 100 of all males are in such jobs (5).

This pattern is to be seen in the Federal government, where special efforts have been made recently to insure equal employment opportunity for Negroes. These efforts have been notably successful in Departments such as Labor, where some 19 percent of employees are now Negro. (A not disproportionate percentage, given the composition of the work force in the areas where the main Department offices are located.) However, it may well be that these efforts

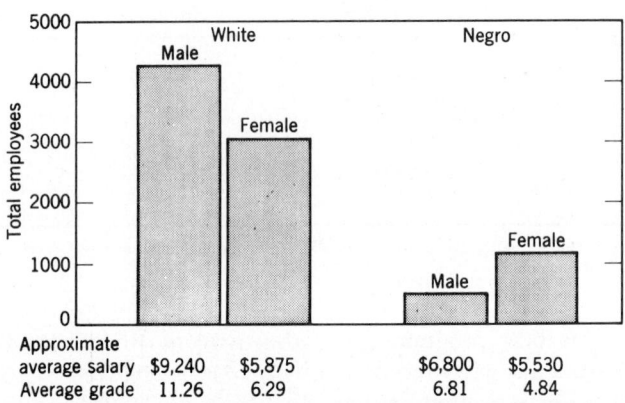

have redounded mostly to the benefit of Negro women, and may even have accentuated the comparative disadvantage of Negro men. Seventy percent of the Negro employees of the Department of Labor are women, as contrasted with only 42 percent of the white employees.

Among nonprofessional Labor Department employees—where the most employment opportunities exist for all groups—Negro women outnumber Negro men 4 to 1, and average almost one grade higher in classification.

The testimony to the effects of the patterns in Negro family structure is widespread, and hardly to be doubted.

Whitney Young:

Historically, in the matriarchal Negro society, mothers made sure that if one of their children had a chance for higher education the daughter was the one to pursue it (6).

The effect on family functioning and role performance of this historical experience [economic deprivation] is what you might predict. Both as a husband and as a father the Negro male is made to feel inadequate, not because he is unlovable or unaffectionate, lacks intelligence or even a gray flannel suit. But in a society that measures a man by the size of his pay check, he doesn't stand very tall in a comparison with his white counterpart. To this situation he may react with withdrawal, bitterness toward society, aggression both within the family and racial group, self-hatred, or crime. Or he may escape through a number of avenues that help him to lose himself in fantasy or to compensate for his low status through a variety of exploits (7).

Thomas Pettigrew:

The Negro wife in this situation can easily become disgusted with her financially dependent husband, and her rejection of him further alienates the male from family life. Embittered by their experiences with men, many Negro mothers often act to perpetuate the mother-centered pattern by taking a greater interest in their daughters than their sons (8).

Deton Brooks:

In a matriarchal structure, the women are transmitting the culture (9).

Dorothy Height:

If the Negro woman has a major underlying concern, it is the status of the Negro man and his position in the community and his need for feeling himself an important person, free and able to make his contribution in the whole society, in order that he may strengthen his home (10).

Duncan M. MacIntyre:

The Negro illegitimacy rate always has been high—about eight times the white rate in 1940 and somewhat higher today even though the white illegitimacy rate also is climbing. The Negro statistics are symtomatic of some old socio-economic problems, not the least of which are under-employment among Negro men and compensating higher labor force propensity among Negro women. Both operate to enlarge the mother's role, undercutting the status of the male and making many Negro families essentially matriarchal. The Negro man's uncertain employment prospects, matriarchy, and the high cost of divorces combine to encourage desertion (the poor man's divorce), increases the number of couples not married, and thereby also increases the Negro illegitimacy rate. In the meantime, higher Negro birth rates are increasing the nonwhite population, while migration into cities like Detroit, New York, Philadelphia, and Washington, D.C. is making the public assistance rolls in such cities heavily, even predominantly, Negro (11).

Robin M. Williams, Jr. in a study of Elmira, New York:

Only 57 percent of Negro adults reported themselves as married—spouse present, as compared with 78 percent of native white American gentiles, 91 percent of Italian-American, and 96 percent of Jewish informants. Of the 93 unmarried Negro youths interviewed, 22 percent did not have their mother living in the home with them, and 42 percent reported that their father was not living in their home. One-third of the youths did not know their father's present occupation, and two-thirds of a sample of 150 Negro adults did not know what the occupation of their father's father had been. Forty percent of the youth said that they had brothers and sisters living in other communities: another 40 percent reported relatives living in their home who were not parents, siblings, or grandparent (12).

THE FAILURE OF YOUTH

Williams' account of Negro youth growing up with little knowledge of their fathers, less of their fathers' occupations, still less of family occupational traditions, is in sharp contrast to the experience of the white child. The white family, despite many variants, remains a powerful agency not only for transmitting property from one generation to the next, but also for transmitting no less valuable contracts with the world of education and work. In an earlier age, the Carpenters, Wainwrights, Weavers, Mercers, Farmers, Smiths acquired their names as well as their trades from their fathers and grandfathers. Children today still learn the patterns of work from their fathers even though they may no longer go into the same jobs.

White children without fathers at least perceive all about them the pattern of men working.

Negro children without fathers flounder—and fail.

Not always, to be sure. The Negro community produces its share, very possibly more than its share, of young people who have the something extra that carries them over the worst obstacles. But such persons are always a minority. The common run of young people in a group facing serious obstacles to success do not succeed.

A prime index of the disadvantage of Negro youth in the United States is their consistently poor performance on the mental tests that are a standard means of measuring ability and performance in the present generation.

There is absolutely no question of any genetic differential: Intelligence potential is distributed among Negro infants in the same proportion and pattern as among Icelanders or Chinese or any other group. American society, however, impairs the Negro potential. The statement of the HARYOU report that "there is no basic disagreement over the fact that central Harlem students are performing poorly in school" (13) may be taken as true of

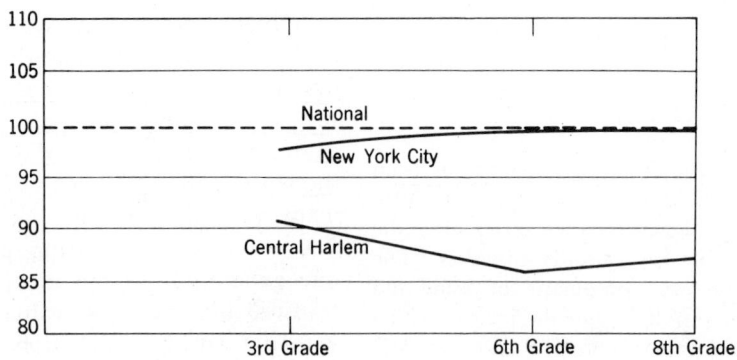

Negro slum children throughout the United States.

Eighth grade children in central Harlem (see Figure 2) have a median IQ of 87.7, which means that perhaps a third of the children are scoring at levels perilously near to those of retardation. IQ *declines* in the first decade of life, rising only slightly thereafter.

The effect of broken families on the performance of Negro youth has not been extensively measured, but studies that have been made show an unmistakable influence.

Martin Deutch and Bert Brown, investigating intelligence test differences between Negro and white 1st and 5th graders of different social classes, found that there is a direct relationship between social class and IQ. As the one rises so does the other: but more for whites than Negroes. This is surely a result of housing segregation, referred to earlier, which makes it difficult for middle-class Negro families to escape the slums.

The authors explain that "it is much more difficult for the Negro to attain identical middle- or upper-middle-class status with whites, and the social class gradations are less marked for Negroes because Negro life in a caste society is considerably more homogeneous than is life for the majority group" (14).

Therefore, the authors look for background variables other than social class which might explain the difference: "One of the most striking differences between the Negro and white groups is the consistently higher frequency of broken homes and resulting family disorganization in the Negro group" (15).

FATHER ABSENT FROM THE HOME

Lowest social class level		*Middle social class level*		*Highest social class level*	
Percent of White Negro		*Percent of White Negro*		*Percent of White Negro*	
15.4	43.9	10.3	27.9	0.0	13.7

(Adapted from authors' table.)

Further, they found that children from homes where fathers are present have significantly higher scores than children in homes without fathers.

	Mean Intelligence Scores
Father Present	97.83
Father Absent	90.79

The influence of the father's presence was then tested *within* the social classes and school grades for Negroes alone. They found that "a consistent trend within both grades at the lower SES [social class] level appears, and in no case is there a reversal of this trend: for males, females, and the combined group, the IQ's of children with fathers in the home are always higher than

Mean Intelligence Scores of Negro Children by School, Grade, Social Class, and by Presence of Father

Social Class and School Grade	Father Present	Father Absent
Lowest social class level:		
Grade 1	95.2	87.8
Grade 5	92.7	85.7
Middle social class level:		
Grade 1	98.7	92.8
Grade 5	92.9	92.0

(Adapted from authors' table.)

Percent of Nonwhite Males Enrolled in School, by Age and Presence of Parents, 1960

Age	Both Parents Present	One Parent Present	Neither Parent Present
5 years	41.7	44.2	34.3
6 years	79.3	78.7	73.8
7 to 9 years	96.1	95.3	93.9
10 to 13 years	96.2	95.5	93.0
14 and 15 years	91.8	89.9	85.0
16 and 17 years	78.0	72.7	63.2
18 and 19 years	46.5	40.0	32.3

Source: 1960 Census, School Enrollment, PC (2) 5A, Table 3, p. 24.

those who have no father in the home (16).

The authors say that broken homes "may also account for some of the differences between Negro and white intelligence scores" (17).

The scores of fifth graders with fathers absent were lower than the scores of first graders with fathers absent, and while the authors point out that it is cross sectional data and does not reveal the duration of the father's absence, "What we might be tapping is the cumulative effect of father-less years" (18).

This difference in ability to perform has its counterparts in statistics on actual school performance. Nonwhite boys from families with both parents present are more likely to be going to school than boys with only one parent present, and enrollmen rates are even lower when neither parent is present.

When the boys from broken homes are in school, they do not do as well as the boys from whole families. Grade retardation is higher when only one parent is present, and highest when neither parent is present.

The loneliness of the Negro youth in making fundamental decisions about education is shown in a 1959 study of Negro and white dropouts in Connecticut high schools.

Only 29 percent of the Negro male dropouts discussed their decision to drop out of school with their fathers, compared with 65 percent of the white males (38 percent of the Negro males were from broken homes). In fact, 26 percent of the Negro males did not discuss this major decision in their lives with anyone at all, compared with only 8 percent of white males.

A study of Negro apprenticeship by the New York State Commission Against Discrimination in 1960 concluded:

Negro youth are seldom exposed to influences which can lead to apprenticeship. Negroes are not apt to have relatives, friends, or neighbors in skilled occupations. Nor are they likely to be in secondary schools where they receive encouragement and direction from alternate role models. Within the minority community, skilled Negro 'models' after whom the Negro youth might pattern himself are rare, while substitute sources which could provide the direction, encouragement, resources, and information needed to achieve skilled craft standing are nonexistent.[19]

DELINQUENCY AND CRIME

The combined impact of poverty, failure, and isolation among Negro youth has had the predictable outcome in a disastrous delinquency and crime rate.

In a typical pattern of discrimination, Negro children in all public and private orphanages are a smaller proportion of all children than their proportion of the population although their needs are clearly greater.

Percent of Nonwhite Males Enrolled in School Who are 1 or More Grades Below Mode for Age, by Age Group and Presence of Parents, 1960

Age Group	Both Parents Present	One Parent Present	Neither Parent Present
7–9 year	7.5	7.7	9.6
10–13 years	23.8	25.8	30.6
14–15 years	34.0	36.3	40.9
16–17 years	37.6	40.9	44.1
18–19 years	60.6	65.9	46.1

Source: 1960 Census, *School Enrollment,* PC(2) 5A, Tabe 3, p. 24.

On the other hand Negroes represent a third of all youth in training schools for juvenile delinquents.

Children in Homes for Dependent and Neglected Children, 1960

	Number	Percent
White	64,807	88.4
Negro	6,140	8.4
Other races	2,359	3.2
All races	73,306	100.0

Source: 1960 Census, *Inmates of Institutions,* PC(2) 3A, Table 31, p. 44.

It is probable that at present, a majority of the crimes against the person, such as rape, murder, and aggravated assault are committed by Negroes. There is, of course, no absolute evidence; inference can only be made from arrest and prison population statistics. The data that follow unquestionably are biased against Negroes, who are arraigned much more casually than are whites, but it may be doubted that the bias is great enough to affect the general proportions.

Again on the urban frontier the ratio is worse: 3 out of every 5 arrests for these crimes were of Negroes.

In Chicago in 1963, three-quarters of the persons arrested for such crimes were Negro; in Detroit, the same proportions held.

Number of Arrests in 1963

	White	Negro
Offenses charged total	31,988	38,549
Murder and nonnegligent manslaughter	2,288	2,948
Forcible rape	4,402	3,935
Aggravated assault	25,298	31,666

Source: *Crime in the United States* (Federal Bureau of Investigation, 1963) Table 25, p. 111.

In 1960, 37 percent of all persons in Federal and State prisons were Negro. In that year, 56 percent of the homicide and 57 percent of the assault offenders committed to State institutions were Negro.

Number of City Arrests in 1963 [a]

	White	Negro
Offenses charged total	24,805	35,520
Murder and nonnegligent manslaughter	1,662	2,593
Forcible rape	3,199	3,570
Aggravated assault	19,944	29,357

[a] In 2,892 cities with population over 2,500.

Source: *Crime in the United States* (Federal Bureau of Investigation, 1963) Table 31, p. 117.

The overwhelming number of offenses committed by Negroes are directed toward other Negroes: the cost of crime to the Negro community is a combination of that to the criminal and to the victim.

Some of the research on the effects of broken homes on delinquent behavior recently surveyed by Thomas F. Pettigrew in *A Profile of the Negro American* is summarized below, along with several other studies of the question.

Mary Diggs found that three-fourths—twice the expected ratio—of Philadelphia's Negro delinquents who came before the law during 1948 did not live with both their natural parents (20).

In predicting juvenile crime, Eleanor and Sheldon Glueck also found that a higher proportion of delinquent than non-delinquent boys came from broken homes. They identified five critical factors in the home environment that made a difference in whether boys would become delinquents: discipline of boy by father, supervision of boy by mother, affection of father for boy, affection of mother for boy, and cohesiveness of family.

In 1952, when the New York City Youth Board set out to test the validity of these five factors as predictors of delinquency, a problem quickly emerged. The Glueck sample consisted of white boys of mainly Irish, Italian, Lithuanian, and English descent. However, the Youth Board group was 44 percent Negro and 14 percent Puerto Rican, and the frequency of broken homes within these groups was out of proportion to the total number of delinquents in the population (21).

In the majority of these cases, the father was usually never in the home at all, absent for the major proportion of the boy's life, or was present only on occasion.

(The final prediction table was reduced to three factors: supervision of boy by mother, discipline of boy by mother, and family cohesiveness within what family, in fact, existed, but was, nonetheless, 85 percent accurate in predicting delinquents and 96 percent accurate in predicting nondelinquents.)

Researchers who have focused upon the "good" boy in high delinquency neighborhoods noted that they typically come from exceptionally stable, intact families, (22).

Recent psychological research demonstrates the personality effects of being reared in a disorganized home without a father. One study showed that children from fatherless homes seek immediate gratification of their desires far more than children with fathers present (23). Others revealed that children who hunger for immediate gratification are more prone to delinquency, along with other less social behavior (24). Two psychologists, Pettigrew says, maintain that inability to delay gratification is a critical factor in immature, criminal, and neurotic behavior (25).

Finally, Pettigrew discussed the evidence that a stable home is a crucial factor in counteracting the effects of racism upon Negro personality.

A warm, supportive home can effectively compensate for many of the restrictions the Negro child faces outside of the ghetto; consequently, the type of home life a Negro enjoys as a child may be far more crucial for governing the influence of segregation upon his personality than the form the segregation takes—legal or informal, Southern or Northern (26).

A Yale University study of youth in the lowest socio-economic class in New Haven in 1950 whose behavior was followed through their 18th year revealed that among the delinquents in the group, 38 percent came from broken homes, compared with 24 percent of nondelinquents (27).

The President's Task Force on Manpower Conservation in 1963 found that of young men rejected for the draft for failure to pass the mental tests, 42 percent of those with a court record came from broken homes, compared with 30 percent of those without a court record. Half of all the nonwhite rejectees in the study with a court record came from broken homes.

An examination of the family background 44,448 delinquency cases in Philadelphia between 1949 and 1954 documents the frequency of broken homes among delinquents. Sixty-two percent of the Negro delinquents and 36 percent of white delinquents were not living with both parents. In 1950, 33 percent of nonwhite children and 17 percent of white children in Philadelphia were living in homes without both parents. Repeaters were even more likely to be from broken homes than first offenders (28).

Juvenile Delinquents—Philadelphia by Presence of Parents, 1949–1954

	White			Negro		
	All Court Cases	First Offenders	Recidivists	All Court Cases	First Offenders	Recidivists
Number of Cases	20,691	13,220	4,612	22,695	11,442	6,641
Number not living with both parents	7,422	4,125	2,047	13,980	6,586	4,298
Percent not living with both parents	35.9	31.2	44.4	61.6	57.6	64.7

Source: Adapted from Table 1, p. 255, "Family Status and the Delinquent Child," Thomas P. Monahan, *Social Forces*, March 1957.

REFERENCES

1. E. Franklin Frazier, *Black Bourgeoisie*, (New York, Collier Books, 1962.)
2. Robert O. Blood, Jr. and Donald M. Wolfe, *Husbands and Wives: The Dynamics of Married Living*, (Illinois, The Free Press of Glencoe, 1960), p. 34.
3. Ibid., p. 35.
4. Ibid.
5. Based on preliminary draft of a report by the President's Committee on Equal Employment Opportunity.
6. Whitney Young, *To Be Equal*, (New York, McGraw Hill Book Company, 1964), p. 25.
7. Ibid., p. 175.
8. Thomas F. Pettigrew, op. cit., p. 16.
9. Deton Brooks, quoted in *The New Improved American* by Bernard Asbell, (New York, McGraw Hill Book Company, 1965), p. 76.
10. Dorothy Height, in the Report of Consultation of Problems of Negro Women, President's Commission on the Status of Women, April 19, 1963, p. 35.
11. Duncan M. MacIntyre, *Public Assistance: Too Much or Too Little?* (New York, New York State School of Industrial Relations, Cornell University, Bulletin 53-1, December 1964), pp. 73–74.
12. Robin M. Williams, Jr., *Strangers Next Door*, (Englewood Cliffs, New Jersey, Prentice-Hall, Inc., 1964), p. 240.
13. *Youth in the Ghetto*, op. cit., p. 195.
14. Martin Deutch and Bert Brown, "Social Influences in Negro-White Intelligence Differences," *Social Issues*, April 1964, p. 27.
15. Ibid., p. 29
16. Ibid.
17. Ibid., p. 31.
18. Ibid.
19. "Negroes in Apprenticeship, New York State," *Monthly Labor Review*, September 1960, p. 955.
20. Mary H. Diggs, "Some Problems and Needs of Negro Children as Revealed by Comparative Delinquency and Crime Statistics," *Journal of Negro Education*, 1950, 19, pp. 290–297.
21. Maude M. Craig and Thelma J. Glick, "Ten Years Experience with the Glueck Social Prediction Table," *Journal of Crime and Delinquency*, July 1963, p. 256.
22. F. R. Scarpitti, Ellen Murray, S. Dinitz and W. C. Reckless, "The 'Good' Boy in a High Delinquency Area: Four Years Later," *American Sociological Review*, 1960, 25, pp. 555–558.
23. W. Mischel, "Father-Absence and Delay of Gratification: Cross-Cultural Comparisons," *Journal of Abnormal and Social Psychology*, 1961, 63, pp. 116–124.
24. W. Mischel, "Preference for Delayed Reinforcement and Social Responsibility," *Journal of Social and Abnormal Psychology*, 1961, 62, pp. 1–7.
"Delay of Gratification, Need for Achievement, and Acquiescense in Another Culture," *Journal of Abnormal and Social Psychology*, 1961, 62, pp. 543–552.
25. O. H. Mowrer and A. D. Ullman, "Time as a Determinant in Integrative Learning," *Psychological Review*, 1945, 52, pp. 61–90.
26. Thomas F. Pettigrew, op. cit., p. 22.
27. Erdman Palmore, "Factors Associated with School Dropouts on Juvenile Delinquency Among Lower Class Children," *Social Security Bulletin*, October 1963, p. 6.
28. Thomas P. Monahan, "Family Status and the Delinquent Child," *Social Forces*, March 1957, p. 254.

44. SOCIAL CLASS AND DELINQUENCY

JOHN P. CLARK
EUGENE P. WENNINGER

UNTIL RECENTLY ALMOST ALL EFFORTS TO discover characteristics that differentiate juveniles who violate legal norms from those who do not have compared institutional and non-institutional populations. Though many researchers still employ a "delinquent" or "criminal" sample from institutions,[1] there is a growing awareness that the process through which boys and girls are selected to populate our "correctional" institutions may cause such comparison studies to distort seriously the true picture of illegal behavior in our society. Therefore, conclusions based upon such studies are subject to considerable criticism[2] if generalized beyond the type of population of the particular institution at the time of the study. Although the study of adjudicated offenders is important, less encumbered studies of the violation of legal norms hold more promise for those interested in the more general concept of deviant behavior.

Though it, too, has methodological limitations, the anonymous-questionnaire procedure has been utilized to obtain results reflecting the rates and patterns of illegal behavior among juveniles from different social classes, ages, sexes, and ethnic groups in the general population.[3] The results of these studies have offered sufficient evidence to indicate that the patterns of illegal behavior among juveniles may be dramatically different than was heretofore thought to be the case.

Some of the most provocative findings have been those that challenge the almost universally-accepted conclusion that the lower socio-economic classes have higher rates of illegal behavior than do the middle or upper classes. For example, neither the Nye-Short study[4] nor that of Dentler and

▶SOURCE: "Socio-Economic Class and Area as Correlates of Illegal Behavior Among Juveniles," *American Sociological Review* (December 1962), 27:6:826–834. Reprinted by permission.

[1] An outstanding example of this type of research design is Sheldon and Eleanor Glueck, *Unraveling Juvenile Delinquency*, New York: The Commonwealth Fund, 1950.

[2] See Marshall B. Clinard, *Sociology of Deviant Behavior*, New York: Rinehart, 1958, p. 124, for his assessment of the validity of the study by Sheldon and Eleanor Glueck, *Unraveling Juvenile Delinquency*.

[3] Most outstanding are those by Austin L. Porterfield, *Youth in Trouble*, Fort Worth, Texas: Leo Potishman Foundation, 1946; F. Ivan Nye and James F. Short, "Scaling Delinquent Behavior," *American Sociological Review*, 22 (June, 1957), pp. 326–331; and Robert A. Dentler and Lawrence J. Monroe, "Early Adolescent Theft," *American Sociological Review*, 26 (October, 1961), 733–743; Fred J. Murphy, Mary M. Shirley, and Helen L. Witmer, "The Incidence of Hidden Delinquency," *American Journal of Orthopsychiatry*, 16 (October, 1946), pp. 686–696.

[4] James F. Short, "Differential Association and Delinquency," *Social Problems*, 4 (January, 1957),

Monroe [5] revealed any significant difference in the incidence of certain illegal or "deviant" behaviors among occupational-status levels—a finding quite at odds with most current explanations of delinquent behavior.

Although most of the more comprehensive studies in the social class tradition have been specifically concerned with a more-or-less well-defined portion of the lower class (i.e., "delinquent gangs," [6] or "culture of the gang," or "delinquent subculture" [7]), some authors have tended to generalize their findings and theoretical formulations rather specifically to the total lower class population of juveniles.[8] These latter authors certainly do not profess that *all* lower class children are equally involved in illegal behavior, but by implication they suggest that the incidence of illegal conduct (whether brought to the attention of law enforcement agencies or not) is more pervasive in this class than others because of some unique but fundamental characteristics of the lower social strata. For example, Miller has compiled a list of "focal concerns" toward which the lower class supposedly is oriented and because of which those in this class violate more legal norms with greater frequency than other classes.[9] Other authors point out that the lower classes are disadvantaged in their striving for legitimate goals and that they resort to deviant means to attain them.[10] Again, the result of this behavior is higher rates of illegal behavior among the lower socio-economic classes.

Therefore, there *appears* to be a direct conflict between the theoretical formulations of Miller, Cohen, Merton, Cloward and Ohlin, and those findings reported by Nye and Short and Dentler and Monroe. This apparent discrepancy in the literature can be resolved, however, if one hypothesizes that the rates of illegal conduct among the social classes vary with the type of community [11] in which they are found. Were this so, it would be possible for studies which have included certain types of communities to reveal differential illegal behavior rates among social classes while studies which have involved other types of communities might fail to detect social class differences.

Whereas the findings and formulations of Merton, Cohen, Cloward and Ohlin, and Miller are oriented, in a sense, toward the "full-range" of social situations, those of Nye-Short and Dentler-Monroe are very specifically limited to the types of populations used in their respective studies. It is important to note that the communities in which these latter studies were conducted ranged only from rural to small city in size. As Nye points out, "They are thus urban but not metropolitan." [12] Yet, most studies of "delinquent gangs" and "delinquent subcultures" have been conducted in metropolitan centers where these phenomena are most apparent. Perhaps, it is only

---

pp. 233–239; F. Ivan Nye, *Family Relationships and Delinquent Behavior*, New York: John Wiley, 1958; James E. Short and F. Ivan Nye, "Reported Behavior as a Criterion of Deviant Behavior," *Social Problems*, 5 (Winter, 1957–1958), pp. 207–213; F. Ivan Nye, James F. Short, and Virgil J. Olson, "Socio-Economic Status and Delinquent Behavior," *American Journal of Sociology*, 63 (January, 1958), pp. 381–389.

[5] Dentler and Monroe, *op. cit.*

[6] Richard A. Cloward and Lloyd E. Ohlin, *Delinquency and Opportunity: A Theory of Delinquent Gangs*, New York: The Free Press of Glencoe, 1961.

[7] Albert K. Cohen, *Delinquent Boys: The Culture of the Gang*, Glencoe, Ill.: Free Press, 1955.

[8] Walter B. Miller, "Lower Class Culture as a Generating Milieu of Gang Delinquency," *Journal of Social Issues*, 14 (No. 3, 1958), pp. 5–19.

[9] *Ibid.* The matter of class differences in "focal concerns" or values will be explored in subsequent articles.

[10] Cohen, *op. cit.*, Cloward and Ohlin, *op. cit.*, and Robert K. Merton, *Social Theory and Social Structure*, Glencoe, Ill.: Free Press, 1957, pp. 146–149.

[11] In this report "type of community" is used to refer in a general way to a geographic and social unit having certain distinctive demographic qualities, such as occupational structure, race, social class, and size. Designations such as "rural farm," or "Negro lower class urban," or "middle class suburbia," have long been utilized to describe such persistent physical-social characteristics.

[12] Nye, Short, and Olson, *op. cit.*, p. 383.

here that there is a sufficient concentration of those in the extreme socio-economic classes to afford an adequate test of the "social class hypothesis."

In addition to the matter of social class concentration and size, there is obviously more than one "kind" of lower class and each does not have rates or types of illegal behavior identical to that of the others. For example, most rural farm areas, in which occupations, incomes, and educational levels are indicative of lower class status, as measured by most social class indexes, consistently have been found to have low rates of misconduct—in fact lower than most urban middle class communities.

Therefore, to suggest the elimination of social class as a significant correlate to the quantity and quality of illegal behavior before it has been thoroughly examined in a variety of community situations, seems somewhat premature. Reiss and Rhodes concluded as a result of study of class and juvenile court rates by school district that "it is clear, that there is no simple relationship between ascribed social status and delinquency." [13] In order to isolate the factor of social class, to eliminate possible effects of class bias in the rate of which juvenile misbehavior is referred to court, as well as to vary the social and physical environs in which it is located, we chose in this study to compare rates of admitted illegal behavior among diverse communities within the northern half of Illinois. Our hypotheses were:

1. Significant differences in the incidence of illegal behavior exist among communities differing in predominant social class composition, within a given metropolitan area.
2. Significant differences in the incidence of illegal behavior exist among similar social class strata located in different types of community.
3. Differences in the incidence of illegal behavior among different social class populations within a given community are not significant.

THE STUDY

The data used to test the above hypotheses were gathered in 1961 as part of a larger exploratory study of illegal behavior (particularly theft) among juveniles, and its relationship to socio-economic class, type of community, age, race, and various attitudinal variables, such as attitude toward law, feelings of alienation, concept of self, and feelings of being able to achieve desired goals. Subsequent reports will deal with other aspects of the study.

A total of 1154 public school students from the sixth through the twelfth grades in the school systems of four different types of communities were respondents to a self-administered, anonymous questionnaire given in groups of from 20 to 40 persons by the senior author. Considerable precaution was taken to insure reliability and validity of the responses. For example, assurances were given that the study was not being monitored by the school administration; questions were pretested to eliminate ambiguity; and the administration of the questionnaire was made as threat-free as possible.

The four communities represented in the study were chosen for the unique social class structure represented by each. The Duncan "Socio-Economic Index for All Occupations" [14] was used to determine the occupational profile of each community by assigning index scores to the occupation of the respondent's fathers. The results are summarized in Table I.

The overwhelming majority of the respondents comprising the *rural farm* population live on farms, farming being by far

---

[13] Albert J. Reiss and Albert L. Rhodes, "The Distribution of Juvenile Delinquency in the Social Class Structure," *American Sociological Review*, 26 (October, 1961), pp. 720–732.

[14] Albert J. Reiss, Jr., Otis Dudley Duncan, Paul K. Hatt, and Cecil C. North, *Occupations and Social Status*, New York: The Free Press of Glencoe, 1961, especially pp. 109–161 prepared by Otis D. Duncan.

Table I. *Duncan Socio-Economic-Index Scores Based on Occupation of Father*

	Type of Community			
Score	Rural Farm %	Lower Urban %	Industrial City %	Upper Urban %
(1) 0–23	75.9	40.4	36.4	5.7
(2) 24–47	9.9	15.5	19.3	4.8
(3) 48–71	4.7	12.5	22.9	43.9
(4) 72–96	1.5	4.2	10.0	34.6
(5) Unclassifiable [a]	8.0	27.4	11.4	11.0
Total	100 (N—274)	100 (N—265)	100 (N—280)	100 (N—335)

[a] This category included those respondents from homes with no father and those respondents who did not furnish adequate information for reliable classification. The 27.4 percent figure in the lower urban community reflects a higher proportion of "father-less" homes rather than greater numbers of responses which were incomplete or vague in other ways.

the most common occupation of their fathers. Many of the fathers who were not listed as farmers were, in fact, "part-time" farmers. Therefore, though the Duncan Index would classify most of the residents in the lower class, most of these public school children live on farms in a prosperous section of the Midwest. The sixth, seventh, and eighth graders were drawn from schools located in very small villages. Grades 9–12 were drawn from the high school which was located in open-farm land.

The *lower urban* sample is primarily composed of children of those with occupations of near-equal ranking but certainly far different in nature from those of the rural farm community. The lower urban sample was drawn from a school system located in a very crowded and largely-Negro area of Chicago. The fathers (or male head of the family) of these youngsters are laborers in construction, waiters, janitors, clean-up men, etc. Even among those who place relatively high on the Duncan Scale are many who, in spite of their occupational title, reside, work, and socialize almost exclusively in the lower class community.

As Table I demonstrates, the occupational structure of the *industrial city* is somewhat more diffuse than the other communities, though consisting primarily of lower class occupations. This city of about 35,000 is largely autonomous, although a small portion of the population commutes daily to Chicago. However, about two-thirds of these students have fathers who work as blue-collar laborers in local industries and services. The median years of formal education of all males age 25 or over is 10.3.[15] The median annual family income is $7,255.[16] The population of this small city contains substantial numbers of Polish and Italian Americans and about fifteen percent Negroes.

Those in the *upper urban* sample live in a very wealthy suburb of Chicago. Nearly three-fourths of the fathers in these families are high-level executives or professionals. The median level of education for all males age 25 or over is 16 plus.[17] The median annual family income is slightly over $20,000—80 percent of the families make $10,000 or more annually.[18]

With two exceptions, representative sampling of the public school children was followed within each of these communities: (1) those who could not read at a fourth grade level were removed in all cases, which resulted in the loss of less than one-half percent of the total sample, and (2) the sixth-

---

[15] *U. S. Census of Population: 1960* Final Report PC (1)–15C, p. 15–296.
[16] *Ibid.*, p. 15–335.
[17] *Ibid.*, p. 15–305.
[18] *Ibid.*, p. 15–344.

Table II. *Percentage of Respondents Admitting Individual Offenses and Significance of Differences Between Selected Community Comparisons*

Offense	Community				Significance of Differences [a]		
	(1) Industrial City $N = 280$	(2) Lower Urban $N = 265$	(3) Upper Urban $N = 335$	(4) Rural Farm $N = 274$	(1–2)	(2–3)	(3–4)
1. Did things my parents told me not to do.	90	87	85	82	X	X	X
2. Minor theft (compilation of such items as the stealing of fruit; pencils, lipstick, candy, cigarettes, comic books, money less than $1, etc.)	79	78	80	73	X	X	X
3. Told a lie to my family, principal, or friends.	80	74	77	74	X	X	X
4. Used swearwords or dirty words out loud in school, church, or on the street so other people could hear me.	63	58	54	51	X	X	X
5. Showed or gave someone a dirty picture, a dirty story, or something like that.	53	39	58	54	1	3	X
6. Been out at night just fooling around after I was supposed to be home.	49	50	51	35	X	X	3
7. Hung around other people who I knew had broken the law lots of times or who were known as "bad" people.	49	47	27	40	X	2	4
8. Threw rocks, cans, sticks, or other things at passing car, bicycle, or person.	41	37	33	36	X	X	X
9. Slipped into a theater or other place without paying.	35	40	39	22	X	X	3
10. Major theft (compilation of such items as the stealing of auto parts, autos, money over $1, bicycles, radios and parts, clothing, wallets, liquor, guns, etc.)	37	40	29	20	X	2	3
11. Gone into another person's house, a shed, or other building without their permission.	31	16	31	42	1	3	4
12. Gambled for money or something else with people other than my family.	30	22	35	26	X	3	3
13. Got some money or something from others by saying that I would pay them back even though I was pretty sure I wouldn't.	35	48	26	14	2	2	3

Table 2—Continued

Offense	Community				Significance of Differences [a]		
	(1) Industrial City N = 280	(2) Lower Urban N = 265	(3) Upper Urban N = 335	(4) Rural Farm N = 274	(2-3)	(1-2)	(3-4)
14. Told someone I was going to beat-up on them unless they did what I wanted them to do.	33	28	24	32	X	X	4
15. Drank beer, wine, or liquor without my parents permission.	38	37	26	12	X	2	3
16. Have been kicked out of class or school for acting up.	27	28	31	22	X	X	3
17. Thrown nails, or glass, or cans in the street.	31	29	21	17	X	X	X
18. Used a slug or other things like this in candy, coke, or coin machines.	24	35	18	12	2	2	3
19. Skipped school without permission.	24	36	18	11	2	2	3
20. Helped make a lot of noise outside a church, or school, or any other place in order to bother the people inside.	17	37	18	15	X	2	X
21. Threw rocks, or sticks or any other thing in order to break a window, or street light, or thing like that.	24	26	22	16	X	X	3
22. Said I was going to tell something on someone unless they gave me money, candy, or something else I wanted.	23	28	17	19	X	2	X
23. Kept or used something that I knew had been stolen by someone else.	29	36	15	16	X	2	X
24. Tampered or fooled with another person's car, tractor, or bicycle while they weren't around.	26	13	19	24	1	3	X
25. Started a fist fight.	26	22	15	18	X	2	X
26. Messed up a restroom by writing on the wall, or leaving the water running to run onto the floor, or upsetting the waste can.	18	33	14	17	X	2	X
27. Hung around a pool hall, bar, or tavern.	21	18	10	23	X	2	4
28. Hung around the railroad tracks and trains.	16	13	23	16	X	3	3
29. Broken down or helped to break down a fence, gate, or door on another person's place.	15	14	8	8	X	2	X
30. Taken part in a "gang fight."	12	18	7	7	X	2	X
31. Ran away from home.	12	12	8	7	X	X	X
32. Asked for money, candy, a cigarette or other things from strangers.	12	12	6	7	X	2	X

Table 2—Continued

	Community				Significance of Differences [a]		
Offense	(1) Industrial City N = 280	(2) Lower Urban N = 265	(3) Upper Urban N = 335	(4) Rural Farm N = 274	(2-3)	(1-2)	(3-4)
33. Carried a razor, switch-blade, or gun to be used against other people.	8	16	3	4	2	2	X
34. "Beat up" on kids who hadn't done anything to me.	8	5	5	6	X	X	X
35. Broke or helped break up the furniture in a school, church, or other public building.	8	4	2	8	X	X	4
36. Attacked someone with the idea of killing them.	3	6	1	3	2	n	n
37. Smoked a reefer or used some sort of dope (narcotics).	3	4	1	3	X	n	n
38. Started a fire or helped set a fire in a building without the permission of the owner.	3	2	1	3	X	n	n

[a] Code: X = No significant difference; 1, 2, 3, or 4 = significant differences at .05 level or higher. The numbers indicate which of the communities in the comparison is higher in incidence of the offense; and n = too few offender cases to determine significant level.

grade sample in the industrial city community was drawn from a predominantly Negro, working class area and was, therefore, non-representative of the total community for that grade-level only. All the students from grades six through twelve were used in the rural farm community "sample."

MEASURE OF ILLEGAL BEHAVIOR

An inventory of 36 offenses was initially assembled from delinquency scales, legal statutes, and the FBI Uniform Crime Reports. In addition to this, a detailed list of theft items, ranging from candy to automobiles, was constructed. The latter list combined into two composite items (minor theft, and major theft) and added to the first list, enlarging the number of items in this inventory to 38 items as shown in Table II. No questions on sex offenses were included in this study, a restriction found necessary in order to gain entrance into one of the school systems.

All respondents were asked to indicate if they had committed each of these offenses (including the detailed list of theft items) *within the past year,* thus furnishing data amenable to age-level analysis.[19] If the respondents admitted commission of an offense, they so indicated by disclosing the number of times (either 1, 2, 3, or 4 or more) they had done so. The first four columns of Table II reveal the percentage of students who admitted having indulged in each specific behavior one or more times *during the past year.*

Specific offense items were arranged in an array from those admitted by the highest percentage of respondents to those admitted by the lowest percentage of respondents. Obviously the "nuisance" offenses appear near the top while the most serious and the more situationally specific fall nearer the end of the listing.[20] Several

[19] Rates of illegal behavior were found to increase until age 14-15 and then to decrease.

[20] Ordinarily, not receiving 100 per cent admission to the first few offenses listed would have raised

offenses are apparently committed very infrequently by school children from the sixth grades regardless of their social environs.

FINDINGS

In order to determine whether significant differences exist in the incidence of illegal behavior among the various types of communities, a two-step procedure was followed. First, each of the four communities was assigned a rank for each offense on the basis of the percentage of respondents admitting commission of that offense. These ranks were totaled across all offenses for each community. The resultant numerical total provided a very crude over-all measure of the relative degree to which the sample population from each community had been involved in illegal behavior during the past year. The results were (from most to least illegal behavior): industrial city, lower urban, upper urban, and rural farm. However, there was little over-all difference in the sum of ranks between upper urban and rural farm and even less difference between the industrial city and lower urban areas.

In the second step the communities were arranged in the order given above and then the significance of the difference between adjacent pairs was determined by applying the Wilcoxon matched-pairs signed-ranks test. Only those comparisons which involve either industrial city or lower urban versus upper urban or rural farm result in any significant differences.[21] This finding is compatible with the above crude ranking procedure.

On the basis of these findings the first hypothesis is supported, while the second hypothesis received only partial support. Lower urban juveniles reported significantly more illegal behavior than did the juveniles of the upper urban community, and the two lower class communities of industrial city and lower urban appear to be quite similar in their high rates, but another class area composed largely of farmers has a much lower rate, similar to that of the upper urban area.

Much more contrast among the rates of juvenile misconduct in the four different communities, than is indicated by the above results, becomes apparent when one focuses on individual offenses. As the last column in Table 2 reveals, and as could be predicted from the above, there are few significant differences in the rates on each offense between the industrial city and lower urban communities. The few differences that do occur hardly fall into a pattern except that the lower urban youth seem to be oriented more toward violence (carrying weapons and attacking persons) than those in the industrial city.

However, 16 of a possible 35 relationships are significantly different in the upper urban-rural farm comparison, a fact that could not have been predicted from the above results. Apparently, variation in one direction on certain offenses tends to be neutralized by variation in the opposite direction on other offenses when the Wilcoxon test is used. There are greater actual differences in the nature of illegal behavior

---

doubt as to the validity of those questionnaires on which these extremely common offenses were not admitted. In the Nye-Short study such questionnaires were discarded. However, since the respondents were asked in this study to admit their offenses during the past year only, it was thought that less than 100 percent admission would be highly possible when one considers the entire age range. Undoubtedly some of the respondents who did not admit these minor offenses were falsifying their questionnaires.

[21] Significance of differences were calculated between pairs of communities across *all* 38 offenses by using the Wilcoxon Matched-Pairs Signed-Ranks test (described in Sidney Siegel, *Non-Parametric Statistics*, New York: McGraw-Hill Book Company, Inc., 1956, pp. 75–83). The results of the procedure were:

1–2—P .35   1–3—P .00006
2–3—P .0034   1–4—P .0006
3–4—P .90   2–4—P .016

between these two communities than is noticeable when considered in more summary terms. (It might be pointed out here, parenthetically, that this type of finding lends support to the suggestion by Dentler and Monroe that the comparison of criterion groups on the basis of "omnibus scales" may have serious shortcomings.) [22]

Rural farm youngsters are more prone than those in the upper urban area to commit such offenses as trespassing, threatening to "beat up" on persons, hanging around taverns and being with "bad" associates—all relatively unsophisticated acts. Although some of the offenses committed more often by those who live in the upper urban community are also unsophisticated (throwing rocks at street lights, getting kicked out of school classes, and hanging around trains), others probably require some skill to perform successfully and probably depend on supportive peer-group relationships. For example, these data reveal that upper urban juveniles are more likely than their rural farm counterparts to be out at night after they are supposed to be at home, drink beer and liquors without parents permission, engage in major theft, gamble, skip school, and slip into theaters without paying. In addition to their likely dependence upon peer-groups, perhaps these offenses are more easily kept from the attention of parents in the urban setting than in open-farm areas.

The greatest differences between rates of illegal conduct occur between the lower urban and upper urban communities, where 21 of a possible 35 comparisons reach statistical significance, the lower urban rates being higher in all except five of these. Although the upper urban youngsters are more likely to pass "dirty pictures," gamble, trespass, hang around trains, and tamper with other people's cars, their cousins in the lower class area are more likely to steal major items, drink, skip school, destroy property, fight, and carry weapons. The latter offenses are those normally thought to be "real delinquent acts" while the upper urban offenses (with the exception of vehicle tampering) are not generally considered to be such.

To summarize briefly, when the rates of juvenile misconduct are compared on individual offenses among communities, it appears that as one moves from rural farm to upper urban to industrial city and lower urban, the incidence of most offenses becomes greater, especially in the more serious offenses and in those offenses usually associated with social structures with considerable tolerance for illegal behavior.

While most emphasis is placed here on the differences, one obvious finding, evident in Table II, is that in most of the nuisance offenses (minor theft, lying to parents, disobeying parents, swearing in public, throwing objects to break things or into the streets) there are no differences among the various communities. Differences appear to lie in the more serious offenses and those requiring a higher degree of sophistication and social organization.

The Reiss-Rhodes findings tend to refute theories of delinquent behavior which imply a high delinquency proneness of the lower class regardless of the "status area" in which it is found.[23] In view of this report, and since Nye-Short and Dentler-Monroe were unable to detect inter-class differences, inter-class comparisons were made within the four community types of this study. Fololwing the technique employed by Nye and Short, only those students age 15 and younger were used in these comparisons in order to neutralize the possible effects of differential school drop-out rates by social classes in the older categories.

With the exception of the industrial city, no significant inter-class differences in illegal behavior rates were found within

---

[22] Dentler and Monroe, op. cit., p. 734.

[23] Reiss and Rhodes, op. cit., p. 729. The concept of "status areas" is used here as it was used by Reiss and Rhodes to designate residential areas of a definite social class composition.

community types when either the Wilcoxon test was used for all offenses or when individual offense comparisons were made.[24] This finding supports hypothesis #3. It could account for the inability of Nye-Short and Dentler-Monroe to find differences among the socio-economic classes from several relatively similar communities in which their studies were conducted. It is also somewhat compatible with the Reiss and Rhodes findings. However, we did not find indications of higher rates of illegal conduct in the predominant socio-economic class within most areas, as the Reiss and Rhodes data suggested.[25] This may have been a function of the unique manner in which the socio-economic categories had to be combined for comparison purposes in this study. These findings, however, are logical in that boys and girls of the minority social classes within a "status area" would likely strive to adhere to the norms of the predominant social class as closely as possible whether these norms were legal or illegal.

Within the industrial city the second socio-economic category (index scores 24–47) was slightly significantly lower than either extreme category when the Wilcoxon test was used. Since the largest percentage of the sample of the industrial city falls in the lowest socio-economic category (0–23) and since this category evidences one of the highest rates of misconduct, the finding for this community is somewhat similar to the Reiss-Rhodes findings.

CONCLUSIONS

The findings of this study tend to resolve some of the apparent conflicts in the literature that have arisen from previous research concerning the relationship between the nature of illegal behavior and socio-economic class. However, some of the results contradict earlier reports.

Our findings are similar to those of Nye-Short and Dentler-Monroe in that we failed to detect any significant differences in illegal behavior rates among the social classes of rural and small urban areas. However, in keeping with the class-oriented theories, we did find significant differences, both in quantity and quality of illegal acts, among communities or "status areas," each consisting of one predominant socio-economic class. The lower class areas have higher illegal behavior rates, particularly in the more serious types of offenses. Differences among the socio-economic classes within these "status areas" were generally insignificant (which does not agree with the findings of Reiss and Rhodes), although when social class categories were compared across communities, significant differences were found. All this suggests some extremely interesting relationships.

1. The pattern of illegal behavior within small communities or within "status areas" of a large metropolitan center is determined by the predominant class of that area. Social class differentiation within these areas is apparently not related to the incidence of illegal behavior. This suggests that there are community-wide norms which are related to illegal behavior and to which juveniles adhere regardless of their social class origins. The answer to the obvious question of how large an urban area must be before socio-economic class becomes a significant variable in the incidence of illegal behavior is not provided by this study. It is quite likely that in addition to size, other considerations such as the ratio

---

[24] Because of small numbers in social classes within certain communities, categories were collapsed or ignored for comparison purposes as shown below. Refer to Table 1 for designation of categories. The Wilcoxon matched-pairs signed-ranks test was used.

Rural farm	category 1 versus 2, 3, 4	insignificant
Lower urban	category 1 versus 2, 3, 4	insignificant
	category 1 versus 5	insignificant
	categories 2, 3, 4 versus 5	insignificant
Industrial city	category 1 versus 2	significant
	category 2 versus 3, 4	significant
	category 1 versus 3, 4	insignificant
Upper urban	category 3 versus 4	insignificant

[25] Reiss and Rhodes, *op. cit.*, p. 729.

of social class representation, ethnic composition, and the prestige of the predominant social class relative to other "status areas" would influence the misconduct rates. The population of 20,000 of the particular upper urban community used in this study is apparently not of sufficient size or composition to provide for behavior autonomy among the social classes in the illegal behavior sense. There is some evidence, however, that an industrial city of roughly 40,000 such as the one included here is on the brink of social class differentiation in misconduct rates.

2. Though the juveniles in all communities admitted indulgence in several nuisance offenses at almost equal rates, serious offenses are much more likely to have been committed by lower class urban youngsters. Perhaps the failure of some researchers to find differences among the social classes in their misconduct rates can be attributed to the relatively less-serious offenses included in their questionnaires or scales. It would seem to follow that any "subculture" characterized by the more serious delinquencies, would be found only in large, urban, lower-class areas. However, the data of this study, at best, can only suggest this relationship.

3. Lastly, these data suggest that the present explanations that rely heavily on socio-economic class as an all-determining factor in the etiology of illegal behavior should be further specified to include data such as this study provides. For example, Cohen's thesis that a delinquent subculture emerges when lower class boys discover that they must satisfy their need for status by means other than those advocated in the middle class public schools should be amended to indicate that this phenomena apparently occurs only in large metropolitan centers where the socio-economic classes are found in large relatively-homogeneous areas. In the same manner, Miller's theory of the relationship between the focal concerns of the lower class culture and delinquency may require closer scrutiny.

If the relationship between focal concerns to illegal behavior that Miller has suggested exists, then those in the lower social classes (as determined by father's occupation) who live in communities or "status areas" that are predominantly of some other social class, are apparently not participants in the "lower class culture;" or, because of their small numbers, they are being successfully culturally intimidated by the predominant class. Likewise, those who are thought to occupy middle class positions apparently take on lower class illegal behavior patterns when residing in areas that are predominantly lower class. This suggests either the great power of prevailing norms within a "status area" or a limitation of social class, as it is presently measured, as a significant variable in the determination of illegal behavior.

RESEARCH QUESTIONS

At least three general questions that demand further research emerge from this study:

1. What dimension (in size and other demographic characteristics) must an urban area attain before socio-economic class becomes a significant variable in the determination of illegal behavior patterns?

2. What are the specific differences between lower class populations and social structures located in rural or relatively small urban areas and those located in large, concentrated areas in metropolitan centers that would account for their differential illegal behavior rates, especially in the more serious offenses?

3. The findings of this study suggest that the criteria presently used to determine social class levels may not be the most conducive to the understanding of variation in the behavior of those who fall within these classes, at least for those within the juvenile ages. A substitute concept is that of "status area" as operationalized by Reiss and Rhodes. For example, the differentiating characteristics of a large, Negro, lower-class, urban "status area" could be established

and would seem to have greater predictive and descriptive power than would the social class category as determined by present methods. Admittedly, this suggestion raises again the whole messy affair of "cultural area typologies" but area patterns of behaviors obviously exist and must be handled in some manner. Research effort toward systematically combining the traditional socio-economic class concept with that of cultural area might prove extremely fruitful by providing us with important language and concepts not presently available.

45. MIDDLE CLASS GANGS

HOWARD L. MEYERHOFF
BARBARA G. MEYERHOFF

THE SOCIOLOGICAL LITERATURE ABOUT GANGS contains at least two sharply conflicting descriptions of the extent of gang structure and the nature of their values. In the most prevalent view, the gang is seen as a kind of primary group, highly structured, relatively permanent and autonomous, possessing a well developed delinquent subculture which is transmitted to new members. The gang is interpreted as meeting strongly felt needs of its members and as providing a collectively derived solution to common problems of adjustment. Different writers who hold this view have stressed different problems, but nearly all have agreed that one of the most important functions of the gang is to establish close bonds of loyalty and solidarity between members of a tightly knit peer group.

Cohen [1] has identified the primary needs met by the gang as those of resolving status frustration for lower class boys, and providing an expression of masculine identification for middle class boys. Parsons [2] has also emphasized the achievement of sexual identity as a problem dealt with by delinquent behavior. Cloward and Ohlin,[3] following Merton's conception, have specified the discrepancy between aspirations toward success goals and opportunities for achieving them as the problem giving rise to gang behavior. Kvaraceus and Miller [4] have stressed the inherent conflict between lower and middle class values and the delinquent's predisposition to the former in explaining gang behavior. Eisenstadt,[5] and Bloch and Niederhoffer [6] have pointed to the gang as a collective response to the adolescent's striving toward the attainment of adulthood and the frustrations attendant on the transition from one age status to another. These authors identify different components of the gang subculture according to their interpretation of its function, but implicit or explicit in all these positions is the view of the gang as an integrated and relatively cohesive group.

A strikingly different interpretation of the structure of gangs describes them as

▶SOURCE: "Field Observations of Middle Class 'Gangs'," *Social Forces (March 1964), 42:3: 328–336.* Reprinted by permission.

[1] Albert K. Cohen, *Delinquent Boys: The Culture of the Gang* (Glencoe: Free Press, 1955).

[2] Talcott Parsons, "Certain Primary Sources and Patterns of Aggression in the Social Structure of the Western World," reprinted in Mullahy (Ed.), *A Study of Interpersonal Relations* (New York: Grove Press, Evergreen Edition, 1949).

[3] Richard A. Cloward and Lloyd E. Ohlin, *Delinquency and Opportunity: A Theory of Delinquent Gangs* (Glencoe: Free Press, 1961).

[4] William C. Kvaraceus and Walter B. Miller, *Delinquent Behavior: Culture and the Individual* (Washington, D. C.: National Education Association, 1959).

[5] S. N. Eisenstadt, *From Generation to Generation: Age Groups and Social Structure* (Glencoe: Free Press, 1956).

[6] Herbert A. Bloch and Arthur Niederhoffer, *The Gang: A Study of Adolescent Behavior* (New York: Philosophical Library, 1958).

informal, short lived, secondary groups without a clear cut, stable delinquent structure. Lewis Yablonsky [7] has suggested a conceptualization of the gang as a "near-group," specifying the following definitive characteristics: diffuse role definitions, limited cohesion, impermanence, minimal consensus on norms, shifting membership, emotionally disturbed leaders, and limited definition of membership expectations. On a continuum of the extent of social organization, Yablonsky locates the gang midway between the mob at one end and the group at the other. The gang is seen as in a state of equilibrium, moving sometimes closer to one end of the continuum and sometimes the other, but never actually becoming completely disorganized like a mob or completely organized like a group. He contends that detached worker programs, by treating the gang as a true group, may actually make it one. When a detached worker acknowledges a gang's leaders, recognizes its territory, membership, name, and purpose, he crystallizes its organization, lending it a structure which it did not previously have. This Yablonsky calls the "group-fulfilling prophecy."

The gangs he has observed are, in actuality, quite different from groups. They are "near-groups" which have a diffuse and malleable structure that enables them to meet the varied and individual needs of the members. For many gang members who are unable to meet the demands and responsibilities of more structured social organizations, it is the gang's very lack of organization and absence of expectations which constitute its primary sources of satisfaction. Youths affiliate with a gang not for a feeling of belonging and solidarity but because it is an organization within which they can relate to others in spite of their limited social abilities. The flexiblity of gang organization means that it can meet diverse, momentary needs of the members who, accordingly, participate in it with varying intensity. Yablonsky suggests that in a gang there are a few core members, surrounded by a large number of peripheral members to whom the gang is much less important and who are more loosely attached to it.

James F. Short, Jr., objects to Yablonsky's description of the gang as a near-group on the grounds that he has overstated the case,[8] but agrees, nevertheless that gangs do not have "the stability of membership, the tightly knit organization and rigid hierarchical structure which is sometimes attributed to them." [9] Most of the groups he has observed have the kind of shifting membership which Yablonsky described.

The supervisor of a large, long lived detached worker program in Los Angeles with many years of gang experience there and in Harlem has given a description much like that of Yablonsky.[10] He observed that delinquent gangs seldom act as a corporate group and that most of their

---

[7] Lewis Yablonsky, "The Delinquent Gang as a Near-Group," *Social Problems,* Vol. 7 (Fall 1959), pp. 108–117.

[8] In a recent article Pfautz raised the question of whether Yablonsky's "near-group" concept is necessary. He suggests that Yablonsky's findings could be more productively recast into the theoretical traditions of collective behavior in general and social movements in particular. Certainly, Pfautz's point that this would widen the theoretical relevance of Yablonsky's findings is well-taken. There are two reasons for the authors' preference for the near-group concept rather than a collective behavior orientation: first, an immediate concern with indicating the point by point similarity between these observations and those reported by Yablonsky, regardless of the conceptual framework he uses in describing them, and second, the authors' feeling that in view of the fragmented and discontinuous state of the literature on the subject, it is at present more important to compare and relate studies of adolescent collective deviant activities to one another than to more general sociological issues and concepts. Harold W. Pfautz, "Near-Group Theory and Collective Behavior: A Critical Reformulation," *Social Problems,* Vol. 9 (Fall 1961), pp. 167–174.

[9] James F. Short, Jr., "Street Corner Groups and Patterns of Delinquency," A Progress Report from National Institute of Mental Health Research Grant, M-3301 (Chicago, March 1961), p. 20.

[10] Alva Collier, Personal Communication (Los Angeles, 1961).

anti-social activities are committed in groups of two's or three's, or by a single person. He found communication between members to be meagre and sporadic, reflecting the same limitations in social abilities that Yablonsky identified. In fact, one of the goals of his detached worker program is the structuring of gangs into social groups, encouraging cooperation and communication between members and a gradual assumption of social responsibilities. When successful, a detached worker is able to form a gang into a club which elects officers, collects dues, arranges activities, and eventually establishes non-delinquent norms and role expectations. Thus by substituting the satisfactions of membership in an organized social group for delinquent activities, the program provides an aspect of socialization which gang members have not previously experienced. The program is able, in this way, to prepare gang members to meet the requirements and responsibilities of conventional, adult social life. The technique is apparently the self-conscious application of what Yablonsky has called "the group-fulfilling prophecy," and seems to be quite a successful one.

The field observations presented here are based on the experiences of a participant-observer who spent two weeks among several groups of deviant and non-deviant middle class youths in a suburb of Los Angeles. These obesrvations are particularly pertinent to the prevailing conflicting interpretations of the extent of gang structure. The middle class youngsters described here were located through lists of "hangouts" provided by local police, school authorities, and probation officers. The observer "hung around" these places and when asked who he was, which was seldom, explained that he was a writer doing a series of articles on teenagers. The youngsters talked freely in front of and to the observer, and after a short time included him in many of their activities, such as house and beach parties, drag races, car club meetings, bull sessions, and bowling. Altogether, about eighty youngsters ranging in age between fifteen and eighteen were observed. All were Caucasian, most in high school, Protestant, and in appearance and manner readily distinguishable from the lower class boys and girls who occasionally mixed with them.

Impressions, activities, and conversations were recorded by the observer in a daily journal, and roughly classified into the following categories: values and peer interactions, deviant activities, and group organization.[11] It should be kept in mind that these comments are observations, not findings. Many authors have lamented the dearth of speculation about as well as empirical observations of gangs, in both the middle and lower classes. Cohen and Short recently said about middle class delinquent subcultures: "The saddest commentary, however, is that we are faced with a poverty of speculation, without which there can be no meaningful research, without which, in turn, there can be no conclusions that are more than speculation." [12] These observations and comments lead to some of the speculation which must precede meaningful empirical research, and their greatest value may prove to be heuristic.

VALUES AND PEER INTERACTIONS

The youngsters observed, like most groups of teenagers, were rather uniform in dress and demeanor. There self-possession and poise, along with elaborate grooming and expensive well tended clothes combined to give an impression of urbanity and sophistication beyond what would normally be expected of this age group.

---

[11] These field observations precisely conform to what Zelditch has called Type I information. This consists of incidents and histories, and treats as data the meanings assigned to and explanations given for activities as well as the behavior itself. Morris Zelditch, Jr., "Some Methodological Problems of Field Studies," *American Journal of Sociology*, Vol. 67 (March 1962), pp. 566–576.

[12] Albert K. Cohen and James F. Short, Jr., "Research in Delinquent Subcultures," *Journal of Social Issues*, Vol. 14, No. 3 (1958), p. 34.

For most events, the girls wore tight capris, blouses or cashmere sweaters, silver fingernail and toenail polish, towering intricate coiffeurs, brush applied iridescent lipstick, and heavy eye make-up. The boys, like the girls, were uniformly clean, and like them preferred their pants as tight as possible; levis were rarely seen. Usually an Ivy League shirt was worn outside the pants and over this a nylon windbreaker. At beaches both boys and girls wore bikinis and apparently no one without a deep and even tan ever dared appear. The overall impression fostered was one of careful, elegant casualness sustained in manner as well as appearance. The complete absence of the social and physical awkwardness usually associated with adolescence was indeed striking.

The content of conversation among these groups did not differ appreciably from what one would expect to find among most teenagers; it concerned clothes, dates, sex, school classes and activities, bridge, sports, and so forth. But no subject dominated the conversation as much as the car, which seemed an object of undying, one might say morbid, fascination. The majority of girls and boys owned their own cars and virtually all had access to a car, usually a late model American or foreign sports car. "Custom jobs" were not rare and cars were often "shaved," "chopped," "channeled," and "pinstriped." All were scrupulously clean and highly polished. The argot concerning the car was as elaborate and subtle as one might expect in view of its importance; such matters as "dual quads,' "turning seven grand," "slicks," "3:7 trans ratio" were frequently discussed with great intensity. Driving skill and mechanical expertise were prized far above mere ownership of a desirable car.

The car, in fact, permeated every aspect of these youngsters social life. The size of groups which gathered was usually limited by the number a single car could hold, and when several cars congregated, at drive-ins for example, youngsters demonstrated a distinct unwillingness to leave the car. Radios in cars were never off and all activities took place against a background of popular music. The car also affected the places frequented, with drive-in movies and restaurants preferred. After school and on weekends, many of these youngsters could be seen slowly cruising in their cars, up and down the neighborhood streets, greeting acquaintances, chatting, taking friends for short rides, all with an air of easy sociability. These cruises in manner and purpose were reminiscent of the Spanish late afternoon *Paseo,* in which young people stroll casually up and down streets closed off for that purpose. The cars were the location for nearly all social events engaged in by these youngsters. They were the site of bull sessions, drinking bouts, and necking parties. In all the car provided a mobile parlor, clubhouse, dining room, and bedroom; it was at once the setting and symbol of much of adolescent deviant and non-deviant sociability and sexuality.

Several writers have emphasized the dominant role of the car in patterns of middle class deviance. Wattenberg and Balistrieri [13] found auto theft to be characteristic of "favored groups," older white boys who had better relations with peers and came from more desirable neighborhoods than did boys charged with other types of offenses. T. C. N. Gibbens [14] studied adolescent car thieves in London and also found them to be a "favored group," not because they lived in better neighborhoods but because they came from homes which were intact and affectionate. All these findings and impressions may be interpreted as supporting the contention of Parsons [15] and Cohen [16] that the primary middle class problem to which delinquency

---

[13] William W. Wattenberg and James Balistrieri, "Automobile Theft: A 'Favored Group' Delinquency," *American Journal of Sociology,* Vol. 57 (May 1952), pp. 575–579.

[14] T. C. N. Gibbens, "Car Thieves," *British Journal of Delinquency,* 7–9 (1957–1959), pp. 257–265.

[15] Parsons, *op. cit.*

[16] Cohen, *op. cit.*

is a response is the establishment of masculine identity. Indeed, the sexual significance of the car has been widely recognized. Gibbens comments that: "In the simplest cases joy-riding is of the common 'proving' type, in which an overprotected lad from a 'good' home commits an offense to prove his masculinity.... The daring act represents a bid for independence, and the car provides a feeling of power in which he feels so lacking...." [17] Certainly, this view is corroborated by the observations of middle class youths offered here, among whom the car, if not a sufficient cause of masculinity, is at least a necessary condition for it.

In view of the importance of the car, it was not surprising to find that the only formal social organizations to which many of these youngsters belonged were car clubs, whose membership often transcended the class and age affiliations typical of the more informal gatherings. These clubs usually consist of about fifteen members and are devoted to the building and legal and illegal racing of cars. In order to be admitted, youngsters' cars must undergo rigorous police safety inspections and members may be expelled or excluded for too many traffic tickets. In marked contrast to the informal groups, these clubs are highly structured. Meetings are regular and frequent, membership is stable, leaders are elected for specified terms, and the clubs have names, plaques and jackets. The meetings are conducted strictly according to Roberts' Rules of Order, fines are levied for infractions of rules, dues are collected, and events are planned in detail and in advance. A well developed pattern of mutual aid and extensive cooperation has been established and it is not unusual for members to pool money, skills, and time to build a car which is entered in races and rallies by the entire group. It is obviously no accident that the only object around with spontaneous, unsupervised yet structured groups form is the car.

[17] Gibbens, *op. cit.*, p. 262.

DEVIANT ACTIVITIES

The deviant behavior of the groups observed varied greatly in seriousness. Some of their activities may be considered deviant only because technically illegal, such as curfew violation and beer drinking, while more serious infractions such as theft and narcotics are less common. The more serious deviant activities seemed to involve the least number of people at one time; youngsters were alone or with a friend or two on these occasions. The less serious infractions were not usually the purpose of a gathering but were rather incidental to another activity. These included spontaneous drag racing, drinking, and much sexual activity.

Of the more serious violations, theft was certainly the most common. Many boys spoke of frequent and regular stealing, often from employers. Ready access rather than need or desire seemed to determine the choice of stolen objects. These items were seldom traded or converted into cash. Great pride was evidenced in the cleverness with which the thefts were executed and a good performance seemed more important than the acquisition of goods. Several boys boasted about never having been caught although they had been engaging in this activity for years. The stolen goods were by no means small, inexpensive, or easily portable, but included such items as tires, car radios, phonographs, tape recorders, and television sets. Great care was taken in order to ensure that stolen goods were not missed. Thefts were timed so as to coincide with events such as inventories, and the filling of orders.

It is not possible on the basis of these observations to estimate the frequency of these thefts but one can say with certainty that they were by no means uncommon. This phenomenon appears to be very similar to "white collar crime" and as such raises questions as to the generalizability of theories of delinquency causation based solely on socio-economic variables. As Wattenberg and Balistrieri have pointed out: "The point of impact of the concept of [white collar crime] lies in its assumption that the form of anti-social or illegal conduct rather than its frequency varies from ... class to class in our society."[18] It may well be that the "white collar delinquent" engages in as many anti-social activities as do lower class youngsters but a combination of factors, particularly the form of delinquency, interact to prevent these activities from coming to the attention of the authorities, or if apprehended, prevent the middle class youngsters from being officially handled and recorded. Indeed, there is already much evidence to suggest this is the case.[19]

The same discretion, judgment, and self-possession which characterized thefts was observed in the homosexual, and to a lesser degree, the heterosexual gatherings. These events were held in private homes and occasionally included slightly older boys from nearby colleges. They were not events which were likely to attract the attention of police or even parents. The homosexual youngsters often met one another at small cabarets, coffee houses, and bars in which few lower class teenagers or adults were to be seen. They also met in several private clubs whose members were primarily upper and middle class teenage homosexuals. These youngsters were typically inconspicuous and did not indulge in egregious displays of homosexuality either in dress or manner. While in the clubs, many were openly solicitous and flirtatious, but upon leaving, their more conventional manners were resumed. The same caution was apparent among those who purchased and used narcotics, usually marijuana. It was smoked at small, quiet parties, rarely while driving or in public places. It was not unusual to hear these poised, well dressed youngsters speak of stealing, using narcotics, and the advantages and disadvantages of their respective college choices in the same tone of voice and conversation.

The middle class group anti-social activities which *do* come to the attention of the authorities are of a rather different nature than those just described. Several examples of these were provided by a local probation officer assigned to the neighborhood. On one occasion, he recalled, a group of about ten boys went back and forth across a busy intersection between 5:30 and 6:30 in the evening, effectively bringing traffic to a complete standstill until dispersed by the police. Another time, a car full of boys drove slowly down a main shopping street spraying the well dressed shoppers with the contents of a fire extinguisher. One incident involved a group of boys who stole an old car and took it to a vacant lot and while one boy drove the car around in circles, the others threw stones at it, until it was nothing but a battered corpse.

There is a mischievous, often amusing overtone to all these incidents; they are not the kind likely to be thought malicious or violent. Rather, they are spontaneous and gratuitous, proving nothing but providing "kicks." This behavior is not the kind which is likely to seriously alarm parents or police and has none of the grim overtones usually associated, correctly or not, with the activities of lower class gangs. In general, the non-violent nature of the deviant activities of these youngsters is salient, and personal aggression rare. The anti-social activities observed among these groups rarely took the form of open defiance of authority; manipulation rather than rebellion appeared to be the preferred technique for handling trouble with authorities. Cohen and Short have postulated just such a difference between lower and middle class delinquency:

---

[18] Wattenberg and Balistrieri, *op. cit.*, p. 575.
[19] A. L. Porterfield, "Delinquency and Its Outcome in Court and College," *American Journal of Sociology*, Vol. 48 (1943), pp. 199–208; Ivan F. Nye and James F. Short, Jr., "Scaling Delinquent Behavior," *American Sociological Review*, Vol. 22 (1957), pp. 326–331.

... we are persuaded that further research will reveal subtle but important differences between working class and middle class patterns of delinquency. It seems probable that the qualities of malice, bellicosity, and violence will be underplayed in the middle class subcultures and that these subcultures will emphasize more the deliberate courting of danger . . . and a sophisticated, irresponsible, 'playboy' approach to activities symbolic in our culture, of adult roles and centering largely around sex, liquor, and automobiles.[20]

How closely that description fits the middle class groups observed is readily apparent.

Interestingly enough, even while engaging in flagrant, frequent infractions of the law, these youngsters sustained the opinion that their activities would in no way interfere with their future plans. They did not define themselves as delinquents or even trouble makers and did not expect others to do so. More likely than not, upon graduating from high school and entering college, as most planned to do, these youngsters will leave their deviant activities behind without a trace in the form of official records, self-definition, or residues of unpleasant experiences with authorities. The police seemed to share this expectation. An incident was observed in which a boy was picked up for drinking and curfew violation. In the patrol car he expressed his concern lest the occasion jeopardize his chances for entering college. The officer, who had until that point been rather surly, hastened to reassure the boy that such a possibility was quite unlikely, and implied that nothing would come of the visit to the station.

The same expectations were shared by the people who worked at the places where these youngsters congregated—waitresses, life guards, theater managers—who did not feel that even as a group they constituted a serious nuisance. Their tolerance is no doubt increased by middle class youngsters' liberal spending habits which make it worth their while to put up with an occasional annoyance. But in addition their attitudes are affected by the usually pleasant relations they have with these boys and girls, whose interpersonal experiences with adults and peers are more harmonious and extensive than those observed among the more socially inadequate lower class gangs observed by Yablonsky and the supervisor of the detached worker program in Los Angeles. This difference in social ability is hardly surprising in view of the middle classes' traditional specialization in entrepeneurial activities. The techniques of smooth social relations are the bread and butter of the middle classes, and middle class teenagers, deviant and non-deviant alike, demonstrate remarkable agility in the manipulation of social situations. Their interpersonal skills enable them to control their social environment to a much greater degree than possible for lower class teenagers who have not had the opportunity to acquire and perfect these techniques.

GROUP ORGANIZATION

It can be seen that the groups observed, with the exception of disturbed leadership, precisely conform to Yablonsky's description of a near-group. Certainly, they do not qualify for the term "gang" as it is usually used, nor do they have well developed delinquent values. On the contrary, the similarity between these youngsters' values and those of the adult, dominant society is conspicuous. Such a continuity has been suggested by Matza and Sykes [21] in a recent article in which they contend that the values underlying much juvenile delinquency are far less deviant than commonly portrayed, due to a prevailing oversimplification of middle class values. The authors argue that exist-

---

[20] Cohen and Short, *op. cit.*, p. 26.

[21] David Matza and Gresham M. Sykes, "Juvenile Delinquency and Subterranean Values," *American Sociological Review*, Vol. 26 (October 1961), pp. 712–719.

ing alongside the official, dominant values in society is another conflicting set which they call subterranean. These are values which are frequently relegated by adults to leisure time pursuits and are not ordinarily allowed to interfere with the regular course of a conventional life. Matza and Sykes point out that the content of these subterranean values has been described by Veblen in his portrayal of the "gentleman of leisure"—disdain for work, identification of masculinity with tough, aggressive behavior, and the search for thrills and adventures. The authors feel that the delinquent emphasizes a society's subterranean values but instead of relegating them to after-hours activities, he makes them a way of life, a code of behavior. The delinquent, then, has not evolved an original set of values but has only taken over one aspect of those held by most people along with their publicly proclaimed, respectable middle class values.

J. A. Pitt-Rivers [22] has suggested the concept "infra-structure" to describe what Matza and Sykes have referred to as subterranean values. The infra-structure is a set of values which exists alongside and in opposition to the official beliefs and behavior required by the formal systems of authority. It is not merely a set of separate beliefs held by one segment of the community but is that part of the social structure consisting of the personal, internalized version of officially endorsed values. The two systems are seen by Pitt-Rivers as interdependent, representing the private and public morals held simultaneously by everyone in the social system. The opposition of the value systems create a structural tension or ambivalence which, though never really sharp enough to seriously endanger the social order, nevertheless provides a predisposition to deviance from officially prescribed behavior. The relation between the two systems is continuous and while certain people or groups are more influenced by one system than the other, both affect all behavior to some degree.

In the light of the observations presented here, one may postulate that just as certain individuals and social groups are closer to one set of these values than the other, so are different age groups. Adolescence may be understood as a period in the life span of the individual when he is closer to deviant or subterranean values than he will be as an adult or has been as a child. Several authors have conceptualized adolescence as a period of license, a time for social and sexual exploration. Benedict [23] has pointed out the expectation that the adolescent will be irresponsible, though as an adult a few years later he can no longer be, and Erikson [24] has described adolescence as a psycho-social moritorium, set aside for experimentation in establishing an identity prior to the assumption of adult roles. One implication which can be drawn from these interpretations is that a teenager's "deviant behavior" may be in actuality a phase in his history when he is allowed and even expected to behave in accord with a set of subterranean values which do not disappear when he becomes an adult but instead are acted upon only on more appropriate occasions.

The adolescent in our culture, it is suggested may be viewed as an aristocrat, a gentleman of leisure who, for a time, is not required to work but is allowed to play, explore, test limits, indulge his pleasures, and little else besides. This description of the delinquent as a kind of aristocrat closely resembles Finestone's characterization of the Negro teenage narcotic addict.[25] The "cat" is an individual

---

[22] J. A. Pitt-Rivers, *The People of the Sierra* (Chicago: University of Chicago Press, Phoenix Edition, 1961).

[23] Ruth Benedict, "Continuities and Discontinuities in Cultural Conditioning," reprinted in Mullahy (Ed.), *A Study of Interpersonal Relations* (New York: Grove Press, Evergreen Edition, 1949).

[24] Erik H. Erikson, *Childhood and Society* (New York: W. W. Norton, 1950).

[25] Harold Finestone, "Cats, Kicks and Color," *Social Problems*, Vol. 5 (July 1957), pp. 3–13.

who has developed an elaborate repertoire of manipulative techniques for dealing with the world, eschewing violence in favor of persuasion and charm. "He seeks through a harmonious combination of charm, ingratiating speech, dress, music, the proper dedication to his "kick" and unrestrained generosity to make of his day to day life itself a gracious work of art." [26] The similarity between this depiction of the "cat" and the youngsters described here is indeed remarkable, especially in light of the differences between them in race, class, and circumstance.

There is, then, much reason to think that Matza and Sykes are justified in urging that delinquency might be better understood as an extension of the adult conforming world rather than as discontinuous with it. One advantage of this interpretation is that it allows for a single explanation of lower and middle class delinquency and thus avoids the inconsistency inherent in theories which specify the influence of socio-economic factors in the etiology of lower class delinquency and psychological factors in the etiology of middle class delinquency. It is likely that much may be gained by exploring the similarity between the delinquent and the rest of society rather than his deviance from it. Certainly these observations suggest that middle class deviants may differ from lower class delinquents not in the frequency of their anti-social activities, but only in the form which they take and the sophistication, social intelligence, judgment, and skill with which they are executed.

SUMMARY

These observations have raised several important issues concerning the structure and values of delinquent groups. It may be that the extent of gang structure is frequently exaggerated and that such groups may not be as cohesive, structured, and stable as they are commonly depicted.

The groups described here manifested all but one of the characteristics (disturbed leadership) described by Yablonsky as those of a near-group. There is a coincidence of opinion based on three sets of observations (Yablonsky's, the supervisor of a detached worker program in Los Angeles, and those reported in this paper) suggesting that the common conception of the gang as a highly organized primary group is not always accurate and may be the result of the gross exaggerations made possible by the dearth of empirical observations of gangs. Exaggeration may also have taken place in the extent of the differences between delinquent values and those of the dominant society. The observations reported in this paper are in accord with the suggestions of Matza and Sykes that the delinquent subculture is an extension of values held by most members of the society but indulged in less openly and less often. Certainly the behavior and beliefs of the middle class youngsters observed are not dramatically different from those of most conventional teenagers or adults.

In view of these three sets of observations, the following questions may be asked: (1) How often and to what extent are gangs primary groups with elaborate delinquent subcultures, and how prevalent are such groups when compared with the loosely structured, secondary, impermanent collectivities with little or no delinquent subculture such as those described here? (2) In view of the conflicting characterizations of the extent of gang structure and the nature of gang values, would not there be more scientific value in describing gangs in terms of at least these two variables rather than primarily on the basis of the content of their deviant activities? (3) To what extent, if any, does adult recognition, particularly in the form of the assignment of detached workers to gangs, legitimize and formalize these groups, lending them a cohesion and solidarity which they previously might not have had? (4) Has the emphasis on the deviant activities of these

---
[26] *Ibid.*, p. 5.

groups obscured their similarity to conventional teenagers and adults, thereby exaggerating the differences between delinquents? And (5) would it not be more fruitful to examine the extent and nature of the similarities rather than differences between deviant and non-deviant teenagers and adults?

The action implications of these questions are far-reaching. If, as Yablonsky suggests, the gang meets different needs for different members, a uniform approach on a gang basis is inappropriate. More suitable would be an attempt to help individual members develop the interpersonal skills which would enable them to participate in structured, socially accepted groups. Or, by deliberately applying techniques such as Yablonsky's "group-fulfilling prophecy," gangs might be made into non-deviant clubs. And, if delinquent values are but a continuation of one aspect of the accepted value system subscribed to by most law abiding people, a program designed to integrate these values into a more appropriate place in deviant youngsters' lives (for example, by providing socially acceptable means of expressing aggression and seeking adventure) would be more honest and effective than attempts to eliminate them altogether.

At this stage, only one firm conclusion is justified. The variables in terms of which gangs can best be understood have not yet been identified and are not likely to be until widespread and systematic empirical observation is conducted. The impressions reported here suggest just how valuable and unsettling such observation may prove.

46. DELINQUENCY AND MIGRATION

LEONARD SAVITZ

ONE MIGHT WELL ASK WHAT IS AN ADEQUATE and realistic definition of delinquency. There is clear consensus that when a child has been formally adjudicated or institutionalized by the Juvenile Court he is a delinquent. There is also some agreement that an "adjusted" case is indicative of delinquency.[1] Problems arise, however, with other dispositions in which the charges are either "dropped" (a very infrequent action), or the juvenile is "discharged" by the court. Discharge, usually, *but not in every case*, indicates the court's belief in the innocence of the child. In some instances, the juvenile while either caught in the act or confessing to active participation in the offense is still discharged. Therefore it does not follow that "discharge" is synonymous with innocence.

For the purposes of this study anyone having a Juvenile Court record, regardless of actual dispositions, will be regarded as a delinquent. It should be kept in mind that almost all dispositions such as "adjudication of delinquency," "adjustment," or "drop" involve delinquent behavior which the child has actually committed. Additionally, one must consider the fact that a boy acquiring a court record of any type typically thinks of himself as a delinquent, as do his family and his peer groups; the subtle legal factors differentiating "adjustment," "discharge," and "adjudication of delinquency" are of small importance to him. What is important is that he was up before the court, that he is now free, and that in his own mind and in that of his reference groups, he *is* a delinquent.

Migration in this study is determined by place of birth. Any person born outside of the city limits of Philadelphia who arrived in Philadelphia at any age after birth will be considered as a migrant.

All boys born between 1939 and 1945, who were pupils in the Philadelphia public school system in 1957, and who resided for at least part of 1957 within that area of Philadelphia bounded by Broad, Sixth, Poplar and Susquehanna streets, were selected for study. The neighborhood selected had one of the four highest delinquency rates in the city; it was serviced by fewer schools than any comparable delinquency area; and it contained a comparatively large number of white and Puerto Rican residents. Public school records were used because it was presumed that

▶SOURCE: *"Delinquency and Migration," Philadelphia: Commission on Human Relations, January, 1960, pp. 1–3, 5–10, 12, 13, 15–17.* (Mimeographed.)

[1] "Adjustment" in Philadelphia usually takes place when the offense is of a minor nature, the victim is somewhat reluctant to prosecute, the offender has a good record, *i.e.*, no previous serious trouble, and even though the child is usually the perpetrator of the act, the intake-interviewer at the Youth Study Center decides that the child need not be brought before the Juvenile Court.

parochial school files would not be available for research of this nature.

The files of the two high schools, two junior high schools, and one special elementary school serving the prescribed area were closely examined in order to secure as much information as possible for those students meeting the above-listed desiderata. The Registration Cards, Rollbook Leafs, Cumulative Records, and Applications for Admission of the Child to School of the 1,062 boys who fell within the scope of the experimental design supplied the subject's name, age, race, place of birth, age entering the school system, home addresses, as well as some parental data.

The 1,062 subjects probably do not constitute the entire universe of individuals meeting all the criteria for selection in this study. By the very structure of this research, an individual would be omitted if his school records indicated an incorrect date of birth or home address in 1957, or if he lived within the prescribed zone but attended a public school which normally serves another section of the city, or if the boy's Registration Card and Pupil Pocket were simultaneously missing from their files.

The four main Municipal Court files were next examined and whenever a Juvenile Court file was located for one of the subjects it was secured. These records contained considerable information on the boy's family structure, as well as on his delinquency record.

The subject population of 1,062 thus consisted of two groups: those who had delinquency records and those who did not. Unfortunately, it is not at all certain that all boys with Juvenile Court records had their files uncovered. If considerable divergence existed between the child's surname at school and his name in the court records it was quite possible that his record might never be discovered. The Municipal Court files are of such a nature, however, that the boy's record might be located on the basis of his home address or his parent's names, as well as his own surname.

Of the 1,062 boys in the subject population, 333 (29%) had Juvenile Court records and were therefore classified as delinquents. The remaining 720 were nondelinquents, although 148 (16% of the total population) while nondelinquent themselves did have delinquent siblings.

The racial composition of the total population was 10% white (109), 84% Negro (890), 5% Puerto Rican (58), and 1% "Other" (5). Negroes were considerably more delinquent (34%) than were whites (22%). Fifty-six percent of the subject population were born in Philadelphia, with 66% of the white, 58% of the Negro and less than 4% of the Puerto Ricans so classified. The bulk of the migrants (65%) were born in southern states.

School records did not permit the ascertainment of age at arrival in Philadelphia for many migrant children. Only if the child came to Philadelphia and entered the school system *after* grade 1A would the school files indicate age at time of arrival. The records of migrant children who *began* their schooling in Philadelphia showed their non-Philadelphia place of birth and indicated that they arrived in Philadelphia "sometime" before entering grade 1A; this could have been anytime from shortly after birth to as late as age 6.

Fifty-two percent of the Negro migrants and only 19% of the "non-Negro" migrants arrived by age 6; by age 13 the percentages of migrants who had arrived in Philadelphia amounted to 90 and 76 respectively.

Negroes were found to be considerably more residentially mobile in Philadelphia than were whites. Little difference was found between the intracity mobility of the Philadelphia-born and the migrant. Fifty-eight percent of the delinquents had moved two or fewer times, whereas 70% of the nondelinquents were in a similar category.

Subsequent textual analyses of tabular data will deal only with the Negro segment of the subject population. The racial composition of the total group might have been handled in at least three other ways. First, the variable of race could have been deliberately overlooked so that all migrants would have been combined into a "total migrant" group. This would, however, constitute a rather meaningless grouping as almost 80% of the migrant population were Negroes so that any fluctuation demonstrated by this group would have been primarily a function of Negro variable, with a very considerable masking of the white and Puerto Rican populations.

Second, the three racial groups could have been analyzed separately. This approach offered a number of difficulties, however. The white population consists of 72 Philadelphia-born and 37 migrants with the majority of the migrants (21) being foreign-born. The introduction of this variable, international immigration, adds a new and gratuitous dimension to an already complex area of investigation; the distinctive problems facing the native-born migrant and foreign-born immigrant require their separate analyses, which would mean, however, that the two white migrant subgroups would be so small in number as to permit only minimal manipulation. It would have been even less profitable to examine separately the Puerto Rican population as only two of 58 Puerto Ricans are Philadelphia-born.

Third, the population might have been dichotomized into "Negro" and "non-Negro" categories. While this might seem to be, *a priori,* a useful division, the "non-Negro" group in actuality is sufficiently artificial and arbitrary in nature that when it is utilized it produces a random, non-systematic series of results.

Regardless of the index or definition of delinquency used ("any Juvenile Court contact," "adjudication of delinquency," or "institutionalization"), the Negro migrant population was considerably less delinquent than the Negro Philadelphia-born population, hereafter referred to as natives. Almost 40% of the natives but only 27% of the migrants had delinquency records. An almost identical pattern emerged when the natives were contrasted to the southern-born migrants. (All differences relating to "any Juvenile Court contact" were statistically significant beyond the .01 level.)

The trouble with these findings is that they fail to take into account variations in length of residence in Philadelphia. The migrant group living in Philadelphia for a shorter period of time should have a lower delinquency rate as they are less exposed to the risk of delinquency in Philadelphia. Attempts to standardize the population for "length of residence" did not meet with easy success. There were few problems with the native group, who had resided in Philadelphia during the entire test period. They were easily grouped by length of residence, ranging from 13 years for those born in 1945 to a full 18 years residence for those born in 1939 or 1940. It was not possible to place the migrants within the same 6 categories, *i.e.,* 13, 14, 15, 16, 17, and 18 years of residence. While the migrants were born in the same years as the natives (1939–1945) they did not all come immediately to Philadelphia after birth. A migrant born in 1945, for example, could have spent from 1 to 12 years in Philadelphia by 1957. The total migrant population, therefore, included individuals who had resided in Philadelphia from one to almost 18 years.

Nor was it possible to construct any rate based on *"total* number of years of residence in Philadelphia" for the entire migrant group, as the school records, it will be recalled, do not disclose the date when a child came to Philadelphia if it was before the age of 6.

In Pennsylvania, the age of culpability is 7 years, which means that any child below that age is legally incapable of committing any offense or delinquency. It was felt that meaningful delinquency rates could be constructed based on "length of

Table I. *Delinquent and Delinquency Exposure Rates for Philadelphia-Born and Migrant Negroes*

Cohort	Total Number	Total Years of Exposure	Total Delinquents	Years of Exposure Per Single Delinquent	Total Delinquencies	Years of Exposure Per Single Delinquency
1. Total natives	517	4,265	200	21.3	537	7.9
2. Total migrants	373	2,685	100	26.9	215	12.4

delinquency exposure," *i.e.*, length of residence in Philadelphia between ages 7 and 18, instead of the unobtainable "total number of years of residence." Therefore the number of years during which each of the 890 boys resided in Philadelphia was determined and a rate based on the "total number of years of delinquency exposure" was computed for the migrant and native groups.

An examination of these data (Table I) shows that the native population (517 boys) produced 200 delinquents during 4,265 years of exposure, or one delinquent for every 21.3 years of exposure. These 200 delinquents committed a total of 537 delinquencies, or one delinquency per 7.9 years of delinquency exposure. The migrant rates were strikingly lower, with one delinquent per 26.9 years and one delinquency per 12.4 years of exposure.

If anything these figures tend to *understate* the negative relationship between migration and delinquency. The data are not standardized for age, and it happens that no one in the total population became delinquent before the age of nine. Thus, for the 517 natives the first two years of delinquency exposure (ages 7 and 8) were void of any delinquency, or a total of 1,034 "delinquency-free years." On the other hand, only 61 percent (227) of the migrants were in Philadelphia by age 7, the remaining 146 came at some later age and, therefore, were considerably more likely to become delinquent in their first two years of exposure. This would tend to inflate artificially the delinquency rates of the migrants compared with the natives.

This type of analysis is once more not entirely satisfactory for a variety of reasons. It was therefore decided to examine the migrant and native groups with length of delinquency exposure held constant. A comparison was made of the 517 natives with 291 migrants who had been exposed to the risk of delinquency for no less than 6 years. (Both groups would then have been exposed to the risk of delinquency for from 6 to 11 years.) The results shown in Table II once more indicate a higher total delinquency rate for the native group (39%) than for a comparable migrant population (28%). Only for those exposed 6 and 7 years did the migrants equal or exceed the native rate; with increasing length of exposure the differentials increased. While the natives demonstrate the expected progressively higher delinquency rates with increasing length of exposure, a similar pattern does not emerge for the migrant group. Most surprisingly, the delinquency rate for the fully exposed (11 years) migrants was exceeded by all but one of the other five migrant groups. Part of this erratic migrant pattern may be due to variations in ages at arrival in Philadelphia and years of birth.

It would be meaningless to control the native and migrant groups for simply year of birth because of the various ages at which the migrants arrived in Philadelphia. It was decided, finally, that both year of birth and length of delinquency exposure could be simultaneously held constant by comparing the native population with a

Table II. *Delinquency Rates of Negro Natives and Negro Migrants (with at Least 6 Years of Delinquency Exposure in Philadelphia) by Length of Delinquency Exposure*

Length of Exposure	Negro Natives	Negro Migrants
6 Years		
Number in group	103	38
Number of delinquents	19	9
% Delinquent	(18.5)	(23.7)
7 Years		
Number in group	101	51
Number of delinquents	27	14
% Delinquent	(26.7)	(27.5)
8 Years		
Number in group	88	44
Number of delinquents	30	10
% Delinquent	(34.1)	(22.7)
9 Years		
Number in group	87	54
Number of delinquents	40	16
% Delinquent	(46.0)	(29.6)
10 Years		
Number in group	65	54
Number of delinquents	38	20
% Delinquent	(58.5)	(37.0)
11 Years		
Number in group	73	50
Number of delinquents	46	13
% Delinquent	(63.0)	(26.0)
TOTAL		
Number in group	517	291
Number of delinquents	200	82
% Delinquency	(38.7)	(27.8)

group of migrants who had arrived in Philadelphia by age 7, by varying years of birth. (This group will be referred to as the migrant-before-seven group.) As a matter of fact, *three* variables: age, length of exposure, and age at time of arrival in Philadelphia (as measured by age entering the public school system), are controlled under these conditions.

Table III reveals, first of all, that the average delinquency rate of the native group was considerably higher than that of the migrant-before-seven group. Migrants arriving in Philadelphia by 7, and born in 1944, were slightly higher in delinquency than the comparable native group, but thereafter the natives were consistently higher in their delinquency rates. *None of the differences was statistically significant.* Of considerable significance is the fact that 59% of all boys exposed to the risk of delinquency for a full 11 years in this section of the city will ultimately succumb to delinquency. No less than 63% of the natives and 50% of the migrant-before-seven boys became delinquent after being fully exposed to the risk of delinquency. A reexamination of Table II reveals that, when the native and migrant-before-seven groups are compared for delinquent and delinquency rates, the migrant-before-seven population is considerably lower on both counts.

The conclusion regarding this crucial point is inescapable. Regardless of index used: gross delinquency rates with delinquency being variously defined as "any Juvenile Court contact," "adjudication of delinquency" or "institutionalization"; delinquency rates measured by varying lengths of delinquency exposure (Table I); length of exposure held constant (Table II); and most importantly, with length of exposure and years of birth both held constant (Table III) a remarkably uniform, clear-cut and consistent *negative* relationship emerges between migration and delinquency. What is important and noteworthy about these differential delinquency rates is not the size of the differences (which are seldom statistically significant) but their regularity and consistency. With surprisingly few exceptions, the Negro native delinquency rate constantly exceeded that of the total Negro migrant and the Negro migrant-before-seven groups.

CONCLUSIONS

The central finding of this study of Negro children in Philadelphia has been that migration does not have the criminogenic effects attributed to it. The Phila-

Table III. *Delinquency Rates of Negroe Natives and Negro Migrants (Residing in Philadelphia by Age 7) by Year of Birth*

Year of Birth	Negro Natives	Negro Migrants
1945		
Number in group	103	34
Number of delinquents	19	6
% delinquent	(18.5)	(17.6)
1944		
Number in group	101	35
Number of delinquents	27	10
% delinquent	(26.7)	(28.6)
1943		
Number in group	88	39
Number of delinquents	30	7
% delinquent	(34.1)	(17.9)
1942		
Number in group	87	45
Number of delinquents	40	14
% delinquent	(46.0)	(31.1)
1941		
Number in group	65	40
Number of delinquents	38	17
% delinquent	(58.5)	(42.5)
1939–40		
Number in group	73	34
Number of delinquents	46	17
% delinquent	(63.0)	(50.0)
TOTAL		
Number in group	517	227
Number of delinquents	200	71
% delinquent	(38.7)	(31.3)

delphia-born population more frequently became delinquent than did the migrant group, though the difference was seldom statistically significant. This positive relationship between nonmigratory status and delinquency persisted regardless of the definition of delinquency used: any Juvenile Court contact, adjustment, adjudication of delinquency, or institutionalization. Similarly, regardless of degree of refinement of the data (total native and migrant delinquency rates, comparative delinquency rates based on years of delinquency exposure, or differential delinquency rates with two variables; year of birth and length of delinquency exposure first separately, and then jointly held constant for the natives and migrants who arrived in Philadelphia before age 7) the Philadelphia-born population produced higher delinquency rates. The last measure, probably the most important of the lot, shows that 39% of the natives and 31% of the migrant-before-seven populations were classified as delinquent.

Additionally, the migrant delinquent, and more importantly, those who migrated before age 7, committed proportionately fewer delinquencies than did the native delinquents; 46% of the migrant-before-seven and 38% of the native delinquents had only one contact with the Juvenile Court.

This lesser migrant delinquency might be attributed to some greater cunning or deviousness on the part of the migrant, so that, while they may equally or even more frequently engage in delinquent activities than the natives, they tend to avoid detection or apprehension more frequently than the native group. There is, however, no evidence to support such a proposition. Another possibility is that of some differential administration of justice whereby the native boys are systematically discriminated against by the Youth Study Center, Juvenile Court, and others. This is a very dubious contention with, once more, no evidence to support it. A third possibility is that the migrant simply commits less delinquency either because of some selectivity in the migratory process of less-delinquency-prone children, or because of the operation of some other sociological phenomenon, such as development of some isolating patterns whereby the migrant child is prevented, perhaps only temporarily, from assimilating northern delinquent values.

The native delinquents also committed somewhat more serious delinquencies (burglary, robbery, homicide) than did the migrants. An examination of the first, second, and third delinquencies, as well as "the most serious offense ever committed," reveals the natives as having a higher proportion of delinquents who at some point in their "careers" engaged in serious delinquencies. As might be expected, the natives received more severe "treatment" in the form of probation or institutionalization from the courts.

The average Negro native delinquent committed his first delinquency at an earlier age (12.9 years) than the average migrant delinquent, or even the Negro migrant who arrived in Philadelphia before the age of 7 (13.8 years). The migrant-before-seven group, on the average, was exposed to the risk of delinquency for over 6½ years before becoming delinquent. It will be noted that the use of this type of comparison, in which the migrants were residing in Philadelphia by age 7, eliminates any problem of delinquencies committed by the migrant child prior to his arrival in the city. When varying definitions of delinquency were used, a similar pattern emerged: that of a younger average age at first delinquency on the part of the native offenders.

It might be, then, that if migrant delinquency is due, in part, to the acculturation of northern subcultural criminal norms, this process is thwarted, temporarily, by some barrier between the migrant and the nonmigrant populations in Philadelphia. There are, as a matter of fact, some scattered indications that this may be the case. Previous studies have indicated that a similar pattern of isolation existed among the new immigrants from Europe, if not for their native-born children. The migrants in this study, however, did not demonstrate the same generational pattern of delinquency as the immigrants, insofar as it has been established that the native-born children of the new immigrants had considerably higher delinquency and crime rates than did the foreign-born immigrant children. While it was not possible to obtain information concerning parental nativity for all the nondelinquents, for 128 Negro boys (nondelinquents with delinquent siblings) court records were available. It is not suggested that these 128 cases are representative of the total nondelinquent universe, but it is interesting to note that, when the parental nativity data of the 128 boys were compared with those of the 300 delinquents, it was found that only 5% of the fathers and 10% of the mothers of the nondelinquents were native-born, whereas 11% of the delinquents had native-born fathers and 19% had native-born mothers. All of this indicates that the children of native parents tend to become delinquent more frequently than do the children of migrant parents.

There was no confirmation of internal migration as a disorganizing process in modern urban life. The migrants not only tended to be lower than the natives in the frequency and seriousness of delinquencies, but also were less likely to come from broken homes, have illegitimate siblings or engage in considerable intracity mobility. It may be that the negative features generally attributed to migration come into play only when the number of migrants in an area is small and/or the creation of some ghetto-like neighborhood is not permitted the migrant population. This was not the case for the area examined in this study where 44% of the entire subject population were migrants.

On the other hand, previous findings regarding the inter-relationship of various negative aspects of the disorganized areas *are* supported by this study. The area investigated had high rates of delinquency, broken homes, illegitimacy, and inter- and intra-city mobility.

Finally, one may ask what is the best index to use in measuring the *real* delinquency rate of a particular geographic area? Some delinquency rates are couched in terms of "percentage of children in the area who become delinquent within a particular year." This, for example, is the type of presentation of data used by the Municipal Court. When the highest category used is "five percent (delinquent) or over," this amounts to an extremely deceptive statement of the true situation. "Only five kids per hundred," someone will say, "delinquency isn't too high even in the worst neighborhood. What's all the fuss about?" Actually, of course, these figures do not take into account either the accumulated percentage of delinquents over a period of years, nor differential demographic features of various sections of the city.

A second, somewhat more realistic approach is the calculation of the *total* percentage of children within Juvenile Court age who have acquired a delinquency record. Such a measurement was used by Shaw and McKay among many others. In the present study, for example, this figure would come to 32%, or, of 1062 boys, 333 had a court record. But this rate, too, tends to understate the situation in so far as it does not account for peculiarities in the age-sex structure of any given population. In areas where a very large proportion of the children are in the younger age groups (below age 12), the total percentage having contact with the courts would offer a fictitiously low picture of the delinquency potential of the neighborhood in that the bulk of the children had not yet attained the high delinquency-risk ages of 12 and over.

Clearly the best measure of delinquency that might be constructed would be relatively independent of the age (or sex) structure of a given group. It is suggested that the most accurate measure of the *real* delinquency of any section of the city would be a rate based on the probability of a child ultimately becoming a delinquent if he remains in the area for a full period of delinquency exposure (from ages 7 through 18). In the present study, the delinquency rate of the age groups born in 1939 and 1940 and who had resided in the selected neighborhood for the full 11 years of delinquency risk, is no less than phenomenal. Over half (59%) of this group (both natives and migrants-before-seven) had acquired delinquency records by the age of 18, with more than 3 out of every 5 native boys (63%) and half of the migrant-before-seven children (50%) ultimately becoming delinquent. This measure, the chance of a child becoming a delinquent if he remains in the neighborhood until his adulthood, it is submitted, is the most accurate indicator of an area's delinquency. With this in mind, when the question is raised: if heavily disorganized areas are indeed conducive to high delinquency, why do only a minority of the boys (5 to 30%) in the very worst sections become delinquent, the answer properly would be: "Give them time. Most of them *will* be delinquent before it's all over."

47. DELINQUENCY, SCHOOL ATTENDANCE AND DROPOUT

DELBERT S. ELLIOTT

THEORETICAL EXPLANATIONS OF DELINQUENT behavior have come to place increasing emphasis upon some form of "status deprivation" as the motivational source of lower-class delinquency.[1] According to these views, the socialization of lower-class boys does not adequately prepare them to compete effectively for status rewards in middle-class-dominated institutions. The intense frustration experienced by these boys consequently motivates them toward delinquent patterns of behavior in an attempt to recoup their loss of self esteem.

Albert Cohen in *Delinquent Boys* suggests that the school in particular awards status upon the basis of middle-class standards. Here, lower- and middle-class youths compete for status in terms of the same set of middle-class criteria, with the result that lower-class youths are relegated to the lowest status positions. As a result of the unequal competition, lower-class youths develop feelings of insecurity, become frustrated, and begin to search for some solution to their status problem.[2]

Delinquency is thus viewed as a by-product of the unequal competition at school. Youth who are denied opportunities to achieve higher status positions because of their lower-class socialization are consequently "provoked" to engage in delinquent behavior in an attempt to avail themselves of illegitimate means to reach legitimate goals[3] or to express their rejection and disdain for middle-class goals which are not available to them.[4]

Delinquency is not the only alternative open to youth who experienced status deprivation in school. Dropping out of school also offers a solution to this problem and is not confined to those lacking intellectual

SOURCE: "Delinquency, School Attendance and Dropout," *Social Problems*, (Winter, 1966), 13:3:307–314. Reprinted by permission.

[1] See David J. Bordua, "Sociological Theories and Their Implications for Juvenile Delinquency: A Report of a Children's Bureau Conference," U.S. Department of Health, Education, and Welfare, 1960; Albert K. Cohen, *Delinquent Boys*, Glencoe, Ill.: The Free Press, 1955; and Richard Cloward and Lloyd Ohlin, *Delinquency and Opportunity*, Glencoe, Ill.: The Free Press, 1960.

[2] Cohen, *op. cit.*, pp. 112–119.

[3] Cloward and Ohlin maintain that some communities have both conventional and criminal opportunity structures. Boys in these communities who experience aspirational blockage in the legitimate opportunity system turn to the illegitimate opportunity system in an effort to achieve their aspirations. This solution is essentially that described by Merton as an innovating mode of adaptation. Robert K. Merton, *Social Theory and Social Structure*, Glencoe, Ill.: The Free Press, 1957, pp. 141–149.

[4] Cohen, on the other hand, maintains that the delinquent subculture engages in behavior which expresses rejection and derogation of middle-class norms and goals. Vandalism, for example, is seen as an expression of the delinquent's disdain of the middle-class norm regarding private property.

ability. Studies of school dropouts suggest that capable youth are leaving school prior to graduation to escape a condition similar to that described by Cohen and Cloward and Ohlin. For example, Lichter and his associates concluded that the capable dropout leaves school because of his desire to escape frustrations encountered in the school milieu:

> The dropouts left school because they were motivated to *run away* from a disagreeable situation; they did not feel impelled to run toward a definite and positive goal. Although they discussed employment, their talk was vague, aimless, or unrealistic. . . . The decision to drop out was the outcome of an accumulation of school problems and the belief that it was too late to correct the difficulties. Dropping out was not only the easiest course to take, but a passive, not an active resolution of the educational problem.[5]

One significant point regarding the decision to drop out of school as an alternative to the status frustration experienced in school is that it should reduce the motivational stimulus to engage in delinquent behavior. The individual who drops out is no longer involved in the competition with middle-class youth at school and the adjustment problem described by Cohen as the motivational source of delinquency it at least partially resolved.[6] If status deprivation experienced at school is causally related to delinquency, it follows that the probability of engaging in delinquent behavior is less for out-of-school youth than for in-school youth.[7] This proposition is examined in this study in the form of two specific hypotheses:

1. The rate of delinquency is greater for boys while in than while out of school.[8]
2. Delinquents who drop out have a higher delinquency rate while in than while out of school.

THE STUDY DESIGN

The study population is composed of 743 tenth grade boys who entered the two largest high schools in a large western city in September, 1959.[9] In this *ex post facto* design, data were gathered on this group of boys for a three year period beginning with their entrance into high school in September, 1959 and ending with their class graduation in June of 1962.[10] The research

---

[5] Solomin Lichter et al., *The Dropouts*, New York: The Free Press of Glencoe, 1962, pp. 247–248.

[6] It is possible, however, that the individual has merely traded the status frustrations encountered at school for those encountered in our economic institutions. The availability of satisfactory employment may well be a necessary condition for the effective resolution of the status deprivation problem.

[7] The hypothesis that delinquency is related to frustrations encountered in the school milieu and that leaving this milieu reduces the motivation for delinquent behavior appears consistent with the fact that offense rates in the U.S. drop significantly after 17, when most lower-class American youth leave school and enter the labor force. Walter Lunden, *Statistics on Delinquents and Delinquency*, Iowa: The Art Press, 1961, p. 28; Jessie Bernard, *Social Problems at Midcentury*, New York: Dryden, 1957, pp. 421–444; William McCord et al., *Origins of Crime*, New York: Columbia University Press, 1959, p. 21; W. H. Dunham and M. E. Knaver, "The Juvenile Court and Its Relationship to Adult Criminality," *Social Forces* (March, 1954), pp. 290–296. In England, the rate of delinquency drops much earlier, at the age of 14 or 15; again, this is when most English youth *leave school* and enter the labor force. John Barron Mays, *Growing Up in the City*, Liverpool: University Press, 1954.

[8] It is recognized that leaving school may not reduce the likelihood of a boy who is already delinquent committing another delinquent act. The delinquent's identification and involvement with an existing delinquent group may lead him to continue his delinquent activities, as a requirement of group membership, even though the original motivational stimulus for this kind of behavior has been eliminated. However, if the dropout is not a member of a delinquent group prior to leaving school, the probability of his joining this kind of group or committing another delinquent act should be reduced.

[9] The total number of males entering these two schools in 1959 was 821. Seventy-eight of this original group transferred out of the area during the three year study period and were dropped from the analysis, leaving 743 subjects.

[10] Police contacts during the summer months of 1960 and 1961 were not considered in this analysis. Almost all of the subjects were out of school during

design specified a comparison of the delinquency rates of these boys while in and out of school. The "in-school" and "out-of-school" distinction requires that each boy be classified as a graduate or dropout. Boys who graduated in June, 1962 or were in school throughout the entire study period were classified as graduates. All those who left school (during the three years) were classified as dropouts. The dropout category thus includes those who were "pushed" out of school for disciplinary problems as well as those who left voluntarily. Those who left to move to another geographical area were excluded from the analysis.[11] All boys classified as graduates were in school during the entire study period and consequently contributed *only* to the in-school delinquency rate. Boys classified as dropouts were in-school for some part of the study period and out of school for the remainder of the period, contributing to *both* the in-school and out-of-school delinquency rates.[12] Of the 743 boys in the study, 182 were classified as dropouts and 561 were classified as graduates.

The comparison of in- and out-of-school delinquency rates also required that these rates be calculated upon a common base. Consequently, it was necessary to determine the actual number of days graduates and dropouts were attending school and the number of days the dropouts were out of school. The number of in-school days for graduates was constant. The number of in-school days for dropouts varied, depending upon the date they left school. School records were examined to determine this date, and an attempt was made to contact each dropout during September and October of 1962 to determine the number of days he was out of school and in the study area. This information was secured for 132 or 73 percent of the 182 dropouts. For the remainder, an estimate of their out-of-school time in the area was made after examining all available records. The latest date the subject was *known* to be in the area was used to calculate the length of time this subject was out-of-school and in the study area. The estimate of the number of out-of-school days is therefore a conservative one.[13]

Official contact reports by police, sheriff, and other law enforcement agencies constitute the measure of delinquency. The date and nature of each offense, as stated on the contact report (referral), were recorded.[14] The use of official statistics as a measure

---

this period of time and there was no practical way of determining how many subjects left the area and for what periods of time. During the school year, all graduates were in school and only dropouts had to be contacted to determine their whereabouts. The official referral rate declines during the summer months. [San Diego Police Department—Juvenile Division, Monthly Reports, 1960, 1961, and 1962.] Had contacts reported during the summer months been included, the most probable effect would have been a decrease in the out-of-school referral rate. Since this works in favor of the hypothesis, it was decided to exclude summer time contacts from the analysis.

[11] This was determined by a "request for transcript" received by the school of origin. In several cases boys indicated they were moving but no request for transcript was received. In this event, they were classified as dropouts and an attempt was made to locate them in the local area.

[12] There were two boys who dropped out of school for a period of time and then re-entered school. The number of days they were out of school contributed to the calculation of the out-of-school rate and *both* their in-school periods contributed to the in-school rate. Neither boy had an official contact.

[13] A conservative estimate works against the hypothesis in this case, since it maximized the out-of-school delinquency rate.

[14] Kobrin asserts that police "complaint records" or contact reports are probably the most inclusive measure of delinquency obtainable though he recognizes that they are not an accurate measure of delinquent behavior. Solomon Kobrin, "The Conflict of Values in Delinquency Areas," *The American Sociological Review,* 16, 1951, pp. 652–661. Since a comparison of in- and out-of-school delinquent offense rates is made, truancy offenses were excluded. The calculation of the total number of in- and out-of-school days does not include any days after an individual's eighteenth birthday since an individual is generally not treated as a juvenile after his eighteenth birthday and only juvenile records were consulted.

of delinquent behavior has been questioned by many.[15] Certainly a direct measure of actual behavior which violates legal statutes would provide a more adequate test of the hypothesis. Short and Nye have suggested the use of a self-reported measure of delinquency to more closely approximate a direct measure of delinquent behavior, but the nature of this study precluded the use of such a measure of delinquency.[16] However, an indirect assessment of delinquent behavior can be obtained from official referrrals of law enforcement agencies. The definition of a delinquent act in terms of official referrals is comprised of two essential elements: (1) it involves behavior which violates legal statutes and (2) it involves the initiation of official proceedings by law enforcement agencies.[17] While the legal definition includes an illegal behavior component, official records are an inaccurate measure of this behavior since the second component requires that the illegal act be known officially and that some action be initiated against the offender. When an official definition of delinquency is used, therefore, any differences in rates of delinquency noted may be attributed to (1) differences in actual behavior, (2) differences in the knowledge or reaction of official agencies to the offender, or (3) both of these elements. If the design of the study permits the investigator to rule out the second possibility, then tests of theoretically derived hypotheses will not be biased by the use of an official definition of delinquency. The crucial question, therefore, is what determines the behavior of official agents and how will these factors affect the tests of these hypotheses.

Since the comparison is between dropouts and graduates there are some logical grounds for assuming that, to the extent differences in knowledge or reaction of official agencies are operating, they would work *against* the hypothesis being tested, i.e., the effect of these biases would be to increase the magnitude of the *out-of-school* delinquency rate. On the basis of available research evidence, it would appear that a major factor influencing the action of official agents is the social class of the offender. Not only is the surveillance likely to be greater in lower-class neighborhoods, but the risk of formal action after detection appears to be greater for those living in these neighborhoods.[18] Since the research evidence also indicates that dropouts come disportionately from lower-class neighborhoods, the effect of this type of official bias on a comparison of in- and out-of-school delinquency rates would be to accentuate

---

[15] Thorsten Sellin, "The Significance of Records of Crime," *The Law Quarterly Review*, 67, 1951, pp. 489–504; and "Culture Conflict and Crime," *Social Science Research Council*, Bulletin 41, 1938, pp. 17–32; James F. Short, Jr. and F. Ivan Nye, "Reported Behavior as a Criterion of Deviant Behavior," *Social Problems*, 5, 1957, pp. 207–213; Sophia Robison, *Can Delinquency Be Measured?*, New York: Columbia University Press, 1936; John I. Kitsuse and Aaron V. Cicourel, "A Note on the Use of Statistics," *Social Problems*, 11, 1963, pp. 131–139.

[16] Short and Nye, *op. cit.* While these authors are aware of the limitations of official statistics when used in etiological research they do not suggest that this type of data is inappropriate for etiological studies. "No other system of data collection seems practicable on a continuing basis. Much etiological research must remain in the manipulation of officially defined problems and statistics. . . . We are inclined to accept Tappan's point regarding the validity of legal norms as a unit of study in preference to nebulous extra-legal concepts." (p. 48)

[17] Cloward and Ohlin, *op. cit.*, p. 3; Kitsuse & Cicourel, *op. cit.*, pp. 131–137.

[18] Clifford R. Shaw and Henry D. McKay, *Juvenile Delinquency and Urban Areas*, Chicago: The University of Chicago Press, 1942; William C. Kvaraceus, "Juvenile Delinquency and Social Class," *Journal of Educational Sociology*, 18, 1944, pp. 51–54; Ernest W. Burgess, "The Economic Factor in Juvenile Delinquency," *Journal of Criminal Law, Criminology and Political Science*, 43, 1952, pp. 29–42; Ivan F. Nye, *Family Relationships and Delinquent Behavior*, New York: John Wiley and Sons, 1958; Short and Nye, *op. cit.*; Martin Gold, *Status Forces in Delinquent Boys*, Ann Arbor: The University of Michigan, 1963, ch. 1; Edwin Sutherland and Donald Cressey, *Principles of Criminology* (6th ed.), New York: J. B. Lippincott & Co., 1960, ch. 15.

the out-of-school rate and increase the likelihood of rejecting the hypothesis.[19]

It might be argued that those in school are more "visible" to law enforcement agents than are those out-of-school. One way the police may learn about delinquent behavior is through reports from school officials. To the extent schools make such reports to law enforcement agencies, the delinquent acts of those in school are more visible than are those of out-of-school youth. In connection with another study, contact reports filed in the county during 1963 and 1964 were reviewed to determine the source of each referral.[20] After excluding truancy offenses, it was found that less than one half of one percent of the referrals identified the school as the source of the referral. Clearly the school is not a significant source for delinquency referrals in this community.

One other factor which might account for a different response on the part of law enforcement agents is the offense. If offenses committed while in school are characteristically different from those committed while out-of-school, this could account for a differential response on the part of law enforcement agents and a higher in-school delinquency rate. The relatively small number of offenses involved in this study precluded the use of a detailed offense breakdown, but the in- and out-of-school offense patterns were compared with respect to (1) property offenses, (2) offenses against persons, and (3) control offenses.[21] The proportions of in- and out-of-school offenses falling into these three categories were as follows: property offenses, 48 percent compared to 50 percent; offenses against persons, 4 percent and 0 percent; control offenses, 36 percent and 25 percent. The major difference noted was in the control offenses where the greater in-school proportion was due to a relatively greater number of curfew offenses. In terms of seriousness of offense, a greater proportion of out-of-school than in-school offenses would be classified as felonies. If there are differences in reactions of officials based on the seriousness of the offense, this would tend to operate against the hypotheses in this study. In general, the observed differences in offense patterns do not appear great enough to

---

[19] R. A. Tesseneer and L. M. Tesseneer, "Review of the Literature on School Dropouts," *Bulletin of the National Association of Secondary School Principals* (May, 1958), pp. 141–153; August B. Hollingshead, *Elmtown's Youth*, New York: John Wiley and Sons, 1949; Edith G. Neisser, *School Failures and Dropouts*, Public Affairs Pamphlet No. 346, July, 1963, pp. 4–6; Division for Youth, *The School Dropout Problem: Rochester, Part I*, State of New York, May, 1962, pp. 9–10; Daniel Schreiber, "The Dropout and the Delinquent: Promising Practices Gleaned From a Year of Study," *Phi Delta Kappan*, 44 (February, 1963), pp. 215–221; Bernard A. Kaplan, "Issues in Educating the Culturally Disadvantaged," *Phi Delta Kappan*, 45 (November, 1963), pp. 70–76; and Starke R. Hathaway and Elio D. Monachesi, *Adolescent Personality and Behavior: MMPI Patterns of Normal, Delinquent, Dropout, and Other Outcomes*, Minneapolis: University of Minnesota Press, 1963, pp. 92–98. This class differential was in fact observed in this study with 85 percent of the dropouts compared to 69 percent of the graduates residing in areas classified as lower SES areas. The measure of socio-economic status (SES) is a social area measure based upon U.S. Census block data. Four block characteristics were considered: 1) average house value, 2) average contract rent, 3) percent homes owner occupied, and 4) percent deterioration and dilapidation. Blocks where two or more of these housing characteristics were below the city average were classified as lower SES areas. All remaining blocks were classified as higher SES areas.

[20] These data were gathered in connection with a five year longitudinal study on delinquency and dropout supported by a Public Health Service Research Grant No. MH 07173 from the National Institute of Mental Health.

[21] The offenses as listed on the police contact report were classified as follows: 1) Property Offenses—Auto Theft, Burglary, Petty Theft, Other Theft, Vandalism; 2) Offenses against Persons—Sex Offenses, Assault and Battery; and 3) Control Offenses,—Runaway, Dangerous Drugs, Drunkenness and Possession of Alcohol, Incorrigible, Beyond Control, & Curfew. Other offenses were classified as miscellaneous. Twelve percent of the in-school and 25 percent of the out-of-school offenses were classified as miscellaneous.

evoke a systematic difference in response on the part of law enforcement agents.

In the light of the above discussion, it is argued that the use of official referrals as a measure of delinquency should result in a conservative test of the hypotheses since the kinds of distortions or biases introduced by the knowledge and reaction of official agents would tend to work against the hypotheses. If the rates of actual delinquent behavior among boys in and out of school were in fact equal, the most probable effect of using official police contacts to measure these rates would be to overestimate the out-of-school delinquency rate among the dropouts who are more likely to be drawn from a lower-class background.

FINDINGS

The comparison of the in- and out-of-school delinquency referral rates is presented in Table I. The overall in-school referral rate is 4.95 compared to an out-of-school rate of 2.75. This difference is substantial and in the direction hypothesized. Table I also presents the in-school delinquency rates for both graduates and future dropouts and for those residing in lower and higher socio-economic (SES) neighborhoods. The highest delinquency rate was observed among lower SES dropouts prior to their leaving school. It is quite possible that their involvement in this kind of activity was responsible for some of them being pushed out of school. What is surprising is that this same group of boys had the lowest referral rate after dropping out of school. Their out-of-school rate is less than one-third their in-school rate. These data clearly support the hypothesis.

Cohen's explanation of delinquency applies specifically to working class boys and the status deprivation variable automatically incorporated the class variable. Since there was no attempt to obtain a measure of this independent variable in this study, it seemed important to calculate separate rates for those from lower and higher SES areas. While the in-school rate for boys from higher SES areas is greater than their out-of-school rate, the difference is quite small and may be of little substantive significance. In fact, there appears to be little difference in any of the rates shown for boys from higher SES areas. The in-school rates for dropouts and graduates are almost identical and are only slightly greater than the out-of-school rates. It would appear that leaving school does not have the same impact on boys from higher SES areas as it does on those from lower SES areas. One might expect that leaving school would affect boys from these two SES areas differently. While leaving school should help to eliminate the status frustration of boys from lower-class areas, it would not necessarily solve the adjustment problem of those from middle- and upper-class areas. Boys from lower-class areas can retreat into the lower-class community where they may seek employment in the unskilled or semi-skilled occupations which are available to them. Their parents and other adult members of their community are willing to accept these occupations as legitimate endeavors for young men.

Table I. *Delinquent Referral Rate*[a] *Among Boys In and Out of School*

SES Areas	In School			Out of School
	Graduates	Dropouts [b]	Sub-total	Dropouts [b]
Lower	4.13	8.70	4.96	2.42
Higher	4.92	4.95	4.92	4.63
Total	4.34	8.03	4.95	2.75

[a] Number of referrals per 10,000 in- or out-of-school days.
[b] These are the same individuals during two different time periods.

Boys from middle-class areas who leave school subsequently find themselves limited to lower-class occupations while their parents and other adult members of their community continue to hold middle-class expectations for them. They are unable or unwilling to meet the formal expectations of school and are equally unable to meet the expectations of their parents if they drop out of school.

A separate but related issue involves the effect of leaving school on the referral rate of boys who were known officially as delinquents while in school. Although the rate of delinquent referral is less for boys while out of school than while in school, it does not necessarily follow that those who have official referrals while in school will have fewer referrals after leaving school. To test the hypothesis that delinquents who drop out have a higher referral rate while in school, in- and out-of-school referral rates were calculated for this group. (Table II)

The data in Table II supports this hypothesis. The in-school referral rate for delinquents is almost twice their out-of-school referral rate. This relationship holds for delinquents from both lower and higher SES areas. The rates in Table II also suggest that delinquents from lower SES neighborhoods have a higher referral rate than do delinquents from higher SES neighborhoods. This is particularly interesting since there is little difference in the proportions (.112 and .118) of boys from each of these two areas who are delinquent, i.e., who had one or more official referrals on file. It appears that delinquents from lower SES neighborhoods are more frequent offenders than are those from higher SES areas.

CONCLUSION

Cohen suggests that delinquency on the part of lower-class boys is a response to the unequal competition encountered at school. Delinquency is thus associated with frustration and failure particularly experienced in school, for it is in this milieu that youth from disparate cultural backgrounds are forced to compete for middle-class success goals.

There are several alternatives available to those who experience frustration at school. They may remain in school and attempt to deal with their frustration by attacking the system of norms and values which they believe to be the source of their difficulties. Delinquent behavior may thus be viewed as an expression of their resentment toward this system and those who attempt to enforce its norms. On the other hand, those experiencing failure may leave school making a "retreatist" adaptation in an effort to escape from the situation which produces the frustrations. No longer frustrated by the unequal competition at school, there is little or no need to attack the school or the normative system it represents.

It was hypothesized, therefore, that (1) the rate of delinquency referral is greater for boys while in school than while out of school; and (2) delinquents who drop out have a higher referral rate while in school

Table II. *Offense Rates[a] for Delinquent Dropouts Before and After Leaving School*

SES Areas	Before	After
Lower	64.96	34.52
Higher	40.12	23.75
Total	60.78	31.01

[a] Number of delinquent referrals per 10,000 student-days.

than while out of school. The data supported both hypotheses. The small difference between in- and out-of-school offense rates for boys from higher SES neighborhoods suggests that dropping out of school may not constitute a solution to problems of status deprivation for boys from higher SES areas. One might infer that dropout is a satisfactory solution for those from lower SES areas for the delinquency rate of such youth is lower after leaving school than it was while they were in school.

48. THE BROKEN HOME AND MALE DELINQUENCY

LAWRENCE ROSEN

There are perhaps three major (but not necessarily independent) approaches that can be used to implicate the family in an understanding of delinquency. They are (1) deviant structure (2) deviant family relationships and (3) transfer of deviant norms.

In the *deviant structure* approach an ideal family structure is postulated (usually the most frequently occurring type in the society) and any deviation from this ideal structure is viewed as "bad" and producing "bad" consequences (such as delinquency).[1] In American society the structurally ideal family is the nuclear family with both natural parents present. The "broken" (or deviant) family may result in an inability for the remaining parent or parent surrogates to "control" the child, fail to provide proper "role models," or fail to contribute sufficient maternal or paternal love. The basic assumption in the *deviant family relationship* approach is that a certain ideal "quality" of parent-child, sibling-sibling, or husband-wife relationship will more likely result in conforming behavior. Thus, lack of love or too much love, an "unhappy home," a too harsh or too lax father, an authoritarian or permissive parent, lack of family solidarity, parental inconsistency, parental discrimination for a favorite child, are all seen as resulting in rebellion, personality problems, defective "generalized other", etc. with a resultant increased probability of delinquency. The *transfer of deviant norms* approach, assumes a "normal" or non-pathological socialization process with differences between delinquents and nondelinquents being attributed to the *content* of the norms internalized by the youths during the years of family socialization. In other words, delinquents had been taught norms and values by family members which favor the violation of juvenile statutes, while the nondelinquent has acquired norms and values which are unfavorable to the violation of laws (as in Sutherland's "differential association"). In this context one investigates the nature and content of the norms rather than the nature of the socialization process.

The purpose of this paper is to evaluate

▶SOURCE: *"The 'Broken Home' and Male Delinquency," paper prepared for this reader based on Ph.D. dissertation: The Delinquent and Non-Delinquent in a High Delinquent Area, Temple University, 1968.*

[1] The danger in this type of logic is that one can easily commit the "evil causes evil" fallacy. (If an event is "bad" or "evil", then all events associated with A are *ipso facto* "bad" or "evil".) See Gwynn Netler, "Good Men, Bad Men, and the Perception of Reality," *Sociometry*, 24 (September 1961) pp. 279–294.

one aspect of *deviant structure*,[2] namely the relationship between "broken home" and male delinquency.[3]

CONCEPT OF "BROKEN HOME"

The most popular definition of "broken home" encountered in the delinquency literature is the absence of at least one "natural" parent because of death, desertion, divorce or separation. One does, however, find some variation in this traditional definition of "broken home." Some may use the absence of *any* parent, natural or step, or restrict the broken home to those which might be termed "indicators of strain and conflict," (desertion, divorce or separation) or even expand them to include temporary absence due to institutionalization, occupation, etc. The adequacy of the traditional definition of "broken home" can be questioned primarily because of its multidimensional character.

The "broken home" concept includes two major dimensions or properties: (1) absence of parent or parents and (2) reason for the break. Each of these two dimensions can be partitioned into three and four states respectively. For parental absence there can be an absent father, absent mother or the absence of both parents. If one were to consider only the absence of "natural" parents and include the possibility of stepparents, then there would be six possible types of parental patterns (e.g., mother-present, no step father; mother present,

---

[2] There are, of course, other structural issues that can be considered, such as family size, ordinal position and extended family relationship.

[3] Because of limitation of time, it was decided to exclude any discussion of female delinquency (which does receive less attention in the literature on delinquency). It seems widely accepted that "broken home" is more important for females than males in producing delinquency. (For example, see Jackson Toby, "The Differential Impact of Family Disorganization," *American Sociological Reivew*, 22 (October 1957), pp. 502–512.) Since a systematic and intensive evaluation of the relationship between broken home and delinquency for females has not been conducted by the present author, the above assertion can not be questioned in this paper.

step father present). For the second dimension four possible states are possible; (1) death, (2) desertion, (3) divorce and (4) separation. Excluded from this list are other possible reasons for prolonged parental absence such as institutionalization of a parent or a family never completed (i.e. mother with illegitimate children). Consequently it is possible to have one of the absent parent configurations, previously mentioned, included in the category of a nonbroken home. If parental absence was the key dimension for delinquency then quite obviously the traditional definitions would be inappropriate.

The combining of the two dimensions would yield 12 types of "broken homes." (In actuality a large number is possible if one were to consider listing a separate reason for each parent in the case of two absent parents.) Not all 12 types need to be considered. Some can be eliminated or combined with others because of rare occurrence or some *a priori* basis. However, since litle is known about the actual mechanisms, if any, that relate "broken home" to delinquency it seems quite unreasonable at this time to collapse all of these types into one omnibus definition. Under conditions of limited knowledge an omnibus definition could be of limited value. For example, the finding of no relationship between delinquency and "broken home" may be due to one of these conditions: (1) not a single type of broken home being important, (2) some types operate in opposite directions to cancel the effects of each other, or (3) the possible importance of one or two types may be masked or "washed out" by the non-importance of the other types.

Until more is known about family structure and delinquency it seems reasonable to aim for a simpler (i.e. undimensional) definition of broken home. One possible definition would be the absence of at least one parent (natural or step). Whether one still labels such a concept "broken home" is of little importance. However, if one wants to avoid confusion with the traditional notion of "broken home," then another label is suggested, for example "altered family."

REVIEW OF THE LITERATURE

The literature in delinquency exhibits a fair amount of controversy on the issue of importance of "broken home" for male delinquency. For example, Peterson and Becker argue strongly for its importance:

> ... the substantial relationship between delinquency and broken homes remains as one of the overriding facts any conception of delinquency must take into account.[4]

On the other hand, there is the biting criticism by Mannheim:

> No other term in the history of criminological thought has been so much overworked, misused, and discredited as this. For many years universally proclaimed as the most obvious explanation of both juvenile delinquency and adult crime, it is now often regarded as the "black sheep" in the otherwise respectable family of criminological theories, and most writers shamefacedly turn their backs to it.[5]

It seems, however, that most writers consider the "broken home" of secondary importance for delinquency.[6]

The major problem in conducting a review of empirical findings is to find an adequate base for comparison. Perhaps the most adequate way of evaluating a relationship is to determine the degree or strength of the relationship. What devices or procedures should be employed to assess the strength of a relationship? One cannot simply look at the difference between the percentage of delinquents from "broken homes" and intact homes because there is no precise and unambiguous way of interpreting the size of the difference in strength of relationship terms. (The primary reason for this limitation is because one is unable to weigh the effect of the relative proportion of boys from "broken homes" and intact homes—a critical component for ascertaining the degree of relationship.)[7] The demonstration of statistical significance by itself is also inappropriate because it tells nothing about the strength of relationship. With a sufficiently large sample, it would be easy to achieve significance for a very weak or trivial relationship. Thus, comparing Chi square values is inappropriate because such values are a function of sample size, which, of course, varies from study to study. What is required is a measure which has a precise and unambiguous interpretation of strength of relationship; such a measure is Goodman and Kruskal's Tau b.[8] The value of this measure varies between 0 and 1 and can be interpreted as the proportionate reduction of total error in the dependent variable (the error made in assigning youth to delinquent or nondelinquent categories without knowledge of the independent variable) produced by having knowledge of the independent variable.[9] A Tau b was computed for each of the studies selected for the review.

---

[4] Donald R. Peterson and Wesley C. Becker, "Family Interaction and Delinquency" In Herbert C. Quay (Ed.), *Juvenile Delinquency*, Princeton, New Jersey; D. Van Nostrand Company, 1965, p. 69.

[5] Herman Mannheim, *Comparative Criminology*, Boston: Houghton-Mifflin Company, 1965, p. 618.

[6] This evaluation is a subjective one based on an unsystematic review of eight major textbooks in crime and delinquency.

[7] One major review of empirical studies (Peterson and Becker, *op. cit.*) did employ such a procedure by noting the differences in the proportion of "broken homes" between delinquents and nondelinquents. This is a questionable procedure since it violates the fundamental notion that one should percentage off the base of the independent variable (i.e., type of family structure). (See Hans Zeisel, *Say It With Figures*, New York: Harper and Brothers, 1957; for an example of possible errors produced by incorrect percentaging, see Travis Hirschi and Hanan C. Selvin, *Delinquency Research: An Appraisal of Analytic Methods*, New York: Free Press, 1967.)

[8] Leo A. Goodman and William H. Kruskal, "Measures of Association for Cross Classification," *Journal of the American Statistical Association* **49** (December 1954), pp. 732–764.

[9] Herbert L. Costner, "Criteria for Measures of Association," *American Sociological Review*, **30** (June 1965), pp. 341–353.

In choosing studies to be included, the following criteria were used:

1. The sample must include only males or the data be presented in such a manner as to allow males to be selected out of the population;
2. a. control group of nondelinquents (however defined) was part of the research design;
3. the data must be presented in sufficient detail so that a Tau b could be computed.
4. The delinquent group did not consist solely of institutionalized males. (There is some evidence that family structure is a factor in the judicial decision to commit a youth to a "correctional institution." Therefore, it is possible that the use of institutional population would tend to inflate the proportion of "broken homes" among delinquents.) [10]

A total of eleven Studies met these criteria and are summarized in Table I.

Despite the variation in date, locale, sample size, nature of population, definition of both delinquency and "broken home", and in basic research design, the conclusion is clear: the strength of the relationship is very small (even though in eight studies a significant level of at least .05 was reached).

A word is in order concerning the two studies, (the Gluecks and the Browning) which seem to have atypically high Tau b values (although both values were below 0.10). The Glueck's study, using 500 institutionalized boys as its delinquents may well have involved an administrative bias of disproportionate commitments from "broken homes" to juvenile institutions. A second possible reason for the relatively high association stems from the matching design employed by the researchers (thus giving them an equal number of delinquents and nondelinquents). Tau b is affected by the marginals in such a manner that its values are maximized when there is a 50–50 split. A reordering of the Glueck's data to give a split of 30 percent delinquents and 70 percent nondelinquents (which is closer to the other studies listed in Table I) yields a Tau b of .018 (still significant at the .001 level).[11] The Browning study seemed to employ the least systematic procedure of all studies used. The nondelinquents were not selected on a probability basis, and the delinquents chosen were only those who had either committed a truancy (a "less serious" offense) or auto theft (a "serious" offense). The weakness of the sample thus casts grave doubts on the results of the study.

DISCUSSION

What accounts for the lack of a strong relationship between broken homes and delinquency? One possible explanation may be that family structure is of far less importance than the "quality" of family interaction. Thus delinquency-producing interactions (stress, conflict, strain, etc.) may be as likely to occur in "broken homes" as intact homes.[12] Another possibility is

---

[10] Richard S. Sterne, *Delinquent Conduct and Broken Homes*, New Haven: College and University Press, 1964, p. 45; P. M. Smith, "Broken Homes and Juvenile Delinquency," *Sociology and Social Research*, 39 (May-June 1955), pp. 307-311. The Gluecks' study, although utilizing an institutional population of delinquents, was included because it is widely cited.

[11] A similar reordering for all the other studies in Table I not having approximately a 30–70 split on the dependent variable, although producing some changes in the Tau b, failed to effect the conclusion of a very weak relationship between the two variables. (Not a single recomputed Tau b value exceeded 0.025.)

[12] Studies which have questioned the general assertion that "broken home" is detrimental to children are Lee G. Burchinal, "Characteristics of Adolescents from Unbroken, Broken and Reconstituted Families," *Journal of Marriage and Family Living*, 26 (February 1964), pp. 44–51; Alan J. Crain and Caroline S. Stamm, "Intermittent Absence of Fathers and Children's Perceptions of Parents," *Journal of Marriage and Family Living*, 27 (August 1965) pp. 344–347; William Goode, *After Divorce*, Glencoe, Illinois: The Free Press, 1956, pp. 307–329; F. Ivan Nye, "Child Adjustment in Broken and Unhappy Unbroken Homes," *Marriage and Family Living*, 19 (November 1957), pp. 366–361.

Table I. *Summary of Studies Investigating "Broken Home" and Delinquency*

Researcher	Year Published	N	Association Tau b	x^2 [1]
(A) Shaw and McKay [2]	1932	8953	.004	40.28
(B) Weeks and Smith [3]	1939	2449	.012	24.49
(C) Carr-Saunders, et al [4]	1944	3925	.019	74.57
(D) Glueck and Glueck [5]	1950	1000	.078	78.50
(E) Nye [6]	1958	1160	.005	5.80
(F) Browning [7]	1960	164	.096	15.69
(G) Hardt [8]	1965	164	.022	3.66
(H) Hardt [9]	1965	191	.015	2.92
(I) Tennyson [10]	1967	294	<.001	.06
(J) Koval and Polk [11]	1967	873	.009	7.60
(K) Rosen [12]	1968	866	.012	10.13

[1] All Chi Square values are for one degree of freedom. Significant values are: For .001 level, 10.83; for .01 level, 6.64; and for .05 level, 3.84.

[2] Clifford Shaw and H. D. McKay, "Are Broken Homes a Causative Factor in Juvenile Delinquency?" *Social Forces*, 10 (May, 1932), pp. 514–524. Delinquents are from Juvenile Court in Chicago, 1929–1930. The non-delinquents, ages 10–17, were sampled from public schools in Chicago. The delinquency rate of the control group was not checked; therefore, it is not known how many delinquents were in the control group. "Broken home" defined as at least one parent absent because of death, desertion, divorce, separation or confinement in an institution.

[3] H. A. Weeks and Margaret G. Smith, "Juvenile Delinquency and Broken Homes in Spokane, Washington," *Social Forces*, 18 (October, 1939), pp. 48–59. Delinquents are from Juvenile Court in Spokane, Washington. The nondelinquents are a random sample of public secondary school students, Spokane, Washington, 1937, having no court record. The age of delinquency is from 7-18. Definition of "broken home" same as that given by Shaw and McKay (Note 2).

[4] A. M. Carr-Saunders, H. Mannheim and E. Rhodes, *Young Offenders*, New York: MacMillan, 1944. Delinquents (ages 7–17) are taken from those *appearing* before court in 1938 in selected cities in England (including London). The nondelinquents were chosen by asking the head teacher at the school at which the delinquent attended for a youth who would be similar to the delinquent youth. The matching variables were age and residence. "Broken home" defined as at least one natural parent absent because of death, separation or divorce.

[5] Sheldon Glueck and Eleanor Glueck, *Unraveling Juvenile Delinquency*, New York: Commonwealth Fund, 1950. The sample of delinquents was taken from correctional schools and the nondelinquents from Boston public schools in 1939. The delinquents and nondelinquents were matched for age, intelligence and ethnicity. "Broken home" is one "broken by separation, divorce, death, or prolonged absence of a parent."

[6] F. Ivan Nye, *Family Relationships and Delinquent Behavior*, New York: John Wiley and Sons, 1958. The sample was selected from high school students in three "medium-sized" towns in Washington in 1955. The measurements of delinquent group being those scoring highest on the delinquency scale. The association values noted include step-parents in the intact family; a reconstruction of the broken home definition to exclude step-parents yields a Tau b of less than .001 and X^2 of 1.16.

[7] Charles J. Browning, "Differential Impact of Family Disorganization on Male Adolescents," *Social Problems*, 8 (Summer, 1960), pp. 37-44. The youths were chosen from a population that was white, at least third generation Americans, Protestant, Catholic or no religion, enrolled in public schools, and living in a common court jurisdiction within Los Angeles, (No date given). The mean age of the youths in the sample was 15. The delinquents were defined as those having a court record and whose most serious offence was auto theft or truancy (the analysis divided delinquency into most serious and least serious). The nondelinquents were those who had no record or truancy for the year of the study. The proportion of delinquents was 66.5%. A "broken home" defined as a "boy not living with both of his natural parents."

[8] Robert H. Hardt, "Delinquency and Social Class: Studies of Juvenile Deviations or Police Dispositions," Unpublished paper presented at Eastern

that the family may *not* be a major independent variable for delinquency. The fact that the dominant emphasis for American sociologists since the 1930's has been with nonfamilial concerns (e.g., delinquent values, gangs, peer group, opportunity structure, subculture, etc.) [13] may suggest that the family plays a secondary role as a factor in delinquency.

Finally, one must criticize the crude nature of almost all of the studies of broken home and delinquency. For the most part these studies have failed to refine the notion of broken home by controlling for such factors as the nature of the break, its duration, the age of the youth at time of the break, adjustments to the break, etc. In an attempt to investigate one of these dimensions, Jackson Toby, after reexamination of the Shaw and McKay data, argues that the "broken home" is *only* important for younger males.[14] Toby apparently reaches this conclusion by a simple inspection of the differences in percent of "broken homes" between delinquents and nondelinquents for each age group. There are several things wrong with this procedure; one, the data is percentaged in the wrong direction; it should be the percentage of delinquents within "broken" and intact homes. Second, the marginals are extremely skewed. The youngest age group (10-year-olds) which had the largest percentage difference for "broken homes" included only twelve delinquents and 1387 nondelinquents. (For 11-year-olds, there were 55 delinquents and 1409 nondelinquents.) Statements about differences in percentages involving such large discrepancies in sample size should be made with extreme caution, if made at all. Finally, as already mentioned, differences in percentages are poor indices of strength of relationship between two variables. A computation of separate Tau b's for the 10–12 [15] year old

---

Sociological Meetings, New York, 1965. The study was conducted in 1963 in a city of 250,000 located in "the center of one of the major metropolitan areas in a Middle Atlantic state." Delinquents were defined as having a record or a "suspected" or "alleged" delinquency in the Central Registry of Juvenile Police Contacts. Both the delinquents and nondelinquents were seventh, eighth and ninth grade students attending parochial and public schools. "Broken home" defined as father absent.

[9] *Ibid.* The sample is the same as noted above (note 8) except that delinquency was defined as self-report.

[10] Ray A. Tennyson, "Family Structure and Delinquent Behavior," in Malcolm W. Klein (Ed.), *Juvenile Gangs in Context,* Englewood Cliffs, New Jersey, Prentice-Hall, 1967, pp. 57–69. Delinquency was membership in a gang defined as "troublesome" by the "Program for Detached Workers of the YMCA of Chicago". The nongang members were lower-class Negro boys. (This sample was not a random one.) The non-gang members were suggested by the YMCA workers. An intact home was a response by the youth of either "both parents continuously" or "mostly both parents" to the question, "Whom did you live with when growing up?"

[11] John P. Koval and Kenneth Polk, "Problem Youth in a Small City", in Malcolm W. Klein (Ed.), *Juvenile Gangs in Context,* Englewood Cliffs, New Jersey, Prentice-Hall, 1967, pp. 123–138. Sample taken from one high school and a non-probability selection of "drop-outs" residing in a "small city" in Lane County, Oregon (no date given). Delinquency was defined as a court or police record with family structure being characterized only as "natural family intact".

[12] Lawrence Rosen, *The Delinquent and Non-Delinquent in a High Delinquent Area,* Unpublished doctoral dissertation, Temple University, 1968. Sample of Negro youths, 13–15, drawn by an area sampling technique, residing in a low income, high delinquent, predominantly Negro area of Philadelphia in the summer of 1963. Delinquency was defined as at least one apprehension by the juvenile authorities. "Broken home" was simply the absence of at least one parent.

[13] David J. Bordua, Delinquency Theory and Research in the United States: Major Trends Since 1930," *Kölner Zietschrift für Soziologie und Sozialpsychologie, Sonderheft,* 2 (1957).

[14] Jackson Toby, *op. cit.*

[15] This age group is, one assumes, what Toby means by pre-adolescent (he never actually defined the age range) when he characterized the association between "broken homes" and delinquency as "considerable" for "pre-adolescents." A computation of a Tau b for the 10–11 year old group would have been unfeasible because of the extremely small

and 13–17 year old groups yields identical values of .005. Consequently, there seems to be no differential effect of age on the relationship between "broken home" and delinquency.[16]

In conclusion, the empirical evidence to date indicates quite conclusively that the "broken home," no matter how defined or measured, accounts by itself for little of male delinquency. This is not to say necessarily that family structure is unimportant in the aetology of male delinquency. As has already been indicated, there are problems in conceptualizing and measuring "broken home," and controlling for significant variables (time and duration of break, reasons for break, subsequent arrangements for child rearing, etc.) which the studies, for the most part, have failed to meet. Until these reservations are resolved and tested, the importance of the "broken home" for male delinquency has not been definitely "disproven." The most one can say at this time is that the empirical evidence has failed to support the thesis that the broken home is a substantial factor in male delinquency.

---

proportion (2.7 percent) of delinquents in that group.

[16] This generalization is true only for the Shaw and McKay data with its given age distribution and differential delinquency rates by age. (The rates were about 5 percent for the 10–12 year olds and 32 percent for the 13–17 year olds.) One may well ask what the relationship between delinquency and "broken home" would be if the delinquency rates were the same for both age groups. Reconstructing the data for the 10–12 year olds to yield an identical delinquency rate as the 13–17 year old group (the effect is similar to standardizing the age distribution of the delinquents on the basis of the nondelinquents, a procedure that Toby argues Shaw and McKay should have followed) gives a Tau b of .019. Although this finding now supports Toby's assertion of a differential age effect, the value of Tau b for the younger group is still quite less than the "considerable association" claimed by Toby.

49. WORKING MOTHERS AND DELINQUENCY

SHELDON and ELEANOR GLUECK

IN "UNRAVELING JUVENILE DELINQUENCY"[1] we matched, pair by pair, 500 persistent delinquents with 500 true non-delinquents, not only in respect to general intelligence, ethnico-racial derivation and age but also with regard to residence in culturally and economically under-privileged urban areas. In considering the problem of the working mother in a matched sample of such design we are enabled to hold constant the factor of low economic status (dependency or marginality), thus getting closer to the pure influence of the mother's working, in the complex of traits and forces involved in delinquency.

From the significant fact that three of the five factors most markedly differentiating the 500 delinquents from the 500 non-delinquents encompassed in the Social Prediction Table[2] presented in *Unraveling Juvenile Delinquency (affection of mother for boy, supervision of boy by mother* and *family cohesiveness)*[3] involve the maternal role in the rearing of children, one might

▶SOURCE: *"Working Mothers and Delinquency," Mental Hygiene (July, 1957), 41:329–333. (Editorial adaptations.) Reprinted by permission.*

[1] New York, Commonwealth Fund, 1950.

[2] See *Unraveling Juvenile Delinquency, op. cit.,* 261.

[3] *Unraveling Juvenile Delinquency, op. cit.,* 261. The other two factors in this predictive device, which has come to be known in the literature as the Glueck Social Prediction Table, are *dicipline of boy by father* and *affection of father for boy.*

reasonably incline to the hypothesis that absence of the mother from the home for lengthy stretches is markedly implicated in the complex of criminogenic influences. Since we had in our files the verified raw materials from *Unraveling Juvenile Delinquency* to test this hypothesis, we have developed the present data to meet a growing interest in the subject of working mothers.

METHOD OF ANALYSIS OF DATA

First, what was found in *Unraveling Juvenile Delinquency* regarding working mothers? We reproduce the relevant table: It is evident that in the lower economic ranks from which both our delinquents and the control group were drawn a considerable number of mothers, not only of delinquents but also of non-delinquents, were employed either regularly or occasionally. It is further evident that equal proportions of mothers of non-delinquents and of delinquents were regularly employed but that a greater proportion of mothers of delinquents than of non-delinquents worked irregularly.

The types of work engaged in by all the working mothers were cleaning and scrubbing, domestic service by hour or day, factory work, running a store or lodging house (or helping husbands do so), waiting on table, entertaining in cafes and restaurants.

From these initial findings in *Unraveling*

Table I. *Usual Occupation of Mother**

	Delinquents		Non-Delinquents		Difference
	No.	%	No.	%	%
Total	496	100.0	497	100.0	—
Housewife	263	53.0	333	67.0	−14.0
Regularly employed	101	20.4	91	18.3	2.1
Occasionally employed	132	26.0	73	14.7	11.9
				$X^2 = 25.72$:	$P<.01$

* *Unraveling Juvenile Delinquency*, Table X-9.

Table II. *Supervision by Mother Unsuitable**

	Delinquents		Non-Delinquents		Difference	
	No.	%	No.	%	No.	%
Total	314	63.5	61	12.5	253	51.0
Housewife	126	48.1	23	7.0	103	41.1
Regularly employed	85	84.2	25	28.0	60	56.2
Occasionally employed	103	78.6	13	18.6	90	60.0
Significance of Differences						
Housewife vs. regularly employed	.01		.02		—	
Housewife vs. occasionally employed	.01		.10		.05	
Regularly employed vs. occasionally employed	—		—		—	

* *Unraveling Juvenile Delinquency*, Table X–10. The mother, whether in the home or absent from the home, is careless in her supervision in that she leaves the boy to his own devices without guidance or in the care of an irresponsible person.

Juvenile Delinquency it may be deduced (subject to more definitive information) that more of the children in the families of delinquents than in those of the controls are deprived of necessary maternal care and that this fact has a bearing on the development of delinquency.

To illustrate the method of analysis we present a sample table, in which the factor *unsuitable supervision of boy by mother* is related to the incidence of *housewives* (non-working mothers), *regularly working mothers* and *occasionally employed mothers* among both delinquents and non-delinquents.

The factor involved in Table II—*unsuitable supervision of boy by mother*—so markedly differentiates delinquents as a whole from the total control group of non-delinquents (irrespective of whether or not the mother works outside the home) that we had used it as one of five factors in the construction of the social prediction table in *Unraveling Juvenile Delinquency*.[4]

A word regarding definitions: A mother designated as a *regular* worker is one who has been gainfully employed for all or most of the time since the birth of the particular child included among the cases of *Unraveling Juvenile Delinquency*. She

---

[4] For a description of the social prediction table and its validations on various samples of cases, see Eleanor T. Glueck, "Predicting Potential Delinquency: Can It Be Done?" *Federal Probation*, 20 (September 1956).

need not necessarily have been on a job from 9 to 5; she may have worked on an afternoon shift or a night shift or for part of the day only. But she has been regularly away from home for several hours a day five to seven days a week, so that her absence is an accepted part of the family routine. An *occasional* worker is one who has been gainfully employed now and then. There has been no fixed pattern in her employment. She has drifted from one job to another with unpredictable frequency, laying off at will and resuming at will. Although it can be surmised that sheer necessity forces some mothers to work regularly in order to supplement an all-too-slender family income, the mother who works sporadically can hardly be looked upon as a "provider" because her earnings cannot regularly be counted upon to prop the family budget.

Turning to an analysis of the illustrative table, we find that it shows, first, that a significantly greater proportion of the mothers of the *non-delinquents* who worked (whether regularly or occasionally) than of those who were housewives neglected to give or provide suitable supervision to their children. Thus entirely apart from the problem of delinquency there is a strong hint that working mothers, at least of low-income groups, are not as conscientious about arranging for the supervision of their children as are those who remain at home. Secondly, the illustrative table shows that supervision of those children who actually became *delinquent* was far less suitable on the part of working mothers (whether they were employed regularly or occasionally) than on the part of the mothers who were housewives. Thirdly, from the column labeled *Difference,* it is learned that a boy who is carelessly supervised and who has a mother who is of the kind who works occasionally is far more likely to become a delinquent than is the poorly supervised son of a mother who does not go to work.

50. RELIGIOUS CONTROL AND DELINQUENT BEHAVIOR

THOMAS M. GANNON

THE EXAMINATION OF THE EFFECTS OF religion on individuals and groups, as well as the specific relationship of religion to delinquency and crime, has long intrigued social scientists. Probably no subject is mentioned more often in discussions of delinquent behavior.[1] Unfortunately, these discussions have shed little light on what the impact of religion is or can be in rehabilitating the offender or in preventing deviance. Part of the difficulty, as Martin and Fitzpatrick indicate, is a lack of agreement on defining religion.[2] Is religion to be identified by church affiliation or by observable religious practice, or does not religion penetrate beyond mere statements of membership or attendance into intensity of a person's commitment to religious belief and practice as they relate to his behavior?[3] There is also the dispute whether religion transcends society defining what society's ultimate values are, or whether, as Durkheim thought, religion is simply the projection onto the plane of the sacred of the natural values already inherent in society.[4]

▶SOURCE: "Religious Control and Delinquent Behavior," *Sociology and Social Research* (July, 1967), 51:418-431. Reprinted by permission.

[1] One of the earliest statements on the question was offered by the French philosopher, M. DeBaets: "Now, go to the poor and unhappy, and ask them what prevents them from quickly slipping downhill into crime, and you will find in their mouths the expression, naive but strong, of the idea of duty; and this idea of duty you will find precisely and clearly only in that submission to an absolute, incontestable, unconditioned authority, that of God." (*Les influences de la misère sur la criminalite*, Paris: Grand, 1895, 18-20). See also, Raffaele Garofalo, *Criminology* (Boston: Little, Brown, and Co., 1914), 142; E. J. Cooley, *Probation and Delinquency* (New York: Thomas Nelson and Sons, 1927), 14.

[2] John M. Martin and Joseph P. Fitzpatrick, *Delinquent Behavior* (New York: Random House, 1964), 91. See also, Thomas F. O'Dea, *The Sociology of Religion* (Englewood Cliffs, New Jersey: Prentice-Hall, Inc., 1966, 11-12.

[3] Cf. Gordon W. Allport, *The Nature of Prejudice* (Garden City, New York: Doubleday and Co., Inc., 1958), 420-25. In identifying the relationship of religion to prejudice, Allport indicates that most studies were really measuring historical background, ethnic characteristics, family traditions, etc., rather than specifically religious influence. He insists that the significant variable is not religious affiliation or religious practice, but the quality of religious commitment. The person of deep spiritual motivation was not prejudiced, while the person who clung to religious symbols and practices for personal security generally was. Charles Glock and Rodney Stark's more recent study, *Christian Beliefs and Anti-Semitism* (New York: Harper and Row, 1966), has been criticized precisely for having failed to take into account the "quality of commitment" Allport insisted upon. This distinction is important in discussions of the relation of religion to delinquency, as will become evident later in this paper.

[4] Cf. Emile Durkheim, *The Elementary Forms of Religious Life* (New York: Collier Books, 1961); also *Moral Education* (New York: The Free Press, a

In terms of the relationship between religion and delinquent behavior, some writers have asserted that religion is the most vital influence in developing the character of youth and, if delinquency takes place, the most effective means for reforming the young offender.[5] Other sociologists have taken the position that because of the insincerity of church leaders, stringent laws imposed by the church, the ethnocentrism that evolves from denominationalism, and the identification of the church with the power structure of society, religion provokes and facilitates delinquent behavior.[6]

A major factor hindering the resolution of these controversies has been the lack of empirical evidence. What is needed are studies which discriminate between religion and such variables as social class or cultural background, and studies which attempt to detail the quality of a person's religious commitment, his religious practice in matters other than mere Church attendance, and his religious values as these relate to his everyday behavior.

METHOD

The present study focuses on this second area of religious commitment and values in the attitudes and behavior of a group of officially labeled, but not institutionalized, delinquents. The findings are based on questionnaires and interviews with a random sample of Catholic boys drawn from among those processed by the Intake Department of the juvenile detention home in Cook County, Illinois (the Chicago area).[7]

Given the paucity of available data, the study design involved an essentially exploratory analysis of religious influence patterns. The research aims were threefold. (1) to select a sample of boys who had been officially judged delinquent but not yet formally placed in a correctional setting; (2) to relate patterns of religious influence to the group's attitudes and behavior; (3) to gain insight into the ways in which religion exercised or did not exercise influence.

The study was concerned with specific attitudes, values, and religious practices, not merely with general religious orientation; thus, the sample was restricted to a single religious denomination, and it was decided to select a group of more serious

---

Division of the Macmillan Co., 1961), 102. For a more detailed discussion of religion as transcendent vis-a-vis social values, see, J. V. Langmead Casserley, *Morals and Man in the Social Sciences* (New York: Longmans, Green, and Co., 1951).

[5] For example, Cooley, *op. cit.*, 14; John E. Coogan, "Religion and the Criminologist," *American Catholic Sociological Review*, 6 (October, 1945), 154–59; "The Myth Mind in an Engineer's World," *Federal Probation*, 16 (March, 1952), 26–30; Mary Hronek, "An Experiment in Penetrating the Spiritual Milieu of the Juvenile Delinquent," *Religious Education*, 50 (1955), 98; William C. Kvaraceus, *The Community and the Delinquent* (New York: World Book, Co., 1954), 408; Robert Lee, "The Church and the Problem of Delinquency," *Religious Education*, 52 (1957), 125–29; Martin H. Neumeyer, *Juvenile Delinquency in Modern Society* (Princeton, New Jersey: D. Van Nostrand, Co., 1961), 236–37; Robert and Muriel Webb, "How Churches Can Help in the Prevention and Treatment of Juvenile Delinquency," *Federal Probation*, 21 (December, 1957), 22.

[6] For example, Cesare Lombroso, *Crime: Its Causes and Remedies* (Boston: Little, Brown, and Co., 1918), 144; Walter C. Reckless and Napheus Smith, *Juvenile Delinquency* (New York: McGraw-Hill Book Co., 1932), 151; Harry Elmer Barnes and Negley K. Teeters, *New Horizons in Criminology* (Englewood Cliffs, New Jersey: Prentice-Hall, Inc., 1951), 184; Sophia M. Robinson, *Juvenile Delinquency: Its Nature and Control* (New York: Henry Holt and Co., 1960), 164; Donald R. Taft, *Criminology* (New York: The Macmillan Co., 1956), 278; Milton L. Barron, *The Juvenile in Delinquent Society* (New York: Alfred A. Knopf, 1954), 169–70; Paul W. Tappan, *Juvenile Delinquency* (New York: McGraw-Hill Book Co., 1949), 518.

[7] As a result of the over-crowded conditions at the detention home, the county established the Intake Department in 1937 for the explict purpose of screening each child's need for detention, and whenever possible, of providing alternatives to detention. Actually, detention follows for slightly over one-half of the Intake referrals. In 1955–57, for instance, the total male admissions in the Intake Department averaged 8,218. Of these, 53.2 percent were transferred to the detention home itself prior to their court hearing.

offenders.[8] The Intake Department was chosen as the location of the study because it offered an accessible group which would include the more serious delinquents, and at the same time, provide a minimally institutionalized setting. The boys were interviewed on the day of their arrival before any decision was made either to release them to parental custody or to retain them in the adjacent detention home to await a delinquency hearing in the Family Court.

It was impossible to interview all the delinquent Catholic boys received during the period allotted for the study. There was a continual flow of youngsters to be processed, and no one could predict how many boys would be brought in on a given day. Most of the delinquents were fourteen to sixteen years old. During the initial pilot study it became apparent that the boys in this age bracket possessed more defined attitude and behavior patterns than the younger boys. Thus, the sample was limited to Catholic boys, fourteen to sixteen years old; every second boy, as the names appeared on the admission list, was interviewed, comprising a random sample of 150 delinquents out of 290 cases admitted during the same period (51.7 percent).

Since no satisfactory method existed for measuring the items as we conceived them, a specific instrument was devised for the study. After pretesting for reliability, the final questionnaire involved items dealing with the delinquent's social and religious background, religious beliefs, values, and practices, related attitudes toward stealing, sex, fighting, and peer-group values, as well as L. L. Thurstone's standardized "Scale of Attitudes Toward God—Form D." The administration of the questionnaire was followed by an in-depth interview lasting about one hour. These interviews served more to interpret the data of the questionnaires than to provide additional quantitative information.

FINDINGS

In the broad sense, delinquency is one result of the inability of family, school, church, police, and other adult-managed groups to communicate to youngsters how society thinks they ought to behave and to induce them to conform to these expectations. Since religion is only one instrument of social control, it is important at the outset to view the present delinquent sample in relation to this larger context of controls before narrowing our analysis to religion.

Family and Environmental Control. The majority of the delinquents studied (67.3 percent) came from the lower socio-economic strata as measured by Hollingshead's "Two-Factor Index of Social Position." Half of them (50.7 percent) were intermediate children in medium-sized families, while 25.3 percent were the oldest children. The theory that there is a close association between physically or legally broken homes and delinquency was supported not by its incidence within the sample (41.3 percent), but by the almost doubled proportion of broken homes as compared with the national average.[9] The number of employed mothers (53.3 percent) was also higher than the national average.

On the level of internal family relationships, the delinquents felt that their parents were generally happy, fair in their regulations and discipline—except with regard to choice of companions. Correlatively, the

---

[8] It seemed desirable to focus attention on the more serious delinquent in order to obtain a group that, in terms of their public behavior, most clearly cuts against both the expectations of the larger society and their church. There is danger that if the group contained mostly occasional offenders, it would be even more difficult to sort out patterns of religious influence and control.

[9] See, Gordon H. Barker, "Family Factors in the Sociology of Juvenile Delinquency," *Journal of Criminal Law and Criminology*, 30 (January-February, 1940), 681–91; Sheldon and Eleanor Glueck, *Unraveling Juvenile Delinquency* (New York: Commonwealth Fund, 1950), 123–25; F. Ivan Nye, *Family Relationships and Delinquent Behavior* (New York: John Wiley and Sons, 1958).

parents' regulations on companions, as reported by the group, were less strict than those regarding curfew and church attendance. The data reveal that the boys seldom sought advice or information from their parents, especially in religious matters. Still, over half the group (52.4 percent) felt that their parents knew a great deal about religion. The point seems to be that the delinquent rarely thought about religion or, when he did, he did not feel there was any need to question or discuss it.

Since the entire sample was within the required school age, virtually all the boys attended school during the academic year. Almost one-third of them (32.7 percent), however, were enrolled in one of the "continuation" schools in the city demanding only one day of attendance per week. It is fair to assume that these boys will drop from school at the end of their sixteenth year. More to the point within the context of social control, almost half of the group (47 percent) reported they had attended school in three to five communities; over a third (34.7 percent) reported attendance in more than five communities. Over three-fourths of the boys (77 percent) had received some formal Catholic education, and 67.2 percent had attended a total of three to five different schools. The average number of years at a Catholic school for the entire sample was 3.5, and this usually in the primary grades.

Most of the delinquents had at least three contacts with the police in terms of station arrests; 43.2 percent had previously been processed by the Intake Department, and about one-third (32.2 percent) had experience in a correctional institution.

Religious Control Factors. Turning to specifically religious variables, we begin with the factor of church attendance. For Catholic adolescents, regular attendance at Sunday Mass is probably most directly related to their religious behavior, especially in view of the strict rule of the church regarding it. Parents and other adults provide the models in this instance, and when control is exercised, one would expect it to be in the direction of conformity to the church's regulation.

As is clear from Table I, although most of the parents were Catholic (80 percent of the mothers, 67 percent of the fathers), they did not offer conforming models of regular church attendance. It is surprising that the delinquents should be more church-going than their parents, with over half the group claiming Mass attendance once or twice a month and just over one-quarter saying that they went to church every Sunday.

More crucial than attendance figures would be whether or not the values generated in the delinquent by his parents' regulations are more influential than their conduct. In this connection we find that among the delinquents who attended church every week 63 percent have parents who were equally faithful to their obligations, while among the delinquents who seldom or never went to church only one-third had parents who set this example. Yet in

Table I. *Parental and Personal Church Attendance as Reported by the Delinquents*

Church Attendance	Mothers (N = 120)	Fathers (N = 101)	Delinquents (N = 150)
	Percent	Percent	Percent
Never	10.7	25.3	12.2
Once or twice a year	14.6	17.4	8.0
Once or twice a month	26.7	28.0	52.7
Every Sunday	48.0	29.3	27.1

both instances, the majority of parents (91.2 percent and 82.5 percent, respectively) told their children that they ought to attend church. Interestingly, over three-fourths of the boys themselves (77.2 percent) felt they also should attend church every Sunday; 13.8 percent were uncertain, and only nine percent felt they should not attend.

Second only to church attendance as a basic indicator of Catholic worship and belief is the reception of Holy Communion. Over a third of the group (38.7 percent) reported that they received Communion about every two or three months, with a slightly larger number (41.3 percent) seldom, if ever, receiving. Generally, a lower frequency of Eucharistic reception was expected; as other studies have shown, the normal communion rate among practicing Catholics is usually less than their rate of church attendance.[10]

When asked how often they prayed, 40.1 percent said they prayed often, and only four boys reported that they never prayed. The reason given for praying by most of the group (59.3 percent) was the need they felt for help and guidance. The second reason, lagging for behind the first, was the desire for forgiveness (20.7 percent). As would be expected, more boys prayed since they had gotten into trouble than before. Probing to test the intensity of the delinquent's experience of prayer, the question was asked whether they ever made up their own prayers, ever just "talked things over" with God. The largest number (48.3 percent) said they did so every now and then, while about the same number of boys reported they often prayed spontaneously as the number saying they never prayed (24.5 percent and 27.2 percent). The fact that over half the group indicated they were not taught to pray at home supports the pattern beginning to emerge that these boys had parents who felt strongly that their children should go to church on Sundays, but this was practically all the religion they taught them.

At the root of one's religious experience is the particular concept a person has of God. For the adolescent of sixteen years, Gesell, Ilg, and Ames found that

> Sixteen shows belief in a divinity more than at any preceding age. The great majority . . . believe in some sort of power greater than man. But the Deity is conceived as being less human-like in form than earlier. Some define God simply as "a spirit," but the largest number give a more complex definition, involving some kind of power, force, feeding, "intangible Being" or "something eternal."[11]

Since the pilot study indicated that a direct question about the delinquent's concept of God was too ambiguous and misleading to require answer in writing, the question was asked in the interview. Our findings square exactly with those of Gesell, Ilf, and Ames. None of the boys in the sample expressed an initial idea of God as a person, or as one who is personally interested in them individually.

To probe the delinquent's idea of God further we employed the Thurstone scale for measuring one's sense of the reality of God. According to the usages of the scale, a favorable attitude is indicated by a low numerical score. As Table II indicates, the majority of the present samples (69 percent) showed positive attitudes toward God, 12 percent were noncommittal, while 19 percent revealed a negative attitude. The mean score of the group was 4.2, meaning that, as a whole, the group was "slightly affected by the idea of God," only one level above the noncommittal.[12]

---

[10] Cf. Joseph H. Fichter, "The Marginal Catholic," *Social Forces*, 32 (1953), 167–73; Joseph B. Schuyler, *Northern Parish* (Chicago: Loyola University Press, 1960), 197–215, 230.

[11] Arnold Gesell, Francis L. Ilg, and Louise B. Ames, *Youth: The Years from Ten to Sixteen* (New York: Harper and Brothers, Inc., 1956), 502.

[12] Cf. Albert K. Cohen, *Deinquent Boys* (New York: The Free Press, a Division of the Macmillan Co., 1955), 127–37; James F. Short, Jr. and Fred L. Strodtbeck, *Group Processes and Gang Delinquency* (Chicago: University of Chicago Press, 1965), 47–76.

Table II. The Delinquents' Attitude Toward God

Attitude Score		(N = 150)
		Percent
0–2.9	(Strong religious attitude toward God)	32.0
3.0–3.9	(Definite recognition of God affecting conduct)	20.0
4.0–4.9	(Slightly affected by idea of God)	17.3
5.0–5.9	(Noncommital, neutral, or agnostic attitude)	12.0
6.0–6.9	(Disbelief but attitude not yet strongly set)	8.0
7.0–7.9	(Definite denial of God influencing conduct)	2.7
8.0–11.0	(Strong atheistic attitude)	8.0

Religious Attitudes in Practice. Given the level of religious commitment described above, it is important to ask how the delinquents scored on other questions of belief and what their response was to attitude and behavior questions related to religious commitment. Four specific areas were investigated; sex, stealing, fighting, and peer-group relations.

None of the boys in the present study showed that they were ignorant of the church's position on sex; of the total number, 63.4 percent agreed with the church's regulations, while over one-third (36.6 percent) thought the church's position was too strict. A slightly different pattern emerges, however, when we compare the boys' attitude toward sex and their reported sexual practices. The most common practice is masturbation, with well over half the group (60.7 percent) admitting frequent masturbation, even despite their apparently negative attitudes towards the practice (58.7 percent strongly negative, 28.7 percent mostly negative). Formal homosexuality and "gang sex parties" were more infrequent, with 83.5 percent reporting they had never participated in them. Sexual intercourse was more widespread, with over half the group (54.2 percent) saying they had performed the act at least twice, although habitual intercourse was low in comparison with masturbation.

Table III illustrates the lack of consistency between moral attitudes and sexual practices. Even though the majority of those strongly opposed to homosexuality, masturbation, and extra-marital intercourse indulged in the practice only once or twice or not at all, the number of those reporting frequent practice is high, especially when all of these delinquents expressed strong negative attitudes toward the same actions.

The second item tested was the delinquent's attitude toward stealing. Only a small fraction of the group felt that stealing was all right, and the majority showed little hesitation in establishing the rightness or wrongness of the act. But when reporting actual stealing experiences, most of the group (68.7 percent) indicated they had stolen items on several occasions, ranging in value from $5 to $50. The inconsistency becomes clearer when we select those who "mostly" or "totally" disapproved of stealing and compare these attitudes with their practice. Of the 86.7 percent who generally disapproved of stealing, 30.8 percent had stolen items worth from $5 to $50 several times, and over one-third (36.9 percent) had stolen items worth over $50 several times. Over half the group (58.9 percent) stated they would not hesitate to "borrow" a car and have done so with some regularity.

The question of gang fighting presents a more complicated phenomenon in view of the differing patterns of legitimate and imagined defensive fighting and sheer aggressive warfare. It interests us here precisely as it reveals a general attitude of respect for the dignity, rights, and well being of others. The reported attitude of the delinquents here followed the trend of the sex and stealing attitudes. Over three-fourths of the boys said it was certainly wrong to fight or to beat someone up if "you wanted to get something" or "just wanted to get even." Understandably, most of the group

Table III. *Sexual Attitudes and Practices Reported by the Delinquents (Percent)*

Specific Sexual Practice	Those Who "Mostly" or "Completely" Disagreed wtih the Specific Practice (N = 150)	The Reported Practice of Those Whose Attitudes Were Strongly Negative Toward the Practice		
		Never	A Few Times	A Number of Times
Homosexuality	93.1	90.3	6.0	4.0
Masturbation	92.0	16.3	24.6	59.1
Illicit intercourse	62.6	53.2	20.3	26.5

felt is was all right to fight to defend oneself or the group. The practices of the group generally conformed to these values, with only 22.3 percent reporting they had fought often and over a quarter (26.8 percent) a few times. Very few of the boys fought others merely "for the fun of it," and hardly any had inflicted pain on someone "just to see a person squirm."

The last item concerned the relationship between values operating within the delinquent's own peer group and his own value judgments. Interestingly, the boys felt that their group was generally indifferent to whether they attended church or not and would not make fun of them for participating in church activities. The same thing cannot be said for the group's invitation to delinquency. Here the boys' response shows a stronger commitment to the group and its expectations then to any moral or religious values. While almost three-fourths (72.3 percent) stated that if the group wanted them to go along with something they knew was wrong or sinful they would always or usually refuse, still almost half the boys (48.4 percent) usually or always had gone along when the group went stealing, fighting, or causing general disorder. Table IV provides illustration of some specific patterns of attitude and behavior inconsistency. In the light of studies of gang delinquency, these findings were to be expected, but they only partially explain the inconsistency between the moral and religious values the delinquents proclaim and the ones they actually live by.

DISCUSSION

In light of the above findings, certain patterns begin to emerge regarding the relation between religion and delinquency which raise important questions about the concept of religion as a social control.

Even if it is fair to assume that delinquency is the result of a breakdown or absence of social controls, it is simply false to say that these boys have no interest in religion. Over half the group attended church; frequently they attended more often than their parents, although parental example is still the most important element in frequent attendance. Most of the group felt they ought to go to church every Sunday.

The scores on the Thurstone scale show a slight, marginal commitment to religious belief and values. In this the delinquents share the same attitudes they report for their comrades, and, it would seem, show little difference from nondelinquents in their attitude toward God.[13] In terms of religious practice, there seems to be no

---

[13] Using a similar Thurstone scale, Middleton and Wright found in studying a delinquent and nondelinquent group that both samples showed a positive belief in God—two levels above a neutral attitude on the scale. Interestingly, the nondelinquents were more favorable toward the law and the church than the delinquents, but there was no difference in their attitudes toward the reality of God. Cf. Warren C. Middleton and Robert R. Wright, "A Comparison of a Group of Ninth and Tenth Grade Delinquents and Non-Delinquent Boys and Girls on Certain Attitude Scales," *Journal of Genetic Psychology*, 58 (March, 1941), 149.

Table IV. *Sample Items Regarding Attitudes of the Group Versus Individual Response (Percent)*

Attitude Statement (N = 150)	Always	Usually	Seldom	Never
Have you ever stopped doing something/ refused that you knew was wrong or was a sin?	24.0	37.0	30.8	8.2
If the fellows wanted you to go along with them in doing something wrong, would you refuse?	24.3	47.0	23.0	4.7
Have you ever gone against your group because they wanted you to do something wrong or "sinful"?	10.7	33.3	38.7	17.3
If the fellows wanted you to go stealing with them, would you refuse?	9.4	17.0	63.6	11.0
If the fellows wanted you to go fighting with them, would you go along?	38.4	42.0	12.6	7.0

conflict arising from a type of "dual allegiance" of the boy of his own group and the church. The data suggest, in other words, that religious commitment as expressed by this group has controlling influence only if supported by other factors more immediately crucial to the delinquent.

Nevertheless, with the exception of car-theft, the delinquents have no doubt about the morality of their actions, the sin factor involved, and the apparent betrayal of their religious values. On tests of religious and moral orthodoxy the group revealed a basic theoretical knowledge of the doctrines of their faith, except for their lack of awareness of God as a person who is interested in them individually.[14]

Regarding the inconsistency revealed in the data between the boys' reported religious values and related behavior, what is most striking is that this inconsistency did not appear as such to the delinquent. In many ways this lack of tension, or inner conflict, could be seen as a logical consequence of what Becker has termed "commitment by default."[15] This kind of commitment is one that has been made without the realization that it has been made. Or, as Becker points out, it can arise through a series of acts no one of which is crucial, but which taken together constitute for the individual interests of such importance that he is unwilling to lose them. A commitment by default can also arise through an act made by another in my name. The marginal commitment noted above would coincide with Becker's notion both because in the present sample all the boys were born-Catholics whose initial religious commitment was made for them by their parents, and because religion itself, which perhaps not crucially influencing them, is important to these boys and is something they do not want to throw aside.[16] If the delinquent's commitment is such a commitment by default, then there is little reason why tension should arise between the nominal values of religion and the realized values

---

[14] These findings resemble those found in studying another group of delinquents regarding religious attitude and behavior change. Cf. Thomas M. Gannon, S. J., "Religious Attitude and Behavior Changes of Institutional Delinquents," *Sociological Analysis,* forthcoming.

[15] Howard S. Becker, "Notes on the Concept of Commitment," *American Journal of Sociology,* 66 (July, 1960), 38.

[16] Another factor to be considered here is the relationship between the adolescent's concept of God and initial religious commitment, and the stages of adolescent interpersonal growth. Cf. Pierre Babin, *Faith and the Adolescent* (New York: Herder and Herder, 1965), 23–105.

of street life. The former are grasped as true; the latter are experienced as desirable.

Moreover, as Goode has remarked, commitments are social acts which are supported by social rewards and censures.[17] In addition to the delinquent's marginal commitment, the data show that the group associates with adolescents equally apathetic toward religion and is surrounded by generally noncensuring, related outsiders—parents who provide ineffectual conformity models and no priests, religious, or religiously-oriented adults with whom the delinquents have identified.

A final factor involved in this failure to transpose a commitment by default into personal decision would seem to arise from the nature of religious control. Religion exerts its strongest influence by means of the religious experience—the personal, felt, relation of the individual with God. The data reveals no such personally experienced relationship. In a way this is to be expected from ambiguous parental influence, limited formal Catholic education, and negligence in regular religious practice. But what appears missing in the delinquent's attitudes is precisely what is lacking in his total religious orientation. There is little question that the Catholic church has long recognized the functional importance of an underlying experience of religious commitment. It has always been more indulgent to the sinner than to the heretic. And, as the data show, the group's commitment by default was not entirely a matter of "not caring" what the demands of the church were.

The sermon outlines used in the churches during this time, the catechism approach to religion used in the primary grades when the delinquents were in them or later in religious instruction classes—all these stressed an intellectualistic grasp of creed and moral principles. It was almost as if the church were telling these youngsters that once the truth and inevitability of a doctrinal or ethical propostiion were grasped, conformity would follow automatically. Any doubts about these dogmatic propositions were temptations against the faith; deviations from the code, sinful. Although the methods of pulpit and classroom have shifted in very recent years, the attitudes of the delinquents reflect, more accurately than was expected, this previous approach.

At the same time, it would seem that many of the delinquents interviewed tended to conform to the demands of the church insofar as these did not threaten their social role or their self-image Thus, for example, the chance to demonstrate manliness by illicit sex is difficult to pass by, even though they know it is wrong or sinful. Stealing, on the other hand, does not have the same significance, and this difference shows up in their responses. Then, too, many of these youngsters cannot conceive of themselves as worthy of a personalized relationship with God. To them His demands are simply the measure of their shortcomings, and they haven't the optimism or the strength to make a real effort to conform.[18]

This only intensifies the problem of how to raise an initially nominal commitment to the level of experience, self-awareness, and conviction. As Goode has indicated, few if any specific techniques can be used to sanction an individual's failure in emotion alone; the normal techniques of socialization and social control do not aim at

---

[17] William J. Goode, "Norm Commitment and Conformity to Role-Status Obligations," *American Journal of Sociology*, 66 (November, 1960), 246–58.

[18] As Babin has observed, regarding the adolescent one can speak of a sensitive state of conscience, but only with difficulty of a state of religious consciousness. The adolescent profoundly experiences his own personality, his failures, and judgments of the world around him, and he reflects on these experiences. Only when he surpasses the simple and affective "pampering of his ego," and awakens to his own potential and a more objective self image, can genuine religious growth take place. (Cf. Babin, 120.)

action and emotional conformity as separable goals.[19]

CONCLUSIONS

The principal difficulty in assessing the relation between religion and delinquency is similar to that encountered in evaluating any institutional factor. What we are really studying is the problem of human motivation in its relationship to social structure. The futility of mere correlation of statistics is indicated by the tendency to establish relationships between such items as church attendance or religious affiliation and the extent of delinquency.

But the effectiveness of religion depends upon the internalization of standards during the critical formative years of childhood and is developed through close identification with parents, family members, and other significant primary groups. Much of this control is exercised unconsciously and depends largely upon behavioral examples and religious experience rather than on precept. Only later does it reach the level of conscious decision and personal commitment.

If other supporting controlling agencies are missing, this simply means that the church has encountered a difficulty in coping with factors in modern life that tend to neutralize the fundamental tenets of religious teaching. It also means that the church will have to develop a new dimension to its teaching, particularly for the lower class youngster, and that it will have to assume wider community responsibility in communicating its message.

Our findings suggest that if religion is only one instrument of social control, as Martin and Fitzpatrick have pointed out, it is not a necessary one if other techniques can be used to prevent delinquency or to cure it.[20] This is not to say that religion is of little importance. But as long as it is perceived with the context of social control, the relationship of religion to delinquency will not be very different from any other source of motivation and control.

---

[19] Goode, 257.

[20] Martin and Fitzpatrick, 93.

51. MASS MEDIA AND REPORTED DELINQUENT BEHAVIOR: A NEGATIVE CASE

ERDWIN H. PFUHL, JR.

USING A MODIFICATION OF SUTHERLAND'S theory of differential association, the present study is an effort to lend clarity to the unresolved issue of the presumed influence of exposure to mass media on delinquent behavior.

Various writers have made much of this relationship. Whether engaging in speculation or relying on empirical evidence, almost every shade of opinion has been registered. Running throughout this argument are several key elements. First, there is the dispute over whether the media serve as predisposing (i.e., media are viewed as primary causal agents) or precipitating (i.e., the psychological orientation of the subject determines his reaction to media content, thereby reducing media content to the level of secondary cause) agents. Earlier research, principally that of Fenton,[1] Healy,[2] Burt,[3] and Blumer and Hauser,[4] though employing different theoretical viewpoints, tended to favor the predisposing argument. More current research, such as that of Rowland,[5] Lewin,[6] Ricutti,[7] Himmelweit, Oppenheim and Vince,[8] Bailyn,[9] Maccoby,[10] and Riley and Riley,[11] is inclined to the precipitant viewpoint.

The second major element contained in the literature, whether of distant or recent vintage, is the presumption that mass media influence learning and shape behavior. This is evident whether one refers to Fenton's concern with media's promotion of anti-social standards,[12] Healy's reliance

▶SOURCE. Original paper prepared for this book.

---

[1] F. Fenton, *The Influence of Newspaper Presentations Upon the Growth of Crime and Other Anti-Social Activity* (Chicago: University of Chicago Press, 1911).

[2] W. Healy, *The Individual Delinquent* (Boston: Little, Brown and Co., 1915).

[3] C. Burt, *The Young Delinquent* (New York: D. Appleton Co., 1925).

[4] H. Blumer and P. Hauser, *Movies, Delinquency and Crime* (New York: Macmillan Co., 1933).

[5] H. Rowland, "Radio Crime Dramas," *Educational Research Bulletin*, Vol. XXIII (November 15, 1944), pp. 210–217.

[6] H. S. Lewin, "Facts and Fears About the Comics," *The Nation's Schools*, Vol. LII (July, 1953), pp. 46–48.

[7] E. A. Ricutti, "Children and Radio: A Study of Listeners and Non-Listeners to Various Types of Radio Programs in Terms of Selected Ability, Attitudes, and Behavior Measures," *Genetic Psychology Monographs*, Vol. XLIV (August, 1951), pp. 69–143.

[8] H. T. Himmelweit, A. N. Oppenheim, and P. Vince, *Television and the Child* (London: Oxford University Press, 1958).

[9] L. Bailyn, "Mass Media and Children: A Study of Exposure Habits and Cognitive Effects," *Psychological Monographs*, Vol. LXXIII, No. 1 (1958), pp. 1–48.

[10] E. E. Maccoby, "Television: Its Impact on School Children," *Public Opinion Quarterly*, Vol. XV (Fall, 1951), pp. 421–444.

[11] M. W. Riley and J. W. Riley, Jr., "A Sociological Approach to Communication Research," *Public Opinion Quarterly*, Vol. XV (Fall, 1951), pp. 444–460.

[12] F. Fenton, *op. cit.*

on the process of projection,[13] Burt's notion of imitation,[14] or Blumer and Hauser's reference to suggestion.[15] Moreover, this reliance on an at least implicit presumption of learning is present whether the author is inclined to the predisposing or the precipitant point of view. What is lacking is a theoretical framework which would, if the facts were available, permit a meaningful, substantive interpretation of the facts.

Related to this is the need to explore the *causal nexus* whereby exposure to mass media may be expected to result in learning—particularly the roles, attitudes, rationalizations and techniques of delinquent behavior. The need for such an orientation has been pointed out by Merton and others.[16] It has been suggested that more than a simplified consideration of "cause" must be employed in assessing the mechanism by which media influence behavior. More is needed than a simple recount of the content of these media and a demonstration of the similarity (or lack thereof) between their content and the behavior under consideration. It is the purpose of this research to effect a theoretical framework that will simultaneously accommodate both the predisposing and precipitant arguments and provide a substantive link between the causal variable and its presumed effect.

Finally, a major element in previous research is the tendency to rely on the ranks of "official" delinquents for case subjects. The fact that such a procedure constitutes a bias needs little elaboration.[17] Not the least of the problems engendered by the use of such subjects was recognized by Burt. In commenting on those who criticize the movies, Burt noted ... perhaps none is so eager to [condemn the cinema] as the young culprit himself, who ... sees in such derivation of his deeds a chance to deflect blame and attention from his own moral laxity to that of the producer of films."[18] More recently, Halloran made the same point.[19]

It is with respect to the above considerations that the present study represents a contrast. First, a principal working assumption of this effort will be that sociopsychological conditions of the audience underlie its receptivity to the behavioral cues presented by the media. That is, rather than presuming that audience receptivity stems solely from personal traits, media influence will be viewed as a consequence of the interplay of sociological factors. Learning is a consequence not simply of what is presented, but is also related to those things which compel attention.[20]

Second, unlike previous research, subjects will be drawn from a noninstitutionalized delinquent population, thereby eliminating the problem of subject bias and providing the added advantage of demonstrating concurrence between the independent and dependent variables under study.

THEORY

The theory of differential association, concerned with the transmission of behavioral patterns, provides a theoretical baseline for consideration of the present problem.[21] Accordingly, one acquires an

---

[13] W. Healy, *op. cit.*, p. 339.

[14] C. Burt, *op. cit.*, p. 137.

[15] H. Blumer and P. Hauser, *op. cit.*, pp. 27 ff.

[16] R. Merton, *Mass Persuasion* (New York: Harper and Brothers, 1946), pp. 24–25; J. T. Klapper, *The Effects of Mass Communications* (Glencoe: Free Press, 1960), pp. 159–160.

[17] J. F. Short, Jr. and F. I. Nye, "Reported Behavior as a Criterion of Deviant Behavior," *Social Problems*, Vol. V (Winter, 1957), pp. 207–213.

[18] C. Burt, *The Young Delinquent* (4th ed.; London: University of London Press, 1944), p. 143.

[19] J. D. Halloran, "Television and Violence," in O. Larsen, editor, *Effects of Mass Media and Violence* (Harper and Row, 1968), p. 143.

[20] W. Schramm, "The Effects of Mass Communication: A Review," *Journalism Quarterly* (December, 1949), cited in, G. Lundberg, C. Schrag, and O. Larsen, *Sociology* (rev. ed., New York: Harper and Brothers, 1958), p. 456 ff.

[21] E. H. Sutherland and D. Cressy, *Principles of Criminology*, 7th ed., (New York: J. B. Lippincott Co., 1966), Chapter 4.

excess of either law-abiding or law-violating definitions of situations as a consequence of the varying content of one's learning experience. In view of the breadth of opportunity for exposure to both of these sets of definitions, there exists a need to specify the conditions under which one acquires (learns) one set of definitions as opposed to the other. Partial clarification of this matter lies in Sutherland's notion of differential organization by which he sought to account for variations in crime rates. However, even when accompanied by differential organization, differential association has been less than optimally successful in explaining how individuals acquire criminal and delinquent roles.[22] On this basis a reformulation of differential association, linking it to modern learning theory, would seem to be called for.[23]

Reduced to its basic elements, the process of association consists of *identification* and *reinforcement*. That is, the learning of criminal or delinquent roles, values, techniques and rationalizations is not the result of association in the sense of personal affiliation, but (as Glaser indicates) is the result of identification with group definitions.[24] However, in the absence of reinforcement, identification may be expected to be shallow and transitory.[25] It is the concept of reinforcement with which we shall be primarily concerned.

Based on Hull's theory, learning is need-oriented in the sense that it is preceded by drive or motivation. The direction that learning takes depends on the actor's milieu and the relevant cues it provides. When the organism responds to cues in a way that produces change in the preceding state of bodily tension (a process of drive reduction via rewards), learning may be said to have occurred.[26] While an oversimplification of the learning process, the significance of this for explaining the previously mentioned persuasive effect of mass communication and the learning of criminal and delinquent roles may be substantial.

Speculatively, this formulation may lend itself to the present problem in that mass media contain cues to which the actor may respond and thereby achieve reinforcement or drive reduction. Thus, the learning of deviant roles is not the result of association or identification as these terms are ordinarily understood, but is the result of the reinforcing or need satisfying capacity of these behavioral responses. It is on the basis of such differential reinforcing properties and the sociological conditions in which they operate that we may explain why learning variously takes a deviant or nondeviant direction.

The capacity of inanimate objects (mass communications) to serve as reinforcing agents and the method by which this may

---

[22] R. L. Burgess and R. L. Akers, "A Differential Association-Reinforcement Theory of Criminal Behavior," *Social Problems,* Vol. XIV, No. 2 (Fall, 1966), pp. 128 ff.

[23] Although predating the reformulation of the Sutherland theory by Burgess and Akers, the theoretical considerations which follow bear resemblance to the Burgess and Akers propositions. See *ibid.*; also see E. H. Pfuhl, Jr., *The Relationship of Mass Media to Reported Delinquent Behavior* (unpublished Ph.D. dissertation, Washington State University, 1960), Chapter 2.

[24] D. Glaser, "Criminality Theories and Behavioral Images," *American Journal of Sociology,* Vol. LXI, No. 5 (March, 1956), pp. 433 ff.

[25] Burgess and Akers, *op. cit.,* pp. 143–144.

[26] The concept of reinforcement refers strictly to the process of drive reduction as indicated by Clark Hull. Drive reduction may be translated into the more general term "need satisfaction" as this latter relates to the basic postulate of Hull's learning theory. The fundamental elements of the learning process, according to Hull, are: drive, response, cue, and reward. Drives are stimuli which impel action, the responses are elicited by cues which, in turn, determine when, where, and which response one will make. The operation of drives brings about responses to certain cues. Learning such responses will occur if they are rewarded. "Rewards produce reduction in drives; drive reduction is, in fact, what makes them rewarding." See E. R. Hilgard, *Theories of Learning* (New York: Appleton-Century-Crofts, Inc., 1948), pp. 76–79.

occur must be considered to achieve theoretical sufficiency.[27] It is contended here that media may serve in this capacity and thereby promote learning not through *real* rewards but through *anticipated* rewards. Schramm has noted that learning from mass media hinges in part on the degree to which one may *anticipate* rewards. These rewards "... may be immediate or remote, real or psychic, ... a release from tension, the kind of prestige that comes from belonging to an in-group, or information that will be useful in future problem situations." [28]

In summary, the direction (content) of learning is seen as a consequence of the available cues in one's milieu and their relative reinforcing capacity. Such reward or drive reduction is likely effected primarily through intimate affiliation with reference groups but, secondarily, may result from expected or fancied rewards or the relating of the individual to the characters and situations being portrayed in the mass media.

It follows from the above that *in and of themselves* mass media are relatively unimportant influences in the initiation (predisposing) of delinquent behavior. Any influence they might have would stem from a lack of need satisfaction (reinforcement) in the primary realms of human interaction—family, peer group, school, for example—and the seeking after alternative sources of satisfaction. Thus, any relationship between mass media and delinquent behavior would be viewed as spurious in the sense that these variables are hypothesized to be related only through the operation of the contingent factor of need deprivation. It remains to consider the role of need satisfaction/deprivation in the etiology of delinquency. Two considerations will be treated: family dislocation and psychosomatic illness.

The role of need deprivation in the etiology of delinquency has been frequently stressed.[29] It has been given special emphasis with regard to deprivation of needs within the family circle, involving physical, economic, or emotional rejection among its members, culture conflict, intergenerational rifts, or the more classically defined "broken home." Failure to achieve need satisfaction within the bounds of the legitimized family group—needs such as adequacy, worthiness, gratification, security [30]—may result in nonlegitimate efforts to obtain satisfaction, including a resort to delinquency. However, not all need deprivation results in aggressive or antisocial behavior. In discussing psychosomatic illness, Sontag indicates that unmet needs may manifest themselves in psychosomatic complaints of either a passive or an aggressive type. In the passive pattern is the conforming, shy, regressive or compulsive type of behavior, while the aggressive mode results in expression of hostility due to frustration in the striving for need satisfaction.[31]

In summary, it has been suggested that if a statistical relationship between exposure to crime themes in the mass media and delinquency is to be understood in substantive and causal terms, it may be done on the basis of a reconceptualization of the theory of differential association.

---

[27] The rleative ineffectiveness of mass media to function in this capacity has been noted both by Sutherland and Cressy and Burgess and Akers. See Sutherland and Cressy, *op. cit.*, p. 81; Burgess and Akers, *op. cit.*, pp. 139–140.

[28] Schramm, *op. cit.*, p. 458.

[29] J. H. S. Bossard, *The Sociology of Child Development* (New York: Harper and Brothers, 1948), pp. 334–339; F. I. Nye, *Family Relationships and Delinquent Behavior* (New York: John Wiley and Sons, Inc., 1958), p. 8; W. and J. McCord, *Origins of Crime* (New York: Columbia University Press, 1959), pp. 100, 104, and 116; A. Cohen, *Delinquent Boys: The Culture of the Gang* (Glencoe: Free Press, 1955), Chapters 3 and 4.

[30] H. C. Bredemeir and J. Toby, *Social Problems in America* (New York: John Wiley and Sons, 1960), Chapter 1.

[31] L. W. Sontag, "The Genetic Differences in Psychosomatic Patterns in Childhood," *American Journal of Orthopsychiatry*, Vol. XX, No. 3 (July, 1950), p. 484.

It has also been suggested that such a relationship be examined in the light of contingent conditions, specifically need satisfaction/deprivation, as they affect learning. Thus stated, this theoretical formulation rests on both levels of the person-situation complex.[32] Such considerations provide a clear operational formulation concerning the supposed influence of mass media on behavior.

Based on the foregoing considerations the following hypotheses will be tested:[33]

1. Without controlling other variables, a positive relationship will be found between (1) interest in mass media crime themes and delinquent behavior, and (2) exposure to mass media crime themes and delinquent behavior.

Following this, and consistent with the theoretical framework, it may be expected that the relationship between the main variables would increase in a positive direction when calculated for those individuals rejecting their parents and remain stable or decrease for those accepting their parents. Accordingly:

2. A higher positive relationship will be found between interest in and exposure to mass media crime themes and delinquent behavior among youth having rejected their parents than among youth not having rejected their parents.

Finally, in terms of the broader context of personal maladjustment, the relationship between the main variables will be calculated when subjects are ranked on the basis of reported psychosomatic complaints. Consistent with the foregoing theoretical considerations, the final hypothesis to be tested is:

3. A higher positive relationship will be found between interest in and exposure to mass media crime themes and delinquent behavior among youth displaying a high degree of psychosomatic complaints than among those youth having few or no psychosomatic complaints.

In addition to the above, other variables will be introduced for purposes of establishing whether they play a role in the mass media-delinquency configuration. These variables are: age and sex of subject, socioeconomic status, area of residence, sibling position, family size, and church attendance of mothers, fathers, and subjects.

METHOD

By means of a systematic random sample, data were gathered from all ninth- through twelfth-grade students in attendance in the high schools of three contiguous communities on the days data were collected. At the time of data collection these communities were in the 10,000 to 40,000 population class. The resulting sample ($N = 792$) consisted of 402 males (51 percent) and 390 females (49 percent).

Using a five-part questionnaire, information was gathered concerning biographical matters, exposure to and interest in mass media dealing with crime themes, parent-child relationships, psychosomatic complaints, and delinquent behavior.

Questions to measure extent of exposure to and interest in comic magazines, radio, motion picture, and television presentations dealing with crime, and to assess the subjects' reading interests of a noncomic type permitted the establishment of 14 separate measures of the independent variable. Response patterns were used to

---

[32] Sutherland and Cressy, *op. cit.*, p. 80.

[33] Chi-square was used in this study to test for the *existence* but not for the degree or directionality of relationships assumed to be present. All statements concerning the significance of differences encountered in this research must therefore be interpreted in light of this fact. Numerous statements are made herein concerning the direction of relationships and are based on the relative frequencies found in the contingency tables. To denote the direction of these relationships, not in a strict mathematical sense, but only as a convenient way of noting the general direction of the association shown in the table, the terms positive and negative are used or implied.

classify subjects into "high," "intermediate," and "low" categories according to their professed interests and frequency of exposure.

Parental rejection, a major contingent condition, was measured by a 22-item Guttman scale, with 11 items concerning each parent. Employing the Cornell and Israel Gamma techniques a Coefficient of Reproducibility of .92 was obtained for the "mother" items and CR of .94 was obtained for the "father" items.[34] Scale types were trichotomized into rejecting, intermediate, and accepting groups for ease of analysis.

The second major contingent variable, psychosomatic complaints, was measured by the Psychosomatic Complaint Inventory developed during World War II for the screening of neurotics from among inductees.[35] Initially composed of 15 items, this instrument was reduced to nine items for boys and 11 items for girls and yielded CR's of .98 and .99, respectively. Subjects were again categorized on the basis of scale type into "high," "moderate," and "low" levels of psychosomatic complaints.

Delinquent behavior was measured by the technique of reported behavior employing a 21-item Guttman scale.[36] Of the initial items, seven yielded a CR of .98 for boys 14 and 15 years of age, and a CR of .97 for boys 16 and 17 years of age.

These same items, when scaled for girls, produced an unduly skewed distribution requiring that they be used in the form of a quasi-scale.

All scales were examined for validity by the method of "internal validity."[37] In addition, the method of "known groups" was used to check the validity of the delinquency scale.[38] In each case the criteria of validity were satisfied. The psychosomatic complaint inventory satisfied the criterion of face or logical validity. Further, using the technique of "known groups," Guttman and his associates demonstrated the discriminative capacity of these same items.[39] Finally, support for the validity of the Psychosomatic Complaint Inventory derives from reliability tests made using other samples.[40]

In view of the sensitivity of the areas under investigation and to effect the highest possible level of validity in these data, additional extensive precautions were taken to guard against falsification of responses. In assessing the subjects' reported interest in and exposure to mass media crime themes, efforts were made to detect those who would seek to impress the investigator with their virtuosity. Using fictitious book titles and annotations, several titles were included that would have little genuine appeal but that would, if one chose to read them, give the impression of virtuosity. While admittedly arbitrary, it was decided that a questionnaire would be investigated for consistency

---

[34] Scaling was effected by use of the Israel Gamma Image Analysis technique. See M. W. Riley et al., *Sociological Studies in Scale Analysis* (New Brunswick: Rutgers University Press, 1954), Chapter 18.

[35] S. Stouffer et al., *Measurement and Prediction*, Vol. IV of *Studies in Social Psychology in World War II* (4 Vols.; Princeton: Princeton University Press, 1950), Chapter 13.

[36] For an extended treatment of the technique of reported behavior for measuring delinquency among noninstitutionalized subjects and the technical aspects of the specific scale employed in the present research, see: F. I. Nye and J. F. Short, Jr., "Scaling Delinquent Behavior," *American Sociological Review*, Vol. XXII (June, 1956), pp. 326–331; F. I. Nye, *Family Relationships and Delinquent Behavior, op. cit.*, p. 10 ff; and J. F. Short, Jr. and F. I. Nye, "Reported Behavior as a Criterion of Deviant Behavior," *op. cit.*

[37] S. Stouffer et. al., *op. cit.*, p. 57.

[38] F. I. Nye, "The Rejected Parent and Delinquency—Rejoinder," *Marriage and Family Living*, Vol. XXVIII, No. 4 (November, 1956), pp. 299–300.

[39] S. Stouffer et al., *op. cit.*, pp. 494–500.

[40] Ordinarily the terms reliability and validity are kept distinct. However, the relationship between the two is greater than is sometimes realized. Thus, an unreliable measure lacks validity. See: C. Selltiz, et al., *Research Methods in Social Relations* (2d ed. revised; New York: Henry Holt and Co., 1959), p. 178. It is defensible to conclude that a scale with reliability is more likely to have validity than one without reliability. Also, see S. Stouffer et al., *op. cit.*, p. 503.

and perhaps eliminated from this phase of the analysis if four of the seven "trap" titles were chosen as books the subject wished to read. Using this criterion, 44 questionnaires (14 male and 30 female) were eliminated from present consideration.

Such "trap" items were also included in the delinquency and psychosomatic illness checklists. In the former, items concerning disobeying parents and telling lies were included to detect the overconformist who might ignore the universality of at least minimal behavior of that sort and thereby seek to mislead. Oppositely, careful scrutiny was given those who reported themselves as having committed every offense in the checklist to the maximum frequency allowed by the answer categories. It was felt that such a person would have little chance of avoiding institutionalization and, hence, become the subject of intensive scrutiny for determination of honesty and consistency of response.

Finally, two "trap" items were included among the balance of the psychosomatic illness items. These concerned such universal maladies as headcolds and sore throats. It was felt that those who indicated "never" having experienced such conditions deserved extra scrutiny for response consistency and honesty. In all, such precautions, together with problems arising from slow reading, lack of interest, etc., resulted in the total elimination of seven, or about 1 percent, of the 799 questionnaires originally distributed.

Lacking data above the ordinal level of measurement, tests of significance will be limited to chi-square with the level of alpha set at .05. Association will be measured by Contingency Coefficient derived directly from chi-square and corrected according to the method indicated by Peters and Van Voorhis.[41]

TEST RESULTS

To avoid the possibility of accepting spurious relationships, a series of 126 tests were made to determine the influence of the previously mentioned 9 factors on each of the 14 measures that constituted the independent variable. Of the 9 variables investigated, few were found to have an influence sufficient to warrant further concern.

Among males, the factors of sibling position, family size, area of residence (rural or urban), and the frequency of parents' church attendance failed to produce significant differences more frequently than could be expected by chance. According to Davies,[42] in 14 tests employing the 5 percent level of significance, three significant differences may occur 2.6 percent of the time by chance, two significant differences may occur 12.3 percent of the time by chance, and one significant difference may occur 35.9 percent of the time by chance. In none of the fourteen sets of tests mentioned were more than two significant differences found for boys. Therefore, no systematic influence may be attributed to these factors. Age and sex may also be discounted as contributory to spurious relationships due to the determination of delinquency scale positions by age and sex groups taken separately. Thus, for boys, only the factors of subjects' church attendance, yielding four significant differences in 14 tests, and socioeconomic position, yielding six significant differences out of 14 tests, appear as possibly influential factors.

Turning to tests on girls' data, the factors of family size, place of residence, mother's church attendance, and socioeconomic status failed to yield a sufficient number of significant differences to warrant further concern. Eliminating age and sex for the reasons stated above, only birth order, father's frequency of church attend-

---

[41] C. C. Peters and W. R. Van Voorhis, *Statistical Procedures and Their Mathematical Bases* (New York: McGraw-Hill Book Co., 1940), pp. 393–399.

[42] V. Davies, "A Table of the Probability of n Tests Reaching the Five Percent Level of Significance in a Series of m Tests" (unpublished).

ance, and subject's frequency of church attendance resulted in a sufficient number of differences to warrant their being regarded as potentially critical.

Exclusive of the factors of age and sex, preliminary analysis also entailed the investigation of the influence of the same variables on delinquent behavior. Significant differences in delinquency among girls were found in two of the seven areas investigated. Girls who were either the youngest or between the youngest and oldest child in their families displayed significantly more delinquency than did other girls. It was also found that as the frequency of girl's church attendance increased involvement in delinquency decreased.

Among male subjects, three of the seven variables yielded significant differences when cross-tabulated with degree of delinquent behavior. It was found that as frequency of father's, mother's and subject's attendance at church increased delinquent involvement decreased.

In summary, of the test variables investigated, only religious activity (principally of the subjects themselves) appeared to be significantly related in any consistent manner to both major variables. Of 58 significant differences found between the test variables and the independent variable, 21 (or 36.2 percent) were found in the area of religious participation. Other differences were scattered among the remaining variables tested. Investigation of the influence of these test variables on delinquency revealed five significant differences, four (or 80 percent) of which were in these same religious areas. It is thus concluded that with the exception of subject's church attendance, the variables investigated do not constitute a systematic bias that would negate the data of this study. However, when significant differences are found between the main variables, tests will be recalculated holding subject's religious participation constant.

Testing the first hypothesis required cross-tabulating subjects by degree of delinquent involvement and their professed degree of interest in and exposure to crime themes. A total of 28 tests were conducted, 26 being devoted to the four major media and two concerning noncomic literature. The results of these tests are shown in Table I.

As noted in Table I, data for males yielded statistically significant differences in three of 14 tests. In each case boys rated as having high interest in or exposure to these media reported more delinquency than did other boys. Among girls, two of 14 tests revealed significant differences; girls with a high frequency of movie attendance and high exposure to crime comics reported significantly more delinquency than other girls.

These five tests were recalculated holding religious participation constant.[43] Subjects continued to be differentiated by sex. As noted in Tables II and III, two of the three initially significant tests retained significance under these more refined conditions. Males highly exposed to movies and crime comics were found to have a higher rate of delinquency than other boys.

Recalculation of the initially significant tests for girls resulted in no change in the findings. As frequency of motion picture attendance and exposure to crime comics increased, so too did reported delinquency. These data are shown in Table IV and V.

In summary, of 28 initial and five secondary tests of the first hypothesis, four tests were found to be statistically significant. On the basis of these findings, the first hypothesis is held to be untenable (two significant tests out of 14 tests, using

---

[43] Control was effected by a process of subsampling which equalized the distribution of subjects when categorized by "high," "intermediate," and "low" religious participation and arranged, simultaneously, into "high," or "low" interest or exposure categories. Through this process the influence of religious participation was equalized while avoiding the problem of overreduction of sample (and cell value) size. However, this process resulted in unequal N's between the various tests conducted.

Table I. *Tests of the Significance of Differences between Patterns of Interest in and Exposure to Mass Media and Delinquency, by Sex*

Measure of Interest	Boys		Girls	
	P	C [a]	P	C [a]
Frequency of attendance at motion pictures	.001	.29	.05	.21
Favorite type of movie	.10	—	.30	—
Crime movies seen	.01	.24	.20	—
Time spent watching television	.30	—	.90	—
Favorite type of television program	.90	—	.90	—
Regular exposure to TV crime dramas	.20	—	.95	—
Time spent listening to radio	.30	—	.20	—
Favorite type of radio program	.10	—	.30	—
Regular exposure to radio crime programs	.30	—	.30	—
Time spent reading comic magazines	.50	—	.90	—
Exposure to horror comics	.30	—	.10	—
Exposure to crime comics	.90	—	.001	.32
Interest in crime and mystery novels	.01	.23	.50	—
Number of crime and mystery novels read	.30	—	.50	—

[a] C coefficient has been computed only for those items reaching the stipulated level of alpha.

Table II. *Frequency of Movie Attendance by Delinquent Scale Types with Religion Held Constant—Boys*

Rate of Movie Attendance	Delinquent Involvement					
	High		Intermediate		Low	
	No.	Percent	No.	Percent	No.	Percent
High (twice weekly or more)	72	35.8	62	30.8	67	33.3
Low (three times/ month or less)	25	20.3	45	36.6	53	43.1

$\chi^2 = 8.78$; at 2 df, $P < .02$ $\overline{C} = .24$

Table III. *Exposure to Crime Movies by Delinquent Scale Types with Religion Held Constant—Boys*

Exposure to Crime Movies	Delinquent Involvement					
	High		Intermediate		Low	
	No.	Percent	No.	Percent	No.	Percent
High	101	32.3	105	33.5	107	34.2
Low	9	22.5	9	22.5	22	55.0

$\chi^2 = 6.56$; at 2 df, $P < .05$ $\overline{C} = .19$

Table IV. *Frequency of Movie Attendance by Delinquent Scale Types with Religion Held Constant—Girls*

Rate of Movie Attendance	Delinquent Involvement					
	High		Intermediate		Low	
	No.	Percent	No.	Percent	No.	Percent
High (twice weekly or more)	69	31.8	104	47.9	44	20.3
Low (three times/ month or less)	22	19.5	59	52.2	32	28.3

$\chi^2 = 6.402$; at 2 df, P < .05 $\overline{C} = .20$

the .05 level of alpha, could be obtained 12.3 percent of the time by chance). Further evidence for rejecting this hypothesis arises from examination of the pattern of relationships between the main variables in the balance of the tests calculated. Seven of those tests for boys and three of those for girls revealed relationships contrary to the direction stipulated by the first hypothesis. This, together with the paucity of significant findings, necessitates rejection of the first hypothesis.

For purposes of testing the second hypothesis, subjects were grouped into two broad categories: those who rejected their parents and those who accepted their parents. In this process, rejection and/or acceptance of both parents was considered simultaneously due to the reduction of cell values in contingency tables when acceptance and rejection were considered for each parent separately. Simultaneous consideration of both parents was accomplished by broadly grouping subjects according to tercile divisions of previously established scale types. According to this tercile division, subjects could be placed in one of three categories: accepting, intermediate, and rejecting. Taking both parents into account resulted in six combinations. In the present analysis, the four most extreme combinations were employed. Subjects who rejected both parents or who rejected one and ranked "intermediate" for the other were given a classification of rejecting. Those who accepted both parents, or who accepted one and ranked "intermediate" on the other, received a classification of accepting. The remaining combinations were not employed in this analysis. Cross-tabulations were made between subject's parental attitude and degree of delinquent involvement. Results of these tests are shown in Table VI.

Considering male subjects, Table VI reveals that of ten pairs of tests, none revealed statistical significance. Further, regardless of level of significance, only six

Table V. *Exposure to Crime Comics by Delinquent Scale Types with Religion Held Constant—Girls*

Exposure to Crime Comics	Delinquent Involvement					
	High		Intermediate		Low	
	No.	Percent	No.	Percent	No.	Percent
High (30 minutes/day or more)	33	42.9	34	44.2	10	13.0
Low (15 minutes/day or less)	36	22.0	84	51.2	44	26.8

$\chi^2 = 12.965$; at 2 df, P < .01 $\overline{C} = .33$

Table VI. *Tests of the Significance of Differences Between Patterns of Interest in and Exposure to Mass Media and Delinquency by Parental Attitude and Sex*

	Boys				Girls			
	Reject Parents		Accept Parents		Reject Parents		Accept Parents	
Measure of Interest or Exposure	P	$\bar{C}$	P	$\bar{C}$	P	$\bar{C}$	P	$\bar{C}$
Favorite type of movie	.50	—	.90	—	—[a]	—	.90	—
Crime movies seen	.10	—	.90	—	.05	.37	.90	—
Favorite type television program	.90	—	.90	—	.50	—	.20	—
Regular exposure to television crime dramas	.90	—	.90	—	.50	—	.50	—
Favorite type radio program	.90	—	.30	—	.90	—	.30	—
Regular exposure to radio crime programs	—[a]	—	.50	—	.30	—	.99	—
Exposure to horror comics	.50	—	.90	—	.30	—	.01	.48
Exposure to crime and adventure comics	.30	—	.90	—	.20	—	.01	.47
Interest in crime and mystery novels	.50	—	.20	—	.90	—	.50	—
Number of crime and murder mysteries read	.90	—	.99	—	.90	—	.90	—

[a] Chi-square not computed due to small expected frequencies.

tests revealed relationships consistent with the directional nature of the hypothesis. On this basis the second hypothesis is rejected for males.

Among girls, three of 19 tests revealed statistical significance. However, only one of these conformed to the directional nature of the hypothesis. Holding religious participation constant and recalculating the one relevant test resulted in the elimination of the initial statistical significance. On the basis of these findings the second hypothesis is rejected for girls. These data are shown in Tables VII and VIII.

The third and final hypothesis predicted a higher positive relationship between interest in and exposure to mass media crime themes for maladjusted youth than for adjusted youth. Scale types established on the basis of psychosomatic complaints were dichotomized into "high" and "low" categories, designating maladjustment and adjustment, respectively. Cross tabulations were run in the manner described above. The results of these tests are shown in Table IX.

Two of the ten tests calculated for males were found to be statistically significant. In one case, however, that of favorite type of radio program, the relationship was contrary to the directional nature of the hypothesis. That is, non-crime radio programs were more popular among the highly delinquent boys than among those low in delinquency, and little proportional difference existed between the three delinquency groups as to preference for radio crime programs. Thus, of ten tests, only one was supportive of the hypothesis. These data are shown in Table X, where it is noted that boys reporting high psychosomatic complaints and a high interest in crime and mystery novels are significantly more delinquent than boys with a low interest in mystery and crime novels.

Turning to data for females, three of the initial tests yielded statistically sig-

Table VII. *Exposure ot Crime Movies by Delinquent Scale Types—Girls*

Exposure to Crime Movies	Delinquent Involvement					
	High		Intermediate		Low	
	No.	Percent	No.	Percent	No.	Percent
High	41	47.7	36	41.9	9	10.5
Low	4	16.7	17	70.8	3	12.5

$\chi^2 = 7.733$; at 2 df, $P < .05$ $\overline{C} = .37$

nificant results. However, as noted in Table IX, only one of these was in the direction stipulated in the hypothesis.

Overall, then, of twenty pairs of tests, only two were statistically and directionally supportive of the third hypothesis. These two tests were recalculated holding religious participation constant. In these retests the initial level of significance for boys was eliminated and among girls the directional nature of the data was reversed to a degree sufficient to permit retention of statistical significance. These data are shown in Tables XI and XII.

In summary, prior to holding religious participation constant, tests of the third hypothesis yielded two signicant differences in the direction stipulated in the hypothesis. Retesting, holding religious participation constant, led to a reversal of the initial relationships and the elimination of statistical significance consistent with the hypothesis. On this basis the final hypothesis must be rejected.

SUMMARY AND CONCLUSIONS

Employing a reinforcement-learning theory modification of the differential association theory, the present study assumed that *in and of themselves* mass media crime themes play an insignificant role in the genesis of delinquent behavior. It was felt that these media, viewed as cues operating within the milieu of the actor, might interact with other forces and thereby come to be regarded as significant etiological factors. Beginning with this proposition, and the idea that delinquent behavior is learned and need satisfying, it was predicted that for individuals experiencing need deprivation in legitimized settings such media might offer promise of need satisfaction, either immediate or remote, tangible or intangible, by presenting models after which they might pattern their own behavior.

Three hypotheses were subjected to extensive testing. Initial statistically significant differences were further examined holding the factor of frequency of religious

Table VIII. *Exposure to Crime Movies by Delinquent Scale Types with Religion Held Constant—Girls*

Exposure to Crime Movies	Delinquent Involvement					
	High		Intermediate		Low	
	No.	Percent	No.	Percent	No.	Percent
High	41	48.2	36	42.4	8	9.4
Low	4	23.5	12	70.6	1	5.9

$\chi^2 = 4.539$; at 2 df, $P < .20$

Table IX. *Tests of the Significance of Differences between Patterns of Interest in and Exposure to Mass Media and Delinquency by Psychosomatic Complaints and Sex*

	Boys				Girls			
	High Complaints		Low Complaints		High Complaints		Low Complaints	
Measure of Interest or Exposure	P	$\bar{C}$	P	$\bar{C}$	P	$\bar{C}$	P	$\bar{C}$
Favorite type movie	.30	—	.90	—	.30	—	.90	—
Crime movies seen	.30	—	.50	—	.90	—	.05	.28
Favorite type television program	.30	—	.90	—	.50	—	.90	—
Regular exposure to television crime dramas	.20	—	.50	—	.10	—	.20	—
Favorite type radio program	.001	.59	.95	—	.90	—	.50	—
Regular exposure to radio crime programs	.30	—	.50	—	.10	—	.90	—
Exposure to horror comics	.50	—	.30	—	.90	—	.001	—
Exposure to crime and adventure comics	.95	—	.50	—	.01	.54	.20	—
Interest in crime and mystery novels	.01	.39	.40	—	.20	—	.02	.34
Crime and murder mysteries read	.30	—	.50	—	.10	—	.50	—

participation constant. The resulting overall paucity of significant findings, both before and after holding religious participation constant, and the inconsistent directional relationship between the major variables demanded rejection of each hypothesis.

Within the limitations of the present study,[44] these data throw considerable doubt on the notion that mass media dealing with crime and violence are an inducement to criminal and delinquent behavior, or that techniques of criminal behavior displayed in the media will be adopted by youth, thus promoting a delinquent career. Indeed, one might conclude from these data that the two phenomena —delinquency, on the one hand, and interest in and exposure to such crime themes, on the other—are quite independent of each other.

A second conclusion from these findings is that there is no consistently significant difference between those who are more delinquent and those who are less delinquent in patterns of interest in or exposure to crime themes in mass media, and that the kinds of need deprivation ordinarily regarded as influential elements in the genesis of delinquency neither significantly nor consistently influence these same interest or exposure patterns. Somewhat broader speculative issues emerge from these findings.

The discrepancy between these findings and popular belief regarding mass media may be reconciled by suggesting (1) that these subjects experienced only limited identification with the characters and situations portrayed in the media to which they had access due to (2) a lack of reinforcement in that direction. In turn, we may postulate that the lack of reinforcement may well have been due to the lack of opportunity for these subjects to affiliate themselves with a truly delinquent subculture. Hence, an explanation for the findings of this study that would be consistent with the position of Sutherland and

---

[44] Space does not permit expansion of these matters in this article. For a full discussion, see E. H. Pfuhl, Jr., *op. cit.*, pp. 114 ff.

Table X. *Interest in Crime and Mystery Novels and Delinquency for Boys Having High Psychosomatic Complaints*

Interest in Crime Novels	Delinquent Involvement					
	High		Immediate		Low	
	No.	Percent	No.	Percent	No.	Percent
High	34	47.2	26	36.1	12	16.7
Low	12	24.0	19	38.0	19	38.0

$\chi^2 = 9.516$; at 2 df, $P < .01$ $\bar{C} = .39$

Table XI. *Interest in Crime and Mystery Novels and Delinquency for Boys Having High Psychosomatic Complaints with Religion Held Constant*

Interest in Crime Novels	Delinquent Involvement					
	High		Immediate		Low	
	No.	Percent	No.	Percent	No.	Percent
High	12	30.8	14	35.9	13	33.3
Low	28	47.5	20	33.9	11	18.6

$\chi^2 = 3.694$; at 2 df, $P < .20$

Table XII. *Exposure to Crime Comics and Delinquency for Girls Having High Psychosomatic Complaints with Religion Held Constant*

Exposure to Crime Comics	Delinquent Involvement			
	High		Low	
	No.	Percent	No.	Percent
High	13	37.1	22	62.9
Low	17	77.3	5	22.7

$\chi^2 = 8.721$; at 1 df, $P < .01$ $\bar{C} = .18$

Cressy [45] and the more recent theoretical position of Burgess and Akers [46] is that the contents of these media do not bear significance, in the sense of reinforcement properties, relative to the milieu of these subjects. Stated differently, it may be that a precondition for mass media to provide promise of reward—either immediate or remote—is the content of the personal and social background of the audience. In short, such media may be incapable of reinforcement in the absence of actual opportunity for identification. It is therefore suggested that future research give simultaneous consideration to the concepts of identification and reinforcement.

Further support for this interpretation stems from previous research by the present writer. In seeking to determine the conditions under which exposure to crime and violence in comic magazines might have a significant relationship to delinquent behavior, it was predicted that a significant relationship between these variables would be found among youth having delinquent associates but not among youth lacking such associates. The hypothesis was given limited support by correlations of .12 and .25 for boys and girls, respectively, having delinquent associates, and .04 and .11 for boys and girls, respectively, not having

---
[45] Sutherland and Cressy, *op. cit.*
[46] Burgess and Akers, *op. cit.*

delinquent associates.[47] While these correlations are not entirely within the realm of statistical significance, they are in the direction predicted and serve only to suggest that the milieu of those youth having delinquent associates might well have provided the degree of reinforcement necessary for the media to provide meaningful models. In short, if the media are to be defined as learning mechanisms, this function may be said to depend on the ability of the audience to perceive its characters and situations as "true to life" as they know and experience it.[48] The data of this study do not suggest the existence of such a condition.

This position presents something of a paradox, in that the subjects of this study, by their own admission, were engaged in some delinquent behavior. This paradox may be reconciled by the fact that these subjects are only marginally delinquent. Thus, none of these subjects were institutionalized delinquents, indicating relatively minor and/or infrequent offenses. Only 10.5 percent of these male subjects were classified as being as seriously delinquent as the majority of training school boys.[49] If we are correct in the assumption that 90 percent of these subjects are only marginally delinquent we may conclude that these findings reflect their predominantly nondelinquent orientation (an orientation that persists despite the sometimes high degree of interest in and exposure to crime themes in the media). Furthermore, it may be suggested that delinquency varies in its rationale and motivation as well as its frequency and seriousness and that delinquents vary in the personality patterns displayed.[50] All of these differentials would influence the frame of reference or "ground" employed by persons to structure their perceptions. It is only by including such differentials as those mentioned that we may exhaust the process of investigating a causal relationship between exposure to criminal suggestion in the media and delinquent behavior. However, in the final analysis, these data suggest that efforts to predict delinquency by investigation and other factors would prove more rewarding.

---

[47] E. H. Pfuhl, Jr., "The Relationship of Crime and Horror Comics and Juvenile Delinquency," *Proceedings of the Pacific Sociological Society* (1956) published as Vol. XXIV, No. 2 of *Research Studies of the State College of Washington* (1956), pp. 170–177.

[48] P. Cressey, "The Motion Picture Experience," *American Sociological Review*, Vol. III, No. 4 (August, 1938), p. 521.

[49] Nye and Short, "Scaling Delinquent Behavior," *op. cit., p.* 330.

[50] A. J. Reiss, "Social Correlates of Psychological Types of Delinquency," *American Sociological Review*, Vol. XVII, No. 6 (December, 1952), pp. 710–718.

SECTION

VI

Selected Patterns of Criminal Activity

ALTHOUGH THERE HAVE BEEN MANY ATTEMPTS TO CLASSIFY CRIMINAL OFFENDERS by the types of activities in which they engage, these efforts have not been very satisfactory or successful. This section provides several descriptive analyses and research studies of distinct varieties of criminal behavior ranging from what Sutherland called "white collar crime" through organized crime, professional thieves, homicide offenders, drug addicts, and sex offenders. We are not suggesting that these offense types should represent a continuum of any kind ranging from the least to the most serious or from the accidental to the persistent offender. The studies and analyses that appear in this section merely represent some of the more insightful and empirical descriptions that are available.

Perhaps there are some adjectival phrases which call attention to the distinguishing characteristics of certain kinds of criminal offenders relative to the degree of development of their criminal roles, their self conceptions as criminals, their patterns of association with others who are criminal, their personality traits, and behavior systems. Generally, efforts to find a common denominator or a high degree of homogeneity have proved futile. The difficulties of overcoming the lack of mutual exclusiveness of subcategories in any classification of criminal behavior have resulted in confusing typologies. Clinard [1] has suggested that offenders can be classified according to the degree to which they make a long-term career out of crime, with the criminally insane at one end and the professional criminal at the other; in between may be ranged extreme sex deviates, homosexuals and prostitutes, occasional offenders, habitual petty criminals, white collar criminals, those with ordinary criminal careers, and organized criminals. However, it is obvious that a sex offender may commit crime only occasionally and, consequently, could be classified under sex deviate and occasional offender; prostitutes may also be classified as petty criminals, and white collar criminals may commit their offenses occasionally.

If it is the dominant social role in crime that is to be used as the most important criterion for identification of a specific criminal type, we would

---

[1] Marshall Clinard, *Sociology of Deviant Behavior,* New York: Rinehart and Company, 1958, p. 201.

then be required to collect empirical data that will ascertain the amount and kinds of all violations each offender commits before we could properly classify him. Moreover, there is the additional problem of determining what kind of, and at what point in, a life career, participation in a criminal act identifies one as having the status of a criminal. It may be true that the man who commits a single murder, but no other type of crime, both is socially identified as, and has a self-conception of, being a murderer. But he has been essentially a law-abiding citizen, is governed and guided by the predominant legal and communal conduct norms, and is perhaps best conceived as an episodic offender, not an occasional offender or any of the other types which Clinard mentions. On the other hand, there is little doubt that many offenders make a career of crime and are committed to a value system that is in direct conflict with the predominant values system embodied in the legal and general communal norms. Most of these offenders are professional or organized criminals and form an extreme type that can be readily recognized by their own individual identification with crime, their status recognition among other similar offender types, their knowledge of criminal techniques, and their development of criminal social roles.

Thus, without creating a rigid theoretical taxonomy or continuum that might suggest a progression from one form of criminal deviance to another, the following studies are presented to provide some understanding of the phenomena associated with each of the following specific selected forms of criminal behavior. This kind of analysis, sometimes referred to as *phenomenological*, may use a variety of research methods and techniques to describe the patterns, uniformities, regularities, or correlations which characterize certain kinds of criminal activity. References to causative factors are usually minimal, suggestive, or implied because of the necessity of theoretically analyzing or providing empirical data of the types of criminal phenomena and criminal offenders being investigated. The object of study is limited and microscopic, but the perspective both on the variables analyzed and on their etiological implications is macroscopic and sociological.

The electrical conspiracy described in the first selection is one of the most fabulous cases of "white collar crime" to have appeared in criminal court. The extent and recency of this case makes it especially useful for sociological analysis of this type of violation of the legal norms. (Unfortunately, there are no equally good descriptions or researches concerned with "blue collar crime" committed by skilled, semiskilled, and unskilled laborers in the normal pursuit of their occupations.) The most violent form of organized crime is represented in a vivid description of "Murder, Inc.," and the reader is reminded of Bell's previous article on "Crime As an American Way of Life" (Selection 18, Section IV) for a succinct and perceptive discussion that refers to the similarities of contemporary organized and white collar crime. Sutherland's famous study of the thief who makes crime a way of life is summarized in a selection from *The Professional*

Thief. The homicide victim who precipitates has own victimization is a special type described by Wolfgang, based upon his larger study on *Patterns in Criminal Homicide.*

After decades of inexplicable indifference, organized crime, in recent years, has finally come under the careful scrutiny of Congress, the National Crime Commission, and successive Attorneys General. As has been indicated before (Selection No. 19, Section IV), the President's Commission on Law Enforcement and Administration of Justice has argued forcefully for the existence of La Cosa Nostra. They further contend, in "Organized Crime: The Code and Its Functions", that organized criminals are tied together by a code based on loyalty, rationality, honor, reliability, and "class." The history of Wincanton is a fascinating, if somber, case history of an eastern gambling empire and the inevitable corrupting influence it exercised over one municipal government. The economic consequences of criminal enterprises, whether in the form of black market operations (monopolistic or cartels), criminal monopolies or extortions, represent an almost insupportable burden for our society; Schelling's thoughtful appraisal of some possible social advantages to organized crime is, however, worthy of serious consideration.

Most examinations of sex offenses and sex offenders are conducted by psychologists or psychiatrists. Wheeler's article remains an excellent example of a sociological perspective with which to approach this topic. "Forcible Rape" is a clear, careful, nondramatic example of sociological research about one of the most dramatic crimes. Amir has helped to put to rest many misconceptions and folk superstitions about the crime of rape.

Whether the possession and use of marihuana and other "soft" drugs should continue to be legally prohibited is an important issue in America today. Lindesmith concludes that although marihuana is not habit-forming, federal penalties have, nevertheless, risen in recent years with almost no rational reasons offered for this increased severity. Finally, the recent introduction of L.S.D., "speed," and other psychotropic drugs among various adolescent and young adult populations has produced a new "Hierarchy of Drug Users" involving the "Crystal Freak," the "Weed Head," the "Acid Freak," and the "Garbage Junkies." These selections on drugs represent detailed and colorful descriptions by social scientists who have searched for the best available evidence.

52. THE INCREDIBLE ELECTRICAL CONSPIRACY

RICHARD AUSTIN SMITH

AS BEFITTED THE BIGGEST CRIMINAL CASE IN the history of the Sherman Act, most of the forty-five defendants arrived early, knocking the snow of Philadelphia's Chestnut Street from their shoes before taking the elevator to federal courtroom No. 3. Some seemed to find it as chill inside as out, for they kept their coats on and shifted from one foot to another in the corridor, waiting silently for the big mahogany doors to open. On the other side of those doors was something none of them relished: judgment for having conspired to fix prices, rig bids, and divide markets on electrical equipment valued at $1,750,000,000 annually. The twenty indictments, under which they were now to be sentenced, charged they had conspired on everything from tiny $2 insulators to multimillion-dollar turbine generators and had persisted in the conspiracies for as long as eight years.

As a group, they looked like just what they were: well-groomed corporation executives in Ivy League suits, employed by companies ranging in size from Joslyn Manufacturing & Supply Co., whose shop space is scarcely larger than the courtroom itself, to billion-dollar giants like General Electric and Westinghouse. There was J. E. Cordell, ex-submariner, sales vice president of Southern States Equipment Corp., pillar of the community in a small Georgia town, though his net worth never exceeded $25,000, and urbane William S. Ginn, G.E. vice president at $135,000 a year, a man once thought to be on his way to the presidency of the corporation. There was old, portly Fred F. Loock, president of Allen-Bradley Co., who found conspiring with competitors quite to his taste ("It is the only way a business can be run. It is free enterprise."), and G.E.'s Marc A. deFerranti, who pocketed his repugnance on orders from his boss. There was M. H. Howard, a production manager of Foster Wheeler, who found it hard to stay in the conspiracy (his company's condenser business ran in the red during two years of it), and C. H. Wheeler Manufacturing's President Thomas, who found it hard to quit—he'd been told his firm couldn't survive if he left the cartel.

At nine-thirty the courtroom doors opened and everyone trooped in. It was a huge room, paneled in mahogany with carved pilasters that reached up thirty feet or more to a white ceiling; yet big as it was it very soon filled with tension. What the defendants were thinking of was not hard to guess: the possibility of prison; the careers ruined after decades of service; the agile associates who weren't there, the

▶SOURCE: *"The Incredible Electrical Conspiracy,"* Fortune (April, 1961), pp. 132–180; (May, 1961), pp. 161–224. (abridged and with editorial adaptations) Reprinted by special permission of Time-Life Inc.

ones who had saved their hides by implicating others.

Shortly after ten o'clock, Judge J. Cullen Ganey, chief judge of the U.S. District Court, entered the courtroom. He had earned a reputation in his twenty years on the bench for tolerance and moderation. But it was clear almost immediately that he took a stern view of this conspiracy: "This is a shocking indictment of a vast section of our economy, for what is really at stake here is the survival of the kind of economy under which this country has grown great, the free-enterprise system." The first targets of his censure were the twenty-nine corporations and their top management. He acknowledged that the Justice Department did not have enough evidence to convict men in the highest echelons of the corporations before the court, but in a broader sense the "real blame" should be laid at their doorstep: "One would be most naive indeed to believe that these violations of the law, so long persisted in, affecting so large a segment of the industry and finally involving so many millions upon millions of dollars, were facts unknown to those responsible for the corporation and its conduct..." Heavy fines, he said, would be imposed on the corporations themselves.

Next he turned a cold blue eye on the forty-five corporation executives who had not escaped the nets of Antitrust. Many of the individual defendants he saw "torn between conscience and an approved corporate policy... the company man, the conformist, who goes along with his superiors and finds balm for his conscience in additional comforts and the security of his place in the corporate setup." The judge said that individuals "with ultimate responsibility for corporate conduct, among those indicted," were going to jail.

By midafternoon of that first day E. R. Jung, Clark Controller vice president, was ashen under a thirty-day prison sentence and a $2,000 fine. Gray-haired Westinghouse Vice President J. H. Chiles Jr., vestryman of St. John's Episcopal Church in Sharon, Pennsylvania, got thirty days in prison, a $2,000 fine; his colleague, Sales Manager Charles I. Mauntel, veteran of thirty-nine years with the corporation, faced thirty days and a $1,000 fine; Ginn of G.E. (indicted in two conspiracies), thirty days and a $12,500 fine; G.E. Divisional Manager Lewis Burger, thirty days plus a $2,000 fine; G.E. Vice President George Burens, $4,000 and thirty days. "There goes my whole life," said this veteran of forty years with G.E., waving his arm distractedly as he waited to telephone his wife. "Who's going to want to hire a jailbird? What am I going to tell my children?"

By lunchtime the second day it was all over. The little game that lawyers from G.E. and Westinghouse had been playing against each other—predicting sentences and total fines—was ended. G.E. had "lost," receiving $437,500 in total fines to Westinghouse's $372,500. All told, $1,924,500 worth of fines were levied, seven jail sentences and twenty-four suspended jail sentences handed down. But sentencing, far from closing the case, has raised it to new importance.

THE PROBLEMS OF PREDOMINANCE

No thoughtful person could have left that courtroom untroubled by the problems of corporate power and corporate ethics. We live in a corporate society. Big business determines institutionally our rate of capital formation, technological innovation, and economic growth; it establishes the kind of competition that is typical of our system and sets the moral tone of the market place. The streets of every city in the U.S. are crowded with small businesses that take their cue from great corporations, whether in trickles down from what some executives tells a crop of college graduates about free enterprise or the way he himself chooses to compete. Their lawyers pleaded that the way the electrical-equipment executives did compete was not collusion at its *worst*. To be sure, it was not so vulgar as the strong-arm price fixing of the Gulf Coast shrimpers or the rough stuff employed by a certain Philadelphia linen-supply company. But by flouting the law, the executives of the great companies set an example that was bound to make small companies feel they had similar license, and never mind the kid gloves. As Robert A. Bicks, then head of Antitrust, declared early in the proceedings, "These men and companies have in a true sense mocked the image of that economic system which we profess to the world."

This being so, it is highly important to understand what went wrong with the electrical-equipment industry and with General Electric, the biggest company of them all and the one without which the conspiracies could not have existed.

"SECURITY, COMPLACENCY, MEDIOCRITY"

When Ralph Cordiner took over the presidency of G.E. from Charles E. Wilson in December of 1950, it was clear from the outset that the corporation was in for some teeth-rattling changes. Cordiner had spent the previous five years working up a reorganization plan that would give G.E. the new plants, the new additions to capital, and the new management setup he thought essential to its revitalization. Moreover, he had long made plain his distaste for running any big company the way G.E. had been run by his predecessors, with authority tightly concentrated in the president's office. *De*centralization was a thing with him: he had never forgotten how the "layers of fat" in a centralized G.E. had slowed his own incessant drive for recognition to a point where he'd once quit to take the presidency of Schick. The simple fact was that intellectually and temperamentally a centralized organization went against his grain, whether it be run with Electric Charlie Wilson's relaxed conviviality or the clockwork autocracy of Gerard ("You have four minutes") Swope.

The corporation at large learned almost immediately what the new boss had in store for it and from Cordiner himself. Within six weeks he rode circuit from New York to Bridgeport, Chicago, Lynn-Boston, Schenectady, spreading the word to some 6,000 G.E. executives. The gist of his message could be divided into three parts. First, G.E. was in sorry shape. It was dedicated principally to "security, complacency, and mediocrity." Second, decentralization and rewards based on performance were going to be relied on in the rapid transformation of his "sinecure of mediocrity" into a dynamic corporation. G.E. would be split into twenty-seven autonomous divisions comprising 110 small companies. The 110 would be run just as if they were individual enterprises, the local boss setting his own budget, even making capital expenditures up to $200,-000. But with authority and responsibility would go accountability and measurement, measurement by higher, harder standards. Third, G.E.'s new philosophy of decentralized management specifically prohibited meeting with competitiors on prices, bids, or market shares. Charlie Wilson's General Instruction 2.35 [1] on compliance with the antitrust laws, first issued in 1946 and reissued in 1948 and 1950, would remain very much in force.

There was good reason for stressing this last point. Antitrust was then a very sore subject at G.E. In the decade just ended (1940–50), the corporation had been involved in thirteen antitrust cases, the offenses ranging from production limitation and patent pooling to price fixing and division of markets. Moreover, G.E. had long been something of a battleground for two divergent schools of economic thought. One school was straight Adam Smith and

---

[1] "It has been and is the policy of this Company to conform strictly to the antitrust laws . . . special care should be taken that any proposed action is in conformity with the law as presently interpreted. If there is any doubt as to the legality of any proposed action . . . the advice of the Law Department must be obtained."

dedicated to the classical concept that corporate progress, like national progress, was best secured by freedom of private initiative within the bonds of justice. Its advocates believed that nothing was less intelligent than entering into price restrictions with competitors, for this just put G.E. on a par with companies that had neither its research facilities not its market power. Ralph Cordiner, the company's most articulate advocate of this viewpoint, prided himself on the fact that it was at his insistence that the three G.E. employees implicated in illegal price fixing got the sack in 1949; his philosophy, at its most eloquent, was simply: "Every company and every industry—yes, and every country—that is operated on a basis of cartel systems is liquidating its present strength and future opportunities."

The second school of thought held that competition, particularly price competition, was for the birds. Getting together with competitors was looked on as a way of life, a convention, "just as a manager's office always had a desk with a swivel chair." It was considered easier to negotiate market percentages than fight for one's share, less wearing to take turns on rigged bids than play the rugged individualist. Besides, the rationale went, they were all "gentlemen" and no more inclined to gouge the consumer than to crowd a competitor. Admittedly, all of them knew they were breaking the law—Section 1 of the Sherman Act is as explicit as a traffic ordinance. Their justification was on other grounds. "Sure, collusion was illegal," explained an old G.E. hand, "but it wasn't *unethical*. It wasn't any more unethical than if the companies had a summit conference the way Russia and the West meet. Those competitor meetings were just attended by a group of distressed individuals who wanted to know where they were going."

A WAY OF LIFE FOR CLARENCE BURKE

One of the more attentive listeners to what the incoming president had to say about antitrust was Clarence Burke, a hard-driving, tenacious executive in his middle forties (who was to become the $42,000-a-year general manager of the High Voltage Switchgear Department and one of fifteen G.E. executives sentenced in Philadelphia). Burke had come to the heavy-equipment end of G.E. in 1926, fresh from the Georgia Institute of Technology (B.S. in electrical engineering), and his entire corporate life had been spent there. The heavy-equipment division was more than just the group that accounted for some 25 percent of G.E. sales; it was the oldest division, and the foundation upon which the whole company had been built. Moreover, it was the stronghold of the collusionists. All of the nineteen indictments to which G.E. pleaded either guilty or no contest in Philadelphia sprang from price fixing, bid rigging, market division in heavy equipment.

Burke's introduction of the heavy-equipment conspiracies was easy as falling off a log. It occurred when he reported to Pittsfield, Massachusetts, on June 1, 1945, as sales manager of distribution transformers. A month or so after Burke's arrival, H. L. "Buster" Brown, sales manager of the whole Transformer Department, called the new man in and told him he'd be expected to attend a Pittsburgh meeting of the transformer section of the National Electrical Manufacturers' Association. It was a regularly scheduled affair, held during OPA days, in what is now the Penn-Sheraton Hotel, and it was attended by thirty or forty industry people plus the N.E.M.A. secretaries from New York. But after adjournment—when the N.E.M.A. secretaries had departed—the company men reassembled within the hour for a cozier meeting. The talk this time was about prices, OPA-regulated prices, and how the industry could best argue Washington into jacking up the ceilings. Burke didn't consider this illegal, and he took part in several subsequent monthly meetings before OPA was abolished.

The convenient price klatsches following the regular N.E.M.A. meetings continued after OPA's demise. But instead of discussing pricing under government controls, the conspirators turned to fixing prices among themselves. "In that conspiracy," Burke recalled this winter, "we didn't try to divide up the market or prorate the sealed-bid business. We only quoted an agreed-upon price—to the penny." Nor did the post-OPA agreements seem to some of the participants like Burke to put them any more outside the law than agreements under the OPA. "We gradually grew into it. Buster Brown assured us that [the company's antitrust directive] didn't mean the kind of thing we were doing, that Antitrust would have to say we had *gouged* the public to say we were doing anything illegal. We understood this was what the company wanted us to do."

For a while this comfortable rationale sustained Burke and any conspirators who had qualms about the matter, but in 1946 it was demolished by the company lawyers. Teams of them made the rounds of G.E. departments, no doubt in response to federal probings that were to result in the successful antitrust prosecutions of G.E. two years later. The lawyers put everyone in G.E. on notice that it certainly was illegal to discuss prices with competitors, whether the public was gouged or not. Then the head office followed this up by barring anybody who had anything to do with pricing from attending N.E.M.A. meetings. Engineering personnel were substituted for people like Buster Brown and Clarence Burke. The G.E. conspirators called such enforced withdrawal from active participation "going behind the iron curtain." This situation continued for about nine months, during which everyone received a copy of Electric Charlie's antitrust admonition and during which G.E.'s competitors kept the Pittsfield shut-ins informed by telephone of their own price agreements. Then, abruptly, the iron curtain was raised.

"Word came down to start contacting competitors again," Burke remembers. "It came to me from my superior, Buster Brown, but my impression was that it came to him from higher up. I think the competitive situation was forcing them to do something, and there were a lot of old-timers who thought collusion was the best way to solve the problems. That is when the hotel-room meetings got started. We were cautioned at this time not to tell the lawyers what we were doing and to cover our trails in our expense-account reports." Part of Burke's camouflage: transportation entries never showed fares to the actual city where the meeting was held but to some point of equivalent distance from Pittsfield.

By 1951, however, at the time Burke was listening to Ralph Cordiner's antitrust exhortations, the Pittsfield conspiracy had closed down—to make matters simpler if, as everyone correctly suspected, Cordiner was going to clamp down on such cabals. But bigger and better conspiracies were in the offing. In September, 1951, not very long after the Cordiner meeting, Clarence Burke walked into a new job at G.E.—and into membership in probably the oldest conspiracy then extant. The conspiracy was in circuit breakers[2] and it had been operative over the span of a quarter-century. Burke's new job was manager of all switchgear marketing, which included circuit breakers, switchgear, and other items of heavy electrical equipment. This particular spot was open because the previous incumbent had been troubled ever since signing a restatement of Charlie Wilson's "Policy Concerning the Antitrust Laws" the year before. As Burke got the

---

[2] Like their household counterparts, circuit breakers are used to interrupt the flow of electricity when it reaches dangerous voltages. The industrial versions are sometimes forty feet long, twenty-six feet high, and weigh eight-five tons.

story from Robert Tinnerholm, who interviewed him for the job: "I was to replace a man who took a strictly religious view of it; who, because he had signed this slip of paper [the Wilson directive] wouldn't contact competitors or talk to them—even when they came to his home." Burke got the job, an important step up the G.E. ladder, because he had become something of a conspiratorial wheel by then: "They knew I was adept at this sort of thing. I was glad to get the promotion. I had no objections." No objections then or subsequently, as it turned out, for he had found it easy to persuade himself that what he was doing in defiance of the letter of the antitrust directive was not done in defiance of its spirit.

Burke's boss when he first went to switchgear in 1951 was Henry V. Erben, to whom Buster Brown had reported in the cozy old days at Pittsfield. Erben had risen to the No. 3 spot in G.E.—executive vice president, Apparatus Group—and as Burke recalls, "he was saying then that he had talked to Cordiner about this policy, that Cordiner was not pleased with [the idea of getting together with competitors] but that he, Erben, had said he would do it in a way that would not get the company into trouble. And I'd been told by others that Erben had said things like this earlier than that."

Burke's initial assignment in Philadelphia was to get to know the local marketing executives of Westinghouse, Allis-Chalmers, and Federal Pacific, and then to see they met the other new members of G.E.'s switchgear management. (This department has been restaffed in anticipation of being split into three parts, the separate companies called for by Cordiner's decentralization plan.) He was also expected to take a hand at indoctrination in conspiracy. "Erben's theory had been live and let live, contact the competitors. He gave us that theory at every opportunity and we took it down to other levels and had no trouble getting the most innocent persons to go along. Mr. Erben thought it was all right, and if they didn't want to do it, they knew we would replace them. Not replace them for that reason, of course. We would have said the man isn't *broad* enough for this job, he hasn't grown into it yet."

One man, ironically enough, who had not yet "grown" into the job was George Burens, the new boss of the whole switchgear operation. Burens had started out in G.E. as a laborer; he had the additional disadvantage of being a junior-high-school man in a corporate world full of college men, but during the next thirty years he had steadily risen by sheer competitive spirit. Part of his zest for competition had been acquired in the Lamp Division, where he had spent the bulk of his career. Lamps had long been noted as the most profitable of G.E. divisions and the most independent, a constant trial to Gerald Swope in the days when he tried to centralize all administrative authority in G.E.'s New York headquarters. But most of Burens' competitive spirit was simply in the nature of the man. "He had grown up hating competitors," was the way a colleague put it. "They were the enemy."

"THIS IS BOB, WHAT IS 7'S BID?"

Burens arrived on the scene in September of 1951 and busied himself solely with the job of splitting switchgear into three independent companies (high, medium, and low voltage), each with a general manager and himself as general manager of the division. Once decentralization was accomplished, he was content for a time to let his new departmental general managers like Clarence Burke run the conspiracy. And some conspiracy it was.

Some $650 million in sales was involved, according to Justice Department estimates, from 1951 through 1958. The annual total amounted to roughly $75 million and was broken down into two categories, sealed bids and open bids. The sealed-bid business (between $15 million and $18 million per year) was done with public agencies, city, state, and federal. The private-sector business was conducted with private utilities and totaled some $55 million to $60 million per annum.

The object of the conspiracy, in so far as the sealed-bid business was concerned, was to rotate that business on a fixed-percentage basis among four participating companies, then the only circuit-breaker manufacturers in the U.S. G.E. got 45 percent, Westinghouse 35, Allis-Chalmers 10, Federal Pacific 10. Every ten days to two weeks working-level meetings were called in order to decide whose turn was next. Turns were determined by the "ledger list," a table of who had got what in recent weeks, and after that the only thing left to decide was the price that the company picked to "win" would submit at the lowest bid.

Above this working-level group was a second tier of conspirators who dealt generally with the over-all scheme of rigging the sealed bids but whose prime purpose was maintenance of book prices (quoted prices) and market shares in the yearly $55 million to $60 million worth of private-sector business. Once each week, the top executives (general managers and vice presidents) responsible for carrying out the conspiracy would get the word to each other via intercompany memo. A different executive would have the "duty" over each thirty-day period. That involved initiating the memos, which all dealt with the same subject matter: the jobs coming up that week, the book price each company was setting, comments on the general level of equipment prices.

The conspiracies had their own lingo and their own standard operating procedures. The attendance list was known as the "Christmas-card list," meetings as "choir practices." Companies had code numbers —G.E. 1, Westinghouse 2, Allis-Chalmers 3, Federal Pacific 7—which were used in conjunction with first names when calling a conspirator at home for price information ("This is Bob, what is 7's bid?"). At the hotel meeting it was S.O.P. not to list one's employer when registering and not to have breakfast with fellow conspirators in the dining room. The G.E. men observed two additional precautions: never to be the ones who kept the records and never to tell G.E.'s lawyers anything.

WHERE TO CUT THROATS

But things were not always smooth even inside this well-oiled machine, for the conspirators actually had no more compunction at breaking the rules of the conspiracy than at breaching the Sherman Act. "Everyone accused the others of not living up to the agreement," Clarence Burke recalled, "and the ones they complained about tried to shift the blame onto someone else." The most constant source of irritation occurred in the sealed-bid business, where chiseling was difficult to detect. But breaks in book price to the utilities in the open-bid business also generated ill will and vituperation. Indeed, one of the many ironies of the whole affair is that the conspiracy couldn't entirely suppress the competitive instinct. Every so often some company would decide that cutthroat competition outside was preferable to the throat-cutting that went on in the cartel; they would break contact and sit out the conspiracy for a couple of years.

What prompted their return? Chronic overcapacity, for one thing, overcapacity that put a constant pressure on prices. Soon after he went to Washington as defense mobilization chief in 1950, Electric Charlie Wilson announced that the nation's electric-power capacity needed to be increased 30 percent over the next three years. The equipment industry jumped to match that figure, and added a little more as well. Thus an executive, who ebulliently increased capacity one year, a few years later might join a price conspiracy to escape the consequences of that increase.

"This is a feast or famine business," summed up Clarence Burke. "At one time everybody was loaded with orders, and ever since they wanted to stay that way. When utilities decide they need more generating capacity, they start buying and we have three years of good business—and then three years of bad. The decision to build capacity was delegated down to the managers [under decentralization]."

A more human explanation of why the conspiracy snarled on for eight years was corporate pressure, the pressure to perform. "All we got from Lexington Avenue," said Burke, "was 'get your percentage of available business up, the General Electric Co. is slipping.'" Cordiner himself has remarked: "I would say the company was more than slightly nervous in 1951–52–53."

Certainly corporate pressure no more exculpates an executive who enters into an illegal conspiracy than the relatively low pay of a bank clerk justifies his dipping into the till. But that is not to say it didn't carry weight with the conspirators from G.E. For the company was not only experiencing the increased pressure that goes with new presidents but was adjusting to a whole new organizational setup. Said one observer of the scene, Vice President Harold Smiddy, G. E.'s management expert: "Some thought . . . that he was going too fast. But Cordiner's asset is stretching men. He can push them and he did." Said another observer, G.E. director Sidney Weinberg: "If you did something wrong, Cordiner would send for you and tell you you were through. That's all there would be to it."

Down the line, where the pressure must have been intense, Clarence Burke had this to say of it as a factor in continuing the conspiracy: "We did feel that this was the only way to reach part of our goals as managers. Each year we had to budget for more profits as a percent of net sales, as well as for a larger percentage of available business. My boss, George Burens, wouldn't approve a budget unless it was a 'reach' budget. We couldn't accomplish a greater percent of net profit to sales without getting together with competitors. Part of the pressure was the will to get ahead and the desire to have the good will of the man above you. He had only to get the approval of the man above *him* to replace you, and if you wouldn't cooperate he could find lots of other faults to use to get you out."

CORDINER TAKES THE PLUNGE

By May of 1953, Clarence Burke had been promoted to general manager of one of the three new switchgear departments (high voltage), a post that made him in effect the president of a small company with some $25 million worth of sales. He felt he had a bellyful of the cartel because "No one was living up to the agreements and we at G.E. were being made suckers. On every job some one would cut our throat; we lost confidence in the group." So he got out.

The G.E. boycott of that cartel continued on through 1954. To be sure, Westinghouse, Allis-Chalmers, and the other competitors would still call Royce Crawford, Burke's marketing man, to tell him the prices that the high-level group had decided on, and express the heartfelt hope he would honor it. Crawford did honor it pretty much, though maintaining a free hand to go after all the business available.

This was the situation when, in mid-September 1954, Ralph Cordiner replaced the Wilson directive of antitrust compliance with a stronger one of his own. Far more explicit than Wilson's directive, Cordiner's Directive Policy 20.5 went beyond the compliance required by the law and blanketed the subject with every conceivable admonition.

But 1954 was a bad year for the industry and for G.E. The company's sales slumped for the first time since Cordiner had taken the helm, dropping almost $176 million. Moreover, profits as a percent of sales were still well below the 8 percent achieved by Charlie Wilson in 1950. The result was that Cordiner and Robert Paxton, executive vice president for industrial products, began putting more heat on one division after another.

"We were told," as one general manager remembered it, "that G.E. was losing business and position because our prices weren't competitive." Then, in the latter part of 1954, Paxton heard a report that moved him from words to the action his blunt Scottish temperament favored. Westinghouse had beaten G.E. out of a big turbine order and had done it at considerably off book price. Determined that no more of the big ones were going to get away, Paxton decided he'd instruct the fieldmen personally. Thus, when the next big job came along, $5-million affair for transformers and switchgear with Ebasco, the New York district manager knew he was not to let the competition underbid him. But Westinghouse and the others were hungry too, and the price breaks came so fast it was difficult to keep track of them: one day the price was 10 percent off book, the next day 20 percent, finally 40 percent.

So began the celebrated "white sales" of 1954-55. Before it was over, the electrical industry was discounting price as much as 40 to 45 percent off book. Delivery dates began stretching out, got as far as five years away from date of sale. This of course meant that the impact of 1955's giveaway prices was not confined to that one year; the blight they put on profits persisted down to 1960.

THE MALIGN CIRCLE

McGregor ("Mac") Smith, chairman of the Florida Power & Light Co., personally handled some of the buying for his dynamic utility. As he went marketing for equipment, it struck him that the manufacturers had set artificially high profit goals for themselves, had priced their products accordingly, and then had got together to see that the prices stuck. In other words, a malign circle of manufacturers was short-circuiting what Ralph Cordiner liked to call the "benign circle of power producers and power consumers." Smith was buying a lot of transformers, switchgear, and other equipment in 1957, but the manufacturers were defending book price as if life depended on it and, despite heavy pressure from Mac Smith and his purchasing agents, were giving little in the way of discounts.

Then one Monday, Smith closed his transformer purchases with a number of companies, including G.E. and Westinghouse; on Tuesday Clarence Burke got a worried report from one of his switchgear salesmen in Miami: Westinghouse had proposed to Florida Power that it add all its circuit-breaker order (about a million dollars worth) to its order for Westinghouse transformers. In return, Westinghouse would take 4 percent off circuit-breaker book and hide the discount in the transformer order. Telling his man to be sure of the facts first, Burke gave him authority to meet the Westinghouse terms. A grateful Mac Smith then decided to split the circuit-breaker order, half to Westinghouse, which had broken the price, and half to G.E., which had matched the break.

This unexpected turn of the wheel brought the Westinghouse salesman boiling into Florida Power's executive suite. There he raised Mac Smith's hackles to a point where the latter called G.E. and asked it to do him the favor of taking the whole order. G.E. naturally obliged.

Retaliation was not long coming. "Westinghouse went to Baltimore Gas & Electric," says Burke, shaking his head in recollection of the chaos that ensued, "and said they'd give them 5 percent off on switchgear and circuit breakers, and a week later Allis-Chalmers gave Potomac Electric 12 percent off. A week after *that*, Westinghouse gave Atlantic City Electric 20 percent off, and it went on down to much worse than the 'white sale'—in the winter of 1957-58 prices were 60 percent off book."

That was the end of that cartel. It did not, of course, mean the end of the other conspiracies G.E. was involved in. Far from it. Each general manager of a division or department took a strictly personal view of his participation in any cartel. Thus while circuit breakers was a daggers drawn, industrial controls was enjoying an amiable conspiracy.

CORDINER'S "PIECES OF PAPER"

G.E. was involved in at least seven other conspiracies during the time the circuit-breaker cartel was inoperative. The one in power transformers (G.E. Vice President Raymond W. Smith) was going, for G.E. had yet to develop the "black box" (a design breakthrough using standard components to produce tailor-made transformers), which two years later would enable it to take price leadership away from Westinghouse. The one in turbine generators (G.E. Vice President William S. Ginn) was functioning too. In the fall of 1957 it was agreed at the Barclay Hotel [3] to give G.E. "position" in bidding on a 500,000-kilowatt TVA unit.

The question that naturally arises, the cartels being so numerous, is why didn't G.E.'s top management stop them? Cordiner has been criticized within the company, and rightly so, for sitting aloofly in New York and sending out "pieces of paper" —his 20.5 antitrust directive—rather than having 20.5 personally handed to the local staff by the local boss. But there was also a failure in human relations. A warmer man might have been close enough to his people to divine what was going on. According to T.K. Quinn (*I Quit Monster Business*), the G.E. vice president who had helped him up the ladder, Ralph Cordiner, was "first class in every aspect of management except human relations."

After the conspiracy case broke, the question of top-level complicity came up. G.E. hired Gerhard Gesell of the Washington law firm of Covington & Burling to come to a conclusion one way or another as to whether Cordiner, Paxton, or any other member of the Executive Office had knowledge of the cartels. No corroborated evidence ever came to light that Cordiner knew of them; quite the opposite. As Clarence Burke put it last month: "Cordiner was sincere but under-sold by people beneath him who rescinded his orders."

Robert Paxton, however, is something else again. The fifty-nine-year-old G.E. president, who resigned this February for reasons of health, was in the unenviable position of having worked most of his corporate life in those vineyards of G.E. where cartels thrived. He was in switchgear for twenty-one years, five of them as works manager, went to Pittsfield with his close friend Ray Smith (later one of the convicted conspirators), and eventually became manager of the Transformer and Allied Product Division there. A conspiracy had started before he got to Pittsfield and one was operating (first under Ginn, then under Smith) after he left. Paxton was not then *responsible* for marketing, as G.E. points out, but he has always shown a lively interest in the subject: "I found myself, even as a very young engineer working for General Electric, dealing with the very practical daily problem of how to minimize cost and how to maximize profit."

Gesell discovered there was violent disagreement within G.E. about Paxton and the cartels: "Things were said about his having knowledge. I interviewed Ray Smith and made every effort to pin down what he thought he had, but it was always atmospheric. The government investigated and didn't have any better luck."

Judge Ganey, however, expressed a more definite view: "I am not naive enough to

---

[3] On February 2, 1960, the hotel jocularly described its spécialité de maison in a small New York Times ad: "Antitrust-corporation secrets are best discussed in the privacy of an executive suite at the Barclay. It's convenient, attractive, and financially practical."

believe General Electric didn't know about it and it didn't meet with their hearty approbation." In Ganey's opinion, Directive 20.5 was "observed in its breach rather than in its enforcement." To say the least, there was a serious management failure at G.E.

COLD TURKEY AND THE PRESSURE FOR PROFITS

In 1958 the circuit breaker-switchgear conspiracy started up again. George Burens and his three departmental general managers, Burke, H. F. Hentschel, and Frank Stehlik, were all dead set against resumption. But the pressure was too great. Pressure had already produced some profound changes in Burke. "He used to be hail fellow well met," said a colleague who witnessed the transformation over the years, "until he was put under that great pressure for profits. Then he simply shrank into himself; everything got to be cold turkey with him—without any warmth at all." Now the pressure was redoubling, as it always did after the market went to pieces. Burens and some of the other apparatus executives were summoned to New York in 1958 for a talk with the boss, Group Executive Arthur F. Vinson. This affair became known to Burens' subordinates as the "Beat Burens" meeting, for at it were aired angry complaints by G.E.'s customers that, the switchgear selling at 40 to 45 percent off book, other G.E. departments should be offering their products at substantial discounts. The solution: stabilize switchgear prices; in other words, get back in the cartel.

Burens returned to Philadelphia, battered but unshaken in his resolve to keep clear of the cartel. He expected to do it by keeping up quality and efficiency, and by pricing the product so that there was a fair profit. Ironically enough, in view of his subsequent indictment, he was firmly of the belief that, given six months time, he could bring prices up in the free market without messing around with any conspiracy. But at the annual business-review meeting of apparatus people, held on July 30 and 31 in Philadelphia, he underwent a further hammering from other divisional general managers about the way switchgear prices were hurting them. He seemed morose at the following banquet, held in a private dining room at the Philadelphia Country Club; indeed, he got into a heated argument about prices with Paxton, who had succeeded Ralph Cordiner as president that April.

What happened next to change George Burens' mind about getting back into the conspiratorial rat race is a matter of great controversy. It concerns whether he got a direct order to rejoin the cartel from Arthur Vinson. If Vinson did so instruct Burens, and others, then General Electric's complicity extended to the highest corporate level, for Vinson was a member of the fifteen-man Executive Office, a group that included Cordiner and Paxton.

Suffice it to say here that Burens did rejoin and was confronted by a delicate problem of face. He didn't want to have to crawl back, particularly after having given everyone such a hard time when he quit. But as matters turned out, G.E. was holding its quadrennial Electric Utility Conference in California that fall and there Burens ran into Fischer Black, the amiable editor of *Electrical World*. Black reported that a lot of people in the industry were sour on G.E. in general and Burens in particular because Burens had refused to go along with new pricing agreements. To end this insalubrious state of affairs, Black would be happy to set up a meeting—if Burens would just attend. The latter agreed.

On October 8, 1958, the cartel set gathered at the Astor Hotel in New York. The G.E. contingent was there, headed by Burens and Burke, Landon Fuller for Westinghouse, Harry Buck for I-T-E Circuit Breaker, Frank Roby for Federal Pacific. L. W. "Shorty" Long had called in to say he couldn't make it but anything they decided was O.K. with Allis-Chalmers. Black himself popped in to chirp that he was paying for the suite and to be sure and order up lunch. Then he left them to business. Not much of it was transacted. There was a lot of crape-hanging over what had happened in the past and a number of hopeful ideas for the future were discussed. The net of it was that everybody agreed to go home, check their records, and come up with proposals on November 9, at the Traymore hotel in Atlantic City.

A PARTY FOR BURENS

Whatever watery cordiality prevailed at the Astor vanished into the steam of conflict at the Traymore. Circuit-breaker prices had been dropping alarmingly ever since September, so much so that G.E., Westinghouse, Allis-Chalmers, and Federal Pacific extended options to some utilities to purchase large numbers of circuit breakers at 40 to 55 percent below book. Moreover, I-T-E Circuit Breaker had got into the business via the purchase of Kelman Electric and wanted a slice of the sealed-bid market; Federal Pacific had a slice but wanted a fatter one.

Deciding what to do about prices was not particularly trying; an agreement was reached to keep them substantially identical at book. The real trouble came over changing the percentages of sealed-bid business. G.E., Westinghouse, and Allis-Chalmers knew that anything done to accommodate the demands of Federal Pacific and I-T-E would have to come out of their hides. But at the end of ten hours of angry argument they decided the only way to get the cartel going again was to submit to the knife: General Elecric's percentage was sliced from 45 to 40.3, Westinghouse's from 35 to 31.3, Allis-Chalmers from 10 to 8.8. I-T-E was cut in for 4 percent and Federal Pacific got a 50 percent boost, its percentage of the market was raised from 10 to 15.6.

So began the final circuit-breaker cartel, born in recrimination and continued in mistrust. George Burens struggled with it for the next three months, a round of meetings at the old hotels and some swanky new places. Circuit-breaker prices inched up. Then in January, 1959, Burens was promoted out. It was a gay party that celebrated his departure to head up G.E.'s Lamp Division, and nobody was gayer than Burens, the tough competitor returning to free competition. Paxton was on hand with an accolade; the Lamp Division, he said, needed Buren's admirable talents to get it back where it belonged.

But there was no gay party for the incoming general manager of switchgear. Lewis Burger was simply told his job was "at risk" for the next two years. If he performed, he could keep it and become a vice president to boot. If he was found wanting, he wouldn't be able to go back to his old job. He'd just be out. Burger promptly joined the circuit-breaker conspiracy. But the day was not far off, indeed it was only nine months away, when a phone call would set in motion the forces that would shatter the conspiracy and send Burger along with Burens off to prison.

Shortly before ten o'clock on the morning of September 28, 1959, an urgent long-distance call came in to G.E.'s vast Transformer Division at Pittsfield, Massachusetts. It was for Edward L. Dobbins, the divisional lawyer, and the person on the line was another attorney, representing Lapp Insulator Co. He just wanted to say that one of Lapp's officers had been subpoened by a Philadelphia grand jury and was going to tell the whole story. "What story?" said Dobbins pleasantly, then listened to an account that sent him, filled with concern, into the office of the divisional vice president, Raymond W. Smith.

At that time, Vice President Smith was a big man in G.E., veteran of twenty-eight years with the corporation, and one of President Robert Paxton's closest personal friends; he was also a big man in Pittsfield, where the Transformer Division employs 6,000 people out of a population of 57,000, director of a local bank, active member of the hospital building board. Smith heard Dobbins out, his six-foot-five frame suddenly taut in the swivel chair and a frown deepening on his forehead; he got up and began pacing back and forth. "It's bad," he said, "very bad." Then he added, shaking his head grimly, "You just don't know how bad it is!"

The story Dobbins had, which the man from Lapp was about to spill before a Philadelphia grand jury, was that Paul Hartig, one of Ray Smith's departmental general managers, had been conspiring with Lapp Insulator and a half-dozen other manufacturers to fix prices on insulators. Such news was unsettling enough to any boss, but Smith's alarm had its roots in something deeper than the derelictions of a subordinate. He was himself "Mr. Big" of another cartel, one involving $210 million worth of transformers a year, and he didn't need the gift of prescience to sense the danger to his own position. Nevertheless, Smith concluded that he had no choice but to report the trouble to Apparatus Group Vice President Arthur Vinson, in New York.

That very night Vinson flew up to Pittsfield. A cool, dynamic executive, boss of G.E.'s nine apparatus divisions, Vinson was used to hearing the word "trouble" from his general managers, but the way Smith had used it permitted of no delay, even for a storm that made the flight a hazardous one. He had dinner with the Smiths at a nearby inn, and then back in Smith's study, heard the story. Vinson's concern centered immediately on the extent of G.E.'s involvement. His recollection today is that after discussing Hartig, he asked Ray Smith whether the Transformer Division was itself involved in a cartel and received assurances to the contrary. Hartig's case appeared to be just that of a young manufacturing executive whose inexperience in marketing matters had got him compromised.

By sheer coincidence, G.E. Chairman Ralph Cordiner showed up in Pittsfield the next day. He had come, ironically enough, to hear an account of the new market approach by means of which Smith's Transformer Division expected to beat the ears off the competition, foreign and domestic. G.E. had worked out a method of cutting the formidable costs of custom-made transformers by putting them together from modular (standard) components. Westinghouse, long the design and cost leader in the transformer field, had been put on notice only the previous month that new prices reflecting the 20 percent cost reduction were in the making.

Told of Hartig's involvement in the insulator cartel, Cordiner reacted with shock and anger. Up until then he had reason to think his general managers were making "earnest efforts" to comply with both the spirit and the letter of the antitrust laws; he had so testified in May before a congressional antitrust subcommittee. When the Tennessee Valley Authority had complained that is was getting identical bids on insulators, transformers, and other equipment, and the Justice Department had begun to take an active interest in this charge, he had sent G.E.'s amiable trade-regulation counsel, Gerard Swope Jr., son of the company's former chief executive, to Pittsfield. Swope considered it his mission to explore "a more dynamic pricing policy to get away from the consistent identity of prices." He had, however ventured to say, "I assume none of you have agreed with competitors on prices," and when nobody contested this assumption, he came away with the feeling that any suspicion of pricing agreements boiled down to a competitor's voicing a single criticism at a cocktail party. Cordiner had been further reassured by a report from G.E.'s outside counsel, Gerhard Gesell of Covington & Burling, who had burrowed through mountains of data and couldn't find anything incriminating. Gesell's conclusion, accepted by the top brass, was that G.E. was up against nothing more than another government attack on "administered" prices such as he and Thomas E. Dewey had beaten off earlier that year in the Salk vaccine case.

It was no wonder, then, that Cordiner was upset by what he heard about the insulator department. And this was only the beginning. G.E.'s general counsel, Ray Luebbe, was brought into the case, and within a matter of days Paul Hartig was in Luebbe's New York office implicating Vice President Ray Smith. Smith made a clean breast of things, detailing the operation of the transformer cartel (bids on government contracts were rotated to ensure that G.E. and Westinghouse each got 30 percent of the business, the remaining 40 being split among four other manufacturers; book prices were agreed upon at meetings held everywhere from Chicago's Drake Hotel to the Homestead at Hot Springs, Virginia; secrecy was safeguarded by channeling all phone calls and mail to the homes, destroying written memoranda upon receipt).

Then Smith implicated a second G.E. vice president, William S. Ginn. Head of the Turbine Division at forty-one, Ginn was considered a comer in the company. Unfortunately for him, he was just as much of a wheel in conspiracy, an important man in *two* cartels, the one in transformers, which he had passed on to Ray Smith, and the one in turbine generators, which only the year before had aroused the suspicions of TVA by bringing about some very rapid price increases.

The involvement of divisional Vice Presidents Smith and Ginn put G.E.'s whole fifteen-man executive Group—a group including Cordiner and Paxton—in an understandable flap. By now, the corporation was plainly implicated in four cartels, and an immense number of questions had to be answered, questions of how to ferret out other conspiracies, what legal defense to make, whether there was any distinction between corporate and individual guilt. For the next few weeks—from early October to late November—the executive office was to devote itself almost exclusively to searching for dependable answers.

BIG FISH IN SMALL COMPANIES

The Justice Department was also looking for answers. It had got started on the case because of TVA's suspicions and because Senator Estes Kefauver had threatened an investigation of the electrical industry, putting the executive branch of government on notice that if it didn't get on with the job, the legislative branch would. Robert A. Bicks, the most vigorous chief of Antitrust since Thurman Arnold, certainly had plenty of will to get on with the job, but the way was clouded. The Antitrust Division had once before—in 1951–52—tried to find a pattern of collusive pricing in the maze of transformer bids, but had wound up with no indictments. Now, as Bicks and William Maher, the head of the division's Philadelphia office, moved into the situation, proof seemed as elusive as ever.

The tactics of the Antitrust Division were based on using the Philadelphia grand jury to subpoena individuals—the corporation executives who would logically have been involved if a conspiracy existed. The ultimate objective was to determine whether the biggest electrical manufacturers and their top executives had participated in a cartel, but the approach had to be oblique. As Maher put it: "Even if we had proof of a meeting where Paxton [president of G.E.] and Cresap [president of Westinghouse] had sat down and agreed to fix prices, we would still have to follow the product lines down through to the illegal acts. You have to invert it, start with what happened at a lower level and build it up step by step. The idea is to go after the biggest fish in the *smallest* companies, then hope to get enough information to land the biggest fish in the biggest companies."

In mid-November a second Philadelphia grand jury was empaneled, and Justice Department attorneys began ringing doorbells across the land. As more of these rang and the trust busters took more testimony (under grand-jury subpoena), a sudden shiver of apprehension ran through the industry. The grapevine, probably the most sensitive in American business, began to buzz with talk that the feds were really on to something—moreover, that jail impended for the guilty. Everyone by then was only too well aware that an Ohio judge had just clapped three executives behind bars for ninety days for participating in a hand-tool cartel.

CORDINER'S COMMAND DECISION

Back at G.E., meanwhile, Cordiner had issued instructions that all apparatus general managers, including those few who so far had been implicated, were to be interviewed by company attorneys about participation in cartels. Most of the guilty lied, gambling that the exposures would not go any further than they had. Cordiner, accepting their stories, began to formulate what he thought would be G.E.'s best defense. It would have two principal salients: first, the company itself was not guilty of the conspiracies; what had occurred was without the encouragement or even the knowledge of the chairman, the president, and the Executive Office. G.E.'s corporate position on antitrust compliance was a matter of record, embodied in Directive 20.5, which Cordiner had personally written and promulgated five years before. Furthermore, illegal conduct of any individuals involved was clearly beyond the authority granted to them by the company, and therefore the company, as distinguished from the individuals, should not be held criminally responsible. Second, those employees who had violated Directive 20.5 were in for corporate punishment. "Stale offenses" were not to be counted, but a three-year company "statute of limitations" would govern liability (the federal limitation: five years).

Punishment of necessity had to go hand in hand with a corporate not-guilty stance. If G.E.'s defense was to be that the conspiracies had taken place in contravention of written policy (Directive 20.5), then unpunished offenders would be walking proof to a jury that 20.5 was just a scrap of paper. On the other hand, here was a clear management failure on the part of the Executive Office—a failure to detect over a period of almost a decade the cartels that were an open secret to the rest of the industry. As G.E. was to learn to its sorrow, lots of people who approved of punishment for the offenders did not think this permitted G.E. to wash its hands of responsibility. Westinghouse's president, Mark W. Cresap Jr., spoke for many executives both inside the industry and out when he stated his position this January: "Corporate punishment of these people ... would only be self-serving on my part ... this is a management failure."

But aside from the moral question, the legal basis of G.E.'s not-guilty stance was shaky to say the least. Its lawyers felt bound to inform the Executive Office: "The trend of the law appears to be that a business corporation will be held criminally liable for the acts of an employee so long as these acts are reasonably related to the area of general responsibility entrusted to him notwithstanding the fact that such acts are committed in violation of instructions issued by the company in good faith ..." Under the decentralization policy, distinguishing between an "innocent" corporation and its "guilty" executives would be tough, for Cordiner himself had given the general managers clear pricing powers.

The Cordiner position had another weakness: it was based on the assumption that G.E. was involved in only four cartels—at the most. Yet wider involvement could reasonably have been expected. That very month general counsel Luebbe (who retired on October 1, 1960) had been warned by one of the general managers who had confessed that collusion would be found to have spread across the whole company front. ("I tried to tell Luebbe to stop the investigation," reflected the general manager, "and try to make a deal with the government. I told him in November, 1959, that this thing would go right across the board. He just laughed at me. He said, 'You're an isolated case—only you fellows would be stupid enough to do it.'") Thus when wider involvement actually did come to light—the four cartels multiplied into nineteen and accounted for more than 10 percent of G.E.'s total sales—the company found itself in the ludicrous position of continuing to proclaim its corporate innocence while its executives were being implicated by platoons.

THE AX FALLS

But vulnerable or not, G.E.'s posture was officially established in November, and management moved to put it into effect. Ray Smith was summoned to Arthur Vinson's big, handsome office and told he was going to be punished. His job was forfeit and his title too. There was a spot for him abroad, at substantially less money, if he wanted to try to rebuild his career in General Electric. Smith was stunned. Once implicated, he had leveled with the company to help it defend itself, and there'd been no hint of punishment then or in the succeeding two months. He decided he'd had it, at fifty-four, and would just take his severance pay and resign.

It was probably a wise move. Those conspirators who didn't quit on the spot had a very rough go of it. Initial punishment (demotion, transfer, pay cuts) was eventually followed by forced resignation, as we shall see. But the extra gall in the punishment was the inequality of treatment. William Ginn had been implicated at the same time as Ray Smith, and his case fell well within G.E.'s statute of limitations. Yet he was allowed to continue in his $135,000 job as vice president of the Turbine Division—until he went off to jail for that conspiracy, loaded with the biggest fine ($12,500) of any defendant.

Widespread resentment over this curious partiality to Ginn and over the meting out of discipline generally was destined to have its effect: willing G.E. witnesses soon began to turn up at the trust buster's camp; among them was an angry Ray Smith, who claimed he had been acting on orders from above. His mood, as a government attorney described it, was that of a man whose boss had said: "I can't get you a raise, so why don't you just take $5 out of petty cash every week. Then the man gets fired for it and the boss does nothing to help him out."

There was, however, an interval of some three months between Smith's resignation in November and his appearance in Philadelphia with his story. And eventful months they were. The first grand jury was looking into conspiracies in insulators, switchgear, circuit breakers, and several other products. The second grand jury was hearing four transformer cases and one on industrial controls. With a score of Justice men working on them, cases proliferated, and from December on lawyers began popping up trying to get immunity for their clients in return for testimony. Scarcely a week went by that Bicks and company didn't get information on at least two new cases. But what they still needed was decisive data that would break a case wide open. In January, 1960, at just about the time Ralph Cordiner was making an important speech to G.E.'s management corps ("every company and every industry—yes, and every country—that is operated on a basis of cartel systems is liquidating its present strength and future opportunities"), the trust busters hit the jackpot in switchgear.

"THE PHASES OF THE MOON"

Switchgear had been particularly baffling to the Antitrust Division, so much so that in trying to establish a cartel in the jumble of switchgear prices the trust busters got the bright idea they might be in code. A cryptographer was brought in to puzzle over the figures and try to crack the secret of how a conspirator could tell what to bid and when he'd win. But the cryptographer was soon as flummoxed as everyone else One of the government attorneys in the case, however, made a point of dropping in on a college classmate who was the president of a small midwestern electrical-equipment company. This executive didn't have chapter and verse on the switchgear cartel but what he did have was enough for Justice to throw a scare into a bigger company, I-T-E Circuit Breaker. Indicating that subpoenas would follow, antitrust investigators asked I-T-E's general counsel, Franklyn Judson, to supply the names of sales managers in specific product lines. Judson decided to conduct an investigation of his own. When the subpoenas did come, a pink-cheeked blond young man named Nye Spencer, the company's sales manager for switchgear, was resolutely waiting—his arms loaded with data. He had decided he wasn't about to commit another crime by destroying the records so carefully laid away in his cellar.

There were pages on pages of notes taken during sessions of the switchgear conspiracy—incriminating entries like "Potomac Light & Power O.K. for G.E." and "Before bidding on this, check with G.E."; neat copies of the ground rules for meetings of the conspirators: no breakfasting together, no registering at the hotel with company names, no calls to the office, no papers to be left in hotel-room wastebaskets. Spencer, it seems, had been instructed to handle some of the secretarial work of the cartel and believed in doing it right; he'd hung onto documents to help in training an assistant. But the most valuable windfall from the meticulous record keeper was a pile of copies of the "phases of the moon" pricing formula for as far back as May, 1958.

Not much to look at—just sheets of paper, each containing a half-dozen columns of figures—they immediately resolved the enigma of switchgear prices in commercial contracts. One group of columns established the bidding order of the seven switchgear manufacturers—a different company, each with its own code number, phasing into the priority position every two weeks (hence "phases of the moon"). A second group of columns, keyed into the company code numbers, established how much each company was to knock off the agreed-upon book price. For example, if it were No. 1's (G.E.'s) turn to be low bidder at a certain number of dollars off book, then all Westinghouse (No. 2), or Allis-Chalmers (No. 3) had to do was look for their code number in the second group of columns to find how many dollars they were to bid *above* No. 1. These bids would then be fuzzed up by having a little added to them or taken away by companies 2, 3, etc. Thus there was not even a hint that the winning bid had been collusively arrived at.

With this little device in hand, the trust busters found they could light up the whole conspiracy like a switchboard. The new evidence made an equally profound impression on the grand juries. On February 16 and 17, 1960, they handed down the first seven indictments. Forty companies and eighteen individuals were charged with fixing prices or dividing the market on seven electrical products. Switchgear led the list.[4]

A LEG UP FROM ALLIS-CHALMERS

These initial indictments brought about two major turning points in the investigation. The first was a decision by Allis-Chalmers to play ball with the government. This move came too late to save L. W.

---

[4] The other six: oil circuit breakers, low-voltage power circuit breakers, insulators, open-fuse cutouts, lightning arresters, bushings. Each indictment covered one product and listed all the corporations and individuals charged with conspiracy to fix prices on that product.

(Shorty) Long, an assistant general manager—he was one of the eighteen already indicted—but the trust busters were willing to go easier on Allis-Chalmers if the company came up with something solid. It did. Thousands upon thousands of documents were turned over to the government. Further, the testimony of Vice President J. W. McMullen, and others was so helpful (attorney Edward Mullinix had coached them many hours on the importance of backing up allegations with receipted hotel bills, expense-account items, memorandums, telephone logs, etc.) that a number of new cases were opened up. Only two of those first seven indictments retained their Justice Department classification as "major" cases. To them were added five new major indictments—power transformers, power switching equipment, industrial controls, turbine generators, and steam condensers—culled from thirteen to follow that spring and fall.

The second major turning point came through a decision in March by Chief Federal Judge J. Cullen Ganey, who was to try all the cases. That decision concerned whether the individuals and companies involved in the first seven indictments would be permitted to plead *nolo contendere* (no contest) to the charges. The matter was of vital importance to the companies, which might well be faced by treble-damage suits growing out of the conspiracies. (A G.E. lawyer had advised the Executive Office: "If a criminal case can be disposed of by a *nolo* plea, the prospective damage claimant is given no assistance in advancing a claim; it must be built from the ground up.) The matter was also of great importance to a determined Robert Bicks, who argued that *nolo* pleas would permit the defendants "the luxury of a 'Maybe we did it; maybe we didn't do it' posture. 'Oh, yes, technically before Judge Ganey we admitted this, but you know we weren't guilty. You know we didn't do this.'"

Actually, in the opinion of one veteran antitrust lawyer, everybody in the industry and 99 percent of the government thought the court would accept *nolos*. Indeed, the Justice Department was so worried about the matter, and so anxious to forfend such a development, that for the first time in the history of the department an attorney general sent a presiding judge an affidavit urging rejection of *nolos*.

"Acceptance of the *nolo* pleas tendered in these cases," William Rogers deposed to Judge Ganey, "would mean [that] . . . insistence on guilty pleas or guilty verdicts would never be appropriate in any antitrust case—no matter the predatory nature of the violation or the widespread adverse consequences to governmental purchasers. This result would neither foster respect for the law nor vindicate the public interest. These interests require, in the cases at bar here, either a trial on the issues of pleas of guilty."

But Judge Ganey didn't need to be impressed with the seriousness of the cases. He ruled that *nolo contendere* pleas were inacceptable (unless, of course, the Justice Department had no objections). The corporations and individuals would either have to plead guilty or stand trial. At the arraignment in April, Allis-Chalmers and its indicted employees promptly pleaded "guilty"; most others, including G.E. and its employees, pleaded "not guilty." They intended at that time to take their chances before a jury, no matter how bleak the prospects.

G.E. pleaded "guilty" to all the major indictments against it, and with the government's consent, *nolo contendere* to the thirteen "minor" ones. The other major companies followed suit. The way thus cleared, judgment was swift in coming. On February 6, executives from every major manufacturer in the entire electrical-equipment industry sat in a crowded courtroom and heard Judge Ganey declare: "What is really at stake here is the survival of the kind of economy under which this country has grown great, the free-enterprise system." Seven executives went off to a

Pennsylvania prison; twenty-three others, given suspended jail sentences, were put on probation for five years; and fines totaling nearly $2 million were handed out.

Twenty-nine companies received fines ranging from $437,500 for G.E. down to $7,500 each for Carrier Corp. and Porcelain Insulator Corp. The others, for the record, were Allen-Bradley Co., Allis-Chalmers Manufacturing Co., A. B. Chance Co., Clark Controller Co., Cornell-Dubilier Electric Corp., Cutler-Hammer, Inc., Federal Pacific Electric Co., Foster Wheeler Corp., Hubbard & Co., I-T-E Circuit Breaker Co., Ingersoll-Rand Co., Joslyn Manufacturing & Supply Co., Kuhlman Electric Co., Lapp Insulator Co., McGraw-Edison Co., Moloney Electric Co., Ohio Brass Co., H. K. Porter Co., Sangamo Electric Co., Schwager-Wood Corp., Southern States Equipment Corp., Square D Co., Wagner Electric Corp., Westinghouse Electric Corp., C. H. Wheeler Manufacturing Co., and Worthington Corp.

IS THE LESSON LEARNED?

So ended the incredible affair—a story of cynicism, arrogance, and irresponsibility. Plainly there was an egregious management failure. But there was also a failure to connect ordinary morals and business morals; the men involved apparently figured there was a difference.

The consent decrees now being hammered out by the Justice Department are partial insurance that bid rigging and price fixing won't happen again. Yet consent decrees are only deterrents, not cures. The fact is that the causes which underlay the electrical conspiracies are still as strong as they ever were. Chronic overcapacity continues to exert a strong downward pressure on prices. The industry's price problem—outgrowth of an inability to shift the buyer's attention from price to other selling points like higher quality, better service, improved design—could hardly be worse: many items of electrical equipment are currently selling for less than in the ruinous days of the "white sale." Corporate pressure is stronger than ever on executives, who must struggle to fulfill the conflicting demands of bigger gross sales on the one hand and more profit per dollar of net sales on the other. These are matters that require careful handling if conspiracy is not to take root again in the electrical-equipment industry.

The antitrust laws also confront the largest corporations with a special dilemma: how to compete without falling afoul of Section 2 of the Sherman Act, which makes it unlawful to "monopolize, or attempt to monopolize." It will take plenty of business statesmanship to handle this aspect of the law; one way, of course, is simply to refrain from going after every last piece of business. If G.E. were to drive for 50 percent of the market, even strong companies like I-T-E Circuit Breaker might be mortally injured.

Has the industry learned any lessons? "One thing I've learned out of all this," said one executive, "is to talk to only one other person, not to go to meetings where there are lots of other people." Many of the defendants FORTUNE interviewed both before and after sentencing looked on themselves as the fall guys of U.S. business. They protested that they should no more be held up to blame than many another American businessman, for conspiracy is just as much "a way of life" in other fields as it was in electrical equipment. "Why pick on us?" was the attitude. "Look at some of those other fellows."

This attitude becomes particularly disturbing when one considers that most of the men who pleaded guilty in Judge Ganey's court (to say nothing of the scores given immunity for testifying before the grand juries) are back at their old positions, holding down key sales and marketing jobs. Only G.E. cleaned house; out went Burens, Burke, Hentschel, and Stehlik, plus ten others, including the heretofore unpunished William S. Ginn. (Although the confessed conspirators at G.E. had been assured that the transfers, demotions, and pay cuts received earlier would be the end of the corporate punishment, this was not the case. In mid-March they were told they could either quit or be fired, and were given anywhere from a half hour to a few days to make their decision.)

DISJOINTED AUTHORITY, DISJOINTED MORALS

But top executive officers of the biggest companies, at least, have come out of their antitrust experience determined upon strict compliance programs and possessed now of enough insight into the workings of a cartel to make those programs effective. Allis-Chalmers has set up a special compliance section. G.E. and Westinghouse, without which cartels in the industry could never endure, are taking more elaborate preventive measures. Both are well aware that any repetition of these conspiracies would lay them open to political pressure for dismemberment; size has special responsibilities in our society, and giants are under a continuous obligation to demonstrate that they have not got so big as to lose control over their far-flung divisions.

This case has focused attention on American business practices as nothing else has in many years. Senator Kefauver says he intends to probe further into the question of conspiracy at the top levels of management. Justice Department investigations are proliferating. Said Attorney General Robert Kennedy: "We are redoubling our efforts to convince anyone so minded that conspiracy as 'a way of life' must mean a short and unhappy one."

The problem for American business does not start and stop with the scofflaws of the electrical industry or with antitrust. Much was made of the fact that G.E. operated under a system of disjointed authority, and this was one reason it got into trouble. A more significant factor, the disjointment of morals, is something for American executives to think about in all aspects of their relations with their companies, each other, and the community.

53. NEWSPAPER PUBLICITY AND THE ELECTRICAL CONSPIRACY

NEWS REPORTS CONCERNING CORPORATE CRIME, if they are covered at all, are generally relegated to "a brief paragraph on an inner page" and even then they are phrased either in terms of the individuals involved or in vague terms of "proceedings" or "suits" against the corporation. [see Sutherland, *White Collar Crime* (1949), p. 50]. The nature and extent of the newspaper coverage in the *General Electric* case—a case which probably received more publicity than any corporate crime case in recent history—was revealing. Newspaper surveys were conducted at two key points in the case.

The first survey conducted by New Republic Magazine studied the following representative newspapers which account for fifteen percent of all newspapers sold in the United States: Atlanta Constitution (circulation 198,028); Boston Globe (340,374); Boston Herald (173,063); Chicago Sun Times (527,675); Chicago Tribune (882,837); Christian Science Monitor (179,839); Cleveland Plane Dealer (513,714); Des Moines Register (224,337); Detroit Free Press (459,265); Indianapolis Star (206,501); Kansas City Times (337,804); Los Angeles Times (497,873); Minneapolis Tribune (215,175); New York Herald Tribune (350,966); N.Y. News (2,025,229); N.Y. Times (673,974); Phila. Inquirer (605-007); Pittsburgh Post Gazette (271,885); St. Louis Democrat (336,137); St. Louis Post Dispatch (411,440); San Francisco Chronicle (236,480); Wash. Post (393,503). See New Republic, Feb. 20, 1961, p. 7. These newspapers were read on December 8 and 9, 1960, the days immediately following the original admissions of guilt by the indicted corporations. Only sixteen percent (weighted according to circulation) of the surveyed newspapers placed the story on page one, each with a single column headline. Eleven per cent used less than a column of print on an inside page. Forty-three percent used less than half of a column on an inside page. And a full *thirty percent* of the surveyed newspapers entirely omitted any reference to the story. "In nearly every report, the only firms named were General Electric and Westinghouse, although twenty-nine companies in all were involved, with plants throughout the nation." New Republic, Feb. 20, 1961, p. 7.

Following the sentencing, this writer made a survey of the following thirty representative newspapers which account for more than twenty percent of all newspapers sold in the United States: Atlantic Constitution; Baltimore Sun (413,299); Chicago Tribune; Christian Science Monitor; Cleveland Plane Dealer; Denver Post (252,748); Detroit News (475,873); Hartford Courant (107,120); Indianapolis Star; Los Angeles Times; Louisville Courier Journal

▶SOURCE: *"Notes and Comment" Corporate Crime, Yale Law Journal, (December, 1961), 71: 288–289.*

(216,539); Memphis Commercial Appeal (212,757); Milwaukee Journal (369,669); Minneapolis Tribune; N.Y. Herald Tribune; N.Y. Mirror (836,810); N.Y. News; N.Y. Post (351,700); N.Y. Times; Phila. Inquirer; Pitts. Post Gazette; St. Louis Post Dispatch; San Francisco Chronicle; Seattle Times (221,549); Springfield Union (80,581); Wall Street Journal (582,491); Wash. Post; Wash. Star (264,717); and New Haven Register (101,244). Although this was the largest criminal antitrust prosecution in the history of the United States, and one of the first in which actual prison sentences were imposed, forty-five percent of the newspapers in the survey kept the story of the sentencing off the front page. Fewer than a handful of the surveyed papers mentioned the names of any of the sentenced corporations other than General Electric and Westinghouse, and most of the papers devoted substantially all their headline space and coverage to the executives who received prison sentences. None of the newspapers emphasized that the *corporations* were actually guilty of committing *crimes*. The language of criminality—words like "guilty," "sentences," and "criminal"—was generally reserved for the executives. More neutral language—words like "proceedings," "antitrust suits" and "penalties"—was employed in reference to the corporate defendants. On the basis of the nature and extent of this coverage, the editorialist who reported on February 8th that "seldom if ever have so many corporate images been so thoroughly tarnished, Denver Post, Feb. 8, 1961, p. 16, may be commended for his wishful thinking; but the writer who observed that because of the "negligible and emasculated reporting of this issue by the bulk of the nations press [the] reaction of the American public to the largest antitrust suit in our history has generally been that of mute acquiescence, New Republic, March 13, 1961, p. 30, deserves the kudos for accuracy of analysis.

One can speculate that had no corporate executives been indicted, or had no prison sentences been imposed, even the newspapers which did publicize the recent case would have relegated the story to a small column on the financial page. Apparently therefore little moral opprobrium attaches to the convicted corporation except in the highly unusual case because few members of the general public are ever aware of such conviction. Moreover, even in the unusual case, like *General Electric,* the opprobrium is shunted away from the corporation and focused upon the convicted individuals. It is unlikely, therefore, that the threat of "tarnishing" moral opprobrium is significant to the endocratic corporation in terms of profit diminution or effective deterrence.

Even if the general public is mutely acquiescent toward the convicted corporation, it has been suggested that certain designated representatives of the public may vent their opprobrium by informal blacklisting of convicted corporations which may result in the reduction of government contracts allocated to these corporations, an unwillingness to extend credit or loans to such corporations or a wide range of other informal but coercive denial of privileges. There is, of course, no available evidence of this practice in the public record. Informed sources insist that although such blacklisting is frequently mentioned, in practice it is never employed. Commenting on its practical inapplicability in relation to the large endocratic corporation Professor Manning of the Yale Law School observed that "if the government stopped buying its electrical equipment from the corporations who pleaded guilty in the *General Electric* Case, it would either have to do without electrical equipment or it would have to import all such equipment from Japan."

54. MURDER, INC.

MEYER BERGER

FOUR MONTHS AGO SHERIFF MANGANO OF Brooklyn delivered "Happy" Maione and "Dasher" Abbandando to Sing Sing Prison. "Two for the back," he told the keeper. "The back" is the death-cell block.

The sheriff removed the gyves from Happy and Dasher. "So long," he said. Abbandando didn't answer. The sheriff squeezed Maione's arm. "Well," he said, "so long, Happy." Maione tried to say "So long, Sheriff," but the words wedged in his throat. His eyes filled.

This emotionalism would have astonished Happy Maione's co-workers in Murder Inc. Maione had killed at least ten—probably 20—men, all most untidily. The George Rudnick murder, for example, for which he and Abbandando got their death sentence, had been done with a meat cleaver and ice pick. With Happy, if it wasn't the cleaver, it was apt to be the ice pick or both. He used a gun only on short-order jobs.

If matters take their normal course, Happy Maione and Dasher Abbandando will be electrocuted within the next few months. Before then they will be joined in "the back" by two of their onetime colleagues in Murder Inc.: Harry ("Pittsburgh Phil") Strauss and Martin ("Buggsy") Goldstein. Goldstein and Strauss, whose trial for the murder of "Puggy" Feinstein

▶SOURCE: *"Murder, Inc.," Life (September 30, 1940), pp. 86–88, 92–96. Reprinted by permission.*

ended in Brooklyn last week, are, like Maione and Abbandando, victims of assiduous prosecution by Brooklyn's District Attorney William O'Dwyer. When O'Dwyer took the lid off Murder Inc. a year ago, he gave the U.S. its most startling crime story of the century.

Although by now a majority of U.S. citizens have heard of Murder Inc., the war has undoubtedly deprived it of the attention to which in normal time it would be entitled. Murder Inc. killed at least 63 men in and around New York in the past nine years. As many again were probably accounted for elsewhere by its talented personnel working on call in Newark, Jersey City, Chicago, St. Louis, Los Angeles and Florida among other places. Concerned primarily with New York killings, District Attorney O'Dwyer thinks extermination of the murder troop may take all of his four-year term which is to end in December 1943.

Mr. O'Dwyer was a Brooklyn policeman from 1917 to 1925. Even with this enlightening background he was startled by the murder troop's extraordinary scope, once he started to research the subject. According to O'Dwyer, six men dominate Murder Inc. in New York's metropolitan district. Six more men run a Chicago branch. In Los Angeles the management is made up mostly of expatriate New Yorkers. These big shots do not murder. They assign the homicide to earnest craftsmen like Happy, Dasher, Pittsburgh Phil and Buggsy, who worked on salary. The executives draw their profits from multiple interests. Through dummy fronts, for example, they control a great part of the country's liquor distribution. They control labor unions through union officers who use their organization to shake down employers. The various branches own night clubs and many of the busier gambling houses. Sometimes they operate bawdy-house chains on the side but there is less of this than most people think. The organization engages in many legitimate enterprises, and has shouldered its way into many heretofore honest firms with years of solid tradition.

Chain store, or corporate, homicide started in the pre-dawn of Repeal; roughly, about nine years ago. Around this time major big city bootleggers, labor-union racketeers and other important criminals realized that under Repeal the public might expect comparative quiet; fewer gang brawls, less freehand killing. In order successfully to apply their liquor profits to new enterprises, the head men from different cities met and agreed to adopt new rules for the conduct of murder under a loosely formed national syndicate known among its founders as "The Combination." The name "Murder Inc.," as applied to The Combination, is a bit of journalistic license. Murder is not The Combination's business. It does no murder for outsiders and no killing for a fee. Indeed, its revised rules sharply restrict the uses of homicide to business needs and have probably reduced rather than increased the total number of U. S. murders committed annually. The new handbook sternly forbids murder for personal or romantic reasons, or even for revenge. Executive heads of The Combination dispassionately debate each murder before causing it to occur, much as a Wall Street syndicate might discuss a maneuver in the stock market.

When The Combination setup was first proposed there was need for a national framework. This was at hand in the Unione Siciliane which was controlled by "Lucky" Luciano, but Lucky and his advisers were concerned about some of the Union's older members. These men were conservatives, in a way; they saw no need for modernizing murder. They were inclined to be stubborn about innovations. The more stubborn ones began to die off with remarkable rapidity. Joe ("The Boss") Masseria, who had borne a charmed life, was probably the most ornery. He died in a dingy Coney Island *estaminet* one spring morning of multiple revolver wounds. The other conservatives began to catch on. They moved hastily for modernization.

THE COMBINATION FUNCTIONS SMOOTHLY

Complications developed, though, as The Combination began to function. One young Brooklyn trooper, for example, was sent on an out-of-town job. The fellow came back with his assignment unfinished. It seems the finger man for The Combination's out-of-town branch was of the older Unione Siciliane group. He spoke no English. The Brooklyn gunman made a second trip, this time with an interpreter and the job came off all right. To keep down the budget, thereafter, The Combination found out beforehand whether a contract called for a linguist.

Because out-of-town kills are expensive, a Combination will rarely call for talent from another city unless the murder subject is some one important and entitled to special honors. Removal of disloyal or untrustworthy punks, eradication of informers and even liquidation of secondary Combination executives is left to home talent. On exchange kills spade work is done beforehand in the host city. When the visiting trooper arrives, he is met by a finger man whose only function is to point out the victim. A visiting trooper does not identify himself by name to a finger man. The finger man, by the same token, remains anonymous. These precautions make sense if there is a slip-up on the kill. Should the police grab either the visiting trooper or the finger man, neither can identify the other.

Before a kill the party or parties who have contracted for the murder establish an alibi. They may take a short cruise. The passenger list and testimony of fellow passengers would clear them in court. They may go to some neighboring State and visit public places—night clubs or theaters—where they can be seen. One out-of-town Combination boss, a proud father, arranged a kill to take place while he and his wife attended a benefit performance of his daughter's dancing class.

On out-of-town kills a trooper does not know whom he has murdered unless the killing makes the newspapers. Professional pride may tempt a trooper to tarry in a strange city to see how local journals review his work. But this is strictly forbidden under the new rules. When a kill is done the trooper immediately leaves the city. He is over the border and speeding home before the police are rounding up obvious—but alibi-proofed—suspects.

An order to murder in the delicate phraseology of The Combination is "a contract." The order reaches the salaried gunman through the troop boss who in turn gets it from some Combination executive. (There is method in this indirection. If someone blunders in commission of a contract, the police find it difficult to trace the murder order to its original source.) If a contract calls for something especially fancy, the troop boss may take it on himself, with or without assistants. Murderers' apprentices—"punks," to the trade—go on the payroll at $50 a week. They start with piddling chores—steal cars to transport corpses after murders, swipe extra license plates for these cars to make identification more difficult. They take courses in crowding convoy machines before and behind these murder transports so that policemen at cross streets cannot read the license plates. The curriculum covers techniques in "schlamming" (severe beating) and "skulling" (assault just short of murder), and conduct at police line-ups in event of arrest. Serious students, if they show aptitude, are privileged in their senior year to attend undergraduate murder clinics; to watch *cum laude* men like Happy Maione or Pittsburg Phil operate with ice pick, bludgeon and cleaver. Talented young men can advance rapidly. A hard-working, conscientious trooper, first class, subject to call at any hour of day or night for professional duty gets from $100 to $150 a week. Real artists, like Maione, get around $100. Troop bosses, like Strauss, command $250 and pickings.

Troop chiefs keep looking for new murder-school pupils. They watch local striplings who are trying their hand at neighborhood stick-ups, general bullying and at cutting in on smalltime card games and dice meetings. The talent scouts choose those who show promise. The new pupil must give up extracurricular activities after he goes on The Combination payroll. The Combination does not want its punks arrested in non-profitable hold-ups, as they easily might be. The new boys, exposed to police massage treatment while they are still greenhorns in homicide, might babble about their Combination murder-car stealing.

IT BECOMES ITS OWN LAW

A freshman in murder school can, however, take on certain "personal jobs" but these operations are limited. The new pupil can, for example, hijack loot taken by independent stick-up men. He may strip burglars or street moneylenders of their profits, on the theory that burglars and independent stick-up men are not apt to complain to the police. This gives the murder-school student something to augment his Combination salary. The troop boss, or headmaster, if he likes the new boy, may even throw him a minor neighborhood slot-machine concession. Early in its history The Combination set up geographical limits for each unit's range of operations. It sternly forbade its troops to murder except on executive contract. While The Combination, like Civil Service, pays pensions to widows of deceased workers, it laid down the principle that no one in The Combination, executive or punk, could retire or withdraw. A trooper's refusal to fulfill a murder contract, once assigned, was designated as disloyal. Double-crossing was written in as a cardinal sin. Misappropriation of Combination profits was defined as one form of double cross. Informers, naturally, were to be put out of the way. To simplify matters, conviction on any count carried a death sentence.

In order to regulate its members The Combination set up its own judicial system, including a high or supreme court, whose verdicts were monotonously adverse to defendants. Each Combination's executive board was bench and jury. Every offender had the right to hearing. For punks, troops and troop chiefs, the local court's verdict was final. Executives were entitled to appeal to the high or national court, made up of Combination leaders from different parts of the country.

Inarticulate defendants were allowed counsel; not a real attorney, but some gifted member of The Combination to plead their cause. Abe ("Kid Twist") Reles, for example, though he lacked academic background, fancied himself as a mouthpiece. He had, by intently listening to lawyers who had delivered him from justice in the 43 times he had stood prisoner before city and county courts, acquired an astonishing hash of legalistic flubdub. He liked to utter courtroom cliches like "If it please the Court," or "I respectfully except."

In the role of counsel The Kid last spring pleaded "Pretty" Levine's case before a Combination Court. Pretty is a tall, rather handsome man, dark, with pale blue eyes; son of a quiet Brownsville shop owner. Reles had adopted him as a protégé and had enlisted him in the Brownsville troop. After he had stolen a few murder cars, though, Pretty decided he didn't like the homicide business. He had married and had become a father. He thought he would give up his troop apprenticeship, buy a motor truck and try a more prosaic way of earning a living. At Pretty's hearing, Kid Twist unloaded his full repertoire of legalistic bombast. Hoarsely fervent, he asserted Pretty's right to leave The Combination. He offered to guarantee, if it pleased the court, that his client would keep all Combination secrets. The Kid is still proud of that dramatic plea, but it was indiscreet. He and his wistful punk were marked for ice-pick and cleaver dismissal. They fled to the District Attorney for protection.

The visit of Kid Twist to O'Dwyer was historic. It was this that brought Murder Inc. to the attention first of the perplexed Mr. O'Dwyer and then to the general public. It was also directly responsible for the present predicament of Messrs. Maione, Abbandando, Strauss and Goldstein.

DISCOVERING NEW WAYS TO KILL

The murder of Puggy Feinstein, an insignificant loan shark, for which Buggsy Goldstein was convicted last week, was an interesting one. It sheds light on one department of Murder Inc.'s activities of which the efficiency leaves something to be desired. Perfectionists on its faculty, headed by Mr. Albert Anastasia who is currently on the lam, had worked out to the ultimate degree the cunning business of decoying, fingering and doing-in murder subjects. Their department for out-of-town, or exchange, murders surpassed anything previously developed. Research men for The Combination had not, however, figured out a perfect method of disposing of victims. They were still hard at work on this when Mr. O'Dwyer interrupted.

Actually, there have been two perfect disposal jobs in recent murder annals, but these were awkward and could not be adopted by The Combination for routine purposes. The late Jack ("Legs") Diamond, who was a whimsical fellow anyway, is supposed to have figured out one of these. Diamond put the body of Harry Westone, a business competitor, in an unguarded concrete mixer one night and Westone became—and still is—part of Kingston highway in upstate New York. This disposal system has obvious drawbacks. Murder Inc. never considered it. The other disposal masterpiece was the sinking of "Bo" Weinberg, who had been in "Dutch" Schultz's entourage. Bo's feet were encased in fresh concrete. When the concrete hardened into a block Bo was put into East River. This system is too cumbersome. It means a truck haul and trucks are too slow for murder jobs.

In their disposal experiments The Combination's homicide staff patiently tried to improve on crude orthodox systems. In the summer of 1937 they used Walter Sage as a laboratory subject. Sage was a Strauss protégé, a reliable worker until he tried to hold out a portion of Strauss's slot-machine profits. Walter fell under the ice pick. The research men surmised that the pick thrusts would puncture vital organs and keep the corpse on the bed of Swan Lake where they dumped it. They chained a 30-lb. rock to the legs and a 60-lb slot machine to the neck to make sure. The body came up in two weeks. This puzzled the research men. They finally decided they would have to brush up on anatomy and learn how to apply the pick in the proper places.

In April 1938 the research staff tried another disposal experiment. This time their subject was Hyman Yuran, potential witness against the New York Combination executive, Louis ("Lepke") Buchalter. They dug a grave 4 ft. deep, hard by the messy banks of Loch Sheldrake in the rural Catskills and lined it with quick lime. They figured that the lime would destroy all identification marks; leave the State without a corpus delicti, even if police did locate the burial place. The theory was all right but the lime did not act on Yuran's dental work. This established identification.

PUGGY FEINSTEIN BITES THE DUST

The research department was disappointed but pushed further experiment with scholarly zeal. In September 1939 they tried disposal by fire. Puggy Feinstein—suspected, as Yuran was, of disloyalty to Lepke—was chosen as the subject of their test. Puggy had no special dental work so the research staff didn't bother to dig a grave. Proceeding on the hypothesis that fire would destroy fingerprints and birthmarks, they used gasoline and, after they left the body in a lot at East 51st Street and Fillmore Avenue in Brooklyn, anxiously awaited results. Anastasia, the faculty adviser, was particularly interested in this experiment and only the best men worked on it. It turned out a failure, though. Police fingerprint experts identified Puggy.

All through the trial for the Puggy Feinstein murder, Headmaster Strauss feigned insanity. He mumbled, shadowboxed with imaginary little men, loosely pivoted his neck as if trying to shake something off. Buggsy Goldstein got completely out of hand when Seymour ("Blue Jaw") Magoon, his old partner, testified against him. He stood up in the courtroom, fingers interlocked in extreme supplication. Tears rolled down his cheeks. He cried out: "For God's sake, Seymour, that's some story you're telling. . . . You're burning me, Seymour."

Professional murderers, through some perversity of Mother Nature, are also apt to be sentimentalists. The grow starry-eyed over fireside themes and death-house audiences cry when soloists render *Your Mother Is Your Best Pal After All* at prison concerts. Buggsy's tender appeal caused Blue Jaw to weep too but he bravely turned his face away and continued with his account of how Puggy was put to the torch. Judge Fitzgerald reassured the jurors when they came in with a "Guilty!" verdict. He confided that Mr. O'Dwyer had told him, out of court, that Strauss alone had killed 28 men in the past ten years.

Murder Inc.'s troops take inordinate pride in their work. In dull seasons, when there is no schlamming or skulling to do, they sit around their hangouts and gravely discuss homicide technique. It was generally conceded in Brooklyn that Happy Maione was born gifted and had red thumb, so to speak, as one gifted in gardening is said to have green thumb. Even more than those of his confreres, Happy's career, now so close to its conclusion, can be regarded as a kind of scale model or cameo portrait of Murder Inc. as a whole. Maione was christened Harry after he was born in Brooklyn on Oct. 7, 1908. His nickname, Happy, was a misnomer. He was a sneering, sadistic bully even as a kid. His father, a sickly tailor, died of a heart attack four years ago. His mother, a quiet, devout little woman, lives in a five-room third-floor flat where the rent is $27 a month. She gets work relief for the two youngest and a widow's pension.

HAPPY MAIONE WORKS HIS WAY UP

Happy did not like school. He left in the seventh grade when he was 15. He could read and write, but his academic attainments didn't go much beyond that. He worked six months as errand boy in a small clothes shop in Manhattan. Later he polished boots in a shoeshine and hat-cleaning store in Williamsburg. He left this to try his hand at bricklaying, but his heart wasn't in the job. He never got his union card. At 16 he was arrested for assault and robbery, a neighborhood job. He tried to knock down the cop and take the cop's service revolver. The cop laid Happy out, but this episode gave Happy a sinister reputation in Ocean Hill poolrooms in Brownsville. About this time he ran into a girl who had fled the House of Good Shepherd. He set up as panderer in partnership with a man quaintly called "Bow-wow" Mercurio. "Maione's sex history," the probation officer sadly wrote after the Rudnick murder conviction, "is very bad." Two rapes were written against Maione's record.

Happy was arrested 35 times before he was 31 years old. The record included virtually everything except arson. Happy ran a racehorse book in a small way, shook down shopkeepers, had part interest with one of his brothers in a small florist shop. He and The Dasher met up with Abe Reles twelve years ago and helped Reles wipe out the three Brothers Shapiro—Willie, Irving and Meyer—and other business competitors. They buried Willie alive in a sand pit in Canarsie in July 1934. Maione performed a series of kills in subjugation of a local plasterers' union. One of his best jobs, incidentally, was the murder of Anthony Siciliano and Caesar Lattoro in a basement on Bergen St., Brooklyn, during his plasterers' series. The victims were wary, difficult to approach. A big police dog warned them when prowlers got close. Happy got around the two men on Feb. 6, 1939, dressed as a woman. The clothes belonged to the spouse of Victor Gurino, one of his associates. Happy painted and powdered his face, swished around in front of the plasterers' flat and was invited inside. He shot and killed both men. Before he left he put two spare bullets in the police dog. At this point in his career Happy rode high. He kept a mistress, according to a probation report, in the house where one of his married sisters lived, and had another woman in Ocean Hill. The mistress, the report gravely recorded, was a girl named Renee. The other woman was written down as "a concubine named Mildred." Happy was one of the big shots in the troop. He rated second only to Pittsburgh Phil Strauss. Dasher Abbandando and Goldstein rated perhaps a grade lower.

The George Rudnick murder, for which Happy and The Dasher got the death sentence, was one of their earlier Combination contracts. Rudnick, a drug addict, had turned stool pigeon. Around the end of March 1937, Pittsburgh Phil Strauss met Kid Twist for a business conference in a hangout at Saratoga and Livonia Avenues in Brooklyn. The Rudnick assignment was fresh. Kid Twist and Strauss adjourned to a nearby drinking spot. Strauss outlined the assignment. He said, "Rudnick is a stoolie. We got to kill him." He arranged to do the job, Happy and Dasher Abbandando assisting. Pittsburgh Phil wanted this to be an extra-fancy bit of handiwork. He said: "We will put a note in Rudnick's pocket. It will say he gave information to Dewey. It will be a favor for Lepke."

PITTSBURGH PHIL WRITES A LETTER

Strauss assigned a Combination punk to borrow a typewriter. The machine was delivered to Kid Twist's home. Pittsburgh Phil typed the note under difficulties. Neither he nor the Kid knew how to put in the typewriter ribbon. Kid Twist finally held the ribbon in his fingers and the job was done that way. The note was smudged and untidy. On the face of the envelope Strauss typed: "Mr. George Rudnick." He bogged down on the note. He did not know how to spell "friend." There was a scholarly argument over this. Reles was almost certain it was "f-r-i-e-n-d." Strauss said "No." Finally started the note: "Friend George." This looked okay to him. The note was rewritten three times. The last version said: "Firend George. Will you please meet me in Ny some day in reference to what you told me last week. Also I will have that certain powder that I promised you the last time I seen you. PS I hope you found this in your letterbox sealed. I remain your firend "YOU KNOW FROM DEWEY'S OFFICE."

Pretty Levine and Anthony ("The Duke") Maffatore, another freshman in the murder college, were told off to steal a murder car. The punks picked a black Buick sedan. Strauss fetched a set of stolen license plates. The Duke and Levine put these on the Buick. Happy checked the new plates to see if they were on tight. The Dasher smashed the car's original license plates.

Everything now was ready for the kill. Rudnick sensed this. He stayed indoors most of the time. If he had to venture out he would come home just before daybreak. He always moved close to the building line. He figured they would be less apt to see him in the deep building shadows. Dasher Abbandando and Kid Twist tried to find him but they did not have much luck. On the night of May 24, 1937, they finally got word that Rudnick was out somewhere. They passed the word along, Happy and Pittsburgh Phil, Dasher Abbandando and Kid Twist, met, according to testimony, in the Sunrise Garage. They figured this might be the night. By an odd coincidence, it happened that on this night, in a flat opposite the Sunrise Garage, Happy's grandmother was dying. She was past 70. She had helped raise Happy. All his family were at her house, kneeling in prayer, but he had the Rudnick job and could not go.

A little before midnight a scream came from the flat across the street from the Sunrise Garage. Happy's grandmother had died. Happy's brothers and sisters kept on wailing for hours but Happy, detailed to wait at the garage until his colleagues returned, could not leave his post. Meanwhile at about 4:30 on the morning of May 25, Kid Twist and The Dasher were still waiting for the stollie in a little tan Ford car in Saratoga Avenue near Livonia. The Dasher had borrowed the Ford from a boyhood chum who was not in Murder Inc. "I want to take out a girl," Abbandando had told him. A few minutes later a little figure moved cautiously along the building line, up Saratoga Avenue toward Livonia.

Kid Twist said: "That's him. That's George." Abbandando peered into the shadows by the building line. He said:

"You are crazy," but he looked a second time. "You are right," he said. He started the tan Ford. Rudnick stopped. He tried to run back but the tan Ford caught up with him. They put the gun on him and he crept into the tan Ford. He shook with sudden palsy. Abbandando drove toward the Sunrise Garage and Kid Twist followed slowly, in another car. He did not want to be in on this kill. He was stalling.

The Dasher drove the tan Ford up on the sidewalk, with the front of the hood against the door. The door opened and he rolled in, with Rudnick. When Kid Twist came up, five minutes later, Happy Maione and Pittsburgh Phil Strauss were standing over the body. Happy said: "The works finished. You are not needed." Dasher Abbandando had Rudnick by the shoulders, keeping him in sitting position. Strauss tied a rope around Rudnick's neck. They tied the body in a jackknife pose.

The black Buick was in this case used as a hearse. Strauss and Maione got Rudnick's body by the legs. Abbandando held the head. They put Rudnick on the floor behind the front seat. The body made a noise through one of the wounds. It startled the troops. Strauss swore. He said: "The sonofabitch ain't dead yet." Strauss used the pick again. Maione said: "We got to finish him." He hit Rudnick on the head, just under the hair line. He stepped back. "We got to clean up the floor," he said. He filled a water bucket. Abbandando got a broom and swept toward the sewer drain. They washed the broom, the cleaver and the pick.

Maione spoke to a Murder Inc. chauffeur named Julie Catalano, "Drive this over into the Wilson Avenue precinct," he said. "Take it easy over the bumps. Take your time." Maione got into the back seat in Kid Twist's car. Catalano abandoned the black Buick in front of 1190 Jefferson Ave., in a quiet residential street. He walked to the corner and got in with Kid Twist and Maione. They let him out at Atlantic Avenue and Eastern Parkway.

Catalano, The Duke, Pretty Levine, Kid Twist and a whole line-up of witnesses told this story when Mr. O'Dwyer brought Happy and The Dasher to trial last May. Happy's lawyers put 14 of his relatives on the stand. They swore Happy was in his grandmother's house all through the night she was dying, but Burton Turkus, Mr. O'Dwyer's assistant, was prepared for this. He proved through the undertaker and the embalmer that Happy was not in his grandmother's house, as they testified.

The jury did not stay out long. On May 27, 1940, County Judge Franklin Taylor passed sentence. On the Maione complaint, under "Disposition," he wrote: "Sing Sing Prison, there to suffer death by electrocution during the week of July 7, 1940." He wrote the same for The Dasher.

On the morning of May 28, Sheriff Mangano called for the prisoners in Raymond Street jail. Happy tried to be debonair when the Sheriff put on the handcuffs. "You got here early," he said. When Maione and Abbandando got in the Black Maria in the prison yard, Happy's mother and his married sister, Jennie, were by the gate. They waved to him. Maione tried to stand up. He hollered, "Good-by momma," but he choked on the words. His face was wet with tears. At the 10:30 train that takes prisoners out of Grand Central to Sing Sing Prison, Renee was waiting. She kissed him. All the way up the Hudson, Happy stared at the Palisades. He littered the floor with cigarets. The Dasher was glumly silent. Maione cursed Kid Twist Reles. "He is a yella rat," he told the Sheriff. "He is a squealer."

Sheriff Mangano got his charges into a black taxi that was waiting at Ossining station. It moved up the serpentine road. The Sheriff walked the two men through the prison reception room to the high-ceilinged room at the left. The Sheriff took off the cuffs. He nodded to the keeper.

"Two for the back," he said.

55. THEFT AS A WAY OF LIFE

EDWIN H. SUTHERLAND

THE ESSENTIAL CHARACTERISTICS OF THE PROfession of theft are technical skill, status, consensus, differential association, and organization. Two significant conclusions may be derived from analysis of these characteristics. The first is that the characteristics of the profession of theft are similar to the characteristics of any other permanent group. The second is that certain elements run through these characteristics which differentiate the professional thieves sharply from other groups. The similarities and differences will be indicated in the following elaboration of these characteristics and of the implications which may be derived from them.

I. THE PROFESSION OF THEFT AS A COMPLEX OF TECHNIQUES

The professional thief has a complex of abilities and skills, just as do physicians, lawyers, or bricklayers. The abilities and skills of the professional thief are directed to the planning and execution of crimes, the disposal of stolen goods, the fixing of cases in which arrests occur, and the control of other situations which may arise in the course of the occupation. Manual dexterity and physical force are a minor

▶SOURCE: *The Professional Thief*, Chicago: University of Chicago Press, 1937, pp. 197–219. (Editorial adaptations.) Copyright 1937 by the University of Chicago Press. Reprinted by permission.

element in these techniques. The principal elements in these techniques are wits, "front," and talking ability. The thieves who lack these general abilities or the specific skills which are based on the general abilities are regarded as amateurs, even though they may steal habitually.[1] Also, burglars, robbers, kidnapers, and others who engage in the "heavy rackets" are generally not regarded as professional thieves, for they depend primarily on manual dexterity or force. A few criminals in the "heavy rackets" use their wits, "front," and talking ability, and these are regarded by the professional thieves as belonging to the profession.

The division between professional and non-professional thieves in regard to this complex of techniques is relatively sharp. This is because these techniques are developed to a high point only by education, and the education can be secured only in association with professional thieves; thieves do not have formal educational

[1] Several statistical studies of habitual thieves, defined in terms of repeated arrests, have been published. Some of these are excellent from the point of view of the problems with which they deal, but they throw little light on professional thieves because they do not differentiate professional thieves from other habitual thieves. See Roland Grassberger, *Gewerbs-und Berufsverbrechertum in den Vereinigten Staaten von Amerika* (Vienna, 1933); Fritz Beger, *Die rückfälligen Betrüger* (Leipzig, 1929); Alfred John, *Die Rückfallsdiebe* (Leipzig, 1929).

institutions for the training of recruits.[2] Also, these techniques generally call for co-operation which can be secured only in association with professional thieves. Finally, this complex of techniques represents a unified preparation for all professional problems in the life of the thief. Certain individuals, as lone wolves, develop to a high point the technique of executing a specific act of theft—e.g., forgery—but are quite unprepared in plans, resources, and connections to deal with emergencies such as arrest.

Because some of the techniques are specific, professional thieves tend to specialize on a relatively small number of rackets that are related to one another. On the other hand, because of the contacts in the underworld with criminals of all kinds and because of the generality of some of the techniques of crime, professional thieves frequently transfer for longer or shorter periods from their specialty to some other racket. In some cases they like the new racket better than the old and remain in the new field. In many cases they dislike the new racket. Hapgood's thief was primarily a pickpocket; he participated occasionally in burglaries but never liked burglary and remained at heart a pickpocket; he wrote regarding burglary: "It is too dangerous, the come-back is too sure, you have to depend too much on the nerve of your pals, the 'bits' [prison sentences] are too long, and it is very difficult to 'square' it."[3]

The evidence is not adequate to determine whether specialization has increased or decreased. Cooper asserts that it has decreased and explains the decrease as due to the war, prohibition, and the depression. He asserts specifically that confidence men, who, a generation ago would have been ashamed to engage in any theft outside of their own specialty, are now engaging in banditry, kidnaping, and other crimes, and he gives a detailed description of a conference of confidence men held in Chicago in which they attempted to formulate a code which would prohibit their colleagues from excursions outside their own field.[4] Byrnes showed in 1886 in his history of professional criminals in America that many thieves participated for longer or shorter times in crimes outside their own special field.[5]

II. THE PROFESSION OF THEFT AS STATUS

The professional thief, like any other professional man, has status. The status is based upon his technical skill, financial standing, connections, power, dress, manners, and wide knowledge acquired in his migratory life. His status is seen in the attitudes of other criminals, the police, the court officials, newspapers, and others. The term "thief" is regarded as honorific and is used regularly without qualifying adjectives to refer to the professional thief. It is so defined in a recent dictionary of criminal slang: "Thief, n. A member of the underworld who steals often and successfully. This term is applied with reserve and only to habitual criminals. It is considered a high compliment."[6]

Professional thieves are contemptuous of

---

[2] Stories circulate at intervals regarding schools for pickpockets, confidence men, and other professional thieves. If formal schools of this nature have ever existed, they have probably been ephemeral.

[3] Hutchins Hapgood, *Autobiography of a Thief* (New York, 1903), p. 107.

[4] Courtney R. Cooper, *Ten Thousand Public Enemies* (Boston, 1935), pp. 271–72; "Criminal America," *Saturday Evening Post,* CCVII (April 27, 1935), 6. A confidence man, when asked regarding this conference of confidence men in Chicago, said that Cooper's writings regarding it should have been entitled "Mythologies of 1935."

[5] Thomas Byrnes, *Professional Criminals of America* (New York, 1886). Grassberger (*op. cit.*) has several ingenious methods of measuring the extent of specialization, but the conclusions apply to habitual criminals in general rather than to professional thieves, and the habitual criminals in general probably have less tendency to specialize than do the professional thieves.

[6] Noel Ersine, *Underworld and Prison Slang* (Upland, Indiana, 1935).

amateur thieves and have many epithets which they apply to the amateurs. These epithets include "snatch-and-grab thief," "boot-and-shoe thief," and "best-hold cannon." Professional thieves may use "raw-jaw" methods when operating under excellent protection, but they are ashamed of these methods and console themselves with the knowledge that they could do their work in more artistic manner if necessary. They will have no dealings with thieves who are unable to use the correct methods of stealing.

Professional thieves disagree as to the extent of gradations within the profession. Some thieves divide the profession into "big-time" and "small-time" thieves on the basis of the size of the stakes for which they play, on the preparations for a particular stake, and on connections. A confidence man who regarded himself as "big-time" wrote as follows regarding a shoplifter:

> While he is undoubtedly a professional thief, I should a few years ago [before he was committed to prison] have been ashamed to be seen on the street with him. I say this not out of a spirit of snobbishness but simply because for business reasons I feel that my reputation would have suffered in the eyes of my friends to be seen in the company of a booster [shoplifter].

On the other hand, the thief who wrote this document insisted that there are no essential gradations within the profession:

> I have never considered anyone a small-time thief. If he is a thief, he is a thief—small-time, big-time, middle-time, eastern standard, or Rocky Mountain, it is all the same. Neither have I considered anyone big-time. It all depends on the spot and how it is handled. I recall a heel touch [sneak theft] at ten one morning which showed $21 and three hours later the same troupe took off one for $6,500 in the same place. Were they small-time in the morning and big-time in the afternoon? The confidence men who play against a store [using a fake gambling club or brokerage office] expect to get large amounts. But there is considerable interchange, some working for a time at short con and then at elaborate con rackets. Those who play against a store know those who engage in short con; if not, they have mutual friends.

This difference in opinion is quite similar to the difference that would emerge if lawyers or doctors were discussing the gradations within their professions. In any case there is pride in one's own position in the group. This pride may be illustrated by the action of Roger Benton, a forger, who was given a signed blank check to fill out the amount of money he desired; Benton wrote a big "Void" across the face of the check and returned it to the grocer who gave it to him. He explains, "I suppose I had too much professional pride to use it—after all I was a forger who took smart money from smart banks, not a thief who robbed honest grocerymen."[7]

III. THE PROFESSION OF THEFT AS CONSENSUS

The profession of theft is a complex of common and shared feelings, and overt acts. Pickpockets have similar reactions to prospective victims and to the particular situations in which victims are found. This similarity of reactions is due to the common background of experiences and the similarity of points of attention. These reactions are like the "clinical intuitions" which different physicians form of a patient or different lawyers form of a juryman on quick inspection. Thieves can work together without serious disagreements because they have these common and similar attitudes. This consensus extends throughout the activities and lives of the thieves, culminating in similar and common reactions to the law, which is regarded as the common enemy. Out of this consensus, moreover, develop the codes, the attitudes of helpfulness, and the loyalties of the underworld.

The following explanation of the emphasis which thieves place on punctuality

---

[7] *Where Do I Go from Here?* (New York: Lee Furman, Inc., 1936 [by permission]), p. 62.

is an illustration of the way consensus has developed:

> It is a cardinal principle among partners in crime that appointments shall be kept promptly. When you "make a meet" you are there on the dot or you do not expect your partner to wait for you. The reason why is obvious. Always in danger of arrest the danger to one man is increased by the arrest of the other; and arrest is the only legitimate excuse for failing to keep an appointment. Thus, if the appointment is not kept on time, the other may assume arrest and his best procedure is to get away as quickly as possible and save his own skin.[8]

One of the most heinous offenses that a thief can commit against another thief is to inform, "squeal," or "squawk." This principle is generally respected even when it is occasionally violated. Professional thieves probably violate the principle less frequently than other criminals for the reason that they are more completely immune from punishment, which is the pressure that compels an offender to inform on others. Many thieves will submit to severe punishment rather than inform. Two factors enter into this behavior. One is the injury which would result to himself in the form of loss of prestige, inability to find companions among thieves in the future, and reprisals if he should inform. The other is loyalty and identification of self with other thieves. The spontaneous reactions of offenders who are in no way affected by the behavior of the squealer, as by putting him in coventry, are expressions of genuine disgust, fear, and hatred.[9] Consensus is the basis of both of these reactions, and the two together explain how the rule against informing grows out of the common experiences of the thieves.

Consensus means, also, that thieves have a system of values and an *esprit de corps* which support the individual thief in his criminal career. The distress of the solitary thief who is not a member of the underworld society of criminals is illustrated in the following statement by Roger Benton at the time he was an habitual but not a professional forger:

> I had no home, no place to which I could return for sanctuary, no friend in the world to whom I could talk freely. . . . I was a lone man, my face set away from those of my fellows. But I didn't mind—at least I didnt think I minded. [A little later he became acquainted in St. Louis with Nero's place, which was a rendezvous for theatrical people.] I liked Nero. I liked the crowd that gathered in his place and I wanted my evening entertainment there to continue. And I found that I was hungrier for human companionship than I had known. Here I found it. . . . It was a gay interlude and I enjoyed it thoroughly, and neglected my own work [forgery] while I played and enjoyed the simple, honest friendships of these children of the stage. [Still later.] I could not rid myself of the crying need for the sense of security which social recognition and contact with one's fellows and their approval furnishes. I was lonely and frightened and wanted to be where there was someone who knew me as I had been before I had become a social outcast.[10]

Among the criminal tribes of India the individual was immersed almost completely in a consistent culture and felt no distress in attacking an outsider because this did not make him an enemy in any group which had significance for him. Nowhere in America, probably, is a criminal so completely immersed in a group that he does not feel his position as an enemy of the larger society. Even after Roger Benton became a member of the underworld as a professional forger, he felt lonely and ill at ease: "I was sick of the whole furtive business, of the constant need to be a fugitive among my fellows, of the impossibility of settling down and making a home for myself, and of the fear of imprisonment."[11]

---

[8] *Ibid.*, p. 269 (by permission).

[9] Philip S. Van Cise, *Fighting the Underworld* (Boston, 1936), p. 321; Josiah Flynt Willard, *Tramping with Tramps* (New York, 1899), pp. 23–24, and *My Life* (New York, 1908), pp. 331–40

[10] *Op. cit.*, pp. 62, 66–67, 80–81 (by permission).
[11] *Ibid.*, p. 242 (by permission).

The professional thief in America feels that he is a social outcast. This is especially true of the professional thieves who originated in middle-class society, as many of them did. He feels that he is a renegade when he becomes a thief. Chic Conwell states that the thief is looking for arguments to ease his conscience and that he blocks off considerations about the effects of his crimes upon the victims and about the ultimate end of his career. When he is alone in prison, he cannot refrain from thought about such things, and then he shudders at the prospect of returning to his professional activities. Once he is back in his group, he assumes the "bravado" attitudes of the other thieves, his shuddering ceases, and everything seems to be all right. Under the circumstances he cannot develop an integrated personality, but the distress is mitigated, his isolation reduced, and his professional life made possible because he has a group of his own in which he carries on a social existence as a thief, with a culture and values held in common by many thieves. In this sense, also, professional theft means consensus.

IV. THE PROFESSION OF THEFT AS DIFFERENTIAL ASSOCIATION

Differential association is characteristic of the professional thieves, as of all other groups. The thief is a part of the underworld and in certain respects is segregated from the rest of society. His place of residence is frequently in the slums or in the "white-light" districts where commercial recreations flourish. Even when he lives in a residential hotel or in a suburban home, he must remain aloof from his neighbors more than is customary for city dwellers who need not keep their occupations secret. The differential element in the association of thieves is primarily functional rather than geographical. Their personal association is limited by barriers which are maintained principally by the thieves themselves. These barriers are based on their community of interests, including security or safety. These barriers may easily be penetrated from within; since other groups also set up barriers in their personal association, especially against known thieves, the thieves are, in fact, kept in confinement within the barriers of their own groups to a somewhat greater extent than is true of other groups. On the other hand, these barriers can be penetrated from the outside only with great difficulty. A stranger who enters a thieves' hangout is called a "weed in the garden." When he enters, conversation either ceases completely or is diverted to innocuous topics.

Many business and professional men engage in predatory activities that are logically similar to the activities of the professional thief. But the widow-and-orphan swindler does not regard himself as a professional thief and is not so regarded by professional thieves. Each regards the other with contempt. They have no occasion to meet and would have nothing to talk about if they did meet. They are not members of the same group.

The final definition of the professional thief is found within this differential association. The group defines its own membership. A person who is received in the group and recognized as a professional thief is a professional thief. One who is not so received and recognized is not a professional thief, regardless of his methods of making a living.

Though professional thieves are defined by their differential association, they are also a part of the general social order. It would be a decided mistake to think of professional thieves as absolutely segregated from the rest of society. They live in the midst of a social order to which they are intimately related and in many ways well adjusted. First, the thief must come into contact with persons in legitimate society in order to steal from them. While, as a pickpocket, he may merely make physical contact with the clothes and pocketbooks of victims, as a confidence man he must enter into intimate association with them.

This intimacy is cold-blooded. The feelings are expressed as by an actor on a stage, with calculations of the results they will produce. He is like a salesman who attempts to understand a prospective customer only as a means of breaking down sales resistance and realizing his own objective of increased sales.

Second, he has some personal friends who are law-abiding in all respects. He is generally known to these friends as a thief. In his relations with these friends the reciprocity of services does not involve criminality on either side.

Third, he receives assistance from persons and agencies which are regarded as legitimate or even as the official protectors of legitimate society. In such persons and agencies he frequently finds attitudes of predatory control [12] which are similar to his own. The political machine which dominates the political life of many American cities and rural districts is generally devoted to predatory control. The professional thief and the politician, being sympathetic in this fundamental interest in predatory control, are able to co-operate to mutual advantage. This involves co-operation with the police and the courts to the extent that these agencies are under control of the political machine or have predatory interests independent of the machine. The thief is not segregated from that portion of society but is in close and initmate communication with it not only in his occupational life but in his search for sociability as well. He finds these sympathizers in the gambling places, cabarets, and houses of prostitution, where he and they spend their leisure time.

Fourth, the professional thief has the fundamental values of the social order in the midst of which he lives. The public patterns of behavior come to his attention as frequently as to the attention of others.

[12] I am indebted for this term, "predatory control," to my colleague, Dr. A. B. Hollingshead. It seems to be a proper term to apply to the salesman, described above, to the thief, to many politicians, and to others.

He reads the newspapers, listens to the radio, attends the picture shows and ball games, and sees the new styles in store windows. He is affected just as are others by the advertisements of dentifrices, cigarettes, and automobiles. His interest in money and in the things that money will buy and his efforts to secure "easy money" fit nicely into the pattern of modern life. Though he has consensus within his own profession in regard to his professional activities, he also has consensus with the larger society in regard to many of the values of the larger society.

V. THE PROFESSION OF THEFT AS ORGANIZATION

Professional theft is organized crime. It is not organized in the journalistic sense, for no dictator or central office directs the work of the members of the profession. Rather it is organized in the sense that it is a system in which informal unity and reciprocity may be found. This is expressed in the *Report of the* [Chicago] *City Council Committee on Crime* as follows:

> While this criminal group is not by any means completely organized, it has many of the characteristics of a system. It has its own language; it has its own laws; its own history; its traditions and customs; its own methods and techniques; its highly specialized machinery for attack upon persons and particularly upon property; its own highly specialized modes of defense. These professional criminals have interurban, interstate and sometimes international connections.[13]

The complex of techniques, status, consensus, and differential association which have been described previously may be regarded as organization. More specifically, the organization of professional thieves consists in part of the knowledge which becomes the common property of the profession. Every thief becomes an information bureau. For instance, each professional thief is known personally to a large pro-

[13] P. 164.

portion of the other thieves, as a result of their migratory habits and common hangouts. Any thief may be appraised by those who know him, in a terse phrase, such as "He is O.K.," "He is a no-good bastard," or "Never heard of him." The residue of such appraisals is available when a troupe wishes to add a new member, or when a thief asks for assistance in escaping from jail.

Similarly, the knowledge regarding methods and situations becomes common property of the profession. "Toledo is a good town," "The lunch hour is the best time to work that spot," "Look out for the red-haired saleslady—she is double-smart," "See Skid if you should get a tumble in Chicago," "Never grift on the way out," and similar mandates and injunctions are transmitteed from thief to thief until everyone in the profession knows them. The discussions in the hangouts keep this knowledge adjusted to changing situations. The activities of the professional thieves are organized in terms of this common knowledge.

Informal social services are similarly organized. Any thief will assist any other thief in a dangerous situation. He does this both by positive actions, such as warning, and by refraining from behavior that would increase the danger, such as staring at a thief who is working. Also, collections are taken in the hangouts and elsewhere to assist a thief who may be in jail or the wife of a thief who may be in prison. In these services reciprocity is assumed, but there is no insistence on immediate or specific return to the one who performs the service.

The preceding description of the characteristics of the profession of theft suggests that a person can be a professional thief only if he is recognized and received as such by other professional thieves. Professional theft is a group-way of life. One can get into the group and remain in it only by the consent of those previously in the group. Recognition as a professional thief by other professional thieves is the absolutely necessary, universal, and definite characteristic of the professional thief. This recognition is a combination of two of the characteristics previously described, namely, status and differential association. A professional thief is a person who has the status of a professional thief in the differential association of professional thieves.

Selection and tutelage are the two necessary elements in the process of acquiring recognition as a professional thief. These are the universal factors in an explanation of the genesis of the professional thief. A person cannot acquire recognition as a professional thief until he has had tutelage in professional theft, and tutelage is given only to a few persons selected from the total population.

Selection and tutelage are continuous processes. The person who is not a professional thief becomes a professional thief as a result of contact with professional thieves, reciprocal confidence and appreciation, a crisis situation, and tutelage. In the course of this process a person who is not a professional thief may become first a neophyte and then a recognized professional thief. A very small percentage of those who start on this process ever reach the stage of professional theft, and the process may be interrupted at any point by action of either party.

Selection is a reciprocal process, involving action by those who are professional thieves and by those who are not professional thieves. Contact is the first requisite, and selection doubtless lies back of the contacts. They may be pimps, amateur thieves, burglars, or they may be engaged in legitimate occupations as clerks in hotels or stores. Contacts may be made in jail or in the places where professional thieves are working or are spending their leisure time. If the other person is to become a professional thief, the contact must develop into appreciation of the professional thieves. This is not difficult, for professional thieves in general are very attractive. They have had wide experience, are interesting conversationalists, know human nature, spend money lavishly, and have great power. Since some persons are not attracted even by these characteristics, there is doubtless a selective process involved in this, also.

The selective action of the professional thieves is probably more significant than the selective action of the potential thief. An inclination to steal is not a sufficient explanation of the genesis of the professional thief. Everyone has an inclination to steal and expresses this inclination with more or less frequency and with more or less finesse. The person must be appreciated by the professional thieves. He must be appraised as having an adequate equipment of wits, front, talking ability, honesty, reliability, nerve, and determination. The comparative importance of these several characteristics cannot be determined at present, but it is highly probable that no characteristic is valued more highly than honesty. It is probably regarded as more essential than mental ability. This, of course, means honesty in dealings within their own group.

An emergency or crisis is likely to be the occasion on which tutelage begins. A person may lose a job, get caught in amateur stealing, or may need additional money. If he has developed a friendly relationship with professional thieves, he may request or they may suggest that he be given a minor part in some act of theft. He would, if accepted, be given verbal instructions in regard to the theory of the racket and the specific part he is to play. In his first efforts in this minor capacity he may be assisted by the professional thieves, although such assistance would be regarded as an affront by one who was already a professional. If he performs these minor duties satisfactorily, he is promoted to more important duties. During this probationary period the neophyte is assimilating the general standards of morality, propriety, etiquette, and rights which characterize the profession, and is acquiring "larceny sense." He is learning the general methods of disposing of stolen goods and of fixing cases. He is building up a personal acquaintance with other thieves, and with lawyers, policemen, court officials, and fixers. This more general knowledge is seldom transmitted to the neophyte as formal verbal instructions but is assimilated by him without being recognized as instruction. However, he is quite as likely to be dropped from participation in further professional activities for failure to assimilate and use this more general culture as for failure to acquire the specific details of the techniques of theft.

As a result of this tutelage during the probationary period, he acquires the techniques of theft and consensus with the thieves. He is gradually admitted into differential association with thieves and given tentative status as a professional thief. This tentative status under probation becomes fixed as a definite recognition as a professional thief. Thereby he enters into the systematic organization which constitutes professional theft.

A person who wished to become a professional thief might conceivably acquire some knowledge of the techniques and of the codes by reading the descriptions of theft in newspapers, journals, and books. Either alone or in the company of two or three others he might attempt to use these techniques and to become a self-made professional thief. Even this, of course, would be tutelage. Aside from the fact that hardly ever is the technique of a theft described in such manner that it can be applied without personal assistance, this part of the skill of the thief is only a part of the requirements for a successful career. This person would not have that indefinite body of appreciation which is called "larceny sense," nor would he have the personal acquaintances with and confidence of fences, fixers, and policemen which are necessary for security in professional theft. He would quickly land in prison, where he would have a somewhat better opportunity to learn how to steal.

A person who is a professional thief may

cease to be one. This would generally result from a violation of the codes of the profession or else from inefficiency due to age, fear, narcotic drugs, or drink. Because of either failure he would no longer be able to find companions with whom to work, would not be trusted by the fixer or by the policemen, and therefore he would not be able to secure immunity from punishment. He is no longer recognized as a professional thief, and therefore he can no longer be a professional thief. On the other hand, if he drops out of active stealing of his own volition and retains his abilities, he would continue to receive recognition as a professional thief. He would be similar to a physician who would be recognized as a physician after he ceased active practice.

It may be worth while to consider very briefly whether theft is really a profession. Carr-Saunders and Wilson list the following as the characteristics of the learned professions: technical skill, formal association as in medical and legal societies, state regulation of the conditions of admission to the profession by examinations and licenses, a degree of monopoly growing out of the formal association and of the regulations by the state, and ethical standards which minimize the pecuniary motive and emphasize the social welfare motive.[14]

The profession of theft has most of these characteristics. It has technical skill, an exclusive group, immunity from punishment which almost amounts to a license from the state to steal, a degree of monopoly growing out of their exclusive group relationship and of their recognition by the agents of the state. Each of these is less formal than in the other professions. They do not have written constitutions for their groups or licenses which they may hang on their office walls. They do have the informal equivalents of constitutions and licenses.

[14] A. W. Carr-Saunders and P. A. Wilson, *The Professions* (Oxford, 1933).

The one characteristic listed by Carr-Saunders and Wilson which they lack is the ethical standards which minimize the pecuniary motive. When this point was mentioned to a professional thief, he admitted that his profession did not have this characteristic, but he added that the medical and legal professions would have very few members if that were used as a criterion of membership.

The learned professions do have a huge body of knowledge in written form, and a long period of formal training in sciences which are basic to their vocational activities. The profession of theft, also, has a body of knowledge, not nearly so large and not in written form, which has been accumulating over several centuries. It includes articulate formulation of the principles of the different rackets. This body of traditional knowledge is transmitted to the student by apprenticeship methods rather than through a professional school. For this reason professional theft should not be regarded as a learned profession. It is probably more nearly on the level of professional athletics, so far as learning is concerned.

The profession of theft, with the characteristics which have been described, is organized around the effort to secure money with relative safety. In this respect, also, the profession of theft is similar to other professions and to other permanent groups. For money and safety are values inherent in Western civilization, and the methods which are used to realize these objectives are adjusted to the general culture.

The thief is relatively safe in his thefts for three reasons: First, he selects rackets in which the danger is at a minimum. The shakedown (extortion from homosexuals and certain other violators of law) is safe because the victims, being themselves violators of the law, cannot complain to the police. The confidence game is safe for the same reason, for the victims have entered into collusion with the thieves to defraud someone else and were themselves defrauded in the attempt. Stealing from stores is relatively safe because the stores are reluctant to make accusations of theft against persons who appear to be legitimate customers. Picking pockets is relatively safe because the legal rules of evidence make it almost impossible to convict a pickpocket. The professional thief scrupulously avoids the types of theft which are attended with great danger and especially those which involve much publicity. The theft of famous art treasures, for instance, is never attempted by professional thieves. It would probably not be especially difficult for them to steal the treasures, but it would be practically impossible, because of the publicity, for them to sell the treasures. It is significant that the two most famous thefts of art treasures in the last century—Gainsborough's "Duchess of Devonshire" and Da Vinci's "Mona Lisa"—were not motivated by the expectation of financial gain.

Second, by training and experience the professional thief develops ingenious methods and the ability to control situations. A thief is a specialist in manipulating people and achieves his results by being a good actor. Third, he works on the principle that he can "fix" practically every case in which he may be caught.

Because of the importance of "the fix" for a general interpretation of professional theft, it is elaborated at this point. Cases are fixed in two ways: first, by making restitution to the victim in return for an agreement not to prosecute; second, by securing the assistance of one or more public officials by payment of money or by political order or suggestion. These two methods are generally combined in a particular case.

The victim is almost always willing to accept restitution and drop the prosecution. This is true not only of the individual victim but also of the great insurance companies, which frequently offer rewards for the return of stolen property with an agreement not to prosecute and are thus the best fences for stolen property. The length of time required for the prosecution of a case is one of the reasons for the willingness of the victim to drop the prosecution. At any rate, the victim is more interested in the return of his stolen property than he is in maintaining a solid front of opposition against theft. He tries to get what he can, just as the thief tries to get what he can; neither has much interest in the general social welfare.

56. VICTIM-PRECIPITATED CRIMINAL HOMICIDE

MARVIN E. WOLFGANG

IN MANY CRIMES, ESPECIALLY IN CRIMINAL homicide, the victim is often a major contributor to the criminal act. Except in cases in which the victim is an innocent bystander and is killed in lieu of an intended victim, or in cases in which a pure accident is involved, the victim may be one of the major precipitating causes of his own demise.

Various theories of social interactions, particularly in social psychology, have established the framework for the present discussion. In criminological literature, however, probably von Hentig in *The Criminal and His Victim*, has provided the most useful theoretical basis for analysis of the victim-offender relationship. In Chapter XII, entitled "The Contribution of the Victim to the Genesis of Crime," the author discusses this "duet frame of crime" and suggests that homicide is particularly amenable to analysis.[1] In *Penal Philosophy*, Tarde[2] frequently attacks the "legislative mistake" of concentrating too much on premeditation and paying too little attention to motives, which indicate an important interrelationship between victim and offender. And in one of his satirical essays, "On Murder Considered as One of the Fine Arts," Thomas DeQuincey[3] shows cognizance of the idea that sometimes the victim is a would-be-murderer. Garofalo,[4] too, noted that the victim may provoke another individual into attack, and though the provocation be slight, if perceived by an egoistic attacker it may be sufficient to result in homicide.

Besides these theoretical concepts, the law of homicide has long recognized provocation by the victim as a possible reason for mitigation of the offense from murder to manslaughter, or from criminal to excusable homicide. In order that such reduction occur, there are four prerequisites.[5]

▶ SOURCE: "Victim-Precipitated Criminal Homicide," *Journal of Criminal Law, Criminology and Police Science* (June, 1957), 48:1–11. Copyright 1957 by Northwestern University School of Law. Reprinted by special permission.

[1] Von Hentig, Hans, The Criminal and His Victim, New Haven: Yale University Press, 1948, pp. 383–385.

[2] Tarde, Gabriel, Penal Philosophy, Boston: Little, Brown, and Company, 1912, p. 466.

[3] De Quincey, Thomas, *On Murder Considered as One of the Fine Arts*, The Arts of Cheating, Swindling, and Murder, Edward Bulwer-Lytton, and Douglas Jerrold, and Thomas De Quincey, New York: The Arnold Co., 1925, p. 153.

[4] Garofalo, Baron Raffaele, Criminology, Boston: Little, Brown, and Company, 1914, p. 373.

[5] For an excellent discussion of the rule of provocation, from which these four requirements are taken, see: Rollin M. Perkins, *The Law of Homicide*, Jour. of Crim. Law and Criminol., (March-April, 1946), 36:412–427; and Herbert Wechsler and Jerome Michael, A Rationale of the Law of Homicide, pp. 1280–1282. A general review of the rule of provocation, both in this country and abroad, may be found in The Royal Commission on Capital Punishment, *1949–1952 Report* Appendix II, pp. 453–458.

(1) There must have been adequate provocation.

(2) The killing must have been in the heat of passion.

(3) The killing must have followed the provocation before there had been a reasonable opportunity for the passion to cool.

(4) A causal connection must exist between provocation, the heat of passion, and the homicidal act. Such, for example, are: adultery, seduction of the offender's juvenile daughter, rape of the offender's wife or close relative, etc.

Finally (4), a causal connection must exist between provocation, the heat of passion, and the homicidal act. Perkins claims that "the adequate provocation must have engendered the heat of passion, and the heat of passion must have been the cause of the act which resulted in death." [6]

DEFINITIONS AND ILLUSTRATION

The term *victim-precipitated* is applied to those criminal homicides in which the victim is a direct, positive precipitator in the crime. The role of the victim is characterized by his having been the first in the homicide drama to use physical force directed against his subsequent slayer. The victim-precipitated cases are those in which the victim was the first to show and use a deadly weapon, to strike a blow in an altercation—in short, the first to commence the interplay or resort to physical violence.

In seeking to identify the victim-precipitated cases recorded in police files it has not been possible always to determine whether the homicides strictly parallel legal interpretations. In general, there appears to be much similiarity. In a few cases included under the present definition, the nature of the provocation is such that it would not legally serve to mitigate the offender's responsibility. In these cases the victim was threatened in a robbery, and either attempted to prevent the robbery, failed to take the robber seriously, or in some other fashion irritated, frightened, or alarmed the felon by physical force so that the robber, either by accident or compulsion, killed the victim. Infidelity of a mate or lover, failure to pay a debt, use of vile names by the victim, obviously means that he played an important role in inciting the offender to overt action in order to seek revenge, to win an argument, or to defend himself. However, mutual quarrels and wordy altercations do not constitute sufficient provocation under law, and they are not included in the meaning of victim-precipitated homicide.

Below are sketched several typical cases to illustrate the pattern of these homicides. Primary demonstration of physical force by the victim, supplemented by surrilous language, characterizes the most common victim-precipitated homicides. All of these slayings were listed by the Philadelphia Police as criminal homicides, none of the offenders was exonerated by a coroner's inquest, and all the offenders were tried in criminal court.

A husband accused his wife of giving money to another man, and while she was making breakfast, he attacked her with a milk bottle, then a brick, and finally a piece of concrete block. Having had a butcher knife in hand, she stabbed him during the fight.

A husband threatened to kill his wife on several occasions. In this instance, he attacked her with a pair of scissors, dropped them, and grabbed a butcher knife from the kitchen. In the ensuing struggle that ended on their bed, he fell on the knife.

In an argument over a business transaction, the victim first fired several shots at his adversary, who in turn fatally returned the fire.

The victim was the aggressor in a fight, having struck his enemy several times. Friends tried to interfere, but the victim persisted. Finally, the offender retaliated with blows, causing the victim to fall and

---

[6] *Ibid.*, p. 425. The term "cause" is here used in a legal and not a psychological sense.

hit his head on the sidewalk, as a result of which he died.

A husband had beaten his wife on several previous occasions. In the present instance, she insisted that he take her to the hospital. He refused, and a violent quarrel followed, during which he slapped her several times, and she concluded by stabbing him.

During a lover's quarrel, the male (victim) hit his mistress and threw a can of kerosene at her. She retaliated by throwing the liquid on him, and then tossed a lighted match in his direction. He died from the burns.

A drunken husband, beating his wife in their kitchen, gave her a butcher knife and dared her to use it on him. She claimed that if he should strike her once more, she would use the knife, whereupon he slapped her in the face and she fatally stabbed him.

A victim became incensed when his eventual slayer asked for money which the victim owed him. The victim grabbed a hatchet and started in the direction of his creditor, who pulled out a knife and stabbed him.

A victim attempted to commit sodomy with his girlfriend, who refused his overtures. He struck her several times on the side of her head with his fists before she grabbed a butcher knife and cut him fatally.

A drunken victim with knife in hand approached his slayer during a quarrel. The slayer showed a gun, and the victim dared him to shoot. He did.

During an argument in which a male called a female many vile names, she tried to telephone the police. But he grabbed the phone from her hands, knocked her down, kicked her, and hit her with a tire gauge. She ran to the kitchen, grabbed a butcher knife, and stabbed him in the stomach.

THE PHILADELPHIA STUDY

Empirical data for analysis of victim-precipitated homicides were collected from the files of the Homicide Squad of the Philadelphia Police Department, and include 588 consecutive cases of criminal homicide which occurred between January 1, 1948 and December 31, 1952. Because more than one person was sometimes involved in the slaying of a single victim, there was a total of 621 offenders responsible for the killing of 588 victims. The present study is part of a much larger work that analyzes criminal homicide in greater detail. Such material as relevant to victim-precipitation is included in the present analysis. The 588 criminal homicides provide sufficient background information to establish much about the nature of the victim-offender relationship. Of these cases, 150, or 26 percent, have been designated, on the basis of the previously stated definition, as VP cases.[7] The remaining 438, therefore, have been designated as non-VP cases.

Thorough study of police files, theoretical discussions of the victim's contribution, and previous analysis of criminal homicide suggest that there may be important differences between VP and non-VP cases. The chi-square test has been used to test the significance in proportions between VP and non-VP homicides and a series of variables. Hence, any spurious association which is just due to chance has been reduced to a minimum by application of this test, and significant differences of distributions are revealed. Where any class frequency of less than five existed, the test was not applied; and in each tested association, a correction for continuity was used, although the difference resulting without it was only slight. In this study a value of P less than .05, or the 5 percent level of significance, is used as the minimal level of significant association. Throughout the subsequent discussion, the term *significant* in italics is used to indicate that a chi-square test of significance of association

[7] In order to facilitate reading of the following sections, the *victim-precipitated* cases are referred to simply as VP cases or VP homicides. Those homicides in which the victim was not a direct precipitator are referred to as non-VP cases.

Table I. *Victim-Precipitated and Non-Victim-Precipitated Criminal Homicide by Selected Variables, Philadelphia, 1948–1952*

	Total Victims		Victim-Precipitated		Non-Victim-Precipitated	
	Number	Percent of Total	Number	Percent of Total	Number	Percent of Total
Race and Sex of Victim						
Both Races	588	100.0	150	100.0	438	100.0
Male	449	76.4	141	94.0	308	70.3
Female	139	23.6	9	6.0	130	29.7
Negro	427	72.6	119	79.3	308	70.3
Male	331	56.3	111	74.0	220	50.2
Female	96	16.3	8	5.3	88	20.1
White	161	27.4	31	20.7	130	29.7
Male	118	20.1	30	20.0	88	20.1
Female	43	7.3	1	0.7	42	9.6
Age of Victim						
Under 15	28	4.8	0	—	28	6.4
15–19	25	4.3	7	4.7	18	4.1
20–24	59	10.0	18	12.0	41	9.4
25–29	93	15.8	17	11.3	76	17.3
30–34	88	15.0	20	13.3	68	15.5
35–39	75	12.8	25	16.7	50	11.4
40–44	57	9.7	23	15.3	34	7.8
45–49	43	7.3	13	8.7	30	6.8
50–54	48	8.2	11	7.3	37	8.5
55–59	26	4.4	6	4.0	20	4.6
60–64	18	3.1	7	4.7	11	2.5
65 and over	28	4.7	3	2.0	25	5.7
Total	588	100.0	150	100.0	438	100.0
Method						
Stabbing	228	38.8	81	54.0	147	33.6
Shooting	194	33.0	39	26.0	155	35.4
Beating	128	21.8	26	17.3	102	23.3
Other	38	6.4	4	2.7	34	7.7
Total	588	100.0	150	100.0	438	100.0
Place						
Home	301	51.2	80	53.3	221	50.5
Not Home	287	48.8	70	46.7	217	49.5
Total	588	100.0	150	100.0	438	100.0
Interpersonal Relationship						
Relatively close friend	155	28.2	46	30.7	109	27.3
Family relationship	136	24.7	38	25.3	98	24.5
(Spouse)	(100)	(73.5)	(33)	(86.8)	(67)	(68.4)
(Other)	(36)	(26.5)	(5)	(13.2)	(31)	(31.6)
Acquaintance	74	13.5	20	13.3	54	13.5
Stranger	67	12.2	16	10.7	51	12.8

Table I—*Continued*

	Total Victims		Victim-Precipitated		Non-Victim-Precipitated	
	Number	Percent of Total	Number	Percent of Total	Number	Percent of Total
Paramour, Mistress, Prostitute	54	9.8	15	10.0	39	9.8
Sex rival	22	4.0	6	4.0	16	4.0
Enemy	16	2.9	6	4.0	10	2.5
Paramour of Offender's mate	11	2.0	1	.7	10	2.5
Felon or police officer	6	1.1	1	.7	5	1.3
Innocent bystander	6	1.1	—	—	6	1.5
Homosexual partner	3	.6	1	.7	2	.5
Total	550	100.0	150	100.0	400	100.0
Presence of alcohol during Offense						
Present	374	63.6	111	74.0	263	60.0
Not Present	214	36.4	39	26.0	175	40.0
Total	588	100.0	150	100.0	438	100.0
Presence of alcohol in the victim						
Present	310	52.7	104	69.3	206	47.0
Not Present	278	47.3	46	30.7	232	53.0
Total	588	100.0	150	100.0	438	100.0
Previous Arrest record of victim						
Previous arrest record	277	47.3	93	62.0	184	42.0
Offenses against the person	150	25.5(54.2)	56	37.3(60.2)	94	21.4(50.1)
Other offenses only	127	21.6(45.8)	37	4.7(39.8)	90	20.5(49.9)
No previous arrest record	311	52.7	57	38.0	254	58.0
Total	588	100.0	150	100.0	438	100.0
Previous arrest record of Offender						
Previous arrest record	400	64.4	81	54.0	319	67.7
Offenses against person	264	42.5(66.0)	49	32.7(60.5)	215	45.6(67.4)
Other offenses only	136	21.8(34.0)	32	21.3(39.5)	104	22.1(32.6)
No previous arrest record	221	35.6	69	(46.0)	152	32.3
Total	621	100.0	150	100.0	471	100.0

has been made and that the value of P less than .05 has been found. The discussion that follows (with respect to race, sex, age, etc.) reveals some interesting differences and similarities between the two. (Table I.)

Race. Because Negroes and males have been shown by their high rates of homicide, assaults against the person, etc., to be more criminally aggressive than whites and females, it may be inferred that there are more Negroes and males among VP victims than among non-VP victims. The data confirm this inference. Nearly 80 percent of VP cases compared to 70 percent of non-VP cases involve Negroes, a proportional difference that results in a *significant* association between race and VP homicide.

Sex. As victims, males comprise 94 percent of VP homicides, but only 72 percent of non-VP homicides, showing a *significant* association between sex of the victim and VP homicide.

Since females have been shown by their low rates of homicide, assaults against the person, etc., to be less criminally aggressive than males, and since females are less likely to precipitate their own victimization than males, we should expect more female *offenders* among VP homicides than among non-VP homicides. Such is the case, for the comparative data reveal that females are twice as frequently offenders in VP slayings (29 percent) as they are in non-VP slayings (14 percent)—a proportional difference which is also highly *significant.*

The number of white female offenders (16) in this study is too small to permit statistical analysis, but the tendency among both Negro and white females as separate groups is toward a much higher proportion among VP than among non-VP offenders. As noted above, analysis of Negro and white females as a combined group does result in the finding of a *significant* association between female offenders and VP homicide.

Age. The age distributions of victims and offenders in VP and non-VP homicides are strikingly similar; study of the data suggests that age has no apparent effect on VP homicide. The median age of VP victims is 33.3 years, while that of non-VP victims is 31.2 years.

Methods. In general, there is a *significant* association between method used to inflict death and VP homicide. Because Negroes and females comprise a larger proportion of offenders in VP cases, and because previous analysis has shown that stabbings occurred more often than any of the other methods of inflicting death,[8] it is implied that the frequency of homicides by stabbing is greater among VP than among non-VP cases. The data support such an implication and reveal that homicides by stabbing account for 54 percent of the VP cases but only 34 percent of non-VP cases, a difference which is *significant.* The distribution of shootings, beatings, and "other" methods of inflicting death among the VP and non-VP cases shows no significant differences. The high frequency of stabbings among VP homicides appears to result from an almost equal reduction in each of the remaining methods; yet the lower proportions in each of these three other categories among VP cases are not separately very different from the proportions among non-VP cases.

Place and Motive. There is no important difference between VP and non-VP homicides with respect to a home/not-home dichotomy, nor with respect to motives listed by the police. Slightly over half of both VP and non-VP slayings occurred in the home. General altercations (43 percent) and domestic quarrels (20 percent) rank highest among VP cases, as they do among non-VP cases (32 and 12 percent), although with lower frequency. Combined, these two motives account for a slightly larger share of the VP cases (3 out of 5) than of the non-VP cases (2 out of 5).

---

[8] Of 588 victims, 228, or 39 percent, were stabbed; 194, or 33 percent, were shot; 128, or 22 percent were beaten; and 38, or 6 percent, were killed by other methods.

Victim-Offender Relationships.[9] Intraracial slayings predominate in both groups, but inter-racial homicides comprise a larger share of VP cases (8 percent) than they do of non-VP cases (5 percent). Although VP cases make up one-fourth of all criminal homicides, they account for over one-third (35 percent) of all inter-racial slayings. Thus it appears that a homicide which crosses race lines is often likely to be one in which the slayer was provoked to assault by the victim. The association between inter-racial slayings and VP homicides, however, is not statistically significant.

Homicides involving victims and offenders of opposite sex (regardless of which sex is the victim or which is the offender) occur with about the same frequency among VP cases (34 percent) as among non-VP cases (37 percent). But a *significant* difference between VP and non-VP cases does emerge when determination of the sex of the victim, relative to the sex of his specific slayer, is taken into account. Of all criminal homicides for which the sex of both victim and offender is known, 88 involve a male victim and a female offender; and of these 88 cases, 43 are VP homicides. Thus, it may be said that 43, or 29 percent, of the 150 VP homicides, compared to 45, or only 11 percent, of the 400 non-VP homicides, are males slain by females.

It seems highly desirable, in view of these findings, that the police thoroughly investigate every possibility of strong provocation by the male victim when he is slain by a female—and particularly, as noted below, if the female is his wife, which is also a strong possibility. It is, of course, the further responsibility of defense counsel, prosecuting attorney, and subsequently the court, to determine whether such provocation was sufficient either to reduce or to eliminate culpability altogether.

The proportion that Negro male/Negro male [10] and white male/white male homicides constitute among VP cases (45 and 13 percent) is similar to the proportion these same relationships constitute among non-VP cases (41 and 14 percent). The important contribution of the Negro male as a victim-precipitator is indicated by the fact that Negro male/Negro female homicides are, proportionately, nearly three times as frequent among VP cases (25 percent) as they are among non-VP cases (9 percent). It is apparent, therefore, that Negroes and males not only are the groups most likely to make positive and direct contributions to the genesis of their own victimization, but that, in particular, Negro males more frequently provoke females of their own race to slay them than they do members of their own sex and race.

For both VP and non-VP groups, close friends, relatives, and acquaintances are the major types of specific relationships between victims and offenders. Combined, these three relationships constitute 69 percent of the VP homicides and 65 percent of the non-VP cases. Victims are relatives of their slayers in one-fourth of both types of homicide. But of 38 family slayings among VP cases, 3 are husband-wife killings; while of 98 family slayings among non-VP cases, only 67 are husband-wife killings. This proportional difference results in a *significant* association between mate slayings and VP homicide.

Finally, of VP mate slayings, 28 victims are husbands and only 5 are wives; but of non-VP mate slayings, only 19 victims are husbands while 48 are wives. Thus there is a *significant* association between husbands who are victims in mate slayings and VP homicide. This fact, namely, that *significantly* more husbands than wives are victims in VP mate slayings—means that (1) husbands actually may provoke their wives more often than wives provoke their hus-

---

[9] Only 550 victim-offender relationships are identified since 38 of the 588 criminal homicides are classified as unsolved, or those in which the perpetrator is unknown.

[10] The diagonal line represents "killed by". Thus, Negro male/Negro male means a Negro male killed by a Negro male; the victim precedes the offender.

bands to assault their respective mates; or, (2) assuming that provocation by wives is as intense and equally as frequent, or even more frequent, than provocation by husbands, then husbands may not receive and define provocation stimuli with as great or as violent a reaction as do wives; or (3) husbands may have a greater felt sense of guilt in a marital conflict for one reason or another, and receive verbal insults and overt physical assaults without retaliation as a form of compensatory punishment; or (4) husbands may withdraw more often than wives from the scene of marital conflict, and thus eliminate, for the time being, a violent overt reaction to their wives' provocation. Clearly, this is only a suggestive, not an exhaustive, list of probable explanations. In any case, we are left with the undeniable fact that husbands more often than wives are major, precipitating factors in their own homicidal deaths.

Alcohol. In the larger work of which this study is a part, the previous discovery of an association between the presence of alcohol in the homicide situation and Negro male offenders, combined with knowledge of the important contribution Negro males make to their own victimization, suggests an association (by transitivity) between VP homicide and the presence of alcohol. Moreover, whether alcohol is present in the victim or offender, lowered inhibitions due to ingestion of alcohol may cause an individual to give vent more freely to pent up frustrations, tensions, and emotional conflicts that have either built up over a prolonged period of time or that arise within an immediate emotional crisis. The data do in fact confirm the suggested hypothesis above and reveal a *significant* association between VP homicide and alcohol in the homicide situation. Comparison of VP to non-VP cases with respect to the presence of alcohol in the homicide situation (alcohol present in either the victim, offender, or both), reveals that alcohol was present in 74 percent of the VP cases and in 60 percent of the non-VP cases. The proportional difference results in a *significant* association between alcohol and VP homicide. It should be noted that the association is not necessarily a causal one, or that a causal relationship is not proved by the association.

Because the present analysis is concerned primarily with the contribution of the victim to the homicide, it is necessary to determine whether an association exists between VP homicide and presence of alcohol in the victim. No association was found to exist between VP homicide and alcohol in the offender. But victims had been drinking immediately prior to their death in more VP cases (69 percent) than in non-VP cases (47 percent). A positive and *significant* relationship is, therefore, clearly established between victims who had been drinking and who precipitated their own death. In many of these cases the victim was intoxicated, or nearly so, and lost control of his own defensive powers. He frequently was a victim with no intent to harm anyone maliciously, but who, nonetheless, struck his friend, acquaintance, or wife, who later became his assailant. Impulsive, aggressive, and often dangerously violent, the victim was the first to slap, punch, stab, or in some other manner commit an assault. Perhaps the presence of alcohol in this kind of homicide victim played no small part in his taking his first and major physical step toward victimization. Perhaps if he had not been drinking he would have been less violent, less ready to plunge into an assaultive stage of interaction. Or, if the presence of alcohol had no causal relation to his being the first to assault, perhaps it reduced his facility to combat successfully, to defend himself from retaliatory assault and, hence, contributed in this way to his death.

Previous Arrest Record. The victim-precipitator is the first actor in the homicide drama to display and to use a deadly weapon; and the description of him thus far infers that he is in some respects an offender in reverse. Because he is the first to assume an aggressive role, he probably has engaged previously in similar but less serious physical assaults. On the basis of these assumptions several meaningful hypotheses were established and tested. Each hypothesis is supported by empirical data, which in some cases reach the level of statistical significance accepted by this study; and in other cases indicate strong associations in directions suggested by the hypotheses. A summary of each hypothesis with its collated data follows:

(1) In VP cases, the victim is more likely than the offender to have a previous arrest, or police, record. The data show that 62 percent of the victims and 54 percent of the offenders in VP cases have a previous record.

(2) A higher proportion of VP victims than non-VP victims have a previous police record. Comparison reveals that 62 percent of VP victims but only 42 percent of non-VP victims have a previous record. The association between VP victims and previous arrest record is a *significant* one.

(3) With respect to the percentage having a previous arrest record, VP victims are more similar to non-VP offenders than to non-VP victims. Examination of the data reveals no significant difference between VP victims and non-VP offenders with a previous record. This lack of a significant difference is very meaningful and confirms the validity of the proposition above. While 62 percent of VP victims have a police record, 68 percent of non-VP offenders have such a record, and we have already noted in (2) above that only 42 percent of non-VP victims have a record. Thus, the existence of a statistically *significant* difference between VP victims and non-VP victims and the *lack* of a statistically significant difference between VP victims and non-VP offenders indicate that the victim of VP homicide is quite similar to the offender in non-VP homicide—and that the VP victim more closely resembles the non-VP offender than the non-VP victim.

(4) A higher proportion of VP victims than of non-VP victims have a record of offenses against the person. The data show a *significant* association between VP victims and a previous record of offenses against the person, for 37 percent of VP victims and only 21 percent of non-VP victims have a record of such offenses.

(5) Also with respect to the percentage having a previous arrest record of offenses against the person, VP victims are more similar to non-VP offenders than non-VP victims. Analysis of the data indicates support for this assumption, for we have observed that the difference between VP victims (37 percent) and non-VP victims (21 percent) is *significant;* this difference is almost twice as great as the difference between VP victims (27 percent) and non-VP offenders (46 percent), and this latter difference is not significant. The general tendency again is for victims in VP homicides to resemble offenders in non-VP homicides.

(6) A lower proportion of VP offenders have a previous arrest record than do non-VP offenders. The data also tend to support this hypothesis, for 54 percent of offenders in VP cases, compared to 68 percent of offenders in non-VP cases have a previous police record.

In general, the rank order of recidivism —defined in terms of having a previous arrest record and of having a previous record of assaults—for victims and offenders involved in the two types of homicide is as follows:

	Percent with Previous Arrest Record	*Percent with Previous Record of Assault*
(1) Offenders in non-VP Homicide	68	46
(2) Victims in VP Homicide	62	37
(3) Offenders in VP Homicide	54	33
(4) Victims in non-VP Homicide	42	21

Because he is the initial aggressor and has provoked his subsequent slayer into killing him, this particular type of victim (VP) is likely to have engaged previously in physical assaults which were either less provoking than the present situation, or which afforded him greater opportunity to defer attacks made upon him. It is known officially that over one-third of them assaulted others previously. It is not known how many formerly provoked others to assault them. In any case, the circumstances leading up to the present crime in which he plays the role of victim are probably not foreign to him since he has, in many cases, participated in similar encounters before this, his last episode.

SUMMARY

Criminal homicide usually involves intense personal interaction in which the victim's behavior is often an important factor. As Porterfield has recently pointed out, "the intensity of interaction between the murderer and his victim may vary from complete non-participation on the part of the victim to almost perfect cooperation with the killer in the process of getting killed.... It is amazing to note the large number of would-be murderers who become the victim." [11] By defining a VP homicide in terms of the victim's direct, immediate, and positive contribution to his own death, manifested by his being the first to make a physical assault, it has been possible to identify 150 VP cases.

Comparison of the VP group with non-VP cases reveals *significantly* higher proportions of the following characteristics among VP homicide:

(1) Negro victims;
(2) Negro offenders;
(3) male victims;
(4) female offenders;
(5) stabbings;
(6) victim-offender relationship involving male victims of female offenders;
(7) mate slayings;
(8) husbands who are victims in mate slayings;
(9) alcohol in the homicide situation;
(10) alcohol in the victim;
(11) victims with a previous arrest record;
(12) victims with a previous arrest record of assault.

In addition, VP homicides have slightly higher proportions than non-VP homicides of altercations and domestic quarrels; interracial slayings, victims who are close friends, relatives, or acquaintances of their slayers.

Empirical evidence analyzed in the present study lends support to, and measurement of, von Hentig's theoretical contention that "there are cases in which they (victim and offender) are reversed and in the long chain of causative forces the victim assumes the role of a determinant." [12]

In many cases the victim has most of the major characteristics of an offender; in some cases two potential offenders come together in a homicide situation and it is probably often only chance which results in one becoming a victim and the other an offender. At any rate, connotations of a victim as a weak and passive individual, seeking to withdraw from an assaultive situation, and of an offender as a brutal, strong, and overly aggressive person seeking out his victim, are not always correct. Societal attitudes are generally positive toward the victim and negative toward the offender, who is often feared as a violent and dangerous threat to others when not exonerated. However, data in the present study—especially that of previous arrest record—mitigate, destroy, or reverse these connotations of victim-offender roles in one out of every four criminal homicides.

---

[11] Porterfield, Austin L. and Talbert, Robert H., Mid-Century Crime in Our Culture: Personality and Crime in the Cultural Patterns of American States, Fort Worth: Leo Potishman Foundation, 1954, pp. 47–48.

[12] Von Hentig, *op. cit.*, p. 383.

57. ORGANIZED CRIME: THE CODE AND ITS FUNCTIONS

We have already indicated that the managers of the big American businesses selling illicit goods and services must also be governors. The illegal nature of the American crime cartel turns that cartel into a confederation, a governmental organization as well as a commercial organization. The formal division of labor which we have sketched out is the structure of a government as well as of a business. Even the titles used by the participants for two principal positions in the division of labor —Lieutenant and Soldier—are governmental titles rather than business titles.

The fundamental basis of any government, legal or illegal, is a code of conduct. Governmental structure is always closely associated with the code of behavior which its members are expected to follow. The legislative and judicial processes of government are concerned with the specification and the enforcement of this code, whether or not it is clearly set down in a set of rules precise enough to be called "law." A behavioral code, such as the Ten Commandments, becomes "law" only when it is officially adopted by a state, a political organization. Yet the distinction between a state and other organizations such as a church, an extended family, or a trade union is quite arbitrary. The distinction is most difficult to maintain when attention is turned to societies where patriarchal power is found.[1] The problem can be illustrated by gypsies, who have no territorial organization and no written law, but who do have customs, taboos, and a semi-judicial council which makes decisions about the propriety of behavior and, on the basis of these decisions, assesses damages and imposes penalties. The problem also can be illustrated by the "families" of Italian-Sicilian criminals in America, and by the confederation they have formed. Behavior in these "families," like behavior of members of the Sicilian Mafia, is controlled by a government which is substituting for the state, even if the code being enforced can in no sense be considered "criminal law" or "civil law."

THE CODE

We have been unable to locate even a summary statement of the code of conduct which is used in governing the lives of the members of American criminal "families." There are a number of summaries of the Sicilian Mafia's code of *"omerta"* or "manliness," and the popular assumption seems to be that such statements also summarize the code of American organized criminals. While this assumption is not in itself improper, the implication is that the American code was simply borrowed from the Mafia. This is not correct, any more than

▶SOURCE: *Task Force Report: Organized Crime, President's Commission on Law Enforcement and Administration of Justice, Appendix A, Washington, D. C.: 1967, pp. 40–50.*

[1] See E. Adamson Hoebel, *The Law of Primitive Man: A Study in Comparative Legal Dynamics* (Cambridge: Harvard University Press, 1954).

it is correct to believe that the "family" structure and the confederation structure were simply borrowed from the Mafia.

The matter is complicated, of course, by the fact that the code of conduct for "family" members is unwritten. The snippets of information we have been able to obtain have convinced us that there is a striking similarity between both the code of conduct and the enforcement machinery used in the confederation of organized criminals and the code of conduct and enforcement machinery which governs the behavior of prisoners. This is no coincidence for, as indicated earlier, both the prisoner government and the confederation government are responses to strong official governments which are limited in their means for achieving their control objectives. In order to maintain their status as governors of illegal organizations, the leaders of the two types of organizations must promulgate and enforce similar behavioral codes.

We will first discuss the code of prisoners and then will summarize the code of American organized criminals. One summary of the many descriptions of life in a wide variety of prisons has suggested that the chief tenets of the inmate code can be classified roughly into five major groups.[2] Sutherland and Cressey have shortened and re-written this summary of the code as follows:

First, there are those maxims that caution: *Don't interfere with inmate interests*. These center on the idea that inmates should serve the least possible time while enjoying the greatest possible number of pleasures and privileges. Included are such directives as: *Never rat on a con; Don't be nosy; Don't have a loose lip; Keep off a man's back; Don't put a guy on the spot*. Put positively: *Be loyal to your class, the cons*.

Second, a set of behavioral rules asks inmates to refrain from quarrels or arguments with fellow prisoners: *Don't lose your head; Play it cool; Do your own time; Don't bring heat*.

Third, prisoners assert that inmates should not take advantage of one another by means of force, fraud, or chicanery: *Don't exploit inmates*. This injunction sums up several directives: *Don't break your word; Don't steal from cons; Don't sell favors; Don't be a racketeer; Don't welsh on debts. Be right*.

Fourth, some rules have as their central theme the maintenance of self: *Don't weaken; Don't whine; Don't cop out* (plead guilty). Stated positively: *Be tough; Be a man*.

Fifth, prisoners express a variety of maxims that forbid according prestige or respect to the guards or the world for which they stand: *Don't be a sucker; Skim it off the top; Never talk to a screw* (guard); *Have a connection; Be sharp*.[3]

Prison inmates as a group do not give the warden and his staff their consent to be governed. By withholding this consent and developing their own unofficial government they accomplish precisely what prison officials say they do not want them to accomplish—legally-obtained status symbols, power, and an unequal share of goods and services in short supply. Organized criminals, like prisoners, live outside the law, and in response to this outlaw status they, like prisoners, develop a set of norms and procedures for controlling conduct within their organization. The five general directives making up the prisoners' code are, in fact, characteristic of the code of good thieves everywhere.[4] Specifically, the chief tenets of this thieves' code as it is found among organized criminals can be summarized and briefly illustrated as follows:

1. *Be loyal to members of the organization. Do not interfere with each other's interests. Do not be an informer*. This directive, with its correlated admonitions,

---

[2] Gresham M. Sykes and Sheldon L. Messinger, "The Inmate Social System," Chapter I in Richard A. Cloward, Donald R. Cressey, George H. Grosser, Richard McCleery, Lloyd E. Ohlin, Gresham M. Sykes and Sheldon R. Messinger, *Theoretical Studies in Social Organization of the Prison* (New York: Social Science Research Council, 1960), pp. 5–9.

[3] Edwin H. Sutherland and Donald R. Cressey, *Principles of Criminology*, Seventh Edition (Philadelphia: Lippincott, 1966), pp. 559–560.

[4] See John Irwin and Donald R. Cressey, "Thieves, Convicts and the Inmate Culture," *Social Problems*, 10:142–155, Fall, 1962.

is basic to the internal operations of the confederation. It is a call for unity, for peace, for maintenance of the status quo, and for silence. We have already discussed the decision for peace, based on this directive, which followed the 1930–1931 war. The need for secrecy is obvious.

2. *Be rational. Be a member of the team. Don't engage in battle if you can't win.* What is demanded here is the corporate rationality necessary to conducting illicit businesses in a quiet, safe, profitable manner. The directive extends to personal life. Like a prisoner, the man occupying even the lowest position in a "family" unit is to be cool and calm at all times. This means, as examples, that he is not to use narcotics, that he is not to be drunk on duty, that he is not to get into fights, and that he is not to commit any crimes without first checking with his superiors. A leader of an Italian-Sicilian "family" in a large city, accompanied by a low-status member of the family, passed a law-enforcement officer on the street. The low-status man spat on the officer. The leader apologized profusely and, presumably, took punitive action against his worker. The low-status man was not, in the language of inmates, "playing it cool." The ruler of a different Italian-Sicilian "family" at one time temporarily stopped all lottery operations in his city because the business was drawing the attention of the police to the even more lucrative criminal activities of the "family." As Tyler has observed:

In this era of the "organization man," the underworld—like most institutions that prosper within an established culture—has learned to conform. Its internal structure provides status for those who would plod along in workaday clothes. In its external relations, it affects all the niceties of a settled society, preferring public relations and investment to a punch in the nose or pickpocketing.[5]

3. *Be a man of honor. Respect womanhood and your elders. Don't rock the boat.*

[5] Gus Tyler, *Organized Crime in America* (Ann Arbor: University of Michigan Press, 1962), p. 116.

This emphasis on "honor" and "respect" helps determine who obeys whom, who attends what funerals and weddings, who opens the door for whom, who takes a tone of deference in a telephone conversation, who rises when another walks into a room. Later we will show that emphasis on honor actually functions to enable despots to exploit their underlings.

4. *Be a stand-up guy. Keep your eyes and ears open and your mouth shut. Don't sell out.* A "family" member, like a prisoner, must be able to withstand frustrating and threatening situations without complaining or resorting to subservience. The "stand-up guy" shows courage and "heart." He does not whine or complain in the face of adversity, including punishment, because "If you can't pay, don't play." In his testimony before the McClellan Committee, Mr. Valachi reported that juvenile delinquents appearing in police stations or jails are watched and assessed to determine whether they possess the "manliness" so essential to membership in the Italian-Sicilian confederation of criminals. This tenet of the code will later be discussed in more detail, in the section on recruitment.

5. *Have class. Be independent. Know your way around the world.* Two basic ideas are involved here, and both of them prohibit the according of prestige to law-enforcement officials or other respectable citizens. One is expressed in the saying, "To be straight is to be a victim." A man who is committed to regular work and submission to duly-constituted authority is a sucker. When one "family" member intends to insult and cast aspersion on the competence of another, he is likely to say, "Why don't you get out and get a job?" The world seen by organized criminals is a world of graft, fraud, and corruption, and they are concerned with their own honesty and manliness as compared with the hypocrisy of corrupt policemen and corrupt political figures. A criminal who

plays the role of Corrupter is superior to a criminal who plays the role of Corruptee.

Vague, general, and overlapping as the tenets of the code are, they form the foundation of the legal order of the confederation. One's standing in the status hierarchy depends in part on his ability to bring in profits, and in part upon his not being caught violating the code. Serious violators of the prohibitions against informing and against interfering with another criminal's interest are killed. Since conformity to or deviation from the code is so important in the lives of family members, it is probable that argot terms have been developed for various kinds of conforming and deviating behavior. We are not familiar with any such argot terms which are unique to the confederation, however. "Stand-up guy," "rat," "fink," "stool pigeon," and variants of these terms are used, but these terms are not significantly different from those used by the members of other systems, legal and illegal.

Both Strong and Schrag have suggested that groups characterize members in relation to the problems, lines of interest, and focal concerns of the group, and then attach distinctive names to these types.[6] Since the problems, focal concerns, and lines of interest of prisoners and members of the criminal confederation are almost identical, it would not be surprising if the distinctive names attached to some types of organized criminals were not similar to the distinctive names attached to some types of prisoners. Before turning to an examination of the functions the code has in the governing of confederation members, we would like to suggest that investigators with access to criminals' conversations should be able to find among confederation members the three principal deviant roles found among prison inmates. Our preliminary examination indicates that these roles are indeed present among organized criminals, despite the fact that we have heard no argot terms for them. We are convinced that the functions the code serves for the confederation will not really be understood until the relationships between the three informal roles are understood.

Prisoners who exhibit highly aggressive behavior against other inmates or against officials are likely to be called "toughs," "hoods," "gorillas" or some similar name, depending on the prison they are in. The terms are all synonyms, and they refer to men likely to be diagnosed as "psychopaths," who hijack their fellow inmates when the latter are returning from the commissary, who attack guards and fellow inmates verbally and physically, who run any kangaroo court, who force incoming inmates to pay for cell and job assignments, who smash up the prison at the beginning of a riot. Precisely the same type is found among organized criminals. Mr. Arthur Flegenheimer (Dutch Schultz), one of the last prohibition gangsters to hold out against "The Italian Society" that formed just prior to the 1930–31 inter-family war, exemplified this type. The following description of a murder committed by Mr. Flegenheimer was written by his lawyer, Corrupter, and Money Mover. It reveals the "tough" characters of both the murderer and the victim:

Dutch Schultz was ugly; he had been drinking and suddenly he had his gun out. The Dutchman wore his pistol under his vest, tucked inside his pants, right against his belly. One jerk at his vest and he had it in his hand. All in the same quick motion he swung it up, stuck it in Jules Martin's mouth, and pulled the trigger. It was as simple and undramatic as that—just one quick motion of the hand. The Dutchman did that murder just as casually as if he were picking his teeth . . . Julie was the bigmouthed ape who ran the restaurant racket for Schultz. He had two big labor unions terrorized and in two years he had shaken down $2,000,000 from the eating places in the Broadway section, in-

---

[6] Samuel M. Strong, "Social Types in a Minority Group," *American Journal of Sociology*, 48:563–573, March, 1943; Clarence Schrag, "Leadership Among Prison Inmates," *American Sociological Review*, 19:37–42, February, 1954; and "A Preliminary Criminal Typology," *Pacific Sociological Review*, 4:11–16, Spring, 1961.

cluding Jack Dempsey's. Once I had seen Julie with his bare hands beat up a man horribly... Julie was saying that he had stolen only $20,000 and the Dutchman was insisting he had stolen $70,000 and they were fighting over the difference.[7]

Currently, "toughs" in criminal syndicates are likely to occupy the position provided for an "Enforcer" and one or more of the positions provided for "Executioner." Enforcers, who are not necessarily the men who actually inflict the punishment or commit the murder ordered by a Boss or the Commission, are high-status men whose function is something like that of penal administrators in legitimate government. They carry out punishments, including executions, ordered by a judicial authority. The process of "carrying out" a judicial order does not require that the penal administrator personally inflict the punishment or perform the execution. In the confederation of organized criminals there are positions for Executioners, including a position for "setting up" the victim, a position for the actual killer, and others. The men who occupy these positions resemble the prisoners called "toughs," "hoods," and "gorillas" by their fellow prisoners, both when they are performing their duties and when they are off duty.

In the criminal confederation, as in prison, the man who plays the role of the "tough" is both an asset and a threat to other types of leaders. He is a leader because he stands above the ordinary run of Soldiers or Buttons, and he is an asset because he readily follows orders to control by "muscle." But the fact that he controls by "muscle" also makes him a threat to whoever uses him. Raymond V. Martin, former Assistant Chief of the Brooklyn South Detectives, has described the "Gallo-Profaci war" that developed in 1961–62 when a faction of "toughs" in a Brooklyn "family" tried to overthrow their leaders because they believed they were being cheated.[8]

A second type of prisoner role is identified in prison argot as the "merchant," "peddler," or "con politician." Prisoners playing this role do favors for their fellow prisoners in direct exchange for favors from them, or in exchange for payment in cigarettes, the medium of exchange in most prisons. Many, if not most, of the "favors" involve distribution of goods and services which should go to inmates without cost—the "merchant" demands a price for dental care, laundry, food, library books, a good job assignment, etc. Thus the "merchant," like the "tough" or "gorilla," actually exploits other inmates while seeming to help make prison life easier for them.

The criminal confederation also has positions for "merchants" who make their way in the world by manipulating and "dealing" with their fellow criminals. One criminal occupational position occupied by "merchants" is that of loan-shark. While these persons loan money at usurious rates (now five percent per week) to respectable victims outside the confederation, they also take advantage of their fellow-criminals' misfortunes by helping and assisting them, at usurious rates. Prison inmates make a distinction between the "real man" or "right guy" (to be discussed below) who might "score" for food occasionally, and the "merchant" who sells stolen food on a "route." The man who "scores" may distribute part of the loot to his friends, with no definite obligation to repay, but the man with the "route" gives nothing away. The loan-shark (sometimes called a "shylock," "shy" or "shell") by analogy, is the man with the "route"—he is out to make money wherever he can make it. Since loan-sharks stand by to loan money to gamblers in need, and since organized criminals are frequently gamblers in need, it may be presumed that usurious loans often are made to members of the organi-

---

[7] J. Richard Davis, "Things I Couldn't Tell Till Now," *Collier's*, July 22, 1939.

[8] Raymond V. Martin, *Revolt in the Mafia* (New York: Duell, Sloan and Pearce, 1963).

zation. Here, as among prison "merchants," there is no discount to friends. In hearings on loan-sharking held by the New York State Commission of Investigation, Sergeant of Detectives Ralph Salerno of the Criminal Intelligence Bureau of the New York City Police Department testified, in effect, that the organized criminal's need for the services of the loan-shark makes it possible for the loan-shark to exploit him:

> It is a demonstration of power. You have something which, I think, is unique in criminal fields in loansharking to a height and to a degree in their own criminal circles that I have never seen duplicated anywhere. It seems to be an unwritten law that even if you are a criminal, even if you are a top guy, you always pay the shylock . . . You borrow money, you pay it back. [The members of the Gallo gang] weren't afraid of the shylock. But they didn't know when they might need him again. So they very diligently paid the shylock.[9]

The Buffer position in confederation "families" also is a position for a "merchant." As we indicated earlier, men occupying the position of "Buffer" are carefully selected and highly trusted by the Boss or by a Lieutenant. The duties of the Buffer are to be aware of all the operations of his immediate superior and to keep that superior officer informed, while at the same time keeping him insulated from police and prosecuting attorneys. In practice, however, these duties require him to gather information about his fellow criminals and to report his findings to a man who has the power of life and death over the underlings. Accordingly, in return for "favors," he allocates "favors," such as interviews with the Boss or Lieutenant, which in a different system the lower-status worker would be able to get for himself, free of charge.

The "right guy" or the "real man" is the third principal type of inmate role identified in prison argot. Men who play this role are the highest status men in any prison. This is no accident, for the prisoner's code of behavior summarized above is really the code of a "right guy," the epitome of the "good prisoner." Because the "right guy" in prison closely resembles the "stand-up guy" in confederated crime, it also may be said that the confederation code summarized earlier is the code of the "stand-up guys" who have the highest status in the hierarchy of a "family" or of the confederation itself. If the Boss or Underboss of a "family" were asked to describe an ideal underling, or if a Soldier were asked to describe his Boss or Underboss, they probably would use many of the phrases used to describe the "right guy" in prison. The following is one such description. We quote at some length because later we will show how the "right guys" of organized crime, the Bosses and Underbosses, use the "right guy" code to protect themselves from both the police and underlings.

A *right guy* is always loyal to his fellow prisoners. He never lets you down no matter how rough things get. He keeps his promises; he's dependable and trustworthy. He isn't nosey about your business and doesn't fall all over himself to make friends either—he has a certain dignity. The *right guy* never interferes with other inmates who are conniving against the officials. He doesn't go around looking for a fight, but he never runs away from one when he is in the right. Anybody who starts a fight with a *right guy* has to be ready to go all the way. When he's got or can get extras in prison—like cigarettes, food stolen from the mess hall, and so on—he shares with his friends. He doesn't take advantage of those who don't have much. He doesn't strong-arm other inmates into punking or fagging for him; instead, he acts like a man.

In his dealings with the prison officials, the *right guy* is unmistakably against them, but he doesn't act foolishly. When he talks about the officials with other inmates, he's sure to say that even the hacks with the best intentions are stupid, incompetent, and not to be trusted; that the worst thing a con can do is give the hacks

---

[9] New York State Commission of Investigation, *An Investigation of the Loan Shark Racket* (New York: Author, 1965).

information—they'll only use it against you when the chips are down. A *right guy* sticks up for his rights, but he doesn't ask for pity: he can take all the lousy screws can hand out and more. He doesn't suck around the officials, and the privileges that he's got are his because he deserves them. Even if the *right guy* doesn't look for trouble with the officials, he'll go to the limit if they push him too far. He realizes that there are just two kinds of people in the world, those in the know skim it off the top; suckers work.[10]

If there were no violations of the code of organized criminals, everyone would be a "stand-up guy" or, to use the prisoner's term, a "right guy." For this reason, the Bosses, Underbosses and other high-status men promulgate both the code and its corollary, the notion that all members should be "stand-up guys" like themselves. Were the code never violated, every member would be a "stand-up guy" and the illicit government's operations would be a complete mystery to the police and other representatives of legitimate government. Further, if every member were a "stand-up guy" the Lieutenant would never be a threat to the Underboss, and the Underboss would never be a threat to the Boss. That is not the case. The code is violated, obviously, by men acting the role of "tough" and the role of "merchant," for they are exploiting fellow criminals and thereby interfering with their interests.

The fact that a code of conduct calling for honor and silence is violated, even frequently, does not mean that it is unimportant in the control of conduct. Our legitimate "code" regarding the right to private property has been put into the precise form of the criminal law, and the "code" as well as the law is violated whenever a larceny is committed. Nevertheless, this "code" determines, directly or indirectly, a broad range of social interactions among both honest and dishonest citizens. The important problem for one who would understand a society or group guided by a code is not that of determining whether the code is violated. It is the problem of determining the code's function in the preservation of order.

SOME FUNCTIONS OF THE CODE

We suggest that the code of honor and silence which asks every member of the confederation to be a "stand-up guy," and which underlies the entire structure of our criminal cartel, serves the same important function that the "rule of law" once served for absolute monarchs—protection of personal power. Although implementing the idea of "a government of law, not of men" is now viewed as basic to protection of man's freedom from tyrants, the idea was once used for maintaining the conditions of tyranny. One who displeased the monarch by revolting against him in the name of democracy was taking the law into his own hands. As democracy developed, so did the prohibitions against *ex post facto* legislation, ideas about the right of revolution, and similar systems of government by the law of the people rather than by the law of the monarch. Whether or not a "government by law" insures basic freedoms to a greater degree than does a "government by men" depends upon who makes, and enforces, the law. In organized crime, the rule of law is the rule of a despot.

The principal function of the code of organized criminals seems to be the same as the principal function of "the law" when the latter protected the monarch from the people. Since the Boss of a "family" has the most to lose if the organization is weakened through an attack by outsiders, he enthusiastically promotes the notion that an offense against one is an offense against all. Moreover, by promoting this idea he makes the subordinates his "boys," who henceforth are dependent upon his paternalism. A Boss who can establish that he will assist his followers when they are in need or when they have

---

[10] Sykes and Messinger, *op. cit.*, note 30, at pp. 10–11.

been offended has gained control over these men. They are obligated to reciprocate, in the name of "honor," thus enhancing his privileged position.

Those aspects of the code which prohibit appealing to outside authorities for justice while at the same time advocating great loyalty, respect and honor are probably most essential to the concentration of power in the hands of a few and, hence to exploitation of lower-status men by their leaders. The ruler of an organized crime unit, whether it be an entire Italian-Sicilian "family" or a thirty-man lottery enterprise, has three classes of enemies—law-enforcement agencies, outsiders who want his profits, and his underlings. Of these, the law-enforcement agencies seem to be the least threatening, for they are hampered by lack of enthusiasm on the part of the governments which support them, by the lack of coordinated intelligence information, and by a commitment to due process of law. The leader's organization has been rationally designed to insulate him from the law-enforcement process. Some evidence of this rationality is seen in the fact that the leaders order their lives so as to take full advantage of the legal safeguards guaranteed by the Constitution. They know the rules of evidence and exploit them to the fullest. A thirty-day jail sentence imposed on a Boss creates consternation on the streets because it demonstrates that the entire illicit government is in danger. The leaders promote a code of honor which makes it impossible for the police to get witnesses to testify against the leaders, a code of honor which is enforced by the death penalty.

More threatening than the police are competitors, who are sometimes called "Indians" by the members of the establishment. Puerto Rican groups in New York and Mexican-American groups in Los Angeles are now giving the confederation a little competition, especially in the narcotics business. Competition among members has been reduced by fair trade agreements, by arbitration and judicial procedures, and by the code which prohibits one criminal from interfering with the business of another. But competition from the outside must be reduced by other means. One method is assassination and another is the coercive power of the legitimate government—the illegal activities of competitive outsiders are reported to the police. It is not necessary that one be honorable with respect to outsiders. Although Tyler presents no evidence in support of his statement, he probably is correct when he says, "Police are glad to cooperate [with older ethnic groups] because the 'Indian' is a disturbance, a source of violence, a disruption to old ties, a threat to the monthly stipend." [11] If the technique of betrayal fails, the outsiders are threatened, maimed, or killed.

Most threatening of all to the governor of an organized crime unit such as a family" are his own underlings, especially when the governor is old and the underlings are young. The charismatic qualities attributed to a leader by his contemporaries are not likely to be attributed to him by the next generation, including his own children. Oldsters are under almost constant threat from the younger generation, and if they are to survive, they must organize their defenses. As Bolitho observed over three decades ago, "The heraldic crest of the underworld is a double-cross. The ultimate secret of almost every criminal and gangster is that he is a traitor, willingly, or by force, or just by stupidity. It is also the chief trade secret of crime detection." [12] The first line of defense used by organized crime rulers against such double-crossers is the code of conduct we have summarized above. The second line of defense is a gun. As McCleery has said,

---

[11] Gus Tyler, "The Roots of Organized Crime", *Crime and Delinquency*, 8:325–338, October, 1962, at p. 336.

[12] William Bolitho, "The Natural History of Graft," The Survey, 63:138–140 ff., April, 1931.

Systems of power differ most significantly in the type and intensity of means employed to extract the consent of the governed ... Just as responsible democratic government rests on freedom of communication and open access to officials, an authoritarian system of power requires procedures which retain initiative for the ruling class, minimize reciprocity, and prevent the communication of popular values to the ruling elite. Authoritarian control does not rest basically on the imposition of punitive sanctions. It rests, instead, on the definition, in a system of authority, of a role for the ruler which makes the use of punitive sanctions superfluous. Thus, the heart of custodial controls in traditional prisons lies in the daily regimentation, routines, and rituals of domination which bend the subjects into a customary posture of silent awe and unthinking acceptance.[13]

A "posture of silent awe and unthinking acceptance" is, after all, what inspires conformity to the criminal law in most members of democratic societies. A "sense of morality," or a "sense of duty," or a "sense of decency" keep the crime rate low. It is this kind of "sense" which constitutes "consent to be governed" in a democracy. Similarly, in the government of criminal organizations, a "posture of silent awe and unthinking acceptance" is the objective of rulers who would inspire in their subjects a different "sense of morality," "duty," or "decency." The code of honor asks the underlings to be honest, moral, and straightforward in their relationships with the men of high status whose positions of power would be severely threatened should the lower-status men subscribe only to the more general societys moral and legal code. Without honor, respect, and honesty there could not be, among the underlings, the "posture of silent awe and unthinking acceptance" which enables rulers to acquire vast fortunes through the hard work and even suffering (in the case of imprisonment) of the underlings.

Yet even a democratic government must constantly be seeking to maintain among its members the consent to be governed. Further, even in a democracy, government must constantly be seeking measures for the control of those members whose "sense of morality" and decency" does not stop them from violating the criminal law. When an individual citizen's consent to be governed has been lost, as indicated by the fact that he has committed a crime, "force" must be used to coerce conformity. But force usually is not physical control; it is *ex post facto* infliction of pain for deviation. If such intentional infliction of suffering is to be accepted by the recipients and by citizens generally, it must be made "justly," in measures suitable to correcting deviation without stimulating rebellion. Maintaining "consent of the government" then, requires that punishments for deviation be accepted as legitimate by those being governed.

This is the basic meaning of "justice" in criminal cases. One who believes that criminals should be dealt with "justly" believes, among other things, that punishments can be inflicted on criminals without great danger of revolt or rebellion, providing sufficient *advance notice* is given in the form of rules. Especially in the Western societies with long traditions of barring *ex post facto* legislation, elaborate systems for *warning* citizens that non-conformity of certain kinds will have punishment as its consequence stimulate rather docile acceptance of official punishments when they are in fact ordered by the courts and executed by prison officials and others. In other words, democratic states operate on the basic assumption that conformity can be maximized only if the punitive system has a rational base. If punishments were imposed irrationally or capriciously, the citizen would be unable to determine to which rules he should conform. Moreover,

---

[13] Richard H. McCleery, "The Governmental Process and Informal Social Control," Chapter IV in Donald R. Cressey, Editor, *The Prison: Studies in Institutional Organization and Change* (New York: Holt, Rinehart and Winston, 1961), pp. 153-154.

the infliction of punishments in an apparently arbitrary way would be viewed as "unjust" and would, then, contribute to divisiveness in the society.

An important function of the criminal law, so far as maintaining consent of the governed is concerned, is providing the "advance notice" necessary for justice. The carefully-stated and precisely-stated prohibitions stipulated in criminal laws give advance notice that wrongdoers will be punished, thus contributing to the maintenance of the consent of the governed even when the latter are punished. In addition, since it is not correct to assume that all criminal laws are perfectly clear, the police are utilized to give additional advance notice that whoever violates a criminal law risks punishment—police discretion often means that the police are to issue warnings that *further violations* will have punishment as a consequence. In the long run, then, the consent of the governed and, thus, a maximum degree of conformity, rests at least in part on a public belief that punishments will be imposed only for deliberate violations or regulations clearly stipulated in advance.

In this regard, the code of the "stand-up guy" is in organized crime the functional equivalent of the criminal law. As indicated, conformity to the code is expected of all members, and severe punishments are meted out to nonconformists. But there is one significant respect in which this code of honor differs significantly from the criminal law of democratic society: It is unwritten. Since the code is unwritten, it can be said by the rulers to provide for whatever the rulers want and to prohibit whatever the rulers do not want.[14] The

rules of the criminal law, and even the rules contained in the procedural manuals of business firms, control the actions of high-status as well as low-status personnel. But the organized criminals' code, being oral, lacks the precision necessary to identifying the violations of high-status personnel who do not want them identified. Note, for example, that the code prohibits interference with the interests of fellows and asks that fellows be loyal to each other. As indicated earlier, this rule is somewhat comparable to the law of larceny, which asks that citizens not interfere with each other's rights to private property. But while the law of larceny is stated precisely, the rule for organized criminals is stated so imprecisely that very few underlings can appreciate the fact that the rulers are actually rule violators.

If an underling is told that he cannot establish a lottery enterprise in a certain part of town because a lottery operation already is being conducted there, he can rationalize the decision as an honorable one that is based on the principle that one should not interfere with the interests of a fellow organized criminal. But when the ruler makes an honorable decision that he henceforth will be in a kind of partnership with all bookmakers in a certain area, the bookmakers are not quick to note that both the ruler's decision and his action are in violation of the code. Similarly, if one criminal starts competing with another criminal, the ruler may find it expedient to have him killed, thus enforcing the rule against interfering with another criminal's interests. But in ordering the killing the ruler is by no means being guided by the code saying that one should not interfere with the interests of another. The "law of larceny" does not apply to him; the king can do no wrong.

Similarly, the lack of precision in the code enables the leader to run his "fam-

---

[14] Compare a Nazi law of June 28, 1935: "Whoever commits an action which the law declares to be punishable or which is deserving of punishment according to the fundamental idea of a penal law and the sound perception of the people, shall be punished. If no determinate penal law is directly applicable to the action, it shall be punished according to the law, the basic idea of which fits it best." This law is discussed in Lawrence Preuss, "Punishment by Analogy in Nationalist Socialist Penal Law," *Journal of Criminal Law and Criminology*, 26:847, March-April, 1936.

ily" organization primarily on the basis of information received from informers, while at the same time enforcing with a gun the idea that informers are the lowest form of life. The role of the Buffer, which we described earlier, is partly the role of an informer. The Buffer, like the Underboss and other couriers, gets information about any defections or suspected defections in the organization from other informers and passes it on to his Boss, thus allowing the Boss to interfere with the interests of his fellow criminals.

The rulers' positions of power are also protected by the confederation's judicial system, which has been devised to give advance notice that violators of the code will be punished. There are two basic systems, one referring to conflicts in which both disputants are members of the same "family," the other to disputes between two men who each report, through a hierarchy of ranks, to a different Boss. In either case, the distinction between tort and crime is unclear. One who claims that another is interfering with his criminal interests is at once a plaintiff in a civil suit and a complainant in a criminal case. If two members of the same "family" are quarreling, it is expected that they will follow the admonition to settle their differences quietly, without violence, so as not to antagonize the citizenry. If they cannot come to an agreement, one of them lodges a complaint with their Lieutenant, who makes a judgment on the matter. The accused is sometimes permitted to present his defense, sometimes not, depending on the conclusiveness of the evidence and the seriousness of the charge. The judgment has the function of the warning given to the general public by the criminal law. Thus, it is advance notice to all concerned that henceforth the arrangements will be adjudicated. If one of the parties to the quarrel does not heed the "notice," he is punished or executed by the man making the decision, not by the man with whom he has been quarrelling. The punishment can be a public reprimand, a slap in the face, a roughing up, or a beating. Reprimands and corporal punishments are administered in the presence of the offender's close friends and associates, as a demonstration of his weakness. Economic sanctions are also involved, through a system of guilt by association—"If he has done something so bad that Johnny slaps him, he will bring heat, so I don't want to be a business associate of his."

When the disputants are members of different "families," the procedure is essentially the same. Each is required to report his problem to his Lieutenant. The two Lieutenants confer at a meeting called a "sit down," and if they can come to an agreement, they issue a "notice" regarding subsequent arrangements. If they cannot come to an agreement, they refer the case to each of their Bosses, who then meet, reach an agreement, and issue the notice. If the two Bosses cannot agree, the matter is a very serious one and it is referred to the Commission, which issues the notice. The notice gives the adjudicating body (be it Lieutenant, Boss of Commission), but not the disputants, the "right" to order the execution of violators.

By giving the rulers of the illegal government the power to assist and reward him, then, the member also gives the rulers the right to kill him. This is the basic meaning of "illicit government," when viewed from the perspective of the participants. Because the operations of bookmakers and other low-echelon personnel are illegal, these men cannot call upon the police and courts for prosecution of criminal activities in which they are victims. The strong emphasis in the code on being loyal, on being rational, on being honorable, and on being inconspicuous, is an emphasis which gives the rulers a monopoly on violence. The code denies to the individual his right to legitimate use of the coercive power of the state, while at the same time conferring upon his superiors the "right" to use illegitimate power to control him. This is one of the most insidious aspects of organized crime, especially because representatives of the legitimate government are induced, for a fee, to subscribe to the same code. A policeman or political figure who plays a role in organized crime transfers his allegiance from one government to another. Sometimes the allegiance of entire police departments and of all the political figures in a ward are transferred in this way. Corrupt officials, like other organized criminals, both deny and are denied access to the judicial processes of legitimate government, while at the same time condoning, in the name of honor, the coercive power of totalitarian government.

In summary, the "men of honor" and "stand-up guys" who have assumed positions of power in the confederation of criminals have done so with the assistance of a code of conduct stipulating that no underling should interfere with their interests, that underlings should not go to the police for protection, that underlings should be "stand-up guys" who go to prison in order that the Bosses may amass fortunes. All the processes of government within organized crime are devoted to enforcing the code so that profit can be maximized. The code, in turn, is the code of a despot bent on securing conformity to his demand that he be left alone to enrich himself at the expense of men who shower him with honor and respect. The leaders are men who have secured their high status and wealth by virtue of a code which gives them exploitive authoritarian power, and they are bent on enforcing the mandates and injunctions of the code so that their power to exploit is maintained.

THE MAFIA CODE

Since there is great similarity between the structure of the Italian-Sicilian Mafia and the structure of the American confederation of criminals, it should not be surprising to find great similarity in the values, norms, and other behavior patterns of the members of the two organizations. As mentioned earlier, any organizational structure, at least in its governmental aspects, is related to the kind of code of behavior members are expected to follow. The code of behavior of the Mafia and the code of behavior of American organized criminals, in turn, are likely to be similar because not any code will do if an organization is to operate outside the law for any length of time. Two succinct summaries of the Mafia code show the resemblance to the code of American organized criminals. One statement was made in 1892; the other in 1900.

1. Reciprocal aid in case of any need whatever. 2. Absolute obedience to the chief. 3. An offense received by one of the members to be considered an offense against all and avenged at any cost. 4. No appeal to the state's authorities for justice. 5. No revelation of the names of members or any secrets of the association.[15]

1. To help one another and avenge every injury of a fellow member. 2. To work with all means for the defense and freeing of any fellow member who has fallen into the hands of the judiciary. 3. To divide the proceeds of thievery, robbery and extortion with certain consideration for the needy as determined by the *capo*. 4. To keep the oath and maintain secrecy on pain of death within twenty-four hours.[16]

The two statements differ very little. The first spells out the dictatorial character of the government, and the second mentions criminal activities. These variations could well be the consequence of the perspectives of the two summarizers, rather than differences in codes themselves. Both statements indicate that the Mafia creed asks the mem-

---

[15] Ed Reid, *Mafia* (New York: New American Library, 1964), p. 31. The same rules appear in *The Chambers Journal* of 1892.

[16] Antonio Cutrera, *La Mafia e mafiosi: origini e manifestazioni, studio di sociologia criminale* (Palermo: Alberto Reber, 1900); cited by Robert T. Anderson, "From Mafia to Cosa Nostra," *American Journal of Sociology*, 61:302–310, November, 1965, at p. 308.

bers for the same kind of behavior asked by the American organized criminals' creed—loyalty, honor, secrecy, honesty, and consent to be governed, which may mean consent to be executed. Except for the last item, these are the attributes of honorable men everywhere, and even honorable men agree, as a part of their citizenship, to the death penalty for traitors. Tyler only exaggerated slightly when he said the rules very well might have been written for the Three Musketeers (one for all and all for one), for the Industrial Workers of the World (an injury to one is an injury to all), for the Irish Republican Army, for the Mau Mau, for the Hatfields or the McCoys, or for delinquent gangs struggling over turf or waging a battle against officialdom.[17] The code expresses hostility toward the authority in power while at the same time recognizing the need to acknowledge its might.

Despite the clear evidence that the Sicilian Mafia has a structure similar to that of any rationally devised bureaucracy, authorities are not convinced that the organization was, or is, much more than an informal agreement to abide by the behavioral code. Mosca reports that a Sicilian-Italian dictionary of 1868 defines the Mafia as a neologism denoting any sign of bravado, a bold show, while a dictionary of 1876 defines it as a word of Piedmontese origin somewhat equivalent to "gang." [18] Thus, in the nineteenth century the term was defined both as an attitude and as a group of men. This pattern has been carried forward by Barzini, who says that in one of its meanings the word should be spelled with a lower-case "m," while in the other meaning the word should be capitalized.

The lower-case mafia is a state of mind, a philosophy of life, a conception of society, a moral code, a particular susceptibility, prevailing among all Sicilians . . . They are taught in the cradle, or are born already knowing, that they must aid each other, side with their friends and fight common enemies even when the friends are wrong and the enemies right; each must defend his dignity at all costs and never allow the smallest slights and insults to go unavenged; they must keep secrets, and always beware of official authority and laws . . . A Sicilian who does not feel these compulsions should no longer consider himself a Sicilian . . . Mafia, in the second and more specialized meaning of the word, is the world-famous illegal organization. It is not strictly an organized association, with hierarchies, written statutes, headquarters, ruling elite and an undisputed chief. It is a spontaneous formation like an art-colony or a beehive, a loose and haphazard collection of single men and heterogeneous groups, each man obeying his entomological rules, each group uppermost in its tiny domain, independent, submitted to the will of its own leader, each group locally imposing its own rigid form of primitive justice. Only in rare times of emergency does the Mafia mobilize and become one loose confederation.[19]

The notion that the Mafia is more of an attitude than an organization was also taken by Premier Mussolini's Chief of Police, Cesare Mori, who was in charge of the drive against the Sicilian Mafia in the 1920's:

The Mafia, as I am describing it, is a peculiar way of looking at things and of acting which, through mental and spiritual affinities, brings together in definite, unhealthy attitudes men of particular temperament, isolating them from their surroundings into a kind of caste. It is a potential state which normally takes concrete form in a system of local oligarchies closely interwoven, but each autonomous in its own district.[20]

In this short statement, there are at least six words or phrases ("caste," "potential state," "concrete form," "system,"

---

[17] Tyler, "The Roots of Organized Crime," *supra* note 11, at p. 333.

[18] Gaetano Mosca, *Encyclopedia of the Social Sciences* (New York: Macmillan, 1933), Vol. X, p. 36.

[19] Luigi Barzini, *The Italians* (New York: Atheneum, 1964), pp. 253–254.

[20] Cesare Mori, *The Last Struggle with the Mafia* (London: Putnam, 1933), pp. 39–40.

"oligarchies," "autonomous") which refer to structural or organizational aspects of the Mafia, not to attitudes. This kind of oversight could occur in two ways. First, many writers are not aware that there can be organization without the written rules, formal procedures and organizational charts similar to those of a governmental bureau or department. Second, police must necessarily be more interested in capturing individual criminals than in worrying about the structure of organizations. Since attitudes belong to individuals, while "hierarchies" belong to organizations, even Mussolini's prefect of police overlooked some of the evidence he needed to help him in his organized crime drive. A number of men—with common attitudes, a hierarchy of authority and power, a system for accepting or rejecting applicants, and a system for policing the behavior of the participants—is an organization, even if the goals are not precisely stated. Formal fraternal organizations invent positions, roles and rituals in order to maximize the commitment of the members, and in that way they develop attitudes of brotherhood and kinship. The Sicilian Mafia started with brotherhood and kinship and developed the structure necessary to a government and business organization as well as to a fraternity.

In the previous sections we have stressed the notion that the code of *"omerta,"* like the code of "right guys" everywhere, supports extra-legal principalities by making it seem chivalrous to comply with the wishes of strong men seeking out their own interests in a particular territory. The basic principle of justice in the Sicilian Mafia, as in American organized crime, is deterrence from deviation by means of the threat of certain, swift, uniform and severe punishment. Another principle, usually overlooked because it does not mesh with observations of the "typical" American gangster of the 1920's and early 1930's, is humility and "understatement" in relationships of power. Again there is an analogy with American upper-class culture, which decries ostentation. A Mafia Don in Sicily, a ruler of a New York "family" of organized criminals, and a New England blueblood have one thing in common—they are all "above" the petty rules which demand conspicuous consumption for those who would climb the social ladder.

In the Sicilian Mafia, a man's rank is determined by the amount of fear he can generate, but the man with the clearest halo of fear around him is not distinguishable, in manner of living, from those who fear him. His manner is majestic, but humble. When in 1943 American soldiers met the Mafia chief of the area being invaded, if not of all Sicily, they probably expected to find him well manicured, diamond studded, and dressed in a $400 silk suit and alligator shoes. They found an old illiterate man, dressed in his shirt sleeves and suspenders, whose whole game seemed to be that of de-emphasizing appearances. He did not change even when the Allies nicknamed him "General Mafia." In almost direct contrast, a bandit enlisted by this Mafia chief to help in a political fight a few years later was a twenty-three year old "tough" who came to a meeting bedecked with a calendar wristwatch, a golden belt buckle, and a diamond solitaire ring. He was said to dress better than businessmen or lawyers, and the press referred to him as "the King of Montelepre."

The same kind of understatement on the part of the leaders, and the same kind of contrast with the demeanor of the underlings, is found in American organized crime. Mr. Vito Genovese, head a New York "family" and, before his current incarceration, leader of the nine-man All-American "Commission," had at the time of the Apalachin meeting in 1957 been invested with charismatic qualities by his followers. He was almost revered, while at the same time being feared, like an Old Testament divine. Even his name had a somewhat sacred quality, with the result that he was sometimes referred to as "a certain party," rather than by name. There was, in short, more than the kind of envy, awe, or even fear commanded by an ordinary immigrant who has accumulated twenty-five to thirty million dollars. Yet at the time of the Apalachin meeting Mr. Genovese lived in a modest house in Atlantic Highlands, New Jersey, drove a two-year-old Ford, and owned not more than ten suits, none of which had been purchased for more than about a hundred dollars. On the dusty top of a dresser in his bedroom stood cheap plaster statues of saints. His children and eight grandchildren visited him frequently, and he personally cooked meals for them.

The contrast with the demeanor of underlings who ostentatiously display their new-found wealth is obvious. The police in one city were unaware of the importance of a man who was in fact a highly placed Underboss until they were able to observe his participation in a meeting. First a dozen men, known to be quite high-ranking, arrived in their air-conditioned automobiles, some of them with chauffeurs. Their manners and style of dress were not "flashy," but they were impeccable. After they had been assembled for a few minutes, a small man, dressed in a shiny-seated black suit and carrying a bag of his wife's home-made peppers, entered the room. All those in attendance jumped to their feet and whipped off their hats. The man addressed the group in Italian, haranguing them about their behavior on a particular issue. After speaking for about fifteen minutes he left the room abruptly and walked to the nearest subway station, where he took the next train home. The meeting broke up upon his departure, the remainder of the group driving off in their expensive automobiles.

Ostentatious display of wealth or power is generally frowned upon in the brotherhood. Big houses such as Joe Barbara's are rare. A mafioso may have a substantial fortune tucked away, as a good many have, but the ancient tradition requires him to live an outwardly modest life. He has his Cadillac or his Chrysler, bought for cash, and almost always at least one mistress; the number depends on his standing in the brotherhood. Home, however, is often a two-family house with overstuffed furniture, antimacassars on the chairs, five-and-ten ceramics and all the other trappings of a stuffy middle-class European household. Here he is the soul of respectability—an affectionate husband, a kind father, usually temperate and a faithful worshipper at his church.[21]

Lewis attributes the fashion of understatement in the demeanor of Sicilian Mafia leaders to linguistic confusion arising out of the similarity between the words *"omerta"* and *"umila"*—manliness and humility. "Many illiterate Sicilians have combined the two words to produce a hybrid of mixed pagan and Christian significance. The virtuous man is in Mafia fashion 'manly' and silent, and as a Christian humble."[22] The matter probably is not so simple, even in Sicily. Certainly the incidence of great humility among top American rulers is much less than the incidence among Sicilian Mafia leaders in the past. Humble men like the two described above are rare, either inside or outside American criminal organizations.

The similarities in the behavior of some American rulers and the typical Sicilian Mafia ruler make it tempting to conclude that the Americans have merely transplanted a Sicilian behavior pattern, complete with the confusion of manliness and humility. The differences, as indicated by the lavish displays of wealth on the part of other American leaders, challenge this conclusion. A more plausible explanation can be found in the observation that most of the American men have not yet "arrived." Since their power and positions of high status are not yet secure, they behave more like the newly-rich than like the old New England families constituting the upper

---

[21] Frederic Sondern, Jr., *Brotherhood of Evil: The Mafia* (New York: Farrar, Straus and Cudahy, 1959), p. 55.

[22] Norman Lewis, *The Honored Society* (New York: G. P. Putnam's Sons, 1964), p. 37.

class. One can afford to neglect a personal display of power only if his position of power is secure. On the other hand, ostentatious display is a sign that one is only climbing the status ladder, as indicated in the behavior of underlings everywhere.

Taken as a group, American rulers of organized crime are still on the way up, as compared with Sicilian Mafia rulers. The former are non-joiners. As respectable citizens have moved to the suburbs, they have moved with them. They live quiet lives with their families. They do not participate extensively in the activities of the residential communities where they live. Perhaps their non-participation is not all a matter of choice. Probably some of them are excluded from sailing weekends and debutante balls not because of their illegal activities but because they do not have the social graces and social background which make them eligible to participate. As the old leaders attempt to show exclusiveness by means of understatement, the new leaders are as yet excluded by means of understatement. But some of them are making the adjustment; they have reached the top of the illegitimate social ladder and are using the wealth and status acquired there to get them near the top of the legitimate social ladder. One New York leader even went to a psychiatrist to try to overcome his inferiority feelings about his inadequacy in social situations. As such feelings are overcome among the rulers—as they gain more power, as they extend their influence to wider and wider circles of economic, social, and political activities—they will attain the self-confidence and poise necessary to refrain from displaying one's wealth to the world.

American leaders are not far away from this condition. They do not have the "humility" that requires them to dress and act like Sicilian peasants, because they have not seized power over Sicilian peasants, as the humble rulers of the Sicilian Mafia have done. But most of them do have the "humility" that requires them to dress and act like American businessmen, rather than like characters in a "B" movie about Chicago gangsters, because they have seized, and are continuing to seize, power from American businessmen. As we will show later, underlings in American organized crime are beginning to follow the Bosses because the latter are men of wealth, rather than revering them as divines or fearing their guns. The danger to America is that respectable businessmen will follow the same men, on the assumption that they are deserving of respect because they are wealthy. As time goes on, Bosses and underlings alike will try to facilitate our support by adopting the system of understatement used by American upper-class citizens, rather than the system of understatement used to impress working-class groups, as Mr. Genovese did, and, before him, the crime bosses now given the derogatory title, "the moustaches."

We repeat that immigrants living together in close association are likely to retain their homeland characteristics, especially those of a psychological nature, for greater periods of time than are immigrants who scatter through a city or nation. After about fifty years in America, Sicilian and Italian groups have been absorbed by the culture of America. Their need and their desire to interact and cooperate with groups and individuals outside their own circle in order to gain a larger share of the good things of American life have been factors in this acculturation process. This generalization applies to those Sicilian-Americans and Italian-Americans who occupy positions in criminal organizations as well as those who do not. What appear to be Sicilian Mafia behavior patterns can be seen in the behavior of those older American organized criminals who came from Sicily or Italy. But the same behavior patterns can also be seen in the behavior of Americans who are not of Sicilian or Italian extraction, be they organized criminals, unorganized criminals, or completely respectable citizens. The Mafia behavior patterns observed among organized criminals are, at most, adaptations of old behavior patterns to the American scene. They might even be independent inventions. They are not importations. They are essential to any established order, authority, or institution. American organized crime is dominated by men of Sicilian and Italian origin, but it is a lineal descendant not a branch of the Sicilian Mafia.

58. GAMBLING AND CORRUPTION

THE STERN EMPIRE

THE HISTORY OF WINCANTON GAMBLING AND corruption since World War II centers around the career of Irving Stern. Stern is an immigrant who came to the United States and settled in Wincanton at the turn of the century. He started as a fruit peddler, but when Prohibition came along, Stern became a bootlegger for Heinz Glickman, then the beer baron of the State. When Glickman was murdered in the waning days of Prohibition, Stern took over Glickman's business and continued to sell untaxed liquor after repeal of Probibition in 1933. Several times during the 1930's, Stern was convicted in Federal court on liquor charges and spent over a year in Federal prison.

Around 1940, Stern announced to the world that he had reformed and went into his family's wholesale produce business. While Stern was in fact leaving the bootlegging trade, he was also moving into the field of gambling, for even at that time Wincanton had a "wide-open" reputation, and the police were ignoring gamblers. With the technical assistance of his bootlegging friends, Stern started with a numbers bank and soon added horse betting, a dice game, and slot machines to his organization. During World War II, officers from a nearby Army training base insisted

▶SOURCE: *Wincanton Gambling and Corruption, Task Force Report: Organized Crime, President's Commission on Law Enforcement and Administration of Justice, Appendix B, Washington, D.C.: 1967, pp. 64–74.*

that all brothels be closed, but this did not affect Stern. He had already concluded that public hostility and violence, caused by the houses, were, as a side effect, threatening his more profitable gambling operations. Although Irv Stern controlled the lion's share of Wincanton gambling throughout the 1940's, he had to share the slot machine trade with Klaus Braun. Braun, unlike Stern, was a Wincanton native and a Gentile, and thus had easier access to the frequently anti-Semitic club stewards, restaurant owners, and bartenders who decided which machines would be placed in their buildings. Legislative investigations in the early 1950's estimated that Wincanton gambling was an industry with gross receipts of $5 million each year; at that time Stern was receiving $40,000 per week from bookmaking, and Braun took in $75,000 to $100,000 per year from slot machines alone.

Irv Stern's empire in Wincanton collapsed abruptly when legislative investigations brought about the election of a reform Republican administration. Mayor Hal Craig decided to seek what he termed "pearl gray purity"—to tolerate isolated prostitutes, bookies, and numbers writers—but to drive out all forms of organized crime, all activities lucrative enough to make it worth someone's while to try bribing Craig's police officials. Within 6 weeks after taking office, Craig and District Attorney Henry Weiss had raided enough of Stern's gambling parlors and seized enough of Braun's slot machines to convince both men that business was over—for 4 years at least. The Internal Revenue Service was able to convict Braun and Stern's nephew, Dave Feinman, on tax evasion charges; both were sent to jail. From 1952 to 1955 it was still possible to place a bet or find a girl. But you had to know someone to do it, and no one was getting very rich in the process.

By 1955 it was apparent to everyone that reform sentiment was dead and that the Democrats would soon be back in office. In the summer of that year, Stern met with representatives of the east coast syndicates and arranged for the rebuilding of his empire. He decided to change his method of operations in several ways; one way was by centralizing all Wincanton vice and gambling under his control. But he also decided to turn the actual operation of most enterprises over to others. From the mid-1950's until the next wave of reform hit Wincanton after elections in the early 1960's, Irv Stern generally succeeded in reaching these goals.

The financial keystone of Stern's gambling empire was numbers betting. Records seized by the Internal Revenue Service in the late 1950's and early 1960's indicated that gross receipts from numbers amounted to more than $100,000 each month, or $1.3 million annually. Since the numbers are a poor man's form of gambling (bets range from a penny to a dime or quarter), a large number of men and a high degree of organization are required. The organizational goals are three: have the maximum possible number of men on the streets seeking bettors, be sure that they are reporting honestly, and yet strive so to decentralize the organization that no one, if arrested, will be able to identify many of the others. During the "pearl gray purity" of Hal Craig, numbers writing was completely unorganized—many isolated writers took bets from their friends and frequently had to renege if an unusually popular number came up; no one writer was big enough to guard against such possibilities.

When a new mayor took office in the mid-1950's, however, Stern's lieutenants notified each of the small writers that they were now working for Stern—or else. Those who objected were "persuaded" by Stern's men, or else arrested by the police, as were any of the others who were suspected of holding out on their receipts. Few objected for very long. After Stern completed the reorganization of the numbers business, its structure was roughly something like this: 11 subbanks reported to Stern's central accounting office. Each subbank employed from 5 to 30 numbers writers. Thirty-five percent of the gross receipts went to the writers. After deducting for winnings and expenses (mostly protection payoffs), Stern divided the net profits equally with the operators of the subbanks. In return for his cut, Stern provided protection from the police and "laid off" the subbanks, covering winnings whenever a popular number "broke" one of the smaller operators.

Stern also shared with out-of-State syndicates in the profits and operation of two enterprises—a large dice game and the largest still found by the Treasury Department since Prohibition. The dice game employed over 50 men—drivers to "lug" players into town from as far as 100 miles away, doormen to check players' identities, loan sharks who "faded" the losers, croupiers, food servers, guards, etc. The 1960 payroll for these employees was over $350,000. While no estimate of the gross receipts from the game is available, some indication of its size can be obtained from the fact that $50,000 was found on the tables and in the safe when the FBI raided the game in 1962. Over 100 players were arrested during the raid; one businessman had lost over $75,000 at the tables. Stern received a share of the game's profits plus a $1,000 weekly fee to provide protection from the police.

Stern also provided protection (for a fee) and shared in the profits of a still, erected in an old warehouse on the banks of the Wincanton River and tied into the city's water and sewer systems. Stern arranged for clearance by the city council and provided protection from the local police after the $200,000 worth of equipment was set up. The still was capable of producing $4 million worth of alcohol each year, and served a five-State area, until Treasury agents raided it after it had been in operation for less than 1 year.

The dice game and the still raise questions regarding the relationship of Irv Stern to out-of-State syndicates. Republican politicians in Wincanton frequently claimed that Stern was simply the local agent of the Cosa Nostra. While Stern was regularly sending money to the syndicates, the evidence suggests that Stern was much more than an agent for outsiders. It would be more accurate to regard these payments as profit sharing with coinvestors and as charges for services rendered. The east coasters provided technical services in the operation of the dice game and still and "enforcement" service for the Wincanton gambling operation. When deviants had to be persuaded to accept Stern's domination, Stern called upon outsiders for "muscle"—strong-arm men who could not be traced by local police if the victim chose to protest. In the early 1940's, for example, Stern asked for help in destroying a competing dice game; six gunmen came in and held it up, robbing and terrifying the players. While a few murders took place in the struggle for supremacy in the 1930's and 1940's, only a few people were roughed up in the 1950's and no one was killed.

After the mid-1950's, Irv Stern controlled prostitution and several forms of gambling on a "franchise" basis. Stern took no part in the conduct of these businesses and received no share of the profits, but exacted a fee for protection from the police. Several horse books, for example, operated regularly; the largest of these paid Stern $600 per week. While slot machines had permanently disappeared from the Wincanton scene after the legislative investigations of the early 1950's, a number of men began to distribute pinball machines, which paid off players for games won. As was the case with numbers writers, these pinball distributors had been unorganized during the Craig administration. When Democratic Mayor Gene Donnelly succeeded Craig, he immediately announced that all pinball machines were illegal and would be confiscated by the police. A Stern agent then contacted the pinball distributors and notified them that if they employed Dave Feinman (Irv Stern's nephew) as a "public relations consultant," there would be no interference from the police. Several rebellious distributors formed an Alsace County Amusement Operators Association, only to see Feinman appear with two thugs from New York. After the association president was roughed up, all resistance collapsed, and Feinman collected $2,000 each week to promote the "public relations" of the distributors. (Stern, of course, was able to offer no protection against Federal action. After the Internal Revenue Service began seizing the pinball machines in 1956, the owners were forced to purchase the $250 Federal gambling stamps as well as paying Feinman. Over 200 Wincanton machines bore these stamps in the early 1960's, and thus were secure from Federal as well as local action.)

After the period of reform in the early 1950's, Irv Stern was able to establish a centralized empire in which he alone determined which rackets would operate and who would operate them (he never, it might be noted, permitted narcotics traffic in the city while he controlled it). What were the bases of his control within the criminal world? Basically, they were three: First, as a business matter, Stern controlled access to several very lucrative operations, and could quickly deprive an uncooperative gambler or numbers writer of his source of income. Second, since he controlled the police department he could arrest any gamblers or bookies who were not paying tribute. (Some of the local gambling and prostitution arrests which took place during the Stern era served another purpose—to placate newspaper demands for a crackdown. As one police chief from this era phrased it, "Hollywood should have given us an Oscar for some of our performances when we had to pull a phony raid to keep the papers happy.") Finally, if the mechanisms of fear of financial loss and fear of police arrest failed to command obedience, Stern was always able to keep alive a fear of physical violence. As we have seen, numbers writers, pinball distributors, and competing gamblers were brought into line after outside enforcers put in an appearance. Stern's regular collection agent, a local tough who had been convicted of murder in the 1940's, was a constant reminder of the virtues of cooperation. Several witnesses who told grand juries or Federal agents of extortion attempts by Stern, received visits from Stern enforcers and tended to "forget" when called to testify against the boss.

Protection. An essential ingredient in Irv Stern's Wincanton operations was protection against law enforcement agencies. While he was never able to arrange freedom from Federal intervention (although, as in the case of purchasing excise stamps for the pinball machines, he was occasionally able to satisfy Federal requirements without disrupting his activities), Stern was able in the 1940's and again from the mid-1950's through the early 1960's to secure freedom from State and local action. The precise extent of Stern's network of protection payments is unknown, but the method of operations can be reconstructed.

Two basic principles were involved in the Wincanton protection system—pay top personnel as much as necessary to keep them happy (and quiet), and pay something to as many others as possible to implicate them in the system and to keep them from talking. The range of payoffs thus went from a weekly salary for some public officials to a Christmas turkey for the patrolman on the beat. Records from the numbers bank listed payments totaling $2,400 each week to some local elected officials, State legislators, the police chief, a captain in charge of detectives, and persons mysteriously labeled "county" and "State." While the list of persons to be paid remained fairly constant, the amounts paid varied according to the gambling activities in operation at the time; payoff figures dropped sharply when the FBI put the dice game out of business. When the dice game was running, one official was receiving $750 per week, the chief $100, and a few captains, lieutenants, and detectives lesser amounts.

While the number of officials receiving regular "salary" payoffs was quite restricted (only 15 names were on the payroll found at the numbers bank), many other officials were paid off in different ways. (Some men were also silenced without charge—low-ranking policemen, for example, kept quiet after they learned that men who reported gambling or prostitution were ignored or transferred to the midnight shift; they didn't have to be paid.) Stern was a major (if undisclosed) contributor during political campaigns—sometimes giving money to all candidates, not caring who won, sometimes supporting a "regular" to defeat a possible reformer, sometimes paying a candidate not to oppose a preferred man. Since there were few legitimate sources of large contributions for Democratic candidates, Stern's money was frequently regarded as essential for victory, for the costs of buying radio and television time and paying poll-watchers were high. When popular sentiment was running strongly in favor of reform, however, even Stern's contributions could not guarantee victory. Bob Walasek, later to be as corrupt as any Wincanton mayor, ran as a reform candidate in the Democratic primary and defeated Stern-financed incumbent Gene Donnelly. Never a man to bear grudges, Stern financed Walasek in the general election that year and put him on the "payroll" when he took office.

Even when local officials were not on the

regular payroll, Stern was careful to remind them of his friendship (and their debts). A legislative investigating committee found that Stern had given mortgage loans to a police lieutenant and the police chief's son. County Court Judge Ralph Vaughan recalled that shortly after being elected (with Stern support), he received a call from Dave Feinman, Stern's nephew. "Congratulations, judge. When do you think you and your wife would like a vacation in Florida?"

"Florida? Why on earth would I want to go there?"

"But all the other judges and the guys in City Hall—Irv takes them all to Florida whenever they want to get away."

"Thanks anyway, but I'm not interested."

"Well, how about a mink coat instead. What size coat does your wife wear? * * *"

In another instance an assistant district attorney told of Feinman's arriving at his front door with a large basket from Stern's supermarket just before Christmas. "My minister suggested a needy family that could use the food," the assistant district attorney recalled, "but I returned the liquor to Feinman. How could I ask a minister if he knew someone that could use three bottles of scotch?"

Campaign contributions, regular payments to higher officials, holiday and birthday gifts—these were the bases of the system by which Irv Stern bought protection from the law. The campaign contributions usually ensured that complacent mayors, councilmen, district attorneys, and judges were elected; payoffs in some instances usually kept their loyalty. In a number of ways, Stern was also able to reward the corrupt officials at no financial cost to himself. Just as the officials, being in control of the instruments of law enforcement, were able to facilitate Stern's gambling enterprises, so Stern, in control of a network of men operating outside the law, was able to facilitate the officials' corrupt enterprises. As will be seen later, many local officials were not satisfied with their legal salaries from the city and their illegal salaries from Stern and decided to demand payments from prostitutes, kickbacks from salesmen, etc. Stern, while seldom receiving any money from these transactions, became a broker: bringing politicians into contact with salesmen, merchants, and lawyers willing to offer bribes to get city business; setting up middlemen who could handle the money without jeopardizing the officials' reputations; and providing enforcers who could bring delinquents into line.

From the corrupt activities of Wincanton officials, Irv Stern received little in contrast to his receipts from his gambling operations. Why then did he get involved in them? The major virtue, from Stern's point of view, of the system of extortion that flourished in Wincanton was that it kept down the official's demands for payoffs directly from Stern. If a councilman was able to pick up $1,000 on the purchase of city equipment, he would demand a lower payment for the protection of gambling. Furthermore, since Stern knew the facts of extortion in each instance, the officials would be further implicated in the system and less able to back out on the arrangements regarding gambling. Finally, as Stern discovered to his chagrin, it became necessary to supervise official extortion to protect the officials against their own stupidity. Mayor Gene Donnelly was cooperative and remained satisfied with his regular "salary." Bob Walasek, however, was a greedy man, and seized every opportunity to profit from a city contract. Soon Stern found himself supervising many of Walasek's deals to keep the mayor from blowing the whole arrangement wide open. When Walasek tried to double the "take" on a purchase of parking meters, Stern had to step in and set the contract price, provide an untraceable middleman, and see the deal through to completion. "I told Irv," Police Chief Phillips later testified, "that Walasek wanted $12 on each meter instead of the $6 we got on the last meter deal. He became furious. He said, 'Walasek is going to fool around and wind up in jail. You come and see me. I'll tell Walasek what he's going to buy.' "

Protection, it was stated earlier, was an essential ingredient in Irv Stern's gambling empire. In the end, Stern's downfall came not from a flaw in the organization of the gambling enterprises but from public exposure of the corruption of Mayor Walasek and other officials. In the early 1960's Stern was sent to jail for 4 years on tax evasion charges, but the gambling empire continued to operate smoothly in his absence. A year later, however, Chief Phillips was caught perjuring himself in grand jury testimony concerning kickbacks on city towing contracts. Phillips "blew the whistle" on Stern, Walasek, and members of the city council, and a reform administration was swept into office. Irv Stern's gambling empire had been worth several million dollars each year; kickbacks on the towing contracts brought Bob Walasek a paltry $50 to $75 each week.

OFFICIAL CORRUPTION

Textbooks on municipal corporation law speak of at least three varieties of official corruption. The major categories are nonfeasance (failing to perform a required duty at all), malfeasance (the commission of some act which is positively unlawful), and misfeasance (the improper performance of some act which a man may properly do). During the years in which Irv Stern was running his gambling operations, Wincanton officials were guilty of all of these. Some residents say that Bob Walasek came to regard the mayor's office as a brokerage, levying a tariff on every item that came across his desk. Sometimes a request for simple municipal services turned into a game of cat and mouse, with Walasek sitting on the request, waiting to see how much would be offered, and the petitioner waiting to see if he could obtain his rights without having to pay for them. Corruption was not as lucrative an enterprise as gambling, but it offered a tempting supplement to low official salaries.

NONFEASANCE

As was detailed earlier, Irv Stern saw to it that Wincanton officials would ignore at least one of their statutory duties, enforcement of the State's gambling laws. Bob Walasek and his cohorts also agreed to overlook other illegal activities. Stern, we noted earlier, preferred not to get directly involved in prostitution; Walasek and Police Chief Dave Phillips tolerated all prostitutes who kept up their protection payments. One madam, controlling more than 20 girls, gave Phillips et al. $500 each week; one woman employing only one girl paid $75 each week that she was in business. Operators of a carnival in rural Alsace County paid a public official $5,000 for the privilege of operating gambling tents for 5 nights each summer. A burlesque theater manager, under attack by high school teachers, was ordered to pay $25 each week for the privilege of keeping his strip show open.

Many other city and county officials must be termed guilty of nonfeasance, although there is no evidence that they received payoffs, and although they could present reasonable excuses for their inaction. Most policemen, as we have noted earlier, began to ignore prostitution and gambling completely after their reports of offenses were ignored or superior officers told them to mind their own business. State policemen, well informed about city vice and gambling conditions, did nothing unless called upon to act by local officials. Finally, the judges of the Alsace County Court failed to exercise their power to call for State Police investigations. In 1957, following Federal raids on horse bookies, the judges did request an investigation by the State Attorney General, but refused to approve his suggestion that a grand jury be convened to continue the investigation. For each of these instances of inaction, a tenable excuse might be offered—the beat patrolman should not be expected to endure harassment from his superior officers, State police gambling raids in a hostile city might jeopardize State-local cooperation on more serious crimes, and a grand jury probe might easily be turned into a "whitewash" in the hands of a corrupt district attorney. In any event, powers available to these law enforcement agencies for the prevention of gambling and corruption were not utilized.

MALFEASANCE

In fixing parking and speeding tickets, Wincanton politicians and policemen committed malfeasance, or committed an act they were forbidden to do, by illegally compromising valid civil and criminal actions. Similarly, while State law provides no particular standards by which the mayor is to make promotions within his police department, it was obviously improper for Mayor Walasek to demand a "political contribution" of $10,000 from Dave Phillips before he was appointed chief in 1960.

The term "political contribution" raises a serious legal and analytical problem in classifying the malfeasance of Wincanton officials, and indeed of politicians in many cities. Political campaigns cost money; citizens have a right to support the candidates of their choice; and officials have a right to appoint their backers to noncivil service positions. At some point, however, threats or oppression convert legitimate requests for political contributions into extortion. Shortly after taking office in the mid-1950's, Mayor Gene Donnelly notified city hall employees that they would be expected "voluntarily" to contribute 2 percent of their salary to the Democratic Party. (It might be noted that Donnelly never forwarded any of these "political contributions" to the party treasurer.) A number of salesmen doing business with the city were notified that companies which had supported the party would receive favored treatment; Donnelly notified one salesman that in light of a proposed $81,000 contract for the purchase of fire engines, a "political contribution" of $2,000 might not be inappropriate. While neither the city hall employees nor the salesmen had rights to their positions of their contracts, the "voluntary" quality of their contributions seems questionable.

One final, in the end almost ludicrous, example of malfeasance came with Mayor Donnelly's abortive "War on the Press." Following a series of gambling raids by the Internal Revenue Service, the newspapers began asking why the local police had not participated in the raids. The mayor lost his temper and threw a reporter in jail. Policemen were instructed to harass newspaper delivery trucks, and 73 tickets were written over a 48-hour period for supposed parking and traffic violations. Donnelly soon backed down after national news services picked up the story, since press coverage made him look ridiculous. Charges against the reporter were dropped, and the newspapers continued to expose gambling and corruption.

MISFEASANCE

Misfeasance in office, says the common law, is the improper performance of some act which a man may properly do. City officials must buy and sell equipment, contract for services, and allocate licenses, privileges, etc. These actions can be improperly performed if either the results are improper (e.g., if a building inspector were to approve a home with defective wiring or a zoning board to authorize a variance which had no justification in terms of land usage) or a result is achieved by improper procedures (e.g., if the city purchased an acceptable automobile in consideration of a bribe paid to the purchasing agent). In the latter case, we can usually assume an improper result as well—while the automobile will be satisfactory, the bribe giver will probably have inflated the sale price to cover the costs of the bribe.

In Wincanton, it was rather easy for city officials to demand kickbacks, for State law frequently does not demand competitive bidding or permits the city to ignore the lowest bid. The city council is not required to advertise or take bids on purchases under $1,000, contracts for maintenance of streets and other public works, personal or professional services, or patented or copyrighted products. Even when bids must be sought, the council is only required to award the contract to the lowest responsible bidder. Given these permissive provisions, it was relatively easy for council members to justify or disguise contracts in fact based upon bribes. The exemption for patented products facilitated bribe taking on the purchase of two emergency trucks for the police department (with a $500 campaign contribution on a $7,500 deal), three fire engines ($2,000 was allegedly paid on an $81,000 contract), and 1,500 parking meters (involving payments of $10,500 plus an $880 clock for Mayor Walasek's home). Similar fees were allegedly exacted in connection with the purchase of a city fire alarm system and police uniforms and firearms. A former mayor and other officials also profited on the sale of city property, allegedly dividing $500 on the sale of a crane and $20,000 for approving the sale, for $22,000, of a piece of land immediately resold for $75,000.

When contracts involved services to the city, the provisions in the State law regarding the lowest responsible bidder and excluding "professional services" from competitive bidding provided convenient loopholes. One internationally known engineering firm refused to agree to kickback in order to secure a contract to design a $4.5 million sewage disposal plant for the city; a local firm was then appointed, which paid $10,700 of its $225,000 fee to an associate of Irv Stern and Mayor Donnelly as a "finder's fee." Since the State law also excludes public works maintenance contracts from the competitive bidding requirements, many city paving and street repair contracts during the Donnelly-Walasek era were given to a contributor to the Democratic Party. Finally, the franchise for towing illegally parked cars and cars involved in accidents was awarded to two garages which were then required to kickback $1 for each car towed.

The handling of graft on the towing contracts illustrates the way in which minor violence and the "lowest responsible bidder" clause could be used to keep bribe payers in line. After Federal investigators began to look into Wincanton corruption, the owner of one of the garages with a towing franchise testified before the grand jury. Mayor Walasek immediately withdrew his franchise, citing "health violations" at the garage. The garageman was also "encouraged" not to testify by a series of "accidents"—wheels would fall off towtrucks on the highway, steering cables were cut, and so forth. Newspaper satirization of the "health violations" forced the restoration of the towing franchise, and the "accidents" ceased.

Lest the reader infer that the "lowest responsible bidder" clause was used as an escape valve only for corrupt purposes, one incident might be noted which took place under the present reform administration. In 1964, the Wincanton School Board sought bids for the renovation of an athletic field. The lowest bid came from a construction company owned by Dave Phillips, the corrupt police chief who had served formerly under Mayor Walasek. While the company was presumably competent to carry out the assignment, the board rejected Phillips' bid "because of a question as to his moral responsibility." The board did not specify whether this referred to his prior corruption as chief or his present status as an informer in testifying against Walasek and Stern.

One final area of city power, which was abused by Walasek et al., covered discretionary acts, such as granting permits and allowing zoning variances. On taking office, Walasek took the unusual step of asking that the bureaus of building and plumbing inspection be put under the mayor's control. With this power to approve or deny building permits, Walasek "sat on" applications, waiting until the petitioner contributed $50 or $75, or threatened to sue to get his permit. Some building designs were not approved until a favored architect was retained as a "consultant." (It is not known whether this involved kickbacks to Walasek or simply patronage for a friend.) At least three instances are known in which developers were forced to pay for zoning variances before apartment buildings or supermarkets could be erected. Businessmen who wanted to encourage rapid turnover of the curb space in front of their stores were told to pay a police sergeant to erect "10-minute parking" signs. To repeat a caveat stated earlier, it is impossible to tell whether these kickbacks were demanded to expedite legitimate requests or to approve improper demands, such as a variance that would hurt a neighborhood or a certificate approving improper electrical work.

All of the activities detailed thus far involve fairly clear violations of the law. To complete the picture of the abuse of office by Wincanton officials, we might briefly mention "honest graft." This term was best defined by one of its earlier practitioners, State Senator George Washington Plunkitt who loyally served Tammany Hall at the turn of the century.

> There's all the difference in the world between [honest and dishonest graft]. Yes, many of our men have grown rich in politics. I have myself.
>
> I've made a big fortune out of the game, and I'm getting richer every day, but I've not gone in for dishonest graft—backmailin' gamblers, saloonkeepers, disorderly people, etc.—and neither has any of the men who have made big fortunes in politics.
>
> There's an honest graft, and I'm an example of how it works. I might sum up the whole thing by sayin': "I seen my opportunities and I took 'em."
>
> Let me explain by examples. My party's in power in the city, and it's goin' to undertake a lot of public improvements. Well, I'm tipped off, say, that they're going to lay out a new park at a certain place.
>
> I see my opportunity and I take it. I go to that place, and I buy up all the land I can in the neighborhood. Then the board of this or that makes its plan public, and there is a rush to get my land, which nobody cared particular for before.
>
> Ain't it perfectly honest to charge a good price and make a profit on my investment and foresight? Of course, it is. Well, that's honest graft.[1]

While there was little in the way of land purchasing—either honest or dishonest—going on in Wincanton during this period, several officials who carried on their own businesses while in office were able to pick up some "honest graft." One city councilman with an accounting office served as bookkeeper for Irv Stern and the major bookies and prostitutes in the city.

Police Chief Phillips' construction firm received a contract to remodel the exterior of the largest brothel in town. Finally one councilman serving in the present reform administration received a contract to construct all gasoline stations built in the city by a major petroleum company; skeptics say that the contract was the quid pro quo for the councilman's vote to give the company the contract to sell gasoline in the city.

How Far Did It Go? This cataloging of acts of nonfeasance, malfeasance, and misfeasance by Wincanton officials raises a danger of confusing variety with universality, of assuming that every employee of the city was either engaged in corrupt activities or was being paid to ignore the corruption of others. On the contrary, both official investigations and private research lead to the conclusion that there is no reason whatsoever to question the honesty of the vast majority of the employees of the city of Wincanton. Certainly no more than 10 of the 155 members of the Wincanton police force were on Irv Stern's

---

[1] William L. Riordan, "Plunkitt of Tammany Hall" (New York: E. P. Dutton. 1963), p. 3.

payroll (although as many as half of them may have accepted petty Christmas presents —turkeys or liquor.) In each department, there were a few employees who objected actively to the misdeeds of their superiors, and the only charge that can justly be leveled against the mass of employees is that they were unwilling to jeopardize their employment by publicly exposing what was going on. When Federal investigators showed that an honest (and possibly successful) attempt was being made to expose Stern-Walasek corruption, a number of city employees cooperated with the grand jury in aggregating evidence which could be used to convict the corrupt officials.

Before these Federal investigations began, however, it could reasonably appear to an individual employee that the entire machinery of law enforcement in the city was controlled by Stern, Walasek, et al., and that an individual protest would be silenced quickly. This can be illustrated by the momentary crusade conducted by First Assistant District Attorney Phil Roper in the summer of 1962. When the district attorney left for a short vacation, Roper decided to act against the gamblers and madams in the city. With the help of the State Police, Roper raided several large brothels. Apprehending on the street the city's largest distributor of punchboards and lotteries, Roper effected a citizen's arrest and drove him to police headquarters for proper detention and questioning. "I'm sorry, Mr. Roper," said the desk sergeant, "we're under orders not to arrest persons brought in by you." Roper was forced to call upon the State Police for aid in confining the gambler. When the district attorney returned from his vacation, he quickly fired Roper "for introducing politics into the district attorney's office."

If it is incorrect to say that Wincanton corruption extended very far vertically—into the rank and file of the various departments of the city—how far did it extend horizontally? How many branches and levels of government were affected? With the exception of the local Congressman and the city treasurer, it seems that a few personnel at each level (city, county, and State) and in most offices in city hall can be identified either with Stern or with some form of free-lance corruption. A number of local judges received campaign financing from Stern, although there is no evidence that they were on his payroll after they were elected. Several State legislators were on Stern's payroll, and one Republican councilman charged that a high-ranking State Democratic official promised Stern first choice of all Alsace County patronage. The county chairman, he claimed, was only to receive the jobs that Stern did not want. While they were later to play an active role in disrupting Wincanton gambling, the district attorney in Hal Craig's reform administration feared that the State Police were on Stern's payroll, and thus refused to use them in city gambling raids.

Within the city administration, the evidence is fairly clear that some mayors and councilmen received regular payments from Stern and divided kickbacks on city purchases and sales. Some key subcouncil personnel frequently shared in payoffs affecting their particular departments—the police chief shared in the gambling and prostitution payoffs and received $300 of the $10,500 kickback on parking meter purchases. A councilman controlling one department, for example, might get a higher percentage of kickbacks than the other councilmen in contracts involving that department.

LEGAL PROTECTION AGAINST CORRUPTION

Later in this report, Wincanton's gambling and corruption will be tied into a context of social and political attitudes. At this point, however, concluding the study of official corruption, it might be appropriate to consider legal reforms which might make future corruption more difficult. Many of the corrupt activities of

Wincanton officials are already covered sufficiently by State law—it is clearly spelled out, for example, that city officials must enforce State gambling and prostitution laws, and no further legislation is needed to clarify this duty. The legal mandate of the State Police to enforce State laws in all parts of the State is equally clear, but it has been nullified by their informal practice of entering cities only when invited; this policy only facilitates local corruption.

The first major reform that might minimize corruption would involve a drastic increase in the salaries of public officials and law enforcement personnel. During the 1950's Wincanton police salaries were in the lowest quartile for middle-sized cities in the Nation, and were well below the median family income ($5,453) in the city. City councilmen then were receiving only slightly more than the median. Since that time, police salaries have been raised to $5,400 (only slightly below the median) and council salaries to $8,500. Under these circumstances, many honest officials and employees were forced to "moonlight" with second jobs; potentially dishonest men were likely to view Stern payoffs or extortionate kickbacks as a simpler means of improving their financial status. Raising police salaries to $7,000 or $8,000 would attract men of higher quality, permit them to forego second jobs, and make corrupt payoffs seem less tempting. The same considerations apply to a recommendation that the salaries of elected officials be increased to levels similar to those received in private industry. A recent budget for the city of Wincanton called for expenditures of $6 million; no private corporation of that size would be headed by a chief executive whose salary was $9,500 per year.

A second type of recommendation would reduce the opportunities available to officials to extort illegal payoffs or conceal corruption. First, the civil service system should be expanded. At the time this report was written, Wincanton policemen could not be discharged from the force unless formal charges were brought, but they could be demoted from command positions or transferred to "punishment" details at the discretion of the chief or mayor. The latter option is probably a proper disciplinary tool, but the former invites policemen to seek alliances with political leaders and to avoid unpopular actions. Promotions within the force (with the possible exception of the chief's position) should be made by competitive examination, and demotions should be made only for proven cause. (While research for this report was being conducted, a full 18 months before the next local election, police officers reported that politicking had already begun. Men on the force had already begun making friends with possible candidates for the 1967 elections, and police discipline was beginning to slip. Command officers reported that the sergeants were becoming unwilling to criticize or discipline patrolmen. "How can I tell someone off?" one captain asked. "I'll probably be walking a beat when the Democrats come back into power, and he may be my boss.") A comprehensive civil service system would also give command officers control over informal rewards and punishments, so that they could encourage "hustlers" and harass slackers, but formal review of promotions and demotions is essential to guard against the politicking, which has been characteristic of the Wincanton police force.

Second, opportunities for corruption could be reduced by closing the loopholes in State laws on bidding for municipal contracts. While a city should be free to disregard a low bid received from a company judged financially or technically unable to perform a contract, the phrase "lowest responsible bidder" simply opens the door to misfeasance—either to accepting under-the-table kickbacks or to rewarding political friends. In this regard, the decision to ignore the bid of former Police Chief Phillips is just as reprehensible as the decision to give paving contracts to a major party contributor. Furthermore, there is no reason why service contracts should be excluded from the competitive bidding; while the professions regard it as undignified to compete for clients, there is no reason why road repair or building maintenance contracts could not be judged on the basis of bids (with a proviso regarding some level of competence). Finally, the exclusion of "patented or copyrighted products" is untenable—it is well known that distributors of say, automobiles, vary widely in their profit margins, or allowances for trade-ins, etc. City officials should be forced therefore to seek the best possible deal.

One mechanism, which is often suggested to guard against official misconduct, is an annual audit of city books by a higher governmental agency, such as those conducted of local agencies (e.g., urban renewal authorities) administering Federal programs. The evidence in Wincanton, however, seems to indicate that even while official corruption was taking place, the city's books were in perfect order. When a kickback was received on a city purchase, for example, the minutes of council meetings would indicate that X was the "lowest responsible bidder," if bids were required, and X would slip the payoff money to a "bagman," or contactman, on a dark street corner. The books looked proper and auditors would have had no authority to force acceptance of other bids. It would seem that revision of the bidding laws would be more significant than an outside audit.

Finally, the problem of campaign contributions must be considered. As was stressed earlier, contributions to political candidates are regarded in this country as both a manifestation of free speech and the best alternative to government sponsorship of campaigns. The use of political contributions as a disguise for extortion and bribery could be curtailed, however, by active enforcement of the "full reporting of receipts" provision of State campaign laws (in Wincanton, candidates filed reports of receipts, but of course, neglected to mention the money received from Irv Stern). Second, city hall employees should be protected against the type of voluntary assessment imposed by Mayor Donnelly. Third, State and local laws might more clearly prohibit contributions, from persons doing business with the city, which can be identified as payoffs for past or future preferment on city contracts. Tightening of bidding requirements, of course, would make such activities less profitable to the contractors.) [2]

GAMBLING AND CORRUPTION: THE GENERAL PUBLIC

THE LATENT FUNCTIONS OF GAMBLING AND CORRUPTION

I feel as though I am sending Santa Claus to jail. Although this man dealt in gambling devices, it appears that he is religious man having no bad habits and is an unmeasurably charitable man.
—a Federal judge sentencing slot machine king Klaus Braun to jail in 1948.

When I was a kid, the man in the corner grocery wrote numbers. His salary was about $20 a week and he made $25 more on book.
—a reform candidate for the Wincanton City Council, early 1960's.

The instances of wrongdoing cataloged in earlier sections seem to paint an easily censurable picture. Irv Stern, Gene Donnelly, Bob Walasek—these names conjure up an image of such total iniquity that one wonders why they were ever allowed to operate as they did. While gambling and corruption are easy to judge in the abstract, however, they, like sin, are never en-

---
[2] See the excellent discussion of political campaign contributions in Alexander Heard, "The Costs of Democracy" (Chapel Hill: University of North Carolina Press, 1960), and Herbert Alexander, "Regulation of Political Finance" (Berkeley: Institute of Governmental Studies, and Princeton: Citizens' Research Foundation, 1966).

countered in the abstract—they are encountered in the form of a slot machine which is helping to pay off your club's mortgage, or a chance to fix you son's speeding ticket, or an opportunity to hasten the completion of your new building by "overlooking" a few violations of the building code. In these forms, the choices seem less clear. Furthermore, to obtain a final appraisal of what took place in Wincanton one must weigh the manifest functions served—providing income for the participants, recreation for the consumers of vice and gambling, etc.—against the latent functions, the unintended or unrecognized consequences of these events.[3] The automobile, as Thorstein Veblen noted, has both a manifest function, transportation, and a latent function, affirming the owner's social status. To balance the picture presented in earlier sections, and thus to give a partial explanation of why Wincanton has had its unusual history, this section explores the latent functions, the unintended and unexpected consequences, of gambling and corruption.

Latent Social Functions. The social life of Wincanton is organized around clubs, lodges, and other voluntary associations. Labor unions have union halls. Businessmen have luncheon groups, country clubs, and service organizations, such as the Rotary, Kiwanis, the Lions, etc. Each nationality group has its own meetinghouse—the Ancient Order of Hibernians, the Liederkranz, the Colored Political Club, the Cristoforo Colombo Society, etc. In each neighborhood, a PTA-type group is organized around the local playground. Each firehall is the nightly gathering place of a volunteer fireman's association. Each church has the usual assortment of men's, women's, and children's groups.

A large proportion of these groups profited in one way or another from some form of gambling. Churches sponsored lotteries, bingo, and "Las Vegas nights." Weekly bingo games sponsored by the playground associations paid for new equipment, Little League uniforms, etc. Business groups would use lotteries to advertise "Downtown Wincanton Days." Finally, depending upon the current policy of law enforcement agencies, most of the clubs had slot machines, payoff pinball machines, punchboards, lotteries, bingo, poker games, etc. For many of these groups, profits from gambling meant the difference between financial success and failure. Clubs with large and affluent membership lists could survive with only fees and profits from meals and drinks served. Clubs with few or impecunious members, however, had to rely on other sources of revenue, and gambling was both lucrative and attractive to nonmembers.

The clubs therefore welcomed slots, pinball machines, punchboards, and so forth, both to entertain members and to bring in outside funds. The clubs usually diivded gambling profits equally with machine distributors such as Stern or Klaus Braun. Some clubs owed even more to gamblers; if Braun heard that a group of men wanted to start a new volunteer fireman's association, he would lend them mortgage money simply for the opportunity to put his slot machines in the firehall. It is not surprising, therefore, to find that the clubs actively defended Stern, Braun, and the political candidates who favored open gambling.

Gambling in Wincanton also provided direct and indirect benefits to churches and other charitable organizations. First, like the other private groups, a number of these churches and charities sponsored bingo, lotteries, etc., and shared in the profits. Second, leading gamblers and racketeers have been generous supporters of Wincanton charities. Klaus Braun gave away literally most of his gambling income, aiding churches, hospitals, and the underprivileged. In the late 1940's, Braun provided 7,000 Christmas turkeys to the poor, and

---

[3] See the classic examination of manifest and latent functions in Robert K. Merton, "Social Theory and Social Structures," revised edition (New York: Free Press, 1957), pp. 19–87.

frequently chartered buses to take slum children to ball games. Braun's Prospect Mountain Park offered free rides and games for local children (while their parents were in other tents patronizing the slot machines). Irv Stern gave a $10,000 stained glass window to his synagogue, and aided welfare groups and hospitals in Wincanton and other cities. (Since the residents of Wincanton refuse to be cared for in the room that Stern gave to Community Hospital, it is now used only for the storage of bandages.) When Stern came into Federal court in the early 1960's to be sentenced on tax evasion charges, he was given character references by Protestant, Catholic, and Jewish clergy, and by the staff of two hospitals and a home for the aged. Critics charge that Stern never gave away a dime that wasn't well publicized; nevertheless, his contributions benefited worthwhile community institutions.

(Lest this description of the direct and indirect benefits of gambling be misleading, it should also be stressed that many ministers protested violently against gambling and corruption, led reform movements and launched pulpit tirades against Stern, Walasek, et al.)

One final social function of Wincanton gambling might be termed the moderation of the demands of the criminal law. Bluntly stated, Irv Stern was providing the people with what at least a large portion of them wanted, whether or not State lawmakers felt they should want it. It is, of course, axiomatic that no one has the right to disobey the law, but in fairness to local officials it should be remembered that they were generally only tolerating what most residents of the city had grown up with—easily accessible numbers, horsebetting, and bingo. When reform mayor Ed Whitton ordered bingo parlors closed in 1964, he was ending the standard form of evening recreation of literally thousands of elderly men and women. One housewife interviewed recently expressed relief that her mother had died before Whitton's edict took effect; "It would have killed her to live without bingo," she said.

In another sense, Wincanton law enforcement was also moderated by the aid that the gambling syndicate gave, at no cost to the public, to persons arrested by the police for gambling activity. Stern provided bail and legal counsel during trials, and often supported families of men sent to jail. A large portion of the payments that Stern sent to the east coast syndicates (as discussed earlier) was earmarked for pensions to the widows of men who had earlier served in the Stern organization. In light of the present interest in the quality of legal services available to the poor, this aspect of Wincanton gambling must be regarded as a worthy social function.

In these ways, Wincanton gambling provided the financial basis for a network of private groups, filling social, service, and quasi-governmental functions. Leading the list of latent functions of gambling, therefore, we must put the support of neighborhood and other group social life and the provision of such important services as recreation and fire protection. Providing these services through private rather than public mechanisms not only reduced tax burdens but also integrated the services into the social structure of the neighborhood served. While it is hard to give profits from gambling sole credit for maintaining these clubs, it must be noted that a number of firemen's and political associations were forced to close their doors when law enforcement agencies seized slot and pinball machines.

Latent Economic Functions. Just as the proceeds from gambling made possible, or at least less expensive, an extensive series of social relationships and quasi-public services, so also did gambling and corruption affect the local economy, aiding some businesses while hindering others. Their manifest function, of course, was to increase the incomes of the providers of illicit services (members of the Stern syndicate, individual number writers and pinball machine distributors, madams, prostitutes, etc.), the recipients of payoffs (elected officials and policemen, for whom these payments were a welcome addition to low salaries), and the businessmen who secured unwarranted contracts, permits, variances, etc. On the other hand, these arrangements provided entertainment for the consumers of gambling and prostitution.

In describing the latent functions of Wincanton illegality, we can begin with two broad phenomena. First, gambling permitted a number of outmoded businesses to survive technological change. As a quotation at the beginning of this chapter indicated, a "mom and pop" grocery store or a candy and cigar store could make more from writing numbers or taking horse bets than they did from their nominal source of support. When reform mayors cracked down on betting, many of these marginal shops went out of business, not being able to compete with the larger, more efficient operations solely on the basis of sales. Second, the system provided an alternate ladder of social mobility for persons who lacked the educational or status prerequisites for success in the legitimate world. Irv Stern came to this country as a fruit peddler's son and is believed by the Internal Revenue Service to be worth several millions of dollars. Gene Donnelly was a bartender's son; Bob Walasek grew up in a slum, although he was able to attend college on an athletic scholarship. Many Wincantonites believe that each of these men collected at least a quarter of a million dollars during his 4 years in city hall. As Daniel Bell has pointed out,[4] and as these men illustrate, organized crime in America has provided a quick route out of the slums, a means of realizing the Horatio Alger dream.

A number of legitimate enterprises in Wincanton profited directly or indirectly when gambling was wide open. Eight or ten major bingo halls provided a large nighttime business for the local bus company. In one year, for example, 272,000 persons paid to play bingo, and most of them were elderly men and women who were brought to the games on regular or chartered buses. Prizes for the bingo games were purchased locally; one department store executive admitted that bingo gift certificates brought "a sizeable amount" of business into his store. Several drugstores sold large quantities of cosmetics to the prostitutes. As in Las Vegas, one Wincanton hotel offered special weekend rates for the gamblers at the dice game, who would gamble at night and sleep during the daytime. Finally, several landlords rented space to Stern for his bookie parlors and accounting offices. Worried that legislative investigations might terminate a profitable arrangement, one landlord asked the investigating committee, "Who else would pay $150 a month for that basement?" Being the center of gambling and prostitution for a wide area also meant increased business for the city's restaurants, bars, and theaters. One man declared that business at his Main Street restaurant was never as good as when gamblers and bingo players were flocking to the downtown area. (Many of these restaurants and bars, of course, provided gambling as well as food and drink for their customers.)

Corruption, like gambling, offered some businessmen opportunities to increase sales and profits. If minor building code violations could be overlooked, houses and office buildings could be erected more cheaply. Zoning variances, secured for a price, opened up new areas in which developers could build high-rise apartment buildings and shopping centers. In selling to the city, businessmen could increase profits either by selling inferior goods or by charging high prices on standard goods when bidding was rigged or avoided. Finally, corruptible officials could aid profits simply by speeding up decisions on city contracts, or by forcing rapid turnover

---

[4] Daniel Bell, "The End of Ideology" (New York: Free Press, 1960), ch. 7, "Crime as an American Way of Life."

of city-owned curb space through either "10-minute parking" signs or strict enforcement of parking laws. (Owners of large stores, however, sought to maximize profits by asking the police to ignore parking violations, feeling that customers who worried about their meters would be less likely to stay and buy.)

This listing of the latent benefits of gambling and corruption must be juxtaposed against the fact that many Wincanton businessmen were injured by the Stern-Walasek method of operations and fought vigorously against it. Leaders of the Wincanton business community—the bankers, industrialists, Chamber of Commerce, etc. —fought Walasek and Stern, refusing to kickback on anything, and regularly called upon State and Federal agencies to investigate local corruption.

It is somewhat misleading, however, to use the single term "business" in analyzing responses to corruption. It will be more fruitful to classify businesses according to the nature of their contact with the city of Wincanton. Some industries had a national market, and only called upon the city for labor and basic services—water, sewage, police and fire protection, etc. Other companies such as sales agencies or construction firms did business directly with city hall and thus were intimately concerned with the terms upon which the city government did business. Because of the looseness of State bidding procedures, these businesses had to be careful, however, not to alienate officials. A third group, while not doing business with the city, had primarily a local clientele. Under these conditions, businesses in this group were frequently interested in corruption and gambling policies.

Official corruption affected each of these groups differently. Businesses whose markets lay primarily outside the city usually had to be concerned only with the possibility that Walasek might force them to pay for building permits. Companies dealing with City Hall, however, were exposed to every extortionate demand that the mayor might impose. As an example, agencies usually able to underbid their competitors were ignored if they refused to abide by the unofficial "conditions" added to contracts. Businessmen in the third category were in an intermediate position, both in terms of their freedom to act against the system and in terms of the impact that it had upon them. Like the others, they suffered when forced to pay for permits or variances. Legitimate businesses, such as liquor stores, taverns, and restaurants, whose functions paralleled those of the clubs, lost revenue when the clubs were licensed to have gambling and slot machines. Those businesses, such as banks, whose success depended upon community growth, suffered when the community's reputation for corruption and gambling drove away potential investors and developers. (Interestingly, businessmen disagree as to whether it is the reputation for corruption or for gambling that discourages new industry. Several Wincanton bankers stated that no investor would run the risk of having to bribe officials to have building plans approved, permits issued, and so forth. One architect, however, argued that buisnessmen assume municipal corruption, but will not move into a "sin town," for their employees will not want to raise children in such circumstances.)

The last detrimental aspect of gambling and corruption seems trivial in comparison with the factors already mentioned, but it was cited by most of the business leaders interviewed. Simply stated, it was embarassing to have one's hometown known throughout the country for its vice and corruption. "I'd go to a convention on the west coast," one textile manufacturer recalled, "and everyone I'd meet would say, 'You're from Wincanton? Boy, have I heard stories about that place!' I would try to talk about textiles or opportunities for industrial development, but they'd keep asking about the girls and the gambling."

An Air Force veteran recalled being ridiculed about his hometown while in boot camp. Finally, some insiders feel that a Wincanton judge was persuaded to act against Irv Stern when he found that his daughter was being laughed at by her college friends for being related to a Wincanton official.

59. ECONOMICS AND CRIMINAL ENTERPRISE

THOMAS C. SCHELLING

AT THE LEVEL OF NATIONAL POLICY, IF NOT always of local practice, the dominant approach to organized crime is through indictment and conviction. This is in striking contrast to the enforcement of anti-trust or food-and-drug laws, or the policing of public utilities, which work through regulation, accommodation, and the restructuring of markets. For some decades, anti-trust problems have received the sustained professional attention of economists concerned with the structure of markets, the organization of business enterprise, and the incentives toward collusion or price-cutting. Racketeering and the provision of illegal goods (like gambling) have been conspicuously neglected by economists. (There exists no analysis of the liquor industry under prohibition that begins to compare with the best available studies of the aluminum or steel industries, air transport, milk distribution, or public-utility pricing.) Yet a good many economic and business principles that operate in the "upperworld" must, with suitable modification for change in environment, operate in the underworld as well—just as a good many economic principles that operate in an advanced compctititve economy operate as well in a socialist or a primitive economy.

▶SOURCE: *"Economics and Criminal Enterprise,"* The Public Interest (Spring, 1967), 7:61–78. Reprinted by permission.

In addition to the sheer satisfaction of curiosity, there are good policy reasons for encouraging a "strategic" analysis of the criminal underworld. Such an analysis, in contrast to "tactical" intelligence aimed at the apprehension of individual criminals, could help in identifying the incentives and disincentives to organize crime, in evaluating the costs and losses due to criminal enterprises, and in restructuring laws and programs to minimize the costs, wastes, and injustices that crime entails.

What market characteristics determine whether a criminal activity becomes "organized"? Gambling, by all accounts, invites organization; abortion, by all accounts, does not. In the upperworld, automobile manufacture is characterized by large firms, but not machine-tool production; collusive price-fixing occurs in the electrical-machinery industry, but not in the distribution of fruits and vegetables. The reasons for these differences are not entirely understood, but they are amenable to study. The same should not be impossible for gambling, extortion, and contraband cigarettes.

How much does organized crime depend on at least one major market in which the advantages of large scale are great enough to support a dominant monopoly firm or cartel? Not all businesses lend themselves to centralized organization; some do, and these may provide the nucleus of capital and entrepreneurial talent for extension into other businesses that would not, alone, support or give rise to an organized monopoly or cartel. Do a few "core" criminal markets provide the organizational stimulus for organized crime? If the answer turns out to be yes, then a critical question is whether the particular market so essential for the "economic development" of the underworld is a "black market," whose existence is dependent on the prohibition of legal competition, or instead is an inherently criminal activity. Black markets always offer to the policy maker, in principle, the option of restructuring the market—of increasing legal competition, of compromising the original prohibition, of selectively relaxing either the law itself or the way it is enforced. If, alternatively, that central criminal enterprise is one that rests on violence, relaxation of the law is likely to be both ineffectual and unappealing.

Since one of the interesting questions is why some underworld business becomes organized and some not, and another, what *kinds* of organization should be expected, a classification of these enterprises has to cover more than just "organized crime" and to distinguish types of organization. A tentative typology of underworld business might be as follows.

BLACK MARKETS

A large part of organized crime is the selling of commodities and services contrary to law. In what we usually consider the underworld this includes dope, prostitution, gambling, liquor (under prohibition), abortions, pornography, and contraband or stolen goods. Most of these are consumer goods.

In what is not usually considered the underworld, black markets include gold, contraceptives in some states, rationed commodities and coupons in wartime, loans and rentals above controlled prices, theater tickets in New York, and a good many similar commodities that, though not illegal per se, are handled outside legitimate markets or diverted from subsidized uses.

In some cases (gambling) the law bans the commodity from all consumers; in others (cigarettes), some consumers are legitimate and some (minors) not. In some cases what is illegal is that the tax or duty has not been paid; in some, it is the price of the transaction that makes it illegal. In some (child labor, illegal immigrant labor), it is buying the commodity, not selling it, that is proscribed.

RACKETEERING

Racketeering includes two kinds of business, both based on intimidation. One is *criminal monopoly*, the other *extortion*.

"Criminal monopoly" means the use of criminal means to destroy competition. Whether a competitor is actually destroyed or merely threatened with violence to make him go out of business, the object is to get protection from competition when the law will not provide it (by franchise or tariff protection) and when it cannot be legally achieved (through price wars, control of patents, or preclusive contracts).

We can distinguish altogether three kinds of "monopoly": those achieved through legal means, those achieved through means that are illegal only because of anti-trust and other laws intended to make monopoly difficult, and monopolies achieved through means that are criminal by any standards—means that would be criminal whether or not they were aimed at monopolizing a business. It is also useful to distinguish between firms that, in an excess of zeal or deficiency of scruple, engage when necessary in ruthless and illegal competition, and the more strictly "racketeering" firms whose profitable monopoly rests entirely on criminal violence. The object of law enforcement in the former case is not to destroy the firm but to curtail its illegal practices. If the whole basis of success in business, though, is strong-arm methods that keep competition destroyed or scare it away, it is a pure "racket".

"Extortion" means living off somebody else's business by the threat of violence or of criminal competition. A protection racket lives off its victims, letting them operate and pay tribute. If one establishes a chain of restaurants and destroys competitors or scares them out of business, that is "monopoly"; if he merely threatens to destroy people's restaurant business, taking part of their profits as the price for leaving them alone, he is an extortionist and likes to see them prosper so that his share will be greater.

For several reasons it is difficult to distinguish "extortion" that, like a parasite, wants a healthy host, from "criminal monopoly" that is dedicated to the elimination of competitors. First, one means of extortion is to threaten to cut off the supply of a monopolized commodity—labor on a construction site, trucking, or some illegal commodity provided through the black market. That is to say, one can use a monopoly at one stage for extortionate leverage at the next. Second, extortion itself can be used to secure a monopoly privilege: instead of taking tribute in cash, for example, a victim signs a contract for the high-priced delivery of beer or linen supplies. The result looks like monopoly, but arose out of extortion.

It is evident that extortion can be organized or not, but in important cases it has to be. Vulnerable victims, after all, have to be protected from other extortionists. A monopolistic laundry service, deriving from a threat to harm the business that does not subscribe, has to destroy or to intimidate not only competing legitimate laundry services but other racketeers who would muscle in on the same victim. Thus, while criminal monopoly may not depend on extortion, organized extortion always needs an element of monopoly.

BLACK-MARKET MONOPOLY

Any successful black marketeer enjoys a "protected" market in the way of domestic industry is protected by a tariff, or butter is protected by a law against margarine. The black marketeer gets protection from the law against all competitors unwilling to pursue a criminal career. But there is a difference between a "protected industry" and a "monopolized industry." Abortion is a black market commodity but not a monopoly; a labor racket is a local monopoly but not a black-market one; a monopoly in dope has both elements—it is a "black-market monopoly."

CARTEL

A "conspiracy in restraint of trade" that does not lead to single-firm monopoly but to collusive price-fixing, and that maintains itself by criminal action, gives rise to a cartel that is not in, but depends on, the underworld. If the garment trade eliminates competition by an agreement on prices and wages, hiring thugs to enforce the agreement, it is different from the monopoly racket discussed above. If the government would make such agreements legally enforceable (as it does with retail-price-maintenance laws in some states), the business would be in no need of criminally enforcing discipline on itself. Similarly, a labor union can use criminal means to discipline its members, even to the presumed benefit of its members, who may be better off working as a bloc rather than as competing individuals. If the law permits enforceable closed-shop agreements, the criminal means becomes unnecessary.

ORGANIZED CRIMINAL SERVICES

A characteristic of the businesses listed above is that they usually involve relations between the underworld and the upperworld. But as businesses in the upperworld need legal services, financial advice, credit, enforcement of contract, places to conduct their business, and communication facilities, so in the underworld there has to be a variety of business services that are "domestic" to the underworld itself. These can be organized or unorganized. They are *in* the underworld, but not because they exploit the underworld as the underworld exploits the legitimate world.

THE INCENTIVES TO CRIMINAL ORGANIZATION

The simplest explanation of a large-scale firm, in the underworld or anywhere else, is high overhead costs or some other element of technology that makes small-scale operation more costly than large-scale. The need to keep equipment or specialized personnel fully utilized often explains at least the lower limit to the size of the firm.

A second explanation is the prospect of monopolistic prices. If most of the business can be cornered by a single firm, it can raise the price at which it sells its illegal services. Like any business, it does this at some sacrifice in size of the market; but if the demand is inelastic, the increase in profit margin will more than compensate for the reduction in output. Of course, decentralized individual firms would have as much to gain by pushing up the price, but without discipline it will not work; each will undercut its competitors. Where entry can be denied to newcomers, centralized price-setting will yield monopoly rewards to whoever can organize the market. With discipline, a cartel can do it; in the absence of discipline a merger may do it; but intimidation, too, can lead to the elimination of competition and the conquest of a monopoly position by a single firm.

Third, the larger the firm, and especially the larger its share of the whole market, the more will formerly "external" costs become costs internal to the firm. "External costs" are those that fall on competitors, customers, bystanders, and others outside the firm itself. Collection of all the business within a single firm causes the costs that individual firms used to inflict on each other to show up as costs (or losses) to the larger centralized firm now doing the business. This is an advantage. The costs were originally there but disregarded; now there is an incentive to take them into account.

Violence is one such external cost. Racketeers have a collective interest in restricting violence, so as to avoid trouble with the public and the police—but the individual racketeer has little or no incentive to reduce the violence connected with his own crime. There is an analogy here with the whaling industry, which has a collective interest in not killing off the whales although an individual whaler has no incentive to consider what he is doing to the future of the industry when he maximizes his own catch. A large organization can afford to impose discipline, holding down violence if the business is crime, holding down the slaughter of females if the business is whaling.

There are also "external economics" that can become internalized, to the advantage of the centralized firm. Lobbying has this character, as does cultivating relations with the police. No small bookie can afford to spend money to influence gambling legislation, but an organized trade association or monopoly among those who live off illegal gambling can. Similarly with labor discipline; the small firm cannot afford to teach a lesson to the labor force of the industry, since most of the lesson is lost on other people's employees, but a single large firm can expect the full benefit of its labor policy. Similarly with cultivating the market; if one cultivates the market for dope, by hooking some customers, or cultivates a market for gambling in a territory where the demand is still latent, he cannot expect much of a return on his investment if opportunistic competitors will take advantage of the market he creates. Anything that requires a long investment in cultivating a consumer interest, a labor market, ancillary institutions, or relations with the police, can be undertaken only by a fairly large firm that has reason to expect that it can enjoy most of the market and get a satisfactory return on the investment.

Finally, there is the attraction of not only monopolizing a market but achieving a dominant position in the underworld itself, and participating in its governing. To the extent that large criminal business firms provide a governmental structure to the underworld, helping to maintain peace, setting rules, arbitrating disputes, and enforcing discipline, they are in a position to set up their own businesses and exclude competition. Constituting a "corporate state," they can give themselves the franchise for various "state-sponsored monopolies." They can do this either by denying the benefits of underworld government to their competitors or by using the equivalent of their "police power" to prevent competition.

MARKET STRUCTURE

In evaluating crime, an accounting approach gives at best a benchmark as to magnitudes, and not even that for the distribution of economic and social gains and losses. The problem is like that of estimating the comparative incidence of profits taxes and excise taxes, or the impact of a minimum-wage law on wage differentials. Especially if we want to know who bears the cost, or to compare the costs to society with the gains to the criminals, an analysis of *market adjustments* is required. Even the pricing practices of organized crime need to be studied.

Consider the illegal wire-service syndicate in Miami that received attention from Senator Kefauver's committee. The magnitude that received explicit attention was the loss of state revenues due to the diversion of gambling from legal race tracks, which were taxable, to illegal bookmakers, whose turnover was not taxable. No accounting approach would yield this magnitude; it depended (as was pointed out in testimony) on what economists call the "elasticity of substitution" between the two services—on the fraction of potential race track business that patronized bookmakers.

Similar analysis is required to determine *at whose expense* the syndicate operated, or what the economic consequences of the syndicate's removal would have been. The provision of wire-service was of small economic significance. It accounted, on a cost basis, for less than 5% of the net income of bookmakers (of which the syndicate took approximately 50%). And cheaper wire service to the bookies might have been available in the absence of the syndicate, whose function was not to provide wire service but to eliminate wire-service competitors.

The essential business of the syndicate was to practice *extortion against bookmakers*. It demanded half their earnings, against the threat of reprisals. The syndicate operated like a taxing authority (as well as providing some reinsurance on large bets); it apparently did not limit the number of bookmakers so long as they paid their "taxes".

How much of this tax was passed along to the customer (on the analogy of a gasoline or a sales tax) and how much was borne by the bookie (on the analogy of an income or profits tax) is hard to determine. If we assume (a) that bookmakers' earnings are approximately proportionate to the volume of turnover, (b) that their customers, though sensitive to the comparative odds of different bookmakers, are not sensitive to the profit margin, (c) that they tend, consciously or implicitly, to budget their total bets and not their rate of loss, we can conclude that the tax is substantially passed along to the customer. In that case the bookmaker, though nominally the victim of extortion, is victimized only into raising the price to his customers, somewhat like a filling station that must pay a tax on every gallon sold. The bookmaker is thus an intermediary between an extortionate syndicate and a customer who pays his tribute voluntarily on the price he is willing to pay for his bets.

The syndicate in Miami relied on the police as their favorite instrument of intimidation. It could have been the other way around, with the police using the syndicate as their agency to negotiate and collect from the bookmakers, and if the police had been organized and disciplined as a monopoly, it would have been the police, not the syndicate, that we should put at the top of our organizational pyramid. From the testimony, though, it is evident that the initiative and entrepreneurship came from the syndicate, which had the talent and organization for this kind of business, and that the police lacked the centralized authority for exploiting to their own benefit the power they had over the bookmakers. Presumably—though there were few hints of this in the hearings—the syndicate could have mobilized other techniques for intimidating the bookmakers; the police were the chosen instrument only so long as the police's share in the proceeds was competitive with alternative executors of the intimidating threats.

Any attempt to estimate the long-term effect on police salaries would have to take into account how widespread and non-discriminatory the police participation was, especially by rank and seniority in service. Recruiting would be unaffected if police recruits were unaware of the illegal earnings that might accrue to them; senior members of the force who might otherwise have quit the service, or lobbied harder for pay increases, would agitate less vigorously for high wages if their salaries were augmented by the racket. One cannot easily infer that part of the "tax" paid by the bookmaker's customer subsidized the police force to the benefit of non-betting taxpayers; mainly they supported a more discriminatory and irregular earnings pattern among the police —besides contributing, unwittingly, to a demoralization of the police that would have made it a bad bargain for the taxpayer anyway.

This is just a sketch, based on the skimpy evidence available, of the rather complex structure of "organized gambling" in one city. (It is not, of course, the gambling that is organized; the organization is an extortionate monopoly that nominally provides a wire-service but actually imposes a tribute on middlemen who pass most of the cost along to their voluntary customers.) Similar analysis would be required to identify the incidence of costs and losses (and gains, of course) of protection rackets everywhere (e.g., monopoly-priced beer deliveries to bars or restaurants, vending machines installed in bars and restaurants under pain of damage or nuisance, etc.).

INSTITUTIONAL PRACTICES

Institutional practices in the underworld need to be better understood. What, for example, is the effect of the tax laws on extortion? Why does an extortionist put cigarette machines in a restaurant or provide linen service? Do the tax laws make it difficult to disguise the payment of tribute in cash but easy to disguise it (and make it tax deductible) if the tribute takes the form of a concession or the purchase of high-priced services? Why does a gambling syndicate bother to provide "wire service" when evidently its primary economic function is to shake down bookies by the threat of hurting their businesses or their persons, possibly with the collusion of the police?

The Kefauver hearings indicate that the wire-service syndicate in Miami took a standard 50% from the bookies. The symmetry of the 50% figure is itself remarkable. Equally remarkable is that the figure was uniform. But most remarkable of all is that the syndicate went through the motions of providing a wire service when it perfectly well could have taken cash tribute instead. There is an analogy here with the car salesman who refuses to negotiate the price of a new car, but is willing to negotiate quite freely the "allowance" on the used car that one turns in. The underworld seems to need institutions, conventions, traditions, and recognizable standard practices much like the upperworld of business. A better understanding of these practices might lead not only to a better evaluation of crime itself but also to a better understanding of the role of tax laws and regulatory laws on the operation of criminal business.

The role of vending machines, for example, appears to be that they provide a tax-deductible, non-discriminatory, and "respectable" way of paying tribute. Pinball and slot machines installed by a gang in somebody's small store may be only half characterized when identified as "illegal gambling"; they are equally a conventionalized medium for the exaction of tribute from the store owner. Effective enforcement of a ban on the machines will take care of the "gambling" part of the enterprise; what happens to the extortion racket depends then on how readily some other lucrative concession, some exclusive delivery contract, or some direct cash tribute can be imposed on the store owner.

Even the resistance to crime would be affected by measures designed to change the cost structure. Economists make an important distinction between a lump-sum tax, a profits tax, and a specific or ad valorum tax on the commodity an enterprise sells. The manner in which a criminal monopolist or extortionist prices his service, or demands his tribute, should have a good deal to do with whether the cost is borne by the victim or passed along by the customer. The "tax" levied by the racketeer uniformly on all his customers—monopoly-priced beer or linen supplies—may merely be passed along in turn to their customers, with little loss to the immediate victims, if the demand in their own market is inelastic. A bar that has to pay an extortionate price for its beer can seek relief in either of two ways. It can try to avoid paying the extortionate or monopolized price; alternatively, it can insist that its supplier achieve similar concessions from all competing bars, to avoid a competitive disadvantage. An individual bar suffers little if the price of wholesale beer goes up; it suffers when competitors' prices do not go up.

Similarly, legal arrangements that make it difficult to disguise illegal transactions, and that make it a punishable offense to pay tribute, might help to change the incentives. In a few cases, the deliberate stimulation of competing enterprises could be in the public interest: loan-sharking, for example, might be somewhat mitigated by the deliberate creation of new and specialized lending enterprises. Loan-sharking appears to involve several elements, only one of which is the somewhat outmoded notion—outmoded by a few centuries—that people so much in need of cash that they'd pay high interest rates should be protected from "usury" even if it means merely that they are protected by being denied any access to credit at all. A second element is that, now that debtors' prison has been liberally abolished, people who cannot post collateral have no ready way to assure their own motivation to repay—attachment of wages has also been liberally made illegal—so that those without assets who need cash must pledge life and limb in the underworld. Thus when the law has no way of enforcing contract, the underworld provides it: a man submits to the prospect of personal violence as the last resort in contract enforcement. Finally, the borrower whose prospects of repayment are so poor that even the threat of violence cannot hold him to repayment is enticed into an arrangement that makes him a victim of perpetual extortion, one who cannot go to the law because he is already party to a criminal transaction. Evidently there is some part of this racket that thrives on a void in our legal and financial institutions.

EVALUATING COSTS AND LOSSES

Crime is bad, as cancer is bad; but even for cancer, one can distinguish among death, pain, anxiety, the cost of treatment, the loss of earnings, the effects on the victim and the effects on his family. Similarly with crime. It is offensive to society that the law be violated. But crime can involve a transfer of wealth from the victim to the criminal, a net social loss due to the inefficient mode of transfer, the creation of fear and anxiety, violence from which nobody profits, the corruption of the police and other public officials, cost of law enforcement and private protection, high prices to customers, unfairness of competition, loss of revenue to the state, and even loss of earnings to the criminals themselves who in some cases may be ill-suited to their trade.

There are important "trade-offs" among these different costs and losses due to crime, and in the different ways that government can approach the problem of crime. There will be choices between reducing the incidence of crime and reducing the consequences of crime, and other choices that require a more explicit indentification and evaluation of the magnitude and distribution of the gains and losses.

If there were but one way to wage war against crime, and the only question how vigorously to do it, there would be no need to identify the different objectives (costs and consequences) in devising the campaign. But if this is a continual campaign to cope with some pretty definite evils, without any real expectation of "total victory" or "unconditional surrender" resources have to be allocated and deployed in a way that maximizes the value of a compromise.

In the black-markets it is especially hard to identify just what the evils are. In the first place, a law-abiding citizen is not obliged to consider the procurement and consumption of illegal commodities inherently sinful. We have constitutional procedures for legislating prohibitions; the outvoted minority is bound to abide by the law but not necessarily to agree with it, and can even campaign to become a majority and legalize liquor after a decade of prohibition, or legalize contraceptives in states where they have been prohibited. Even those who vote to ban gambling or saloons or dope can do so, not because they consider the consumption sinful, but because *some* of the consequences are bad; and if it is infeasible to prohibit the sale of alcohol only to alcoholics, or gambling only to minors, we have to forbid all of it to forbid the part we want to forbid.

The only reason for rehearsing these arguments is to remind ourselves that the evil of gambling, drinking, or dope, is not necessarily proportionate to how much of it goes on. The evil can be greater or less than suggested by any such figure. One might, for example, conclude that the consumption of narcotics that actually occurs is precisely the consumption that one wanted to prevent, and that it is the more harmless consumption that has been eliminated; or one might conclude that the gambling laws eliminate the worst of gambling, that what filters through the laws is fairly innocuous (or would be, if its being illegal per se were not harmful to society), and that gambling laws thus serve the purpose of selective discrimination in their enforcement if not in their enactment.

The evils of abortion are particularly difficult to evaluate, especially because it is everybody's privilege to attach his own moral value to the commodity. Are the disgust, anxiety, humiliation, and physical danger incurred by the abortionists' customers part of the "net cost" to society, or are they positively valued as punishment for the wicked? If a woman gets an abortion, do we prefer she pay a high price or a low one? Is the black-market price a cost to society, a proper penalty inflicted on the woman, or merely an economic waste? If a woman gets a safe cheap abortion abroad, is this a legitimate bit of "international trade," raising the national income like any gainful trade, or is it even worse than her getting an expensive, more disagreeable, more dangerous abortion at home, because she evaded the punishment and the sense of guilt?

These are not academic questions. There are issues of policy in identifying what it is we dislike about criminal activity, especially in deciding where and how to compromise. The case of prostitution is a familiar example. Granting the illegality of prostitution, and efforts to enforce the law against it, one may still discover that one particular evil of prostitution is a hazard to health—the spread of venereal disease, a spread that is not confined to the customers but transmitted even to those who had no connection with the illicit commodity. Yet there is some incompatibility between a campaign to eradicate venereal disease and a campaign to eradicate prostitution, and one may prefer to legislate a public health service for prostitutes and their customers even at the expense of "diplomatic recognition" of the enemy. The point is that a hard choice can arise and ideology gives no answer. If two of the primary evils connected with a criminal activity are negatively correlated, one has to distinguish them, separately evaluate them, and then make up one's mind.

Similarly with abortion. At the very least, one can propose clinical help to women seeking abortion for the limited purpose of eliminating from the market those who are actually *not* pregnant, providing them the diagnosis that an abortionist might have neglected or preferred to withhold. Going a step further, one may want to provide reliable advice about postabortion symptoms to women who may become infected or who may hemorrhage or otherwise suffer from ignorance. Still a step further, one may like to provide even abortionists with a degree of immunity so that if a woman needs emergency treatment he can call for it without danger of self-incrimination. None of these suggestions compromises the principle of illegality; they merely apply to abortion some of the principles that would ordinarily be applied to hit-and-run driving or to an armed robber who inadvertently hurt his victim and preferred to call an ambulance.

One has to go a step further, though, on the analogy with contraception, and ask about the positive or negative value of scientific discovery, or research and development, in the field of abortion itself. Cheap, safe and reliable contraceptives are now considered a stupendous boon to mankind. What is the worth of a cheap, safe and reliable technique of abortion, one that involves no surgery, no harmful or addicting drugs, no infection, and preferably not even reliance on a professional abortionist? Suppose some of the new techniques developed in Eastern Europe and elsewhere for performing safer and more convenient abortions become technically available to abortionists in this country, with the consequence that fewer patients suffer—but also with the consequence that more abortions are procured? How do we weigh these consequences against each other? Each of us may have his own answer, and a political or judicial decision is required if we want an official answer. But the questions cannot be ignored.

The same questions arise in the field of firearm technology. Do we hope that nonlethal weapons become available to criminals, so that they kill and damage fewer victims, or would we deplore it on grounds that any technological improvement available to criminal enterprise is against the public interest? Do we hope to see less damaging narcotics become available, perhaps cheaply available through production and marketing techniques that do not lend themselves to criminal monopoly, to compete with the criminally monopolized and more deleterious narcotics? Or is this a "compromise" with crime itself?

SHOULD CRIME BE ORGANIZED OR DISORGANIZED?

It is usually implied, if not asserted, that organized crime is a menace and has to be fought. But if the alternative is "disorganized crime"—if the criminals and their opportunities will remain, with merely a lesser degree of organization than before—the choice is not an easy one.

There is one argument for favoring the "organization" of crime. It is that organization would "internalize" some of the costs that fall on the underworld itself but go unnoticed, or ignored, if criminal activity is decentralized. The individual hijacker may be tempted to kill a truck driver to destroy a potential witness—to the dismay of the underworld, which suffers from public outrage and the heightened activity of the police. A monopoly or a trade association could impose discipline. This is not a decisive argument, nor does it apply to all criminal industries if it applies to a few; but it is important.

If abortion, for example, will not be legalized and cannot be eliminated, one can wish it were better organized. A large organization could not afford to mutilate so many women. It could impose higher standards. It would have an interest in quality control and the protection of its "goodwill" that the petty abortionist is unlikely to have. As it is, the costs external to the enterprise—the costs that fall not on the abortionist but on the customer or on the reputation of other abortionists—are of little concern to him and he has no incentive to minimize them. By all accounts, criminal abortion is conducted more incompetently and more irresponsibly than illegal gambling.

COMPROMISING WITH ORGANIZED CRIME

It is customary to deplore the "accommodation" that the underworld reaches, sometimes, with the forces of law and order, with the police, with the prosecutors, with the courts. Undoubtedly there is corruption of public officials, bad not only because it frustrates justice but also because it lowers standards of morality. On the other hand, officials concerned with law enforcement are inevitably in the front line of diplomacy between the legitimate world and the underworld. Aside from the approved negotiations by which criminals are induced to testify, to plead guilty, to surrender themselves, or to tip off the police, there is always a degree of accommodation between the police and the criminals—tacit or explicit understandings analogous to what in military affairs would be called the limitations of war, the control of armament, and the delineation of spheres of influence.

In criminal activity by legitimate firms—such as conspiracy in restraint of trade, tax evasion, illegal labor practices, or the marketing of dangerous drugs—regulatory agencies can deal specifically with the harmful practices. One does not have to declare war on the industry itself, only on the illegal practices. Regulation, even negotiation, are recognized techniques for coping with those practices. But when the business itself is criminal, it is harder to have an acknowledged policy of regulation and negotiation. For this involves a kind of "diplomatic recognition."

In the international field, one can coldbloodedly limit warfare and come to an understanding about the kinds of violence that will be resisted or punished, the activities that will be considered non-aggressive, and the areas within the other side's sphere of influence. Maybe the same approach is necessary in dealing with crime itself. And if we cannot acknowledge it at the legislative level, it may have to be accomplished in an unauthorized or unacknowledged way by the people whose business—law enforcement—requires it of them.

THE RELATION OF ORGANIZED CRIME TO ENFORCEMENT

We have to distinguish the "black market monopolies," dealing in forbidden goods—gambling, dope, smuggling, prostitution—from the racketeering enterprises. It is the black market monopolies that depend on the law itself. Without the law and some degree of enforcement, there is no presumption that the organization can survive competition—or, if it could survive competition once it is established, that the organization could have arisen in the first place in the face of competition.

There must be an "optimum degree of enforcement" from the point of view of the criminal monopoly. With no enforcement—either because enforcement is not attempted or because enforcement is not feasible—the black market could not be profitable enough to invite criminal monopoly (at least not any more than any other market, legitimate or criminal). With wholly effective enforcement, and no collusion with the police, the business would be destroyed. Between these extremes, there may be an attractive black market profitable enough to invite monopoly.

Organized crime could not, for example, possibly corner the market on cigarette sales to minors. Every 21-year-old is a potential source of supply. No organization, legal or illegal, could keep a multitude of 21-year-olds from buying cigarettes and passing them along to persons under 21. No black-market price differential, great enough to make organized sale to minors profitable, could survive the competition. And no organization, legal or illegal, could so intimidate every adult that he would not be a source of supply to the youngsters. Without there being any way to enforce the law, organized crime would get no more out of selling cigarettes to children than out of selling them soft drinks.

The same is true of contraceptives in those states where their sale is nominally illegal. If the law is not enforced, there is no scarcity out of which to make profits. And if one is going to try to intimidate every drugstore that sells contraceptives, in the hope of monopolizing the business, he may as well monopolize toothpaste, which would be more profitable. The intervention of the law is needed to intimidate the druggists with respect to the one commodity that organized crime is trying to monopolize.

What about abortions? Why is it not "organized"? The answer is not easy, and there may be too many special characteristics of this market to permit a selection of the critical one. The consumer and the product have unusual characteristics. Nobody is a "regular" consumer the way a person may regularly gamble, drink, or take dope. (A woman may repeatedly need the services of an abortionist, but each occasion is once-for-all.) The consumers are more secret about dealing with this black market, secret among intimate friends and relations, than are the consumers of most banned commodities. It is a dirty business, and too many of the customers die; and while organized crime might drastically reduce fatalities, it may be afraid of getting involved with anything that kills and maims so many customers in a way that could be blamed on the criminal himself rather than just on the commodity that is sold.

BLACK MARKETS AND COMPETITION

I have emphasized that a difference between black-market crimes and most others, like racketeering and robbery, is that they are "crimes" only because we have legislated against the commodity they provide. We single out certain goods and services as harmful or sinful; for reasons of history and tradition, and for other reasons, we forbid dope but not tobacco, gambling in casinos but not on the stock-market, extramarital sex but not gluttony, erotic stories but not mystery stories. We do all this for reasons different from those behind the laws against robbery and tax evasion.

It is policy that determines the black markets. Cigarettes and firearms are borderline cases. We can, as a matter of policy, make the sales of guns and cigarettes illegal. We can also, as a matter of policy, make contraceptives and abortion illegal. Times change, policies change, and what was banned yesterday can become legitimate today; what was freely available yesterday, can be banned tomorrow. Evidently there are changes under way in policy on birth control; there may be changes on abortion and homosexuality, and there may be legislation restricting the sale of firearms.

The pure black markets reflect some moral tastes, economic principles, paternalistic interests, and notions of personal freedom in a way that the rackets do not. And these tastes and principles change. We can revise our policy on birth control (and we are changing it) in a way that we could not change our policy on armed robbery. The usury laws may to some extent be a holdover from medieval economics; and some of the laws on prostitution, abortion, and contraception were products of the Victorian era and reflect the political power of various church groups. One cannot even deduce from the existence of abortion laws that a majority of the voters, even a majority of enlightened voters, oppose abortion; and the wise money would probably bet that the things that we shall be forbidding in fifty years will differ substantially from the things we forbid now.

What happens when a forbidden industry is subjected to legitimate competition? Legalized gambling is a good example. What has happened to Las Vegas is hardly reassuring. On the other hand, the legalization of liquor in the early 1930's swamped the criminal liquor industry with competition. Criminals are alleged to have moved into church bingo, but they have never got much of a hold on the stockmarket. Evidently criminals cannot always survive competition, evidently sometimes they can.

The question is important in the field of narcotics. We could easily put insulin and antibiotics into the hands of organized crime by forbidding their sale; we could do the same with a dentist's novocaine. (We could, that is, if we could sufficiently enforce the prohibition. If we cannot enforce it, the black market would be too competitive for any organized monopoly to arise.) If narcotics were not illegal, there could be no black market and no monopoly profits; the interest in "pushing" it would not be much greater than the pharmaceutical interest in pills to reduce the symptoms of common colds. This argument cannot by itself settle the question of whether (and which) narcotics (or other evil commodities) ought to be banned, but it is an important consideration.

The greatest gambling enterprise in the United States has not been significantly touched by organized crime. That is the stock market. (There has been criminal activity in the stock market, but not monopoly by what we usually call "organized crime.") Nor has organized crime succeeded in controlling the foreign currency black markets around the world. The reason is that the market works too well. Federal control over the stock market, designed mainly to keep it honest and informative and aimed at maximizing the competitiveness of the market and the information of the consumer, makes it a hard market to tamper with.

Ordinary gambling ought to be one of the hardest industries to monopolize. Almost anybody can compete, whether in taking bets or providing cards, dice, or racing information. "Wire services" could not stand the ordinary competition of radio and Western Union; bookmakers could hardly be intimidated if the police were not available to intimidate them. If ordinary brokerage firms were encouraged to take horse-racing accounts, and buy and sell bets by telephone for their customers, it is hard to see how racketeers could get any kind of grip on it. And when any restaurant, bar, country club or fraternity house can provide tables and sell fresh decks of cards, it is hard to see how gambling can be monopolized any more than the soft-drink or television business, or any other.

We can still think gambling is a sin, and try to eliminate it; but we should probably try not to use the argument that it would remain in the hands of criminals if we legalized it. Both reason and evidence seem to indicate the contrary.

The decisive question is whether the goal of somewhat reducing the consumption of narcotics, gambling, prostitution, abortion or anything else that is forced by law into the black market, is or is not outweighed by the costs to society of creating a criminal industry. The costs to society of creating these black markets are several.

First, it gives the criminal the same kind of protection that a tariff gives to a domestic monopoly. It guarantees the absence of competition from people who are unwilling to be criminal, and an advantage to those whose skill is in evading the law.

Second, it provides a special incentive to corrupt the police, because the police not only may be susceptible to being bought off but can even be used to eliminate competition.

Third, a large number of consumers who are probably not ordinary criminals—the conventioneers who visit prostitutes, the housewives who bet on horses, the women who seek abortions—are taught contempt, even enmity, for the law by being obliged to purchase particular commodities and services from criminals in an illegal transaction.

Fourth, dope addiction may so aggravate poverty for certain desperate people that they are induced to commit crimes, or can be urged to commit crimes, because the law arranges that the only (or main) source for what they desperately demand will be a criminal (high-priced) source.

Fifth, these big black markets may guarantee enough incentive and enough profit for organized crime so that large-scale criminal organization comes into being and maintains itself. It may be—this is an important question for research—that without these important black markets, crime would be substantially decentralized, lacking the kind of organization that makes it enterprising, safe, and able to corrupt public officials. In economic-development terms, these black markets may provide the central core (or "infra-structure") of underworld business.

A good economic history of prohibition in the 1920's has never been attempted, so far as I know. By all accounts, though, prohibition was a mistake. It merely turned the liquor industry over to organized crime. In the end we gave up, probably because not everybody agreed drinking was bad (or, if it was bad, that it was anybody's political business), but also because the attempt was an evident failure and a costly one in its social by-products. It may have propelled underworld business in the United States into what economic developers call the "take-off" into self-sustained growth.

60. SEX OFFENSES: A SOCIOLOGICAL CRITIQUE

STANTON WHEELER

ISSUES RAISED BY SEX OFFENDER LEGISLATION cut across a number of problems that are of interest to law, psychiatry, and the social sciences. Three problems are selected for brief review in this paper. The first concerns the basis for deciding what types of sex relationships should be subject to legal restraint. Second, the paper will review objective evidence regarding social attitudes toward various forms of sex conduct between consenting partners. Problems posed by more serious sex offenders will be examined in the closing section, with special attention directed to sex psychopath statutes and to possible sociogenic factors in the development of sex offenders. For reasons of space, the special problems posed by prostitution are not considered. Since other contributions to this symposium deal with experience in other societies and with the special problems of juveniles, the concern in this article is limited primarily to social norms and laws relevant to adult sexual relationships in the United States.

▶SOURCE: *"Sex Offenses: A Sociological Critique," Law and Contemporary Problems (Sex Offenses), (Spring, 1960), 25:258-278.* Reprinted by permission.

I
PROBLEMS IN THE DEFINITION OF SEX OFFENSES [1]

A. Sex Relationships Subject to Legal Restraint

Most of our sex laws are designed to govern one or more of four aspects of sexual relationships. Strongest legal sanctions are directed to control of the *degree of consent* in the relationship, with many states allowing the death penalty for forcible rape. Other bodies of sex law place limits on the *nature of the object*. Currently, most states restrict legitimate objects to humans, of the opposite sex, of roughly the same age, and of a certain social distance in kinship terms. Thus, sodomy or bestiality statutes prohibit relations with animals, parts of the sodomy statutes prohibit relations with members of the same sex, statutory rape and indecent liberties or

[1] Statutes defining sex offenses have been reviewed in a number of publications and will not be discussed in detail here. Major sources on which this discussion is based include Robert V. Sherwin, Sex and the Statutory Law (1949); Morris Ploscowe, Sex and the Law (1951); Bensing, *A Comparative Study of American Sex Statutes*, 42 J. Crim. L., & P.S. 57 (1951). See also Ploscowe, *Sex Offenses: The American Legal Context, supra* pp. 217-24.

child-molestation statutes restrict the legitimate age range of the partner, and incest statutes prohibit relationships with relatives other than the spouse. In addition, many jurisdictions, through fornication and adultery laws, limit legitimate objects to marriage partners. Legal restrictions are also placed on the *nature of the sexual act*. Full legitimacy is restricted largely to acts of heterosexual intercourse. Even if the object is a legitimate sexual object, the act may be subject to severe legal sanction. Thus oral-genital contacts, digital manipulation, and common-law sodomy are legally deviant acts, although they may occur by consent between a married pair. Finally, the law attempts to control the *setting in which the act occurs*. Relationships that occur otherwise subject to no restraints may become so when they occur publicly or when carried on in such a manner that the public may easily be aware of the relationship. States that do not punish single or even repetitive acts of fornication or adultery may do so if there is evidence of "notorious" show of public indecency. Public solicitation statutes as well as indecent exposure laws are likewise oriented to control of the setting, rather than the act itself.

B. Aims of the Criminal Law

If there were an explicit and articulate rationale underlying the criminal law's attempts to control sex conduct, one might expect that the legal sanctions attached to the various relationships would show an orderly pattern. That nothing could be further from the case is a frequently-noted and often-condemned fact.[2] The wide disparity in definitions of sex offenses and in severity of sanctions reflects, in part, the differential judgment of the seriousness of all sex offenses. In addition, it reflects differing judgements of the *relative* seriousness of differing types of sex relationships. Some understanding of the sources of disparity emerges from consideration of the various and conflicting aims of the criminal law as it applies to sex offenses.

A traditional emphasis views the criminal law as reflecting the moral condemnation of the community. Emile Durkheim's discussion of the universal elements in crime stressed the feature of moral condemnation. Crimes "shock sentiments which, for a given social system, are found in all healthy consciences."[3] Crimes consist "in acts universally disapproved of by members of each society."[4] The image of a homogeneous community reacting through the collective conscience was forcefully presented as the characteristic reaction to crime. A vigorous statement of a similar position has recently been made from a legalistic perspective. Henry M. Hart has defined crime as "conduct which, if duly shown to have taken place, will incur the formal and solemn pronouncement of the moral condemnation of the community."[5] He has voiced the fear that this element may be lost in sentencing procedure, even if retained in the definition of crime, if corrective and rehabilitative emphases predominate.

The element of moral condemnation in sex laws is vividly portrayed in statutes defining "crimes against nature." The very use of such a vague and ill-defined concept is related to the revolting nature of the behavior. Ploscowe has noted a judge's ruling in such a case:[6]

---

[2] Morris Ploscowe, Sex and the Law 136–55 (1951).

[3] Emile Durkheim, On the Division of Labor in Society 73 (George Simpson transl. 1933).

[4] *Ibid.*

[5] Hart, *The Aims of the Criminal Law*, 23 Law & Contemp. Prob. 401, 405 (1958). Hart also has emphasized the obligations imposed by community life, although these obligations are only indirectly caught up in his formal definition. See *id.* at 413, 426.

[6] Morris Ploscowe, Sex and the Law 197 (1951).

It was never the practice to describe the particular manner of the details of the commission of the crime, but the offense was treated in the indictment as the abominable crime not fit to be named among Christians. The existence of such an offense is a disgrace to human nature. The legislature has not seen fit to define it further than by the general term, and the records of the courts need not be defiled with the details of the different acts which may go to constitute it. A statement of the offense in the language of the statute is all that is required.

A different basis for the definition and grading of crimes is reflected in the conception that the criminal law should punish only those acts that are socially dangerous, independent of their moral character. The American Law Institute's Model Penal Code [7] and the Wolfenden Report [8] in England have been strongly influenced by this conception in the drafting of recommendations regarding sex offender laws. In recommending the restriction of the crime of fornication to open and notorious acts and those involving adoptive parents and children, the draftsmen of the Model Penal Code justify their position as follows: [9]

The code does not attempt to use the power of the state to enforce purely moral or religious standards. We deem it inappropriate for the government to attempt to control behavior that has no substantial significance except as to the morality of the action.

Throughout the discussion of code provisions, emphasis is clearly placed on control of behavior that appears to show some immediate social harm, either through the use of violence, through the exploitation of children, or through the nuisance value of public indecency.

The Wolfenden Report reflects a similar concern. It has been noted that "the yardstick applied throughout was utilitarian. If it could be proved that the behavior of an individual was socially injurious, he or she must be restrained." [10] Sex offenses are to be distinguished from sins and controlled in accordance with their objective social danger, rather than the degree of moral arousal they bring about.

A third criterion for the establishment of sex legislation has emerged during the past two decades. It is part of the growing influence of rehabilitative concerns on the administration of criminal law. This criterion reflects neither the moral condemnation nor the social danger of the offense; rather, the stress is on the degree of psychopathology charaterizing the offender. The influence of this conception has been extended from sentencing and treatment considerations to the definition of antisocial acts. Some of the sex psychopath statutes have allowed commitment up to life for persons showing such characteristics as "emotional instability, impulsiveness, lack of good judgment, failure to see consequences of act, irresponsibility in sex matters . . ." [11] Clearly, the emphasis is on personal qualities of the offender, rather than on the seriousness of any particular act.

Finally, there is increasing recognition of the important practical criterion of enforceability. The lack of visibility of most forms of sexual relations between consenting partners means that detection and arrest are nearly impossible for the vast number of cases. Such lack of enforceability may become another basis for judgment of selection of legal sanctions. Practical problems of enforcement are reflected in Model Penal Code recommendations concerning adultery and in discussion of the possible withdrawal of penal sanctions of deviate

---

[7] Model Penal Code art. 207 (Tent. Draft. No. 4, 1955: Tent. Draft No. 9, 1959.)

[8] Committee on Homosexual Offenses and Prostitution, *Report*, Cmnd No. 247 (1957).

[9] Model Penal Code § 207.1, comment at 207 (Tent. Draft No. 4, 1955).

[10] Eustace Chesser, Live and Let Live 116 (1958).

[11] From a 1949 Indiana statute, as described in California Dep't of Mental Hygiene, Final Report on California Sexual Deviation Research 45 (1954).

sexual intercourse between consenting adults.[12]

Current sex statutes reflect these varying aims of the criminal law. They do not fit a single dimension of social evaluation, but instead catch up in differing degrees the aims of expressing (a) the community's sense of moral condemnation or revulsion; (b) the degree of social harm resultant from the act; (c) the degree of psychopathology characterizing the offender; or (d) by omission, the practical problem of enforcement. Thus, it is no surprise that our sex laws are inconsistent and contradictory. A consistent criminal code for sex offenders is unlikely to emerge until there is agreement on the fundamental aims of the criminal law in this area.

C. Trends and Problems

The Model Penal Code and the Wolfenden Report give evidence of a movement toward a consistent framework for the criminal law regarding sex offenses. As noted, this framework places the social-danger criterion at the apex of the aims of the criminal law, assigns a lesser but important role to the aim of enforceability, and restricts the expression of the moral condemnation of the community to such cases as are also viewed as socially dangerous. This shift away from a moral emphasis presents some problems that deserve brief mention.

A chief difficulty in implementing a criterion of moral condemnation lies in the diversity of moral sentiment in modern communities. Durkheim's conception of a universal response to deviance was perhaps overdrawn, even for primitive communities. It seems particularly unrealistic in application to contemporary western societies. The very changes that were indexed by the growth of restitutive law have brought about also a change in the collective response to criminals. Increasing social differentiation makes it difficult to find acts that are universally condemned.

To speak of moral condemnation of *the community* is to use the term community in a very loose sense. It may apply to certain acts of violence and to crimes against children. Beyond these areas are many actions where no single community opinion can be said to exist. Responses to gambling laws, to white-collar violations, or to sex offenses between consenting partners depend heavily on the cultural background of the offender or of the person making the judgment. These influences play upon processes of adjudication and help to produce the great disparity in sentencing policies in different jurisdictions. Thus, the conception of a homogeneous community response, as implied by the moral condemnation argument, fails to square with contemporary life.[13]

In the face of these problems, the aim of limiting criminal sanctions to socially dangerous acts has great appeal. It purports to avoid the problem of differing moral judgments by establishing an objective standard of social danger; if acts surpass a certain minimal level, they are to be defined as crimes and graded as to severity according to the degree of danger involved.

The difficulties in working out such a formulation are evident in parliamentary response to the Wolfenden Report recommendations on homosexuality. There appeared to be general acceptance of the argument that conduct not injurious to society falls outside the legitimate concerns of the criminal law. But members of the House of Commons were uncertain that homosexuality between consenting adults was not injurious. There was fear that others might easily be corrupted if the act is not criminal—that persons will be willing to experiment with homosexual relations.[14]

---

[12] Model Penal Code 277-78 (Tent. Draft. No. 4, 1955).

[13] *Cf.* Fuller, *Morals and the Criminal Law*, 32 J. Crim. L. & C. 624 (1942). Evidence on variation in sentences comes from a variety of sources and is summarized in Glueck, *Predictive Devices and the Individualization of Justice*, 23 Law & Contemp. Prob. 463 (1958).

[14] Murray, *Commons Debate on the Wolfenden Report*, 122 Just. P. 816 (1958).

There was also the fear that removing the legal sanctions might imply condonation of homosexuality.[15]

Thus, even though there is no clear and present danger of bodily harm or corruption of morals in acts between consenting adults, there is always the possibility of long-term harmful consequences. Arguments to this effect can always be made and are hard to refute on empirical grounds, especially where the effects, if any, are likely to be subtle and only shown over a long time span. Although the history of legal control of sex conduct is largely one of failure,[16] this fact is a commentary on the problem of enforceability of the law; it does not, of itself, establish anything about the degree of social danger of the conduct. It is always possible to argue, as members of Parliament did, that conditions could be worse were the laws not on the books.[17]

This suggests something of the circular relationship likely to be maintained between social danger and moral condemnation as factors influencing public discussions and legislative decisions. The shift to an emphasis on the secular harms of various acts withdraws attention from their moral character. But in the absence of any clear-cut criterion of social danger, moral considerations will enter into and influence the perception of what is or is not socially dangerous. Until the consequences for society of various types of sex relationships are better known, changes in sex legislation will have to be based largely on changes in attitude and ideology, rather than on compelling evidence.

II
SOCIAL NORMS AND SEXUAL CONDUCT

The Kinsey volumes provided the first detailed account of sexual practices in the United States.[18] Public interest in the reports revealed the high degree of curiosity and anxiety aroused by the topic. But precisely because the subject of sex calls forth anxieties and fears, there has been a tendency for behavioral scientists to shy away from the systematic study of sexual attitudes and norms. No study of social norms regarding sexual conduct comes close to matching in quantitative detail the knowledge about sex contained in the Kinsey volumes. The result is that we have

---

[15] *Wolfenden Report in Parliament*, 1959 Crim. L. Rev. (Eng.) 38. The recommendations of the Wolfenden Committee are discussed in greater detail elsewhere in this symposium. Hall Williams, *Sex Offenses: The British Experience, infra* pp. 334–60.

[16] All authorities are in agreement on the failures of legal controls, and the evidence is well known. Most states have almost no prosecutions under fornication, seduction, or adultery statutes. To quote Ploscowe, "Nowhere are the disparities between law in action and law on the books so great as in the control of sex crimes." Morris Ploscowe, Sex and the Law 155 (1951). Nor is this a recent phenomenon. Geoffrey May cites data for the town of Groton, Mass., showing extremely high rates of fornication during the height of puritanism in the colonies. Geoffrey May, Social Control of Sex Expression 254 (1930). When the Model Penal Code discussions review problems of enforceability, fairly good evidence for the claims is presented. When the discussions concern possible secular harms, claims are based largely on argument and opinion. See, *e.g.*, the discussion of adultery. Model Penal Code § 207.1, comment at 204–10 (Tent. Draft No. 4, 1955).

[17] A similar problem is evident in discussions about the effectiveness of correctional techniques. It is fashionable to think of the "new penology" as based on rational, scientific investigation; yet, there is little evidence that current techniques are any more effective than those used in the past. Increasingly, evaluative research is carried out to test the effectiveness of various programs. Even the best of the studies are subject to methodological weaknesses that make for ambiguity in results, so that interpretations may be made consistent with the ideology of the interpreter. See Cressey, *The Nature and Effectiveness of Correctional Techniques*, 23 Law & Contemp. Prob. 754 (1958).

[18] Alfred C. Kinsey, Wardell B. Pomeroy & Clyde E. Martin, Sexual Behavior in the Human Male (1948) [hereinafter cited as Kinsey Male Report]; Alfred C. Kinsey, Wardell B. Pomeroy, Clyde E. Martin & Paul H. Gebhard, Sexual Behavior in the Human Female (1953) [hereinafter cited as Kinsey Female Report].

only meager evidence concerning the social evaluation of sexual conduct, as distinguished from the conduct itself.

Such evidence as is available comes from a variety of sources. The Roper Fortune Surveys have included a few items on sex attitudes in their national sample surveys over the past twenty-five years. Attitude questionnaires have been administered to select samples of individuals, primarily college students. Some case studies of particular communities or subcultures yields a modicum of data on normative patterns. Finally, inferences can be drawn from certain gross features of societal concern for sex relationships.

The data bear upon three questions frequently raised in discussions of sex mores: Is there evidence of a trend toward increasing permissiveness? Are there widespread subcultural differences in social norms regarding sexual conduct? Do the norms bear a close relationship to sexual behavior?

A. Trends in Values

Changes in American values during the twentieth century point to a widespread increase in sexual permissiveness, at least as gauged by the increasing freedom and lack of restraint in discussing sexual matters. Instead of the "Society for Sanitary and Moral Prophylaxis," the mid-twentieth century has a "Society for the Scientific Study of Sex." The pervasive influence of Freudian conceptions and the interest generated by the studies of Havelock Ellis are indicators of the same trend. The change has received support in modifications of obscene literature statutes, as brought forth most vividly in the recent case involving *Lady Chatterly's Lover*.[19] Although commentaries speaking darkly of a "sex revolution" pervading every aspect of social life seem highly overdrawn,[20] there is abundant evidence of increasing public attention and discussion of sexual codes.[21]

There is a vast difference, however, between the change in mores allowing greater freedom of discussion and a change reflecting either greater approval or a higher incidence of particular types of sex relationships. It is more difficult to find solid evidence for the latter type of change. Kinsey's data suggested, for instance, that the major change in rates of premarital intercourse for females occurred with those born between 1900 and 1910. Women born during the period from 1910 to 1930 had roughly the same pattern as those born during the first decade of the twentieth century.[22] And while younger-generation males had slightly higher rates of premarital intercourse with companions, the difference was largely offset by relatively more frequent contacts with prostitutes among the older-generation males.[23] The incidence of homosexuality and adultery remained relatively constant, although suggesting slight intergenerational changes for different segments of the population.[24]

Caution must be used in interpreting these findings, for there are well-known methodological problems in the Kinsey volumes, the most important being the use of nonprobability sampling, volunteer subjects, problems of recall among the older respondents, and the possible differences between reported and actual be-

---

[19] Kingsley Int'l Picture Corp. v. Regents, 360 U.S. 684 (1959).

[20] Pitirim A. Sorokin, The American Sex Revolution (1956).

[21] A major review of changes in American values shows increasing discussion of sex and a rising interest in extramarital relationships revealed in content analyses of best sellers. See Kluckhohn, *Have There Been Discernible Shifts in American Values During the Past Generation?* in Elting E. Morrison, The American Style 145 (1958). For changes of a similar sort during earlier decades, see Newcomb, *Recent Changes in Attitudes Toward Sex and Marriage*, 2 Am. Soc. Rev. 659 (1937). For interesting essays on the subject, see Abram Kardiner, Sex and Morality (1954).

[22] Kinsey Female Report 242–46.

[23] Kinsey Male Report 411–13.

[24] Id. at 413–17.

havior.[25] Within these limitations, the findings give no indication of significant changes in the gross features of sexual conduct since the 1920's.

Studies of the social evaluation of sexual conduct reveal a similar pattern. Impressionistic accounts of changes in the mores suggest that intercourse outside of marriage is increasingly viewed as an acceptable form of conduct. Unfortunately, there is no solid empirical evidence that can be used to evaluate this claim over a long time span, for objective methods of attitude and opinion assessment were not in use prior to the 1930's. The best available evidence for a more recent period consists in responses of national samples to an item asked in 1937 and again in 1959 by the Roper polling agency. If major changes in attitudes have occurred during the past twenty years, this fact should be revealed in the Roper data.

The question asked on both polls was: "Do you think it is all right for either or both parties to a marriage to have had previous sexual experience?"[26] Responses are indicated in Table I. The results show a surprisingly stable pattern over the past two decades. When it is remembered that the period spanned included publication and widespread discussion of the two Kinsey volumes, it is apparent that the fears voiced in some quarters—that knowledge of the Kinsey results may have widespread effect on sexual standards—have not materialized.

It is, indeed, risky to base a conclusion on such limited evidence. Other interpretations than that of stability could be given. There may have been widespread shifts in opposite directions for different segments of the population, such that they cancel out in the summary findings. There may have been important changes of such a subtle nature that they are not reflected by a single item on an opinion poll. The results may be reliable, but may have caught the population at particular points in a cycle of sexual attitudes, thus giving a false appearance of stability. All of these interpretations are possible and cannot be refuted without further evidence. The simplest interpretation, however, is that there has been little over-all change in attitudes toward this form of sexual conduct over the period spanned by the studies.[27]

Table I. *"Do You Think It Is All Right for Either or Both Parties to a Marriage to Have Had Previous Sexual Intercourse?"*

	1937	1959
All right for both	22	22
All right for men only	8	8
All right for neither	56	54
Don't know or refused to answer	14	16
	100	100

---

[25] An excellent review of the methodological problems in the Kinsey report on males is provided by William G. Cochran, Frederick Mosteller & John Tukey, Statistical Problems of the Kinsey Report (1954). These authors discuss the problem of establishing the stability of sexual patterns and caution against drawing more than tentative conclusions. *Id.* at 141.

[26] The 1937 data are from *The Fortune Quarterly Survey: VIII*, Fortune, April 1937, pp. 111, 188–90. The 1959 results were supplied to the writer by Phillip K. Hastings, Director, The Roper Public Opinion Research Center, Williams College, Williamstown, Mass. Results from these surveys demonstrate the dangers in inferring trends from comparison of older and younger generations at a single point in time. In both surveys, the older generation were somewhat less approving. The trend data suggest that this is largely a function of age, rather than a changing climate of opinion.

[27] Studies of moral values among samples of college students provide some evidence of change over recent decades. One study compared the responses of students in 1939 and in 1956 on an instrument designed to assess the perceived importance of certain characteristics in the ideal marriage mate. It found a decline in the importance attributed to chastity consistent with an assumed change from traditional to romantic and companionship factors as bases for mate selection. McGinnis, *Campus Values in Mate Selection: A Repeat Study*, 36 Social Forces 368 (1958). A similar study, however, notes an increase in the severity of moral judgment regarding forms of promiscuity. See Rettig & Pasa-

B. Socioeconomic Status and Sex Attitudes

One argument frequently raised in support of a change in legal controls is that communities are no longer homogeneous with respect to sexual standards—that the wide range of standards held in different segments of the population precludes application of universalistic legal standards. Kinsey's data are usually cited in support of this contention.[28] The most important of Kinsey's findings for present purposes are the variations in rates of premarital intercourse and in techniques of sexual arousal. Kinsey found that rates of premarital intercourse for males were highest at low educational levels and were considerably lower among the college-educated segment of his population.[29] At the same time, he found that lower-level couples were likely to restrict their sexual contacts to the most direct form of sexual union, while upper-level couples employed a wide variety of coital techniques, mouth and breast stimulation, and manual and oral forms of genital stimulation. For example, oral stimulation of female genitalia was found in sixty percent of the college-educated segment, but in only twenty and eleven percent of the high-school and grade-school histories, respectively.[30] The direction of these relationships suggests that sex statutes limiting premarital intercourse are most frequently violated by lower-class members, while statutes defining various forms of heterosexual perversions are more likely to be violated by middle- and upper-level persons.

There is little systematic evidence to determine whether the normative patterns are consistent with the differential incidence rates for perversions. Kinsey suggests that his lower-class respondents viewed with disgust some of the petting and coital practices of middle- and upper-level persons, although systematic evidence is lacking. The pattern, if verified, is an interesting reversal of the usual view that legal standards of sexual conduct reflect a middle-class morality.

More evidence is available concerning the social evaluation of premarital intercourse at differing socioeconomic levels. Between 1939 and 1943, the Roper agency asked questions about sexual attitudes in three of their sample surveys.[31] Typical results are reported in Tables II and III. The question for Table II was: "Do you consider it all right, unfortunate or wicked when young men (women) have sexual relations before marriage?" For Table III, the question was: "Should men (women) require virginity in a girl (man) for marriage?" Variation in response by socioeconomic status is similar in both tables, although the strength of the relationship varies with the wording of the question.[32] The relationship is also found when occupation is used as the relevant variable. Among males, the proportion who felt such activity was wicked increased from twenty-six percent among white-collar and professional workers to thirty, thirty-five, and thirty-six percent among blue-collar, unemployed, and farmers, respectively.

---

manick, *Changes in Moral Values Among College Students: A Factorial Study*, 24 Am. Soc. Rev. 856 (1959). While the increase in severity of judgment on three items dealing with sex was less than that for many other items, the values are still quite strong. For instance, "having illicit sex relations after marriage" was judged a more severe moral transgression than "nations at war using poison gas on the homes and cities of its enemy behind the lines"; or "a legislator, for a financial consideration, using his influence to secure the passage of a law known to be contrary to public interest."

[28] Model Penal Code § 207.1, comment at 206–07 (Tent. Draft No. 4, 1955).

[29] Kinsey Male Report 347.

[30] *Id.* at 576–77.

[31] I wish to acknowledge the aid of the Roper Public Opinion Research Center in making the data available for analysis. Unfortunately, evidence on class distribution of responses for the 1959 item was not yet available for study.

[32] The socioeconomic labels are interpreted from an index used by the Roper agency and may not match the distinctions made in other studies. These distributions probably fail to catch the extreme top and bottom of the socioeconomic scale, where different patterns might emerge. Data are for white respondents only.

Table II. *"Do You Consider It All Right, Unfortunate or Wicked When Young Men (Women) Have Sexual Relations Before Marriage?" (Women Only; N = 5220) (Percent)*

Socioeconomic Status	Wicked for Men	Wicked for Women
Upper	28	36
Upper-Middle	34	43
Lower-Middle	40	50
Lower	53	62

Table III. *"Should Men (Women) Require Virginity in a Girl (Man) for Marriage?" (Women Only; N = 2570) (Percent)*

Socioeconomic Status	Men Should Require in Women	Women Should Require in Men
Upper	64	42
Upper-Middle	66	47
Lower-Middle	71	53
Lower	72	52

What is surprising about the Roper results is not the degree of variation by social class, but its direction. Those in lower social strata are more likely to express disapproval of intercourse outside of marriage than are those in middle and upper positions. This is precisely the reverse of the direction for the behavioral record as found by Kinsey and others. The discrepancy could be due to such factors as a greater tendency among lower-class respondents to give what they perceive as socially desirable responses to middle-class interviewers, or the correlation of social class with religion or other variables. Certainly, the data are not strong enough to accept the finding as confirmed; yet, it does call into question the inference, frequently drawn by Kinsey's interpreters, that the social-class differences in rates are strongly supported by class differences in sex attitudes and values.[33]

There are reasons to believe that the relationship between overt sex acts and cultural values is much more complex than is usually presumed. Thus, a growing body of research has documented the higher degree of intolerance for deviant behavior among those of low education and socioeconomic position.[34] The response to sex may be part of the broader tendency to see the world in a good-evil dichotomy. The tendency is reinforced by the dogmatism of fundamentalist religious groups likely to flourish and have greatest appeal to those in lower social strata.[35] Class differentials in tolerance for sexual expression are also indicated in recent studies of child-rearing patterns. Working-class mothers are found to be far less permissive and to use more punitive measures for preventing sexual exploration.[36] These findings would lead one to expect greater rather than less disapproval at lower socioeconomic levels.

At the same time, the objective life situation of lower socioeconomic groups may predispose them to greater pressure for engaging in the activity. Thus, studies of lower-class urban areas point to the frequency of female-based households in which if the mother is to have any normal sexual outlet, it becomes, by definition, adultery.[37] The greater amount of premarital intercourse among lower-class girls may reflect less a difference in stated values than the

---

[33] Kinsey's own interpretations frequently were based on this assumption. Other examples are included in Jerome Himelhoch & Sylvia Fava, Sexual Behavior in American Society 175–205 (1955).

[34] Samuel A. Stouffer, Communism, Conformity, and Civil Liberties 89–108 (1955); Lipset, *Democracy and Working Class Authoritarianism,* 24 Am. Soc. Rev. 482 (1959).

[35] See Liston Pope, Millhands and Preachers (1942).

[36] Robert R. Sears, Eleanor E. Maccoby & Harry Levin, Patterns of Child Rearing 428 (1957).

[37] See Miller, *Implications of Urban Lower-Class Culture for Social Work,* 23 Soc. Serv. Rev. 225 (1959); see also Allison Davis & John Dollard, Children of Bondage 272–90 (1940).

use of sex as a means of attaching males of higher status, in the absence of alternative qualities of attraction.[38] A related and important feature concerns differences in the use and effectiveness of social-control techniques. For example, the more punitive methods of child-rearing used in lower socioeconomic strata may be less effective in producing long-term internal controls, even though parental attitudes may be similar to those in other strata.

All of these features may operate to suppress the effect of cultural values on overt conduct. One of the reasons the relationships between socioeconomic status, sex attitudes, and sex behavior are not yet clearly understood is that they are probably quite complex, involving differential pressures for engaging in the behavior and different mechanisms of control. A particular pattern of conduct emerges from many social influences and is rarely a simple reflection of stated cultural values. These influences are frequently neglected in drawing conclusions from the Kinsey research.[39]

C. Other Structural Characteristics and Sex Attitudes

Considerable variation in sex attitudes is revealed when characteristics other than social class are studied. Even a single question on a public opinion poll reveals important differences in attitude by race. Where roughly fifteen percent of the white females said that premarital intercourse for males was "all right," twenty-nine per cent of the Negro females gave that response. The differences in tolerance for women who engaged in the same behavior ranged from roughly five percent for white respondents to seventeen percent for Negroes.[40] Evidence on sex behavior leaves no doubt that the attitudinal differences are carried out in action. A study of army recruits located seven virgins among 500 Negro draftees.[41] Studies of illegitimate birth point to the extremely high rates for Negro girls in urban areas.

Kinsey's results revealed the influence of religious affiliation on sexual attitudes and behavior. Increasing rates of premarital intercourse are observed as one moves from Jewish to Catholic to Protestant groups. For each religious grouping, the proportion of women voicing regret for having premarital intercourse was greatest among the most active believers.[42]

Regional and rural-urban differences are revealed in recent opinion poll results: permissive attitudes are highest in the urban Northeast (twenty-eight percent), followed by the Far West (twenty-six percent), the South (twenty-three percent), and the Mid-west (fifteen percent).[43] The same data also indicate that the double standard applies most clearly to Southern manhood. Thirteen percent of the Southern respondents, compared to about five percent in the other areas, say that premarital sex is "Okay for men only."

The above review of variation in social norms in differing sectors of society is probably a conservative statement of the

---

[38] See Kanin & Howard, *Postmarital Consequences of Premarital Sex Adjustments*, 23 Am. Soc. Rev. 558 (1958); see also Ehrmann, *Influence of Comparative Social Class of Companion Upon Premarital Heterosexual Behavior*, 17 Marriage & Family Living 48 (1955).

[39] A related point of misinterpretation hinges on Kinsey's use of an accumulative-incidence curve, which reflects single acts engaged in only during childhood, or perhaps on only one occasion as an adult. One can hardly assume that because an act has been committed at least once by the majority of the population, it is, therefore, regarded as culturally acceptable. Yet, this argument has apparently been used in court cases. See Himelhoch & Fava, *op. cit. supra* note 33, at 244–50. On this basis, one would withdraw a large proportion of penal legislation, at least as it applies to males, including that governing tax evasion, malicious mischief, auto misdemeanors, disorderly conduct, and larceny. See Wallerstein & Wyle, *Our Law Abiding Law-Breakers*, 25 Probation 107 (1947).

[40] In response to the question reported in Table II *supra*.

[41] Hohman & Schaffner, *The Sex Lives of Unmarried Men*, 52 Am. J. Soc. 501 (1947).

[42] Kinsey Female Report 319.

[43] From the 1959 Roper survey reported in Table I *supra*.

actual variation, for it has been impossible to assess the combined effect of the several characteristics. At the same time, citation of percentages engaging in this or that conduct or holding particular attitudes tends to obscure the general lack of clarity of sex codes. With the exception of certain extremes found among particular ethnic or religious subcultures, it is probably fair to say that no single normative pattern is institutionalized in any large segment of the population, let alone the society as a whole. The wide variation in response to the Kinsey volumes gives abundant testimony to this fact.[44]

In part, the lack of clarity of sex codes is due to the specificity of sex attitudes. Whether premarital intercourse is viewed as acceptable or not depends on many features of the relationship between the couple. The sociologist William F. Whyte noted that Italian street-corner boys made a clear differentiation between "good girls," with whom intercourse was prohibited, and "lays" with whom it was highly desirable.[45] Studies of college students and middle-class sexual patterns suggest that intercourse is more acceptable to girls if part of a love relationship, while males are less likely to view it as acceptable under those conditions (although at any point, of course, premarital intercourse for males is considered more acceptable than for females.)[46] Until recently, the social scientists' concern with sexual attitudes and conduct was limited largely to the gross features of such conduct as revealed by frequency counts and general opinion. The meaningful context of the behavior or attitude was seldom studied in detail. The growth of a body of knowledge about the meaning of the activity for participants should provide a more useful set of empirical findings on the social distribution of sex attitudes and behavior.[47]

A more pervasive influence is the lack of visibility of sex attitudes and behavior. To an important degree, no one knows what standards others are employing. Enough life remains in the puritan ethic to prevent persons from expressing their attitudes openly. This quite naturally produces a condition of pluralistic ignorance. Without this element, it would be hard to account for the amazing public interest in the Kinsey reports. And so long as the condition remains, it will be impossible to achieve any genuine normative consensus.

D. Homosexuality

Little can be said about attitudes toward other forms of sexual relations between consenting adults. While much has been written about the homosexual problem, there is almost no objective information on the degree of public tolerance for homosexuals or on conceptions of the desirability of penal sanctions as a means of control. Although mass responses are still shrouded in mystery and fear, the trend is surely toward a more enlightened, dispassionate perspective.[48]

---

[44] See Palmore, *Published Reactions to the Kinsey Report,* 31 Social Forces 165 (1952).

[45] Whyte, *A Slum Sex Code,* 49 Amer. J. Soc. 24 (1943).

[46] Ehrmann, *Premarital Sexual Behavior and Sex Codes of Conduct with Acquaintances, Friends and Lovers,* 38 Social Forces 158 (1959).

[47] One of the major complaints in popular literature about the Kinsey research was the overly biological orientation and lack of attention to love and affection as basis for sex relationships. Some of Kinsey's results as well as those of other investigators suggest, however, that where the abstinence standard no longer exists, the emerging standard permits coitus when part of a stable, affectionate relationship. See Reiss, *The Treatment of Pre-Marital Coitus in "Marriage and the Family" Texts,* 4 Social Problems 334 (1957). An interesting recent study finds a high degree of ego involvement in premarital sexual relationships, particularly among middle-class women, and suggests some of the conditions that encourage intimacies for females in the middle and upper socioeconomic strata. See Vincent, *Ego-Involvement in Sexual Relations: Implications for Research on Illegitimacy,* 65 Am. J. Soc. 287 (1959).

[48] Contributing to and reflecting this trend is an increasing willingness on the part of some homosexuals to make their problems a matter for public concern. See, *e.g.,* Peter Wildeblood, Against the Law (1956). And note the signs of incipient pressure-group formation in the following quotation

Some inferences as to sources of changing perspectives can be drawn from other studies of tolerance toward deviance. As noted above, an increasing body of research suggests that tolerance toward nonconforming behavior may be a relatively general trait that may cut across many specific forms of deviation.[49] Tolerance is greatest among the younger generation and those with most education. The sociologist Samuel Stouffer's report on political nonconformity found tolerance also greater among community leaders.[50]

Whether these results hold for attitudes toward sexual nonconformity can only be determined by further study. The findings at least suggest the important sectors of the population that may be least resistive to changes of the type recommended by the Wolfenden Report in England. While such proposals are probably still in advance of public opinion, the forces making for greater tolerance are likely to remain and should be a sign of hope for supporters of more liberal legislation regarding homosexuals.[51]

E. Need for more Adequate Information

Review of objective data on social norms and sexual conduct reveals above all else the paucity of useful information. Aside from an occasional item in an opinion poll, a handful of studies of college students, and one or two anthropological accounts, there is nothing that even makes for intelligent speculation as to the sources and types of community reaction to sexual deviations between consenting adults. Such evidence as is available suggests that while there has been no great change in *standards* of sexual conduct at least over the past twenty years, there is a general trend toward greater *tolerance* of various *forms* of sexual relationships. Some of the more recent proposals for change in legislation invoke distinctions between mental illness, crime, and sin that major segments of the public are probably not yet prepared to understand or accept. Perhaps the single most important factor making for public recognition of these distinctions is the increase in average level of education.

The outstanding fact remains that no major study has been made of attitudes and norms regarding sex conduct. Any conclusions must be tempered by awareness of the flimsy evidence on which they are based. Within this arena of ignorance, the American Law Institute is attempting to design new legislation concerning sexual behavior. Important recommendations are being decided at least partially on the basis of guesses as to how the public or legislative officials will react.[52] Consideration of con-

---

from the trade journal, One, published in Los Angeles: "No American Politician regards as humorous a millions votes. . . . Let's say the membership dues are . . . fifty cents a month . . . six dollars a year . . . multiply that by a million and you have the gigantic fighting strength . . . $6,000,000. . . . Nobody will care whose money it is . . . that of screaming pansies, delicate decorators or professional wrestlers. Nobody will give a damn because this is the U.S.A. and money talks. . . ." From the Sept. 1953 issue of One, as quoted in James M. Reinhardt, Sex Perversions and Sex Crimes 32 (1957).

[49] See authorities cited, note 34 *supra*. These results refer largely to response to behavior clearly defined as deviant. Whether a given pattern of behavior is recognized as deviant in the first place is a related, but separate, issue. At least in regard to mental illness, there is some evidence that lower-class persons with little education are less likely to recognize a particular behavior pattern as that of a mentally-ill person than are more educated, middle-class persons. See August B. Hollingshead & F. C. Redlich, Social Class and Mental Illness 171–93 (1958).

[50] Stouffer, *op. cit. supra* note 34, at 26–57.

[51] Trends consistent with those noted above have been found for one item on sex criminals taken

from a national survey. In response to the question: "What do you think is the best thing to do with sex criminas, send them to a hospital or a jail?," the younger and more educated were much more likely to choose the hospital. Significantly, a majority at all educational levels favored the hospital, as did a majority in all age groups up to age 45. See Woodward, *Changing Ideas on Mental Illness and Its Treatment*, 16 Am. Soc. Rev. 443 (1951).

[52] See the discussion of proposed changes in legislation regarding deviate sexual intercourse. Model Penal Code § 207.5, comment at 276–81 (Tent. Draft No. 4, 1955).

troversial proposals could benefit from more adequate information on public attitudes.[53]

III
THE SEX OFFENDER

Certain types of sex offenders are either a danger to the community or a nuisance that the community need not tolerate. Their offenses include rape, indecent liberties, exhibitionism, and incest, as well as a variety of related acts. The conception that sex offenders are different from any other types of law violators has led to legislation that results in a placement of sex offenders in a kind of limbo, somewhere between the criminal and the mentally ill. The remainder of this paper directs attention to the problems raised by sex offender legislation and to some possible socio-cultural factors in the genesis of sex deviation.

A History and Critique of Sex Offender Laws

Legislation defining sex psychopaths and establishing administrative procedures for their custody, treatment, and release was passed by some thirteen states between 1937 and 1950, and has been extended to other states since that time. Procedures leading up to the legislation were similar in the different jurisdictions. In a review of the development of sex psychopath laws, the late criminologist Edwin Sutherland noted a sequence characterized by (a) arousal in a community of a state of fear as a result of a few serious sex crimes, (b) agitated community response, leading to (c) the appointment of a committee that gathered information and made recommendations that generally were uncritically accepted by state legislatures.[54] The work of the committees proceeded largely in the absence of facts. Sutherland noted that the laws embodied a set of implicit assumptions that were explicit in much of the popular literature on sex offenses. These included the notion that all sex offenders were potentially dangerous, that they were very likely to repeat their offenses, that they can be accurately diagnosed and efficiently treated by psychiatrists. The laws were passed in the name of science, although there was little scientific evidence as to the validity of the assumptions underlying the statutes.

The act of passing the statutes set in motion the kind of data-gathering process that was needed to establish adequate legislation in the first place. Some of the legislation required study of the effectiveness of the statutes along with studies of sex offenders. These studies drew attention to the weaknesses of the legislation.

Many of the criticisms have been presented in reports prepared for state legislatures and will be mentioned only briefly here.[55] The label "sex psychopath" is so

---

[53] To be sure, there are weaknesses and pitfalls in the gathering and interpretation of opinions on controversial issues. But these problems are well known to experts in opinion-research and are subject to increasing control. One need not suggest that public opinion replace legislative and judicial opinion in order to see the value that can come from knowledge of public attitudes, especially in areas where presumed public response is explicitly considered in making important decisions. For a recent study and discussion of the use of opinion surveys and their application to one area of legal concern, see Julius Cohen, Reginald A. H. Robson & Alan Bates, Parental Authority: The Community and the Law (1958). This is not to suggest that public opinion studies are the only or necessarily the most appropriate means of establishing the relationship of public opinion to legal process. The University of Chicago Jury Project is one instance of a much different approach that promises to reveal some of the areas of agreement and disagreement between the response of judge and of jury to certain types of offenses. See Broeder, *The University of Chicago Jury Project*, 38 Neb. L. Rev. 744 (1959).

[54] Sutherland, *The Diffusion of Sexual Psychopath Laws*, 56 Am. J. Soc. 142 (1950).

[55] Reports with detailed analyses of sex offender statutes and experience in their use include Paul W. Tappan, The Habitual Sex Offender (1950) (prepared for the state of New Jersey); California Dep't of Mental Hygiene, Final Report on California Sexual Deviation Research (1954) [hereinafter cited as California Report]; Governor's Study Comm'n, Report on the Deviated Criminal Sex Offender (1951) (Michigan).

vague as to make administration of statutes unreliable.[56] Sex offenders are less likely to repeat their crimes than are other types of offenders.[57] Very few sex offenders present a grave social danger.[58] Current diagnostic techniques are incapable of distinguishing reliably between the potentially dangerous and those that are not dangerous.[59] There has been no test of the assumption that treatment techniques are effective in rehabilitation of sex offenders.[60]

Given these findings, it is not surprising that members of the legal profession were reluctant to approve of the usual procedures for administration of the statutes. Significantly, the opposition was not along lines usually assumed to separate legal from psychiatric viewpoints: a free-will, punitive orientation *versus* deterministic, permissive orientation. Rather, the criticism has been directed to the possible denial of due process to offenders. Since the statutes typically called for commitment up to life, even for minor offenses, the usual safeguard of a maximum sentence was missing. In addition, the administrative procedure for release, frequently requiring certification that the offender was no longer a danger to the community, made release very difficult. Administrators were understandably reluctant to assert that the patient was cured.[61]

While these problems signify dissatisfaction with many of the procedures built into the earlier statutes, there is still no common agreement on the most appropriate solutions. Some states have dropped the label "sex psychopath" from their statutes, have restricted the scope of the statutes to more serious offenders, and have required that the offender be held no longer than the maximum sentence under traditional criminal provisions. One of the problems posed by these changes is illustrated by the experience in Massachusetts. Massachusetts revised its psychopathic personality statute in 1954. The new law discarded the term "psychopath" and included the requirement that an offender must be released at the expiration of his maximum sentence. The law was deemed inadequate after a double murder was committed by an offender whose release from the state reformatory could not be prevented by provisions of the 1954 act. The law was quickly amended to allow for indefinite commitment up to life for certain types of sex offenders.[62]

The case points to a familiar problem in the visibility of mistakes in the processing of offenders. Errors made in releasing men too early are publicly observable. Under a statute allowing commitment up to life, however, errors made in keeping men who may, in fact, be cured cannot be tested, because by the nature of the procedure, they are not given a chance either to succeed or to fail. While every failure of early release may come to public attention, errors of keeping men too long cannot be detected. Such errors may be quite frequent in the absence of accurate diagnostic procedures. There is always the danger of undue restriction of civil liberties in attempts to provide adequate protection to the community.

---

[56] Tappan, *op. cit. supra* note 55, at 36–42; California Report 20–38.

[57] Tappan, *op. cit. supra* note 55, at 22–25. Tappan cites a New York study that found that only 7% of convicted sex offenders were re-arrested for sex offenses over a 12-year period. A recent California study also found 7% sex recidivism among sex offenedrs. See Frisbie, *The Treated Sex Offender*, Fed. Prob., March 1958, p. 18.

[58] Tappan, *op. cit. supra* note 55, at 20–22. See also Albert Ellis & Ralph Brancale, The Psychology of Sex Offenders 32 (1956).

[59] For a beginning in this direction, see California Report 142–47.

[60] Tappan, *op. cit. supra* note 55, at 15–16. Of course, a major problem has been that treatment has been almost totally lacking. Many states have passed laws requiring treatment without establishing treatment facilities. Beyond this, however, any treatment technique will have to be very effective if it is to reduce significantly the rate of recidivism, for the rate is already quite low.

[61] Tappan, *op. cit. supra* note 55, at 34.

[62] Edwin Powers, The Basic Structure of the Administration of Criminal Justice in Massachusetts 15–17 (United Prison Ass'n of Mass., Res. Div. Rep. No. 5, 1957).

B. Developmental Careers of Sex Offenders

Perhaps the single most important outgrowth of recent experience with sex statutes is that we are now aware of how little reliable knowledge is available. Until recently, the major source of ideas about sex offenders stemmed from clinical reports on a wide variety of sex deviants. The case materials have filled most of the books written on sexual deviation.[63] Although the cases may enrich clinical understanding, they do not provide an adequate basis for the development of sound administrative procedures. The clinical interpretations stand logically not as fact, but as hypotheses requiring test.[64] Since the cases are drawn from an unknown population of offenders, there is no adequate basis for generalization. And since adequate control groups are not employed, any claims as to therapeutic effectiveness are claims, and no more. They remain untested.

The impetus to research provided by the sex psychopath statutes has resulted in knowledge that calls into question some of the earlier clinical findings. While the research is still at a descriptive rather than an experimental stage, it has been effective in casting doubt on assertions that all or almost all sex offenders are highly disturbed. Systematic study of 300 offenders committed to the diagnostic facility in New Jersey showed that on the basis of psychiatric diagnoses, fully forty-three percent of the offenders were classified as normal or only mildly neurotic.[65] This raises the question of what distinguishes the psychiatrically normal from the abnormal sex offender. More broadly, are there systematic differences in the developmental careers of different types of sex offenders? Suggestions of such differences are apparent in recent research.

A distinction can be made between aggressive and passive offenders. The former usually commit offenses involving attempted or completed intercourse with a legitimate sexual object—i.e., a person of the opposite sex beyond the age of puberty. Most rapes and sexual assaults fall in this category. The passive offenses include exhibitionism and noncoital sex play with children. In terms of physical danger, the former category presents the most serious social problem. The sex statutes were passed largely to control the violent acts of rape and sexual assault. Yet, available evidence suggests that as a group, such offenders are less likely to exhibit clear-cut pathological symptoms and may have more in common with nonsexual offenders than with the passive sex deviants.

The report on sex offenders processed through the New Jersey diagnostic center provides information on the characteristics of offenders classified by type of offense. Selected findings from the study are reproduced in Table IV for the offense categories falling most clearly at the aggressive and passive poles.[66]

---

[63] Benjamin Karpman, The Sexual Offender and His Offenses (1954); Joseph Paul De River, The Sexual Criminal (1950); Reinhardt, *op. cit. supra* note 48.

[64] For a clear, concise statement of the needs and uses of controls in psychiatric research, see Comm. on Research, Group for the Advancement of Psychiatry, Rep No. 42, Some Observations on Controls in Psychiatric Research (1959). Neglect of the distinction between fact and hypothesis is illustrated in the following exchange in a discussion of a paper on sex psychopaths wirtten by the psychiatrist Benjamin Karpman. One of the discussants, Albert Ellis, suggested that Karpman's propositions should be regarded as hypotheses rather than facts, and that evidence for some of them was lacking; to which Karpman replied: "I deny these allegations in toto. All of my statements are based on *actual clinical material;* I do not have one bit of theory." Karpman, *op. cit. supra* note 63, at 511–12, 525.

[65] Ellis & Brancale, *op. cit. supra* note 58, at 94.

[66] See *id.* at 34, 38, 42, 46, 49, 56, 62. Two of the major categories excluded from the above review are statutory rape and incest. Ellis and Brancale provide convincing evidence of the essential normality of statutory rape offenders, and support the conclusions of Ploscowe and others that the age limit in such cases should be reduced. Evidence on incest cases suggests, as would be expected, that offenders are more like the aggressive than the passive offenders in terms of social and criminal background.

Table IV. *Differences Between Aggressive and Passive Sex Offenders on Selected Characteristics*[a]

	Diagnosed Normal or Mildly Neurotic	Commitable to Mental Institution	Overinhibited	Severe Emotional Disturbance
Aggressive offenders				
Sex assault	48	24	48	48
Forcible rape	38	25	50	63
Passive offenders				
Noncoital sex play with children	20	45	66	66
Exhibitionists	30	29	72	63
	Previous Arrest for Sex Offenses	Previous Non-Sex Arrests	Underlying Hostility	(No. of Subjects)
Aggressive offenders				
Sex assault	14	48	72	21
Forcible rape	12	50	75	8
Passive offenders				
Noncoital sex play with children	51	43	35	51
Exhibitionists	34	23	25	89

[a] Each column contains the percentages of each type of offender characterized as indicated by column headings. Thus 30% of the exhibitionists were diagnosed normal or only mildly neurotic. Number of cases on which the percentages are based appear in the lower right column.

The aggressive offenders are more likely to be judged normal by psychiatric diagnosis. They are less inhibited sexually and tend to give fewer indications of severe emotional disturbance. Fewer of them are judged to have been exposed to severe emotional deprivation during childhood. Significantly, their prior arrest histories show few sexual offenses, but many nonsexual offenses. The ratio of non-sexual to sexual offenses is much higher for the aggressive than for the passive offenders. Finally, they are much more likely to show signs of hostility, a characteristic most common among property offenders from delinquent or criminal subcultures.[67]

Evidence from the California studies of sexual deviation supports the pattern noted above. Case descriptions of the most serious and aggressive sex offenses committed by delinquents in San Francisco revealed that over half of the cases were gang-motivated. Furthermore, of the thirty-seven serious offenders studied, half had previous records for nonsexual offenses, only three had previous sex arrests. Reading of the case descriptions further shows that the gang attacks were more frequently directed toward girls in middle or late adolescence, while the offenses against very young sexual objects were more likely to be committed by lone offenders.[68]

Ethnic differences in rates of sex offenses give further support to this pattern. The California research showed that Negroes and Mexicans were overpresented in the

[67] The findings of the New Jersey study are, of course, subject to many weaknesses commonly found in sex offender research. As the authors of the study note, there is no way of knowing how their sample differs in background from sex offenders sentenced to state prisons or from those who are undetected. The number of cases is much too small, especially for the rapists, to place much confidence in the results. The characterizations of offenders, with the exception of prior arrest data, are undoubtedly colored by knowledge of which type of offense they committed.

[68] California Report 132–35.

rape category, underrepresented in offenses against children.[69] The New Jersey experience suggested that Negro sex offenders were less emotionally disturbed than their white counterparts.[70] Both of these findings are consistent with studies of racial differences in homicide rates and suggest the influence of cultural differences in restraints on the use of violence to resolve interpersonal affairs.[71]

The evidence thus suggests that the typical aggressive sex offender may be less "sick" than is usually supposed. Their backgrounds have much in common with nonsexual offenders who come from crime-inducing cultural settings. Instead of conceiving of their conduct as resulting from a highly specific and grossly deviant sexual motivation, it is perhaps more valid to view their offenses as part of a broader behavior system in which force may be used to attain their goals. It is the use of force rather, than any specifically deviant sexual motivation, that distinguishes these offenders from those who fall within the law.[72]

Psychiatric study has revealed the frequency with which sexual motivations underlie such non-sexual crimes as arson and certain types of burglary. The suggestion here is that the reverse may hold for certain types of aggressive sex offenders. In a society stressing active mastery of the environment over passive acquiescence, perhaps it is not surprising that the aggressive sex offender who overresponds is judged less disturbed than the passive exhibitionist.[73]

Brief mention may be made of two additional points where sociological conceptions usually applied to nonsexual offenses may have bearing on deviant modes of sexual response. One of these points concerns the way in which the social structure exerts pressure on persons to use deviant means of achieving culturally acceptable goals. High rates of deviance are presumed to occur among those segments of the population that are least fortunately situated in terms of their abilities to achieve valued goals by legitimate means.[74] The same conception is applicable to the achievement of sexual gratification. Prisons are, of course, an extreme case of a structure that promotes deviant means of sexual outlet. But less extreme instances are in evidence as well. Thus, two studies note high rates of incest in rural populations, where the choice of alternatives to the wife, given dissatisfaction with her performance, is

---

[69] *Id.* at 101-02.

[70] Ellis, Doorbar & Johnston, *Characteristics of Convicted Sex Offenders*, 40 J. Soc. Psych. 14 (1954).

[71] Marvin E. Wolfgang, Patterns in Criminal Homicide 329 (1958).

[72] The psychiatrist Richard L. Jenkins has observed that "the difference between the law-abiding man and the rapist lies typically not in a difference of sex impulse, but in a difference of inhibition and consideration for the personality of others." Jenkins, *The Making of a Sex Offender*, in Cylde B. Vedder, Samuel Koenig & Robert E. Clark, Criminology 293, 295 (1953). The above observations seem consistent with this view, but are at variance with psychiatric analyses, which see even statutory rape as fundamentally tied up with the oedipus complex, representing an unconscious attack upon the parent. See, *e.g.*, David Abrahamsen, Who Are the Guilty? 184-85 (1952). Any theory that seeks to interpret sex aggression as a highly neurotic or psychopathic act must consider the prevalence of aggressive sexual acts among presumably normal populations of college students. See Kanin, *Male Aggression in Dating-Courtship Relations*, 63 Am. J. Soc. 197 (1957). The Kanin article points to some of the factors that may prevent these cases from becoming officially labeled as felonious aggressions.

[73] The culture of prison inmates provides insight into the differences between aggressive and passive sex offenders. No special status is conferred on aggressive offenders or those convicted of statutory rape. In fact, the latter are viewed as having "bum beefs" as a result of "pick on your own size" laws designed to allow promiscuous teenagers to get off the hook when they become pregnant. Offenders who engage in a nonviolent sex acts with children, on the other hand, are relegated to the bottom of the social structure and referred to in derogatory terms as "rapos"—so afraid of women they had to pick on children.

[74] See Robert K. Merton, Social Theory and Social Structure 131-94 (rev. ed. 1957).

severely limited.[75] And prostitution flourishes in lumber and mining areas, and in the central sectors of cities, where the sex ratio is abnormally high. These illustrations remind us that the availability of legitimate sexual outlets is itself socially-structured; resort to deviant outlets will reflect these structural features and need not be conceived solely as a result of faulty personality makeup.

Second, the dyadic character of many types of crime means that the victim may play more than a passive role. Wolfgang's recent study of Philadelphia homicides revealed that fully twenty-six per cent were victim-precipitated.[76] Similar findings might result from careful study of those convicted of rape, where the offense frequently follows an evening of drinking and mutual sexual arousal. Consideration of the victim's role means that the offense can be viewed as a product of a social situation; its explanation cannot easily be reduced to a search for the childhood emotional disorders of the party who becomes labeled the offender.[77]

These observations suggest some ways in which sociocultural and situational features may be related to deviant sexual behavior. Assumptions that direct attention solely to psychogenic factors may lead to an inaccurate conception of the causal processes involved, and hence to treatment programs that neglect important sources of the deviation. Specifically, further research may reveal that many aggressive sex offenders are responding to culturally learned patterns of aggression and to situational factors that are unlikely to be relieved by the usual methods of clinical psychotherapy. Patterns of cultural learning as well as psychogenic disorders may be reflected in their offenses. This may partially explain why such offenders are deemed generally less amenable to treatment than the less dangerous but more disturbed passive offenders.[78]

Sociological conceptions of crime are heavily influenced by the sociologist's concern for the impact of culture and social organization. These elements are revealed most clearly in such types of offenses as professional crime, white-collar crime, and gang delinquency. Some of the evidence reviewed above suggests that there may be important sociogenic features in the development of certain types of sex offenders, and that further study could profit from an interdisciplinary approach to the problems posed by such offenders. The growing need for systematic knowledge should lead to research designed to reveal the combined influence of sociogenic and psychogenic sources of sexual deviation. Such research may suggest inadequacies in the conception that most sex offenders are a special breed of criminal requiring unique laws and administrative procedures for their control.

[75] John Lewis Gillen, The Wisconsin Prisoner 107–16 (1946); Reimer, *The Background of Incestuous Relationship*, in Vedder, Koenig & Clark, *op. cit. supra* note 72, at 301.

[76] Wolfgang, *op. cit. supra* note 71, at 245.

[77] The Model Penal Code expresses recognition of these elements in suggesting that where a woman loses capacity to control her own conduct by voluntary use of intoxicants or drugs, any resulting intercourse cannot be charged as rape, although it can be under most existing statutes. Model Penal Code § 207.4, comment at 248–49 (Tent. Draft No. 4, 1955).

[78] Ellis & Brancale, *op. cit. supra* note 58 at 78.

61. FORCIBLE RAPE

MENACHEM AMIR

THE TERM "RAPE" AROUSES HOSTILE AND aggressive feelings in many societies and in many countries. In a number of jurisdictions it is punishable by death. There is sympathy for the victim and hostility toward the offender. Since the crime of rape includes many elements other than sex, judicial decisions relating to punishment and treatment are difficult to render.

This article is based on an empirical study which was designed to explore and disclose the patterns of forcible rape among 646 cases occurring in Philadelphia, Pennsylvania, from January 1 to December 31, 1958, and from January 1 to December 31, 1960. The cases were those in the files of the Morals Squad of the Philadelphia Police Department where all complaints about rapes are recorded and centrally filed.

The emphasis in this study has not been on the psychological dynamics underlying the behavior of the individual offender and his victim but rather on their social characteristics, social relationships, and on the act itself, that is, the modus operandi of the crime and the situations in which rape is likely to occur.

The patterns which emerged were derived from a study of 646 victims and 1,292 offenders who were involved in single and

▶SOURCE: *"Forcible Rape,"* Federal Probation (March, 1967), 31:1:51–58. Reprinted with permission.

multiple rape.[1] Patterns were sought regarding race, marital status, and employment differences, as well as seasonal and other temporal patterns, spatial patterns, the relationships between forcible rape and the presence of alcohol, and the previous arrest record of victims and offenders.

Further questions were raised relating to rape during the commission of another felony, the relationship between the victim and offender, Victim-precipitated rape, and unsolved cases of rape. Finally, all of these aspects were related to group rape and to leadership functions in such situations.

METHOD OF STUDY

While we approached the study from a sociological viewpoint, i.e., crimes as learned behavior committed within socio-culturally defined situations, we were not guided by a specific theoretical system for explaining the offense studied. Nor did we attempt to find specific causes and explanations for the offense. Rather, we undertook to learn what we could about the characteristics of the offense, the offenders, and the victims separately, but also as mutually interacting participants. The

---

[1] The term "multiple rape" refers to cases where two or more offenders rape one victim. It includes the following two categories: "pair rape" where two offenders rape one victim, and "group rape" where three or more offenders rape one victim.

suggested associations were tested primarily by the chi-square test of significance.

At the outset of the study our hypothesis was that criminal behavior is a patterned and structured event. However, some unexpected empirical uniformities appeared, and the study was able to refute some of the misconceptions surrounding the crime of rape.

SOME MISCONCEPTIONS ABOUT RAPE

Following are some misconceptions about rape disclosed in this study:

1. *Negroes are more likely to attack white women than Negro women.* Rape, we found, is an intraracial act, especially between Negro men and women.

2. *Rape reflects a demographic strain due to sex-marital status imbalance in the community.* This theory was refuted, along with the derivative assumption about age-sex imbalance which might exist within the general populations.

3. *Rape is predominantly a hot-season crime.* The "thermic law of delinquency" was not confirmed by the present study.

4. *Rape usually occurs between total strangers.* This assumption was challenged by the analysis of several variables.

5. *Rape is associated with drinking.* In two thirds of our cases alcohol was absent from the rape situation.

6. *Rape victims are innocent persons.* One fifth of the victims had a police record, especially for sexual misconduct. Another 20 percent had "bad" reputations.

7. *Rape is predominantly an explosive act.* In almost three-quarters of the cases rape was found to be a planned event.

8. *Rape is mainly a dead-end street or dark alley event.* Rape was found to occur in places where the victim and offender initially met each other (especially when the meeting was in the residence of one of the participants).

9. *Rape is a violent crime in which brutality is inflicted upon the victim.* In a large number of cases (87 percent) only temptation and verbal coercion were used initially to subdue the victim.

10. *Victims generally do not resist their attackers.* As it is commonly believed that almost no woman wants to be deprived of her sexual self-determination, it was surprising to find that over 50 percent of the victims failed to resist their attackers in any way.

11. *Victims are responsible for their victimization either consciously or by default.* The proportion of rape precipitated by the victim and the characteristics of such acts refute this claim.

FINDINGS OF THIS STUDY

In the following pages are discussed the major significant patterns emerging from the study:

Race. A significant association was found between forcible rape and the race of both victims and offenders. Negroes exceed whites both among victims and offenders in absolute numbers as well as in terms of their proportion in the general population. Negroes have four times their expected number of victims, and the proportion of Negro offenders was four times greater than their proportion in the general population of Philadelphia.

We have used Sellin's [2] concept of "potential population," that is, the members of each race whose age and sex are such that they could be an offender or a victim, respectively, and from which the involvement of the participants can be presumed.

When specific rates by age and sex were calculated on the basis of the "potential" population of each race, it was found that the rates for the Negro victims (on the basis of total Negro female population) is almost 12 times higher than that of the white women who were victims (on the basis of total white female population).

---

[2] Thorsten Sellin, "The Significance of Records of Crime," *Law Quarterly Review,* October 1951, pp. 496–504.

Similarly, for offenders, when the rates were computed on the basis of male population in each racial group, the proportion of Negro offenders was 12 times greater than that of white offenders. Furthermore, when the rates were figured on the basis of the "potential" race populations, the rate for Negro offenders turned out to be three times greater than that of Negro victims, a difference found to hold also for white offenders as compared to white victims.

The data on racial differences reveals that forcible rape is mainly an intraracial event. In this sample, forcible rape occurred significantly more often between Negroes than between whites.

Age. A statistical association existed between age and forcible rape, the age group 15-19 years having the highest rates among offenders and among victims. In examining the relative ages of the offenders and the victims, we found that the higher the age of the offender, the more likely it was that the victim would be in a lower age group. When the differences were broken down further by race it appeared that, regardless of the population basis, the top "risk" age group for Negro and white offenders is the same (15 to 19, and 20 to 25 years of age), but the rates for Negroes in these age levels are higher than for whites. For each age group, however, the rates show a greater proportion of Negro than of white males involved in forcible rape.

The age pattern for victims was found to be somewhat different from that of offenders. For victims there is a wider range of "critical" age groups, with the Negro victim rate exceeding that of the white victims in all age groups.

Examination of age differences according to race of victims and offender showed that mainly in Negro and white intraracial rape events, offenders and victims were at the same age level. However, white victims tend to be younger than their white assailants by at least 10 years, while Negro offenders tend to be at least 10 years younger than their white victims. (The majority of cases of the latter description were felony-rape events.)

Marital Status. After examination of the marital status of both offenders and victims, it was found that both generally were unmarried. The highest rates for victims were in the "dependent" category (below marriageable age and still unmarried).

Offenders as a group, but Negroes more than whites, show the highest rate in the "single" group (above the age of marriage but not married and still living at parents' home) and the second highest rate in the "dependent" group. These results coincide with the age distribution of victims and offenders noted above.

Negro victims showed a greater concentration in the "single" and "dependent" groups than did white victims who were, however, also concentrated in these groups.

Demographic imbalance. An attempt was made to check Von Hentig's [3] demographic explanation of forcible rape, i.e., a disturbed sex ratio for unmarried persons age 19 to 49 years resulting in a surplus of males, leads to rape as a solution to their problem of securing sexual partners. We found that the marital demographic structure of Philadelphia cannot explain the extent to which males, especially Negroes, resort to forcible rape. The same applies when marital status, age, and sex ratio were analyzed together.

Occupational Status. Examination of the occupational status of the offenders indicated that 90 percent of the offenders of both races belonged to the lower part of the occupational scale. The rate of Negro offenders in the unemployed category was twice as high as the rate of unemployed Negroes in Philadelphia at that time, and five times as high as that of white offenders.

Season. Although the number of forcible rapes tended to increase during the hot summer months, there was no significant association either with the season or with

---
[3] Hans Von Hentig, "The Sex Ratio," *Social Forces*, March 1951.

the month of the year. While Negro intraracial rapes were spread over the year, white intraracial events showed a more consistent increase during the summer. Summer was also found to be the season when multiple rapes were most likely to occur.

Days of the Week. Forcible rape was found to be significantly associated with days of the week. We found the highest concentration of rapes (53 percent) to be on weekends, with Saturday being the peak day.

Time of Day. A study of the distribution of forcible rapes by hours of the day found the top "risk" hours to be between 8:00 p.m. and 2:00 a.m. Almost half of all the rape events occurred during these hours. Finally, the highest number of weekend rapes occurred on Friday between 8:00 p.m. and midnight.

Ecological Patterns. The analysis of the ecology of forcible rape reveals that in various areas of Philadelphia there was a correspondence between high rates of crime against the person and the rates of forcible rape. Moreover, those police districts where Negroes are concentrated were also the areas where the rates of forcible rape were highest.

A check was made to determine whether the offenders lived in the vicinity of the victims or the offense. In the majority of cases (82 percent) offenders and victims lived in the same area, while in 68 percent a "neighborhood triangle" was observed, i.e., offenders lived in the vicinity of victim and offense. Also observed are the pattern of "residence mobility triangle," i.e., instances in which the site of the crime was in the area of the residence of the offender but not that of the victim. A new concept used in this study was a "crime mobility triangle." In 4 percent of the cases the offenders lived in the victim's vicinity, while the crime was committed outside the boundaries of their residential area. When correlating these ecological patterns with race and age factors we found that forcible rape was an interracial event between victims and offenders who were at the same age level and who were ecologically bound, i.e., victims and offenders lived in the same area, which tended also to be the area of the offense. This was especially true for Negro intraracial rapes.

Drinking. Unlike previous studies the present one examined the consumption of alcohol by the offender and the victim separately and together. Alcohol was found only in one-third of all the rape events. In 63 percent of the 217 cases in which alcohol was present, it was present in both the victim and the offender.

The presence of alcohol in the rape situation appeared to be statistically associated with whites—both victims and offenders—and with Negro victims who had consumed alcohol alone before the offense. Alcohol was frequently found to be present in the victim, offender, or both in white intraracial rape events. Of the various combinations of drinking patterns, alcohol in the victim alone and in both victim and offender has stronger implications of causal relationships with the crime of rape than other drinking patterns.

Alcohol is a factor found to be strongly related to violence used in the rape situation, especially when present in the offender only. In terms of race, it was drinking Negro victims or the offenders who were involved most frequently in violent rapes. Also, alcohol was found to be significantly associated with sexual humiliation forced upon a drinking victim.

Finally, weekend rapes were found to be associated with the presence of alcohol in either the victim, the offender, or both. As an explanation, we offered (as did Wolfgang in his homicide study [4]) the fact that Friday is a payday with greater purchase of alcohol and the more intense social and leisure activities.

Previous Arrest Records of Offenders and Victims. A relatively high proportion of

---

[4] Marvin E. Wolfgang, *Patterns in Criminal Homicide*. Philadelphia: University of Pennsylvania Press, 1958, pp. 142–143.

rapists in Philadelphia (50 percent) had previous arrest records. Contrary to past impressions, it was found that there are slight differences between the races, for offenders or victims, in terms of police or arrest record, although Negro offenders had a statistically significant higher proportion of two or more offenses in their past than white offenders.

When cases of persistence in violating the law were examined, it was found that over 50 percent of those who had an arrest record as adults also had a record as juveniles.

Analysis of the type of previous offenses committed by the offenders revealed that only 20 percent of those who had a past arrest record had previously committed a crime against the person, with Negro offenders outnumbering the whites in this respect. Among offenders with criminal records, 9 percent had committed rape in the past, and 4 percent had been arrested before for sexual offenses other than rape. When examining the continuity and persistence of offenses from juvenile to adult age, we found that the highest proportion in continuity was in offenses against the person. Thus, adults arrested for rape were found to be less likely first offenders than adults arrested for other types of offenses.

The analysis of the victim's criminal records revealed that 19 percent had an arrest record, the highest proportion of these arrests being for sexual misconduct (56 percent).

The victim's "bad" reputation was explored. It was found that 128, or 20 percent, of the 646 victims had such reputations, with significantly higher proportion of Negro victims having such a reputation. The assumption was made, and later confirmed, that a "bad" reputation, together with other factors such as ecological proximity, was a factor in what was termed "victim-precipitated" forcible rape.

Modus Operandi. The analysis of the modus operandi was made in terms of processes and characteristics of the rape situation, i.e., sequences and conjunctions of events which enter into the perpetration of the offense. Five phases were distinguished according to offender's behavior, victim's reaction, and situational factors which finally set the stage for the rape event.

In phase one we were concerned with the initial interaction between victim and offender, and the relevant problems such as the place meeting and the degree of planning of the offense. It was found that the most dangerous meeting places were the street, and the residence of the victims or offenders or place of sojourn. In one-third of the cases, the offender met the victim at and committed the offense in the victim's home or place where she stayed. Such was especially the case in intraracial rape situations.

Planning of the Act. On the basis of the description of the event by the victim and offender, three degrees of planning were distinguished. Contrary to past impression, the analysis revealed that 71 percent of the rapes were planned. Most planned events were intraracial events when the meeting place was the residence of one of the participants or when the rape was a group affair. Explosive rapes were characterized as being single interracial rapes, with the street as the meeting place.

Location of the Event. Phase two concerned itself with the location of the offense and was found to be associated with the place of initial meeting. Thus, when the meeting place was outside the participant's residence or place of sojourn, the offense also took place there. Movement of the crime scene was mainly from outdoors to inside. The automobile, which was already found as a vehicle of crime commission, was revealed to be the location of the offense in only 15 percent of the cases, and more often when white offenders were involved. A significant association was also found between the location of the rape in the participant's place and use of violence in the commission of the offense, as well as the subjection of the victim to sexually humiliating practices.

Degrees of Violence. In phase three we examined various aspects in the actual commission of the offense: Nonphysical methods used to manipulate the victim into submission, the degrees of violence used against her, and sexual humiliating practices which she was forced to endure.

Besides temptation, three forms of nonphysical methods were distinguished: Verbal coercion, intimidation by physical gestures, and intimidation with a weapon or other physical object to force the victim into submission. Combined with verbal coercion, nonphysical aggression was used in the majority of cases (87 percent), with Negroes in significant proportion using both forms of intimidation against their Negro victims. No differences were found between intra- and interracial events in this respect.

Degrees of violence were classified into three main groups: roughness, beatings (brutal and nonbrutal), and choking. In 15 percent of the 646 rapes, no force was used. Of the cases in which force was used, 29 percent took the form of roughness, one-quarter were nonbrutal beatings, one-fifth were brutal beatings, and 12 percent involved choking the victim. Violence, especially in its extreme forms, was found to be significantly associated with Negro intraracial events and with cases in which the offender was Negro and the victim white. Also, a significant association was found between multiple rape and the use of force in the rape situation and between the latter and the outside as the place of rape.

Sexual Humiliation. It was not merely to forced intercourse that the female was subjected in rape, but also to various forms of sexual practices usually defined as sexual deviations. It was found that sexual humiliation existed in 27 percent of all rape cases, especially in the forms of fellatio, cunnilingus, or both, or in the form of repeated intercourse. Sexual humiliation was found to be significantly associated with white intraracial rapes, where the victims were subjected most frequently to fellatio and pederasty, and with Negro intraracial rapes where Negro victims were forced more often to repeated intercourse by their Negro assaulters. Sexual humiliation was found also to be significantly associated with multiplicity of offenders and with the presence of alcohol in the offender only or both by the offender and the victim. In these cases sexual humiliation appeared mainly in the form of fellatio.

Victim Behavior. The behavior of the victim—that is, whether she "consented" or resisted the offender—was, and still is, the basis in determining in the court whether the offender is guilty of forcible rape. This problematic dimension was, therefore, analyzed in the present work.

The varieties of victim behavior have been divided into three groups—submission, resistance, and fight. The analysis revealed that in over half of the rapes the victims displayed only submissive behavior; in 173, or 27 percent, victims resisted the offender; and in 116, or 18 percent, the victims put up a strong fight against their attackers.

In both intra- and interracial rapes Negroes and white victims displayed the same proportion of either one of these forms of behavior. The highest proportion of the instances of submissive behavior were cases in which the victim was white and the offender Negro. These cases included almost all felony-rape situations. In most situations the victim was older than her attacker.

In terms of age the younger the age, the more submissive was the victim—mainly those 10 to 14 years. In the adult age (30 and over), victims showed significantly more resistance. Victims tended to fight more when they were more intimate in the initial encounter with the offender, or when force was used against them by the offenders. As expected, the presence of alcohol in the victim diminished her capacity to resist, and in such cases her behavior was found to be mainly submissive.

Multiple Rape. The phenomenon of multiple rape (see footnote 1), mentioned sometimes in the literature but nowhere analyzed, was given special attention in this study. We suggested a tentative theory, borrowing heavily from Redl's [5] theory, which emphasizes the role of the leader in group deviant behavior.

Multiple rape situations were divided into "pair rapes," in which two offenders rape one victim, and "group rapes," in which three or more males rape one victim. Of the 646 cases of forcible rape, 276 cases, or 43 percent, were multiple rapes. Of these cases, 105 were pair rapes and 171 were group rapes. Of 1,292 offenders, 210, or 16 percent, were involved in pair rapes and 712, or 55 percent, participated in group rapes.

The analysis of multiple rapes revealed the following characteristics: More white than Negro offenders participated in pair rapes and more Negro than white offenders were involved in group rapes. Multiple-rape situations were found to be mainly an intraracial affair, with no differences in proportions between Negro and white intraracial events.

The younger the offender, the less likely he is to participate in multiple rape. All of the offenders of ages 10 to 14 participated either in pair rapes or group rapes. The highest proportion of pair rapes or group rapes were perpetuated by offenders between ages 14 to 19. Group rapes were also found to be characterized by victims being in the same age level as the offender.

Group rape shows a tendency to occur more on weekends and to occur in the evening as well as late at night.

In group rapes, alcohol was more likely to be present, especially in the victim only, while in pair rapes it was more often present only in the offender who was the leader.

A significant proportion of participants in multiple rapes, compared with single-rape offenders, had a previous arrest record either for offenses against the person, for sex offenses other than rape, or for forcible rape. This was true for pair-rape leaders, as compared to their partners, but not for group-rape vis-a-vis their followers.

Turning to the modus operandi aspect in multiple-rape situations, it was observed that multiple-rape offenders are most likely to attack victims who live in their area (neighborhood or delinquency triangles). The initial interaction between victims and offenders usually occurred in the street, where the rape also took place. There was little "mobility of crime scene" in multiple-rape situations.

Multiple rapes, especially group rapes, were found to be planned events. Compared to group rapes, pair rapes showed a high proportion of cases of explosiveness or partial planning.

Turning to the problems of intimidation and coercion, it was found that multiple-rape situations, especially group rapes, are characterized by temptation and coercion, with intimidation more used in pair-rape events. The leader was found to be the initiator of the manipulating acts, i.e., he was the first to tempt or to intimidate the victim into submission.

A significant association existed between violence and multiple rapes, especially group rapes. Multiple rapes also are characterized by the greater use of nonbrutal beatings. Extreme violence and brutality characterize the single-rape events, since the lone offender must constantly subdue the victim alone. The leader in pair and group rapes was more violent than his followers, and he was also the one to initiate the beatings.

Group rapes were also found to be characterized by tormenting the victim with perverted sexual practices. Testing the theory of "magical seduction" [6] we found that only the pair-rape leader inflicted sexual humiliation upon the victim.

When the association between leadership

---

[5] Fritz Redl, "Group Emotion and Leadership," *Psychiatry*, July 1942, pp. 573–596.

[6] Redl, *op. cit.*

functions, such as "initiator" or "magical seducer" were tested, it was found that both are significantly associated, i.e., those who first attacked the victim were also the first to rape her. However, "magical seduction" was found to be the more important role of the leader. Introducing another leadership function, that of "commanding" and organizing the situation, we found that in group rape the "true" leader was the one who performed all three functions. However, if the three functions were not performed by the same person, the one who first raped the victim was also likely to be the one who commanded the event.

The futility of resistance and fight by the group-rape victim is revealed by the fact that in group-rape situations the victim was more submissive or lightly resisted the offender but was less inclined to put up a strong fight. Pair-rape victims showed no definite pattern in this respect.

For many variables pair rapes and group rapes show some variations from the cluster of patterns which distinguished the multiple-rape situations. We found that in many instances pair rape resembled single rape more than group rape. Thus, it may be better to see pair rapes not as a form of group event but rather as a form of criminal "partnership."

Felony Rape. In 76 cases, or 4 percent, of the 646 rape situations, a felony in the form of burglary or robbery was committed in addition to the rape. These cases were mainly single rapes, and especially Negro intraracial rapes. A special trait of felony rape is the age disparity between victim and offender. In more than half of these cases the offender was at least 10 years younger than the victims, especially when the offender was Negro and the victim white.

Examination of the previous record of felony-rapists showed them to be more often recidivists than the offenders in rape generally. Felony rapes also were characterized by a greater proportion of cases in which sexual humiliation was inflicted upon the victim. Because of the age differences between victim and offenders, it was expected and, indeed, found that victims of felony rapes were more inclined to be submissive than victims of rape generally.

Victim-Offender Relationships. Almost half (48 percent) of the identified victim-offender relationships conformed to our definition of "primary" relationships. When the types of primary contacts were further divided into "acquaintanceship" and more "intimate" contacts, the former constituted 34 percent and the latter contributed 14 percent of all types of victim-offender relationships.

A detailed analysis of victim-offender relationships revealed that when primary relationships existed, a relatively large proportion of cases involved Negro victims whose assailants were their close neighbors, or victims who were drinking acquaintances of their white assaulters.

As expected, Negro intraracial events involved mainly close neighbors. White intraracial events occurred mainly between acquaintances who established their relations just before the offense. Again, as expected, acquaintanceships were formed mainly between victims and offenders who were at the same level.

Neighbors met initially in the residence of one of the participants and the rape also took place there. The automobile was the place of rape for those who were intimate.

Although nonphysical means of coercion in its light forms were used between acquaintances, the closer the relationship was between victim and offender the greater was the use of physical force against the victim, and neighbors and acquaintances were found to be the most dangerous people so far as brutal rape was concerned.

As hypothesized, a greater proportion of multiple than single rape was found to take place between strangers. In general, the analysis of the interpersonal relations between victim and offender lent support to those who reject the myth of the offender who attacks victims unknown to him. But, equally rejected is the notion that rape is generally an affair between, or a result of, intimate relations between victims and offenders.

Vulnerable Situations in which Rape Occurred. After discussing the psychological approach to victim proneness and victim selection, we found it more fruitful to deal with vulnerable or "risk" situations rather than with psychological concepts like "victim proneness." We noted those factors which emerged in significant proportions as constituents of such situations. It is probable that women entering these risk situations will more likely become victims of rape regardless of their own psychological characteristics.

The following were the main features of vulnerable situations in which rape occurred:

1. Where victims and offenders of single and multiple-rape events were either of the same race or age or both;
2. Where victims of felony rape, who tended to be at least 10 years older than their assailants (Negro and white), lived as neighbors or acquaintances in the same area as their assailants, which tended to be also the area where the offense was committed;
3. Where offenders and victims of the same race and age level met during the summer months, mainly on weekends and/or during the evening and night hours, in places which allowed or encouraged the development of an acquaintanceship or relations between neighbors;
4. Where alcohol was present in both white offender and white victim, or in white offender and Negro victim, or in the victim only, especially when her assailant was white;
5. Where Negro victims with a "bad" reputation lived in the neighborhood of their Negro attackers, and where groups of offenders who planned the rape of victim of their own race live in the same vicinity;
6. When victims and offenders were neighbors of the same race and age, between whom primary relations existed, and where victims and offenders established drinking relations just prior to the offense; and
7. Where a drinking victim was accosted in the street by a stranger, usually of her own race.

Victim-Precipitated Rape. The term "victim-precipitated," initiated by Wolfgang in his study of homicide,[7] was introduced to refer to those rape cases in which the victims actually—or so it was interpreted by the offender—agreed to sexual relations but retracted before the actual act or did not resist strongly enough when the suggestion was made by the offenders. The term applies also to cases in which the victim enters vulnerable situations charged with sexuality, especially when she uses what could be interpreted as indecent language and guestures or makes what could be taken as an invitation to sexual relations.

Philadelphia data revealed several significant factors associated with the 122 victim-precipitated rapes, which comprised 19 percent of all forcible rapes studied. These factors are:

1. White victims; white intraracial rapes; alcohol in the rape situation, particularly in the victim or both in offenders and victims;
2. Victims with a bad reputation; victims who live in residential proximity to the offenders and/or the area of offense; victims who meet their offenders in a bar, picnic, or party;
3. Victims who were in "primary" relationships with the offenders but who were not their relatives.
4. Victims who were raped outside their or the offender's home or place of sojourn; and
5. Victims subjected to sexual humiliation.

Solved and Unsolved Rape. We distinguished two types of "unsolved" cases: the "undetected"—those cases in which the police could not attribute the recorded offense to any identifiable offender(s), and

---

[7] Wolfgang, *op. cit.*, chap. 14, pp. 245–269.

the "vanished"—those cases about which the police had some information on suspected, identified, or alleged offenders but which suspects were still at large. In 124, or 19 percent, of the rape events the offenders were classified as "undetected" and in 24, or 4 percent, as "vanished." Of 1,292 offenders, 405, or 33 percent, were classified as undetected.

In unsolved cases of rape in Philadelphia there was:

1. A higher proportion of Negro offenders involved in Negro intraracial rape than in solved cases;
2. A higher average age among the offenders than among offenders in general;
3. A higher proportion of explosive types of rape;
4. A higher proportion of cases in which alcohol was present in the victim only or in the offender only;
5. A higher proportion of single-rape situations; and
6. A higher proportion where there was delay by the victim or others in reporting the offense to the police, especially because of fear of the offender or an inability to adequately describe him.

CONCLUSION

Discussing various theoretical explanations for the crime of forcible rape, a subculture theory of violence emerged as a possible interpretation of the patterns discerned in this study.

There can be little doubt that more studies are needed to give us more systematic and comparative knowledge of the characteristics of rapists and victims and of social conditions which may explain more accurately the crime of rape.

62. THE MARIHUANA PROBLEM

ALFRED R. LINDESMITH

THE PRIMARY FACT ABOUT MARIHUANA which ought to be taken into account by legislators but is not, is that it is not a habit-forming drug. By this is meant that the regular use of marihuana does not produce tolerance, and its abrupt cessation does not lead to withdrawal distress. As a consequence the problem of controlling or regulating its use is sharply different from that presented by the genuine drugs of addiction, i.e., the opiates such as heroin and morphine and their synthetic equivalents. Nevertheless, by federal legislation in 1951 and 1956, the increased penalties imposed on opiate users and peddlers were also applied to the users and distributors of marihuana. This extension was made casually with little discussion or investigation and with no apparent appreciation that the use of marihuana is something almost totally different from the use of heroin.

EFFECTS OF SMOKING MARIHUANA

Marihuana is ordinarily used in this country by smoking. The effects it produces are experienced as exhilaration, loss of inhibitions, a changed sense of time, and other psychological effects which have sometimes been described and extravagantly praised by those who have experienced them. These effects are in a general way comparable to the stimulating effects produced by alcohol in the sense that they are intoxicating, although they differ qualitatively from those of alcohol.

Intrinsically, however, marihuana is less dangerous and less harmful to the human body than is alcohol. It is, for example, not habit-forming, whereas alcohol is. While the alcoholic commonly substitutes alcohol for food, marihuana sharply stimulates the appetite. Chronic alcoholism is associated with various psychotic conditions and diseases such as Korsakoff's psychosis and cirrhosis of the liver. In comparison, the smoking of marihuana produces relatively trivial physical effects, although it does appear that immoderate use of the more concentrated products of the hemp plant also produce deleterious bodily effects. Such effects, however, are not conspicuous among American reefer smokers, probably because of the relatively small quantities of the essential drug that are ingested from the poor quality marihuana ordinarily consumed in this country. The American marihuana smoker who inadvertently uses too much when he switches, let us say, to the more potent ganja plant raised in Mexico and the West Indies is likely to experience nothing more alarming than going to sleep and waking up hungry.

▶SOURCE: *The Addict and the Law*, Bloomington: Indiana University Press, 1965, pp. 222-242. Reprinted by permission.

USE OF MARIHUANA IN OTHER COUNTRIES

Marihuana consists of the dried and crumbled stems, leaves, and seed pods of a plant known as Indian hemp or *Cannabis sativa*. These materials are often mixed with tobacco and in the United States are ordinarily smoked. In many other parts of the world a special type of hemp plant of unusual potency, known commonly as *ganja*, is used in a similar manner or it may be brewed and drunk as ganja tea—a common practice in the West Indies, where this drink is prized for its alleged therapeutic efficacy. In India the uncultivated hemp plant is smoked as marihuana is here and is also drunk. It is known there as *bhang*. The essential drug of the hemp plant is *cannabis indica* or *cannabinol* and it, of course, can be taken in this form. This essential drug is derived primarily from the resin of the female hemp plant. This concentrated hemp resin is commonly known as *hashish* and is immensely more powerful than either ganja or marihuana. The comparison of hashish and marihuana is like that between pure alcohol and beer. Lurid accounts of the psychological effects and dangers of hemp are often based upon observations made by and upon hashish users. The mixture smoked as marihuana ordinarily contains very small quantities of the drug and its effects are correspondingly less spectacular, less dangerous, and less harmful than those of hashish.[1]

The medical use of *cannabis indica* has declined in Western medicine but it is still extensively used in the Ayurvedic and Unani systems of indigenous medicine in India. In various parts of the world folk beliefs attribute great therapeutic and even divine virtues to the drug. In Jamaica it is known to many persons of the lower classes as "the wisdom weed" and it is alleged that it stimulates good qualities in the person who uses it and brings him closer to God. The use of ganja there is supported by references to various Biblical passages which recommend the "herbs of the field." The same passages, incidentally, are taken by the devotees of peyote (a cactus containing mescaline) to refer to that plant. A back-to-Africa protest cult in Jamaica, known as the Ras Tafari, has adopted ganja as a symbol of the movement and its members sometimes refer to themselves as the "herb men." In defiance of the Government, members of this cult, and others who are simply impressed by the fact that ganja is a more profitable crop than any other, grow and harvest the plant and use some of it themselves. Ganja tea is regarded as a prime ameliorative agent in the folk treatment of many diseases including asthma, tuberculosis, venereal disease, and many others, especially all types of respiratory ailments. Ganja cigarettes are extensively used by the workers in the sugar cane fields and some foremen of the sugar producing companies state that, were it not for ganja, they would have difficulty finding workingmen to harvest their crops.[2]

On the book jacket of Professor Robert P. Walton's 1938 book entitled, *Marihuana: America's New Drug Problem,* Frederick T. Merrill and Mr. Anslinger are quoted. The latter observed: "It is a new peril—in some ways the worst we have met, and it concerns us all." Merrill was even more emphatic and alarmed: "If the abuse of this narcotic drug is not stamped out at once, the cost in crime waves, wasted human lives, and insanity will be enormous." Quoting Walton, Merrill notes that marihuana often produces "uncontrollable irritability and violent rages, which in most advanced forms cause assault and murder." He continues: "Amnesia often occurs, and the mania is frequently so acute that the heavy smoker becomes temporarily insane. Most authori-

---

[1] For general discussions of marihuana see: Robert P. Walton, *Marihuana: America's New Drug Problem* (Philadelphia: Lippincott, 1938), and Norman Taylor, *Flight from Reality* (New York: Duell, Sloan and Pearce, 1949).

[2] From observations and interviews with Jamaicans by the writer during a visit to that island.

ties agree that permanent insanity can result from continual over-indulgence." Marihuana has had no noticeable effect in increasing the population of our mental institutions and whatever crimes of violence it may instigate are as nothing when compared to those that are linked with the use of alcohol.

Norman Taylor notes that the hemp plant, called *Cannabis sativa* by Linnaeus in the eighteenth century, probably originated in Central Asia or in China, where it was described in a book on pharmacy written by one Shen Nung nearly three thousand years before the birth of Christ.[3] The euphoric potential of the resinous female plant was known then and troubled Chinese moralists, who called it the "Liberator of Sin." Nung, however, recommended the medicine from this plant for "female weakness, gout, rheumatism, malaria, beri-beri, constipation and absent-mindedness." From China the use of hemp spread westward to India, to the Middle East, and along both sides of the Mediterranean, and ultimately reached Europe and the Western hemisphere. Nowhere has its use been eradicated, even after thousands of years of effort in some instances. Recent publications of the United Nations comment on the apparent continued spread of the practice.

The evil reputation of hemp was enhanced when, during the eleventh century, it became linked with a cult headed by one Hasan which initiated a new political tactic of secret assassination to cleanse the Moslem world of false prophets. Hasan's full name was Hashishin and he was called the Old Man of the Mountain. The term *hashish* and *assassin* are linked with the name of Hasan and his cult.

USE BY LOWER CLASSES

It is possible that the bad reputation of marihuana and other forms of this drug reflects in part the bias of upper classes against an indulgence of the lower strata. Since hemp grows luxuriantly without cultivation in many parts of the world, it is available to many of its devotees at extremely low cost—in India, for example, at about one-twentieth the price of good quality whiskey in 1894, when the English carried out an extensive inquiry into the subject.[4] Denunciations of the weed come characteristically from persons of those classes which prefer whiskey, rum, gin, and other alcoholic beverages and who do not themselves use marihuana. Such persons, overlooking the well-known effects of alcohol, commonly deplore the effects of hemp upon the lower classes and often believe that it produces murder, rape, violence, and insanity.

Despite the prevalence of these beliefs among the drinkers of rum and whiskey and the upper classes generally, impartial investigations invariably have shown no such results. The moderate use of hemp, according to the Indian Hemp Drug Commission in 1894, does not produce significant mental or moral injuries, does not lead to disease, nor does it necessarily or even usually lead to excess any more than alcohol does. Excess, the Commission said, is confined to the idle and dissipated.[5] Many years later in New York City similar conclusions were stated on the basis of experimental study and from an examination of violent crimes committed in that city over a period of years.[6]

In Jamaica, where the lower classes regard the drug with favor, persons of high social status commonly assert that ganja is a potent cause of much of the personal violence which is relatively frequent there among the working classes. This is

---

[3] N. Taylor, *Flight from Reality*, p. 27.

[4] *Report of the Indian Hemp Drug Commission* (7 vols.; Simla, Inida, 1894), cited by N. Taylor, *Flight from Reality*, p. 34.

[5] N. Taylor, *Flight from Reality*, pp. 34-35.

[6] *The Marihuana Problem in the City of New York: Sociological, Medical, Psychological and Pharmacological Studies* by the Mayor's Committee on Marihuana, George B. Wallace, Chairman (Lancaster, Pa.: Jaques Cattell Press, 1945).

staunchly denied by the ganja users, who contend that the effects are usually in the opposite direction but admit that ganja may bring out the evil in some persons who are already evil. Police examination of violent crimes in Jamaica suggest that ganja has little connection with them and that they arise rather from sexual jealousy and the highly informal manner in which sexual matters are arranged on that island among the simpler people of the lower classes.

MARIHUANA AND ALCOHOL

In general, virtually all of the charges that are made against marihuana tend to shrink or dissolve entirely when they are closely examined by impartial investigators. The present tendency of the rank-and-file policeman, despite the enormous penalties attached to handling marihuana, is to regard it as a minor problem hardly deserving serious attention except for those who handle the weed in large amounts for mercenary purposes or who promote its use among the uninitiated.

Ironically, the accusations that are leveled at marihuana are all applicable to alcohol, as has been demonstrated by innumerable investigations. These studies indicate that much murder, rape, and homicide is committed by persons under the influence. The special psychoses and ailments of alcoholics are numerous and well delineated in countless scientific and literary productions. The menace of the drinking driver of automobiles is well understood by all and is more or less accepted as one of the inevitable hazards of life in the modern world. It is well known, too, that the manufacturers of alcoholic beverages advertise their products and seek to enlarge their markets and that the use of alcohol spreads from those who already have the practice to those who do not. Why, then, so much excitement about marihuana? It is said that marihuana sometimes causes girls and women to lose their virtue and innocence, but the role of alcohol in this respect is infinitely more important. It seems inconsistent, therefore, that while the decision to drink or not to drink is viewed as a personal moral decision, the use of marihuana should be viewed as a heinous crime subject to long prison sentences.

Among those who have never used hemp or seen it used by others the belief is often found that marihuana acts as a sexual stimulant or aphrodisiac. Actually its effects, like those of opiates, are in exactly the opposite direction, tending to cause the user to lose interest in the opposite sex. Users more frequently than not report the absence of ideas of sex or say that Venus herself could not tempt them when they are under the influence of this drug.

THE EFFECTS OF ANTI-MARIHUANA LEGISLATION

In 1937 the Congress passed a Marihuana Tax Act, modeled after the Harrison Act. It was designed to curb the use of marihuana by the use of the federal police power, and like the Harrison Act imposed penalties upon both buyers and sellers. This Act was the result of a publicity campaign staged by the Federal Bureau of Narcotics under Mr. Anslinger's direction and leadership. The bill was passed with little discussion after brief hearings on the ground that marihuana was a highly dangerous drug inciting its users to commit crimes of violence and often leading to insanity.[7]

The beliefs concerning marihuana which led to this legislation may be represented in a pure and extreme form by turning to the writing of a hyperactive reformer and

---

[7] See *Taxation of Marihuana:* Hearings before the Committee on Ways and Means, U.S. House of Representatives, 75th Cong., 1st sess., April and May, 1937 (hereafter called *House Marihuana Hearings, 1937*); and *Taxation of Marihuana:* Hearings before a Subcommittee of the Committee on Finance, U.S. Senate, 75th Cong., 1st sess., on H.R. 6906 (hereafter called *Senate Marihuana Hearings, 1937*).

alarmist of the period, Earle Albert Rowell.[8] He claimed in 1939 that he had spent fourteen years campaigning against this weed, delivering more than four thousand lectures in forty states and personally pulling up and destroying many flourishing hemp fields. Mr. Rowell's zealous opposition to marihuana was only slightly less intense than his disapproval of alcohol and tobacco. The use of tobacco, he correctly observed, invariably precedes the smoking of the deadly reefer. Mr. Rowell came into disfavor with the Bureau of Narcotics around 1938 and this agency spent considerable energy and manpower in an attempt to silence and discredit him. This may have been because of Mr. Rowell's view that opiate addiction is a disease or perhaps because of his repeated allegations that the police were not sufficiently diligent in destroying marihuana.

Mr. Rowell summarized the effects of marihuana as follows:

We know that marihuana—
1. Destroys will power, making a jellyfish of the user. He cannot say no.
2. Eliminates the line between right and wrong, and substitutes one's own warped desires or the base suggestions of others as the standard of right.
3. Above all, causes crime; fills the victim with an irrepressible urge to violence.
4. Incites to revolting immoralities, including rape and murder.
5. Causes many accidents both industrial and automobile.
6. Ruins careers forever.
7. Causes insanity as its specialty.
8. *Either in self-defense or as a means of revenue, users make smokers of others, thus perpetuating evil.* [Italics in original.] [9]

In 1939 when Rowell published his book, marihuana was regarded as a relatively new drug menace in the United States. Mr. Rowell thought that he had already detected an increase of the population of mental hospitals because of it:

Asylums and mental hospitals in this country are beginning to see and feel the influence of marihuana, and are awaking to its deleterious effects on the brain. As we traveled through the various states, superintendents of these institutions told us of cases of insanity resulting from marihuana.[10]

"The baleful mental effects of marihuana," he said, "begin soon after the first reefer is smoked. . . ." [11]

When Mr. Anslinger appeared before the Senate subcommittee which was investigating the illicit drug traffic in 1955 under the guidance of Senator Price Daniel, there were only a few offhand discussions of marihuana. Mr. Anslinger observed that the Bureau in its national survey was "trying to keep away from the marihuana addict, because he is not a true addict." The real problem, he said, was the heroin addict. Senator Daniel thereupon remarked:

"Now, do I understand it from you that, while we are discussing marihuana, the real danger there is that the use of marihuana leads many people eventually to the use of heroin, and the drugs that do cause complete addiction; is that true?" [12]

Mr. Anslinger agreed:

"That is the great problem and our great concern about the use of marihuana, that eventually if used over a long period, it does lead to heroin addiction." [13]

Senators Welker and Daniel pursued the subject, and Mr. Anslinger, when prompted, agreed that marihuana was dangerous. Senator Welker finally asked this question:

---

[8] Earle Albert Rowell and Robert Rowell, *On the Trail of Marihuana, the Weed of Madness* (Mountain View, Cal.: Pacific Press Publishing Association, 1939). See also Earle Albert Rowell, *Dope: Adventures of David Dare* (Nashville, Tenn.: Southern Publishing Association, 1937).

[9] E. A. Rowell and R. Rowell, *On the Trail of Marihuana*, p. 33.

[10] *Ibid.*, p. 51.
[11] *Ibid.*
[12] *Daniel Subcommittee Hearings*, Part 5, 1955, p. 16.
[13] *Ibid.*

"Is it or is it not a fact that the marihuana user has been responsible for many of our most sadistic, terrible crimes in this nation, such as sex slayings, sadistic slayings, and matters of that kind?"

Mr. Anslinger hedged:

"There have been instances of that, Senator. We have had some rather tragic occurrences by users of marihuana. It does not follow that all crime can be traced to marihuana. There have been many brutal crimes traced to marihuana, but I would not say that it is a controlling factor in the commission of crimes." [14]

Eighteen years earlier, in 1937, the year in which the federal antimarihuana law was passed, Mr. Anslinger had presented a very different picture of marihuana. Prior to 1937 Mr. Anslinger and the Bureau of Narcotics had spearheaded a propaganda campaign against marihuana on the ground that it produced an immense amount of violent crime such as rape, mayhem, and murder, and that many traffic accidents could be attributed to it. During the 1937 hearings before a House subcommittee, Representative John Dingell of Michigan asked Mr. Anslinger: "I am just wondering whether the marihuana addict graduates into a heroin, an opium, or a cocaine user."

Mr. Anslinger replied: "No sir; I have not heard of a case of that kind. I think it is an entirely different class. The marihuana addict does not go in that direction." [15]

A few months later in the same year, before a Senate subcommittee which was considering the antimarihuana law which the Bureau of Narcotics had asked for Mr. Anslinger commented: "There is an entirely new class of people using marihuana. The opium user is around 35 to 40 years old. These users are 20 years old and know nothing of heroin or morphine." [16]

The theme stated by the Commissioner of Narcotics in 1955, that the main threat in marihuana is that it leads to the use of heroin, is now ordinarily cited as the principal justification for applying to it the same severe penalties that are applied in the case of heroin. Reformer Rowell in 1939 was more logical and consistent than either the Senators or the Commissioner when he emphasized that cigarette smoking invariably preceded reefer smoking. Mr. Rowell told of a shrewd gangster whom he engaged in what now appears as a prophetic discussion of the prospects of the dope industry.[17]

The gangster remarked: "Marihuana is the coming thing."

"But," I protested in surprise, "marihuana is not a habit-forming drug like morphine or heroin; and besides, it's too cheap to bother with."

He laughed. "You don't understand. Laws are being passed now by various states against it, and soon Uncle Sam will put a ban on it. The price will then go up, and that will make it profitable for us to handle."

The gangster, according to Mr. Rowell, then commented on the shrewd manner in which the tobacco companies had popularized cigarettes among the soldiers of the First World War and on the enormous increase in cigarette consumption by young persons. He grew eloquent: "Every cigarette smoker is a prospect for the dope ring via the marihuana road. Millions of boys and girls now smoke. Think of the unlimited new market!"

Mr. Rowell got the idea and commented as follows to his readers: "Slowly, insidiously, for over three hundred years, Lady Nicotine was setting the stage for a grand climax. The long years of tobacco using were but an introduction and training for marihuana use. Tobacco, which was first smoked in a pipe, then as a cigar, and at last as a cigarette, demanded more and more of itself until its supposed pleasures palled, and some of the tobacco victims looked about for something stronger. Tobacco was no longer potent enough."

---

[14] *Ibid.*, p. 18.
[15] *House Marihuana Hearings, 1937*, p. 24.
[16] *Senate Marihuana Hearings, 1937*, pp. 14–15.
[17] E. A. Rowell and R. Rowell, *On the Trail of Marihuana*, pp. 69–74.

Mr. Rowell was not optimistic about the future: "Marihuana will continue to be a problem for both police and educators, because it is so easy to grow, to manufacture, and to peddle, and is such a quick source of easy money. The plant can be grown anywhere; it can be harvested secretly, prepared in twenty-four years without a penny of investment for equipment; and every cigarette user is a prospect. As our laws are enforced and the weed becomes scarcer and the price rises, organized crime will step in and establish a monopoly."[18]

While Mr. Rowell, in the manner of reforming alarmists, exaggerated the evil with which he was preoccupied, the above appraisal of the effects of the Marihuana Tax Act has been reasonably well borne out by subsequent events. Certainly it was a more realistic assessment of the law's effects than any that were made by the legislators who passed the bill or by the officials who promoted it. Mr. Rowell was also completely right in pointing out that virtually every marihuana smoker graduated to this practice from cigarette smoking. His gangster informant was correct in his calculation that state and federal laws prohibiting marihuana would make the weed more expensive and more profitable for peddlers to handle, and also correctly foresaw that with the same merchants handling both marihuana and heroin it would become a simple matter for marihuana users to switch from the less to the more dangerous drug, as they have done.

In the United States during the nineteenth century, and the early decades of the twentieth, addiction to opiates frequently developed from the abuse of alcohol. This still occurs to some extent and is frequently reported from other parts of the world, for morphine provides a potent means of relieving the alcoholic hangover. An American doctor once advocated as a cure of alcoholism that alcohol addicts be deliberately addicted to morphine, arguing with considerable plausibility that of the two habits the latter was obviously the lesser evil.[19] Moreover, he practiced what he preached and recommended his technique with considerable enthusiasm for use by others.

The truth of the matter, of course, is that very few cigarette smokers go on to marihuana, very few marihuana users go on to heroin, and very few alcohol users graduate to the use of heroin. Since some barbiturate and amphetamine users progress to heroin it should be added that it is also only a very small proportion who do. If all of these substances were to be prohibited because they are sometimes involved in the progression toward heroin addiction there is little doubt that the illicit traffic in marihuana and heroin would be expanded to include the other offending substances and that the movement from less to more serious habits would be greatly facilitated.

No one, of course, recommends the use of marihuana nor does anyone deny that there are evil effects and consequences associated with using it. The fact that the use of marihuana is outlawed, for example, means that it is often obtained through association with unsavory types, often used in an underworld environment, and the user takes the risk of criminal prosecution. It is also undeniable that marihuana intoxication may sometimes lead to automobile accidents and to irresponsible or criminal acts. The controversy with respect to marihuana is solely concerning the relative prevalence or frequency of such results in comparison to similar consequences following from the use of alcoholic beverages. All empirical investigations indicate that alcohol constitutes a far greater social danger than does marihuana.

---

[18] *Ibid.*, pp. 88–89.

[19] J. R. Black, "Advantages of Substituting the Morphia Habit for the Incurably Alcoholic," *Cincinnati Lancet-Clinic*, XXII, n.s. (1889), Part I, 537–41.

MAYOR LAGUARDIA'S COMMITTEE ON MARIHUANA

Mayor LaGuardia's Committee on Marihuana, on the basis of a close examination of the matter in New York City, stressed the relative triviality of the effects of marihuana use in a report published in 1945.[20] In the July 1943 issue of the *Military Surgeon,* the editor, Colonel J. M. Phalen, commented as follows in an editorial on "The Marihuana Bugaboo":

> The smoking of the leaves, flowers and seeds of *Cannabis sativa* is no more harmful than the smoking of tobacco or mullein or sumac leaves. ... The legislation in relation to marihuana was ill-advised ... it branded as a menace and a crime a matter of trivial importance. ... It is hoped that no witch hunt will be instituted in the military service over a problem that does not exist.[21]

Similar statements have been made by many other competent investigators and observers.

On the other hand, as has been pointed out, a sharply divergent view has been presented by law enforcement officials, particularly by the Federal Bureau of Narcotics, and also by many individual writers. The sharp divergence of views among the scientifically oriented evidently depends upon the manner in which the research is done. Investigators who rely on the opinions of high echelon officials, who have no direct acquaintance with the use of marihuana and who base their opinions on ancedotes rather than actual statistical data, usually reach the conclusion that marihuana is a highly dangerous drug which produces much violent crime and insanity. These conclusions, as we have suggested, may be a reflection of upper-class hostility toward an unfamiliar lower-class indulgence. More critical and skeptical investigators, who look for basic statistical evidence, invariably fail to find it and end up writing debunking articles for which they are roundly abused by the moralists.

It is often felt that, even if the dangers of marihuana are exaggerated, these exaggerations and misstatements should be allowed to stand so that they may frighten adolescents away from the drug. The implication that adolescents are influenced to any appreciable degree by articles appearing in scientific journals is probably absurd. Those who use marihuana probably come to do so on the basis of personal associations and direct observations of their own.

The deliberate circulation of false information is self-defeating in that the adventurous, experimentally inclined youth can quickly discover for himself, by trying the weed or talking to those who have smoked it, that much of the officially circulated view is false. He is then prepared to believe that everything he has been told about narcotics is equally wrong.

When Mayor LaGuardia's Committee on Marihuana made its report, it was strongly attacked by those committed to a belief in the marihuana menace. The *Journal of the American Medical Association* in 1943 published a letter from Mr. Anslinger in which he criticized an article by Drs. Allentuck and Bowman on findings derived from the New York study in which they had participated.[22] There were rumors that the New York marihuana study was to be suppressed, but after considerable delay, it was ultimately released in 1945. On April 28, 1945, the *Journal of the American Medical Association* editorially assailed the report, using language and arguments of a type not ordinarily found in learned journals:

> For many years medical scientists have considered cannabis a dangerous drug. Nevertheless, a book called "Marihuana Problems" by the New York City Mayor's Committee on Marihuana submits an analysis by seventeen doctors of tests on 77 prisoners and, on this narrow and thoroughly unscientific foundation, draws

---

[20] *The Marihuana Problem in the City of New York.*
[21] Cited by N. Taylor, *Flight from Reality,* p. 36.
[22] *J.A.M.A.,* 121, No. 3 (Jan. 16, 1943), 212–13.

sweeping and inadequate conclusions which minimize the harmfulness of marihuana. Already the book has done harm. One investigator has described some tearful parents who brought their 16 year old son to a physician after he had been detected in the act of smoking marihuana. A noticeable mental deterioration had been evident for some time even to their lay minds. The boy said he had read an account of the LaGuardia Committee report and that this was his justification for using marihuana. He read in *Down Beat,* a musical journal, an analysis of this report under the caption "Light Up, Gates, Report Finds Tea a Good Kick."

A criminal lawyer for marihuana drug peddlers has already used the LaGuardia report as a basis to have defendants set free by the court. . . .

The book states unqualifiedly to the public that the use of this narcotic does not lead to physical, mental or moral degeneration and that permanent deleterious effects from its continued use were not observed on 77 prisoners. This statement has already done great damage to the cause of law enforcement. Public officials will do well to disregard this unscientific, uncrucial study, and continue to regard marihuana as a menace wherever it is purveyed.[23]

Despite the fact that this editorial continues to be cited and reproduced to discredit the New York study, the conclusions of the report enjoy considerable status and are undoubtedly far closer to the realities of the situation than is the view represented by the A.M.A. editorial. Indeed, if one judges the law enforcement agencies by their actions rather than their words, it appears that even the police, to a considerable extent, have swung over to the viewpoint of the Mayor's Committee.

MARIHUANA ARRESTS

After 1951 the budget and field force of the Federal Bureau of Narcotics were substantially enlarged. Nevertheless, the number of marihuana arrests has steadily declined and by 1960 it was close to the vanishing point, with only 169 such cases.

In previous years the numbers of federal marihuana violations were reported as follows: [24]

1952	1,288
1954	508
1956	403
1958	179

Of the 169 federal marihuana violations reported in 1960, 88 occurred in California, 16 in Maryland, and 13 in Kentucky. No other state had as many as ten, and no violations were reported from 28 states. We have already noted that the Bureau does not bother to count marihuana users in its national survey of addiction and does not regard marihuana as an addicting drug. The above figures on enforcement suggest that, at the federal level at least, the marihuana laws are being largely ignored since it is not claimed that the use of marihuana is diminishing.

Statistics on marihuana prosecutions as such are extremely difficult to obtain and data that are available are very unreliable and incomplete. The Federal Narcotics Bureau presented to the Daniel Subcommittee a summary of marihuana prosecutions for the year 1954, giving both federal and nonfederal cases. It is not claimed that the latter are complete; they are merely figures from some of the main cities in the indicated states (Table I).

From this table it will be seen that 3,263 of the total of 3,918 arrests were made in the six states of California, Texas, Illinois, Michigan, New York, and Louisiana. These states are, in one way or another, centers of the marihuana traffic. High arrest rates in California, Texas, and Louisiana no doubt arise from the fact that considerable quantities of marihuana are smuggled into the country there from Mexico and the Caribbean area. The rates in Illinois,

---

[23] *J.A.M.A.*, 127, No. 17 (April 28, 1945), 1129.

[24] From the annual reports of the Bureau of Narcotics for the years indicated. In 1962 the number of marihuana cases was 242. (*Traffic in Opium and Other Dangerous Drugs, 1962,* p. 62.)

Table I. *Marihuana Arrests—Federal and Local by States—1954*[25]

State	Arrests Federal	Arrests Local	State	Arrests Federal	Arrests Local
Alabama	2	6	New Hampshire	0	0
Arizona	25	4	New Jersey	5	26
Arkansas	2	0	New Mexico	23	10
California	51	1,101	New York	5	407
Colorado	28	1	North Carolina	0	0
Connecticut	2	6	North Dakota	0	0
Delaware	0	1	Ohio	25	23
District of Columbia	3	17	Oklahoma	2	13
			Oregon	1	8
Florida	4	30	Pennsylvania	3	50
Georgia	4	1	Rhode Island	0	0
Idaho	0	2	South Carolina	4	0
Illinois	13	327	South Dakota	0	0
Indiana	0	14	Tennessee	11	1
Iowa	0	8	Texas	325	612
Kansas	2	0	Utah	4	0
Kentucky	39	8	Vermont	0	0
Louisiana	17	105	Virginia	0	1
Maine	0	0	Washington	22	10
Maryland	2	30	West Virginia	0	0
Massachusetts	5	1	Wisconsin	0	47
Michigan	30	270	Wyoming	4	0
Minnesota	0	5	Alaska	5	0
Mississippi	0	1	Hawaii	14	23
Missouri	9	15	Totals	713	3,205
Montana	0	6			
Nebraska	1	13			
Nevada	16	2	Grand Total		3,918

Michigan, and New York reflect mainly police activity in the three large cities of Detroit, Chicago, and New York, all of them narcotics distribution centers. Heroin arrests are also highest in the states of California, New York, Illinois, and Michigan, while Texas and Louisiana are farther down on the list.

The penalty provisions applicable to marihuana users under state and federal law are about the same as those applied to heroin users. These penalties are entirely disproportionate to the seriousness of the offending behavior and lead to gross injustice and undesirable social consequences. For example, it is well known that many jazz musicians and other generally inoffensive persons use or have used marihuana.

To send these persons to jail is absurd and harmful and serves no conceivable useful purpose. The moderate or occasional marihuana user is not a significant social menace. Jails and prisons, chronically overcrowded, should be used for those who present a genuine threat to life and property. The absurdity is compounded when an occasional judge, ignorant of the nature of marihuana, sends a marihuana user to prison to cure him of his nonexistent addiction. The writer was once in court when a middle-aged Negro defendant appeared before the judge charged with having used

[25] *Daniel Subcommittee Hearings*, 1955, pp. 267–71, exhibit 7. Note the unexplained discrepancy between the federal total given here and that of the preceding citation.

and had in his possession one marihuana cigarette during the noon hour at the place where he had worked for a number of years. This man had no previous criminal record and this fact was stated before the court. Nevertheless, a two-year sentence was imposed to "dry up his habit."

The President's Advisory Commission which reported on narcotic and drug abuse in 1963 took cognizance of the relatively trivial nature of the marihuana evil by suggesting that all mandatory sentences be eliminated for crimes involving it and that judges be granted full discretionary power in dealing with offenders.[26] These suggestions are excessively timid and not entirely logical, for there is no good reason why a mere user of marihuana should be subjected to a jail sentence at all. The marihuana user probably ought to be dealt with by the law along the same lines that are used with persons who drink alcohol.

If it is deemed in the public interest to punish smokers of marihuana, such punishments should ordinarily consist of fines only, up to some maximum of perhaps $500.00, depending upon the offense and the defendant's ability to pay. These fines might be scaled down or eliminated entirely for persons who provided information concerning their source of supply. Police efforts should be focused primarily on the traffic rather than on the user. Persons driving automobiles under the influence of the drug might be fined and deprived of their driving licenses for a period of time. Crimes which could be shown to the satisfaction of a court of law to be linked with the use of marihuana ought to be dealt with about the way that crimes arising from the use of alcohol are handled.

Laws such as this, with penalties of a reasonable nature, would probably be more effective than those now in effect because they would be more enforceable and more in accord with the nature of the problem being dealt with. They would have the effect of reducing the discrepancy that now exists between the laws as written and the laws as they are actually enforced. A more matter-of-fact and realistic handling of the marihuana problem would also probably reduce the aura of sensationalism which now surrounds the subject and diminish the illicit glamor which is now attached to the hemp plant.

It is argued by some that the marihuana industry should be brought under control by legalization, taxation, licensing, and other devices like those used to control alcohol—and to exploit it as a source of revenue. Advocates of this view might well argue that there should be no unfair discrimination among vices; that if the greater evil of alcohol use is legal, the lesser one of marihuana smoking should be so as well. Since the smoking of marihuana will undoubtedly continue regardless of legislation against it, it can also be argued that it would be better to accept the inevitable than to wage war for a lost cause.

In opposition to this extremely permissive position, the more conservative reformer can call attention to the fact that, outside of a few Asian and African countries, the use of this substance is everywhere disapproved of and subject to legal restrictions. It is possible that legal sanctions exercise some deterrent effect and that without them the use of this drug might spread even more rapidly and assume more virulent forms. Should the use of marihuana become anywhere nearly as widespread as that of alcohol it might be too late to talk of effective restrictions since the users would command too many votes. A legal marihuana or ganja industry which advertised its produce and sought to improve it through research and experimentation would be a distinct embarrassment to the nation as a whole as well as being a direct economic threat to the alcoholic beverage industries and possibly to the tobacco industry. A final and decisive argument seems to be that public opinion is not likely in

---

[26] *Final Report:* The President's Advisory Commission on Narcotic and Drug Abuse, p. 42.

the foreseeable future to accept indulgence in marihuana as an equivalent of, or substitute for, indulgence in alcohol.

The long history of the use of marihuana, the spread of the practice throughout the world in the face of determined and sometimes fanatical opposition, and the persistence of the practice once it is established —all suggest that the smoking of marihuana will continue in the United States for some time to come. The practical question seems to be one of minimizing and controlling the practice while avoiding the extreme tactics of prohibitionists. A comprehensive, impartial public inquiry into the matter, based on the assumption that marihuana is *not* the same as heroin, might help to bring about a more sober and rational approach to an indulgence which merits some concern but which is far less serious than is presently suggested by the harsh inflexibility of current laws.

63. A HIERARCHY OF DRUG USERS

ALAN G. SUTTER

PRESTIGE HIERARCHY: DRUG USER TYPES

PRESTIGE IN THE HIERARCHY OF A DOPE FIEND's world is allocated by the size of a person's habit and his success as a hustler. One who is able to carry on a habit as a luxury without letting it interfere with his hustling schemes, will be the "Father" to all other dope fiends on the "set." All dope fiends dream of having a lifetime supply of heroin. All hustlers dream of living a life of luxury where they can openly display their wealth and occupational success. A "righteous" hustler" who is at the same time a "righteous dope fiend," combines the attributes of Marx's entrepreneur and Veblen's pecuniary man who seeks a Utopian existence: "There is hope with dope in the land of Nod."

The dope fiend does not "trip" in the same sense as other types of drug users "trip." By observing how other drugs effect the social demeanor and hustling style of other people, the dope fiend concludes that opiate use is top; other drug users must be content with a less expensive chemical and a lower class existence. He "downgrades" all other "freaks" on the drug scene who will never "know where it's at," who merely clutter up the hustling scene, and create havoc by attracting the police. The only drug user respected by a righteous dope fiend is a "weed head" who can "maintain his cool" and will "hold his mug" (not turn informer).

The introduction of new amphetamine compounds on the streets during the past five years [1] has changed the character of the hustling world, and has altered the pattern of drug use among adolescents; however, the "righteous dope fiend" is hardly impressed by any other drug but heroin. While a number of people being released from prisons are experimenting with "crystals" (methedrine), few dope fiends are converted to the "crystal trip." Opiate users will only shoot crystal when they want to "speed-ball" the heroin effect by mixing it with an amphetamine compound, when they are forced to "clean up" before taking a Nalline test while on parole, or when their habit gets beyond their ability to support and it is necessary to "kick" before starting "fresh." The same tendency is apparent in the case of pills. Only while on parole, or when trying to

▶SOURCE: "The Righteous Dope Fiend," Issues in Criminology (Fall, 1966), 2:2:200–213. Reprinted by permission.

[1] See: J. W. Rawlin, "'Street Level' Abusage of Amphetamines," *A presentation to the Conferees Attending the First National Institute on Amphetamine Abuse at Southern Illinois University*, February 21–25, 1966; S. Fiddle, "Circles Beyond the Circumference: Some Hunches about Amphetamine and Addiction," *A Presentation to the Conferees Attending the First National Institute on Amphetamine Abuse at Southern Illinois University*, February 21–25, 1966

"kick the opiate habit will a righteous dope fiend use drugs in rotation by interspersing opiate and non-opiate drugs. The reason for this behavior does not simply lie in the addict's personality disposition. Once a person has experienced "being hooked," only morphine-like agents will "fix" him or satisfy his "craving." The sharp contrast between the misery of withdrawal symptoms and the ease of eliminating them with a "fix" makes the dope fiend generalize his conception of the opiates and attribute magical power to them. Thus, dope fiends claim that "crystal is much weaker" than heroin. Another reason why dope fiends will not use other drugs regularly lies in the image they have of other types of users. The regular use of "crystal," "pills" or "acid" (LSD-25) will transform the identity of a righteous dope fiend into one of a "freak." Return to or beginning a regular pattern of marijuana use indicates a regression to childhood behavior. And the practice of rotating the use of different drugs when heroin is available carries the most severe stigma of a "garbage junkie" who cannot afford any habit.

THE "CRYSTAL FREAK"

Anyone who regularly uses methedrine or other methamphetamines "for the trip," is a "crystal freak" in the eyes of a righteous dope fiend. This type excludes good hustlers who use crystal instrumentally for a particular scheme;[2] although, even these people are watched carefully for signs of erratic behavior and paranoia. The "crystal freak" will attend freak parties and go on a rapid journey into the space of his own mind. Because of the stimulating effect on the central nervous system, those who "trip behind crystal" are seen by dope fiends as "jitter bugs who like to hassle all the time," as "frantic nuts, jerking, twitching, talking a mile-a-minute with diarrhea." Because of such erratic behavior, a crystal user can be singled out easily in public places. He is therefore dangerous to have around when hustling. Similarly, the rapid flight of a crystal user's associations, and the intensity of his speech pattern leads the dope fiend to suspect that such a "freak" may "snitch" if pressure is put on him.

"Crystal freaks" have their own chemists and the illicit market intensified after the recent California law making it a felony to possess or sell "dangerous drugs." The drug is increasingly in demand by adolescent "players" and other "hustlers." There are also elements in the "crystal freak's" life which parallel the life of a dope fiend. The procedures of "fixing," the recent necessity to "score" from a "connection" on the illegal market, and the increasing amount of use by "righteous hustlers," ranks the drug second to heroin in the dope fiend's eyes. It is interesting to hear "crystal freaks" talk about their drug taking art in jargon originally coined in dope fiend circles:

> When I first fixed, I was scared to death of the spike see. But now you know I'm more intrigued by sticking the needle in my arm and going through the intricate things, watching the blood registrar, booting it, and triping on that than anything else. . . . If you cook it up it detracts from the effect. Just dissolve it in cold water and stir it into a jellitine substance until it dissolves. Then drop the cotton in it, draw it up and shoot it up . . . .

As was pointed out earlier, the practice of "playing with the needle" is frowned upon in dope fiend circles. Other crystal users report frequent episodes of paranoid thinking even after being off the drug. Most crystal "freaks" do not like heroin:

---

[2] There is evidence that the drug increases performance and delays fatigue-induced performance without serious adverse effects. R. B. Payne and G. T. Hauty, "The Effects of Experimentally Induced Attitudes Upon Task Performance," *Journal of Experimental Psychology*, 47:267–273, April, 1954. Also see: J. D. Griffiith, "Psychiatric Implications of Amphetamine Drug Use," *A Presentation to the Conferees Attending the First National Institute on Amphetamine Abuse At Southern Illinois University, February 21–25, 1966.*

... I never approached anyone with stuff. I don't like the high in the first place. I'm also afraid of stuff, won't associate with people who use it. Most of your hyps just have their own little trip anyway and I don't care much for it. ...

"THE WEED HEAD"

The next level on the "dope fiend's" stratification system is occupied by "the weed head." Although dope fiends "rank" the majority of weed heads as "young kids" who have little experience, a "righteous pot head" is respected for his *potential value*. For the most part there is very little association between "weed heads" and "dope fiends," except through family contacts, during casual parties, or when a "weed head" is dealing marijuana, pills, or heavy narcotics. "Weed heads" are notoriously "cool people" who "know what's happening on the set." As opposed to many adolescents who "get loaded on weed to be sociable," the "weed head" consciously seeks out marijuana, scores his own drugs, and may deal on a small-time basis for a "connection" who handles larger quantities.[3]

Through the eyes of a "weed head" the dope fiend appears to have "blown his cool." He is untrustworthy, "doesn't care about anything but his dope," "plays chicken shit with his friends," and specializes in "burning people." Thus, many "weed heads" are fearful of dope fiends unless they slowly establish a close relationship with a few good hustlers who happen to be "hooked." A "weed head" believes that morphine-like agents are for "fools" and "rowdy people" who "don't know what's happening." But a smart dope fiend will often jump at a chance to have a "weed head" deal narcotics for him in the role of a "runner." Dope fiends often view "weed heads" as "cool little dudes who can hold their mugs and ride the beef (accept legal responsibility) in case a bust goes down" (arrest). Also many dope fiends "get loaded on weed" periodically, especially if they have recently "kicked the habit."

... He (a particular 'weed head') gave me a half-can when I was sick man, helped a little bit but not much ... you got to respect this dude because someday he may have a connection when you need one in a minute. If you give him a bad time, someday this young kid may have stuff and he'll freeze on you. So you say 'well he's just another weed head,' and tell him to get the hell out, but tomorrow he may start dealing stuff and then where am I. I'm sick and he's put the freeze on ....

"THE PILL FREAK"

When a person begins to use pills on a repetitive and continuous basis,[4] he acquires the status of a "drug store hyp" or "pill freak" in the eyes of a righteous dope fiend. The "pill freak" is not able to hustle on a level par to the dope fiend, and he cannot afford to maintain a respectable habit. Although there is a full market structure for the illicit distribution of pills, a "pill freak" does not have to involve himself in the same world as a dope fiend. In fact, most "pill freaks" quickly withdraw from the hustling world out of fear. Some would rather burglarize a drug store than involve themselves with a dealer and other dope fiends. Most "pill freaks" will be exploited by dope fiends who can usually "con" them out of money and fail to return with their pills. As a result of being unable to hustle, the "croaker" or doctor is often the main source for a "pill freak's" supply, and people divert their conning ability into simulating bodily illnesses, depression, and severe headaches in order to "make the croaker." In the eyes of a righteous dope fiend, the pill user is somewhat pathetic when he involves himself in the games of stealing prescription pads, forging signatures, and making croakers.

---

[3] See: H. S. Becker, *Outsiders: Studies in the Sociology of Deviance*, New York, 1963, pp. 42–78.

[4] See: S. Fiddle, "'The Pills' and the Heroin Addict," Statement prepared for the Joint Legislative Committee on Health Insurance Plans, *Hearing on the Public Health Laws and Penal Laws to regulate the sale and possession of dangerous drugs* March 26, 1965.

Dope fiends are quick to make the distinction between those who abuse pills, or "pill freaks," and those who use pills *legitimately* for the purpose of increasing their hustling efficiency or for the purpose of kicking a long-run habit. The practice of mixing various amphetamine compounds with marijuana is perfectly legitimate. If one is casually enjoying himself by dropping a few pills, smoking a little "grass," and going about the business of hustling, a dope fiend hardly comments on this pervasive pattern of drug use. This type of pill user gains his status in dope fiend circles by his ability to "fake," "boost," burglarize, or "deal dope." But there are important features of this pattern which make even an instrumental pill user inferior to a righteous dope fiend.

The same suspicions of a person who hustles on "crystal" apply to those who use a variety of amphetamine compounds in pill form: loud and excessive talking, excitability, paranoia, and likelihood of turning "snitch." Those who use barbiturates and hypnotic drugs to deaden their fear when anticipating a violent crime, are looked upon with contempt.[5] "Thugs" have an inferior status to "hustlers," although they are used by hustlers. "Anyone can drop a roll of reds and play Al Capone man. That ain't where it's at." Finally, the "cornmeal mush freak," or "Perk freak," is a label applied to those who involve themselves in theft of percadon and codein pills to feed an opiate habit. "Cornmeal mush" refers to the arduous process of soaking percadon pills in water for a long time until the solution looks like cornmeal mush. A cotton is dropped into the solution and the drug is drawn up through a "spike" to be injected in the same way as other narcotics. "You know," thought one dope fiend, "I never could understand why those guys go to all that trouble to get something out of a drug store that they get hooked on, they pulling a burglary, get busted for possession and burglary; why don't they do something for straight cash and shoot real stuff?"

"THE ACID FREAK"

The response of many dope fiends to the recent influx of LSD use among high school and college students is rather interesting.[6] In the dope fiend's world, the only drug user who warrants the status of being a "head" is one who regularly "gets loaded" on marijuana, the "weed head." The type of user designated as an "acid head" around artistic, intellectual, and "hippie" circles is merely a euphemism for another "freak" drug user on the scene. In dope fiend circles, the LSD user is hardly acknowledged and very little is known about the drug or the people who use it. An older dope fiend noted that "acid people don't figure in much, don't know anybody who's even been on acid. We don't know much about them people. Hear about it and their weird trips, but I don't see nobody on it." A younger dope fiend commented that LSD users "were too much. The trip is too serious for me. I don't mess with them people man. I'm a dope fiend, I love that gow man." A righteous dope fiend does not embark on voyages of discovery through the depths of his own mind in the hope of returning a more authentic human being.[7] He feels the best when he does not feel. When he is "on the nod," he is temporarily suspended in oblivion.

"GARBAGE JUNKIES AND WINOS"

The lowest level of drug user through the eyes of a dope fiend is the "garbage junkie," who can only set up a "shooting

---

[5] See: H. A. Davidson, "Confessions of a Goof Ball Addict," *The American Journal of Psychiatry*, 120:8:750—756, Feb. 1964.

[6] J. Larner, "The College Drug Scene," *Atlantic Monthly*, 216:127-130, November, 1965, and R. Goldstein, *1 in 7: Drugs on Campus*, New York, 1966.

[7] See: D. Solomon, (ed.) *LSD: The Consciousness-expanding Drug*, New York, 1964; and R. Blum, *The Utopiates*, New York, 1964.

gallery" to make enough money to "fix." Dope fiends seldom carry around their "outfits" while running in the street, and a garbage junkie will rent a cheap hotel room and loan out four or five outfits in exchange for a few "drops" or used "cottons" from another man's "stuff?" The garbage junky will also use any substance which is available to him at the time. The range of substances used includes Caffeine, Winamite, Valo inhalers and Dristan, Vicks vapor rubs, pills, wine, etc. Whether a "wino" has less respect than a garbage junkie is mooted, but there is almost universal agreement among dope fiends that a "lush" is not much better than a "garbage junkie" in the general hierarchy of respectable drug users. One righteous dope fiend was known to have asked for "help" at a Synanon House, where he would be associating with some alcoholics and garbage junkies. The opinion of his clique was that he "hit rock bottom and copped out on his soul as a dope fiend."

PRESTIGE HIERARCHY: HUSTLERS ON THE SET

A "player" becomes a "hustler" when his "games" are converted into the polished "works" of a craftsman. Commitment to his action gradually shifts from "play" and preoccupation with the immediate present to "serious business" and preoccupation with a master crime scheme for the future. The changing criminal commitment is illustrated linguistically: A "player" runs down a variety of "games"; a "hustler" goes to "work" at specialized schemes for making money. Changes in the market structure for non-opiate drugs and coincident changes in the types of drug users on the hustling scene demands that the retreatist idea of drug involvement be radically altered. Furthermore, the notion that addicts are "snatch-and-grab junkies," "petty thieves and petty operators" who, status-wise, are at the bottom of the criminal population may apply to certain addicts but not to "righteous dope fiends." Dope fiends use the term "square" to indicate *addicts who are unaware of different hustles*, non-opiate users unable to support a respectable habit, and finally to indicate "conventional people who do not use drugs." (A rare breed when one considers the amount of alcohol consumed in the United States.) If a person has never been a "righteous hustler" as well as an addict, he can never make the claim to fame as a "righteous dope fiend."

Many people "get hooked" on opiates after they have become successful hustlers; others may increase their hustling skill after they recognize a *need* to hustle in order to maintain a respectable habit. Still others hustle well without using drugs. But the common notion that addicts are *forced* into crime to support a habit is overdrawn and far-fetched. It presumes that anyone with a habit can commit profitable crimes at will. I did speak with one addict who was "forced" into crime after he realized his addiction. He was arrested eight times inside of a two-year period and hardly had time to develop a habit. Being quite miserable, he referred to himself as a "freak dope fiend" who "didn't even fit in dope fiend circles." Righteous dope fiends appear more like respected professional men who boast of drinking a fifth of Scotch each day, not like bums who lay in the gutter drinking wine. To be sure, after a dope fiend has struggled in the "rat race" for many years, he may become a "snatch-and-grab junkie" or a "gutter-hyp," but the term *"hope to die dope fiend,"* not "righteous dope fiend," indicates the way some addicts come to terms with a miserable existence in the "rat race."

It is true that many dope fiends are arrested for petty crimes, but if a person himself makes five "stings" each day and has only two or three women who give him about forty dollars each day, within a month his profit will exceed that gained from a systematic robbery, and this type of hustling is considered small-time in the eyes of successful men. Furthermore, the risk of serving penitentiary time is reduced by one's hustling skill. Out of a number of dope fiends who were not on parole, two were "fixing" an average of two grams daily (one "spoon" selling at $40 to $60 depending on the quality of heroin). Another was temporarily abstaining while trying to develop a city-wide burglary operation. One "fixed" a $20 half-spoon daily while selling life and disability insurance to ghetto residents; a thirty-year-old woman fixed five spoons daily ($150) and claimed that her "old man" had a three-year-run behind a daily heroin consumption of fourteen grams of heroin. Out of a number of dope fiends who were under parole supervision, many were "snatch-and-grab" junkies trying to find a "slave" (legitimate employment), "fixing $10 balloons on weekends, and preventing themselves from "getting hooked" by "using crystal to come down off stuff," (interspersing heroin and methedrine to prevent tolerance and physical dependence).

Hustlers are ranked on a fixed hierarchy of prestige based on their "money-making power," ingenuity, and versatility. People who go after "straight cash," hold the top positions in the hierarchy. Those who deal heroin and crystal by the ounce, "mackmen" and "fakes" (short con men) rank highest. Till tappers and money burglars also demand respect. Those who go after property (boosters, merchandise burglars and fences) occupy the second level in the hierarchy. Game artists and gamblers rank third on the hustling scale; while strong arm robbers and thugs are not respected. Those who burglarize drug stores or operate shooting galleries aren't even discussed.

A good hustler knows from experience that "life is a racket" and "everyone has a front." Any man who laboriously works for a regular salary is not only a "fool" but a legitimate "vick" for a "sting," (victim to be exploited). All hustlers desire a life of conspicuous wealth, luxury, and leisure time. Visible evidence of a hustler's success is communicated by first showing no visible means of income. At the same time, the hustler will drive an expensive car, wear gold watches, diamond rings, alligator skin shoes, mohair and silk suits which are changed twice daily. He carries a large bank-roll of one-hundred dollar bills, and a bodyguard protects him. He is always alert for new techniques which can be incorporated into his working games. His preferable hustles are those schemes which yield the most cash profit and also carry the shortest jail sentences; however the "big time dope dealer" holds the top position in close competition with the "mackman" and "con artist." A successful hustler who owns a number of apartment buildings, may have two or three parties at his home each month. During such exclusive parties a variety of dugs are "served" to guests. A match box of marijuana and a role of pills for each guest is not uncommon.

GRADUAL FALL

One new initiate into the hustling world described a recent "hustlers ball" with great enthusiasm:

. . . You know I was the youngest one on the set. That was a cold thing (exceptionally good). . . . Get there and see what you can get out of it you know. Runnin them games down, trying to get them games from the fakes. People just kicked it around and cut up different dudes. Pool sharks, gamblers, boosters, dealers, all together man. It was out a sight, out a sight. They were talking about cocaine and morphine, triping yeah. . . . This is what's happening man . . . .

Some hustlers overplay their role by attempting to shoot heroin as a luxury, but even after "getting hooked," (which they will not admit to anyone for a long time) confidence in their ability to make money and support a habit is rarely shaken. However, there is a consensus among dope fiends that if a person lets his women get hooked also, he will eventually "start going down." One young hustler reported the experience of an intimate friend:

... This big mack I was taking care of, dressing you know. (The youth was a booster who fenced his merchandise with a particular mackman who needed 'working clothes' for himself and his women). He had a gang of holes, (women) a gang of holes. And you know what man? He lost everything man. His apartment buildings, his car, and all his holes. He was down see and it hurt me to see him like that man. All he could do was sit there and talk that stuff. He'd say, 'I'm a dope fiend, and she's a dope fiend, and they all dope fiends and we ain't doin nothin but making a little change to support our habit, man. Don't get in that bag man, don't get in that bag.' But it was too late. I told him it was too late. I'm in that bag deep . . . .

The above "player" was convinced that he would be on the street for years without "going down." When a hustler begins to fall, the last thing he neglects will be his car payments, and only when he begins to pawn his clothes does he think about actually "going to work" himself. Early in the morning, dope fiends gather in selected areas of the city in order to pick up hustling partners for the day. The big time hustler may appear on the scene and ask, "Hey, anybody goin to work today?" Others glance at him with amusement, "Yeah, hey what are you doin man? I didn't know you was out there gamin." "Well, you know how it is," he replies with a slight feeling of embarrassment. He now has to make his own money. If he stops dealing and loses a few of his "bitches," "playing con" will be his next hustle, not "boosting"; for he doesn't want too many people knowing that he is "running." When he begins hustling every day, the risk of arrest is greatly increased, invariably he "gets a case." Almost immediately after "kicking the habit" in a county jail, the hustler begins planning how he will regain his position on the set and learn how to control a healthy habit without letting his "bitches" get hooked.

THE BIG-TIME DOPE DEALER

Dealing heavy narcotics is an extremely lucrative enterprise and a preferred activity among hustlers. The "big-time dope dealer" will buy "stuff" in pound units ($3,500 to $4,000/pound) from "runners" who bring heroin to the Bay Area from Los Angeles. The heroin is "cut" with milk sugar at approximately two to six percent pure heroin and distributed to other dealers at $250 per ounce. The term "pusher" is seldom, if ever, used in dope fiend circles. The term is most often used by early adolescent drug users and scholars who probably pick the term up from newspaper accounts, T.V. and law enforcement personnel. Anyone who sells dope is a *dealer;* the level of traffic in which he operates is determined by the amount of dope handled. Thus, a "piece man" deals in ounces to a "spoon man" who cuts the ounces and deals to a "bag man," who in turn may cut the spoons into $10 balloons ($1/4$ to $1/2$ gram). The majority of dope fiends on the street deal in "big bags" or spoons containing two grams of heroin at a cost of $40 to $60 depending on the percentage of pure heroin. If a dope fiend is temporarily "down" and needs an immediate "fix" he will often pitch in his money with three or four other "hyps" in order to purchase a "spoon" which is later portioned out and "fixed" in a shooting gallery, hotel room, or rooming house. A dealer may, in the course of a year, slide up and down the scale from pieces to small bags, but the prestige rests with the "piece man":

. . . Well, for a while I was up there. Had three dudes dealing for me; that' all I was concerned with. They each had guys running for them. I was making good bread with about three hundred a day coming in from stuff, but then I starting using it like a hog when I met my old lady and most of the money went in both our arms. . . .

The "stuff man" seldom deals anything but heroin and crystal; although at lower levels of traffic, dope fiends may act in the capacity of a "connector" to other drug markets, especially marijuana. A dope fiend moves so fast in the street that he may pass several people looking for "weed."

In such cases he may take their money, score a quarter pound for a friend, bring back his weed, and use the extra money to buy "stuff" for his habit. For the most part however, dope fiends do not make it a practice to handle marijuana; it's bulk is too large, the profit is relatively small compared to "stuff," the prison sentence is almost the same if arrested.

THE MACKMAN

Few people are qualified to become "mackmen," although nearly all young "players," aspire to reach the position of a "righteous pimp." The image of a passive, parasitic individual who lives off a few down and out prostitutes hardly depicts the time consuming, dangerous, and competitive enterprise of a successful pimp. Typical activities of a "mack" includes a number of different hustles. He may have a few "hookers" (prostitutes) in the street "turning tricks" and taking care of customers. Older women in their late thirties, young college girls, school teachers, secretaries, post office employees, often desire sexual gratification from a superior male. If the "mackman" satisfies this demand, he will share the woman's monthly salary in the fashion of a male prostitute. Some "mackmen" have three or four children out of wedlock from different women who often receive county welfare assistance. "Mother's day" is twice a month, and the "mack" makes his rounds by picking up the welfare checks from his "bitches." Good pimps also have women "boosting" merchandise for them. A skillful female booster can be a gold mine.

The "mackman" faces a number of problems and the strain involved in his action often requires that he go for days without sleep. Other aspiring pimps are continuously trying to "steal his holes," take merchandise from his "boosters," and make love to his working women. His life is frequently in danger of being "snuffed" by a jealous husband or another hustler.

Thus, few have the skill to reach higher than the position of a "popcorn pimp."

... Around 1960 this dude came here from New York and had two skinny holes, and all they could do was make popcorn money see, and the dude's name was Willie, and he was supposed to be a Pimp. You know the kind who'd walk around giving everybody the high sign: 'I'm a pimp,' you know. Everybody says, 'Yeah Willie you're cool man,' shining him on. He was a trip man. From then on, everybody that's a pimp that ain't a pimp that tries to be a pimp, that's a Willie popcorn. I'm a Willie popcorn with three lously holes.

It is difficult to describe the power of a "mackman's conversation, and his easiest mark is a "square broad," willing to make great sacrifices out of love for him. A girl raised on the streets "knows what's happening behind the game," and doesn't go for the con so easy. The requirements of a "mackman's" job has caused the widespread use of "crystals" which enable pimps to work around the clock "taking care of business," and seeing that his "bitches" are protected against the onslaughts of competing hustlers. Many righteous dope fiends are also "mackmen"; but if a pimp can help it he will stay clear of narcotics and "keep his bitched wired on crystal." The only drawback in the widespread crystal use lies in the tendency of "hookers" to "get strung out," exhausted and rundown from lack of proper food and sleep. Ideally a woman must be kept healthy, well dressed, well fed, and attractive to be profitable.

THE DOPE FIEND BROAD AS A "HOOKER AND BOOSTER"

A young girl in high school who wants a little extra spending money for the weekends, can start to "play" if she is "cool people." Similarly, a college girl, secretary, or office worker may realize how she can use her body profitably and be a little different from a middle class housewife using her body to manipulate a tightwad husband or a respectable single girl who sleeps around with different men in the hope of finding a loveable husband. But a "hooker" has a full "bag of tricks" and relies on her ingenuity and versatility to make money. Most "dope fiend broads" are "hookers" *before* they become addicted to narcotics, unless a woman falls in love with a "mackman" or a "dealer" and they both "get hooked" together before she consents to "turn tricks." However, once a woman begins to hustle her role expectations seem to include the use of drugs:

... Everybody just knew I had to be shooting dope because when you're hustling, people just expected you to use anyway. I hustled for a long time before I got strung out. Money was my first desire before anything. My old man was dealer and I was hustling right along with him . . .

... I started hustling first; for quite a while as a matter of fact. You know I turned down quite a few fixes before I started chippying around. This dude messed with me and I didn't go for it. When he tried to split with the money I made at a month's work, I said later with you man. But I already hustled so I kept hustling you know. . . .

Few men can develop as much skill at shoplifting as a good female booster. But women usually team up with an "old man" while using this particular hustle. It is very unusual and also difficult for a woman to support her habit by her own hustling skill. It is much more profitable and less trouble to have an "old man" protect her from the normal exigencise of the hustling world. The career of a "dope fiend broad" is usually short, but it is common knowledge that when a hustler has a few trustworthy women capable of boosting and turning tricks, his financial success will skyrocket. Behind a good hustler there are four or five good women.

THE CON ARTIST

When it comes to "playing con" few people can match the skill and versatility of a righteous dope fiend. A good "fake" will often be seen with a crowd of people surrounding him; virtually every hustler is trying to "get his game." But a "righteous fake" very seldom "let's go of his game," unless another fake has a better game to exchange, or until he loses his polish with age and literally *sells* his game to young hustlers for dope. It takes years of practice to become a good "pocket stinger," and usually one can only learn the art by gradually picking up bits of information in the course of trial and error:

... See you'll never let your game go and when you're coming up the older cons will just tell you enough to help them off, polish off a sting, but that's all. Then when you go out and try it on your own, another con may spot you and think you know more than you really do. Pretty soon you'll get the game. That's the way I got the game . . . .

A description of the assortment of different short con games and their variations would exceed the length of a book. It is sufficient to note that few dope fiends have the time to travel around the country and set up a "mark" for a big "take." Most will concentrate on "pocket stings" and be satisfied with what a man is carrying in his pocket.

Closely related to the short con game is a practice of "palming hoops and blocks." This is usually a fly-by-night hustle engaged in by many "players" trying to practice their conversation. Different wholesale houses distribute watches, rings, and other types of jewelry by the dozen. On a good night, a hustler will sell eight or nine items at a profit ranging from 5% to 200% depending on the victims willingness to buy hot merchandise and the hustler's sales pitch. Some hustlers are even able to sell cut glass rings across the counter to jewelers; other can walk into a jewelry store wearing a thirty dollar watch and walk out wearing a solid gold Omega. The jewelry is then resold.

TILL TAPPERS AND MONEY BURGLARS

Till tapping includes a number of different methods to "take off" a cash register. The targets for a till tapper are usually liquor stores, hardware stores, etc., wherever a fat cash register is within reach. The hustler may walk into the store, ask for an item, do something to distract the storekeeper and "take off" the till. In the meantime his partners have distracted the attention of customers. Burglary is often the systematic operation of a small group. Because of the skill involved and the equipment needed, burglars enjoy a great deal of status in the hustling world, especially burglars who will steal nothing but cash.

BOOSTERS, MERCHANDISE BURGLARS AND FENCES

Boosting is another lucrative activity aided by the use of amphetamine compounds. A good booster, especially a female, who is "wired on crystals," can "take off" a number of dress shops, and department stores inside of a few hours. Many professional shop lifters who work in groups of three or four can almost make as much money as a burglar; the risk of arrest is slight, the prison sentence is light. Merchandise burglars, as well as boosters, will often "work" in one city and "fence" the stolen property in another city to avoid being seen "in public" (by police) with stolen property which can be checked within the confines of a city area. Probably one half of all the boosters in Oakland are drug users of some kind, especially righteous dope fiends who are attracted to the boosting craft. There is great demand for clothes and jewelry by "mackmen" "hookers" and "fences" who specialize in receiving and selling stolen property from boosters and merchandise burglars. The relationships between different hustlers become apparent in the following comments:

... I draw my respect from the mackman. He wants to keep sharp so he can get out there and steal them holes. So I get out there and dress the rest of them and keep them in business, then stand out there doin the same thing they doin, nothin to worry about see. ... Then I draw respect from the dope man because I'm so young and I can get out there and make money from the weed man, the crystal man, and money from the gow man too. Can get out there and get anything I want and nobody can game on me see ....

GAME ARTISTS

For the most part "game artists" concentrate on activities in which their own skill and proficiency may be wagered on, and a variety of gambling games which float around different parts of Oakland and San Francisco. Pool halls, gambling houses, selected dance halls, and small apartment houses make up the "set" for the game artist. Drugs most commonly used are marijuana and amphetamines ("weed," "whites," and "cartwheels"); although many "pool sharks," "crap hustlers," and gamblers do not use drugs during working hours. Dope fiends seldom have time for games after they get hooked; however most have passed through an adolescent phase where "gaming" was their primary hustle.

STRONGARMERS AND THUGS

Strongarm robbers and thugs are most often recruited from adolescent gangs. Those who "never seem to get off the rowdy trip," are attracted to violent crime. Few dope fiends engage in such activity; the money to be gained is not worth the risk of a long sentence or an "accidental murder," and violent crimes do not involve the ingenuity and finesse required for a booster, con artist, mackman, or dealer. Nevertheless, a thug is in demand by hustlers who need protection and is often called on to enforce the laws against "snitching."

SQUARE INVESTORS AND REGULAR SLAVES

During the course of this study, it was hardly a surprise to discover that two respectable businessmen in the community were investing sizeable amounts of capital in some dope dealers who in turn purchased heroin from "runners." Both of the businessmen were known "squares" because they were unfamiliar with the hustling world and seldom used drugs. They seem to be living proof of a hustler's working philosophy: "Everybody's got a front, and everybody's running a game." It is not uncommon for dope fiends to have a legitimate "slave" as a "front" while they go about the business of hustling. For example, one dope fiend was working as an insurance salesman during the day; while he supervised three women turning tricks on the street. Another young hustler found legitimate employment when he began promoting encyclopedias for a well-known company. After finding that he could make more money by selling encyclopedias than by selling "hoops," he "tucked in that game and fell off into the selling slave." To be sure these cases are not unusual. Similar findings in the future should purge the fantastic idea that people become addicts because they are failures who choose a retreatist role adaptation as an expression of withdrawal.

The various hustles in the world of a righteous dope fiend are not mutually exclusive. A good hustler may engage in three or four games at the same time. Thus, a young "weed head," who thinks of himself as a "game artist" may spend most of the day in a local pool hall, have two girls working part time for him, and may deal "weed" on a small time basis. Similarly, a righteous dope fiend may boost up and down a particular street with three women during the day, burglarize a warehouse at night, and collect money from his "bitches" in the morning. In spite of the prestige allocated to a hustler, a large part of the hustling enterprise is anything but pleasurable and romantic. The entire scene is often viewed as one big "rat race," and few dope fiends see themselves as living the Utopian existence they often dream about.